Psychology

Sixth Edition
AP® Edition

Saundra K. Ciccarelli
Gulf Coast State College

J. Noland White
Georgia College & State University

AP® and Advanced Placement Program are trademarks registered and/or owned by the College Board, which was not involved in the production of, and does not endorse, this product.

Copyright © 2021, 2015, 2011 by Pearson Education, Inc., 221 River Street, Hoboken, NJ 07030, or its affiliates. All Rights Reserved. Printed in the United States of America. This publication is protected by copyright, and permission should be obtained from the publisher prior to any prohibited reproduction, storage in a retrieval system, or transmission in any form or by any means, electronic, mechanical, photocopying, recording, or otherwise. For information regarding permissions, request forms and the appropriate contacts within the Pearson Education Global Rights & Permissions department, please visit www.pearsoned.com/permissions/.

We would like to thank all of the students who allowed us to use their photos in our book. Acknowledgments of third-party content appear on the appropriate page within the text.

Cover Image: Natthawut Nungsanther/EyeEm/Getty Images

PEARSON, ALWAYS LEARNING, and MYLAB are exclusive trademarks in the U.S. and/or other countries owned by Pearson Education, Inc. or its affiliates.

Unless otherwise indicated herein, any third-party trademarks that may appear in this work are the property of their respective owners and any references to third-party trademarks, logos or other trade dress are for demonstrative or descriptive purposes only. Such references are not intended to imply any sponsorship, endorsement, authorization, or promotion of Pearson's products by the owners of such marks, or any relationship between the owner and Pearson Education, Inc. or its affiliates, authors, licensees or distributors.

Library of Congress Cataloging-in-Publication Data:

Names: Ciccarelli, Saundra K., author. | White, J. Noland, author.
Title: Psychology / Saundra K. Ciccarelli, Gulf Coast State College, J. Noland White, Georgia College & State University.
Description: AP edition. | Hoboken, NJ : Pearson, [2020] | Includes bibliographical references and index.
Identifiers: LCCN 2019052327 (print) | LCCN 2019052328 (ebook) | ISBN 9780135218211 (hardcover) | ISBN 9780135263082 (epub)
Subjects: LCSH: Psychology—Textbooks.
Classification: LCC BF121 .C52 2020 (print) | LCC BF121 (ebook) | DDC 150—dc23
LC record available at https://lccn.loc.gov/2019052327
LC ebook record available at https://lccn.loc.gov/2019052328

7 2023

ISBN 10: 0-13-521821-7 (High School Binding)
ISBN 13: 978-0-13-521821-1 (High School Binding)

Contents

For Advanced Placement Psychology	viii
AP Correlation Guide	xi
Preface	xx

Psychology in Action Secrets for Surviving AP Psychology and Improving Your Grades — PIA-2

Study Skills	PIA-4
Managing Time and Tasks	PIA-5
Reading the Text: Textbooks Are Not Meatloaf	PIA-8
Survey	PIA-9
Question	PIA-9
Read	PIA-9
Recite	PIA-9
Recall/Review	PIA-10
Getting the Most Out of Lectures	PIA-11
Studying for Exams: Cramming Is Not an Option	PIA-12
Improving Your Memory	PIA-16
Writing Papers	PIA-17
Your Ethical Responsibility as a Student	PIA-19
Psychology in Action Summary	PIA-20
Test Yourself: Preparing for the AP Exam	PIA-21

1 The Science of Psychology — 2

The History of Psychology	4
In the Beginning: Wundt, Titchener, and James	4
Three Influential Approaches: Gestalt, Psychoanalysis, and Behaviorism	7
The Field of Psychology Today	11
Modern Perspectives	11
Psychological Professionals and Areas of Specialization	15
Scientific Research	17
Thinking Critically About Critical Thinking	18
The Scientific Approach	19
Descriptive Methods	23
Correlations: Finding Relationships	26
The Experiment	28
Experimental Hazards and Controlling for Effects	31
APA Goal 2: Scientific Inquiry and Critical Thinking: A Sample Experiment	34
What Are Statistics?	35
Descriptive Statistics	36
Frequency Distributions	36
Measures of Central Tendency	38
Measures of Variability	40
Inferential Statistics	43
Looking at Differences: Statistical Significance	43
The Correlation Coefficient	44
Ethics of Psychological Research	46
The Guidelines for Doing Research with People	46
Animal Research	48
Applying Psychology to Everyday Life: Critical Thinking and Social Media	49
Chapter Summary	50
Test Yourself: Preparing for the AP Exam	52

2 The Biological Perspective — 54

Neurons and Neurotransmitters	56
Structure of the Neuron: The Nervous System's Building Block	56
Generating the Message Within the Neuron: The Neural Impulse	58
Neurotransmission	60
Looking Inside the Living Brain	65
Methods for Studying Specific Regions of the Brain	66
Neuroimaging Techniques	68
From the Bottom Up: The Structures of the Brain	73
The Hindbrain	74
Structures Under the Cortex: The Limbic System	76
The Cortex	78
The Association Areas of the Cortex	81
Classic Studies in Psychology: Through the Looking Glass—Spatial Neglect	82
The Cerebral Hemispheres	83
The Nervous System: The Rest of the Story	86
The Central Nervous System: The "Central Processing Unit"	86
The Peripheral Nervous System: Nerves on the Edge	89
The Endocrine Glands	93
The Pituitary: Master of the Hormonal Universe	93
Other Endocrine Glands	95
APA Goal 2: Scientific Inquiry and Critical Thinking: Phineas Gage and Neuroplasticity	96
Applying Psychology to Everyday Life: Minimizing the Impact of Adult Attention-Deficit/Hyperactivity Disorder	98
Chapter Summary	98
Test Yourself: Preparing for the AP Exam	101

3 Sensation and Perception — 102

The ABCs of Sensation	104
Transduction	104
Sensory Thresholds	104
Habituation and Sensory Adaptation	106

iii

The Science of Seeing	107
Light and the Eye	108
The Visual Pathway	111
Perception of Color	112
The Hearing Sense: Can You Hear Me Now?	116
Sound Waves and the Ear	116
Perceiving Pitch	118
Types of Hearing Impairments	118
Chemical Senses: It Tastes Good and Smells Even Better	120
Gustation: How We Taste the World	120
The Sense of Scents: Olfaction	122
The Other Senses: What the Body Knows	124
Somesthetic Senses	124
Body Movement and Position	126
The ABCs of Perception	129
How We Organize Our Perceptions	129
Depth Perception	131
Perceptual Illusions	134
APA Goal 2: Scientific Inquiry and Critical Thinking: Perceptual Influences on Metacognition	139
Applying Psychology to Everyday Life: Using Your Senses to Be More Mindful	140
Chapter Summary	140
Test Yourself: Preparing for the AP Exam	142

4 Consciousness — 144

What Is Consciousness?	146
Definition of Consciousness	146
Altered States of Consciousness	146
Sleep	148
The Biology of Sleep	148
Why We Sleep	150
The Stages of Sleep	153
Sleep Disorders	156
APA Goal 2: Scientific Inquiry and Critical Thinking: Weight Gain and Sleep	161
Dreams	162
Why Do We Dream?	162
What Do People Dream About?	164
Hypnosis	166
How Hypnosis Works	166
Theories of Hypnosis	167
The Influence of Psychoactive Drugs	169
Dependence	169
Stimulants: Up, Up, and Away	171
Down in the Valley: Depressants	174
Hallucinogens: Higher and Higher	177
Applying Psychology to Everyday Life: Can You Really Multitask?	181
Chapter Summary	182
Test Yourself: Preparing for the AP Exam	183

5 Learning — 186

Definition of Learning	188
It Makes Your Mouth Water: Classical Conditioning	188
Pavlov and the Salivating Dogs	188
Classical Conditioning Applied to Human Behavior	194
What's in It for Me? Operant Conditioning	198
The Contributions of Thorndike and Skinner	198
The Concept of Reinforcement	199
Schedules of Reinforcement: Why the One-Armed Bandit Is so Seductive	202
The Role of Punishment in Operant Conditioning	206
Other Aspects of Operant Conditioning	209
Applications of Operant Conditioning: Shaping and Behavior Modification	210
Classic Studies in Psychology: Biological Constraints on Operant Conditioning	211
APA Goal 2: Scientific Inquiry and Critical Thinking: Spare the Rod, Spoil the Child?	215
Cognitive Learning Theory	216
Tolman's Maze-Running Rats: Latent Learning	217
Köhler's Smart Chimp: Insight Learning	218
Seligman's Depressed Dogs: Learned Helplessness	219
Observational Learning	221
Bandura and the Bobo Doll	221
The Four Elements of Observational Learning	223
Applying Psychology to Everyday Life: Conditioning in the Real World	224
Chapter Summary	225
Test Yourself: Preparing for the AP Exam	226

6 Memory — 228

What Is Memory?	230
Three Processes of Memory	230
Models of Memory	230
The Information-Processing Model: Three Memory Systems	233
Sensory Memory: Why Do People Do Double Takes?	233
Classic Studies in Psychology: Sperling's Iconic Memory Test	234
Short-Term Memory	236
Long-Term Memory	239
Getting It Out: Retrieval of Long-Term Memories	245
Retrieval Cues	245
Recall and Recognition	246
Classic Studies in Psychology: Elizabeth Loftus and Eyewitnesses	248
Automatic Encoding: Flashbulb Memories	249
The Reconstructive Nature of Long-Term Memory	
Retrieval: How Reliable Are Memories?	250
APA Goal 2: Scientific Inquiry and Critical Thinking: Effects of Supplements on Memory	254
What Were We Talking About? Forgetting	256
Ebbinghaus and the Forgetting Curve	256
Reasons We Forget	257

Neuroscience of Memory	259
The Biological Bases of Memory	260
When Memory Fails: Organic Amnesia	261
Applying Psychology to Everyday Life: Using Elaborative Rehearsal to Make Memories More Memorable	**265**
Chapter Summary	266
Test Yourself: Preparing for the AP Exam	267

7 Cognition: Thinking, Intelligence, and Language — 270

How People Think	272
Mental Imagery	272
Concepts and Prototypes	273
Problem-Solving and Decision-Making Strategies	275
Problems with Problem Solving and Decision Making	278
Creativity	279
Intelligence	282
Theories of Intelligence	282
Measuring Intelligence	285
Test Construction: Good Test, Bad Test?	286
Individual Differences in Intelligence	292
Classic Studies in Psychology: Terman's "Termites"	**294**
The Nature/Nurture Issue Regarding Intelligence	297
Language	301
The Levels of Language Analysis	301
Development of Language	303
The Relationship between Language and Thought	304
Animal Studies in Language	305
APA Goal 2: Scientific Inquiry and Critical Thinking: A Cognitive Advantage for Bilingual Individuals?	**308**
Applying Psychology to Everyday Life: Recognizing Cognitive Biases	**309**
Chapter Summary	310
Test Yourself: Preparing for the AP Exam	312

8 Development Across the Life Span — 314

Studying Human Development	316
Research Designs	316
Nature and Nurture	316
The Basic Building Blocks of Development	318
Prenatal Development	321
Fertilization	321
Three Stages of Development	322
Infancy and Childhood Development	325
Physical Development	325
Classic Studies in Psychology: The Visual Cliff	**328**
Cognitive Development	329
Psychosocial Development	335
Classic Studies in Psychology: Harlow and Contact Comfort	**337**
APA Goal 2: Scientific Inquiry and Critical Thinking: The Facts About Immunizations	**341**
Gender Development and Sexual Orientation	342
Gender Roles	342
Theories of Gender-Role Development	343
Sexual Orientation	344
Adolescence	346
Physical Development	346
Cognitive Development	346
Psychosocial Development	348
Adulthood and Aging	350
Physical Development: Use It or Lose It	350
Cognitive Development	351
Psychosocial Development	352
Theories of Physical and Psychological Aging	353
Stages of Death and Dying	354
Death and Dying in Other Cultures	355
Applying Psychology to Everyday Life: Not an Adolescent, but Not Yet an Adult?	**357**
Chapter Summary	358
Test Yourself: Preparing for the AP Exam	360

9 Motivation and Emotion — 362

Understanding Motivation	364
Defining Motivation	364
Early Approaches to Understanding Motivation	364
Different Strokes for Different Folks: Psychological Needs	366
Arousal and Incentive Approaches	368
Humanistic Approaches	369
APA Goal 2: Scientific Inquiry and Critical Thinking: Cultural Differences in the Use of Praise as a Motivator	**373**
What, Hungry Again? Why People Eat	374
Physiological and Social Components of Hunger	374
Obesity	377
Emotion	379
The Three Elements of Emotion	380
Early Theories of Emotion	385
Cognitive Theories of Emotion	387
Classic Studies in Psychology: The Angry/Happy Man	**388**
Applying Psychology to Everyday Life: What Is Holding You Back from Keeping Track?	**392**
Chapter Summary	393
Test Yourself: Preparing for the AP Exam	394

10 Stress and Health — 396

Stress and Stressors	398
The Relationship Between Stress and Stressors	398
Environmental Stressors: Life's Ups and Downs	399
Psychological Stressors: What, Me Worry?	403
Physiological Factors: Stress and Health	408
The General Adaptation Syndrome	408
The Immune System and Stress	409
Health Psychology	413
Cognitive Factors in Stress	414
Personality Factors in Stress	416
Social and Cultural Factors in Stress: People Who Need People	420

APA Goal 2: Scientific Inquiry and Critical Thinking: Homeopathy: An Illusion of Healing … 424
Coping with Stress … 425
  Coping Strategies … 425
  How Social Support Affects Coping … 428
  How Culture Affects Coping … 429
  How Religion Affects Coping … 430
Applying Psychology to Everyday Life: Coping with Stress in College … 431
  Chapter Summary … 432
  Test Yourself: Preparing for the AP Exam … 434

11 Social Psychology … 436

Social Influence … 438
  Conformity … 438
  Group Behavior … 440
  Compliance … 443
  Obedience … 444
APA Goal 2: Scientific Inquiry and Critical Thinking: Cults and the Failure of Critical Thinking … 449
Social Cognition … 450
  Attitudes … 450
  Attitude Change: The Art of Persuasion … 453
  Cognitive Dissonance: When Attitudes and Behavior Clash … 454
  Impression Formation … 456
  Attribution … 458
Social Interaction … 461
  Prejudice and Discrimination … 461
  How People Learn and Overcome Prejudice … 463
Classic Studies in Psychology: Brown Eyes, Blue Eyes … 463
  Interpersonal Attraction … 466
  Love Is a Triangle—Robert Sternberg's Triangular Theory of Love … 468
  Aggression … 469
  Prosocial Behavior … 474
Applying Psychology to Everyday Life: Looking at Groups … 478
  Chapter Summary … 479
  Test Yourself: Preparing for the AP Exam … 482

12 Theories of Personality … 484

Theories of Personality … 486
Psychodynamic Perspectives … 486
  Freud's Conception of Personality … 487
  Stages of Personality Development … 489
  The Neo-Freudians … 492
  Current Thoughts on Freud and the Psychodynamic Perspective … 494
The Behavioral and Social Cognitive View of Personality … 496
  Learning Theories … 497
  Current Thoughts on the Behavioral and Social Cognitive Learning Views … 499
The Third Force: Humanism and Personality … 500
  Carl Rogers and the Humanistic Perspective … 500
  Current Thoughts on the Humanistic View of Personality … 502
Trait Theories: Who Are You? … 504
  Allport and Cattell: Early Attempts to List and Describe Traits … 504
  Modern Trait Theories: The Big Five … 505
  Current Thoughts on the Trait Perspective … 506
Personality: Genetics, Neuroscience, and Culture … 508
  The Biology of Personality: Behavioral Genetics … 508
  The Biology of Personality: Neuroscience … 510
  Current Thoughts on the Heritability and Neuroscience of Personality … 512
Classic Studies in Psychology: Geert Hofstede's Four Dimensions of Cultural Personality … 512
APA Goal 2: Scientific Inquiry and Critical Thinking: Personality, Family, and Culture … 514
Assessment of Personality … 515
  Interviews, Behavioral Assessments, and Personality Inventories … 516
  Projective Tests … 519
Applying Psychology to Everyday Life: Informally Assessing Personality … 522
  Chapter Summary … 522
  Test Yourself: Preparing for the AP Exam … 524

13 Psychological Disorders … 526

What Is Abnormality? … 528
  Changing Conceptions of Abnormality … 528
  Models of Abnormality … 530
  Diagnosing and Classifying Disorders … 533
Disorders of Mood: The Effect of Affect … 539
  Major Depressive Disorder and Bipolar Disorders … 539
  Causes of Disordered Mood … 542
Disorders of Anxiety, Trauma, and Stress: What, Me Worry? … 544
  Anxiety Disorders … 545
  Other Disorders Related to Anxiety … 547
  Causes of Anxiety, Trauma, and Stress Disorders … 549
Dissociative Disorders: Altered Identities … 552
  Types of Dissociative Disorders … 552
  Causes of Dissociative Disorders … 553
Eating Disorders … 555
  Eating Disorders … 555
Personality Disorders: I'm Okay, It's Everyone Else Who's Weird … 558
  Categories of Personality Disorders … 559
  Causes of Personality Disorders … 560
Schizophrenia: Altered Reality … 561
  Symptoms of Schizophrenia … 561
  Causes of Schizophrenia … 562

APA Goal 2: Scientific Inquiry and Critical Thinking: Learning More: Psychological Disorders — 566

Applying Psychology to Everyday Life: Taking the Worry Out of Exams — 567
    Chapter Summary — 567
    Test Yourself: Preparing for the AP Exam — 569

14 Psychological Therapies — 572

Treatment of Psychological Disorders: Past to Present — 574

Insight Therapies: Psychodynamic and Humanistic Approaches — 576
    Psychotherapy Begins: Freud's Psychoanalysis — 576
    Humanistic Therapy: To Err Is Human — 578

Action Therapies: Behavior Therapies and Cognitive Therapies — 582
    Behavior Therapies: Learning One's Way to Better Behavior — 583
    Cognitive Therapies: Thinking Is Believing — 588

Group Therapies: Not Just for the Shy — 592
    Types of Group Therapies — 592
    Evaluation of Group Therapy — 593

Does Psychotherapy Really Work? — 595
    Studies of Effectiveness — 595
    Characteristics of Effective Therapy — 596

APA Goal 2: Scientific Inquiry and Critical Thinking: Does It Work? Psychological Treatment — 601

Biomedical Therapies — 602
    Psychopharmacology — 602
    ECT and Psychosurgery — 607
    Emerging Techniques — 610

Lifestyle Factors: Fostering Resilience — 612

Applying Psychology to Everyday Life: How to Help Others: Reducing the Stigma of Seeking Help — 614
    Chapter Summary — 615
    Test Yourself: Preparing for the AP Exam — 617

Appendix Applied Psychology and Psychology Careers — A-1

Glossary — G-1

References — R-1

Name Index — NI-1

Subject Index — SI-1

For Advanced Placement Psychology

Our goals with this new AP Edition were to create the most useful tool possible to introduce AP students to the study of psychology and to prepare them for success on the Advanced Placement (AP) Psychology Exam. For this AP Edition, we have retained the approach of the sixth edition, and we have made specific changes and additions to tailor the text to AP Psychology classes. We have paid special attention to the presentation, adjusting it throughout to be more relevant, appropriate, clear, and understandable for high school AP students. In addition, we have created specific tools to help AP students prepare for the AP Psychology Exam.

Correlation to the College Board's AP Topics and Learning Objectives

In the AP Psychology Course and Exam Description booklet (AP Central on the AP Psychology homepage), the College Board provides a list of nine units, or major content areas, that are covered on the AP Psychology Exam. Each unit is broken down into topics. Each topic area is accompanied by several learning objectives that AP students should be able to meet in order to succeed on the AP Exam. This new AP Edition addresses each of the topics and learning objectives described in the AP Psychology Course and Exam Description. With AP students in mind, this text utilizes several organizational features that readily identify the specific content areas that correlate with the key AP Psychology topics and learning objectives. These features include:

Comprehensive AP Correlation Guide

On pages xi–xix you will find a comprehensive correlation guide that provides the page reference indicating where this text addresses each of the AP Psychology topics and the associated learning objectives.

Advanced Placement Psychology Topics	Advanced Placement Psychology Learning Objectives	Ciccarelli/White, Psychology, AP Edition, 6th Edition, Chapter/Page Citations
Unit 1: Scientific Foundations of Psychology		
Topic 1.1: Introducing Psychology		Chapter 1
	1.A: Recognize how philosophical and physiological perspectives shaped the development of psychological thought.	1.1–1.2 The History of Psychology, 4; Concept Map, 10
	1.B: Identify the research contributions of major historical figures in psychology.	1.1–1.2 The History of Psychology, 4-10; Concept Map 10; Chapter Summary, 50
	1.C: Describe and compare different theoretical approaches in explaining behavior.	1.1–1.2 The History of Psychology, 4-10; 1.3–1.4 The Field of Psychology Today, 11-14; Table 1.1, 14; Concept Map 16-17; Chapter Summary, 50
	1.D: Recognize the strengths and limitations of applying theories to explain behavior.	1.5–1.10 Scientific Research, 17-20
	1.E: Distinguish the different domains of psychology.	1.4 Psychological Professionals and Areas of Specialization, 15-17; Figure 1.2, 15; Concept Map 16-17; Chapter Summary, 50
Topic 1.2: Research Methods in Psychology		Chapters 1, 8
	1.F: Differentiate types of research with regard to purpose, strengths, and weaknesses.	1.7 Descriptive Methods, 23-26; 1.8 Correlations: Finding Relationships, 26-28; 1.9 The Experiment, 28-31; Concept Map 32-33; Chapter Summary, 50-51; 8.1 Research Designs, 316; Table 8.1, 317; Concept Map, 320; Chapter Summary, 358
	1.G: Discuss the value of reliance on operational definitions and measurement in behavioral research.	The Variables, 29; Concept Map 32-33
Topic 1.3: The Experimental Method		Chapter 1
	1.H: Identify independent, dependent, confounding, and control variables in experimental designs.	1.9 The Experiment, 28-31; Concept Map 32-33; A Sample Experiment, 34-35; Chapter Summary, 51

AP 2.F Identify basic processes and systems in the biological bases of behavior, including parts of the neuron.

AP Icons

Integrated into each chapter, these icons call out where we address each AP Psychology learning objective.

Built-In Preparation and Practice for the AP Psychology Exam

AP students will benefit from plenty of practice with questions formatted and styled like those on the AP Exam: multiple-choice questions with five answer choices and free-response questions. This text provides numerous opportunities for AP students to test their understanding and to practice and develop good test-taking skills.

Practice Quiz   How much do you remember?

Pick the best answer.

1. Which part of the neuron carries messages to other cells?
   - **a.** synaptic vesicles
   - **b.** axon
   - **c.** dendrite
   - **d.** soma
   - **e.** myelin

2. Which one of the following is NOT a function of glial cells?
   - **a.** cleaning up the remains of dead neurons
   - **b.** generating myelin
   - **c.** providing structural support for neurons
   - **d.** generating action potentials
   - **e.** getting nutrients to the neurons

3. When a neuron's resting potential is occurring, the neuron is _____ charged on the inside.
   - **a.** both positively and negatively
   - **b.** neutrally
   - **c.** positively
   - **d.** not
   - **e.** negatively

Practice Quiz: Preparing for the AP Exam

Multiple-choice quizzes are included in each chapter at the end of every major section to help students think critically and apply their understanding of crucial content. These multiple-choice quizzes are presented in the same five-answer format used on the AP Exam.

Test Yourself: Preparing for the AP Exam

PART I: MULTIPLE-CHOICE QUESTIONS

Directions for Part I: Read each of the questions or incomplete sentences below. Then choose the response that best answers the question or completes the sentence.

1. In the structure of the neuron, the _____ receives messages from other cells.
   a. dendrite
   b. vesicle
   c. soma
   d. axon
   e. myelin

2. Oligodendrocytes and Schwann cells generate a fatty substance known as _____.
   a. glial
   b. soma
   c. myelin
   d. neurilemma
   e. stasis

3. When a neuron is in the resting potential state, the neuron is negatively charged on the _____ and positively charged on the _____.
   a. output, input
   b. top, bottom
   c. inside, outside
   d. bottom, top
   e. outside, inside

4. Which neurotransmitter stimulates skeletal muscle cells to contract but slows contractions of the heart?
   a. serotonin
   b. acetylcholine (ACh)
   c. GABA
   d. glutamate
   e. endorphin

9. Which part of the brain is involved in the creation of declarative memories and is often linked to Alzheimer's
   a. thalamus
   b. amygdala
   c. hypothalamus
   d. hippocampus
   e. cingulate

10. Loretta suffered a severe blow to the back of her head was thrown from her horse. Subsequently, her occipital been injured. Which of her senses has the highest affected?
    a. touch
    b. hearing
    c. taste
    d. smell

11. Jillian is recovering from a brain injury. She is able to but often uses incorrect words in a sentence. In one friend's birthday party, she said, "I would like something have some battery?" Jillian's problem may be a symptom
    a. Wernicke's aphasia
    b. visual agnosia
    c. anterograde amnesia
    d. spatial ne
    e. Broca's a

Test Yourself: Preparing for the AP Exam

A sample test is found at the end of every chapter. The chapter test contains multiple-choice questions and a free-response question, both styled after AP Exam format. Answers to all practice quizzes and end-of-chapter tests are in the Answer Key found Instructor Resource section of the MyLab. The Answer Key also includes criteria for a successful free-response essay. Use of proper psychological terminology is required in your answer.

PART II: FREE-RESPONSE QUESTION

Directions for Part II: Read the essay question that follows. Then respond to the question in a clear, concise essay. Do not simply list facts. Instead, present a thorough argument based on your critical consideration of the topic. Use of proper terminology is necessary.

While walking to the pencil sharpener during class, Alonso painfully stubbed his toe on his desk. He jerked his foot back and hopped on one leg, and just as he was about to yell a swear word, he noticed his teacher watching. He stopped himself from saying something inappropriate and said, "Ouch!" instead. Later on in the class, Alonso stops feeling the pain from his sore toe.

For each of the following terms, explain how they play a role in Alonso's behavior:
- prefrontal cortex
- cerebellum
- efferent neurons
- Broca's area
- endorphins
- somatosensory cortex
- spinal cord
- afferent neurons

Correlation Guide to the Advanced Placement Psychology Curriculum Framework Topics and Learning Targets (Fall 2019)

Advanced Placement Psychology Topics	Advanced Placement Psychology Learning Objectives	Ciccarelli/White, Psychology, AP Edition, 6th Edition, Chapter/Page Citations
Unit 1: Scientific Foundations of Psychology		
Topic 1.1: Introducing Psychology		Chapter 1
	1.A: Recognize how philosophical and physiological perspectives shaped the development of psychological thought.	1.1–1.2 The History of Psychology, 4; Concept Map, 10
	1.B: Identify the research contributions of major historical figures in psychology.	1.1–1.2 The History of Psychology, 4-10; Concept Map 10; Chapter Summary, 50
	1.C: Describe and compare different theoretical approaches in explaining behavior.	1.1–1.2 The History of Psychology, 4-10; 1.3–1.4 The Field of Psychology Today, 11-14; Table 1.1, 14; Concept Map 16-17; Chapter Summary, 50
	1.D: Recognize the strengths and limitations of applying theories to explain behavior.	1.5–1.10 Scientific Research, 17-20
	1.E: Distinguish the different domains of psychology.	1.4 Psychological Professionals and Areas of Specialization, 15-17; Figure 1.2, 15; Concept Map 16-17; Chapter Summary, 50
Topic 1.2: Research Methods in Psychology		Chapters 1, 8
	1.F: Differentiate types of research with regard to purpose, strengths, and weaknesses.	1.7 Descriptive Methods, 23-26; 1.8 Correlations: Finding Relationships, 26-28; 1.9 The Experiment, 28-31; Concept Map 32-33; Chapter Summary, 50-51; 8.1 Research Designs, 316; Table 8.1, 317; Concept Map, 320; Chapter Summary, 358
	1.G: Discuss the value of reliance on operational definitions and measurement in behavioral research.	The Variables, 29; Concept Map 32-33
Topic 1.3: The Experimental Method		Chapter 1
	1.H: Identify independent, dependent, confounding, and control variables in experimental designs.	1.9 The Experiment, 28-31; Concept Map 32-33; A Sample Experiment, 34-35; Chapter Summary, 51
	1.I: Describe how research design drives the reasonable conclusions that can be drawn.	1.8 Correlations: Finding Relationships, 26-28; The Experiment, 28-31; 1.10 Experimental Hazards and Controlling for Effects, 31-32; Concept Map 32-33; Chapter Summary, 51
	1.J: Distinguish between random assignment of participants to conditions in experiments and random selection of participants, primarily in correlational studies and surveys.	The Importance of Randomization, 30-31; Concept Map 32-33; Chapter Summary, 51
Topic 1.4: Selecting a Research Method		Chapter 1
	1.K: Predict the validity of behavioral explanations based on the quality of research design.	1.6 The Scientific Approach, 19-23; 1.7 Descriptive Methods, 23-26; 1.10 Experimental Hazards and Controlling for Effects, 31-32
Topic 1.5: Statistical Analysis in Psychology		Chapter 1
	1.L: Apply basic descriptive statistical concepts, including interpreting and constructing graphs and calculating simple descriptive statistics.	1.11 What Are Statistics?, 35-36; 1.12–1.14 Descriptive Statistics, 36-42; Figure 1.4, 36; Figure 1.5, 36; Concept Map, 42; Chapter Summary, 51
	1.M: Distinguish the purposes of descriptive statistics and inferential statistics.	1.12–1.14 Descriptive Statistics, 36-42; Concept Map, 42; 1.15–1.16 Inferential Statistics, 43-45; Concept Map, 45; Chapter Summary, 51
Topic 1.6: Ethical Guidelines in Psychology		Chapter 1
	1.N: Identify how ethical issues inform and constrain research practices.	1.17–1.18 Ethics of Psychological Research, 46-48; Concept Map, 48; Chapter Summary 51-52
	1.O: Describe how ethical and legal guidelines protect research participants and promote sound ethical practice.	1.17–1.18 Ethics of Psychological Research, 46-48; Concept Map, 48; Chapter Summary 51-52

Advanced Placement Psychology Topics	Advanced Placement Psychology Learning Objectives	Ciccarelli/White, Psychology, AP Edition, 6th Edition, Chapter/Page Citations
Unit 2: Biological Bases of Behavior		
Topic 2.1: Interaction of Heredity and Environment		Chapters 1, 2, 7, 8, 12
	2.A: Discuss psychology's abiding interest in how heredity, environment, and evolution work together to shape behavior.	Biopsychological Perspective, 13; Evolutionary Perspective, 13-14; Table 1.1, 14; Concept Map, 16; Chapter Summary, 50; 7.10 The Nature/Nurture Issue Regarding Intelligence, 297-299; Concept Map, 300-301; Chapter Summary, 311; 8.2 Nature and Nurture 316-318; Concept Map, 320; 8.9–8.11 Gender Development and Sexual Orientation, 342-344; Concept Map, 345; Chapter Summary, 358-359; Instincts and the Evolutionary Approach, 364-365; Concept Map, 372; The Behavior of Emotion: Emotional Expression, 382-384; Chapter Summary, 393; 12.13 The Biology of Personality: Behavioral Genetics, 508–510; 12.15 Current Thoughts on the Heritability and Neuroscience of Personality, 512; Concept Map, 514
	2.B: Identify key research contributions of scientists in the area of heredity and environment.	William James and Functionalism, 5-7; Table 1.1, 14; The Behavior of Emotion: Emotional Expression, 382-384; The Facial Feedback Hypothesis: Smile, You'll Feel Better, 386-387
	2.C: Predict how traits and behavior can be selected for their adaptive value.	Evolutionary Perspective, 13-14; Table 1.1, 14; Chapter Summary, 50; 12.12 Current Thoughts on the Trait Perspective, 506-507
Topic 2.2: The Endocrine System		Chapter 2
	2.D: Discuss the effect of the endocrine system on behavior.	2.13–2.14 The Endocrine Glands, 93-95; Concept Map, 96; Chapter Summary, 100
Topic 2.3: Overview of the Nervous System and the Neuron		Chapter 2
	2.E: Describe the nervous system and its subdivisions and functions.	2.11–2.12 The Nervous System: The Rest of the Story, 86-92; Figure 2.14, 86; Figure 2.16, 89; Figure 2.17, 90; Concept Map, 92; Chapter Summary, 100
	2.F: Identify basic processes and systems in the biological bases of behavior, including parts of the neuron.	2.1 Structure of the Neuron: The Nervous System's Building Block, 56-58; Figure 2.1, 56; Concept Map, 65; Chapter Summary, 98-99
Topic 2.4: Neural Firing		Chapter 2
	2.G: Identify basic process of transmission of a signal between neurons.	2.2 Generating the Message within the Neuron: The Neural Impulse, 58–60; Figure 2.2, 59; 2.3 Neurotransmission, 60-64; Concept Map, 65; Chapter Summary, 99
Topic 2.5: Influence of Drugs on Neural Firing		Chapters 2, 14
	2.H: Discuss the influence of drugs on neurotransmitters.	Neurotransmitters: Messengers of the Network, 61-63; Cleaning Up the Synapse: Reuptake and Enzymes, 63-64; Concept Map, 65; 14.10 Psychopharmacology, 602-607; Figure 14.1, 603; Figure 14.2, 605
Topic 2.6: The Brain		Chapter 2
	2.I: Describe the nervous system and its subdivisions and functions in the brain.	2.6–2.10 From the Bottom Up: The Structures of the Brain, 73-85; Figure 2.9, 74; Figure 2.10, 76; Figure 2.11, 78; Figure 2.12, 79; Concept Map, 85; Chapter Summary, 99-100
	2.J: Identify the contributions of key researchers to the study of the brain.	Broca's Area, 81; Wernicke's Area, 81; Through the Looking Glass—Spatial Neglect, 82
Topic 2.7: Tools for Examining Brain Structure and Function		Chapter 2
	2.K: Recount historic and contemporary research strategies and technologies that support research.	2.4–2.5 Looking Inside the Living Brain, 65-71; Concept Map, 72; Chapter Summary, 99
	2.L: Identify the contributions of key researchers to the development of tools for examining the brain.	Split-Brain Research, 83-84
Topic 2.8: The Adaptable Brain		Chapters 1, 2, 4
	2.M: Discuss the role of neuroplasticity in traumatic brain injury.	Damage to the Central Nervous System, Neuroplasticity, and Neurogenesis, 88–89; Phineas Gage and Neuroplasticity, 96-97; Chapter Summary, 100
	2.N: Identify the contributions of key researchers to the study of neuroplasticity.	Split-Brain Research, 83-84
	2.O: Describe various states of consciousness and their impact on behavior.	4.1–4.2 What Is Consciousness?, 146-147; Concept Map, 147; Chapter Summary, 182

AP Correlation Guide xiii

Advanced Placement Psychology Topics	Advanced Placement Psychology Learning Objectives	Ciccarelli/White, Psychology, AP Edition, 6th Edition, Chapter/Page Citations
	2.P: Identify the major psychoactive drug categories and classify specific drugs, including their psychological and physiological effects.	4.11–4.14 The Influence of Psychoactive Drugs, 169-180; Table 4.4, 176; Table 4.5, 180; Concept Map, 180; Chapter Summary, 183
	2.Q: Discuss drug dependence, addiction, tolerance, and withdrawal.	4.11 Dependence, 169-171; Concept Map, 180, Chapter Summary, 183
	2.R: Identify the contributions of major figures in consciousness research.	William James and Functionalism, 5; Sigmund Freud's Theory of Psychoanalysis, 8; 4.1 Definition of Consciousness, 146; 4.7 Why Do We Dream?, 162-164
Topic 2.9: Sleep and Dreaming		Chapter 4
	2.S: Discuss aspects of sleep and dreaming.	4.3–4.6 Sleep, 148-160; Concept Map, 160; 4.7–4.8 Dreams, 162-165; Concept Map, 165; Chapter Summary, 182
Unit 3: Sensation and Perception		
Topic 3.1: Principles of Sensation		Chapter 3
	3.A: Describe general principles of organizing and integrating sensation to promote stable awareness of the external world.	3.1–3.3 The ABCs of Sensation, 104-107; Concept Map, 107; 3.14–3.16 The ABCs of Perception, 129-138; Chapter Summary, 140-141
	3.B: Discuss basic principles of sensory transduction, including absolute threshold, difference threshold, signal detection, and sensory adaptation.	3.1–3.3 The ABCs of Sensation, 104-107; Concept Map, 107; Chapter Summary, 140-141
	3.C: Identify the research contributions of major historical figures in sensation and perception.	3.2 Sensory Thresholds, 104-106; 3.6 Perception of Color, 112-115; 3.8 Perceiving Pitch, 118; 3.16 Perceptual Illusions, 134-138
Topic 3.2: Principles of Perception		Chapter 3
	3.D: Discuss how experience and culture can influence perceptual processes.	3.14–3.16 The ABCs of Perception, 129-138
	3.E: Discuss the role of attention in behavior.	3.2 Sensory Thresholds, 104-106; 3.3 Habituation and Sensory Adaptation, 106-107; Applying Psychology to Everyday Life, 140; Chapter Summary, 142
Topic 3.3: Visual Anatomy		Chapter 3
	3.F: Describe the vision process, including the specific nature of energy transduction, relevant anatomical structures, and specialized pathways in the brain for each of the senses.	3.4–3.6 The Science of Seeing, 107-115; Figure 3.3, 108; Figure 3.6, 111; Concept Map, 115; Chapter Summary, 141
	3.G: Explain common sensory conditions.	3.1 Transduction, 104; The Structure of the Eye, 109; Figure 3.4, 109; Color Blindness, 114–115; 3.9 Types of Hearing Impairments, 118–119; Pain Disorders, 126; Chapter Summary, 141
Topic 3.4: Visual Perception		Chapter 3
	3.H: Explain the role of top-down processing in producing vulnerability to illusion.	Other Factors That Influence Perception, 137; Chapter Summary, 142
Topic 3.5: Auditory Sensation and Perception		Chapter 3
	3.I: Describe the hearing process, including the specific nature of energy transduction, relevant anatomical structures, and specialized pathways in the brain for each of the senses.	3.7–3.9 The Hearing Sense: Can You Hear Me Now?, 116–119; Figure 3.12, 117; Concept Map, 119; Chapter Summary, 141
Topic 3.6: Chemical Senses		Chapter 3
	3.J: Describe taste and smell processes, including the specific nature of energy transduction, relevant anatomical structures, and specialized pathways in the brain for each of the senses.	3.10–3.11 Chemical Senses: It Tastes Good and Smells Even Better, 120–123; Figure 3.14, 121; Figure 3.16, 123; Concept Map, 123; Chapter Summary, 141
Topic 3.7: Body Senses		Chapter 3
	3.K: Describe sensory processes, including the specific nature of energy transduction, relevant anatomical structures, and specialized pathways in the brain for each of the body senses.	3.12–3.13 The Other Senses: What the Body Knows, 124-128; Figure 3.17, 125; Concept Map, 128; Chapter Summary, 141-142
Unit 4: Learning		
Topic 4.1: Introduction to Learning		Chapters 1, 5
	4.A: Identify the contributions of key researchers in the psychology of learning.	Pavlov, Watson, and the Dawn of Behaviorism, 8; Behavioral Perspective, 11; Table 1.1, 14; 5.2 Pavlov and the Salivating Dogs, 188-194, 5.3 Classical Conditioning Applied to Human Behavior, 194-196; 5.4 The Contributions of Thorndike and Skinner, 198-199; Biological Constraints on Operant Conditioning, 211-212; Concept Map, 214; 5.10 Tolman's Maze-Running Rats: Latent Learning, 217-218; 5.11 Köhler's Smart Chimp: Insight Learning, 218-219; 5.12 Seligman's Depressed Dogs: Learned Helplessness, 219-220; Concept Map, 221; 5.13 Bandura and the Bobo Doll, 221-223; Chapter Summary, 225-226

Advanced Placement Psychology Topics	Advanced Placement Psychology Learning Objectives	Ciccarelli/White, Psychology, AP Edition, 6th Edition, Chapter/Page Citations
	4.B: Interpret graphs that exhibit the results of learning experiments.	Figure 5.5, 198; Figure 5.6, 204; Figure 5.9, 218
	4.C: Describe the essential characteristics of insight learning, latent learning, and social learning.	5.10–5.12 Cognitive Learning Theory, 217-220; Concept Map, 221; 5.13–5.14 Observational Learning, 221-223; Concept Map, 223; Chapter Summary, 226
	4.D: Apply learning principles to explain emotional learning, taste aversion, superstitious behavior, and learned helplessness.	5.3 Classical Conditioning Applied to Human Behavior, 194-196; Seligman's Depressed Dogs: Learned Helplessness, 219-220; Chapter Summary, 225–226
	4.E: Provide examples of how biological constraints create learning predispositions.	Biological Constraints on Operant Conditioning, 211–212
Topic 4.2: Classical Conditioning		Chapter 5
	4.F: Describe basic classical conditioning phenomena.	5.2–5.3 It Makes Your Mouth Water: Classical Conditioning, 188-196; Concept Map, 197; Biological Constraints on Operant Conditioning, 211-212; Chapter Summary, 225
	4.G: Distinguish general differences between principles of classical conditioning, operant conditioning, and observational learning.	5.2–5.3 It Makes Your Mouth Water: Classical Conditioning, 188-196; 5.4–5.9 What's in It for Me? Operant Conditioning, 198-214; 5.13–5.14 Observational Learning, 221-223; Chapter Summary, 225–226
Topic 4.3: Operant Conditioning		Chapter 5
	4.H: Predict the effects of operant conditioning.	5.4–5.9 What's in It for Me? Operant Conditioning, 198-214; Concept Map, 214; Chapter Summary, 225-226
	4.I: Predict how practice, schedules of reinforcement, other aspects of reinforcement, and motivation will influence quality of learning.	5.6 Schedules of Reinforcement: Why the One-Armed Bandit Is So Seductive, 202-206; Concept Map, 214; Chapter Summary, 225
Topic 4.4: Social and Cognitive Factors in Learning		Chapter 5
	4.J: Suggest how behavior modification, biofeedback, coping strategies, and self-control can be used to address behavioral problems.	5.9 Applications of Operant Conditioning: Shaping and Behavior Modification, 210-214; Concept Map, 214; Chapter Summary, 226
Unit 5: Cognitive Psychology		
Topic 5.1: Introduction to Memory		Chapter 6
	5.A: Compare and contrast various cognitive processes.	6.1 Three Processes of Memory, 230; Concept Map, 232; 6.3–6.5 The Information-Processing Model: Three Memory Systems, 233-244; Concept Map, 244; 6.7 Recall and Recognition, 246-248; 6.8 Automatic Encoding: Flashbulb Memories, 249-250; Concept Map, 253; Chapter Summary, 266
	5.B: Describe and differentiate psychological and physiological systems of memory.	The Information-Processing Model: Three Memory Systems, 233-244; Concept Map, 244; Chapter Summary, 266
	5.C: Identify the contributions of key researchers in cognitive psychology.	Sperling's Iconic Memory Test, 234; Capacity: The Magical Number Seven, Or Five, Or Four, 237; Elizabeth Loftus and Eyewitnesses, 248-249; 6.10 Ebbinghaus and the Forgetting Curve, 256-257; Chapter Summary, 267
Topic 5.2: Encoding		Chapter 6
	5.D: Outline the principles that underlie construction and encoding of memories.	Putting It In: Encoding, 230; Encoding Specificity: Context Effects on Memory Retrieval, 245-246; Encoding Specificity: State-Dependent Learning, 246; 6.8 Automatic Encoding: Flashbulb Memories, 249-250; Concept Map, 253; Encoding Failure, 257; Concept Map, 259; Using Elaborative Rehearsal to Make Memories More Memorable, 265; Chapter Summary, 266
Topic 5.3: Storing		Chapter 6
	5.E: Outline the principles that underlie effective storage of memories.	Keeping It In: Storage, 230; Elaborative Rehearsal, 240; 6.6–6.9 Getting It Out: Retrieval of Long-Term Memories, 245-253
Topic 5.4: Retrieving		Chapter 6
	5.F: Describe strategies for retrieving memories.	6.6–6.9 Getting It Out: Retrieval of Long-Term Memories, 245-253; Concept Map, 253; Chapter Summary, 266
Topic 5.5: Forgetting and Memory Distortion		Chapter 6
	5.G: Describe strategies for memory improvement and typical memory errors.	Elaborative Rehearsal, 240; 6.6–6.9 Getting It Out: Retrieval of Long-Term Memories, 245-253; Concept Map, 253; 6.10–6.11 What Were We Talking About? Forgetting, 256-259; Concept Map, 259; Using Elaborative Rehearsal to Make Memories More Memorable, 265; Chapter Summary, 266-267

Advanced Placement Psychology Topics	Advanced Placement Psychology Learning Objectives	Ciccarelli/White, Psychology, AP Edition, 6th Edition, Chapter/Page Citations
Topic 5.6: Biological Bases of Memory		Chapter 6
	5.H: Describe and differentiate psychological and physiological systems of short- and long-term memory.	6.3–6.5 The Information-Processing Model: Three Memory Systems, 233-244; Concept Map, 244; 6.12–6.13 Neuroscience of Memory, 259-264; Concept Map, 264; Chapter Summary, 266-267
Topic 5.7: Introduction to Thinking and Problem Solving		Chapter 7
	5.I: Identify problem-solving strategies as well as factors that influence their effectiveness.	7.3 Problem-Solving and Decision-Making Strategies, 275–278; 7.4 Problems with Problem-Solving and Decision-Making, 278–279; 7.5 Creativity, 279–281; Table 7.1, 280; Concept Map, 281; Recognizing Cognitive Biases, 309-310; Chapter Summary, 310
	5.J: List the characteristics of creative thought and creative thinkers.	7.5 Creativity, 279–281; Table 7.1, 280; Concept Map, 281; Chapter Summary, 310
Topic 5.8: Biases and Errors in Thinking		Chapter 7
	5.K: Identify problem-solving strategies as well as factors that create bias and errors in thinking.	7.3 Problem-Solving and Decision-Making Strategies, 275–278; 7.4 Problems with Problem-Solving and Decision-Making, 278–279; Concept Map, 281; Recognizing Cognitive Biases, 309-310; Chapter Summary, 310-311
Topic 5.9: Introduction to Intelligence		Chapter 7
	5.L: Define intelligence and list characteristics of how psychologists measure intelligence.	7.6–7.10 Intelligence, 282-299; Table 7.3, 287; Concept Map, 300-301; Chapter Summary, 310-311
	5.M: Discuss how culture influences the definition of intelligence.	7.2 Concepts and Prototypes, 273-275; Divergent Thinking, 280; Concept Map, 281; IQ Tests and Cultural Bias, 289-290; Emotional Intelligence, 296-297; The Bell Curve and Misinterpretation of Statistics, 299
	5.N: Compare and contrast historic and contemporary theories of intelligence.	7.6 Theories of Intelligence, 282-; Table 7.2, 283; Figure 7.7, 284; Concept Map, 300-301; Chapter Summary, 310-311
	5.O: Identify the contributions of key researchers in intelligence research and testing.	7.6 Theories of Intelligence, 282-; Table 7.2, 283; Figure 7.7, 284; 7.7 Measuring Intelligence, 285-286; Terman's "Termites", 294-295; Emotional Intelligence, 296-297; Concept Map, 300-301; Chapter Summary, 310-311
Topic 5.10: Psychometric Principles and Intelligence Testing		Chapters 1, 7
	5.P: Explain how psychologists design tests, including standardization strategies and other techniques to establish reliability and validity.	7.7 Measuring Intelligence, 285-286; 7.8 Test Construction: Good Test, Bad Test?, 286-291; Table 7.3, 287; Concept Map, 300; Chapter Summary, 311
	5.Q: Interpret the meaning of scores in terms of the normal curve.	The Normal Curve, 37; Figure 1.6, 37; 1.14 Measures of Variability, 40-42; Figure 1.11, 41; Norms, 288; Figure 7.8, 288; The Bell Curve and Misinterpretation of Statistics, 299; Concept Map, 300-301; Chapter Summary, 311
	5.R: Describe relevant labels related to intelligence testing.	7.9 Individual Differences in Intelligence, 292-297; Concept Map, 300-301; Chapter Summary, 311
Topic 5.11: Components of Language and Language Acquisition		Chapter 7
	5.S: Synthesize how biological, cognitive, and cultural factors converge to facilitate acquisition, development, and use of language.	7.11–7.14 Language, 301-307; Concept Map, 307; Chapter Summary, 311
	5.T: Debate the appropriate testing practices, particularly in relation to culture-fair test uses.	IQ Tests and Cultural Bias, 289-290; The Bell Curve and Misinterpretation of Statistics, 299
Unit 6: Developmental Psychology		
Topic 6.1: The Lifespan and Physical Development in Childhood		Chapter 8
	6.A: Explain the process of conception and gestation, including factors that influence successful pre-natal development.	8.4–8.5 Prenatal Development, 321-324; Table 8.2, 324; Concept Map, 325; Chapter Summary, 358
	6.B: Discuss the interaction of nature and nurture (including cultural variations), specifically physical development, in the determination of behavior.	8.2 Nature and Nurture, 316-318; 8.3 The Basic Building Blocks of Development, 318-320; Concept Map, 320; 8.9–8.11 Gender Development and Sexual Orientation, 342-344; Concept Map, 345; Chapter Summary, 358-359
	6.C: Discuss maturation of motor skills.	8.6 Physical Development, 325-328; Figure 8.6, 327; Concept Map, 340; Chapter Summary, 358

Advanced Placement Psychology Topics	Advanced Placement Psychology Learning Objectives	Ciccarelli/White, Psychology, AP Edition, 6th Edition, Chapter/Page Citations
Topic 6.2: Social Development in Childhood		Chapters 8, 12
	6.D: Describe the influence of temperament and other social factors on attachment and appropriate socialization.	8.8 Psychosocial Development, 335-339; Harlow and Contact Comfort, 337-338; Table 8.4, 339; Concept Map, 340; Chapter Summary, 358
	6.E: Identify the contributions of major researchers in developmental psychology in the area of social development in childhood.	Attachment Styles, 336-337; Harlow and Contact Comfort, 337-338; Erikson's Theory, 338-339; Table 8.4, 339; Concept Map, 340; Chapter Summary, 358; 12.3 Stages of Personality Development, 489-492
	6.F: Discuss the interaction of nature and nurture (including cultural variations), specifically social development, in the determination of behavior.	8.2 Nature and Nurture, 316-318; Concept Map, 320; 8.9–8.11 Gender Development and Sexual Orientation, 342-344; Concept Map, 345; Chapter Summary, 358-359
	6.G: Explain how parenting styles influence development.	8.8 Psychosocial Development, 335-339; Concept Map, 340; Erikson's Generativity Versus Stagnation: Parenting, 352-353
Topic 6.3: Cognitive Development in Childhood		Chapter 8
	6.H: Explain the maturation of cognitive abilities (Piaget's stages, Information process).	8.7 Cognitive Development, 329-334; Table 8.3, 330; Figure 8.8, 331; Concept Map, 340; Chapter Summary, 358
	6.I: Identify the contributions of major researchers in the area of cognitive development in childhood.	8.7 Cognitive Development, 329-334; Concept Map, 340; Chapter Summary, 358
Topic 6.4: Adolescent Development		Chapter 8
	6.J: Discuss maturational challenges in adolescence, including related family conflicts.	8.12–8.14 Adolescence, 346-349; Concept Map, 349; Chapter Summary, 359
Topic 6.5: Adulthood and Aging		Chapter 8
	6.K: Characterize the development of decisions related to intimacy as people mature.	8.17 Psychosocial Development, 352–353; Chapter Summary, 359
	6.L: Predict the physical and cognitive changes that emerge through the lifespan, including steps that can be taken to maximize function.	8.15–8.20 Adulthood and Aging, 350-355; Concept Map, 356; Chapter Summary, 359
	6.M: Identify the contributions of key researchers in the area of adulthood and aging.	8.17 Psychosocial Development, 352–353; Chapter Summary, 359
Topic 6.6: Moral Development		Chapter 8
	6.N: Identify the contributions of major researchers in the area of moral development.	Moral Development, 347-348; Table 8.5, 348; Chapter Summary, 359
	6.O: Compare and contrast models of moral development.	Moral Development, 347-348; Table 8.5, 348; Chapter Summary, 359
Topic 6.7: Gender and Sexual Orientation		Chapter 8
	6.P: Describe how sex and gender influence socialization and other aspects of development.	8.9–8.11 Gender Development and Sexual Orientation, 342-344; Concept Map, 345; Chapter Summary, 358-359
Unit 7: Motivation, Emotion, and Personality		
Topic 7.1: Theories of Motivation		Chapters 8, 9, 10, 12
	7.A: Identify and apply basic motivational concepts to understand the behavior of humans and other animals.	9.1–9.5 Understanding Motivation, 364-372; Concept Map, 372; Chapter Summary, 393; Bandura's Reciprocal Determinism and Self-Efficacy, 497-498
	7.B: Compare and contrast motivational theories, including the strengths and weaknesses of each.	9.1–9.5 Understanding Motivation, 364-372; Concept Map, 372; Chapter Summary, 393; 10.7 Cognitive Factors in Stress, 415-416
	7.C: Describe classic research findings in specific motivations.	9.6–9.7 What, Hungry Again? Why People Eat, 374-378
	7.D: Identify contributions of key researchers in the psychological field of motivation and emotion.	Harlow and Contact Comfort, 337-338; 9.3 Different Strokes for Different Folks: Psychological Needs, 366-367; 9.5 Humanistic Approaches, 369-372; 9.9 Early Theories of Emotion, 385-387; 9.10 Cognitive Theories of Emotion, 387-390; The Angry/Happy Man, 388-389; Chapter Summary, 393-394; 10.4 The General Adaptation Syndrome, 408-409; Concept Map, 422-423; Chapter Summary, 432-433
Topic 7.2: Specific Topics in Motivation		Chapter 9
	7.E: Discuss the biological underpinnings of motivation, including needs, drives, and homeostasis.	9.2 Early Approaches to Understanding Motivation, 364-366; Concept Map, 372; Chapter Summary, 393

Advanced Placement Psychology Topics	Advanced Placement Psychology Learning Objectives	Ciccarelli/White, Psychology, AP Edition, 6th Edition, Chapter/Page Citations
Topic 7.3: Theories of Emotion		Chapters 9, 10
	7.F: Compare and contrast major theories of emotion.	9.8–9.10 Emotion, 379-390; Figure 9.12, 390; Concept Map, 391; Chapter Summary, 393-394; 10.7 Cognitive Factors in Stress, 415-416; Concept Map, 422-423; Chapter Summary, 433
	7.G: Describe how cultural influences shape emotional expression, including variations in body language.	The Behavior of Emotion: Emotional Expression, 382-384; Subjective Experience: Labeling Emotion, 384; Chapter Summary, 393; How Culture Affects Stress, 421-422; Concept Map, 422-423; 10.12 How Culture Affects Coping, 429-430; Concept Map, 431; Chapter Summary, 433
Topic 7.4: Stress and Coping		Chapter 10
	7.H: Discuss theories of stress and the effects of stress on psychological and physical well-being.	10.1–10.3 Stress and Stressors, 398-406, Concept Map, 407; 10.4–10.9 Physiological Factors: Stress and Health, 408-422; Concept Map 422-423; 10.10–10.13 Coping with Stress, 425-430; Concept Map, 431; Chapter Summary, 432-433
Topic 7.5: Introduction to Personality		Chapter 12
	7.I: Describe and compare research methods that psychologists use to investigate personality.	12.13–12.15 Personality: Genetics, Neuroscience, and Culture, 508-512; Concept Map, 514; 12.16–12.17 Assessment of Personality, 515-521; Table 12.5, 516; Concept Map, 521; Informally Assessing Personality, 522; Chapter Summary, 524
	7.J: Identify the contributions of major researchers in personality theory.	12.2 Freud's Conception of Personality, 487-489; 12.4 The Neo-Freudians, 492-494; Concept Map 495-496; 12.6 Learning Theories, 497-499; Concept Map, 500; 12.8 Carl Rogers and the Humanistic Perspective, 500-502; 12.10 Allport and Cattell: Early Attempts to List and Describe Traits, 504; 12.11 Modern Trait Theories: The Big Five, 505-506; Concept Map, 507; Chapter Summary, 522-523
Topic 7.6: Psychoanalytic Theories of Personality		Chapter 12
	7.K: Compare and contrast the psychoanalytic theories of personality with other theories of personality.	12.2–12.5 Psychodynamic Perspectives, 486-495; Concept Map, 495-496; Chapter Summary, 522-523
Topic 7.7: Behaviorism and Social Cognitive Theories of Personality		Chapter 12
	7.L: Compare and contrast the behaviorist and social cognitive theories of personality with other theories of personality.	12.6–12.7 The Behavioral and Social Cognitive View of Personality, 496-499; Concept Map, 500; Chapter Summary, 523
Topic 7.8: Humanistic Theories of Personality		Chapter 12
	7.M: Compare and contrast humanistic theories of personality with other theories of personality.	12.8–12.9 The Third Force: Humanism and Personality, 500-503; Concept Map, 503; Chapter Summary, 523
	7.N: Speculate how cultural context can facilitate or constrain personality development, especially as it relates to self-concept.	Geert Hofstede's Four Dimensions of Cultural Personality, 512-513; Personality, Family, and Culture, 514-515
Topic 7.9: Trait Theories of Personality		Chapter 12
	7.O: Compare and contrast trait theories of personality with other theories of personality.	12.10–12.12 Trait Theories: Who Are You?, 504-507; Concept Map, 507; Chapter Summary, 523-524
Topic 7.10: Measuring Personality		Chapter 12
	7.P: Identify frequently used assessment strategies, and evaluate relative test quality based on reliability and validity of the instruments.	12.16–12.17 Assessment of Personality, 515-521; Table 12.5, 516; Concept Map, 521; Informally Assessing Personality, 522; Chapter Summary, 524
Unit 8: Clinical Psychology		
Topic 8.1: Introduction to Psychological Disorders		Chapter 13
	8.A: Recognize the use of the most recent version of the *Diagnostic and Statistical Manual of Mental Disorders (DSM)* published by the American Psychiatric Association as the primary reference for making diagnostic judgments.	13.3 Diagnosing and Classifying Disorders, 533–537; Concept Map, 538; Chapter Summary, 568
	8.B: Describe contemporary and historical conceptions of what constitutes psychological disorders.	13.1 Changing Conceptions of Abnormality, 528-530; Chapter Summary, 567
	8.C: Discuss the intersection between psychology and the legal system.	A Working Definition of Abnormality, 529-530; Chapter Summary, 567

Advanced Placement Psychology Topics	Advanced Placement Psychology Learning Objectives	Ciccarelli/White, Psychology, AP Edition, 6th Edition, Chapter/Page Citations
Topic 8.2: Psychological Perspectives and Etiology of Disorders		Chapters 13
	8.D: Evaluate the strengths and limitations of various approaches to explaining psychological disorders.	13.2 Models of Abnormality, 530-532; Concept Map, 538; Chapter Summary, 567-568
	8.E: Identify the positive and negative consequences of diagnostic labels.	The Pros and Cons of Labels, 537–520
Topic 8.3: Neurodevelopmental and Schizophrenic Spectrum Disorders		Chapters 6, 8, 13
	8.F: Discuss the major diagnostic categories, including neurodevelopmental disorders, neurocognitive disorders, schizophrenia spectrum, and other psychotic disorders, and their corresponding symptoms.	Anterograde Amnesia, 262; Autism Spectrum Disorder, 334; 13.14–13.15 Schizophrenia: Altered Reality, 561-565; Concept Map, 565; Chapter Summary, 569
Topic 8.4: Bipolar, Depressive, Anxiety, and Obsessive-Compulsive and Related Disorders		Chapter 13
	8.G: Discuss the major diagnostic categories, including anxiety disorders, bipolar and related disorders, depressive disorders, obsessive-compulsive and related disorders, and their corresponding symptoms.	13.4–13.5 Disorders of Mood: The Effect of Affect; 539-544; Concept Map, 544; 13.6–13.8 Disorders of Anxiety, Trauma, and Stress: What, Me Worry?, 544-551; Table 13.2, 547; Concept Map, 551; Chapter Summary, 568
Topic 8.5: Trauma- and Stressor-Related, Dissociative, and Somatic Symptom and Related Disorders		Chapter 13
	8.H: Discuss the major diagnostic categories, including dissociative disorders, somatic symptom and related disorders, and trauma- and stressor-related disorders and their corresponding symptoms.	Acute Stress Disorder (ASD) and Posttraumatic Stress Disorder (PTSD), 548-549; Concept Map, 551; 13.9–13.10 Dissociative Disorders: Altered Identities, 552-554; Concept Map, 554; Chapter Summary, 568
Topic 8.6: Feeding and Eating, Substance and Addictive, and Personality Disorders		Chapters 9, 13
	8.I: Discuss the major diagnostic categories, including feeding and eating disorders, personality disorders, and their corresponding symptoms.	9.7 Obesity, 377-379; Concept Map, 379; 13.11 Eating Disorders, 555-557; Concept Map, 558; 13.12–13.13 Personality Disorders: I'm Okay, It's Everyone Else Who's Weird, 558-560; Concept Map, 560; Chapter Summary, 569
Topic 8.7: Introduction to Treatment of Psychological Disorders		Chapter 14
	8.J: Describe the central characteristics of psychotherapeutic intervention.	14.1 Treatment of Psychological Disorders: Past to Present, 574-575; Concept Map, 575; Chapter Summary, 615
	8.K: Identify the contributions of major figures in psychological treatment.	14.2–14.3 Insight Therapies: Psychodynamic and Humanistic Approaches, 576- 581; Concept Map, 581–582; 14.4–14.5 Action Therapies: Behavior Therapies and Cognitive Therapies, 583-591; Table 14.2, 591; Chapter Summary 615-616
Topic 8.8: Psychological Perspectives and Treatment of Disorders		Chapter 14
	8.L: Describe major treatment orientations used in therapy and how those orientations influence therapeutic planning.	14.2–14.3 Insight Therapies: Psychodynamic and Humanistic Approaches, 576- 581; Concept Map, 581–582; 14.4–14.5 Action Therapies: Behavior Therapies and Cognitive Therapies, 583-591; Table 14.2, 591; 14.10–14.12 Biomedical Therapies, 602-610; Concept Map, 611; Chapter Summary 615-617
	8.M: Summarize effectiveness of specific treatments used to address specific problems.	Evaluation of Psychoanalysis and Psychodynamic Approaches, 577-578; Evaluation of the Humanistic Therapies, 581; Concept Map, 581-582; Evaluation of Behavior Therapies, 587–588; Evaluation of Cognitive and Cognitive-Behavioral Therapies, 590; Concept Map, 591; 14.7 Evaluation of Group Therapy, 593-594; Concept Map, 594; 14.8–14.9 Does Psychotherapy Really Work?, 595–600; Concept Map, 600; Does It Work? Psychological Treatment, 601-602; 14.10–14.12 Biomedical Therapies, 602-610; Chapter Summary, 615-617
	8.N: Discuss how cultural and ethnic context influence choice and success of treatment (e.g., factors that lead to premature termination of treatment)	Cultural, Ethnic, and Gender Concerns in Psychotherapy, 598-600; Concept Map, 600; How to Help Others: Reducing the Stigma of Seeking Help, 614-615; Chapter Summary, 616
	8.O: Describe prevention strategies that build resilience and promote competence.	14.6–14.7 Group Therapies: Not Just for the Shy, 592-594; Concept Map, 594; 14.13 Lifestyle Factors: Fostering Resilience, 612-613; Concept Map, 613; Chapter Summary, 616-617

Advanced Placement Psychology Topics	Advanced Placement Psychology Learning Objectives	Ciccarelli/White, Psychology, AP Edition, 6th Edition, Chapter/Page Citations
Topic 8.9: Treatment of Disorders from the Biological Perspective		Chapter 14
	8.P: Summarize effectiveness of specific treatments used to address specific problems from a biological perspective.	14.12 Biomedical Therapies, 602-610; Concept Map, 611; Chapter Summary, 616-617
Topic 8.10: Evaluating Strengths, Weaknesses, and Empirical Support for Treatments of Disorders		Chapter 14
	8.Q: Compare and contrast different treatment methods.	Evaluation of Psychoanalysis and Psychodynamic Approaches, 577-578; Evaluation of the Humanistic Therapies, 581; Concept Map, 581–582; Evaluation of Behavior Therapies, 587–588; Evaluation of Cognitive and Cognitive-Behavioral Therapies, 590; Concept Map, 591; 14.7 Evaluation of Group Therapy, 593-594; Concept Map, 594; 14.8–14.9 Does Psychotherapy Really Work?, 595–600; Concept Map, 600; Does It Work? Psychological Treatment, 601-602; 14.10–14.12 Biomedical Therapies, 602-610; Chapter Summary, 615-617
Unit 9: Social Psychology		
Topic 9.1: Attribution Theory and Person Perception		Chapters 1, 8, 11, 12
	9.A: Apply attribution theory to explain motives.	11.9 Attribution, 458–460; Concept Map, 460; Chapter Summary, 480; Evaluating Behavioral Assessments, Interviews, and Personality Inventories, 518-519
	9.B: Articulate the impact of social and cultural categories on self-concept and relations with others.	Sociocultural Perspective, 12; Who Am I? The Development of the Self-Concept, 338; 11.10–11.15 Social Interaction, 461-477; Concept Map, 477-478; Chapter Summary, 480-481
	9.C: Anticipate the impact of self-fulfilling prophecy on behavior.	Stereotype Vulnerability, 464-465; Chapter Summary, 481
Topic 9.2: Attitude Formation and Attitude Change		Chapter 11
	9.D: Identify important figures and research in the areas of attitude formation and change.	11.7 Cognitive Dissonance: When Attitudes and Behavior Clash, 454-456
	9.E: Discuss attitude formation and change, including persuasion strategies and cognitive dissonance.	11.5–11.9 Social Cognition, 450-460; Concept Map, 460; Chapter Summary, 480
Topic 9.3: Conformity, Compliance, and Obedience		Chapter 11
	9.F: Identify the contributions of key researchers in the areas of conformity, compliance, and obedience.	11.1–11.4 Social Influence, 438-448; Concept Map, 448; Chapter Summary, 479
	9.G: Explain how individuals respond to expectations of others, including groupthink, conformity, and obedience to authority.	11.1–11.4 Social Influence, 438-448; Table 11.1, 441; Concept Map, 448; Chapter Summary, 479
Topic 9.4: Group Influences on Behavior and Mental Processes		Chapter 11
	9.H: Describe the structure and function of different kinds of group behavior.	11.2 Group Behavior, 440-443; Concept Map, 448; Chapter Summary, 479
	9.I: Predict the impact of the presence of others on individual behavior.	11.2 Group Behavior, 440-443; 11.3 Compliance, 443-444; 11.4 Obedience, 444-448; Concept Map, 448; 11.15 Prosocial Behavior, 474-477; Concept Map, 477-478; Chapter Summary, 479-481
Topic 9.5: Bias, Prejudice, and Discrimination		Chapter 11
	9.J: Describe processes that contribute to differential treatment of group members.	11.10 Prejudice and Discrimination, 461-463; 11.11 How People Learn and Overcome Prejudice, 463-466; Concept Map, 477-478; Chapter Summary, 480-481
Topic 9.6: Altruism and Aggression		Chapter 11
	9.K: Describe the variables that contribute to altruism and aggression.	11.14 Aggression, 469-474; 11.15 Prosocial Behavior, 474-477; Concept Map, 477-478; Chapter Summary, 481
Topic 9.7: Interpersonal Attraction		Chapter 11
	9.L: Describe the variables that contribute to attraction.	11.12 Interpersonal Attraction, 466-468; Concept Map, 477-478; Chapter Summary, 481

Preface

Content Highlights

Our goal is to awaken students' curiosity and energize their desire to learn by having them read and engage with the material. The sixth edition builds upon the strengths of previous editions, with particular focus on the application of psychological principles to students' lives. A completely revised feature, *Applying Psychology to Everyday Life*, features students describing in their own words the intersection of concepts in psychology with their personal experiences in daily life. A new appendix, *Applied Psychology and Psychology Careers*, examines the research findings and methods of industrial-organizational psychologists. It also provides resources for learning more about a career in the I-O field with a focus on APA Goal 5: Professional Development. With the dynamic learning aids of previous editions as a foundation, digital materials for this edition allow students to experience figures, graphs, and tables as part of an active learning process. Instead of simply looking and reading, the student is *doing* things with the digital materials. This format will truly help students engage in the learning process and will also help instructors make classroom presentations more vivid and attention grabbing.

DYNAMIC VIDEOS AND ARTWORK

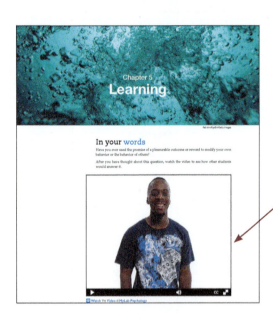

Chapter-Opening Student Voice Videos
Chapters open with videos in which psychology students share personal stories about how the chapter theme directly applies to their lives.

Applying Psychology to Everyday Life Pearson Originals Video Series
Fifteen new videos have been filmed for this edition. These videos show current college students discussing where they see a variety of key concepts from introductory psychology in their own lives, from being conditioned by their cell phones to overcoming test anxiety to finding mental health resources on campus. This new Pearson Originals video series invites students to reflect on how psychology applies to their everyday experiences.

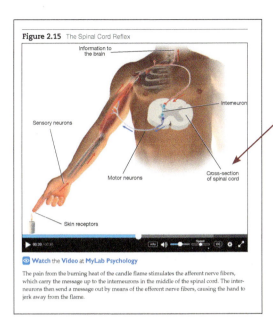

Biological Artwork and Animations
Biological artwork is designed in a contemporary aesthetic and includes detailed reference figures as well as animations of key biological processes.

EMPHASIS ON APA LEARNING GOALS

We have used the APA goals and assessment recommendations as guidelines for structuring our content. For the sixth edition, we have placed even greater emphasis on these goals.

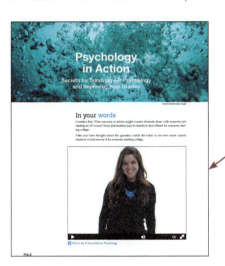

Psychology in Action Chapter
Structured around eight modules, this chapter addresses many of the APA learning goals for the undergraduate major. Each module is accompanied by a study tip video.

Chapter Feature on APA Goal 2: Scientific Inquiry and Critical Thinking
Each chapter includes a special feature that reinforces scientific inquiry and critical thinking skills. Students are introduced to a psychological topic and then encouraged to practice their skills using a hands-on example.

EMBEDDED INTERACTIVE CONTENT

Interactive content has been fully incorporated into all aspects of the title, allowing students a more direct way to access and engage with the material.

Figure 5.11 Bandura's Bobo Doll Experiment

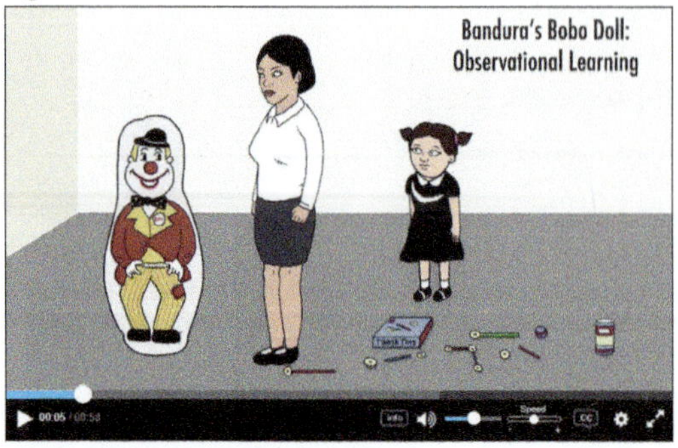

Watch the **Video** at **MyLab Psychology**

In Albert Bandura's famous Bobo doll experiment, the doll was used to demonstrate the impact of observing an adult model performing aggressive behavior on the later aggressive behavior of children.

Watch **Videos** of topics as they are explained.

Figure 5.5 Graph of the Time to Learn in Thorndike's Experiment

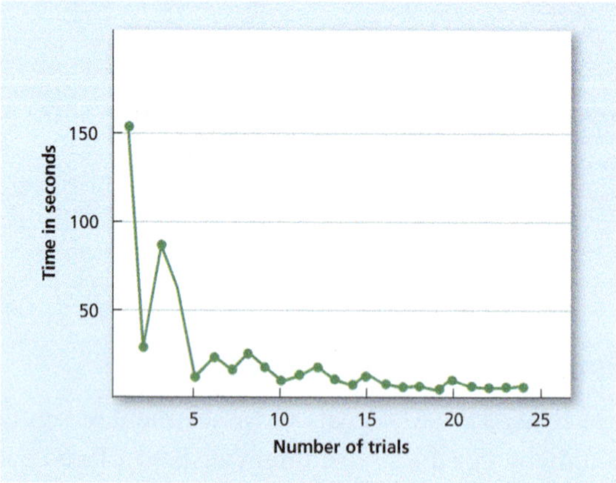

This is one of the earliest "learning curves" in the history of the experimental study of conditioning. The time required by one of Thorndike's cats to escape from the puzzle box gradually decreased with trials but with obvious reversals.

Interactive Figures and Tables walk students through some of the more complex processes in psychology and offer students the ability to evaluate their knowledge of key topics.

Survey Do You Fly or Fight?

Take the **Survey** at **MyPsychLab**

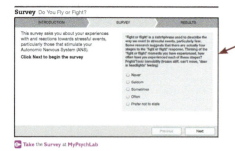

Simulate **experiments** and answer **surveys** right from the narrative.

Concept Map L.O. 2.4, 2.5

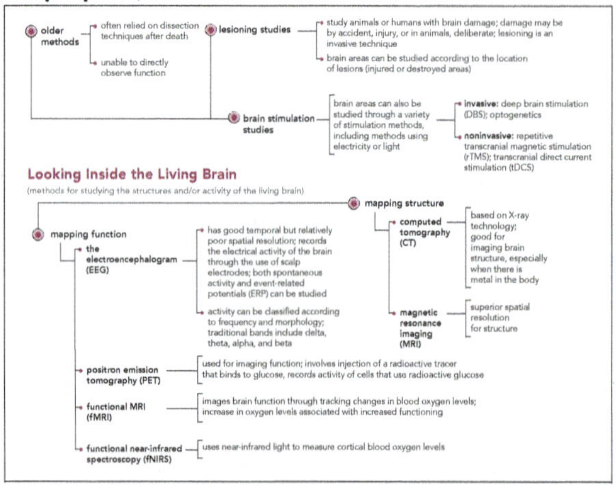

Reinforce connections across topics with **Concept Maps**.

Teaching and Learning Resources

It is increasingly true today that as valuable as a good textbook is, it is still only one element of a comprehensive learning package. The teaching and learning package that accompanies *Psychology*, 6e, AP edition, is the most comprehensive and integrated on the market. We have made every effort to provide high-quality instructor resources that will save you preparation time and will enhance the time you spend in the classroom.

MYLAB PSYCHOLOGY

MyLab Psychology is an online homework, tutorial, and assessment program that truly engages students in learning. It helps students better prepare for classes, quizzes, and exams—resulting in better performance in the course—and provides educators with a dynamic set of tools for gauging individual and class progress. MyLab Psychology comes from Pearson, your partner in providing the best digital learning experience.

INSTRUCTOR RESOURCES

A robust set of instructor resources and multimedia accompanies the text and can be accessed through MyLab Psychology.

Lecture PowerPoint Slides These accessible PowerPoint slides provide an active format for presenting concepts from each chapter and feature relevant figures and tables from the text.

Art PowerPoint Slides These slides contain only the photos, figures, and line art from the textbook.

Instructor's Resource Manual offers learning objectives, chapter rapid reviews, detailed chapter lecture outlines, lecture launchers, activities, assignments, and handouts.

Test Bank The Test Bank contains more than 5,000 questions and each chapter includes a Total Assessment Guide (TAG), an easy-to-reference grid that organizes all test questions by Learning Objective and Skill Level. Each question is mapped to the textbook by learning objective and the major text section, or topic. Questions are additionally assigned with the appropriate skill level and difficulty level and the American Psychological Association (APA) learning objective.

Pearson MyTest The Test Bank is also available through Pearson MyTest, a powerful assessment generation program that helps instructors easily create and print quizzes and exams. Questions and tests can be authored online, allowing instructors ultimate flexibility. For more information, go to **www.PearsonMyTest.com**.

STUDENT RESOURCES

Pearson's Test Prep Series for AP Psychology This student workbook contains concise content summaries of each chapter, AP-style multiple-choice and free-response practice questions tied to the learning objectives for each chapter, and two full practice exams, including scoring guidelines. An innovative Study Hints section helps students with the most difficult to understand concepts from every chapter. Available for purchase.

PREVIEW AND ADOPTION PROCESS

Upon textbook purchase, students and teachers are granted access to MyLab Psychology with Pearson eText. High school teachers can obtain preview or adoption access in one of the following ways:

Preview Access

- Teachers can request preview access by visiting Savvas.com/Access_Request. Select Initial Access then using Option 2, select your discipline and title from the drop-down menu and complete the online form. Preview Access information will be sent to the teacher via email.

Adoption Access

- Upon purchase teachers can request course adoption access by visiting Savvas.com/Access_Request. Select Initial Access then using Option 3, select your discipline and title from the drop-down menu and complete the online form. Access codes and registration instructions will be sent to the requester via email.

OR

- Ask your Account General Manager for an Adoption Access Code Card (ISBN: 0-13-034391-9)

Students, ask your teacher about access

Pearson reserves the right to change and/or update technology platforms, including possible edition updates to customers during the term of access. This will allow Pearson to continue to deliver the most up-to-date content and technology to customers. Customer will be notified of any change prior to the beginning of the new school year.

Learning Outcomes and Assessment

LEARNING OBJECTIVES

Based on APA recommendations, each chapter is structured around detailed learning objectives. All of the instructor and student resources are also organized around these objectives, making the text and resources a fully integrated system of study. The flexibility of these resources allows instructors to choose which learning objectives are important in their courses as well as the content on which they want their students to focus.

About the Authors

SAUNDRA K. CICCARELLI is a professor emeritus of psychology at Gulf Coast State College in Panama City, Florida. She received her Ph.D. in developmental psychology from George Peabody College of Vanderbilt University, Nashville, Tennessee. She is a member of the American Psychological Association and the Association for Psychological Science. Originally interested in a career as a researcher in the development of language and intelligence in developmentally delayed children and adolescents, Dr. Ciccarelli had publications in the *American Journal of Mental Deficiency* while still at Peabody. However, she discovered a love of teaching early on in her career. This led her to the position at Gulf Coast State College, where she taught Introductory Psychology and Human Development for more than 30 years. Her students loved her enthusiasm for the field of psychology and the many anecdotes and examples she used to bring psychology to life for them. Before writing this title, Dr. Ciccarelli authored numerous ancillary materials for several introductory psychology and human development texts.

J. NOLAND WHITE is a professor of psychology at Georgia College & State University (Georgia College), Georgia's Public Liberal Arts University, located in Milledgeville. He received his A.A. in psychology from Macon State College and both his B.S. and M.S. in psychology from Georgia College. After receiving his Ph.D. in counseling psychology from the University of Tennessee, he joined the faculty of Georgia College in 2001. He teaches Introductory Psychology, Psychology of Adjustment, Behavioral Neuroscience, Advanced Behavioral Neuroscience, Counseling and Clinical Psychology, Senior Seminar, and a section of Advanced Research Methods focusing on psychophysiology. He has an active lab and, with his students, is investigating the psychophysiological characteristics and neuropsychological performance of adults with and without ADHD. Outside of the lab, Dr. White is engaged in collaborative research examining the effectiveness of incorporating various technologies in and out of the college classroom to facilitate student learning. He also serves as a mentor for other faculty wanting to expand their use of technology with their classes. In April 2008, he was a recipient of the Georgia College Excellence in Teaching Award. Dr. White is also a licensed psychologist and has worked with adolescents and adults in a variety of clinical and community settings.

Acknowledgments

I have to thank my husband, Joe Ciccarelli, for his love and support while I spent many long hours writing and editing this textbook. My children, Al and Liz, also put up with my odd working hours and frequent trips and deserve my thanks as well.

There are so many people to thank for their support! Erin Mitchell supported and advised me—thank you so much.

We are grateful to all of the instructors and students who have contributed to the development of this title and package over the last six editions. We thank the hundreds of folks who have reviewed content, participated in focus groups, evaluated learning tools, appeared in videos, and offered their feedback and assistance in numerous other ways. We thank you.

Special thanks to Carolyn Schweitzer, our development editor, who fit right into our editing process and has been a wonderful addition to the team. Thanks, Carolyn! Thanks also to Jennifer Stevenson, who did a great job of herding cats and keeping us all sane in the process. Thanks, Jen!

And, of course, I can't forget Noland White, my coauthor, pal, and Grand High Expert. His expertise in neuropsychology and clinical psychology is a valuable resource, and his revisions of half of the chapters and all of the chapter maps have once again made this edition a real standout. I owe a huge debt of gratitude to Noland for his support during this process. Hurricane Michael struck the Florida Panhandle in October 2018, devastating our area and damaging or destroying nearly every single home and business in its path. Noland was my rock while we worked to finish this edition and I simply cannot thank him enough. You are one in a million, and I bless the day we met! Thank you from the bottom of my heart, buddy! And give my foster "grands" a hug from Nana Sandy.

Sandy Ciccarelli
Gulf Coast State College
Panama City, Florida
sandy243@comcast.net

I want to thank personally:

My wife and best friend, Leah, and our wonderful children, Sierra, Alexis, and Landon, thank you for your love and patience through the long hours and many absences. I would not be able to do any of this without you;

My lead author and collaborator, Sandy Ciccarelli, for making all of this possible—and for your friendship, encouragement, assistance, advice, and continuing to be the most amazing mentor and writing partner with whom I could ever hope to work! Thank you for your support and your trust;

My students, for your inspiration, encouragement, and for all of the things you continue to teach me;

The student and faculty users and reviewers of this text, for your support and ever-helpful comments and suggestions;

My friends and colleagues in the Department of Psychological Science at Georgia College, for your encouragement, frequent discussions, and feedback, with special thanks to Lee Gillis, John Lindsay, and Greg Jarvie for your input and support along the way. And to Walt Isaac, Kristina Dandy, and Diana Young, thank you for your contributions and continuing willingness to be "on call" reviewers!

Erin Mitchell, Jen Stevenson, and Kelli Strieby, for your guidance, collaboration, and awesomeness!

Denise Forlow, for doing such a fantastic job getting the AP Edition ready, and Stephen Foley for all of your contributions, work on the FRQ's, and for sharing your AP Psychology expertise!

All of the Pearson and associated staff, for your contributions and continuing to make this such a great experience!

Noland White
Georgia College & State University
Milledgeville, Georgia
noland.white@gcsu.edu

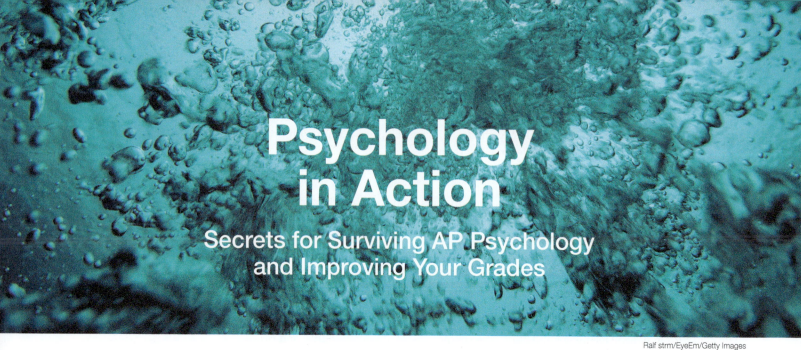

Psychology in Action

Secrets for Surviving AP Psychology and Improving Your Grades

Ralf strm/EyeEm/Getty Images

In your words

Consider this: What concerns or advice might current students share with someone just starting an AP course? Some information may be similar to that offered for someone starting college.

After you have thought about the question, watch the video to see how some current students would answer it for someone starting college.

Watch the Video at MyLab Psychology

Why study how to study?

Many students entering an AP course have developed a system of taking notes, reading the textbook, and reviewing for exams that may have worked pretty well in the past; but what worked in past classes may not be enough in an AP class, where the expectations from teachers are higher and the workload is far greater. Students should develop skills in the following areas in order to do their absolute best in any college-level course: study methods, time and task management, effective reading of course materials, active listening and note taking, studying for exams, memory strategies, and writing papers. One final aspect of being a successful student involves being an ethical student—exactly how can you use the materials you find for your research paper, for example, without committing the sin of *plagiarism* (claiming the work of someone else as your own)?

This introduction presents various techniques and information aimed at maximizing knowledge and skills in each of these eight areas. In addition, brief videos are available on each of these topics. These topics address aspects of the American Psychological Association's (APA) undergraduate learning goals. APA Goal 2 (Scientific Inquiry and Critical Thinking) is addressed in Chapter One and is the basis of a feature in every chapter.

Learning Objectives

PIA.1 Identify four methods of studying.

PIA.2 Describe some strategies for time and task management.

PIA.3 Describe how to read a textbook so that you get the most out of your reading efforts.

PIA.4 Identify the best methods for taking notes and listening in class.

PIA.5 Describe how to approach studying for exams.

PIA.6 Explain how using mnemonics can help you improve your memory for facts and concepts.

PIA.7 Describe the key steps in writing papers.

PIA.8 Identify some of the key ethical considerations you'll face as a student.

PIA.1 Study Skills

PIA.1 Identify four methods of studying.

Some students find it helpful to hear the content in addition to reading it. This is especially true when learning a new language. This woman is listening to an audio recording from her textbook as she follows along and looks at the figures and photos.

💬 I want to make better grades, but sometimes it seems that no matter how hard I study, the test questions turn out to be hard and confusing and I end up not doing very well. Is there some trick to getting good grades?

Many students would probably say their grades are not what they want them to be. They may make the effort, but they still don't seem to be able to achieve the higher grades they wish they could earn. A big part of the problem is that despite many different educational experiences, students are rarely taught how to study.

We learn many different kinds of things during our lives, and using only one method of learning probably isn't going to work for everyone. Students may have preferences for a particular study method or may find it useful to use a combination of different methods. *Verbal study methods* involve the use of words, expressed either through writing or speaking. For instance, after you read about a topic, you might put it into your own words, or you might write out longer, more detailed versions of the notes you took in class. *Visual learning methods* involve the use of pictures or images. Students using these methods may look at or create charts, diagrams, and figures to master the content. There are also those who prefer to learn by hearing the information (*auditory learning methods*). Listening to a recording of a lecture is a good example. Finally, there are people who use the motion of their own bodies to help them remember key information (*action learning methods*). For instance, you might construct a three-dimensional model to gain a better understanding of a topic.

THINKING CRITICALLY PIA.1

Describe some other ways in which the various study methods can be put to use.

Table PIA.1 lists just some of the ways in which you can study. All of the methods listed in this table are good for students who wish to improve both their understanding of a subject and their grades on tests.

Watch Study Methods

👁 Watch the Video at MyLab Psychology

Table PIA.1 Multiple Study Methods

Verbal Methods (involve speaking or writing)	Visual Methods (involve pictures, images)	Auditory Methods (involve listening)	Action Methods (involve physical activity)
Use flash cards to identify main points or key terms.	Make flash cards with pictures or diagrams to aid recall of key terms.	Join or form a study group or find a study partner so you can discuss concepts and ideas.	Sit near the front of the classroom. If online, give yourself room to walk around while studying. Take notes by making pictures or charts to help you remember key terms and ideas.
Write out or recite key information in whole sentences or phrases in your own words.	Make charts and diagrams and sum up information in tables.	Take advantage of the various videos and audio recordings in MyLab Psychology.	Read out loud, or use the audio feature in your eText while walking around.
When looking at diagrams, write out a description.	Use different colors of highlighter for different sections of information in text, e-text, or notes.	Make speeches.	Study with a friend.
Use physical or electronic "sticky" notes to remind yourself of key terms and information.	Visualize charts, diagrams, and figures.	Record class lectures (with permission). Take notes on the lecture sparingly, using the recording to fill in parts you might have missed.	While exercising, listen to recordings of important information, either your own or those in your eText.
Practice spelling words or repeating facts to be remembered.	Trace letters and words to remember key facts.	Read notes, text, or study materials out loud into a digital recorder, and listen to them while exercising or doing chores.	Write out key concepts on a large board or poster.
Rewrite things from memory.	Use the interactive simulations, activities, and videos available in MyLab Psychology.	When learning something new, state or explain the information in your own words out loud or to a study partner.	Make your own flash cards, using different colors and diagrams, and lay them out in order on a large surface.
	Redraw things from memory.	Use musical rhythms as memory aids, or put information to a rhyme or a tune.	Make a three-dimensional model.
			Spend extra time in the lab.
			Go to off-campus areas such as a museum or historical site to gain information.

Concept Map L.O. PIA.1

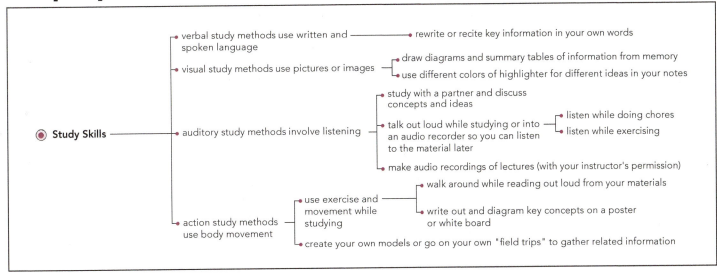

Practice Quiz   How much do you remember?

Pick the best answer.

1. In an episode of a popular television program, a detective reconstructs a crime scene by using various foods from his dinner table. He uses ears of corn to represent the cars, mashed potatoes to form the sides of the road, and so on. What method of learning best fits the method this character seems to be using to think about the events of the crime?
   a. verbal
   b. visual
   c. auditory
   d. olfactory
   e. action

2. Jace has been advised by a learning expert to study employing techniques like using flash cards, writing out important points in his own words and then reciting them, using sticky notes to emphasize important points, and creating descriptions of figures and images. Jace's tutor is recommending the use of _____ study methods.
   a. auditory
   b. action
   c. visual
   d. kinesthetic
   e. verbal

PIA.2 Managing Time and Tasks

PIA.2 Describe some strategies for time and task management.

One of the biggest failings of students (and many others) is managing the time for all the tasks involved. Procrastination, the tendency to put off tasks until some later time that often does not arrive, is the enemy of time management. There are some strategies to defeating procrastination (The College Board, 2011):

- Make a map of your long-term goals. If you are starting here, what are the paths you need to take to get to your ultimate goal?
- Use a calendar to keep track of class times, time devoted to studying, time for writing papers, work times, social engagements, everything! Use the calendar app on your phone, tablet, or computer—or all three.
- Before you go to bed, plan your next day, starting with when you get up and prioritizing your tasks for that day. Mark tasks off as you do them.
- Go to bed. Getting enough sleep is a necessary step in managing your tasks. Eating right and walking or stretching between tasks is a good idea, too.

- If you have big tasks, break them down into smaller, more manageable pieces. For example, if you have to write a paper, divide the task into smaller ones, such as making an outline or writing the introductory paragraph. How do you eat an elephant? One bite at a time.
- Do small tasks, like taking a practice quiz or writing the first paragraph of a paper, in those bits of time you might otherwise dismiss: riding the bus to school or work, waiting in a doctor's office, and so on.
- Build in some play time—all work and no play pretty much ensures you will fail at keeping your schedule. Use play time as a reward for getting tasks done.
- If your schedule falls apart, don't panic—just start again the next day. Even the best time managers have days when things don't go as planned.

Another problem that often interferes with time management is the enduring myth that we can effectively multitask. In today's world of technological interconnectedness, people tend to believe they can learn to do more than one task at a time. The fact, however, is that the human mind is not meant to multitask, and trying to do so not only can lead to car wrecks and other disasters but also may result in changes in how individuals process and retain different types of information, and not for the better. One study challenged college students to perform experiments that involved task switching, selective attention, and working memory (Ophir et al., 2009). The expectation was that students who were experienced at multitasking would outperform those who were not, but the results were just the opposite: The "chronic multitaskers" failed miserably at all three tasks. The results seemed to indicate that frequent multitaskers use their brains less effectively, even when focusing on a single task. Other research supports observations that chronic, or heavy media multitaskers, individuals who frequently use multiple media simultaneously, have difficulty ignoring distracting information, even when instructed to do so (Cain & Mitroff, 2011). Heavy media multitaskers also have reduced performance on tasks requiring working memory, or keeping things in mind, which subsequently has a negative effect on long-term memory, affecting both encoding and retrieval of information (Uncapher et al., 2016). See Learning Objectives 6.1, 6.4, 6.5.

Yet other studies have found that students who multitask while studying or in class tend to have lower grade point averages or performance than students who do not multitask (Junco & Cotton, 2012; Rosen et al., 2013; Uncapher et al., 2017; Wood et al., 2012). Furthermore, multitasking during class has a negative impact on those around the multitasker. Not only do students who multitask with laptops in class have impaired comprehension of the class material, but students who can see the students' screens also have lower performance (Sana et al., 2013). Researchers also have found that people who think they are good at multitasking are actually not (Sanbonmatsu et al., 2013), while still another study indicates that video gamers, who often feel their success at gaming is training them to be good multitaskers in other areas of life such as texting or talking while driving, are just as unsuccessful at multitasking as nongamers (Donohue et al., 2012). In short, it's better to focus on one task and only one task for a short period of time before moving on to another than to try to do two things at once.

Besides being aware of how to best manage your available time, what else can you do to make sure you complete the tasks you need to finish or address the commitments you've made? Many students find it difficult to keep track of all of their class assignments and projects and to remember all of the things they are supposed to do—and when to do them. Keeping on task can be especially challenging when you might not be exactly thrilled about doing some of them in the first place. Common pitfalls such as distractions, being too busy, and being overloaded can also wreak havoc on the best of intentions (Allen et al., 2018).

Watch Managing Time

Watch the Video at MyLab Psychology

The book *Getting Things Done: The Art of Stress-Free Productivity* by David Allen and his "Getting Things Done" (or GTD) methodology can provide a useful structure for a wide range of people who need help in, well, getting things done (Allen, 2001, 2008).

The GTD method consists of five stages of processing your "stuff" into actual outcomes, identifying "next actions" you can actually take to gain and maintain control of your tasks and commitments. The five stages of the GTD method are:

1. Capture anything and everything that has your attention by writing it down or entering it into your phone, tablet, or computer, getting it out of your head and collected in one place. This place can be a digital location like an app on your phone or computer or a paper-based spot such as a folder, a notebook, a set of index cards, or the like.

2. Process and define what you can take action on and identify the next steps. For example, instead of "do my research paper," identify actionable next steps such as "pinpoint topic, collect articles, schedule meeting to discuss ideas with classmates." Use the "two-minute rule"; if whatever you need to do takes less than 2 minutes, go ahead and do it.

3. Organize information and reminders into categories or contexts, based on how and when you need them. For example, if you need to send an email or text message to your group partners, you probably need to have your phone or computer to do so; "phone" or "computer" might be a context that you use.

4. Complete weekly reviews of your projects, next actions, and new items. To get things done, you need to review what you need to do.

5. Do your next actions in the appropriate context or time frame for doing so.

Adapted from David Allen's *Getting Things Done: The Art of Stress-Free Productivity* (2001) and *Making It All Work* (2008), and from *Getting Things Done for Teens: Take Control of Your Life in a Distracting World* (Allen et al., 2018).

Watch the video *The GTD Method* to learn more.

Watch The GTD Method

Watch the Video at MyLab Psychology

Concept Map L.O. PIA.2

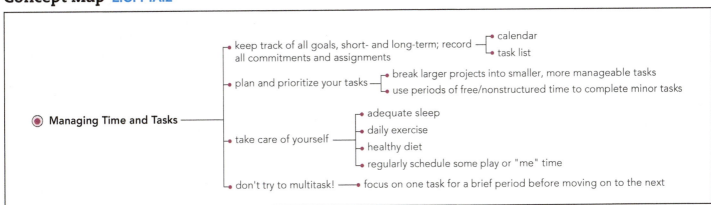

Practice Quiz — How much do you remember?

Pick the best answer.

1. Which of the following is *not* a question that students should ask themselves in order to maximize their studying effectiveness?
   a. How can I spread out my study periods to take advantage of distributed practice?
   b. How can I make sure I get enough sleep, exercise, and proper nutrition to maximize my study efforts?
   c. How can I improve my memory for facts and concepts?
   d. How can I best manage my time and avoid procrastination?
   e. How can I write good term papers?

2. Which of the following is a suggestion to help you with time management skills?
   a. Only look at the syllabus at the beginning of the semester. If an assignment or deadline is important, you will remember it.
   b. When you have a big project to complete, try to complete it all at once rather than breaking it down into smaller pieces so that you don't put it off until later.
   c. Try to focus only on short-term goals, since looking at long-term goals can be defeating and upsetting.
   d. Build in some play time, using it as a reward for getting tasks done.
   e. If your schedule falls apart, make sure to panic immediately!

3. What does the research indicate regarding multitasking?
   a. Chronic multitaskers have developed strategies that allow them to use their brains more effectively.
   b. Chronic multitasking may be related to less effective ways of processing different types of information.
   c. Multitasking is effective, but only if you limit the number of tasks to five or fewer.
   d. Video gamers are better at multitasking in all areas of life.
   e. Students who multitask while studying tend to have higher grades than students who do not multitask.

PIA.3 Reading the Text: Textbooks Are Not Meatloaf

PIA.3 Describe how to read a textbook so that you get the most out of your reading efforts.

No matter what the study method, students must read the textbook or other assigned course materials to be successful in the course. (While that might seem obvious to some, many students today seem to think that just taking notes on lectures or slide presentations will be enough.) This section deals with how to read textbooks—whether in print or online—for understanding rather than just to "get through" the material.

Students make two common mistakes in regard to reading a textbook. The first mistake is simple: Many students don't bother to read the textbook *before* watching the lecture that will cover that material. Trying to get anything out of a lecture without having read the material first is like trying to find a new, unfamiliar place without using a GPS or any kind of directions. It's easy to get lost. This is especially true because of the assumption that most instructors make when planning their lectures: They take for granted that the students have already read the assignment. The instructors then use the lecture to go into detail about the information the students supposedly got from the reading. If the students have not done the reading, the instructor's lecture isn't going to make a whole lot of sense.

The second mistake most students make when reading textbook material is to try to read it the same way they would read a novel: They start at the beginning and read continuously. With a novel, it's easy to do this because the plot is usually interesting and people want to know what happens next, so they keep reading. It isn't necessary to remember every little detail—all they need to remember are the main plot points. One could say that a novel is like meatloaf—some meaty parts with lots of filler. Meatloaf can be eaten quickly, without even chewing for very long.

With a textbook, the material may be interesting but not in the same way that a novel is interesting. A textbook is a big, thick steak—all meat, no filler. Just as a steak has to be chewed to be enjoyed and to be useful to the body, textbook material has to be "chewed" with the mind. You have to read slowly, paying attention to every morsel of meaning.

So how do you do that? Probably one of the best-known reading methods is called SQ3R, first used by F. P. Robinson in a 1946 book *Effective Study*. The letters S-Q-R-R-R stand for:

Survey

Look at the chapter you've been assigned to read. Read the outline, learning objectives, or other opening materials. Then scan the chapter and read the headings of sections, and look at tables and figures. Quickly read through the chapter summary if one is provided.

It might sound like it takes too much time to do this, but you should just be skimming at this point—a couple of minutes is all it should take. Why do this at all? Surveying the chapter, or "previewing" it, as some experts call it, helps you form a framework in your head around which you can organize the information in the chapter when you read it in detail. Organization is one of the main ways to improve your memory for information. See Learning Objective 6.5.

Before reading any chapter in a text, survey the chapter by reading the outline and the section headings.

Question

After previewing the chapter, read the heading for the first section. *Just* the first section! Try to think of a question based on this heading that the section should answer as you read. For example, in Chapter One there's a section titled "Pavlov, Watson, and the Dawn of Behaviorism." You could ask yourself, "What did Pavlov and Watson do for psychology?" or "What is behaviorism?" In this text, we've presented a list of learning objectives for the key concepts in the chapter that can be used with the SQ3R method. There are also student questions highlighted throughout the chapters that can serve the same purpose. Now when you read the section, you aren't *just* reading—you're reading to *find an answer*. That makes the material much easier to remember later on.

Read

Now read the section, looking for the answers to your questions. As you read, take notes by making an outline of the main points and terms in the section. This is another area where some students make a big mistake. They assume that highlighting words and phrases is as good as writing notes. One of the author's former students conducted research on the difference between highlighting and note taking, and her findings were clear: Students who wrote their own notes during the reading of a text or while listening to a lecture scored significantly higher on their exam grades than students who merely highlighted the text (Boyd & Peeler, 2004). Highlighting requires no real mental effort (no "chewing," in other words), but writing the words down yourself requires you to read the words in depth and to understand them. When we study memory, you'll learn more about the value of processing information in depth. See Learning Objective 6.2.

As you read, take notes. Write down key terms and try to summarize the main points of each paragraph and section in the chapter. These notes will be useful when you later review the chapter material.

Recite

It may sound silly, but reciting out loud what you can remember from the section you've just read is another good way to process the information more deeply and completely. How many times have you thought you understood something, only to find that when you tried to explain it to someone, you didn't understand it at all?

Recitation forces you to put the information in your own words—just as writing it in notes does. Writing it down accesses your visual memory; saying it out loud gives you an auditory memory for the same information. If you have ever learned something well by teaching it to someone else, you already know the value of recitation. If you feel self-conscious about talking to yourself, talk into a digital recorder—it's a great way to review later.

Now repeat the Question, Read, and Recite instructions for each section, taking a few minutes' break after every two or three sections. Why take a break? There's a process that has to take place in your brain when you are trying to form a permanent memory for information, and that process takes a little time. When you take a break every 10 to 20 minutes, you are giving your brain the time to accomplish this process. A break will help you avoid a common problem in reading texts—finding yourself reading the same sentence over and over again because your brain is too overloaded from trying to remember what you just read.

Recall/Review

Finally, you've finished reading the entire chapter. If you've used the guidelines listed previously, you'll only have to read the chapter as thoroughly this one time instead of having to read it over and over throughout the semester and just before exams. Once you've read the chapter, take a few minutes to try to remember as much of what you learned while reading it as you can. A good way to do this is to take any practice quizzes that might be available. For this text, we offer both practice quizzes within the print text and online quizzes and study materials in the e-text. If there are no quizzes, read the chapter summary in detail, making sure that you understand everything in it. If there's anything that's confusing, go back to that section in the chapter and read again until you understand it.

Some educators and researchers now add a fourth R: *Reflect*. To reflect means to try to think critically about what you have read by trying to tie the concepts into what you already know, thinking about how you can use the information in your own life, and deciding which of the topics you've covered interests you enough to look for more information on that topic (Richardson & Morgan, 1997). For example, if you have learned about the genetic basis for depression, you might better understand why that disorder seems to run in your best friend's family. See Learning Objective 13.5.

Reading textbooks in this way means that, when it comes time for the final exam, all you will have to do is carefully review your notes to be ready for the exam—you won't have to read the entire textbook all over again. What a time saver! Recent research suggests that the most important steps in this method are the three Rs: Read, recite, and review. In two experiments with college students, researchers found that when compared with other study methods such as rereading and note-taking study strategies, the 3R strategy produced superior recall of the material (McDaniel et al., 2009).

After reading a chapter section, take time to reflect on what the information means and how it might relate to real-world situations.

Watch Reading the Text

Watch the Video at MyLab Psychology

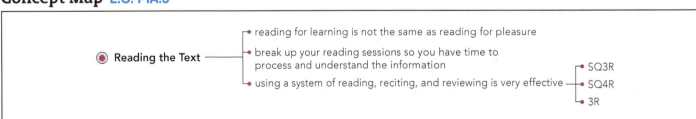

Practice Quiz   How much do you remember?

Pick the best answer.

1. What does the S in SQ3R stand for?
   a. stand
   b. synthesize
   c. supplement
   d. study
   e. survey

2. As you read the text material, you should _____
   a. use a highlighter so that you don't waste time writing notes.
   b. avoid taking notes while reading so that you can concentrate on the material.
   c. ignore boxes, charts, and other features.
   d. make an outline of the main points and key terms.
   e. read the entire chapter all at once.

3. Peyton has surveyed the material, developed questions to consider, and begun reading the material to find the answers to her questions. What should she do next?
   a. Rewrite the material verbatim to help commit it to memory.
   b. Review the material from the chapter that she has read.
   c. Retain the material by storing her notes in a folder.
   d. Reread the material a second time.
   e. Recite out loud what she can remember from the section she just read.

PIA.4 Getting the Most Out of Lectures

PIA.4 Identify the best methods for taking notes and listening in class.

As mentioned earlier, mastering course content means you have to attend the lectures. Even if lectures are online, you have to read or watch them. But just attending or reading or watching is not enough; you have to process the information just as you have to process the text material. To get the most out of lectures, you need to take notes on the content, and taking notes involves quite a bit more than just writing down the words the instructor says or printing out the PowerPoint slides.

One very important fact you must remember: PowerPoint slides are not meant to be notes at all; they are merely talking points that help the instructor follow a particular sequence in lecturing. Typically, the instructor will have more to say about each point on the slide, and that is the information students should be listening to and writing down. In Table PIA.1, the suggestion to use highlighters of different colors is not meant to replace taking notes but instead to supplement the notes you do take.

How should you take notes? As stated earlier, you should try to take notes while reading the chapter (*before* attending the lecture) by writing down the main points and the vocabulary terms (*in your own words* as much as possible). This forces you to think about what you are reading. The more you think about it, the more likely it is that the concepts will become a part of your permanent memory. See Learning Objective 6.5.

Taking notes while listening to the lecture is a slightly different procedure. First, you should have your notes from your earlier reading in front of you, and it helps to leave plenty of space between lines to add notes from the lecture. A major mistake made by many students is to come to the lecture without having read the material first. This is an EXTREMELY BAD IDEA. If you come to the lecture totally unprepared, you will have no idea what is important enough to write down and what is just the instructor's asides and commentary. Reading the material first gives you a good idea of exactly what is important in the lecture and reduces the amount of notes you must take.

THINKING CRITICALLY PIA.2

What are some reasons why not relying on the instructor's PowerPoints might be beneficial in committing information to memory?

There is an art to really listening to someone, too, often called *active listening*. Active listeners make eye contact with the speaker and sit facing the speaker in a place where they can easily hear and see the speaker. Active listeners focus on what is being said rather than how the speaker looks or sounds (not always an easy task) and ask

Here are two things that instructors love to see: attentive looks and note taking during the lecture. And for the student who learns better just listening, a small digital recorder (used with permission) can help for later review of the lecture. How should these students have prepared before coming to this class?

Watch Lecture Notes

Watch the Video at MyLab Psychology

questions when they do not understand something or need a clarification. Asking questions during a lecture is a good way to stay engaged in actively processing the speaker's message.

Ask your instructor if you can bring a digital recorder to class to record the lecture. You will then be able to listen during the class and use the recording to take notes from later. Some students may prefer to jot down diagrams, charts, and other visual aids along with their written notes. When you have good notes, taken while reading the text and from the lectures, you will also have ready-made study aids for preparing to take exams. The next section deals with the best ways to study for exams.

Concept Map L.O. PIA.4

- Getting the Most Out of Lectures
  - read your textbook and take notes before class so you can focus on the lecture–in the lecture only take notes on the most important ideas
  - take notes and write information in your own words; create diagrams or charts
  - engage in active listening; focus on what is being discussed and ask questions for clarification

Practice Quiz   How much do you remember?

Pick the best answer.

1. To maximize success, which method of note taking should José use?
   a. He should not take any notes, relying solely on reading the text.
   b. He should take notes in his own words as much as possible.
   c. He should write down every word from the PowerPoint slides used in class.
   d. He should highlight the text rather than write his own notes.
   e. He should make sure that his notes contain the exact words used by his instructor.

2. Violet maintains eye contact when listening to her instructors. She also places herself so that she can see and hear the instructors. Additionally, she works to listen to the content of the lecture instead of focusing on how they look or what they are wearing. Violet would be described as a(n)
   a. non-listener.
   b. passive listener.
   c. social listener.
   d. active listener.
   e. marginal listener.

PIA.5 Studying for Exams: Cramming Is Not an Option

PIA.5 Describe how to approach studying for exams.

Inevitably, the time will come when your instructor wants some hard evidence that you have truly learned at least some of the material to which you have been exposed. There is a right way to study for a test, believe it or not. Here are some good things to remember when preparing for an exam, whether it's a quiz, a unit test, a midterm, or a final (Carter et al., 2005; Reynolds, 2002):

Could this be you? The early morning sunlight peeking in, the scattered materials, the remnants of multiple doses of caffeine, and the general look of fatigue and despondence are all hallmarks of that hallowed yet useless student tradition, cramming. Don't let this happen to you.

- **Timing is everything.** One of the worst things students can do is to wait until the last minute to study for an exam. Remember the analogy about "chewing" the steak? (Just as a steak has to be chewed to be enjoyed and to be useful to the body, textbook material has to be "chewed" with the mind.) The same concept applies to preparing for an exam: You have to give yourself enough time. If you've read your text material and taken good notes as discussed in the previous sections, you'll be able to save a lot of time in studying for the exam, but you still need to give yourself ample time to go over all of those notes. The time management tips given earlier in this chapter will help you prioritize your studying.

- **Find out as much as you can about the type of test and the material it will cover.** The type of test can affect the way in which you want to study the material. Since you are already aware of the fact that the AP exam consists of only multiple choice questions and free response questions, you are a step ahead in terms of how to best learn the material.

The AP exam includes three types of multiple choice questions:

- **Factual:** Questions that ask you to remember a specific fact from the text material. For example, "Who built the first psychological laboratory?" requires that you recognize a person's name. (The answer is Wilhelm Wundt.)
- **Applied:** Questions that ask you to use, or apply, information presented in the text. For example, consider the following question:

    Ever since she was scared by a dog as a young child, Angelica has been afraid of all dogs. The fact that she is afraid not only of the original dog but of all types of dogs is an example of

    a. stimulus generalization.
    b. stimulus discrimination.
    c. spontaneous recovery.
    d. shaping.
    e. extinction.

    This question requires you to take a concept (in this case, generalization) and apply it to a real-world example.
- **Conceptual:** Questions that demand that you think about the ideas or concepts presented in the text and demonstrate that you understand them by answering questions like the following: "Freud is to _____ as Watson is to _____." (The answers could vary, but a good set would be "the unconscious" and "observable behavior.")

Notice that although memorizing facts might help on the first type of question, it isn't going to help at all on the last two. Memorization doesn't always help on factual questions either because the questions are sometimes worded quite differently from the text. It is far better to understand the information rather than be able to "spit it back" without understanding it. "Spitting it back" is memorization; understanding it is true learning. See Learning Objective 6.2. There are different levels of analysis for information you are trying to learn, and the higher the level of analysis, the more likely you are to remember (Anderson et al., 2001; Bloom, 1956). *Factual questions* are the lowest level of analysis: knowledge. *Applied questions* are a higher level and are often preferred by instructors for that reason—it's hard to successfully apply information if you don't really understand it. *Conceptual questions* are a kind of analysis, a level higher than either of the other two. Not only do you have to understand the concept, you have to understand it well enough to compare and contrast it with other concepts. They might be harder questions to answer, but in the long run, you will get more "bang for your buck" in terms of true learning.

The AP exam also includes two free response questions (FRQs). But don't be fooled by the seemingly small number of questions—these two FRQs are worth one-third of your total score! The FRQ is considered a subjective test, as it requires you to not only recall and understand the information from the course, but also to organize it in your own words. To study for a subjective test means that you need to be familiar with the material *and* that you need to be able to write it down. Make outlines of your notes. Rewrite both reading and lecture notes and make flash cards, charts, and drawings. Practice putting the flash cards in order. Talk out loud or study with someone else and discuss the possible questions that could be on an essay test. You might find that only a few of these methods work best for you, but the more ways in which you try to study, the better you will be able to retrieve the information when you need it. It may sound like a big investment of your time, but most students vastly underestimate how long it takes to study—and fail to recognize that many of these techniques are doable when first reading the textbook assignment and preparing for the classroom lecture. DON'T CRAM!

Once you've prepared for the test, it's time to think about how to answer the FRQs when taking the actual test. Here is a step-by-step guide:

- First, *identify*, or name the term or concept.
- Next, *define* the term in five words or less. (Always define the term, even if it is not required!)
- Finally, *apply* the term, as it relates to the question—this is not the time to "get creative," as points are dependent upon answering the question as stated with complete sentences.

Continue with the next term and answer the question in the order stated. And don't forget—you must use proper psychological terminology in your response!

You might also look at past AP exams (available at **apstudents.collegeboard.org/courses/ap-psychology**) to see what kinds of questions are usually asked. Other helpful advice:

- **Use SQ3R.** You can use the same method you used to read the text material to go over your notes. Skim through your notes, try to think of possible test questions, recite the main ideas and definitions of terms, either out loud, into a digital recorder, or to a friend or study group. Review by summarizing sections of material or by making an outline or flash cards that you can use in studying important concepts.
- **Use the concept maps if provided.** When surveying the chapter, make sure you look over any concept maps. (In this text, they are provided at the end of each major section of the chapters, just before the practice quizzes). **Concept maps** are a visual organization of the key concepts, terms, and definitions found in each section and are an excellent way to "see" how various concepts are linked together (Carnot et al., 2001; Novak, 1995; Wu et al., 2004). They are also a great way to review the chapter once you have finished reading it, just to check for understanding—if the concept maps don't make sense, then you've missed something and need to go back over the relevant section. You can also make your own concept maps as you take notes on the chapter. A good resource for the background behind concept maps and how to use them is at **cmap.ihmc.us/docs/theory-of-concept-maps.php**.
- **Take advantage of all the publisher's test and review materials.** Practice helps, and most textbooks come with a study guide or a Web site. Those materials should have practice quizzes available—take them. The more types of quiz questions you try to answer, the more successful you will be at interpreting the questions on the actual exam. You'll also get a very good idea of the areas that you need to review. And remember, retrieval practice, or actually testing your recall through tests or quizzes, is a great way to improve long-term learning (Karpicke, 2012; Karpicke & Blunt, 2011), even when just thinking about the information or rehearsing it in your mind (Smith et al., 2013)! Retrieval practice works better than simply restudying. The key is testing your retrieval of information, not your recognition of information.

For more information, a variety of excellent resources on effective study strategies, and tips on how to apply them for students and teachers alike, visit the *The Learning Scientists*, **learningscientists.org**, and *Retrieval Practice*, **retrievalpractice.org**. Another great resource is an article written for college students, *Optimizing Learning in College: Tips From Cognitive Psychology* (Putnam et al., 2016), available at **doi.org/10.1177/1745691616645770**

- **Make use of the resources.** If you find that you are having difficulty with certain concepts, go to the instructor well in advance of the exam for help. (This is another good reason to manage your study time so that you aren't trying to do everything in a few hours the night before the exam.)
- **Don't forget your physical needs.** Studies have shown that not getting enough sleep is bad for memory and learning processes (Stickgold et al., 2001; Vecsey et al., 2009). Try to stop studying an hour or so before going to bed at a reasonable time to give your body time to relax and unwind. Get a full night's sleep if possible.

Many students studying for exams ignore one of the most valuable resources to which they have access: the instructor. Most instructors are happy to answer questions or schedule time for students who are having difficulty understanding the material.

Holding your eyes open is not going to help you study when you are this tired. Sleep has been shown to improve memory and performance on tests, so get a good night's sleep before every exam.

concept map
an organized visual representation of knowledge consisting of concepts and their relationships to other concepts.

Do not take sleep-inducing medications or drink alcohol, as these substances prevent normal stages of sleep, including the stage that seems to be the most useful for memory and learning (Davis et al., 2003). Do eat breakfast; hunger is harmful to memory and mental performance. A breakfast heavy on protein and light on carbohydrates is the best for concentration and recall (Benton & Parker, 1998; Dani et al., 2005; Pollitt & Matthews, 1998; Stubbs et al., 1996).

- **Use your test time wisely.** When taking the test, don't allow yourself to get stuck on one question that you can't seem to answer. If an answer isn't clear, skip that question and go on to others. After finishing all of the questions you can answer easily, go back to the ones you have skipped and try to answer them again. This accomplishes several things: You get to experience success in answering the questions you can answer, which makes you feel more confident and relaxed; other questions on the test might act as memory cues for the exact information you need for one of those questions you skipped; and once you are more relaxed, you may find that the answers to those seemingly impossible questions are now clear because anxiety is no longer blocking them. This is a way of reducing stress by dealing directly with the problem, one of many ways of dealing effectively with stress. See Learning Objective 10.10.

Watch Exam Prep

Watch the Video at MyLab Psychology

THINKING CRITICALLY PIA.3

Many elementary and secondary school programs now offer breakfast to their students. What foods would benefit these children the most and why?

Concept Map L.O. PIA.5

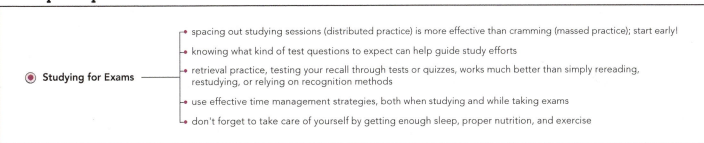

- **Studying for Exams**
  - spacing out studying sessions (distributed practice) is more effective than cramming (massed practice); start early!
  - knowing what kind of test questions to expect can help guide study efforts
  - retrieval practice, testing your recall through tests or quizzes, works much better than simply rereading, restudying, or relying on recognition methods
  - use effective time management strategies, both when studying and while taking exams
  - don't forget to take care of yourself by getting enough sleep, proper nutrition, and exercise

Practice Quiz   How much do you remember?

Pick the best answer.

1. Which category is the following question an example of? *True or False: Psychology is the study of behavior and mental processes.*
   a. factual question
   b. conceptual question
   c. applied question
   d. applied-conceptual question
   e. critical question

2. Which questions are the highest level of analysis and often considered the hardest to answer on a test?
   a. factual
   b. matching
   c. applied
   d. conceptual
   e. true/false

3. Simply spitting information back out on a test is likely more indicative of _____, while truly understanding information is more indicative of actual _____.
   a. memorization, learning
   b. learning, memorization
   c. behavior, action
   d. action, behavior
   e. comprehension, memorization

4. What is the value of retrieval practice?
   a. It allows students more opportunities to study.
   b. It helps increase long-term learning.
   c. It assists only in preparing for essay-based exams.
   d. It is essentially the same as studying for recognition.
   e. No research exists that supports the efficacy of retrieval practice.

5. Henry is studying for his first psychology exam. What should he do to ensure he remembers all that he has studied?
   a. Begin studying many days in advance to give his brain time to commit the material to memory and repeatedly test his retrieval of information.
   b. Rely on highlighting and rereading of the text.
   c. Memorize as much of the information as possible.
   d. Study all night long before the exam—he can sleep after the test.
   e. Wait to study until just before the scheduled exam, so that the information will be fresh in his mind.

PIA.6 Improving Your Memory

PIA.6 Explain how using mnemonics can help you improve your memory for facts and concepts.

mnemonic
a strategy or trick for aiding memory.

Everyone needs a little memory help now and then. Even memory experts use strategies to help them perform their unusual feats of remembering. These strategies may be unique to that individual, but there are many memory "tricks" that are quite simple and available for anyone to learn and use. A memory trick or strategy to help people remember is called a **mnemonic**, from the Greek word for memory. Take a look at **Figure PIA.1** to see examples of a few of the more popular mnemonics, some of which may sound familiar:

Figure PIA.1 Popular Mnemonics

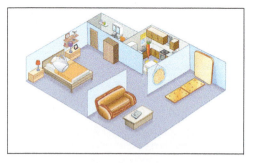

- **Linking.** Make a list in which items to be remembered are linked in some way. If trying to remember a list of the planets in the solar system, for example, a person could string the names of the planets together like this: *Mercury* was the messenger god, who carried lots of love notes to *Venus*, the beautiful goddess who sprang from the *Earth's* sea. She was married to *Mars*, her brother, which didn't please her father *Jupiter* or his father *Saturn*, and his uncle *Uranus* complained to the sea god, *Neptune*. That sounds like a lot, but once linked in this way, the names of the planets are easy to recall in proper order.

- **The peg-word method.** In this method, it is necessary to first memorize a series of "peg" words, numbered words that can be used as keys for remembering items associated with them. A typical series of peg words is:

One is a bun.	Six is bricks.
Two is a shoe.	Seven is heaven.
Three is a tree.	Eight is a gate.
Four is a door.	Nine is a line.
Five is a hive.	Ten is a hen.

To use this method, each item to be remembered is associated with a peg word and made into an image. For instance, if you are trying to remember the parts of the nervous system, you might picture the brain stuck inside a bun, the spinal cord growing out of a shoe or with shoes hanging off of it, and the peripheral nerves as the branches of a tree.

- **The method of loci (LOW-kee or LOW-si).** In this method, the person pictures a very familiar room or series of rooms in a house or other building. Each point of the information is then made into an image and "placed" mentally in the room at certain locations. For example, if the first point was about military spending, the image might be a soldier standing in the doorway of the house throwing money out into the street. Each point would have its place, and all the person would need to do to retrieve the memories would be to take a "mental walk" around the house.

- **Verbal/rhythmic organization.** How do you spell relief? If, when spelling a word with an *ie* or an *ei* in it, you resort to the old rhyme "I before E except after C, or when sounded as A as in neighbor or weigh," you have made use of a verbal/rhythmic organization mnemonic. "Thirty days hath September, April, June, and November ..."

is another example of this technique. Setting information into a rhyme aids memory because it uses verbal cues, rhyming words, and the rhythm of the poem itself to aid retrieval. Sometimes this method is accomplished through making a sentence by using the first letters of each word to be remembered and making them into new words that form a sentence. The colors of the rainbow are ROY G. BIV (red, orange, yellow, green, blue, indigo, and violet). The notes on the musical staff are "Every Good Boy Does Fine." There are countless examples of this technique.

- **Put it to music (a version of the rhythmic method).** Some people have had success with making up little songs, using familiar tunes, to remember specific information. The best example of this? The alphabet song.

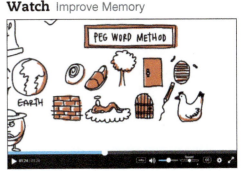

Watch Improve Memory

Watch the Video at MyLab Psychology

Concept Map L.O. PIA.6

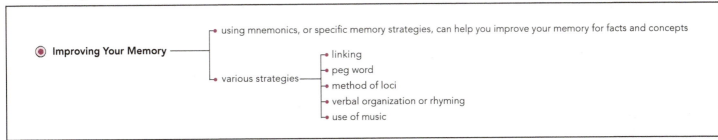

Practice Quiz   How much do you remember?

Pick the best answer.

1. Which of the following is NOT one of the mnemonic techniques described in this chapter?
   a. verbal/rhythmic organization
   b. method of loci
   c. rote memorization
   d. linking
   e. peg-word

2. "My very excellent mother just served us nine pizzas" is a mnemonic for remembering the order of the planets in our solar system (including poor, downgraded Pluto, of course). What kind of mnemonic is this?
   a. method of loci
   b. linking
   c. kinesthetic
   d. peg-word
   e. verbal/rhythmic organization

PIA.7 Writing Papers

PIA.7 Describe the key steps in writing papers.

While papers are not typically written during an AP class prior to the exam, your teacher may ask you to write one after the exam. Several steps are involved in writing a paper, whether it is a short paper or a long one. You should begin all of these steps well in advance of the due date for the paper (not the night before):

1. **Choose a topic.** The first step is to choose a topic for your paper. In some cases, the instructor may have a list of acceptable subjects, which makes your job easier. If that is not the case, don't be afraid to go to your instructor during office hours and talk about some possible topics. Try to choose a topic that interests you—one you would like to learn more about. The most common mistake students make is to choose subject matter that is too broad. For example, the topic "emotions" could fill several books. A narrower focus might discuss a single aspect of emotions in detail. Again, your instructor can help you narrow down your topic choices.

2. **Do the research.** Find as many sources as you can that have information about your topic. Don't limit yourself to textbooks. Go to your school library and ask the librarian to point you in the direction of some good scientific journals that would have useful information on the subject. Be very careful about using the Internet to do research: Not

In earlier times, people actually had to write or type their first, second, and sometimes third drafts on real paper. The advent of computers with word-processing programs that allow simple editing and revision has no doubt saved a lot of trees from the paper mill. This also means there is no good excuse for failing to write a first draft and proofreading one's work.

everything on the Internet is correct or written by true experts—avoid other students' papers and "encyclopedia" Web sites that can be written and updated by darn near anyone.

3. **Take notes.** While reading about your topic, take careful notes to remember key points and write down the reference that will go along with the reading. References for psychology papers are usually going to be in APA (American Psychological Association) style, which can be found at **apastyle.apa.org**.

    Taking good notes helps you avoid using the materials you find in their exact or nearly exact form, a form of cheating we'll discuss more in a later module of this chapter.

4. **Decide on the thesis.** The thesis is the central message of your paper—the message you want to communicate to your audience—which may be your instructor, your classmates, or both, depending on the nature of the assignment. Some papers are persuasive, which means the author is trying to convince the reader of a particular point of view, such as "Autism is not caused by immunizations." Some papers are informative, providing information about a topic to an audience that may have no prior knowledge, such as "Several forms of autism have been identified."

5. **Write an outline.** Using your notes from all your readings, create an outline of your paper—a kind of "road map" of how the paper will go. Start with an introduction (e.g., a brief definition and discussion of autism). Then decide what the body of the paper should be. If your paper is about a specific type of autism, your outline might include sections about the possible causes of that type. The last section of your outline should be some kind of conclusion. For example, you might have recommendations about how parents of a child with autism can best help that child develop as fully as possible.

6. **Write a first draft.** Write your paper using the outline and your notes as guides. If using APA style, place citations with all of your statements and assertions. Failure to use citations (which point to the particular reference work from which your information came) is also a common mistake that many students make.

    It is very important that you avoid plagiarism, as discussed in Step 3. When you use a source, you are supposed to explain the information you are using in your own words *and* cite the source, as in the following example:

    In one study comparing both identical and fraternal twins, researchers found that stressful life events of the kind listed in the SRRS were excellent predictors of the onset of episodes of major depression (Kendler & Prescott, 1999).

    Your paper's reference section would have the following citation: Kendler, K. S. & Prescott, C. A. (1999). A population-based twin study of lifetime major depression in men and women. *Archives of General Psychiatry, 56*(1), 39-44. doi:10.1001/archpsyc.56.1.39. [Author's note: The number in front of the parentheses is the volume of the journal, the one inside is the issue number, and the last numbers before the period and the digital object identifier (DOI) are the page numbers of that article.]

7. **Let it sit.** Take a few days (if you have been good about starting the paper on time) to let the paper sit without reading it. Then go back over and mark places that don't sound right and need more explanation, a citation, or any other changes. This is much easier to do after a few days away from the paper; the need to reword will be more obvious.

8. **Write the revised draft.** Some people do more than one draft, while others do only a first draft and a final. In any case, revise the draft carefully, making sure to check your citations—and your spelling!

Watch Paper Writing

Concept Map L.O. PIA.7

- **Writing Papers**
  - quality papers often require timely preparation, research, planning, and outlining; write an initial draft followed by a revised draft
  - don't forget to proofread and to use your spelling and grammar checker

Practice Quiz How much do you remember?

Pick the best answer.

1. Madison has developed and researched a topic for her paper. What should she do next?
   a. Begin writing a rough draft of her paper.
   b. Start writing her conclusion.
   c. Begin writing as if her first draft will be her final draft.
   d. Develop an outline as a road map to help her stay on track when writing her paper.
   e. Let everything sit for a couple of days before beginning her rough draft.

2. Which of the following would be a more manageable topic for a term paper?
   a. mental illness
   b. learning
   c. causes of schizophrenia
   d. the meaning of life
   e. human development

3. Once you have written the first draft, what should you do?
   a. Submit it to the instructor, as your first draft is usually the best effort.
   b. Let it sit a few days before going back over it to make corrections.
   c. Proofread, then start your final draft.
   d. Immediately write the second or final draft before the material gets too stale for you to remember why you wrote it the way you did.
   e. Write the outline of the paper, which is easier to do once the paper is already written.

PIA.8 Your Ethical Responsibility as a Student

PIA.8 Identify some of the key ethical considerations you'll face as a student.

Many students have committed the sin of **plagiarism**, the copying of someone else's ideas or exact words (or a close imitation of the words) and presenting them as your own. When you cite someone else's work in your paper, you have to give them credit for that work. If you don't, you have committed plagiarism, whether you meant to do so or not, and this is theft. In taking credit for someone else's work, you hurt yourself and your reputation in a number of ways. You don't actually learn anything (because if you don't put it in your own words, you haven't really understood it), which means you aren't giving yourself the chance to develop the skills and knowledge you will need in your future career. You also put your integrity and honesty as a person under close scrutiny. Plagiarism shows disrespect for your peers as well—they did their own work and expected you to do the same (Pennsylvania State University, 2014).

How can you avoid plagiarizing? First, remember that if you want to use the actual words from your source, you should put them inside quotation marks and then include the reference or citation, including page numbers. If you want to use the ideas but don't want to plagiarize, try taking brief notes on the source material (preferably from more than one source) and then use your notes—not the actual source—to write the ideas in your own words. See **Table PIA.2** for some helpful resources.

Table PIA.2 Tools and Resources for Avoiding Plagiarism

Turnitin.com Resources for Students: https://www.turnitin.com/resources
Grammar and Plagiarism Checker: https://www.grammarly.com/plagiarism-checker
Purdue Online Writing Lab: https://owl.english.purdue.edu/owl/resource/589/1/
Indiana University Writing Tutorial Service: http://www.indiana.edu/~wts/pamphlets/plagiarism.shtml
Accredited Schools Online: http://www.accreditedschoolsonline.org/resources/preventing-plagiarism/

Another ethical responsibility you have as a student is to not cheat. Most schools have honor codes about academic integrity, and cheating of any kind can have some fairly severe consequences. Cheating can involve copying answers from someone else's test as you look over their shoulder, stealing tests to get the answers before the exam, working collectively with others on assignments that are supposed to be completed individually and independently, or even having someone else take your test for you, among others. Sadly, cheating in school is still very common. A survey of more than 23,000 American

plagiarism
the copying of someone else's exact words (or a close imitation of the words) and presenting them as your own.

Watch Ethics

Watch the Video at MyLab Psychology

high school students (private, public, and charter school students) conducted by the Josephson Institute Center for Youth Ethics (2012) found that in 2012, more than half of the students admitted to cheating on an exam at least once, and more than a fourth said they had cheated more than once. Cheating at the college or university level also happens more often than it should, and even the most prestigious universities are not immune: In 2012, Harvard University investigated more than 125 undergraduates for plagiarism and other forms of cheating (Galante & Zeveloff, 2012). When it does occur, research results suggest many students will not report classmates who are cheating unless there is a cost for remaining silent, such as a lower grade for themselves (Yachison et al., 2018). And even students who individually have negative attitudes toward cheating may see cheating with and for peers to be acceptable (Pulfrey et al., 2018). In the long run, both plagiarism and cheating hurt you far more than they provide any temporary relief.

Concept Map L.O. PIA.8

- Your Ethical Responsibility as a Student
  - maintain academic integrity for yourself and others; take responsibility for your learning and education; do not take shortcuts
  - do your own work and make sure you understand what constitutes academic dishonesty; do not plagiarize someone else's work and do not cheat

Practice Quiz How much do you remember?

Pick the best answer.

1. Grayson is writing a paper for psychology. One of his sources is a text in which the following statement appears: When a deeply depressed mood comes on fairly suddenly and either seems to be too severe for the circumstances or exists without any external cause for sadness, it is called major depressive disorder. Which of the following would NOT be an acceptable way for Grayson to use this material in his paper?
   a. Put the entire sentence in quotation marks and cite the author and textbook information where he found the quote.
   b. Summarize the ideas in the sentence in his own words.
   c. Put the information into his own words and cite the source of the information.
   d. Use only part of the information, but make sure he uses his own language.
   e. All of the answer choices are correct.

2. In the Josephson Center survey, how many students reported cheating at least once?
   a. about one fourth
   b. almost 90% of them
   c. a little more than half
   d. a little more than three fourths
   e. The survey found no reported incidences of cheating.

Psychology in Action Summary

Study Skills

PIA.1 Identify four methods of studying.

- Research has shown that using multiple learning methods to study is a useful and effective strategy.
- Four common learning methods are verbal, visual, auditory, and action methods.

Managing Time and Tasks

PIA.2 Describe some strategies for time and task management.

- Making or using a calendar of prioritized tasks, breaking down tasks into smaller ones, and avoiding multitasking are some ways to improve time management.

- The stages of the Getting Things Done (GTD) method involve capturing, processing, organizing, reviewing, and doing the tasks to which you have committed.

Reading the Text: Textbooks Are Not Meatloaf

PIA.3 Describe how to read a textbook so that you get the most out of your reading efforts.

- Textbooks must be read in a different way from novels or popular books.
- The SQ3R method is an excellent way to approach reading a textbook: survey, question, read, recite, review.

Getting the Most Out of Lectures

PIA.4 Identify the best methods for taking notes and listening in class.

- Notes should be in your own words and written or typed, not highlighted in the text or on handouts.
- When taking notes from a lecture, you should be prepared by having the notes from your reading in front of you; some people may benefit from recording the lecture and taking notes afterward.

Studying for Exams: Cramming Is Not an Option

PIA.5 Describe how to approach studying for exams.

- Don't wait until the last minute to study.
- Find out about the types of questions on the exam.
- Use concept maps, the SQ3R method, and publishers' practice-test materials.
- Engage in retrieval practice; test your recall, not just recognition, of content often.
- Get plenty of sleep and eat breakfast, preferably something with protein.

Improving Your Memory

PIA.6 Explain how using mnemonics can help you improve your memory for facts and concepts.

- There are memory strategies called mnemonics, including methods that use imagery, rhymes, linking, and even music to improve memory.

Writing Papers

PIA.7 Describe the key steps in writing papers.

- Key steps in writing a research paper are to choose a topic, read about the topic, take notes on your reading, decide on the central message of your paper, write an outline, complete a first draft, and allow the paper to sit for a few days before going back and writing the final draft.

Your Ethical Responsibility as a Student

PIA.8 Identify some of the key ethical considerations you'll face as a student.

- Students need to realize that plagiarism and cheating in school are harmful to the students and disrespectful to others.

Test Yourself: Preparing for the AP Exam

Directions: Read each of the questions or incomplete sentences below. Then choose the response that best answers the question or completes the sentence.

1. Lucas learns best whenever he can see things laid out before him. He uses flash cards and concept maps and often tries to redraw charts and figures from memory. What learning method does Lucas seem to prefer?
   - a. verbal
   - b. rhythmic
   - c. visual
   - d. auditory
   - e. action

2. Which of the following is NOT one of the strategies for defeating procrastination?
   - a. Make a map of long-term goals.
   - b. Use a calendar.
   - c. Stay up all night to finish your task.
   - d. Break big tasks down into smaller, more manageable pieces.
   - e. Prioritize your tasks when you plan them.

3. The first stage of David Allen's Getting Things Done (GTD) method is _____ anything and everything that has your attention.
   - a. reviewing
   - b. doing
   - c. capturing
   - d. defining
   - e. organizing

4. What learning strategy gives the student the ability to more effectively read and remember material?
   - a. using different colored highlighters
   - b. relying exclusively on chapter summaries
   - c. looking at content maps
   - d. SQ3R
   - e. simple rereading

5. Which of the following is likely the best option when taking notes?
   - a. Rely on a classmate's notes as your sole source of notes.
   - b. Make sure you do not read the chapter before the lecture so the material will be fresher and more memorable.
   - c. Highlight material in the textbook as the instructor lectures.
   - d. Use the instructor's presentation slides as your notes.
   - e. Take notes while reading the chapter before going to the lecture.

6. What type of question requires that you understand the material so well that you are able to compare and contrast it to other material?
   - a. factual
   - b. applied
   - c. fill-in-the-blank
   - d. conceptual
   - e. true/false

7. Zoey is stuck on a question while taking her psychology exam. What should she do?
   - a. Stay on that question until she can figure out what the answer is.
   - b. Go on to the other questions. Maybe she can find a clue to the one she skipped.
   - c. Take a guess as to the correct answer. She probably will get it correct anyway.
   - d. Turn in her exam now, she probably will not be able to get any others either.
   - e. Review the questions she already has answered to find a clue there.

8. Which mnemonic involves first memorizing a series of numbered words?
   - a. linking
   - b. musical
   - c. peg-word
   - d. method of loci
   - e. verbal/rhythmic organization

9. Savannah has finished a draft of her research paper almost 2 weeks before the date it is due. What should she do now?
   - a. Let it sit for a few days before reviewing it.
   - b. Proofread it now, then complete the final draft immediately.
   - c. Complete the final draft immediately while the material is still fresh in her head.
   - d. Hand in her rough draft as if it were the final draft. Most students tend to make their paper worse when they revise it.
   - e. Savannah needs to start again, since papers finished early tend not to be well written.

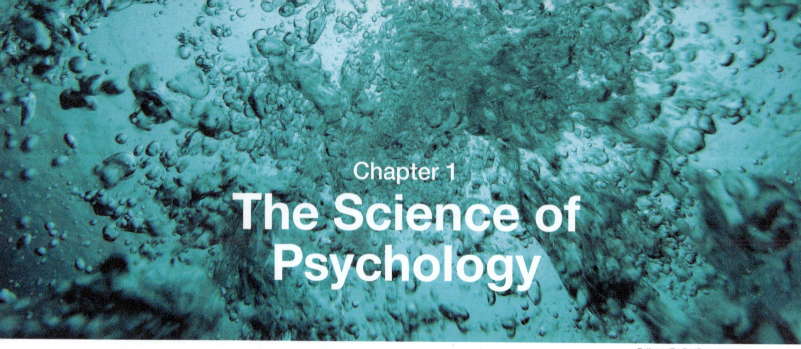

Chapter 1
The Science of Psychology

Ralf strm/EyeEm/Getty Images

In your words

How would you define psychology? What do you hope to learn about psychology, yourself, and others after taking this course?

After you have thought about these questions, watch the video to see how other students would answer them.

👁 Watch the Video at MyLab Psychology

Why study psychology?

Psychology not only helps you understand why people (and animals) do the things they do, but it also helps you better understand yourself and your reactions to other people. Psychology can show you how your brain and body are connected, how to improve your learning abilities and memory, and how to deal with the stresses of life, both ordinary and extraordinary. In studying psychology, a basic understanding of the research methods psychologists use is extremely important because research can be flawed, and knowing how research *should* be done can bring those flaws to light. Finally, the study of psychology and its research methods helps foster critical thinking, which can be used to evaluate not just research but also claims of all kinds, including those of advertisers, fake news stories and social media posts, and politicians.

Learning Objectives

1.1 Describe the contributions of some of the early pioneers in psychology.

1.2 Summarize the basic ideas and the important people behind the early approaches known as Gestalt, psychoanalysis, and behaviorism.

1.3 Summarize the basic ideas behind the seven modern perspectives in psychology.

1.4 Differentiate between the various types of professionals within the field of psychology.

1.5 Recall the basic criteria for critical thinking that people can use in their everyday lives.

1.6 Recall the five steps of the scientific approach.

1.7 Compare and contrast some of the methods used to describe behavior.

1.8 Explain how researchers use the correlational technique to study relationships between two or more variables.

1.9 Identify the steps involved in designing an experiment.

1.10 Recall two common sources of problems in an experiment and some ways to control for these effects.

1.11 Explain why statistics are important to psychologists and psychology majors.

1.12 Describe the types of tables and graphs that represent patterns in data.

1.13 Identify three measures of central tendency and explain how they are impacted by the shape of the distribution.

1.14 Identify the types of statistics used to examine variations in data.

1.15 Describe how inferential statistics can be used to determine if differences in sets of data are large enough to be due to something other than chance variation.

1.16 Explain how statistics are used to predict one score from another.

1.17 Identify some of the common ethical guidelines for doing research with people.

1.18 Explain why psychologists sometimes use animals in their research.

1.19 Identify strategies for critically evaluating news and other information shared on social media.

AP 1.A Recognize how philosophical and physiological perspectives shaped the development of psychological thought.

1.1–1.2 The History of Psychology

Some people believe psychology is just the study of people and what motivates their behavior. Psychologists do study people, but they study animals as well. Psychologists study not only what people and animals do but also what happens in their bodies and in their brains as they do it. The study of psychology is not only important to psychologists: Psychology is a *hub science* and findings from psychological research are cited and used in many other fields as diverse as cancer research, health, and even climate change (Cacioppo, 2013; McDonald et al., 2015; Roberto & Kawachi, 2014; Rothman et al., 2015; van der Linden et al., 2015).

Psychology is the scientific study of behavior and mental processes. *Behavior* includes all of our outward or overt actions and reactions, such as talking, facial expressions, and movement. The term *mental processes* refers to all the internal, covert (hidden) activity of our minds, such as thinking, feeling, and remembering. Why "scientific"? To study behavior and mental processes in both animals and humans, researchers must observe them. Whenever a human being observes anyone or anything, there's always a possibility that the observer will see only what he or she *expects* to see. Psychologists don't want to let these possible biases* cause them to make faulty observations. They want to be precise and to measure as carefully as they can—so they use a systematic** approach to study psychology scientifically.

💬 How long has psychology been around?

Psychology is a relatively new field in the realm of the sciences, only about 140 years old. It's not that no one thought about why people and animals do the things they do before then; on the contrary, there were philosophers,*** medical doctors, and physiologists**** who thought about little else—particularly with regard to people. Philosophers such as Plato, Aristotle, and Descartes tried to understand or explain the human mind and its connection to the physical body (Durrant, 1993; Everson, 1995; Kenny, 1968, 1994). Medical doctors and physiologists wondered about the physical connection between the body and the brain. For example, physician and physicist Gustav Fechner is often credited with performing some of the first scientific experiments that would form a basis for experimentation in psychology with his studies of perception (Fechner, 1860), and physician Hermann von Helmholtz (von Helmholtz, 1852, 1863) performed groundbreaking experiments in visual and auditory perception. See Learning Objectives 3.2, 3.6, and 3.8.

psychology
scientific study of behavior and mental processes.

AP 1.B Identify the research contributions of major historical figures in psychology.

1.1 In the Beginning: Wundt, Titchener, and James

1.1 Describe the contributions of some of the early pioneers in psychology.

It really all started to come together in a laboratory in Leipzig, Germany, in 1879. It was here that Wilhelm Wundt (VILL-helm Voont, 1832–1920), a physiologist, attempted to apply scientific principles to the study of the human mind. In his laboratory, students from around the world were taught to study the structure of the human mind. Wundt believed that consciousness, the state of being aware of external events, could be broken down into thoughts, experiences, emotions, and other basic elements. In order to inspect these nonphysical elements, students had to learn

AP 1.C Describe and compare different theoretical approaches in explaining behavior.

---

*biases: personal judgments based on beliefs rather than facts.
**systematic: according to a fixed, ordered plan.
***philosophers: people who seek wisdom and knowledge through thinking and discussion.
****physiologists: scientists who study the physical workings of the body and its systems.

to think objectively about their own thoughts—after all, they could hardly read someone else's mind. Wundt called this process **objective introspection**, the process of objectively examining and measuring one's own thoughts and mental activities (Rieber & Robinson, 2001). For example, Wundt might place an object, such as a rock, in a student's hand and have the student tell him everything that he was feeling as a result of having the rock in his hand—all the sensations stimulated by the rock. (Objectivity* was—and is—important because scientists need to remain unbiased. Observations need to be clear and precise but unaffected by the individual observer's beliefs and values.)

This was really the first attempt by anyone to bring objectivity and measurement to the concept of psychology. This attention to objectivity, together with the establishment of the first true experimental laboratory in psychology, is why Wundt is known as the father of psychology.

TITCHENER AND STRUCTURALISM IN AMERICA One of Wundt's students was Edward Titchener (1867–1927), an Englishman who eventually took Wundt's ideas to Cornell University in Ithaca, New York. Titchener expanded on Wundt's original ideas, calling his new viewpoint **structuralism** because the focus of study was the structure of the mind. He believed that every experience could be broken down into its individual emotions and sensations (Brennan, 2002). Although Titchener agreed with Wundt that consciousness could be broken down into its basic elements, Titchener also believed that objective introspection could be used on thoughts as well as on physical sensations. For example, Titchener might have asked his students to introspect about things that are blue rather than actually giving them a blue object and asking for reactions to it. Such an exercise might have led to something like the following: "What is blue? There are blue things, like the sky or a bird's feathers. Blue is cool and restful, blue is calm . . ." and so on.

In 1894, one of Titchener's students at Cornell University became famous for becoming the first woman to receive a Ph.D. in psychology (Goodman, 1980; Guthrie, 2004). Her name was Margaret F. Washburn, and she was Titchener's only graduate student for that year. In 1908 she published a book on animal behavior that was considered an important work in that era of psychology, *The Animal Mind* (Washburn, 1908).

Structuralism was a dominant force in the early days of psychology, but it eventually died out in the early 1900s, as the structuralists were busily fighting among themselves over just which key elements of experience were the most important. A competing view arose not long after Wundt's laboratory was established, shortly before structuralism came to America.

WILLIAM JAMES AND FUNCTIONALISM Harvard University was the first school in America to offer classes in psychology in the late 1870s. These classes were taught by one of Harvard's most illustrious instructors, William James (1842–1910). James began teaching anatomy and physiology, but as his interest in psychology developed, he started teaching it almost exclusively (Brennan, 2002). His comprehensive textbook on the subject, *Principles of Psychology*, is so brilliantly written that copies are still in print (James, 1890).

Unlike Wundt and Titchener, James was more interested in the importance of consciousness to everyday life than just its analysis. He believed that the scientific study of consciousness itself was not yet possible. Conscious ideas are constantly flowing in an

objective introspection
the process of examining and measuring one's own thoughts and mental activities.

structuralism
early perspective in psychology associated with Wilhelm Wundt and Edward Titchener, in which the focus of study is the structure or basic elements of the mind.

AP 2.R Identify the contributions of major figures in consciousness research.

---

*objectivity: expressing or dealing with facts or conditions as they really are without allowing the influence of personal feelings, prejudices, or interpretations.

AP 2.B Identify key research contributions of scientists in the area of heredity and environment.

ever-changing stream, and once you start thinking about what you were just thinking about, what you were thinking about is no longer what you *were* thinking about—it's what you *are* thinking about—and . . . excuse me, I'm a little dizzy. I think you get the picture, anyway.

Instead, James focused on how the mind allows people to *function* in the real world—how people work, play, and adapt to their surroundings, a viewpoint he called **functionalism**. James was heavily influenced by Charles Darwin's ideas about *natural selection*, in which physical traits that help an animal adapt to its environment and survive are passed on to its offspring. If physical traits could aid in survival, why couldn't behavioral traits do the same? Animals and people whose behavior helped them to survive would pass those traits on to their offspring, perhaps by teaching or even by some then-unknown mechanism of heredity.* For example, a behavior such as avoiding the eyes of others in an elevator can be seen as a way of protecting one's personal space—a kind of territorial protection that may have its roots in the primitive need to protect one's home and source of food and water from intruders (Manusov & Patterson, 2006) or as a way of avoiding what might seem like a challenge to another person (Brown et al., 2005; Jehn et al., 1999).

It is interesting to note that one of James's early students was Mary Whiton Calkins, who completed every course and requirement for earning a Ph.D. but was denied that degree by Harvard University because she was a woman. She was allowed to take classes as a guest only. Calkins eventually established a psychological laboratory at Wellesley College. Her work was some of the earliest research in the area of human memory and the psychology of the self. In 1905, she became the first female president of the American Psychological Association (Furumoto, 1980, 1991; Zedler, 1995). Unlike Washburn, Calkins never earned the elusive Ph.D. degree despite a successful career as a professor and researcher (Guthrie, 2004).

Women were not the only disadvantaged group to make contributions in the early days of psychology. In 1920, for example, Francis Cecil Sumner became the first African American to earn a Ph.D. in psychology at Clark University. He eventually became the chair of the psychology department at Howard University and is assumed by many to be the father of African American psychology (Guthrie, 2004). Kenneth and Mamie Clark worked to show the negative effects of school segregation on African American children (Lal, 2002). In the 1940s, Hispanic psychologist George (Jorge) Sanchez conducted research in the area of intelligence testing, focusing on the cultural biases in such tests (Tevis, 1994). Other names of noted minorities include Dr. Charles Henry Thompson, the first African American to receive a doctorate in educational psychology in 1925; Dr. Albert Sidney Beckham, senior assistant psychologist at the National Committee for Mental Hygiene at the Illinois Institute for Juvenile Research in the early 1930s; Dr. Robert Prentiss Daniel, who became president of Shaw University in North Carolina and finally the president of Virginia State College; Dr. Inez Beverly Prosser (1897–1934), who was the first African American woman to earn a Ph.D. in educational psychology; Dr. Howard Hale Long, who became dean of administration at Wilberforce State College in Ohio; and Dr. Ruth Howard, who was the first African American woman to earn a Ph.D. in psychology (not educational psychology) in 1934 from the University of Minnesota (Guthrie, 2004).

Since those early days, psychology has seen an increase in the contributions of women and minorities, although the percentages are still small when compared to the

functionalism

early perspective in psychology associated with William James, in which the focus of study is how the mind allows people to adapt, live, work, and play.

---

*heredity: the transmission of traits and characteristics from parent to offspring through the actions of genes.

population at large. The American Psychological Association's Office of Ethnic Minority Affairs features notable psychologists as part of their *Ethnicity and Health in America Series*. Their Web site provides brief biographies of ethnic minority psychologists and work or research highlights particularly related to chronic health conditions for several ethnic groups: African American, Asian American, Hispanic–Latino, and Native American. For more information, visit **apa.org/pi/oema/resources/ethnicity-health/psychologists/**.

💬 Is functionalism still an important point of view in psychology?

In the new field of psychology, functionalism offered an alternative viewpoint to structuralism. But like so many of psychology's early ideas, it is no longer a major perspective. Instead, one can find elements of functionalism in the modern fields of *educational psychology* (studying the application of psychological concepts to education) and *industrial/organizational psychology* (studying the application of psychological concepts to businesses, organizations, and industry), as well as other areas in psychology. See Learning Objective A.6. Functionalism also played a part in the development of one of the more modern perspectives, evolutionary psychology, discussed later in this chapter.

1.2 Three Influential Approaches: Gestalt, Psychoanalysis, and Behaviorism

1.2 Summarize the basic ideas and the important people behind the early approaches known as Gestalt, psychoanalysis, and behaviorism.

While the structuralists and functionalists argued with each other and among themselves, some psychologists were looking at psychology in several other ways.

GESTALT PSYCHOLOGY: THE WHOLE IS GREATER THAN THE SUM OF ITS PARTS Max Wertheimer (VERT-hi-mer), like James, objected to the structuralist point of view, but for different reasons. Wertheimer believed that psychological events such as perceiving* and sensing** could not be broken down into any smaller elements and still be properly understood. For example, you can take a smartphone apart, but then you no longer have a smartphone—you have a pile of unconnected bits and pieces. Or, just as a melody is made up of individual notes that can only be understood if the notes are in the correct relationship to one another, so perception can only be understood as a whole, entire event. Hence the familiar slogan, "The whole is greater than the sum of its parts." Wertheimer and others believed that people naturally seek out patterns ("wholes") in the sensory information available to them.

Wertheimer and others devoted their efforts to studying sensation and perception in this new perspective, **Gestalt psychology**. *Gestalt* (Gesh-TALT) is a German word meaning "an organized whole" or "configuration," which fit well with the focus on studying whole patterns rather than small pieces of them. See **Figure 1.1** for an example of Gestalt perceptual patterns. Today, Gestalt ideas are part of the study of *cognitive psychology*, a field focusing not only on perception but also on learning, memory, thought processes, and problem solving; the basic Gestalt principles of perception are still taught within this newer field (Ash, 1998; Köhler, 1925, 1992; Wertheimer, 1982).

Gestalt psychology
early perspective in psychology focusing on perception and sensation, particularly the perception of patterns and whole figures.

Figure 1.1 A Gestalt Perception

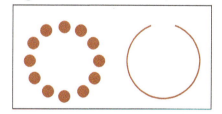

The eye tends to "fill in" the blanks here and sees both of these figures as circles rather than as a series of dots or a broken line.

---

*perceiving: becoming aware of something through the senses.
**sensing: seeing, hearing, feeling, tasting, or smelling something.

AP 2.R Identify the contributions of major figures in consciousness research.

AP 7.J Identify the contributions of major researchers in personality theory.

AP 8.K Identify the contributions of major figures in psychological treatment.

See Learning Objective 3.14. The Gestalt approach has also been influential in psychological therapy, becoming the basis for a therapeutic technique called *Gestalt therapy*. See Learning Objective 14.3.

SIGMUND FREUD'S THEORY OF PSYCHOANALYSIS It should be clear by now that psychology didn't start in one place and at one particular time. People of several different viewpoints were trying to promote their own perspective on the study of the human mind and behavior in different places all over the world. Up to now, this chapter has focused on the physiologists who became interested in psychology, with a focus on understanding consciousness but little else. The medical profession took a whole different approach to psychology.

💬 What about Freud? Everybody talks about him when they talk about psychology. Are his ideas still in use?

Sigmund Freud had become a noted physician in Austria while the structuralists were arguing, the functionalists were specializing, and the Gestaltists were looking at the big picture. Freud was a neurologist, a medical doctor who specializes in disorders of the nervous system; he and his colleagues had long sought a way to understand the patients who were coming to them for help.

Freud's patients suffered from nervous disorders for which he and other doctors could find no physical cause. Therefore, it was thought, the cause must be in the mind, and that is where Freud began to explore. He proposed that there is an *unconscious* (unaware) mind into which we push, or *repress*, all of our threatening urges and desires. He believed that these repressed urges, in trying to surface, created the nervous disorders in his patients (Freud et al., 1990). See Learning Objective 12.2.

Freud stressed the importance of early childhood experiences, believing that personality was formed in the first 6 years of life; if there were significant problems, those problems must have begun in the early years.

Some of his well-known followers were Alfred Adler, Carl Jung, Karen Horney, and his own daughter, Anna Freud. Anna Freud began what became known as the ego movement in psychology, which produced one of the best-known psychologists in the study of personality development, Erik Erikson. See Learning Objective 8.8.

Freud's ideas are still influential today, although in a somewhat modified form. He had a number of followers in addition to those already named, many of whom became famous by altering Freud's theory to fit their own viewpoints, but his basic ideas are still discussed and debated. See Learning Objective 12.4.

While some might think that Sigmund Freud was the first person to deal with people suffering from various mental disorders, the truth is that mental illness has a fairly long (and not very pretty) history. For more on the history of mental illness, see Learning Objective 13.1.

psychoanalysis

an insight therapy based on the theory of Freud, emphasizing the revealing of unconscious conflicts; Freud's term for both the theory of personality and the therapy based on it.

Freudian **psychoanalysis**, the theory and therapy based on Freud's ideas, has been the basis of much modern *psychotherapy* (a process in which a trained psychological professional helps a person gain insight into and change his or her behavior), but another major and competing viewpoint has actually been more influential in the field of psychology as a whole.

AP 4.A Identify contributions of key researchers in the psychology of learning.

PAVLOV, WATSON, AND THE DAWN OF BEHAVIORISM Ivan Pavlov, like Freud, was not a psychologist. He was a Russian physiologist who showed that a *reflex* (an involuntary reaction) could be caused to occur in response to a formerly unrelated stimulus. While working with dogs, Pavlov observed that the salivation reflex (which is normally produced by actually having food in one's mouth) could be caused to occur in response to a totally new stimulus, in this case, the sound of a ticking metronome. At the onset of his experiment, Pavlov would turn on the metronome and give the dogs food, and they would salivate. After several repetitions, the dogs would salivate to the sound of the metronome *before* the food was presented—a learned (or "conditioned") reflexive response (Klein & Mowrer, 1989). This process was called *conditioning*. See Learning Objective 5.2.

By the early 1900s, psychologist John B. Watson had tired of the arguing among the structuralists; he challenged the functionalist viewpoint, as well as psychoanalysis, with his own "science of behavior," or **behaviorism** (Watson, 1924). Watson wanted to bring psychology back to a focus on scientific inquiry, and he felt that the only way to do that was to ignore the whole consciousness issue and focus only on *observable behavior*—something that could be directly seen and measured. He had read of Pavlov's work and thought that conditioning could form the basis of his new perspective of behaviorism.

Watson was certainly aware of Freud's work and his views on unconscious repression. Freud believed that all behavior stems from unconscious motivation, whereas Watson believed that all behavior is learned. Freud had stated that a *phobia*, an irrational fear, is really a symptom of an underlying, repressed conflict and cannot be "cured" without years of psychoanalysis to uncover and understand the repressed material. Watson believed that phobias are learned through the process of conditioning and set out to prove it.

Along with his colleague Rosalie Rayner, he took a baby, known as "Little Albert" and taught him to fear a white rat by making a loud, scary noise every time the infant saw the rat until finally just seeing the rat caused the infant to cry and become fearful (Watson & Rayner, 1920). Even though "Little Albert" was not afraid of the rat at the start, the experiment worked very well—in fact, he later appeared to be afraid of other fuzzy things including a rabbit, a dog, and a sealskin coat. See Learning Objective 5.3.

💬 This sounds really bizarre—what does scaring a baby have to do with the science of psychology?

Watson wanted to prove that all behavior was a result of a stimulus–response relationship such as that described by Pavlov. Because Freud and his ideas about unconscious motivation were becoming a dominant force, Watson felt the need to show the world that a much simpler explanation could be found. Although scaring a baby sounds a little cruel, he felt that the advancement of the science of behavior was worth the baby's relatively brief discomfort.

A graduate student of Watson's named Mary Cover Jones later decided to repeat Watson and Rayner's study but added training that would "cancel out" the phobic reaction of the baby to the white rat. She duplicated the "Little Albert" study with another child, "Little Peter," successfully conditioning Peter to be afraid of a white rabbit (Jones, 1924). She then began a process of *counterconditioning*, in which Peter was exposed to the white rabbit from a distance while eating a food that he really liked. The pleasure of the food outweighed the fear of the faraway rabbit. Day by day, the situation was repeated with the rabbit being brought closer each time, until Peter was no longer afraid of the rabbit. Jones went on to become one of the early pioneers of behavior therapy. Behaviorism is still a major perspective in psychology today. It has also influenced the development of other perspectives, such as *cognitive psychology*.

American psychologist John Watson is known as the father of behaviorism. Behaviorism focuses only on observable behavior.

Mary Cover Jones, one of the early pioneers of behavior therapy, earned her master's degree under the supervision of John Watson. Her long and distinguished career also included the publication in 1952 of the first educational television course in child development (Rutherford, 2000).

behaviorism

the science of behavior that focuses on observable behavior only.

Concept Map L.O. 1.1, 1.2

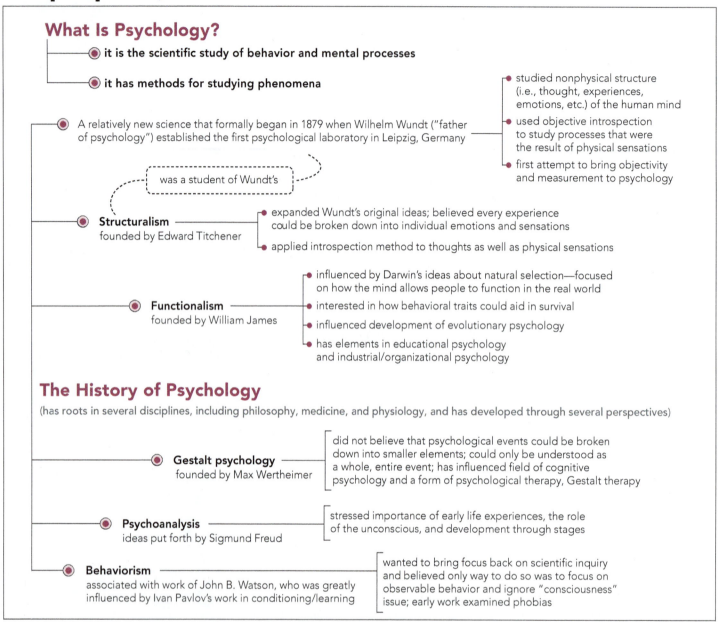

Practice Quiz   How much do you remember?

Pick the best answer.

1. In the definition of psychology, the term *mental processes* means
   a. only human behavior.
   b. only animal behavior.
   c. outward or overt actions and reactions.
   d. unconscious processes.
   e. internal, covert processes.

2. Which early psychologist was the first to try to bring objectivity and measurement to the concept of psychology?
   a. Edward Titchener
   b. Sigmund Freud
   c. William James
   d. John Watson
   e. Wilhelm Wundt

3. Which of the following early psychologists would have been most likely to agree with the statement, "The study of the mind should focus on how it functions in everyday life"?
   a. Sigmund Freud
   b. William James
   c. John Watson
   d. Wilhelm Wundt
   e. Margaret Washburn

4. Who was the first woman to complete the coursework for a doctorate at Harvard University?
   a. Ruth Howard
   b. Margaret Washburn
   c. Beverly Prosser
   d. Mary Whiton Calkins
   e. Mary Cover Jones

5. Which early perspective tried to return to a focus on scientific inquiry by ignoring the study of consciousness?
   a. functionalism
   b. structuralism
   c. behaviorism
   d. psychoanalysis
   e. Gestalt

1.3–1.4 The Field of Psychology Today

Even in the twenty-first century, there isn't one single perspective that is used to explain all human behavior and mental processes. There are actually seven modern perspectives.

AP 1.C Describe and compare different theoretical approaches in explaining behavior.

1.3 Modern Perspectives

1.3 Summarize the basic ideas behind the seven modern perspectives in psychology.

Two of psychology's modern perspectives are updated versions of psychoanalysis and behaviorism, while the others focus on people's goals, thought processes, social and cultural factors, biology, and genetics. Watch the video *Diverse Perspectives* to get a quick overview of the perspectives before we continue.

Watch Diverse Perspectives

Watch the Video at MyLab Psychology

PSYCHODYNAMIC PERSPECTIVE Freud's theory is still used by many professionals in therapy situations. It is far less common today than it was a few decades ago, however, and even those who use his techniques modify them for contemporary use. In the more modern **psychodynamic perspective**, the focus may still include the unconscious mind and its influence over conscious behavior and on early childhood experiences, but with less of an emphasis on sex and sexual motivations and more emphasis on the development of a sense of self, social and interpersonal relationships, and the discovery of other motivations behind a person's behavior. See Learning Objective 12.4. Some modern psychodynamic practitioners have even begun to recommend that the link between neurobiology (the study of the brain and nervous system) and psychodynamic concepts should be more fully explored (Glucksman, 2006).

BEHAVIORAL PERSPECTIVE Like modern psychodynamic perspectives, behaviorism is still also very influential. When its primary supporter, John B. Watson, moved on to greener pastures in the world of advertising, B. F. Skinner became the new leader of the field.

Skinner not only continued research in classical conditioning, but he also developed a theory called *operant conditioning* to explain how voluntary behavior is learned (Skinner, 1938). In this theory, *behavioral* responses that are followed by pleasurable consequences are strengthened, or *reinforced*. For example, a child who cries and is rewarded by getting his mother's attention will cry again in the future. Skinner's work is discussed later in more depth. See Learning Objective 5.4. In addition to the psychodynamic and behavioral perspectives, there are five newer perspectives that have developed within the last 60 years.

HUMANISTIC PERSPECTIVE Often called the "third force" in psychology, humanism was really a reaction to both psychoanalytic theory and behaviorism. If you were a psychologist in the early to mid-1900s, you were either a psychoanalyst or a behaviorist—there weren't any other major viewpoints to rival those two.

In contrast to the psychoanalytic focus on sexual development and behaviorism's focus on external forces in guiding personality development, some professionals began to develop a perspective that would allow them to focus on people's ability to direct their own lives. Psychologists with a **humanistic perspective** held the view that people have *free will*, the freedom to choose their own destiny, and strive for *self-actualization*, the achievement of one's full potential. Two of the earliest and most famous founders of this view were Abraham Maslow (1908–1970) and Carl Rogers (1902–1987). Today, humanism exists as a form of psychotherapy aimed at self-understanding and self-improvement. See Learning Objective 14.3.

Behaviorist B. F. Skinner puts a rat through its paces. What challenges might arise from applying information gained from studies with animals to human behavior?

psychodynamic perspective

modern version of psychoanalysis that is more focused on the development of a sense of self and the discovery of motivations behind a person's behavior other than sexual motivations.

humanistic perspective

the "third force" in psychology that focuses on those aspects of personality that make people uniquely human, such as subjective feelings and freedom of choice.

COGNITIVE PERSPECTIVE Cognitive psychology, which focuses on how people think, remember, store, and use information, became a major force in the field in the 1960s. It wasn't a new idea, as the Gestalt psychologists had themselves supported the study of mental processes of learning. Swiss psychologist Jean Piaget proposed a theory of cognitive development in infants, children, and adolescents in the middle of the twentieth century, a theory still influential in education (Piaget, 1952, 1962, 1983). See Learning Objective 8.7. The development of computers (which just happened to make pretty good models of human thinking) and discoveries in biological psychology all stimulated an interest in studying the processes of thought. The **cognitive perspective** with its focus on memory, intelligence, perception, thought processes, problem solving, language, and learning has become a major force in psychology. See Chapter Seven: Cognition.

Within the cognitive perspective, the relatively new field of **cognitive neuroscience** includes the study of the physical workings of the brain and nervous system when engaged in memory, thinking, and other cognitive processes. Cognitive neuroscientists use tools for imaging the structure and activity of the living brain, such as magnetic resonance imaging (MRI), functional magnetic resonance imaging (fMRI), and positron emission tomography (PET). See Learning Objective 2.5. The continually developing field of brain imaging is important in the study of cognitive processes.

SOCIOCULTURAL PERSPECTIVE Another modern perspective in psychology is the **sociocultural perspective**, which actually combines two areas of study: *social psychology*, which is the study of groups, social roles, and rules of social actions and relationships, and *cultural psychology*, which is the study of cultural norms,* values, and expectations. These two areas are related in that they are both about the effect that people have on one another, either individually or in a larger group such as a culture (Bronfenbrenner, 1979; Peplau & Taylor, 1997). See Chapter Eleven: Social Psychology. Think about it: Don't you behave differently around your family members than you do around your friends? Would you act differently in another country than you do in your native land? Russian psychologist Lev Vygotsky (1978) also used sociocultural concepts in forming his sociocultural theory of children's cognitive development. See Learning Objective 8.7.

The sociocultural perspective is important because it reminds people that the way they and others behave (or even think) is influenced not only by whether they are alone, with friends, in a crowd, or part of a group but also by the social norms, fads, class differences, and ethnic identity concerns of the particular culture in which they live. *Cross-cultural research* also fits within this perspective. In cross-cultural research, the contrasts and comparisons of a behavior or issue are studied in at least two or more cultures. This type of research can help illustrate the different influences of environment (culture and training) when compared to the influence of heredity (genetics, or the influence of genes on behavior).

For example, in a classic study covered in Chapter Eleven: Social Psychology, researchers Dr. John Darley and Dr. Bibb Latané (1968) found that the presence of other people actually *lessened* the chances that a person in trouble would receive help. This phenomenon** is called the "bystander effect," and it is believed to be the result of *diffusion of responsibility*, which is the tendency to feel that someone else is responsible for taking action when others are present. But would this effect appear in other cultures? There have been incidents in India that meet the criteria for the bystander effect: In 2002, a man under the influence of alcohol sexually assaulted a girl who was mentally

---

cognitive perspective

modern perspective in psychology that focuses on memory, intelligence, perception, problem solving, and learning.

cognitive neuroscience

study of the physical changes in the brain and nervous system during thinking.

sociocultural perspective

perspective that focuses on the influence of social interactions, society, and culture on an individual's thinking and behavior; in psychopathology, approach that examines the impact of social interactions, community, and culture on a person's thinking, behavior, and emotions.

---

*norms: standards or expected behavior.
**phenomenon: a situation that is seen to exist and for which an explanation may be needed.

challenged while the two were traveling on a train with five other passengers who did nothing to stop the attack; and in 2012, a 20-year-old woman was molested outside a bar in Guwahati for thirty minutes in view of many witnesses who did nothing (Tatke, 2012). India is a country that is culturally quite different from the United States, and individuals in India are typically expected to act for the greater good of others, yet the bystander effect apparently exists even there (Hofstede, 1980; Hofstede et al., 2002). Questions about how human behavior differs or is similar in different social or cultural settings are exactly what the sociocultural perspective asks and attempts to answer, using cross-cultural research.

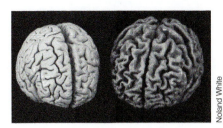

Compare the two preserved brains above. A "normal" brain is on the left while the one on the right is from someone diagnosed with Alzheimer's disease. Note the narrowed gyri (bulges) and widened sulci (grooves) in the brain on the right. This is due to progressive brain cell loss associated with Alzheimer's disease. In the case of dementia and other progressive diseases, one focus of the biological perspective is examining how thinking and behavior changes over time as the brain changes. You may also notice the brains are not identical in size. This is due to slight differences between individuals and how individual specimens respond to the preservation and plastination processes.

BIOPSYCHOLOGICAL PERSPECTIVE *Biopsychology*, or the study of the biological bases of behavior and mental processes, isn't really as new a perspective as one might think. Also known as physiological psychology, biological psychology, psychobiology, and behavioral neuroscience, biopsychology is part of the larger field of *neuroscience*: the study of the physical structure, function, and development of the nervous system. Also, the previously discussed field of cognitive neuroscience often overlaps with biopsychology.

In the **biopsychological perspective**, human and animal behavior is seen as a direct result of events in the body. Hormones, heredity, brain chemicals, tumors, and diseases are some of the biological causes of behavior and mental events. See Chapter Two: The Biological Perspective. Some of the topics researched by biopsychologists include sleep, emotions, aggression, sexual behavior, and learning and memory—as well as disorders. While disorders may have multiple causes (family issues, stress, or trauma, for example), research in biopsychology points clearly to biological factors as one of those causes.

For example, research suggests that human sexual orientation may be related to the developing baby's exposure in the womb to testosterone, especially in females (Breedlove, 2010; Grimbos et al., 2010), as well as the birth order of male children (Puts et al., 2006). The birth order study suggests that the more older brothers a male child has, the more likely he is to have a homosexual orientation (Puts et al., 2006). The biopsychological perspective plays an even greater role in helping us understand psychological phenomena in other areas. There is clear evidence that genetics play a role in the development of *schizophrenia*, a mental disorder involving delusions (false beliefs), hallucinations (false sensory impressions), and extremely distorted thinking, with recent research pointing to greater risk for those who inherit variants of a gene that plays a role in removing extra connections between neurons in the brain (Flint & Munafò, 2014; Schizophrenia Working Group of the Psychiatric Genomics, 2014; Sekar et al., 2016). See Learning Objectives 2.1 and 13.16. In still another example, the progressive brain changes associated with Alzheimer's disease may begin more than 20 years prior to the onset of the clinical symptoms of dementia (Bateman et al., 2012). To date, no cure exists, and treatments only temporarily assist with some cognitive and behavioral symptoms. Early identification and tracking of cognitive performance in individuals at risk for Alzheimer's disease is one vital component of researchers' efforts to identify potential interventions and treatments for this devastating disease (Amariglio et al., 2015).

EVOLUTIONARY PERSPECTIVE The **evolutionary perspective** focuses on the biological bases for universal mental characteristics that all humans share. It seeks to explain general mental strategies and traits, such as why we lie, how attractiveness influences mate selection, why fear of snakes is so common, or why people universally like music and dancing. This approach may also overlap with biopsychology and the sociocultural perspective.

In this perspective, the mind is seen as a set of information-processing machines, designed by the same process of natural selection that Darwin (1859) first theorized, allowing

biopsychological perspective

perspective that attributes human and animal behavior to biological events occurring in the body, such as genetic influences, hormones, and the activity of the nervous system.

evolutionary perspective

perspective that focuses on the biological bases of universal mental characteristics that all humans share.

AP 2.A Discuss psychology's abiding interest in how heredity, environment, and evolution work together to shape behavior.

human beings to solve the problems faced in the early days of human evolution—the problems of the early hunters and gatherers. For example, *evolutionary psychologists* (psychologists who study the evolutionary origins of human behavior) would view the human behavior of not eating substances that have a bitter taste (such as poisonous plants) as an adaptive* behavior that evolved as early humans came into contact with such bitter plants. Those who ate the bitter plants would die, while those who spit them out survived to pass on their "I-don't-like-this-taste" genes to their offspring, who would pass on the genes to *their* offspring, and so on, until after a long period of time, there is an entire population of humans that naturally avoids bitter-tasting substances.

> That explains why people don't like bitter stuff, like the white part of an orange peel, but that's really a physical thing. How would the evolutionary perspective help us understand something psychological like relationships?

You may have realized as you read through the various perspectives that no one perspective has all the answers. Some perspectives are more scientific (e.g., behavioral and cognitive), while others are based more in thinking about human behavior (e.g., psychodynamic and humanistic). Some, like sociocultural, biopsychological, and evolutionary perspectives, are related to each other. Psychologists will often take an *eclectic* perspective—one that uses the "bits and pieces" of several perspectives that seem to best fit a particular situation. For a look at all seven modern perspectives, their major concepts, and some of the major "players" in each, see **Table 1.1**.

Table 1.1 The Seven Modern Perspectives in Psychology

Perspective	Major Focus and Concepts	Major Theorists
Psychodynamic	Development of sense of self, motivation for social/interpersonal relationships	Sigmund Freud, Carl Gustav Jung, Alfred Adler, Karen Horney, Erik Erikson, Anna Freud
Behavioral	Classical and operant conditioning, concept of reinforcement, focus on observable behavior	Ivan Pavlov, John B. Watson, Edward L. Thorndike, B. F. Skinner
Humanistic	The ability of the individual to direct and control his or her own life, free will, self-actualization	Abraham Maslow, Carl Rogers, Natalie Rogers
Cognitive	Perception, memory, intelligence, thought processes, problem solving, language, learning, the role of the brain and nervous system	Jean Piaget, Noam Chomsky, Elizabeth Loftus, Howard Gardner, Fergus I. M. Craik, Raymond Cattell, Eleanor Rosch
Sociocultural	Relationship between social behavior and the contexts of family, social groups, and culture	Lev Vygotsky, John Darley, Bibb Latané, Albert Bandura, Leon Festinger, Henri Tajfel, Philip Zimbardo, Stanley Milgram
Biopsychological	Influences of genetics, hormones, and the activity of the nervous system on human and animal behavior	Paul Broca, Charles Darwin, Michael Gazzaniga, Roger Sperry, Carl Wernicke, S. Marc Breedlove, Lisa Feldman Barrett
Evolutionary	The biological bases for universal mental characteristics that are shared by all humans	David Buss, Richard Dawkins, Leda Cosmides, Robert Trivers, David C. Geary, Todd K. Shackelford, Daved F. Bjorklund, Anne Campbell, Susan Oyama

THINKING CRITICALLY 1.1

Do you believe that violence is a part of human nature? Is violent behavior something that can someday be removed from human behavior or, at the very least, be controlled? Think about this question from each of the perspectives discussed in this chapter.

---

*adaptive: having the quality of adjusting to the circumstances or need; in the sense used here, a behavior that aids in survival.

1.4 Psychological Professionals and Areas of Specialization

1.4 Differentiate between the various types of professionals within the field of psychology.

Psychology is a large field, and the many professionals working within it have different training, different focuses, and may have different goals from the typical psychologist.

A **psychologist** has no medical training but has a doctorate degree. Psychologists undergo intense academic training, learning about many different areas of psychology before choosing a specialization. Because the focus of their careers can vary so widely, psychologists work in many different vocational* settings. **Figure 1.2a** shows the types of settings in which psychologists work. It is important to realize that not all psychologists are trained to do counseling, nor are all psychologists actually counselors. Psychologists who are in the counseling specialization must be licensed to practice in their states.

In contrast, a **psychiatrist** has a medical degree and is a physician who specializes in the diagnosis and treatment (including the prescription of medications) of psychological disorders. A **psychiatric social worker** is trained in the area of social work and usually possesses a master's degree in that discipline. These professionals focus more on the environmental conditions that can have an impact on mental disorders, such as poverty, overcrowding, stress, and drug abuse. There are also *licensed professional counselors* and *licensed marriage and family therapists* who may have a master's or doctoral degree in a variety of areas and provide counseling services relative to their area of training. See Learning Objective A.3.

AP 1.E Distinguish the different domains of psychology.

psychologist
a professional with an academic degree and specialized training in one or more areas of psychology.

psychiatrist
a physician who specializes in the diagnosis and treatment of psychological disorders.

Psychiatric social workers help many kinds and ages of people. The woman on the right might be going through a divorce, dealing with the loss of a spouse, or even recovering from drug abuse.

Figure 1.2 Work Settings and Subfields of Psychology

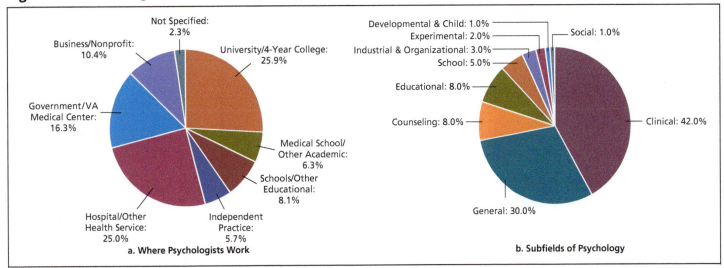

a. Where Psychologists Work

b. Subfields of Psychology

(a) There are many different work settings for psychologists. Although not obvious from the chart, many psychologists work in more than one setting. For example, a clinical psychologist may work in a hospital setting and teach at a university or college. (b) This pie chart shows the specialty areas of psychologists who recently received their doctorates.

Source: American Psychological Association. (2016). Psychology Master's and Doctoral Degrees Awarded by Broad Field, Subfield, Institution Type and State (2004–2013): Findings from the Integrated Postsecondary Education Data System. Washington, DC: Author

💬 You said not all psychologists do counseling. But I thought that was all that psychologists do—what else is there?

Although many psychologists do participate in delivering therapy to people who need help, there is a nearly equal number of psychologists who do other tasks:

psychiatric social worker
a social worker with training in therapy methods who focuses on the environmental conditions that can have an impact on mental disorders, such as poverty, overcrowding, stress, and drug abuse.

---

*vocational: having to do with a job or career.

Watch Careers in Psychology

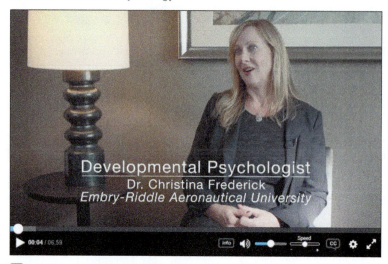

Watch the Video at MyLab Psychology

basic research
research focused on adding information to the scientific knowledge base.

applied research
research focused on finding practical solutions to real-world problems.

researching, teaching, designing equipment and workplaces, and developing educational methods, for example. Also, not every psychologist is interested in the same area of human—or animal—behavior, and most psychologists work in several different areas of interest, as shown in **Figure 1.2b**, "Subfields of Psychology."

Those psychologists who do research have two types of research to consider: basic research versus applied research. **Basic research** is research for the sake of gaining scientific knowledge. For example, a researcher might want to know how many "things" a person can hold in memory at any one time. The other form of research is **applied research**, which is research aimed at answering real-world, practical problems. An applied researcher might take the information from the basic researcher's memory study and use it to develop a new study method for students. Some of the subfields in Figure 1.2b tend to do more basic research, such as experimental and developmental psychologists, while others may focus more on applied research, such as educational, school, and industrial/organizational psychologists.

There are many other areas of specialization: Psychology can be used in fields such as health; sports performance; legal issues; business concerns; and even in the design of equipment, tools, and furniture. For a more detailed look at some of the areas in which psychological principles can be applied and a listing of careers that can benefit from a degree in psychology, watch the video *Careers in Psychology* and see the Appendix: Applied Psychology and Psychology Careers.

Concept Map L.O. 1.3, 1.4

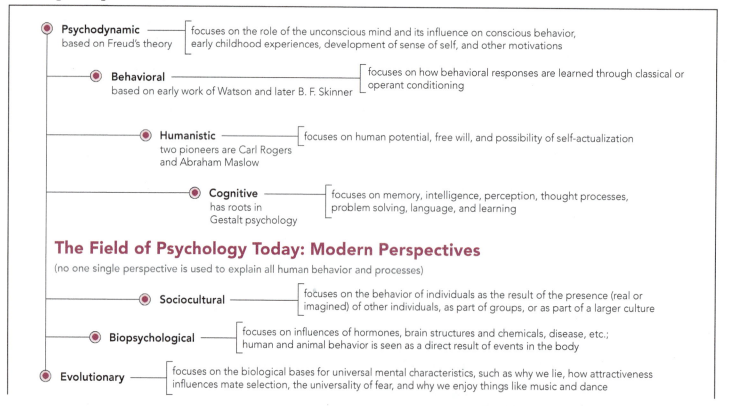

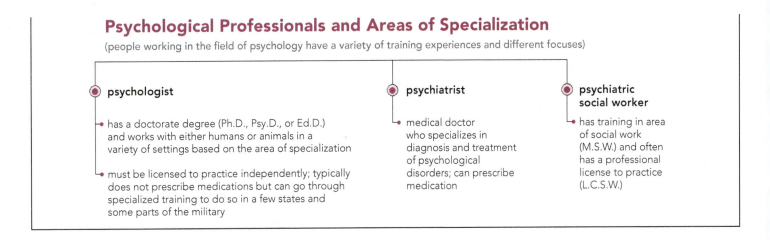

Practice Quiz — How much do you remember?

Pick the best answer.

1. Which of the following perspectives focuses on the biological bases of universal mental characteristics?
   a. humanistic
   b. Gestalt
   c. evolutionary
   d. behavioral
   e. psychodynamic

2. Which perspective offers the best explanation for schizophrenia?
   a. evolutionary
   b. behavioral
   c. psychodynamic
   d. biopsychological
   e. humanistic

3. Carter has learned that if he cries with his mother in public, she will often get him a new toy or a piece of candy so as to quiet him. Which of the following perspectives explains Carter's behavior?
   a. biopsychological
   b. psychodynamic
   c. cognitive
   d. behavioral
   e. sociocultural

4. Which perspective would a researcher be taking if she were studying a client's early childhood experiences and his resulting development of self?
   a. psychodynamic
   b. cognitive
   c. humanistic
   d. behavioral
   e. evolutionary

5. Which of the following professionals in psychology has a doctoral degree that is not in medicine?
   a. psychiatrist
   b. master's-level counselor
   c. psychiatric social worker
   d. psychiatric nurse
   e. psychologist

6. If Dr. Stevenson is like most psychologists, where does she probably work?
   a. business/nonprofit
   b. independent practice
   c. business/profit
   d. government/VA medical center
   e. university/college

1.5–1.10 Scientific Research

Have you ever played the "airport game"? You sit at the airport (bus terminal, mall, or any other place where people come and go) and try to guess what people do for a living based only on their appearance. Although it's a fun game, the guesses are rarely correct. People's guesses also sometimes reveal the biases that they may have about certain physical appearances: men with long hair are musicians, people wearing suits are executives, and so on. Psychology is about trying to determine facts, reducing uncertainty and bias, and promoting scientific thinking.

You have hopefully noticed that there are questions designed to help you think a little differently scattered throughout this chapter. Some are actually labeled as "thinking critically" while others appear as part of the captions for the pictures in the chapter. The ability to look carefully and with a critical eye at the information and statements to which we are exposed on a daily basis—in news sources, on the Internet, on the television, or even our phones—is an extremely important one. Let's take a look at why and how *critical thinking* should be emphasized in every aspect of our lives.

AP 1.D Recognize the strengths and limitations of applying theories to explain behavior.

1.5 Thinking Critically About Critical Thinking

1.5 Recall the basic criteria for critical thinking that people can use in their everyday lives.

The real world is full of opportunities for scientific, well-reasoned thinking. Think about all the commercials on television for miracle weight loss, hair restoration, or herbal remedies for arthritis, depression, and a whole host of physical and mental problems. Wouldn't it be nice to know how many of these claims people should believe? Wouldn't you like to know how to evaluate statements like these and possibly save yourself some time, effort, and money? That's exactly the kind of "real-world" problem that critical thinking can help sort out.

Critical thinking means making reasoned judgments (Beyer, 1995; McLaughlin & McGill, 2017). The word *reasoned* means that people's judgments should be logical and well thought out. Critical thinking also includes the ability to ask and seek answers for critical questions at the right time (Browne & Keeley, 2009). An example of a critical question might be, "Is someone paying you to do this research/sell this product, and is this a conflict of interest?" or "Do you have any good evidence for the claims you are making, or are you just giving your opinion?" Critical thinking can also help us avoid false beliefs that may lead to poor decisions or even prove dangerous to our mental and physical health.

While the word *critical* is often viewed as meaning "negative," that is not the use of this term here. Instead, it's more related to the word *criteria*,* as in thinking that meets certain high criteria or standards (Nosich, 2008). There are four basic criteria for critical thinking that people should remember when faced with statements about the world around them (Browne & Keeley, 2009; Gill, 1991; Shore, 1990):

1. **There are very few "truths" that do not need to be subjected to testing.** Although people may accept religious beliefs and personal values on faith, everything else in life needs to have supporting evidence. Questions that can be investigated empirically (i.e., verified by observations and gathering of evidence) should be examined using established scientific approaches. One shouldn't accept anything at face value but should always ask, "How do you know that? What is the evidence? Can you be more specific in your terms?" For example, many people still believe that astrology, the study of the supposed influence of the stars and planets on the birth of an infant, can be used to make predictions about that infant's personality and life events as he or she grows. But scientific investigations have shown us, time after time, that astrology is without any basis in truth or scientific fact (Dean & Kelly, 2000; Hines, 2003; Kelly, 1980; Narlikar, 2013; Wiseman, 2007).

2. **All evidence is not equal in quality.** One of the most important, often overlooked steps in critical thinking is evaluating how evidence is gathered before deciding that it provides good support for some idea. For example, there are poorly done experiments, incorrect assumptions based on the wrong kind of data gathering, studies that could not be repeated, and studies in which there were major design flaws. There are also studies that have been deliberately manipulated to produce the findings that the researcher (or whoever is paying the researcher) would prefer. For example, the results of a study on the effectiveness of a particular drug would be immediately suspect if the researcher is being paid by the company making the drug. As a critical thinker, you should be aware that the wilder the claim, the better the evidence should be: For example, I have not yet seen any evidence that convinces me of alien visitations or abductions!

critical thinking
making reasoned judgments about claims.

---

*criteria: standards on which a judgment or decision may be based.

3. **Just because someone is considered to be an authority or to have a lot of expertise does not make everything that person claims automatically true.** One should always ask to see the evidence rather than just take some expert's word for anything. How good is the evidence? Are there other alternative explanations? Is the alternative explanation simpler? If there are two explanations for some phenomenon and both account for the phenomenon equally well, the *simplest* explanation is *more often* the best one—a rule of thumb known as *the law of parsimony*. For example, let's look at crop circles, those geometric patterns of flattened crop stalks that have at times been discovered in farmers' fields. Two possible explanations for crop circles exist: Either they are made by aliens in spaceships—as is the claim by many alleged experts—or they are made by human beings as a hoax.* Which explanation is simpler? Obviously, the hoax rationalization is the simplest, and it turned out to be correct for the crop circles that appeared in England in the late 1970s and 1980s: David Bower and Doug Chorley, two British men, confessed to creating the crop circles as a prank, thought up in a barroom and meant to make fun of people who believe in alien visitations (Nickell, 1995; M. Ridley, 2002; Schnabel, 1994).

4. **Critical thinking requires an open mind.** Although it is good to be a little skeptical, people should not close their minds to things that are truly possible. At the same time, it's good for people to have open minds but not so open that they are gullible** and apt to believe anything. Critical thinking requires a delicate balance between skepticism and the willingness to consider possibilities—even possibilities that contradict previous judgments or beliefs. For example, scientists have yet to find any convincing evidence that there was once life on Mars. That doesn't mean that scientists totally dismiss the idea, just that there is no convincing evidence *yet*. I don't believe that there are Martians on Mars, but if I were shown convincing evidence, I would have to be willing to change my thinking—as difficult as that might be.

Watch Critical Thinking

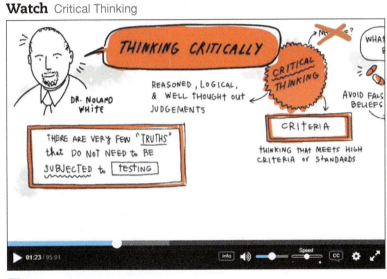

👁 **Watch** the **Video** at **MyLab Psychology**

THINKING CRITICALLY 1.2

Why do you think some people (even very smart people) sometimes avoid thinking critically about issues such as politics, the existence of ESP, or the supernatural?

AP 1.F Differentiate types of research with regard to purpose, strengths, and weaknesses.

1.6 The Scientific Approach

1.6 Recall the five steps of the scientific approach.

In psychology, researchers want to see only what is really there, not what their biases might lead them to see. They must apply all the principles of critical thinking, and this can be achieved best by using the **scientific approach**, an approach to research intending to reduce the likelihood of bias and error in the measurement of data.

PSYCHOLOGY'S GOALS Every science has the common goal of learning how things work. The goals specifically aimed at uncovering the mysteries of human and animal behavior are description, explanation, prediction, and control. The scientific approach is a way to accomplish these goals of psychology.

AP 1.G Discuss the value of reliance on operational definitions and measurement in behavioral research.

AP 1.K Predict the validity of behavioral explanations based on the quality of research design.

scientific approach

system of gathering data so that bias and error in measurement are reduced.

---

*hoax: something intended to fool people, a trick or lie.
**gullible: easily fooled or cheated.

- **Description: What Is Happening?** The first step in understanding anything is to describe it. *Description* involves observing a behavior and noting everything about it: what is happening, where it happens, to whom it happens, and under what circumstances it seems to happen.

  For example, a psychologist might wonder why so many computer scientists seem to be male. She makes further observations and notes that many "nontechies" stereotypically perceive the life and environment of a computer scientist as someone who lives and breathes at the computer and surrounds himself with computer games, junk food, and science-fiction gadgets—characteristics that add up to a very masculine ambiance.

  That's what *seems* to be happening. The psychologist's observations are a starting place for the next goal: Why do females seem to avoid going into this environment?

- **Explanation: Why Is It Happening?** Based on her observations, the psychologist might try to come up with a tentative explanation, such as "women feel they do not belong in such stereotypically masculine surroundings." In other words, she is trying to understand or find an *explanation* for the lower proportion of women in this field. Finding explanations for behavior is a very important step in the process of forming theories of behavior. A **theory** is a general explanation of a set of observations or facts. The goal of description provides the observations, and the goal of explanation helps build the theory.

  The preceding example comes from a real experiment conducted by psychologist Sapna Cheryan and colleagues (Cheryan et al., 2009). Professor Cheryan (who teaches psychology at the University of Washington in Seattle) set up four experiments with more than 250 female and male student participants who were not studying computer science. In the first experiment, students came into a small classroom that had one of two sets of objects: either Star Trek® posters, video-game boxes, and Coke™ cans, or nature posters, art, a dictionary, and coffee mugs (among other things). Told to ignore the objects because they were sharing the room with another class, the students spent several minutes in the classroom. While still sitting in the classroom, they were asked to fill out a questionnaire asking about their attitude toward computer science. While the attitudes of male students were not different between the two environments, women exposed to the stereotypically masculine setup were less interested in computer science than those who were exposed to the nonstereotypical environment. The three other similar experiments yielded the same results. Later studies found that when women were exposed to role models who dressed and acted according to the computer science stereotyped image, those women showed decreased interest in computer science as a career as well as decreased expectation of success in that field (Cheryan et al., 2011; Cheryan et al., 2013). In two similar follow-up studies with high school students, the researchers found that providing adolescent girls with an educational environment that did not fit current computer science stereotypes seemed to increase their interest in computer science courses (Master et al., 2015).

Is this an environment that you would want to work in? Some researchers have wondered if your answer might be influenced by gender.

- **Prediction: When Will It Happen Again?** Determining what will happen in the future is a *prediction*. In the original Cheryan et al., study, the prediction is clear: If we want more women to go into computer science, we must do something to change either the environment or the perception of the environment typically associated with this field. This is the purpose of the last of the four goals of psychology: changing or modifying behavior.

- **Control: How Can It Be Changed?** The focus of control, or the modification of some behavior, is to change a behavior from an undesirable one (such as

theory

a general explanation of a set of observations or facts.

women avoiding a certain academic major) to a desirable one (such as more equality in career choices). Professor Cheryan suggests that changing the image of computer science may help increase the number of women choosing to go into this field.

Not all psychological investigations will try to meet all four of these goals. In some cases, the main focus might be on description and prediction, as it would be for a personality theorist who wants to know what people are like (description) and what they might do in certain situations (prediction). Some psychologists are interested in both description and explanation, as is the case with experimental psychologists who design research to find explanations for observed (described) behavior. Therapists may be more interested in controlling or influencing behavior and mental processes, although the other three goals would be important in achieving this objective.

STEPS IN THE SCIENTIFIC APPROACH The first step in any investigation is to have a question to investigate, right? So the first step in the scientific approach is this:

1. **Perceiving the Question:** You notice something interesting happening in your surroundings for which you would like to have an explanation. An example might be that you've noticed that your children seem to get a little more aggressive with each other after watching a particularly violent children's cartoon program on Saturday morning. You wonder if the violence in the cartoon could be creating the aggressive behavior in your children. This step is derived from the goal of *description*: What is happening here?

    Once you have a question, you want an answer. The next logical step is to form a tentative* answer or explanation for the behavior you have seen. This tentative explanation is known as a **hypothesis**.

2. **Forming a Hypothesis:** Based on your initial observations of what's going on in your surroundings, you form an educated guess about the explanation for your observations, putting it into the form of a statement that can be tested in some way. Testing hypotheses is the heart of any scientific investigation and is the primary way in which support for theories is generated. In fact, a good theory should lead to the formation of hypotheses (predictions based on the theory). It might be helpful to think of an "if–then" statement: If the world is round, then a person should be able to sail in a straight line around the world and come back to where he or she started. "If the world is round" is the theory part of this statement, a theory based on many observations and facts gathered by observers, like observing that when a ship sails toward the horizon, it seems to "disappear" from the bottom up, indicating a curvature of the surface of the water. The "then" part of the statement is the hypothesis, a specific, *testable* prediction based on the theory. While it would be nice if all of our assumptions about what we observe are always correct, that isn't what happens and isn't necessarily what we want to happen—the scientific approach means you have to seek out information even though it might not agree with what you believed you would find. As odd as it might seem, hypotheses must be *falsifiable*: there must be a way not just to prove a hypothesis is true but also to prove a hypothesis is false. This is what being "testable" means: You have to be able to see if your hypothesis is true or false. In the example, the "then" part of the statement is testable because, as Christopher Columbus attempted to do, you actually can sail in a straight (more or less) line and see if your prediction comes true. Going

The scientific approach can be used to determine if children who watch violence on television are more likely to be aggressive than those who do not.

hypothesis

tentative explanation of a phenomenon based on observations.

---

*tentative: something that is not fully worked out or completed as yet.

back to the previous example, you might say, "If exposure to violence leads to increased aggression in children, then children who watch violent cartoons will become more aggressive." The last part of that statement is the hypothesis to be tested. (Forming a hypothesis based on observations is related to the goals of *description* and *explanation*.)

How do researchers go about testing the hypothesis? People have a tendency to notice only things that agree with their view of the world, a kind of selective perception called *confirmation bias*. See Learning Objective 7.4. For example, if a person is convinced that all men with long hair smoke cigarettes, that person will tend to notice only those long-haired men who are smoking and ignore all the long-haired men who don't smoke. As mentioned in the previous paragraph, the scientific approach is designed to overcome the tendency to look at only the information that confirms people's biases by forcing them to actively seek out information that might *contradict* their biases (or hypotheses). So when you test your hypothesis, you are trying to determine if the factor you suspect has an effect and that the results weren't due to luck or chance. That's why psychologists keep doing research over and over—to get more evidence that hypotheses are "supported" or "not supported." When you have a body of hypotheses that have been supported, you can build your theory around those observations.

3. **Testing the Hypothesis:** The approach you use to test your hypothesis will depend on exactly what kind of answer you think you might get. You could make more detailed observations or do a survey in which you ask questions of a large number of people, or you might design an experiment in which you would deliberately change one thing to see if it causes changes in the behavior you are observing. In the example, the best approach would probably be an experiment in which you select a group of children, show half of them a cartoon with violence and half of them a cartoon with no violence, and then find some way of measuring aggressive behavior in the two groups.

What do you do with the results of your testing? Of course, testing the hypothesis is all about the goal of getting an *explanation* for behavior, which leads to the next step.

4. **Drawing Conclusions:** Once you know the results of your hypothesis testing, you will find that either your hypothesis was supported—which means that your experiment worked and that your measurements supported your initial observations—or that they weren't supported, which means that you need to go back to square one and think of another possible explanation for what you have observed. (Could it be that Saturday mornings make children a little more aggressive? Or Saturday breakfasts?)

The results of any form of hypothesis testing won't be just the raw numbers or measurements. Any data that come from your testing procedure will be analyzed with some kind of statistical method that helps to organize and refine the data. Drawing conclusions can be related to the goal of *prediction*: If your hypothesis is supported, you can make educated guesses about future, similar scenarios.

5. **Report Your Results:** You have come to some conclusion about your investigation's success or failure, and you want to let other researchers know what you have found.

 Why tell anyone what happened if it failed?

Just because one experiment or study did not find support for the hypothesis does not necessarily mean that the hypothesis is incorrect. Your study could have been poorly designed, or there might have been factors out of your control that interfered with the study.

But other researchers are asking the same kinds of questions that you might have asked. They need to know what has already been found out about the answers to those questions so that they can continue investigating and adding more knowledge about the answers to those questions. Even if your own investigation didn't go as planned, your report will tell other researchers what *not* to do in the future. So the final step in any scientific investigation is reporting the results.

At this point, you would want to write up exactly what you did, why you did it, how you did it, and what you found. If others can **replicate** your research (meaning, do exactly the same study over again and get the same results), it gives much more support to your findings. A research study that cannot be replicated successfully is a poor quality of evidence, as discussed in the second criterion for critical thinking in the previous section. A study that can be replicated successfully allows others to predict behavior based on your findings and to use the results of those findings to modify or *control* behavior, the last goal in psychology. Replication of a study's results is not always an easy task, and some evidence suggests editors of peer-reviewed journals have tended to publish positive research results overall and not embrace direct replications of "old" knowledge (Nosek et al., 2012). Even when direct replication studies have been published, some results have not been as strong or did not reach the same level of statistical significance as the originals (Open Science Collaboration, 2015). While these and related concerns have been referred to as a *replicability crisis* in psychology, the field is responding to the challenge (Frankenhuis & Nettle, 2018; Washburn et al., 2018). There are focused and continued efforts of researchers to test and retest "what we think we know," providing additional evidence for many areas and suggesting we still have much work to do in other areas of psychology (Open Science Collaboration, 2015).

This might be a good place to make a distinction between questions that can be scientifically or empirically studied and those that cannot. For example, "What is the meaning of life?" is not a question that can be studied using the scientific or empirical approach. Empirical questions are those that can be tested through direct observation or experience. For example, "Has life ever existed on Mars?" is a question that scientists are trying to answer through measurements, experimentation, soil samples, and other methods. Eventually they will be able to say with some degree of confidence that life could have existed or could not have existed. That is an empirical question, because it can be supported or disproved by gathering real evidence. The meaning of life, however, is a question of belief for each person. One does not need proof to *believe*, but scientists need proof (in the form of objectively gathered evidence) to *know*. Questions that involve beliefs and values are best left to philosophy and religion.

In psychology, researchers try to find the answers to empirical questions. They can use a variety of research methods depending on the scientific question to be answered, as seen in the video *Research Methods*.

replicate
in research, repeating a study or experiment to see if the same results will be obtained in an effort to demonstrate reliability of results.

Watch Research Methods

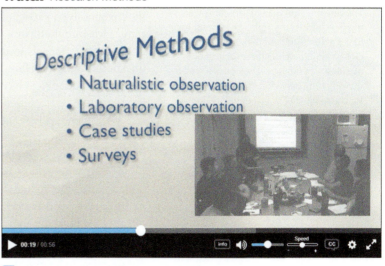

Watch the Video at MyLab Psychology

1.7 Descriptive Methods

1.7 Compare and contrast some of the methods used to describe behavior.

There are a number of different ways to investigate the answers to research questions, and which one researchers use depends on the kind of question they want to answer. If they only want to gather information about what has happened or what is happening, they would select a method that gives them a detailed description.

AP 1.K Predict the validity of behavioral explanations based on the quality of research design.

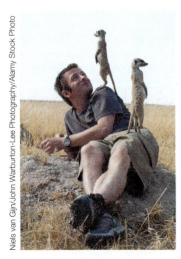

This researcher is studying the behavior of a group of meerkats. Is this naturalistic observation? Why or why not?

The researcher in the foreground is watching the children through a one-way mirror to get a description of their behavior. Observations such as these are just one of many ways that psychologists have of investigating behavior. Why is it important for the researcher to be behind a one-way mirror?

observer effect
tendency of people or animals to behave differently from normal when they know they are being observed.

participant observation
a naturalistic observation in which the observer becomes a participant in the group being observed.

observer bias
tendency of observers to see what they expect to see.

NATURALISTIC OBSERVATION Sometimes all a researcher needs to know is what is happening to a group of animals or people. The best way to look at the behavior of animals or people is to watch them behave in their normal environment. That's why animal researchers go to where the animals live and watch them eat, play, mate, and sleep in their own natural surroundings. With people, researchers might want to observe them in their workplaces, in their homes, or on playgrounds. For example, if someone wanted to know how adolescents behave with members of the opposite sex in a social setting, that researcher might go to a major shopping area on a weekend night.

What is the advantage of naturalistic observation? It allows researchers to get a realistic picture of how behavior occurs because they are actually watching that behavior in its natural setting. In a more controlled, arranged environment, like a laboratory, they might get behavior that is contrived or artificial rather than genuine. Of course, precautions must be taken. An observer should have a checklist of well-defined and specific behavior to record, perhaps using their phone, tablet, or a special handheld computer to log each piece of data. In many cases, animals or people who know they are being watched will not behave normally—a process called the **observer effect**—so often the observer must remain hidden from view. When researching humans, remaining hidden is often a difficult thing to do. In the earlier example of the shopping area with the teenagers, a researcher might find that sitting on a bench pretending to read a book is a good disguise, especially if one wears glasses to hide the movement of the eyes. Using such a scenario, researchers would be able to observe what goes on between the teens without them knowing that they were being watched. In other cases, researchers might use one-way mirrors, or they might actually become participants in a group, a technique called **participant observation**.

Are there disadvantages to this method? Unfortunately, yes. One of the disadvantages of naturalistic observation is the possibility of **observer bias**. That happens when the person doing the observing has a particular opinion about what he or she expects to see. If that is the case, sometimes that person recognizes only those actions that support the preconceived expectation and ignores actions that contradict it. For example, if you think girls initiate flirting, you might not see the boys who initiate flirting. One way to avoid observer bias is to use *blind observers*: people who do not know what the research question is and, therefore, have no preconceived notions about what they "should" see. It's also a good idea to have more than one observer so that the various observations can be compared.

Another disadvantage is that each naturalistic setting is unique and unlike any other. Observations that are made at one time in one setting may not hold true for another time, even if the setting is similar, because the conditions are not going to be identical time after time—researchers don't have that kind of control over the natural world. For example, famed gorilla researcher Dian Fossey had to battle poachers who set traps for the animals in the area of her observations (Mowat, 1988). The presence and activities of the poachers affected the normal behavior of the gorillas she was trying to observe.

LABORATORY OBSERVATION Sometimes observing behavior in animals or people is just not practical in a natural setting. For example, a researcher might want to observe the reactions of infants to a mirror image of themselves and to record the reactions with a camera mounted behind a one-way mirror. That kind of equipment might be difficult to set up in a natural setting. In a laboratory observation, the researcher would bring the infant to the equipment, controlling the number of infants and their ages, as well as everything else that goes on in the laboratory.

As mentioned previously, laboratory settings have the disadvantage of being an artificial situation that might result in artificial behavior—both animals and people often react differently in the laboratory than they would in the real world. The main advantage of this method is the degree of control that it gives to the observer.

Both naturalistic and laboratory observations can lead to the formation of hypotheses that can later be tested.

CASE STUDIES Another descriptive technique is called the **case study**, in which one individual is studied in great detail. In a case study, researchers try to learn everything they can about that individual. For example, Sigmund Freud based his entire theory of psychoanalysis on case studies of his patients in which he gathered information about their childhoods and relationships with others from the very beginning of their lives to the present. See Learning Objective 12.3.

The advantage of the case study is the tremendous amount of detail it provides. It may also be the only way to get certain kinds of information. For example, one famous case study was the story of Phineas Gage, who, in an accident, had a large metal rod driven through his head and survived but experienced major personality and behavioral changes during the time immediately following the accident (Damasio et al., 1994; Ratiu et al., 2004; Van Horn et al., 2012). Researchers couldn't study that with naturalistic observation, and an experiment is out of the question. Imagine anyone responding to an ad in the newspaper that read:

> *Wanted: 50 people willing to suffer nonfatal brain damage for scientific study of the brain. Will pay all medical expenses.*

You certainly wouldn't get many volunteers. Case studies are good ways to study things that are rare.

The disadvantage of the case study is that researchers can't really apply the results to other similar people. In other words, they can't assume that if another person had the same kind of experiences growing up, he or she would turn out just like the person in their case study. People are unique and have too many complicating factors in their lives to be that predictable (Think about the uniqueness of the case of Phineas Gage, for example). So what researchers find in one case won't necessarily apply or generalize to others. Another weakness of this method is that case studies are a form of detailed observation and are vulnerable to bias on the part of the person conducting the case study, just as observer bias can occur in naturalistic or laboratory observation.

SURVEYS Sometimes what psychologists want to know about is pretty personal. The only way to find out about very private (covert) behavior is to ask questions.

In the survey method, researchers will ask a series of questions about the topic they are studying. Surveys can be conducted in person in the form of interviews or on the phone, through the Internet, or with a written questionnaire. The questions used in interviews or on the phone can vary, but usually the questions in a survey are all the same for everyone answering the survey. In this way, researchers can ask lots of questions and survey literally hundreds of people.

That is the big advantage of surveys: Aside from their ability to get at private information, researchers can also get a tremendous amount of data on a very large group of people. Of course, there are disadvantages. For one, researchers have to be very careful about the group of people they survey. If they want to find out what college freshmen think about politics, for example, they can't really ask every single college freshman in the entire United States. But they can select a **representative sample** from that group. They could randomly* select a certain number of college freshmen from several different

AP 2.K Recount historic and contemporary research strategies and technologies that support research.

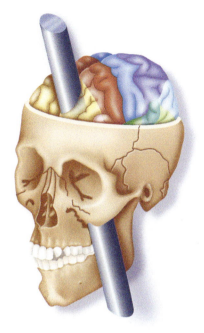

Phineas Gage survived a steel tamping rod going through his head after some explosive powder went off unexpectedly. The steel tamping rod entered above the left side of his mouth, passed through his left frontal lobe, and exited through the top of his skull.

AP 1.J Distinguish between random assignment of participants to conditions in experiments and random selection of participants, primarily in correlational studies and surveys.

case study
study of one individual in great detail.

representative sample
randomly selected sample of participants from a larger population of participants.

---

*randomly: in this sense, selected so that each member of the group has an equal chance of being chosen.

population
the entire group of people or animals in which the researcher is interested.

colleges across the United States, for example. Why randomly? Because the sample has to be *representative* of the **population**, which is the entire group in which the researcher is interested. If researchers selected only freshmen from Ivy League schools, for example, they would certainly get different opinions on politics than they might get from small community colleges. But if they take a lot of colleges and select their *participants* (people who are part of the study) randomly, they will be more certain of getting answers that a broad selection of college students would typically give.

Getting a representative sample is not always easy (Banerjee & Chaudhury, 2010). Many researchers (even more so in the past than now) use people who are readily available for their samples. Since many researchers work in educational settings, that means that they often use college students. College students aren't really good representatives of the general population even if you sampled many different kinds of schools as in the previous example—they are mostly white and well educated (and, in the early days of psychology, nearly all men). The general population is not all of those things, obviously. Random sampling can be accomplished by assigning potential participants a number and then using an electronically generated table of random numbers to select the participants, for example.

Another major disadvantage of the survey technique occurs because people aren't always going to give researchers accurate answers. The fact is, people tend to misremember things or distort the truth, and some may lie outright—even if the survey is an anonymous* questionnaire. Remembering is not a very accurate process sometimes, especially when people think that they might not come off sounding very desirable or socially appropriate. Some people deliberately give the answer they think is more socially correct rather than their true opinion so that no one gets offended in a process called *courtesy bias*. Researchers must take their survey results with a big grain of salt**—they may not be as accurate as they would like them to be.

Both the wording of survey questions and the order in which they appear can affect the outcome. It is difficult to find a wording that will be understood in exactly the same way by all those who read the question. Questions can be worded in a way that the desired answer becomes obvious (often resulting in courtesy bias-type answers). For example, "Do you agree that the new procedures for registering for classes are too complicated?" is obviously looking for a confirmation, while "What is your opinion of the new procedures for registering for classes?" is much more open to differing responses. Even the order of questions in a survey matters: A question about how much should be spent on public safety might have a very different answer at the beginning of a survey than after a long list of questions about crimes and criminal activity.

1.8 Correlations: Finding Relationships

1.8 Explain how researchers use the correlational technique to study relationships between two or more variables.

The methods discussed so far only provide descriptions of behavior. There are really only two methods that allow researchers to know more than just a description of what has happened: correlations and experiments. Correlation is actually a statistical technique, a particular way of organizing numerical information so that it is easier to look for patterns in the information. This method will be discussed here rather than in the statistics section later in this chapter because correlation, like the experiment, is about finding

AP 1.1 Describe how research design drives the reasonable conclusions that can be drawn.

---
*anonymous: not named or identified.
**grain of salt: a phrase meaning to be skeptical; to doubt the truth or accuracy of something.

relationships. In fact, the data from the descriptive methods just discussed are often analyzed using the correlational technique.

A **correlation** is a measure of the relationship between two or more variables. A *variable* is anything that can change or vary—scores on a test, temperature in a room, gender, and so on. For example, researchers might be curious to know whether cigarette smoking is connected to life expectancy—the number of years a person can be expected to live. Obviously, the scientists can't hang around people who smoke and wait to see when those people die. The only way (short of performing a very unethical and lengthy experiment) to find out if smoking behavior and life expectancy are related to each other is to use the medical records of people who have already died. (For privacy's sake, the personal information such as names and social security numbers would be removed, with only the facts such as age, gender, weight, and so on available to researchers.) Researchers would look for two facts from each record: the number of cigarettes the person smoked per day and the age of the person at death.

Now the researcher has two sets of numbers for each person in the study that go into a mathematical formula (see Learning Objective 1.16) to produce a number called the **correlation coefficient**. The correlation coefficient represents two things: the direction of the relationship and its strength.

 Direction? How can a mathematical relationship have a direction?

Whenever researchers talk about two variables being related to each other, what they really mean is that knowing the value of one variable allows them to predict the value of the other variable. For example, if researchers found that smoking and life expectancy are indeed related, they should be able to predict how long someone might live if they know how many cigarettes a person smokes in a day. But which way does that prediction work? If a person smokes a lot of cigarettes, does that mean that he or she will live a longer life or a shorter one? Does life expectancy go up or down as smoking increases? That's what is meant by the *direction* of the relationship.

In terms of the correlation coefficient (represented by the small letter r), the number researchers get from the formula will either be a positive number or a negative number. If positive, the two variables increase in the same direction—as one goes up, the other goes up; as one decreases, the other also decreases. If negative, the two variables have an inverse* relationship—as one increases, the other decreases. If researchers find that the more cigarettes a person smoked, the younger that person was when he or she died, it would mean that the correlation between the two variables is negative. (As smoking goes up, life expectancy goes down—an inverse relationship.)

The strength of the relationship between the variables will be determined by the actual number itself. That number will always range between +1.00 and −1.00.

The reason that it cannot be greater than +1.00 or less than −1.00 has to do with the formula and an imaginary line on a graph around which the data points gather, a graph called a scatterplot (see **Figure 1.3**). If the relationship is a strong one, the number will be closer to +1.00 or to −1.00. A correlation of +.89 for example, would be a very strong positive correlation. That might represent the relationship between scores on the SAT and an IQ test, for example. A correlation of −.89 would be equally strong but negative. That would be more like the correlation researchers would probably find between smoking cigarettes and the age at which a person dies.

Notice that the closer the number is to zero, the weaker the relationship becomes. Researchers would probably find that the correlation coefficient for the relationship between people's weight and the number of freckles they have is pretty close to zero, for example.

---

*inverse: opposite in order.

correlation

a measure of the relationship between two variables.

correlation coefficient

a number that represents the strength and direction of a relationship existing between two variables; number derived from the formula for measuring a correlation.

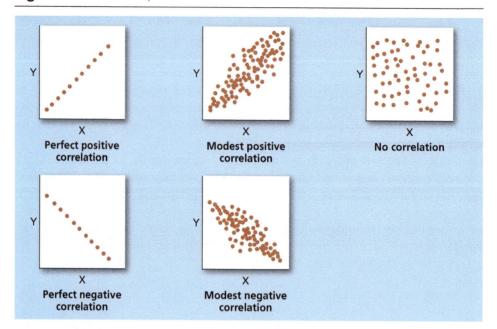

Figure 1.3 Five Scatterplots

These scatterplots show direction and strength of correlation. It should be noted that perfect correlations, whether positive or negative, rarely occur in the real world.

💬 Go back to the cigarette thing—if we found that the correlation between cigarette smoking and life expectancy was high, does that mean that smoking causes your life expectancy to be shortened?

Not exactly. The biggest error that people make concerning correlation is to assume that it means one variable is the cause of the other. Remember that *correlation does not prove causation*. Although adverse health effects from cigarette smoking account for approximately 480,000 deaths each year in the United States alone, correlation by itself cannot be used to prove causation (U.S. Department of Health and Human Services, 2014). Just because two variables are related to each other, researchers cannot assume that one of them causes the other one to occur. They could both be related to some other variable that is the cause of both. For example, cigarette smoking and life expectancy could be linked only because people who smoke may be less likely to take care of their health by eating right and exercising, whereas people who don't smoke may tend to eat healthier foods and exercise more than smokers do.

To sum up, a correlation will tell researchers if there is a relationship between the variables, how strong the relationship is, and in what direction the relationship goes. If researchers know the value of one variable, they can predict the value of the other. If they know someone's IQ score, for example, they can predict approximately what score that person should get on the SAT—not the exact score, just a reasonable estimate. Also, even though correlation does not prove causation, it can provide a starting point for examining causal relationships with another type of study, the experiment.

1.9 The Experiment

1.9 Identify the steps involved in designing an experiment.

The only method that will allow researchers to determine the cause of a behavior is the **experiment**. In an experiment, researchers deliberately manipulate (change in some purposeful way) the variable they think is causing some behavior while holding all the other variables that might interfere with the experiment's results constant and unchanging. That way, if they get changes in behavior (an effect, in other words), they

experiment
a deliberate manipulation of a variable to see if corresponding changes in behavior result, allowing the determination of cause-and-effect relationships.

know that those changes must be due to the manipulated variable. For example, remember the discussion of the steps in the scientific approach. It talked about how to study the effects of watching violent cartoons on children's aggressive behavior. The most logical way to study that particular relationship is by an experiment.

SELECTION First, researchers might start by selecting the children they want to use in the experiment. The best way to do that is through random selection of a sample of children from a "population" determined by the researchers—just as a sample would be selected for a survey. Ideally, researchers would decide on the age of child they wanted to study—say, children who are 3–4 years old. Then researchers would go to various day care centers and randomly select a certain number of children of that age. Of course, that wouldn't include the children who don't go to a day care center. Another way to get a sample in the age range might be to ask several pediatricians to send out letters to parents of children of that age and then randomly select the sample from those children whose parents responded positively.

The act of pushing each other could be part of an operationalization of aggressive behavior.

THE VARIABLES Another important step is to decide on the variable the researchers want to manipulate (which would be the one they think causes changes in behavior) and the variable they want to measure to see if there are any changes (this would be the effect on behavior of the manipulation). Often deciding on the variables in the experiment comes before selection of the participants.

In the example of aggression and children's cartoons, the variable that researchers think causes changes in aggressive behavior is the violence in the cartoons. Researchers would want to manipulate that in some way, and in order to do that they have to decide the meaning of the term *violent cartoon*. They would have to find or create a cartoon that contains violence. Then they would show that cartoon to the participants and try to measure their aggressive behavior afterward. In measuring the aggressive behavior, the researchers would have to describe exactly what they mean by "aggressive behavior" so that it can be measured. This description is called **operationalization** because it specifically names the operations (steps or procedures) that the experimenter must use to control or measure the variables in the experiment (Lilienfeld et al., 2015a). An operationalization of aggressive behavior might be a checklist of very specific actions such as hitting, pushing, and so on that an observer can mark off as the children do the items on the list. If the observers were just told to look for "aggressive behavior," the researchers would probably get half a dozen or more different interpretations of what aggressive behavior is.

The name for the variable that is manipulated in any experiment is the **independent variable** because it is *independent* of anything the participants do. The participants in the study do not get to choose or vary the independent variable, and their behavior does not affect this variable at all. In the preceding example, the independent variable would be the presence or absence of violence in the cartoons.

The response of the participants to the manipulation of the independent variable *is* a dependent relationship, so the response of the participants that is measured is known as the **dependent variable**. Their behavior, if the hypothesis is correct, should *depend* on whether or not they were exposed to the independent variable, and in the example, the dependent variable would be the measure of aggressive behavior in the children. The dependent variable is always the thing (response of participants or result of some action) that is measured to see just how the independent variable may have affected it. Watch the video *Experiments: Independent versus Dependent Variables* to learn more about variables in experiments.

AP 1.G Discuss the value of reliance on operational definitions and measurement in behavioral research.

AP 1.H Identify independent, dependent, confounding, and control variables in experimental designs.

operationalization

specific description of a variable of interest that allows it to be measured.

independent variable

variable in an experiment that is manipulated by the experimenter.

dependent variable

variable in an experiment that represents the measurable response or behavior of the participants in the experiment.

Watch Experiments: Independent versus Dependent Variables

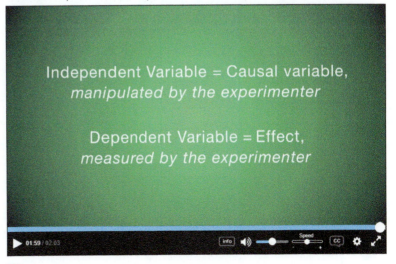

Watch the Video at MyLab Psychology

THE GROUPS

> 💬 If researchers do all of this and find that the children's behavior is aggressive, can they say that the aggressive behavior was caused by the violence in the cartoon?

No, what has been described so far is not enough. The researchers may find that the children who watch the violent cartoon are aggressive, but how would they know if their aggressive behavior was caused by the cartoon or was just the natural aggression level of those particular children or the result of the particular time of day they were observed? Those sorts of *confounding variables* (variables that interfere with each other and their possible effects on some other variable of interest) are the kind researchers have to control for in some way. For example, if most children in this experiment just happened to be from a fairly aggressive family background, any effects the violent cartoon in the experiment might have had on the children's behavior could be confused (confounded) with the possible effects of the family background. The researchers wouldn't know if the children were being aggressive because they watched the cartoon or because they liked to play aggressively anyway.

The best way to control for confounding variables is to have two groups of participants: those who watch the violent cartoon and those who watch a nonviolent cartoon for the same length of time. Then the researchers would measure the aggressive behavior in both groups. If the aggressive behavior is significantly greater in the group that watched the violent cartoon (statistically speaking), then researchers can say that in this experiment, violent cartoon watching caused greater aggressive behavior.

The group that is exposed to the independent variable (the violent cartoon in the example) is called the **experimental group** because it is the group that receives the experimental manipulation. The other group that gets either no treatment or some kind of treatment that should have no effect (like the group that watches the nonviolent cartoon in the example) is called the **control group** because it is used to *control* for the possibility that other factors might be causing the effect that is being examined. If researchers were to find that both the group that watched the violent cartoon and the group that watched the nonviolent cartoon were equally aggressive, they would have to assume that the violent content did not influence their behavior at all.

Many experiments involve more than just two groups. A researcher who wants to determine the effect of different levels of a particular independent variable (such as different dosages of a drug) would need multiple experimental groups. Other studies have multiple independent variables, such as a study looking at how age, gender, and exposure to video-game playing affect scores on a test of memory. If you also tested anxiety levels in that last example, you'd have more than one dependent variable as well. (Is your head hurting yet? Sorry about that.) Watch the video *Experiments: Experimental Group versus Control Group* to learn more about the function of groups in experiments.

AP 1.I Describe how research design drives the reasonable conclusions that can be drawn.

AP 1.J Distinguish between random assignment of participants to conditions in experiments and random selection of participants, primarily in correlational studies and surveys.

experimental group
participants in an experiment who are subjected to the independent variable.

control group
participants in an experiment who are not subjected to the independent variable and who may receive a placebo treatment.

random assignment
process of assigning participants to the experimental or control groups randomly, so that each participant has an equal chance of being in either group.

Watch Experiments: Experimental Group versus Control Group

👁 Watch the Video at MyLab Psychology

THE IMPORTANCE OF RANDOMIZATION As mentioned previously, random selection is the best way to choose the participants for any study. Participants must then be assigned to either the experimental group or the control group. Not surprisingly, **random assignment** of participants to one or the other condition is the best way to ensure control over other interfering, or *extraneous*, variables. Random assignment means that each participant has an equal chance of being assigned to each condition. If researchers simply looked at the children and put all of the children from one day care center or one pediatrician's recommendations into the experimental group and the same for the control group, they would run the risk of biasing their research. Some day care centers may have more naturally aggressive children, for example, or some pediatricians may have a particular client base in which the children are very passive. So researchers want to take the entire participant group and assign each person randomly to one or the other of the groups in the study. Sometimes this is as simple as picking names out of a hat.

1.10 Experimental Hazards and Controlling for Effects

1.10 Recall two common sources of problems in an experiment and some ways to control for these effects.

There are a few other problems that might arise in any experiment, even with the use of control groups and random assignment. These problems are especially likely when studying people instead of animals, because people are often influenced by their own thoughts or biases about what's going on in an experiment.

THE PLACEBO EFFECT AND THE EXPERIMENTER EFFECT For example, say there is a new drug that is supposed to improve memory in people who are in the very early stages of *Alzheimer's disease* (a form of mental deterioration that occurs in some people as they grow old). See Learning Objective 6.13. Researchers would want to test the drug to see if it really is effective in helping improve memory, so they would get a sample of people who are in the early stages of the disease, divide them into two groups, give one group the drug, and then test for improvement. They would probably have to do a test of memory both before and after the administration of the drug to be able to measure improvement.

placebo effect

the phenomenon in which the expectations of the participants in a study can influence their behavior.

> 💬 Let me see if I've got this straight. The group that gets the drug would be the experimental group, and the one that doesn't is the control group, right?

Right, and getting or not getting the drug is the independent variable, whereas the measure of memory improvement is the dependent variable. But there's still a problem with doing it this way. What if the researchers do find that the drug group had greater memory improvement than the group that received nothing? Can they really say that the drug itself caused the improvement? Or is it possible that the participants who received the drug *knew* that they were supposed to improve in memory and, therefore, made a major effort to do so? The improvement may have had more to do with participants' *belief* in the drug than the drug itself, a phenomenon known as the **placebo effect**: The expectations and biases of the participants in a study can influence their behavior. In medical research, the control group is often given a harmless substitute for the real drug, such as a sugar pill or an injection of salt water, and this substitute (which has no medical effect) is called the *placebo*. If there is a placebo effect, the control group will show changes in the dependent variable even though the participants in that group received only a placebo.

Another way that expectations about the outcome of the experiment can influence the results, even when the participants are animals rather than people, is called the **experimenter effect**. It has to do with the expectations of the experimenter, not the participants.

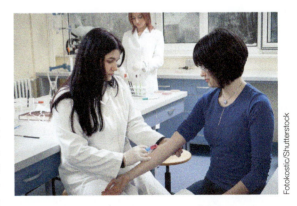

This woman suffers from chronic pain. If she were given a new pain-killing drug, the researcher could not be certain that any improvement in her pain was caused by the drug rather than by the woman's belief that the drug would work. The expectations of any person in an experimental study can affect the outcome of the study, a phenomenon known as the placebo effect.

experimenter effect

tendency of the experimenter's expectations for a study to unintentionally influence the results of the study.

As discussed earlier in the section about naturalistic observations, sometimes observers are biased—they see what they expect to see. Observer bias can also happen in an experiment. When the researcher is measuring the dependent variable, it's possible that he or she could give the participants clues about how they are supposed to respond—through the use of body language, tone of voice, or even eye contact. Although not deliberate, it does happen. It could go something like this in the memory drug example mentioned earlier: You, the Alzheimer's patient, are in the experimenter's office to take your second memory test after trying the drug. The experimenter seems to pay a lot of attention to you and to every answer that you give in the test, so you get the feeling that you are supposed to have improved a lot. So you try harder, and any improvement you show may be caused only by your own increased effort, not by the drug. That's an example of the experimenter effect in action: The behavior of the experimenter caused the participant to change his or her response pattern.

SINGLE-BLIND AND DOUBLE-BLIND STUDIES There are ways to control these effects. The classic way to avoid the placebo effect is to give the control group an actual placebo—some kind of treatment that doesn't affect behavior at all. In the drug experiment, the placebo would have to be some kind of sugar pill or saline (salt) solution that looks like and is administered just like the actual drug. The participants in both the experimental and the control groups would not know whether they got the real drug or the placebo. That way, if their expectations have any effect at all on the outcome of the experiment, the experimenter will be able to tell by looking at the results for the control group and comparing them to the experimental group. Even if the control group improves a little, the drug group should improve significantly more if the drug is working. This is called a **single-blind study** because the participants are "blind" to the treatment they receive.

For a long time, that was the only type of experiment researchers carried out in psychology. But researchers found that when teachers were told that some students had a high potential for success and others a low potential, the students showed significant gains or decreases in their performance on standardized tests depending on which "potential" they were supposed to have (Rosenthal & Jacobson, 1968). Actually, the students had been selected randomly and were randomly assigned to one of the two groups, "high" or "low." Their performances on the tests were affected by the attitudes of the teachers concerning their potential. This study and similar ones after it highlighted the need for the experimenter to be "blind" as well as the participants in research. So in a **double-blind study**, neither the participants nor the person or persons measuring the dependent variable know who got what. That's why every element in a double-blind experiment gets coded in some way, so that only after all the measurements have been taken can anyone determine who was in the experimental group and who was in the control group.

single-blind study
study in which the participants do not know if they are in the experimental or the control group.

double-blind study
study in which neither the experimenter nor the participants know if the participants are in the experimental or the control group.

Concept Map L.O. 1.5, 1.6, 1.7, 1.8, 1.9, 1.10

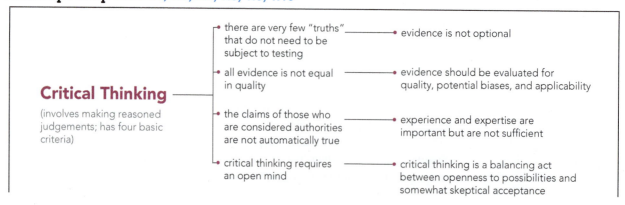

- psychology has four primary goals
  - describe
  - explain
  - predict
  - control

- steps in the scientific approach
  - perceiving the question about some empirical event for which you would like an explanation; can be derived from the goal of description: What is happening here?
  - forming a hypothesis, a tentative explanation about an event
  - testing the hypothesis by collecting data, analyzing results
  - drawing conclusions about investigation's success or failure to explain event
  - reporting your results; share exactly what, why, and how you did it, which provides means for replication

Scientific Research
(psychology uses the scientific approach to try to determine facts and reduce uncertainty)

- descriptive data collection methods
  - **naturalistic observation:** observe people or animals in natural environment ← can lead to formation of hypotheses that can later be tested
  - **laboratory observation:** observe people or animals in laboratory setting ← can lead to formation of hypotheses that can later be tested
  - **case studies:** individual is studied in greater detail, researchers try to learn everything they can about the individual
  - **surveys:** ask questions about topic researchers are studying via telephone, Internet, or a questionnaire

Correlation
- is a measure of relationship between two or more variables (anything that can change or vary)
- produces a value called the *correlation coefficient* that represents both direction and strength of relationship
- does not prove causation—variables can be related but you cannot assume that one of them causes the other to occur

The Experiment
(the only research method that will allow researchers to determine the cause of a behavior by deliberately manipulating some variable and measuring changes in the variable of interest)

- **selection:** researchers often aim to identify participants through random selection of a sample from the population of interest
- the process of **operationalization** specifically names the steps or procedures used to control or measure the variables in the experiment
  - **independent variable** is the variable that is manipulated, it is independent of anything participants do
  - **dependent variable** is the measure used to evaluate the manipulation of the independent variable
- groups
  - **experimental:** gets the independent variable or experimental manipulation ← random assignment to conditions is the best way to assure control over extraneous variables or confounding variables, variables that interfere with each other and/or on the variable of interest
  - **control:** receives no treatment or treatment that should not have an effect
- hazards
  - **placebo effect:** beliefs or expectations about a study can influence their behavior ← can be controlled through single-blind (participant "blind" to treatment/condition) and double-blind studies where both the participants and the experimenter measuring the dependent variable do not know the treatment/condition associated with the data
  - **experimenter effect:** experimenter's biases can affect or influence participants' behavior

Practice Quiz — How much do you remember?

Pick the best answer.

1. A common and very dangerous misconception often seen on the Internet is the idea that a childhood immunization, the MMR vaccine, causes autism. This is completely false, but began when a man published a falsified and now discredited paper making that claim. He was later found to have received money from lawyers representing parents of children with autism who wanted to sue the vaccine companies. Which criterion of critical thinking is most clearly being violated by those who accepted the false claim?
   a. Authority or claimed expertise does not make something true.
   b. All evidence is not equal in quality.
   c. Very few "truths" do not need to be tested.
   d. Keep an open mind.
   e. All evidence is equal in quality.

2. Dr. White noticed something odd happening to the behavior of his students as midterm exams neared. He decided to take notes about this behavior to find out exactly what was happening and the circumstances surrounding the behavior. His goal is clearly _____
   a. prediction
   b. explanation
   c. testing
   d. description
   e. control

3. Which of the following would indicate the weakest relationship and thus be close to complete randomness?
   a. −0.98
   b. +0.18
   c. +1.04
   d. −0.12
   e. +0.01

4. Which of the following is an example of observer bias?
   a. You develop an opinion of what you expect to see in an experiment.
   b. You do not allow a student to quit an experiment simply because he or she is bored.
   c. You ask your fellow students to be participants in a study of adult memory.
   d. You ask people from your church to participate in a study of family values.
   e. You allow a student to quit an experiment simply because he or she is bored.

5. In an experiment to examine the effects of sleep deprivation on completion of a puzzle, one group is allowed to sleep 8 hours while another group is made to stay awake. In this experiment, the control group is _____
   a. the group that remains awake.
   b. the group that gets to sleep.
   c. the puzzle.
   d. the difference in time for each group to complete the puzzle.
   e. the difference in time each group sleeps.

6. In a _____ study, the participants do not know if they are part of the control group or the experimental group. Only the experimenter knows who is in each group.
   a. triple-blind
   b. placebo
   c. correlational
   d. double-blind
   e. single-blind

APA Goal 2: Scientific Inquiry and Critical Thinking

A Sample Experiment

Addresses APA Learning Objective 2.4: Interpret, design, and conduct basic psychological research.

Many people have a somewhat negative stereotype of college athletes' academic abilities—believing that they are graded and promoted based on their athletic performance rather than their classroom performance. Evidence does exist for poorer performance on academic tests of athletes when compared to nonathletes in college (National Collegiate Athletic Association, 2002; Purdy et al., 1982; Upthegrove et al., 1999). But is this negative performance the result of poor academic ability, or could it be the effect of the negative stereotype itself? The following experiment (Jameson et al., 2007) was designed to examine the latter possibility.

In the experiment, 72 male college athletes from the sports teams of a university were given an intellectual test. Half of the athletes answered a brief questionnaire *before* taking the test, whereas the other half received the same questionnaire *after* taking the test. The questionnaire asked three questions, with the third question being, "Rate your likelihood of being accepted to the university without the aid of athletic recruiting." This item was designed to bring the negative stereotype of athletes ("dumb jocks") to the forefront of students' minds, *operationalizing* a "high threat" for that stereotype. The difference in threat level between the two groups before taking the intellectual test represents the *independent variable* in this experiment.

Those students who answered the "high threat" question *before* the intellectual test (the *experimental* group) scored significantly lower on that test (the measurement of the *dependent* variable) than those who answered the question *after* the test (the *control* group). The researchers also found a correlation between the students' exposure to the "high threat" stereotype condition and accuracy on the intellectual test: The more students believed that they got into college primarily because of their ability in sports (based on their rating of that third question), the worse they performed on the subsequent test. The researchers concluded that obvious negative stereotypes in higher education may be an important cause underlying the tendency of college athletes to underperform in academics.

APA Goal 2 A Sample Experiment

> **Fill in the blanks with the correct element of the experiment.**
> Feeling of stereotype threat ....
> Intellectual test scores ....
> Group answering questionnaire before taking intellectual test ....
> Group answering questionnaire after taking intellectual test ....
>
> **Word Bank:** Experimental group; Control group; Independent variable; Dependent variable

---

1.11 What Are Statistics?

1.11 Explain why statistics are important to psychologists and psychology majors.

Many students in psychology wonder why the field uses such seemingly complicated mathematics. The answer is easy. Psychologists base their field on research findings. Data are collected, and they have to be analyzed. *Statistics* is the field that gives us the tools to do that.

Psychologists have to be able to do two things with the data they collect. The first is to summarize the information from a study or experiment. The second is to make judgments and decisions about the data. We are interested if groups differ from each other. We are also interested in how one group of variables is related to another.

Statistics is the branch of mathematics concerned with the collection and interpretation of data from samples (Agresti & Finlay, 1997; Aron et al., 2005). A **sample** is a group of people selected, usually randomly, from a larger population of people. If you asked what the average height of teenage males was, and you calculated the average from just your high school, that average would be a statistic.

Statistical analysis is a way of trying to account for the error that exists in almost any body of data. Psychology is only one of many fields that use the following types of statistics.

In this section, we will take a look at describing data—seeing if groups differ from each other and seeing if two variables are related to each other. Those are the basic ideas of psychological statistics. The more advanced techniques are just bigger and better versions of these ideas. Many psychology students sometimes panic at the thought of taking statistics. However, it is crucial to the field and not really that hard if you put your mind to it and don't freeze yourself up. Why is it so important? Even if you are not the kind of psychologist who uses statistics on a daily basis, all psychologists have to be able to read and understand the research others are doing, and understanding what the statistical

statistics

branch of mathematics concerned with the collection and interpretation of numerical data.

sample

group of subjects selected from a larger population of subjects, usually selected randomly.

descriptive statistics
a way of organizing numbers and summarizing them so that patterns can be determined.

frequency distribution
a table or graph that shows how often different numbers or scores appear in a particular set of scores.

AP 1.L Apply basic descriptive statistical concepts, including interpreting and constructing graphs and calculations simple descriptive statistics.

AP 1.M Distinguish the purposes of descriptive statistics and inferential statistics.

analyses of that research is really saying is crucial. Here's a practical hint: Students with good research and statistical skills are much more employable and make more money than those who don't try to master research skills. It's nice to care about people, but you need all the skills you can get in today's world. Statistics and research design is one really profitable set of skills.

1.12–1.14 Descriptive Statistics

Descriptive statistics are a way of organizing numbers and summarizing them so that they can be understood. There are two main types of descriptive statistics:

- **Measures of Central Tendency.** Measures of central tendency are used to summarize the data and give you one score that seems typical of your sample.
- **Measures of Variability.** Measures of variability are used to indicate how spread out the data are. Are they tightly packed or are they widely dispersed?

The actual descriptive statistics are best understood after we explain the concept of a frequency distribution.

One way psychologists get started in a research project is to look at their data, but just looking at a list of numbers wouldn't do much good. So, we make a graph or chart. Then we can look for patterns.

1.12 Frequency Distributions

1.12 Describe the types of tables and graphs that represent patterns in data.

A **frequency distribution** is a table or graph that shows how often different numbers, or scores, appear in a particular set of scores. For example, let's say that you have a sample of 30 people, the size of some psychology classes. You ask them how many glasses of water they drink each day. You could represent the answers as shown in **Table 1.2**. Just by looking at this table, it is clear that typical people drink between four and eight glasses of water a day.

Tables can be useful, especially when dealing with small sets of data. Sometimes a more visual presentation gives a better "picture" of the patterns in a data set, and that is when researchers use graphs to plot the data from a frequency distribution. One common graph is a **histogram**, or a bar graph. **Figure 1.4** shows how the same data from Table 1.2 would look in a bar graph. Another type of graph used in frequency distributions is the **polygon**, a line graph. **Figure 1.5** shows the same data in a polygon graph.

Table 1.2 A Frequency Distribution

Number of Glasses Per Day	Number of People Out of 30 (Frequency)
1	0
2	1
3	2
4	4
5	5
6	6
7	5
8	4
9	2
10	1

Figure 1.4 A Histogram

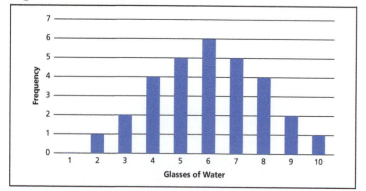

Histograms, or bar graphs, provide a visual way to look at data from frequency distributions. In this graph, for example, the height of the bars indicates that most people drink between four and eight glasses of water (represented by the five highest bars in the middle of the graph).

Figure 1.5 A Polygon

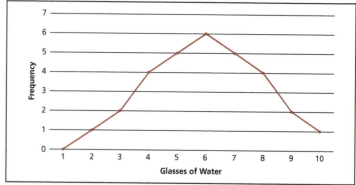

A polygon is a line graph that can represent the data in a frequency distribution in much the same way as a bar graph but allows the shape of the data set to be easily viewed.

THE NORMAL CURVE Frequency polygons allow researchers to see the shape of a set of data easily. For example, the number of people drinking glasses of water in Figure 1.5 is easily seen to be centered around six glasses (central tendency) but drops off below four glasses and above eight glasses a day (variability). Our frequency polygon has a high point, and the frequency decreases on both sides.

A common frequency distribution of this type is called the **normal curve**. It has a very specific shape and is sometimes called the *bell curve*. Look at **Figure 1.6**. This curve is almost a perfectly normal curve, and many things in life are not that perfect. The normal curve is used as a model for many things that are measured, such as intelligence, height, or weight, but even those measures only come close to a perfect distribution (provided large numbers of people are measured). One of the reasons why the normal curve is so useful is that it has very specific relationships to measures of central tendency and a measurement of variability, known as the standard deviation.

OTHER DISTRIBUTION TYPES: SKEWED AND BIMODAL Distributions aren't always normal in shape. Some distributions are described as *skewed*. This occurs when the distribution is not even on both sides of a central score with the highest frequency (like in our example). Instead, the scores are concentrated toward one side of the distribution. For example, what if a study of people's water-drinking habits in a different class revealed that most people drank around seven to eight glasses of water daily, with no one drinking more than eight? The frequency polygon shown in **Figure 1.7** reflects this very different distribution.

In this case, scores are piled up in the high end, with most people drinking seven or eight glasses of water a day. The graphs in **Figure 1.8** show a **skewed distribution**. Skewed distributions are called positively or negatively skewed, depending on where the scores are concentrated. A concentration in the high end would be called **negatively skewed**. A concentration in the low end would be called **positively skewed**. The direction of the extended tail determines whether it is positively (tail to right) or negatively (tail to left) skewed. Here's an example. What do you think about the distribution of heights of Hobbits (the little guys from *The Lord of the Rings*) and NBA basketball players (who are usually tall)? Might not these frequency distributions of height in Figure 1.8 be appropriate?

histogram
a bar graph showing a frequency distribution.

polygon
line graph showing a frequency distribution.

normal curve
a special frequency polygon, shaped like a bell, in which the scores are symmetrically distributed around the mean, and the mean, median, and mode are all located on the same point on the curve, with scores decreasing as the curve extends from the mean.

skewed distribution
frequency distribution in which most of the scores fall to one side or the other of the distribution.

negatively skewed
a distribution of scores in which scores are concentrated in the high end of the distribution.

positively skewed
a distribution of scores in which scores are concentrated in the low end of the distribution.

Figure 1.6 The Normal Curve

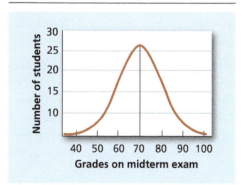

The normal curve, also known as the bell curve because of its unique shape, is often the way in which certain characteristics such as intelligence or weight are represented in the population. The highest point on the curve typically represents the average score in any distribution.

Figure 1.7 A Frequency Polygon

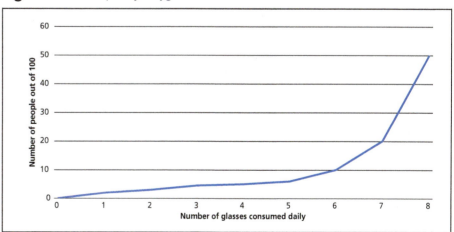

Skewed distributions are those in which the most frequent scores occur at one end or the other of the distribution, as represented by this frequency polygon, in which most people are seen to drink at least seven to eight glasses of water each day.

Figure 1.8 Skewed Distribution

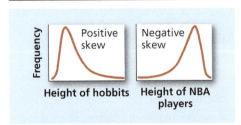

These frequency polygons show how distributions can be skewed in two different directions. The graph on the left represents the frequency of heights among Hobbits (the little people from the fantasy *The Lord of the Rings*) and is positively skewed because the long "tail" goes to the right, or positive direction. The graph on the right shows the frequency of heights among NBA basketball players and is negatively skewed—the tail points to the left.

Figure 1.9 A Bimodal Distribution

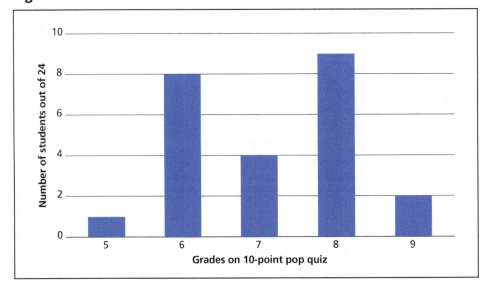

When a distribution is bimodal, it means that there are two high points instead of just one. For example, in the pop-quiz scores represented on this graph, there are two "most frequent" scores—6 and 8. This most likely represents two groups of students, with one group being less successful than the other.

Some frequency polygons show two high points rather than just one (see **Figure 1.9**) and are called **bimodal distributions**. In this example, we have a distribution of scores from a 10-point pop quiz, and we see that one group of students seemed to do well and one group didn't. Bimodal distributions usually indicate that you have two separate groups being graphed in one polygon. What would the distribution of height for men and women look like?

1.13 Measures of Central Tendency

1.13 Identify three measures of central tendency and explain how they are impacted by the shape of the distribution.

A frequency distribution is a good way to look at a set of numbers, but there's still a lot to look at—isn't there some way to sum it all up? One way to sum up numerical data is to find out what a "typical" score might be, or some central number around which all the others seem to fall. This kind of summation is called a **measure of central tendency**, or the number that best represents the central part of a frequency distribution. There are three different measures of central tendency: the mean, the median, and the mode.

MEAN The most commonly used measure of central tendency is the **mean**, the arithmetic average of a distribution of numbers, which simply indicates that you add up all the numbers in a particular set and then divide them by how many numbers there are. This is usually the way teachers get the grade point average for a particular student, for example. If Rochelle's grades on the tests she has taken so far are 86, 92, 87, and 90, then the teacher would add 86 + 92 + 87 + 90 = 355, and then divide 355 by 4 (the number of scores) to get the mean, or grade point average, of 88.75. Here is the formula for the mean:

$$\text{Mean} = \Sigma X/N$$

What does this mean?

- Σ is a symbol called sigma. It is a Greek letter, also called the summation sign.
- X represents a score. Rochelle's grades are represented by X.

bimodal distribution
frequency distribution in which there are two high points rather than one.

measure of central tendency
numbers that best represent the most typical score of a frequency distribution.

mean
the arithmetic average of a distribution of numbers.

- ΣX means add up or sum all the X scores or $\Sigma X = 86 + 92 + 37 + 90 = 355$.
- N means the number of scores. In this case, there are four grades.
- We then divide the sum of the scores (ΣX) by N to get the mean or

$$\text{Mean} = \Sigma X / N = \frac{355}{4} = 88.75$$

The mean is a good way to find a central tendency, if the set of scores clusters around the mean with no extremely different scores that are either far higher or far lower than the mean.

You may hear or read about a concept called "regression to the mean." This is a concept that describes the tendency for measurements of a variable to even out over the course of the measurements (Stigler, 1997). If a measurement is fairly high at first, subsequent measurements will tend to be closer to the mean, the average measurement, for example. This is one of the reasons that researchers want to replicate measurements many times rather than relying on the first results, which could cause them to draw incorrect conclusions from the data.

> 💬 I remember that sometimes my teacher would "curve" the grades for a test, and it was always bad when just one person did really well and everyone else did lousy—is that what you mean about extremely different scores?

MEDIAN Yes, the mean doesn't work as well when there are extreme scores, as you would have if only two students out of an entire class had a perfect score of 100 and everyone else scored in the 70s or lower. If you want a truer measure of central tendency in such a case, you need one that isn't affected by extreme scores. The **median** is just such a measure. A median is the score that falls in the middle of an *ordered* distribution of scores. Half of the scores will fall above the median, and half of the scores will fall below it. If the distribution contains an odd number of scores, it's just the middle number, but if the number of scores is even, it's the average of the two middle scores. The median is also the 50th percentile. Look at **Table 1.3** for an example of the median.

The mean IQ of this group would be 114.6, but the median would be 101 (the average between Evan with 102 and Fethia with 100, the two middle numbers). This may not look like much of a difference, but it's really a change of about 13.6 IQ points—a big difference. Also, think about measures of income in a particular area. If most people earn around $35,000 per year in a particular area, but there are just a few extremely wealthy people in the same area who earn $1,000,000 a year, a mean of all the annual incomes would no doubt make the area look like it was doing much better than it really is economically. The median would be a more accurate measure of the central tendency of such data.

MODE The **mode** is another measure of central tendency, in which the most frequent score is taken as the central measure. In the numbers given in Table 1.3, the mode would be 100 because that number appears more times in the distribution than any other. Three people have that score. This is the simplest measure of central tendency and is also more useful than the mean in some cases, especially when there are two sets of frequently appearing scores. For example, suppose a teacher notices that on the last exam, the scores

median
the middle score in an ordered distribution of scores, or the mean of the two middle numbers; the 50th percentile.

mode
the most frequent score in a distribution of scores.

Table 1.3 Intelligence Test Scores for 10 People

Name	Allison	Ben	Carol	Denise	Evan	Fethia	George	Hal	Inga	Jay
IQ	160	150	139	102	102	100	100	100	98	95

Figure 1.10 Positively Skewed Distribution

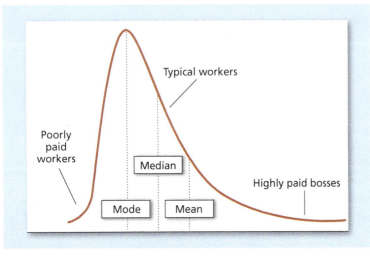

In a skewed distribution, the high scores on one end will cause the mean to be pulled toward the tail of the distribution, making it a poor measure of central tendency for this kind of distribution. For example, in this graph, many workers make very little money (represented by the mode), while only a few workers make a lot of money (the tail). The mean in this case would be much higher than the mode because of those few high scores distorting the average. In this case, the median is a much better measure of central tendency because it tends to be unaffected by extremely high or extremely low scores such as those in this distribution.

fell into two groups, with about 15 students making a 95 and another 14 students making a 67. The mean *and* the median would probably give a number somewhere between those two scores—such as 80. That number tells the teacher a lot less about the distribution of scores than the mode would because in this case the distribution is **bimodal**—there are two very different yet very frequent scores. (Refer to Figure 1.9 for another example.)

MEASURES OF CENTRAL TENDENCY AND THE SHAPE OF THE DISTRIBUTION When the distribution is normal or close to it, the mean, median, and mode are the same or very similar. There is no problem. When the distribution is not normal, then the situation requires a little more explanation.

SKEWED DISTRIBUTIONS If the distribution is skewed, then the mean is pulled in the direction of the tail of the distribution. The mode is still the highest point, and the median is between the two. Let's look at an example. In **Figure 1.10**, we have a distribution of salaries at a company. A few people make a low wage, most make a mid-level wage, and the bosses make a lot of money. This gives us a positively skewed distribution with the measures of central tendency placed as in the figure. As mentioned earlier, with such a distribution, the median would be the best measure of central tendency to report. If the distribution were negatively skewed (tail to the left), the order of the measures of central tendency would be reversed.

BIMODAL DISTRIBUTIONS If you have a bimodal distribution, then none of the measures of central tendency will do you much good. You need to discover why you appear to have two groups in your one distribution.

1.14 Measures of Variability

1.14 Identify the types of statistics used to examine variations in data.

Descriptive statistics can also determine how much the scores in a distribution differ, or vary, from the central tendency of the data. These **measures of variability** are used to discover how "spread out" the scores are from each other. The more the scores cluster around the central scores, the smaller the measure of variability will be, and the more widely the scores differ from the central scores, the larger this measurement will be.

Variability is measured in two ways. The simpler method is by calculating the **range** of the set of scores, or the difference between the highest score and the lowest score in the set of scores. The range is somewhat limited as a measure of variability when there are extreme scores in the distribution. For example, if you look at Table 1.3, the range of those IQ scores would be 160 – 95, or 65. But if you just look at the numbers, you can see there really isn't that much variation except for the three highest scores of 139, 150, and 160.

The other measure of variability commonly used is the one related to the normal curve, the **standard deviation**. This measurement is simply the square root of the average squared difference, or deviation, of the scores from the mean of the distribution. The mathematical formula for finding the standard deviation looks complicated, but it is really nothing more than taking each individual score, subtracting the mean from it, squaring that number (because some numbers will be negative and squaring them gets rid of the negative value), and adding up all of those squares. Then, this total is divided by the number of scores, and the

bimodal
condition in which a distribution has two modes.

measures of variability
measurement of the degree of differences within a distribution or how the scores are spread out.

range
the difference between the highest and lowest scores in a distribution.

standard deviation
the square root of the average squared deviations from the mean of scores in a distribution; a measure of variability.

square root of that number is the standard deviation. In the IQ example, it would go like this:

Standard Deviation Formula $SD = \sqrt{[\Sigma(X - M)^2/N]}$

The mean (M) of the 10 IQ scores is 114.6. To calculate the standard deviation, we

1. Subtract the mean from each score to get a deviation score → $(X - M)$
2. Square each deviation score → $(X - M)^2$
3. Add them up. Remember that's what the sigma (Σ) indicates → $\Sigma(X - M)^2$
4. Divide the sum of the squared deviation by N (the number of scores) → $\Sigma(X - M)^2/N$
5. Take the square root ($\sqrt{\ }$) of the sum for our final step. $\sqrt{[\Sigma(X - M)^2/N]}$

The process is laid out in **Table 1.4**, resulting in a standard deviation of 23.5. What that tells you is that this particular group of data deviates, or varies, from the central tendencies quite a bit—there are some very different scores in the data set or, in this particular instance, three noticeably different scores.

Table 1.4 Finding the Standard Deviation

Score	Deviation from the Mean ($X - M$)	Squared Deviation ($X - M)^2$
160.00	45.40	2,061.16
	(ex. 160 − 114.60 = 45.40)	(45.40^2 = 2,061.16)
150.00	35.4	1,253.16
139.00	24.4	595.36
102.00	−12.60	158.76
102.00	−12.60	158.76
100.00	−14.60	213.16
100.00	−14.60	213.16
100.00	−14.60	213.16
98.00	−16.60	275.56
95.00	−19.60	384.16
Sum of Scores (ΣX) = 1,146.00 Mean = (ΣX)/N = 1,146/10 = 114.60	$\Sigma(X - M) = 0.00$	$\Sigma(X - M)^2 = 5,526.40$ Standard Deviation = $\sqrt{[\Sigma(X - M)^2/N]}$ = $\sqrt{5,526.40/10}$ = 23.5

This procedure may look very complicated. Let us assure you that computers and inexpensive calculators can figure out the standard deviation simply by entering the numbers and pressing a button. No one does a standard deviation by hand anymore. How does the standard deviation relate to the normal curve? Let's look at the classic distribution of IQ scores. It has a mean of 100 and a standard deviation of 15 as set up by the test designers. It is a bell curve. With a true normal curve, researchers know exactly what percentage of the population lies under the curve between each standard deviation from the mean. For example, notice that in the percentages in **Figure 1.11**, one standard deviation above the mean has 34.13 percent of the population represented by the graph under that section. These are the scores between the IQs of 100 and 115. One standard deviation below the mean (−1) has exactly the same percent, 34.13, under that section—the scores between 85 and 100. This means that 68.26 percent of the population falls within one standard deviation from the mean, or one average "spread" from the center of the distribution. For example, "giftedness" is normally defined as having an IQ score two standard deviations *above* the mean. On the Wechsler Intelligence Scales, this means having an IQ of 130 or greater because the Wechsler's standard deviation is 15. But if the test a person took to determine giftedness was the Stanford-Binet Fourth Edition (the previous version of the test), the IQ score must have been 132 or greater because the standard deviation of that test was 16, not 15. The current version, the

Figure 1.11 IQ Normal Curve

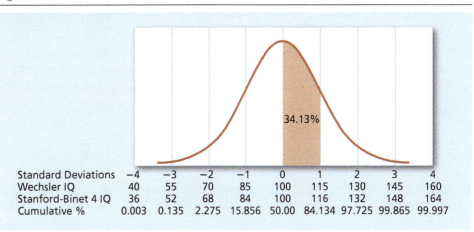

Standard Deviations	−4	−3	−2	−1	0	1	2	3	4
Wechsler IQ	40	55	70	85	100	115	130	145	160
Stanford-Binet 4 IQ	36	52	68	84	100	116	132	148	164
Cumulative %	0.003	0.135	2.275	15.856	50.00	84.134	97.725	99.865	99.997

Scores on intelligence tests are typically represented by the normal curve. The vertical lines each represent one standard deviation from the mean, which is always set at 100. For example, an IQ of 116 on the Stanford-Binet Fourth Edition (Stanford-Binet 4) represents one standard deviation above the mean, and the area under the curve indicates that 34.13 percent of the population falls between 100 and 116 on that test. The Stanford-Binet Fifth Edition was published in 2003 and it now has a mean of 100 and a standard deviation of 15 for composite scores.

Stanford-Binet Fifth Edition, was published in 2003, and it now has a mean of 100 and a standard deviation of 15 for composite scores.

Although the "tails" of this normal curve seem to touch the bottom of the graph, in theory they go on indefinitely, never touching the base of the graph. In reality, though, any statistical measurement that forms a normal curve will have 99.72 percent of the population it measures falling within three standard deviations either above or below the mean. Because this relationship between the standard deviation and the normal curve does not change, it is always possible to compare different test scores or sets of data that come close to a normal curve distribution. This is done by computing a **z score**, which indicates how many standard deviations you are away from the mean. It is calculated by subtracting the mean from your score and dividing by the standard deviation. For example, if you had an IQ of 115, your z score would be 1.0. If you had an IQ of 70, your z score would be −2.0. So on any exam, if you had a positive z score, you did relatively well. A negative z score means you didn't do as well. The formula for a z score is:

$$Z = (X - M)/SD$$

z score
a statistical measure that indicates how far away from the mean a particular score is in terms of the number of standard deviations that exist between the mean and that score.

Concept Map L.O. 1.11, 1.12, 1.13, 1.14

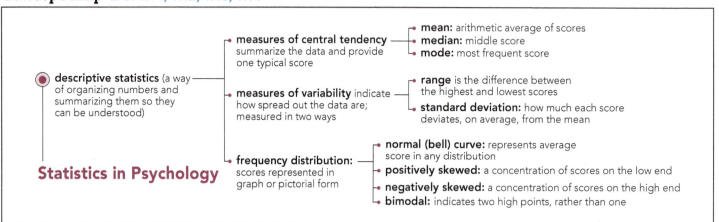

Practice Quiz   How much do you remember?

Pick the best answer.

1. Dr. Lindsay has just given an examination to his Introduction to Psychology class. Because this is a class of more than 500 students, it would be difficult for him to assess the results looking at each score one at a time. If he wants to know how many students earned an A, a B, and so on, which of the following might be the best for him to program his computer to provide?
   a. a correlation coefficient
   b. a measure of central tendency
   c. a mean
   d. a frequency distribution
   e. a z score

2. Because of its very specific shape, a "normal" distribution is also often described as a _____ curve.
   a. positively skewed
   b. bell
   c. negatively skewed
   d. multimodal
   e. bimodal

3. Alyce has just received her grade on the third exam of her chemistry class. She earned a 90 on this test. She is happy because her grades have been steadily increasing since the start of the term. On the first exam she earned an 80, and on the second exam she earned an 85. Which of the following represents the approximate mean of the three exam scores?
   a. 80
   b. 88
   c. 85
   d. 198.3
   e. 255

4. Which of the following would be most useful if you want to know how many standard deviations from the mean a single score in a data set falls?
   a. a t-score
   b. a z score
   c. the mode
   d. a deviation coefficient
   e. a variance determination

1.15–1.16 Inferential Statistics

Descriptive methods of statistics are useful for organizing and summarizing numbers or scores. But what method is useful when it comes to comparing sets of numbers or scores to see if there are differences between them great enough to be caused by something other than chance variation?

> **AP** 1.M Distinguish the purposes of descriptive statistics and inferential statistics.

1.15 Looking at Differences: Statistical Significance

1.15 Describe how inferential statistics can be used to determine if differences in sets of data are large enough to be due to something other than chance variation.

Inferential statistics consist of statistical techniques that allow researchers to determine the difference between results of a study that are meaningful and those that are merely due to chance variations. Inferential statistics also allow researchers to draw conclusions, or make *inferences*, about the results of research and about whether those results are only true for the specific group of animals or people involved in the study or whether the results can be applied to, or *generalized* to, the larger population from which the study participants were selected.

For example, in the Cheryan (Cheryan et al., 2009) study of the difference in male and female students' attitudes toward computer science when exposed to environments that were either stereotypically masculine or nonstereotypical, a lot of variables simply could not be controlled completely, even with the random assignment of participants to the two conditions. See Learning Objective 1.6. For example, there was no guarantee that random assignment would account for the interfering effects of female participants who might have really liked the science fiction toys, posters, and pizza they saw in one of the test conditions. Maybe any difference found between the males and females was due to pure luck or chance and not to the variables under study.

In any analysis that compares two or more sets of data, there's always the possibility of error in the data that comes either from within the group (all participants in one group, for example, will not be exactly like each other) or differences between groups (the experimental group and the control group are formed with different people, so there are differences between the two groups that have nothing to do with the manipulations of the experimenter). When researchers want to know if the differences they find in the data that come from studies like the Cheryan experiment are large enough to be caused by the experimental manipulation and *not* just by the chance differences that exist within and between groups, they have to use a kind of statistical technique that can take those chance variations into account. These kinds of statistical analyses use inferential statistics.

Inferential statistical analysis also allows researchers to determine how much confidence they should have in the results of a particular experiment. As you might remember, results from other kinds of studies that look for relationships—observations, surveys, and case studies—are often analyzed with descriptive statistics, especially correlations. But experiments look for *causes* of relationships, and researchers want to have some evidence that the results of their experiments really mean what they think they mean.

There are many different kinds of inferential statistical methods. The method used depends on the design of the experiment such as the number of independent and dependent variables or the number of experimental groups. All inferential statistics have one thing in common—they look for differences in group measurements that are **statistically significant**. Statistical significance is a way to test differences to see how likely those

inferential statistics

statistical analysis of two or more sets of numerical data to reduce the possibility of error in measurement and to determine if the differences between the data sets are greater than chance variation would predict.

statistically significant

referring to differences in data sets that are larger than chance variation would predict.

differences are to be real and not just caused by the random variations in behavior that exist in everything animals and people do.

For example, in a classic study investigating the effects of intrinsic versus extrinsic motivation on children's creativity, Dr. Teresa Amabile's 1986 study showed that the collages of the children who were promised prizes (an extrinsic reward) were judged to be less creative than those of the children who created collages just for fun. See Learning Objective 9.1. But was that difference between the creativity scores of the two groups a real difference, or was it merely due to chance variations in the children's artistic creations? Dr. Amabile used an inferential test on her results that told her that the difference was too big to be just chance variations, which means her results were *significant*—they were most likely to be real differences. How likely? Tests of significance give researchers the probability that the results of their experiment were caused by chance and not by their experimental manipulation. For example, in one test called a ***t*-test**, the scores of the children's artwork would have been placed into a formula that would result in a single number (t) that evaluates the probability that the difference between the two group means is due to pure chance or luck. That number would be compared to a value that exists in a table of possible t values, which tells researchers the probability that the result is due to chance or luck. If the number obtained by the calculation is bigger than the value in the table, there will be a probability associated with that number in the table. The probability, symbolized by the letter p, will tell researchers the probability that the difference was due to chance. In Dr. Amabile's case, the probability was $p < 0.05$, which means the probability that the results were due to chance alone was less than 5 out of 100. Another way of stating the same result is that Dr. Amabile could be 95 percent certain that her results were real and not due to chance. Dr. Amabile would, thus, report that the study found a **significant difference**, which means a difference thought not to be due to chance.

There are several statistical techniques to test if groups are different from each other. Here are some common ones you might encounter if you read journal articles:

- *t*-test—determines if two means are different from each other.
- *F*-test or analysis of variance—determines if three or more means are different from each other. Can also evaluate more than one independent variable at a time.
- chi-square—compares frequencies of proportions between groups to see if they are different. For example, the proportion of women hired at a company is too low and might indicate discrimination. *Chi* is pronounced like the beginning of the word *kite*. Don't say "chee." It will be ugly.

If you take a statistics course, you will find out that most analyses are done by computers, and you don't have to manually go through the long formulas.

We've already talked about the correlation coefficient. Let's see how psychologists can predict one variable from another by using it.

1.16 The Correlation Coefficient

1.16 Explain how statistics are used to predict one score from another.

Remember that a correlation is a measure of the relationship between two or more variables. For example, if you wanted to know if scores on the SAT are related to grade point averages, you could get SAT scores and GPAs from a group of people and enter those numbers into a mathematical formula, which will produce a number

t-test
type of inferential statistical analysis typically used when two means are compared to see if they are significantly different.

significant difference
a difference between groups of numerical data that is considered large enough to be due to factors other than chance variation.

called the correlation coefficient. And as we discussed, the correlation coefficient represents the direction of the relationship and its strength. See Learning Objective 1.8.

 Is the formula for the correlation coefficient really complicated?

Actually, the definitional formula for finding a correlation coefficient is not very complicated. Here it is:

$$r = \frac{\Sigma Z_x Z_y}{n}$$

The r is the correlation coefficient, the number representing the strength and direction of the relationship between the two variables. Z_x and Z_y are the z scores for each score. If you remember, the z score tells you how many standard deviations a score is away from the mean. You would calculate the Z_x and Z_y for each subject, multiply, and add them up. Then divide by the number of subjects. There is a very complicated-looking formula based on the raw scores.

$$r = \frac{\Sigma XY - \frac{\Sigma X \Sigma Y}{N}}{\sqrt{\left(\Sigma X^2 - \frac{(\Sigma X)^2}{N}\right)\left(\Sigma Y^2 - \frac{(\Sigma Y)^2}{N}\right)}}$$

Don't worry. You can do all this work on inexpensive calculators or on computers using common statistical programs or spreadsheets. Let's take the following example of two sets of scores, one on a test of drawing ability with scores from 1 (poor) to 5 (excellent) and the other on a test of writing ability using the same scale (see **Table 1.5**).

If we plugged our data set into our calculator or spreadsheet, we would find that r (the correlation coefficient) equals 0.86. That would indicate a fairly strong correlation. If you continue studies in statistics, you will find out how to see if the correlation coefficient we calculated is statistically significant or, if you recall, not due to just dumb luck when we picked our subjects. In our case, the r is very significant and would happen by chance only 1 in 100 times!

Remember that the correlation coefficient has values that range between +1.0 and −1.0. The closer the r is to these values, the stronger the relationship. A positive r means a positive relationship, whereas a negative r means a negative relationship. See Learning Objective 1.8; see Figure 1.3.

Our example had us trying to see if two scores were related. It is also possible to see if three or more scores are related with various techniques. The most common one is called multiple regression.

Table 1.5 Drawing and Writing Ability Test Scores

	Drawing (X)	Writing (Y)
Student 1	3	5
Student 2	1	2
Student 3	2	3
Student 4	4	4
Student 5	1	3
Student 6	4	6
Student 7	2	3
Student 8	3	4
Student 9	5	5
Student 10	1	2

Concept Map L.O. 1.15, 1.16

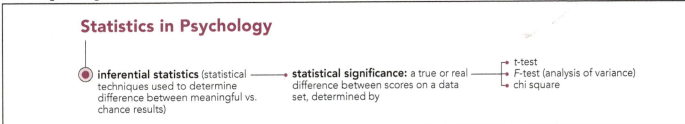

Practice Quiz — How much do you remember?

Pick the best answer.

1. _____ statistics consist of techniques that allow researchers to determine the difference between results of a study that are meaningful and those that are merely due to chance variations.
   - **a.** Descriptive
   - **b.** Parametric
   - **c.** Predictive
   - **d.** Inferential
   - **e.** Correlational

2. Leilani is conducting a test in which she has three different participant groups, and she wants to analyze the variance among the three groups. In other words, she wants to know whether the means of each group are significantly different from each other. Which of the following would she want to calculate?
   - **a.** an F-test
   - **b.** a z-test
   - **c.** a t-test
   - **d.** a chi-square test
   - **e.** a point-biserial correlation

3. Isaiah is conducting a correlational study that examines the frequency with which it rains in his town and the atmospheric pressure at noon on each day. When he is done, he calculates a correlation coefficient that will summarize the relationship between these two variables. This coefficient is going to be summarized by the lowercase letter _____.
   - **a.** p
   - **b.** c
   - **c.** r
   - **d.** e
   - **e.** z

4. If researchers want to demonstrate that their findings depict a significant difference between participant groups, which of the following statistical statements would need to be made?
   - **a.** $r = \pm 1.00$
   - **b.** $p \leq .05$
   - **c.** $t \geq 2.50$
   - **d.** $z \leq 100$
   - **e.** $p \geq .05$

1.17–1.18 Ethics of Psychological Research

💬 The study that John Watson and Rosalie Rayner did with "Little Albert" and the white rat seems pretty cruel when you think about it. Do researchers today do that kind of study?

AP 1.N Identify how ethical issues inform and constrain research practices.

AP 1.O Describe how ethical and legal guidelines protect research participants and promote sound ethical practice.

Actually, as the field and scope of psychology began to grow and more research with people and animals was being done, psychologists began to realize that some protections had to be put in place. No one wanted to be thought of as a "mad scientist," and if studies were permitted that could actually harm people or animals, the field of psychology might die out pretty quickly. See Learning Objectives 5.3 and 11.4.

1.17 The Guidelines for Doing Research with People

1.17 Identify some of the common ethical guidelines for doing research with people.

Scientists in other areas of research were also realizing that ethical treatment of the participants in studies had to be ensured in some way. Ethical treatment, of course, means that people who volunteer for a study will be able to expect that no physical or psychological harm should come to them. The video *The Ethics of Psychological Research with People* explains how researchers in the field of psychology draw the line between what is ethical and what is not and explains some of the safeguards in place today.

Universities and colleges (where most psychological research is carried out) usually have *institutional review boards*, groups of psychologists or other professionals who look over each proposed study and judge it according to its safety and consideration for the research participants. These review boards look at all aspects of the projected study, from the written materials that explain the research to the potential participants to the equipment that may be used in the study itself.

Watch The Ethics of Psychological Research with People

Watch the Video at MyLab Psychology

There are quite a few ethical concerns when dealing with human participants in an experiment or other type of study. Here is a list of some of the most common ethical guidelines:

1. **Rights and well-being of participants must be weighed against the study's value to science.** In other words, people come first, research second.
2. **Participants must be allowed to make an informed decision about participation.** This means that researchers have to explain the study to the people they want to include before they do anything to them or with them—even children—and it has to be in terms that the participants can understand. If researchers are using infants or children, their parents have to be informed and give their consent, a legal term known as *informed consent*. Even in single- or double-blind studies, it is necessary to tell the participants that they may be members of either the experimental or the control group—they just won't find out which group they were actually in until after the experiment is concluded.
3. **Deception must be justified.** In some cases, it is necessary to deceive the participants because the study wouldn't work any other way. For example, if you intend to give the participants a test of memory at the end but don't want them to know about the test beforehand, you would have to withhold that part of the experiment. The participants have to be told after the study exactly why the deception was important. This is called *debriefing*.
4. **Participants may withdraw from the study at any time.** The participants must be allowed to drop out for any reason. For example, sometimes people get bored with the study, decide they don't have the time, or don't like what they have to do. Children participating in studies often decide to stop "playing" (play is a common part of studies of children). Researchers have to release them, even if it means having to get more participants.
5. **Participants must be protected from risks or told explicitly of risks.** For example, if researchers are using any kind of electrical equipment, care must be taken to ensure that no participant will experience a physical shock from faulty electrical equipment.
6. **Investigators must debrief participants, telling the true nature of the study and expectations of results.** This is important in all types of studies but particularly in those involving a deception.
7. **Data must remain confidential.** Freud recognized the importance of confidentiality, referring to his patients in his books and articles with false names. Likewise, psychologists and other researchers today tend to report only group results rather than results for a single individual so that no one could possibly be recognized.
8. **If for any reason a study results in undesirable consequences for the participant, the researcher is responsible for detecting and removing or correcting these consequences.** Sometimes people react in unexpected ways to the manipulations in an experiment, despite the researcher's best efforts to prevent any negative impact on participants. If this happens, the researcher must find some way of helping the participant overcome that impact (American Psychological Association, 2002).

THINKING CRITICALLY 1.3

You are testing a new drug to treat a serious, often fatal medical condition. Before your experiment is over, it becomes obvious that the drug is working so well that the people in the experimental group are going to recover completely. Should you stop the experiment to give the drug to the people in the control group?

1.18 Animal Research

1.18 Explain why psychologists sometimes use animals in their research.

Psychologists also study animals to find out about behavior, often drawing comparisons between what the animals do and what people might do under similar conditions.

But why not just study people in the first place?

Some research questions are extremely important but difficult or impossible to answer by using human participants. Animals live shorter lives, so looking at long-term effects becomes much easier. Animals are also easier to control—the scientist can control diet, living arrangements, and even genetic relatedness. The white laboratory rat has become a recognized species different from ordinary rats, bred with its own kind for many decades until each white rat is essentially a little genetic "twin" of all the others. Animals also engage in much simpler behavior than humans do, making it easier to see the effects of manipulations. But the biggest reason that researchers use animals in some research is that animals can be used in ways that researchers could never use people. For example, it took a long time for scientists to prove that the tars and other harmful substances in tobacco cause cancer, because they had to do correlational studies with people and experiments only with animals. There's the catch—researchers can do many things to animals that they can't do to people. That might seem cruel at first, but when you think that without animal research there would be no vaccines for deadly diseases, no insulin treatments for diabetics, no transplants, and so on, then the value of the research and its benefits to humankind far outweigh the hazards to which the research animals are exposed. Still, some animal rights activists disagree with this point of view.

There are also ethical considerations when dealing with animals in research, just as there are with humans. With animals, though, the focus is on avoiding exposing them to any *unnecessary* pain or suffering. So if surgery is part of the study, it is done under anesthesia. If the research animal must die for the effects of some drug or other treatment to be examined in a necropsy (autopsy performed on an animal), the death must be accomplished humanely. Animals are used in only about 7 percent of all psychological studies (Committee on Animal Research and Ethics, 2012).

Concept Map L.O. 1.17, 1.18

Ethics of Psychological Research
(psychological scientists have a primary goal of protecting the health and welfare of their animal or human participants)

- **guidelines for research with humans**
  - rights and well-being of participants must be weighed against the study's value to science
  - participants must be allowed to make an informed decision about participating (informed consent)
  - deception must be justified
  - participants may withdraw from the study at any time
  - participants must be protected from risks or told explicitly of risks
  - investigator must debrief participants, telling the true nature of the study and expectations of results
  - data must remain confidential

- **research with animals**
  - any animal research is also covered by ethical considerations; primary focus is on avoiding any unnecessary pain or suffering
  - why use animals?
    - some research questions are important but can be difficult or dangerous to answer with human participants
    - animals are easier to control
    - animals have shorter lives; easier to study long-term effects

Practice Quiz   How much do you remember?

Pick the best answer.

1. What is the first guideline for doing research with people?
   a. Participants have to give informed consent.
   b. Participants may withdraw from the study at any time.
   c. The rights and well-being of the participants must come first.
   d. Deception cannot be used in any studies with human beings.
   e. Data must remain confidential.

2. What happens when the results of a study create an undesirable outcome for the participant?
   a. The participant is institutionalized for further study.
   b. The participants signed permission forms and must take their chances.
   c. The researcher must find some way of helping the participant deal with the negative impact.
   d. The researcher simply adds an addendum to the report of the study's results.
   e. The only action required is for the researcher to remove the individual's data from the data analysis.

3. What is the biggest reason we use animals in research?
   a. We can do things to animals that we can't do to people.
   b. Animals have simple behavior that makes it easy to see changes.
   c. Outcomes from animal research are identical to human studies.
   d. Animals don't live as long as humans.
   e. Animals are easier to control.

4. Which of the following is an ethical consideration when using animals in research?
   a. There are no ethical considerations when using animals in research.
   b. If possible, animals should be used in all experiments.
   c. Animals cannot be killed during the course of an experiment.
   d. Animals must not experience any pain during an experiment.
   e. Avoiding exposing them to unnecessary pain.

Applying Psychology to Everyday Life

Critical Thinking and Social Media

1.19 Identify strategies for critically evaluating news and other information shared on social media.

Twitter and other social media make it very easy to hear about many different things: new products, new information about some celebrity or political figure, and so on. Think back to the information on critical thinking discussed earlier in the chapter. How do you know that what you read about in these venues is actually true? Take a look at the following video to see how some students try to sort through the possible facts and fictions of life in cyberspace.

Applying Psychology to Everyday Life Critical Thinking and Social Media

▶ **Watch** the **Video** at **MyLab Psychology**

After watching the video, answer the following questions:

1. What were two strategies highlighted in the video for critically evaluating news and other information shared on social media?
2. Beyond the strategies shared by the students in the video, what are some ways you might critically evaluate a topic of news or some other information shared on social media?

Chapter Summary

The History of Psychology

1.1 Describe the contributions of some of the early pioneers in psychology.

- Psychology is the scientific study of behavior and mental processes.
- In 1879, psychology began as a science of its own in Germany with the establishment of Wundt's psychology laboratory. He developed the technique of objective introspection.
- Titchener, a student of Wundt, brought psychology in the form of structuralism to America. Structuralism died out in the early twentieth century.
- William James proposed a countering point of view called functionalism, which stressed the way the mind allows us to adapt.
- Functionalism influenced the modern fields of educational psychology, evolutionary psychology, and industrial/organizational psychology.
- Many of psychology's early pioneers were minorities such as Hispanic and African Americans who, despite prejudice and racism, made important contributions to the study of human and animal behavior.

1.2 Summarize the basic ideas and the important people behind the early approaches known as Gestalt, psychoanalysis, and behaviorism.

- Wertheimer and others studied sensation and perception, calling the new perspective Gestalt (an organized whole) psychology.
- Freud proposed that the unconscious mind controls much of our conscious behavior in his theory of psychoanalysis.
- Watson proposed a science of behavior called behaviorism, which focused only on the study of observable stimuli and responses.
- Watson and Rayner demonstrated that a phobia could be learned by conditioning a baby to be afraid of a white rat.
- Mary Cover Jones, one of Watson's more famous students in behaviorism and child development, later demonstrated that a learned phobia could be counterconditioned.

The Field of Psychology Today

1.3 Summarize the basic ideas behind the seven modern perspectives in psychology.

- Modern Freudians such as Anna Freud, Jung, and Adler changed the emphasis in Freud's original theory into a kind of neo-Freudianism, which led to the psychodynamic perspective.
- Skinner's operant conditioning of voluntary behavior became a major force in the twentieth century. He introduced the concept of reinforcement to behaviorism.
- Humanism, which focuses on free will and the human potential for growth, was developed by Maslow and Rogers, among others, as a reaction to the deterministic nature of behaviorism and psychoanalysis.
- Cognitive psychology is the study of learning, memory, language, and problem solving and includes the field of cognitive neuroscience.
- Biopsychology emerged as the study of the biological bases of behavior, such as hormones, heredity, chemicals in the nervous system, structural defects in the brain, and the effects of physical diseases.
- The principles of evolution and the knowledge we currently have about evolution are used in the evolutionary perspective to look at the way the mind works and why it works as it does. Behavior is seen as having an adaptive or survival value.

1.4 Differentiate between the various types of professionals within the field of psychology.

- Psychologists have academic doctoral degrees and can do counseling, teaching, and research, and may specialize in any one of a large number of areas within psychology.
- There are many different areas of specialization in psychology, including clinical, counseling, developmental, social, and personality, as areas of work or study.
- Psychiatrists are medical doctors who provide diagnosis and treatment for persons with mental disorders.
- Psychiatric social workers are social workers with special training in the influences of the environment on mental illness.
- Besides social workers, other psychology professions, such as licensed professional counselors and licensed marriage and family therapists, may only require a master's degree.

Scientific Research

1.5 Recall the basic criteria for critical thinking that people can use in their everyday lives.

- Critical thinking is the ability to make reasoned judgments. The four basic criteria of critical thinking are that there are few concepts that do not need to be tested, evidence can vary in quality, claims by experts and authorities do not automatically make something true, and keeping an open mind is important.

1.6 Recall the five steps of the scientific approach.

- The four goals of psychology are description, explanation, prediction, and control.
- The scientific approach is a way to determine facts and control the possibilities of error and bias when observing behavior. The five steps are perceiving the question, forming a hypothesis, testing the hypothesis, drawing conclusions, and reporting the results.

1.7 Compare and contrast some of the methods used to describe behavior.

- Naturalistic observations involve watching animals or people in their natural environments but have the disadvantage of lack of control.
- Laboratory observations involve watching animals or people in an artificial but controlled situation, such as a laboratory.

- Case studies are detailed investigations of one participant, whereas surveys involve asking standardized questions of large groups of people that represent a sample of the population of interest.
- Information gained from case studies cannot be applied to other cases. People responding to surveys may not always tell the truth or remember information correctly.

1.8 Explain how researchers use the correlational technique to study relationships between two or more variables.

- Correlation is a statistical technique that allows researchers to discover and predict relationships between variables of interest.
- Positive correlations exist when increases in one variable are matched by increases in the other variable, whereas negative correlations exist when increases in one variable are matched by decreases in the other variable.
- Correlations cannot be used to prove cause-and-effect relationships.

1.9 Identify the steps involved in designing an experiment.

- Experiments are tightly controlled manipulations of variables that allow researchers to determine cause-and-effect relationships.
- The independent variable in an experiment is the variable that is deliberately manipulated by the experimenter to see if related changes occur in the behavior or responses of the participants and is given to the experimental group.
- The dependent variable in an experiment is the measured behavior or responses of the participants.
- The control group receives either a placebo treatment or nothing.
- Random assignment of participants to experimental groups helps control for individual differences both within and between the groups that might otherwise interfere with the experiment's outcome.

1.10 Recall two common sources of problems in an experiment and some ways to control for these effects.

- Experiments in which the participants do not know if they are in the experimental or control groups are single-blind studies, whereas experiments in which neither the experimenters nor the participants know this information are called double-blind studies.
- An experiment studying the effect of negative stereotypes on test performance of athletes found that exposure to negative stereotypes prior to taking a test resulted in poorer performance by athletes than the performance of athletes whose exposure came after the test.

What Are Statistics?

1.11 Explain why statistics are important to psychologists and psychology majors.

- Statistics is a branch of mathematics that involves the collection, description, and interpretation of numerical data.
- Students who understand the process of research and the statistical methods used in research are more desirable to many university and business institutions than those who lack such skills.

Descriptive Statistics

- Descriptive statistics are ways of organizing numbers and summarizing them so that they can be understood.

1.12 Describe the types of tables and graphs that represent patterns in data.

- Frequency distributions are tables or graphs that show the patterns in a set of scores and can be a table, a bar graph or histogram, or a line graph or polygon.
- The normal curve is a special frequency polygon that is symmetrical and has the mean, median, and mode as the highest point on the curve.

1.13 Identify three measures of central tendency and explain how they are impacted by the shape of the distribution.

- Measures of central tendency are ways of finding numbers that best represent the center of a distribution of numbers and include the mean, median, and mode.

1.14 Identify the types of statistics used to examine variations in data.

- Measures of variability provide information about the differences within a set of numbers and include the range and the standard deviation.

Inferential Statistics

1.15 Describe how inferential statistics can be used to determine if differences in sets of data are large enough to be due to something other than chance variation.

- Inferential statistics involves statistical analysis of two or more sets of numerical data to reduce the possibility of error in measurement and determine statistical significance of the results of research.

1.16 Explain how statistics are used to predict one score from another.

- The correlation coefficient is a number that represents the strength and direction of a relationship existing between two variables.

Ethics of Psychological Research

1.17 Identify some of the common ethical guidelines for doing research with people.

- Ethical guidelines for doing research with human beings include the protection of rights and well-being of participants, informed consent, justification when deception is used, the right of participants to withdraw at any time, protection of participants from physical or psychological harm, confidentiality, and debriefing of participants at the end of the study. Researchers are also responsible for correcting any undesirable consequences that may result from the study.

1.18 Explain why psychologists sometimes use animals in their research.

- Animals in psychological research make useful models because they are easier to control than humans, they have simpler behavior, and they can be used in ways that are not permissible with humans.

Applying Psychology to Everyday Life: Critical Thinking and Social Media

1.19 Identify strategies for critically evaluating news and other information shared on social media.

- Strategies for evaluating claims or information posted on social media involve various aspects of critical thinking. Of the questions you might ask, some might be in evaluating the qualifications of the person making the claim, what kind of evidence is being presented, how many studies have provided evidence, and whether the information suggests a correlational or causal relationship.

Test Yourself: Preparing for the AP Exam

PART I: MULTIPLE-CHOICE QUESTIONS

Directions for Part I: Read each of the questions or incomplete sentences below. Then choose the response that best answers the question or completes the sentence

Pick the best answer.

1. In the definition of psychology, the term *behavior* means _____.
   a. internal, covert processes
   b. only human behavior
   c. overt actions and reactions
   d. outward behavior
   e. only animal behavior

2. Who is considered to be the father of African American psychology?
   a. Robert V. Guthrie
   b. Charles Henry Thompson
   c. Francis Cecil Sumner
   d. Howard Hale Long
   e. Robert Prentiss Daniel

3. Sigmund Freud's psychoanalysis focused on _____.
   a. free will
   b. introspection
   c. observable behavior
   d. Gestalt perceptions
   e. early childhood experiences

4. Imagine that the following is a set of grades from your class's first psychology exam: 71, 71, 71, 73, 75, 76, 81, 86, 97. What is the median score?
   a. 9
   b. 71
   c. 75
   d. 701
   e. 73

5. Which perspective is often referred to as the "third force" in psychology and focuses on people's freedom of choice in determining their behavior?
   a. biopsychological perspective
   b. behaviorism
   c. humanism
   d. biopsychosocialism
   e. cognitive psychology

6. Which perspective best explains the bystander effect whereby individuals will be less likely to help someone in need because of the presence of others close by?
   a. sociocultural
   b. Gestalt psychology
   c. psychoanalysis
   d. behaviorism
   e. cognitive psychology

7. A researcher finds that as her participants increased the number of hours they spent exercising, the overall weight of her participants decreased. This would be an example of a _____ correlation.
   a. causal
   b. positive
   c. zero
   d. negative
   e. median

8. If Dr. Patel uses an eclectic approach in her clinical treatment of children, what is it that she is doing?
   a. She is relying primarily on one psychological perspective to treat all her patients.
   b. She is using a combination of perspectives to treat different clients.
   c. She relies heavily on play therapy to help children with anxiety.
   d. She is using medications with all her patients, especially those suffering from depression.
   e. She relies heavily on the Freudian psychodynamic perspective to help children who show abnormal behavior.

9. Dr. Jarvie identifies himself with the largest subfield of psychology. What kind of psychologist is he?
   a. school
   b. counseling
   c. social
   d. clinical
   e. experimental

10. _____ is a way of organizing numbers and summarizing them so that they can be understood, whereas _____ allow(s) researchers to draw conclusions about the results of research.
    a. Descriptive statistics, inferential statistics
    b. Inferential statistics, descriptive statistics
    c. Correlational research, mean statistics
    d. Inferential statistics, the mean, median, and mode
    e. Descriptive statistics, correlational research

11. A psychologist is interested in finding out why married couples seemingly begin to look like each other after several years of marriage. This psychologist is most interested in the goal of _____.
    a. analysis
    b. prediction
    c. description
    d. explanation
    e. control

12. Patrice wants to find an explanation for the behavior of her lab rats in her study. Which step in the scientific approach is she currently focusing on?
    a. testing a hypothesis
    b. perceiving the question
    c. replication
    d. drawing conclusions
    e. reporting her results

13. Which psychologist dared to ignore the whole consciousness issue and return to a study of scientific inquiry by focusing on observable behavior?
    a. Sigmund Freud
    b. Max Wertheimer
    c. Ivan Pavlov
    d. John Watson
    e. William James

14. A researcher asks an assistant to conduct a study on her behalf. She specifically tells her assistant only to share the results anonymously and not to include the names of the students along with their scores. Such an experiment would be considered a _____.
    a. case study
    b. laboratory observation
    c. single-blind experiment
    d. correlational study
    e. double-blind experiment

15. Dr. Calvin needs just one more participant to complete her experiment. Lisa, a student of Dr. Calvin, has almost completed the experiment when she announces she wants to quit because the experiment is boring. What options does Dr. Calvin have?
    a. Dr. Calvin can make Lisa stay since she is a student of hers and she requires students to take part in her experiments.
    b. Dr. Calvin cannot make Lisa stay since she is a student of hers, but Lisa has to identify and bring in another student as a replacement.
    c. Dr. Calvin can require that Lisa finish because students don't have the same rights to quit an experiment as the general public does.
    d. Dr. Calvin can require that Lisa finish because boredom is not an acceptable excuse for quitting.
    e. Dr. Calvin must let Lisa go and find another participant.

16. A researcher wants to study the effects of texting on driving. Students in Group A drive a car in a computer game and see how many virtual accidents they have. Students in Group B are asked to drive the same virtual car but they must respond to and send at least three texts. The number of virtual accidents is measured for each group. What is the independent variable?
    a. the virtual car
    b. the computer
    c. texting
    d. the number of virtual accidents
    e. the group assignment

17. Imagine that the following is a set of grades from your first psychology exam: 71, 71, 71, 73, 75, 76, 81, 86, 97. What is the mode?
    a. 701
    b. 75
    c. 9
    d. 71
    e. 73

18. A famous golfer advertises a new golf bracelet that helps minimize fatigue while playing. If Maureen decides to order the bracelet because she believes that such a well-known personality should know if it works or not, she has made an error in which of the following criteria for critical thinking?
    a. Authority or expertise does not make the claims of the authority or expert true.
    b. Forming a hypothesis is the first step.
    c. Few "truths" do not need to be tested.
    d. All evidence is not equal in quality.
    e. Critical thinking requires an open mind.

PART II: FREE-RESPONSE QUESTION

Directions for Part II: Read the essay question that follows. Then respond to the question in a clear, concise essay. Do not simply list facts. Instead, present a thorough argument based on your critical consideration of the topic. Use of proper terminology is necessary.

In an experimental study of how taste influences people's moral judgment, researchers took volunteers from their introductory psychology course, completed an informed consent process, and randomly assigned them into two conditions. The experimenters gave the experimental group a disgusting tasting bitter liquid and gave the control group a pleasant tasting sweet liquid. After this manipulation, all participants were asked to rate their judgment of 5 hypothetical scenarios for how morally wrong they were on a scale from 0 (not at all wrong) to 100 (extremely wrong). Once they completed the moral judgment survey, participants were given a debriefing that discussed all participants' individual results from the study.

The graph below shows the results of the experiment. Assume the difference is significant.

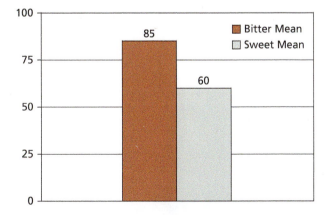

a. Identify the operational definition of the dependent variable in this study.
b. Explain why the researchers cannot generalize their findings.
c. Explain why the study is not a correlational study.
d. Describe how to correct the ethical flaw in this study.
e. Explain why this research belongs to the cognitive perspective on psychology.
f. Explain why the researchers cannot conclude that tasting the bitter liquid caused the participants to judge the hypothetical scenarios as more morally wrong.
g. Explain how to correct the study so that the researchers could test whether bitter taste causes harsher moral judgment.

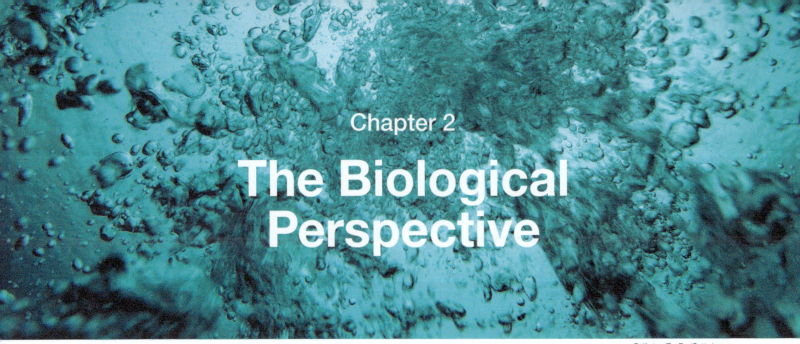

Chapter 2
The Biological Perspective

Ralf strm/EyeEm/Getty Images

In your words

What do you see as the brain's role in our behavior? How much do you think your behavior is influenced by hormones and chemicals in the nervous system?

After you have thought about these questions, watch the video to see how other students would answer them.

Watch the Video at MyLab Psychology

Why study the nervous system and the glands?

How could we possibly understand any of our behavior, thoughts, or actions without knowing something about the incredible organs that allow us to act, think, and react? If we can understand how the brain, the nerves, and the glands interact to control feelings, thoughts, and behavior, we can begin to truly understand the complex organism called a human being.

Learning Objectives

2.1 Identify the parts of a neuron and the function of each.

2.2 Explain the action potential.

2.3 Describe how neurons use neurotransmitters to communicate with each other and with the body.

2.4 Describe how lesioning studies and brain stimulation are used to study the brain.

2.5 Compare and contrast neuroimaging techniques for mapping the brain's structure and function.

2.6 Identify the different structures of the hindbrain and the function of each.

2.7 Identify the structures of the brain that are involved in emotion, learning, memory, and motivation.

2.8 Identify the parts of the cortex that process the different senses and those that control movement of the body.

2.9 Recall the function of association areas of the cortex, including those especially crucial for language.

2.10 Explain how some brain functions differ between the left and right hemispheres.

2.11 Describe how the components of the central nervous system interact and how they may respond to experiences or injury.

2.12 Differentiate the roles of the somatic and autonomic nervous systems.

2.13 Explain why the pituitary gland is known as the "master gland."

2.14 Recall the role of various endocrine glands.

2.15 Identify potential strategies for positively coping with attention-deficit/hyperactivity disorder.

2.1–2.3 Neurons and Neurotransmitters

This chapter will explore a complex system of cells, organs, and chemicals that work together to produce behavior, thoughts, and actions. The first part of this complex arrangement is the **nervous system**, a network of cells that carries information to and from all parts of the body. The field of **neuroscience** is a branch of the life sciences that deals with the structure and functioning of the brain and the neurons, nerves, and nervous tissue that form the nervous system. **Biological psychology, or behavioral neuroscience**, is the branch of neuroscience that focuses on the biological bases of psychological processes, behavior, and learning, and it is the primary area associated with the biological perspective in psychology.

AP 2.F Identify basic processes and systems in the biological bases of behavior, including parts of the neuron.

2.1 Structure of the Neuron: The Nervous System's Building Block

2.1 Identify the parts of a neuron and the function of each.

In 1887, Santiago Ramón y Cajal, a doctor studying slides of brain tissue, first theorized that the nervous system was made up of individual cells (Ramón y Cajal, translation, 1995). Although the entire body is composed of cells, each type of cell has a special purpose and function and, therefore, a special structure. For example, skin cells are flat, but muscle cells are long and stretchy. Most cells have three things in common: a nucleus, a cell body, and a cell membrane holding it all together. The **neuron** is the specialized cell in the nervous system that receives and sends messages within that system. Neurons are one of the messengers of the body, meaning they have a very special structure, which we will explore in **Figure 2.1**.

The parts of the neuron that receive messages from other cells are called the **dendrites**. The name *dendrite* means "tree-like," or "branch," and this structure does indeed look like the branches of a tree. The dendrites are attached to the cell body, or **soma**, which is the part of the cell that contains the nucleus and keeps the entire cell alive and functioning. The word *soma* means "body." The **axon** (from the Greek for "axis") is a

nervous system
an extensive network of specialized cells that carries information to and from all parts of the body.

neuroscience
a branch of the life sciences that deals with the structure and function of neurons, nerves, and nervous tissue.

biological psychology, or behavioral neuroscience
branch of neuroscience that focuses on the biological bases of psychological processes, behavior, and learning.

neuron
the basic cell that makes up the nervous system and that receives and sends messages within that system.

dendrites
branchlike structures of a neuron that receive messages from other neurons.

soma
the cell body of the neuron responsible for maintaining the life of the cell.

axon
tubelike structure of neuron that carries the neural message from the cell body to the axon terminals, for communication with other cells.

Figure 2.1 The Structure of a Neuron

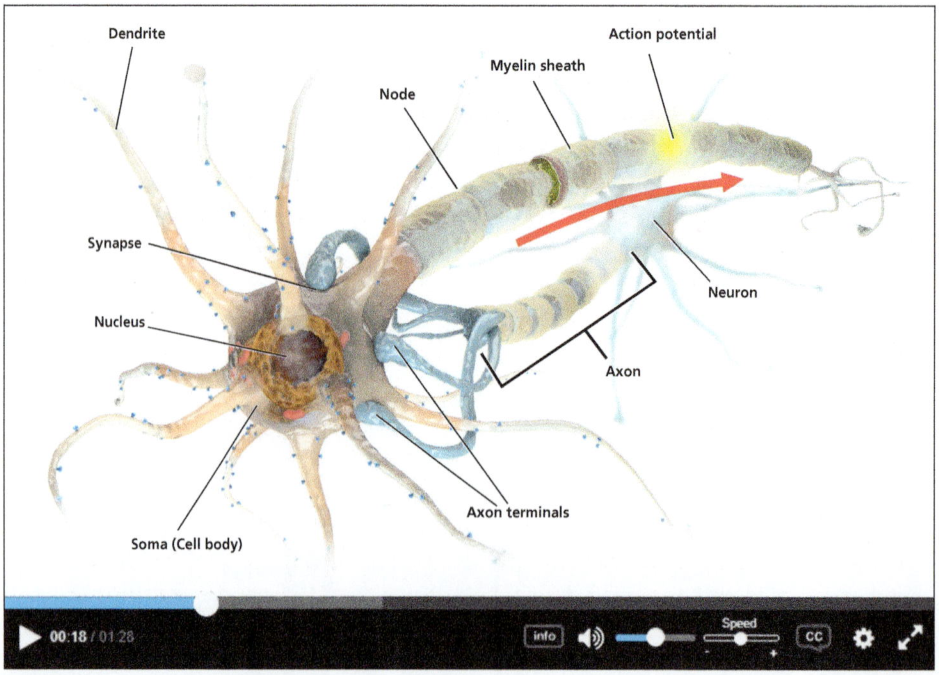

Watch the Video at MyLab Psychology

fiber attached to the soma, and its job is to carry messages out to other cells. The end of the axon branches out into several shorter fibers that have swellings or little knobs on the ends called **axon terminals** (may also be called *presynaptic terminals, terminal buttons,* or *synaptic knobs*), which are responsible for communicating with other nerve cells.

Neurons make up a large part of the brain, but they are not the only cells that affect our thinking, learning, memory, perception, and all of the other facets of life that make us who we are. The other primary cells are called glia, or **glial cells**, which serve a variety of functions. While historically viewed as support cells for neurons, the expanded roles of glia are still being discovered. And while they help maintain a state of *homeostasis*, or sense of balance in the nervous system, they are increasingly being better understood as partner cells, not just support cells (Kettenmann & Ransom, 2013; Verkhratsky et al., 2014). Some glia serve as a sort of structure on which the neurons develop and work and that hold the neurons in place. For example, during early brain development, radial glial cells (extending from inner to outer areas like the spokes of a wheel) help guide migrating neurons to form the outer layers of the brain. Other glia are involved in getting nutrients to the neurons, cleaning up the remains of neurons that have died, communicating with neurons and other glial cells, and insulating the axons of some neurons.

Glial cells affect both the functioning and structure of neurons, and specific types also have properties similar to stem cells, which allow them to develop into new neurons, both during prenatal development and in adult mammals (Bullock et al., 2005; Gotz et al., 2015; Kriegstein & Alvarez-Buylla, 2009). Glial cells are also being investigated for their possible role in a variety of neurodevelopmental diseases like *autism spectrum disorder*, degenerative disorders such as Alzheimer's disease, and psychiatric disorders including *major depressive disorder* and *schizophrenia* (Molofsky et al., 2012; Peng et al., 2015; Sahin & Sur, 2015; Verkhratsky et al., 2014; Yamamuro et al., 2015). See Learning Objectives 8.7, 13.5, and 13.14. Glial cells also play important roles in learning, behavior, and neuroplasticity by affecting synaptic connectivity and facilitating communication between neurons in specific neural networks (Hahn et al., 2015; Martín et al., 2015).

Two special types of glial cells, called *oligodendrocytes* and *Schwann cells*, generate a layer of fatty substances called **myelin**. Oligodendrocytes produce myelin for the neurons in the brain and spinal cord (the central nervous system); Schwann cells produce myelin for the neurons of the body (the peripheral nervous system). Myelin wraps around the shaft of the axons, forming an insulating and protective sheath. Bundles of myelin-coated axons travel together as "cables" in the central nervous system called *tracts*, and in the peripheral nervous system bundles of axons are called **nerves**. Myelin from Schwann cells has a unique feature that can serve as a tunnel through which damaged nerve fibers can reconnect and repair themselves. That's why a severed toe might actually regain some function and feeling if sewn back on in time. Unfortunately, myelin from oligodendrocytes covering axons in the brain and spinal cord does not have this feature, and these axons are more likely to be permanently damaged.

The myelin sheath is a very important part of the neuron. It not only insulates and protects the neuron, it also speeds up the neural message traveling down the axon. As shown in Figure 2.1, sections of myelin bump up next to each other on the axon, similar to the way sausages are linked together. The places where the myelin seems to bump are actually small spaces on the axon called nodes, which are not covered in myelin. Myelinated and unmyelinated sections of axons have slightly different electrical properties. There are also far more ion channels at each node. Both of these features affect the speed at which the electrical signal is conducted down the axon. When the electrical impulse that is the neural message travels down an axon coated with myelin, the electrical impulse is regenerated at each node and appears to "jump" or skip rapidly from node to node down the axon (Koester & Siegelbaum, 2013; Schwartz et al., 2013). That makes the message go

axon terminals

enlarged ends of axonal branches of the neuron, specialized for communication between cells.

glial cells

cells that provide support for the neurons to grow on and around, deliver nutrients to neurons, produce myelin to coat axons, clean up waste products and dead neurons, influence information processing, and, during prenatal development, influence the generation of new neurons.

myelin

fatty substances produced by certain glial cells that coat the axons of neurons to insulate, protect, and speed up the neural impulse.

nerves

bundles of axons coated in myelin that travel together through the body.

much faster down the coated axon than it would down an uncoated axon of a neuron in the brain. In the disease called *multiple sclerosis* (MS), the myelin sheath is destroyed (possibly by the individual's own immune system), which leads to diminished or complete loss of neural functioning in those damaged cells. Early symptoms of MS may include fatigue; changes in vision; balance problems; and numbness, tingling, or muscle weakness in the arms or legs. Just as we are learning more about the expanded roles of glial cells, our knowledge about the structure and function of myelin is also expanding far beyond myelin simply being an insulator of axons. Myelin thickness varies, and myelin distribution may vary along the length of an axon, likely affecting communication properties of those neurons and impacting larger neural networks (Fields, 2014; Tomassy et al., 2014).

AP 2.F Identify basic processes and systems in the biological bases of behavior, including parts of the neuron.

2.2 Generating the Message Within the Neuron: The Neural Impulse

2.2 Explain the action potential.

 Exactly how does this "electrical message" work inside the cell?

A neuron that's at rest—not currently firing a neural impulse or message—is actually electrically charged. Inside and outside of the cell is a semiliquid (jelly-like) solution in which there are charged particles, or *ions*. Although both positive and negative ions are located inside and outside of the cell, the relative charge of ions inside the cell is mostly negative, and the relative charge of ions outside the cell is mostly positive due to both **diffusion**, the process of ions moving from areas of high concentration to areas of low concentration, and *electrostatic pressure*, the relative balance of electrical charges when the ions are at rest. The cell membrane itself is *semipermeable*, meaning some molecules may freely pass through the membrane while others cannot. Some molecules outside the cell enter through tiny protein openings, or *channels*, in the membrane, while molecules inside the cell can pass through the same channels to the outside of the cell. Many of these channels are gated—they open or close based on the electrical potential of the membrane—more about that in a minute. Inside the cell is a concentration of both smaller positively charged potassium ions and larger negatively charged protein ions. The negatively charged protein ions, however, are so big that they can't get out, which leaves the inside of the cell primarily negative when at rest. Outside the cell are lots of positively charged sodium ions and negatively charged chloride ions, but they are unable to enter the cell membrane when the cell is at rest because the ion channels that would allow them in are closed. But because the outside sodium ions are positive and the inside ions are negative, and because opposite electrical charges attract each other, the sodium ions will cluster around the membrane. This difference in charges creates an electrical potential.

Clustering outside the neuron, the sodium ions are primed to enter the cell. When the cell is resting (the electrical potential is in a state called the **resting potential**, because the cell is at rest), the sodium ions are stuck outside. The sodium ions cannot enter when the cell is at rest, because even though the cell membrane has all these channels, the *particular channels* for the sodium ions aren't open yet. But when the cell receives a strong enough stimulus from another cell (at the dendrites or soma), the cell membrane opens those particular channels, one after the other in a chain reaction, all down its surface, allowing the sodium ions to rush into the cell. That causes the inside of the cell to become mostly positive because many of the positive sodium ions are now inside the cell—at the point where the first ion channel opened. This electrical charge reversal will start at the part of the axon closest to the soma, the *axon hillock*, and proceed down the

---

diffusion
process of molecules moving from areas of high concentration to areas of low concentration.

resting potential
the state of the neuron when not firing a neural impulse.

axon sequentially opening ion channels. This electrical charge reversal is known as the **action potential** because the electrical potential is now in action rather than at rest. Each action potential sequence takes about one-thousandth of a second, so the neural message travels very fast—from 2 miles per hour in the slowest, shortest neurons to 270 miles per hour in other neurons.

Now the action potential is traveling down the axon. When it gets to the end of the axon, something else happens: The message will get transmitted to another cell (that step will be discussed momentarily). Meanwhile, what is happening to the parts of the cell that the action potential has already left behind? Remember, the action potential means the cell is now positive inside and negative outside at the point where the channel opened. Several things happen to return the cell to its resting state. First, the sodium ion channels close immediately after the action potential has passed, allowing no more sodium ions to enter. Small, positively charged potassium ions inside the neuron also move rapidly out of the cell after the action potential passes, helping to restore the inside of the cell to a negative charge, and then the potassium channels too close. Once the neuron has returned to its normal resting potential, the sodium channels reset and the neuron is now poised and ready to fire again. However, the potassium ions leaving the cell results in a brief period of *hyperpolarization* where the membrane charge goes beyond its original resting potential. It returns to its normal resting level when particular membrane structures come into play, transporting any remaining sodium ions back outside the cell and potassium ions back in (see **Figure 2.2**).

To sum up, when the cell is sufficiently stimulated, the first ion channel opens and the electrical charge of the membrane *at that ion channel* is reversed. Then the next ion channel opens and *that* charge is reversed, but the *first* ion channel immediately closes and the membrane potential at that channel returns to its resting level. The action potential is the *sequence* of ion channels opening and membrane potential reversing, ion channels closing and resetting all along the length of the cell's axon.

> 💬 So if the stimulus that originally causes the neuron to fire is very strong, will the neuron fire more strongly than it would if the stimulus were weak?

Neurons actually have a threshold for firing, and all it takes is a stimulus just strong enough to get past that threshold to make the neuron fire. Here's a simple version of how this works: Each neuron is receiving many signals from other neurons. Some of these signals are meant to cause the neuron to fire, whereas others are meant to prevent the neuron from firing. The neuron constantly adds together the effects of the "fire" messages and subtracts the "don't fire" messages, and if the "fire" messages are great enough, the threshold is crossed and the neuron fires. When a neuron does fire, it fires in an **all-or-none** fashion. That is, neurons are either firing at full strength or not firing at all—there's no

action potential
the release of the neural impulse, consisting of a reversal of the electrical charge within the axon.

all-or-none
referring to the fact that a neuron either fires completely or does not fire at all.

Figure 2.2 The Neural Impulse Action Potential

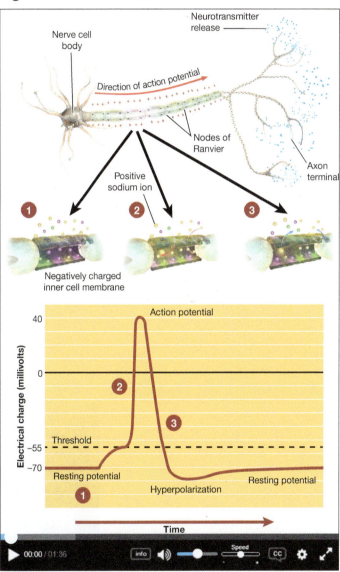

▶ Watch the Video at MyLab Psychology

Voltage is graphed at a given axonal node over 2 to 3 milliseconds (thousandths of a second). From an initial resting state, enough stimulation is received that the threshold of excitation is reached and an action potential is triggered. The resulting rapid depolarization, repolarization, brief hyperpolarization, and return to resting potential coincide with movement of sodium and potassium ions across the cell membrane.

such thing as "partial" firing of a neuron. It would be like turning on a light switch—it's either on or it's off.

So, what's the difference between strong stimulation and weak stimulation? A strong message will cause the neuron to fire repeatedly (as if someone flicked the light switch on and off as quickly as possible), and it will also cause more neurons to fire (as if there were a lot of lights going on and off instead of just one).

2.3 Neurotransmission

AP 2.G Identify basic process of transmission of a signal between neurons.

2.3 Describe how neurons use neurotransmitters to communicate with each other and with the body.

> 🗨 Now that we know how the message travels within the axon of the cell, what is that "something else" that happens when the action potential reaches the end of the axon?

Once a neural signal reaches the axon terminals of a neuron, several events take place to allow neurons to communicate with each other. These events depend on key structures within a neuron and on the surface of adjacent neurons.

SENDING THE MESSAGE TO OTHER CELLS: THE SYNAPSE Look at the axon terminals in Figure 2.1 again and then look at the enlarged axon terminal shown in **Figure 2.3**. Notice the presynaptic terminal is not empty. It has a number of little sac-like structures in it called **synaptic vesicles**. The word *vesicle* is Latin and means a "little blister" or "fluid-filled sac."

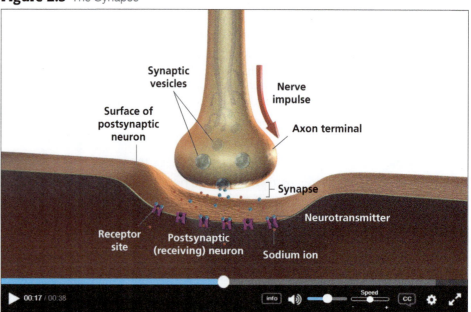

Figure 2.3 The Synapse

👁 Watch the Video at MyLab Psychology

The nerve impulse reaches the axon terminal, triggering the release of neurotransmitters from the synaptic vesicles. The molecules of neurotransmitter cross the synaptic gap to fit into the receptor sites that fit the shape of the molecule, opening the ion channel and allowing sodium ions to rush in.

synaptic vesicles
saclike structures found inside the synaptic knob containing chemicals.

neurotransmitter
chemical found in the synaptic vesicles that, when released, has an effect on the next cell.

Inside the synaptic vesicles are chemicals suspended in fluid, which are molecules of substances called **neurotransmitters**. The name is simple enough—they are inside a neuron and they are going to transmit a message. (Neurons have traditionally been viewed as containing a single type of neurotransmitter, but it is now accepted that neurons may release more than one neurotransmitter. For simplicity and unless otherwise specified, our discussion throughout the text will assume a single, predominant neurotransmitter is being released.) Next to the axon terminal is the dendrite of another neuron (see Figure 2.3). Between them is a fluid-filled space called the **synapse** or the **synaptic gap**. Instead of an electrical charge, the vesicles at the end of the axon (also called the presynaptic membrane) contain the molecules of neurotransmitters, and the surface of the dendrite next to the axon (the postsynaptic membrane) contains ion channels that have **receptor sites**, proteins that allow only particular molecules of a certain shape to fit into it, just as only a particular key will fit into a keyhole. Synapses can also occur on the soma of the postsynaptic cell, as the surface membrane of the soma also has receptor sites.

How do the neurotransmitters get across the gap? Recall the action potential making its way down the axon after the neuron has been stimulated. When that action potential, or electrical charge, reaches the synaptic vesicles, the synaptic vesicles release their neurotransmitters into the synaptic gap. The molecules then float across the synapse, and many of them fit themselves into the receptor sites, opening the ion channels and allowing sodium to rush in, activating the next cell. It is this very activation that stimulates, or releases, the action potential in that cell. It is important to understand that the "next cell" may be a neuron, but it may also be a cell on a muscle or a gland. Muscles and glands have special cells with receptor sites on them, just like on the dendrite or soma of a neuron.

So far, we've been talking about the synapse as if neurotransmitters always cause the next cell to fire its action potential (or, in the case of a muscle or gland, to contract or start secreting its chemicals). But the neurons must have a way to be turned *off* as well as on. Otherwise, when a person burns a finger, the pain signals from those neurons would not stop until the burn was completely healed. Muscles are told to contract or relax, and glands are told to secrete or stop secreting their chemicals. The neurotransmitters found at various synapses around the nervous system can either turn cells on (called an *excitatory* effect) or turn cells off (called an *inhibitory* effect), depending on exactly what synapse is being affected. Although some people refer to neurotransmitters that turn cells on as *excitatory* neurotransmitters and the ones that turn cells off as *inhibitory* neurotransmitters, it's really more correct to refer to **excitatory synapses** and **inhibitory synapses**. In other words, it's not the neurotransmitter itself that is excitatory or inhibitory, but rather it is the effect of that neurotransmitter that is either excitatory or inhibitory at the receptor sites of a particular synapse.

NEUROTRANSMITTERS: MESSENGERS OF THE NETWORK The first neurotransmitter to be identified was named *acetylcholine* (ACh). It is found at the synapses between neurons and muscle cells. Acetylcholine stimulates the skeletal muscles to contract but actually slows contractions in the heart muscle. If acetylcholine receptor sites on the muscle cells are blocked in some way, then the acetylcholine can't get to the site and the muscle will be incapable of contracting—paralyzed, in other words. This is exactly what happens when *curare*, a drug used by South American Indians on their blow darts, gets into the nervous system. Curare's molecules are just similar enough to fit into the receptor site without actually stimulating the cell, making curare an **antagonist** (a chemical substance that blocks or reduces the effects of a neurotransmitter) for ACh.

What would happen if the neurons released too much ACh? The bite of a black widow spider does just that. Its venom stimulates the release of excessive amounts of ACh and causes convulsions and possible death. Black widow spider venom is an **agonist** (a chemical substance that mimics or enhances the effects of a neurotransmitter) for ACh.

synapse (synaptic gap)
microscopic fluid-filled space between the axon terminal of one cell and the dendrites or soma of the next cell.

receptor sites
three-dimensional proteins on the surface of the dendrites or certain cells of the muscles and glands, which are shaped to fit only certain neurotransmitters.

excitatory synapse
synapse at which a neurotransmitter causes the receiving cell to fire.

inhibitory synapse
synapse at which a neurotransmitter causes the receiving cell to stop firing.

antagonists
chemical substances that block or reduce a cell's response to the action of other chemicals or neurotransmitters.

agonists
chemical substances that mimic or enhance the effects of a neurotransmitter on the receptor sites of the next cell, increasing or decreasing the activity of that cell.

AP 2.H Discuss the influence of drugs on neurotransmitters.

The venom of the black widow spider causes a flood of acetylcholine to be released into the body's muscle system, causing convulsions.

ACh also plays a key role in memory, arousal, and attention. For example, ACh is found in the hippocampus, an area of the brain that is responsible for forming new memories, and low levels of ACh have been associated with Alzheimer's disease, the most common type of dementia. See Learning Objective 6.13. We will focus more on agonists and antagonists later in the chapter. *Dopamine* (DA) is a neurotransmitter found in the brain, and like some of the other neurotransmitters, it can have different effects depending on the exact location of its activity. For example, if too little DA is released in a certain area of the brain, the result is Parkinson's disease—the disease that is currently being battled by actor Michael J. Fox and that affected the late former boxing champ Muhammad Ali (Almasy, 2016; Ahlskog, 2003). If too much DA is released in other areas, the result is a cluster of symptoms that may be part of schizophrenia (Akil et al., 2003). See Learning Objective 13.15.

Serotonin (5-HT) is a neurotransmitter originating in the lower part of the brain that can have either an excitatory or inhibitory effect, depending on the particular synapses being affected. It is associated with sleep, mood, anxiety, and appetite. For example, low levels of 5-HT activity have been linked to depression. See Learning Objective 13.5.

Although ACh was the first neurotransmitter found to have an excitatory effect at the synapse, the nervous system's major excitatory neurotransmitter is *glutamate*. Like ACh, glutamate plays an important role in learning and memory and may also be involved in the development of the nervous system and in synaptic plasticity (the ability of the brain to change connections among its neurons). However, an excess of glutamate results in overactivation and neuronal damage and may be associated with the cell death that occurs after stroke or head injury or in degenerative diseases like Alzheimer's disease and Huntington's disease (Julien et al., 2011; Siegelbaum et al., 2013).

Another neurotransmitter is *gamma-aminobutyric acid* or GABA. Whereas glutamate is the major neurotransmitter with an excitatory effect, GABA is the most common neurotransmitter producing inhibition in the brain. GABA can help calm anxiety, for example, by binding to the same receptor sites that are affected by tranquilizing drugs and alcohol. In fact, the effect of alcohol is to enhance the effect of GABA, which causes the general inhibition of the nervous system associated with getting drunk. This makes alcohol an agonist for GABA. See Learning Objective 4.13. **Table 2.1** below lists some neurotransmitters and their functions.

Table 2.1 Some Neurotransmitters and Their Functions

Neurotransmitters	Functions
Acetylcholine (ACh)	Excitatory or inhibitory; involved in arousal, attention, memory, and controls muscle contractions
Norepinephrine (NE)	Mainly excitatory; involved in arousal and mood
Dopamine (DA)	Excitatory or inhibitory; involved in control of movement and sensations of pleasure
Serotonin (5-HT)	Excitatory or inhibitory; involved in sleep, mood, anxiety, and appetite
Gamma-aminobutyric acid (GABA)	Major inhibitory neurotransmitter; involved in sleep and inhibits movement
Glutamate	Major excitatory neurotransmitter; involved in learning, memory formation, nervous system development, and synaptic plasticity
Endorphins	Inhibitory neural regulators; involved in pain relief

A group of substances known as *neuropeptides* can serve as neurotransmitters or hormones or influence the action of other neurotransmitters (Schwartz & Javitch, 2013). You may have heard of the set of neuropeptides called *endorphins*—pain-controlling chemicals in the body. When a person is hurt, a neurotransmitter that signals pain is released. When the brain gets this message, it triggers the release of endorphins. The endorphins bind to receptors that open the ion channels on the axon. This causes the cell to be unable to fire its pain signal, and the pain sensations eventually lessen. For example, you might bump your elbow and experience a lot of pain at first, but the pain will quickly subside to a much lower level. Athletes may injure themselves during an event and yet not feel the pain until after the competition is over, when the endorphin levels go down.

The name *endorphin* comes from the term *endogenous morphine*. (*Endogenous* means "native to the area"—in this case, native to the body.) Scientists studying the nervous system found receptor sites that fit morphine molecules perfectly and decided that there must be a natural substance in the body that has the same effect as morphine. Endorphins are one reason that heroin and the other drugs derived from opium are so addictive—when people take morphine or heroin, their bodies neglect to produce endorphins. When the drug wears off, they are left with no protection against pain at all, and *everything* hurts. This pain is one reason most people want more heroin, creating an addictive cycle of abuse. See Learning Objective 4.11.

> If the neurotransmitters are out there in the synaptic gap and in the receptor sites, what happens to them when they aren't needed anymore?

CLEANING UP THE SYNAPSE: REUPTAKE AND ENZYMES The neurotransmitters have to get out of the receptor sites before the next stimulation can occur. Some just drift away through the process of diffusion, but most will end up back in the presynaptic neuron to be repackaged into the synaptic vesicles in a process called **reuptake**. (Think of a little suction tube, sucking the chemicals back into the presynaptic neuron.) That way, the synapse is cleared for the next release of neurotransmitters. Some drugs, like cocaine, affect the nervous system by blocking the reuptake process, as shown in **Figure 2.4**.

Figure 2.4 Neurotransmitters: Reuptake

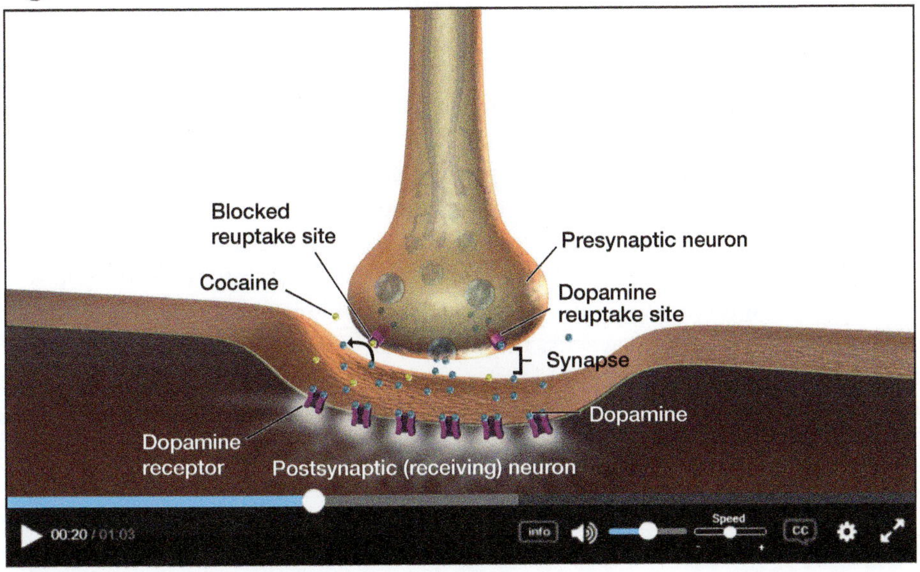

Watch the Video at MyLab Psychology

Dopamine is removed from the synapse by reuptake sites. Cocaine acts by blocking dopamine reuptake sites, allowing dopamine to remain active in the synapse longer.

One neurotransmitter is not taken back into the vesicles, however. Because ACh is responsible for muscle activity, and muscle activity needs to happen rapidly and continue happening, it's not possible to wait around for the "sucking up" process to occur. Instead,

reuptake
process by which neurotransmitters are taken back into the synaptic vesicles.

an enzyme* specifically designed to break apart ACh clears the synaptic gap very quickly (a process called **enzymatic degradation**). There are enzymes that also break down other neurotransmitters.

> 💬 I think I understand the synapse and neurotransmitters now, but how do I relate that to the real world?

Knowing how and why drugs affect us can help us understand why a physician might prescribe a particular drug or why certain drugs are dangerous and should be avoided. Because the chemical molecules of various drugs, if similar enough in shape to the neurotransmitters, can fit into the receptor sites on the receiving neurons just like the neurotransmitters do, drugs can act as agonists or antagonists. Drugs acting as agonists, for example, can mimic or enhance the effects of neurotransmitters on the receptor sites of the next cell. This can result in an increase or decrease in the activity of the receiving cell, depending on what the effect of the original neurotransmitter (excitatory or inhibitory) was going to be. So, if the original neurotransmitter was excitatory, the effect of the agonist will be to increase that excitation. If it was inhibitory, the effect of the agonist will be to increase that inhibition. Another deciding factor is the nervous system location of the neurons that use a specific neurotransmitter.

For example, some antianxiety medications, such as diazepam (Valium®), are classified as benzodiazepines (see Learning Objective 14.10) and are agonists for GABA, the primary inhibitory neurotransmitter in the brain. Areas of the brain that you will learn about later that play a role in controlling anxiety, agitation, and fear include the amygdala, orbitofrontal cortex, and the insula (LeDoux & Damasio, 2013; Zilles & Amunts, 2012). By increasing the inhibitory (calming) action of GABA, the benzodiazepines directly calm these specific brain areas (Advokat et al., 2019; Preston et al., 2017; Stahl, 2013, 2017).

Other drugs act as antagonists, blocking or reducing a cell's response to the action of other chemicals or neurotransmitters. Although an antagonist might sound like it has only an inhibitory effect, it is important to remember that if the neurotransmitter that the antagonist affects is inhibitory itself, the result will actually be an *increase* in the activity of the cell that would normally have been inhibited; the antagonist *blocks* the inhibitory effect.

Lastly, some drugs yield their agonistic or antagonistic effects by impacting the amount of neurotransmitter in the synapse. They do so by interfering with the regular reuptake or enzymatic degradation process. Remember that the neurotransmitter serotonin helps regulate and adjust people's moods, but in some people the normal process of adjustment is not working properly. Some of the drugs used to treat depression are called SSRIs (selective serotonin reuptake inhibitors). SSRIs block the reuptake of serotonin, leaving more serotonin available in the synapse to bind with receptor sites. Over several weeks, the individual's mood improves. Although the reason for this improvement is not as simple as once believed (i.e., low levels of serotonin = low levels of mood) or fully understood, SSRIs are effective for depression, anxiety, and obsessive-compulsive disorder (Advokat et al., 2019; Hyman & Cohen, 2013; Preston et al., 2017; Stahl, 2013, 2017). Again, although SSRIs are effective, it is not just a case of low levels of serotonin resulting in low or depressed levels of mood, or the reverse; increasing serotonin in and of itself is not the sole reason for the changes in mood.

This section covered the neuron and how neurons communicate. The next section looks at different methods for examining the structure and function of the brain.

enzymatic degradation
process by which the structure of a neurotransmitter is altered so it can no longer act on a receptor.

---

*enzyme: a complex protein that is manufactured by cells.

Concept Map L.O. 2.1, 2.2, 2.3

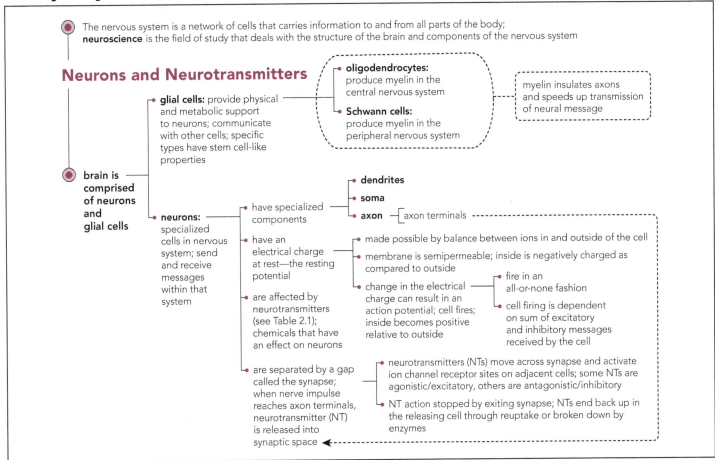

Practice Quiz   How much do you remember?

Pick the best answer.

1. Which part of the neuron carries messages to other cells?
   a. synaptic vesicles
   b. axon
   c. dendrite
   d. soma
   e. myelin

2. Which one of the following is NOT a function of glial cells?
   a. cleaning up the remains of dead neurons
   b. generating myelin
   c. providing structural support for neurons
   d. generating action potentials
   e. getting nutrients to the neurons

3. When a neuron's resting potential is occurring, the neuron is _____ charged on the inside.
   a. both positively and negatively
   b. neutrally
   c. positively
   d. not
   e. negatively

4. Neurotransmitters must pass from an axon terminal to the next dendrite by crossing a fluid-filled space called the _____.
   a. synapse
   b. vesicle
   c. neuron
   d. glial cell
   e. reuptake inhibitor

5. The venom of a black widow spider acts as a(n) _____ by mimicking the effects of acetylcholine.
   a. enzyme
   b. glial cell
   c. antagonist
   d. agonist
   e. protagonist

6. Which of the following is associated with pain relief?
   a. acetylcholine
   b. endorphins
   c. GABA
   d. serotonin
   e. glutamate

2.4–2.5 Looking Inside the Living Brain

AP 2.K Recount historic and contemporary research strategies and technologies that support research.

Scientists can't be sure what brain tissue really looks like when it's inside the skull of a living person—nor can they be certain that it looks identical to that of a brain sitting on a dissecting table. How can scientists find out if the brain is intact, if parts are missing or damaged, or what the various parts of the brain do?

2.4 Methods for Studying Specific Regions of the Brain

2.4 Describe how lesioning studies and brain stimulation are used to study the brain.

Researchers are able to learn about the brain through accidental damage or through intentional manipulation of brain tissue. When appropriate, such manipulation can be accomplished through lesioning or stimulation methods.

LESIONING STUDIES One way to get some idea of the functions that various areas of the brain control is to study animals or people with damage in those areas. In animals, that may mean researchers will deliberately damage a part of the brain, after which they test the animal to see what has happened to its abilities. In such an experiment, the test animal is anesthetized and given medication for pain. An electrode, a thin wire or probe insulated everywhere but at its tip, is then surgically inserted into the brain. An electrical current is passed through the electrode, heating the tip and destroying the intended brain tissue. This procedure is called **lesioning**.

It should be obvious that researchers cannot destroy areas of brains in living human beings. One method they can use is to study and test people who already have brain damage. However, this is not an ideal way to study the brain. No two case studies of humans are likely to present damage in exactly the same area of the brain, nor would the cases involve exactly the same amount of damage.

BRAIN STIMULATION In contrast to lesioning, a less harmful way to study the brain is to temporarily disrupt or enhance the normal functioning of specific brain areas through electrical stimulation and then study the resulting changes in behavior or cognition. The procedure of stimulating a specific area of the brain is much the same as in lesioning, but the much milder current in this research does no damage to the neurons. It does cause the neurons to react as if they had received a message. This is called *electrical stimulation of the brain*, or *ESB*. It has become an important technique in psychology as its use in animals (and humans under very special circumstances such as testing before surgery to address seizure disorders) has informed us in many areas of investigation, including new directions for therapy.

INVASIVE TECHNIQUES: STIMULATING FROM THE INSIDE A specific type of ESB called *deep brain stimulation (DBS)* has been shown to be very helpful in some disorders in humans. In this procedure, neurosurgeons place electrodes in specific deep-brain areas and then route the electrode wires to a pacemaker-like device called an impulse generator that is surgically implanted under the collarbone. The impulse generator then sends impulses to the implanted electrodes, stimulating the specific brain areas of interest. DBS has been widely used as a treatment for Parkinson's disease and may play an important role in the treatment of seizure disorder, chronic pain, and possibly some treatment-resistant psychiatric disorders, including depression, obsessive compulsive disorders, and Tourette syndrome (Kohl et al., 2014; Laxpati et al., 2014; McDonald et al., 2017; Miocinovic et al., 2013; Morishita et al., 2014), among other areas. Also, using DBS for specific disorders allows researchers to learn about other effects DBS may have on the brain, such as affecting an individual's mood or memory. Techniques such as DBS are typically only used after all other less intrusive treatments have been shown to be ineffective or have side effects that have been deemed undesirable. For example, DBS is being investigated for the treatment of anorexia nervosa in individuals for whom other treatments have not been effective (Lee et al., 2018; Lipsman et al., 2013).

One of the newest and fastest developing areas in brain stimulation is *optogenetics*, where neurons can be activated by light rather than electricity. While currently only used in animal models, it is employed across a variety of areas to enhance our understanding

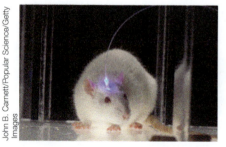

Optogenetics involves modifying the genes of neurons so they are sensitive to light and then using light devices inserted in the brain to modify the activity of those neurons (e.g., increase or decrease their rate of firing).

lesioning
insertion of a thin, insulated electrode into the brain through which an electrical current is sent, destroying the brain cells at the tip of the wire.

of the brain, cognition, and behavior (Burguière et al., 2013; Miocinovic et al., 2013; Nurminen et al., 2018). Furthermore, the technique is not only used to refine existing DBS methods, it is also being paired with other methods, such as *fMRI*, to further enhance our understanding of brain function in both normal and disordered behavior (Creed et al., 2015; Ferenczi et al., 2016; Leong et al., 2018).

NONINVASIVE TECHNIQUES: STIMULATING FROM THE OUTSIDE Noninvasive brain stimulation (NIBS) techniques also contribute to research and our knowledge of the brain in a variety of areas. In *transcranial magnetic stimulation* (TMS), magnetic pulses are applied to the cortex (outer areas of the brain) using special copper wire coils positioned over the head. The resulting magnetic fields stimulate neurons in the targeted area of the cortex. Longer lasting stimulation results when the pulses are administered in a repetitive fashion and is referred to as *repetitive TMS* (rTMS). Another procedure, called *transcranial direct current stimulation* (tDCS), uses scalp electrodes to pass very low amplitude direct current to the brain to change the excitability of cortical neurons directly below the electrodes.

This woman is receiving repetitive transcranial magnetic stimulation (rTMS) as an experimental treatment for migraine headaches. This procedure uses magnetic pulses to stimulate specific areas of the cortex. rTMS is being used in both the exploration of new potential treatments for a variety of psychological, pain, and movement disorders and in studies of cognition.

NIBS methods are proving useful in studies of learning and cognition. For example, tDCS has been used to stimulate parts of the frontal lobe to reduce the impacts of stress on working memory (Bogdanov & Schwabe, 2016). See Learning Objectives 2.8, 6.3. Another interesting study used TMS to investigate brain mechanisms related to perceived object stiffness, such as determining how ripe a piece of fruit is by squeezing it (Leib et al., 2016). NIBS techniques are also being used to investigate brain plasticity (Hirtz et al., 2018) and as possible treatment options for a variety of symptoms and disorders including impulsivity in adult attention-deficit/hyperactivity disorder (ADHD), reducing cravings and improving impulse control in substance use disorders, augmenting cognitive therapy in posttraumatic stress disorder (PTSD), management of depression, and to assist rehabilitation efforts following a stroke (Allenby et al., 2018; D'Agata et al., 2016; Kelly et al., 2017; Kozel et al., 2018; Meille et al., 2017; Trojak et al., 2017; Wang et al., 2017).

Beyond learning, cognition, and treatment, NIBS are also being used to assist researchers in understanding ways in which the brains of individuals with various psychological disorders may function differently than individuals without a specific disorder and how treatments may change brain function or structure. For example, what structural brain changes may be taking place during effective treatments of depression, such as changes in the cingulate cortex (Boes et al., 2018). See Learning Objective 2.7. TMS has also been used to help understand excitatory and inhibitory functions of the cortex in adolescents with a history of suicidal behavior (Lewis et al., 2018). See Learning Objective 2.8. The study suggested some cortical inhibition changes may be related to variations in a specific type of GABA activity, possibly different than the type of GABA activity noted in adults with a history of suicidal behavior. See Learning Objective 2.3.

Bear in mind that stimulating the cortex may facilitate specific functions or behaviors but impair others. For example, if someone is counting from 1 to 20 and the brain is stimulated in the correct location of the motor cortex, the person's speech would be disrupted, but perhaps stimulating in other areas of the frontal lobe may assist the person in attending to the counting task. Furthermore, the brain has widespread connections, so stimulation in one area is likely to affect other areas. In one study, inhibitory stimulation of the left prefrontal cortex resulted in reduced blood oxygenation on both the left and right sides of the prefrontal cortex (Tupak et al., 2013).

Note: tDCS is NOT the same as electroconvulsive therapy, which uses much higher levels of current through the entire brain, resulting in a grand mal seizure that appears to normalize brain chemistry and function in the treatment of severe depression. See Learning Objective 14.11.

2.5 Neuroimaging Techniques

2.5 Compare and contrast neuroimaging techniques for mapping the brain's structure and function.

All of these methods of stimulation yield important information about the brain, thinking, and behavior, but they do not allow us to see what is going on with the brain as a whole. Instead, various neuroimaging techniques can do this, either by directly imaging the brain's structure (the different parts) or its function (how the parts work). These methods also vary in their degree of spatial resolution (ability to see fine detail) and temporal resolution (ability to time lock a recorded event).

MAPPING STRUCTURE As hinted at earlier, aside from observing the person's behavior, scientists had to wait until a person died to fully investigate if there were changes or damage to the individual's brain. Fortunately, modern neuroimaging allows us to image the brain's structure while the person is still alive (see **Figure 2.5**).

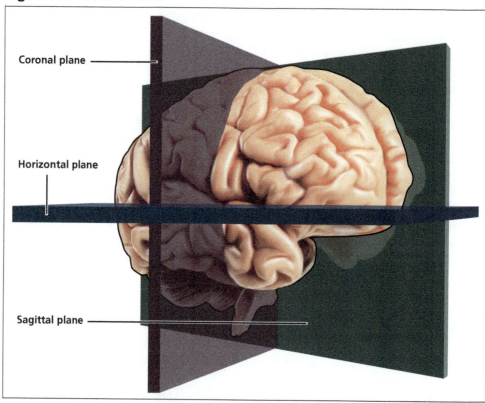

Figure 2.5 Planes of Section

Medical professionals often divide the brain in terms of anatomical planes of section. These planes are imaginary vertical or horizontal slices drawn through an upright head. These divisions are used to help describe the location of brain structures.

computed tomography (CT)
brain-imaging method using computer-controlled X-rays of the brain.

magnetic resonance imaging (MRI)
brain-imaging method using radio waves and magnetic fields of the body to produce detailed images of the brain.

COMPUTED TOMOGRAPHY (CT) Scientists have several ways to look inside the human brain without causing harm to the person. One way is to take a series of X-rays of the brain, aided by a computer. This is accomplished during a **CT** scan **(computed tomography** involves mapping "slices" of the brain by computer). CT scans can show stroke damage, tumors, injuries, and abnormal brain structure (see **Figure 2.6a**). A CT scan is also the structural imaging method of choice when there is metal in the body (e.g., a bullet or surgical clips) and useful for imaging possible skull fractures (see **Figure 2.6b**).

MAGNETIC RESONANCE IMAGING (MRI) As useful as a CT scan can be for imaging the skull, it doesn't show very small details within the brain. The relatively newer technique of **magnetic resonance imaging**, or **MRI**, provides much more detail (see **Figure 2.6c** and **Figure 2.6d**), even allowing doctors to see the effects of very small strokes. The person getting an MRI scan is placed inside a machine that generates a powerful magnetic field to align hydrogen atoms in the brain tissues (these normally spin in a random fashion); then radio pulses are used to make the atoms spin at a particular frequency and direction. The time it takes for the atoms to return to their normal spin allows a computer to create a three-dimensional image of the brain and display "slices" of that image on a screen.

Using MRI as a basis, researchers have developed several techniques to study other aspects of the brain. *MRI spectroscopy* allows researchers to estimate the concentration of specific chemicals and neurotransmitters in the brain. Another fascinating technique is called *DTI*, or *diffusion tensor imaging*. The brain has two distinct color regions, *gray matter*, the outer areas consisting largely of neurons with unmyelinated axons, and *white matter*, the fiber tracts consisting of myelinated axons (the myelin is responsible for the lighter color). DTI uses MRI technology to provide a way to measure connectivity in the brain by imaging these white matter tracts. DTI has been used to investigate normal function, such as structural changes associated with different levels of semantic learning, memory performance, and brain changes during normal aging, and with various disorders and conditions including Alzheimer's disease, MS, and traumatic brain injury (de Mooij et al., 2018; Hayes et al., 2016; Ly et al., 2016; Muthuraman et al., 2016; Ripollés et al., 2017; Wang et al., 2016).

MAPPING FUNCTION In addition to imaging the different parts of the brain to understand what may or may not be present, examining the function of the brain is also important in understanding behavior and mental processes.

THE ELECTROENCEPHALOGRAM (EEG) As important as imaging brain structure is, it is sometimes important to know how different brain areas function. A fairly harmless way to study the activity of the living brain is to record the electrical activity of the cortex just below the skull using a device called an *electroencephalograph*. The first **electroencephalogram (EEG)** recording in humans was accomplished in 1924 by Hans Berger (Niedermeyer, 2005). Recording the EEG involves using small metal disks or sponge-like electrodes placed directly on the scalp and a special solution to help conduct the electrical signals from the cortex just below. These electrodes are connected to an amplifier and then to a computer to view the information. The resulting electrical output forms waves that indicate many things, such as stages of sleep, seizures, and even the presence of tumors. The EEG can also be used to help determine which areas of the brain are active during various mental tasks that involve memory and attention. EEG activity can be classified according to appearance and frequency, and different waves are associated with different brain activity. For example, *alpha waves* in the back of the brain are one indication of relaxed wakefulness (seen in bottom two lines in **Figure 2.7a**). EEG waveforms are covered in more detail in Chapter Four. See Learning Objective 4.5.

Another common EEG-based technique focuses on *event-related potentials*, or *ERPs*. In ERP studies, multiple presentations of a stimulus are measured during an EEG and then averaged to remove variations in the ongoing brain activity that is normally recorded during the EEG. The result is a measurement of the response of the brain

Figure 2.6 Mapping Brain Structure

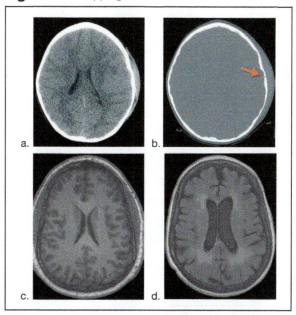

Fig 2.6a: CT scan from a 5-year-old girl with a head injury and skull fracture, depicting the brain and swelling associated with the injury. Fig 2.6b: Same CT scan highlighting the skull fracture (indicated by the red arrow). Contrast the brain detail of Fig 2.6a with the MRI scan in Fig 2.6c (different, adult individual). Note the scans are in the horizontal plane, separating the brain into upper and lower portions (also see Figure 2.8). Fig 2.6d: Different type of MRI image from an older adult, with cortical cell loss (atrophy) and white matter changes. Notice the enlarged ventricles and widening of the grooves (sulci) in the outer cortex as compared to 2.6c.

Source: Noland White; Figs 2.6a, b, c, and d images created with OsiriX software.

electroencephalogram (EEG)
a recording of the electrical activity of large groups of cortical neurons just below the skull, most often using scalp electrodes.

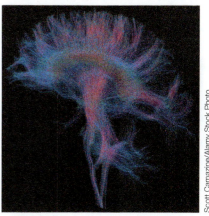

Diffusion tensor imaging (DTI) uses MRI data to estimate the location and orientation of the brain's white matter tracts. The different colors in this image highlight different white matter pathways in the brain.

Figure 2.7 Mapping Brain Function

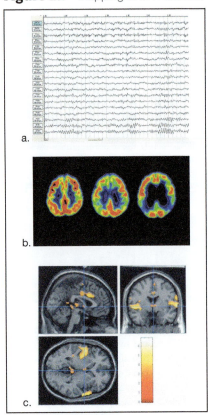

Various methods for mapping brain function. An EEG record is shown in 2.7a, a PET scan image in 2.7b, and an image from an fMRI study in 2.7c.

Sources: a) Noland White; b) Science Source/Getty Images; c) Philippe Psaila/Science Source

positron emission tomography (PET) brain-imaging method in which a radioactive sugar is injected into the subject and a computer compiles a color-coded image of the activity of the brain.

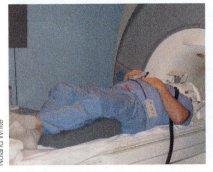
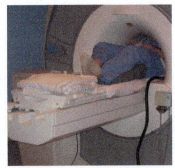

As part of an fMRI study on attention, one of your authors is fitted with headphones, an angled mirror, and a hand response pad. During the study, the headphones will allow him to hear audio instructions and stimuli, and the mirror will allow him to view task items projected on a rear screen placed outside of the scanner. The response pad is used to indicate answers for the various tasks.

related to the stimulus event itself, or an event-related potential. ERPs allow the study of different stages of cognitive processing. For example, the use of ERPs has allowed researchers to investigate differences in brain processing associated with verbal working memory in individuals with and without schizophrenia and attention problems common in women with bipolar disorder and women with ADHD (Kustermann et al., 2018; Michelini et al., 2018). In other studies, ERPs are being studied as a possible method of lie detection (Lu et al., 2018; Labkovsky & Rosenfeld, 2014; Rosenfeld et al., 2017; Rosenfeld et al., 2008).

MAGNETOENCEPHALOGRAPHY (MEG) While the EEG alone does not allow for the direct identification of areas of brain activation, a closely related technique does. *Magnetoencephalography* (MEG) detects small magnetic fields generated by the electrical activity of neurons. MEG has many applications and is being used to explore information processing differences in language disorders like aphasia and emotional processing of faces, including why humans identify some emotions faster than others and seem to identify angry faces more quickly than happy faces (Dima et al., 2018; Kielar et al., 2018).

POSITRON EMISSION TOMOGRAPHY (PET) The functional neuroimaging methods discussed so far rely on the electrical activity of the brain. Other techniques make use of other indicators of brain activity, including energy consumption or changes in blood oxygen levels (if areas of the brain are active, they are likely using fuel and oxygen). In **positron emission tomography (PET)**, the person is injected with a radioactive glucose (a kind of sugar). The computer detects the activity of the brain cells by looking at which cells are using up the radioactive glucose and projecting the image of that activity onto a monitor. The computer uses colors to indicate different levels of brain activity. For example, lighter colors may indicate greater activity (see **Figure 2.7b**). With this method, researchers can actually have the person perform different tasks while the computer shows what his or her brain is doing during the task. A related technique is *single photon emission computed tomography (SPECT)*, which measures brain blood flow and uses more easily obtainable radioactive tracers than those used for PET (Bremmer, 2005).

FUNCTIONAL MRI (FMRI) Although traditional MRI scans only show structure, **functional MRI (fMRI)**, in which the computer tracks changes in the oxygen levels of the blood (see **Figure 2.7c**), provides information on the brain's function as well. By superimposing information about where oxygen is used in the brain over an image of the brain's structure, researchers can identify what areas of the brain are most active during specific tasks. By combining such images taken over a period of time, a sort of "movie" of the brain's functioning can be made (Lin et al., 2007). Functional MRIs can give more detail, tend to be clearer than PET scans, and are an incredibly useful tool for research into the workings of the brain. For example, in association with genetics and other measures, resting-state fMRI has been used to demonstrate how brain connectivity impacts individuals at risk for, or with mild symptoms of, Alzheimer's disease. Patients with higher levels of connectivity between left frontal areas of the brain and the brain as a whole showed slower declines in memory and other cognitive symptoms associated with the progression of Alzheimer's disease (Franzmeier et al., 2018). Interestingly, greater levels of left frontal connectivity have also been associated with more years of education, another indicator of potential cognitive reserve (Franzmeier et al., 2017). Functional neuroimaging is also helping researchers understand

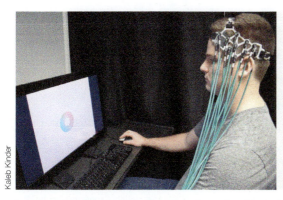 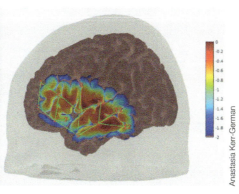

Left: An adult participant performs a color-estimation task while wearing an fNIRS probe targeting left frontal and temporal cortical regions. Right: A depiction of the cortical surface to which this fNIRS probe is sensitive, where cool colors indicate areas where the probe is least sensitive and warm colors indicate areas where the probe is most sensitive.

how various types of treatment and therapy affect the brain in a variety of disorders (Ball et al., 2014; Fournier & Price, 2014; Miller et al., 2015).

NEAR-INFRARED SPECTROSCOPY (NIRS) Another non-invasive brain imaging technique that capitalizes on changes in blood oxygen levels is **near-infrared spectroscopy** (NIRS; also referred to as functional **NIRS** or fNIRS). fNIRS uses near-infrared light to measure cortical changes in the concentration of oxygenated and deoxygenated hemoglobin, the protein in red blood cells that carries oxygen (Ferrari & Quaresima, 2012). Near-infrared light can penetrate the skin and skull and is absorbed differently by oxygenated versus deoxygenated hemoglobin. fNIRS can be used to monitor brain blood oxygen level changes in some parts of the brain during the performance of various tasks. The primary advantages of fNIRS are that it is much quieter than fMRI and it does not require the participant to lie still in a confined space. However, unlike fMRI, which can measure activity of the entire brain, fNIRS is limited to only recording from a couple of centimeters in depth from the cortical surface. For example, fNIRS is being used to measure cognitive development in children and temporal lobe activation during speech perception in adults (Defenderfer et al., 2017; Kerr-German & Buss, under review).

NIRS has been used to demonstrate the potential negative consequences of partial sleep deprivation in college students (Yeung et al., 2018). Based on self-reported sleep duration from the night before, a sample of college students was split into those with sufficient sleep (greater than 7 hours) and those with insufficient sleep (less than or equal to 7 hours). See Learning Objective 4.4. They were then asked to perform a demanding test of working memory. See Learning Objective 6.4. While both groups performed about the same on the test, only those with sufficient sleep demonstrated frontal brain activation patterns similar to those seen in previous studies. The students with insufficient sleep did not demonstrate the same pattern of frontal activation. And while the researchers noted it sometimes requires total sleep deprivation, or five or more consecutive nights of partial sleep deprivation before failures in working memory appear, there were other areas of concern. The pattern of brain activation in these students resembled those seen in some psychological disorders, such as depression, and posed questions about the possible long-term effects of sleep deprivation on frontal lobe functions. (Yeung et al., 2018).

functional magnetic resonance imaging (fMRI)
MRI-based brain-imaging method that allows for functional examination of brain areas through changes in brain oxygenation.

near-infrared spectroscopy (NIRS)
a functional brain imaging method that measures brain activity by using infrared light to determine changes in blood oxygen levels in the brain.

THINKING CRITICALLY 2.1

You may see a lot of brain imaging studies in the news or on the Internet. Thinking back to the research methods, statistics, and ethics discussed in Chapter One (Learning Objectives 1.6 through 1.18), what kinds of questions should you ask about these studies before accepting the findings as valid?

Concept Map L.O. 2.4, 2.5

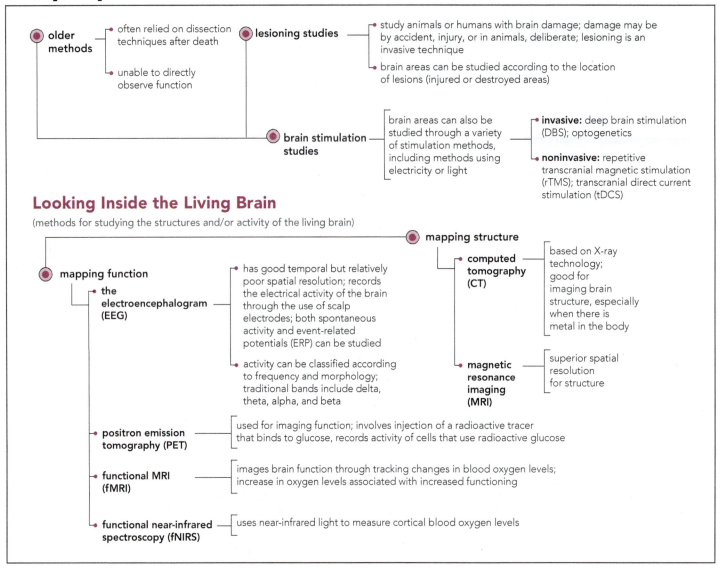

Practice Quiz — How much do you remember?

Pick the best answer.

1. Which of the following techniques involves passing a mild current through the brain to activate certain structures without damaging them?
   a. electroconvulsive tomography (ECT)
   b. electrical stimulation of the brain (ESB)
   c. optogenetics
   d. deep brain lesioning
   e. magnetic resonance imaging (MRI)

2. Which of the following techniques analyzes blood oxygen levels to look at the functioning of the brain?
   a. PET
   b. MRI
   c. EEG
   d. CT
   e. fMRI

3. Dr. Ahn is conducting a research study. She wants to measure the physical connectivity in the research participants' brains by imaging their white matter. Which of the following methods will she use?
   a. functional magnetic resonance imaging (fMRI)
   b. diffusion tensor imaging (DTI)
   c. functional near-infrared spectroscopy (fNIRS)
   d. computed tomography (CT)
   e. MRI spectroscopy

4. If you were suffering from neurological problems and your neurologist wanted to have a study done of your brain and its electrical functioning, which of the following techniques would be most appropriate?
   a. EEG
   b. fMRI
   c. DTI
   d. PTI
   e. PET

2.6–2.10 From the Bottom Up: The Structures of the Brain

AP 2.1 Describe the nervous system and its subdivisions and functions in the brain.

💬 Okay, now I understand a little more about how we look inside the brain. What exactly IS inside the brain?

Now it's time to look at the various structures of the brain, starting from the bottom and working up to the top. This text won't be discussing every single part of the brain, only major areas of interest to psychologists as explorers of thinking and behavior. Many areas also have multiple roles, but a full understanding of the brain is not possible within one chapter of an introductory psychology text. We will examine general functions for these areas and science-based principles for brain function in general. For example, while there may be behavior and subtle brain differences according to sex or gender, despite what you may have read in the popular press, there is little evidence of people having a "female" versus a "male" brain (Joel et al., 2015). Human brains can simply not be categorized that way. Neuroanatomy is an area where each structure can have multiple names, and structures can be identified or described by location, or in relation to other structures. For example, the *dorsolateral prefrontal cortex (DLPFC)* refers to portions of the prefrontal cortex toward the top and away from the midline. Before going further, it may be helpful if you understand some of the directional terms used to describe locations within the brain and nervous system. See **Figure 2.8** for more information. The video *Parts of the Brain* describes the major parts of the brain and their functions.

Figure 2.8 Anatomical Directions

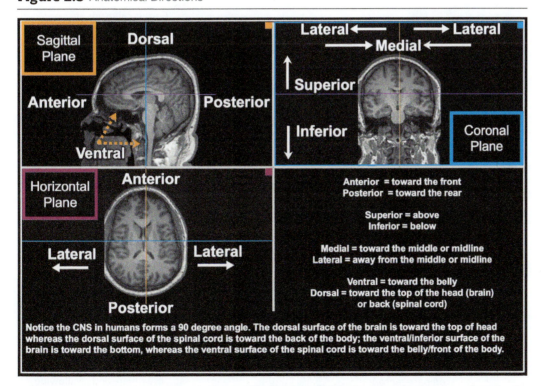

These terms are used relative to other structures. For example, when standing upright, the ears are lateral to the midline of the head and the eyes are superior to the nose. Images created with OsiriX software.

Source: Images created with OsiriX software; MRI data courtesy of Noland White.

Watch Parts of the Brain

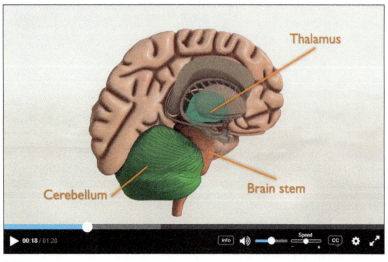

Watch the Video at MyLab Psychology

medulla
the first large swelling at the top of the spinal cord, forming the lowest part of the brain, which is responsible for life-sustaining functions such as breathing, swallowing, and heart rate.

2.6 The Hindbrain

2.6 Identify the different structures of the hindbrain and the function of each.

The brain can be divided into three main divisions early in our development that later subdivide into smaller divisions. The three primary divisions are the forebrain, the midbrain, and the hindbrain. The forebrain includes the cortex, the basal ganglia, and the limbic system. The midbrain is important for both sensory and motor functions. The hindbrain includes the medulla, pons, and cerebellum.

MEDULLA The **medulla** is located at the top of the spinal column. In **Figure 2.9**, it is the first "swelling" at the top of the spinal cord, just at the very bottom of the brain. This is the part of the brain that a person would least want to have damaged, as it controls life-sustaining functions such as heartbeat, breathing, and swallowing. It is in the medulla that the sensory nerves coming from the left and right sides of the body cross over, so that sensory information from the left side of the body goes to the right side of the brain and vice versa.

PONS The **pons** is the larger "swelling" just above the medulla. This term means "bridge," and the pons is indeed the bridge between the cerebellum and the upper sections of the brain. As in the medulla, there is a crossover of nerves, but in this case it is

Figure 2.9 Major Structures of the Human Brain

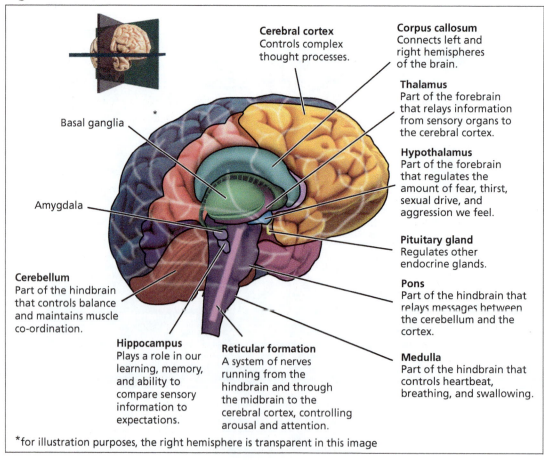

*for illustration purposes, the right hemisphere is transparent in this image

the motor nerves carrying messages from the brain to the body. This allows the pons to coordinate the movements of the left and right sides of the body. (It will be useful to remember these nerve crossovers when reading about the functions of the left and right sides of the brain in a later part of this chapter.) The pons also influences sleep, dreaming, and arousal. The role that the pons plays in sleep and dreams will be discussed in more detail in Chapter Four. See Learning Objective 4.7.

THE RETICULAR FORMATION The **reticular formation (RF)** is a network of neurons running through the middle of the medulla and the pons and slightly beyond. These neurons are responsible for people's ability to generally attend to certain kinds of information in their surroundings. Basically, the RF allows people to ignore constant, unchanging information (such as the noise of an air conditioner) and become alert to changes in information (for example, if the air conditioner stopped, most people would notice immediately).

The reticular formation is also the part of the brain that helps keep people alert and aroused. One part of the RF is called the *reticular activating system* (RAS), and it stimulates the upper part of the brain, keeping people awake and alert. When a person is driving and someone suddenly pulls out in front of the vehicle, it is the RAS that brings that driver to full attention. It is also the system that lets a mother hear her baby cry in the night, even though she might sleep through other noises.

Studies have shown that when the RF of rats is electrically stimulated while they are sleeping, they immediately awaken. If the RF is destroyed (by deep lesioning, for example), they fall into a sleeplike coma from which they never awaken (Moruzzi & Magoun, 1949; Steriade & McCarley, 1990). The RF is also implicated in comas in humans (Plum & Posner, 1985).

CEREBELLUM At the base of the skull, behind the pons and below the main part of the brain, is a structure that looks like a small brain (see **Figure 2.9**). This is the **cerebellum** (meaning "little brain"). The cerebellum is the part of the lower brain that controls all involuntary, rapid, fine motor movement. People can sit upright because the cerebellum controls all the little muscles needed to keep them from falling out of their chair. It also coordinates voluntary movements that have to happen in rapid succession, such as walking, skating, dancing, playing a musical instrument, and even the movements of speech. Learned reflexes, skills, and habits are also stored here, which allows them to become more or less automatic. Because of the cerebellum, people don't have to consciously think about their posture, muscle tone, and balance.

💬 So if your cerebellum is damaged, you might be very uncoordinated?

Yes. In fact, in a disease called *spinocerebellar degeneration*, the first symptoms are tremors, an unsteady walk, slurred speech, dizziness, and muscle weakness. The person suffering from this disease will eventually be unable to walk, stand, or even get a spoon to his or her own mouth (Schöls et al., 1998). These symptoms are similar to what one might see in a person who is suffering from alcohol intoxication. Alcohol actually appears to impact various areas of the brain and connections between the areas differently in acute versus chronic alcohol users. After the equivalent of approximately three drinks, and using fMRI to measure brain activity, disruptions in motor function were associated with changes in the thalamus for heavy drinkers, namely a portion responsible for relaying motor information to the cortex. But in normal males, declines in motor performance after drinking were associated with activity changes in the cerebellum (Shokri-Kojori et al., 2017). Brain area and activity differences were also found for declines in cognitive performance between the two groups.

Just like we are starting to better understand the various roles of glial cells, researchers and scientists are still working to better understand other functions of the cerebellum. Research suggests the cerebellum is involved in much more than motor control and may be involved with a variety of higher functions, with parts of the cerebellum activated during sensorimotor tasks and other parts involved in higher cognitive, perceptual, and emotional

pons
the larger swelling above the medulla that connects the top of the brain to the bottom and that plays a part in sleep, dreaming, left-right body coordination, and arousal.

reticular formation (RF)
an area of neurons running through the middle of the medulla and the pons and slightly beyond that is responsible for general attention, alertness, and arousal.

cerebellum
part of the lower brain located behind the pons that controls and coordinates involuntary, rapid, fine motor movement and may have some cognitive functions.

This gymnast must count on her cerebellum to help her balance and coordinate the many involuntary and voluntary motor movements that allow her to perform on this narrow balance beam. What other kinds of professions depend heavily on the activity of the cerebellum?

tasks (Adamaszek et al., 2017; Baumann et al., 2015; Hoche et al., 2016; Koziol et al., 2014; Stoodley & Schmahmann, 2009). Research continues to investigate the role of the cerebellum in these and other functions once believed to be the domain of other lobes of the brain, in a large part by examining the connections between the cerebellum and other functional areas and patterns of brain activation during resting states, specific tasks, and in both seemingly normal individuals and among individuals with various disorders (Gong et al., 2017; Kellerman et al., 2012; Strick et al., 2009; Stoodley et al., 2012; Voogd & Ruigrok, 2012).

2.7 Structures Under the Cortex: The Limbic System

2.7 Identify the structures of the brain that are involved in emotion, learning, memory, and motivation.

The forebrain includes the two cerebral hemispheres of the brain, including the cortex, which is discussed in detail later in this chapter, and a number of important structures located under the cortex in each hemisphere. These subcortical structures (the prefix *sub* means "under" or "below") play a part in our thinking and behavior. While there are subcortical structures that influence motor control and the learning of motor skills, the *basal ganglia*, and white matter fiber pathways that connect the cortex to other parts of the brain and spinal cord, we will focus on the subcortical structures that have been collectively referred to as the *limbic system* (see **Figure 2.10**).

Figure 2.10 The Limbic System

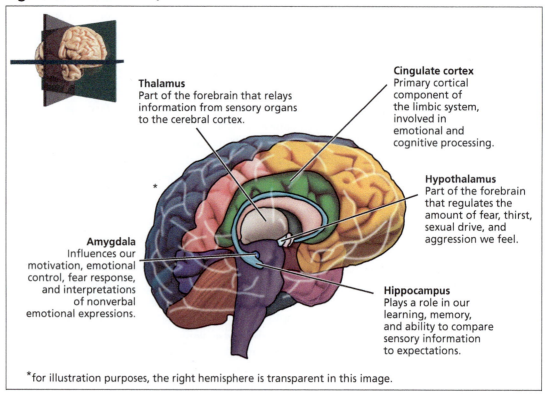

*for illustration purposes, the right hemisphere is transparent in this image.

limbic system
a group of several brain structures located primarily under the cortex and involved in learning, emotion, memory, and motivation.

thalamus
part of the limbic system located in the center of the brain, this structure relays sensory information from the lower part of the brain to the proper areas of the cortex and processes some sensory information before sending it to its proper area.

The **limbic system** (the word *limbic* means limbus or "margin," referring to a border around something, and these structures are found between the upper brain and brain stem) includes the thalamus, hypothalamus, hippocampus, amygdala, and the cingulate cortex. In general, the limbic system is involved in emotions, motivation, memory, and learning.

THALAMUS The **thalamus** ("inner chamber") is in some ways similar to a triage* nurse. This somewhat round structure in the center of the brain acts as a kind of relay station for

---

*triage: a process for sorting injured people into groups based on their need for, or likely benefit from, immediate medical treatment.

incoming sensory information. Like a nurse, the thalamus might perform some processing of that sensory information before sending it on to the part of the cortex that deals with that kind of sensation—hearing, sight, touch, or taste. Damage to the thalamus might result in the loss or partial loss of any or all of those sensations. Recent research has also suggested the thalamus may affect the functioning of task-specific regions of the cortex. For example, a study of children with dyslexia found abnormal connections between the thalamus and brain areas associated with reading behavior (Fan et al., 2014).

The sense of smell is unique in that signals from the neurons in the sinus cavity go directly into special parts of the brain called **olfactory bulbs**, just under the front part of the brain. Smell is the only sense that does not have to first pass through the thalamus.

This biker's thirst is regulated by her hypothalamus.

HYPOTHALAMUS A very small but extremely powerful part of the brain is located just below and in front of the thalamus (see Figure 2.10). The **hypothalamus** ("below the inner chamber") regulates body temperature, thirst, hunger, sleeping and waking, sexual activity, and emotions. It sits right above the pituitary gland. The hypothalamus controls the pituitary, so the ultimate regulation of hormones lies with the hypothalamus.

HIPPOCAMPUS Like many structures in the brain, the **hippocampus** was named based on its appearance. Hippocampus is the Greek word for "seahorse," and it was given to this brain structure because the first scientists who dissected the brain thought it looked like a seahorse. The hippocampus is located within the medial temporal lobe on each side of the brain (medial means "toward the middle"). Research has shown that the hippocampus is instrumental in forming long-term (permanent) declarative memories that are then stored elsewhere in the brain (Squire & Kandel, 2009). See Learning Objective 6.12. As mentioned earlier, ACh, the neurotransmitter involved in muscle control, is also involved in the memory function of the hippocampus. People who have Alzheimer's disease, for example, have much lower levels of ACh in that structure than is normal, and the drugs given to these people boost the levels of ACh.

AMYGDALA The **amygdala** ("almond") is another area of the brain named for its shape and appearance. It is located near the hippocampus. The amygdala is involved in fear responses and memory of fear. Information from the senses goes to the amygdala before the upper part of the brain is even involved, so that people can respond to danger very quickly, sometimes before they are consciously aware of what is happening. In 1939 researchers found that monkeys with large amounts of their temporal lobes removed—including the amygdala—were completely unafraid of snakes and humans, both normally fear-provoking stimuli (Klüver & Bucy, 1939). This effect came to be known as the *Klüver-Bucy syndrome*. Rats that have damaged amygdala structures will also show no fear when placed next to a cat (Maren & Fanselow, 1996). Case studies of humans with damage to the amygdala also show a link to decreased fear response (Adolphs et al., 2005). Although the amygdala plays a vital role in forming emotional memories, it is still unclear if the memories are stored in the amygdala (Squire & Kandel, 2009). One study has suggested activity in the amygdala impacts hippocampal neuroplasticity by facilitating structural changes in the hippocampus, possibly underlying the influence of stress on fear memories (Giachero et al., 2015).

CINGULATE CORTEX The *cingulate cortex* is the limbic structure that is actually found in the cortex. It is found right above the corpus callosum in the frontal and parietal lobes and plays an important role in both emotional and cognitive processing. The cingulate cortex can be divided into up to four regions that play different roles in processing emotional, cognitive, and autonomic information (Vogt & Palomero-Gallagher, 2012). It has been shown to be active during a variety of cognitive tasks such as selective attention, written word recognition, and working memory (Cabeza & Nyberg, 2000) and has been implicated in a variety of psychological and mental disorders including ADHD disorder (Bush et al., 1999; Bush et al., 2008; Castellanos & Proal, 2012; Konrad et al., 2018; Rubia, 2018), schizophrenia, major depressive disorder, and bipolar disorder (Brugger & Howes, 2017; Maggioni et al., 2017; Samara et al., 2018). The next section further explores the cortex and its functions.

olfactory bulbs

two bulb-like projections of the brain located just above the sinus cavity and just below the frontal lobes that receive information from the olfactory receptor cells.

hypothalamus

small structure in the brain located below the thalamus and directly above the pituitary gland, responsible for motivational behavior such as sleep, hunger, thirst, and sex.

hippocampus

curved structure located within each temporal lobe, responsible for the formation of long-term declarative memories.

amygdala

brain structure located near the hippocampus, responsible for fear responses and memory of fear.

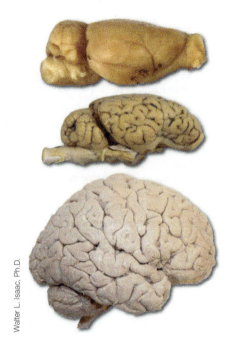

From top to bottom, a rat brain, sheep brain, and human brain (not to scale!). Note the differences in the amount of corticalization, or wrinkling, of the cortex between these three brains. Greater amounts of corticalization are associated with increases in size and complexity.

2.8 The Cortex

2.8 Identify the parts of the cortex that process the different senses and those that control movement of the body.

As stated earlier, the **cortex** ("rind" or outer covering) is the outermost part of the brain, which is the part of the brain most people picture when they think of what the brain looks like. It is made up of tightly packed neurons and actually is only about one tenth of an inch thick on average (Fischl et al., 2001; MacDonald et al., 2000; Zilles, 1990). The cortex has very recognizable surface anatomy because it is full of wrinkles.

💬 Why is the cortex so wrinkled?

The wrinkling of the cortex allows a much larger area of cortical cells to exist in the small space inside the skull. If the cortex were to be taken out, ironed flat, and measured, it would be about 2 to 3 square feet. (The owner of the cortex would also be dead, but that's fairly obvious, right?) As the brain develops before birth, it forms a smooth outer covering on all the other brain structures. This will be the cortex, which will get more and more wrinkled as the brain increases in size and complexity. This increase in wrinkling is called "corticalization."

CEREBRAL HEMISPHERES The **cerebrum** is the upper part of the brain. It is divided into two sections called the **cerebral hemispheres**, which are covered by cortex and connected by a thick, tough band of neural fibers (axons) called the **corpus callosum** (literally meaning "hard body," as calluses on the feet are hard). (Refer to Figure 2.9.) The corpus callosum allows the left and right hemispheres to communicate with each other. Each hemisphere can be roughly divided into four sections or lobes by looking at the deeper wrinkles, or fissures, in its surface. The lobes are named for the skull bones that cover them (see **Figure 2.11**).

Figure 2.11 Lobes and Cortical Areas of the Brain

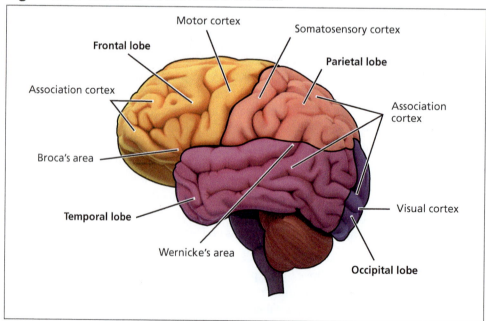

cortex
outermost covering of the brain consisting of densely packed neurons, responsible for higher thought processes and interpretation of sensory input.

cerebrum
the upper part of the brain consisting of the two hemispheres and the structures that connect them.

cerebral hemispheres
the two sections of the cortex on the left and right sides of the brain.

corpus callosum
thick band of neurons that connects the right and left cerebral hemispheres.

Another organizational feature of the cortex is that for specific regions, each hemisphere is responsible for the opposite side of the body, either for control, or for receiving information. For example, the motor cortex controls the muscles on the opposite side of the body. If we are writing with our right hand, the motor cortex in the left hemisphere is responsible for controlling those movements. This feature, referred to as *contralateral organization*, plays a role in information coming from many of the sense organs to the brain, and in the motor commands originating in the brain going to the rest of the body.

Information from our body can also be transmitted to both sides of the brain, or *bilaterally* (as in hearing and vision), or to only one side of the brain, or *ipsilaterally* (as in taste and olfaction). These aspects are also important in the study of *brain lateralization*, which we will come back to later in the chapter. Why do we have this arrangement for some functions and not for others? No one really knows, but at least for some information, it assists with identifying where information from the environment is coming from. For auditory information from the ears, having sensory information projected to both hemispheres allows us to localize sounds by comparing the slightly different information coming from each ear.

OCCIPITAL LOBES At the base of the cortex, toward the back of the brain, is an area called the **occipital lobe**. This area processes visual information from the eyes in the *primary visual cortex*. The *visual association cortex*, also in this lobe and in parts of the temporal and parietal lobes, helps identify and make sense of the visual information from the eyes. The famed neurologist Oliver Sacks once had a patient who had a tumor in his right occipital lobe area. He could still see objects and even describe them in physical terms, but he could not identify them by sight alone. When given a rose, the man began to describe it as a "red inflorescence" of some type with a green tubular projection. Only when he held it under his nose (stimulating the sense of smell) did he recognize it as a rose (Sacks, 1990). Each area of the cortex has these association areas that help people make sense of sensory information.

PARIETAL LOBES The **parietal lobes** are at the top and back of the brain, just under the parietal bone in the skull. This area contains the **somatosensory cortex**, an area of neurons (see **Figure 2.12**) at the front of the parietal lobes on either side of the brain. This area

occipital lobe

section of the brain located at the rear and bottom of each cerebral hemisphere containing the primary visual centers of the brain.

parietal lobes

sections of the brain located at the top and back of each cerebral hemisphere containing the centers for touch, temperature, and body position.

somatosensory cortex

area of cortex at the front of the parietal lobes responsible for processing information from the skin and internal body receptors for touch, temperature, and body position.

Figure 2.12 The Motor and Somatosensory Cortex

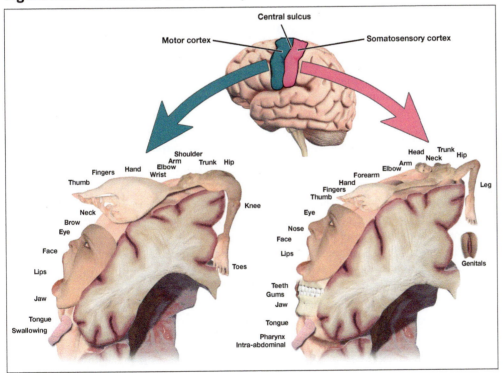

The motor cortex in the frontal lobe controls the voluntary muscles of the body. Cells at the top of the motor cortex control muscles at the bottom of the body, whereas cells at the bottom of the motor cortex control muscles at the top of the body. Body parts are drawn larger or smaller according to the number of cortical cells devoted to that body part. For example, the hand has many small muscles and requires a larger area of cortical cells to control it. The somatosensory cortex, located in the parietal lobe just behind the motor cortex, is organized in much the same manner and receives information about the sense of touch and body position.

This boxer must rely on her parietal lobes to sense where her body is in relation to the floor of the ring and her training partner, her occipital lobes to see her targets, and her frontal lobes to guide her hand and arm into the punch.

processes information from the skin and internal body receptors for touch, temperature, and body position. The somatosensory cortex is laid out in a rather interesting way—the cells at the top of the brain receive information from the bottom of the body, and as one moves down the area, the signals come from higher and higher in the body. It's almost as if a little upside-down person were laid out along this area of cells.

TEMPORAL LOBES The beginning of the **temporal lobes** are found just behind the temples of the head. These lobes contain the *primary auditory cortex* and the *auditory association area*. Also found in the left temporal lobe is an area that in most people is particularly involved with language. We have already discussed some of the medial structures of the temporal lobe, the amygdala and hippocampus, that are involved in aspects of learning and memory. There are also parts of the temporal lobe that help us process visual information.

FRONTAL LOBES These lobes are at the front of the brain, hence, the name **frontal lobes**. (It doesn't often get this easy in psychology; feel free to take a moment to appreciate it.) Found here are all the higher mental functions of the brain—planning, personality, memory storage, complex decision making, and (again in the left hemisphere in most people) areas devoted to language. The frontal lobe also helps in controlling emotions by means of its connection to the limbic system. The most forward part of the frontal lobes is called the prefrontal cortex (PFC). The PFC is linked to cognitive control, and especially the *executive functions*, or our ability to consider future outcomes and control of our current behavior to accomplish goals (Barkley, 2017; Gazzaley et al., 2018; Yuan & Raz, 2014). These include self-awareness, inhibition or self-restraint, working memory, time management, self-organization, and emotional self-control (Barkley, 2017). This is also an area associated with disorders of executive function such as ADHD (Barkley, 2015, 2017). The middle area toward the center (medial prefrontal cortex) and bottom surface above the eyes (orbitofrontal prefrontal cortex—right above the orbits of the eye) have strong connections to the limbic system. Phineas Gage, who was mentioned in Chapter One, suffered damage to his left frontal lobe (Ratiu et al., 2004). He lacked emotional control for some time immediately after the accident because of the damage to his prefrontal and orbitofrontal cortex and to the connections with limbic system structures. Overall, he had connections damaged from the left frontal cortex to many other parts of the brain (Ratiu et al., 2004; Van Horn et al., 2012). People with damage to the frontal lobe may also experience problems with performing mental or motor tasks, such as getting stuck on one step in a process or on one wrong answer in a test and repeating it over and over again, or making the same movement over and over, a phenomena called *perseveration* (Asp & Tranel, 2013; Luria, 1965).

The frontal lobes also contain the **motor cortex**, a band of neurons located at the back of each lobe (see Figure 2.12). These cells control the movements of the body's voluntary muscles by sending commands out to the somatic division of the peripheral nervous system. The motor cortex is laid out just like the somatosensory cortex, which is right next door in the parietal lobes.

This area of the brain has been the focus of a great deal of research, specifically as related to the role of a special type of neuron. These neurons are called **mirror neurons**, which fire when an animal performs an action—but they also fire when an animal observes that same action being performed by another animal. Neuroimaging studies in humans suggest that we too have neurons with mirroring functions in this area of the brain (Buccino et al., 2001; Buccino et al., 2004; Iacoboni et al., 1999; Kilner et al., 2009; Kilner & Lemon, 2013; Molenberghs et al., 2012). However, single-cell and multi-cell recordings in humans have demonstrated neurons with mirroring functions are found not only in motor regions but also in parts of the brain involved in vision, audition, emotion, and memory, suggesting such neurons provide much more information than previously thought, about our own actions as compared to the actions of others (Hafri et al., 2017; Molenberghs et al., 2012; Mukamel et al., 2010). These findings may have particular relevance for better understanding or treating specific clinical conditions that are believed to

temporal lobes
areas of the cortex located along the side of the brain, starting just behind the temples, containing the neurons responsible for the sense of hearing and meaningful speech.

frontal lobes
areas of the brain located in the front and top, responsible for higher mental processes and decision making as well as the production of fluent speech.

motor cortex
rear section of the frontal lobe, responsible for sending motor commands to the muscles of the somatic nervous system.

mirror neurons
neurons that fire when an animal or person performs an action and also when an animal or person observes that same action being performed by another.

involve a faulty mirror system in the brain, such as autism (Fishman et al., 2014; Oberman & Ramachandran, 2007; Rizzolatti et al., 2009). See Learning Objective 8.7.

2.9 The Association Areas of the Cortex

2.9 Recall the function of association areas of the cortex, including those especially crucial for language.

> You've mentioned association cortex a few times. Do the other lobes of the brain also contain an association cortex?

Association areas are made up of neurons in the cortex devoted to making connections between the sensory information coming into the brain and stored memories, images, and knowledge. In other words, association areas help people make sense of the incoming sensory input. Although association areas in the occipital and temporal lobes have already been mentioned, much of the brain's association cortex is in the frontal lobes. Furthermore, some special association areas are worth talking about in more detail.

BROCA'S AREA In the left frontal lobe of most people is an area of the brain associated with the production of speech. (In a small portion of the population, this area is in the right frontal lobe.) More specifically, this area allows a person to speak smoothly and fluently. It is called *Broca's area* after nineteenth-century neurologist Paul Broca, who first provided widely accepted clinical evidence that deficits in fluent and articulate speech result from damage to this area (Finger, 1994). However, it appears that Broca's area is not responsible for the production of speech itself but rather for the interaction between frontal, temporal, and motor areas responsible for speech production (Flinker et al., 2015). Damage to Broca's area causes a person to be unable to get words out in a smooth, connected fashion. People with this condition may know exactly what they want to say and understand what they hear others say, but they cannot control the actual production of their own words. Speech is halting and words are often mispronounced, such as saying "cot" instead of "clock" or "non" instead of "nine." Some words may be left out entirely, such as "the" or "for." This is called **Broca's aphasia**. *Aphasia* refers to an inability to use or understand either written or spoken language (Goodglass et al., 2001). (Stuttering is a somewhat different problem in getting words *started*, rather than mispronouncing them or leaving them out, but it may also be related to Broca's area.)

WERNICKE'S AREA In the left temporal lobe (again, in most people) is an area called *Wernicke's area*, named after Broca's contemporary, physiologist Carl Wernicke, who first studied problems arising from damage in this location. This area of the brain appears to be involved in understanding the meaning of words (Goodglass et al., 2001). And just as with Broca's area, research continues to improve our understanding of brain areas and associated functions. Besides the area first described by Carl Wernicke, there are other parts of the surrounding area, additional white matter tracts, and other brain areas that are important to the comprehension of words and sentences (Mesulam et al., 2015; Poeppel et al., 2012; Tremblay & Dick, 2016), and damage to these areas can cause problems. A person with **Wernicke's aphasia** would be able to speak fluently and pronounce words correctly, but the words would be the wrong ones entirely. For example, Elsie suffered a stroke to the temporal lobe, damaging this area of the brain. As the ER nurse inflated a blood pressure cuff, Elsie said, "Oh, that's so Saturday hard." Elsie *thought* she was making sense. She also had trouble understanding what the people around her were saying to her. In another instance, Ernest suffered a stroke at the age of 80 and showed signs of Wernicke's aphasia. For example, he asked his wife to get him some milk out of the air conditioner. Right idea, wrong word.

As this boy imitates the motions his father goes through while shaving, certain areas of his brain are more active than others, areas that control the motions of shaving. But even if the boy were only *watching* his father, those same neural areas would be active—the neurons in the boy's brain would *mirror* the actions of the father he is observing.

AP 2.J Identify the contributions of key researchers to the study of the brain.

association areas

areas within each lobe of the cortex responsible for the coordination and interpretation of information, as well as higher mental processing.

Broca's aphasia

condition resulting from damage to Broca's area, causing the affected person to be unable to speak fluently, to mispronounce words, and to speak haltingly.

Wernicke's aphasia

condition resulting from damage to Wernicke's area, causing the affected person to be unable to understand or produce meaningful language.

Classic Studies in Psychology

Through the Looking Glass—Spatial Neglect

Dr. V. S. Ramachandran reported in his fascinating book, *Phantoms in the Brain* (Ramachandran & Blakeslee, 1998), the case of a woman with an odd set of symptoms. When Ellen's son came to visit her, he was shocked and puzzled by his formerly neat and fastidious* mother's appearance. The woman who had always taken pride in her looks, who always had her hair perfectly done and her nails perfectly manicured, looked messy and totally odd. Her hair was uncombed on the left side. Her green shawl was hanging neatly over her right shoulder but hanging onto the floor on the left. Her lipstick was neatly applied to the right side of her lips, and *only to the right side—the left side of her face was completely bare of makeup!* Yet her eyeliner, mascara, and blush were all neatly applied to the right side of her face.

What was wrong? The son called the doctor and was told that his mother's stroke had left her with a condition called **spatial neglect**, or unilateral neglect, in which a person with damage to the right parietal and occipital lobes of the cortex will ignore everything in the left visual field. Damage to areas of the frontal and temporal lobes may also play a part along with the parietal damage. Spatial neglect can affect the left hemisphere, but this condition occurs less frequently and in a much milder form than right-hemisphere neglect (Corbetta et al., 2005; Heilman et al., 1993; Springer & Deutsch, 1998).

As this woman applies makeup to the right side of her face, is she really "seeing" the left side? If she has spatial neglect, the answer is "no." While her eyes work just fine, her damaged right hemisphere refuses to notice the left side of her visual field.

When the doctor examined this woman, he tried to get her to notice her left side by holding up a mirror (remember, she was not blind—she just would not notice anything on her left side unless her attention was specifically called to it). She responded correctly when asked what the mirror was and she was able to describe her appearance correctly, but when an assistant held a pen just within the woman's reach, reflected in the mirror on her left side, she tried to reach *through the mirror* to get the pen with her good right hand. When the doctor told her that he wanted her to grab the real object and not the image of it in the mirror, she told him that the pen was *behind* the mirror and even tried to reach around to get it.

Clearly, persons suffering from spatial neglect can no longer perceive the world in the same way as other people do. For these people, the left sides of objects, bodies, and spaces are somewhere "through the looking glass."

Questions for Further Discussion

1. If a person with spatial neglect only eats the food on the right side of the plate, what could caregivers do to help that person get enough to eat?
2. What other odd things might a person with spatial neglect do that a person with normal functioning would not? What other things might a person with spatial neglect fail to do?

---

*fastidious: having demanding standards, difficult to please.

spatial neglect
condition produced most often by damage to the parietal lobe association areas of the right hemisphere, resulting in an inability to recognize objects or body parts in the left visual field.

2.10 The Cerebral Hemispheres

2.10 Explain how some brain functions differ between the left and right hemispheres.

> 💬 I've heard that some people are right brained and some are left brained. Are the two sides of the brain really that different?

Most people tend to think of the two cerebral hemispheres as identical twins. Both sides have the same four lobes and are arranged in much the same way. But language seems to be confined to the left hemisphere in about 90 percent of the population (Toga & Thompson, 2003). What other special tasks do the two halves of the cerebrum (the upper part of the brain consisting of the two hemispheres and the structures connecting them) engage in, and how do researchers know about such functions? Participate in the experiment simulation *Hemispheric Specialization* to test the language abilities of the two hemispheres.

SPLIT-BRAIN RESEARCH Roger Sperry was a pioneer in the field of hemisphere specialization. He won a Nobel Prize for his work in demonstrating that the left and right hemispheres of the brain specialize in different activities and functions (Sperry, 1968). In looking for a way to cure epilepsy (severe muscle spasms or seizures resulting from brain damage), Sperry cut through the corpus callosum, the thick band of neural fibers that joins the two hemispheres. In early research with animals, this technique worked and seemed to have no side effects. The first people to have this procedure done also experienced relief from their severe epileptic symptoms, but testing found that (in a sense) they now had two brains in one body.

The special testing involves sending messages to only one side of the brain, which is now possible because the connecting tissue, the corpus callosum, has been cut. Remember that each hemisphere is largely responsible for controlling, or receiving information from, the opposite side of the body. **Figure 2.13** shows what happens with a typical split-brain patient.

AP 2.K Recount historic and contemporary research strategies and technologies that support research.

AP 2.L Identify the contributions of key researchers to the development of tools for examining the brain.

AP 2.N Identify the contributions of key researchers to the study of neuroplasticity.

Figure 2.13 The Split-Brain Experiment

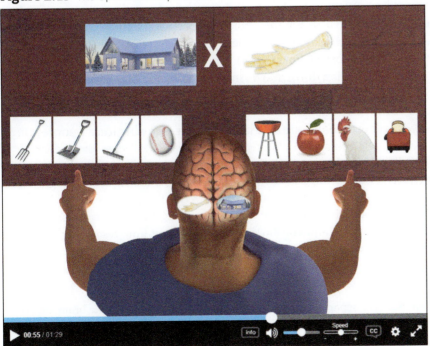

👁 **Watch** the **Video** at **MyLab Psychology**

Building off methods developed by Roger Sperry, Michael Gazzaniga and Joseph LeDoux used this simultaneous concept test to further investigate functions of the left and right hemispheres of the brain.

In a split-brain patient, if a picture of a ball is flashed to the right side of the screen, the image of the ball will be sent to the left occipital lobe. The person will be able to say he or she sees a ball. If a picture of a hammer is flashed to the left side of the screen, the person will not be able to *verbally* identify the object or be able to state with any certainty that something was seen. But if the left *hand* (controlled by the right hemisphere) is used, the person can point to the hammer he or she "didn't see." The right occipital lobe clearly saw the hammer, but the person could not *verbalize* that fact (Sperry, 1968). By doing studies such as these, researchers have found that the left hemisphere specializes in language, speech, handwriting, calculation (math), sense of time and rhythm (which is mathematical in nature), and basically any kind of thought requiring analysis. The right hemisphere appears to specialize in more global (widespread) processing involving perception, visualization, spatial perception, recognition of patterns, faces, emotions, melodies, and expression of emotions. It also comprehends simple language but does not produce speech. (See **Table 2.2**.)

Table 2.2 Specialization of the Two Hemispheres

Left Hemisphere	Right Hemisphere
Controls the right hand	Controls the left hand
Spoken language	Nonverbal
Written language	Visual–spatial perception
Mathematical calculations	Music and artistic processing
Logical thought processes	Emotional thought and recognition
Analysis of detail	Processes the whole
Reading	Pattern recognition
	Facial recognition

In general, the left hemisphere processes information in a sequence and is good at breaking things down into smaller parts, or performing analysis (Springer & Deutsch, 1998). The right hemisphere, by contrast, processes information all at once and simultaneously, a more global or holistic* style of processing. Remember the discussion in Chapter One of the early days of psychology, the structuralists, and the Gestalt psychologists? One could almost say that the left hemisphere of the brain is a structuralist who wants to break everything down into its smallest parts, and the right side of the brain is a Gestaltist, who wants to study only the whole.

 So there really are left-brained and right-brained people?

Actually, unless one is a split-brain patient, the two sides of the brain are always working together as an integrated whole. For example, the right side might recognize someone's face, while the left side struggles to recall the person's name. People aren't really left- or right-brained, they are "whole-brained." Michael Gazzaniga was one of Roger Sperry's students and collaborators and is a long-time researcher in the area of brain asymmetry and cognitive neuroscience. Gazzaniga's continuing contributions have led to insights of the integrated mind, human consciousness, perception, and neuroethics (Doron et al., 2012; Gazzaniga, 2006, 2009, 2015, 2018).

HANDEDNESS The separate functions of the left and right sides of the brain are often confused with handedness, or the tendency to use one hand for most fine motor skills. Roughly 90% of individuals are right handed, and handedness appears to be influenced largely through genetics (Corballis, 2009; Ocklenburg et al., 2013). While most right-handed people also have their left hemisphere in control of their other fine motor skills, such as speech, a

AP 2.N Identify the contributions of key researchers to the study of neuroplasticity.

---

*holistic: relating to or concerned with complete systems or wholes.

few right-handers actually have their language functions in the right hemisphere, in spite of the dominance of the left hemisphere for controlling the right hand. Among left-handed people, there are also many who, although right-brain dominant for motor control, still have their language functions on the left side of the brain. One study suggests approximately 4% of right-handed, 15% of ambidextrous, and 27% of left-handed people have language functions in the right hemisphere (Knecht et al., 2000).

Concept Map L.O. 2.6, 2.7, 2.8, 2.9, 2.10

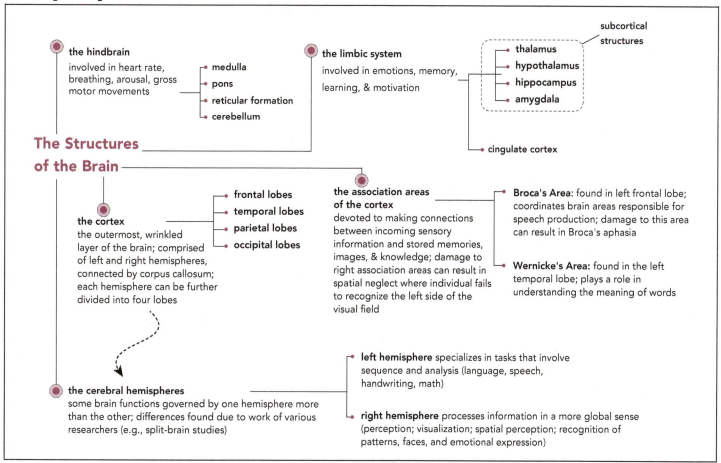

Practice Quiz   How much do you remember?

Pick the best answer.

1. Which brain structure relays incoming sensory information?
   a. reticular formation
   b. thalamus
   c. hippocampus
   d. hypothalamus
   e. pons

2. If you were to develop a rare condition in which you were not able to remember to be afraid of certain situations, animals, or events, which part of the brain would most likely be damaged?
   a. amygdala
   b. hypothalamus
   c. cingulate cortex
   d. thalamus
   e. medulla

3. What part of the brain can sometimes be referred to as the "rind" or outer covering?
   a. cingulate
   b. cortex
   c. thalamus
   d. medulla
   e. corpus callosum

4. In which of the following lobes of the cortex would you find the primary visual cortex?
   a. parietal
   b. limbic
   c. temporal
   d. frontal
   e. occipital

5. You have a dream in which you wake up to find that people around you are using words that make no sense. What's more, your friends don't seem to understand you when you speak. At one point in your dream, your mom tells you that you almost forgot your tree limb today. When you give her a puzzled look, she holds up your lunchbox and repeats, "You know, your tree limb." Your predicament in your dream is most like which of the following disorders?
   a. spatial neglect
   b. amnesia
   c. Broca's aphasia
   d. Wernicke's aphasia
   e. apraxia

AP 2.E Describe the nervous system and its subdivisions and functions.

2.11–2.12 The Nervous System: The Rest of the Story

Now that we have looked at the cells that make up the nervous system, ways in which they process and communicate information, and roles of different parts of the brain, take a look at **Figure 2.14**. This figure shows the organization of the various parts of the nervous system and will help in understanding how all the different parts work together in controlling the way people and animals think, act, and feel.

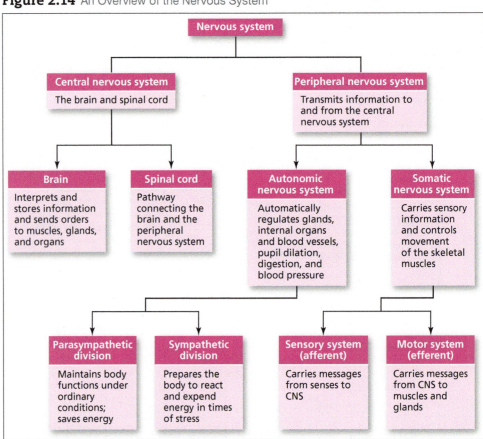

Figure 2.14 An Overview of the Nervous System

2.11 The Central Nervous System: The "Central Processing Unit"

2.11 Describe how the components of the central nervous system interact and how they may respond to experiences or injury.

The brain and the spinal cord make up the **central nervous system (CNS)**. Both the brain and the spinal cord are composed of the neurons and glial cells discussed earlier that control the life-sustaining functions of the body as well as all thought, emotion, and behavior.

THE BRAIN The brain is the core of the nervous system, the part that makes sense of the information received from the senses, makes decisions, and sends commands out to the muscles and the rest of the body, if needed. Many different areas of the brain are involved in preparing us for an appropriate response to the information received, and as you have read, the brain is responsible for cognition and thoughts, including learning, memory, and language. While the neurons in each of the different areas work in much the same way, it is the groups of cells and the connections between them and other parts of the

central nervous system (CNS)
part of the nervous system consisting of the brain and spinal cord.

brain or components of the nervous system, and our experiences, that influence the various functions found in specific brain areas (Amaral & Strick, 2013; Heimer, 1995; Sporns, 2014; Squire & Kandel, 2009).

THE SPINAL CORD The **spinal cord** is a long bundle of neurons that serves two vital functions for the nervous system. Look at the cross-section of the spinal cord in **Figure 2.15**. Notice that it seems to be divided into two areas, a lighter outer section and a darker inner section. If it were a real spinal cord, the outer section would appear to be white and the inner section would seem gray. That's because the outer section is composed mainly of myelinated axons and nerves, which appear white, whereas the inner section is mainly composed of cell bodies of neurons, which appear gray. The purpose of the outer section is to carry messages from the body up to the brain and from the brain down to the body. In some ways, it serves as a message "pipeline."

The look on this young woman's face clearly indicates that she has experienced pain in her shoulder. Pain is a warning signal that something is wrong. What might be some of the problems encountered by a person who could feel no pain at all?

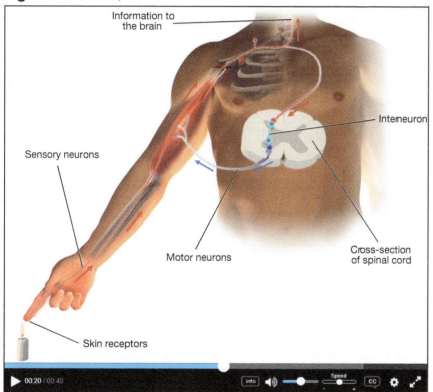

Figure 2.15 The Spinal Cord Reflex

Watch the Video at MyLab Psychology

The pain from the burning heat of the candle flame stimulates the afferent nerve fibers, which carry the message up to the interneurons in the middle of the spinal cord. The interneurons then send a message out by means of the efferent nerve fibers, causing the hand to jerk away from the flame.

The inside section, which is made up of cell bodies separated by glial cells, is actually a primitive sort of "brain." This part of the spinal cord is responsible for certain reflexes—very fast, lifesaving reflexes. To understand how the spinal cord reflexes work, it is important to know there are three basic types of neurons: **afferent (sensory) neurons** that carry messages from the senses to the spinal cord, **efferent (motor) neurons** that carry messages from the spinal cord to the muscles and glands, and **interneurons** that connect the afferent neurons to the efferent neurons (and make up the inside of the spinal cord and much of the brain itself) (see **Figure 2.15**). Touch a flame or a hot stove with your finger, for example, and an afferent neuron will send the pain message up to the spinal column, where it enters into the central area of the spinal cord. The interneuron in that central area will then receive the message and send out a response along an efferent neuron, causing your finger to pull back. This all happens

spinal cord
a long bundle of neurons that carries messages between the body and the brain and is responsible for very fast, lifesaving reflexes.

afferent (sensory) neuron
a neuron that carries information from the senses to the central nervous system.

efferent (motor) neuron
a neuron that carries messages from the central nervous system to the muscles of the body.

interneuron
a neuron found in the center of the spinal cord that receives information from the afferent neurons and sends commands to the muscles through the efferent neurons. Interneurons also make up the bulk of the neurons in the brain.

very quickly. If the pain message had to go all the way up to the brain before a response could be made, the response time would be greatly increased and more damage would be done to your finger. So having this kind of **reflex arc** controlled by the spinal cord alone allows for very fast response times. (A good way to avoid mixing up the terms *afferent* and *efferent* is to remember "afferent neurons access the spinal cord, efferent neurons exit." The pain message does eventually get to the brain, where other motor responses may be triggered, like saying "Ouch!" and putting the finger in your mouth.

DAMAGE TO THE CENTRAL NERVOUS SYSTEM, NEUROPLASTICITY, AND NEUROGENESIS

AP 2.M Discuss the role of neuroplasticity in traumatic brain injury.

Damage to the central nervous system was once thought to be permanent. Neurons in the brain and spinal cord were not seen as capable of repairing themselves. When people recovered from a stroke, for example, it was assumed that it was primarily due to healthy brain cells taking over the functions of the damaged ones. Scientists have known for a while now that some forms of central nervous system damage can be repaired by the body's systems, and in recent years great strides have been made in repairing spinal cord damage. The brain actually exhibits a great deal of **neuroplasticity**, the ability to constantly change both the structure and function of many cells in the brain in response to trauma or experience (Fulford et al., 2017; Kaas & Bowes, 2014; Pauwels et al., 2018; Stevens & Neville, 2014). For example, dendrites grow and new synapses are formed in at least some areas of the brain as people learn new things throughout life (Sanes & Jessell, 2013a, 2013b). The video *Overview of Neuroplasticity* explains some aspects of neuroplasticity in more detail.

Watch Overview of Neuroplasticity

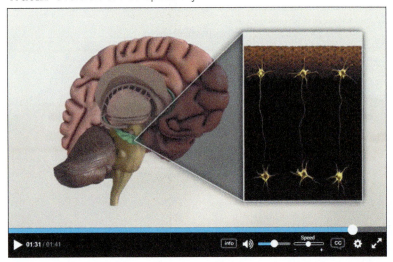

Watch the Video at MyLab Psychology

The brain may also change through **neurogenesis**, the formation of new neurons, an important process during the development of our nervous system. The greatest period of neurogenesis takes place prior to birth, during the prenatal period. And while not at the same level as during early development, the brains of most mammals continue to produce neurons well into adulthood, primarily in the *hippocampus* and *olfactory bulb*. Humans are an exception. We do not appear to have any new neurons produced in our olfactory bulbs as we grow older (Bergmann et al., 2012). The occurrence and prevalence of neurogenesis in the human hippocampus and other brain areas is less clear. Researchers have found strong but preliminary evidence of human adult neurogenesis in the *striatum* (Ernst et al., 2014; Ernst & Frisen, 2015), an important area of the brain related to motor control, voluntary movement, and other functions. And until relatively recently, research has suggested that humans continue to generate new neurons in the hippocampus throughout adulthood (Eriksson et al., 1998; Knoth et al., 2010; Spalding et al., 2013). However, some very recent studies suggest humans might be different than other mammals, and neurogenesis in the hippocampus may actually stop in childhood (Dennis et al., 2016; Sorrells et al., 2018).

Scientists are exploring ways to facilitate both neurogenesis and neuroplasticity. In efforts to repair spinal cord damage, they are examining the application of special proteins that are typically involved in the development and survival of new neurons and in the maintenance of existing neurons (Harvey et al., 2015). Researchers are examining the effects of implanting Schwann cells from the peripheral nervous system to the central nervous system to aid in treating spinal cord injuries (Bastidas et al., 2017; Deng et al., 2013; Deng et al., 2015; Kanno et al., 2015; Kanno et al., 2014).

Researchers are constantly looking for new ways to repair the brain. One avenue of research has involved scientists investigating the possibility of transplanting **stem cells** to repair damaged or diseased brain tissue. Stem cells can become any cell in the body and may offer promise for addressing diseases such as Parkinson's and Alzheimer's or the repair of

reflex arc
the connection of the afferent neurons to the interneurons to the efferent neurons, resulting in a reflex action.

neuroplasticity
the ability within the brain to constantly change both the structure and function of many cells in response to experience or trauma.

neurogenesis
the formation of new neurons; occurs primarily during prenatal development but may also occur at lesser levels in some brain areas during adulthood.

stem cells
special cells found in all the tissues of the body that are capable of becoming other cell types when those cells need to be replaced due to damage or wear and tear.

damaged spinal cords or brain tissue. If stem cells can be implanted into areas that have been damaged, the newly developed neurons may assume the roles that the original (now damaged) neurons can no longer perform. Besides transplantation, researchers are also examining the feasibility of activating stem cells through electrical stimulation (Huang et al., 2015).

Efforts to promote neurogenesis and neuroplasticity, or to aid in rehabilitation, have also examined a variety of other areas, including sleep, cognitive training, pharmacological intervention, and physical activity. Research with animals suggests sustained aerobic activity increases neurogenesis in the hippocampus, at least for some that are genetically inclined to benefit from aerobic exercise (Nokia et al., 2016). Physical exercise also appears to benefit neuroplasticity in humans (Mueller et al., 2015; Prakash et al., 2015). Sleep is another important factor. Brain wave activity changes have been recorded during sleep following specific learning experiences, and changes have been noted to coincide with symptoms observed in some psychological disorders (Tesler et al., 2016; Wilhelm et al., 2014). Brain stimulation, such as through implanted electrodes, can also be used to impact brain plasticity. By inducing changes in the excitability of specific regions of the brain, functional changes can occur, which can subsequently influence change at other functional and anatomical sites near the site of stimulation (Keller et al., 2018). See Learning Objective 2.4.

While not a rehabilitative approach, ongoing research is investigating how neuroplasticity and functioning of the nervous system are influenced through **epigenetics**, or the interaction between genes and environmental factors that influence gene activity. Such factors include our physical environment, nutritional status, and life experiences. We cannot reverse time, but new life experiences can influence our brain, impact future behavior, and impact our resiliency and ability to cope with life's challenges (Caldji et al., 1998; Goossens et al., 2015; McEwen et al., 2015; Tammen et al., 2013). Furthermore, research in epigenetics is revealing specific ways in which adverse life events, such as maltreatment in childhood, impact the nervous system in long-lasting ways and possibly increase vulnerability to psychological disorders like depression in adulthood (Lutz et al., 2017). See Learning Objective 13.1.

epigenetics

the interaction between genes and environmental factors that influence gene activity; environmental factors include diet, life experiences, and physical surroundings.

peripheral nervous system (PNS)

all nerves and neurons that are not contained in the brain and spinal cord but that run through the body itself.

somatic nervous system

division of the PNS consisting of nerves that carry information from the senses to the CNS and from the CNS to the voluntary muscles of the body.

autonomic nervous system (ANS)

division of the PNS consisting of nerves that control all of the involuntary muscles, organs, and glands.

sensory pathway

nerves coming from the sensory organs to the CNS consisting of afferent neurons.

motor pathway

nerves coming from the CNS to the voluntary muscles, consisting of efferent neurons.

2.12 The Peripheral Nervous System: Nerves on the Edge

2.12 Differentiate the roles of the somatic and autonomic nervous systems.

💬 Okay, that takes care of the central nervous system. How does the central nervous system communicate with the rest of the body?

The term *peripheral* refers to things not in the center or on the edges of the center. The **peripheral nervous system** or **PNS** (see **Figure 2.16** and refer to Figure 2.15) is made up of all the nerves and neurons not contained in the brain and spinal cord. This system allows the brain and spinal cord to communicate with the sensory systems and enables the brain and spinal cord to control the muscles and glands of the body. The PNS can be divided into two major systems: the **somatic nervous system**, which consists of nerves that control the voluntary muscles of the body, and the **autonomic nervous system (ANS)**, which consists of nerves that control the involuntary muscles, organs, and glands.

THE SOMATIC NERVOUS SYSTEM One of the parts of a neuron is the soma, or cell body (remember that the word *soma* means "body"). The somatic nervous system is made up of the **sensory pathway**, which involves the nerves carrying messages from the senses to the central nervous system (those nerves containing afferent neurons), and the **motor pathway**, which involves the nerves carrying messages from the central nervous system to the voluntary, or skeletal,* muscles of the body—muscles that allow people

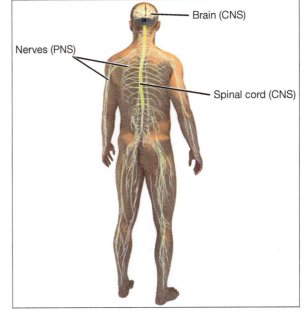

Figure 2.16 The Peripheral Nervous System

---

*skeletal: having to do with the bones of the body, or skeleton.

to move their bodies (those nerves composed of efferent neurons). When people are walking, raising their hands in class, lifting a flower to smell, or directing their gaze toward the person they are talking to or to look at a pretty picture, they are using the somatic nervous system. (As seen in the discussion of spinal cord reflexes, although these muscles are called the voluntary muscles, they can move involuntarily when a reflex response occurs. They are called "voluntary" because they *can* be moved at will but are not limited to only that kind of movement.)

Involuntary* muscles, such as the heart, stomach, and intestines, together with glands such as the adrenal glands and the pancreas are all controlled by clumps of neurons located on or near the spinal column. See Learning Objective 2.14. The words *on or near* are used quite deliberately here. The neurons *inside* the spinal column are part of the central nervous system, not the peripheral nervous system. These large groups of neurons near the spinal column make up the *autonomic nervous system*.

THE AUTONOMIC NERVOUS SYSTEM The word *autonomic* suggests that the functions of this system are more or less automatic, which is basically correct. Whereas the somatic division of the peripheral nervous system controls the senses and voluntary muscles, the autonomic division controls everything else in the body—organs, glands, and involuntary muscles. The autonomic nervous system is divided into two systems, the *sympathetic division* and the *parasympathetic division* (see **Figure 2.17**; for a schematic representation of how all the various sections of the nervous system are organized, refer back to Figure 2.14).

Figure 2.17 Functions of the Parasympathetic and Sympathetic Divisions of the Nervous System

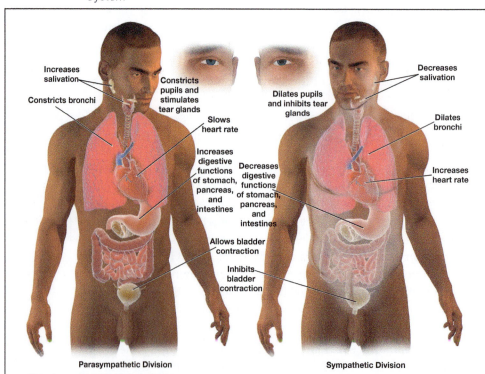

sympathetic division (fight-or-flight system)
also called the sympathetic nervous system (SNS), part of the ANS that is responsible for reacting to stressful events and bodily arousal.

THE SYMPATHETIC DIVISION The **sympathetic division** of the autonomic nervous system is primarily located on the middle of the spinal column—running from near the top of the ribcage to the waist area. It may help to think of the name in these terms:

*involuntary: not under deliberate control.

The *sympathetic* division is in *sympathy* with one's emotions. In fact, the sympathetic division is usually called the "fight-or-flight system" because it allows people and animals to deal with all kinds of stressful events. See Learning Objective 10.4. Emotions during these events might be anger (hence the term *fight*) or fear (that's the "flight" part, obviously) or even extreme joy or excitement. Yes, even joy can be stressful. The job of the sympathetic division, or *sympathetic nervous system* (SNS), is to get the body ready to deal with the stress. Many of us have experienced a fight-or-flight moment at least once in our lives.

What are the specific ways in which this division readies the body to react (see Figure 2.17)? The pupils seem to get bigger, perhaps to let in more light and, therefore, more information. The heart starts pumping faster and harder, drawing blood away from nonessential organs such as the skin (so at first the person may turn pale) and sometimes even the brain itself (so the person might actually faint). Blood needs lots of oxygen before it goes to the muscles, so the lungs work overtime, too (the person may begin to breathe faster). One set of glands in particular receives special instructions. The adrenal glands will be stimulated to release certain stress-related chemicals (members of a class of chemicals released by glands called *hormones*) into the bloodstream. These stress hormones will travel to all parts of the body, but they will only affect certain target organs. Just as a neurotransmitter fits into a receptor site on a cell, the molecules of the stress hormones fit into receptor sites at the various target organs—notably, the heart, muscles, and lungs. This further stimulates these organs to work harder. But not every organ or system will be stimulated by the activation of the sympathetic division. Digestion of food and excretion* of waste are not necessary functions when dealing with stressful situations, so these systems tend to be "shut down" or inhibited. Saliva, which is part of digestion, dries right up (ever try whistling when you're scared?). Food that was in the stomach sits there like a lump. Usually, the urge to go to the bathroom will be suppressed, but if the person is really scared, the bladder or bowels may actually empty (this is why some people who experience extreme stress may wet or soil themselves, such as soldiers in intense combat, or everyday folks in unexpected life-or-death circumstances). The sympathetic division is also going to demand that the body burn a tremendous amount of fuel, or blood sugar.

Now, all this bodily arousal is going on during a stressful situation. If the stress ends, the activity of the sympathetic division will be replaced by the activation of the parasympathetic division. If the stress goes on too long or is too intense, the person might actually collapse (as a deer might do when being chased by another animal). This collapse occurs because the parasympathetic division overresponds in its inhibition of the sympathetic activity. The heart slows, blood vessels open up, blood pressure in the brain drops, and fainting can result.

THE PARASYMPATHETIC DIVISION If the sympathetic division can be called the fight-or-flight system, the **parasympathetic division**, or *parasympathetic nervous system* (PNS), might be called the "eat-drink-and-rest" system. The neurons of this division are located at the top and bottom of the spinal column, on either side of the sympathetic division neurons (*para* means "beyond" or "next to" and in this sense refers to the neurons located on either side of the sympathetic division neurons).

In looking at Figure 2.17, it might seem as if the parasympathetic division does pretty much the opposite of the sympathetic division, but it's a little more complex. The parasympathetic division's job is to return the body to normal functioning after a stressful situation ends. It slows the heart and breathing, constricts the pupils, and reactivates digestion and excretion. Signals to the adrenal glands stop because the parasympathetic division isn't connected to the adrenal glands. In a sense, the parasympathetic division allows

Many people find in-person interviews and other such evaluations to be particularly stressful. Which part of this young woman's autonomic nervous system is most likely to be activated at this moment?

parasympathetic division (eat-drink-and-rest system)

also called the parasympathetic nervous system (PNS), part of the ANS that restores the body to normal functioning after arousal and is responsible for the day-to-day functioning of the organs and glands.

---

*excretion: in this sense, the act of eliminating waste products from the body.

the body to restore all the energy it burned—which is why people are often very hungry *after* the stress is all over.

The parasympathetic division does more than just react to the activity of the sympathetic division. It is the parasympathetic division that is responsible for most of the ordinary, day-to-day bodily functioning, such as regular heartbeat and normal breathing and digestion. People spend the greater part of their 24-hour day eating, sleeping, digesting, and excreting. So, the parasympathetic division is typically active. At any given moment, then, one or the other of these divisions, sympathetic or parasympathetic, will determine whether people are aroused or relaxed.

Concept Map L.O. 2.11, 2.12

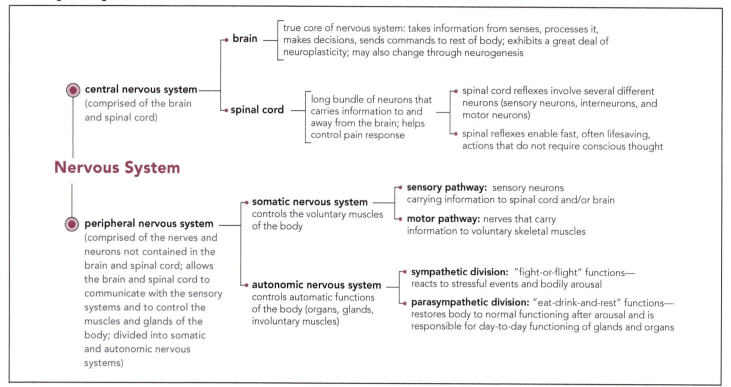

Practice Quiz How much do you remember?

Pick the best answer.

1. If you touch a hot stove, your spinal cord can prompt you to withdraw your hand without having to send the message all the way to the brain. This is due to what scientists call _____.
   a. the sympathetic nervous system
   b. the reflex arc
   c. the neuroplastic response
   d. the "fight-or-flight" system
   e. the parasympathetic nervous system

2. What is the process whereby the structure and function of brain cells change in response to trauma, damage, or even learning?
   a. deep lesioning
   b. neuroplasticity
   c. reuptake
   d. cell regeneration
   e. shallow lesioning

3. The neurons of the sensory pathway contain _____.
   a. voluntary muscle fibers
   b. automatic muscle fibers
   c. efferent neurons
   d. both efferent and afferent neurons
   e. afferent neurons

4. Yvonne's ability to reach for and pick up her book is largely due to the functions of the _____ pathway of the _____ nervous system.
   a. sympathetic, autonomic
   b. sensory, somatic
   c. parasympathetic, autonomic
   d. motor, somatic
   e. autonomic, peripheral

5. Which of the following would be active if you have just had an automobile accident?
   a. motor division
   b. somatic division
   c. sensory division
   d. sympathetic division
   e. parasympathetic division

2.13–2.14 The Endocrine Glands

AP 2.D Discuss the effects of the endocrine system on behavior.

💬 How do the glands fit into all of this? Aren't there more glands than just the adrenal glands? How do they affect our behavior?

Earlier, we addressed neurons and how they release neurotransmitters into the synapse to communicate with postsynaptic neurons. This type of chemical communication is fairly specific, primarily affecting neurons in the immediate vicinity of the originating neuron, and also very fast (almost immediate). Other structures also use chemical communication but at a different rate and act in a more far-reaching manner. For example, glands are organs in the body that secrete chemicals. Some glands, such as salivary glands and sweat glands, secrete their chemicals directly onto the body's tissues through tiny tubes, or ducts. This kind of gland affects the functioning of the body but doesn't really affect behavior. Other glands, called **endocrine glands**, have no ducts and secrete their chemicals directly into the bloodstream (see **Figure 2.18**). The chemicals secreted by this type of gland are called **hormones**. As mentioned when talking about the sympathetic division of the autonomic nervous system, these hormones flow into the bloodstream, which carries them to their target organs. The molecules of these hormones then fit into receptor sites on those organs to fulfill their function, affecting behavior as they do so. As compared to synaptic communication, endocrine communication is generally slower due to the time it takes hormones to travel to target organs, and the behaviors and responses they affect may not occur until hours, weeks, or years later.

The hormones affect behavior and emotions by stimulating muscles, organs, or other glands of the body. Some theories of emotion state that the surge in certain hormones actually triggers the emotional reaction (Izard, 1988; Zajonc, 1980, 1984). See Learning Objective 9.9. Some of the hormones produced by endocrine glands also influence the activity of the brain, producing excitatory or inhibitory effects (Schwartz & Javitch, 2013).

endocrine glands
glands that secrete chemicals called hormones directly into the bloodstream.

hormones
chemicals released into the bloodstream by endocrine glands.

pituitary gland
gland located in the brain that secretes human growth hormone and influences all other hormone-secreting glands (also known as the master gland).

2.13 The Pituitary: Master of the Hormonal Universe

2.13 Explain why the pituitary gland is known as the "master gland."

The **pituitary gland** is located just below the brain and is connected to the hypothalamus. The hypothalamus controls the glandular system by influencing the pituitary because the pituitary gland is the *master gland*—the one that controls or influences all of the other endocrine glands.

Part of the pituitary secretes several hormones that influence the activity of the other glands. One of these hormones is a *growth hormone* that controls and regulates the increase in size as children grow from infancy to adulthood. There are also hormones that stimulate the gonads (ovaries and testes) to release female or male sex hormones, which in turn influence the development and functioning of the reproductive organs, development of secondary sex characteristics in puberty, and reproductive behavior in general. Male and female sex hormones have also been implicated in cognitive changes as we grow older. One study has

Figure 2.18 The Endocrine Glands

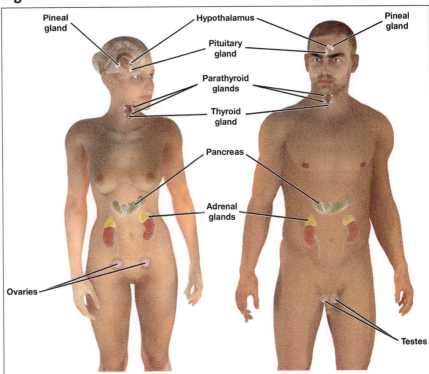

The endocrine glands secrete hormones directly into the bloodstream, which carries them to organs in the body, such as the heart, pancreas, and sex organs.

found a correlation between lower levels of the male sex hormone androgen and cognitive decline in older men (Hsu et al., 2015), and for females, hormonal therapy during a limited postmenopausal time window may lower the risk of mild cognitive impairment later in their lives (Scott et al., 2012).

> **THINKING CRITICALLY 2.2**
>
> Some people think that taking human growth hormone (HGH) supplements will help reverse the effects of aging. If this were true, what would you expect to see in the news media or medical journals? How would you expect HGH supplements to be marketed as a result?

Another part of the pituitary controls things associated with pregnancy and levels of water in the body. The hormone that controls aspects of pregnancy is called **oxytocin**, and it is involved in a variety of ways with both reproduction and parental behavior. It stimulates contractions of the uterus in childbirth. The word itself comes from the Greek word *oxys*, meaning "rapid," and *tokos*, meaning "childbirth," and injections of oxytocin are frequently used to induce or speed up labor and delivery. It is also responsible for the *milk letdown reflex*, which involves contraction of the mammary gland cells to release milk for the nursing infant. The hormone that controls levels of water in our body is called *vasopressin*, and it essentially acts as an antidiuretic, helping the body to conserve water.

You may have seen oxytocin covered in the news lately, as its role in human social behavior has been making headlines. Sometimes referred to in the media as the "love hormone" or the "trust hormone," it is prompting a great deal of research. While the role of oxytocin and vasopressin has been demonstrated in the formation of social bonds in nonhuman animals such as prairie voles, the exact role of these hormones in human social behavior is still under investigation (Algoe et al., 2017; Ferguson et al., 2001; Lim & Young, 2006; Miller, 2013; Stoesz et al., 2013; Winslow et al., 1993).

From investigations of receptor genes to direct impact on social behaviors, both of these hormones are gathering a lot of attention (Donaldson & Young, 2008; Poulin et al., 2012; Scheele et al., 2012). One study has suggested men in monogamous relationships were more likely to keep a greater distance between themselves and an attractive female during their first meeting after receiving oxytocin (Scheele et al., 2012). In turn, this suggests oxytocin may help men in heterosexual monogamous relationships remain faithful to their partners. Recent research has also examined how oxytocin may influence human boding. Specifically, in romantic partners, it appears larger amounts of oxytocin may influence how one perceives gratitude and love from their partner (Algoe et al., 2017).

There is additional evidence that oxytocin may have different effects for different individuals under different conditions. Men less socially proficient at recognizing social cues performed better on a task of empathic accuracy after receiving nasal administration of oxytocin, whereas more socially proficient males did not (Bartz et al., 2010). Especially in light of growing interest in the potential role of oxytocin as a treatment for a variety of psychiatric behaviors where social behavior is impacted (e.g., autism, social anxiety), researchers need to be aware of the different impacts oxytocin may have on different individuals in different situations (Bartz et al., 2011). Oxytocin's effects depend on what people believe about themselves in relation to other people and what they believe about achieving close social relationships (Bartz et al., 2015). In addition to the prosocial affects most often studied, some researchers have suggested it may be tied more to increasing the importance of social stimuli. As such, administration of oxytocin has also been tied to increased aggressive responses (Ne'eman et al., 2016). New research is also examining ways in which oxytocin interacts with

oxytocin
hormone released by the posterior pituitary gland that is involved in reproductive and parental behaviors.

other brain systems in impacting social behavior. For example, recent animal studies are investigating the interaction between oxytocin and other neuromodulators, such as serotonin (Lefevre et al., 2017).

2.14 Other Endocrine Glands

2.14 Recall the role of various endocrine glands.

As the master gland, the pituitary forms a very important part of a feedback system, one that includes the hypothalamus and the organs targeted by the various hormones. The balance of hormones in the entire endocrine system is maintained by feedback from each of these "players" to the others.

THE PINEAL GLAND The **pineal gland** is located in the brain, toward the rear and above the brain stem. It plays an important role in several biological rhythms. The pineal gland secretes a hormone called *melatonin*, which helps track day length (and seasons). In some animals, this influences seasonal behaviors such as breeding and molting. In humans, melatonin levels are more influential in regulating the sleep–wake cycle. See Learning Objective 4.3.

THE THYROID GLAND The **thyroid gland** is located inside the neck and secretes hormones that regulate growth and metabolism. One of these, a hormone called *thyroxine*, also known as T4 or *thyroxin*, regulates metabolism (how fast the body burns its available energy). As related to growth, the thyroid plays a crucial role in body and brain development.

THE PANCREAS The **pancreas** controls the level of blood sugar in the body by secreting *insulin* and *glucagon*. If the pancreas secretes too little insulin, it results in *diabetes*. If it secretes too much insulin, it results in *hypoglycemia*, or low blood sugar, which causes a person to feel hungry all the time and often become overweight as a result. See Learning Objective 9.6.

THE GONADS The **gonads** are the sex glands, including the **ovaries** in the female and the **testes** in the male. They secrete hormones that regulate sexual behavior and reproduction. They do not control all sexual behavior, though. In a very real sense, the brain itself is the master of the sexual system—human sexual behavior is not controlled totally by instincts and the actions of the glands as in some parts of the animal world, but it is also affected by psychological factors such as attractiveness.

THE ADRENAL GLANDS Everyone has two **adrenal glands**, one on top of each kidney. The origin of the name is simple enough; *renal* comes from a Latin word meaning "kidney" and *ad* is Latin for "to," so *adrenal* means "to or on the kidney." Each adrenal gland is actually divided into two sections, the *adrenal medulla* and the *adrenal cortex*. It is the adrenal medulla that releases epinephrine and norepinephrine when people are under stress and aids in sympathetic arousal.

The adrenal cortex produces more than 30 different hormones called *corticoids* (also called steroids) that regulate salt intake and help initiate* and control stress reactions; it also provides a source of sex hormones in addition to those provided by the gonads. One of the most important of these adrenal hormones is *cortisol*, released when the body experiences stress, both physical stress (such as illness, surgery, or extreme heat or cold) and psychological stress (such as an emotional upset). See Learning Objective 9.5. Cortisol is important in the release of glucose into the bloodstream during stress, providing energy for the brain itself, and the release of fatty acids from the fat cells that provide the muscles with energy.

When the pancreas does not secrete enough insulin, the result is diabetes. A person with diabetes must keep a close watch on blood sugar levels. Some people test more than once a day while others are able to test only a few times a week. Devices such as the one in use here make it much easier—and far less painful—to test blood sugar levels than in years past.

pineal gland
endocrine gland located near the base of the cerebrum; secretes melatonin.

thyroid gland
endocrine gland found in the neck; regulates metabolism.

pancreas
endocrine gland; controls the levels of sugar in the blood.

gonads
sex glands; secrete hormones that regulate sexual development and behavior as well as reproduction.

ovaries
the female gonads or sex glands.

testes (testicles)
the male gonads or sex glands.

adrenal glands
endocrine glands located on top of each kidney that secrete over 30 different hormones to deal with stress, regulate salt intake, and provide a secondary source of sex hormones affecting the sexual changes that occur during adolescence.

---

*initiate: begin or start.

Concept Map L.O. 2.13, 2.14

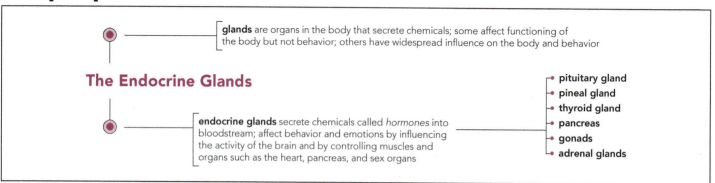

Practice Quiz — How much do you remember?

Pick the best answer.

1. Your friend Belinda has suffered from diabetes for her entire life. She regularly tests her blood to make sure her sugar levels are not too high or low. Which gland in her endocrine system is responsible for regulating her blood sugar?
   a. pituitary
   b. thyroid
   c. pancreas
   d. adrenal
   e. pineal

2. Hector has always been thin. In fact, he often seems to be able to eat whatever he wants without gaining weight. The doctor told his parents that Hector's _____ gland is the cause of his fast metabolism.
   a. thyroid
   b. adrenal
   c. pancreas
   d. pituitary
   e. pineal

3. Although oxytocin has been tied to a variety of prosocial behaviors such as "love" and "trust," some researchers believe that in humans, it may actually work to increase _____.
   a. the release of glucose
   b. social loafing
   c. negative pair bonding
   d. heart rate and empathy
   e. the importance of some social stimuli

4. Which gland(s) have the greatest influence over other components of the endocrine system?
   a. pituitary
   b. ovaries
   c. testes
   d. pineal
   e. pancreas

AP 2.K Recount historic and contemporary research strategies and technologies that support research.

AP 2.M Discuss the role of neuroplasticity in traumatic brain injury.

APA Goal 2: Scientific Inquiry and Critical Thinking

Phineas Gage and Neuroplasticity

Addresses APA Learning Objective 2.2: Demonstrate psychology information literacy.

Earlier in the chapter, you read about neuroplasticity and the role of the frontal lobes in the case of Phineas Gage. There is little question about the significant changes that likely occurred in Phineas's behavior and personality immediately following the accident and trauma to his brain. However, based on what you know about the brain, his injury, and neuroplasticity and recovery, what questions might you have regarding his behavior and personality immediately before and after the injury and later in his life?

With regard to initial changes, it was reported that Gage went from being well balanced, energetic, and a smart businessman to being fitful, irreverent, and impatient to the point that those who knew him said he was "no longer Gage" (Harlow, 1848). In turn, many reports in psychology (including many psychology textbooks!) have previously suggested Gage's behavior and personality were permanently altered (Griggs, 2015; Macmillan, 2000; Macmillan & Lena, 2010). It is also important to note that at the time of Gage's accident, not as much was known about specific aspects of brain function and injury, much less recovery from brain injury.

As you have read, the actual amount of brain damage was not as well understood until relatively recently. Recent investigations using reconstructions of his skull and other methods have identified the most likely areas of brain damage. These studies have revealed

APA Goal 2 Relevant Brain Areas in Phineas Gage's Accident

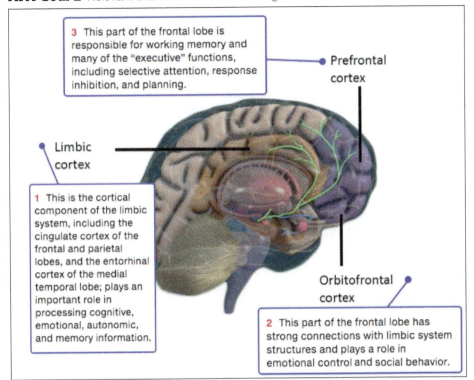

Phineas Gage experienced behavioral and personality changes immediately following his accident. Explore some of the brain areas that were either injured or affected by his accident.

damage to the left frontal lobe, primarily the prefrontal and orbitofrontal areas, and the white matter connections between the left frontal lobe and other parts of the brain (Ratiu et al., 2004; Van Horn et al., 2012). Given these brain areas' involvement in goal-directed behavior, planning, personality, emotional control, and the connections to other brain areas, it is easy to imagine the profound changes initially reported in Gage's behavior.

But what about his behavior later in life? Although he has historically been portrayed as being permanently altered, there has been some evidence to suggest he experienced a fair amount of recovery. After a period of time in which he exhibited himself and the tamping iron at least twice, there has not been any confirmation that he was actually in a "freak show," and in contrast, he traveled throughout the New England area of the United States, found employment in a horse stable, and later traveled to Chile for work to drive a horse-drawn coach (Harlow, 1868; Macmillan & Lena, 2010). This was not a single horse-and-buggy setup, but rather a six-horse stagecoach that was loaded with passengers and luggage. Although some may consider the work menial, it certainly had to provide some challenges as he had to take care of the horses, tend to the needs of his passengers, and most likely learn something about local customs (Macmillan & Lena, 2010; Van Horn et al., 2012).

There has also been an image of Phineas discovered although the date is not known. What does the portrait suggest with regard to Phineas's confidence, demeanor, etc.?

From this information and what you know in your study of psychology thus far, can you answer the following questions?

THINKING CRITICALLY 2.3

1. What type of questions should you ask yourself when referring to case studies? Do the questions differ based on the case studies being modern or historical?
2. What kind of supports and structure might have been provided to Phineas through his post-accident jobs that would have possibly helped him with his recovery?
3. How might the modern study of psychology help us better understand other historical case studies?

Applying Psychology to Everyday Life

Minimizing the Impact of Adult Attention-Deficit/Hyperactivity Disorder

2.15 Identify potential strategies for positively coping with attention-deficit/hyperactivity disorder.

Attention-deficit/hyperactivity disorder (ADHD) is a developmental disorder involving behavioral and cognitive aspects of inattention, impulsivity, and hyperactivity. Despite what many people have been told over the years, it is not due to bad parenting, too much junk food, or certain types of food coloring, and while symptoms may change somewhat, people do not necessarily outgrow the disorder. ADHD is a biological disorder that is related to genetics, environmental influences, and variations in brain structure and function. Some of the symptoms of ADHD are associated with brain areas responsible for the *executive functions*. See Learning Objective 2.8. Given ADHD is a brain-based disorder, aside from medication and other interventions, specific behavioral and cognitive strategies may prove useful. For example, using a daily assignment calendar, coupled with automatic phone or computer reminders, to stay on top of tasks and assignments. Also, alternating required or more difficult classes with electives, or those classes that are more fun (Barkley, 2017). What might you do to help yourself, or someone you care about, to be successful in school, work, or personal relationships? Watch the following video to see how other students try to help themselves or people they care about proactively manage some of the impacts of ADHD.

Applying Psychology to Everyday Life Minimizing the Impact of Adult Attention-Deficit/Hyperactivity Disorder

👁 **Watch** the **Video** at **MyLab Psychology**

After watching the video, answer the following questions:

1. In addition to specific cognitive and behavioral strategies, what external supports can individuals with ADHD use as a positive coping strategy?
2. Beyond the strategies shared by the students in the video, what are some ways you, or someone you care about, might proactively manage some of the impacts of ADHD?

Chapter Summary

Neurons and Neurotransmitters

2.1 Identify the parts of a neuron and the function of each.

- The nervous system is a complex network of cells that carries information to and from all parts of the body.
- The brain is made up of two types of cells, neurons and glial cells.
- Neurons have four primary components: dendrites that receive input, a soma or cell body, axons that carry the neural message to other cells, and axon terminals that are the site of neurotransmitter release.

- Glial cells separate and support neurons, both functionally and structurally; glia influence thinking, memory, and other forms of cognition.
- Specific types of glia produce myelin. Myelin insulates and protects the axons of some neurons. Some axons bundle together in "cables" called nerves. Myelin also speeds up the neural message.

2.2 Explain the action potential.

- A neuron contains charged particles called ions. When at rest, the neuron is negatively charged on the inside and positively charged on the outside. When stimulated, this reverses the charge by allowing positive sodium ions to enter the cell. This is the action potential.
- Neurons fire in an all-or-nothing manner. It is the speed and number of neurons firing that tell researchers the strength of the stimulus.
- Synaptic vesicles in the end of the axon terminal release neurotransmitter chemicals into the synapse, or gap, between one cell and the next. The neurotransmitter molecules fit into receptor sites on the next cell, stimulating or inhibiting that cell's firing. Neurotransmitters may be either excitatory or inhibitory.

2.3 Describe how neurons use neurotransmitters to communicate with each other and with the body.

- The first known neurotransmitter was acetylcholine (ACh). It stimulates muscles, helps in memory formation, and plays a role in arousal and attention.
- GABA is the major inhibitory neurotransmitter; high amounts of GABA are released when drinking alcohol.
- Serotonin (5-HT) is associated with sleep, mood, and appetite.
- Dopamine (DA) is associated with Parkinson's disease and schizophrenia.
- Endorphins are neural regulators that control our pain response.
- Most neurotransmitters are taken back into the synaptic vesicles in a process called reuptake.
- ACh is cleared out of the synapse by enzymes that break up the molecules.

Looking Inside the Living Brain

2.4 Describe how lesioning studies and brain stimulation are used to study the brain.

- We can study the brain by using lesioning techniques to destroy certain areas of the brain in laboratory animals or by electrically stimulating those areas (ESB).
- We can use case studies of human brain damage to learn about the brain's functions but cannot easily generalize from one case to another.
- rTMS and tDCS are noninvasive methods for stimulating the brain.

2.5 Compare and contrast neuroimaging techniques for mapping the brain's structure and function.

- Different neuroimaging methods allow scientists to investigate the structure or the function of the living brain.
- The electroencephalograph allows researchers to look at the electroencephalogram (EEG), or electrical activity of the surface of the brain, through the use of electrodes placed on the scalp that are then amplified and viewed using a computer. ERPs allow researchers to look at the timing and progression of cognitive processes.
- CT scans are computer-aided X-rays of the brain and show the skull and brain structure.
- MRI scans use a magnetic field, radio pulses, and a computer to give researchers an even more detailed look at the structure of the brain.
- PET scans use a radioactive sugar injected into the bloodstream to track the activity of brain cells, which is enhanced and color-coded by a computer. SPECT allows for the imaging of brain blood flow.
- fMRI allows researchers to look at the activity of the brain over a time period.
- NIRS use infrared light to measure changes in blood oxygen levels in the brain, reflecting increases and decreases in brain activity.

From the Bottom Up: The Structures of the Brain

2.6 Identify the different structures of the hindbrain and the function of each.

- The medulla is at the very bottom of the brain and at the top of the spinal column. It controls life-sustaining functions such as breathing and swallowing. The nerves from each side of the body also cross over in this structure to opposite sides.
- The pons is above the medulla and acts as a bridge between the cerebellum and the cerebrum. It influences sleep, dreaming, arousal, and coordination of movement on the left and right sides of the body.
- The reticular formation runs through the medulla and the pons and controls our general level of attention and arousal.
- The cerebellum is found at the base and back of the brain and coordinates fine, rapid motor movement, learned reflexes, posture, and muscle tone. It may also be involved in some cognitive and emotional functions.

2.7 Identify the structures of the brain that are involved in emotion, learning, memory, and motivation.

- The limbic system consists of the thalamus, hypothalamus, hippocampus, and amygdala.
- The thalamus is the relay station that sends sensory information to the proper areas of the cortex.
- The hypothalamus controls hunger, thirst, sexual behavior, sleeping and waking, and emotions. It also controls the pituitary gland.
- The hippocampus is the part of the brain responsible for the formation of long-term declarative memories.
- The amygdala controls our fear responses and memory of fearful stimuli.
- The cingulate cortex is important in both emotional and cognitive processing.

2.8 Identify the parts of the cortex that process the different senses and those that control movement of the body.

- The cortex is the outer covering of the cerebrum and consists of a tightly packed layer of neurons about one-tenth of an inch in thickness. Its wrinkles, or corticalization, allow for greater cortical area and are associated with greater brain complexity.

- The cortex is divided into two cerebral hemispheres connected by a thick band of neural fibers called the corpus callosum.
- The occipital lobes at the back and base of each hemisphere process vision and contain the primary visual cortex.
- The parietal lobes at the top and back of the cortex contain the somatosensory area, which processes our sense of touch, temperature, and body position.
- The temporal lobes contain the primary auditory area and are also involved in understanding language.
- The frontal lobes contain the motor cortex, which controls the voluntary muscles, and are also where all the higher mental functions occur, such as planning, language, and complex decision making.

2.9 Recall the function of association areas of the cortex, including those especially crucial for language.

- Association areas of the cortex are found in all the lobes but particularly in the frontal lobes. These areas help people make sense of the information they receive from primary sensory areas and the lower areas of the brain.
- A region called Broca's area in the left frontal lobe coordinates brain areas that are important for producing fluent, understandable speech. If damaged, the person has Broca's aphasia, in which words will be halting and pronounced incorrectly.
- Other regions of the brain, including Wernicke's area in the left temporal lobe and related structures and pathways, play a role in understanding language. Brain injuries in this area may result in Wernicke's aphasia, in which speech is fluent but nonsensical; the wrong words are used.

2.10 Explain how some brain functions differ between the left and right hemispheres.

- Studies with split-brain patients, in which the corpus callosum has been severed to correct epilepsy, reveal that the left side of the brain seems to control language, writing, logical thought, analysis, and mathematical abilities. The left side also processes information sequentially.
- The right side of the brain processes information globally and controls emotional expression, spatial perception, recognition of faces, patterns, melodies, and emotions. Information presented only to the left hemisphere can be verbalized, but information only sent to the right cannot.

The Nervous System: The Rest of the Story

2.11 Describe how the components of the central nervous system interact and how they may respond to experiences or injury.

- The central nervous system consists of the brain and the spinal cord.
- The spinal cord serves two functions. The outer part of the cord transmits messages to and from the brain, whereas the inner part controls lifesaving reflexes such as the pain/withdrawal response.
- Spinal cord reflexes involve afferent neurons, interneurons, and efferent neurons, forming a simple reflex arc.
- Neuroplasticity refers to the brain's ability to modify its structure and function as the result of experience or injury; researchers are examining ways to capitalize on this feature to assist individuals with brain injury or disease.

2.12 Differentiate the roles of the somatic and autonomic nervous systems.

- The peripheral nervous system is all the neurons and nerves that are not part of the brain and spinal cord and that extend throughout the body.
- There are two systems within the peripheral nervous system: the somatic nervous system and the autonomic nervous system.
- The somatic nervous system contains the sensory pathway, or neurons carrying messages to the central nervous system, and the motor pathway, or neurons carrying messages from the central nervous system to the voluntary muscles.
- The autonomic nervous system consists of the parasympathetic division and the sympathetic division. The sympathetic division is our fight-or-flight system, reacting to stress, whereas the parasympathetic division is our eat-drink-and-rest system that restores and maintains normal day-to-day functioning of the organs.

The Endocrine Glands

2.13 Explain why the pituitary gland is known as the "master gland."

- Endocrine glands secrete chemicals called hormones directly into the bloodstream, influencing the activity of the muscles and organs.
- The pituitary gland is found in the brain just below the hypothalamus. Among its many functions, it helps us conserve water and controls oxytocin, a hormone involved in the onset of labor and lactation. The pituitary also regulates growth hormone and influences the activity of the other glands.

2.14 Recall the role of various endocrine glands.

- The pineal gland is also located in the brain. It secretes melatonin, a hormone that regulates the sleep–wake cycle, in response to changes in light.
- The thyroid gland is located inside the neck. It controls metabolism (the burning of energy) by secreting thyroxine.
- The pancreas controls the level of sugar in the blood by secreting insulin and glucagons. Too much insulin produces hypoglycemia, whereas too little causes diabetes.
- The gonads are the ovaries in women and testes in men. They secrete hormones to regulate sexual growth, activity, and reproduction.
- The adrenal glands, one on top of each kidney, control the stress reaction through the adrenal medulla's secretion of epinephrine and norepinephrine. The adrenal cortex secretes more than 30 different corticoids (hormones), controlling salt intake, stress, and sexual development.

Applying Psychology to Everyday Life: Minimizing the Impact of Adult Attention-Deficit/Hyperactivity Disorder

2.15 Identify potential strategies for positively coping with adult attention-deficit/hyperactivity disorder.

- Attention-deficit/hyperactivity disorder (ADHD) involves behavioral and cognitive aspects of inattention, impulsivity, and hyperactivity that people likely do not outgrow. Some symptoms are associated with brain areas responsible for the *executive functions*. Positive coping strategies may include both behavioral and cognitive strategies.

Test Yourself: Preparing for the AP Exam

PART I: MULTIPLE-CHOICE QUESTIONS

Directions for Part I: Read each of the questions or incomplete sentences below. Then choose the response that best answers the question or completes the sentence.

1. In the structure of the neuron, the _____ receives messages from other cells.
   a. dendrite
   b. vesicle
   c. soma
   d. axon
   e. myelin

2. Oligodendrocytes and Schwann cells generate a fatty substance known as _____.
   a. glial
   b. soma
   c. myelin
   d. neurilemma
   e. stasis

3. When a neuron is in the resting potential state, the neuron is negatively charged on the _____ and positively charged on the _____.
   a. output, input
   b. top, bottom
   c. inside, outside
   d. bottom, top
   e. outside, inside

4. Which neurotransmitter stimulates skeletal muscle cells to contract but slows contractions of the heart?
   a. serotonin
   b. acetylcholine (ACh)
   c. GABA
   d. glutamate
   e. endorphin

5. Heroin mimics the actions of endorphins, inhibiting pain signals. Heroin is an example of a(n) _____.
   a. enzyme
   b. glial cell
   c. antagonist
   d. agonist
   e. protagonist

6. Sandy is a subject in a study on memory and problem solving. The researcher is applying magnetic pulses to her brain through copper wire coils positioned directly above her scalp. Sandy's study would best be described as a(n) _____ technique.
   a. noninvasive stimulation
   b. invasive stimulation
   c. EEG
   d. PET
   e. optogenetic

7. Nicole and Camille are synchronized swimmers for their school swim team. They often work long hours to ensure the movements in their routine are perfectly timed. What part of their brains must Camille and Nicole rely most upon?
   a. cerebellum
   b. pons
   c. medulla
   d. reticular formation
   e. temporal lobes

8. Your psychology professor refers to this as the great relay station of the brain. What part is he or she referring to?
   a. medulla
   b. amygdala
   c. hippocampus
   d. thalamus
   e. hypothalamus

9. Which part of the brain is involved in the creation of long-term, declarative memories and is often linked to Alzheimer's disease?
   a. thalamus
   b. amygdala
   c. hypothalamus
   d. hippocampus
   e. cingulate cortex

10. Loretta suffered a severe blow to the back of her head when she was thrown from her horse. Subsequently, her occipital lobe has been injured. Which of her senses has the highest chance of being affected?
    a. touch
    b. hearing
    c. taste
    d. smell
    e. vision

11. Jillian is recovering from a brain injury. She is able to speak fluently but often uses incorrect words in a sentence. In one instance at a friend's birthday party, she said, "I would like something to drink. Can I have some battery?" Jillian's problem may be a symptom of _____.
    a. Wernicke's aphasia
    b. visual agnosia
    c. anterograde amnesia
    d. spatial neglect
    e. Broca's aphasia

12. Although the brain works largely as a whole, which of the following is *not* a correct pairing of hemisphere and function?
    a. left: reading
    b. right: recognition of faces
    c. right: control of right-handed motor functions
    d. right: global processing
    e. left: control of right-handed motor functions

13. As you take notes, your heart beats at a normal rate. Your breathing is normal and your stomach slowly digests your earlier meal. What part of the peripheral nervous system is currently in action?
    a. autonomic division
    b. efferent division
    c. somatic division
    d. sympathetic division
    e. parasympathetic division

14. Which gland(s) influence all other glands within the endocrine system?
    a. pituitary
    b. thyroid
    c. pineal
    d. adrenal
    e. gonads

15. Aidan has had difficulty sleeping for the past 6 months, and his body seemingly no longer differentiates between night and day. His doctor believes the problem lies with Aidan's endocrine system. What gland will Aidan's physician focus on?
    a. testes
    b. pituitary
    c. pineal
    d. thyroid
    e. adrenal

PART II: FREE-RESPONSE QUESTION

Directions for Part II: Read the essay question that follows. Then respond to the question in a clear, concise essay. Do not simply list facts. Instead, present a thorough argument based on your critical consideration of the topic. Use of proper terminology is necessary.

While walking to the pencil sharpener during class, Alonso painfully stubbed his toe on his desk. He jerked his foot back and hopped on one leg, and just as he was about to yell a swear word, he noticed his teacher watching. He stopped himself from saying something inappropriate and said, "Ouch!" instead. Later on in the class, Alonso stops feeling the pain from his sore toe.

For each of the following terms, explain how they play a role in Alonso's behavior:
- prefrontal cortex
- cerebellum
- efferent neurons
- Broca's area
- endorphins
- somatosensory cortex
- spinal cord
- afferent neurons

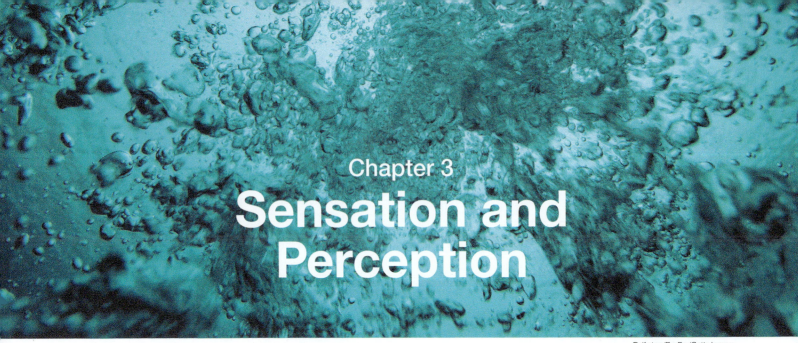

Chapter 3
Sensation and Perception

Ralf strm/EyeEm/Getty Images

In your words

Which of your sensory abilities do you rely on most during a typical day? Are certain senses more important than others, depending on the social context or setting?

After you have thought about these questions, watch the video to see how other students would answer them.

Watch the Video at MyLab Psychology

Why study sensation and perception?

Without sensations to tell us what is outside our own mental world, we would live entirely in our own minds, separate from one another and unable to find food or any other basics that sustain life. Sensations are the mind's window to the world that exists around us. Without perception, we would be unable to understand what all those sensations mean—perception is the process of interpreting the sensations we experience so that we can act upon them.

Learning Objectives

3.1 Describe how we get information from the outside world into our brains.

3.2 Describe the difference and absolute thresholds.

3.3 Explain why some sensory information is ignored.

3.4 Describe how light travels through the various parts of the eye.

3.5 Explain how light information reaches the visual cortex.

3.6 Compare and contrast two major theories of color vision, and explain how color-deficient vision occurs.

3.7 Explain the nature of sound, and describe how it travels through the various parts of the ear.

3.8 Summarize three theories of how the brain processes information about pitch.

3.9 Identify types of hearing impairment and treatment options for each.

3.10 Explain how the sense of taste works.

3.11 Explain how the sense of smell works.

3.12 Describe how we experience the sensations of touch, pressure, temperature, and pain.

3.13 Describe the systems that tell us about balance and position and movement of our bodies.

3.14 Describe how perceptual constancies and the Gestalt principles account for common perceptual experiences.

3.15 Explain how we perceive depth using both monocular and binocular cues.

3.16 Identify some common visual illusions and the factors that influence our perception of them.

3.17 Describe how mindfulness and paying attention to our senses, thoughts, and feelings can impact perceptions, personal experiences, and overall sense of well-being.

AP 3.B Discuss basic principles of sensory transduction, including absolute threshold, difference threshold, signal detection, and sensory adaptation.

3.1–3.3 The ABCs of Sensation

Information about the world has to have a way to get into the brain, where it can be used to determine actions and responses. The way into the brain is through the sensory organs and the process of sensation.

3.1 Transduction

3.1 Describe how we get information from the outside world into our brains.

Sensation occurs when special receptors in the sense organs—the eyes, ears, nose, skin, and taste buds—are activated, allowing various forms of outside stimuli to become neural signals in the brain. This process of converting outside stimuli, such as light, into neural activity is called **transduction**.

The *sensory receptors* are specialized forms of neurons, the cells that make up the nervous system. Instead of receiving neurotransmitters from other cells, these receptor cells are stimulated by different kinds of energy—for example, the receptors in the eyes are stimulated by light, whereas the receptors in the ears are activated by vibrations. Touch receptors are stimulated by pressure or temperature, and the receptors for taste and smell are triggered by chemical substances. Each receptor type transduces the physical information into electrical information in different ways, which then either depolarizes or hyperpolarizes the cell, causing it to fire more or to fire less based on the timing and intensity of information it is detecting from the environment (Gardner & Johnson, 2013).

In some people, the sensory information gets processed in unusual, but fascinating ways. Taria Camerino is a pastry chef who experiences music, colors, shapes, and emotions as taste; Jamie Smith is a sommelier, or wine steward, who experiences smells as colors and shapes; and James Wannerton is an information technology consultant who experiences sounds, words, and colors as tastes and textures (Carlsen, 2013, March 18). All three of these individuals have a condition known as **synesthesia**, which literally means "joined sensation." Studies suggest at least 4 to 5 percent of the population may experience some form of synesthesia, with nearly equivalent representation across females and males (Hubbard & Ramachandran, 2005; Simner, 2013; Simner & Carmichael, 2015; Simner et al., 2006). While the causes of synesthesia are still being investigated, it appears that in some forms, signals that come from the sensory organs, such as the eyes or the ears, either go to places in the brain where they weren't originally meant to be or they are processed differently. Some research suggests synesthesia is not purely a sensory phenomenon. For example, some forms of synesthesia may not be developmental, as synesthesia-like experiences can be learned (Bor et al., 2014). Other research suggests some aspects are universal—many people with grapheme-color synesthesia report that the first grapheme is red (see **Figure 3.1**) (Root et al., 2018).

sensation
the process that occurs when special receptors in the sense organs are activated, allowing various forms of outside stimuli to become neural signals in the brain.

transduction
the process of converting outside stimuli, such as light, into neural activity.

AP 3.G Explain common sensory conditions.

synesthesia
condition in which the signals from the various sensory organs are processed differently, resulting in the sense information being interpreted as more than one sensation.

AP 3.C Identify the research contributions of major historical figures in sensation and perception.

3.2 Sensory Thresholds

3.2 Describe the difference and absolute thresholds.

Ernst Weber (1795–1878) did studies trying to determine the smallest difference between two weights that could be detected. His research led to the formulation known as Weber's law of **just noticeable differences (JND**, or the **difference threshold)**. A JND is the smallest difference between two stimuli that is detectable 50 percent of the time, and Weber's law simply means that whatever the difference between stimuli might be, it is always a *constant*. If to notice a difference in the amount of sugar a person would need to add to a cup of coffee already sweetened with 5 teaspoons is 1 teaspoon, then the percentage of

just noticeable difference (JND or the difference threshold)
the smallest difference between two stimuli that is detectable 50 percent of the time.

Figure 3.1 Grapheme-Color Synesthesia

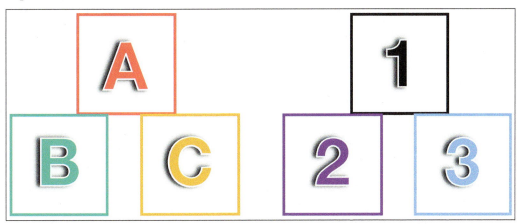

Both alphabetical letters and numerical digits are graphemes. In grapheme-color synesthesia, individuals consistently perceive specific letters and numbers as having associated colors, as illustrated in the figure. Putting aside the immediate experience, how might having synesthesia impact someone's memory?

change needed to detect a just noticeable difference is one fifth, or 20 percent. So, if the coffee has 10 teaspoons of sugar in it, the person would have to add another 20 percent, or 2 teaspoons, to be able to taste the difference half of the time. Most people would not typically drink a cup of coffee with 10 teaspoons of sugar in it, let alone 12 teaspoons, but you get the point.

Gustav Fechner (1801–1887) expanded on Weber's work by studying something he called the **absolute threshold** (Fechner, 1860). An absolute threshold is the lowest level of stimulation that a person can consciously detect 50 percent of the time the stimulation is present. (Remember, the JND is detecting a difference *between two* stimuli.) For example, assuming a very quiet room and normal hearing, how far away can someone sit and you might still hear the tick of their analog watch on half of the trials? For some examples of absolute thresholds for various senses, see **Table 3.1**.

Table 3.1 Examples of Absolute Thresholds

Sense	Threshold
Sight	A candle flame at 30 miles on a clear, dark night
Hearing	The tick of a mechanical watch 20 feet away in a quiet room
Smell	One drop of perfume diffused throughout a three-room apartment
Taste	1 teaspoon of sugar in 2 gallons of water
Touch	A bee's wing falling on the cheek from 1 centimeter above

💬 I've heard about people being influenced by stuff in movies and on television, things that are just below the level of conscious awareness. Is that true?

Stimuli below the level of conscious awareness are called *subliminal stimuli*. (The word *limin* means "threshold," so *sublimin* means "below the threshold.") These stimuli are just strong enough to activate the sensory receptors but not strong enough for people to be consciously aware of them. Many people believe these stimuli act on the unconscious mind, influencing behavior in a process called *subliminal perception*.

absolute threshold
the lowest level of stimulation that a person can consciously detect 50 percent of the time the stimulation is present.

At one time, many people believed that a market researcher named James Vicary had demonstrated the power of subliminal perception in advertising. In 1957, Vicary claimed that over a 6-week period, 45,699 patrons at a movie theater in Fort Lee, New Jersey, were shown two advertising messages, *Eat Popcorn* and *Drink Coca-Cola*, while they watched the film *Picnic*. According to Vicary, these messages were flashed for 3 milliseconds once every 5 seconds. Vicary claimed that over the 6-week period the sales of popcorn rose 57.7 percent and the sales of Coca-Cola rose 18.1 percent. It was 5 years before Vicary finally admitted that he had never conducted a real study (Merikle, 2000; Pratkanis, 1992). Furthermore, many researchers have gathered scientific evidence that subliminal perception does not work in advertising (Bargh et al., 1996; Broyles, 2006; Moore, 1988; Pratkanis & Greenwald, 1988; Trappey, 1996; Vokey & Read, 1985).

This is not to say that subliminal perception does not exist—there is a growing body of evidence that we process some stimuli without conscious awareness, especially stimuli that are fearful or threatening (LeDoux & Phelps, 2008; Öhman, 2008). In this effort, researchers have used *event-related potentials* (ERPs) and functional magnetic resonance imaging (fMRI) to verify the existence of subliminal perception and associated learning in the laboratory (Babiloni et al., 2010; Bernat et al., 2001; Fazel-Rezai & Peters, 2005; King et al., 2016; Sabatini et al., 2009; Victor et al., 2017). See Learning Objective 2.5. The stimuli used in these studies are detectable by our sensory systems but below the level of full conscious perception. Participants are not aware or conscious that they have been exposed to the stimuli due to masking or manipulation of attention. Furthermore, the stimuli typically influence automatic reactions (such as an increase in facial tension) rather than direct voluntary behaviors (such as going to buy something suggested by advertising).

Another useful way of analyzing what stimuli we respond to is based on signal detection theory. **Signal detection theory** is used to compare our judgments, or the decisions we make, under uncertain conditions. The ability to detect any physical stimulus is based on how strong it is and how mentally and physically prepared the individual is. It was originally developed to help address issues associated with research participants guessing during experiments and is a way to measure accuracy (Green & Swets, 1966; Macmillan & Creelman, 1991).

For example, a stimulus can be either present or absent. In turn, an individual can either detect a stimulus when present, a "hit," or say it is not there, a "miss." He or she can also falsely report a stimulus as present when it actually isn't, a "false alarm," or correctly state it isn't there, a "correct rejection."

3.3 Habituation and Sensory Adaptation

3.3 Explain why some sensory information is ignored.

Some of the lower centers of the brain filter sensory stimulation and "ignore" or prevent conscious attention to stimuli that do not change. The brain is primarily interested in changes in information. That's why people don't really "hear" the noise of the air conditioner unless it suddenly cuts off or the noise made in some classrooms unless it gets very quiet or someone else directs their attention toward it. Although they actually are *hearing* it, they aren't paying attention to it. This is called **habituation**, and it is the way the brain deals with unchanging information from the environment.

> 💬 Sometimes I can smell the odor of the garbage can in the kitchen when I first come home, but after a while the smell seems to go away—is this also habituation?

Although different from habituation, **sensory adaptation** is another process by which constant, unchanging information from the sensory receptors is effectively ignored. In habituation, the sensory receptors are still responding to stimulation, but the lower centers of the

---

AP 3.E Discuss the role of attention in behavior.

signal detection theory
provides a method for assessing the accuracy of judgments or decisions under uncertain conditions; used in perception research and other areas. An individual's correct "hits" and rejections are compared against their "misses" and "false alarms."

habituation
tendency of the brain to stop attending to constant, unchanging information.

sensory adaptation
tendency of sensory receptor cells to become less responsive to a stimulus that is unchanging.

brain are not sending the signals from those receptors to the cortex. The process of sensory adaptation differs because the receptor cells *themselves* become less responsive to an unchanging stimulus—garbage odors included—and the receptors no longer send signals to the brain.

For example, when you eat, the food you put in your mouth tastes strong at first, but as you keep eating the same thing, the taste does fade somewhat, doesn't it? Generally speaking, all of our senses are subject to sensory adaptation.

You might think, then, that if you stare at something long enough, it would also disappear, but the eyes are a little different. Even though the sensory receptors in the back of the eyes adapt to and become less responsive to a constant visual stimulus, under ordinary circumstances, the eyes are never entirely still. There's a constant movement of the eyes, tiny little vibrations called "microsaccades" or "saccadic movements," that people don't consciously notice. These movements keep the eyes from adapting to what they see. (That's a good thing because otherwise many students would no doubt go blind from staring off into space.)

This young woman does not feel the piercings on her ears and nose because sensory adaptation allows her to ignore a constant, unchanging stimulation from the metal rings. What else is she wearing that would cause sensory adaptation?

Concept Map L.O. 3.1, 3.2, 3.3

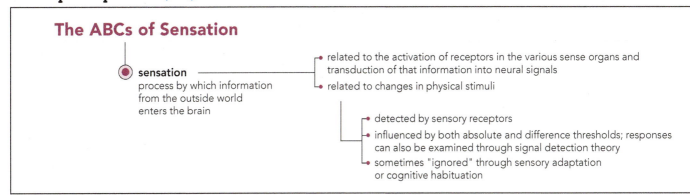

Practice Quiz   How much do you remember?

Pick the best answer.

1. _____ involves the detection of physical stimuli from our environment and is made possible by the activation of specific receptor cells.
   a. Sublimation
   b. Sensation
   c. Perception
   d. Habituation
   e. Adaptation

2. The lowest level of stimulation that a person can consciously detect 50 percent of the time the stimulation is present is the _____.
   a. sensation baseline
   b. just noticeable difference
   c. absolute threshold
   d. difference threshold
   e. sensory adaptation

3. After being in class for a while, _____ is a likely explanation for not hearing the sound of the fan in the LCD projector above you until someone says something about it.
   a. accommodation
   b. adaptation
   c. sublimation
   d. acclimation
   e. habituation

4. You are drinking a strong cup of coffee that is particularly bitter. After a while, the coffee doesn't taste as strong as it did when you first tasted it. What has happened?
   a. perceptual accommodation
   b. habituation
   c. sensory adaptation
   d. perceptual defense
   e. subliminal perception

3.4–3.6 The Science of Seeing

AP 3.F Describe the vision process, including the specific nature of energy transduction, relevant anatomical structures, and specialized pathways in the brain for each of the senses.

💬 I've heard that light is waves, but I've also heard that light is made of particles—which is it?

Light is a complicated phenomenon. Although scientists have long argued over the nature of light, they finally have agreed that light has the properties of both waves and particles. The following section gives a brief history of how scientists have tried to "shed light" on the mystery of light.

Figure 3.2 The Visible Spectrum

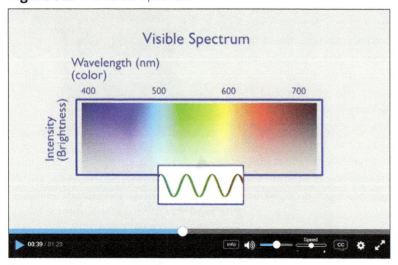

▶ Watch the Video at MyLab Psychology

3.4 Light and the Eye

3.4 Describe how light travels through the various parts of the eye.

It was Albert Einstein who first proposed that light is actually tiny "packets" of waves. These "wave packets" are called *photons* and have specific wavelengths associated with them (Lehnert, 2007; van der Merwe & Garuccio, 1994).

When people experience the physical properties of light, they are not really aware of its dual, wavelike and particle-like, nature. With regard to its psychological properties, there are three aspects to our perception of light: *brightness, color,* and *saturation*.

Brightness is determined by the amplitude of the wave—how high or how low the wave actually is. The higher the wave, the brighter the light appears to be. Low waves are dimmer. *Color*, or hue, is largely determined by the length of the wave. Short wavelengths (measured in nanometers) are found at the blue end of the *visible spectrum* (the portion of the whole spectrum of light visible to the human eye; see **Figure 3.2**), whereas longer wavelengths are found at the red end.

Saturation refers to the purity of the color people perceive: A highly saturated red, for example, would contain only red wavelengths, whereas a less-saturated red might contain a mixture of wavelengths. For example, when a child is using the red paint from a set of poster paints, the paint on the paper will look like a pure red, but if the child mixes in some white

Figure 3.3 Structure of the Eye

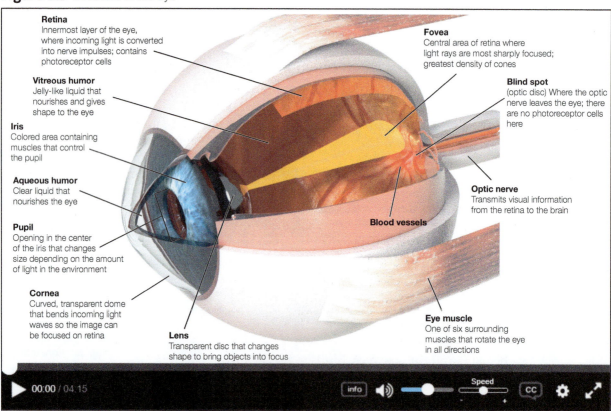

▶ Watch the Video at MyLab Psychology

Light enters the eye through the cornea and pupil. The iris controls the size of the pupil. From the pupil, light passes through the lens to the retina, where it is transformed into nerve impulses. The nerve impulses travel to the brain along the optic nerve.

paint, the paint will look pink. The hue is still red, but it will be less of a saturated red because of the presence of white wavelengths. Mixing in black or gray would also lessen the saturation. (Note that when combining different colors, light works differently than pigments or paint. We will look at this distinction when we examine perception of color.)

THE STRUCTURE OF THE EYE The best way to talk about how the eye processes light is to talk about what happens to an image being viewed as the photons of light from that image travel through the eye. Refer to **Figure 3.3** to follow the path of the image.

FROM FRONT TO BACK: THE PARTS OF THE EYE Light enters the eye directly from a source (such as the sun) or indirectly by reflecting off of an object. To see clearly, a single point of light from a source or reflected from an object must travel through the structures of the eye and end up on the retina as a single point. Light bends as it passes through substances of different densities, through a process known as refraction. For example, have you ever looked at a drinking straw in a glass of water through the side of the glass? It appears that the straw bends, or is broken, at the surface of the water. That optical illusion is due to the refraction of light. The structures of the eye play a vital role in both collecting and focusing light so we can see clearly.

This photo illustrates an optical illusion caused by the refraction of light. The straw is not really broken, although it appears that way.

The surface of the eye is covered in a clear membrane called the *cornea*. The cornea not only protects the eye but also is the structure that focuses most of the light coming into the eye. The cornea has a fixed curvature, like a camera that has no option to adjust the focus. However, this curvature can be changed somewhat through vision-improving techniques that change the shape of the cornea. For example, ophthalmologists, physicians who specialize in medical and surgical treatment of eye problems, can use both *photoreactive keratectomy (PRK)* and *laser-assisted in situ keratomileusis (LASIK)* procedures to remove small portions of the cornea, changing its curvature and thus the focus in the eye. The next visual layer is a clear, watery fluid called the *aqueous humor*. This fluid is continually replenished and supplies nourishment to the eye. The light from the visual image then enters the interior of the eye through a hole, called the *pupil*, in a round muscle called the *iris* (the colored part of the eye). The iris can change the size of the pupil, letting more or less light into the eye. That also helps focus the image; people try to do the same thing by squinting.

Behind the iris, suspended by muscles, is another clear structure called the *lens*. The flexible lens finishes the focusing process begun by the cornea. In a process called **visual accommodation**, the lens changes its shape from thick to thin, enabling it to focus on objects that are close or far away. The variation in thickness allows the lens to project a sharp image on the retina. People lose this ability as the lens hardens through aging (a disorder called *presbyopia*). Although people try to compensate* for their inability to focus on things close to them, eventually they usually need bifocals because their arms just aren't long enough anymore. In nearsightedness, or *myopia*, visual accommodation may occur, but the shape of the eye causes the focal point to fall short of the retina. In farsightedness, or *hyperopia*, the focus point is beyond the retina (see **Figure 3.4**). Glasses,

AP 3.G Explain common sensory conditions.

visual accommodation
the change in the thickness of the lens as the eye focuses on objects that are far away or close.

Figure 3.4 Nearsightedness and Farsightedness

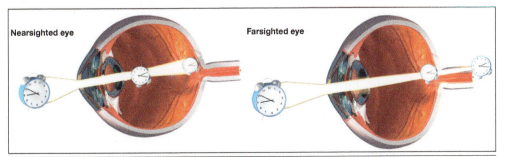

Source: Adapted from St. Luke's Cataract & Laser Institute

*compensate: to correct for an error or defect.

Watch Rods and Cones

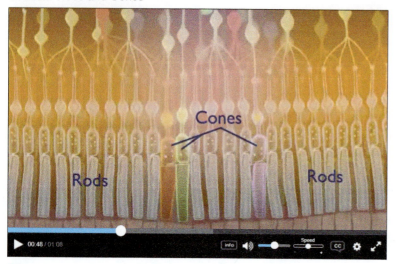

Watch the Video at MyLab Psychology

Figure 3.5 The Blind Spot

Hold the image in front of you. Close your right eye and stare at the picture of the dog with your left eye. Slowly bring the image closer to your face. The picture of the cat will disappear at some point because the light from the picture of the cat is falling on your blind spot. If you cannot seem to find your blind spot, try moving the image more slowly.

rods
visual sensory receptors found at the back of the retina, responsible for non-color sensitivity to low levels of light.

cones
visual sensory receptors found at the back of the retina, responsible for color vision and sharpness of vision.

blind spot
area in the retina where the axons of the retinal ganglion cells exit the eye to form the optic nerve; insensitive to light.

contacts, or corrective surgery like LASIK or PRK can correct these issues.

Once past the lens, light passes through a large, open space filled with a clear, jelly-like fluid called the *vitreous humor*. This fluid, like the aqueous humor, also nourishes the eye and gives it shape.

THE TRANSDUCTION OF LIGHT The final stop for light within the eye is the *retina*, a light-sensitive area at the back of the eye containing three layers: ganglion cells, bipolar cells, and the **rods** and **cones**, special receptor cells (*photoreceptors*) that respond to the various wavelengths of light. The video *Rods and Cones* provides an overview.

While the retina is responsible for absorbing and processing light information, the rods and the cones are the business end of the retina—the part that actually receives the photons of light and turns them into neural signals for the brain, sending them first to the *bipolar cells* (a type of interneuron; called bipolar or "two-ended" because they have a single dendrite at one end and a single axon on the other; see Learning Objective 2.1) and then to the retinal *ganglion cells* whose axons form the optic nerve.

The rods and cones are responsible for different aspects of vision. There are 6 million cones in each eye, and while they are located all over the retina, cones are more concentrated at its very center (the area called the *fovea*) where there are no rods. Some cones have a private line to the optic nerve (one bipolar cell for each cone). This means that the cones are the receptors for visual acuity, or the ability to see fine detail. Cones require a lot more light to function than the rods do and work best in bright light, which is also when people see things most clearly. Cones are also sensitive to different wavelengths of light, so they are responsible for color vision.

Rods are found all over the retina except the *fovea* but are concentrated in the periphery and responsible for peripheral vision. They are sensitive to changes in brightness but only for a narrow band of wavelengths, so they see in black and white and shades of gray. Many rods connect to a single bipolar cell. If only one rod in a region is stimulated, the brain perceives the whole area as stimulated. But because the brain doesn't know exactly what part of the region is actually sending the message, visual acuity is quite low. That's why in low levels of light, such as twilight or a dimly lit room, things tend to appear less distinct and dark or grayish.

The eyes don't adapt to constant stimuli under normal circumstances because of saccadic movements. But if people stare with one eye at one spot long enough, small objects that slowly cross their visual field may at one point disappear briefly because there is a "hole" in the retina—the place where all the axons of those ganglion cells leave the retina to become the optic nerve, the *optic disk*. There are no rods or cones here, so this is referred to as the **blind spot**. You can demonstrate the blind spot for yourself by following the directions in **Figure 3.5**.

3.5 The Visual Pathway

3.5 Explain how light information reaches the visual cortex.

You may want to first look at **Figure 3.6** for a moment before reading this section. Light entering the eyes can be separated into the left and right visual fields. Light from the right visual field falls on the left side of each eye's retina; light from the left visual field falls on the right side of each retina. Light travels in a straight line through the cornea and lens, resulting in the image projected on the retina actually being upside down and reversed from left to right as compared to the visual fields. Thank goodness our brains can compensate for this!

Figure 3.6 Crossing of the Optic Nerve

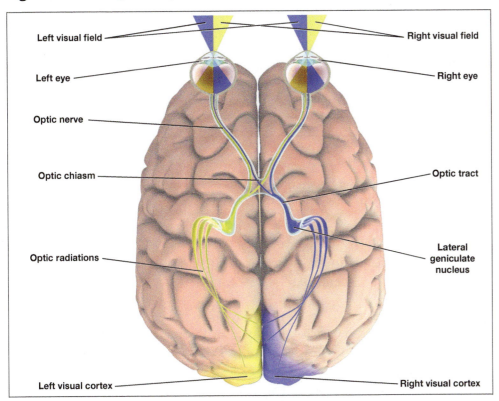

Light falling on the left side of each eye's retina (from the right visual field, shown in yellow) will stimulate a neural message that will travel along the optic nerve to the thalamus and then on to the visual cortex in the occipital lobe of the left hemisphere. Notice that the message from the temporal half of the left retina goes to the left occipital lobe, while the message from the nasal half of the right retina crosses over to the left hemisphere (the optic chiasm is the point of crossover). The optic nerve tissue from both eyes joins together to form the left optic tract before going on to the lateral geniculate nucleus of the thalamus, the optic radiations, and then the left occipital lobe. For the left visual field (shown in blue), the messages from both right sides of the retinas will travel along the right optic tract to the right visual cortex in the same manner.

The areas of the retina can be divided into halves, with the halves toward the temples of the head referred to as the temporal retinas and the halves toward the center, or nose, called the nasal retinas. Look at Figure 3.6 again. Notice that the information from the left visual field (falling on the right side of each retina) goes to the right visual cortex, while the information from the right visual field (falling on the left side of each retina) goes to the left visual cortex. This is because the axons from the temporal halves of each retina project to the visual cortex on the same side of the brain, while the axons from the nasal halves cross over to the visual cortex on the opposite side of the brain. The optic chiasm is the point of crossover.

dark adaptation
the recovery of the eye's sensitivity to visual stimuli in darkness after exposure to bright lights.

light adaptation
the recovery of the eye's sensitivity to visual stimuli in light after exposure to darkness.

Because rods work well in low levels of light, they are also the cells that allow the eyes to adapt to low light. **Dark adaptation** occurs as the eye recovers its ability to see when going from a brightly lit state to a dark state. (The light-sensitive pigments that allow us to see are able to regenerate or "recharge" in the dark.) The brighter the light was, the longer it takes the rods to adapt to the new lower levels of light (Bartlett, 1965). This is why the bright headlights of an oncoming car can leave a person less able to see for a while after that car has passed. Fortunately, this is usually a temporary condition because the bright light was on so briefly and the rods readapt to the dark night relatively quickly. Full dark adaptation, which occurs when going from more constant light to darkness, such as turning out one's bedroom lights, takes about 30 minutes. As people get older this process takes longer, causing many older persons to be less able to see at night and in darkened rooms (Klaver et al., 1998). This age-related change can cause *night blindness*, in which a person has difficulty seeing well enough to drive at night or get around in a darkened room or house. Some research indicates that taking supplements such as vitamin A can reverse or relieve this symptom in some cases (Jacobson et al., 1995). When going from a darkened room to one that is brightly lit, the opposite process occurs. The cones have to adapt to the increased level of light, and they accomplish this **light adaptation** much more quickly than the rods adapt to darkness—it takes a few seconds at most (Hood, 1998).

3.6 Perception of Color

3.6 Compare and contrast two major theories of color vision, and explain how color-deficient vision occurs.

AP 3.C Identify the research contributions of major historical figures in sensation and perception.

💬 Earlier you said the cones are used in color vision. There are so many colors in the world—are there cones that detect each color? Or do all cones detect all colors?

Although experts in the visual system have been studying color and its nature for many years, at this point in time there is an ongoing theoretical discussion about the role the cones play in the sensation of color.

trichromatic ("three colors") theory
theory of color vision that proposes three types of cones: red, blue, and green.

TRICHROMATIC THEORY Two theories about how people see colors were originally proposed in the 1800s. The first is called the **trichromatic ("three colors") theory**. First proposed by Thomas Young in 1802 and later modified by Hermann von Helmholtz in 1852, this theory proposed three types of cones: red cones, blue cones, and green cones, one for each of the three primary colors of light.

Most people probably think that the primary colors are red, yellow, and blue, but these are the primary colors when talking about *painting*—not when talking about *light*. Paints *reflect* light, and the way reflected light mixes is different from the way direct light mixes. For example, if an artist were to blend red, yellow, and blue paints together, the result would be a mess—a black mess. The mixing of paint (reflected light) is subtractive, removing more light as you mix in more colors. As all of the colors are mixed, more light waves are absorbed and we see black. But if the artist were to blend a red, green, and blue light together by focusing lights of those three colors on one common spot, the result would be white, not black (see **Figure 3.7**). The mixing of direct light is additive, resulting in lighter colors, more light, and when mixing red, blue, and green, we see white, the reflection of the entire visual spectrum.

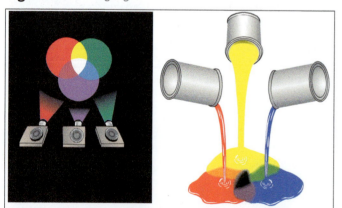

Figure 3.7 Mixing Light

The mixing of direct light is different than the mixing of reflected light. The mixing of red, blue, and green light is additive, resulting in white light. The mixing of multiple colors of paint (reflected light) is subtractive, resulting in a dark gray or black color.

In the trichromatic theory, different shades of colors correspond to different amounts of light received by each of these three types of cones. These cones then fire their message to the brain's vision centers. The combination of cones and the rate at which they are firing determine the color that will be seen. For example, if the red and green cones are firing in response to a stimulus at fast enough rates, the color the person sees is yellow. If the red and blue cones are firing fast enough, the result is magenta. If the blue and green cones are firing fast enough, a kind of cyan color (blue-green) appears.

Paul K. Brown and George Wald (1964) identified three types of cones in the retina, each sensitive to a range of wavelengths, measured in nanometers (nm), and a peak sensitivity that roughly corresponds to three different colors (although hues/colors can vary depending on brightness and saturation). The peak wavelength of light the cones seem to be most sensitive to turns out to be just a little different from Young and von Helmholtz's original three corresponding colors: Short-wavelength cones detect what we see as blue-violet (about 420 nm), medium-wavelength cones detect what we see as green (about 530 nm), and long-wavelength cones detect what we see as green-yellow (about 560 nm). Interestingly, none of the cones identified by Brown and Wald have a peak sensitivity to light where most of us see red (around 630 nm). Keep in mind, though, each cone responds to light across a range of wavelengths, not just its wavelength of peak sensitivity. Depending on the intensity of the light, both the medium- and long-wavelength cones respond to light that appears red, as shown in **Figure 3.8**.

OPPONENT-PROCESS THEORY The trichromatic theory would, at first glance, seem to be more than adequate to explain how people perceive color. But there's an interesting phenomenon that this theory cannot explain. If a person stares at a picture of the American flag for a little while—say, a minute—and then looks away to a blank white wall or sheet of paper, that person will see an afterimage of the flag. **Afterimages** occur when a visual sensation persists for a brief time even after the original stimulus is removed. The person would also notice rather quickly that the colors of the flag in the afterimage are all wrong—green for red, black for white, and yellow for blue. If you follow the directions for **Figure 3.9**, in which the flag is yellow, green, and black, you should see a flag with the usual red, white, and blue.

> Hey, now the afterimage of the flag has normal colors! Why does this happen?

The phenomenon of the color afterimage is explained by the second theory of color perception, called the **opponent-process theory** (De Valois & De Valois, 1993; Hurvich & Jameson, 1957), based on an idea first suggested by Edwald Hering in 1874 (Finger, 1994). In opponent-process theory, there are four primary colors: red, green, blue, and yellow. The colors are arranged in pairs, with each member of the pair as opponents. Red is paired with its opponent green, and blue is paired with its opponent yellow. If one member of a pair is strongly stimulated, the other member is inhibited and cannot be working—so there are no reddish-greens or bluish-yellows.

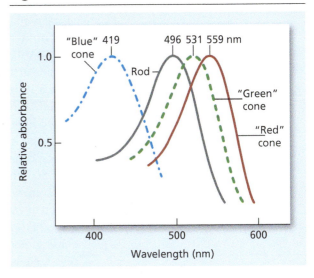

Figure 3.8 Absorbance of Light from Rods and Cones

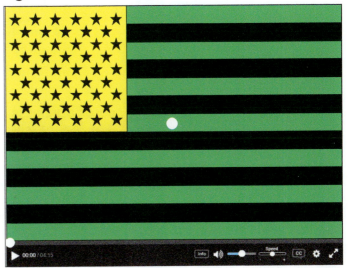

Figure 3.9 Color Afterimage

Stare at the white dot in the center of this oddly colored flag for about 30 seconds. Now look at a white piece of paper or a white wall. Notice that the colors are now the normal, expected colors of the American flag. They are also the primary colors that are opposites of the colors in the picture and provide evidence for the opponent-process theory of color vision.

afterimages
images that occur when a visual sensation persists for a brief time even after the original stimulus is removed.

opponent-process theory
theory of color vision that proposes visual neurons (or groups of neurons) are stimulated by light of one color and inhibited by light of another color.

So how can this kind of pairing cause a color afterimage? From the level of the bipolar and ganglion cells in the retina, all the way through the thalamus, and on to the visual cortical areas in the brain, some neurons (or groups of neurons) are stimulated by light from one part of the visual spectrum and inhibited by light from a different part of the spectrum. For example, let's say we have a red-green ganglion cell in the retina whose baseline activity is rather weak when we expose it to white light. However, the cell's activity is increased by red light, so we experience the color red. If we stimulate the cell with red light for a long enough period of time, the cell becomes fatigued. If we then swap out the red light with white light, the fatigued cell responds even less than the original baseline. Now we experience the color green, because green is associated with a decrease in the responsiveness of this cell.

So which theory is the right one? Both theories play a part in color vision. Trichromatic theory can explain what is happening with the raw stimuli, the actual detection of various wavelengths of light. Opponent-process theory can explain afterimages and other aspects of visual perception that occur after the initial detection of light from our environment. In addition to the retinal bipolar and ganglion cells, opponent-process cells are contained inside the thalamus in an area called the lateral geniculate nucleus (LGN). The LGN is part of the pathway that visual information takes to the occipital lobe. It is when the cones in the retina send signals through the retinal bipolar and ganglion cells that we see the red versus green pairings and blue versus yellow pairings. Together with the retinal cells, the cells in the LGN appear to be the ones responsible for opponent-processing of color vision and the afterimage effect.

> So which theory accounts for color blindness? I've heard there are two kinds of color blindness, when you can't tell red from green and when you can't tell blue from yellow.

AP 3.G Explain common sensory conditions.

COLOR BLINDNESS From the mention of red-green and yellow-blue color blindness, one might think that the opponent-process theory explains this problem. But in reality, "color blindness" is caused by defective cones in the retina of the eye and, as a more general term, *color-deficient vision* is more accurate, as most people with "color blindness" have two types of cones working and can see many colors.

There are really three kinds of color-deficient vision. In a very rare type, *achromatopsia* or *monochromatic vision*, people have cones, but they are not functioning correctly as the result of one or more genetic mutations. Essentially, everything looks the same to the brain—black, white, and shades of gray. The other types of color-deficient vision, or *dichromatic vision*, are caused by the same kind of problem—having one cone that does not work properly. So instead of experiencing the world with normal vision based on combinations of three cones or colors, trichromatic vision, individuals with dichromatic vision experience the world with essentially combinations of two cones or colors. Red-green color deficiency (as in *protanopia* or *deuteranopia*) is due to red or green cones not functioning correctly. In both of these, the individual confuses reds and greens, seeing the world primarily in blues, yellows, and shades of gray. In one real-world example, a November 2015 professional American football game had one team in all green uniforms and the other in all red uniforms. The combination caused problems for some viewers, who were unable to tell the teams apart! An actual lack of functioning blue cones is much less common and causes blue-yellow color deficiency (*tritanopia*). These individuals see the world primarily in reds, greens, and shades of gray. To get an idea of what someone with color-deficient vision might experience, look at **Figure 3.10**.

Figure 3.10 Types of Color-Deficient Vision

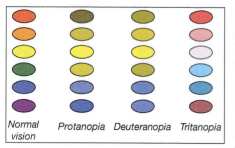

Compare the colors perceived by someone with normal color vision on the left with three types of color-deficient vision. *Protanopia* is linked to red cone cells not working properly, *deuteranopia* is caused by deficient functioning of green cone cells, and *tritanopia* is tied to a lack of blue cone cells.

Source: Timonina/Shutterstock

💬 **Why are most of the people with color-deficient vision men?**

Color-deficient vision involving one set of cones is inherited in a pattern known as *sex-linked inheritance*. The gene for color-deficient vision is *recessive*. To inherit a recessive trait, you normally need two of the genes, one from each parent. See Learning Objective 8.3. But the gene for color-deficient vision is attached to a particular chromosome (a package of genes) that helps determine the sex of a person. Men have one X chromosome and one smaller Y chromosome (named for their shapes), whereas women have two X chromosomes. The smaller Y has fewer genes than the larger X, and one of the genes missing is the one that would suppress the gene for color-deficient vision. For a woman to have color-deficient vision, she must inherit two recessive genes, one from each parent, but a man only needs to inherit *one* recessive gene—the one passed on to him on his mother's X chromosome. His odds are greater; therefore, more males than females have color-deficient vision.

Concept Map L.O. 3.4, 3.5, 3.6

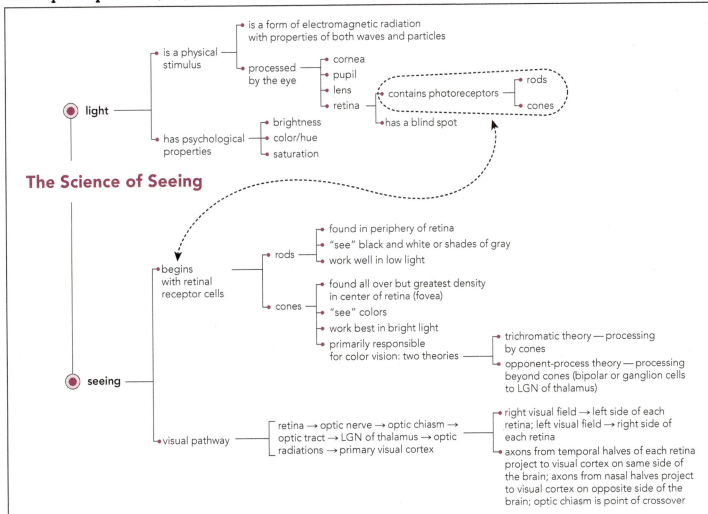

Practice Quiz   How much do you remember?

Pick the best answer.

1. Which of the following is largely determined by the length of a light wave?
   a. direction
   b. saturation
   c. duration
   d. brightness
   e. color

2. Aside from the lens, damage to the _____ can affect the eye's ability to focus light.
   a. pupil
   b. cornea
   c. retina
   d. iris
   e. rods

3. In farsightedness, also known as _____, the focal point is _____ the retina.
   a. hyperopia, beyond
   b. myopia, in front of
   c. myopia, beyond
   d. presbyopia, above
   e. hyperopia, in front of

4. Grace stares at a fixed spot in her bedroom using only one eye. After a while, what might happen to her vision?
   a. Objects will become more focused the longer she looks at them.
   b. Objects will become brighter the longer she looks at them.
   c. Any small object that crosses her visual field very slowly may at one point briefly disappear.
   d. Objects will become more distorted the longer she looks at them.
   e. Any object that she focuses on will begin to rotate, first clockwise, then counterclockwise.

5. What are the three primary colors as proposed by the trichromatic theory?
   a. white, black, brown
   b. red, yellow, blue
   c. white, black, red
   d. red, green, blue
   e. yellow, blue, green

6. Which of the following best explains afterimages?
   a. myopia
   b. color-deficient vision
   c. opponent-process theory
   d. monochrome color blindness
   e. trichromatic theory

AP 3.1 Describe the hearing process, including the specific nature of energy transduction, relevant anatomical structures, and specialized pathways in the brain for each of the senses.

3.7–3.9 The Hearing Sense: Can You Hear Me Now?

💬 If light works like waves, then do sound waves have similar properties?

Both the seeing and hearing senses rely on waves. But the similarity ends there, as the physical properties of sound are different from those of light.

3.7 Sound Waves and the Ear

3.7 Explain the nature of sound, and describe how it travels through the various parts of the ear.

Sound waves do not come in little packets the way light comes in photons. Sound waves are simply the vibrations of the molecules of air that surround us. Sound waves do have the same properties of light waves though—wavelength, amplitude, and purity. Wavelengths are interpreted by the brain as frequency or *pitch* (high, medium, or low). Amplitude is interpreted as *volume*, how soft or loud a sound is (see **Figure 3.11**). Finally, what would correspond to saturation or purity in light is called *timbre* in sound, a richness in the tone of the sound. And just as people rarely see pure colors in the world around us, they also seldom hear pure sounds. The everyday noises that surround people do not allow them to hear many pure tones.

Just as a person's vision is limited by the visible spectrum of light, a person is also limited in the range of frequencies he or she can hear. Frequency is measured in cycles (waves) per second, or **hertz (Hz)**. Human limits are between 20 and 20,000 Hz, with the most sensitivity from about 2,000 to 4,000 Hz—very important for conversational speech. (In comparison, dogs can hear between 50 and 60,000 Hz, and dolphins can hear up to 200,000 Hz.) To hear the higher and lower frequencies of a piece of music on their iPhone, for example, a person would need to increase the amplitude or volume—which explains why some people like to "crank it up."

hertz (Hz)
cycles or waves per second, a measurement of frequency.

Figure 3.11 Sound Waves and Decibels

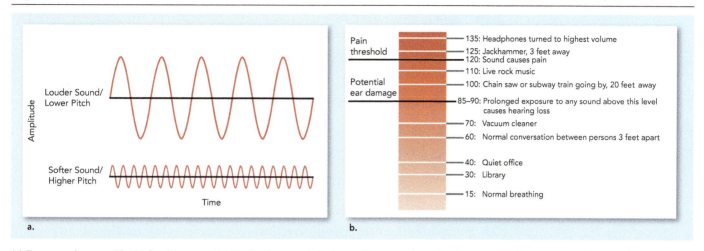

(a) Two sound waves. The higher the wave, the louder the sound; the lower the wave, the softer the sound. If the waves are close together in time (high frequency), the pitch will be perceived as a high pitch. Waves that are farther apart (low frequency) will be perceived as having a lower pitch. (b) Decibels of various stimuli. A *decibel* is a unit of measure for loudness. Psychologists study the effects that noise has on stress, learning, performance, aggression, and psychological and physical well-being.

THE STRUCTURE OF THE EAR: FOLLOW THE VIBES The ear is a series of structures, each of which plays a part in the sense of hearing, as shown in **Figure 3.12**.

THE OUTER EAR The **pinna** is the visible, external part of the ear that serves as a kind of concentrator, funneling* the sound waves from the outside into the structure of the ear. The pinna is also the entrance to the **auditory canal** (or ear canal), the short tunnel that runs down to the *tympanic membrane*, or eardrum. When sound waves hit the eardrum, they cause three tiny bones in the middle ear to vibrate.

THE MIDDLE EAR: HAMMER, ANVIL, AND STIRRUP The three tiny bones in the middle ear are known as the hammer (*malleus*), anvil (*incus*), and stirrup (*stapes*), each name stemming from the shape of the respective bone. Collectively, they are referred to as the *ossicles* and they are the smallest bones in the human body. The vibration of these three bones amplifies the vibrations from the eardrum. The stirrup, the last bone in the chain, causes a membrane covering the opening of the inner ear to vibrate. This membrane is called the *oval window*, and its vibrations set off another chain reaction within the inner ear.

Figure 3.12 The Structure of the Ear

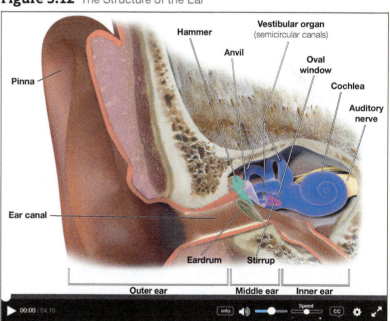

Watch the Video at MyLab Psychology

THE TRANSDUCTION OF SOUND In our previous discussion of vision, we discussed the special role the retina and the photoreceptors play in the transduction of light. In hearing, specific structures in the inner ear are involved in the transduction of sounds, they are the *hair cells* found on the *organ of Corti*.

The inner ear is a snail-shaped structure called the **cochlea**, which is filled with fluid. When the oval window vibrates, it causes the fluid in the cochlea to vibrate. This fluid surrounds a membrane running through the middle of the cochlea called the *basilar membrane*.

The *basilar membrane* is the resting place of the organ of Corti, which contains the receptor cells for the sense of hearing. When the basilar membrane vibrates, it vibrates

pinna
the visible part of the ear.

auditory canal
short tunnel that runs from the pinna to the eardrum.

cochlea
snail-shaped structure of the inner ear that is filled with fluid.

---

*funneling: moving to a focal point.

the organ of Corti, causing it to brush against a membrane above it. On the organ of Corti are special cells called hair cells, which are the receptors for sound. When these auditory receptors or hair cells are bent up against the other membrane, it causes them to send a neural message through the **auditory nerve** (which contains the axons of all the receptor neurons) and into the brain, where after passing through the thalamus, the auditory cortex will interpret the sounds (the transformation of the vibrations of sound into neural messages is transduction). The louder the sound in the outside world, the stronger the vibrations that stimulate more of those hair cells—which the brain interprets as loudness.

> 💬 I think I have it straight—but all of that just explains how soft and loud sounds get to the brain from the outside. How do we hear different kinds of sounds, like high pitches and low pitches?

3.8 Perceiving Pitch

3.8 Summarize three theories of how the brain processes information about pitch.

Pitch refers to how high or low a sound is. For example, the bass beats in the music pounding through the wall of your apartment from the neighbors next door are low pitch, whereas the scream of a 2-year-old child is a very high pitch. *Very* high. There are three primary theories about how the brain receives information about pitch.

PLACE THEORY The oldest of the three theories, **place theory**, is based on an idea proposed in 1863 by Hermann von Helmholtz and elaborated on and modified by Georg von Békésy, beginning with experiments first published in 1928 (Békésy, 1960). In this theory, the pitch a person hears depends on where the hair cells that are stimulated are located on the organ of Corti. For example, if the person is hearing a high-pitched sound, all of the hair cells near the oval window will be stimulated, but if the sound is low pitched, all of the hair cells that are stimulated will be located farther away on the organ of Corti.

FREQUENCY THEORY **Frequency theory**, developed by Ernest Rutherford in 1886, states that pitch is related to how fast the basilar membrane vibrates. The faster this membrane vibrates, the higher the pitch; the slower it vibrates, the lower the pitch. (In this theory, all of the auditory neurons would be firing at the same time.)

So which of these first two theories is right? It turns out that both are right—up to a point. For place theory to be correct, the basilar membrane has to vibrate unevenly—which it does when the frequency of the sound is *above* 1,000 Hz. For frequency theory to be correct, the neurons associated with the hair cells would have to fire as fast as the basilar membrane vibrates. This only works up to 1,000 Hz, because neurons don't appear to fire at exactly the same time and rate when frequencies are faster than 1,000 times per second. Not to mention the maximum firing rate for neurons is approximately 1,000 times per second due to the refractory period. See Learning Objective 2.2.

VOLLEY PRINCIPLE Frequency theory works for low pitches, and place theory works for moderate to high pitches. Is there another explanation? Yes, and it is a third theory, developed by Ernest Wever and Charles Bray, called the **volley principle** (Wever, 1949; Wever & Bray, 1930), which appears to account for pitches from about 400 Hz up to about 4,000 Hz. In this explanation, groups of auditory neurons take turns firing in a process called *volleying*. If a person hears a tone of about 3,000 Hz, it means that three groups of neurons have taken turns sending the message to the brain—the first group for the first 1,000 Hz, the second group for the next 1,000 Hz, and so on.

3.9 Types of Hearing Impairments

3.9 Identify types of hearing impairment and treatment options for each.

Hearing impairment is the term used to refer to difficulties in hearing. A person can be partially hearing impaired or totally hearing impaired, and the treatment for hearing loss will vary according to the reason for the impairment.

---

auditory nerve
bundle of axons from the hair cells in the inner ear.

pitch
psychological experience of sound that corresponds to the frequency of the sound waves; higher frequencies are perceived as higher pitches.

place theory
theory of pitch that states that different pitches are experienced by the stimulation of hair cells in different locations on the organ of Corti.

frequency theory
theory of pitch that states that pitch is related to the speed of vibrations in the basilar membrane.

volley principle
theory of pitch that states that frequencies from about 400 Hz to 4,000 Hz cause the hair cells (auditory neurons) to fire in a volley pattern, or take turns in firing.

AP 3.G Explain common sensory conditions.

CONDUCTION HEARING IMPAIRMENT *Conduction hearing impairment*, or conductive hearing loss, refers to problems with the mechanics of the outer or middle ear and means that sound vibrations cannot be passed from the eardrum to the cochlea. The cause might be a damaged eardrum or damage to the bones of the middle ear (usually from an infection). In this kind of impairment, the causes can often be treated, for example, hearing aids may be of some use in restoring hearing.

NERVE HEARING IMPAIRMENT In *nerve hearing impairment*, or sensorineural hearing loss, the problem lies either in the inner ear or in the auditory pathways and cortical areas of the brain. This is the most common type of permanent hearing loss. Normal aging causes loss of hair cells in the cochlea, and exposure to loud noises can damage hair cells. *Tinnitus* is a fancy word for an extremely annoying ringing in one's ears, and it can also be caused by infections or loud noises—including loud music in headphones. Prolonged exposure to loud noises further leads to permanent damage and hearing loss, so you might want to turn the volume down!

Because the damage is to the nerves or the brain, nerve hearing impairment cannot typically be helped with ordinary hearing aids, which are basically sound amplifiers, or the hearing aids are not enough. A technique for restoring some hearing to those with irreversible nerve hearing impairment makes use of an electronic device called a *cochlear implant*. This device sends signals from a microphone worn behind the ear to a sound processor worn on the belt or in a pocket, which then translates those signals into electrical stimuli that are sent to a series of electrodes implanted directly into the cochlea, allowing transduction to take place and stimulating the auditory nerve (see **Figure 3.13**). The brain then processes the electrode information as sound.

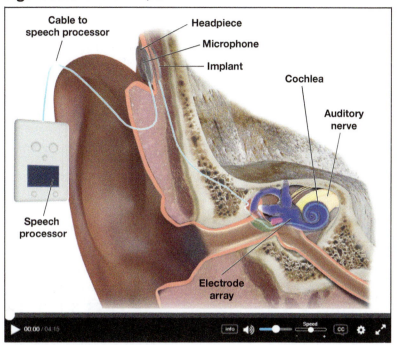

Figure 3.13 Cochlear Implant

Watch the **Video** at **MyLab Psychology**

In a cochlear implant, a microphone implanted just behind the ear picks up sound from the surrounding environment. A speech processor, attached to the implant and worn outside the body, selects and arranges the sound picked up by the microphone. The implant itself is a transmitter and receiver, converting the signals from the speech processor into electrical impulses collected by the electrode array in the cochlea and then sent to the brain.

THINKING CRITICALLY 3.1

How might someone who has had total hearing loss from birth react to being able to hear?

Concept Map L.O. 3.7, 3.8, 3.9

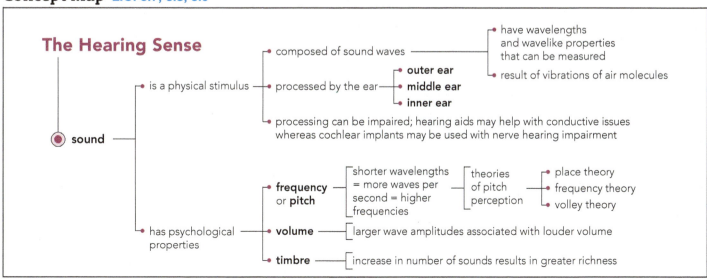

Practice Quiz How much do you remember?

Pick the best answer.

1. The part of the ear that can be seen is also called the _____.
   a. cochlea
   b. oval window
   c. pinna
   d. tectorial membrane
   e. organ of Corti

2. The oval window is found in what part of the ear?
   a. middle ear
   b. inner ear
   c. The oval window is not a structure of the ear.
   d. pinna
   e. outer ear

3. Which theory of hearing cannot adequately account for pitches above 1,000 Hz?
   a. volley
   b. habituation
   c. frequency
   d. adaptive
   e. place

4. Imari has suffered minor damage to the bones in his left middle ear. What treatment, if any, might help restore his hearing?
   a. None; the bones of the middle ear cannot be damaged.
   b. Such damage is permanent and cannot be remedied.
   c. A cochlear implant might help restore his hearing.
   d. Both a hearing aid and a cochlear implant will be needed.
   e. A hearing aid might help restore his hearing.

5. Which is considered the most common type of permanent hearing loss?
   a. frequency-based hearing loss
   b. conductive hearing loss
   c. location-based hearing loss
   d. sensorineural hearing loss
   e. psychological hearing loss

AP 3.J Describe taste and smell processes, including the specific nature of energy transduction, relevant anatomical structures, and specialized pathways in the brain for each of the senses.

3.10–3.11 Chemical Senses: It Tastes Good and Smells Even Better

The sense of taste (taste in food, not taste in clothing or friends) and the sense of smell are very closely related. As Dr. Alan Hirsch, a researcher on smell and taste, explains in the video *Smell and Taste*, about 90 percent of what we deem taste is really smell. Have you ever noticed that when your nose is all stopped up, your sense of taste is affected, too? That's because the sense of taste is really a combination of taste and smell.

More on that later; for now let's start with the taste buds.

3.10 Gustation: How We Taste the World

3.10 Explain how the sense of taste works.

Our food preferences, or aversions, start to form very early in life. Taste is one of our earliest developed senses. Research suggests developing babies are exposed to substances the mother inhales or digests, and these impart flavor to the amniotic fluid, which the baby also ingests. Along with exposure to different flavors early in life after we are born, these experiences may affect food choices and nutritional status, that is, picking certain foods over others, for a long time to come (Beauchamp & Mennella, 2011; Mennella & Trabulsi, 2012).

TASTE BUDS *Taste buds* are the common name for the taste receptor cells, special kinds of neurons found in the mouth that are responsible for the sense of taste, or **gustation**. Most taste buds are located on the tongue, but there are a few on the roof of the mouth, the cheeks, under the tongue, and in the throat. How sensitive people are to various tastes depends on how many taste buds they have; some people have only around 500, whereas others have 20 times that number. The latter are called "supertasters" and need far less seasoning in their food than those with fewer taste buds (Bartoshuk, 1993).

Watch Smell and Taste

👁 **Watch** the **Video** at **MyLab Psychology**

gustation
the sensation of a taste.

💬 So taste buds are those little bumps I can see when I look closely at my tongue?

No, those "bumps" are called *papillae*, and the taste buds line the walls of these papillae (see **Figure 3.14**).

Each taste bud has about 20 receptors that are very similar to the receptor sites on receiving neurons at the synapse. See Learning Objective 2.3. In fact, the receptors on taste buds work exactly like receptor sites on neurons—they receive molecules of various substances that fit into the receptor like a key into a lock. Taste is often called a chemical sense because it works with the molecules of foods people eat in the same way the neural receptors work with neurotransmitters. When the molecules (dissolved in saliva) fit into the receptors, a signal is fired to the brain, which then interprets the taste sensation.

💬 What happens to the taste buds when I burn my tongue? Do they repair themselves? I know when I have burned my tongue, I can't taste much for a while, but the taste comes back.

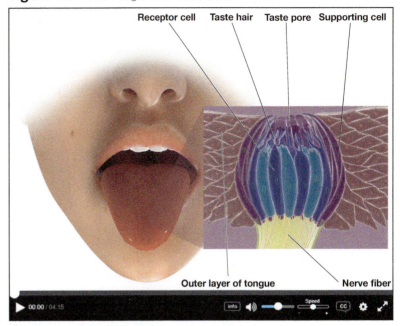

Figure 3.14 The Tongue and Taste Buds

▶ Watch the Video at MyLab Psychology

Taste buds are located inside the papillae of the tongue and are composed of small cells that send signals to the brain when stimulated by molecules of food.

In general, the taste receptors get such a workout that they have to be replaced every 10 to 14 days (McLaughlin & Margolskee, 1994). And when the tongue is burned, the damaged cells no longer work. As time goes on, those cells get replaced and the taste sense comes back.

THE FIVE BASIC TASTES In 1916, German psychologist Hans Henning proposed that there are four primary tastes: sweet, sour, salty, and bitter. Lindemann (1996) supported the idea of a fifth kind of taste receptor that detects a pleasant "brothy" taste associated with foods like chicken soup, tuna, kelp, cheese, and soy products, among others. Lindemann proposed that this fifth taste be called *umami*, a Japanese word first coined in 1908 by Dr. Kikunae Ikeda of Tokyo Imperial University to describe the taste. Dr. Ikeda had succeeded in isolating the substance in kelp that generated the sensation of umami—glutamate (Beyreuther et al., 2007). See Learning Objective 2.3. Glutamate not only exists in the foods listed earlier but is also present in human breast milk and is the reason that the seasoning MSG—monosodium *glutamate*—adds a pleasant flavor to foods. Although not yet widely accepted, researchers have recently suggested there may be yet another basic taste. The proposed name for this potential sixth taste is *oleogustus*, the taste of fatty acids in the food we eat (Running et al., 2015; Running et al., 2017).

Although researchers used to believe that certain tastes were located on certain places on the tongue, it is now known that all of the taste sensations are processed all over the tongue (Bartoshuk, 1993). The taste information is sent to the gustatory cortex, found in the front part of the *insula* and the *frontal operculum* (see **Figure 3.15**). These areas are involved in the conscious perception of taste, whereas the texture, or "mouth-feel," of foods is processed in the somatosensory cortex of the parietal lobe (Buck & Bargmann, 2013; Pritchard, 2012; Shepherd, 2012). The cortical taste areas also project to parts of the limbic system, which helps explain why tastes can be used for both positive and negative reinforcement (Pritchard, 2012). See Learning Objective 5.5. The five taste sensations work

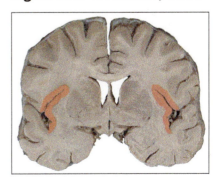

Figure 3.15 The Gustatory Cortex

The gustatory cortex is found in the anterior insula and frontal operculum. The insula is an area of cortex covered by folds of overlying cortex, and each fold is an operculum. In the coronal section, see Figure 2.5, of a human brain above the gustatory cortex is found in the regions colored a light red.

together, along with the sense of smell and the texture, temperature, and "heat" of foods, to produce thousands of taste sensations, which are further affected by our culture, personal expectations, and past learning experiences. For example, boiled peanuts are not an uncommon snack in parts of the southern United States, but the idea of a warm, soft and mushy, slightly salty peanut may not be appealing in other parts of the country. Males and females respond differently to taste, and there are differences in perceived taste intensity among different ethnic groups (Bartoshuk et al., 1994; Williams et al., 2016). Why might this be relevant? As the researchers pointed out, taste perception and individual preferences influence what we choose to eat and the choices we make when modifying our diet, such as in the prevention or treatment of obesity (Williams et al., 2016).

Just as individuals and groups can vary on their food preferences, they can also vary on level of perceived sweetness. For example, obese individuals have been found to experience less sweetness than individuals who are not obese; foods that are both sweet and high in fat tend to be especially attractive to individuals who are obese (Bartoshuk et al., 2006). Such differences (as well as genetic variations like the supertasters) complicate direct comparison of food preferences. One possible solution is to have individuals rate taste in terms of an unrelated "standard" sensory experience of known intensity, such as the brightness of a light or loudness of a sound or preference in terms of all pleasurable experiences, and not just taste (Bartoshuk et al., 2005; Snyder & Bartoshuk, 2009).

Turning our attention back to how things taste for us as individuals, have you ever noticed that when you have a cold, food tastes very bland? Everything becomes bland or muted because you can taste only sweet, salty, bitter, sour, and umami—and because your nose is stuffed up with a cold, you don't get all the enhanced variations of those tastes that come from the sense of smell.

3.11 The Sense of Scents: Olfaction

3.11 Explain how the sense of smell works.

Like the sense of taste, the sense of smell is a chemical sense. The ability to smell odors is called **olfaction**, or the **olfactory sense**.

The outer part of the nose serves the same purpose for odors that the pinna and ear canal serve for sounds: Both are merely ways to collect the sensory information and get it to the part of the body that will translate it into neural signals.

The part of the olfactory system that transduces odors—turns odors into signals the brain can understand—is located at the top of the nasal passages. This area of olfactory receptor cells is only about an inch square in each cavity yet contains about 10 million olfactory receptors (see **Figure 3.16**).

OLFACTORY RECEPTOR CELLS The *olfactory receptor cells* each have about a half dozen to a dozen little "hairs," called *cilia*, that project into the cavity. Like taste buds, there are receptor sites on these hair cells that send signals to the brain when stimulated by the molecules of substances that are in the air moving past them.

> 💬 Wait a minute—you mean that when I can smell something like a skunk, there are little particles of skunk odor IN my nose?

Yes. When a person is sniffing something, the sniffing serves to move molecules of whatever the person is trying to smell into the nose and into the nasal cavities. That's okay when it's the smell of baking bread, apple pie, flowers, and the like, but when it's skunk, rotten eggs, dead animals—well, try not to think about it too much.

Olfactory receptors are like taste buds in another way, too. Olfactory receptors also have to be replaced as they naturally die off, about every 5–8 weeks. Unlike the taste buds, there are many more than 5 types of olfactory receptors—in fact, there are at least 1,000 of them.

olfaction (olfactory sense)
the sensation of smell.

Figure 3.16 The Olfactory Receptors

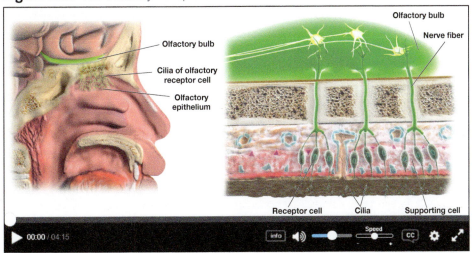

👁 Watch the Video at MyLab Psychology

(Left) A cross-section of the nose and mouth. This drawing shows the nerve fibers inside the nasal cavity that carry information about smell directly to the olfactory bulb just under the frontal lobe of the brain (shown in green). (Right) A diagram of the cells in the nose that process smell. The olfactory bulb is on top. Notice the cilia, tiny hairlike cells that project into the nasal cavity. These are the receptors for the sense of smell.

Signals from the olfactory receptors in the nasal cavity do not follow the same path as the signals from all the other senses. Vision, hearing, taste, and touch all pass through the thalamus and then on to the area of the cortex that processes that particular sensory information. But the sense of smell has its own special place in the brain—the olfactory bulbs.

THE OLFACTORY BULBS The **olfactory bulbs** are located right on top of the sinus cavity on each side of the brain directly beneath the frontal lobes. (Refer to Figure 3.16.) The olfactory receptors send their neural signals directly up to these bulbs, bypassing the thalamus, the relay center for all other sensory information. The olfactory information is then sent from the olfactory bulbs to higher cortical areas, including the primary olfactory cortex (the *piriform cortex*), the orbitofrontal cortex, and the amygdala (remember from Chapter Two that the orbitofrontal cortex and amygdala play important roles in emotion). See Learning Objectives 2.7 and 2.8.

olfactory bulbs
two bulb-like projections of the brain located just above the sinus cavity and just below the frontal lobes that receive information from the olfactory receptor cells.

Concept Map L.O. 3.10, 3.11

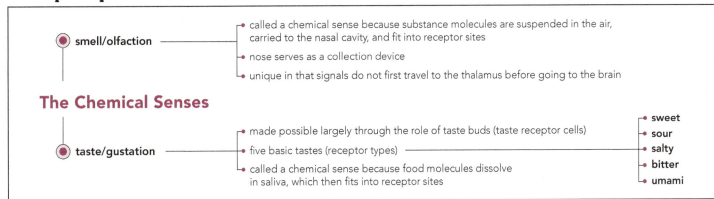

Practice Quiz How much do you remember?

Pick the best answer.

1. Taste is often called a(n) _____ sense because it works with the molecules of foods that people eat.
   a. chemical
   b. psychological
   c. physical
   d. electrical
   e. mechanical

2. Research has found that taste information is sent to the _____.
   a. medial occipital lobe
   b. pons and medulla
   c. insula and frontal operculum
   d. cerebellum and parietal lobe
   e. suprachiasmatic nucleus

3. How often are olfactory receptors replaced by new olfactory receptors?
   a. every 30 days
   b. every 5–8 weeks
   c. every 2–3 days
   d. every 12–24 hours
   e. every 120 days

4. Olfactory receptors project directly to the _____ and are unique in that signals do not first connect to the thalamus.
   a. sensory association cortex
   b. hypothalamus
   c. occipital lobe
   d. gustatory cortex
   e. olfactory bulbs

AP 3.K Describe sensory processes, including the specific nature of energy transduction, relevant anatomical structures, and specialized pathways in the brain for each of the body senses.

3.12–3.13 The Other Senses: What the Body Knows

So far, this chapter has covered vision, hearing, taste, and smell. That leaves touch. What is thought of as the sense of touch is really several sensations, originating in several different places in—and on—the body. It's really more accurate to refer to these as the body senses, or **somesthetic senses**. The first part of that word, *soma*, means "body" (as mentioned in Chapter Two); the second part, *esthetic*, means "feeling," hence the name. We will discuss four somesthetic sense systems.

3.12 Somesthetic Senses

3.12 Describe how we experience the sensations of touch, pressure, temperature, and pain.

Here's a good trivia question: What organ of the body is about 20 square feet in size? The answer is the skin. Skin is an organ. Its purposes include more than simply keeping bodily fluids in and germs out; skin also receives and transmits information from the outside world to the central nervous system (specifically, to the somatosensory cortex). See Learning Objective 2.8. Information about light touch, deeper pressure, hot, cold, and even pain is collected by special receptors in the skin's layers.

TYPES OF SENSORY RECEPTORS IN THE SKIN There are about half a dozen different receptors in the layers of the skin (see **Figure 3.17**). Some of them will respond to only one kind of sensation. For example, the *Pacinian corpuscles* are just beneath the skin and respond to changes in pressure. There are nerve endings that wrap around the ends of the hair follicles, a fact people may be well aware of when they tweeze their eyebrows or when someone pulls their hair. These nerve endings are sensitive to both pain and touch. There are *free nerve endings* just beneath the uppermost layer of the skin that respond to changes in temperature and to pressure—and to pain.

💬 How exactly does pain work? Why is it that sometimes I feel pain deep inside? Are there pain receptors there, too?

Yes, there are pain nerve fibers in the internal organs as well as receptors for pressure. How else would people have a stomachache or intestinal* pain—or get that full feeling of pressure when they've eaten too much or their bladder is full?

The sense of touch allows individuals that are blind to "read" a Braille book with their fingers. The fingertips are extremely sensitive to fine differences in texture, allowing readers to distinguish between small dots representing the different letters of the alphabet.

somesthetic senses
the body senses consisting of the skin senses, the kinesthetic sense, and the vestibular senses.

---

*intestinal: having to do with the tubes in the body that digest food and process waste material.

There are actually different types of pain. There are receptors that detect pain (and pressure) in the organs, a type of pain called *visceral pain*. Pain sensations in the skin, muscles, tendons, and joints are carried on large nerve fibers and are called *somatic pain*. Somatic pain is the body's warning system that something is being or is about to be damaged and tends to be sharp and fast. Another type of somatic pain is carried on small nerve fibers and is slower and more of a general ache. This somatic pain acts as a kind of reminder system, keeping people from further injury by reminding them that the body has already been damaged. For example, if you hit your thumb with a hammer, the immediate pain sensation is of the first kind—sharp, fast, and bright. But later the bruised tissue simply aches, letting you know to take it easy on that thumb.

PAIN: GATE-CONTROL THEORY One explanation for how the sensation of pain works is called *gate-control theory*, first proposed by Ronald Melzack and Patrick Wall (1965) and later refined and expanded (Melzack & Wall, 1996). In this theory, the pain signals must pass through a "gate" located in the spinal cord. The activity of the gate can be closed by nonpain signals coming into the spinal cord from the body and by signals coming from the brain. The gate is not a physical structure but instead represents the relative balance in neural activity of cells in the spinal cord that receive information from the body and then send information to the brain. Additional research has revealed that the activity of relay centers in the brain can also be influenced, and the exact locations and mechanisms are still being investigated. The video *Gate-Control Theory* provides a simulation of how pain signals travel along the spinal cord.

Stimulation of the pain receptor cells releases a neurotransmitter and neuromodulator called *substance P* (for peptide, not "pain"). Substance P released into the spinal cord activates other neurons that send their messages through spinal gates (opened by the pain signal). From the spinal cord, the message goes to the brain, activating cells in the thalamus, somatosensory cortex, areas of the frontal lobes, and the limbic system. The brain then interprets the pain information and sends signals that either open the spinal gates farther, causing a greater experience of pain, or close them, dampening the pain. Of course, this decision by the brain is influenced by the psychological aspects of the pain-causing stimulus. Anxiety, fear, and helplessness intensify pain, whereas laughter, distraction, and a sense of control can diminish it. (This is why people might bruise themselves and not know it if they were concentrating on something else.) Pain can also be affected by competing signals from other skin senses, which is why rubbing a sore spot can reduce the feeling of pain.

Those same psychological aspects can also influence the release of the *endorphins*, the body's natural version of morphine. See Learning Objective 2.3. Endorphins can inhibit the transmission of pain signals in the brain, and in the spinal cord they can inhibit the release of substance P.

Figure 3.17 Cross Section of the Skin and Its Receptors

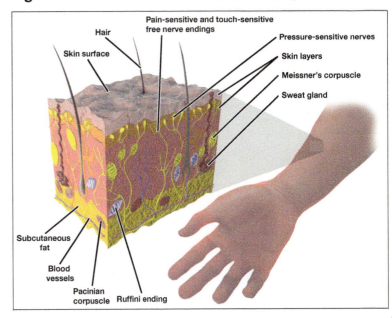

The skin is composed of several types of cells that process pain, pressure, and temperature. Some of these cells are wrapped around the ends of the hairs on the skin and are sensitive to touch on the hair itself, whereas others are located near the surface and still others just under the top layer of tissue.

Watch Gate Control Theory of Pain

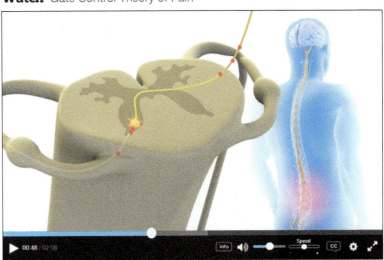

Watch the Video at MyLab Psychology

💬 I've always heard that women are able to stand more pain than men. Is that true?

It depends. Some research has suggested women report and subjectively feel some types of pain more intensely than men, along with greater subjective functional impairment (Gautschi et al., 2016). However, when objective measures are used, those differences disappear (Gautschi et al., 2016). One systematic review of 10 years of laboratory research suggests there still hasn't been a clear and consistent pattern of sex differences identified, even when using experimental methods that best mimic chronic types of pain (Racine et al., 2012). When differences are present, it appears that social and cognitive factors may help explain at least some reported differences (McGraw, 2016; Racine et al., 2012). For example, men have been shown to cope better with many kinds of pain, possibly because men are often found to have a stronger belief than women that they can (or should) control their pain by their own efforts (Jackson et al., 2002).

PAIN DISORDERS People may not like pain, but its function as a warning system is vitally important. There are people who are born without the ability to feel pain, rare conditions called *congenital analgesia* and *congenital insensitivity to pain with anhidrosis (CIPA)*. Children with these disorders cannot feel pain when they cut or scrape themselves, leading to an increased risk of infection when the cut goes untreated (Mogil, 1999). They fear nothing—which can be a horrifying trial for the parents and teachers of such a child. These disorders affect the neural pathways that carry pain, heat, and cold sensations. (Those with CIPA have an additional disruption in the body's heat–cold sensing perspiration system [*anhidrosis*], so that the person is unable to cool off the body by sweating.)

A condition called *phantom limb pain* occurs when a person who has had an arm or leg removed sometimes "feels" pain in the missing limb (Nikolajsen & Jensen, 2001; Woodhouse, 2005). As many as 50 to 80 percent of people who have had amputations experience various sensations: burning, shooting pains, or pins-and-needles sensations where the amputated limb used to be. Once believed to be a psychological problem, some now believe it is caused by the traumatic injury to the nerves during amputation (Ephraim et al., 2005). Other research suggests it may be due to maladaptive neuroplasticity, or reorganization of some parts of the somatosensory cortex (Flor et al., 1995; Karl et al., 2001; Raffin et al., 2016), and yet others suggest this may not be the cause for the pain, at least not in all individuals (Makin et al., 2015).

THINKING CRITICALLY 3.2

What kinds of changes in your life would you have to make if you suddenly could not feel pain?

3.13 Body Movement and Position

3.13 Describe the systems that tell us about balance and position and movement of our bodies.

Besides the systems already covered, other senses tell us about our body. *Kinesthesia* and *proprioception*, awareness of body movement and position, are based on somesthetic information. Information affecting our balance comes from the vestibular system, which informs us about head and whole-body movement and position.

KINESTHETIC AND PROPRIOCEPTIVE SENSES Special receptors located in the muscles, tendons, and joints provide information about body movement and the movement and location of the arms, legs, and so forth in relation to one another. Some of these receptors increase awareness of the body's own movements, or **kinesthesia**, from the Greek words *kinein* ("to move") and *aesthesis* ("sensation"). Changes in the skin stretching as body parts move also provide kinesthetic information.

These special receptors also provide proprioceptive information, letting us know where our body parts are and their position in space. This awareness is called **proprioception**. When you close your eyes and raise your hand above your head, you know where your hand is because these receptors, called proprioceptors, tell you about joint movement or the muscles stretching or contracting.

If you have ever gotten sick from traveling in a moving vehicle, it has not been because of these proprioceptors. The culprits are actually special structures in the ear that tell us about the position of the body in relation to the ground and movement of the head that make up the **vestibular sense**—the sense of balance.

THE VESTIBULAR SENSE The name of this particular sense comes from a Latin word that means "entrance" or "chamber." The structures for this sense are located in the innermost chamber of the ear. There are two kinds of vestibular organs, the otolith organs and the semicircular canals.

The *otolith organs* are tiny sacs found just above the cochlea. These sacs contain a gelatin-like fluid within which tiny crystals are suspended (much like pieces of fruit in a bowl of Jell-O). The head moves and the crystals cause the fluid to vibrate, setting off some tiny hairlike receptors on the inner surface of the sac, telling the person that he or she is moving forward, backward, sideways, or up and down. (It's pretty much the way the cochlea works but with movement being the stimulus instead of sound vibrations.)

The *semicircular canals* are three somewhat circular tubes that are also filled with fluid that will stimulate hairlike receptors when rotated. Having three tubes allows one to be located in each of the three planes of motion. Remember learning in geometry class about the x-, y-, and z-axes? Those are the three planes through which the body can rotate, and, when it does, it sets off the receptors in these canals. When you spin around and then stop, the fluid in the horizontal canal is still rotating and will make you feel dizzy because your body is telling you that you are still moving, but your eyes are telling you that you have stopped. The horizontal canals are also critical in helping us navigate our environments, as they provide important information about which direction we are facing (Valerio & Taube, 2016).

This disagreement between what the eyes say and what the body says is pretty much what causes *motion sickness*, the tendency to get nauseated when in a moving vehicle, especially one with an irregular movement. Normally, the vestibular sense coordinates with the other senses. But for some people, the information from the eyes may conflict a little too much with the vestibular organs, and dizziness, nausea, and disorientation are the result. This explanation of motion sickness is known as **sensory conflict theory** (Oman, 1990; Reason & Brand, 1975). The dizziness is the most likely cause of the nausea. Many poisons make a person dizzy, and the most evolutionarily adaptive thing to do is to expel the poison. Even without any poison in a case of motion sickness, the nausea occurs anyway (Treisman, 1977).

One way some people overcome motion sickness is to focus on a distant point or object. This provides visual information to the person about how he or she is moving, bringing the sensory input into agreement with the visual input. This is also how ballerinas and ice skaters manage not to get sick when turning rapidly and repeatedly—they focus their eyes at least once on some fixed object every so many turns.

Astronauts, who travel in low-gravity conditions, can get a related condition called space motion sickness (SMS). This affects about 60 percent of those who travel in space,

kinesthesia

the awareness of body movement

proprioception

awareness of where the body and body parts are located in relation to each other in space and to the ground.

vestibular sense

the awareness of the balance, position, and movement of the head and body through space in relation to gravity's pull.

sensory conflict theory

an explanation of motion sickness in which the information from the eyes conflicts with the information from the vestibular senses, resulting in dizziness, nausea, and other physical discomfort.

typically for about the first week of space travel. After that time of adjustment, the astronauts are able to adapt and the symptoms diminish. Repeated exposure to some environment that causes motion sickness—whether it is space, a car, a train, or some other vehicle—is actually one of the best ways to overcome the symptoms (Hu & Stern, 1999). Researchers are also looking at ways to help individuals learn to control their physiological responses to help prevent motion sickness. Both sympathetic and parasympathetic nervous system activity changes have been noted in motion sickness. See Learning Objective 2.12. By teaching astronauts to control their physiological responses through *autogenic training*, a specific relaxation technique, and **biofeedback** training, they may be less susceptible to motion sickness. See Learning Objective 5.9. For example, the United States National Aeronautics and Space Administration (NASA) has identified a set of potential risk factors for astronauts during reentry and landing of the newly proposed Orion spacecraft, including spatial disorientation, motion sickness, and impaired performance. In turn, researchers are exploring the use of Autogenic-Feedback Training Exercise (AFTE), a combination of biofeedback and autogenic training, as a possible strategy for Orion astronauts and have found positive results after a single two-hour training session (Cowings et al., 2018).

biofeedback
using feedback about biological conditions to bring involuntary responses, such as blood pressure and relaxation, under voluntary control.

Concept Map L.O. 3.12, 3.13

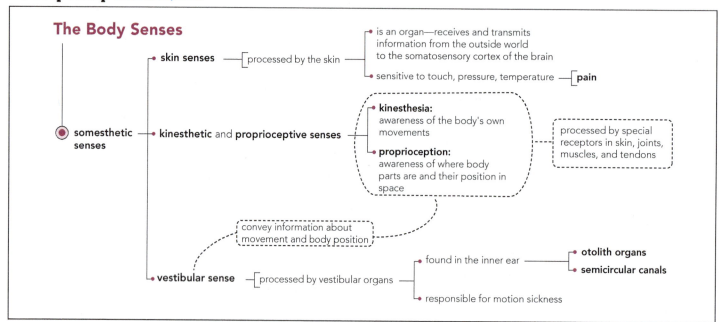

Practice Quiz   How much do you remember?

Pick the best answer.

1. _____ are tactile receptors that are located just beneath the skin and respond to changes in pressure.
   a. Visceral receptors
   b. Free nerve endings
   c. Oligodendrocytes
   d. Pacinian corpuscles
   e. Tactile interneurons

2. In gate-control theory, substance P _____.
   a. is unrelated to pain
   b. opens the spinal gates for pain
   c. is responsible for phantom limb pain
   d. is similar in function to endorphins
   e. closes the spinal gates for pain

3. When you close your eyes and raise your hand above your head, you know where your hand is due to information from _____.
   a. semicircular canals
   b. visceral receptors
   c. horizontal canals
   d. otolith organs
   e. proprioceptors

4. Motion sickness often results from conflicting signals sent from the _____ and from the _____.
   a. extremities, brain
   b. conscious, unconscious
   c. eyes, vestibular organs
   d. brain, internal organs
   e. eyes, visceral organs

3.14–3.16 The ABCs of Perception

Perception is the method by which the brain takes all the sensations a person experiences at any given moment and allows them to be interpreted in some meaningful fashion. Perception has some individuality to it. For example, two people might be looking at a cloud, and while one thinks it's shaped like a horse, the other thinks it's more like a cow. They both *see* the same cloud, but they *perceive* that cloud differently.

3.14 How We Organize Our Perceptions

3.14 Describe how perceptual constancies and the Gestalt principles account for common perceptual experiences.

As individual as perception might be, some similarities exist in how people perceive the world around them. As such, there are some circumstances during which stimuli are seemingly automatically perceived in almost the same way by various individuals.

THE CONSTANCIES: SIZE, SHAPE, AND BRIGHTNESS One form of perceptual constancy* is **size constancy**, the tendency to interpret an object as always being the same size, regardless of its distance from the viewer (or the size of the image it casts on the retina). So if an object normally perceived to be about 6 feet tall appears very small on the retina, it will be interpreted as being very far away.

Another perceptual constancy is the tendency to interpret the shape of an object as constant, even when it changes on the retina. This **shape constancy** is why a person still perceives a coin as a circle even if it is held at an angle that makes it appear to be an oval on the retina. Dinner plates on a table are also seen as round, even though from the angle of viewing they are oval (see **Figure 3.18**).

A third form of perceptual constancy is **brightness constancy**, the tendency to perceive the apparent brightness of an object as the same even when the light conditions change. If a person is wearing black pants and a white shirt, for example, in broad daylight the shirt will appear to be much brighter than the pants. But if the sun is covered by thick clouds, even though the pants and shirt have less light to reflect than previously, the shirt will still appear to be just as much brighter than the pants as before—because the different amount of light reflected from each piece of clothing is still the same difference as before (Zeki, 2001).

THE GESTALT PRINCIPLES Remember the discussion of the Gestalt theorists in Chapter One? Their original focus on human perception can still be seen in certain basic principles today, including the Gestalt tendency to group objects and perceive whole shapes.

FIGURE–GROUND RELATIONSHIPS Take a look at the drawing of the cube in **Figure 3.19**. Which face of the cube is in the front? Look again—do the planes and corners of the cube seem to shift as you look at it?

This is called the "Necker cube." It has been around officially since 1832, when Louis Albert Necker, a Swiss scientist who was studying the structure of crystals, first drew it in his published papers. The problem with this cube is that there are conflicting sets of depth cues, so the viewer is never really sure which plane or edge is in the back and which is in the front—the visual presentation of the cube seems to keep reversing its planes and edges.

A similar illusion can be seen in **Figure 3.20**. In this picture, the viewer can switch perception back and forth from two faces looking at each other to the outline of a goblet in the middle. Which is the figure in front and which is the background?

Figure–ground relationships refer to the tendency to perceive objects or figures as existing on a background. People seem to have a preference for picking out figures from backgrounds even as early as birth. The illusions in Figures 3.19 and 3.20 are **reversible figures**, in which the figure and the ground seem to switch back and forth.

---

*constancy: something that remains the same; the property of remaining stable and unchanging.

AP 3.A Describe general principles of organizing and integrating sensation to promote stable awareness of the external world.

Figure 3.18 Shape Constancy

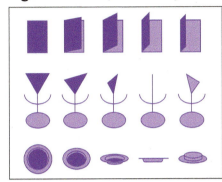

Three examples of shape constancy are shown here. The opening door is actually many different shapes, yet we still see it as basically a rectangular door. We do the same thing with a triangle and a circle—and, although when we look at them from different angles they cast differently shaped images on our retina, we experience them as a triangle and a circle because of shape constancy.

perception
the method by which the sensations experienced at any given moment are interpreted and organized in some meaningful fashion.

size constancy
the tendency to interpret an object as always being the same actual size, regardless of its distance.

shape constancy
the tendency to interpret the shape of an object as being constant, even when its shape changes on the retina.

brightness constancy
the tendency to perceive the apparent brightness of an object as the same even when the light conditions change.

figure–ground
the tendency to perceive objects, or figures, as existing on a background.

reversible figures
visual illusions in which the figure and ground can be reversed.

Figure 3.19 The Necker Cube

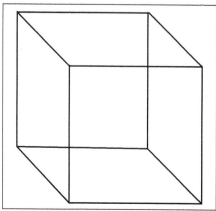

This is an example of a reversible figure. It can also be described as an ambiguous figure, since it is not clear which pattern should predominate.

Figure 3.20 Figure-Ground Illusion

What do you see when you look at this picture? Is it a wine goblet? Or two faces looking at each other? This is an example in which the figure and the ground seem to "switch" each time you look at the picture.

PROXIMITY Another very simple rule of perception is the tendency to perceive objects that are close to one another as part of the same grouping, a principle called **proximity**, or "nearness" (see **Figure 3.21**).

SIMILARITY **Similarity** refers to the tendency to perceive things that look similar as being part of the same group. When members of a sports team wear uniforms that are all the same color, it allows people viewing the game to perceive them as one group even when they are scattered around the field or court.

CLOSURE **Closure** is the tendency to complete figures that are incomplete. A talented artist can give the impression of an entire face with just a few cleverly placed strokes of the pen or brush—the viewers fill in the details.

CONTINUITY The principle of **continuity** is easier to see than it is to explain in words. It refers to the tendency to perceive things as simply as possible with a continuous pattern rather than with a complex, broken-up pattern. Look at Figure 3.21 for an example of continuity. Isn't it much easier to see the figure on the left as two wavy lines crossing each other than as the little sections in the diagrams to the right?

CONTIGUITY **Contiguity** isn't shown in Figure 3.21 because it involves not just nearness in space but also nearness in time. Basically, contiguity is the tendency to perceive two things that happen close together in time as related. Usually, the first occurring event is seen as causing the second event. Ventriloquists* make vocalizations without appearing to move their own mouths but move their dummy's mouth instead. The tendency to believe that the dummy is doing the talking is due largely to contiguity.

COMMON REGION AND ELEMENT CONNECTEDNESS There are other principles of perceptual grouping that were not one of the original principles. At least two have been added (and can be seen in Figure 3.21) by Stephen Palmer and colleagues (Palmer, 1992; Palmer & Rock, 1994). In *common region*, the tendency is to perceive objects that are in a common area or region as being in a group. In Figure 3.21, people could perceive the stars as one group and the circles as another on the basis of similarity. But the colored backgrounds so visibly define common regions that people instead perceive three groups—one of which has both stars and circles in it.

In *element connectedness*, the tendency to perceive objects that are connected overrides both elements of similarity and proximity (Brooks, 2015; Palmer & Rock, 1994). See the bottom of Figure 3.21.

*ventriloquist: an entertainer who, through the use of misdirection and skill, makes other objects, such as a dummy, appear to talk.

proximity
a Gestalt principle of perception; the tendency to perceive objects that are close to each other as part of the same grouping; physical or geographical nearness.

similarity
a Gestalt principle of perception; the tendency to perceive things that look similar to each other as being part of the same group.

closure
a Gestalt principle of perception; the tendency to complete figures that are incomplete.

continuity
a Gestalt principle of perception; the tendency to perceive things as simply as possible with a continuous pattern rather than with a complex, broken-up pattern.

contiguity
a Gestalt principle of perception; the tendency to perceive two things that happen close together in time as being related.

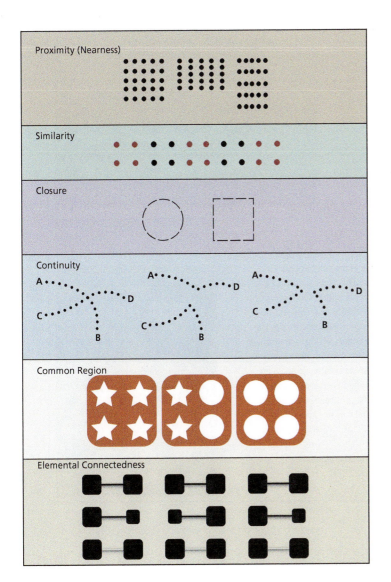

Figure 3.21 Gestalt Principles of Grouping

The Gestalt principles of grouping are shown here. These are the human tendency to organize isolated stimuli into groups on the basis of six characteristics: proximity, similarity, closure, continuity, common region, and elemental connectedness.

Proximity: The dots on the left can be seen as horizontal or vertical rows—neither organization dominates. But just by changing the proximity of certain dots, as in the other two examples, we experience the dots as vertical columns (middle) or horizontal rows (right).

Similarity: The similarity of color here makes you perceive these dots as forming black squares and color squares rather than two rows of black and colored dots.

Closure: Even though the lines are broken, we still see these figures as a circle and a square—an example of how we tend to "close" or "fill in" missing parts from what we know of the whole.

Continuity: Because of continuity, we are much more likely to see the figure on the left as being made up of two lines, A to B and C to D, than we are to see it as a figure made up of lines A to D and C to B or A to C and B to D.

Common Region: Similarity would suggest that people see two groups, stars and circles. But the colored backgrounds define a visible common region, and the tendency is to perceive three different groups.

Elemental Connectedness: Connecting the blocks forms pairs of items, overrides both the principles of proximity and similarity, and as you can see in the bottom set, is not dependent upon items being the same color.

Source: Based on Brooks (2015) and Palmer & Rock (1994).

3.15 Depth Perception

3.15 Explain how we perceive depth using both monocular and binocular cues.

The capability to see the world in three dimensions is called **depth perception**. It's a handy ability because without it you would have a hard time judging how far away objects are. How early in life do humans develop depth perception? It seems to develop very early in infancy, if it is not actually present at birth. People who have had sight restored have almost no ability to perceive depth if they were blind from birth. Depth perception, like the constancies, seems to be present in infants at a very young age. See Learning Objective 8.6.

Various cues exist for perceiving depth in the world. Some require the use of only one eye (**monocular cues**) and some are a result of the slightly different visual patterns that exist when the visual fields of both eyes are used (**binocular cues**).

MONOCULAR CUES Monocular cues are often referred to as **pictorial depth cues** because artists can use these cues to give the illusion of depth to paintings and drawings. Examples of these cues are discussed next and can be seen in **Figure 3.22**.

1. **Linear perspective:** When looking down a long interstate highway, the two sides of the highway appear to merge together in the distance. This tendency for lines that are actually parallel to *seem* to converge* on each other is called **linear perspective**.

depth perception
the ability to perceive the world in three dimensions.

monocular cues (pictorial depth cues)
cues for perceiving depth based on one eye only.

binocular cues
cues for perceiving depth based on both eyes.

linear perspective
monocular depth perception cue; the tendency for parallel lines to appear to converge on each other.

---
*converge: come together.

Figure 3.22 Examples of Pictorial Depth Cues

(a) Both the lines of the trees and the sides of the road appear to come together or converge in the distance. This is an example of *linear perspective*. (b) Notice how the larger pebbles in the foreground seem to give way to smaller and smaller pebbles near the middle of the picture. *Texture gradient* causes the viewer to assume that as the texture of the pebbles gets finer, the pebbles are getting farther away. (c) In *aerial* or *atmospheric perspective*, the farther away something is the hazier it appears because of fine particles in the air between the viewer and the object. Notice that the shed and grassy area in the foreground are in sharp focus while the mountain ranges are hazy and indistinct. (d) The depth cue of *relative size* appears in this photograph. Notice that the flowers in the distance appear much smaller than those in the foreground. Relative size causes smaller objects to be perceived as farther away from the viewer.

Sources: a) Grant Faint/ The Image Bank/Getty Images; b) Cherrill Rance/Shutterstock; c) Popova Valeriya/Shutterstock; d) Creative Eye/Mira.com

relative size
monocular depth perception cue; perception that occurs when objects that a person expects to be of a certain size appear to be small and are, therefore, assumed to be much farther away.

interposition
monocular depth perception cue; the assumption that an object that appears to be blocking part of another object is in front of the second object and closer to the viewer.

aerial (atmospheric) perspective
monocular depth perception cue; the haziness that surrounds objects that are farther away from the viewer, causing the distance to be perceived as greater.

texture gradient
monocular depth perception cue; the tendency for textured surfaces to appear to become smaller and finer as distance from the viewer increases.

It works in pictures because people assume that in the picture, as in real life, the converging lines indicate that the "ends" of the lines are a great distance away from where the people are as they view them.

2. **Relative size:** The principle of size constancy is at work in **relative size**, when objects that people expect to be of a certain size appear to be small and are, therefore, assumed to be much farther away. Movie makers use this principle to make their small models seem gigantic but off in the distance.

3. **Overlap:** If one object seems to be blocking another object, people assume that the blocked object is behind the first one and, therefore, farther away. This cue is also known as **interposition**.

4. **Aerial (atmospheric) perspective:** The farther away an object is, the hazier the object will appear to be due to tiny particles of dust, dirt, and other pollutants in the air, a perceptual cue called **aerial (atmospheric) perspective**. This is why distant mountains often look fuzzy, and buildings far in the distance are blurrier than those that are close.

5. **Texture gradient:** If there are any large expanses of pebbles, rocks, or patterned roads (such as a cobblestone street) nearby, go take a look at them one day. The pebbles or bricks close to you are very distinctly textured, but as you look farther off into the distance, their texture becomes smaller and finer. **Texture gradient** is another trick used by artists to give the illusion of depth in a painting.

6. **Motion parallax:** The next time you're in a car, notice how the objects outside the car window seem to zip by very fast when they are close to the car, and objects in

the distance, such as mountains, seem to move more slowly. This discrepancy in motion of near and far objects is called **motion parallax**.

7. **Accommodation:** A monocular cue that is not one of the pictorial cues, **accommodation** makes use of something that happens inside the eye. The lens of the human eye is flexible and held in place by a series of muscles. The discussion of the eye earlier in this chapter mentioned the process of visual accommodation as the tendency of the lens to change its shape, or thickness, in response to objects near or far away. The brain can use this information about accommodation as a cue for distance. Accommodation is also called a "muscular cue."

BINOCULAR CUES As the name suggests, these cues require the use of two eyes.

1. **Convergence:** Another muscular cue, **convergence**, refers to the rotation of the two eyes in their sockets to focus on a single object. If the object is close, the convergence is pretty great (almost as great as crossing the eyes). If the object is far, the convergence is much less. Hold your finger up in front of your nose, and then move it away and back again. That feeling you get in the muscles of your eyes is convergence (see **Figure 3.23**, left).

2. **Binocular disparity: Binocular disparity** is a scientific way of saying that because the eyes are a few inches apart, they don't see exactly the same image. The brain interprets the images on the retina to determine distance from the eyes. If the two images are very different, the object must be pretty close. If they are almost identical, the object is far enough away to make the retinal disparity very small. You can demonstrate this cue

motion parallax
monocular depth perception cue; the perception of motion of objects in which close objects appear to move more quickly than objects that are farther away.

accommodation
as a monocular cue of depth perception; the brain's use of information about the changing thickness of the lens of the eye in response to looking at objects that are close or far away.

convergence
binocular depth perception cue; the rotation of the two eyes in their sockets to focus on a single object, resulting in greater convergence for closer objects and lesser convergence if objects are distant.

binocular disparity
binocular depth perception cue; the difference in images between the two eyes, which is greater for objects that are close and smaller for distant objects.

Figure 3.23 Binocular Cues to Depth Perception

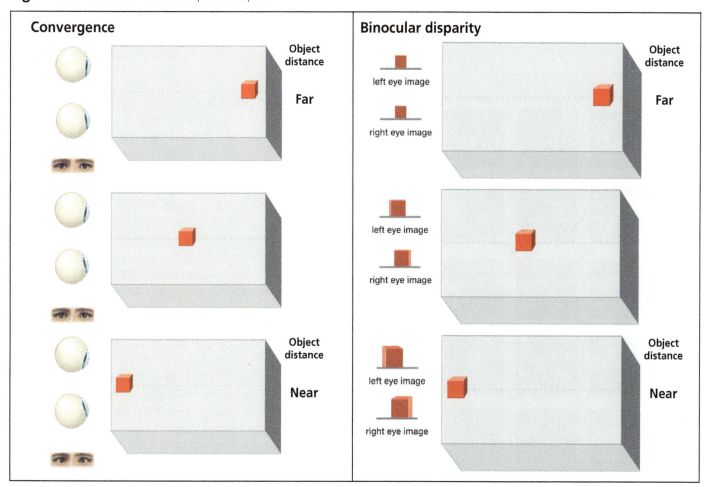

(Left) Convergence is a depth cue that involves the muscles of the eyes. When objects are far away, some eye muscles are more relaxed; when objects are closer or near, those muscles activate and the eyes rotate inward, or converge. (Right) Binocular disparity. Because your eyes are separated by several centimeters, each eye sees a slightly different image of the object in front of you. When an object is far away, that difference is small. When the object is closer or near, there is a greater difference between what each eye sees. The brain interprets this difference to determine the distance of the object.

for yourself by holding an object in front of your nose. Close one eye, note where the object is, and then open that eye and close the other. There should be quite a difference in views. But if you do the same thing with an object that is across the room, the image doesn't seem to "jump" or move nearly as much, if at all (see Figure 3.23, right).

In spite of all the cues for perception that exist, even the most sophisticated perceiver can still fail to perceive the world as it actually is, as the next section demonstrates.

3.16 Perceptual Illusions

3.16 Identify some common visual illusions and the factors that influence our perception of them.

AP 3.A Describe general principles of organizing and integrating sensation to promote stable awareness of the external world.

> 💬 You've mentioned the word *illusion* several times. Exactly what are illusions, and why is it so easy to be fooled by them?

An *illusion* is a perception that does not correspond to reality: People *think* they see something when the reality is quite different. Another way of thinking of illusions is as visual stimuli that "fool" the eye. (Illusions are not hallucinations: An illusion is a distorted perception of something that is really there, but a hallucination originates in the brain, not in reality.)

Research involving illusions can be very useful for both psychologists and neuroscientists. These studies often provide valuable information about how the sensory receptors and sense organs work and how humans interpret sensory input.

Sometimes, illusions are based on early sensory processes, subsequent processing, or higher-level assumptions made by the brain's visual system (Eagleman, 2001; Macknik et al., 2008).

AP 3.C Identify the research contributions of major historical figures in sensation and perception.

We've already discussed one visual illusion, color afterimages, which is due to opponent-processes in the retina or lateral geniculate nucleus (LGN) of the thalamus after light information has been detected by the rods and cones. Another postdetection but still rather early process has been offered for yet another illusion.

Figure 3.24 Hermann Grid

Look at this matrix of squares. Do you notice anything interesting at the white intersections? What happens if you focus your vision directly on one of the intersections?

THE HERMANN GRID Look at the matrix of squares in **Figure 3.24**. Notice anything interesting as you look at different parts of the figure, particularly at the intersections of the white lines? You probably see gray blobs or diamonds that fade away or disappear completely when you try to look directly at them. This is the Hermann grid.

One explanation for this illusion is attributed to the responses of neurons in the primary visual cortex that respond best to bars of light of a specific orientation (Schiller & Carvey, 2005). Such neurons are called "simple cells" and were first discovered by David Hubel and Torsten Wiesel (Hubel & Wiesel, 1959). They also discovered other cells including "complex cells," which respond to orientation and movement, and "end-stopped cells," which respond best to corners, curvature, or sudden edges. Collectively these cells have been referred to as *feature detectors* because they respond to specific features of a stimulus. Hubel and Wiesel were later awarded the Nobel Prize for extensive work in the visual system. Other research into the Hermann grid illusion has documented that straight edges are necessary for this illusion to occur, as the illusion disappears when the edges of the grid lines are slightly curved, and further suggests that the illusion may be due to a unique function of how our visual system processes information (Geier et al., 2008).

Figure 3.25 Müller-Lyer Illusion

The Müller-Lyer optical illusion features two lines, with one appearing to be longer than the other. In reality, both lines are equal in length.

MÜLLER-LYER ILLUSION One of the most famous visual illusions, the **Müller-Lyer illusion**, is shown in **Figure 3.25**. The distortion happens when the viewer tries to determine if the two lines are exactly the same length. They are identical, but one line looks longer than the other. (It's always the line with the angles on the end facing outward.)

Why is this illusion so powerful? The explanation is that most people live in a world with lots of buildings. Buildings have corners. When a person is outside a building, the corner of the building is close to that person, while the walls seem to be moving away (like the line with the angles facing inward). When the person is inside a building, the corner of the room seems to move away from the viewer while the walls are coming closer (like the line with the angles facing outward). In their minds, people "pull" the inward-facing angles toward them like the outside corners of a building, and they make the outward-facing angles "stretch" away from them like the inside corners of the room (Enns & Coren, 1995; Gregory, 1990).

Marshall Segall and colleagues (Segall et al., 1966) found that people in Western cultures, having carpentered buildings with lots of straight lines and corners (Segall and colleagues refer to this as a "carpentered world"), are far more susceptible to this illusion than people from non-Western cultures (having round huts with few corners—an "uncarpentered world"). Richard Gregory (1990) found that Zulus, for example, rarely see this illusion. They live in round huts arranged in circles, use curved tools and toys, and experience few straight lines and corners in their world.

EBBINGHAUS ILLUSION Another famous visual illusion is the *Ebbinghaus illusion*, shown in **Figure 3.26**. The challenge lies in determining if the central circles in each group are identical in size. They are the same size but the one surrounded by larger circles appears to be smaller.

This illusion is based on one facet of our visual system, namely the tendency to

AP 3.D Discuss how experience and culture can influence perceptual processes.

Müller-Lyer illusion

illusion of line length that is distorted by inward-turning or outward-turning corners on the ends of the lines, causing lines of equal length to appear to be different.

Figure 3.26 The Ebbinghaus Illusion

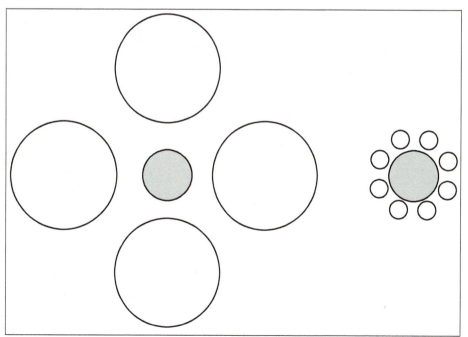

Which of the two gray circles in the center of each cluster is larger? The visual context effects of the surrounding circles influence our perception.

The moon illusion. When this moon is high in the night sky, it will still be the same size to the eye as it is now. Nevertheless, it is perceived to be much larger when on the horizon. In the sky, there are no objects for comparison, but on the horizon, objects such as this tree are seen as being in front of a very large moon.

use context, or surrounding information, to determine the size of objects. In the Ebbinghaus illusion, the central circles are the *target* elements being compared and the surrounding large or small circles are *inducer* elements influencing our perception (Axelrod et al., 2017).

As with other perceptual illusions, culture and the environment in which we grow up and develop can influence how these figures are perceived. In a comparison of individuals living in a remote village, the Himba of Northern Namibia, and groups of urbanized Himba, urban British, and urban Japanese, the traditional Himba were less susceptible to this illusion, suggesting a strong local bias in processing visual information (Caparos et al., 2012). In contrast, exposure to an urban environment increased susceptibility to this illusion or a tendency to process visual information from a more global bias.

In this study, urbanized Himba, urban British, and urban Japanese groups were more likely to report the circles were not the same size (Caparos et al., 2012). In other words, the traditional Himba focused on the central circles more than the surrounding circles in making their judgments. Other research has demonstrated such cross-cultural biases in processing visual information emerge in early childhood (Bremner et al., 2016) and brief exposures to nature can change the way we attend to and perceive the world around us (Berman et al., 2008).

THE MOON ILLUSION Another common illusion is the *moon illusion*, in which the moon on the horizon* appears to be much larger than the moon in the sky (Plug & Ross, 1994). One explanation for this is that the moon high in the sky is all alone, with no cues for depth surrounding it. But on the horizon, the moon appears behind trees and houses, cues for depth that make the horizon seem very far away. The moon is seen as being behind these objects and, therefore, farther away from the viewer. Because people know that objects that are farther away from them yet still appear large are very large indeed, they "magnify" the moon in their minds—a misapplication of the principle of size constancy. This explanation of the moon illusion is called the *apparent distance hypothesis*. This explanation goes back to the second century A.D., first written about by the Greek–Egyptian astronomer Ptolemy and later further developed by an eleventh-century Arab astronomer, Al-Hazan (Ross & Ross, 1976).

Figure 3.27 Perceived Motion

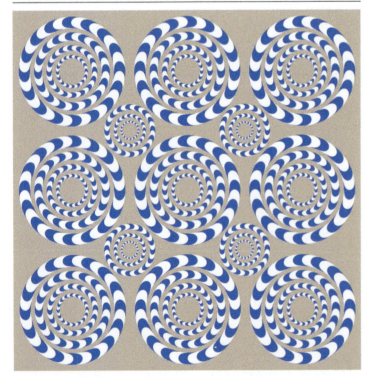

Notice anything as you move your eyes over this image? The image is not moving; seeing the circles move is due at least in part to movements of your eyes.

Source: Vonuk/Fotolia

ILLUSIONS OF MOTION Sometimes, people perceive an object as moving when it is actually still. One example of this takes place as part of a famous experiment in conformity called the *autokinetic effect*. In this effect, a small, stationary light in a darkened room will appear to move or drift because there are no surrounding cues to indicate that the light is *not* moving. Another is the *stroboscopic motion* seen in motion pictures, in which a rapid series of still pictures will seem to be in motion. Many a student has discovered that drawing little figures on the edges of a notebook and then flipping the pages quickly will also produce this same illusion of movement.

Another movement illusion related to stroboscopic motion is the *phi phenomenon*, in which lights turned on in sequence appear to move. For example, if a light is turned on in a darkened room and then turned off, and then another light a short distance away is flashed on and off, it will appear to be

---

*horizon: the place where the earth apparently meets the sky.

one light moving across that distance. This principle is used to suggest motion in many theater marquee signs, flashing arrows indicating direction that have a series of lights going on and off in a sequence, and even in strings of decorative lighting, such as the "chasing" lights seen on houses at holiday times.

What about seeing motion in static images? There are several examples, both classic and modern, of illusory movement or apparent motion being perceived in a static image. The debate about the causes for such illusions, whether they begin in the eyes or the brain, has been going on for at least 200 years (Troncoso et al., 2008).

Look at **Figure 3.27**. What do you see?

There have been a variety of explanations for this type of motion illusion, ranging from factors that depend on the image's luminance and/or the color arrangement to possibly slight differences in the time it takes the brain to process this information. When fMRI and equipment used to track eye movements were used to investigate participants' perception of a similar illusion, researchers found that there was an increase in brain activity in a visual area sensitive to motion. However, this activity was greatest when accompanied by guided eye movements, suggesting eye movements play a significant role in the perception of the illusion (Kuriki et al., 2008).

Eye movements have also been found to be a primary cause for the illusory motion seen in images based on a 1981 painting by Isia Levant, *Enigma*. Look at the center of **Figure 3.28**; notice anything within the green rings? Many people will see the rings start to "sparkle" or the rings rotating. Why does this occur? By using special eye-tracking equipment that allowed them to record even the smallest of eye movements, researchers found that tiny eye movements called *microsaccades*, discussed earlier in the chapter, are directly linked to the perception of motion in *Enigma* and are at least one possible cause of the illusion (Troncoso et al., 2008).

OTHER FACTORS THAT INFLUENCE PERCEPTION Human perception of the world is obviously influenced by things such as culture and misinterpretations of cues. Following are other factors that cause people to alter their perceptions.

People often misunderstand what is said to them because they were expecting to hear something else. People's tendency to perceive things a certain way because their previous experiences or expectations influence them is called **perceptual set** or **perceptual expectancy**. Although expectancies can be useful in interpreting certain stimuli, they can also lead people down the wrong path. What you see depends upon what you expect to see.

The way in which people *interpret* what they perceive can also influence their perception. For example, people can try to understand what they perceive by using information they already have (as is the case of perceptual expectancy). But if there is no existing information that relates to the new information, they can look at each feature of what they perceive and try to put it all together into one whole.

Anyone who has ever worked on a jigsaw puzzle knows that it's a lot easier to put it together if there is a picture of the finished puzzle to refer to as a guide. It also helps to have worked the puzzle before—people who have done that already know what it's going to look like when it's finished. In the field of perception, this is known as **top-down processing**—the use of existing knowledge to organize individual features into a unified whole. This is also a form of perceptual expectancy.

If the puzzle is one the person has never worked before or if that person has lost the top of the box with the picture on it, he or she would have to start with a small section, put it together, and keep building up the sections until the recognizable picture appears. This analysis of smaller features and building up to a complete perception is called **bottom-up processing** (Cave & Kim, 1999). In this case, there is no expectancy to help organize the perception, making bottom-up processing more difficult in some respects. Fortunately, the two types of processing are often used together in perceiving the surrounding world.

Figure 3.28 "Reinterpretation of Enigma"

As in Figure 3.27, the motion you see in this static image is because of movements of your eyes, this time due more to tiny movements called *microsaccades*.

Source: Created by and courtesy of Jorge Otero-Millan, Martinez-Conde Laboratory, Barrow Neurological Institute.

The Ames Room illusion. This illusion is influenced by our past experiences and expectancies. The viewer perceives the room as a rectangle, but in reality, it is actually a trapezoid with angled walls and floor.

AP 3.H Explain the role of top-down processing in producing vulnerability to illusion.

perceptual set (perceptual expectancy)

the tendency to perceive things a certain way because previous experiences or expectations influence those perceptions.

top-down processing

the use of preexisting knowledge to organize individual features into a unified whole.

bottom-up processing

the analysis of the smaller features to build up to a complete perception.

AP 3.D Discuss how experience and culture can influence perceptual processes.

Figure 3.29 Devil's Trident

At first glance, this seems to be an ordinary three-pronged figure. But a closer look reveals that the three prongs cannot be real as drawn. Follow the lines of the top prong to see what goes wrong.

Would people of different cultures perceive objects differently because of different expectancies? Some research suggests this is true. For example, refer back to the section on the Ebbinghaus illusion and the potential impact of an urban environment on perception. Also, take a look at **Figure 3.29**. This figure is often called the "devil's trident." Europeans and North Americans insist on making this figure three dimensional, so they have trouble looking at it—the figure is impossible if it is perceived in three dimensions. But people in less technologically oriented cultures have little difficulty with seeing or even reproducing this figure because they see it as a two-dimensional drawing, quite literally a collection of lines and circles rather than a solid object (Deregowski, 1969). By contrast, if you give Europeans and North Americans the task of reproducing a drawing of an upside-down face, their drawings tend to be more accurate as compared to drawing regular, upright faces, because the upside-down face has become a "collection of lines and circles." That is, they draw what they actually see in terms of light and shadow rather than what they "think" is there three dimensionally.

Concept Map L.O. 3.14, 3.15, 3.16

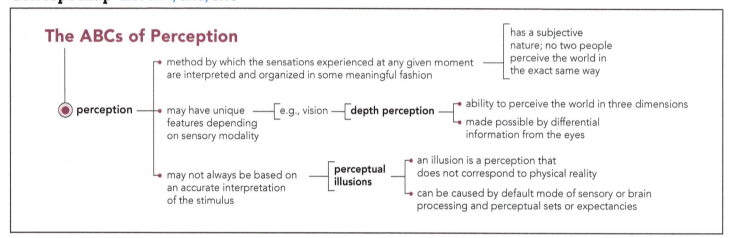

Practice Quiz How much do you remember?

Pick the best answer.

1. When opening a door, the actual image on your retina changes drastically, but you still perceive the door as a rectangle. This is an example of _____ constancy.
   a. material
   b. color
   c. brightness
   d. size
   e. shape

2. Hunters who wear camouflage so that they can blend in with their surroundings are relying on which principle of perception?
   a. subliminal perception
   b. figure–ground relationships
   c. shape constancy
   d. depth perception
   e. expectancy

3. What monocular depth cue can best explain why railroad tracks appear to come together in the distance?
   a. motion parallax
   b. texture gradient
   c. linear perspective
   d. convergence
   e. overlap

4. The Müller-Lyer illusion occurs more frequently in _____.
   a. children than adults
   b. people living in a Western culture
   c. men than women
   d. individuals living in poverty
   e. Zulu culture

5. Jason's uncle claimed to have seen a black panther in the trees beside the highway, although no one else saw it. Knowing that his uncle has been looking for a black panther for years, Jason attributes his uncle's "sighting" to _____.
   a. bottom-up processing
   b. perceptual defense
   c. cognitive convergence
   d. perceptual dissonance
   e. perceptual set

6. The first time Megan had to install a ceiling fan in her new home, it took a long time. But later when she helped install a ceiling fan in her best friend's home, she completed the job very quickly. Her improved speed and skill can partially be attributed to _____.
   a. top-down processing
   b. bottom-up processing
   c. the phi phenomenon
   d. the autokinetic effect
   e. cognitive dissonance

APA Goal 2: Scientific Inquiry and Critical Thinking

Perceptual Influences on Metacognition

Addresses APA Learning Objective 2.3: Engage in innovative and integrative thinking and problem-solving.

As you can see, what we perceive as being real does not always match the actual visual stimulus we are presented with. Perceptual information can also influence how we think about a given object. For example, many of us assume things that are larger weigh more than things that are smaller. The color of an object can also have an influence (De Camp, 1917). Darker objects are often appraised to be heavier than comparable objects that are lighter in color (Walker et al., 2010). Both of these are examples of stimulus influences on perceptual expectations. But what about stimulus influences on expectations for a cognitive task, like assessing how well we will be able to remember something?

Metacognition is thinking about thinking. It includes being aware of our own thought processes, such as evaluating how well we actually understand something or how well we will remember something. For example, the font size of a given word appears to have an effect. In one study, words that were printed in a larger font were rated as being more memorable than words appearing in a smaller font (Rhodes & Castel, 2008). In other words, when evaluated as part of a sequential list, Psychology might be rated as being more memorable than macroeconomics. At least it was for one of your authors during college. Despite the initial ratings on memorability, when tested later, word font size did not yield significant effects on recall (Rhodes & Castel, 2008).

Research also suggests that students often report using study strategies, such as focusing primarily on **bold** or *italicized* terms in a textbook (Gurung, 2003, 2004), or over-reliance on strategies such as highlighting. These are methods that have less of an overall positive impact on retention of material, especially when compared to more robust study and memory strategies. See PIA.6 and Learning Objectives 6.5, 6.6.

APA Goal 2 Perceptual Influences on Metacognition

Which of the following is a better way to study, assess, and improve learning? Look at the two example questions following the study techniques below and think about which would be more effective.

1) Memorizing key terms:
similarity a Gestalt principle of perception; the tendency to perceive things that look similar to each other as being part of the same group.

2) Taking practice quizzes:
Of the Gestalt principles, the tendency to perceive things that look similar as being part of the same group is known as _____.

a. proximity   b. similarity   c. closure   d. continuity   Correct answer: b

As compared to relying on memorization of the key term or glossary word as in the first item, research suggests repeated quizzing or testing as in #2 is the better way to study, assess, and improve learning.

Applying Psychology to Everyday Life
Using Your Senses to Be More Mindful

3.17 Describe how mindfulness and paying attention to our senses, thoughts, and feelings can impact perceptions, personal experiences, and overall sense of well-being.

Being mindful, or maintaining full or focused awareness of the sensations, feelings, and thoughts we experience at any given moment, can enhance our perceptions and a variety of personal experiences. For example, distracted eating can result in eating when you are not hungry, overeating for a given meal or snack, and eating more food in later meals. Mindfulness can also impact how we feel in a given situation. By focusing on our breath or specific bodily sensations, we can shift an experience of nervousness during an exam to one of calm and control. Watch the following video to see how some students practice mindfulness in different situations.

Applying Psychology to Everyday Life Using Your Senses to Be More Mindful

👁 **Watch** the **Video** at **MyLab Psychology**

After watching the video, answer the following questions:

1. As discussed in the video, people who eat emotionally, eat too fast, or have a difficult time with portion control can use mindfulness to increase awareness of their eating behaviors. What are two of the strategies for mindful eating that were highlighted in the video?
2. The video highlighted various applications of mindfulness to experiences such as eating and walking in nature or noticing our immediate environment. What are some other situations in which paying attention to your senses, thoughts, and feelings can impact your perceptions?

Chapter Summary

The ABCs of Sensation

3.1 Describe how we get information from the outside world into our brains.

- Sensation is the activation of receptors located in the eyes, ears, skin, nasal cavities, and tongue.
- Sensory receptors are specialized forms of neurons activated by different stimuli such as light and sound.

3.2 Describe the difference and absolute thresholds.

- A just noticeable difference is the point at which a stimulus is detectable half the time it is present.
- Weber's law of just noticeable differences states that the just noticeable difference between two stimuli is always a constant.
- Absolute thresholds are the smallest amount of energy needed for conscious detection of a stimulus at least half the time it is present.

- Subliminal stimuli are stimuli presented just below the level of conscious awareness, and subliminal perception has been demonstrated in the laboratory. It has not been shown to be effective in advertising.

3.3 Explain why some sensory information is ignored.
- Habituation occurs when the brain ignores a constant stimulus.
- Sensory adaptation occurs when the sensory receptors stop responding to a constant stimulus.

The Science of Seeing

3.4 Describe how light travels through the various parts of the eye.
- Brightness corresponds to the amplitude of light waves, whereas color corresponds to the length of the light waves.
- Saturation is the psychological interpretation of wavelengths that are all the same (highly saturated) or varying (less saturated).
- Light enters the eye and is focused through the cornea, passes through the aqueous humor, and then through the hole in the iris muscle called the pupil.
- The lens also focuses the light on the retina, where it passes through ganglion and bipolar cells to stimulate the rods and cones.

3.5 Explain how light information reaches the visual cortex.
- Visual pathway = retina –> optic nerve –> optic chiasm –> optic tract –> LGN of thalamus –> optic radiations –> primary visual cortex.
- Light from right visual field projects to left side of each retina; light from left visual field projects to right side of each retina.
- Axons from temporal halves of each retina project to visual cortex on same side of the brain; axons from nasal halves of each retina project to visual cortex on opposite side of the brain; optic chiasm is point of crossover.

3.6 Compare and contrast two major theories of color vision, and explain how color-deficient vision occurs.
- Cones are sensitive to colors and work best in bright light. They are responsible for the sharpness of visual information and are found in the fovea.
- Rods detect changes in brightness but do not see color and function best in low levels of light. They are found everywhere in the retina except the center, or fovea.
- Trichromatic theory of color perception assumes three types of cones: red, green, and blue. All colors would be perceived as various combinations of these three.
- Opponent-process theory of color perception assumes four primary colors of red, green, blue, and yellow. Colors are arranged in pairs, and when one member of a pair is activated, the other is not.
- Color blindness is a total lack of color perception, whereas color-deficient vision refers to color perception limited primarily to yellows and blues or reds and greens only.

The Hearing Sense: Can You Hear Me Now?

3.7 Explain the nature of sound, and describe how it travels through the various parts of the ear.
- Sound has three aspects: pitch (frequency), loudness, and timbre (purity).
- Sound enters the ear through the visible outer structure, or pinna, and travels to the eardrum and then to the small bones of the middle ear.
- The bone called the stirrup rests on the oval window, causing the cochlea and basilar membrane to vibrate with sound.
- The organ of Corti on the basilar membrane contains the auditory receptors, which send signals to the brain about sound qualities as they vibrate.

3.8 Summarize three theories of how the brain processes information about pitch.
- Place theory states that the locations of the hair cells on the organ of Corti correspond to different pitches of sound. This can explain pitch above 1,000 Hz.
- Frequency theory states that the speed with which the basilar membrane vibrates corresponds to different pitches of sound. This can explain pitch below 1,000 Hz.
- The volley principle states that neurons take turns firing for sounds above 400 Hz and below 4,000 Hz.

3.9 Identify types of hearing impairment and treatment options for each.
- Conduction hearing impairment is caused by damage to the outer or middle ear structures, whereas nerve hearing impairment is caused by damage to the inner ear or auditory pathways in the brain.
- Hearing aids may be used for those with conductive hearing impairment, while cochlear implants may restore some hearing to those with nerve hearing impairment.

Chemical Senses: It Tastes Good and Smells Even Better

3.10 Explain how the sense of taste works.
- Gustation is the sense of taste. Taste buds in the tongue receive molecules of substances, which fit into receptor sites.
- Gustation is a chemical sense that involves detection of chemicals dissolved in saliva.
- The five basic types of taste are sweet, sour, salty, bitter, and umami (brothy).

3.11 Explain how the sense of smell works.
- Olfaction is the sense of smell. The olfactory receptors in the upper part of the nasal passages receive molecules of substances and create neural signals that then go to the olfactory bulbs under the frontal lobes.
- Olfaction is a chemical sense that involves detection of chemicals suspended in the air.

The Other Senses: What the Body Knows

3.12 Describe how we experience the sensations of touch, pressure, temperature, and pain.
- The skin senses are one part of our somesthetic senses.
- Pacinian corpuscles respond to pressure, certain nerve endings around hair follicles respond to pain and pressure, and free nerve endings respond to pain, pressure, and temperature.
- The gate-control theory of pain states that when receptors sensitive to pain are stimulated, a neurotransmitter and neuromodulator called substance P is released into the spinal cord, activating other pain receptors by opening "gates" in the spinal column and sending the message to the brain.

3.13 Describe the systems that tell us about balance and position and movement of our bodies.

- The kinesthetic sense allows the brain to know about movement of the body.
- Proprioception, or information about where the body and its parts are in relation to each other and the ground, comes from the activity of special receptors responsive to movement of the joints and limbs.
- The vestibular sense also contributes to the body's sense of spatial orientation and movement through the activity of the otolith organs (up-and-down movement) and the semicircular canals (movement through arcs).
- Motion sickness is explained by sensory conflict theory, in which information from the eyes conflicts with information from the vestibular sense, causing nausea.

The ABCs of Perception

3.14 Describe how perceptual constancies and the Gestalt principles account for common perceptual experiences.

- Perception is the interpretation and organization of sensations.
- Size constancy is the tendency to perceive objects as always being the same size, no matter how close or far away they are.
- Shape constancy is the tendency to perceive objects as remaining the same shape even when the shape of the object changes on the retina of the eye.
- Brightness constancy is the tendency to perceive objects as a certain level of brightness, even when the light changes.
- The Gestalt psychologists developed several principles of perception that involve interpreting patterns in visual stimuli. The principles are figure–ground relationships, closure, similarity, continuity, contiguity, common region, and elemental connectedness.

3.15 Explain how we perceive depth using both monocular and binocular cues.

- Depth perception is the ability to see in three dimensions.
- Monocular cues for depth perception include linear perspective, relative size, overlap, aerial (atmospheric) perspective, texture gradient, motion parallax, and accommodation.
- Binocular cues for depth perception include convergence and binocular overlap.

3.16 Identify some common visual illusions and the factors that influence our perception of them.

- Illusions are perceptions that do not correspond to reality or are distortions of visual stimuli.
- Perceptual set or expectancy refers to the tendency to perceive objects and situations in a particular way because of prior experiences or our expectations in a given situation.
- Top-down processing involves the use of existing knowledge to organize individual features into a unified whole.
- Bottom-up processing involves the analysis of smaller features, building up to a complete perception.

Applying Psychology to Everyday Life: Using Your Senses to Be More Mindful

3.17 Describe how mindfulness and paying attention to our senses, thoughts, and feelings can impact perceptions, personal experiences, and overall sense of well-being.

- Being mindful, or being fully aware of and paying attention to our breathing, sensory experiences, feelings, and thoughts, can help us establish a sense of peace and control, benefiting our overall sense of well-being.
- Paying closer attention to our senses can enhance both perceptions and personal experiences. For example, mindful eating consists of paying closer attention to the various tastes, colors, and smells of food; chewing more slowly; and enjoying smaller portions to fully appreciate the experience of eating.

Test Yourself: Preparing for the AP Exam

PART I: MULTIPLE-CHOICE QUESTIONS

Directions for Part I: Read each of the questions or incomplete sentences below. Then choose the response that best answers the question or completes the sentence.

1. In making a large pot of chili for a family reunion, you find that you have to add 1 onion to your pot of chili that already has 5 onions mixed in it to notice a difference. According to Weber's law, how many onions would you have to add to notice a difference if you are making twice as much chili with 10 onions?
   a. 3   b. 2   c. 1   d. 4   e. 15

2. You detect the strong smell of cedar when you enter a furniture store. However, after a short while in the store, you no longer can detect the smell. This is likely due to _____.
   a. perceptual constancy
   b. accommodation
   c. habituation
   d. olfactory dissonance
   e. sensory adaptation

3. Which of the following terms refers to the amplitude of a light wave such as how high or low the wave is?
   a. timbre
   b. hue
   c. pitch
   d. brightness
   e. color

4. What part of the eye hardens as we age, thus causing many to suffer from presbyopia?
   a. rods
   b. fovea
   c. lens
   d. vitreous humor
   e. cones

5. When going from a brightly lit room to a darkened room, the rods play a role in the process of _____, or our ability to adjust to seeing in low levels of light.
   a. dark adaptation
   b. top-down processing
   c. afterimage
   d. light adaptation
   e. opponent-process theory

6. The hammer, the anvil, and the stirrup are part of the _____.
   a. cochlea
   b. otolith organs
   c. outer ear
   d. inner ear
   e. middle ear

7. Studies show that taste preference can typically begin _____.
   a. in the first 3 to 6 months after birth
   b. before a baby is born
   c. by age 1
   d. during preschool
   e. during elementary school

8. Alec is suffering from a severe cold. His nose has been stopped up for several days. What effect, if any, might his cold have on his sense of taste?
   a. His sense of taste will be decreased for sweet and salty but increased for bitter, sour, umami, and enhanced variations of all of the tastes.
   b. His sense of taste will get better but not until 48 hours after he loses his sense of smell.
   c. His sense of taste will be increased since he isn't receiving additional sensory input from his sense of smell.
   d. His sense of taste will be dulled since taste and smell often work together.
   e. His sense of taste will be no better or worse since the senses of taste and smell are completely separate.

9. If a child suffers from congenital analgesia, why must he or she be careful when outside playing?
   a. The child often cannot hear sounds unless he or she is within 3 feet of the source.
   b. The child lacks the ability to react to a dangerous situation.
   c. The child has increased pain sensitivity.
   d. The child's sense of smell does not work properly.
   e. The child cannot feel pain and can suffer injuries without even knowing it.

10. A child may sometimes play by quickly turning around in a circle. When the child stops, he or she often feels like his or her head is still spinning. What is responsible for this sensation?
    a. disruption of the otolith crystals
    b. information from the eyes being processed in the somatosensory cortex
    c. fluid still rotating in the semicircular canals
    d. proprioceptors
    e. compression of the otolith organs

11. Little Aida is with her mother at the docks waiting for her daddy to return from his naval deployment. While the boat is still a way out, her mother says, "There is daddy's boat." Aida is confused. She cannot understand how her dad can be on a boat that is so small that she can hold up her thumb and cover the entire boat. It's safe to assume that Aida does not yet understand _____ constancy.
    a. size
    b. shape
    c. color
    d. depth
    e. brightness

12. XX XX XX   XXXXXX
    XX XX XX   XXXXXX
    XX XX XX   XXXXXX

    In viewing the items above, seeing three columns of Xs on the left versus three rows of Xs on the right can be explained by the Gestalt principle of _____.
    a. common region
    b. similarity
    c. closure
    d. proximity
    e. contiguity

13. The Müller-Lyer illusion is influenced greatly by one's _____.
    a. level of intellect
    b. gender
    c. culture
    d. eyesight
    e. age

14. Emma opened her new jigsaw puzzle but soon realized that she had the same puzzle when she was a child. With her past experience to rely upon, Emma will probably use _____ to help her reassemble the puzzle.
    a. perceptual expectancy
    b. top-down processing
    c. bottom-up processing
    d. perceptual set
    e. accommodation

15. Cade enjoys playing with sparklers on the 4th of July. He loves watching his sisters run with a sparkler and the momentary trail of light that seems to be left behind. Which aspect of our visual system best explains this trail of light?
    a. lateral inhibition
    b. microsaccades of the eyes
    c. achromatopsia
    d. convergence
    e. persistence of vision

PART II: FREE-RESPONSE QUESTION

Directions for Part II: Read the essay question that follows. Then respond to the question in a clear, concise essay. Do not simply list facts. Instead, present a thorough argument based on your critical consideration of the topic. Use of proper terminology is necessary.

Diana is a musician who specializes in playing the violin, which requires deft finger movements. When she performs in the orchestra, she reads sheet music. Lately, she has had difficulty seeing both the music and the orchestra conductor, so her optometrist prescribed her new bifocal lenses.

Part A

Explain how each of the following terms might help Diana as she performs in the orchestra:

- fovea
- proprioception
- place theory
- accommodation

Part B

Explain how each of the following terms might hinder Diana as she performs in the orchestra:

- presbyopia
- tinnitus
- conduction hearing impairment

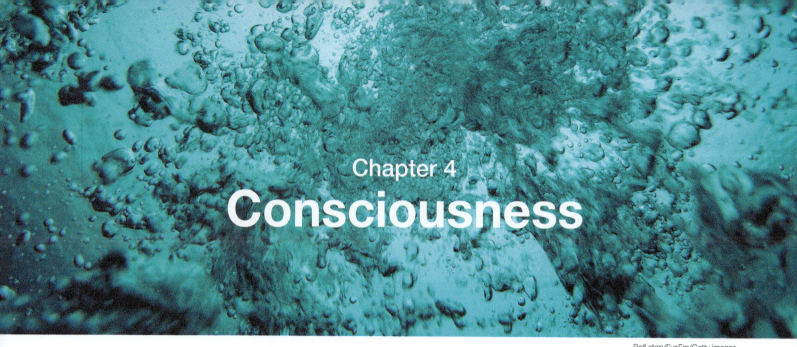

Chapter 4
Consciousness

Ralf strm/EyeEm/Getty Images

In your words

What are some ways in which you multitask throughout the day?

After you have thought about this question, watch the video to see how other students would answer it.

Watch the Video at MyLab Psychology

Why study consciousness?

In a very real sense, to understand consciousness is to understand what it means to be who we are. Waking, sleeping, dreaming, daydreaming, and other forms of conscious awareness make up the better part of the human experience. Lack of sleep may increase the likelihood of diabetes, interfere with the onset of puberty changes, decrease memory for learning, and increase weight gain. Drug use can affect consciousness as well, and not always to our benefit. Clearly, an understanding of the workings of the conscious mind is important to both our mental and our physical well-being.

Learning Objectives

4.1 Define what it means to be conscious.

4.2 Differentiate between the different levels of consciousness.

4.3 Describe the biological process of the sleep–wake cycle.

4.4 Explain why we sleep.

4.5 Identify the different stages of sleep.

4.6 Differentiate among the various sleep disorders.

4.7 Compare and contrast two explanations of why people dream.

4.8 Identify commonalities and differences in the content of people's dreams.

4.9 Explain how hypnosis affects consciousness.

4.10 Compare and contrast two views of why hypnosis works.

4.11 Distinguish between physical dependence and psychological dependence upon drugs.

4.12 Identify the effects and dangers of using stimulants.

4.13 Identify the effects and dangers of using depressants.

4.14 Identify the effects and dangers of using hallucinogens.

4.15 Identify the negative impacts of multitasking.

AP 2.0 Describe various states of consciousness and their impact on behavior.

AP 2.R Identify the contributions of major figures in consciousness research.

4.1–4.2 What Is Consciousness?

💬 What exactly is meant by the term *consciousness*? I've heard it a lot, but I'm not sure that I know everything it means.

Consciousness is one of those terms that most people think they understand until someone asks them to define it. Various sorts of scientists, psychologists, neuroscientists, philosophers, and even computer scientists (who have been trying to develop an artificial intelligence for some time now) have tried to define consciousness, and so there are several definitions—one for nearly every field in which consciousness is studied.

4.1 Definition of Consciousness

4.1 Define what it means to be conscious.

Philosopher Daniel Dennett, in his 1991 book *Consciousness Explained*, asserts that (contrary to the opinion of William James in his 1894 text) there is no single stream of consciousness but rather multiple "channels," each of which is handling its own tasks (Dennett, 1991). All of these channels operate in parallel, a kind of chaos of consciousness. People must somehow organize all this conscious experience, and that organization is influenced by their particular social groups and culture.

Do animals experience consciousness in the same way as people? That is a question too complex to answer fully here, but many researchers of animal behavior, language, and cognition have some reason to propose that there is a kind of consciousness in at least some animals, although its organization would naturally not be the same as human consciousness (Block, 2005; Browne, 2004; Hurley & Nudds, 2006; Koch & Mormann, 2010; Smith et al., 2014). Chapter Seven in this text includes a discussion of animal language that touches on some of these issues. See Learning Objective 7.14.

💬 So where does that leave us in the search for a working definition of consciousness?

For our purposes, a more useful definition of consciousness might be the following: **Consciousness** is your awareness of everything that is going on around you and inside your own head at any given moment, which you use to organize your behavior (Farthing, 1992), including your thoughts, sensations, and feelings. In a cognitive neuroscience view, consciousness is generated by a set of action potentials in the communication among neurons just sufficient to produce a specific perception, memory, or experience in our awareness (Crick & Koch, 1990, 2003; Koch & Mormann, 2010). In other words, your eyes see a dog, the neurons along the optic pathway to the occipital lobe's visual cortex are activated, and the visual association cortex is activated to identify the external stimulus as a "dog." Bam!—consciousness! See Learning Objective 2.8.

consciousness
a person's awareness of everything that is going on around him or her at any given time.

waking consciousness
state in which thoughts, feelings, and sensations are clear and organized and the person feels alert.

4.2 Altered States of Consciousness

4.2 Differentiate between the different levels of consciousness.

Much of people's time awake is spent in a state called **waking consciousness** in which their thoughts, feelings, and sensations are clear and organized, and they feel alert. But there are many times in daily activities and in life when people experience states of consciousness that differ from this organized waking state. These variations are called "altered states of consciousness."

An **altered state of consciousness** occurs when there is a shift in the quality or pattern of your mental activity. Thoughts may become fuzzy and disorganized, and you may feel less alert, or your thoughts may take bizarre turns, as they so often do in dreams. Sometimes being in an altered state may mean being in a state of *increased* alertness, as when under the influence of a stimulant. You may also divide your conscious awareness, as when you drive to work or school and then wonder how you got there—one level of conscious awareness was driving, while the other was thinking about the day ahead, perhaps. This altered state of divided consciousness can be a dangerous thing, as many people who try to drive and talk on a cell phone at the same time have discovered. People are often unaware that there are two kinds of thought processes, *controlled processes* and *automatic processes* (Bargh et al., 2012; Huang & Bargh, 2014). Controlled processes are those that require our conscious attention to a fairly high degree, such as driving, carrying on a conversation, or taking notes in your psychology class (you are taking notes, right?). Automatic processes require far less of a conscious level of attention—we are aware of these actions at a low level of conscious awareness; examples would be brushing one's hair or well-practiced actions such as walking or riding a bicycle. Driving a car along a familiar path can become fairly automatic, hence the experience of driving somewhere and not knowing how you got there—driving is really a control process, not an automatic one, but we often forget to pay attention to this fact.

The driver of this car has several competing demands on her attention: working her cell phone, listening to the passenger read to her, and driving her car. If she manages to get herself and her passenger safely to their destination—and by multitasking while driving she is certainly endangering both of their lives and others as well—it's possible that she won't even remember the trip; she may be driving in an altered state of consciousness.

Controlled processes such as driving or carrying on a conversation should only be done one at a time, while you can do an automatic process and a controlled process at the same time without too much trouble. Talking on a cell phone while brushing your hair is okay, for example, but talking on a cell phone while driving your car is not. Studies have shown that driving while talking on a cell phone, even a hands-free phone, puts a person at the same degree of risk as driving under the influence of alcohol (Alm & Nilsson, 1995; Briem & Hedman, 1995; Caird et al., 2018; Strayer & Drews, 2007; Strayer & Johnston, 2001; Strayer et al., 2006, 2014). Texting while driving is more than risky—it can be murderous (Centers for Disease Control, 2015d; Eastern Virginia Medical School, 2009; He et al., 2018; Wang et al., 2012). See Learning Objective PIA.2.

There are many forms of altered states of consciousness. For example, daydreaming, being hypnotized, or achieving a meditative state are usually considered to be altered states. See Learning Objective 10.10. Being under the influence of certain drugs such as caffeine, tobacco, or alcohol is definitely an example of an altered state. Over several decades, there has been a definite rise in the use of stimulants that would ordinarily be prescribed for children and adolescents with attention-deficit/hyperactivity disorder but are also used by college students and older adults who feel that the drugs give them an "edge" (Partnership for Drug-Free Kids, 2014; Szalavitz, 2009; Zuvekas & Vitiello, 2012). But the most common altered state people experience is the one they spend about a third of their lives in on a nightly basis—sleep.

altered state of consciousness state in which there is a shift in the quality or pattern of mental activity as compared to waking consciousness.

Concept Map L.O. 4.1, 4.2

What Is Consciousness?

- people's awareness of everything that is going on around them at any given moment (thoughts, sensations, and feelings); much of the day is spent in waking consciousness where these are clear and organized
- altered states of consciousness occur when there is a shift in the quality or pattern of mental activity as compared to waking consciousness; alertness, thought content, and focus can vary greatly

Practice Quiz — How much do you remember?

Pick the best answer.

1. A change in the quality or pattern of mental activity, such as increased alertness or divided consciousness, is called a(n) _____.
   a. altered state of consciousness
   b. waking consciousness
   c. hallucination
   d. delusion
   e. transient state of consciousness

2. Consciousness can be defined as a set of action potentials occurring among neurons in which of the following views?
   a. sociocultural
   b. behavioral
   c. evolutionary
   d. cognitive
   e. cognitive neuroscience

3. Which of the following is an example of an automatic process?
   a. taking notes in class
   b. talking on a cell phone
   c. brushing your teeth
   d. doing math problems
   e. driving a car

4. Which of the following statements is false?
   a. Driving while talking on a cell phone is as risky as driving while under the influence of alcohol.
   b. Brushing your hair while talking on the phone is easy to do.
   c. Texting while driving is more dangerous than talking on a cell phone while driving.
   d. Controlled processes should only be done one at a time.
   e. It is safe to drive and talk on a cell phone as long as it is hands free.

AP 2.S Discuss aspects of sleep and dreaming.

4.3–4.6 Sleep

Have you ever wondered why people have to sleep? They could get so much more work done if they didn't have to sleep, and they would have more time to play and do creative things.

4.3 The Biology of Sleep

4.3 Describe the biological process of the sleep–wake cycle.

Sleep was once referred to as "the gentle tyrant" (Webb, 1992). People can try to stay awake, and sometimes they may go for a while without sleep, but eventually they *must* sleep. One reason for this fact is that sleep is one of the human body's *biological rhythms*, natural cycles of activity that the body must go through. Some biological rhythms are monthly, like the cycle of a woman's menstruation, whereas others are far shorter—the beat of the heart is a biological rhythm. But many biological rhythms take place on a daily basis, like the rise and fall of blood pressure and body temperature or the production of certain body chemicals (Moore-Ede et al., 1982; Paul et al., 2016). The most obvious of these is the sleep–wake cycle (Baehr et al., 2000; Ding et al., 2016).

THE RHYTHMS OF LIFE: CIRCADIAN RHYTHMS The sleep–wake cycle is a **circadian rhythm**. The term actually comes from two Latin words, *circa* ("about") and *diem* ("day"). So a circadian rhythm is a cycle that takes "about a day" to complete.

For most people, this means that they will experience several hours of sleep at least once during every 24-hour period. The sleep–wake cycle is ultimately controlled by the brain, specifically by an area within the *hypothalamus*, the tiny section of the brain that influences the glandular system. See Learning Objectives 2.7, 2.13.

💬 There was a big fuss over something called melatonin a few years ago—isn't melatonin supposed to make people sleep?

THE ROLE OF THE HYPOTHALAMUS: THE MIGHTY MITE Beginning several decades ago and continuing to the present, a lot of people were buying supplements of *melatonin* (a hormone normally secreted by the pineal gland) hoping to sleep better and perhaps even slow the effects of aging (Folkard et al., 1993; Herxheimer & Petrie, 2001;

Sleep, according to Webb (1992), is the "gentle tyrant." As this picture shows, when the urge to sleep comes upon a person, it can be very difficult to resist—no matter where that person is at the time. Can you think of a time or place when you fell asleep without meaning to do so? Why do you think it happened?

circadian rhythm
a cycle of bodily rhythm that occurs over a 24-hour period.

Sharma et al., 2018; Young, 1996). The release of melatonin is influenced by a structure deep within the tiny hypothalamus in an area called the *suprachiasmatic* (SOO-prah-ki-AS-ma-tik) *nucleus*, the internal clock that tells people when to wake up and when to fall asleep (Gandhi et al., 2015; Quintero et al., 2003; Yamaguchi et al., 2003; Zisapel, 2001). The suprachiasmatic nucleus, or SCN, is sensitive to changes in light. As daylight fades, the SCN tells the pineal gland (located in the base of the brain) to secrete melatonin (Bondarenko, 2004; Delagrange & Guardiola-Lemaitre, 1997). As melatonin accumulates, it suppresses the neurons in the brain that keep us awake and alert, resulting in sleepiness (Sharma et al., 2018). As the light coming into the eyes increases (as it does in the morning), the SCN tells the pineal gland to stop secreting melatonin, allowing the body to awaken. That's a lot of control for such a small part of the brain.

Melatonin supplements are often used to treat a condition called *jet lag*, in which the body's circadian rhythm has been disrupted by traveling to another time zone. There is some evidence that melatonin may be linked to a healthier metabolism (Cardinali et al., 2013; Gandhi et al., 2015). It may help people who suffer from sleep problems due to shift work. Shift-work sleep problems, often attributed to the custom of having workers change shifts against their natural circadian rhythms (e.g., from a day shift to a night shift, and then back again to an evening shift), have been linked to increased accident rates, increased absence from work due to illness, and lowered productivity rates (Folkard & Tucker, 2003; Folkard et al., 1993; Folkard et al., 2005). In addition to melatonin supplements, it has been found that gradually changing the shifts that workers take according to the natural cycle of the day (e.g., from day shift to evening shift to night shift, rather than from day shift directly to night shift) has significantly reduced these problems (Czeisler et al., 1982; Folkard et al., 2006).

Melatonin is not the whole story, of course. Several neurotransmitters are associated with arousal and sleep regulation, including serotonin. It was once theorized that serotonin promoted sleepiness. However, it is not that simple. Serotonin-producing neurons are most active during wakefulness, less active during deep sleep, and relatively inactive during the type of sleep in which dreams typically occur (Elmenhorst et al., 2012; Hornung, 2012; Siegel, 2011). Furthermore, effects differ based on which serotonin-producing cells are firing and which brain structures are receiving those messages. Last, some serotonin receptors are excitatory and others are inhibitory. For example, some receptors facilitate some stages of sleep, while others inhibit other stages (Siegel, 2011; Zhang et al., 2015).

Body temperature plays a part in inducing sleep, too. The suprachiasmatic nucleus, as part of the hypothalamus, controls body temperature. The higher the body temperature, the more alert people are; the lower the temperature, the sleepier they are. When people are asleep at night, their body temperature is at its lowest level. Be careful: The research on the effects of serotonin and body temperature on sleep is correlational, so we cannot assume causation, and there are many different factors involved in sleep. See Learning Objective 1.8.

In studies in which volunteers spend several days without access to information about day or night, their sleep–wake cycles lengthened (Czeisler, 1995; Czeisler et al., 1980). The daily activities of their bodies—such as sleeping, waking, waste production, blood pressure rise and fall, and so on—took place over a period of 25 hours rather than 24 hours. Our circadian rhythms are synchronized to a 24-hour day consistent with the day-night cycle due to the suprachiasmatic nucleus, which receives direct input from some retinal ganglion cells responding to light (McCormick & Westbrook, 2013).

In the same studies, body temperature dropped consistently even in the absence of light (Czeisler et al., 1980). As body temperature dropped, sleep began, giving further support to the importance of body temperature in the regulation of sleep. It is little wonder that in more industrialized cultures that use artificial light at times and in places where there normally would be little light, people report far higher levels of sleep disturbances and poor sleep quality when compared to cultures using the ordinary light of the sun to regulate their daily activities (Stevens & Zhu, 2015).

4.4 Why We Sleep

4.4 Explain why we sleep.

How much sleep is enough sleep? Traditionally, the answer has varied from person to person because of each person's age and possibly inherited sleep needs (Feroah et al., 2004), and it has generally been suggested that most adults require about 7–9 hours of sleep during each 24-hour period in order to function well (see **Figure 4.1**). Some people seem to be short sleepers, apparently needing only 4 or 5 hours, whereas others seem to be long sleepers and seemingly require more than 9 hours of sleep (McCann & Stewin, 1988). As we age, we seem to sleep less during each night until the average length of sleep approaches only 6 hours. This is not really because we need less sleep as we age, but rather a function of the other consequences of aging: more frequent trips to the bathroom, increased snoring, and changes in the brain's reaction to light, to name just a few (Biello et al., 2018; Mander et al., 2017). Based on a recent global survey of over 10,000 people, it appears the optimal amount of sleep in a single night for adults, regardless of age, is 7–8 hours of restful sleep to perform our best, and this appears to be especially important for higher level cognitive skills such as reasoning, problem solving, and communication (Wild et al., 2018). As sleep researcher Dr. Jerry Siegel describes in the video *How Much Sleep Do We Need?*, the amount of sleep that we get can have an impact on our health.

Figure 4.1 Sleep Patterns of Infants and Adults

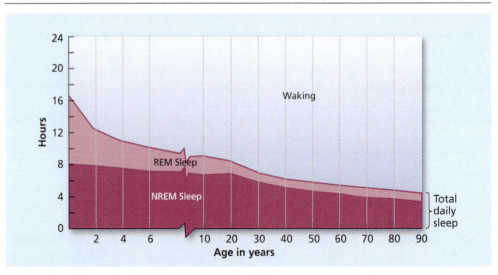

Infants need far more sleep than older children and adults. Both REM sleep and NREM sleep decrease dramatically in the first 10 years of life, with the greatest decrease in REM sleep. Nearly 50 percent of an infant's sleep is REM, compared to only about 20 percent for a normal, healthy adult.

Source: Roffwarg et al. (1966). Ontogenetic development of the human sleep-dream cycle, Science, 152:604-619.

Although people can do without sleep for a while, they cannot do without it altogether. In one experiment, rats were placed on moving treadmills over water. They couldn't sleep normally because they would then fall into the water and be awakened, but they did drift repeatedly into **microsleeps**, or brief sidesteps into sleep lasting only seconds (Goleman, 1982; Konowal et al., 1999). People can have microsleeps, too, and if this happens while they are driving a car or a truck, it's obviously bad news (Åkerstedt et al., 2013; Dinges, 1995; Lyznicki et al., 1998; Thomas et al., 1998). Microsleep periods are no doubt responsible for a lot of car accidents that occur when drivers have had very little sleep.

Watch How Much Sleep Do We Need?

Watch the Video at MyLab Psychology

> Okay, so we obviously need to sleep. But what does it do for us? Why do we have to sleep at all?

THEORIES OF SLEEP While it's clear that sleep is essential to life, theories about *why*—the purpose of sleep—differ.

THE ADAPTIVE THEORY OF SLEEP Sleep is a product of evolution (Webb, 1992) according to the **adaptive theory** of sleep. It proposes that animals and humans evolved different sleep patterns to avoid being present during their predators' normal hunting times, which typically would be at night. For example, if a human or a prey animal (one a predator will eat) is out and about at night, they are more at risk of being eaten. However, if during active hunting hours the prey is in a safe place sleeping and conserving energy, it is more likely to remain unharmed. If this theory is true, then one would expect prey animals to sleep mostly at night and for shorter periods of time than predator animals; you would also expect that predators could sleep in the daytime—virtually as much as they want. This seems to be the case for predators like lions that have very few natural predators themselves. Lions will sleep nearly 15 hours a day, whereas animals such as gazelles that are lions' prey sleep a mere 4 hours a day, usually in short naps. Nocturnal animals such as the opossum can afford to sleep during the day and be active at night (when their food sources are available), because they are protected from predators by sleeping high up in trees (see **Figure 4.2**).

THE RESTORATIVE THEORY OF SLEEP The other major theory of why organisms sleep is called **restorative theory**, which states that sleep is necessary to the physical health of the body. During sleep, chemicals that were used up during the day's activities are replenished, other chemicals that were secreted in excess and could become toxic if left in the system are removed, and cellular damage is repaired (Adam, 1980; Moldofsky, 1995; Xie et al., 2013). As discussed earlier, brain plasticity is enhanced by sleep, and there is evidence that most bodily growth and repair occur during the deepest stages of sleep, when enzymes responsible for these functions are secreted in higher amounts (Saper et al., 2001).

Sleep is also important for forming memories. Studies have shown that the physical changes in the brain that occur when we form memories are strengthened during sleep, and particularly so for children (Cairney et al., 2018; Racsmány et al., 2010; Wilhelm et al., 2013). See Learning Objective 6.14. This memory effect is no doubt due, at least in part, to the finding that sleep enhances the synaptic

microsleeps
brief sidesteps into sleep lasting only a few seconds.

adaptive theory
theory of sleep proposing that animals and humans evolved sleep patterns to avoid predators by sleeping when predators are most active.

restorative theory
theory of sleep proposing that sleep is necessary to the physical health of the body and serves to replenish chemicals and repair cellular damage.

Figure 4.2 Animals and the Adaptive Theory of Sleep

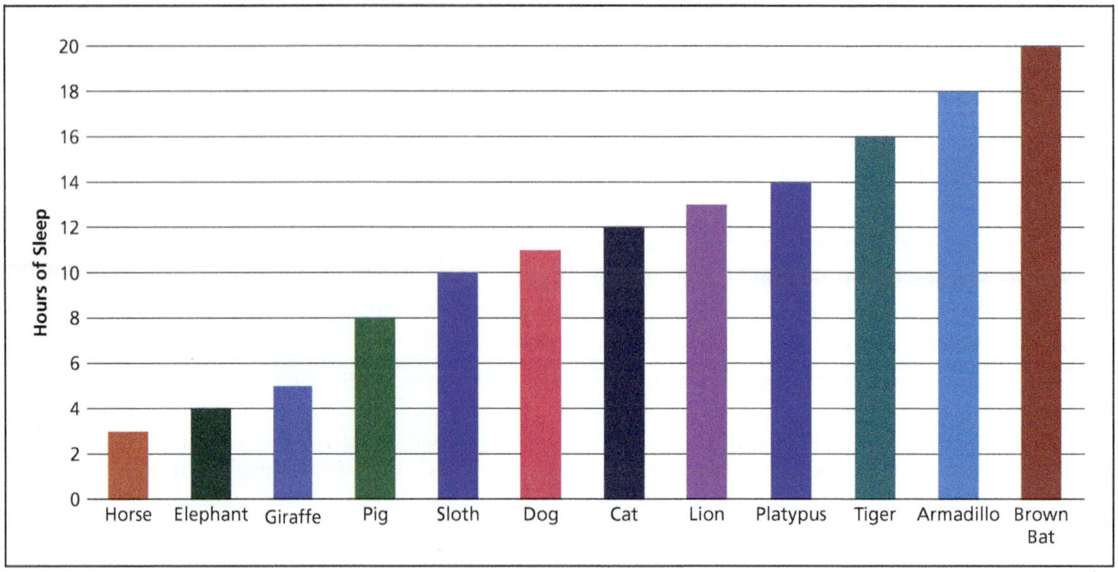

Animal	Hours of Sleep
Horse	3
Elephant	4
Giraffe	5
Pig	8
Sloth	10
Dog	11
Cat	12
Lion	13
Platypus	14
Tiger	16
Armadillo	18
Brown Bat	20

Source: Based on American Academy of Sleep Medicine.

connections among neurons, thus increasing the plasticity of the brain—the brain's ability to adapt to experiences (Aton et al., 2009; Bushey et al., 2011; Cirelli et al., 2012; Frank & Benington, 2006). Sleep may also reduce the activity of neurons associated with forgetting, leading to memory retention (Berry et al., 2015), and people who learn tasks right before they go to sleep are able to both recall and perform those tasks better than if they had not slept after learning (Kurdziel et al., 2013; Stickgold & Ellenbogen, 2008). See Learning Objective 2.7 and 2.11.

Which of these theories is correct? The answer is that both are probably needed to understand why sleep occurs the way it does. Adaptive theory explains why people sleep *when* they do, and restorative theory (including the important function of memory formation) explains why people *need* to sleep.

SLEEP DEPRIVATION While we've already discussed the importance of being able to sleep and the dangers of microsleeps, just how much sleep loss can occur before serious problems start to happen? What will losing out on just one night's sleep do to a person? For most people, a missed night of sleep will result in concentration problems and the inability to do simple tasks that normally would take no thought at all, such as inserting a flash drive into a USB slot. More complex tasks, such as math problems, suffer less than these simple tasks because people *know* they must concentrate on a complex task (Chee & Choo, 2004; Lim et al., 2007).

Even so, **sleep deprivation**, or loss of sleep, is a serious problem, which many people have without realizing it. Students, for example, may stay up all night to study for an important test the next day. In doing so, they will lose more information than they gain, as a good night's sleep is important for memory and the ability to think well (Gillen-O'Neel et al., 2012; Lewis et al., 2018). See Learning Objective PIA.5. Even a few nights of poor sleep have serious consequences for mental and physical functioning (Jackson et al., 2013; Van Dongen et al., 2003). Some typical symptoms of sleep deprivation include trembling hands, inattention, staring off into space, droopy eyelids, and general discomfort (Naitoh et al., 1989), as well as emotional symptoms such as irritability and even depression. See Learning Objective 13.4. Add to that list an increased risk of insulin resistance, which can lead to diabetes (Matthews et al., 2012), an increased risk of obesity

sleep deprivation
any significant loss of sleep, resulting in problems in concentration and irritability.

(Kim et al., 2018), a possible increased risk of Alzhiemer's disease (Shokri-Kojori et al., 2018), depression of the immune system (Watson et al., 2017), and even possible delays in the onset of puberty (Shaw et al., 2012). And if you are a Twitter user, beware—a study found that users suffering from sleep deprivation tend to create more negative tweets, a sign of increased risk for psychological issues (McIver et al., 2015). As you will see in the feature titled "Weight Gain and Sleep" later on in this chapter, one common cause of sleep deprivation is a disturbance of the sleep–wake cycle, something that is a common problem among college students. Some people think they can just sleep longer than normal to make up for those nights of too little sleep, but doing that may increase the risk of dying before the age of 65—we *need* 6 to 7 hours of sleep *each* night not just on average and 7 to 8 hours of good sleep to perform at our very best (Åkerstedt et al., 2018; Wild et al., 2018).

For children and adolescents who are undergoing higher rates of growth and development during sleep, a good quality and quantity of sleep is extremely important. For example, one recent study found that a longer duration of sleep and a better quality of sleep were linked to a healthier heart and a lowered risk of diabetes, heart disease, and stroke (Feliciano et al., 2018). Yet many adolescents report sleeping fewer than 7 hours a night and that much of that sleep loss may be due to spending too many hours online (Twenge et al., 2017). People of all ages are experiencing more exposure to artificial light sources (i.e., cell phones or monitors left on in the room, small lights on clocks or other electronic devices) while they are trying to sleep. Research shows that light exposure interferes with the quality of sleep, and even a single night of light exposure can impact insulin resistance, which if chronic, may increase health risks for metabolic conditions such as type 2 diabetes (Mason et al., 2018).

4.5 The Stages of Sleep

4.5 Identify the different stages of sleep.

💬 So are there different kinds of sleep? Do you go from being awake to being asleep and dreaming—is it instant?

There are actually two kinds of sleep: **rapid eye movement sleep (R; REM)** and **non-rapid eye movement sleep (N; NREM)**. REM sleep is a relatively psychologically active type of sleep when most of a person's dreaming takes place, whereas NREM sleep spans from lighter stages to a much deeper, more restful kind of sleep. In REM sleep, the voluntary muscles are inhibited, meaning that the person in REM sleep moves very little, whereas in NREM sleep the person's body is free to move around (including kicking one's bed partner!). There are also several different stages of sleep that people go through each night in which REM sleep and NREM sleep occur. A machine called an electroencephalograph allows scientists to record the brain-wave activity as a person passes through the various stages of sleep and to determine what type of sleep the person has entered (Aserinsky & Kleitman, 1953).

A person who is wide awake and mentally active will show a brain-wave pattern on the electroencephalogram (EEG) called **beta waves**. Beta waves are very small and very fast. As the person relaxes and gets drowsy, slightly larger and slower **alpha waves** appear. The alpha waves are eventually replaced by even slower and larger **theta waves**. In the deepest stages of sleep, the largest and slowest waves appear, called **delta waves**.

Before moving on to the topic of the stages of sleep, it is worth mentioning that the terminology we now use for the various types and stages of sleep has changed in recent

rapid eye movement sleep (R, REM)
stage of sleep in which the eyes move rapidly under the eyelids and the person is typically experiencing a dream.

non-REM (NREM) sleep
any of the stages of sleep that do not include REM.

beta waves
smaller and faster brain waves, typically indicating mental activity.

alpha waves
brain waves that indicate a state of relaxation or light sleep.

theta waves
brain waves indicating the early stages of sleep.

delta waves
long, slow brain waves that indicate the deepest stage of sleep.

years, replacing older terminology that dated back to the 1960s (Carskadon & Dement, 2011; Iber et al., 2007; Rechtschaffen & Kales, 1968). If you find yourself reading older sleep research and see terms like REM (now R), NREM (now N), or four stages of NREM sleep instead of the three stages we will examine shortly, it is due to this change in the guidelines set forth by the American Academy of Sleep Medicine (Iber et al., 2007).

N1: LIGHT SLEEP As theta wave activity increases and alpha wave activity fades away, people are said to be entering stage N1 sleep, or light sleep. Several rather interesting things can happen in this stage of sleep. If people are awakened at this point, they will probably not believe that they were actually asleep. They may also experience vivid visual events called *hypnogogic images* or *hallucinations* (Kompanje, 2008; Lana-Peixoto, 2014; Liu et al., 2018; Ohayon et al., 1996; Vitorovic & Biller, 2013). (The Greek word *hypnos* means "sleep.") Many researchers now believe that people's experiences of ghostly visits, alien abductions, and near-death experiences may be most easily explained by these hallucinations (Kompanje, 2008; Moody & Perry, 1993). Since people are not aware of having been asleep, they are convinced that whatever happened in the hypnogogic hallucination really happened.

A much more common occurrence is called the *hypnic jerk* (Cuellar et al., 2015; Mahowald & Schenck, 1996; Oswald, 1959). Have you ever been drifting off to sleep when your knees, legs, or sometimes your whole body gives a big "jerk"? Although experts have no solid proof of why this occurs, many believe that it has something to do with the possibility that our ancestors slept in trees: The relaxation of the muscles as one drifts into sleep causes a "falling" sensation, at which point the body jerks awake to prevent the "fall" from the hypothetical tree (Coolidge, 2006; Sagan, 1977).

N2: SLEEP SPINDLES As people drift further into sleep, the body temperature continues to drop. Heart rate slows, breathing becomes more shallow and irregular, and the EEG will show the first signs of *sleep spindles*, brief bursts of activity lasting only a second or two. These bursts of activity may help stimulate neural areas in which recent memories have been stored, leading to better recall of those memories later on (Cairney et al., 2018). Theta waves still predominate in this stage, but if people are awakened during this stage, they will be aware of having been asleep.

N3: DELTA WAVES ROLL IN In the third stage of sleep, the slowest and largest waves make their appearance. These waves are called delta waves. These waves increase during this stage from about 20 percent to more than 50 percent of total brain activity. Now the person is in the deepest stage of sleep, often referred to as slow-wave sleep (SWS) or simply deep sleep (Carskadon & Dement, 2011).

It is during this stage that growth hormones (often abbreviated as GH) are released from the pituitary gland and reach their peak. The body is at its lowest level of functioning. Eventually, the delta waves become the dominant brain activity for this stage of sleep. See **Figure 4.3**, which shows progression, including brain activity, through the sleep stages throughout one night.

People in deep sleep are very hard to awaken. If something does wake them, they may be very confused and disoriented at first. It is not unusual for people to wake up in this kind of disoriented state only to hear the crack of thunder and realize that a storm has come up. Children are even harder to wake up when in this state than are adults. Deep sleep is the time when body growth occurs. This may explain why children in periods of rapid growth need to sleep more and also helps explain why children who are experiencing disrupted sleep (as is the case in situations of domestic violence) suffer delays in growth (Gilmour & Skuse, 1999; Saper et al., 2001; Swanson, 1994).

The fact that children do sleep so deeply may explain why certain sleep disorders are more common in childhood. Indeed, many sleep disorders are more common in boys than in girls because boys sleep more deeply than do girls due to high levels of the male hormone testosterone (Miyatake et al., 1980; Thiedke, 2001).

Figure 4.3 Brain Activity During Sleep

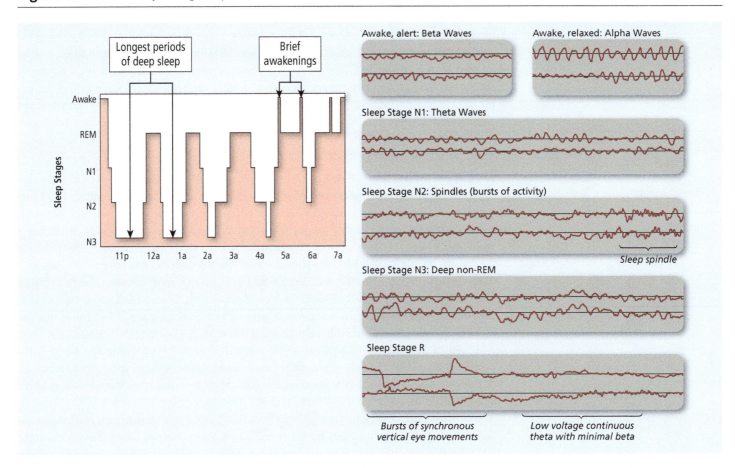

The EEG reflects brain activity during both waking and sleep. This activity varies according to level of alertness while awake (top two segments on the right) and the stage of sleep. Stage N3 of sleep is characterized by the presence of delta activity, which is much slower and accounts for the larger, slower waves on these graphs. R sleep has activity that resembles alert wakefulness but has relatively no muscle activity except rapid eye movement. The graph on the left shows the typical progression through the night of Stages N1–N3 and R. The R sleep periods occur about every 90 minutes throughout the night.

Source: Based on Dement (1974); EEG data and images courtesy of Dr. Leslie Sherlin.

R: RAPID EYE MOVEMENT After spending some time in N3, the sleeping person will go back up through N2 and then into a stage in which body temperature increases to near-waking levels, the eyes move rapidly under the eyelids, the heart beats much faster, and brain waves resemble beta waves—the kind of brain activity that usually signals wakefulness. The person is still asleep but in the stage known as rapid eye movement sleep (R) and sometimes referred to as paradoxical sleep.

REM SLEEP: PERCHANCE TO DREAM? When a person in stage R is awakened, he or she almost always reports being in a dream state (Shafton, 1995). REM sleep is, therefore, associated with dreaming, and 90 percent of dreams actually take place in REM sleep. People do have dreams in the other non-REM sleep stages, but REM sleep dreams tend to be more vivid, more detailed, longer, and more bizarre than the dreams of NREM sleep. NREM sleep dreams tend to be more like thoughts about daily occurrences and far shorter than REM sleep dreams (Foulkes & Schmidt, 1983; Takeuchi et al., 2003). Fortunately, the body is unable to act upon these dreams under normal conditions because the voluntary muscles are paralyzed during REM sleep, a condition known as **sleep paralysis**. (This is why you sometimes have a dream in which you are trying to run or move and can't—you are partially aware of sleep paralysis.) It is this paralysis that is often experienced as part

sleep paralysis

the inability of the voluntary muscles to move during REM sleep.

of a *hypnopompic hallucination*. These experiences, similar to the hypnogogic hallucinations of N1 sleep, typically happen as a person is caught between REM sleep and waking up.

Some people have a rare disorder in which the brain mechanisms that normally inhibit the voluntary muscles fail, allowing the person to thrash around and even get up and act out nightmares. This disorder is called **REM behavior disorder (RBD)**, which is a fairly serious condition (Nihei et al., 2012; Shafton, 1995). Usually seen in men over age 60, it can also happen in younger men and in women. Researchers have found support for the possibility that the breakdown of neural functioning in RBD may be a warning sign for future degeneration of neurons, leading to brain diseases such as Alzheimer's and Parkinson's disorders (Alibiglou et al., 2016; Peever et al., 2014). This has positive implications for early detection and treatment of these disorders.

WHAT IS THE PURPOSE OF REM SLEEP? Why two kinds of sleep? And why would REM sleep ever be considered restful when the body is almost awake and the brain is so active? REM sleep seems to serve a different purpose than does NREM, or deep sleep. After a very physically demanding day, people tend to spend more time in NREM deep sleep than is usual. But an emotionally stressful day leads to increased time in REM sleep (Horne & Staff, 1983). Perhaps the dreams people have in REM sleep are a way of dealing with the stresses and tensions of the day, whereas physical activity would demand more time for recovery of the body in NREM sleep. Also, if deprived of REM sleep (as would occur with the use of sleeping pills or other depressant drugs), a person will experience greatly increased amounts of REM sleep the next night, a phenomenon called **REM rebound** (Lo Bue et al., 2014; Vogel, 1975, 1993).

An early study of REM sleep deprivation (Dement, 1960) seemed to suggest that people deprived of REM sleep would become paranoid, seemingly mentally ill from lack of this one stage of sleep. This is called the *REM myth* because later studies failed to reliably produce the same results (Dement et al., 1969).

Other early research attempted to link REM sleep with the physical changes that occur during storing a memory for what one has recently learned, but the evidence today suggests that no one particular stage of sleep is the "one" in which this memory process occurs; rather, the evidence is mounting for sleep in general as necessary to the formation of memory (Ellenbogen et al., 2006; Kurdziel et al., 2013; Maquet et al., 2003; Seehagen et al., 2015; Siegel, 2001; Stickgold et al., 2001; Walker, 2005).

REM sleep in early infancy differs from adult REM sleep in several ways: Babies spend nearly 50 percent of their sleep in REM sleep as compared to adults' 20 percent, the brain-wave patterns on EEG recordings are not exactly the same in infant REM sleep when compared to adult REM sleep recordings, and infants can and do move around quite a bit during REM sleep (Carskadon & Dement, 2005; Davis et al., 2004; Sheldon, 2002; Tucker et al., 2006). These differences can be explained: When infants are engaged in REM sleep, they are not dreaming but rather forming new connections between neurons (Carskadon & Dement, 2005; Davis et al., 2004; Seehagen et al., 2015; Sheldon, 2002). The infant brain is highly plastic, and much of brain growth and development takes place during REM sleep. See Learning Objective 2.11. As the infant's brain nears its adult size by age 5 or 6, the proportion of REM sleep has also decreased to a more adult-like ratio of REM sleep to NREM sleep. For infants, to sleep is perchance to grow synapses.

While this infant is sleeping, an increased amount of REM sleep (occurring about half of the time she is asleep) allows her brain to make new neural connections.

REM behavior disorder (RBD)
a rare disorder in which the mechanism that blocks the movement of the voluntary muscles fails, allowing the person to thrash around and even get up and act out nightmares.

REM rebound
increased amounts of REM sleep after being deprived of REM sleep on earlier nights.

4.6 Sleep Disorders

4.6 Differentiate among the various sleep disorders.

What happens when sleep goes wrong? Nightmares, sleepwalking, and being unable to sleep well are all examples of sleep disorders.

💬 What would happen if we could act out our dreams? Would it be like sleepwalking?

NIGHTMARES Being able to act out one's dreams, especially nightmares, is a far more dangerous proposition than sleepwalking. **Nightmares** are bad dreams, and some nightmares can be utterly terrifying. Children tend to have more nightmares than adults do because they spend more of their sleep in the REM sleep state, as discussed earlier. As they age, they have fewer nightmares because they have less opportunity to have them. But some people still suffer from nightmares as adults.

NIGHT TERRORS Often seen as a rare disorder, **night terrors** have been found to occur in up to 56 percent of children between the ages of 1½ to 13 years old, with greatest prevalence around 1½ years of age (34.4%) and rapidly decreasing as the child grows older (13.4% at 5 years; 5.3% at 13 years; Petit et al., 2015). A night terror is essentially a state of panic experienced while sound asleep. People may sit up, scream, run around the room, or flail at some unseen attacker. It is also not uncommon for people to feel unable to breathe while they are in this state. Considering that people suffering a night-terror episode are in a deep stage of sleep and breathing shallowly, one can understand why breathing would seem difficult when they are suddenly active. Most people do not remember what happened during a night-terror episode, although a few people can remember vividly the images and terror they experienced.

Nightmares of being chased by a monster or a similar frightening creature are common, especially in childhood.

> But that sounds like the description of a nightmare—what's the difference?

Some very real differences exist between night terrors and nightmares. Nightmares are usually vividly remembered immediately upon waking. A person who has had a nightmare, unlike a person experiencing a night terror, will actually be able to awaken and immediately talk about the bad dream. Perhaps the most telling difference is that nightmares occur during REM sleep rather than deep NREM, slow wave sleep, which is the domain of night terrors, which means that people don't move around in a nightmare as they do in a night-terror experience.

SLEEPWALKING Real **sleepwalking, or somnambulism,** occurs in approximately 29 percent of children overall between the ages of 2½ to 13 years and is most likely between the ages of 10 and 13 years, at about 13 percent (Petit, et al., 2015). Sleepwalking is at least partially due to heredity, with greatest risk for children of parents who are or were sleepwalkers (Kales et al., 1980; Petit et al., 2015). The prevalence for children without parents having a history of sleepwalking is 22.5 percent, increasing to 47.4 percent where one parent did and reaching 61.5 percent for children where both parents were sleepwalkers. In other words, children with one or both parents having a history of sleepwalking are three to seven times more likely to be sleepwalkers themselves (Petit, et al., 2015). A person who is sleepwalking may do nothing more than sit up in bed. But other episodes may involve walking around the house, looking in the refrigerator or even eating, and getting into the car. Most people typically do not remember the episode the next day. One student said that her brother walked in his sleep, and one morning his family found him sound asleep behind the wheel of the family car in the garage. Fortunately, he had not been able to find the keys in his sleep.

Many people with this disorder grow out of their sleepwalking by the time they become adolescents. Many parents have found that preventing sleep loss makes sleepwalking a rare occurrence. This is most likely due to the deeper stage N3 sleep becoming even deeper during sleep loss, which would make fully waking even more difficult (Pilon et al., 2008; Zadra et al., 2008, 2013). The only real precaution that the families of people who sleepwalk should take is to clear their floors of obstacles and to put not-easy-to-reach locks on the doors. And although it is typically not dangerous to wake sleepwalkers, they may strike out before awakening.

nightmares
bad dreams occurring during REM sleep.

night terrors
relatively rare disorder in which the person experiences extreme fear and screams or runs around during deep sleep without waking fully.

sleepwalking (somnambulism)
occurring during deep sleep, an episode of moving around or walking around in one's sleep.

There have been incidents in which people who claimed to be in a state of sleepwalking (or more likely RBD) have committed acts of violence, even murder (Mahowald et al., 2005; Martin, 2004; Morris, 2009). In some cases the sleepwalking defense led to the acquittal of the accused person.

> **THINKING CRITICALLY 4.1**
>
> Do you think that sleepwalking is an adequate defense for someone who has harmed or killed another person? Should a person who has done harm while sleepwalking be forced by the courts to take preventive actions, such as installing special locks on bedroom doors? How might this affect the person's safety, such as in a fire?

INSOMNIA Most people think that **insomnia** is the inability to sleep. Although that is the literal meaning of the term, in reality insomnia is the inability to get to sleep, stay asleep, or get quality sleep (Kryger et al., 1999; Mayo Clinic Staff, 2014). There are many causes of insomnia, both psychological and physiological. Some of the psychological causes are worrying, trying too hard to sleep, or having anxiety. Some of the physiological causes are too much caffeine, indigestion, or aches and pains.

There are several steps people can take to help them sleep. Obvious ones are consuming no caffeinated drinks or foods that cause indigestion before bedtime, taking medication for pain, and dealing with anxieties in the daytime rather than facing them at night. That last bit of advice is easy to say but not always easy to do. Here are some other helpful hints (Kupfer & Reynolds, 1997; Mayo Clinic Staff, 2014; National Sleep Foundation, 2009):

1. **Go to bed only when you are sleepy.** If you lie in bed for 20 minutes and are still awake, get up and do something like reading or other light activity (avoid watching TV or being in front of a computer, tablet, or cell phone screen) until you feel sleepy, and then go back to bed. Studies have shown that the light emitted by television screens and particularly e-readers can be very disruptive to the natural sleep cycle (Chang et al., 2015).

2. **Don't do anything in your bed but sleep.** Your bed should be a cue for sleeping, not for studying or watching television. Using the bed as a cue for sleeping is a kind of learning called *classical conditioning*, or the pairing of cues and automatic responses. See Learning Objective 5.2.

3. **Don't try too hard to get to sleep, and especially do not look at the clock and calculate how much sleep you aren't getting.** That just increases the tension and makes it harder to sleep.

4. **Keep to a regular schedule.** Go to bed at the same time and get up at the same time, even on days that you don't have to go to work or class.

5. **Don't take sleeping pills or drink alcohol or other types of drugs that slow down the nervous system** (see the depressants category later in this chapter). These drugs force you into deep sleep and do not allow you to get any REM sleep or lighter stages of sleep. When you try to sleep without these drugs the next night, you will experience REM rebound, which will cause you to feel tired and sleepy the next day. REM rebound is one way to experience the form of insomnia in which a person sleeps but sleeps poorly.

6. **Exercise.** Exercise is not only good for your health, it's good for your quality of sleep, too. Exercise is particularly useful for combatting *hypersomnia*, or excessive sleepiness in the daytime—one cause of insomnia (Rethorst et al., 2015).

If none of these things seems to be working, there are sleep clinics and sleep experts who can help people with insomnia. The American Academy of Sleep Medicine has an excellent Web site at **www.aasm.org** that provides links to locate sleep clinics in any area.

insomnia

the inability to get to sleep, stay asleep, or get quality sleep.

One treatment that seems to have more success than any kind of sleep medication is the use of cognitive-behavior therapy, a type of therapy in which both rational thinking and controlled behavior are stressed (Bastien et al., 2004; Ellis & Barclay, 2014; Irwin et al., 2006; Morin et al., 2006). See Learning Objective 14.5.

SLEEP APNEA Gerald was a snorer. Actually, that's an understatement. Gerald could give a jet engine some serious competition. Snoring is fairly common, occurring when the breathing passages (nose and throat) get blocked. Most people snore only when they have a cold or some other occasional problem, but some people snore every night and quite loudly, like Gerald. It is this type of snoring that is often associated with a condition called **sleep apnea**, in which the person stops breathing for 10 seconds or more. When breathing stops, there will be a sudden silence, followed shortly by a gasping sound as the person struggles to get air into the lungs. Many people do not wake up while this is happening, but they do not get a good, restful night's sleep because of the apnea.

Apnea is a serious problem. According to the National Institutes of Health (2011), from 5 to 25 percent of adults in the United States suffer from apnea (it is difficult to be precise, as many people are unaware that they have apnea). Apnea can cause heart problems as well as poor sleep quality and depression (Edwards et al., 2015; Flemons, 2002; National Institute of Neurological Disorders and Stroke, 2015) and can also increase the likelihood of experiencing often frightening hypnopompic hallucinations (Lombardi et al., 2009). If a person suspects the presence of apnea, a visit to a physician is the first step in identifying the disorder and deciding on a treatment. While some people can benefit from wearing a nasal opening device, losing weight (obesity is often a primary cause of apnea), or using a nasal spray to shrink the nasal tissues, others must sleep with a device that delivers a continuous stream of air under mild pressure, called a *continuous positive airway pressure (CPAP) device*. Still others undergo a simple surgery in which the *uvula* (the little flap that hangs down at the back of the throat) and some of the soft tissues surrounding it are removed.

Some very young infants also experience a kind of apnea due to immaturity of the brain stem. These infants are typically placed on monitors that sound an alarm when breathing stops, allowing caregivers to help the infant begin breathing again. Although sleep apnea in infants is often associated with sudden infant death syndrome, or SIDS, it is not necessarily caused by it: Many infants who die of SIDS were never diagnosed with sleep apnea (Blackmon et al., 2003). There may be a connection between levels of the neurotransmitter serotonin and sleep apnea in infants (Donnelly et al., 2016).

NARCOLEPSY A disorder affecting 1 in every 2,000 persons, **narcolepsy** is a kind of "sleep seizure." In narcolepsy, the person may slip suddenly into REM sleep during the day (especially when the person experiences strong emotions). Another symptom is excessive daytime sleepiness that results in the person falling asleep throughout the day at inappropriate times and in inappropriate places (Overeem et al., 2001). These sleep attacks may occur many times and without warning, making the operation of a car or other machinery very dangerous for the person with narcolepsy. The sudden REM attacks are especially dangerous because of the symptom of *cataplexy*, or a sudden loss of muscle tone. This sleep paralysis may cause injuries if the person is standing when the attack occurs. The same hypnogogic images that may accompany stage N1 sleep may also occur in the person with narcolepsy. There may be new hope for sufferers of narcolepsy: Researchers have been developing several new drugs to treat narcolepsy, and initial tests with human participants look very promising (Abad & Guilleminault, 2017; Nagahara et al., 2015). **Table 4.1** has a more detailed list of known sleep disorders.

sleep apnea
disorder in which the person stops breathing for 10 seconds or more.

narcolepsy
sleep disorder in which a person falls immediately into REM sleep during the day without warning.

Table 4.1 Sleep Disorders

Name of Disorder	Primary Symptoms
Somnambulism	Sitting, walking, or performing complex behavior while asleep
Night terrors	Extreme fear, agitation, screaming while asleep
Restless leg syndrome	Uncomfortable sensations in legs causing movement and loss of sleep
Nocturnal leg cramps	Painful cramps in calf or foot muscles
Hypersomnia	Excessive daytime sleepiness
Circadian rhythm disorders	Disturbances of the sleep–wake cycle such as jet lag and shift work
Enuresis	Urinating while asleep in bed

Concept Map L.O. 4.3, 4.4, 4.5, 4.6

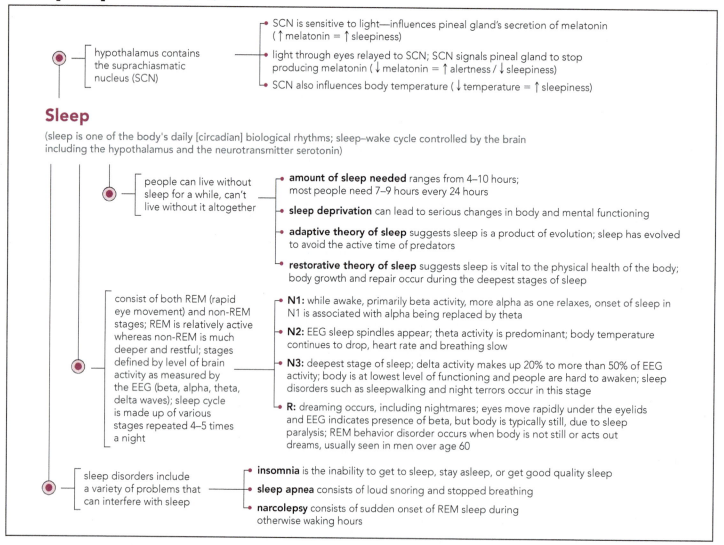

Practice Quiz   How much do you remember?

Pick the best answer.

1. The sleep–wake cycle typically follows a 24-hour cycle and is regulated by the _____.
   a. pituitary gland
   b. temporal lobe
   c. frontal lobe
   d. cerebellum
   e. suprachiasmatic nucleus

2. The pineal gland receives instructions from the _____ to release _____.
   a. thalamus, dopamine
   b. occipital lobe, serotonin
   c. spinal cord, acetylcholine
   d. temporal lobe, glutamate
   e. suprachiasmatic nucleus, melatonin

3. Which of the following is involved in determining when we sleep?
   a. digestion
   b. dopamine
   c. GABA
   d. body position
   e. body temperature

4. Which theory states that sleep is a product of evolution?
   a. REM theory
   b. adaptive theory
   c. circadian theory
   d. reactive theory
   e. restorative theory

5. Which of the following is a characteristic of stage N3, or slow-wave sleep?
   a. increased beta activity
   b. increased body temperature
   c. deepest level of sleep
   d. paralysis of voluntary muscles
   e. increased heart rate

6. Sleepwalking occurs in stage _____ sleep, whereas nightmares occur in stage _____ sleep.
   a. N2, N3
   b. N2, N1
   c. N3, R
   d. N1, N2
   e. R, N3

APA Goal 2: Scientific Inquiry and Critical Thinking

Weight Gain and Sleep

Addresses APA Learning Objective 2.1: Use scientific reasoning to interpret psychological phenomena.

Many people have heard that it's common for young people going off to college or university for the first time to gain weight. There's even a name for it, the "freshman 15." Some of the reasons people have given for this weight gain, citing "common sense" reasoning, include being away from home (and parental supervision) for the first time, more partying than studying, and mass consumption of junk food, among others. But common sense, as we've seen, doesn't always give an accurate picture of what is really happening. For accuracy, we need to determine what science says about the freshman 15.

First we need to ask, do first-year college students really put on weight their first year of school? The answer seems to be yes, but not quite as much as rumor has it. The actual freshman weight gain tends to be about 3.5 to 6 pounds (Holm-Denoma et al., 2008; Roane et al., 2015). Score one for science, not so much for common sense.

Now that we know there is a weight gain, what could be the cause or causes of that gain? We do know that college students probably don't get the amount of sleep recommended by experts, which is a little over 9 hours a night (Dahl & Lewin, 2002; Hirshkowitz et al., 2015). Sleep deprivation can make you eat more, and there's evidence that when teens and young adults are sleep deprived, they tend to go for sweet foods that are high in calories and low in nutrition (Simon et al., 2015).

But is it the fewer hours of sleep or the timing of the amount of sleep freshman do get? Students often get to bed much later when away at school than when at home, and one study has shown that for every hour bedtime was pushed back, there was a gain of about two points in body mass index or BMI, an indicator of how much body fat a person has (Asarnow et al., 2015).

A more recent study suggests that in addition to all of these factors, the weight gain experienced by many freshman college students may also be a result of irregular sleep patterns: Not only do students get less sleep and go to bed later, but they also go to sleep at different times due to different class schedules and social activities. While a person who is working has a schedule of getting up at a certain time and going to bed by a certain time on a regular basis, students may get to bed at midnight and get up at 7 A.M. one night but go to bed at 2 A.M. the following night and get up at 9 A.M. Even though both nights are 7 hours of sleep, the shift in the schedule is what may cause more sleep deprivation symptoms, according to one study (Roane et al., 2015). When your sleep–wake cycle is shifted daily by 2 to nearly 3 hours, it's like having daily jet lag—just like shift workers and frequent flyers.

So the "freshman 15" is real, but more like the "freshman 5," and the causative factors are not as simple as common sense might tell us. The sleep deprivation symptoms brought on by not only less sleep but also frequent variability in sleep cycles lead to fatigue (which leads to less exercise) and eating more sweets for quick energy boosts, eventually leading to weight gain. In the Brown study, this weight gain amounted to about 6 pounds in only 9 weeks!

APA Goal 2 Weight Gain and Sleep

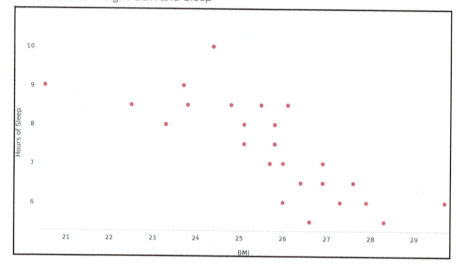

> **AP** 2.S Discuss aspects of sleep and dreaming.

4.7–4.8 Dreams

"To sleep, perchance to dream" is a well-known and often-quoted line from Act II of *Hamlet* by William Shakespeare (Shakespeare & Hubler, 1987). But how important is dreaming? What is the purpose of dreaming?

4.7 Why Do We Dream?

4.7 Compare and contrast two explanations of why people dream.

Dreams have long been a source of curiosity. People of ancient times tried to find meaning in dreams. Some viewed dreams as prophecy, some as messages from the spirits. Aboriginal peoples of Australia, for example, see dreams as intimately tied to their religious and cultural belief systems (James, 2015). But the real inquiry into the process of dreaming began with the publication of Freud's *The Interpretation of Dreams* (1900).

> **AP** 2.R Identify the contributions of major figures in consciousness research.

FREUD'S INTERPRETATION: DREAMS AS WISH FULFILLMENT Sigmund Freud (1856–1939) believed that the problems of his patients stemmed from conflicts and events that had been buried in their unconscious minds since childhood. These early traumas were seen as the cause of behavior problems in adulthood, in which his patients suffered from symptoms such as a type of paralysis that had no physical basis or repetitive, ritualistic* hand washing. One of the ways Freud devised to get at these early memories was to examine the dreams of his patients, believing that conflicts, events, and desires of the past would be represented in symbolic** form in the dreams. Freud believed dreams to be a kind of wish fulfillment for his patients. See Learning Objective 12.2.

---

*ritualistic: referring to an action done in a particular manner each time it is repeated, according to some specific pattern.
**symbolic: having the quality of representing something other than itself.

The *manifest content* of a dream is the actual content of the dream itself. For example, if Chad has a dream in which he is trying to climb out of a bathtub, the manifest content of the dream is exactly that—he's trying to climb out of a bathtub.

But, of course, Freud would no doubt find more meaning in Chad's dream than is at first evident. He believed that the true meaning of a dream was hidden, or *latent*, and only expressed in symbols. In the dream, the water in the tub might symbolize the waters of birth, and the tub itself might be his mother's womb. Using a Freudian interpretation, Chad may be dreaming about being born.

> Seems like quite a stretch. Wouldn't there be lots of other possible interpretations?

Yes, and today many professionals are no longer as fond of Freud's dream analysis as they once were. But there are still some people who insist that dreams have symbolic meaning. For example, dreaming about being naked in a public place is very common, and most dream analyzers interpret that to mean feeling open and exposed, an expression of childhood innocence, or even a desire for sex. Exactly how the dream is interpreted depends on the other features of the dream and what is happening in the person's waking life.

The development of techniques for looking at the structure and activity of the brain (see Learning Objective 2.5) has led to an explanation of why people dream that is more concrete than that of Freud.

THE ACTIVATION-SYNTHESIS HYPOTHESIS Using brain-imaging techniques such as a PET scan (see Chapter Two), researchers have found evidence that dreams are products of activity in the pons (Hobson, 1988; Hobson & McCarley, 1977; Hobson et al., 2000; Weber et al., 2015). This lower area inhibits the neurotransmitters that would allow movement of the voluntary muscles while sending random signals to the areas of the cortex that interpret vision, hearing, and so on (see **Figure 4.4**).

Figure 4.4 The Brain and Activation-Synthesis Theory

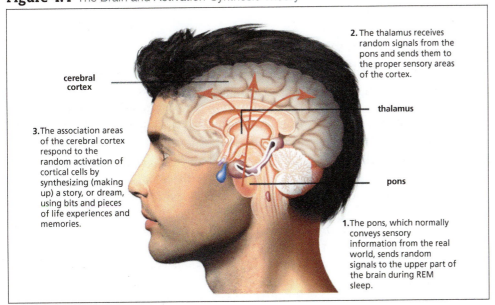

According to the activation-synthesis theory of dreaming, the pons in the brainstem sends random signals to the upper part of the brain during REM sleep. These random signals pass through the thalamus, which sends the signals to the proper sensory areas of the cortex. Once in the cortex, the association areas of the cortex respond to the random activation of these cortical cells by synthesizing (making up) a story, or dream, using bits and pieces of life experiences and memories.

When signals from the pons bombard* the cortex during waking consciousness, the association areas of the cortex interpret those signals as seeing, hearing, and so on. Because those signals come from the real world, this process results in an experience of reality. But when people are asleep, the signals from the brain stem are random and not necessarily attached to actual external stimuli, yet the brain must somehow interpret these random signals. It *synthesizes* (puts together) an explanation of the cortex's activation from memories and other stored information.

In this theory, called the **activation-synthesis hypothesis**, a dream is merely another kind of thinking that occurs when people sleep. It is less realistic because it comes not from the outside world of reality but from within people's memories and experiences of the past. The frontal lobes, which people normally use in daytime thinking, are more or less shut down during dreaming, which may also account for the unrealistic and often bizarre nature of dreams (Macquet & Franck, 1996).

> My dreams can be really weird, but sometimes they seem pretty ordinary or even seem to mean something. Can dreams be more meaningful?

THE ACTIVATION-INFORMATION-MODE (AIM) MODEL There are dream experts who suggest that dreams may have more meaning than Hobson and McCarley originally theorized. A survey questioning participants about their dream content, for example, concluded that much of the content of dreams is meaningful, consistent over time, and fits in with past or present emotional concerns rather than being bizarre, meaningless, and random (Domhoff, 1996; Domhoff, 2005).

Hobson and colleagues have reworked the activation-synthesis hypothesis to reflect concerns about dream meaning, calling it the **activation-information-mode model,** or **AIM** (Hobson et al., 2000). In this newer version, information that is accessed during waking hours can have an influence on the synthesis of dreams. In other words, when the brain is "making up" a dream to explain its own activation, it uses meaningful bits and pieces of the person's experiences from the previous day or the last few days rather than just random items from memory.

4.8 What Do People Dream About?

4.8 Identify commonalities and differences in the content of people's dreams.

Calvin Hall believed that dreams are just another type of cognitive process, or thinking, that occurred during sleep in his *cognitive theory of dreaming* (Hall, 1953). He collected more than 10,000 dreams and concluded that most dreams reflect the events that occur in everyday life (Hall, 1966). Although most people dream in color, people who grew up in the era of black-and-white television sometimes have dreams in black and white. There are gender differences, although whether those differences are caused by hormonal/genetic influences, sociocultural influences, or a combination of influences remains to be seen.

In his book *Finding Meaning in Dreams*, Dr. William Domhoff concluded that across many cultures, men more often dream of other males whereas women tend to dream about males and females equally (Domhoff, 1996). Girls and women tend to dream about people they know, personal appearance concerns, and issues related to family and home. Boys and men also tend to dream about other males in outdoor or unfamiliar settings and these dreams may involve weapons, tools, cars, and roads. Men also report more sexual dreams, usually with unknown and attractive partners (Domhoff, 1996; Domhoff &

---

activation-synthesis hypothesis
premise that states that dreams are created by the higher centers of the cortex to explain the activation by the brain stem of cortical cells during REM sleep periods.

activation-information-mode model (AIM)
revised version of the activation-synthesis explanation of dreams in which information that is accessed during waking hours can have an influence on the synthesis of dreams.

---

*bombard: to attack or press.

Schneider, 2008; Foulkes, 1982; Horikawa et al., 2013; Van de Castle, 1994). Men across various cultures also tend to have more physical aggression in their dreams than do women, and women are more often the victims of such aggression in their own dreams.

Domhoff also concluded that where there are differences in the content of dreams across cultures, the differences make sense in light of the culture's "personality." For example, American culture is considered fairly aggressive when compared to the culture of the Netherlands, and the aggressive content of the dreams in both cultures reflects this difference: There were lower levels of aggression in the dreams of those from the Netherlands when compared to the Americans' dream content. The most common dream topic of German and Chinese students was schools, teachers, and studying (Schredl et al., 2004; Yu, 2008), but for Canadian students the common topic was being chased or pursued (Nielsen et al., 2003).

In dreams people run, jump, talk, and do all of the actions that they do in normal daily life. Nearly 50 percent of the dreams recorded by Hall (Hall, 1966) had sexual content, although later research has found lower percentages (Van de Castle, 1994). Then there are dreams of flying, falling, and of trying to do something and failing—all of which are very common dreams, even in other cultures (Domhoff, 1996). So is that often-recounted dream of being naked in public!

Concept Map L.O. 4.7, 4.8

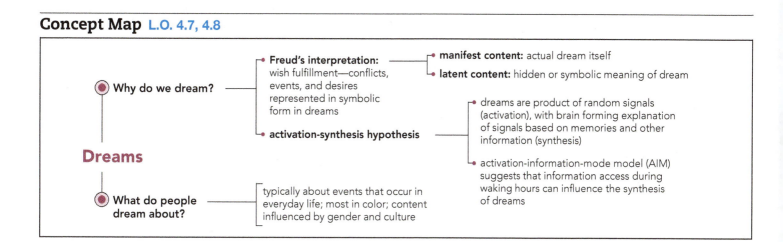

Practice Quiz   How much do you remember?

Pick the best answer.

1. In Freud's theory, the actual content of a dream is called _____ content.
   a. dormant
   b. hidden
   c. symbolic
   d. manifest
   e. latent

2. Rachel finds that most of her dreams are little more than random images that seemingly have been put into a strange storyline. Which theory of dreams best explains this?
   a. Hall's dreams as reflections of everyday life
   b. dreams for survival theory
   c. dreams at random theory
   d. activation-synthesis hypothesis
   e. Freudian dream theory

3. According to Calvin Hall, around what are most dreams centered?
   a. unfulfilled fantasies
   b. everyday life
   c. frightening events
   d. past childhood
   e. personal pets

4. Studies show that most people tend to _____.
   a. dream in color
   b. not dream at all
   c. dream in color but have nightmares in black and white
   d. only have nightmares
   e. dream in black and white

4.9–4.10 Hypnosis

Contrary to what you may have seen in the movies or on television, people who are hypnotized are not in some mystical, supernatural trance (Lynn et al., 2015). **Hypnosis** is simply a state of consciousness in which a person is especially susceptible to suggestion. Although a lot of misunderstandings exist about hypnosis, it can be a useful tool when properly managed.

4.9 How Hypnosis Works

4.9 Explain how hypnosis affects consciousness.

There are four key steps in inducing hypnosis (Druckman & Bjork, 1994):

1. The hypnotist tells the person to focus on what is being said.
2. The person is told to relax and feel tired.
3. The hypnotist tells the person to "let go" and accept suggestions easily.
4. The person is told to use vivid imagination.

The real key to hypnosis seems to be a heightened state of suggestibility.* People can be hypnotized when active and alert, but only if they are willing to be hypnotized. Only 80 percent of all people can be hypnotized, and only 40 percent are good hypnotic participants. The ability to be hypnotized may lie in the way the brain functions. Using brain-scanning techniques, researchers found that two areas in the brains of highly hypnotizable people, areas associated with decision making and attention, seem to be more active and connected when compared to people who cannot be hypnotized (Hoeft et al., 2012; Jiang et al., 2016).

A test of *hypnotic susceptibility*, or the degree to which a person is a good hypnotic participant, often makes use of a series of ordered suggestions. The more suggestions in the ordered list the person responds to, the more susceptible** that person is. (See **Table 4.2** for examples of the types of items on a typical hypnotic susceptibility scale.)

hypnosis
state of consciousness in which the person is especially susceptible to suggestion.

Table 4.2 Examples of Items That Would Appear on a Hypnotic Susceptibility Scale

1. Movement of the body back and forth	5. Responding to posthypnotic suggestion
2. Closing eyes and unable to open them	6. Loss of memory for events during the session
3. Fingers locked together	7. Unable to state one's own name
4. One arm locked into position	8. Seeing or hearing nonexistent stimuli

Source: Based on Hilgard E. R. (1965). Hypnotic susceptibility. New York: Harcourt, Brace & World.

💬 Is it true that people can be hypnotized into doing things that they would never do under normal conditions?

Although the popular view is that the hypnotized person is acting involuntarily, the fact is that the hypnotist may only be a guide into a more relaxed state, while the participant actually hypnotizes himself or herself (Kirsch & Lynn, 1995). People cannot be hypnotized against their will. The tendency to act as though their behavior

---

*suggestibility: being readily influenced.
**susceptible: easily affected emotionally.

is automatic and out of their control is called the *basic suggestion effect* (Kihlstrom, 1985); it gives people an excuse to do things they might not otherwise do because the burden of responsibility for their actions falls on the hypnotist.

For a more detailed discussion of the problems in using hypnosis for memory retrieval, watch the video, *Hypnosis in Therapy and Recovered Memories*. See Learning Objective 6.9.

In general, hypnosis is a handy way to help people relax and/or to control pain. These subjective experiences are very much under people's mental influence, and hypnosis is not the only way to achieve them. The same kind of effects (such as hallucinations, reduction of pain, and memory loss) can be achieved without any hypnotic suggestion (Lynn et al., 2015). Actual physical behavior is harder to change, and that is why hypnosis alone is not as effective at changing eating habits or helping people stop smoking (Druckman & Bjork, 1994; Milling et al., 2018). Hypnosis is sometimes used in psychological therapy to help people cope with anxiety or deal with cravings for food or drugs. For a concise look at what hypnosis can and cannot do, see **Table 4.3**.

Watch Hypnosis in Therapy and Recovered Memories

Watch the Video at MyLab Psychology

Table 4.3 Facts About Hypnosis

Hypnosis Can:	Hypnosis Cannot:
Create amnesia for whatever happens during the hypnotic session, at least for a brief time (Bowers & Woody, 1996; Jamieson et al., 2017).	Give people superhuman strength. (People may use their full strength under hypnosis, but it is no more than they had before hypnosis.)
Relieve pain by allowing a person to remove conscious attention from the pain (Holroyd, 1996; Kihlstrom, 2018).	Reliably enhance memory (Kihlstrom, 2018). (There's an increased risk of false-memory retrieval because of the suggestible state hypnosis creates.)
Alter sensory perceptions. (Smell, hearing, vision, time sense, and the ability to see visual illusions can all be affected by hypnosis.)	Regress people back to childhood (Kihlstrom, 2018). (Although people may *act* like children, they do and say things children would not.)
Help people relax in situations that normally would cause them stress, such as flying on an airplane (Muhlberger et al., 2001; Kihlstrom, 2018).	Regress people to some "past life." There is no scientific evidence for past-life regression (Lilienfeld et al., 2004).

4.10 Theories of Hypnosis

4.10 Compare and contrast two views of why hypnosis works.

There are two views of why hypnosis works. One emphasizes the role of **dissociation**, or a splitting of conscious awareness, whereas the other involves a kind of social role-playing.

HYPNOSIS AS DISSOCIATION: THE HIDDEN OBSERVER Ernest Hilgard (1991; Hilgard & Hilgard, 1994) believed that hypnosis worked only on the immediate conscious mind of a person, while a part of that person's mind (a "hidden observer") remained aware of all that was going on. It's the same kind of dissociation that takes place when people

dissociation
divided state of conscious awareness.

Stage hypnotists often make use of people's willingness to believe that something ordinary is extraordinary. This woman was hypnotized and suspended between two chairs after the person supporting her middle stepped away. The hypnotist led the audience to believe that she could not do this unless hypnotized, but in reality anyone can do this while fully conscious.

social-cognitive theory of hypnosis

theory that assumes that people who are hypnotized are not in an altered state but are merely playing the role expected of them in the situation.

drive somewhere familiar and then wonder how they got there. One part of the mind, the conscious part, is thinking about dinner or a date or something else, while the other part is doing the actual driving. When people arrive at their destination, they don't really remember the actual trip. In the same way, Hilgard believes that there is a hidden part of the mind that is very much aware of the hypnotic participant's activities and sensations, even though the "hypnotized" part of the mind is blissfully unaware of these same things.

In one study (Miller & Bowers, 1993), participants were hypnotized and told to put their arms in ice water, although they were instructed to feel no pain. There had to be pain—most people can't even get an ice cube out of the freezer without *some* pain—but participants reported no pain at all. The participants who were successful at denying the pain also reported that they imagined being at the beach or in some other place that allowed them to dissociate* from the pain.

HYPNOSIS AS SOCIAL ROLE-PLAYING: THE SOCIAL-COGNITIVE EXPLANATION The other theory of why hypnosis works began with an experiment in which participants who were *not* hypnotized were instructed to behave as if they were (Sarbin & Coe, 1972). These participants had no trouble copying many actions previously thought to require a hypnotic state, such as being rigidly suspended between two chairs. The researchers also found that participants who were not familiar with hypnosis and had no idea what the "role" of a hypnotic participant was supposed to be could not be hypnotized.

Add to those findings the later findings that expectancies of the hypnotized person play a big part in how the person responds and what the person does under hypnosis (Kirsch, 2000; Lynn et al., 2012). The **social-cognitive theory of hypnosis** assumes that people who are hypnotized are not in an altered state but are merely playing the role expected of them in the situation. They might believe that they are hypnotized, but in fact it is all a very good performance, so good that even the "participants" are unaware that they are role-playing. Social roles are very powerful influences on behavior, as we'll see in Chapter Eleven.

---

*dissociate: break a connection with something.

Concept Map L.O. 4.9, 4.10

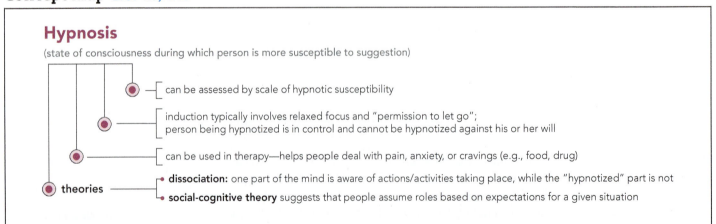

Practice Quiz   How much do you remember?

Pick the best answer.

1. The primary key to hypnosis is finding someone who _____.
   a. easily distracted
   b. is easily distracted
   c. has a vivid imagination
   d. accepts suggestions easily
   e. is already very tired

2. Some researchers have suggested that hypnosis may work due to an individual's personal expectations about what being hypnotized is supposed to be like and the individual's ability to play a particular role in the given social situation. Which theory of hypnosis best accounts for these possible explanations for an individual's behavior while hypnotized?
   a. dissociative theory
   b. social-cognitive theory
   c. expectancy theory
   d. biological theory
   e. psychodynamic theory

3. Your friend tells you she is seeing a therapist who wishes to use hypnosis as part of her therapy. However, your friend is concerned that she might be hypnotized without knowing it. What might you tell her?
   a. You actually hypnotize yourself and you cannot be hypnotized against your will.
   b. Don't worry. Hypnosis is just an illusion and doesn't really work.
   c. Be careful. Hypnotic trances can last far beyond the therapy session.
   d. Don't worry. Hypnotists can only control their patient's behavior about 40 percent of the time.
   e. Be careful. Hypnotists are in control of you while hypnotized.

4. Which theory of hypnosis includes the idea of a "hidden observer"?
   a. social cognitive
   b. dissociative
   c. biological
   d. expectancy
   e. psychodynamic

4.11–4.14 The Influence of Psychoactive Drugs

AP 2.P Identify the major psychoactive drug categories and classify specific drugs, including their psychological and physiological effects.

Whereas some people seek altered states of consciousness in sleep, daydreaming, meditation, or even hypnosis, others try to take a shortcut. They use **psychoactive drugs**, chemical substances that alter thinking, perception, memory, or some combination of those abilities. Many of the drugs discussed in the following sections are very useful and were originally developed to help people. Some put people to sleep so that surgeries and procedures that would otherwise be impossible can be performed, whereas others help people deal with the pain of injuries or disease. Still others may be used in helping to control various conditions such as sleep disorders or attention deficits in children and adults.

4.11 Dependence

4.11 Distinguish between physical dependence and psychological dependence upon drugs.

AP 2.Q Discuss drug dependence, addiction, tolerance, and withdrawal.

The usefulness of these drugs must not blind us to the dangers of misusing or abusing them. When taken for pleasure, to get "high," or to dull psychological pain or when taken without the supervision of a qualified medical professional, these drugs can pose serious risks to one's health and may even cause death. One danger of such drugs is their potential to create either a physical or psychological dependence, both of which can lead to a lifelong pattern of abuse as well as the risk of taking increasingly larger doses, leading to one of the clearest dangers of dependence: a drug overdose. Drug overdoses do not happen only with illegal drugs; even certain additives in so-called natural supplements can have a deadly effect. One survey found that more than 23,000 emergency room visits per year could be attributed to the use and abuse of dietary supplements (Geller et al., 2015).

PHYSICAL DEPENDENCE   Drugs that people can become physically dependent on cause the user's body to crave the drug (Abadinsky, 1989; Fleming & Barry, 1992; Pratt, 1991). After using the drug for some period of time, the body becomes unable to function normally without the drug and the person is said to be dependent or addicted, a condition commonly called **physical dependence**.

Another sign of a physical dependence is that the user experiences symptoms of **withdrawal** when deprived of the drug. Depending on the drug, these symptoms can

psychoactive drugs
chemical substances that alter thinking, perception, and memory.

physical dependence
condition occurring when a person's body becomes unable to function normally without a particular drug.

withdrawal
physical symptoms that can include nausea, pain, tremors, crankiness, and high blood pressure, resulting from a lack of an addictive drug in the body systems.

range from headaches, nausea, and irritability to severe pain, cramping, shaking, and dangerously elevated blood pressure. These physical sensations occur because the body is trying to adjust to the absence of the drug. Many users will take more of the drug to alleviate the symptoms of withdrawal, which makes the entire situation worse. This is actually an example of *negative reinforcement*, the tendency to continue a behavior that leads to the removal of or escape from unpleasant circumstances or sensations. Negative reinforcement is a very powerful motivating factor, and scores of drug-dependent users exist as living proof of that power. See Learning Objective 5.3.

The "high" of drug use often takes place in certain surroundings, with certain other people, and perhaps even using certain objects, such as the tiny spoons used by cocaine addicts. These people, settings, and objects can become cues that are associated with the drug high. When the cues are present, it may be even harder to resist using the drug because the body and mind have become conditioned, or trained, to associate drug use with the cues. This is a form of *classical conditioning*. See Learning Objective 5.2.

This learned behavioral effect has led to nondrug treatments that make use of behavioral therapies such as *contingency-management therapy* (an operant conditioning strategy), in which patients earn vouchers for negative drug tests (Tusel et al., 1994). The vouchers can be exchanged for healthier, more desirable items like food. These behavioral therapies can include residential and outpatient approaches. See Learning Objective 14.4. *Cognitive-behavioral interventions* work to change the way people think about the stresses in their lives and react to those stressors, working toward more effective coping without resorting to drugs.

In addition to learning, the brain itself plays an important part in dependency. Drugs that can lead to dependence tend to activate dopaminergic neurons in specific pathways of the brain. One is called the mesolimbic pathway, which begins in the midbrain area (just above the pons, in an area called the *ventral tegmental area* or *VTA*) and connects to limbic system structures, including the amygdala and hippocampus, and to the *nucleus accumbens*, which is involved in reinforcement. The other is the mesocortical pathway, which connects the VTA to prefrontal areas. Combined, these pathways make up a mesocorticolimbic reward circuit that is heavily involved in drug use behavior (Blum et al., 2012; Gardner, 2011; Koob & Volkow, 2016; Pariyadath et al., 2016; Volkow et al., 2017). See Learning Objective 2.7. While the mesocortical pathway is involved with judgment and control of behavior, the mesolimbic pathway is involved with the reinforcing aspects of a stimulus. When a drug of abuse enters the body, it quickly activates the mesolimbic system, known as the brain's "reward pathway," causing a release of dopamine and intense pleasure (see **Figure 4.5**). The brain tries to adapt to this large amount of dopamine by decreasing the number of synaptic receptors for dopamine. The next time the user takes the drug, he or she needs more of it to get the same pleasure response because of the reduced number of receptors—**drug tolerance** has developed (Koob & Le Moal, 2005; Laviolette et al., 2008; Salamone & Correa, 2012). This system of structures in the reward pathway is tied to all forms of addiction and may be involved in the depression that occurs in some mood disorders (Glangetas et al., 2015; Mahr et al., 2013; Russo & Nestler, 2013). See Learning Objective 13.4.

💬 But not all drugs produce physical dependence, right? For example, some people say that you can't get physically dependent on marijuana. If that's true, why is it so hard for some people to quit smoking pot?

PSYCHOLOGICAL DEPENDENCE Not all drugs cause physical dependence; some cause **psychological dependence**, or the belief that the drug is needed to continue a feeling of emotional or psychological well-being, which is a very powerful factor in continued drug use. The body may not need or crave the drug, and people may not experience the symptoms of physical withdrawal or tolerance, but they will continue to use the drug because they *think* they need it. In this case, it is the rewarding properties of using the drug that cause a dependency to develop. This is an example of *positive reinforcement*, or the

---

AP 2.H Discuss the influence of drugs on neurotransmitters.

drug tolerance
the decrease of the response to a drug over repeated uses, leading to the need for higher doses of drug to achieve the same effect.

psychological dependence
the belief that a drug is needed to continue a feeling of emotional or psychological well-being.

Figure 4.5 The Brain's Reward Pathway

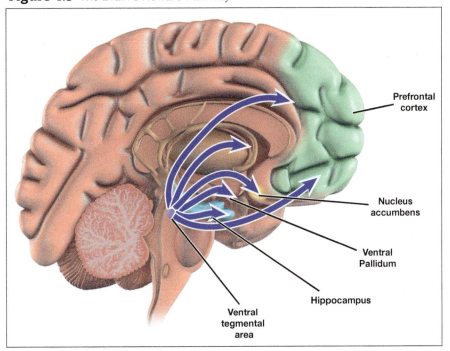

A pleasure center has been discovered in the mesocorticolimbic dopamine system. The cells in this system communicate via the neurotransmitter dopamine. The pathway between the ventral tegmental area and the nucleus accumbens (the mesolimbic pathway) is most likely the site for the rewarding effects of natural rewards (e.g., eating, drinking, sex) and drug effects (e.g., euphoria, pleasure).

tendency of a behavior to strengthen when followed by pleasurable consequences. See Learning Objective 5.5. Negative reinforcement is also at work here, as taking the drug will lower levels of anxiety.

Although not all drugs produce physical dependence, *any* drug can become a focus of psychological dependence. Indeed, because there is no withdrawal to go through or to recover from, psychological dependencies can last forever. Some people who gave up smoking marijuana decades ago still say that the craving returns every now and then (Hasin et al., 2016; Roffman et al., 1988).

The effect of a particular drug depends on the category to which it belongs and the particular neurotransmitter the drug affects. See Learning Objective 2.3. In this current chapter we will describe several of the major drug categories, including **stimulants** (drugs that increase the functioning of the nervous system), **depressants** (drugs that decrease the functioning of the nervous system), and **hallucinogenics** (drugs that alter perceptions and may cause hallucinations).

4.12 Stimulants: Up, Up, and Away

4.12 Identify the effects and dangers of using stimulants.

Stimulants are a class of drugs that cause either the sympathetic division or the central nervous system (or both) to increase levels of functioning, at least temporarily. In simple terms, stimulants "speed up" the nervous system—the heart may beat faster or the brain may work faster, for example. Many of these drugs are called "uppers" for this reason.

AMPHETAMINES **Amphetamines** are stimulants that are synthesized (made) in laboratories rather than being found in nature. Among the amphetamines are drugs like Adderall, Benzedrine, Methedrine, and Dexedrine. A related compound, *methamphetamine*, is sometimes used to treat attention-deficit/hyperactivity disorder or narcolepsy. "Crystal meth"

One of the dangers of psychoactive drugs is that they may lead to physical or psychological dependence.

stimulants
drugs that increase the functioning of the nervous system.

depressants
drugs that decrease the functioning of the nervous system.

hallucinogenics
drugs including hallucinogens and marijuana that produce hallucinations or increased feelings of relaxation and intoxication.

amphetamines
stimulants that are synthesized (made) in laboratories rather than being found in nature.

is a crystalline form that can be smoked and is used by "recreational" drug users, people who do not need drugs but instead use them to gain some form of pleasure.

Like other stimulants, amphetamines cause the sympathetic nervous system to go into overdrive. See Learning Objective 2.12. Some truck drivers use amphetamines to stay awake while driving long hours. Stimulants won't give people any extra energy, but they will cause people to burn up whatever energy reserves they do have. They also depress the appetite, which is another function of the sympathetic division. Many doctors used to prescribe these drugs as diet pills. Today they are only used on a short-term basis and under strict medical supervision, often in the treatment of attention-deficit hyperactivity disorder (Safer, 2015). Diet pills sold over the counter usually contain another relatively mild stimulant, caffeine.

When the energy reserves are exhausted, or the drug wears off, a "crash" is inevitable and the tendency is to take more pills to get back "up." The person taking these pills finds that it takes more and more pills to get the same stimulant effect (drug tolerance). Nausea, vomiting, high blood pressure, and strokes are possible, as is a state called "amphetamine psychosis." This condition causes addicts to become delusional (losing contact with what is real) and paranoid. They think people are out to "get" them. Violence is a likely outcome, against both the self and others (Dickinson, 2015; Kratofil et al., 1996; Paparelli et al., 2011).

COCAINE Unlike amphetamines, **cocaine** is a natural drug found in coca plant leaves. It produces feelings of euphoria (a feeling of great happiness), energy, power, and pleasure. It also deadens pain and suppresses the appetite. It was used rather liberally by both doctors and dentists (who used it in numbing the mouth prior to extracting a tooth, for example) near the end of the nineteenth century and the beginning of the twentieth century, until the deadly effects of its addictive qualities became known. Many patent medicines contained minute traces of cocaine, including the now famous Coca-Cola™ (this popular soft drink was originally marketed as a nerve tonic). The good news is that even in 1902, there wasn't enough cocaine in a bottle of cola to affect even a fly, and by 1929, all traces of cocaine were removed (Allen, 1994).

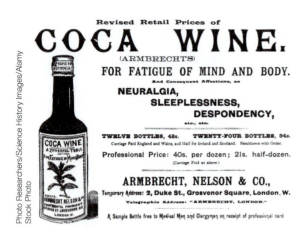

Far from being illegal, cocaine was once used in many drinks and medications.

Cocaine is a highly dangerous drug, not just for its addictive properties. Some people have convulsions and may even die when using cocaine for the first time (Lacayo, 1995). It can have devastating effects on the children born to mothers who use cocaine and has been associated with increased risk of learning disabilities, delayed language development, and an inability to cope adequately with stress, among other symptoms (Cone-Wesson, 2005; Eiden et al., 2009; Kable et al., 2008; Morrow et al., 2006). Laboratory animals have been known to press a lever to give themselves cocaine rather than eating or drinking, even to the point of starvation and death (Chahua et al., 2015; Glangetas et al., 2015; Iwamoto & Martin, 1988; Ward et al., 1996).

Although cocaine users do not go through the same kind of physical withdrawal symptoms that users of heroin, alcohol, and other physically addictive drugs go through, users will experience a severe mood swing into depression (the "crash"), followed by extreme tiredness, nervousness, an inability to feel pleasure, and paranoia. The brain is the part of the body that develops the craving for cocaine because of chemical changes caused by the drug (Glangetas et al., 2015; Hurley, 1989; Schmitt & Reith, 2010). See Learning Objective 2.3.

One way to examine addiction is to consider the number of individuals who become dependent upon it. Another is to examine how hard it is to quit using a substance (Roh, 2018). As addictive as cocaine is, there is one other stimulant that may lead to even greater dependence. Of people who tried nicotine, alcohol, cannabis, or cocaine, the highest likelihood of becoming dependent was for nicotine users (67.5 percent), followed by alcohol users (22.7 percent), cocaine users (20.9 percent), and cannabis users (8.9 percent; Lopez-Quintero, Perez de los Cobos et al., 2011). The same researchers also examined remission rates, or the likelihood individuals who were dependent upon a substance stopped using it. Of those substances, nicotine users had the lowest remission rate, followed by alcohol, cannabis, and cocaine (Lopez-Quintero, Hasin et al., 2011).

cocaine

a natural drug derived from the leaves of the coca plant.

💬 Hasn't nicotine just been the victim of a lot of bad press? After all, it's legal, unlike cocaine and heroin.

NICOTINE Every year, nearly 480,000 people in the United States die from illnesses related to smoking, costing more than $300 billion in health care and productivity losses annually. That's more people than those who die from accidents in motor vehicles, alcohol, cocaine, heroin and other drug abuse, AIDS, suicide, and homicide *combined* (Jamal et al., 2015; U.S. Department of Health and Human Services, 2010). Remember, cocaine, heroin, and many other currently controlled substances or illegal drugs once used to be legal. One has to wonder what would have been the fate of these drugs if as many people had been making money off of them at that time as do those who farm, manufacture, and distribute tobacco products today.

Nicotine is a relatively mild but nevertheless toxic stimulant, producing a slight "rush" or sense of arousal as it raises blood pressure and accelerates the heart, as well as providing a rush of sugar into the bloodstream by stimulating the release of adrenalin in addition to raising dopamine levels in the brain's reward pathway (Kovacs et al., 2010; Rezvani & Levin, 2001). As is the case with many stimulants, it also has a relaxing effect on most people and seems to reduce stress (Pormerleau & Pormerleau, 1994).

AP 2.H Discuss the influence of drugs on neurotransmitters.

Although fewer Americans are smoking (down to about 17% from more than 40% in the 1960s), men are more likely to smoke than women, an incidence of about 19% for men and 15% for women (CDC, 2015b). The heaviest smokers (20%) are those adults aged 25–44 years. This is alarming news when one considers the toxic nature of nicotine: In the 1920s and 1930s it was used as an insecticide and is considered to be highly toxic and fast acting (Gosselin et al., 1984; Mayer, 2014). Although the amount of nicotine in a cigarette is low, first-time smokers often experience nausea as a result of the toxic effects after just a few puffs.

Why is it so difficult to quit using tobacco products? Aside from the powerfully addictive nature of nicotine, the physical withdrawal symptoms can be as bad as those resulting from alcohol, cocaine, or heroin abuse (Epping-Jordan et al., 1998). People don't think of nicotine as being as bad as cocaine because nicotine is legal and easily obtainable, but in terms of its addictive power, it works in a similar fashion to cocaine, is more likely to lead to dependence, and is harder to quit (CDC, 2010; Lopez-Quintero, Hasin et al., 2011; Lopez-Quintero, Perez de los Cobos et al., 2011; Roh, 2018). Using smokeless tobacco (e.g., chewing tobacco, snuff, etc.) may actually be more harmful, as one study found higher levels of exposure to nicotine and toxins in those users than in users of regular tobacco products (Rostron et al., 2015). Electronic cigarettes (e-cigs, vaping, vapes, etc.) are also not safe, as studies have found high and unsafe levels of formaldehyde in these products (Salamanca et al., 2018), as well as an increased risk to heart functioning, blood pressure, and hardening of the arteries that is equal to or greater than that of regular cigarettes (Franzen et al., 2018).

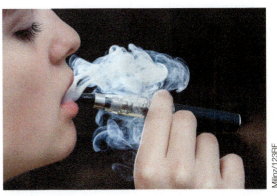

That isn't a cloud of smoke coming from this woman's mouth. She's using an e-cig, or electronic cigarette. There are many different brands of this battery-operated device currently on the market. Each e-cig can deliver nicotine (with flavorings and other chemicals) in the form of a vapor rather than smoke. Often promoted as safer than a regular cigarette, the health risks of using such devices are not yet determined.

THINKING CRITICALLY 4.2

What might happen if the use of nicotine products became illegal?

CAFFEINE Although many people will never use amphetamines or take cocaine, and others will never smoke or will quit successfully, there is one stimulant that almost everyone uses, with many using it every day. This, of course, is **caffeine**, the stimulant found in coffee, tea, most sodas, energy drinks, chocolate, and even many over-the-counter drugs.

Caffeine is another natural substance, like cocaine and nicotine, and is found in coffee beans, tea leaves, cocoa nuts, and at least 60 other types of plants (Braun, 1996). It is a mild stimulant, helps maintain alertness, and can increase the effectiveness of some

nicotine
the stimulant found in tobacco.

caffeine
a mild stimulant found in coffee, tea, and several other plant-based substances.

While most people probably get their caffeine dose in the form of coffee or caffeinated sodas, many people are turning to highly caffeinated energy drinks such as the one pictured here. What problems might arise from using such heavily sweetened beverages?

barbiturates

depressant drugs that have a sedative effect.

benzodiazepines

drugs that lower anxiety and reduce stress.

alcohol

the chemical resulting from fermentation or distillation of various kinds of vegetable matter.

Watch The Physical Effects of Alcohol

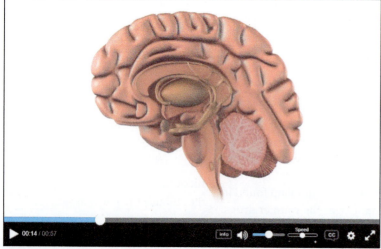

Watch the Video at MyLab Psychology

pain relievers such as aspirin. Caffeine is often added to pain relievers for that reason and is the key ingredient in medications meant to keep people awake.

Contrary to popular belief, coffee does not help induce sobriety. All one would get is a wide-awake drunk. Coffee is fairly acidic, too, and acids are not what the stomach of a person with a hangover needs. (And since the subject has come up, drinking more alcohol or "hair of the dog that bit you" just increases the problem later on—the best cure for a hangover is lots of water to put back all the fluids that alcohol takes out of the body, and sleep.)

Research suggests that, in modest amounts of perhaps two cups a day, coffee may actually be good for you. Studies have found that coffee consumption is associated with lowered risk of Type 2 diabetes and a lower risk of death overall (Ding et al., 2014, 2015).

4.13 Down in the Valley: Depressants

4.13 Identify the effects and dangers of using depressants.

Another class of psychoactive drugs is *depressants*, drugs that slow the central nervous system.

MAJOR AND MINOR TRANQUILIZERS Commonly known as the *major tranquilizers* (drugs that have a strong depressant effect) or sleeping pills, **barbiturates** are drugs that have a sedative (sleep-inducing) effect. Overdoses can lead to death as breathing and heart action are stopped.

The *minor tranquilizers* (drugs having a relatively mild depressant effect) include the **benzodiazepines**. These drugs are used to lower anxiety and reduce stress. Some of the most common are Valium, Xanax, Halcion, Ativan, and Librium.

Both major and minor tranquilizers can be addictive, and large doses can be dangerous, as can an interaction with alcohol or other drugs (Breslow et al., 2015; Olin, 1993).

Rohypnol is a benzodiazepine tranquilizer that has become famous as the "date rape" drug. Unsuspecting victims drink something that has been doctored with this drug, which causes them to be unaware of their actions, although still able to respond to directions or commands. Rape or some other form of sexual assault can then be carried out without fear that the victim will remember it or be able to report it (Armstrong, 1997; Gable, 2004).

ALCOHOL The most commonly used and abused depressant is **alcohol**, the chemical resulting from fermentation or distillation of various kinds of vegetable matter. Anywhere from 10 to 20 million people in the United States suffer from alcoholism.

In 2014, nearly 25 percent of people aged 18 or older reported that they had participated in binge drinking within the past month (National Institute on Alcohol Abuse and Alcoholism [NIAAA], 2016). Aside from the obvious health risks to the liver, brain, and heart (see the video *The Physical Effects of Alcohol*) alcohol is associated with loss of work time, loss of a job, and loss of economic stability.

Many people are alcoholics but deny the fact. They believe that getting drunk, especially in college, is a ritual of adulthood. Many college students and even older adults engage in binge drinking (drinking four or five drinks within a limited amount of time, such as at "happy hour"). Binge drinking quickly leads to being drunk, and drunkenness is a major sign of alcoholism. Some other danger signs are feeling guilty about drinking, drinking in the morning, drinking to recover from drinking, drinking alone, being sensitive about how much one drinks when others mention it, drinking so much that one does and says things one later regrets, drinking enough to have blackouts or memory loss, drinking too fast, lying about drinking, and drinking enough to pass out.

The dangers of abusing alcohol cannot be stressed enough. According to the Centers for Disease Control and Prevention (CDC, 2011a, 2015a), the number of alcohol-related deaths in the period from 2006 to 2010 was around 88,000 deaths. This figure does *not* include deaths due to accidents and homicides that may be related to abuse of alcohol—only those deaths that are caused by the body's inability to handle the alcohol. The National Institute on Alcohol Abuse and Alcoholism (NIAAA, 2016) has statistics showing that nearly 88,000 people *per year* die from alcohol-related causes, a figure that probably *does* include those accidents and homicides, making alcohol the fourth leading cause of death in the United States.

Pregnant women should not drink at all, as alcohol can damage the growing embryo, causing a condition of mental retardation and physical deformity known as fetal alcohol syndrome (Truong et al., 2012; Williams & Smith, 2015). See Learning Objective 8.5. Increased risk of loss of bone density (known as osteoporosis) and heart disease has also been linked to alcoholism (Abbott et al., 1994). These are just a few of the many health problems that alcohol can cause.

If you are concerned about your own drinking or are worried about a friend or loved one, there is a free and very simple online assessment at this site: **alcoholscreening.org**.

Although many young adults see drinking as a rite of passage into adulthood, few may understand the dangers of "binge" drinking, or drinking four to five drinks within a limited amount of time. Inhibitions are lowered and poor decisions may be made, such as driving while intoxicated. Binge drinking, a popular activity on some college campuses, can also lead to alcoholism.

> 💬 I have friends who insist that alcohol is a stimulant because they feel more uninhibited when they drink, so why is it considered a depressant?

Alcohol is often confused with stimulants. Many people think this is because alcohol makes a person feel "up" and euphoric (happy). Actually, alcohol is a depressant that gives the illusion of stimulation, because the very first thing alcohol depresses is a person's natural inhibitions, or the "don'ts" of behavior. Inhibitions are all the social rules people have learned that allow them to get along with others and function in society. Inhibitions also keep people from taking off all their clothes and dancing on the table at a crowded bar—inhibitions are a good thing.

Many people are unaware of exactly what constitutes a "drink." **Table 4.4** explains this and shows the effects of various numbers of drinks on behavior. Alcohol indirectly stimulates the release of a neurotransmitter called GABA, the brain's major depressant (Brick, 2003; Santhakumar et al., 2007). GABA slows down or stops neural activity. As more GABA is released, the brain's functioning actually becomes more and more inhibited, depressed, or slowed down. The areas of the brain that are first affected by alcohol are the areas that control social inhibitions. As the effects continue, motor skills, reaction time, and speech are all affected.

Some people might be surprised that only one drink can have a fairly strong effect. People who are not usually drinkers will feel the effects of alcohol much more quickly than those who have built up a tolerance. Women also feel the effects sooner, as their bodies process alcohol differently than men's bodies do. (Women are typically smaller, too, so alcohol has a quicker impact on women.)

OPIATES: I FEEL YOUR PAIN Opiates are a type of depressant that suppress the sensation of pain by binding to and stimulating the nervous system's natural receptor sites for endorphins (called *opioid receptors*), the neurotransmitters that naturally deaden pain sensations (Levesque, 2014; Olin, 1993). Because they also slow down the action of the nervous

AP 2.H Discuss the influence of drugs on neurotransmitters.

opiates

a class of opium-related drugs that suppress the sensation of pain by binding to and stimulating the nervous system's natural receptor sites for endorphins.

AP 2.H Discuss the influence of drugs on neurotransmitters.

Table 4.4 Blood Alcohol Level and Behavior Associated With Amounts of Alcohol

A drink is a drink. Each contains half an ounce of alcohol.

So a drink is…

- 1 can of beer (12 oz.; 4–5% alcohol)
- 1 glass of wine (4 oz.; 12% alcohol)
- 1 shot of most liquors (1 oz.; 40–50% alcohol)

At times "a drink" is really the equivalent of more than just one drink, like when you order a drink with more than one shot of alcohol in it, or you do a shot followed by a beer.

Average Number of Drinks	Blood Alcohol Level	Behavior
1–2 drinks	0.05%	Feeling of well-being, uninhibited, poor judgment, coordination, and alertness Impaired driving
3–5 drinks	0.10%	Slow reaction time Muscle control, vision, and speech impaired Crash risk greatly increased
6–7 drinks	0.15%	Major increases in reaction time
8–10 drinks	0.20%	Loss of balance, fine motor skills, legally blind and unable to drive for up to 10 hours
10–14 drinks	0.20% and 0.25%	Staggering and severe motor disturbances
10–14 drinks	0.30%	Not aware of surroundings
10–14 drinks	0.35%	Surgical anesthesia Lethal dosage for a small percentage of people
14–20 drinks	0.40%	Lethal dosage for about 50% of people Severe circulatory/respiratory depression Alcohol poisoning/overdose

Source: Adapted from the *Moderate Drinking Skills Study Guide* (2004). Eau-Claire, WI: University of Wisconsin.

system, drug interactions with alcohol and other depressants are possible—and deadly. Psychologically, opiates can have both positive and negative effects on a person's feelings of social connection to others, which might increase the tendency to abuse this type of drug (Inagaki, 2018). All opiates are a derivative of a particular plant-based substance—opium.

OPIUM Opium, made from the opium poppy, has pain-relieving and euphoria-inducing properties that have been known for at least 2,000 years. Highly addictive, it mimics the effects of endorphins, the nervous system's natural painkillers. The nervous system slows or stops its production of endorphins. When the drug wears off, there is no protection against any kind of pain, causing the severe symptoms of withdrawal associated with these drugs. It was not until 1803 that opium was developed for use as a medication by a German physician. The new form—morphine—was hailed as "God's own medicine" (Hodgson, 2001).

MORPHINE Morphine was created by dissolving opium in an acid and then neutralizing the acid with ammonia. Morphine was thought to be a wonder drug, although its addictive qualities soon became a major concern to physicians and their patients. Morphine is still used today to control severe pain, but in carefully controlled doses and for very short periods of time.

HEROIN Ironically, **heroin** was first hailed as the new wonder drug—a derivative of morphine that did not have many of the disagreeable side effects of morphine. The theory was that heroin was a purer form of the drug and that the impurities in morphine were

opium
substance derived from the opium poppy from which all narcotic drugs are derived.

morphine
narcotic drug derived from opium, used to treat severe pain.

heroin
narcotic drug derived from opium that is extremely addictive.

the substances creating the harmful side effects. It did not take long, however, for doctors and others to realize that heroin was even more powerfully addictive than morphine or opium. Although usage as a medicine ceased, it is still used by many people.

The United States has seen an increase in the use of heroin among both men and women in various age groups and levels of income (CDC, 2015c). People are not only using heroin but are combining it with other drugs, particularly cocaine and prescription painkillers containing opiates, which has of course led to an increase in overdose deaths. The rate of heroin-related overdose deaths quadrupled in only an 11-year period, from 2002–2013 (CDC, 2015c).

OPIOIDS Opioids are synthetically created drugs that act like opiates when taken for pain. Some common opioids are *methadone, oxycodone, hydrocodone,* and *fentanyl*. Drugs such as methadone, *buprenorphine,* and *naltrexone* may be used to control withdrawal symptoms and help treat opiate addictions (Kahan & Sutton, 1998; Kakko et al., 2003; Ward et al., 1999). Eventually, as the addicted person is weaned from these drugs, the natural endorphin system starts to function more normally. Unfortunately, opioids are also addictive and are a cause of increasing concern when used recreationally or to excess, resulting in a deadly "opioid crisis" in the United States and elsewhere (Kolodny et al., 2015; Ruhm, 2018; Stevens et al., 2017). In the United States alone, one in five deaths of young adults is opioid-related (Gomes et al., 2018). In the United States, from 1999 to 2017, opioid overdose deaths increased six times, and approximately 130 Americans die every day from an opioid overdose (CDC, 2018f). The most recent increases are associated with synthetic opioids including illicitly manufactured fentanyl; from 2016 to 2017, deaths related to synthetic opioids increased by 45.2 percent (Scholl et al., 2019).

4.14 Hallucinogens: Higher and Higher

4.14 Identify the effects and dangers of using hallucinogens.

Hallucinogens actually cause the brain to alter its interpretation of sensations (Olin, 1993) and can produce sensory distortions very similar to *synesthesia* (see Learning Objective 3.1), in which sensations cross over each other—colors have sound, sounds have smells, and so on. False sensory perceptions, called *hallucinations,* are often experienced, especially with the more powerful hallucinogens. There are two basic types of hallucinogens—those that are created in a laboratory and those that are from natural sources.

MANUFACTURED HIGHS There are several drugs that were developed in the laboratory instead of being found in nature. Perhaps because these drugs are manufactured, they are often more potent than drugs found in the natural world.

LSD **LSD,** or **lysergic acid diethylamide,** is synthesized from a grain fungus called *ergot*. Ergot fungus commonly grows on rye grain but can be found on other grains as well. First manufactured in 1938, LSD is one of the most potent, or powerful, hallucinogens (Johnston et al., 2007; Lee & Shlain, 1986). It takes only a very tiny drop of LSD to achieve a "high."

People who take LSD usually do so to get that high feeling. Some people feel that LSD helps them expand their consciousness or awareness of the world around them. Colors seem more intense, sounds more beautiful, and so on. But the experience is not always a pleasant one, just as dreams are not always filled with positive emotions. "Bad trips" are quite common, and there is no way to control what kind of "trip" the brain is going to decide to take.

One of the greater dangers in using LSD is the effect it has on a person's ability to perceive reality. Real dangers and hazards in the world may go unnoticed by a person "lost" in an LSD fantasy, and people under the influence of this drug may make

opioids
synthetic drugs that mimic the pain-reducing effects of opiates and their addictive properties

hallucinogens
drugs that cause false sensory messages, altering the perception of reality.

LSD (lysergic acid diethylamide)
powerful synthetic hallucinogen.

poor decisions, such as trying to drive while high. A person who has taken LSD can have flashbacks—spontaneous hallucinations—even years after taking the drug, and chronic users of the drug can develop *hallucinogen persisting perception disorder (HPPD)*, an irreversible condition in which hallucinations and altered perceptions of reality can occur repeatedly, accompanied by depression and physical discomfort (Brodrick & Mitchell, 2015; Lerner et al., 2002).

PCP Another synthesized drug was found to be so dangerous that it remains useful only in veterinary medicine as a tranquilizer. The drug is **PCP** (which stands for *p*henyl *c*yclohexyl *p*iperidine, a name which is often contracted as *phencyclidine*) and can have many different effects. Depending on the dosage, it can be a hallucinogen, stimulant, depressant, or an analgesic (painkilling) drug. As with LSD, users of PCP can experience hallucinations, distorted sensations, and very unpleasant effects. PCP can also lead to acts of violence against others or suicide (Brecher, 1988; Cami et al., 2000; Forrest & Kendell, 2018; Johnston et al., 2007; Morris & Wallach, 2014). Users may even physically injure themselves unintentionally because PCP causes them to feel no warning signal of pain.

> **AP** 2.H Discuss the influence of drugs on neurotransmitters.

MDMA The last synthetic drug we will address here is technically an amphetamine, but it is capable of producing hallucinations as well. In fact, both **MDMA** (a "designer drug" known on the streets as *ecstasy, molly,* or simply X) and PCP are now classified as **stimulatory hallucinogenics**, drugs that produce a mixture of psychomotor stimulant and hallucinogenic effects (National Institute on Drug Abuse, 2016; Shuglin, 1986). Although many users of MDMA believe that it is relatively harmless, the fact is that it—like many other substances—can be deadly when misused. MDMA causes the release of large amounts of serotonin and also blocks the reuptake of this neurotransmitter (Hall & Henry, 2006; Liechti & Vollenweider, 2001; Montgomery & Fisk, 2008; United Nations Office on Drugs and Crime [UNODC], 2014). The user feels euphoric, energized, and increased emotional warmth toward others. But there is some evidence that MDMA may damage the serotonin receptors, which could lead to depression. Other negative effects include severe dehydration and raised body temperature, which can lead to excessive intake of liquids—with possible fatal results (Laws & Kokkalis, 2007; Leccese et al., 2000; Meyer, 2013; UNODC, 2014). It should also be noted that since MDMA is illegal, illicit drug manufacturers try to stay ahead of the legal system by manufacturing novel psychoactive substances (NPS) such as "ivory wave" or "bath salts" that are similar in effect to MDMA but just different enough to skirt the law, at least for a while (Baumeister et al., 2015; Bright, 2013; European Monitoring Centre for Drugs and Drug Addiction [EMCDDA], 2015). In recent years, the use of MDMA by adolescents in the United States has taken a somewhat downward trend, possibly because those adolescents see the drug as being harder to obtain than in previous decades (Johnston et al., 2017).

NONMANUFACTURED HIGH: MARIJUANA One of the best known and most commonly abused of the hallucinogenic drugs, **marijuana** (also called "pot" or "weed") comes from the leaves and flowers of the hemp plant called *Cannabis sativa*. (*Hashish* is the concentrated substance made by scraping the resin from these leaves, and both marijuana and hashish contain *cannabinoids*.) The most psychoactive cannabinoid, and the active ingredient in marijuana, is *tetrahydrocannabinol* (THC). Marijuana is best known for its ability to produce a feeling of well-being, mild intoxication, and mild sensory distortions or hallucinations. As of early 2019, ten states have legalized the recreational use of marijuana (Berke & Gould, 2019).

PCP
synthesized drug now used as an animal tranquilizer that can cause stimulant, depressant, narcotic, or hallucinogenic effects.

MDMA (ecstasy or X)
designer drug that can have both stimulant and hallucinatory effects.

stimulatory hallucinogenics
drugs that produce a mixture of psychomotor stimulant and hallucinogenic effects.

marijuana
mild hallucinogen (also known as "pot" or "weed") derived from the leaves and flowers of a particular type of hemp plant.

The effects of marijuana are relatively mild compared to those of the other hallucinogens. In fact, an inexperienced user who doesn't know what to expect upon smoking that first marijuana cigarette may feel nothing at all. Most people do report a feeling of mild euphoria and relaxation, along with an altered time sense and mild visual distortions. Higher doses can lead to hallucinations, delusions, and the all-too-common paranoia. Most studies of marijuana's effects have concluded that while marijuana can create a powerful psychological dependency, it does not produce physical dependency or physical withdrawal symptoms in most people (Gordon et al., 2013). For a small percentage of people, discontinuing use of marijuana does produce physical withdrawal symptoms, a syndrome called marijuana use disorder (Gorelick et al., 2012; Rotter et al., 2013). In either case, after alcohol and nicotine, cannabis dependence is the most common form of drug dependence in the United States, Canada, and Australia (Hall & Degenhardt, 2009). Even at mild doses, it is not safe to operate heavy machinery or drive a car while under the influence of marijuana because it negatively affects reaction time and perception of surroundings; the drug reduces a person's ability to make the split-second decisions that driving a car or other equipment requires. Information processing in general, attention, and memory are all likely to be impaired in a person who has used marijuana.

Marijuana is most commonly smoked like tobacco or vaped like nicotine, but some people have been known to eat it baked into brownies or other foods. This is a kind of double duty for the doctored food, as marijuana stimulates the appetite.

Although no one has ever been known to die from an overdose of marijuana, smoking it is not a healthy habit. Research linking marijuana smoking and lung cancer is not definitive due to the fact that many studies have not been able to control for confounding variables, such as cigarette smoking, alcohol use, or other risk factors (Berthiller et al., 2008; Hall & Degenhardt, 2009), but there is some suggestion that early marijuana use by adolescents may increase their likelihood of nicotine addiction, adding to their cancer risk (Rubinstein et al., 2014). See Learning Objective 1.10. Aside from those previously mentioned, probable adverse effects from chronic nonmedical marijuana use also include increased risk of motor vehicle crashes, chronic bronchitis or other lung problems, and cardiovascular disease. In adolescents who are regular users, psychosocial development, educational attainment, and mental health can be negatively impacted (Borgelt et al., 2013; Gordon et al., 2013; Hall & Degenhardt, 2009; Hirvonen et al., 2011; Madras, 2014). With regard to the possible mental health problems, there appears to be an increased risk for psychotic symptoms and disorders later in life for adolescents who are regular and heavier users (Aguilar et al., 2018; Hall & Degenhardt, 2009; Hirvonen et al., 2011; Madras, 2014; Moore et al., 2007).

This is a medical marijuana dispensary in Ypsilanti, Michigan. How might having marijuana available in such legal stores change the illegal drug business?

There are some legitimate medical uses for marijuana, and 33 states and the District of Columbia have legalized medical marijuana since 1996 (Hasin et al., 2015; Berke & Gould, 2019). Aside from uses in treating the nausea resulting from chemotherapy for both cancer and autoimmune deficiency disease (AIDS), medical marijuana has either proven useful or is showing great promise in treating chronic pain, depression, and posttraumatic stress disorder, for example (Greer et al., 2014; Haj-Dahmane & Shen, 2014; Ware et al., 2015). Despite fears that availability of medical marijuana would lead to an increase of marijuana use among adolescents, studies over the past 28 years have found no evidence of such increases (Cerdá et al., 2018; Hasin et al., 2015; Johnson et al., 2015).

Table 4.5 summarizes the various types of drugs, their common names, and their effects on human behavior.

Table 4.5 How Drugs Affect Consciousness

Drug Classification	Common Names or Forms	Main Effect	Adverse Effects
Stimulants		Stimulation, excitement	
Amphetamines	Methamphetamine, speed, Ritalin, Dexedrine		Risk of addiction, stroke, fatal heart problems, psychosis
Cocaine	Cocaine, crack		Risk of addiction, stroke, fatal heart problems, psychosis
Nicotine	Tobacco		Addiction, cancer
Caffeine	Coffee, tea, energy drinks		Addiction, high blood pressure
Depressants		Relaxation	
Barbiturates (major tranquilizers)	Nembutal, Seconal		Addiction, brain damage, death
Benzodiazepines (minor tranquilizers)	Valium, Xanax, Halcion, Ativan, Rohypnol		Lower risk of overdose and addiction when taken alone
Alcohol	Beer, wine, spirits		Alcoholism, health problems, depression, increased risk of accidents, death
Opiates	Opium, morphine, heroin	Euphoria	Addiction, death
Hallucinogens	LSD, PCP, MDMA (ecstasy), marijuana	Distorted consciousness, altered perception	Possible permanent memory problems, bad "trips," suicide, overdose, and death

Concept Map L.O. 4.11, 4.12, 4.13, 4.14

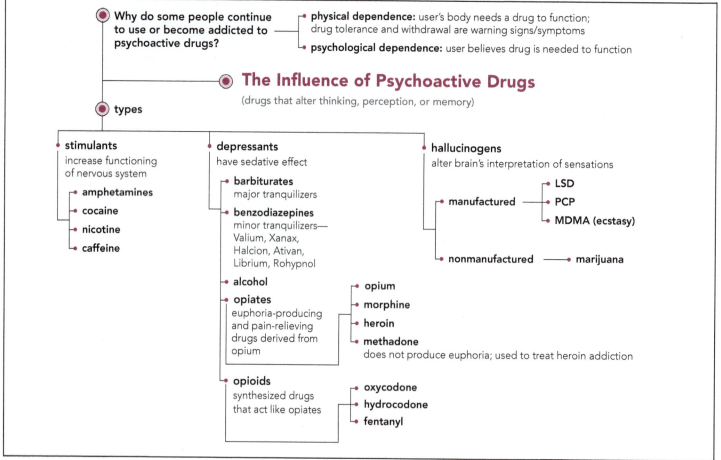

Practice Quiz   How much do you remember?

Pick the best answer.

1. As consequences to stopping drug use, headaches, nausea, shaking, and elevated blood pressure are all signs of _____.
   a. psychoactive reactivity
   b. overdose
   c. psychological dependency
   d. withdrawal
   e. amphetamine toxicity

2. _____ is a tranquilizer that is also known as the "date rape" drug.
   a. Halcion
   b. Rohypnol
   c. Librium
   d. Valium
   e. Xanax

3. Which of the following statements about nicotine is true?
   a. Overall, the number of women and teenagers smoking is on the increase.
   b. In terms of addictive power, nicotine may be more powerful than cocaine or alcohol.
   c. Overall, the number of Americans smoking is on the increase.
   d. Nicotine can slow the heart and therefore create a sense of relaxation.
   e. Nicotine use does not lead to physical dependence, only psychological dependence.

4. What drug's physical withdrawal symptoms include severe mood swings (crash), paranoia, extreme fatigue, and an inability to feel pleasure?
   a. caffeine
   b. heroin
   c. cocaine
   d. alcohol
   e. cannabis

5. Typically, opiates have the ability to _____.
   a. cause deep levels of depression
   b. stimulate the user
   c. be used as insecticides
   d. cause intense hallucinations
   e. suppress the sensation of pain

6. Most studies of marijuana's effects have found that it _____.
   a. produces a slight "rush" or sense or arousal
   b. is easy to overdose on the substance
   c. creates a strong physical dependency
   d. creates a powerful psychological dependency
   e. produces intense withdrawal symptoms

Applying Psychology to Everyday Life
Can You Really Multitask?

4.15 Identify the negative impacts of multitasking.

By now, you've begun to realize that multitasking is not all it's cracked up to be, and that you probably aren't as good at doing it as you thought you were. Yet we continue to try to cram into each day far too many tasks, doing few of them very well. The following video highlights some of the hazards of trying to multitask in our everyday lives.

Applying Psychology to Everyday Life Can You Really Multitask?

👁 **Watch** the **Video** at **MyLab Psychology**

After watching the video, answer the following questions:

1. The video highlighted several negative outcomes of trying to multitask, especially for specific kinds of tasks. What were two situations in which students reported they were not likely to be able to multitask without negative consequences?

2. Students in the video shared some of the negative impacts of attempts to multitask while doing schoolwork and while driving. What are some other areas of your life in which multitasking can have negative outcomes? What negative outcomes are possible for these areas?

Chapter Summary

What Is Consciousness?

4.1 Define what it means to be conscious.
- Consciousness is a person's awareness of everything that is going on at any given moment. Most waking hours are spent in waking consciousness.

4.2 Differentiate between the different levels of consciousness.
- Altered states of consciousness are shifts in the quality or pattern of mental activity.
- Controlled processes are those tasks that require a higher degree of conscious attention, while automatic processes can be done at a far lower level of conscious awareness.

Sleep

4.3 Describe the biological process of the sleep–wake cycle.
- Sleep is a circadian rhythm, lasting 24 hours, and is a product of the activity of the hypothalamus, the hormone melatonin, the neurotransmitter serotonin, and body temperature.

4.4 Explain why we sleep.
- Adaptive theory states that sleep evolved as a way to conserve energy and keep animals safe from predators that hunt at night.
- Restorative theory states that sleep provides the body with an opportunity to restore chemicals that have been depleted during the day as well as the growth and repair of cell tissue.
- The average amount of sleep needed by most adults is about 7 to 9 hours within each 24-hour period.

4.5 Identify the different stages of sleep.
- N1 sleep is light sleep.
- N2 sleep is indicated by the presence of sleep spindles, bursts of activity on the EEG.
- N3 is highlighted by the first appearance of delta waves, the slowest and largest waves, and the body is at its lowest level of functioning.
- R sleep occurs four or five times a night, replacing N1 after a full cycle through N1–N3 and then ascending back to lighter stages of sleep. It is accompanied by paralysis of the voluntary muscles but rapid movement of the eyes.

4.6 Differentiate among the various sleep disorders.
- Sleepwalking and sleeptalking occur in N3, during slow-wave sleep.
- Voluntary muscles are paralyzed during REM sleep.
- Night terrors are attacks of extreme fear that the victim has while sound asleep.
- Nightmares are bad or unpleasant dreams that occur during REM sleep.
- REM behavior disorder is a rare condition in which sleep paralysis fails and the person moves violently while dreaming, often acting out the elements of the dream.
- Insomnia is an inability to get to sleep, stay asleep, or get enough sleep.
- Sleep apnea occurs when a person stops breathing for 10 seconds or more.
- Narcolepsy is a genetic disorder in which the person suddenly and without warning collapses into REM sleep.

Dreams

4.7 Compare and contrast two explanations of why people dream.
- Manifest content of a dream is the actual dream and its events. Latent content of a dream is the symbolic content, according to Freud.
- Without outside sensory information to explain the activation of the brain cells in the cortex by the pons area, the association areas of the cortex synthesize a story, or dream, to explain that activation in the activation-synthesis hypothesis.
- A revision of activation-synthesis theory, the activation-information-mode model (AIM), states that information experienced during waking hours can influence the synthesis of dreams.

4.8 Identify commonalities and differences in the content of people's dreams.
- Calvin Hall believed that dreams are just another type of cognitive process that occurred during sleep, called the cognitive theory of dreaming.
- Common dream content includes normal activities that people do while awake along with more fanciful actions such as flying or being naked in public.

Hypnosis

4.9 Explain how hypnosis affects consciousness.
- Hypnosis is a state of consciousness in which a person is especially susceptible to suggestion.
- The hypnotist will tell the person to relax and feel tired, to focus on what is being said, to let go of inhibitions and accept suggestions, and to use vivid imagination.
- Hypnosis cannot give increased strength, reliably enhance memory, or regress people to an earlier age or an earlier life, but it can produce amnesia, reduce pain, and alter sensory impressions.

4.10 Compare and contrast two views of why hypnosis works.
- Hilgard believed that a person under hypnosis is in a state of dissociation, in which one part of consciousness is hypnotized and susceptible to suggestion, while another part is aware of everything that occurs.

- Other theorists believe that the hypnotized participant is merely playing a social role—that of the hypnotized person. This is called the social-cognitive theory of hypnosis.

The Influence of Psychoactive Drugs

4.11 Distinguish between physical dependence and psychological dependence upon drugs.

- Drugs that are physically addictive cause the user's body to crave the drug. When deprived of the drug, the user will go through physical withdrawal.
- Drug tolerance occurs as the user's body becomes conditioned to the level of the drug. After a time, the user must take more and more of the drug to get the same effect.
- In psychological dependence, the user believes that he or she needs the drug to function well and maintain a sense of well-being. Any drug can produce psychological dependence.

4.12 Identify the effects and dangers of using stimulants.

- Stimulants are drugs that increase the activity of the nervous system, particularly the sympathetic division and the central nervous system.
- Amphetamines are synthetic drugs such as Benzedrine or Dexedrine. They help people stay awake and reduce appetite but are highly physically addictive.
- Cocaine is highly addictive and can cause convulsions and death in some first-time users.
- Nicotine is a mild stimulant and is very physically addictive.
- Caffeine is the most commonly used stimulant, found in coffee, tea, chocolate, and many sodas.

4.13 Identify the effects and dangers of using depressants.

- Barbiturates, also known as major tranquilizers, have a sedative effect and are used as sleeping pills.
- The minor tranquilizers are benzodiazepines such as Valium or Xanax.
- Alcohol is the most commonly used and abused depressant.
- Alcohol can interact with other depressants.
- Excessive use of alcohol can lead to alcoholism, health problems, loss of control, and death.
- Opiates are pain-relieving drugs of the depressant class that are derived from the opium poppy.
- Opium is the earliest form of this drug and is highly addictive because it directly stimulates receptor sites for endorphins. This causes natural production of endorphins to decrease.
- Morphine is a more refined version of opium but is highly addictive.
- Heroin was believed to be a purer form of morphine and, therefore, less addictive but in fact is even more powerfully addictive.
- Drugs such as methadone, *buprenorphine*, and *naltrexone* may be used to control withdrawal symptoms and help treat opiate addictions.

4.14 Identify the effects and dangers of using hallucinogens.

- Hallucinogens are stimulants that alter the brain's interpretation of sensations, creating hallucinations. Three synthetically created hallucinogens are LSD, PCP, and MDMA.
- Marijuana is a mild hallucinogen, producing a mild euphoria and feelings of relaxation in its users. Larger doses can lead to hallucinations and paranoia. It contains substances that may be carcinogenic and impairs learning and memory.
- Many states in the U.S. have now legalized marijuana use for medical purposes, such as treatment of the nausea and other side effects of chemotherapy.

Applying Psychology to Everyday Life: Can You Really Multitask?

4.15 Identify the negative impacts of multitasking.

- Attempts to multitask often result in none of the attempted activities being done well.
- Despite our best efforts to do things simultaneously, tasks are often completed sequentially, and there are multiple costs in time and efficiency as the result of trying to divide attention between different tasks, and as result of switching back and forth.

Test Yourself: Preparing for the AP Exam

PART I: MULTIPLE-CHOICE QUESTIONS

Directions for Part I: Read each of the questions or incomplete sentences below. Then choose the response that best answers the question or completes the sentence.

1. What part of the brain is influential in determining when to sleep?
    a. hippocampus
    b. thalamus
    c. hypothalamus
    d. frontal lobe
    e. medulla

2. As the sun begins to set, Winston finds himself becoming sleepier and sleepier. What structure is sensitive to light and influences when to go to sleep and when to awaken?
    a. occipital lobe
    b. corpus callosum
    c. suprachiasmatic nucleus
    d. thalamus
    e. parietal lobe

3. When Tiana is asked to write down her dreams as a class assignment, she is bothered by the fact that her dreams often seem to jump randomly from scene to scene with little meaning. What theory best explains her dreams?
    a. dreams-for-survival theory
    b. activation-synthesis hypothesis
    c. Freudian theory
    d. sociocultural theory
    e. sleep as a hypnotic trance theory

4. Jaquan is pulling an all-nighter in preparation for his big psychology test tomorrow. According to the research, what is the result on Jaquan's memory when he deprives himself of sleep the night prior to his exam?
   a. Jaquan's memory will not be affected if he eats breakfast before the exam.
   b. Jaquan's memory will not be affected in any way assuming he only stays awake for one all-night study session.
   c. Jaquan will actually remember less if he deprives himself of sleep the night before.
   d. Jaquan will retain information from staying up all night, but only if his test is early in the morning.
   e. The ability to retain information can be influenced by the presence of sunlight. Thus, if the sun is shining, Jaquan will remember more than if it is a cloudy day.

5. After watching television while surfing the Internet on your tablet, you find yourself having trouble falling asleep at night. According to what we know about the biology of sleep, what is the most likely cause of your sleep problem?
   a. Surfing the Internet while watching television is too much for your brain, leading to poor sleep.
   b. Surfing the Internet while watching television is the problem. You should watch television first and then surf the Internet.
   c. The bright light from the TV and tablet is causing your pineal gland to release too much melatonin.
   d. The bright light from the TV and tablet is causing your pineal gland to release too little melatonin.
   e. The TV shows are probably too exciting, making it difficult to calm down for sleep.

6. Studies have found that certain chemicals that help repair damaged cells only function while we sleep. What theory best explains this?
   a. sleep deprivation theory
   b. restorative theory of sleep
   c. Dement's theory of sleep
   d. adaptive theory of sleep
   e. circadian rhythm of sleep

7. Geof has had a very demanding day. Though his work is not physically challenging, it tends to mentally drain him. Which type of sleep will Geof probably require more of?
   a. N2
   b. N1
   c. N1 and N2
   d. R
   e. N3

8. Olivia has difficulty falling off to sleep. Morgan can fall off to sleep easily but often wakes up early. Dina typically sleeps for 10 hours. All three are tired and not rested upon rising. Who seems to be experiencing insomnia?
   a. Dina
   b. Olivia
   c. Morgan
   d. only Olivia and Morgan
   e. All three suffer from insomnia.

9. Which of the following would be bad advice for someone who is suffering from insomnia?
   a. Do not take sleeping pills.
   b. Go to bed only when you are sleepy.
   c. Do not look at the clock.
   d. Do not exercise—it overstimulates the brain.
   e. Keep to a regular sleep schedule.

10. Luis suddenly and without warning slips into REM sleep during the day. He often falls to the ground and is difficult to awaken. Luis may have a condition called _____.
    a. somnambulism
    b. epilepsy
    c. insomnia
    d. sleep apnea
    e. narcolepsy

11. Kaleb had a dream about his dog Buster in which he constantly looked for him but couldn't find him. In reality, Kaleb's dog had died after being hit by a car. According to Sigmund Freud, Kaleb's dream in which he was searching for his dog is an example of _____, while the inner meaning that he misses his dog terribly is an example of _____.
    a. latent content, wish fulfillment
    b. manifest content, latent content
    c. latent content, manifest content
    d. wish fulfillment, manifest content
    e. manifest content, activation synthesis

12. Kevin's therapist is using hypnosis to help him recall the night he was supposedly abducted by aliens. Keanu's therapist is using hypnosis to help him prepare for the pain of dental surgery because Keanu is allergic to the dentist's painkillers. Kyle's therapist is using hypnosis to help him quit drinking and smoking. Who has the highest chance for success?
    a. Kevin
    b. Keanu
    c. All three can benefit from hypnosis because each technique is proven effective.
    d. Kyle
    e. only Kevin and Kyle

13. Destiny has found that when she tries to quit drinking, she gets headaches, has night sweats, and shakes uncontrollably. Such a reaction is an example of _____.
    a. psychological dependence
    b. withdrawal
    c. the placebo effect
    d. overdose
    e. learned behavior

14. What is the most commonly used and abused depressant?
    a. Prozac
    b. tranquilizers
    c. cannabis
    d. alcohol
    e. caffeine

15. Which drug, depending on the dosage, can be a hallucinogen, stimulant, depressant, or painkiller?
    a. marijuana
    b. PCP
    c. caffeine
    d. opium
    e. nicotine

PART II: FREE-RESPONSE QUESTION

Directions for Part II: Read the essay question that follows. Then respond to the question in a clear, concise essay. Do not simply list facts. Instead, present a thorough argument based on your critical consideration of the topic. Use of proper terminology is necessary.

Lexy works late shifts in a paper mill while she goes to college during the day. She drinks coffee and other caffeinated beverages throughout the day and while she is at work. She used to drink two cups per shift, but she now finds she is drinking four or five cups to stay awake. On her days off, she tends not to have as much caffeine, and she gets headaches and feels irritable.

Part A
Explain how the following terms account for Lexy's behavior:

- stimulant
- circadian rhythm
- tolerance
- physical dependence

Part B
Lexy decides she needs to reduce her caffeine intake. Explain how the following terms might affect her attempts to use less caffeine:

- negative reinforcement
- psychological dependence
- withdrawal

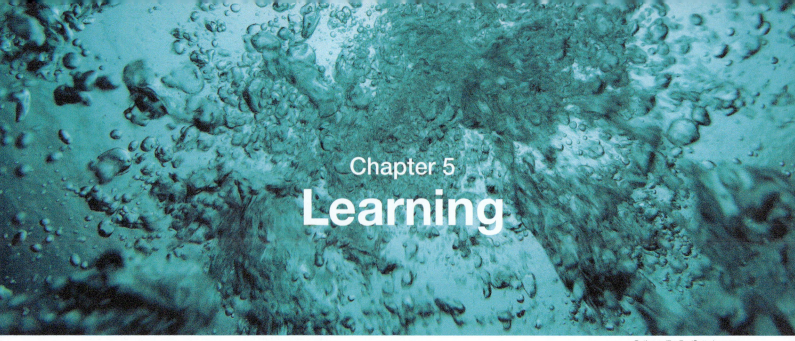

Chapter 5
Learning

Ralf strm/EyeEm/Getty Images

In your words

Have you ever used the promise of a pleasurable outcome or reward to modify your own behavior or the behavior of others?

After you have thought about this question, watch the video to see how other students would answer it.

Watch the Video at MyLab Psychology

Why study learning?

If we had not been able to learn, we would have died out as a species long ago. Learning is the process that allows us to adapt to the changing conditions of the world around us. We can alter our actions until we find the behavior that leads us to survival and rewards, and we can stop doing actions that have been unsuccessful in the past. Without learning, there would be no buildings, no agriculture, no lifesaving medicines, and no human civilization.

Learning Objectives

5.1 Define the term *learning*.

5.2 Identify the key elements of classical conditioning as demonstrated in Pavlov's classic experiment.

5.3 Apply classical conditioning to examples of phobias, taste aversions, and drug dependency.

5.4 Identify the contributions of Thorndike and Skinner to the concept of operant conditioning.

5.5 Differentiate between primary and secondary reinforcers and positive and negative reinforcement.

5.6 Identify the four schedules of reinforcement.

5.7 Identify the effect that punishment has on behavior.

5.8 Explain the concepts of discriminant stimuli, extinction, generalization, and spontaneous recovery as they relate to operant conditioning.

5.9 Describe how operant conditioning is used to change animal and human behavior.

5.10 Explain the concept of latent learning.

5.11 Explain how Köhler's studies demonstrated that animals can learn by insight.

5.12 Summarize Seligman's studies on learned helplessness.

5.13 Describe the process of observational learning.

5.14 List the four elements of observational learning.

5.15 Describe an example of conditioning in the real world.

5.1 Definition of Learning

5.1 Define the term *learning*.

The term *learning* is one of those concepts whose meaning is crystal clear until one has to put it in actual words. "Learning is when you learn something." "Learning is learning how to do something." A more useful definition is as follows: **Learning** is any relatively permanent change in behavior brought about by experience or practice.

> 💬 What does "relatively permanent" mean? And how does experience change what we do?

The "relatively permanent" part of the definition refers to the fact that when people learn anything, some part of their brain is physically changed to record what they've learned (Farmer et al., 2013; Loftus & Loftus, 1980). This is actually a process of memory, for without the ability to remember what happens, people cannot learn anything. Although there is no conclusive proof as yet, research suggests that once people learn something, it may be present somewhere in memory in physical form (Barsalou, 1992; Smolen et al., 2006). They may be unable to "get" to it, but it's there. See Learning Objective 6.5.

As for the role of experience in learning, think about the last time you did something that caused you a lot of pain. Did you do it again? Probably not. You didn't want to experience that pain again, so you changed your behavior to avoid the painful consequence.* This is how children learn not to touch hot stoves. In contrast, if a person does something resulting in a very pleasurable experience, that person is more likely to do that same thing again. This is another change in behavior explained by the law of effect, a topic we will discuss later in the chapter.

Not all change is accomplished through learning. Changes like an increase in height or the size of the brain are another kind of change, controlled by a genetic blueprint. This kind of change is called *maturation* and is due to biology, not experience. For example, practice alone will not allow a child to walk. Children learn to walk because their nervous systems, muscle strength, and sense of balance have reached the point where walking is physically possible for them—all factors controlled by maturation. Once that maturational readiness has been reached, then practice and experience play their important part.

AP 4.F Describe basic classical conditioning phenomena.

AP 4.G Distinguish general differences between principles of classical conditioning, operant conditioning, and observational learning.

AP 4.A Identify contributions of key researchers in the psychology of learning.

learning
any relatively permanent change in behavior brought about by experience or practice.

5.2–5.3 It Makes Your Mouth Water: Classical Conditioning

In the early 1900s, research scientists were unhappy with psychology's focus on mental activity. See Learning Objective 1.2. Many were looking for a way to bring some kind of objectivity and scientific research to the field. It was a Russian *physiologist* (a person who studies the workings of the body) named Ivan Pavlov (1849–1936) who pioneered the empirical study of the basic principles of a particular kind of learning (Pavlov, 1906, 1926).

5.2 Pavlov and the Salivating Dogs

5.2 Identify the key elements of classical conditioning as demonstrated in Pavlov's classic experiment.

Studying the digestive system in his dogs, Pavlov and his assistants had built a device that would accurately measure the amount of saliva produced by the dogs when they

---

*consequence: an end result of some action.

were fed a measured amount of food. Normally, when food is placed in the mouth of any animal, the salivary glands automatically start releasing saliva to help with chewing and digestion. This is a normal **reflex**—an unlearned, involuntary response that is not under personal control or choice—one of many that occur in both animals and humans. The food causes a particular reaction, the salivation. A *stimulus* can be defined as any object, event, or experience that causes a *response*, the reaction of an organism. In the case of Pavlov's dogs, the food is the stimulus and salivation is the response.

Pavlov soon discovered that the dogs began salivating when they weren't supposed to be salivating. Some dogs would start salivating when they saw a lab assistant bringing their food, others when they heard the clatter of the food bowl in the kitchen, and still others when it was the time of day they were usually fed. Switching his focus, Pavlov spent the rest of his career studying what eventually he termed **classical conditioning**, learning to elicit* an involuntary, reflex-like response to a stimulus other than the original, natural stimulus that normally produces the response.

Dr. Ivan Pavlov working in his laboratory. Pavlov, a Russian physiologist, was the first to study and write about the basic principles of classical conditioning.

ELEMENTS OF CLASSICAL CONDITIONING Pavlov eventually identified several key elements that must be present and experienced in a particular way for conditioning to take place.

UNCONDITIONED STIMULUS The original, naturally occurring stimulus is called the **unconditioned stimulus (UCS)**. The term *unconditioned* means "unlearned." This is the stimulus that ordinarily leads to the involuntary response. In the case of Pavlov's dogs, the food is the UCS.

UNCONDITIONED RESPONSE The automatic and involuntary response to the unconditioned stimulus is called the **unconditioned response (UCR)** for much the same reason. It is unlearned and occurs because of genetic "wiring" in the nervous system. For example, in Pavlov's experiment, the salivation to the food is the UCR.

CONDITIONED STIMULUS Pavlov determined that almost any kind of stimulus could become associated with the unconditioned stimulus (UCS) if it is paired with the UCS often enough. In his original study, the sight of the food dish itself became a stimulus for salivation *before* the food was given to the dogs. Every time they got food (to which they automatically salivated), they saw the dish. At first, the dish was a **neutral stimulus (NS)** because it had no effect on salivation. After being paired with the food many times, the sight of the dish also began to produce a salivation response, although a somewhat weaker one than the food itself. When a previously neutral stimulus, through repeated pairing with the unconditioned stimulus, begins to cause the same kind of involuntary response, learning has occurred. The previously neutral stimulus can now be called a **conditioned stimulus (CS)**. (*Conditioned* means "learned," and, as mentioned earlier, *unconditioned* means "unlearned.")

CONDITIONED RESPONSE The response that is given to the conditioned stimulus (CS) is not usually as strong as the original unconditioned response (UCR), but it is essentially the same response. However, because it comes as a learned response to the conditioned stimulus (CS), it is called the **conditioned response (CR)**. (The abbreviations used to discuss classical conditioning can be confusing, so it's not a bad idea to make a little "cheat sheet" to keep handy while reading this chapter, such as **Table 5.1**.)

reflex
an involuntary response, one that is not under personal control or choice.

classical conditioning
learning to make an involuntary response to a stimulus other than the original, natural stimulus that normally produces the response.

unconditioned stimulus (UCS)
in classical conditioning, a naturally occurring stimulus that leads to an involuntary and unlearned response.

unconditioned response (UCR)
in classical conditioning, an involuntary and unlearned response to a naturally occurring or unconditioned stimulus.

neutral stimulus (NS)
in classical conditioning, a stimulus that has no effect on the desired response prior to conditioning.

conditioned stimulus (CS)
in classical conditioning, a previously neutral stimulus that becomes able to produce a conditioned response, after pairing with an unconditioned stimulus.

conditioned response (CR)
in classical conditioning, a learned response to a conditioned stimulus.

Table 5.1 Classical Conditioning Terminology Chart

Full Term	Abbreviation
Unconditioned Stimulus	UCS
Unconditioned Response	UCR
Conditioned Stimulus	CS
Conditioned Response	CR

---

*elicit: to draw forth.

PUTTING IT ALL TOGETHER: PAVLOV'S CANINE CLASSIC, OR TICK TOCK TICK TOCK

Pavlov did a classic experiment in which he paired the ticking sound of a metronome (a simple device that produces a rhythmic ticking sound) with the presentation of food to see if the dogs would eventually salivate at the sound of the metronome (Pavlov, 1927). Since the metronome's ticking did not normally produce salivation, it was a neutral stimulus (NS) before any conditioning took place. The repeated pairing of a NS and the UCS is usually called *acquisition*, because the organism is in the process of acquiring learning. **Figure 5.1** explains how each element of the conditioning relationship worked in Pavlov's experiment.

Figure 5.1 Classical Conditioning

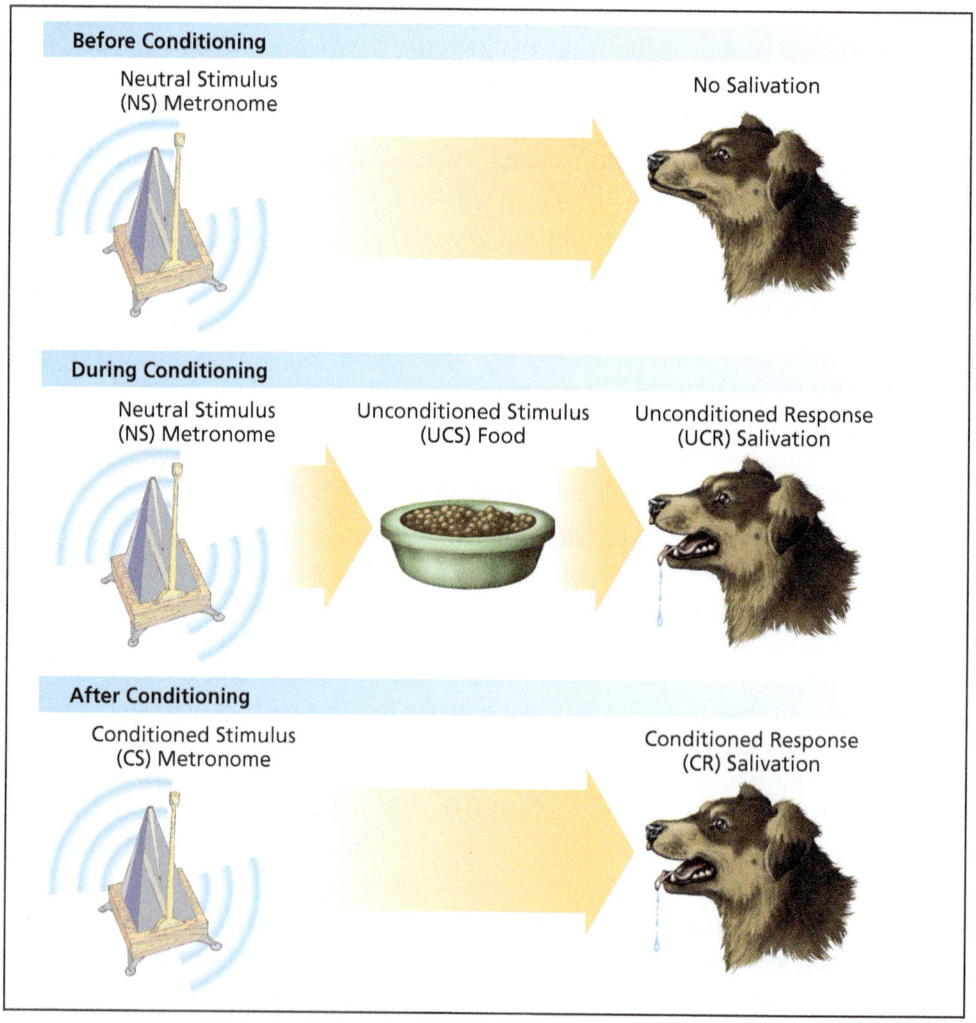

Before conditioning takes place, the sound of the metronome does not cause salivation and is a neutral stimulus, or NS. During conditioning, the sound of the metronome occurs just before the presentation of the food, the UCS. The food causes salivation, the UCR. When conditioning has occurred after several pairings of the metronome with the food, the metronome will begin to elicit a salivation response from the dog without any food. This is learning, and the sound of the metronome is now a CS and the salivation to the metronome is the CR.

Notice that the responses, CR and UCR, are very similar—salivation. However, they differ not only in strength but also in the stimulus to which they are the response. An *unconditioned* stimulus (UCS) is always followed by an *unconditioned* response (UCR), and a *conditioned* stimulus (CS) is always followed by a *conditioned* response (CR).

Classical conditioning is actually one of the simplest forms of learning. It's so simple that it happens to people all the time without them even being aware of it. Does your mouth water when you merely *see* an advertisement for your favorite food on television? Do you feel anxious every time you hear the high-pitched whine of the dentist's drill?

These are both examples of classical conditioning. Over the course of many visits to the dentist, for example, the body comes to associate that sound (the CS) with the anxiety or fear (the UCR) the person has felt while receiving a painful dental treatment (the UCS), and so the sound produces a feeling of anxiety (the CR) whether that person is in the chair or just in the outer waiting area.

Pavlov and his fellow researchers did many experiments with the dogs. In addition to the metronome, whistles, tuning forks, various visual stimuli, and bells were used (Thomas, 1994). Although classical conditioning happens quite easily, Pavlov and his other researchers formulated a few basic principles about the process (although we will see that there are a few exceptions to some of these principles):

1. The CS must come *before* the UCS. If Pavlov sounded the metronome just after he gave the dogs the food, they did not become conditioned (Rescorla, 1988).
2. The CS and UCS must come very close together in time—ideally, no more than 5 seconds apart. When Pavlov tried to stretch the time between the potential CS and the UCS to several minutes, no association or link between the two was made. Too much could happen in the longer interval of time to interfere with conditioning (Pavlov, 1926; Polewan et al., 2006; Ward et al., 2012; Wasserman & Miller, 1997).
3. The neutral stimulus must be paired with the UCS several times, often many times, before conditioning can take place (Pavlov, 1926).
4. The CS is usually some stimulus that is distinctive* or stands out from other competing stimuli. The metronome, for example, was a sound that was not normally present in the laboratory and, therefore, distinct (Pavlov, 1927; Rescorla, 1988).

💬 That seems simple enough. But I wonder—would Pavlov's dogs salivate to other ticking sounds?

STIMULUS GENERALIZATION AND DISCRIMINATION Pavlov did find that similar ticking sounds would (at least at first) produce a similar conditioned response from his dogs. He and other researchers found that the strength of the response to similar sounds was not as strong as it was to the original one, but the more similar the other sound was to the original sound (be it a metronome or any other kind of sound), the more similar the strength of the response was (Siegel, 1969; see **Figure 5.2**). The tendency to respond to a stimulus that is similar to the original conditioned stimulus is called **stimulus generalization**. For example, a person who reacts with anxiety to the sound of a dentist's drill might react with some slight anxiety to a similar-sounding machine, such as an electric coffee grinder.

Of course, Pavlov did not give the dogs any food after the similar ticking sound. They only got food following the correct CS. It didn't take long for the dogs to stop responding (generalizing) to the "fake" ticking sounds altogether. Because only the real CS was followed with food, they learned to tell the difference, or to *discriminate*, between the fake ticking and the CS ticking, a process called **stimulus discrimination**. Stimulus discrimination occurs when an organism learns to respond to different stimuli in different ways. For example, although the sound of the coffee grinder might produce a little anxiety in the dental-drill-hating person, after a few uses that sound will no longer produce anxiety because it isn't associated with dental pain.

EXTINCTION AND SPONTANEOUS RECOVERY What would have happened if Pavlov had stopped giving the dogs food after the real CS? Pavlov did try just that, and the dogs gradually stopped salivating to the sound of the ticking. When the

---

*distinctive: separate, having a different quality from something else.

If you find yourself cringing at the mere sight of a hypodermic needle, your cringing is a CR to the CS of the needle. The pain of the shot would be the original UCS.

stimulus generalization

the tendency to respond to a stimulus that is only similar to the original conditioned stimulus with the conditioned response.

stimulus discrimination

the tendency to stop making a generalized response to a stimulus that is similar to the original conditioned stimulus because the similar stimulus is never paired with the unconditioned stimulus.

Figure 5.2 Strength of the Generalized Response

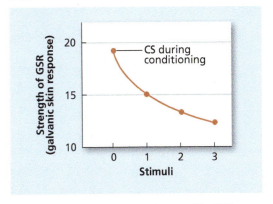

An example of stimulus generalization. The UCS was an electric shock and the UCR was the galvanic skin response (GSR), a measure associated with anxiety. The subjects had been conditioned originally to a CS tone (0) of a given frequency. When tested with the original tone, and with tones 1, 2, and 3 of differing frequencies, a clear generalization effect appeared. The closer the frequency of the test tone to the frequency of tone 0, the greater was the magnitude of the galvanic skin response to the tone.

Source: Hovland, C. I. (1937). The generalization of conditioned responses. I. The sensory generalization of conditioned responses with varying frequencies of tone. Journal of General Psychology, 17, 125–48.

metronome's ticking (the CS) was repeatedly presented in the absence of the food (the UCS, in this case), the salivation (the CR) "died out" in a process called **extinction**.

Why does the removal of an unconditioned stimulus lead to extinction of the conditioned response? One theory is that the presentation of the CS alone leads to new learning. During extinction, the CS–UCS association that was learned is weakened, as the CS no longer predicts the UCS. In the case of Pavlov's dogs, through extinction they learned to not salivate to the metronome's ticking, as it no longer predicted that food was on its way.

Look back at Figure 5.1. Once conditioning is acquired, the conditioned stimulus (CS) and conditioned response (CR) will always come *before* the original unconditioned stimulus (UCS). The UCS, which now comes after the CS and CR link, serves as a strengthener, or reinforcer, of the CS–CR association. Remove that reinforcer, and the CR it strengthens will weaken and disappear—at least for a while.

The term *extinction* is a little unfortunate in that it seems to mean that the original conditioned response is totally gone, dead, never coming back, just like the dinosaurs. (*Jurassic World* is thankfully not real.) Remember the definition of learning is any relatively *permanent* change in behavior. The fact is that once people learn something, it's almost impossible to "unlearn" it. People can learn new things that replace it or lose their way to it in memory, but it's still there. In the case of classical conditioning, this is easily demonstrated.

After extinguishing the conditioned salivation response in his dogs, Pavlov waited a few weeks, putting the conditioned stimulus (i.e., the metronome) away. There were no more training sessions, and the dogs were not exposed to the metronome's ticking in that time at all. But when Pavlov took the metronome back out and set it ticking, the dogs all began to salivate, although it was a fairly weak response and didn't last very long. This brief recovery of the conditioned response proves that the CR is "still in there" somewhere (remember, learning is *relatively permanent*). The CR is suppressed or inhibited by the lack of an association with the UCS of food (which is no longer reinforcing or strengthening the CR). As time passes, this inhibition weakens, especially if the original conditioned stimulus has not been present for a while. In **spontaneous recovery** the conditioned response can briefly reappear when the original CS returns, although the response is usually weak and short lived as it was with Pavlov's dogs. See **Figure 5.3** for a graph showing both extinction and spontaneous recovery.

extinction

the disappearance or weakening of a learned response following the removal or absence of the unconditioned stimulus (in classical conditioning) or the removal of a reinforcer (in operant conditioning).

spontaneous recovery

the reappearance of a learned response after extinction has occurred.

Figure 5.3 Extinction and Spontaneous Recovery

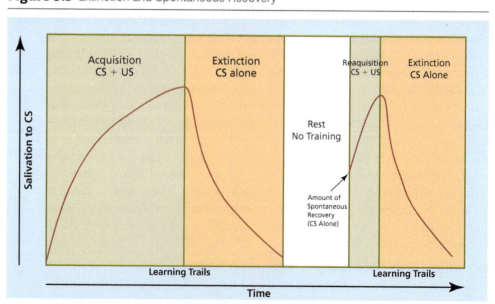

This graph shows the acquisition, extinction, spontaneous recovery, and reacquisition of a conditioned salivary response. Typically, the measure of conditioning is the number of drops of saliva elicited by the CS on each trial. Note that on the day following extinction, the first presentation of the CS elicits quite a large response. This response is due to spontaneous recovery.

HIGHER-ORDER CONDITIONING Another concept in classical conditioning is **higher-order conditioning** (see **Figure 5.4**). This occurs when a strong conditioned stimulus is paired with a neutral stimulus. The strong CS can actually play the part of a UCS, and the previously neutral stimulus becomes a *second* conditioned stimulus.

Figure 5.4 Higher-Order Conditioning

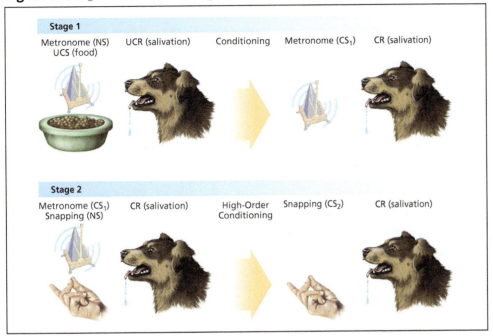

In Stage 1, a strong salivation response is conditioned to occur to the sound of the metronome (CS_1). In Stage 2, finger snapping (NS) is repeatedly paired with the ticking of the metronome (CS_1) until the dog begins to salivate to the finger snapping alone (now CS_2). This is called "higher-order conditioning," because one CS is used to create another, "higher" CS.

For example, let's revisit the point when Pavlov has already conditioned his dogs to salivate at the sound of the metronome. What would happen if, just before Pavlov turned on the metronome, he snapped his fingers? The sequence would now be "snap-ticking-salivation," or "NS–CS–CR" ("neutral stimulus/conditioned stimulus/conditioned response"). If this happens enough times, the finger snap will eventually also produce a salivation response. The finger snap becomes associated with the ticking through the same process that the ticking became associated with the food originally and is now another conditioned stimulus. Of course, the food (UCS) would have to be presented every now and then to maintain the original conditioned response to the metronome's ticking. Without the UCS, the higher-order conditioning would be difficult to maintain and would gradually fade away.

WHY DOES CLASSICAL CONDITIONING WORK? Pavlov believed that the conditioned stimulus, through its association close in time with the unconditioned stimulus, came to activate the same place in the animal's brain that was originally activated by the unconditioned stimulus. He called this process *stimulus substitution*. But if a mere association in time is all that is needed, why would conditioning *fail to happen* when the CS is presented immediately *after* the UCS?

Robert Rescorla (1988) found that the CS has to provide some kind of information about the coming of the UCS in order to achieve conditioning. In other words, the CS must predict that the UCS is coming. In one study, Rescorla exposed one group of rats to a tone and, just after the tone's onset and while the tone was still able to be heard, an electric shock was administered for some of the tone presentations. Soon the rats

AP 4.A Identify contributions of key researchers in the psychology of learning.

higher-order conditioning

occurs when a strong conditioned stimulus is paired with a neutral stimulus, causing the neutral stimulus to become a second conditioned stimulus.

became agitated* and reacted in fear by shivering and squealing at the onset of the tone, a kind of conditioned emotional response. But with a second group of rats, Rescorla again sounded a tone but administered the electric shock only *after* the tone *stopped*, not while the tone was being heard. That group of rats responded with fear to the *stopping* of the tone (Rescorla, 1968; Rescorla & Wagner, 1972).

The tone for the second group of rats provided a different kind of information than the tone in the first instance. For the first group, the tone means the shock is coming, whereas for the second group, the tone means there is no shock while the tone is on. It was the particular *expectancy* created by pairing the tone or absence of tone with the shock that determined the particular response of the rats. Because this explanation involves the mental activity of consciously expecting something to occur, it is an example of an explanation for classical conditioning called the **cognitive perspective**.

5.3 Classical Conditioning Applied to Human Behavior

5.3 Apply classical conditioning to examples of phobias, taste aversions, and drug dependency.

AP 4.D Apply learning principles to explain emotional learning, taste aversion, superstitious behavior, and learned helplessness.

AP 4.A Identify contributions of key researchers in the psychology of learning.

Later scientists took Pavlov's concepts and expanded them to explain not only animal behavior but also human behavior. One of the earliest of these studies showed that even an emotional response could be conditioned.

PHOBIAS In the first chapter of this text, John B. Watson and Rosalie Rayner's classic experiment with "Little Albert" and the white rat was discussed. See Learning Objective 1.2. This study was a demonstration of the classical conditioning of a phobia—an irrational fear response (Watson & Rayner, 1920). See Learning Objective 13.6.

Watson and Rayner paired the presentation of the white rat to the baby with a loud, scary noise. Although the baby was not initially afraid of the rat, he was naturally afraid of the loud noise and started to cry. After only seven pairings of the noise with the rat, every time the baby saw the rat, he started to cry. In conditioning terms, the loud noise was the UCS, the fear of the noise the UCR, the white rat became the CS, and the fear of the rat (the phobia) was the CR. (It should be pointed out that Watson and Rayner didn't really "torture" the baby—Albert's fright was temporary. Still, no ethics committee today would approve an experiment in which an infant experiences psychological distress like this.)

Little Albert remains a topic of interest for many researchers and students of psychology alike. Researchers have suggested his true identity was Douglas Merritte, the neurologically impaired son of a wet nurse at the hospital where the study took place, who died at six years of age (Beck & Irons, 2011; Beck et al., 2009; Fridlund et al., 2012). Others point out that "Albert B." or "Little Albert" was described as normal and healthy, descriptors that do not match up with Douglas Merritte (Griggs, 2015; Powell et al., 2014).

These concerns led many researchers to believe that Little Albert was not Douglas Merritte (Harris, 2011; Powell, 2010; Reese, 2010). With help from a professional genealogist,** researchers now have evidence for the true identity of Little Albert as another infant named Albert Barger (Digdon et al., 2014; Powell et al., 2014). While there are still a few inconsistencies, the similarities between Albert Barger's name and Watson and Rayner's record of Albert B., Albert's age, his mother's occupation at the hospital, his body weight, and a medical record indicating he was well developed and healthy in general, all seem to be more consistent with Albert Barger as the real identity of Little Albert (Digdon et al., 2014; Griggs, 2015; Powell et al., 2014). We may never know for certain why there was such a confusion about who Little Albert really was. People may

After "Little Albert" had been conditioned to fear a white rat, he also demonstrated fear of a rabbit, a dog, and a sealskin coat (although it remains uncertain if stimulus generalization actually occurred, as this fear was of a single rabbit, a single dog, etc.). Can you think of any emotional reactions you experience that might be classically conditioned emotional responses?

cognitive perspective
modern perspective in psychology that focuses on memory, intelligence, perception, problem solving, and learning.

---

*agitated: excited, upset.
**genealogist: someone who specializes in the study of family history and ancestry.

have been overconfident in their original beliefs and possibly victims of *confirmation bias* (Digdon, 2017; Griggs, 2015; Powell et al., 2014). See Learning Objective 7.4.

The learning of phobias is a very good example of a certain type of classical conditioning, the **conditioned emotional response (CER)**. Conditioned emotional responses are some of the easiest forms of classical conditioning to accomplish, and our lives are full of them. It's easy to think of fears people might have that are conditioned or learned: a child's fear of the doctor's office, a puppy's fear of a rolled-up newspaper, or the fear of dogs that is often shown by a person who has been attacked by a dog in the past. But other emotions can be conditioned, too.

It is even possible to become classically conditioned by simply watching someone else respond to a stimulus in a process called **vicarious conditioning** (Bandura & Rosenthal, 1966; Hygge & Öhman, 1976; Jones & Menzies, 1995). For example, one of the authors (we're not saying who, but her name rhymes with "candy") grew up watching her mother react very badly to any stray dog. The mother had been bitten and had to get rabies shots, so her fear was understandable. Her daughter had never been bitten or attacked yet developed an irrational and strong fear of all dogs as a result of watching her mother's reaction.

The next time you watch television, observe the commercials closely. Advertisers often use certain objects or certain types of people in their ads to generate a specific emotional response in viewers, hoping that the emotional response will become associated with their product. Sexy models, cute little babies, and adorable puppies are some of the examples of stimuli the advertising world uses to tug at our heartstrings, so to speak. But advertisers also use vicarious classical conditioning, often showing people reacting emotionally in the ad (either positively or negatively) to a product. They hope that the viewer will become conditioned to experience that same emotion when seeing the same product on store shelves.

conditioned emotional response (CER)

emotional response that has become classically conditioned to occur to learned stimuli, such as a fear of dogs or the emotional reaction that occurs when seeing an attractive person.

Watch Using Classical Conditioning to Treat Disorders

Watch the Video at MyLab Psychology

The good news is that the same learning principles that can contribute to phobias and anxiety disorders can also be used to treat them, as we'll see in the video *Using Classical Conditioning to Treat Disorders*.

CONDITIONED TASTE AVERSIONS Some kinds of associations in classical conditioning seem to be easier to make than others. For example, are there any foods that you just can't eat anymore because of a bad experience with them? Believe it or not, your reaction to that food is a kind of classical conditioning.

AP 4.A Identify contributions of key researchers in the psychology of learning.

vicarious conditioning

classical conditioning of an involuntary response or emotion by watching the reaction of another person.

conditioned taste aversion

development of a nausea or aversive response to a particular taste because that taste was followed by a nausea reaction, occurring after only one association.

Many experiments have shown that laboratory rats will develop a **conditioned taste aversion** for any liquid or food they swallow up to 6 hours before becoming nauseated. Researchers (Garcia et al., 1989; Garcia & Koelling, 1966) found that rats that were given a sweetened liquid and then injected with a drug or exposed to radiation* that caused nausea would not touch the liquid again. In a similar manner, alcoholics who are given a drug to make them violently nauseated when they drink alcohol may learn to avoid drinking any alcoholic beverage. The chemotherapy drugs that cancer patients receive also can create severe nausea, which causes those people to develop a taste aversion for any food they have eaten before going in for the chemotherapy treatment (Berteretche et al., 2004).

> 💬 But I thought that it took several pairings of these stimuli to bring about conditioning. How can classical conditioning happen so fast?

---

*radiation: beams of electromagnetic energy.

AP 2.C Predict how traits and behavior can be selected for their adaptive value.

It's interesting to note that birds, which find their food by sight, will avoid any object or insect that simply *looks* like the one that made them sick. There is a certain species of moth with coloring that mimics the monarch butterfly. That particular butterfly is poisonous to birds, but the moth isn't. The moth's mimicry causes birds to avoid eating it, even though it is quite edible. Researchers have found that some associations between certain stimuli and responses are far easier to form than others and that this is true in both animals and people. This is called **biological preparedness**. While mammals are biologically prepared to associate taste with illness, birds are biologically prepared to associate visual characteristics with illness (Shapiro et al., 1980).

As for phobias, fear is a natural emotional response that has ties to survival—we need to remember what the fear-inducing stimuli are so we can safely avoid them in the future. Nausea and fear are both examples of involuntary reactions that help organisms survive to reproduce and pass on their genetic material, so the innate tendency to make quick and strong associations between stimuli and these reactions has evolutionary importance.

Biological preparedness for fear of objects that are dangerous makes sense for survival, but when objects are not typically dangerous, it turns out to be very difficult to condition a fear of those objects. In one study, monkeys easily learned to be afraid of a toy snake or crocodile by watching videos of other monkeys reacting fearfully to these stimuli (a good example of vicarious classical conditioning). But the monkeys never learned to fear flowers or a toy rabbit by the same means. Snakes and crocodiles are predators; flowers and rabbits are not (Cook & Mineka, 1989; Mineka & Öhman, 2002).

DRUG DEPENDENCY The "high" of drug use, whether it comes from an opiate derivative, a stimulant, or a depressant such as alcohol, often takes place in certain surroundings, with certain other people, and perhaps even using certain objects, such as the tiny spoons used by cocaine addicts. These people, settings, and objects can become conditioned stimuli that are associated with the drug high and can produce a conditioned "high" response. The presence of these cues can make it even harder to resist using the drug because the body and mind have become classically conditioned to associate drug use with the cues.

Conditioned taste aversions in nature. This queen butterfly is not significantly poisonous to birds, but the monarch butterfly whose coloring the queen butterfly imitates is both poisonous and foul tasting to predators. Birds find their food by vision and will generally not eat anything that looks like the monarch.

biological preparedness

referring to the tendency of animals to learn certain associations, such as taste and nausea, with only one or few pairings due to the survival value of the learning.

THINKING CRITICALLY 5.1

Do you think that humans are as controlled by their biology as other animals? Why or why not?

Concept Map L.O. 5.1, 5.2, 5.3

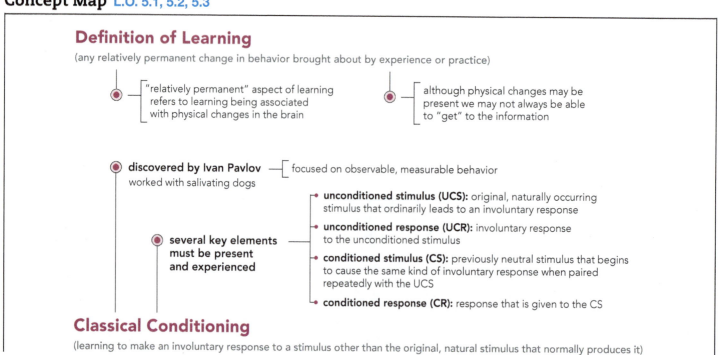

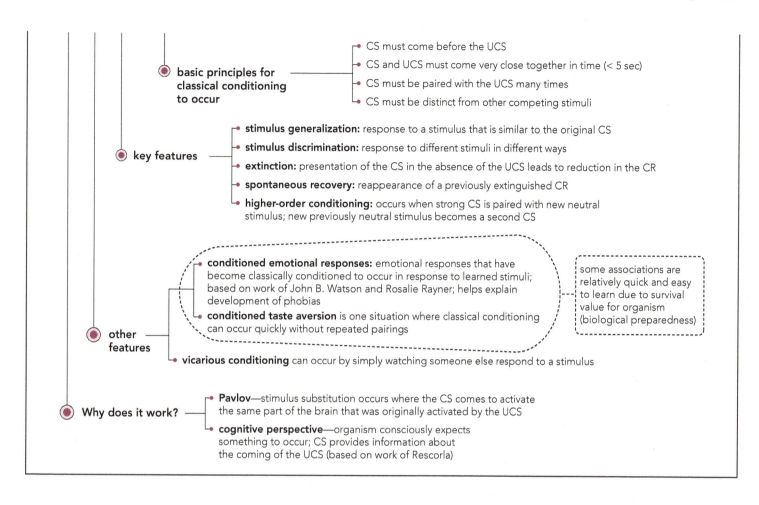

Practice Quiz — How much do you remember?

Pick the best answer.

1. Brendan noticed that whenever he moved his dog's food dish, his dog would come into the kitchen and act hungry and excited. He reasoned that because he feeds the dog using that dish, the sound of the dish had become a(n) _____.
   a. unconditioned response (UCR)
   b. unconditioned stimulus (UCS)
   c. neutral stimulus (NS)
   d. conditioned stimulus (CS)
   e. conditioned response (CR)

2. Ever since she was scared by a dog as a young child, Alexia has been afraid of all dogs. The fact that she is afraid of not only the original dog but all types of dogs is an example of _____.
   a. extinction
   b. stimulus generalization
   c. biological preparedness
   d. spontaneous recovery
   e. stimulus discrimination

3. In Watson and Rayner's experiment with "Little Albert," the conditioned stimulus (CS) was _____.
   a. the loud noise
   b. the white rat
   c. the fear of the noise
   d. the fear of Watson and Rayner
   e. the fear of the rat

4. Which of the following is an example of vicarious classical conditioning?
   a. Angel watches her grandfather check the air pressure in her bike tire and then use a hand pump to add air to the tire. She is later able to check the air pressure and pump up the tire herself.
   b. A pigeon pecks at a disk for a food pellet but only in the presence of other pigeons.
   c. Mason is told about a new product by a close friend and decides to buy it for himself.
   d. A cat responds to the sound of a bell because it sounds similar to a bell it hears on the television.
   e. As a young child, Liam frequently observed his older sisters jump around and scream whenever any of them saw a spider, as they were very afraid of them. Subsequently, Liam experiences feelings of fear when he sees a spider.

5. Hailey had cheesy tacos at a local Mexican restaurant. Later she became terribly ill and suffered bouts of nausea and vomiting. What might we predict based on conditioned taste aversion research?
   a. Hailey will probably be able to eat cheesy tacos with no nausea at all.
   b. Hailey will probably get nauseated the next time she tries to eat cheesy tacos.
   c. Hailey will probably develop a strong liking for cheesy tacos.
   d. Hailey will probably continue to eat cheesy tacos, but only at the same restaurant where she got sick.
   e. Hailey will probably continue to eat cheesy tacos except when she feels nauseous.

6. Rescorla found that the CS must _____ the UCS for conditioning to take place.
   a. come 10 to 15 minutes after
   b. predict
   c. replace
   d. come 10 to 15 minutes before
   e. come at the same time as

AP 4.G Distinguish general differences between principles of classical conditioning, operant conditioning, and observational learning.

5.4–5.9 What's in It for Me? Operant Conditioning

operant conditioning
the learning of voluntary behavior through the effects of pleasant and unpleasant consequences to responses.

law of effect
law stating that if an action is followed by a pleasurable consequence, it will tend to be repeated, and if followed by an unpleasant consequence, it will tend not to be repeated.

💬 So far, all learning seems to involve involuntary behavior, but I know that I am more than just automatic responses. People do things on purpose, so is that kind of behavior also learned?

There are two kinds of behavior that all organisms are capable of doing: involuntary and voluntary. If Inez blinks her eyes because a gnat flies close to them, that's a reflex and totally involuntary. But if she then swats at the gnat to frighten it, that's a voluntary choice. She *had* to blink, but she *chose* to swat.

Classical conditioning is the kind of learning that occurs with automatic, involuntary behavior. In this section we'll describe the kind of learning that applies to voluntary behavior, which is both different from and similar to classical conditioning.

5.4 The Contributions of Thorndike and Skinner

AP 4.A Identify contributions of key researchers in the psychology of learning.

AP 4.B Interpret graphs that exhibit the results of learning experiments.

5.4 Identify the contributions of Thorndike and Skinner to the concept of operant conditioning.

While classical conditioning involves the learning of involuntary, automatic responses, operant conditioning is about how organisms learn voluntary responses. **Operant conditioning** is based on the research of Edward L. Thorndike and B. F. Skinner.

FRUSTRATING CATS: THORNDIKE'S LAW OF EFFECT Thorndike (1874–1949) was one of the first researchers to explore and attempt to outline the laws of learning voluntary responses, although the field was not yet called operant conditioning. Thorndike placed a hungry cat inside a "puzzle box" from which the only escape was to press a lever located on the floor of the box. Thorndike placed a dish of food *outside* the box, so the hungry cat was highly motivated to get out. Thorndike observed that the cat would move around the box, pushing and rubbing up against the walls in an effort to escape. Eventually, the cat would accidentally push the lever, opening the door. Upon escaping, the cat was fed from a dish placed just outside the box. The lever is the stimulus, the pushing of the lever is the response, and the consequence is both escape (good) and food (even better).

The cat did not learn to push the lever and escape right away. After a number of trials (and many errors) in the puzzle box, the cat took less and less time to push the lever that would open the door (see **Figure 5.5**). It's important not to assume that the cat had "figured out" the connection between the lever and freedom—Thorndike kept moving the lever to a different position, and the cat had to learn the whole process over again. The cat would simply continue to rub and push in the same general area that led to food and freedom the last time, each time getting out and fed a little more quickly.

Based on this research, Thorndike developed the **law of effect**: If an action is followed by a pleasurable consequence, it will tend to be repeated. If an action is followed by an unpleasant consequence, it will tend not to be repeated (Thorndike, 1911; 1927). This is the basic principle behind learning voluntary behavior. In the case of the cat in the box, pushing the lever was followed by a pleasurable consequence (getting out and getting fed), so pushing the lever became a repeated response.

Figure 5.5 Graph of the Time to Learn in Thorndike's Experiment

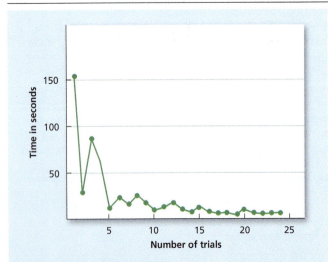

This is one of the earliest "learning curves" in the history of the experimental study of conditioning. The time required by one of Thorndike's cats to escape from the puzzle box gradually decreased with trials but with obvious reversals.

B. F. SKINNER: WATSON'S SUCCESSOR B. F. Skinner (1904–1990) was the behaviorist who assumed leadership of the field after John Watson. He was even more determined than Watson that psychologists should study only measurable, observable behavior. In addition to his knowledge of Pavlovian classical conditioning, Skinner found in the work of Thorndike a way to explain all behavior as the product of learning. He even gave the learning of voluntary behavior a special name: *operant conditioning* (Skinner, 1938). Voluntary behavior is what people and animals do to *operate* in the world. When people perform a voluntary action, it is to get something they want or to avoid something they don't want, right? So voluntary behavior, for Skinner, is **operant** behavior, and the learning of such behavior is operant conditioning.

The heart of operant conditioning is the effect of consequences on behavior. Thinking back to the section on classical conditioning, learning an involuntary behavior really depends on what comes *before* the response—the unconditioned stimulus (UCS) and what will become the conditioned stimulus (CS). These two stimuli are the *antecedent* stimuli (antecedent means something that comes before another thing). But in operant conditioning, learning depends on what happens *after* the response—the consequence. In a way, operant conditioning could be summed up as this: "If I do this, what's in it for me?"

5.5 The Concept of Reinforcement

5.5 Differentiate between primary and secondary reinforcers and positive and negative reinforcement.

AP 4.H Predict the effects of operant conditioning.

"What's in it for me?" represents the concept of **reinforcement**, one of Skinner's major contributions to behaviorism. The word itself means "to strengthen," and Skinner defined reinforcement as anything that, when following a response, causes that response to be more likely to happen again. Typically, this means that reinforcement is a consequence that is in some way pleasurable to the organism, which relates back to Thorndike's law of effect. The "pleasurable consequence" is what's "in it" for the organism. (Keep in mind that a pleasurable consequence might be something like getting food when hungry or a paycheck when you need money, but it might also mean *avoiding* a tiresome chore, like doing the dishes or taking out the garbage. I'll do almost anything to get out of doing the dishes myself!)

This rat is learning to press the bar in the wall of the cage in order to get food (delivered a few pellets at a time in the food trough on the lower left). In some cases, the light on the top left might be turned on to indicate that pressing the bar will lead to food or to warn of an impending shock delivered by the grate on the floor of the cage.

Going back to Thorndike's puzzle-box research, what was in it for the cat? We can see that the escape from the box and the food that the cat received after getting out are both *reinforcement* of the lever-pushing response. Every time the cat got out of the box, it got reinforced for doing so. In Skinner's view, this reinforcement is the reason that the cat learned anything at all. In operant conditioning, reinforcement is the key to learning.

Skinner had his own research device called a "Skinner box" or "operant conditioning chamber." His early research often involved placing a rat in one of these chambers and training it to push down on a bar to get food.

PRIMARY AND SECONDARY REINFORCERS The events or items that can be used to reinforce behavior are not all alike. Let's say that a friend of yours asks you to help her move some books from the trunk of her car to her apartment on the second floor. She offers you a choice of $25 or a candy bar. You'll most likely choose the money, right? With $25, you could buy more than one candy bar. (At today's prices, you might even be able to afford three.)

Now pretend that your friend offers the same deal to a 3-year-old child who lives downstairs for carrying up some of the paperback books: $25 or a candy bar. Which reward will the child more likely choose? Most children at that age have no real idea of the value of money, so the child will probably choose the candy bar. The money and the candy bar represent two basic kinds of **reinforcers**, items or events that when following a response will strengthen it. The reinforcing properties of money must be learned, but candy gives immediate reward in the form of taste and satisfying hunger.

operant

any behavior that is voluntary and not elicited by specific stimuli.

reinforcement

any event or stimulus, that when following a response, increases the probability that the response will occur again.

reinforcers

any events or objects that, when following a response, increase the likelihood of that response occurring again.

A reinforcer such as a candy bar that fulfills a basic need like hunger is called a **primary reinforcer**. Examples would be food (hunger drive), liquid (thirst drive), or touch (pleasure drive). Infants, toddlers, preschool-age children, and animals can be easily reinforced by using primary reinforcers. (It's not a good idea to start thinking of reinforcers as rewards—freedom from pain is also a basic need, so pain itself can be a primary reinforcer when it is *removed*. Removal of a painful stimulus fills a basic need just as eating food when hungry fills the hunger need.)

A **secondary reinforcer** such as money, however, gets its reinforcing properties from being associated with primary reinforcers in the past. A child who is given money to spend soon realizes that the ugly green paper can be traded for candy and treats—primary reinforcers—and so money becomes reinforcing in and of itself. If a person praises a puppy while petting him (touch, a primary reinforcer), the praise alone will eventually make the puppy squirm with delight.

> That sounds very familiar. Isn't this related to classical conditioning?

Secondary reinforcers do indeed get their reinforcing power from the process of classical conditioning. After all, the pleasure people feel when they eat, drink, or get a back rub is an automatic response, and any automatic response can be classically conditioned to occur to a new stimulus. In the case of money, the candy is a UCS (unconditioned stimulus) for pleasure (the UCR or unconditioned response), and the money is present just before the candy is obtained. The money becomes a CS (conditioned stimulus) for pleasure, and people certainly do feel pleasure when they have a lot of that green stuff, don't they?

In the case of the puppy, the petting is the UCS, the pleasure at being touched and petted is the UCR. The praise, or more specifically the tone of voice, becomes the CS for pleasure. Although classical and operant conditioning often "work together," as in the creation of secondary reinforcers, they are two different processes. **Table 5.2** presents a brief look at how the two types of conditioning differ from each other.

While classical and operant conditioning are different processes, the biological aspects of how they both work reside in a single source: the brain.

Table 5.2 Comparing Two Kinds of Conditioning

Operant Conditioning	Classical Conditioning
End result is an increase in the rate of an already-occurring response.	End result is the creation of a new response to a stimulus that did not normally produce that response.
Responses are voluntary, emitted by the organism.	Responses are involuntary and automatic, elicited by a stimulus.
Consequences are important in forming an association.	Antecedent stimuli are important in forming an association.
Reinforcement should be immediate.	CS must occur immediately before the UCS.
An expectancy develops for reinforcement to follow a correct response.	An expectancy develops for UCS to follow CS.

primary reinforcer
any reinforcer that is naturally reinforcing by meeting a basic biological need, such as hunger, thirst, or touch.

secondary reinforcer
any reinforcer that becomes reinforcing after being paired with a primary reinforcer, such as praise, tokens, or gold stars.

THE NEURAL BASES OF LEARNING As new ways of looking at the brain and the workings of neurons advance, researchers are investigating the neural bases of both classical and operant conditioning (Gallistel & Matzel, 2013). One important area involved in learning consists of neurons in the anterior cingulate cortex (ACC), located in the frontal lobe above the front of the corpus callosum (Apps et al., 2015).

The ACC also connects to the nucleus accumbens. Remember our discussion of drug dependence and the reward pathway in Chapter Four? See Learning Objective 4.11. The nucleus accumbens was a part of that pathway, and both of these areas of the brain are involved in the release of dopamine (Gale et al., 2016; Morita et al., 2013; Yavuz et al., 2015).

Given the role it plays in amplifying some input signals and decreasing the intensity of others in the nucleus accumbens (Floresco, 2015), it makes sense that dopamine would be involved in the process of reinforcement. Think about what happens when you hear the particular sound from your cell phone when you have an incoming message, for example. We like getting messages, so much so that we will often ignore the live person we are with to look at the message. Have you ever been accused of being "addicted" to your phone? If you think about it, that little sound—be it a chime, ding, or whatever you have chosen—has become a kind of conditioned stimulus. We find reading the messages themselves pleasurable, so the message could be seen as a kind of unconditioned stimulus for pleasure, and the sound becomes a CS for the CR of pleasure. But what is happening in the brain when you hear that sound followed by rewarding activities is excitatory activity in several areas, accompanied by increased dopamine activity, to signal that the behavior was beneficial and to do it again. Just as dopamine and the reward pathway are involved in drug dependency, they also seem to be heavily involved in our "learned" addictions, too.

POSITIVE AND NEGATIVE REINFORCEMENT   Reinforcers can also differ in the way they are used. Most people have no trouble at all understanding that following a response with some kind of pleasurable consequence (like a reward) will lead to an increase in the likelihood of that response being repeated. This is called **positive reinforcement**, the reinforcement of a response by the *addition* or experience of a pleasurable consequence, such as a reward or a pat on the back.

But many people have trouble understanding that the opposite is also true: Following a response with *the removal or escape* from something *unpleasant* will also increase the likelihood of that response being repeated—a process called **negative reinforcement**. Remember the idea that pain can be a primary reinforcer if it is removed? If a person's behavior gets pain to stop, the person is much more likely to do that same thing again—which is part of the reason people can get addicted to painkilling medication. Watch the video *Negative Reinforcement* for another example.

Let's consider a few examples of each of these types of reinforcement. Getting money for working is an example of *positive reinforcement* because the person *gets* money (an added, pleasurable consequence) for the behavior of working. That one everyone understands. But what about avoiding a penalty by turning one's income tax return in on time? That is an example of *negative reinforcement* because the behavior (submitting the return before the deadline) results in *avoiding* an *unpleasant* stimulus (a penalty). The likelihood that the person will behave that way again (turn it in on time in the future) is therefore *increased*—just as positive reinforcement will increase a behavior's likelihood. It is very important to remember that BOTH positive AND negative reinforcement *increase* the likelihood of the behavior they follow—they *both* have the effect of strengthening, or reinforcing, the behavior. Examples are the best way to figure out the difference between these two types of reinforcement, so try to figure out which of

positive reinforcement
the reinforcement of a response by the addition or experiencing of a pleasurable stimulus.

negative reinforcement
the reinforcement of a response by the removal, escape from, or avoidance of an unpleasant stimulus.

Watch Negative Reinforcement

Watch the Video at MyLab Psychology

the following examples would be positive reinforcement and which would be negative reinforcement:

1. Pedro's father nags him to wash his car. Pedro hates being nagged, so he washes the car so his father will stop nagging.
2. Napoleon learns that talking in a funny voice gets him lots of attention from his classmates, so now he talks that way more often.
3. Allen is a server at a restaurant and always tries to smile and be pleasant because that seems to lead to bigger tips.
4. An Li turns her report in to her teacher on the day it is due because papers get marked down a letter grade for every day they are late.

Here are the answers:

1. Pedro is being negatively reinforced for washing his car because the nagging (unpleasant stimulus) stops when he does so.
2. Napoleon is getting positive reinforcement in the form of his classmates' attention.
3. Allen's smiling and pleasantness are positively reinforced by the customers' tips.
4. An Li is avoiding an unpleasant stimulus (the marked-down grade) by turning in her paper on time, which is an example of negative reinforcement.

THINKING CRITICALLY 5.2

Think back to the "pleasurable outcome" question at the beginning of this chapter. You should now realize that that question was really asking about reinforcement. What type of reinforcement worked best for you when you were in grade school? Positive or negative? Did this change in high school?

We've discussed what reinforcement is and how it affects the behavior that follows the reinforcement as well as the role of the brain in reinforcement. In the next section, we'll discuss the different ways in which reinforcement can be administered as well as the difference between reinforcement and punishment. We'll also look at the role of the stimuli that come *before* the behavior that is to be reinforced and a few other operant conditioning concepts.

AP 4.1 Predict how practice, schedules of reinforcement, other aspects of reinforcement, and motivation will influence quality of learning.

5.6 Schedules of Reinforcement: Why the One-Armed Bandit Is So Seductive

5.6 Identify the four schedules of reinforcement.

The timing of reinforcement can make a tremendous difference in the speed at which learning occurs and the strength of the learned response. However, Skinner (1956) found that reinforcing every response was not necessarily the best schedule of reinforcement for long-lasting learning, as we'll see in the video *Schedules of Reinforcement*.

Watch Schedules of Reinforcement

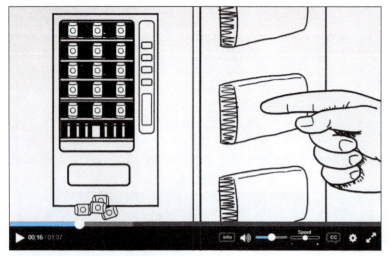

Watch the Video at MyLab Psychology

THE PARTIAL REINFORCEMENT EFFECT Consider the following scenario: Alicia's mother agrees to give her a quarter every night she remembers to put her dirty clothes in the clothes hamper. Bianca's mother agrees to give her a dollar at the end of the week, but only if she has put her clothes in the hamper every night. Alicia learns to put her clothes in the hamper more quickly than does Bianca because responses that are reinforced each time they occur are more easily and quickly learned. After a time, the mothers stop giving the girls the money. Which child is more likely to stop putting her clothes in the hamper?

The answer might surprise you. It is more likely that Alicia, who has expected to get a reinforcer (the quarter) after *every single response*, will stop putting her clothes in the hamper. As soon as the reinforcers stop for her, the behavior is no longer reinforced and is likely to extinguish. In contrast, Bianca has expected to get a reinforcer only after *seven correct responses*. When the reinforcers stop for her, she might continue to put the clothes in the hamper for several more days or even another whole week, hoping that the reinforcer will eventually come anyway. Bianca may have learned more slowly than Alicia, but once she learned the connection between putting her clothes in the hamper and getting that dollar, she is less likely to stop doing it—even when her mother fails to give the dollar as expected.

Bianca's behavior illustrates the **partial reinforcement effect** (Skinner, 1956): A response that is reinforced after some, but not all, correct responses will be more resistant to extinction than a response that receives **continuous reinforcement** (a reinforcer for each and every correct response). Although it may be easier to teach a new behavior using continuous reinforcement, partially reinforced behavior is not only more difficult to suppress but also more like real life. Imagine being paid for every hamburger you make or every report you turn in. In the real world, people tend to receive partial reinforcement rather than continuous reinforcement for their work.

Partial reinforcement can be accomplished according to different patterns or schedules. For example, it might be a certain interval of time that's important, such as an office safe that can only be opened at a certain time of day. It wouldn't matter how many times one tried to open the safe if the effort didn't come at the right *time*. On the other hand, it might be the number of responses that is important, as it would be if one had to sell a certain number of raffle tickets in order to get a prize. When the timing of the response is more important, it is called an *interval schedule*. When it is the number of responses that is important, the schedule is called a *ratio schedule* because a certain number of responses is required for each reinforcer (e.g., 50 raffle tickets for each prize is a 50 to 1 ratio or 50:1). The other way in which schedules of reinforcement can differ is in whether the number of responses or interval of time is *fixed* (the same in each case) or *variable* (a different number or interval is required in each case). So it is possible to have a fixed interval schedule, a variable interval schedule, a fixed ratio schedule, and a variable ratio schedule (Skinner, 1961).

FIXED INTERVAL SCHEDULE OF REINFORCEMENT If you receive a paycheck once a week, you are familiar with what is called a **fixed interval schedule of reinforcement**, in which a reinforcer is received *after* a certain, fixed interval of time has passed. If Professor Conner were teaching a rat to press a lever to get food pellets, she might require it to push the lever *at least once* within a 2-minute time span to get a pellet. It wouldn't matter how many times the rat pushed the bar; the rat would only get a pellet at the end of the 2-minute interval if it had pressed the bar at least once. It is the *first* correct response that gets reinforced at the end of the interval.

As shown in **Figure 5.6**, a fixed interval schedule of reinforcement does not produce a fast rate of responding (notice that the line doesn't go "up" as fast as in the blue fixed ratio line). Since it only matters that at least *one* response is made *during* the specific interval of time, speed is not that important. Eventually, the rat will start pushing the lever only as the interval of time nears its end, causing the *scalloping* effect you see in the graph. The response rate goes up just before the reinforcer and then drops off immediately after, until it is almost time for the next food pellet. This is similar to the way in which workers speed up production just before payday and slow down just after payday (Critchfield et al., 2003).

Paychecks aren't the only kind of fixed schedule that people experience. When do you study the hardest? Isn't it right before a test? If you know when the test is to be given, that's like having a fixed interval of time that is predictable, and you can save your greatest studying efforts until closer to the exam. (Some students save *all* of their studying for the night before the exam, which is not the best strategy.) Another example of a fixed interval schedule would be the way that many people floss and brush their teeth most

partial reinforcement effect
the tendency for a response that is reinforced after some, but not all, correct responses to be very resistant to extinction.

continuous reinforcement
the reinforcement of each and every correct response.

fixed interval schedule of reinforcement
schedule of reinforcement in which the interval of time that must pass before reinforcement becomes possible is always the same.

AP 4.B Interpret graphs that exhibit the results of learning experiments.

Figure 5.6 Schedules of Reinforcement

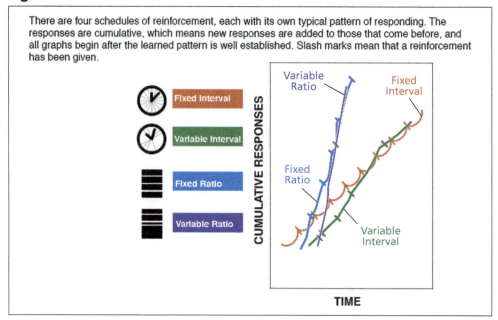

These four graphs show the typical pattern of responding for both fixed and variable interval and ratio schedules of reinforcement. The responses are cumulative, which means new responses are added to those that come before, and all graphs begin after the learned pattern is well established. Slash marks mean that a reinforcement has been given. In both the fixed interval and fixed ratio graphs, there is a pause after each reinforcement as the learner briefly "rests." The "scalloped" shape of the fixed interval curve is a typical indicator of this pause, as is the stair-step shape of the fixed ratio curve. In the variable interval and ratio schedules, no such pause occurs, because the reinforcements are unpredictable. Notice that both fixed and variable interval schedules are slower (less steep) than the two ratio schedules because of the need to respond as quickly as possible in the ratio schedules.

rigorously* for a few days before their next dental exam—especially those who have not been flossing until just before their appointment! In this case, they are probably hoping for negative reinforcement. The cleaner they get their teeth before the appointment, the less unpleasant the time they might have to spend in that chair.

💬 If a scheduled test is a fixed interval, then would a pop quiz be a variable interval schedule?

VARIABLE INTERVAL SCHEDULE OF REINFORCEMENT Pop quizzes are unpredictable. Students don't know exactly what day they might be given a pop quiz, so the best strategy is to study a little every night just in case there is a quiz the next day. Pop quizzes are good examples of a **variable interval schedule of reinforcement**, where the interval of time after which the individual must respond in order to receive a reinforcer (in this case, a good grade on the quiz) changes from one time to the next. In a more basic example, a rat might receive a food pellet when it pushes a lever, every 5 minutes on average. Sometimes the interval might be 2 minutes, sometimes 10, but the rat must push the lever at least once *after* that interval to get the pellet. Because the rat can't predict how long the

variable interval schedule of reinforcement

schedule of reinforcement in which the interval of time that must pass before reinforcement becomes possible is different for each trial or event.

---

*rigorously: strictly, consistently.

interval is going to be, it pushes the bar more or less continuously, producing the smooth graph in Figure 5.6. Once again, speed is not important, so the rate of responding is slow but steady.

Another example of a variable interval schedule might be the kind of fishing in which people put the pole in the water and wait—and wait—and—wait, until a fish takes the bait, if they are lucky. They only have to put the pole in once, but they might refrain from taking it out for fear that just when they do, the biggest fish in the world would swim by. Redialing a busy number, such as a customer service line or a number that keeps going to someone's voicemail and you don't want to leave a message, is also this kind of schedule. People don't know when the call will go through, so they keep redialing.

When people go fishing, they never know how long they may have to dangle the bait in the water before snagging a fish. This is an example of a variable interval schedule of reinforcement and explains why some people, such as this father and child, are reluctant to pack up and go home.

FIXED RATIO SCHEDULE OF REINFORCEMENT In ratio schedules, it is the number of responses that counts. In a **fixed ratio schedule of reinforcement**, the number of responses required to receive each reinforcer will always be the same number.

Notice two things about the fixed ratio graph in Figure 5.6. The rate of responding is very fast, especially when compared to the fixed interval schedule, and there are little "breaks" in the response pattern immediately after a reinforcer is given. The rapid response rate occurs because the rat wants to get to the next reinforcer just as fast as possible, and the number of lever pushes counts. The pauses or breaks come right after a reinforcer, because the rat knows "about how many" lever pushes will be needed to get to the next reinforcer because it's always the same. Fixed schedules—both ratio and interval—are predictable, which allows rest breaks.

In human terms, anyone who does piecework, in which a certain number of items have to be completed before payment is given, is reinforced on a fixed ratio schedule. Some sandwich shops use a fixed ratio schedule of reinforcement with their customers by giving out punch cards that get punched one time for each sandwich purchased. When the card has 10 punches, for example, the customer might get a free sandwich.

VARIABLE RATIO SCHEDULE OF REINFORCEMENT

💬 The purple line in Figure 5.6 is also very fast, but it's so much smoother, like the variable interval graph. Why are they similar?

A **variable ratio schedule of reinforcement** is one in which the number of responses changes from one trial to the next. In the rat example, the rat might be expected to push the bar an *average* of 20 times to get reinforcement. That means that sometimes the rat would push the lever only 10 times before a reinforcer comes, but at other times it might take 30 lever pushes or more.

Figure 5.6 shows a purple line that is just as rapid a response rate as the fixed ratio schedule because the *number* of responses still matters. But the graph is much smoother because the rat is taking no rest breaks. It can't afford to do so because it *doesn't know* how many times it may have to push that lever to get the next food pellet. It pushes as fast as it can and eats while pushing. It is the *unpredictability* of the variable schedule that makes the responses more or less continuous—just as in a variable interval schedule.

In human terms, people who shove money into the one-armed bandit, or slot machine, are being reinforced on a variable ratio schedule of reinforcement (they hope). They put their coins in (response), but they don't know how many times they will have to do this before reinforcement (the jackpot) comes. People who do this tend to sit there until they either win or run out of money. They don't dare stop because the "next one" might hit that jackpot. Buying lottery tickets is much the same thing, as is any kind of gambling. People don't know how many tickets they will have to buy, and they're afraid that if they don't buy the next one, that will be the ticket that would have won, so they keep buying and buying.

Slot machines provide reinforcement in the form of money on a variable ratio schedule, making the use of these machines very addictive for many people. People don't want to stop for fear the next pull of the lever will be that "magic" one that produces a jackpot.

fixed ratio schedule of reinforcement

schedule of reinforcement in which the number of responses required for reinforcement is always the same.

variable ratio schedule of reinforcement

schedule of reinforcement in which the number of responses required for reinforcement is different for each trial or event.

Regardless of the schedule of reinforcement one uses, two additional factors contribute to making reinforcement of a behavior as effective as possible. The first factor is *timing*: In general, a reinforcer should be given as immediately as possible *after* the desired behavior. Delaying reinforcement tends not to work well, especially when dealing with animals and small children. (For older children and adults who can think about future reinforcements, such as saving up one's money to buy a highly desired item, some delayed reinforcement can work—for them, just saving the money is reinforcing as they think about their future purchase.) The second factor in effective reinforcement is to reinforce *only* the desired behavior. This should be obvious, but we all slip up at times; for example, many parents make the mistake of giving a child who has not done some chore the promised treat anyway, which completely undermines the child's learning of that chore or task. And who hasn't given a treat to a pet that has not really done the trick?

AP 4.H Predict the effects of operant conditioning.

5.7 The Role of Punishment in Operant Conditioning

5.7 Identify the effect that punishment has on behavior.

> So I think I get reinforcement now, but what about punishment? How does punishment fit into the big picture?

Let's go back to the discussion of positive and negative reinforcement. These strategies are important for *increasing* the likelihood that the targeted behavior will occur again. But what about behavior that we do not want to recur?

DEFINING PUNISHMENT People experience two kinds of things as consequences in the world: things they like (food, money, candy, sex, praise, and so on) and things they don't like (spankings, being yelled at, and experiencing any kind of pain, to name a few). In addition, people experience these two kinds of consequences in one of two ways: Either people experience them directly (such as getting money for working or getting yelled at for misbehaving) or they don't experience them, such as losing an allowance for misbehaving or avoiding a scolding by lying about misbehavior. These four consequences are named and described in **Table 5.3**.

Table 5.3 Four Ways to Modify Behavior

	Reinforcement	Punishment
Positive (Adding)	Something valued or desirable *Positive Reinforcement* Example: getting a gold star for good behavior in school	Something unpleasant *Punishment by Application* Example: getting a spanking for disobeying
Negative (Removing/Avoiding)	Something unpleasant *Negative Reinforcement* Example: fastening a seat belt to stop the alarm from sounding	Something valued or desirable *Punishment by Removal* Example: losing a privilege such as going out with friends

As you can see from this table, **punishment** is actually the opposite of reinforcement. It is any event or stimulus that, when following a response, causes that response to be *less* likely to happen again. People often confuse negative reinforcement with punishment because "negative" sounds like it ought to be something bad, like a kind of punishment. But reinforcement (no matter whether it is positive or negative) *strengthens* a response, while punishment *weakens* a response.

Just as there are two ways in which reinforcement can happen, there are also two ways in which punishment can happen.

punishment
any event or object that, when following a response, makes that response less likely to happen again.

Punishment by application occurs when something unpleasant (such as a spanking, scolding, or other unpleasant stimulus) is added to the situation or *applied*. This is the kind of punishment that most people think of when they hear the word *punishment*. This is also the kind of punishment that many child development specialists strongly recommend parents avoid using with their children because it can easily escalate into abuse (Dubowitz & Bennett, 2007; Durrant & Ensom, 2012; Gershoff & Grogan-Kaylor, 2016; Gershoff et al., 2017). A spanking might be *physically* harmless if it is only two or three swats with a hand, but if done in anger or with a belt or other instrument, it becomes abuse, both physical and emotional.

Punishment by removal, on the other hand, is the kind of punishment most often confused with negative reinforcement. In this type of punishment, behavior is punished by the removal of something pleasurable or desired after the behavior occurs. "Grounding" a teenager is removing the freedom to do what the teenager wants to do and is an example of this kind of punishment. Other examples would be placing a child in time-out (removing the attention of the others in the room), fining someone for disobeying the law (removing money), and punishing aggressive behavior by taking away Internet privileges. This type of punishment is typically far more acceptable to child development specialists because it involves no physical aggression and avoids many of the problems caused by more aggressive punishments.

This mother is cutting up the daughter's credit card. Is the mother using punishment by application or punishment by removal?

The confusion over the difference between negative reinforcement and punishment by removal makes it worth examining the difference just a bit more. Negative reinforcement occurs when a response is followed by the *removal* of an *unpleasant* stimulus. If something unpleasant has just gone away as a consequence of that response, wouldn't that response tend to happen again and again? If the response increases, the consequence has to be a kind of *reinforcement*. The problem is that the name sounds like it should be some kind of punishment because of the word *negative*, and that's exactly the problem that many people experience when they are trying to understand negative reinforcement. Many people get negative reinforcement mixed up with punishment by removal, in which a *pleasant* thing is removed (like having your driver's license taken away because you caused a bad accident). Because something is removed (taken away) in both cases, it's easy to think that they will both have the effect of punishment, or weakening a response. The difference between them lies in *what* is taken away: In the case of negative reinforcement, it is an *unpleasant* thing; in the case of punishment by removal, it is a *pleasant* or desirable thing. Many textbooks refer to punishment by application as positive punishment and punishment by removal as negative punishment. While technically these terms are correct, they just add to the confusion, and as a result, your authors have chosen to stay with the more descriptive terms. For a head-to-head comparison of negative reinforcement and this particular type of punishment by removal, see **Table 5.4**.

punishment by application
the punishment of a response by the addition or experiencing of an unpleasant stimulus.

punishment by removal
the punishment of a response by the removal of a pleasurable stimulus.

Table 5.4 Negative Reinforcement Versus Punishment by Removal

Example of Negative Reinforcement	Example of Punishment by Removal
Stopping at a red light to avoid getting in an accident.	Losing the privilege of driving because you got into too many accidents.
Fastening your seat belt to get the annoying warning signal to stop.	Having to spend some of your money to pay a ticket for failure to wear a seat belt.
Obeying a parent before the parent reaches the count of "three" to avoid getting a scolding.	Being "grounded" (losing your freedom) because of disobedience.

PROBLEMS WITH PUNISHMENT Although punishment can be effective in reducing or weakening a behavior, it has several drawbacks. The job of punishment is much harder than that of reinforcement. In using reinforcement, all one has to do is strengthen a response that is already there. But punishment is used to weaken a response, and getting rid of a response that is already well established is not that easy. (Ask any parent or pet owner.) Many times punishment only serves to temporarily suppress or inhibit a behavior until enough time has passed. For example, punishing a child's bad behavior doesn't always eliminate the behavior completely. As time goes on, the punishment is forgotten and the "bad" behavior may occur again in a kind of spontaneous recovery of the old (and probably pleasurable for the child) behavior.

Look back at Table 5.3 under the "Punishment" column. Punishment by application can be quite severe, and severe punishment does do one thing well: It stops the behavior immediately (Bucher & Lovaas, 1967; Carr & Lovaas, 1983). It may not stop it permanently, but it does stop it. In a situation in which a child might be doing something dangerous or self-injurious, this kind of punishment is sometimes more acceptable (Duker & Seys, 1996). For example, if a child starts to run into a busy street, the parent might scream at the child to stop and then administer several rather severe swats to the child's rear. If this is NOT typical behavior on the part of the parent, the child will most likely never run into the street again.

Other than situations of immediately stopping dangerous behavior, severe punishment has too many drawbacks to be really useful (Berlin et al., 2009; Boutwell et al., 2011). It should also be discouraged because of its potential for leading to abuse (Afifi et al., 2017; Hecker et al., 2014; Gershoff, 2000, 2010; Lee et al., 2013; MacKenzie et al., 2012; McMillan et al., 1999):

- Severe punishment may cause the child (or animal) to avoid the punisher instead of the behavior being punished, so the child (or animal) learns the wrong response.
- Severe punishment may encourage lying to avoid the punishment (a kind of negative reinforcement)—again, not the response that is desired.
- Severe punishment creates fear and anxiety, emotional responses that do not promote learning (Baumrind, 1997; Gershoff, 2002, 2010). If the point is to teach something, this kind of consequence isn't going to help.
- Hitting provides a successful model for aggression (Afifi et al., 2017; Gershoff, 2000, 2010; Milner, 1992; Österman et al., 2014; Taylor et al., 2010).

That last point is worth a bit more discussion. In using an aggressive type of punishment, such as spanking, the adult is actually modeling (presenting a behavior to be imitated by the child). After all, the adult is using aggression to get what the adult wants from the child. Children sometimes become more likely to use aggression to get what they want when they receive this kind of punishment (Bryan & Freed, 1982; Larzelere, 1986), and the adult has lost an opportunity to model a more appropriate way to deal with parent–child disagreements. Since aggressive punishment does tend to stop the undesirable behavior, at least for a while, the parent who is punishing actually experiences a kind of negative reinforcement: "When I spank, the unpleasant behavior goes away." This may increase the tendency to use aggressive punishment over other forms of discipline and could even lead to child abuse (Dubowitz & Bennett, 2007). There is some evidence that physical punishment that would not be considered abusive (i.e., pushing, shoving, grabbing, hitting) is associated with an increased risk of mental illness for the child in later life (Afifi et al., 2012, 2017; Ma et al., 2012). Finally, some children are so desperate for attention from their parents that they will actually misbehave on purpose. The punishment is a form of attention, and these children will take whatever attention they can get, even negative attention.

Punishment by removal is less objectionable to many parents and educators and is the only kind of punishment that is permitted in many public schools. But this kind of punishment also has its drawbacks—it teaches the child what *not* to do but not what the child should do. Both punishment by removal and punishment by application are usually only temporary in their effect on behavior. After some time has passed, the behavior will most likely return as the memory of the punishment gets weaker, allowing spontaneous recovery.

💬 If punishment doesn't work very well, what can a parent do to keep a child from behaving badly?

The way to make punishment more effective involves remembering a few simple rules:

1. **Punishment should immediately follow the behavior it is meant to punish.** If the punishment comes long after the behavior, it will not be associated with that behavior. (Remember, this is also true of reinforcement.)

2. **Punishment should be consistent.** This actually means two things. First, if the parent says that a certain punishment will follow a certain behavior, then the parent must make sure to follow through and do what he or she promised to do. Second, punishment for a particular behavior should stay at the same intensity or increase slightly but never decrease. For example, if a child is scolded for jumping on the bed the first time, the second time this behavior happens the child should also be punished by scolding or by a stronger penalty, such as removal of a favorite toy. But if the first misbehavior is punished by spanking and the second by only a scolding, the child learns to "gamble" with the possible punishment.

3. **Punishment of the wrong behavior should be paired, whenever possible, with reinforcement of the right behavior.** Instead of yelling at a 2-year-old for eating with her fingers, the parent might pull her hand gently out of her plate while saying something such as, "No, we do not eat with our fingers. We eat with our fork," and then place the fork in the child's hand and praise her for using it. "See, you are doing such a good job with your fork. I'm so proud of you." Pairing punishment (the mild correction of pulling her hand away while saying "No, we do not eat with our fingers") with reinforcement allows parents (and others) to use a much milder punishment and still be effective. It also teaches the desired behavior rather than just suppressing the undesired one.

Watch Alternatives to Using Punishment

👁 Watch the Video at MyLab Psychology

A few examples of these methods are explained in the video *Alternatives to Using Punishment*.

5.8 Other Aspects of Operant Conditioning

5.8 Explain the concepts of discriminant stimuli, extinction, generalization, and spontaneous recovery as they relate to operant conditioning.

We've discussed the role of the antecedent stimulus in classical conditioning, as well as the concepts of extinction, generalization, and spontaneous recovery. These concepts are also important in operant conditioning but in slightly different ways.

STIMULUS CONTROL: SLOW DOWN, IT'S THE COPS You see a police car in your rearview mirror and automatically slow down, even if you weren't speeding. The traffic light turns red, so you stop. When you want to get into a store, you head for the door and push or pull on the handle. All of these things—slowing down, stopping, using the door handle—are learned. But how do you know what learned response to make and when? The police car, the stoplight, and the door handle are all cues, or stimuli, which tell you what behavior will get you what you want.

A **discriminative stimulus** is any stimulus that provides an organism with a cue for making a certain response in order to obtain reinforcement—specific cues would lead to specific responses, and discriminating between the cues leads to success. For example, a police car is a discriminative stimulus for slowing down and a red stoplight is a cue for stopping

discriminative stimulus
any stimulus, such as a stop sign or a doorknob, that provides the organism with a cue for making a certain response in order to obtain reinforcement.

One way to deal with a child's temper tantrum is to ignore it. The lack of reinforcement for the tantrum behavior will eventually result in extinction.

because both of these actions are usually followed by negative reinforcement—people don't get a ticket or don't get hit by another vehicle. A doorknob is a cue for where to grab the door in order to successfully open it. In fact, if a door has a knob, people always turn it, but if it has a handle, people usually pull it, right? The two kinds of opening devices each bring forth a different response from people, and their reward is opening the door.

EXTINCTION, GENERALIZATION, AND SPONTANEOUS RECOVERY IN OPERANT CONDITIONING *Extinction* in classical conditioning involves the removal of the UCS, the unconditioned stimulus that eventually acts as a reinforcer of the CS–CR bond. It should come as no surprise, then, that extinction in operant conditioning involves the removal of the reinforcement. Have you ever seen a child throw a temper tantrum in the checkout line because the little one wanted some candy or toy? Many exasperated* parents will cave in and give the child the treat, positively reinforcing the tantrum. The parent is also being negatively reinforced for giving in, because the obnoxious** behavior stops. The only way to get the tantrum behavior to stop is to remove the reinforcement, which means no candy, no treat, and if possible, no attention from the parent. (Not only is this hard enough to do while enduring the tantrum, but also the tantrum behavior may actually get worse before it extinguishes!)

Just as in classical conditioning, operantly conditioned responses also can be generalized to stimuli that are only *similar* to the original stimulus. For example, what parent has not experienced that wonderful moment when Baby, who is just learning to label objects and people, says "Dada" in response to the presence of her father and is reinforced by his delight and attention to her. But in the beginning, Baby may cause Dad to cringe when she generalizes her "Dada" response to any man. As other men fail to reinforce her for this response, she'll learn to discriminate among them and her father and only call her father "Dada." In this way, the man who is actually her father becomes a discriminative stimulus just like the stoplight or the doorknob mentioned earlier.

Spontaneous recovery (in classical conditioning, the recurrence of a conditioned response after extinction) will also happen with operant responses. Anyone who has ever trained animals to do several different tricks will say that when first learning a new trick, most animals will try to get reinforcers by performing their *old* tricks.

AP 4.J Suggest how behavior modification, biofeedback, coping strategies, and self-control can be used to address behavioral problems.

5.9 Applications of Operant Conditioning: Shaping and Behavior Modification

5.9 Describe how operant conditioning is used to change animal and human behavior.

Operant conditioning is more than just the reinforcement of simple responses. It can be used to modify the behavior of both animals and humans.

💬 How do the circus trainers get their animals to do all those complicated tricks?

shaping
the reinforcement of simple steps in behavior through successive approximations that lead to a desired, more complex behavior.

SHAPING When you see an animal in a circus or in a show at a zoo perform tricks, you are seeing the result of applying the rules of conditioning—both classical and operant—to animals. But the more complex tricks are a process in operant conditioning called **shaping**, in which small steps toward some ultimate goal are reinforced until the goal itself is reached.

For example, if Jody wanted to train his dog to jump through a hoop, he would have to start with some behavior that the dog is already capable of doing on its own. Then he would gradually "mold" that starting behavior into the jump—something the dog is capable of doing but not likely to do on its own. Jody would have to start with

---

*exasperated: irritated or annoyed.
**obnoxious: highly offensive or undesirable.

the hoop on the ground in front of Rover's face and then call the dog through the hoop, using the treat as bait. After Rover steps through the hoop (as the shortest way to the treat), Jody should give Rover the treat (positive reinforcement). Then he could raise the hoop just a little, reward him for walking through it again, raise the hoop, reward him … until Rover is jumping through the hoop to get the treat. The goal is achieved by reinforcing each *successive approximation* (small steps one after the other that get closer and closer to the goal). This process is shaping (Skinner, 1974). Through pairing of a sound such as a whistle or clicker with the primary reinforcer of food, animal trainers can use the sound as a secondary reinforcer and avoid having an overfed learner. Watch the video *Shaping* to see this process in action.

While animals can learn many types of behavior through the use of operant conditioning, it seems that not every animal can be taught *anything*—see the following section on biological constraints for more on this topic.

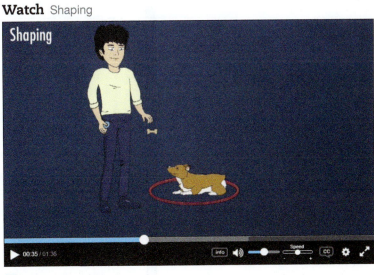

Watch Shaping

Watch the Video at MyLab Psychology

Classic Studies in Psychology
Biological Constraints on Operant Conditioning

AP 4.E Provide examples of how biological constraints create learning predispositions.

Raccoons are fairly intelligent animals and are sometimes used in learning experiments. In a typical experiment, a behaviorist would use shaping and reinforcement to teach a raccoon a trick. The goal might be to get the raccoon to pick up several coins and drop them into a metal container, for which the raccoon would be rewarded with food. The behaviorist starts by reinforcing the raccoon for picking up a single coin. Then the metal container is introduced and the raccoon is now required to drop the coin into the slot on the container in order to get reinforcement.

It is at this point that operant conditioning seems to fail. Instead of dropping the coin in the slot, the raccoon puts the coin in and out of the slot and rubs it against the inside of the container, then holds it firmly for a few seconds before finally letting it go. When the requirement is upped to two coins, the raccoon spends several minutes rubbing them against each other and dipping them into the container without actually dropping them in. In spite of the fact that this dipping and rubbing behavior is not reinforced, it gets worse and worse until conditioning becomes impossible.

Keller and Marian Breland, in their attempt to train a raccoon, found that this problem was not limited to the raccoon (Breland & Breland, 1961). They ran into a similar difficulty with a pig that was being trained to pick up a total of five large wooden coins and put them into a "piggy bank." Although at first successful, the pig became slower and slower at the task over a period of weeks, dropping the coin, rooting (pushing) it around with its nose, picking it up, dropping it again, and rooting some more. This behavior became so persistent that the pig actually did not get enough to eat for the day.

The Brelands concluded that the raccoon and the pig were reverting* to behavior that was instinctual for them. Instinctual behavior is genetically determined and not under the influence of learning. Apparently, even though the animals were at first able to learn the tricks, as the coins became more and more associated with food, the animals began to drift back into the instinctual patterns of behavior that they used with real food. Raccoons rub their food between

Raccoons commonly dunk their food in and out of water before eating. This "washing" behavior is controlled by instinct and difficult to change even using operant techniques.

---

*reverting: to go back in action, thought, speech, and so on.

their paws and dip it in and out of water. Pigs root and throw their food around before eating it. The Brelands called this tendency to revert to genetically controlled patterns **instinctive drift**.

In their 1961 paper describing these and other examples of instinctive drift, the Brelands (both trained by Skinner himself) determined that, contrary to Skinner's original ideas:

1. The animal does NOT come to the laboratory a *tabula rasa*, or "blank slate," and cannot be taught just *any* behavior.
2. Differences between species of animals matter in determining what behavior can or cannot be conditioned.
3. Not all responses are equally able to be conditioned to any stimulus.

As became quickly obvious in their studies with these animals, each animal comes into the world (and the laboratory) with certain genetically determined instinctive patterns of behavior already in place. These instincts differ from species to species, with the result that there are some responses that simply cannot be trained into an animal regardless of conditioning.

Questions for Further Discussion

1. What other kinds of limitations do animals have in learning?
2. What kinds of behavior might people do that would be resistant to conditioning?
3. How can these research findings about animal behavior be generalized to human behavior?

Watch How to Make Healthier Choices

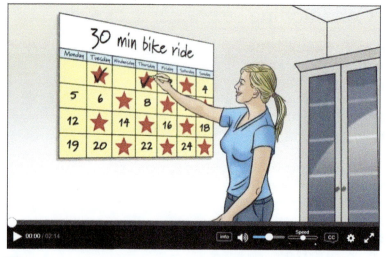

Watch the Video at MyLab Psychology

instinctive drift
tendency for an animal's behavior to revert to genetically controlled patterns.

behavior modification
the use of learning techniques to modify or change undesirable behavior and increase desirable behavior.

token economy
the use of objects called tokens to reinforce behavior in which the tokens can be accumulated and exchanged for desired items or privileges.

BEHAVIOR MODIFICATION Operant conditioning principles such as reinforcement and the process of shaping have been used for many years to change undesirable behavior and create desirable responses in animals and humans—particularly in schoolchildren. The term **behavior modification** refers to the application of operant conditioning (and sometimes classical conditioning) to bring about such changes. The video *How to Make Healthier Choices* describes a sample behavior modification plan for someone who wants to watch less television and exercise more.

As another example, if a teacher wants to use behavior modification to help a child learn to be more attentive during the teacher's lectures, the teacher may do the following:

1. Select a target behavior, such as making eye contact with the teacher.
2. Choose a reinforcer. This may be a gold star applied to the child's chart on the wall, for example.
3. Put the plan in action. Every time the child makes eye contact, the teacher gives the child a gold star. Inappropriate behavior (such as looking out the window) is not reinforced with gold stars.
4. At the end of the day, the teacher gives the child a special treat or reward for having a certain number of gold stars. This special reward is decided on ahead of time and discussed with the child.

The gold stars in this example can be considered *tokens*, secondary reinforcers that can be traded in for other kinds of reinforcers. The use of tokens to modify behavior is called a **token economy**. See Learning Objective 14.4. In the example, the child is collecting gold stars to "buy" the special treat at the end of the day. When one thinks about it, the system of money is very much a token economy. People are rewarded for working with money, which they then trade for food, shelter, and so on. Credit card companies encourage the use of their card by offering reward points that can be exchanged for desirable goods and services, and airlines offer frequent flyer miles. Many fast-food restaurants offer punch cards or stamps that are exchanged for free food when filled up. The points, miles, and punches on the cards are all forms of tokens.

Another tool that behaviorists can use to modify behavior is the process of *time-out*. A time-out is a form of mild punishment by removal in which a misbehaving animal, child, or adult is placed in a special area away from the attention of others. Essentially, the organism is being "removed" from any possibility of positive reinforcement in the form of attention. When used with children, a time-out should be limited to 1 minute for each year of age, with a maximum time-out of 10 minutes (longer than that and the child can forget why the time-out occurred).

Applied behavior analysis (ABA) is the modern term for a form of behavior modification that uses both analysis of current behavior and behavioral techniques to address a socially relevant issue. In ABA, skills are broken down to their simplest steps and then taught to the child through a system of reinforcement. Prompts (such as moving a child's face back to look at the teacher or the task) are given as needed when the child is learning a skill or refuses to cooperate. As the child begins to master a skill and receives reinforcement in the form of treats or praise, the prompts are gradually withdrawn until the child can do the skill independently. Applied behavior analysis is a growing field, with many colleges and universities offering degrees at both the undergraduate and graduate levels. A person graduating from one of these programs may act as a consultant* to schools or other institutions or may set up a private practice. Typical uses for ABA are treating children with disorders, training animals, and developing effective teaching methods for children and adults of all levels of mental abilities (Baer et al., 1968; Du et al., 2015; Klein & Kemper, 2016; Mohammadzaheri et al., 2015).

An example of how ABA can be used is found in the use of shaping to mold desirable, socially acceptable behavior in individuals with *autism spectrum disorder* (ASD). ASD is a disorder in which the person has great difficulty in communicating with others, often refusing to look at another person. People who have ASD may also fail to learn to speak at all, and they normally do not like to be touched. See Learning Objective 8.7. This specific application of ABA can be said to have begun with the work of Dr. O. Ivar Lovaas (1964) and his associates, although the basic general techniques are those first outlined by Skinner. Lovaas used small pieces of candy as reinforcers to teach social skills and language to children with ASD.

Other techniques for modifying responses have been developed so that even biological responses that are normally considered involuntary such as blood pressure, muscle tension, and hyperactivity can be brought under conscious control. For nearly 60 years, scientists have known how to use feedback from a person's biological information (such as heart rate) to create a state of relaxation (Margolin & Kubic, 1944). **Biofeedback** is the traditional term used to describe this kind of biological feedback of information, and through its use many problems can be relieved or controlled.

A relatively newer biofeedback technique called **neurofeedback** involves trying to change brain activity. See Learning Objective 2.5. Although this technique uses the latest in technology, the basic principles behind it are much older. Traditionally, this technique was based on recording the electrical activity of the brain, or EEG. To record the EEG, a person would have to be connected to a stand-alone *electroencephalograph*, a machine that amplifies and records the brain's electrical activity. Modern biofeedback and neurofeedback amplifiers are often connected to a computer that records and analyzes the physiological activity of the brain. Neurofeedback can be integrated with video game–like programs that individuals can use to learn how to produce brain waves or specific types of brain activity associated with specific cognitive or behavioral states (e.g., increased attention, staying focused, relaxed awareness). Individuals learn to make these changes through the principles of operant conditioning (Sherlin et al., 2011). Neurofeedback using the EEG continues to be investigated in specific disorders such as attention-deficit/hyperactivity disorder (ADHD) and in new areas such as

applied behavior analysis (ABA)

modern term for a form of functional analysis and behavior modification that uses a variety of behavioral techniques to mold a desired behavior or response.

biofeedback

using feedback about biological conditions to bring involuntary responses, such as blood pressure and relaxation, under voluntary control.

neurofeedback

form of biofeedback using brain-scanning devices to provide feedback about brain activity in an effort to modify behavior.

---

*consultant: someone who offers expert advice or services.

the control of chronic pain (Arns et al., 2009; Jensen et al., 2013), treatment of antisocial personality disorder (Ewbank et al., 2018), and the treatment of epilepsy (Koberda, 2015; Micoulaud-Franchi et al., 2014; Strehl et al., 2014). Other recent neurofeedback studies have incorporated MRI or fMRI to examine the effects of EEG-based neurofeedback on the brain (Ghaziri et al., 2013; Ros et al., 2013). And in some studies, fMRI is being used as a neurofeedback method in and of itself (Ruiz et al., 2013; Scharnowski et al., 2012; Stoeckel et al., 2014; Sulzer et al., 2013).

Concept Map L.O. 5.4, 5.5, 5.6, 5.7, 5.8, 5.9

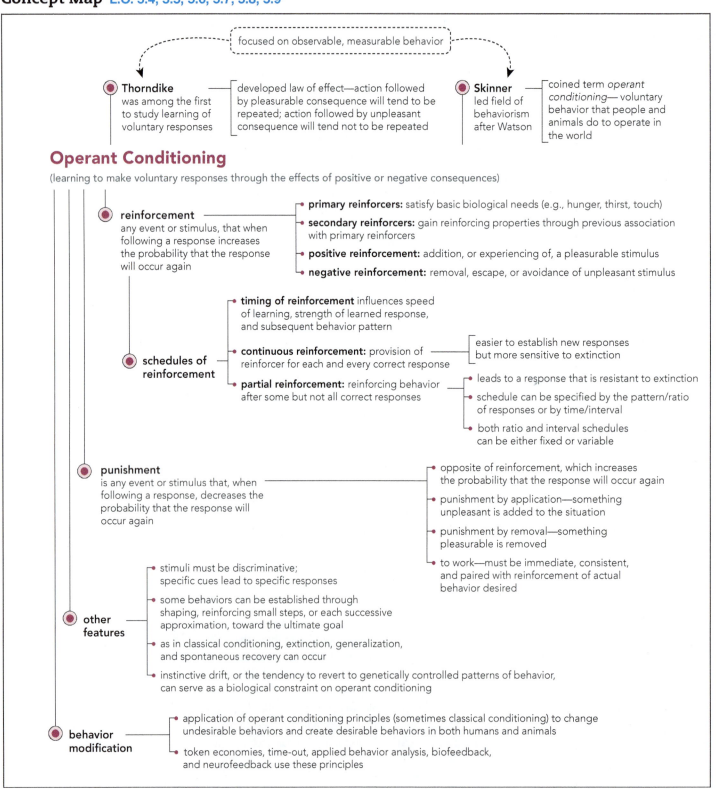

Practice Quiz   How much do you remember?

Pick the best answer.

1. To a dog, _____ is an example of a primary reinforcer, whereas _____ is an example of a secondary reinforcer.
   a. a paycheck, money
   b. dog food, a Frisbee
   c. a bath, a squirrel
   d. dog food, a dog treat
   e. a gold star, candy

2. Cody cannot sleep because he is terribly worried about his research paper. So Cody decides to get out of bed and continue working on the paper. Although he stays up till nearly 3 a.m., he is relieved that it is done and easily falls off to sleep. In the future, Cody will be more likely to finish his work before going to bed so that he can avoid the worry and sleeplessness. Such behavior is an example of _____.
   a. classical conditioning
   b. extinction
   c. positive reinforcement
   d. punishment
   e. negative reinforcement

3. Ian owned a small repair shop. Each day, he would check the mail to see if any of his customers mailed in a payment for the work he had done for them. Some days, he would receive a check or two. At other times, he would have to wait days before getting another payment. What schedule of reinforcement is evident here?
   a. fixed ratio
   b. fixed interval
   c. variable interval
   d. continuous
   e. variable ratio

4. Little Antonio's mother was upset to find that Antonio had not picked up his building blocks after repeated requests to do so. The next morning, Antonio found all his blocks had been picked up and put into a bag on top of the refrigerator. Antonio's mother told him that he couldn't play with his blocks for the next 2 days. Which type of discipline did she use?
   a. positive reinforcement
   b. time out
   c. negative reinforcement
   d. punishment by application
   e. punishment by removal

5. Erin signed up for a new credit card that offers reward miles for every purchase. Erin plans to make as many purchases as she can so that she can accumulate enough miles to go on a trip over spring break. Such an approach is an example of _____.
   a. shaping
   b. a token economy
   c. successive approximations
   d. a schedule of reinforcement
   e. a form of negative reinforcement

6. Which of the following is the best example of applied behavior analysis?
   a. Daniela has children watch her repeatedly so as to understand how a task is to be done. Once they have finished the observation, then they are asked to imitate the behavior.
   b. Gavin says "no" and sprays water from a spray bottle into the face of his pet llama when it spits at him.
   c. Esther works with children by asking them what they want to accomplish and then helping them attain that goal through different forms of classical conditioning.
   d. Sofia observes a child to see what purpose a disruptive classroom behavior serves and identifies a new replacement behavior. She then implements a training program for the new behavior, reinforcing often at the simplest levels and gradually removing reinforcers as the child demonstrates the behavior independently.
   e. Zoe wants children to learn a new behavior and uses punishment as the basis for the behavior change.

APA Goal 2: Scientific Inquiry and Critical Thinking

Spare the Rod, Spoil the Child?

Addresses APA Learning Objectives 2.1: Use scientific reasoning to interpret psychological phenomena; 2.2: Demonstrate psychology information literacy; and 2.5: Incorporate sociocultural factors in scientific inquiry.

To spank or not to spank has been a controversial issue for many years now. In the past, across many cultures, spanking a child for misbehavior was an accepted form of discipline, but with the rise in both awareness and incidence of child abuse, critical thinking demands asking the next question: Does it work, or does it do more harm than good?

Finland was the second country in the world (after Sweden) to enact a law that banned any kind of physical punishment of children, including by their own parents. This law was put into effect in 1983. The results of a survey conducted nearly 30 years later on a sample of 4,609 males and females between the ages of 15 and 80 years of age showed a significant decrease in reports of physical discipline (e.g., being beaten with an object or slapped) among those participants who were born after the law went into effect. There were also far fewer murdered children. Those participants who had been exposed to more physical punishment than average were found to be more likely to abuse alcohol, suffer from mental health issues such as depression, and engage in bullying and were also more likely to be divorced or to have attempted suicide (Khademi et al., 2018; Österman et al., 2014). In other countries where a ban against corporal punishment has been enacted, there has also been a decrease in child abuse (Zolotor & Puzia, 2010). In this case it definitely seems that physical punishment such as spanking actually does more harm.

In the last 45 years in the United States, spanking has decreased as a means of disciplining children but is still used by the parents of about 80 percent of preschool-aged children. While in addition to Finland, Sweden, and most recently France, 53 other countries have officially banned corporal punishment in about the same time period (see **Figure 5.7**), spanking is still common across many cultures (Rettner, 2017; Runyan et al., 2010; Zolotor & Puzia, 2010; Zolotor et al., 2011). Regardless of country of origin, research has found that spanking and other forms of harsh physical discipline are more common in places where income is low and parents are less educated (Runyan et al., 2010).

Figure 5.7 APA Goal 2: Spare the Rod and Spoil the Child? Countries That Have Banned Corporal Punishment

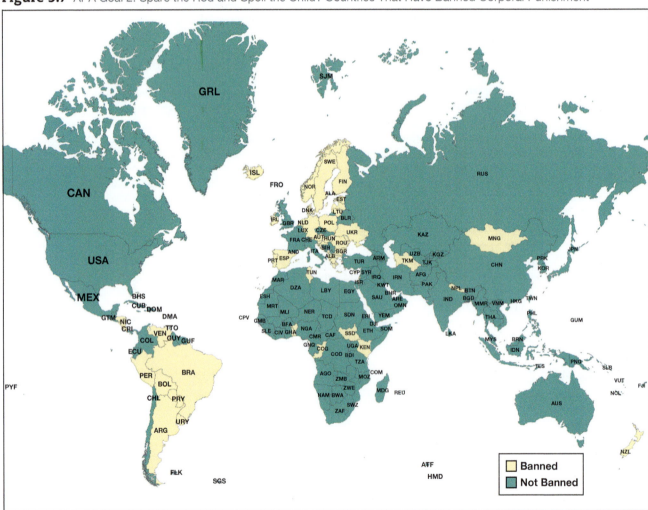

Source: The Global Initiative to End All Corporal Punishment of Children, 2018

5.10–5.12 Cognitive Learning Theory

In the early days of behaviorism, the focus of Watson, Skinner, and many of their followers was on observable, measurable behavior. Anything that might be occurring inside a person's or animal's head during learning was considered to be of no interest to the behaviorist because it could not be seen or directly measured. Other psychologists, however, were still interested in the mind's influence over behavior. Gestalt psychologists, for instance, were studying the way the human mind tried to force a pattern onto stimuli in the world around the person. See Learning Objective 1.2. This continued interest in the mind was followed, in the 1950s and 1960s, by the comparison of the human mind to the workings of those fascinating "thinking machines," computers. Soon after, interest in *cognition*, the mental events that take place inside a person's mind while behaving, began to dominate experimental psychology. Many behavioral psychologists could no longer ignore the thoughts, feelings, and expectations that clearly existed in the mind and that seemed to influence observable behavior and eventually began to develop a cognitive learning theory to supplement the more traditional theories of learning (Kendler, 1985). Three important figures often cited as key theorists in the early days of the development of cognitive learning theory were the Gestalt psychologists Edward Tolman and Wolfgang Köhler and modern psychologist Martin Seligman.

5.10 Tolman's Maze-Running Rats: Latent Learning

5.10 Explain the concept of latent learning.

AP 4.C Describe the essential characteristics of insight learning, latent learning, and social learning.

AP 4.A Identify contributions of key researchers in the psychology of learning.

One of Gestalt psychologist Edward Tolman's best-known experiments in learning involved teaching three groups of rats the same maze, one at a time (Tolman & Honzik, 1930). In the first group, each rat was placed in the maze and reinforced with food for making its way out the other side. The rat was then placed back in the maze, reinforced upon completing the maze again, and so on until the rat could successfully solve the maze with no errors (see **Figure 5.8**).

The second group of rats was treated exactly like the first, except that they never received any reinforcement upon exiting the maze. They were simply put back in again and again, until the 10th day of the experiment. On that day, the rats in the second group began to receive reinforcement for getting out of the maze. The third group of rats, serving as a control group, was also not reinforced and was not given reinforcement for the entire duration of the experiment.

Figure 5.8 A Typical Maze

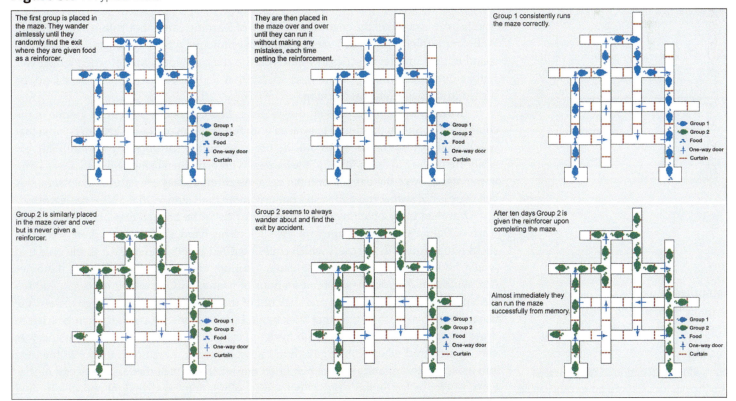

This is an example of a maze such as the one used in Tolman's experiments in latent learning. A rat is placed in the start box. The trial is over when the rat gets to the end box.

Figure 5.9 Learning Curves for Three Groups of Rats

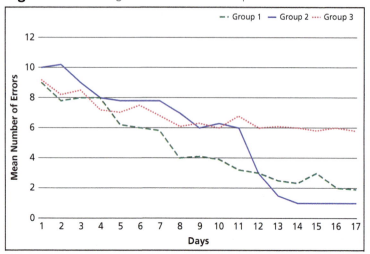

In the results of the classic study of latent learning, Group 1 was rewarded on each day, while Group 2 was rewarded for the first time on Day 10. Group 3 was never rewarded. Note the immediate change in the behavior of Group 2 on Day 12.

Source: Based on Tolman, E. C., & Honzik, C. H. (1930). Introduction and removal of reward and maze learning in rats. University of California Publications in Psychology, 4, 257–275.

A strict Skinnerian behaviorist would predict that only the first group of rats would learn the maze successfully because learning depends on reinforcing consequences. At first, this seemed to be the case. The first group of rats did indeed solve the maze after a certain number of trials, whereas the second and third groups seemed to wander aimlessly around the maze until accidentally finding their way out.

On the 10th day, however, something happened that would be difficult to explain using only Skinner's basic principles. The second group of rats, after receiving the reinforcement for the first time, *should* have then taken as long as the first group to solve the maze. Instead, they began to solve the maze almost immediately (see **Figure 5.9**).

Tolman concluded that the rats in the second group, while wandering around in the first 9 days of the experiment, had learned where all the blind alleys, wrong turns, and correct paths were and stored this knowledge away as a kind of "mental map," or *cognitive map* of the physical layout of the maze. The rats in the second group had learned and stored that learning away mentally but had not *demonstrated* this learning because there was no reason to do so. The cognitive map had remained hidden, or latent, until the rats had a reason to demonstrate their knowledge by getting to the food. Tolman called this **latent learning**. The idea that learning could happen without reinforcement and then later affect behavior was not something traditional operant conditioning could explain.

AP 4.C Describe the essential characteristics of insight learning, latent learning, and social learning.

AP 5.C Identify the contributions of key researchers in cognitive psychology.

5.11 Köhler's Smart Chimp: Insight Learning

5.11 Explain how Köhler's studies demonstrated that animals can learn by insight.

Another exploration of the cognitive elements of learning came about almost by accident. Wolfgang Köhler (1887–1967) was a Gestalt psychologist who became marooned* on an island in the Canaries (a series of islands off the coast of North Africa) when World War I broke out. Stuck at the primate research lab that had first drawn him to the island, he turned to studies of animal learning.

In one of his more famous studies (Köhler, 1925), he set up a problem for one of the chimpanzees. Sultan the chimp was faced with the problem of how to get to a banana that was placed just out of his reach outside his cage. Sultan solved this problem relatively easily, first trying to reach through the bars with his arm, then using a stick that was lying in the cage to rake the banana into the cage. As chimpanzees are natural tool users, this behavior is not surprising and is still nothing more than simple trial-and-error learning.

But then the problem was made more difficult. The banana was placed just out of reach of Sultan's extended arm with the stick in his hand. At this point there were two sticks lying around in the cage, which could be fitted together to make a single pole that would be long enough to reach the banana. Sultan tried first one stick, then the other (simple trial and error). After about an hour of trying, Sultan seemed to have a sudden flash of inspiration. He pushed one stick out of the cage as far as it would go toward the banana and then pushed the other stick behind the first one. Of course, when he tried to draw the sticks back, only the one in his hand came. He jumped up and down and was very excited, and when Köhler gave him the second stick, he sat on the floor of the cage and looked at them carefully. He then fitted one stick into the other and retrieved his banana. Köhler called Sultan's rapid "perception of relationships" **insight** and determined that insight could not be gained through trial-and-error learning alone (Köhler, 1925).

*marooned: in this sense, being placed on an island from which escape is impossible.

latent learning
learning that remains hidden until its application becomes useful.

insight
the sudden perception of relationships among various parts of a problem, allowing the solution to the problem to come quickly.

Although Thorndike and other early learning theorists believed that animals could not demonstrate insight, Köhler's work seems to demonstrate that insight requires a sudden "coming together" of all the elements of a problem in a kind of "aha" moment that is not predicted by traditional animal learning studies. See Learning Objective 7.3. Other research has also found support for the concept of animal insight (Heinrich, 2000; Heyes, 1998; Zentall, 2000), but there is still controversy over how to interpret the results of those studies (Wynne, 1999).

Another of Köhler's chimpanzees, Grande, has just solved the problem of how to get to the banana by stacking boxes. Does this meet the criteria for insight, or was it simple trial-and-error learning?

5.12 Seligman's Depressed Dogs: Learned Helplessness

5.12 Summarize Seligman's studies on learned helplessness.

Martin Seligman is now famous for founding the field of *positive psychology*, a way of looking at the entire concept of mental health and therapy that focuses on the adaptive, creative, and psychologically more fulfilling aspects of human experience rather than on mental disorders. But in the mid- to late-1960s, learning theorist Seligman (1975) and his colleagues were doing classical conditioning experiments on dogs. They accidentally discovered an unexpected phenomenon, which Seligman called **learned helplessness**, the tendency to fail to act to escape from a situation because of a history of repeated failures. Their original intention was to study escape and avoidance learning. Seligman and colleagues presented a tone followed by a harmless but painful electric shock to one group of dogs (Overmier & Seligman, 1967; Seligman & Maier, 1967). The dogs in this group were harnessed so that they could not escape the shock. The researchers assumed that the dogs would learn to fear the sound of the tone and later try to escape from the tone before being shocked.

AP 4.D Apply learning principles to explain emotional learning, taste aversion, superstitious behavior, and learned helplessness.

These dogs, along with another group of dogs that had not been conditioned to fear the tone, were placed in a special box containing a low fence that divided the box into two compartments. The dogs, which were now unharnessed, could easily see over the fence and jump over if they wished—which is precisely what the dogs that had not been conditioned did as soon as the shock occurred (see **Figure 5.10**). Imagine the researchers' surprise when, instead of jumping over the fence when the tone sounded, the previously conditioned dogs just sat there. In fact, these dogs showed distress but didn't try to jump over the fence *even when the shock itself began.*

learned helplessness

the tendency to fail to act to escape from a situation because of a history of repeated failures in the past.

Why would the conditioned dogs refuse to move when shocked? The dogs that had been harnessed while being conditioned had apparently learned in the original tone/shock situation that there was nothing they could do to escape the shock. So when placed in a situation in which escape was possible, the dogs still did nothing because they had learned to be "helpless." They believed they could not escape, so they did not try.

Figure 5.10 Seligman's Apparatus

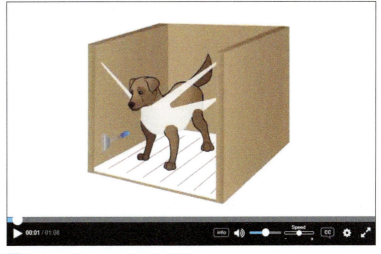

Watch the Video at MyLab Psychology

Seligman's colleague and co-researcher in those early studies, Steven F. Maier, has revisited the phenomenon of learned helplessness from a neuroscientific approach, and this work has provided some new insights. Maier and others have investigated the brain mechanisms underlying this phenomenon, focusing on an area of the brain stem that releases serotonin and can play a role in activating the amygdala (which plays an important role in fear and anxiety) but also participates in decreasing activity in brain areas responsible for the "fight-or-flight" response.

In Seligman's studies of learned helplessness, dogs were placed in a two-sided box. Dogs that had no prior experience with being unable to escape a shock would quickly jump over the hurdle in the center of the box to land on the "safe" side. Dogs that had previously learned that escape was impossible would stay on the side of the box in which the shock occurred, not even trying to go over the hurdle.

This combination of increased fear/anxiety with non-escape or freezing is the very behavior associated with learned helplessness. This part of the brain stem (the dorsal raphe nucleus) is a much older part of the brain and not able to determine what type of stressors are controllable. Their research suggests that a higher-level area, a part of the frontal lobe called the *ventromedial prefrontal cortex* (vmPFC), is able to help determine what is controllable. In turn, the vmPFC inhibits the brain stem area and calms the amygdala's response, allowing an animal to effectively respond to a stressor and exhibit control (Amat et al., 2005; Arulpragasam et al., 2018; Maier et al., 2006; Maier & Watkins, 2005). In other words, it is possible that the dogs in the early studies, rather than learning to be helpless, were *not* learning how to relax and take control of the situation. Maier and colleagues suggest that both training and input from the vmPFC are necessary for animals to learn how to take control (Maier et al., 2006).

> 💬 I know some people who seem to act just like those dogs—they live in a horrible situation but won't leave. Is this the same thing?

Seligman extended the concept of learned helplessness to explain some behaviors characteristic of *depression*. Depressed people seem to lack normal emotions and become somewhat apathetic, often staying in unpleasant work environments or bad marriages or relationships rather than trying to escape or better their situation. Seligman proposed that this depressive behavior is a form of learned helplessness. Depressed people may have learned in the past that they seem to have no control over what happens to them (Alloy & Clements, 1998). A sense of powerlessness and hopelessness is common to depressed people, and certainly this would seem to apply to Seligman's dogs as well. Maier's work also has implications here, especially the focus on the components necessary for learning how to relax and demonstrate control: input from the vmPFC and training (repeated exposures to stressors). This combination provides a mechanism not only for understanding resilience* but also for possibly helping people foster resilience and avoid anxiety or mood disorders such as posttraumatic stress disorder (PTSD) or depression (Maier et al., 2006). See Learning Objectives 13.4 and 13.8. Maier and colleagues are continuing to study the brain foundations of learned helplessness and examining how factors related to control and controllability impact not only immediate events but future stressful events as well (Amat et al., 2010; Rozeske et al., 2011; Varela et al., 2012). Other research suggests the importance of dopamine signals released from the nucleus accumbens—low levels of dopamine are implicated in both a reduced ability to avoid threatening situations and depression (Wenzel et al., 2018).

Think about how learned helplessness might apply to other situations. Perceived control or learned helplessness can play an important role in coping with chronic or acute health conditions, either for the person with the disorder or for the family member making medical decisions for a loved one (Camacho et al., 2013; Sullivan et al., 2012). What about college? There are many students who feel that they are bad at math because they have had problems with it in the past. Is it possible that this belief could make them not try as hard or study as much as they should? Is this kind of thinking also an example of learned helplessness, or is it possible that these students have simply not had enough experiences of success or control?

Cognitive learning is also an important part of a fairly well-known form of learning, often simplified as "monkey see, monkey do." In the next section, we'll take a look at learning through watching the actions of others.

---

*resilience: the ability to recover quickly from change and/or stress.

Concept Map L.O. 5.10, 5.11, 5.12

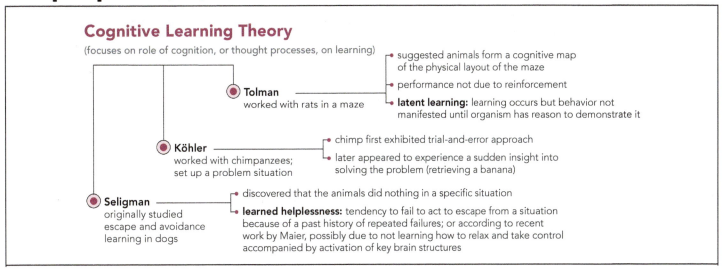

Practice Quiz How much do you remember?

Pick the best answer.

1. In Tolman's maze study, the fact that the group of rats receiving reinforcement only after Day 10 of the study solved the maze far more quickly than did the rats who had been reinforced from the first day can be interpreted to mean that these particular rats _____.
   a. were much smarter than the other rats
   b. had already learned the maze in the first 9 days
   c. were not attending to the task for the first 9 days
   d. had the opportunity to cheat by watching the other rats
   e. were very hungry and, therefore, learned much more quickly

2. Laura's parents have decided to take a 3-week trip to Europe. Consequently, Laura's mother will not be able to make her famous pies for the upcoming bake sale. When her mother encourages Laura to bake the pies herself, Laura panics at first, but then she finds that she knows how to put the recipe together. Her ability to prepare the recipe is an example of _____.
   a. insight learning.
   b. learned helplessness.
   c. learning by proxy
   d. latent learning.
   e. discovery learning.

3. Which theory is commonly referred to as the "aha!" phenomenon?
   a. Seligman's learned helplessness theory
   b. Tolman's latent learning theory
   c. Köhler's insight theory
   d. Thorndike's law of effect
   e. Bandura's observational learning

4. Research by Steven Maier suggests that learned helplessness may be due to a higher-level region of the brain known as the _____, which helps subjects determine what is controllable.
   a. hippocampus
   b. hypothalamus
   c. amygdala
   d. ventromedial prefrontal cortex (vmPFC)
   e. dorsal raphe nucleus

5.13–5.14 Observational Learning

Observational learning is the learning of new behavior through watching the actions of a *model* (someone else who is doing that behavior). Sometimes that behavior is desirable, and sometimes it is not, as the next section describes.

5.13 Bandura and the Bobo Doll

5.13 Describe the process of observational learning.

Albert Bandura's classic study in observational learning involved having a preschool child in a room in which the experimenter and a model interacted with toys in front of the child (Bandura et al., 1961). In one condition, the model interacted with the toys in a nonaggressive manner, completely ignoring the presence of a "Bobo" doll (a punch-bag doll in the shape of a clown). In another condition, the model became very aggressive with the doll, kicking it and yelling at it, throwing it in the air and hitting it with a hammer.

AP 4.C Describe the essential characteristics of insight learning, latent learning, and social learning.

AP 4.G Distinguish general differences between principles of classical conditioning, operant conditioning, and observational learning.

AP 4.A Identify contributions of key researchers in the psychology of learning.

observational learning
learning new behavior by watching a model perform that behavior.

Figure 5.11 Bandura's Bobo Doll Experiment

👁 **Watch** the **Video** at **MyLab Psychology**

In Albert Bandura's famous Bobo doll experiment, the doll was used to demonstrate the impact of observing an adult model performing aggressive behavior on the later aggressive behavior of children.

learning/performance distinction
referring to the observation that learning can take place without actual performance of the learned behavior.

When each child was left alone in the room and had the opportunity to play with the toys, a camera filming through a one-way mirror caught the children who were exposed to the aggressive model beating up on the Bobo doll, in exact imitation of the model (see **Figure 5.11**). The children who saw the model ignore the doll did not act aggressively toward the toy. Obviously, the aggressive children had learned their aggressive actions from merely watching the model—with no reinforcement necessary. The fact that learning can take place without actual performance (a kind of latent learning) is called **learning/performance distinction**.

💬 Ah, but would that child have imitated the model if the model had been punished? Wouldn't the consequences of the model's behavior make a difference?

In later studies, Bandura showed a film of a model beating up the Bobo doll. In one condition, the children saw the model rewarded afterward. In another, the model was punished. When placed in the room with toys, the children in the first group beat up the doll, but the children in the second group did not. But when Bandura told the children in the second group that he would give them a reward if they could show him what the model in the film did, each child duplicated the model's actions. Both groups had learned from watching the model, but only the children watching the successful (rewarded) model imitated the aggression with no prompting (Bandura, 1965). Apparently, consequences do matter in motivating a child (or an adult) to imitate a particular model. The tendency for some movies and television programs to make "heroes" out of violent, aggressive "bad guys" is particularly disturbing in light of these findings. In fact, Bandura began this research to investigate possible links between children's exposure to violence on television and aggressive behavior toward others.

In one nationwide study of youth in the United States, it was found that young people ages 8 to 18 spend, on average, almost 7.5 hours per day 7 days a week involved in media consumption (television, computers, video games, music, cell phones, print, and movies), while a later national survey found over 9 hours of use in the same age group (Common Sense Media, Inc., 2015). Furthermore, given the prevalence of media multitasking (using more than one media device at a time), they are packing in approximately 10 hours and 45 minutes of media during those 7.5 hours (Rideout et al., 2010)! While not all media consumption is of violent media, it is quite easy to imagine that some of that media is of a violent nature.

Hundreds of studies stretching over nearly three decades and involving hundreds of thousands of participants strongly indicate that a link exists between viewing violent media and an increased level of aggression in children and young adults (Allen et al., 2018; Anderson et al., 2015; Bushman & Huesmann, 2001; Groves et al., in press; Huesmann & Eron, 1986). See Learning Objective 1.8. While some of these studies involved correlations, and correlations do not prove that viewing violence on various media is the *cause* of increased violence, one cannot help but be concerned, especially given the continuing rise of media consumption in young people, coupled with the multiple ways young people interact with media. Although still a topic of debate for some (Boxer et al., 2015; Ferguson, 2015; Gentile, 2015; Rothstein & Bushman, 2015; Zendle et al., 2018), there appears to be a strong body of evidence that exposure to media violence does have immediate and long-term effects, increasing the likelihood of aggressive verbal and physical behavior and aggressive thoughts and emotions—and the effects appear to impact children, adolescents, and adults (Anderson et al., 2003, 2015).

Prosocial behavior, which is behavior aimed at helping others, has also been shown to be influenced by media consumption. Studies have shown that when children watch media that models helping behavior, aggressive behavior decreases and prosocial behavior increases (Anderson et al., 2015; Prot et al., 2014). See Learning Objectives 11.15, 11.16.

THINKING CRITICALLY 5.3

Do you think that watching violence on television increases violence and aggression in viewers? Why or why not?

5.14 The Four Elements of Observational Learning

5.14 List the four elements of observational learning.

Bandura (1986) concluded, from his studies and others, that observational learning required the presence of four elements.

ATTENTION To learn anything through observation, the learner must first pay *attention* to the model. For example, a person at a fancy dinner party who wants to know which utensil to use has to watch the person who seems to know what is correct. Certain characteristics of models can make attention more likely. For example, people pay more attention to those they perceive as similar to them and to those they perceive as attractive.

MEMORY The learner must also be able to retain the *memory* of what was done, such as remembering the steps in preparing a dish that was first seen on a cooking show or the order of steps an instructor took in solving an equation in the classroom.

IMITATION The learner must be capable of reproducing, or *imitating*, the actions of the model. A 2-year-old might be able to watch someone tie shoelaces and might even remember most of the steps, but the 2-year-old's chubby little fingers will not have the dexterity* necessary for actually tying the laces. A person with extremely weak ankles might be able to watch and remember how some ballet move was accomplished but will not be able to reproduce it. The mirror neurons discussed in Chapter Two may be willing, but the flesh is weak. See Learning Objective 2.6.

DESIRE Finally, the learner must have the desire or *motivation* to perform the action. That person at the fancy dinner, for example, might not care which fork or which knife is the "proper" one to use. Also, if a person expects a reward because one has been given in the past or has been promised a future reward (like the children in the second group of Bandura's study) or has witnessed a model getting a reward (like the children in the first group), that person will be much more likely to imitate the observed behavior. Successful models are powerful figures for imitation, but rarely would we be motivated to imitate someone who fails or is punished.

(An easy way to remember the four elements of modeling is to remember the letters AMID, which stand for the first letters of each of the four elements. This is a good example of using a strategy to improve memory. See Learning Objective PIA.6.)

Concept Map L.O. 5.13, 5.14

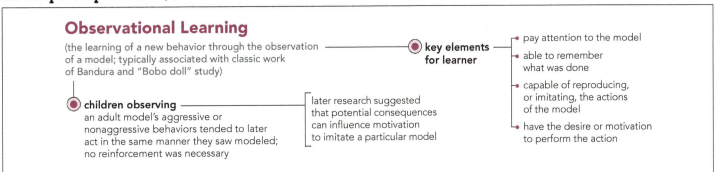

---

*dexterity: skill and ease in using the hands.

Practice Quiz — How much do you remember?

Pick the best answer.

1. Bandura's studies found that learning can take place without actual performance. What is this referred to as?
   a. cognitive learning
   b. memorizing
   c. insight-based learning
   d. AMID
   e. learning/performance distinction

2. Which of the following statements is false?
   a. Prosocial behavior can be positively influenced by the viewing/playing of prosocial media.
   b. When media multitasking, young people spend the equivalent of 10 hours and 45 minutes for every 7.5 hours they are viewing various forms of media.
   c. There is a strong link between viewing violent media and an increase in aggressive behavior among young people.
   d. Adults are not negatively affected by viewing or playing violent media.
   e. Young people spend more than 7 hours a day viewing various forms of media.

3. What is the correct sequence of the four elements of observational learning?
   a. desire, attention, memory, imitation
   b. observe, memorize, desire, imitation, attention
   c. attention, imitation, desire, memory
   d. attention, memory, imitation, desire
   e. memory, attention, desire, imitation

4. Angelina wanted to help her father prepare breakfast. She had watched him crack eggs into a bowl many times, paying careful attention to how he did it. But when she went to crack her own eggs, they smashed into many pieces. Which of the following elements of observational learning was Angelina's problem?
   a. attention
   b. dedication
   c. imitation
   d. memory
   e. desire

Applying Psychology to Everyday Life
Conditioning in the Real World

5.15 Describe an example of conditioning in the real world.

How often do you check your cell phone for texts or other messages? It's almost addictive, isn't it? How do you feel when you see that you have a message? What do you think is happening in the pleasure center of your brain? Think back to the section on conditioned stimuli: Is there any chance you have been conditioned by your cell phone? Watch the following video to see other students describe how their cell phones have conditioned various aspects of their behavior.

Applying Psychology to Everyday Life Conditioning in the Real World

▶ Watch the Video at MyLab Psychology

After watching the video, answer the following questions:

1. Some students reported specific behaviors associated with their cell phones that can be tied to various principles of conditioning. What are two of the principles or examples that were highlighted?

2. In this video, students shared examples of how their behavior has been conditioned by their cell phone use. Identify another area of life in which your behavior has been conditioned by some device or circumstance, and identify what in particular has shaped your behavior.

Chapter Summary

Definition of Learning

5.1 Define the term *learning*.

- Learning is any relatively permanent change in behavior brought about by experience or practice and is different from maturation, which is genetically controlled.

It Makes Your Mouth Water: Classical Conditioning

5.2 Identify the key elements of classical conditioning as demonstrated in Pavlov's classic experiment.

- Pavlov accidentally discovered the phenomenon in which one stimulus can, through pairing with another stimulus, come to produce a similar response. He called this "classical conditioning."
- The unconditioned stimulus (UCS) is the stimulus that is naturally occurring and produces the innate, or involuntary, unconditioned response (UCR). Both are called "unconditioned" because they are not learned.
- The conditioned stimulus (CS) begins as a neutral stimulus, but when paired with the unconditioned stimulus, it eventually begins to elicit an involuntary and automatic behavior on its own. The response to the conditioned stimulus is called the "conditioned response" (CR), and both stimulus and response are learned.
- Pavlov paired a sound with the presentation of food to dogs and discovered several principles for classical conditioning: The neutral stimulus (NS) and UCS must be paired several times, and the CS must precede the UCS by only a few seconds.
- Other important aspects of classical conditioning include stimulus generalization, stimulus discrimination, extinction, spontaneous recovery, and higher-order conditioning.

5.3 Apply classical conditioning to examples of phobias, taste aversions, and drug dependency.

- Watson was able to demonstrate that an emotional disorder called a phobia could be learned through classical conditioning by exposing a baby to a white rat and a loud noise, producing conditioned fear of the rat in the baby.
- Conditioned taste aversions occur when an organism becomes nauseated some time after eating a certain food, which then becomes aversive to the organism.
- Some kinds of conditioned responses are more easily learned than others because of biological preparedness.
- Pavlov believed that the NS became a substitute for the UCS through association in time.
- The cognitive perspective asserts that the CS has to provide some kind of information or expectancy about the coming of the UCS in order for conditioning to occur.

What's in It for Me? Operant Conditioning

5.4 Identify the contributions of Thorndike and Skinner to the concept of operant conditioning.

- Thorndike developed the law of effect: A response followed by a pleasurable consequence will be repeated, but a response followed by an unpleasant consequence will not be repeated.
- B. F. Skinner named the learning of voluntary responses "operant conditioning" because voluntary responses are what we use to operate in the world around us.

5.5 Differentiate between primary and secondary reinforcers and positive and negative reinforcement.

- Skinner developed the concept of reinforcement, the process of strengthening a response by following it with a pleasurable, rewarding consequence.
- A primary reinforcer is something such as food or water that satisfies a basic, natural drive, whereas a secondary reinforcer is something that becomes reinforcing only after being paired with a primary reinforcer.
- The neural bases of both classical and operant conditioning include the anterior cingulate cortex and the nucleus accumbens, areas involved in the release of dopamine.
- In positive reinforcement, a response is followed by the presentation of a pleasurable stimulus, whereas in negative reinforcement, a response is followed by the removal or avoidance of an unpleasant stimulus.
- Shaping is the reinforcement of successive approximations to some final goal, allowing behavior to be molded from simple behavior already present in the organism.
- Extinction, generalization and discrimination, and spontaneous recovery also occur in operant conditioning.

5.6 Identify the four schedules of reinforcement.

- Continuous reinforcement occurs when each and every correct response is followed by a reinforcer.
- Partial reinforcement, in which only some correct responses are followed by reinforcement, is much more resistant to extinction. This is called the partial reinforcement effect.
- In a fixed interval schedule of reinforcement, at least one correct response must be made within a set interval of time to obtain reinforcement.
- In a variable interval schedule of reinforcement, reinforcement follows the first correct response made after an interval of time that changes for each reinforcement opportunity.
- In a fixed ratio schedule of reinforcement, a certain number of responses is required before reinforcement is given.
- In a variable ratio schedule of reinforcement, a varying number of responses is required to obtain reinforcement.

5.7 Identify the effect that punishment has on behavior.

- Punishment is any event or stimulus that, when following a response, makes that response less likely to happen again.
- In punishment by application, a response is followed by the application or experiencing of an unpleasant stimulus, such as a spanking.
- In punishment by removal, a response is followed by the removal of some pleasurable stimulus, such as taking away a child's toy for misbehavior.
- A person who uses aggressive punishment, such as spanking, can act as a model for aggressive behavior. This will increase aggressive behavior in the one being punished, which is an undesirable response.

- Punishment of both kinds normally has only a temporary effect on behavior.
- Punishment can be made more effective by making it immediate and consistent and by pairing punishment of the undesirable behavior with reinforcement of the desirable one.

5.8 Explain the concepts of discriminant stimuli, extinction, generalization, and spontaneous recovery as they relate to operant conditioning.

- Discriminative stimuli are cues, such as a flashing light on a police car or a sign on a door that says "Open," which provide information about what response to make in order to obtain reinforcement.
- Shaping, extinction, generalization and discrimination, and spontaneous recovery are other concepts in operant conditioning.
- Instinctive drift is the tendency for an animal that is being trained by operant conditioning to revert to instinctive patterns of behavior rather than maintaining the trained behavior.

5.9 Describe how operant conditioning is used to change animal and human behavior.

- Operant conditioning can be used in many settings on both animals and people to change, or modify, behavior. This use is termed *behavior modification* and includes the use of reinforcement and shaping to alter behavior.
- Token economies are a type of behavior modification in which secondary reinforcers, or tokens, are used.
- Applied behavior analysis (ABA) is the modern version of behavior modification and makes use of functional analysis and behavioral techniques to change human behavior.
- Neurofeedback is a modified version of biofeedback in which a person learns to modify the activity of his or her brain.

Cognitive Learning Theory

5.10 Explain the concept of latent learning.

- Cognitive learning theory states that learning requires cognition, or the influence of an organism's thought processes.
- Tolman found that rats that were allowed to wander in a maze but were not reinforced still showed evidence of having learned the maze once reinforcement became possible. He termed this hidden learning *latent learning*, a form of cognitive learning.

5.11 Explain how Köhler's studies demonstrated that animals can learn by insight.

- Köhler found evidence of insight, the sudden perception of the relationships among elements of a problem, in chimpanzees.

5.12 Summarize Seligman's studies on learned helplessness.

- Seligman found that dogs that had been placed in an inescapable situation failed to try to escape when it became possible to do so, remaining in the painful situation as if helpless to leave. Seligman called this phenomenon "learned helplessness" and found parallels between learned helplessness and depression.

Observational Learning

5.13 Describe the process of observational learning.

- Observational learning is acquired by watching others perform, or model, certain actions.
- Bandura's famous Bobo doll experiment demonstrated that young children will imitate the aggressive actions of a model even when there is no reinforcement for doing so.

5.14 List the four elements of observational learning.

- Bandura determined that four elements needed to be present for observational learning to occur: attention, memory, imitation, and desire.

Applying Psychology to Everyday Life: Conditioning in the Real World

5.15 Describe an example of conditioning in the real world.

- The chime of an incoming message can act as a conditioned stimulus for a pleasurable response.

Test Yourself: Preparing for the AP Exam

PART I: MULTIPLE-CHOICE QUESTIONS

Directions for Part I: Read each of the questions or incomplete sentences below. Then choose the response that best answers the question or completes the sentence.

1. Mary almost got hit by a car at a street corner because she was too busy texting on her phone. From that day on, Mary looks before she reaches the street corner. Her change in behavior is a result of _____.
   - **a.** motivation
   - **b.** only perception
   - **c.** memory
   - **d.** learning
   - **e.** both sensation and perception

2. At home, you rattle the chain on your dog's leash every time you prepare to take him for a walk. After several episodes like this, you find that your dog comes running to the front door even when you pick up the leash to put it back in the closet. In this example, what is the conditioned stimulus?
   - **a.** the front door
   - **b.** opening the closet door
   - **c.** going for a walk
   - **d.** the sound of the leash
   - **e.** the dog runs to the door

3. During the cold winter, you have stopped taking your dog for walks. What's more, your dog has gotten used to the fact that when you accidentally rattle his leash, he isn't going for a walk, and subsequently he doesn't come running to the front door. What has occurred?
   - **a.** stimulus generalization
   - **b.** extinction
   - **c.** punishment
   - **d.** stimulus discrimination
   - **e.** spontaneous recovery

4. Brooke had tartar sauce with her fish one night. The next morning she was nauseated and sick for much of the day. The next time she was offered the chance to go out for fish, she felt queasy and declined. Her queasiness at the thought of fish with tartar sauce was probably due to _____.
   - **a.** stimulus substitution
   - **b.** extinction
   - **c.** higher-order conditioning
   - **d.** a conditioned taste aversion
   - **e.** stimulus generalization

5. Jada works in the psychology department's rat lab. In her studies, she found that many of her lab rats would develop a conditioned taste aversion to certain foods after as little as one trial. Jada's psychology professor refers to this as a classic example of _____.
   a. stimulus substitution
   b. continuous reinforcement
   c. psychological preparedness
   d. instinctive drift
   e. biological preparedness

6. In classical conditioning, behavior typically is _____, whereas with operant conditioning, behavior is _____.
   a. voluntary, involuntary
   b. effortful, spontaneous
   c. rewarded, punished
   d. biological, internal
   e. involuntary, voluntary

7. Positive reinforcement results in a(n) _____ in the target behavior and negative reinforcement results in a(n) _____ in the target behavior.
   a. increase, decrease
   b. increase, increase
   c. modulation, modification
   d. decrease, decrease
   e. decrease, increase

8. Rita has a terrible headache. If she takes some aspirin to make her headache go away, this would be an example of _____.
   a. punishment
   b. discrimination
   c. positive reinforcement
   d. negative reinforcement
   e. generalization

9. John gets paid every 2 weeks. In one 2-week period, he works a total of 20 hours. During another 2-week period, he works a total of 50 hours. Regardless of the total number of hours he works each week, he is paid every 2 weeks. What schedule of reinforcement is being used?
   a. variable interval
   b. continuous
   c. fixed ratio
   d. variable ratio
   e. fixed interval

10. What is the relationship between negative reinforcement and punishment?
    a. Both tend to weaken a response.
    b. Both will weaken an existing response and strengthen a new response.
    c. Both tend to strengthen a response.
    d. Negative reinforcement strengthens a response, while punishment weakens a response.
    e. Negative reinforcement weakens a response, while punishment strengthens a response.

11. Which of the following is an example of the use of extinction with operant conditioning?
    a. A mother gives a child chocolate prior to him or her asking for it so as to keep a tantrum from occurring in the first place.
    b. A mother gives a child a toy every time they brush their teeth.
    c. A mother gives in to her child's demands for candy by buying the child some chocolate so as to quiet him or her.
    d. A mother spanks a child when he or she starts throwing a tantrum.
    e. A mother ignores her child's temper tantrum so that the behavior ultimately goes away.

12. Studies by Keller and Marian Breland found that many animals exhibit instinctive drift. What does this mean?
    a. The animals studied would learn skills through reinforcement, and they remained that way no matter how much reinforcement they were given.
    b. The animals studied could only learn skills similar to those they observed other animals doing.
    c. The animals studied could not learn any skills even with the use of reinforcement.
    d. The animals studied would learn skills through reinforcement but eventually revert to their genetically controlled patterns of behavior.
    e. The animals studied could only learn skills similar to those found in the wild.

13. David was lying in bed when he suddenly realized how he might deal with a fast-approaching deadline at work. When his co-workers asked how he came up with his idea, he said, "It just came to me out of nowhere." Psychologists would refer to this as _____.
    a. observational learning
    b. AMID
    c. latent learning
    d. learned helplessness
    e. insight learning

14. Amber failed repeatedly in college algebra. Finally, she gave up and was seriously considering dropping out of college. One day, her best friend offered to personally help her if she signed up for college algebra again, but she refused. What concept might explain her reluctance?
    a. insight learning
    b. punishment by application
    c. latent learning
    d. learned helplessness
    e. observational learning

15. Jasmine has noticed how some of her friends have lost weight and gotten trim by exercising 1 to 2 hours each day. However, she has no plans to imitate their behavior. What component of Bandura's model of observational learning will explain why Jasmine has not started a similar weight-loss program?
    a. Jasmine's unconscious does not believe she can achieve the goal.
    b. Jasmine is not motivated, nor does she have the desire to begin the program.
    c. Jasmine has experienced vicarious punishment.
    d. Jasmine's self-esteem must first be addressed.
    e. Jasmine's unwillingness may be the result of media multitasking.

PART II: FREE-RESPONSE QUESTION

Directions for Part II: Read the essay question that follows. Then respond to the question in a clear, concise essay. Do not simply list facts. Instead, present a thorough argument based on your critical consideration of the topic. Use of proper terminology is necessary.

Greg is training his new puppy to not jump onto or sit on the furniture. As Greg trains his puppy, the dog gets on the furniture less frequently, but only when Greg is around. Often when Greg comes home from being away, he finds his puppy on the couch.

Part A

For each of the following terms, explain how Greg could use this concept to train his puppy:

- positive reinforcement
- punishment by application
- shaping
- fixed ratio schedule

Part B

For each of the following terms, explain how this concept explains the puppy's behavior:

- law of effect
- extinction
- discriminative stimulus

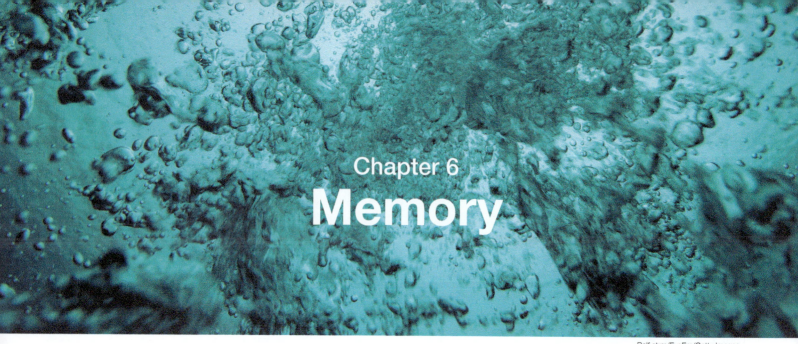

Chapter 6
Memory

Ralf strm/EyeEm/Getty Images

In your words

How is your memory of events? Do you find that you remember events from your past differently than others who were also present at that time?

After you have thought about these questions, watch the video to see how other students would answer them.

Watch the Video at MyLab Psychology

Why study memory?

Without memory, how would we be able to learn anything? The ability to learn is the key to our very survival, and we cannot learn unless we can remember what happened the last time a particular situation arose. Why study forgetting? If we can learn about the ways in which we forget information, we can apply that learning so that unintended forgetting occurs less frequently.

Learning Objectives

6.1 Identify the three processes of memory.

6.2 Explain how the different models of memory work.

6.3 Describe the process of sensory memory.

6.4 Describe short-term memory, and differentiate it from working memory.

6.5 Explain the process of long-term memory, including nondeclarative and declarative forms.

6.6 Identify the effects of cues on memory retrieval.

6.7 Differentiate the retrieval processes of recall and recognition.

6.8 Describe how some memories are automatically encoded into long-term memory.

6.9 Explain how the constructive processing view of memory retrieval accounts for forgetting and inaccuracies in memory.

6.10 Describe the "curve of forgetting."

6.11 Identify some common reasons people forget things.

6.12 Explain the biological bases of memory in the brain.

6.13 Identify the biological causes of amnesia.

6.14 Describe ways in which you can use elaborative rehearsal to make information easier to remember.

6.1–6.2 What Is Memory?

Is memory a place or a process? The answer to that question is not simple. In reading through this chapter, it will become clear that memory is a process but that it also has a "place" in the brain as well. Perhaps the best definition of **memory** is an active system that receives information from the senses, puts that information into a usable form, organizes it as it stores it away, and then retrieves the information from storage (adapted from Baddeley, 1996, 2003).

6.1 Three Processes of Memory

6.1 Identify the three processes of memory.

Although there are several different models of how memory works, all of them involve the same three processes: getting the information into the memory system, storing it there, and getting it back out.

PUTTING IT IN: ENCODING The first process in the memory system is to get sensory information (sight, sound, etc.) into a form that the brain can use. This is called **encoding**. Encoding is the set of mental operations that people perform on sensory information to convert that information into a form that is usable in the brain's storage systems. For example, when people hear a sound, their ears turn the vibrations in the air into neural messages from the auditory nerve (*transduction*), which make it possible for the brain to interpret that sound. See Learning Objective 3.1.

> 💬 It sounds like memory encoding works just like the senses—is there a difference?

Encoding is not limited to turning sensory information into signals for the brain. Encoding is accomplished differently in each of three different storage systems of memory. In one system, encoding may involve rehearsing information over and over to keep it in memory, whereas in another system, encoding involves elaborating on the meaning of the information—but let's elaborate on that later.

KEEPING IT IN: STORAGE The next step in memory is to hold on to the information for some period of time in a process called **storage**. The period of time will actually be of different lengths, depending on the system of memory being used. For example, in one system of memory, people hold on to information just long enough to work with it, about 20 seconds or so. In another system of memory, people hold on to information more or less permanently.

GETTING IT OUT: RETRIEVAL The biggest problem many people have is **retrieval**, that is, getting the information they know they have out of storage. Have you ever handed in an essay test and *then* remembered several other things you could have said? Retrieval problems are discussed thoroughly in a later section of this chapter.

6.2 Models of Memory

6.2 Explain how the different models of memory work.

Exactly how does memory work? When the storage process occurs, where does that information go and why? Memory experts have proposed several different ways of looking at memory. The model that many researchers once felt was the most comprehensive* and has perhaps been the most influential over the last several decades is the **information-processing model**. This approach focuses on the way information

---

*comprehensive: all-inclusive, covering everything.

AP 5.D Outline the principles that underlie construction and encoding of memories.

AP 5.E Outline the principles that underlie effective storage of memories.

memory
an active system that receives information from the senses, puts that information into a usable form, and organizes it as it stores it away, and then retrieves the information from storage.

encoding
the set of mental operations that people perform on sensory information to convert that information into a form that is usable in the brain's storage systems.

storage
holding on to information for some period of time.

retrieval
getting information that is in storage into a form that can be used.

information-processing model
model of memory that assumes the processing of information for memory storage is similar to the way a computer processes memory in a series of three stages.

is handled, or processed, through three different systems of memory. The processes of encoding, storage, and retrieval are seen as part of this model.

While it is common to refer to the three systems of the information-processing model as *stages* of memory, that term seems to imply a sequence of events. While many aspects of memory formation may follow a series of steps or stages, there are those who see memory as a simultaneous* process, with the creation and storage of memories taking place across a series of mental networks "stretched" across the brain (McClelland & Rumelhart, 1988; Plaut & McClelland, 2010; Rumelhart et al., 1986). This simultaneous processing allows people to retrieve many different aspects of a memory all at once, facilitating much faster reactions and decisions. This model of memory, derived from work in the development of artificial intelligence (AI), is called the **parallel distributed processing (PDP) model**. In the AI world, PDP is related to *connectionism*, the use of artificial neural networks to explain the mental abilities of humans (Bechtel & Abrahamsen, 2002; Henderson & McClelland, 2011; Marcus, 2001; Schapiro & McClelland, 2009).

The information-processing model assumes that the length of time that a memory will be remembered depends on the stage of memory in which it is stored. Other researchers have proposed that a memory's duration** depends on the depth (i.e., the effort made to understand the meaning) to which the information is processed or encoded (Cermak & Craik, 1979; Craik & Lockhart, 1972). If the word *BALL* is flashed on a screen, for example, and people are asked to report whether the word was in capital letters or lowercase, the word itself does not have to be processed very much at all—only its visual characteristics need enter into conscious attention. But if those people were to be asked to use that word in a sentence, they would have to think about what a ball is and how it can be used. They would have to process its meaning, which requires more mental effort than processing just its "looks." This model of memory is called the **levels-of-processing model**. Numerous experiments have shown that thinking about the meaning of something is a deeper level of processing and results in longer retention of the word (Cermak & Craik, 1979; Craik & Tulving, 1975; Paul et al., 2005; Watson et al., 1999). Watch the video *Depth of Processing* for an interactive demonstration of how shallow versus deep processing of information can affect memory.

parallel distributed processing (PDP) model
a model of memory in which memory processes are proposed to take place at the same time over a large network of neural connections.

levels-of-processing model
model of memory that assumes information that is more "deeply processed," or processed according to its meaning rather than just the sound or physical characteristics of the word or words, will be remembered more efficiently and for a longer period of time.

💬 So which model is right?

"Which model is right?" is not the correct question. The correct question is, *Which model explains the findings of researchers about how memory works?* The answer to that question is that all of these models can be used to explain some, if not all, research findings. Each of these views of the workings of memory can be seen as speaking to different aspects of memory. For example, the information-processing model provides a "big picture" view of how the various memory systems relate to each other—how the "memory machine" works. The PDP model is less about the mechanics of memory and more about the connections and timing of memory processes. The depth to

Watch Depth of Processing

👁 Watch the Video at MyLab Psychology

---

*simultaneous: all at the same time.
**duration: how long something lasts.

which information is processed can be seen to address the strength of those parallel connections within each of the three memory systems, with strength and duration of the memory increasing as the level of processing deepens.

While the information-processing model is no longer the primary way current memory researchers view the processes of memory, it is historically important and provides a handy way to talk about how memory seems to work. We're going to explore a lot of memory concepts in this chapter and will look at many of these concepts in the framework of this older model just because it's a little easier to talk about these concepts in these terms—terms many of you have probably heard in daily use. If you should decide to specialize in the study of memory, you'll no doubt have a better grasp of the latest memory theories because you understand the historical view from which they arose. Many of those more current ideas will also be covered in later sections of this chapter as well.

Concept Map L.O. 6.1, 6.2

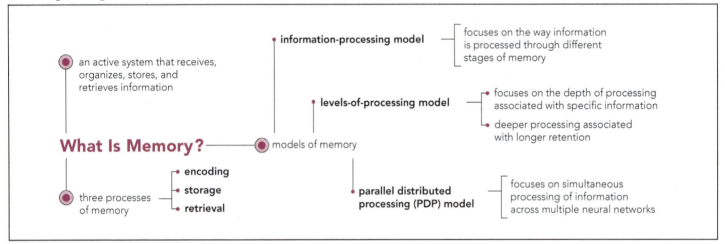

Practice Quiz — How much do you remember?

Pick the best answer.

1. Human memory consists of multiple systems that have the ability to store information for periods of time that range from _____ to _____.
   a. seconds, hours
   b. minutes, decades
   c. seconds, our lifetime
   d. hours, years
   e. hours, our lifetime

2. Anna has just finished her research paper and handed it in. As she walks out of the classroom, she realizes that there were a few more things she should have included in the paper. Anna's problem is in the memory process of _____.
   a. encoding
   b. retrieval
   c. application
   d. storage
   e. retention

3. Which model of memory suggests that memory processes occur throughout a neural network simultaneously?
   a. three-stage model
   b. parallel distributed processing model
   c. levels-of-processing model
   d. information-processing model
   e. three-stage model

4. Research has demonstrated you can enhance your memory for a specific word if you think about its meaning, how it can be used, and by giving a personal example of its use. This is best accounted for by which model of memory?
   a. parallel distributed processing model
   b. levels-of-processing model
   c. working memory model
   d. information-processing model
   e. three-stage model

6.3–6.5 The Information-Processing Model: Three Memory Systems

> **AP** 5.B Describe and differentiate psychological and physiological systems of memory.

The information-processing theory, which looks at how memory and other thought processes work as part of the cognitive perspective (see Learning Objective 1.3), bases its model for human thought on the way that a computer traditionally functions (Massaro & Cowan, 1993). Data are encoded in a manner that the computer can understand and use. The computer stores that information on a disc, a hard drive, or a memory stick, and then the data are retrieved out of storage as needed. It was also information-processing theorists who first proposed that there are three types of memory systems (see **Figure 6.1**), sensory memory, short-term memory, and long-term memory (Atkinson & Shiffrin, 1968).

Figure 6.1 Three-Stage Process of Memory

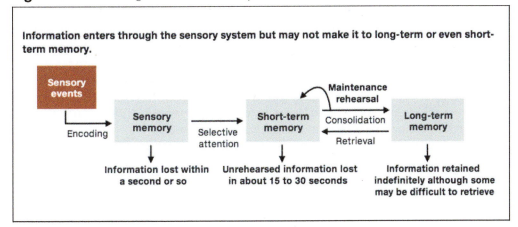

Information enters through the sensory system, briefly registering in sensory memory. Selective attention filters the information into short-term memory, where it is held while attention (rehearsal) continues. If the information receives enough rehearsal (maintenance or elaborative), it will enter and be stored in long-term memory.

6.3 Sensory Memory: Why Do People Do Double Takes?

6.3 Describe the process of sensory memory.

Sensory memory is the first system in the process of memory, the point at which information enters the nervous system through the sensory systems—eyes, ears, and so on. Think of it as a door that is open for a brief time. Looking through the door, one can see many people and objects, but only some of them will actually make it through the door itself. Sensory memory is a kind of door onto the world.

Information is encoded into sensory memory as neural messages in the nervous system. As long as those neural messages are traveling through the system, it can be said that people have a "memory" for that information that can be accessed if needed. For example, imagine that Elaina is driving down the street, looking at the people and cars on either side of her vehicle. All of a sudden she thinks, "What? Was that man wearing any pants?" and she looks back to check. How did she know to look back? Her eyes had already moved past the possibly pantless person, but some part of her brain must have just processed what she saw (most likely it was the reticular formation, which notices new and important information). This is called a "double take" and can only be explained by the presence, however brief, of a memory for what she saw. See Learning Objective 2.6.

There are two kinds of sensory memory that have been studied extensively. They are the iconic (visual) and echoic (auditory) sensory systems.

sensory memory
the very first system of memory, in which raw information from the senses is held for a very brief period of time.

ICONIC SENSORY MEMORY The example of seeing the possibly pantless person is an example of how the visual sensory system works. The visual sensory system is often called **iconic memory**, and it only lasts for a fraction of a second. *Icon* is the Greek word for "image." Iconic memory was studied in several classic experiments by George Sperling (1960), as shown in the *Classic Studies in Psychology* feature.

> AP 5.C Identify the contributions of key researchers in cognitive psychology.

Classic Studies in Psychology
Sperling's Iconic Memory Test

George Sperling had found in his early studies that if he presented a grid of letters using a machine that allowed very fast presentation, his subjects could only remember about four or five of the letters, no matter how many had been presented.

Sperling became convinced that this method was an inaccurate measure of the capacity of iconic memory because the human tendency to read from top to bottom took long enough that the letters on the bottom of the grid may have faded from memory by the time the person had "read" the letters at the top. He developed a technique called the *partial report method,* in which he showed a grid of letters similar to those in **Figure 6.2** but immediately sounded a high, medium, or low tone just after the grid was shown. Participants were told to report the top row of letters if they heard the high tone, the middle row for the medium tone, or the lowest row for the low tone. As they didn't hear the tone until after the grid went away, they couldn't look at just one row in advance.

Figure 6.2 Iconic Memory Test

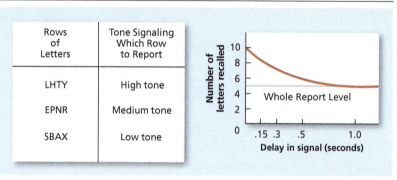

Sample grid of letters for Sperling's test of iconic memory. To determine if the entire grid existed in iconic memory, Sperling sounded a tone associated with each row after the grid's presentation. Participants were able to recall the letters in the row for which they heard the tone. The graph shows the decrease in the number of letters recalled as the delay in presenting the tone increased.

Using this technique, Sperling found that participants could accurately report any of the three rows. This meant that the entire grid was in iconic memory and available to the participants. The capacity of iconic memory is everything that can be seen at one time.

Sperling also found that if he delayed the tone for a brief period of time, after about a second, participants could no longer recall letters from the grid any better than they had during the whole report procedure. The iconic information had completely faded out of sensory memory in that brief time.

Questions for Further Discussion

1. How might the results of the partial report method be different for people from cultures in which text is read from right to left or top to bottom?
2. Would the results be different if more detailed pictures were used instead of letters?

iconic memory

visual sensory memory, lasting only a fraction of a second.

In real life, information that has just entered iconic memory will be pushed out very quickly by new information, a process called *masking* (Cowan, 1988). Research suggests that after only a quarter of a second, old information is replaced by new information.

Although it is rare, some people do have what is properly called **eidetic imagery**, or the ability to access a visual sensory memory over a long period of time. Although the popular term *photographic memory* is often used to describe this rare ability, some people claiming to have photographic memory actually mean that they have an extremely good memory. Having a very good memory and having eidetic imagery ability are two very different things. People with eidetic imagery ability might be able to look quickly at a page in a book, then by focusing on a blank wall or piece of paper, "read" the words from the image that still lingers in their sensory memory. Although it might sound like a great ability to have while in school, it actually provides little advantage when taking tests, because it's just like having an open-book test. If a student can't *understand* what's written on the pages, having the book open is useless. It is unknown why some people have this ability, but it is more common in children and tends to diminish by adolescence or young adulthood (Haber, 1979; Leask et al., 1969; Stromeyer & Psotka, 1971).

These sparklers appear to create trails of light when, in fact, no light continues to exist after passing a given point along its path. The apparent trails of light are due to the brief persistence of light from each sparkler in sensory memory, a concept referred to as *visual persistence*, or *persistence of vision*.

💬 If iconic memory lasts such a brief time, what use is it to us?

Iconic memory actually serves a very important function in the visual system. Chapter Three discussed the way the eyes make tiny little movements called *microsaccades* that keep vision from adapting to a constant visual stimulus, so that what is stared at steadily doesn't slowly disappear. Iconic memory helps the visual system view surroundings as continuous and stable in spite of these saccadic movements. It also allows enough time for the brain stem to decide if the information is important enough to be brought into consciousness—like the possibly pantless person.

ECHOIC SENSORY MEMORY Another type of sensory system is **echoic memory**, or the brief memory of something a person has heard. A good example of echoic memory is the "What?" phenomenon. You might be reading or concentrating on the television, and your parent, roommate, or friend walks up and says something to you. You sit there for a second or two and then say "What? Oh—yes, I'm ready to eat now," or whatever comment is appropriate. You didn't really process the statement from the other person as he or she said it. You heard it, but your brain didn't interpret it immediately. Instead, it took several seconds for you to realize that (1) something was said, (2) it may have been important, and (3) you'd better try to remember what it was. If you realize all this within about 4 seconds (the duration of echoic memory), you will more than likely be able to "hear" an echo of the statement in your head, a kind of "instant replay."

Echoic memory's capacity is limited to what can be heard at any one moment and is smaller than the capacity of iconic memory, although it lasts longer—about 2–4 seconds (Schweickert, 1993).

Echoic memory is very useful when a person wants to have meaningful conversations with others. It allows the person to remember what someone said just long enough to recognize the meaning of a phrase. As with iconic memory, it also allows people to hold on to incoming auditory information long enough for the lower brain centers to determine whether processing by higher brain centers is needed. It is echoic memory that allows a musician to tune a musical instrument, for example. The memory of the tuning fork's tone lingers in echoic memory long enough for the person doing the tuning to match that tone on the instrument.

Tuning a piano requires the use of echoic sensory memory. What other occupations might find a good echoic memory to be an asset?

eidetic imagery
the ability to access a visual memory for 30 seconds or more.

echoic memory
auditory sensory memory, lasting only 2–4 seconds.

💬 What happens if the lower brain centers send the information on to the higher centers?

6.4 Short-Term Memory

6.4 Describe short-term memory, and differentiate it from working memory.

If an incoming sensory message is important enough to enter consciousness, that message will move from sensory memory to the next process of memory, called **short-term memory (STM)**. Unlike sensory memory, short-term memories may be held for up to 30 seconds and possibly longer through *maintenance rehearsal*.

SELECTIVE ATTENTION: HOW INFORMATION ENTERS **Selective attention** is the ability to focus on only one stimulus from among all sensory input (Broadbent, 1958). It is through selective attention that information enters our STM system. In Dr. Donald E. Broadbent's original filter theory, a kind of "bottleneck" occurs between the processes of sensory memory and short-term memory. Only a stimulus that is "important" enough (determined by a kind of "pre-analysis" accomplished by the attention centers in the brain stem) will make it past the bottleneck to be consciously analyzed for meaning in STM. When a person is thinking actively about information, that information is said to be conscious and is also in STM. See Learning Objective 4.1.

> **AP** 5.A Compare and contrast various cognitive processes.

It is somewhat difficult to use Broadbent's selective-attention filter to explain the "cocktail-party effect" that has been long established in studies of perception and attention (Bronkhorst, 2000; Cherry, 1953; Handel, 1989). If you've ever been at a party where there's a lot of noise and several conversations going on in the background but you are still able to notice when someone says your name, you have experienced this effect. In this kind of a situation, the areas of the brain that are involved in selective attention had to be working—even though you were not consciously aware of it. Then, when that important bit of information (your name) "appeared," those areas somehow filtered the information into your conscious awareness—in spite of the fact that you were not paying conscious attention to the other background noise (Hopfinger et al., 2000; Mesgarani & Chang, 2012; Stuss et al., 2002).

Dr. Anne M. Treisman (Treisman, 2006; Triesman & Gelade, 1980) proposed that selective attention operates in a two-stage filtering process: In the first stage, incoming stimuli in sensory memory are filtered on the basis of simple physical characteristics, similar to Broadbent's original idea. Instead of moving to STM or being lost, however, there is only a lessening (*attenuation*) of the "signal strength" of unselected sensory stimuli in comparison to the selected stimuli. In the second stage, only the stimuli that meet a certain threshold of importance are processed. Since the attenuated stimuli are still present at this second stage, something as subjectively important as one's own name may be able to be "plucked" out of the attenuated incoming stimuli. Even when deeply asleep, when the selective attention filter is not working at its peak level, it still functions: A sleeping mother will awake to her infant's cries while sleeping through louder, less important sounds such as a dog barking (LaBerge, 1980).

Each person at this gathering is involved in a conversation with others, with dozens of such conversations going on at the same time all around. Yet if a person in another conversation says the name of one of the people in the crowd, that person in the crowd will be able to selectively attend to his or her name. This is known as the "cocktail-party effect."

What happens when information does pass through the selective attention filter and into short-term memory? Short-term memory tends to be encoded primarily in auditory (sound) form. That simply means that people tend to "talk" inside their own heads. Although some images are certainly stored in STM in a kind of visual "sketchpad" (Baddeley, 1986), auditory storage accounts for much of short-term encoding. Even a dancer planning out moves in her head will not only visualize the moves but also be very likely to verbally describe the moves in her head as she plans. An artist planning a painting certainly has visual information in STM but may also keep up an internal dialogue that is primarily auditory. Research in which participants were asked to recall numbers and letters showed that errors were nearly always made with numbers or letters that *sounded like* the target but not with those that *looked like* the target word or number (Acheson et al., 2010; Conrad & Hull, 1964).

short-term memory (STM)
the memory system in which information is held for brief periods of time while being used.

selective attention
the ability to focus on only one stimulus from among all sensory input.

WORKING MEMORY Some memory theorists use the term *working memory* as another way of referring to short-term memory—they see no difference between the two concepts. Others feel that the two systems are quite different. In this discussion, we will use short-term memory to refer to simple storage and working memory as relating to storage and manipulation of information (Baddeley, 2012). Short-term memory has traditionally been thought of as a thing or a place into which information is put. As mentioned earlier, current memory researchers prefer to think of memory in terms of a more continuous system, where information flows from one form of representation to another, rather than a series of "boxes." **Working memory** is therefore thought of as an active system that processes the information present within short-term memory. Working memory is thought to consist of three interrelated systems: a central executive (a kind of "CEO" or "Big Boss") that controls and coordinates the other two systems, the visuospatial "sketchpad" of sorts that was mentioned earlier, and a kind of auditory action "recorder" or phonological loop (Baddeley, 1986, 2012; Baddeley & Hitch, 1974; Baddeley & Larsen, 2007; Engle & Kane, 2004; Van der Stigchel & Hollingworth, 2018). The central executive acts as interpreter for both the visual and auditory information, and the visual and auditory information are themselves contained in short-term memory. For example, when a person is reading a book, the sketchpad will contain images of the people and events of the particular passage being read, while the recorder "plays" the dialogue in the person's head. The central executive helps interpret the information from both systems and pulls it all together. In a sense, then, short-term memory can be seen as being a part of the working memory system (Acheson et al., 2010; Bayliss et al., 2005; Colom et al., 2006; Kail & Hall, 2001).

Another way to think about short-term memory is as a desk where you do your work. You might pull some files out of storage (permanent memory), or someone might hand you some files (sensory input). While the files are on your desk, you can see them, read them, and work with them (working memory). The "files" are now conscious material and will stay that way as long as they are on the desk. Less important files may get "thrown out" (forgotten as you fail to pay attention to them), while more important files might get stored away (permanent memory), where they are not conscious until they are once again retrieved—brought out of the desk.

CAPACITY: THE MAGICAL NUMBER SEVEN, OR FIVE, OR FOUR George Miller (Miller, 1956) wanted to know how much information humans can hold in short-term memory at any one time (or how many "files" will fit on the "desk"). He reviewed several memory studies, including some using a memory test called the *digit-span test*, in which a series of numbers is read to participants in the study who are then asked to recall the numbers in order. Each series gets longer and longer, until the participants cannot recall any of the numbers in order.

What you will discover is that most everyone you test will get past the first two sequences of numbers, but some people will make errors on the six-digit span, about half of the people you test will slip up on the seven-digit span, and very few will be able to get past the nine-digit span without errors. This led Miller to conclude that the capacity of STM is about seven items or pieces of information, plus or minus two items, or from five to nine bits of information. Miller called this the magical number seven, plus or minus two. Since Miller's review of those early studies and subsequent conclusion about the capacity of STM being about seven items, research methods have improved, as has our knowledge and understanding of memory processes. Current research suggests that working memory capacity can vary from person to person (Engle, 2018; Shipstead et al., 2016). For example, younger adults can hold three to five items of information at a time if a strategy of some type is not being used. When the information is in the form of longer, similar-sounding, or unfamiliar words, however, that capacity reduces until it is only about four items (Cowan, 2001; Cowan et al., 2005; Palva et al., 2010). There is a way to "fool" STM into holding more information than is usual. (Think of it as "stacking" related files on the desk.) If the bits of information are combined into meaningful units, or chunks, more information can be held in STM. If someone were to recode a sequence of

AP 5.C Identify the contributions of key researchers in cognitive psychology.

working memory
an active system that processes the information in short-term memory.

numbers as "654-789-3217," for example, instead of 10 separate bits of information, there would only be three "chunks" that read like a phone number. This process of recoding or reorganizing the information is called *chunking*. Chances are that anyone who can easily remember more than eight or nine digits in the digit-span test is probably recoding the numbers into chunks.

WHY DO YOU THINK THEY CALL IT "SHORT TERM"? How long is the "short" of short-term memory? Research has shown that short-term memory lasts from about 12 to 30 seconds without rehearsal (Atkinson & Shiffrin, 1968; J. Brown, 1958; Peterson & Peterson, 1959). After that, the memory seems to rapidly "decay" or disappear. In fact, the findings of one study with mice suggest that in order to form new memories, old memories must be "erased" by the formation of newly formed neurons (Kitamura et al., 2009). The hippocampus only has so much storage room, and while many of the memories formed there will be transferred to more permanent storage in other areas of the brain, some memories, without rehearsal, will decay as new neurons (and newer memories) are added to the already existing neural circuits.

💬 What do you mean by rehearsal? How long can short-term memories last if rehearsal is a factor?

Most people realize that saying something they want to remember over and over again in their heads can help them remember it longer. We sometimes do this with names we want to remember, or a phone number we want to remember long enough to enter into our phone's contacts. This is a process called **maintenance rehearsal**. With maintenance rehearsal, a person is simply continuing to pay attention to the information to be held in memory, and since attention is how that information got into STM in the first place, it works quite well (Atkinson & Shiffrin, 1968; Rundus, 1971). With this type of rehearsal, information will stay in short-term memory until rehearsal stops. When rehearsal stops, the memory rapidly decays and is forgotten. If anything interferes with maintenance rehearsal, memories are also likely to be lost. For example, if someone is trying to count items by reciting each number out loud while counting, and someone else asks that person the time and interferes with the counting process, the person who is counting will probably forget what the last number was and have to start all over again. Short-term memory helps people keep track of things like counting.

Interference in STM can also happen if the amount of information to be held in STM exceeds its capacity. Information already in STM may be "pushed out" to make room for newer information. This is why it might be possible to remember the first few names of people you meet at a party, but as more names are added, they displace the older names. A better way to remember a person's name is to associate the name with something about the person's appearance, a process that may help move the name from STM into more permanent storage. This more permanent storage is the process of long-term memory, which is the topic of the next section.

Working memory is an important area of research and has implications for understanding not only intelligence but also learning and attention disorders such as attention-deficit/hyperactivity disorder, and various dementia-related memory problems (Alloway et al., 2009; Jafarpour et al., 2017; Kensinger et al., 2003; Martinussen et al., 2005). Researchers have trained mice to improve their working memory and found that the mice become more intelligent with improved working memory (e.g., Light et al., 2010). Other researchers have found that working memory is helpful in solving mathematical problems but may actually hurt the ability to solve creative problems (Wiley & Jarosz, 2012). Creative problem solving seems to benefit from a less focused approach than the focused attention taking place in working memory.

This restaurant server is taking the woman's order without writing it down. Which memory system is she using? Do you think that her capacity for items in this system may be greater than someone who does not try to remember items like this often?

maintenance rehearsal
practice of saying some information to be remembered over and over in one's head in order to maintain it in short-term memory.

6.5 Long-Term Memory

6.5 Explain the process of long-term memory, including nondeclarative and declarative forms.

The third stage of memory is **long-term memory (LTM)**, the system into which all the information is placed to be kept more or less permanently. In terms of capacity, LTM seems to be unlimited for all practical purposes (Bahrick, 1984; Barnyard & Grayson, 1996). In fact, researchers now think the capacity of the human brain may be as much as 10 times greater than previously estimated (Bartol et al., 2015). Think about it: Would there ever really come a time when you could not fit one more piece of information into your head? When you could learn nothing more? If humans lived much longer lives, there might be a finite end to the capacity of LTM stores. But in practical terms, there is always room for more information (in spite of what some students may believe).

DURATION As for duration, the name *long term* says it all. There is a relatively permanent physical change in the brain itself when a memory is formed. That means that many of the memories people have stored away for a long, long time—even since childhood—may still be there. That does not mean that people can always retrieve those memories. The memories may be *available* but not *accessible*, meaning that they are still there, but for various reasons (discussed later under the topic of forgetting) people cannot "get to" them. It's like knowing that there is a certain item on the back of the top shelf of the kitchen cabinet but having no ladder or step stool to reach it. The item is there (available), but you can't get to it (not accessible).

"Long term" also does not mean that *all* memories are stored forever; our personal memories are too numerous to be permanently retained, for example. Nor do we store every single thing that has ever happened to us. We only store long-lasting memories of events and concepts that are meaningful and important to us.

These students are rehearsing for a concert. They will use maintenance rehearsal (repeating the musical passages over and over) until they can play their parts perfectly. The movements of their hands and fingers upon their instruments will be stored in long-term memory. How is this kind of long-term memory different from something like the memorized lines of one's part in a play?

> 💬 I once memorized a poem by repeating it over and over—that's maintenance rehearsal, right? Since I still remember most of the poem, it must be in long-term memory. Is maintenance rehearsal a good way to get information into long-term memory?

Information that is rehearsed long enough may actually find its way into long-term memory. After all, it's how most people learned their Social Security number and the letters of the alphabet (although people cheated a little on the latter by putting the alphabet to music, which makes it easier to retrieve). Most people tend to learn poems and the multiplication tables by maintenance rehearsal, otherwise known as rote learning. *Rote* is like "rotating" the information in one's head, saying it over and over again. But maintenance rehearsal is not the most efficient way of putting information into long-term storage, because to get the information back out, one has to remember it almost exactly as it went in. Try this: What is the 15th letter of the alphabet? Did you have to recite or sing through the alphabet song to get to that letter?

Although many long-term memories are encoded as images (think of the *Mona Lisa*), sounds, smells, or tastes (Cowan, 1988), in general, LTM is encoded in meaningful form, a kind of mental storehouse of the meanings of words, concepts, and all the events that people want to keep in mind. Even the images, sounds, smells, and tastes involved in these events have some sort of meaning attached to them that gives them enough importance to be stored long term. If STM can be thought of as a working "surface" or desk, then LTM can be thought of as a huge series of filing cabinets behind the desk, in which files are stored in an organized fashion, according to meaning. Files have to be placed in the cabinets in a certain organized fashion to be useful—how could anyone ever remember any kind of information quickly if the files were not in some order? The best way to

long-term memory (LTM)
the system of memory into which all the information is placed to be kept more or less permanently.

AP 5.A Compare and contrast various cognitive processes.

AP 5.E Outline the principles that underlie effective storage of memories.

encode information into LTM in an organized fashion is to make it meaningful through *elaborative rehearsal*.

ELABORATIVE REHEARSAL **Elaborative rehearsal** is a way of increasing the number of *retrieval cues* (stimuli that aid in remembering) for information by connecting new information with something that is already well known (Craik & Lockhart, 1972; Postman, 1975; Roberts et al., 2014). For example, the French word *maison* means "house." A person could try to memorize that (using maintenance rehearsal) by saying over and over, "*Maison* means house, *maison* means house." But it would be much easier and more efficient if that person simply thought, "*Maison* sounds like masons, and masons build houses." That makes the meaning of the word tie in with something the person already knows (masons, who lay stone or bricks to build houses) and helps in remembering the French term. In older versions of this concept, elaborative rehearsal was seen as a way of transferring information from STM to LTM, but that makes the two forms of memory sound like boxes. The "memory stores as boxes" idea is one of the main criticisms of the information-processing model because it makes it seem as though there is nothing in between STM and LTM. This is not the case; research has shown that information can exist anywhere along the continuum of actively paying attention to an experience and permanent storage of that experience (Raaijmakers, 1993; Raaijmakers & Shiffrin, 2003).

As discussed in the beginning of this chapter, Craik and Lockhart (1972) theorized that information that is more "deeply processed," or processed according to its meaning rather than just the sound or physical characteristics of the word or words, will be remembered more efficiently and for a longer period of time. As the levels-of-processing approach predicts, elaborative rehearsal is a deeper kind of processing than maintenance rehearsal and so leads to better long-term storage (Craik & Tulving, 1975; Roberts et al., 2014). See the *Applying Psychology to Everyday Life* feature at the end of this chapter for more on elaborative rehearsal.

> 💬 I can remember a lot of stuff from my childhood. Some of it is stuff I learned in school and some of it is more personal, like the first day of school. Are these two different kinds of long-term memories?

Nondeclarative knowledge, such as tying one's shoes, often must be learned by doing, as it is difficult to put into words. Once these children learn how to tie their shoes, the knowledge will likely always be there to retrieve.

TYPES OF LONG-TERM INFORMATION Long-term memories include general facts and knowledge, personal facts, and even skills that can be performed. Memory for skills is a type of *nondeclarative memory*, or *implicit memory*, because the skills have to be demonstrated and not reported. Memory for facts is called *declarative memory*, or *explicit memory*, because facts are things that are known and can be declared (stated outright). These two types of long-term memory are quite different, as the following sections will explain.

NONDECLARATIVE (IMPLICIT) LTM Memories for things that people know how to do, like tying shoes and riding a bicycle, are a kind of LTM called **nondeclarative (implicit) memory**. The fact that people have the knowledge of how to tie their shoes, for example, is *implied* by the fact that they can actually tie them. Nondeclarative memories also include emotional associations, habits, and simple conditioned reflexes that may or may not be in conscious awareness, which are often very strong memories (Mitchell et al., 2018; Schacter & Wagner, 2013; Squire & Kandel, 2009). See Learning Objectives 5.2, 5.3, 5.5. Referring to Chapter Two, the amygdala is the most probable location for emotional associations, such as fear, and the cerebellum in the hindbrain is responsible for storage of memories of conditioned responses, skills, and habits (Dębiec et al., 2010; Kandel & Siegelbaum, 2013; Squire et al., 1993).

Evidence that separate areas of the brain control nondeclarative memory comes from studies of people with damage to the hippocampal area of the brain. This damage causes them to have **anterograde amnesia**, in which new long-term declarative memories cannot be formed. (This disorder is fairly accurately represented by the character

elaborative rehearsal
a way of increasing the number of retrieval cues for information by connecting new information with something that is already well known.

nondeclarative (implicit) memory
type of long-term memory including memory for skills, procedures, habits, and conditioned responses. These memories are not conscious but are implied to exist because they affect conscious behavior.

anterograde amnesia
loss of memory from the point of injury or trauma forward, or the inability to form new long-term memories.

of Lenny in the motion picture *Memento* as well as Dory from *Finding Nemo* and *Finding Dory*.) One of the more famous anterograde amnesia patients, H.M., is discussed in detail later in this chapter.

In one study of nondeclarative memory (Cohen et al., 1985), patients with this disorder were taught how to solve a particular puzzle called the Tower of Hanoi (see **Figure 6.3**). Although the patients were able to learn the sequence of moves necessary to solve the puzzle, when brought back into the testing room at a later time, they could not remember ever having seen the puzzle before—or, for that matter, the examiner. Yet they were able to solve the puzzle even while claiming that they had never seen it before. Their nondeclarative memories for how to solve the puzzle were evidently formed and stored in a part of the brain separate from the part controlling the memories they could no longer form. Even people with Alzheimer's disease, who also suffer from anterograde amnesia, do not forget how to walk, talk, fasten clothing, or even tie shoes (although they do lose motor ability because the brain eventually fails to send the proper signals). These are all implicit, nondeclarative memories. In fact, it would be rare to find someone who has lost nondeclarative memory. Literally, these are the kind of memories people "never forget."

Nondeclarative memories are not easily retrieved into conscious awareness. Have you ever tried to tell someone how to tie shoes without using your hands to show them? The participants in the Tower of Hanoi study also provide a good example of implicit memory, as they could solve the puzzle but had no conscious knowledge of how to do so. Such knowledge is in people's memories because they use this information, but they are often not consciously aware of this knowledge (Roediger, 1990). A memory from one's early childhood of being frightened by a dog, for example, may not be a conscious memory in later childhood but may still be the cause of that older child's fear of dogs. Conscious memories for events in childhood, on the other hand, are usually considered to be a different kind of long-term memory called declarative memory.

DECLARATIVE (EXPLICIT) LTM Nondeclarative memory is about the things that people can *do*, but **declarative (explicit) memory** is about all the things that people can *know*—the facts and information that make up knowledge. People know things such as the names of the planets in the solar system, that adding 2 and 2 makes 4, and that a noun is the name of a person, place, or thing. These are general facts, but people also know about the things that have happened to them personally. For example, I know what I ate for breakfast this morning and what I saw on the way to work, but I don't know what you had for breakfast or what you might have seen. There are two types of declarative long-term memories, *semantic* and *episodic* (Nyberg & Tulving, 1996).

One type of declarative memory is general knowledge that anyone has the ability to know. Most of this information is what is learned in school or by reading. This kind of LTM is called **semantic memory**. The word *semantic* refers to meaning, so this kind of knowledge is the awareness of the meanings of words, concepts, and terms as well as names of objects, math skills, and so on. This is also the type of knowledge that is used on game shows such as *Jeopardy*. Semantic memories, like nondeclarative memories, are relatively permanent. But it is possible to "lose the way" to this kind of memory, as discussed later in the section on forgetting.

The other kind of factual memory is the personal knowledge that each person has of his or her daily life and personal history, a kind of autobiographical* memory (LePort et al., 2012). Memories of what has happened to people each day, certain birthdays, anniversaries that were particularly special, childhood events, and so on are called **episodic memory**, because they represent episodes from their lives. Unlike nondeclarative and semantic long-term memories, episodic memories tend to be updated and revised more or less constantly. You can probably remember what you had for breakfast today, but what

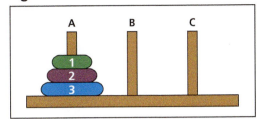

Figure 6.3 Tower of Hanoi

The Tower of Hanoi is a puzzle that is solved in a series of steps by moving one disk at a time. The goal is to move all of the disks from peg A to peg C; the rules are that a larger disk cannot be moved on top of a smaller one and a disk cannot be moved if there are other disks on top of it. Amnesic patients were able to learn the procedure for solving the puzzle but could not remember that they knew how to solve it.

declarative (explicit) memory
type of long-term memory containing information that is conscious and known.

semantic memory
type of declarative memory containing general knowledge, such as knowledge of language and information learned in formal education.

episodic memory
type of declarative memory containing personal information not readily available to others, such as daily activities and events.

---

*autobiographical: the story of a person's life as told by that person.

you had for breakfast 2 years ago on this date is most likely a mystery. Episodic memories that are especially *meaningful*, such as the memory of the first day of school or your first date, are more likely to be kept in LTM (although these memories may not be as exact as people sometimes assume they are). The updating process is a kind of survival mechanism, because although semantic and nondeclarative memories are useful and necessary on an ongoing basis, no one really needs to remember every little detail of every day. As becomes obvious later, the ability to forget some kinds of information is very necessary.

Some evidence suggests that women are a bit better at retrieving episodic memories than are men, while there seems to be no similar gender difference for semantic memories (Fuentes & Desrocher, 2013; Herlitz et al., 1997; Maitland et al., 2004). Women tend to use more verbal descriptions than do men, and perhaps women are using more verbal cues when encoding and retrieving episodic memories, creating an advantage over men who may not be relying as much on verbal cues. As semantic memories are verbal in their very nature, there would be no gender advantage in this memory system—both men and women would be using verbal cues.

Episodic and semantic memories are explicit memories because they are easily made conscious and brought from long-term storage into short-term memory. The knowledge of semantic memories such as word meanings, science concepts, and so on can be brought out of the "filing cabinet" and placed on the "desk" where that knowledge becomes *explicit*, or obvious. The same is often true of personal, episodic memories.

> But sometimes I can't remember all the names of the planets or what I had for breakfast yesterday. Doesn't that make these memories implicit instead of explicit?

The difference between implicit memories, such as how to balance on a bicycle, and explicit memories, such as naming all the planets, is that it is impossible or extremely difficult to bring implicit memories into consciousness. Explicit memories can be forgotten but always have the potential to be made conscious. When someone reminds you of what you had for breakfast the day before, for example, you will remember that you had that knowledge all along—it was just temporarily "mislaid." For a look at the connections among all these types of LTM, see **Figure 6.4**.

Figure 6.4 Types of LTM

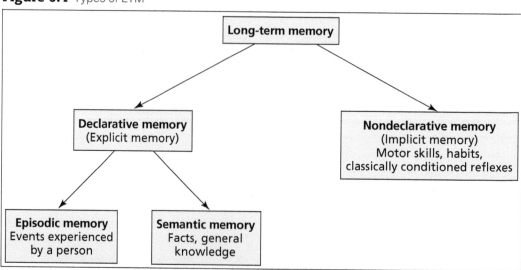

Long-term memory can be divided into declarative memories, which are factual and typically conscious (explicit) memories, and nondeclarative memories, which are skills, habits, and conditioned responses that are typically unconscious (implicit). Declarative memories are further divided into episodic memories (personal experiences) and semantic memories (general knowledge).

LONG-TERM MEMORY ORGANIZATION As stated before, LTM has to be fairly well organized for retrieval to be so quick. Can you remember the name of your first-grade teacher? If you can, how long did it take you to pull that name out of LTM and pull it into STM? It probably took hardly any time at all.

Research suggests that long-term memory is organized in terms of related meanings and concepts (Collins & Loftus, 1975; Collins & Quillian, 1969). In their original study, Allan Collins and M. Ross Quillian (1969) had participants respond "true" or "false" as quickly as possible to sentences such as "a canary is a bird" and "a canary is an animal." Looking at **Figure 6.5**, it is apparent that information exists in a kind of network, with nodes (focal points) of related information linked to each other in a kind of hierarchy.* To verify the statement "a canary is a bird" requires moving to only one node, but "a canary is an animal" would require moving through two nodes and should take longer. This was exactly the result of the 1969 study, leading the researchers to develop the **semantic network model**, which assumes that information is stored in the brain in a connected fashion with concepts that are related to each other stored physically closer to each other than concepts that are not highly related (Collins & Quillian, 1969; Kenett et al., 2017).

Figure 6.5 Example of Semantic Network

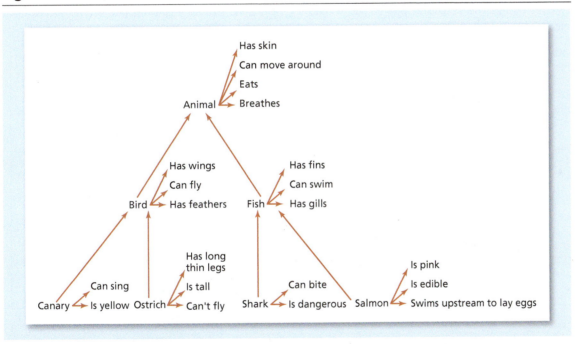

In the semantic network model of memory, concepts that are related in meaning are thought to be stored physically near each other in the brain. In this example, canary and ostrich are stored near the concept node for "bird," whereas shark and salmon are stored near "fish." But the fact that a canary is yellow is stored directly with that concept.

The PDP model (Rumelhart et al., 1986) discussed earlier in this chapter can be used to explain how rapidly the different points on the networks can be accessed. Although the access of nodes within a particular category (for example, *birds*) may take place in a serial fashion, explaining the different response times in the Collins and Quillian (1969) study, access across the entire network may take place in a parallel fashion, allowing several different concepts to be targeted at the same time (for example, one might be able to think about *birds, cats,* and *trees* simultaneously).

semantic network model
model of memory organization that assumes information is stored in the brain in a connected fashion, with concepts that are related stored physically closer to each other than concepts that are not highly related.

---

*hierarchy: a ranked and ordered list or series.

Perhaps the best way to think of how information is organized in LTM is to think about the Internet. A person might go to one Web site and from that site link to many other related sites. Each related site has its own specific information but is also linked to many other related sites, and a person can have more than one site open at the same time. This may be very similar to the way in which the mind organizes the information stored in LTM.

THINKING CRITICALLY 6.1

In thinking about a typical day, how do you use each type of memory: nondeclarative, episodic, and semantic?

Concept Map L.O. 6.3, 6.4, 6.5

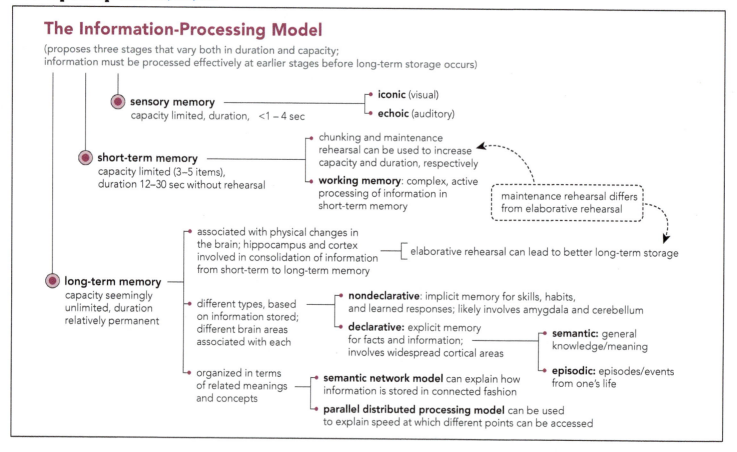

Practice Quiz — How much do you remember?

Pick the best answer.

1. _____ memories are said to linger in the mind for a few seconds, allowing people the chance to keep up with the flow of conversations and remember what was just said.
   a. Long-term
   b. Personal
   c. Iconic
   d. Short-term
   e. Echoic

2. Information enters into short-term memory through a process known as _____.
   a. recency effect
   b. selective attention
   c. consolidation
   d. primacy effect
   e. repetition

3. Of the following, which is the most similar to the concept of long-term memory?
   a. a computer mouse
   b. computer RAM
   c. a computer monitor
   d. a computer hard drive
   e. a computer keyboard

4. Amber meets a cute guy named Carson at a party. She wants to make sure she remembers his name, so she reminds herself that he has the same name as the capital of Nevada (Carson City). This transferring of information from short-term memory to long-term memory is an example of what type of rehearsal?
   a. maintenance
   b. semantic
   c. repetitive
   d. imagery
   e. elaborative

5. Brenda has been able to tie her shoes since she was 4. She now finds it difficult to explain to her baby brother how to tie his shoes, but she can easily demonstrate it for him. Brenda's memory for shoe tying is best characterized as a(n) _____ memory.
   a. episodic
   b. short-term
   c. declarative (explicit)
   d. semantic
   e. nondeclarative (implicit)

6. When you take your final exam in your psychology class, what type of memory will you most certainly need to access to answer each question?
   a. nondeclarative
   b. semantic
   c. sensory
   d. episodic
   e. working

6.6–6.9 Getting It Out: Retrieval of Long-Term Memories

AP 5.E Outline the principles that underlie effective storage of memories.

AP 5.F Describe strategies for retrieving memories.

AP 5.G Describe strategies for memory improvement and typical memory errors.

💬 My problem isn't so much getting information into my head; it's finding it later that's tough.

Oddly enough, most people's problems with getting information stored in LTM back out again have to do with *how* they put that information *into* LTM.

6.6 Retrieval Cues

6.6 Identify the effects of cues on memory retrieval.

Remember the previous discussion about maintenance rehearsal versus elaborative rehearsal? One of the main reasons that maintenance rehearsal is not a very good way to get information into LTM is that saying something over and over gives only one kind of retrieval cue, the sound of the word or phrase. When people try to remember a piece of information by thinking of what it means and how it fits in with what they already know, they are giving themselves multiple cues for meaning in addition to sound. The more retrieval cues stored with a piece of information, the easier the retrieval of that information will be (Karpicke, 2012; Pyc et al., 2014; Robin & Moscovitch, 2017; Roediger, 2000; Roediger & Guynn, 1996), which is the primary reason elaborative rehearsal enhances the formation of a memory. See Learning Objective PIA.6. Furthermore, we are not always aware of what cues are being associated. Remember from the discussion of nondeclarative memory, *priming* can occur where experience with information or concepts can improve later performance. And in many situations, we are not aware the improvement has taken place.

Although most people would assume that cues for retrieval would have to be directly related to the concepts being studied, the fact is that almost anything in one's surroundings is capable of becoming a cue. If you usually watch a particular television show while eating peanuts, for example, the next time you eat peanuts you might find yourself thinking of the show you were watching. This connection between surroundings and remembered information is called *encoding specificity*.

The results of the Godden and Baddeley (1975) study indicated the retrieval of words learned while underwater was higher when the retrieval also took place underwater. Similarly, words learned while out of water (on land) were retrieved at a higher rate out of the water.

AP 5.D Outline the principles that underlie construction and encoding of memories.

ENCODING SPECIFICITY: CONTEXT EFFECTS ON MEMORY RETRIEVAL Have you ever had to take a test in a different classroom than the one in which you learned the material being tested? Do you think that your performance on that test was hurt by being in a different physical context? Researchers have found strong evidence for the concept of **encoding specificity**, the tendency for memory of any kind of information to be improved if retrieval conditions are similar to the conditions under which the information was encoded (Tulving & Thomson, 1973). These conditions, or cues, can be internal or external. *Context-dependent learning* may refer to the physical surroundings a person is in when they are learning specific information. For example,

encoding specificity
the tendency for memory of information to be improved if related information (such as surroundings or physiological state) that is available when the memory is first formed is also available when the memory is being retrieved.

When this bride and groom experience happy moments together later on in their marriage, they will be more likely to recall how happy they were at their wedding. State-dependent learning makes it easier for people to recall information stored while in a particular emotional state (such as the happiness of this couple) if the recall occurs in a similar emotional state.

encoding specificity would predict that the best place to take one's chemistry test is in the same room in which you learned the material. Also, it's very common to walk into a room and know that there was something you wanted, but in order to remember it, you have to go back to the room you started in to use your surroundings as a cue for remembering.

In one study, researchers had students who were learning to scuba dive in a pool also learn lists of words while they were either out of the pool or in the pool under the water (Godden & Baddeley, 1975). Participants were then asked to remember the two lists in each of the two conditions. Words that were learned while out of the pool were remembered significantly better when the participants were out of the pool, and words that were learned underwater were more easily retrieved if the participants were underwater while trying to remember.

ENCODING SPECIFICITY: STATE-DEPENDENT LEARNING Physical surroundings at the time of encoding a memory are not the only kinds of cues that can help in retrieval. In another form of encoding specificity called *state-dependent learning*, memories formed during a particular physiological or psychological state will be easier to remember while in a similar state (Devitt & Schacter, 2018; Girden & Culler, 1937; Jovasevic et al., 2015). For example, when you are fighting with someone, it's much easier to remember all of the bad things that person has done than to remember the good times. In one study (Eich & Metcalfe, 1989), researchers had participants try to remember words that they had read while listening to music. Participants read one list of words while listening to sad music (influencing their mood to be sad) and another list of words while listening to happy music. When it came time to recall the lists, the researchers again manipulated the mood of the participants. The words that were read while participants were in a happy mood were remembered better if the manipulated mood was also happy but far less well if the mood was sad. The reverse was also true.

6.7 Recall and Recognition

6.7 Differentiate the retrieval processes of recall and recognition.

 Why do multiple-choice tests seem so much easier than essay tests?

There are two kinds of retrieval of memories, *recall* and *recognition*. It is the difference between these two retrieval methods that makes some kinds of exams seem harder than others. In **recall**, memories are retrieved with few or no external cues, such as filling in the blanks on an application form. **Recognition**, on the other hand, involves looking at or hearing information and matching it to what is already in memory. A word-search puzzle, in which the words are already written down in the grid and simply need to be circled, is an example of recognition. The following section takes a closer look at these two important processes.

RECALL: HMM ... LET ME THINK When someone is asked a question such as "Where were you born?" the question acts as the cue for retrieval of the answer. This is an example of recall, as are essay, short-answer, and fill-in-the-blank tests that are used to measure a person's memory for information (Borges et al., 1977; Gillund & Shiffrin, 1984; Raaijmakers & Shiffrin, 1992).

Whenever people find themselves struggling for an answer, recall has failed (at least temporarily). Sometimes the answer seems so very close to the surface of conscious thought that it feels like it's "on the tip of the tongue." (If people could just get their tongues out there far enough, they could read it.) This is sometimes called the *tip of the tongue (TOT)* phenomenon (Brown & McNeill, 1966; Burke et al., 1991; Forseth et al., 2018). Although people may be able to say how long the word is or name letters that start or even end the word, they cannot retrieve the sound or actual spelling of the word to allow it to be pulled into the auditory "recorder" of STM so that it can be fully retrieved.

recall
type of memory retrieval in which the information to be retrieved must be "pulled" from memory with very few external cues.

recognition
the ability to match a piece of information or a stimulus to a stored image or fact.

serial position effect
tendency of information at the beginning and end of a body of information to be remembered more accurately than information in the middle of the body of information.

This particular memory problem gets more common as we get older, although it should not be taken as a sign of oncoming dementia unless the increase is sudden (Osshera et al., 2012). Evidence now suggests that TOT may be a function of an area of the brain called the fusiform gyrus, part of the temporal and occipital lobes (Forseth et al., 2018). This is an area of the brain that is involved in several forms of dementia, including Alzheimer's, and people with this type of dementia often have trouble recalling the names of things.

How can a person overcome TOT? The best solution is the one "everyone" seems to know: Forget about it. When you "forget about it," the brain apparently continues to work on retrieval. Sometime later (perhaps when you run across a similar-sounding word in your surroundings), the word or name will just "pop out." This can make for interesting conversations, because when that particular word does "pop out," it usually has little to do with the current conversation.

Another interesting feature of recall is that it is often subject to a kind of "prejudice" of memory retrieval, in which information at the beginning and the end of a list, such as a poem or song, tends to be remembered more easily and accurately. This is called the **serial position effect** (Murdock, 1962).

A good demonstration of this phenomenon involves instructing people to listen to and try to remember words that are read to them that are spaced about 1 or 2 seconds apart. People typically use maintenance rehearsal by repeating each word in their heads. They are then asked to write as many of the words down as they can remember. If the frequency of recall for each word in the list is graphed, it will nearly always look like the graph in **Figure 6.6**.

Words at the very beginning of the list tend to be remembered better than those in the middle of the list. This effect is called the **primacy effect** and is due to the fact that the first few words, when the listener has nothing already in STM to interfere with their rehearsal, will receive far more rehearsal time than the words in the middle, which are constantly being replaced by the next word on the list (Craik, 1970; Murdock, 1962).

At the end of the graph there is another increase in recall. This is the **recency effect**; it is usually attributed to the fact that the last word or two was *just heard* and is still in short-term memory for easy retrieval, with no new words entering to push the most recent word or words out of memory (Bjork & Whitten, 1974; Murdock, 1962). The serial position effect works with many different kinds of information. In fact, business schools often teach their students that they should try not to be "in the middle" for job interviews. Going first or last in the interview process is much likelier to make a person's interview more memorable.

Can knowledge of the serial position effect be of help to students trying to remember the information they need for their classes? Yes—students can take advantage of the recency effect by skimming back over their notes just before an exam. Knowing that the middle of a list of information is more likely to be forgotten means that students should pay more attention to that middle, and breaking the study sessions up into smaller segments helps reduce the amount of "middle to muddle." (Students can also use *mnemonic strategies* to help offset this memory problem, as well as others. See Learning Objective PIA.6.) Watch the video *Methods for Remembering* for additional mnemonic strategies.

primacy effect
tendency to remember information at the beginning of a body of information better than the information that follows.

recency effect
tendency to remember information at the end of a body of information better than the information that precedes it.

These people are waiting to audition for a play. The person who auditioned first and the one who auditioned last have the greatest chance of being remembered when the time comes for the director to choose. The serial position effect will cause the impression made by the actors who come in the "middle" to be less memorable.

Figure 6.6 Serial Position Effect

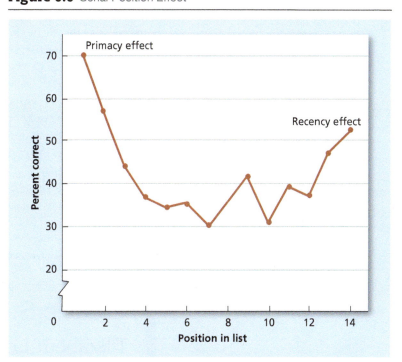

In the serial position effect, information at the beginning of a list will be recalled at a higher rate than information in the middle of the list (primacy effect), because the beginning information receives more rehearsal and may enter LTM. Information at the end of a list is also retrieved at a higher rate (recency effect), because the end of the list is still in STM, with no information coming after it to interfere with retrieval.

Watch Methods for Remembering

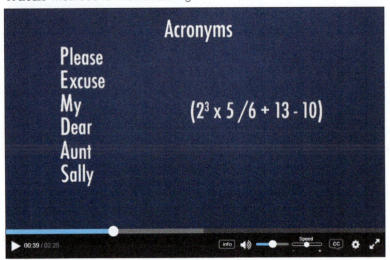

Watch the Video at MyLab Psychology

Speaking of students and classes, practicing retrieval is obviously very important to the process of learning. In education, this is often called the *testing effect*, the fact that long-term memory is increased when students practice retrieving the information to be learned (Karpicke & Blunt, 2011; Karpicke, 2012; Pyc et al., 2014; Roediger & Karpicke, 2006: Yang et al., 2018). Retrieval practice is essentially what testing is all about, so even though you might want to groan over yet another test your instructor hands out, be grateful—it's all in the best interests of memory!

RECOGNITION: HEY, DON'T I KNOW YOU FROM SOMEWHERE? The other form of memory retrieval is *recognition*, the ability to match a piece of information or a stimulus to a stored image or fact (Borges et al., 1977; Gillund & Shiffrin, 1984; Raaijmakers & Shiffrin, 1992). Recognition is usually much easier than recall because the cue is the actual object, word, sound, and so on that one is simply trying to detect as familiar and known. Examples of tests that use recognition are multiple-choice, matching, and true–false tests. The answer is right there and simply has to be matched to the information already in memory.

Recognition tends to be very accurate for images, especially human faces. In one study, more than 2,500 photographs were shown to participants at the rate of one every 10 seconds. Participants were then shown pairs of photographs in which one member of each pair was one of the previously seen photographs. Accuracy for identifying the previous photos was between 85 and 95 percent (Russell et al., 2009; Standing et al., 1970).

Recognition isn't foolproof, however. Sometimes, there is just enough similarity between a stimulus that is not already in memory and one that is in memory so that a *false positive* occurs (Kersten & Earles, 2016; Muter, 1978). A false positive occurs when a person thinks that he or she has recognized (or even recalled) something or someone but in fact does not have that something or someone in memory.

False positives can become disastrous in certain situations. In one case, in a series of armed robberies in Delaware, word had leaked out that the suspect sought by police might be a priest. When police put Father Bernard Pagano in a lineup for witnesses to identify, he was the only one in the lineup wearing a priest's collar. Seven eyewitnesses identified him as the man who had robbed them. Fortunately for Father Pagano, the real robber confessed to the crimes halfway through Pagano's trial (Loftus, 1987). Eyewitness recognition can be especially prone to false positives, although most people seem to think that "seeing is believing." Some research suggests that it is not the original, "pure" memory of the eyewitness that is at fault so much as it is the "contaminating" factors that come during retrieval of those memories, such as improperly managed police lineups or poorly conducted interviews of the eyewitness (Wixted et al., 2018). For more about the problems with eyewitnesses, see the following *Classic Studies in Psychology*.

AP 5.C Identify the contributions of key researchers in cognitive psychology.

Classic Studies in Psychology
Elizabeth Loftus and Eyewitnesses

Elizabeth Loftus is a distinguished professor of social ecology, a professor of law, and a professor of cognitive science at the University of California in Irvine. For more than 30 years, Dr. Loftus has been one of the world's leading researchers in the area of memory. Her focus has been on the accuracy of recall of memories—or rather, the inaccuracies of memory retrieval. She has been an expert witness or consultant in hundreds of trials, including that of Ted Bundy, the serial killer who eventually was executed in Florida (Neimark, 1996).

Loftus and many others have demonstrated time and again that memory is not an unchanging, stable process but rather is a constantly changing one. People continually update and revise their memories of events without being aware that they are doing so, and they incorporate information gained after the actual event, whether correct or incorrect.

Here is a summary of one of Loftus's classic studies concerning the ways in which eyewitness testimony can be influenced by information given after the event in question (Loftus, 1975).

In this experiment, Loftus showed participants a 3-minute video clip taken from the movie *Diary of a Student Revolution*. In this clip, eight demonstrators run into a classroom and eventually leave after interrupting the professor's lecture in a noisy confrontation. At the end of the video, two questionnaires were distributed containing one key question and 90 "filler" questions. The key question for half of the participants was, "Was the leader of the four demonstrators who entered the classroom a male?" The other half were asked, "Was the leader of the twelve demonstrators who entered the classroom a male?" One week later, a new set of questions was given to all participants in which the key question was, "How many demonstrators did you see entering the classroom?" Participants who were previously asked the question incorrectly giving the number as "four" stated an average recall of 6.4 people, whereas those who were asked the question incorrectly giving the number as "twelve" recalled an average of 8.9 people. Loftus concluded that participants were trying to compromise the memory of what they had actually seen—eight demonstrators—with later information. This study, along with the Father Pagano story and many others, clearly demonstrates the heart of Loftus's research: What people see and hear about an event after the fact can easily affect the accuracy of their memories of that event.

Dr. Elizabeth Loftus is an internationally known expert on the accuracy of eyewitness testimony. She is often called on to testify in court cases.

Questions for Further Discussion

1. How might police officers taking statements about a crime avoid getting inaccurate information from eyewitnesses?

2. The Innocence Project (**www.innocenceproject.org**) helps prisoners prove their innocence through DNA testing. More than 300 people in the United States have been freed by this testing, and the average time they served in prison before release is 13 years. Is eyewitness testimony enough, or should DNA evidence be required for sending someone to prison?

6.8 Automatic Encoding: Flashbulb Memories

6.8 Describe how some memories are automatically encoded into long-term memory.

Although some long-term memories need extensive maintenance rehearsal or effortful encoding in the form of elaborative rehearsal to enter from STM into LTM, many other kinds of long-term memories seem to enter permanent storage with little or no effort at all, in a kind of **automatic encoding** (Kvavilashvili et al., 2009; Mandler, 1967; Schneider et al., 1984). People unconsciously notice and seem able to remember a lot of things, such as the passage of time, knowledge of physical space, and frequency of events. For example, a person might make no effort to remember how many times cars have passed down the street but when asked can give an answer of "often," "more than usual," or "hardly any."

A special kind of automatic encoding takes place when an unexpected event or episode in a person's life has strong emotional associations, such as fear, horror, or joy. Memories of highly emotional events can often seem vivid and detailed, as if the person's

AP 5.A Compare and contrast various cognitive processes.

AP 5.D Outline the principles that underlie construction and encoding of memories.

automatic encoding

tendency of certain kinds of information to enter long-term memory with little or no effortful encoding.

Flashbulb memories are as vivid and detailed as if your mind took a snapshot picture of the moment in time. While your cell phone uses a flash, cameras used to use a flashbulb to highlight their subjects, hence the term "flashbulb memory."

flashbulb memories
type of automatic encoding that occurs because an unexpected event has strong emotional associations for the person remembering it.

mind took a "flash picture" of the moment in time. These kinds of memories are called **flashbulb memories** (Hirst & Phelps, 2016; Kraha & Boals, 2014; Neisser, 1982; Neisser & Harsch, 1992; Winningham et al., 2000).

Many people share certain flashbulb memories. People of the "baby boomer" generation remember exactly where they were when the news came that President John F. Kennedy had been shot or the moment that Neil Armstrong first stepped on the surface of the moon. Millennials may remember the horrific events of September 11, 2001 and younger generations the 2018 massacre at Marjory Stoneman Douglas High School in Parkland, Florida. But personal flashbulb memories also exist. These memories tend to be major positive or negative emotional events, such as a first date, graduation, an embarrassing event, or a particularly memorable birthday party.

Why do flashbulb memories seem so vivid and exact? The answer seems to lie in the emotions felt at the time of the event. Emotional reactions stimulate the release of hormones that have been shown to enhance the formation of long-term memories (Dolcos et al., 2005; McEwen, 2000; McGaugh, 2004; Sharot et al., 2004). There may also be certain memory-enhancing proteins released during the formation of this kind of memory (Korneev et al., 2018). But is this kind of memory really all that accurate? Although some researchers have found evidence for a high degree of accuracy in flashbulb memories of *major events*, such as the 2016 presidential election or the tragic death of actress/writer Carrie Fisher in the same year, others have found that while such memories are often convincingly real, they are just as subject to decay and alterations over time as other kinds of memories (Neisser & Harsch, 1992). In fact, the memory of highly stressful events such as experiencing a crime has been shown to be less accurate than other memories (Loftus, 1975). Apparently, no memories are completely accurate after the passage of time. The next section will discuss some of the reasons for faulty memories.

6.9 The Reconstructive Nature of Long-Term Memory Retrieval: How Reliable Are Memories?

6.9 Explain how the constructive processing view of memory retrieval accounts for forgetting and inaccuracies in memory.

> 💬 I think my memory is pretty good, but my brother and I often have arguments about things that happened when we were kids. Why don't we have the same exact memories? We were both there!

People tend to assume that their memories are accurate when, in fact, memories are revised, edited, and altered on an almost continuous basis. The reason for the changes that occur in memory has to do with the way in which memories are formed as well as how they are retrieved.

CONSTRUCTIVE PROCESSING OF MEMORIES Many people have the idea that when they recall a memory, they are recalling it as if it were an "instant replay." As new memories are created in LTM, old memories can get "lost," but they are more likely to be changed or altered in some way (Baddeley, 1988). In reality, memories (including those very vivid flashbulb memories) are never quite accurate, and the more time that passes, the more inaccuracies creep in. The early twentieth-century memory schema theorist Sir Frederic Bartlett (1932) saw the process of memory as more similar to creating a story than reading one already written. He viewed memory as a problem-solving activity in which the person tries to retrieve the particulars of some past event, or the problem, by using current knowledge and inferring from evidence to create the memory or the solution (Kihlstrom, 2002a).

Carrie Fisher died on December 27, 2016, after suffering a medical emergency while on a flight from London to Los Angeles. Events like this are so emotional for many people that the memories for the event are stored automatically, as if the mind had taken a "flash" picture of that moment in time. Such "flashbulb" memories seem to be very accurate but are actually no more accurate than any other memory.

Elizabeth Loftus, along with other researchers (Hyman, 1993; Hyman & Loftus, 1998, 2002), has provided ample evidence for the **constructive processing** view of memory retrieval. In this view, memories are literally "built," or reconstructed, from the information stored away during encoding. Each time a memory is retrieved, it may be altered or revised in some way to include new information or to exclude details that may be left out of the new reconstruction.

An example of how memories are reconstructed occurs when people, upon learning the details of a particular event, revise their memories to reflect their feeling that they "knew it all along." They will discard any incorrect information they actually had and replace it with more accurate information gained after the fact. This tendency of people to falsely believe that they would have accurately predicted an outcome without having been told about it in advance is called **hindsight bias** (Bahrick et al., 1996; Hoffrage et al., 2000; Von der Beck et al., 2017). People who have ever done some "Monday morning quarterbacking" by saying that they knew all along who would win the game have fallen victim to hindsight bias.

AP 5.G Describe strategies for memory improvement and typical memory errors.

These men may engage in "Monday morning quarterbacking" as they apply hindsight to their memories of this game. Their memories of the game may be altered by information they get afterward from the television, social media, or their friends.

THINKING CRITICALLY 6.2

Think about the last time you argued with a family member about something that happened when you were younger. How might hindsight bias have played a part in your differing memories of the event?

MEMORY RETRIEVAL PROBLEMS Some people may say that they have "total recall." What they usually mean is that they feel that their memories are more accurate than those of other people. As should be obvious by now, true total recall is not a very likely ability for anyone to have. Here are some reasons people have trouble recalling information accurately.

THE MISINFORMATION EFFECT Police investigators sometimes try to keep eyewitnesses to crimes or accidents from talking with each other. The reason is that if one person tells the other about something she has seen, the other person may later "remember" that same detail, even though he did not actually see it at the time. Such false memories are created by a person being exposed to information after the event. That misleading information can become part of the actual memory, affecting its accuracy (Loftus et al., 1978). This is called the **misinformation effect**. Loftus, in addition to her studies concerning eyewitness testimony, has also done several similar studies that demonstrate the misinformation effect. In one study, participants viewed a slide presentation of a traffic accident. The actual slide presentation contained a stop sign, but in a written summary of the presentation, the sign was referred to as a yield sign. Participants who were given this misleading information after viewing the slides were far less accurate in their memories for the kind of sign present than were participants given no such information. One of the interesting points made by this study is that information that comes not only after the original event but also in an entirely different format (i.e., written instead of visual) can cause memories of the event to be incorrectly reconstructed.

FALSE MEMORY SYNDROME If memory gets edited and changed when individuals are in a state of waking consciousness, alert and making an effort to retrieve information, how much more might memory be changed when individuals are being influenced by others or in an altered state of consciousness, such as hypnosis? *False-memory syndrome* refers to the creation of inaccurate or false memories through the suggestion of others, often while the person is under hypnosis (Frenda et al., 2014; Hochman, 1994; Laney & Loftus, 2013; Roediger & McDermott, 1995).

For example, research has shown that, although hypnosis may make it easier to recall some real memories, it also makes it easier to create false memories. Hypnosis also has been found to increase the confidence people have in their memories, regardless of whether those memories are real or false (Bowman, 1996). False memories have been accidentally created by therapists' suggestions during hypnotic therapy sessions. See Learning Objective 4.9. Some research even suggests that a simple relaxed state such as mindfulness meditation

constructive processing

referring to the retrieval of memories in which those memories are altered, revised, or influenced by newer information.

hindsight bias

the tendency to falsely believe, through revision of older memories to include newer information, that one could have correctly predicted the outcome of an event.

misinformation effect

the tendency of misleading information presented after an event to alter the memories of the event itself.

can also increase the tendency to experience false memories (Wilson et al., 2015). For more information on false-memory syndrome, visit the Web site at **www.fmsfonline.org**.

Research suggests that false memories are created in the brain in much the same way as real memories are formed, especially when visual images are involved (Gonsalves et al., 2004). Researchers, using fMRI scans, looked at brain activity of individuals who were looking at real visual images and then were asked to imagine looking at visual images. They found that these same individuals were often unable to later distinguish between the images they had really seen and the imagined images when asked to remember which images were real or imagined. This might explain why asking people if they saw a particular person at a crime scene (causing them to imagine the image of that person) might affect the memories those people have of the crime when questioned sometime later—the person they were asked to think about may be falsely remembered as having been present. Other evidence suggests that false memories have much in common with the confabulations (stories that are made up but not intended to deceive) of people with dementia-related memory problems and that both forms of false memories involve a lower-than-normal level of activity in the part of the frontal lobe associated with doubt and skepticism (Mendez & Fras, 2011). Clearly, memories obtained through hypnosis should not be considered accurate without solid evidence from other sources.

> But I've heard about people who under hypnosis remember being abused as children. Aren't those memories sometimes real?

The fact that some people recover false memories under certain conditions does not mean that child molestation does not really happen; nor does it mean that a person who was molested might not push that unwanted memory away from conscious thought. Molestation is a sad fact, with one conservative estimate stating that nearly 20 percent of all females and 7 percent of all males have experienced molestation during childhood (Abel & Osborn, 1992; Finkelhor et al., 2014). There are also many therapists and psychological professionals who are quite skilled at helping clients remember events of the past without suggesting possible false memories, and they find that clients do remember information and events that were true and able to be verified but were previously unavailable to the client (Dalenberg, 1996). False-memory syndrome is not only harmful to the persons directly involved but also makes it much more difficult for genuine victims of molestation to be believed when they do recover their memories of the painful traumas of childhood.

As these young people casually observe the activity outside, they are storing some of the things they see in memory while ignoring others. If they were to witness an accident involving a pedestrian or vehicle, how would investigators know if their memories of the events were accurate? Would hypnotizing either of them to help them remember be effective? Why or why not?

So can we trust any of our memories at all? There is evidence to suggest that false memories cannot be created for just any kind of memory content, and that false memories are harder to construct than real ones. The *memories* must at least be plausible, according to the research of cognitive psychologist and memory expert Kathy Pezdek, who with her colleagues has done several studies demonstrating the resistance of children to the creation of implausible false memories (Hyman et al., 1998; Pezdek et al., 1997; Pezdek & Blandón-Gitlin, 2017; Pezdek & Hodge, 1999).

In the 1999 study, Pezdek and Hodge asked children to read five different summaries of childhood events. Two of these events were false, but only one of the two false events was plausible (e.g., getting lost). Although the children were told that all of the events happened to them as small children, the results indicated that the plausible false events were significantly more likely to be "remembered" as false memories than were the implausible false events (e.g., getting a rectal enema). A second experiment (Pezdek & Hodge, 1999) found similar results: Children were significantly less likely to form a false memory for an implausible false event than for a plausible false event.

The idea that only plausible events can become false memories runs contrary to the earlier work of Loftus and colleagues and to research concerning some very implausible false memories that have been successfully implanted, such as a memory for satanic rituals and alien abductions (Finkelstein, 2017; Mack, 1994). Loftus and colleagues (Mazzoni et al., 2001) conducted several experiments in which they found that implausible events could be made more plausible by having the experimenters provide false feedback to the participants, who read articles telling of the implausible events as if they had actually happened to other people. The false feedback involved telling the participants that their responses to a questionnaire about fears were typical of people who had been through one of the false events (much as a well-meaning therapist might suggest to a client that certain anxieties and feelings are typical of someone who has been abused). These manipulations were so successful that participants not only developed false memories for the events but also even contradicted their own earlier statements in which they denied having these experiences in childhood. The researchers concluded that there are two steps that must occur before people will be likely to interpret their thoughts and fantasies about false events as true memories:

1. The event must be made to seem as plausible as possible.
2. Individuals are given information that helps them believe that the event could have happened to them personally.

The personality of the individual reporting such a memory also matters, it seems. In one study, people who claimed to have been abducted by aliens (an implausible event) were compared to a control group with no such memories on a measure of false-memory recall and false recognition. Those who reported recovered memories of alien abduction were far more likely to recall or recognize items that were false than were the controls (Clancy et al., 2002). Other variables that predicted a higher false recall and recognition response were susceptibility to hypnosis, symptoms of depression, and the tendency to exhibit odd behavior and unusual beliefs (such as past-life regression or the healing ability of crystals).

Concept Map L.O. 6.6, 6.7, 6.8, 6.9

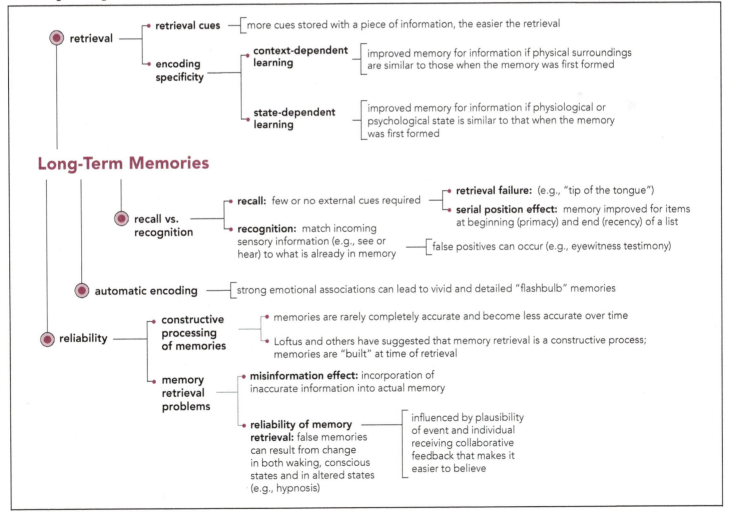

Practice Quiz — How much do you remember?

Pick the best answer.

1. What concept suggests that the best place to study for your psychology final to ensure good retrieval of concepts is your psychology classroom?
   a. serial position effect
   b. tip-of-the-tongue phenomenon
   c. encoding specificity
   d. primacy effect
   e. automatic encoding

2. Kyle had written a grocery list but accidentally left it at home. Trying to remember the list, Kyle remembers what was at the beginning of the list and what was at the end but not those things in the middle. This is an example of _____.
   a. flashbulb memory
   b. the middle-of-the list effect
   c. encoding specificity
   d. the tip-of-the-tongue effect
   e. the serial position effect

3. Multiple-choice test questions typically rely on _____, while essay questions rely on _____.
   a. deep processing, shallow processing
   b. recognition, recall
   c. rehearsal, recall
   d. relearning, rehearsing
   e. recall, recognition

4. Jaycee can recall with great detail the day of her wedding and all that occurred. What might psychologists say about these particular flashbulb memories?
   a. The memories should last up to 15 to 20 years.
   b. The memories were likely enhanced in part by the hormones released during emotional moments.
   c. They are stored as semantic memories.
   d. The memories are unusually accurate.
   e. They are stored as nondeclarative memories.

5. In Loftus's 1978 study, participants viewed a slide presentation of an accident. Later, some of the participants were asked a question about a yield sign when the actual slides contained pictures of a stop sign. When presented with this inaccurate information, how did these participants typically respond?
   a. Participants denied participating in the study.
   b. Many participants' overall accuracy dropped when confronted with conflicting information.
   c. Most corrected Loftus and recalled seeing a stop sign.
   d. Many began seeing both a stop sign and a yield sign.
   e. Participants were confused, but only briefly, at which point their accuracy of recalling the event returned.

6. A key component for any person to believe that a false event is in fact true is to make sure that the false information is _____.
   a. introduced by a source perceived as trustworthy
   b. introduced as soon after the event as possible
   c. as plausible as possible
   d. is obviously not possible
   e. introduced no sooner than 24 hours after the event but no later than 15 days

---

APA Goal 2: Scientific Inquiry and Critical Thinking

Effects of Supplements on Memory

Addresses APA Learning Objectives 2.1: Use scientific reasoning to interpret psychological phenomena, and 2.3: Engage in innovative and integrative thinking and problem solving.

More and more people are turning to various supplements that promise to improve memory, ward off or even alleviate Alzheimer's, and prevent other forms of cognitive decline. But what does science say about the claims of these various supplements? Are they really helpful? Could they be harmful? Here's a look at some of the more popular supplements and the research examining their claims.

Gingko Biloba

The gingko biloba supplement is an extract from the leaf of the gingko biloba tree. The Chinese have used this supplement for thousands of years to improve various aspects of health, and you might think that anything that people have used for that long must work, right? But think about other reasons that people might continue to use a dietary supplement that have little or nothing to do with actual health results. It's a cultural habit and tradition, for example. People may take the supplement and think they feel better or think better because of the placebo effect. See Learning Objective 1.10. The only way to really know if gingko biloba actually has any positive effect on memory is to look at the scientific research.

So what does the research say? There are numerous studies over the past decade that strongly indicate the failure of gingko biloba supplements in improving memory in healthy people or in preventing dementia-related memory problems such as those found in Alzheimer's disease (Birks & Evans, 2009; Cooper et al., 2013; Laws et al., 2012; Mancuso et al., 2012; Snitz et al., 2009). A large review of current research did find that the extract may slow the decline in cognitive abilities, including memory, for people who already have symptoms of dementia (Tan et al., 2015). The conclusion: Don't bother with this supplement unless you actually have dementia, and even then your doctor should be monitoring you for possible side effects. This supplement can change your insulin levels, make bleeding harder to stop, increase bruising, blur vision, cause any number of gastric distress symptoms, affect your sense of taste, cause fluid retention—the list goes on.

Coconut Oil and Fish Oil

Another popular type of supplement is coconut oil, an extract from the meat of coconuts that is high in saturated fat. While there are many health claims for this supplement, the one we will examine is the claim that consuming coconut oil can treat and even cure Alzheimer's disease. This claim is based on the idea that people with Alzheimer's disease have neurons in their brains that cannot use glucose (blood sugar) properly, leading to "starving" brain cells. Coconut oil is supposed to provide an alternative energy source for these cells, but at the present time the scientific evidence has yielded mixed results (Connor et al., 2012; Naqvi et al., 2013). A clinical trial in the United States has just been completed, but the results are not yet available.

So is it safe to take coconut oil? It is a saturated fat, and high cholesterol levels may occur with the accompanying increased risk of stroke, heart disease, and—ironically—dementia. If you do not have Alzheimer's or another dementia, taking coconut oil may not do much of anything except adversely affect your blood work on your next trip to the doctor.

Fish oil supplements have a slightly better track record for helping slow the rates of cognitive decline in people with Alzheimer's disease but may do very little for healthy people or children (Connor et al., 2012; Daiello et al., 2014; Montgomery et al., 2018). The safest advice to improve your memory and possibly prevent or postpone any symptoms of dementia may simply be to remain mentally and physically active (Naqvi et al., 2013). Get some exercise, work crossword puzzles, read, and keep those neurons firing!

APA Goal 2 Effects of Supplements on Memory

Which of the following supplements or activities are supported by science and which are not? Sort each item into the correct column.
- *Physical exercise*
- *Vitamin E*
- *Coenzyme Q10*
- *Word games*
- *Fish oil*
- *Coconut oil*
- *Ginkgo biloba*
- *Crossword puzzles*
- *Ginseng*
- *B vitamins*

Supported by Science	Not Supported by Science

AP 5.G Describe strategies for memory improvement and typical memory errors.

6.10–6.11 What Were We Talking About? Forgetting

💬 Why do we forget things? And why do we forget some things but not others?

Watch Reasons for Forgetting

👁 Watch the Video at MyLab Psychology

Most of us, at some point in our busy lives, have trouble remembering things, especially events from the distant past. What if you could remember nearly every day of your life? This rare ability is possessed by Brad Williams, who is known as the "Human Google." Brad is one of a small group of individuals with a syndrome called *hyperthymesia* (hī-per-thī-mē-sē-uh). A person with hyperthymesia not only has an astonishing and rare ability to recall specific events from his or her personal past but also spends an unusually large amount of time thinking about that personal past. Brad can recall almost any news event or personal event he himself has experienced, particularly specific dates—and even the weather on those dates.

You may think that being able to remember everything like Brad Williams would be wonderful. But it's important to consider that people with hyperthymesia not only have the ability to remember nearly everything but also have the inability to *forget*. The ability to forget may be nearly as vital to human thought processes as the ability to remember. William James, one of the founders of the field of psychology, said, "If we remembered everything, we should on most occasions be as ill off as if we remembered nothing" (James, 1890, 2002). *Adaptive forgetting* is the idea that being able to suppress information that we no longer need makes it easier to remember what we do need (Kuhl et al., 2007; MacLeod, 1998; Nairne, 2015; Wimber et al., 2015.) Learn more about Brad Williams and hyperthymesia in the video *Reasons for Forgetting*.

A similar problem was experienced in the case of A. R. Luria's (1968) famous *mnemonist*, Mr. S. (A mnemonist is a memory expert or someone with exceptional memory ability.) Mr. S. was a performing mnemonist, astonishing his audiences with lists of numbers that he memorized in minutes. But Mr. S. found that he *was unable to forget* the lists. He also could not easily separate important memories from trivial ones, and each time he looked at an object or read a word, images stimulated by that object or word would flood his mind. He eventually invented a way to "forget" things—by writing them on a piece of paper and then burning the paper (Luria, 1968).

The ability to forget seems necessary to one's sanity if the experience of Mr. S. is any indicator. But how fast do people forget things? Are there some things that are harder or easier to forget?

AP 5.C Identify the contributions of key researchers in cognitive psychology.

6.10 Ebbinghaus and the Forgetting Curve

6.10 Describe the "curve of forgetting."

Hermann Ebbinghaus (1913) was one of the first researchers to study forgetting. Because he did not want any verbal associations to aid him in remembering, he created several lists of "nonsense syllables," pronounceable but meaningless (such as GEX and WOL). He memorized a list, waited a specific amount of time, and then tried to retrieve the

Figure 6.7 Curve of Forgetting

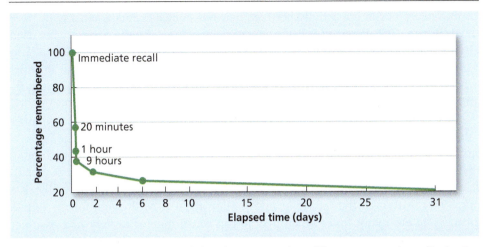

Ebbinghaus found that his recall of words from his memorized word lists was greatest immediately after learning the list but rapidly decreased within the first hour. After the first hour, forgetting leveled off.

list, graphing his results each time. The result has become a familiar graph: the **curve of forgetting**. This graph clearly shows that forgetting happens quickly within the first hour after learning the lists and then tapers off gradually (see **Figure 6.7**). In other words, forgetting is greatest just after learning. This curve can be applied to other types of information as well. Although meaningful material is forgotten much more slowly and much less completely, the pattern obtained when testing for forgetting is similar (Conway et al., 1992).

In his early studies, Ebbinghaus (1885) found that it is also important not to try to "cram" information you want to remember into your brain. Research has found that spacing out one's study sessions, or **distributed practice**, will produce far better retrieval of information studied in this way than does *massed practice*, or the attempt to study a body of material all at once. For example, studying your psychology material for 3 hours may make you feel that you've done some really hard work, and you have. Unfortunately, you won't remember as much of what you studied as you would if you had shorter study times of 30 minutes to an hour followed by short breaks (Cepeda et al., 2006; Dempster & Farris, 1990; Donovan & Radosevich, 1999; Simon & Bjork, 2001). See Learning Objective PIA.5.

6.11 Reasons We Forget

6.11 Identify some common reasons people forget things.

There are several reasons people forget things. We'll examine three theories here.

ENCODING FAILURE One of the simplest is that some things never get encoded in the first place. Your friend, for example, may have said something to you as he walked out the door, and you may have heard him, but if you weren't paying attention to what he said, it would not get past sensory memory. This isn't forgetting so much as it is **encoding failure**, the failure to process information into memory. Researchers (Nickerson & Adams, 1979) developed a test of long-term memory using images of a common object for many people, a penny. Look at **Figure 6.8**. Which view of a stop sign is the correct one? People see stop signs nearly every day, but how many people actually look at them that closely so the information is encoded into long-term memory?

curve of forgetting
a graph showing a distinct pattern in which forgetting is very fast within the first hour after learning a list and then tapers off gradually.

distributed practice
spacing the study of material to be remembered by including breaks between study periods.

encoding failure
failure to process information into memory.

Figure 6.8 Stop!

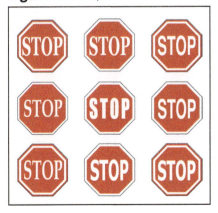

Many people look at stop signs multiple times a day. Which of these stop signs is closest to an actual stop sign? The answer can be found on the next page.

memory trace

physical change in the brain that occurs when a memory is formed.

decay

loss of memory due to the passage of time, during which the memory trace is not used.

disuse

another name for decay, assuming that memories that are not used will eventually decay and disappear.

The fact that these women can remember the events shown in the pictures in these photo albums even after many years makes it unlikely that the memory trace decay theory can explain all forgetting in long-term memory.

MEMORY TRACE DECAY THEORY One of the older theories of forgetting involves the concept of a **memory trace**. A memory trace is some physical change in the brain, perhaps in a neuron or in the activity between neurons, which occurs when a memory is formed (Brown, 1958; Peterson & Peterson, 1959). Over time, if these traces are not used, they may **decay**, fading into nothing. It would be similar to what happens when a number of people walk across a particular patch of grass, causing a path to appear in which the grass is trampled down and perhaps turning brown. But if people stop using the path, the grass grows back and the path disappears.

Forgetting in sensory memory and short-term memory seems easy to explain as decay: Information that is not brought to attention in sensory memory or continuously rehearsed in STM will fade away. But is decay a good explanation for forgetting from long-term memory? When referring to LTM, decay theory is usually called **disuse**, and the phrase "use it or lose it" takes on great meaning (Bjork & Bjork, 1992). Although the fading of information from LTM through disuse sounds logical, there are many times when people can recall memories they had assumed were long forgotten. There must be other factors involved in the forgetting of long-term memories.

INTERFERENCE THEORY A possible explanation of LTM forgetting is that although most long-term memories may be stored more or less permanently in the brain, those memories may not always be accessible to attempted retrieval because other information interferes (Anderson & Neely, 1996). (And even memories that are accessible are subject to constructive processing, which can lead to inaccurate recall.) An analogy might be this: The can of paint that Phillip wants may very well be on some shelf in his storeroom, but there's so much other junk in its way that he can't see it and can't get to it. In the case of LTM, interference can come from two different "directions."

PROACTIVE INTERFERENCE Have you needed to use your new password but had trouble remembering it because you kept remembering bits of the old one? The reason you experience difficulty is called **proactive interference**: the tendency for older or previously learned material to interfere with the learning (and subsequent retrieval) of new material (see **Figure 6.9**).

Another example of proactive interference often occurs when someone gets a new cell phone number. People in this situation often find themselves remembering their old cell phone number or some of its digits instead of the new cell phone number when they are trying to give the new number to friends.

RETROACTIVE INTERFERENCE When newer information interferes with the retrieval of older information, this is called **retroactive interference** (see **Figure 6.9**). What happens if you find you need to remember that old password, maybe to get into an older tablet or phone? You might have trouble remembering the old one, retrieving bits of the newer password instead, because the newer information retroactively interferes with remembering the old information.

How might interference work in each of the following cases?

1. Moving from the United States to England, where people drive on the left instead of the right side of the road.
2. Trying to use your old Amazon Fire TV® remote after having used your newer Roku® remote for a year.
3. Moving from one type of cell phone system to another, such as going from an iPhone® to an Android® system.

The different ways that forgetting occurs are summarized in **Table 6.1**.

Figure 6.9 Proactive and Retroactive Interference

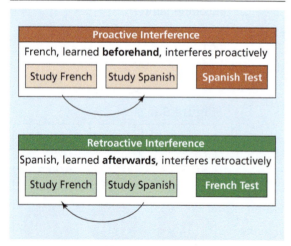

If a student were to study for a French exam and then a Spanish exam, interference could occur in two directions. When taking the Spanish exam, the French information studied first may proactively interfere with the learning of the new Spanish information. But when taking the French exam, the more recently studied Spanish information may retroactively interfere with the retrieval of the French information.

The answer to **Figure 6.8** is the middle right image.

Table 6.1 Reasons for Forgetting

Reason	Description
Encoding Failure	The information is not attended to and fails to be encoded.
Decay or Disuse	Information that is not accessed decays from the storage system over time.
Proactive Interference	Older information already in memory interferes with the learning of newer information.
Retroactive Interference	Newer information interferes with the retrieval of older information.

proactive interference
memory problem that occurs when older information prevents or interferes with the learning or retrieval of newer information.

retroactive interference
memory problem that occurs when newer information prevents or interferes with the retrieval of older information.

Concept Map L.O. 6.10, 6.11

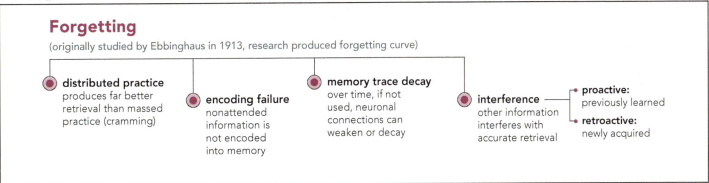

Practice Quiz   How much do you remember?

Pick the best answer.

1. Camille has just finished learning a list of nonsense words given to her by her psychology instructor as part of a class activity. She had 100 percent recall at the end of class. According to Ebbinghaus's curve of forgetting, how quickly will Camille likely forget about 40 percent of the information she has just learned?
   a. within the first day after leaving the class
   b. nearly a week after the class
   c. within the first 20 minutes after leaving the class
   d. nearly 12 months after the class
   e. nearly a month after the class

2. Cade is asked to repeat what his mother just told him. He says he "forgot," but in reality Cade wasn't paying attention to his mother at all. This is an example of the _____ explanation of forgetting.
   a. proactive interference
   b. memory trace
   c. encoding failure
   d. retroactive interference
   e. repression

3. Nicole spent a year living abroad in Spain. During that time, her ability to read and speak Spanish grew tremendously. However, now, 2 years later, Nicole feels she can no longer travel there because she can barely remember a thing. Her problem is most likely due to _____.
   a. encoding failure
   b. decay theory
   c. consolidation failure
   d. retroactive interference
   e. proactive interference

4. Yvonne bought a fancy new smartphone. It was a different brand of phone than her old phone, so she spent quite a few frustrating hours learning to use the new one. The problem was that she kept trying to tap icons on the new phone in the places they had been on her old phone. Yvonne's problem was most likely due to _____.
   a. old age
   b. proactive interference
   c. encoding failure
   d. retroactive interference
   e. decay theory

6.12–6.13 Neuroscience of Memory

Researchers have evidence that specific areas of the brain may be the places in which memories are physically formed and that these areas are different for different types of memory.

AP 5.B Describe and differentiate psychological and physiological systems of memory.

AP 5.H Describe and differentiate psychological and physiological systems of short- and long-term memory.

6.12 The Biological Bases of Memory

6.12 Explain the biological bases of memory in the brain.

Nondeclarative memories seem to be stored in the cerebellum (Boyd & Winstein, 2004; Daum & Schugens, 1996). Research involving PET scanning techniques strongly suggests that short-term memories are stored in the prefrontal cortex (the very front of the frontal lobe) and the temporal lobe (Goldman-Rakic, 1998; Rao et al., 1997). Memories related to fear seem to be stored in the amygdala (Dębiec et al., 2010). Sensory information appears to be temporarily stored in the thalamus for processing before heading for the higher cortical areas of the brain (Mease et al., 2016).

As for semantic and episodic long-term memories, evidence suggests that these memories are also stored in the frontal and temporal lobes but not in exactly the same places, nor in the same location as short-term memories (Binder et al., 2009; Weis et al., 2004). Furthermore, storage and retrieval are aided by other brain areas. For example, episodic memory retrieval seems to be partly a function of the *posterior parietal cortex*, an area at the very back of the parietal lobe (Sestieri et al., 2017), while both encoding and retrieval of episodic memories seem related to activity in the *posterior cingulate cortex*, an area located above and toward the rear of the corpus callosum in each hemisphere (Lega et al., 2017). See Learning Objective 2.7.

💬 All that explains is the "where" of memory. Did scientists ever find out the "what" or the exact physical change that happens in the brain when memories are stored?

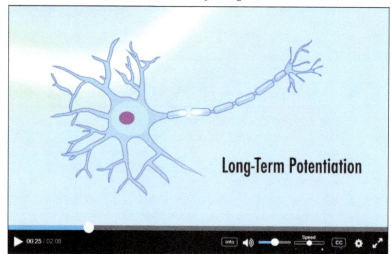

Watch The Neuroscience of Memory: Long-Term Potentiation

👁 Watch the Video at MyLab Psychology

Several studies have offered evidence that memory is not simply one physical change but many: changes in the number of receptor sites, changes in the sensitivity of the synapse through repeated stimulation (called *long-term potentiation*), and changes in the dendrites and specifically in the proteins within the neurons (Alkon, 1989; Kandel & Schwartz, 1982; Squire & Kandel, 1999). The changes underlying synaptic plasticity and memory storage have been attributed to six molecular mechanisms (*cAMP, PKA, CRE, CREB-1* and *CREB-2, CPEB*) that signify information changing from short-term memory to long-term memory, and apply to both explicit and implicit memory (Kandel, 2012). In addition to multiple changes occurring, changes in synaptic function have to occur across collections of neurons as part of a larger circuit (Kandel, 2012). Collectively, the synaptic alterations, changes in neuronal structure, protein synthesis, and other changes that take place as a memory is forming are called **consolidation** (Deger et al., 2012; Fioriti et al., 2015; Griggs et al., 2013; Hill et al., 2015; Krüttner et al., 2012). Consolidation may take only a few minutes for some memories, such as learning a new friend's name, but may take years for others, such as learning a new language (Dudai, 2004). Sleep, particularly N2 sleep in which we first see the appearance of bursts of activity called sleep spindles (see Learning Objective 4.5) may be of significant importance in the consolidation and refinement of recently acquired information (Cairney et al., 2018). For more on long-term potentiation and consolidation, watch the video *The Neuroscience of Memory: Long-Term Potentiation*.

In the discussion of the *hippocampus* (a part of the limbic system) in Chapter Two, it was identified as the part of the brain that is responsible for the formation of new

consolidation

the changes that take place in the structure and functioning of neurons when a memory is formed.

long-term declarative memories. One of the clearest pieces of evidence of this function comes from the study of a man known as H.M. (Milner et al., 1968).

H.M. was 16 when he began to suffer from severe epileptic seizures. Eleven years later, H.M.'s hippocampi and adjacent medial temporal lobe structures were removed in an experimental operation that the surgeon hoped would stop his seizures. The last thing H.M. could remember was being rolled to the operating room, and from then on his ability to form new declarative memories was profoundly impaired. The hippocampus was not the source of his problem (his seizures were reduced but not eliminated), but it was apparently the source of his ability to consolidate and store any new factual information he encountered, because without either hippocampus, he was completely unable to remember new events or facts. Consolidation had become impossible. He had a magazine that he carried around, reading and rereading the stories, because each time he did so the stories were completely new to him. As with most amnesic patients of this type (although H.M.'s case was quite severe), his nondeclarative memory was still intact.* It was only new declarative memory—both semantic and episodic—that was lost. H.M., who can now be revealed as Henry Gustav Molaison, died in December 2008 at the age of 82. His experience and his brain continue to educate students and neuroscientists, as he agreed many years ago that his brain would be donated for further scientific study upon his death. To learn more about the H.M. postmortem project, go to **thebrainobservatory.org/project-hm**

AP 2.K Recount historic and contemporary research strategies and technologies that support research.

There is some evidence that memories of the same event may involve different areas of the hippocampus (Collin et al., 2015). The different areas seem to correspond to different degrees of memory detail for the event, such as remembering reading a specific text message from your partner before going to class (a fine detail) or recalling going out to eat after class (a broader event).

The posterior cingulate cortex also seems to be involved in the formation of long-term memories. See Learning Objective 2.7. This is one of the areas of the brain that shows damage in people with Alzheimer's disease. It is involved in consolidation, as researchers have found evidence that the posterior cingulate is not only activated when engaging in active rehearsal to first remember specific information, but it is also active when retrieving that memory (Bird et al., 2015). Furthermore, improved memory appears to be related to how similar brain activity during retrieval is to the activity in this same area during active rehearsal. It is possible that active rehearsal and activity in the posterior cingulate strengthens memory by helping link both episodic and semantic information (Binder et al., 2009; Bird et al., 2015).

6.13 When Memory Fails: Organic Amnesia

6.13 Identify the biological causes of amnesia.

From movies and TV, many people are familiar with the concept of repression, a type of psychologically motivated forgetting in which a person supposedly cannot remember a traumatic event. See Learning Objective 13.10. But what about an inability to remember brought about by some physical cause? There are two forms of severe loss of memory disorders caused by problems in the functioning of the memory areas of the brain. These problems can result from concussions, brain injuries brought about by trauma, alcoholism (Korsakoff's syndrome), or disorders of the aging brain.

AP 5.B Describe and differentiate psychological and physiological systems of memory.

AP 5.H Describe and differentiate psychological and physiological systems of short- and long-term memory.

RETROGRADE AMNESIA If the hippocampus is that important to the formation of declarative memories, what would happen if it got temporarily "disconnected"?

---

*intact: whole or complete.

retrograde amnesia

loss of memory from the point of some injury or trauma backwards, or loss of memory for the past.

People who are in accidents in which they've received a head injury often are unable to recall the accident itself. Sometimes they cannot remember the last several hours or even days before the accident. This type of amnesia (literally, "without memory") is called **retrograde amnesia**, which is loss of memory from the point of injury backward (Hodges, 1994). What apparently happens in this kind of memory loss is that the consolidation process, which was busy making the physical changes to allow new memories to be stored, gets disrupted and loses everything that was not already nearly "finished."

Think about this: You are working on your computer, trying to finish a history paper that is due tomorrow. Your computer saves the document every 10 minutes, but you are working so furiously that you've written a lot in the last 10 minutes. Then the power goes out—horrors! When the power comes back on, you find that while all the files you had already saved are still intact, your history paper is missing that last 10 minutes' worth of work. This is similar to what happens when someone's consolidation process is disrupted. All memories that were in the process of being stored—but are not yet permanent—are lost.

One of the therapies for severe depression is *ECT*, or *electroconvulsive therapy*, in use for this purpose for many decades. See Learning Objective 14.11. One of the common side effects of this therapy is the loss of memory, specifically retrograde amnesia (Meeter et al., 2011; Sackeim et al., 2007; Squire & Alvarez, 1995; Squire et al., 1975). While the effects of the induced seizure seem to significantly ease the depression, the shock also seems to disrupt the memory consolidation process for memories formed prior to the treatment. While some researchers in the past found that the memory loss can go back as far as three years for certain kinds of information (Squire et al., 1975), later research suggests that the loss may not be a permanent one (Meeter et al., 2011; Ziegelmayer et al., 2017).

ANTEROGRADE AMNESIA Concussions can also cause a more temporary version of the kind of amnesia experienced by H.M. This kind of amnesia is called *anterograde amnesia*, or the loss of memories from the point of injury or illness forward (Squire & Slater, 1978). People with this kind of amnesia, like H.M., have difficulty remembering anything new. One of your authors knows a young man who was struck by lightning in the summer of 2018. He remembers walking behind his brother, pulling a cart they had their tools in. His next memories start about two months later. He cannot remember the lightning strike nor his time in the hospital or other experiences that occurred in the two months following the strike. This is also the kind of amnesia most often seen in people with *dementia*, a *neurocognitive disorder*, or decline in cognitive functioning, in which severe forgetfulness, mental confusion, and mood swings are the primary symptoms. (Dementia patients also may suffer from retrograde amnesia in addition to anterograde amnesia.) If retrograde amnesia is like losing a document in the computer because of a power loss, anterograde amnesia is like discovering that your hard drive has become defective—you can read data that are already on the hard drive, but you can't store any new information. As long as you are looking at the data in your open computer window (i.e., attending to it), you can access it, but as soon as you close that window (stop thinking about it), the information is lost, because it was never transferred to the hard drive (long-term memory). This makes for some very repetitive conversations, such as being told the same story or being asked the same question numerous times in the space of a 20-minute conversation. See **Figure 6.10** for a comparison of retrograde and anterograde amnesia.

ALZHEIMER'S DISEASE Nearly 5.7 million Americans have Alzheimer's disease (Alzheimer's Association, 2018). It is the most common type of dementia found in

Figure 6.10 Retrograde and Anterograde Amnesia

(top) Sometimes a blow to the head, such as might be sustained in an accident like this one, can lead to the loss of memories from the time of the injury backwards—a loss of recent memory which may be only a few minutes to several hours or days, or in some cases, even years of the past. This is called retrograde amnesia, because "retro" means "relating to the recent past. (bottom) Anterograde amnesia involves the loss of the ability to form new memories. Memories of the distant past may still be intact, but newer memories such as the name of the person you just met or whether you took your medication or not seem unable to "stick." That's why a person with this type of amnesia (common in dementia) might not remember a conversation that just took place or a visit from the day before.

Sources: (top) Dmitry Kalinovsky/123RF; (bottom) highwaystarz/Fotolia.

adults and the elderly, accounting for nearly 60 to 80 percent of all cases of dementia. It is estimated that 1 out of 10 people over the age of 65 has Alzheimer's disease. It has also become the sixth-leading cause of death in the United States and the fifth-leading cause of death in people 65 years and older, with only heart disease and cancer responsible for more deaths (Alzheimer's Association, 2018; Antuono et al., 2001; National Center for Health Statistics, 2015).

With Alzheimer's disease, the primary memory problem, at least in the beginning, is anterograde amnesia. Memory loss may be rather mild at first but becomes more severe over time, causing the person to become more and more forgetful about everyday tasks. Eventually more dangerous forgetting occurs, such as taking extra doses of medication or leaving something cooking on the stove unattended. As Alzheimer's disease progresses, memories of the past seem to begin "erasing" as retrograde amnesia also takes hold. It is a costly disease to care for, and caregivers often face severe emotional and financial burdens in caring for a loved one who is slowly becoming a stranger.

What causes Alzheimer's disease is not completely understood. While it is normal for the brain to begin to form beta-amyloid protein deposits (plaques) and for strands of the protein tau to become twisted ("tangles"), people who suffer from Alzheimer's disease are found to have far more of these physical signs of an aging brain (Chen et al., 2012; Lim et al., 2012). One of the neurotransmitters involved in the formation of memories in the hippocampus is acetylcholine, and the neurons that produce this chemical break down in the early stages of the disease (Martyn et al., 2012). While one early-onset form of Alzheimer's appears to be heavily genetically influenced and involves several different genetic variations, this seems to be the case for fewer than 5 percent of the total cases of the disease (Alzheimer's Association, 2010, 2018; Bertram & Tanzi, 2005; Haass et al., 1995). The sad truth is that there is not one cause but many, and even those who do NOT have Alzheimer's disease are not safe from other forms of dementia, such as dementia caused by strokes, dehydration, medications, and so on (Karantzoulis, & Galvin, 2011).

Treatments can slow but not halt or reverse the course of the disease. Six drugs are currently approved for treatment, but as yet only slow down the symptoms for an average of 6 to 12 months. What is known is that the risk factors for Alzheimer's (and many other forms of dementia) are something that can be managed: high cholesterol, high blood pressure, smoking, obesity, Type II diabetes, and lack of exercise all contribute (Alzheimer's Association, 2010; 2018; Baumgart et al., 2015). Keeping the brain mentally active is also a way to help prolong good cognitive health. One study's findings indicate that continued everyday learning stimulates brain-derived neurotrophic factors (BDNF), a key protein involved in the formation of memories (L. Y. Chen et al., 2010). A more recent study suggests that a drug intended for use in treating diabetes, AC253, may be able to restore memory to Alzheimer's-affected brain cells (Kimura et al., 2012), while another new drug, ORM-12741, also shows promise (Rinne et al., 2017; Rouru et al., 2013).

We also know that Alzheimer's is *not* caused by eating food from aluminum pots and pans, using the artificial sweetener aspartame, having silver dental fillings, or getting a flu shot—all myths you may have seen on the Internet or social media. None of these are true (Alz.org®: Alzheimer's Association, 2018).

People with dementia or traumatic brain injuries may end up with both types of amnesia. In a study of a recent case of anterograde amnesia, a musician suffering brain damage from a bad case of encephalitis (brain inflammation) no longer remembers his past life, friends, or relatives (retrograde amnesia) and can no longer learn new information (anterograde amnesia). Yet he can still play his cello, can read music, and can not only play pieces from before his brain injury but can also learn new pieces (Finke et al., 2012). These are nondeclarative skills, and this type of memory is typically unaffected by amnesia, suggesting that a different area of the brain is involved.

> 💬 I've tried to remember things from when I was a baby, but I don't seem to be able to recall much. Is this some kind of amnesia, too?

INFANTILE AMNESIA What is the earliest memory you have? Chances are you cannot remember much that happened to you before age 3. When a person does claim to "remember" some event from infancy, a little investigation usually reveals that the "memory" is really based on what family members have told the person about that event and is not a genuine memory at all. This type of "manufactured" memory often has the quality of watching yourself in the memory as if it were a movie and you were an actor. In a genuine memory, you would remember the event through your own eyes—as if you were the camera.

Why can't people remember events from the first 2 or 3 years of life? One explanation of **infantile amnesia** involves the type of memory that exists in the first few years of life, when a child is still considered an infant. Early memories tend to be implicit, and, as stated earlier in this chapter, implicit memories are difficult to bring to consciousness. Explicit memory, which is the more verbal and conscious form of memory, does not really develop until after about age 2, when the hippocampus is more fully developed and language skills blossom (Carver & Bauer, 2001).

Katherine Nelson (1993) also gives credit to the social relationships that small children have with others. As children are able to talk about shared memories with adults, they begin to develop their **autobiographical memory**, or the memory for events and facts related to one's personal life story.

infantile amnesia
the inability to retrieve memories from much before age 3.

autobiographical memory
the memory for events and facts related to one's personal life story.

Concept Map L.O. 6.12, 6.13

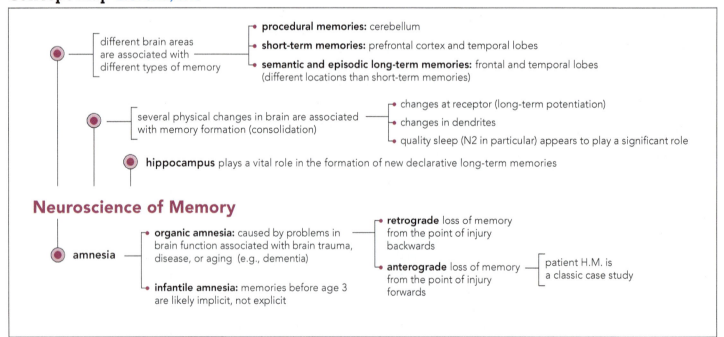

Practice Quiz   How much do you remember?

Pick the best answer.

1. Maya is very afraid of clowns, no doubt because she was frightened by one when she was very young. Maya's memories of that fearful encounter are likely to be associated with the _____.
   a. prefrontal cortex
   b. parietal lobe
   c. cerebellum
   d. amygdala
   e. posterior cingulate cortex

2. Henry Gustav Molaison (H.M.) suffered from profound anterograde amnesia after his _____ were surgically removed in an attempt to control his seizures.
   a. frontal lobes
   b. association cortices
   c. amygdalae
   d. hippocampi
   e. thalami

3. What type of amnesia do you have when you cannot remember things that happened before a traumatic accident?
   a. infantile amnesia
   b. transient global amnesia
   c. anterograde amnesia
   d. psychogenic amnesia
   e. retrograde amnesia

4. Which neurotransmitter is no longer readily produced in Alzheimer's patients?
   a. dopamine
   b. acetylcholine
   c. serotonin
   d. endorphins
   e. GABA

Applying Psychology to Everyday Life
Using Elaborative Rehearsal to Make Memories More Memorable

6.14 Describe ways in which you can use elaborative rehearsal to make information easier to remember.

As a student, you have probably noticed that some things are much easier to remember than others, especially if you are trying to remember concepts and terms for a big exam. There are some good strategies for remembering information (see Learning Objective PIA.6), and in this chapter we talked about elaborative rehearsal—making what you want to remember meaningful in some way. Take a look at the video to see how other students put these strategies to work.

Applying Psychology to Everyday Life Using Elaborative Rehearsal to Make Memories More Memorable

👁 **Watch** the **Video** at **MyLab Psychology**

After watching the video, answer the following questions:

1. What were two of the strategies highlighted in the video for making information that needs to be remembered more meaningful?
2. Beyond the strategies shared by the students in the video, what are some ways you use elaborative rehearsal or other strategies to make information easier to remember?

Chapter Summary

What Is Memory?

6.1 Identify the three processes of memory.

- Memory can be defined as an active system that receives information from the senses, organizes and alters it as it stores it away, and then retrieves the information from storage.
- The three processes are encoding, storage, and retrieval.

6.2 Explain how the different models of memory work.

- In the levels-of-processing model of memory, information that gets more deeply processed is more likely to be remembered.
- In the parallel distributed processing model of memory, information is simultaneously stored across an interconnected neural network that stretches across the brain.

The Information-Processing Model: Three Memory Systems

6.3 Describe the process of sensory memory.

- Iconic memory is the visual sensory memory, in which an afterimage or icon will be held in neural form for about one fourth to one half second.
- Echoic memory is the auditory form of sensory memory and takes the form of an echo that lasts for up to 4 seconds.

6.4 Describe short-term memory, and differentiate it from working memory.

- Short-term memory is where information is held while it is conscious and being used. It holds about three to five items of information and lasts about 30 seconds without rehearsal.
- Whereas STM refers to simple storage of information, working memory involves manipulation of the information within STM; working memory consists of three interrelated systems: a central executive, a visuospatial sketchpad, and a phonological loop.
- STM can be lost through failure to rehearse, decay, interference by similar information, and the intrusion of new information into the STM system, which pushes older information out.

6.5 Explain the process of long-term memory, including nondeclarative and declarative forms.

- Long-term memory is the system in which memories that are to be kept more or less permanently are stored and is unlimited in capacity and relatively permanent in duration.
- Information that is more deeply processed, or processed according to meaning, will be retained and retrieved more efficiently.
- Nondeclarative, or implicit, memories are memories for skills, habits, and conditioned responses. Declarative, or explicit, memories are memories for general facts and personal experiences and include both semantic memories and episodic memories.
- Implicit memories are difficult to bring into conscious awareness, whereas explicit memories are those that a person is aware of possessing.
- LTM is organized in the form of semantic networks, or nodes of related information spreading out from a central piece of knowledge.

Getting It Out: Retrieval of Long-Term Memories

6.6 Identify the effects of cues on memory retrieval.

- Retrieval cues are words, meanings, sounds, and other stimuli that are encoded at the same time as a new memory.
- Encoding specificity occurs when context-dependent information becomes encoded as retrieval cues for specific memories.
- State-dependent learning occurs when physiological or psychological states become encoded as retrieval cues for memories formed while in those states.

6.7 Differentiate the retrieval processes of recall and recognition.

- Recall is a type of memory retrieval in which the information to be retrieved must be "pulled" out of memory with few or no cues, whereas recognition involves matching information with stored images or facts.
- The serial position effect, or primacy or recency effect, occurs when the first items and the last items in a list of information are recalled more efficiently than items in the middle of the list.
- Loftus and others have found that people constantly update and revise their memories of events. Part of this revision may include adding information acquired later to a previous memory. That later information may also be in error, further contaminating the earlier memory.

6.8 Describe how some memories are automatically encoded into long-term memory.

- Automatic encoding of some kinds of information requires very little effort to place information in long-term memory.
- Memory for particularly emotional or traumatic events can lead to the formation of flashbulb memories, memories that seem as vivid and detailed as if the person were looking at a snapshot of the event but that are no more accurate than any other memories.

6.9 Explain how the constructive processing view of memory retrieval accounts for forgetting and inaccuracies in memory.

- Memories are reconstructed from the various bits and pieces of information that have been stored away in different places at the time of encoding in a process called constructive processing.
- Hindsight bias occurs when people falsely believe that they knew the outcome of some event because they have included knowledge of the event's true outcome in their memories of the event itself.
- The misinformation effect refers to the tendency of people who are asked misleading questions or given misleading information to incorporate that information into their memories for a particular event.

- Rather than improving memory retrieval, hypnosis makes the creation of false memories more likely.
- False-memory syndrome is the creation of false or inaccurate memories through suggestion, especially while hypnotized.
- Pezdek and colleagues assert that false memories are more likely to be formed for plausible false events than for implausible ones.

What Were We Talking About? Forgetting

6.10 Describe the "curve of forgetting."
- Ebbinghaus found that information is mostly lost within 1 hour after learning and then gradually fades away. This is known as the curve of forgetting.

6.11 Identify some common reasons people forget things.
- Some "forgetting" is actually a failure to encode information.
- Memory trace decay theory assumes the presence of a physical memory trace that decays with disuse over time.
- Forgetting in LTM is most likely due to proactive or retroactive interference.

Neuroscience of Memory

6.12 Explain the biological bases of memory in the brain.
- Evidence suggests that nondeclarative memories are stored in the cerebellum, whereas short-term memories are stored in the prefrontal and temporal lobes of the cortex.
- Semantic and episodic memories may be stored in the frontal and temporal lobes as well but in different locations than short-term memory, whereas memory for fear of objects is most likely stored in the amygdala.
- Consolidation consists of the physical changes in neurons that take place during the formation of a memory.
- The hippocampus appears to be responsible for the formation of new long-term declarative memories. If it is removed, the ability to store anything new is completely lost.

6.13 Identify the biological causes of amnesia.
- In retrograde amnesia, memory of the past (prior to the injury) is lost, which can be a loss of only minutes or a loss of several years.
- ECT, or electroconvulsive therapy, can disrupt consolidation and cause retrograde amnesia.
- In anterograde amnesia, memory for anything new becomes impossible, although old memories may still be retrievable.
- The primary memory difficulty in Alzheimer's disease is anterograde amnesia, although retrograde amnesia can also occur as the disease progresses.
- Alzheimer's disease has multiple causes, many of which are not yet identified.
- There are various drugs in use or in development for use with the hopes of slowing, or possibly in the future halting, the progression of Alzheimer's disease.
- Most people cannot remember events that occurred before age 2 or 3. This is called infantile amnesia and is most likely due to the implicit nature of infant memory.

Applying Psychology to Everyday Life: Using Elaborative Rehearsal to Make Memories More Memorable

6.14 Describe ways in which you can use elaborative rehearsal to make information easier to remember.
- Elaborative rehearsal is one method for adding meaning to the things we want to remember and for increasing the likelihood of remembering those things later.
- Elaborative rehearsal may involve linking new content to information you already know, putting information into your own words, or making concepts personally relevant by identifying personal examples or applications.

Test Yourself: Preparing for the AP Exam

PART I: MULTIPLE-CHOICE QUESTIONS

Directions for Part I: Read each of the questions or incomplete sentences below. Then choose the response that best answers the question or completes the sentence.

1. According to Sperling, what is the capacity of iconic memory?
   a. everything that can be perceived in a lifetime
   b. everything that can be heard in 1 minute
   c. seven plus or minus two items
   d. everything that can be sensed in 1 second
   e. everything that can be seen at one time

2. For information to travel from either the iconic or echoic sensory system to short-term memory, it must first be _____ and then encoded primarily into _____ form.
   a. biologically chosen, tactile
   b. selectively attended to, visual
   c. unconsciously chosen, auditory
   d. selectively attended to, auditory
   e. biologically chosen, visual

3. You are introduced to someone at a party. While talking with the person, you realize that you have already forgotten the person's name. What amount of time does it typically take before such information is lost from short-term memory?
   a. 12 to 18 months
   b. typically between 12 and 30 seconds
   c. approximately ¼ of a second
   d. usually no more than 4 seconds
   e. Short-term memories typically last a lifetime.

4. Early studies of the capacity of short-term memory suggested that most people could remember approximately _____ bits of information. More recent research suggests it may only be about _____ items.
   a. seven, six
   b. three, two
   c. two, one
   d. ten, eight
   e. seven, four

5. Lynn has just met an attractive man named Ted at a party. She wants to make sure she remembers his name. What should she do?
   a. Lynn should simply write it down on paper and not worry about looking at it again.
   b. Lynn should make it personally relevant and more meaningful. For example, she might remind herself that Ted could be short for her favorite "teddy bear."
   c. Lynn should repeat the name continuously so as to commit it to long-term memory.
   d. Lynn should chunk it by remembering each letter as an individual set.
   e. Lynn should close her eyes and visualize writing his name for about 12 seconds.

6. _____ memory includes what people can do or demonstrate, whereas _____ memory is about what people know and can report.
   a. Episodic, semantic
   b. Semantic, episodic
   c. Declarative, nondeclarative
   d. Semantic, nondeclarative
   e. Nondeclarative, declarative

7. The semantic network model of memory suggests that the _____ nodes you must pass through to access information, the longer it will take for you to recall information.
   a. bigger the
   b. more simple the
   c. fewer
   d. more
   e. more complex the

8. Jesse walks out of his office and into the conference room. However, after he leaves his office, he forgets what he was coming into the conference room for. According to the encoding specificity hypothesis, what should Jesse do to regain his lost memory?
   a. Jesse should return to his office to help him remember what he had forgotten.
   b. Jesse should ask someone else, "What did I come in here for?"
   c. Jesse should remain in the conference room and simply relax so that his memory returns.
   d. Jesse should create a list of items in the conference room.
   e. Jesse should consider seeing a psychologist, since such memory loss can be a sign of more serious issues.

9. When creating a presentation, many public-speaking instructors will tell you to develop a strong opening or attention getter to your presentation as well as a good summary and finish. What aspect of memory best explains these suggestions?
   a. elaborative rehearsal theory
   b. proactive interference
   c. parallel distributed processing model of memory
   d. chunking
   e. serial position effect

10. Research by Elizabeth Loftus shows that eyewitness recognition is very prone to what psychologists call _____.
    a. a flashbulb memory
    b. a primacy effect
    c. automatic encoding
    d. a false positive
    e. a recency effect

11. The ability to remember where you were and what you were doing when the United States was attacked on September 11, 2001, is an example of _____.
    a. encoding specificity hypothesis
    b. elaborative rehearsal
    c. eyewitness testimony
    d. false-memory syndrome
    e. flashbulb memory

12. In Hermann Ebbinghaus's classic study on memory and the forgetting curve, how long after learning the lists did most forgetting happen?
    a. 5 hours
    b. 12 hours
    c. Immediately
    d. 1 hour
    e. 9 hours

13. You are surprised by the fact that you cannot remember if Abraham Lincoln's head faces the left or the right on a penny. This is all the more surprising given the fact that you work with money at your job on nearly a daily basis. What would best explain such an inability to recall this information?
    a. misinformation effect
    b. encoding failure
    c. decay theory
    d. interference theory
    e. distributed practice effect

14. Henry Gustav Molaison, widely known as H.M., was unable to form new declarative memories after a surgical procedure. He suffered from what psychologists call _____ amnesia.
    a. retroactive
    b. infantile
    c. psychogenic
    d. retrograde
    e. anterograde

15. Your English instructor has given you an assignment to write down your favorite memory from when you were 12 months old. What might you tell him?
    a. Students will probably not be able to recall events from such an early age.
    b. Students will write about their first birthday party.
    c. Memories from this time are exceptionally vivid because of the exciting nature of childhood.
    d. Students will not be able to recall such memories if they had yet to develop the ability to walk by age 1.
    e. Students' memories are detailed but often inaccurate.

PART II: FREE-RESPONSE QUESTION

Directions for Part II: Read the essay question that follows. Then respond to the question in a clear, concise essay. Do not simply list facts. Instead, present a thorough argument based on your critical consideration of the topic. Use of proper terminology is necessary.

Jen is studying for her psychology exam. To do well on the test, she will need to match the names and locations of various brain areas, answer multiple choice questions about the nervous system, and write an essay on the biological perspective in psychology.

Part A

Explain how Jen could use each of the following to improve her encoding of information she needs for the test:

- elaborative rehearsal
- levels of processing
- distributed practice

Part B

Explain how Jen could use each of the following to improve her retrieval of information she needs for the test:

- retrieval cues
- recollection

Part C

Describe how the curve of forgetting might predict Jen's performance on the exam.

Chapter 7
Cognition: Thinking, Intelligence, and Language

In your words

Do you tend to rely more on instinctual or deliberate thought processes? How do your thought processes and decision-making strategies vary depending on the situation?

After you have thought about these questions, watch the video to see how other students would answer them.

Watch the Video at MyLab Psychology

Why study the nature of thought?

To fully understand how we do any of the things we do (such as learning, remembering, and behaving), we need to understand how we think. How do we organize our thoughts? How do we communicate those thoughts to others? What do we mean by intelligence? Why are some people able to learn so much faster than others?

Learning Objectives

7.1 Explain how mental images are involved in the process of thinking.

7.2 Describe how concepts and prototypes influence our thinking.

7.3 Identify some methods that people use to solve problems and make decisions.

7.4 Identify three common barriers to successful problem solving.

7.5 Recall some characteristics of creative, divergent thinking.

7.6 Compare and contrast different theories on the nature of intelligence.

7.7 Compare and contrast some methods of measuring intelligence.

7.8 Identify ways to evaluate the quality of a test.

7.9 Define intellectual disability, giftedness, and emotional intelligence.

7.10 Evaluate the influence of heredity and environment on the development of intelligence.

7.11 Identify the different elements and structure of language.

7.12 Explain how language develops.

7.13 Evaluate whether or not language influences how people think.

7.14 Summarize the research on the ability of animals to communicate and use language.

7.15 Identify personal cognitive biases and determine how to prevent them from negatively impacting decision making.

7.1–7.5 How People Think

What does it mean to think? People are thinking all the time and talking about thinking as well: "What do you think?" "Let me think about that." "I don't think so." So, what does it mean to think? **Thinking,** or **cognition** (from a Latin word meaning "to know"), can be defined as mental activity that goes on in the brain when a person is processing information—organizing it, understanding it, and communicating it to others. Thinking includes memory, but it is much more. When people think, they are not only aware of the information in the brain but also are making decisions about it, comparing it to other information, and using it to solve problems.

These two types of thinking, sometimes referred to as System 1 and System 2, characterize much of how we think and process information (Kahneman, 2011; Stanovich & West, 2000). System 1, which involves making quick decisions and using cognitive shortcuts, is guided by our innate abilities and personal experiences. System 2, which is relatively slow, analytical, and rule based, is dependent more on our formal educational experiences. Overall, our thinking has to be governed by the interplay between the two.

Thinking also includes more than just a kind of verbal "stream of consciousness." When people think, they often have images as well as words in their minds.

7.1 Mental Imagery

7.1 Explain how mental images are involved in the process of thinking.

As stated in Chapter Six, short-term memories are encoded in the form of sounds and as visual images, forming a mental picture of the world. Thus, **mental images** (representations that stand in for objects or events and have a picture-like quality) are one of several tools used in the thought process.

Here's an interesting demonstration of the use of mental images. Get several people together and ask them to tell you *as fast as they can* how many windows are in the place where they live. Usually, you'll find that the first people to shout out an answer have fewer windows in their houses than the ones who take longer to respond. You'll also notice that most of them look up, as if looking at some image that only they can see. If asked, they'll say that to determine the number of windows, they pictured where they live and simply counted windows as they "walked through" the image they created in their mind.

> So more windows means more time to count them in your head? I guess mentally "walking" through a bigger house in your head would take longer than "walking" through a smaller one.

That's what researchers think, too. They have found that it does take longer to view a mental image that is larger or covers more distance than a smaller, more compact one (Kosslyn et al., 2001; Ochsner & Kosslyn, 1994). In one study (Kosslyn et al., 1978), participants were asked to look at a map of an imaginary island (see **Figure 7.1**). On this map were several landmarks, such as a hut, a lake, and a grassy area. After viewing the map and memorizing it, participants were asked to imagine a specific place on the island, such as the hut, and then to "look" for another place, like the lake. When they mentally "reached" the second place, they pushed a button that recorded reaction time. The greater the physical distance on the map between the two locations, the longer it took participants to scan the image for the second location. The participants were apparently looking at their mental image and scanning it just as if it were a real, physical map.

People are even able to mentally rotate, or turn, images (Shepard & Metzler, 1971). Kosslyn (1983) asked participants questions such as the following: "Do frogs have lips and a stubby tail?" He found that most participants reported visualizing a frog, starting

---

Figure 7.1 Kosslyn's Fictional Island

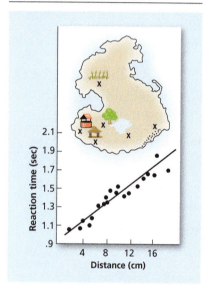

In Kosslyn's 1978 study, participants were asked to push a button when they had imagined themselves moving from one place on the island to another. As the graph below the picture shows, participants took longer times to complete the task when the locations on the image were farther apart.

Source: Kosslyn et al. (1978). Visual Images Preserve Metric Spatial Information: Evidence from Studies of Image Scanning. Journal of Experimental Psychology: Human Perception and Performance, Vol. 4, No. 1, 47-60.

thinking (cognition)
mental activity that goes on in the brain when a person is organizing and attempting to understand information and communicating information to others.

mental images
mental representations that stand for objects or events and have a picture-like quality.

with the face ("no lips"), then mentally rotating the image so it was facing away from them, and then "zooming in" to look for the stubby tail ("yes, there it is"). A very important aspect of the research on mental rotation is that we tend to engage *mental* images in our mind much like we engage or interact with *physical* objects. When we rotate an object in our minds (or in other ways interact with or manipulate mental images), it is not instantaneous—it takes time, just as it would if we were rotating a physical object with our hands.

In the brain, creating a mental image is almost the opposite of seeing an actual image. With an actual image, the information goes from the eyes to the visual cortex of the occipital lobe and is processed, or interpreted, by other areas of the cortex that compare the new information to information already in memory. See Learning Objective 2.8. In creating a mental image, areas of the cortex associated with stored knowledge send information to the visual cortex, where the image is perceived in the "mind's eye" (Kosslyn et al., 1993; Sparing et al., 2002). PET, MEG, and fMRI studies show areas of the visual cortex being activated during the process of forming an image, providing evidence for the role of the visual cortex in mental imagery (Dijkstra et al., 2018; Fulford et al., 2018; Kosslyn et al., 1993, Kosslyn et al., 1999, Kosslyn et al., 2001; Winlove et al., 2018). And although there is overlap between the processes, it takes longer to generate a mental image of an item, a *top-down* process, versus seeing and perceiving a visual stimulus, which is a *bottom-up* process (Dijkstra et al., 2018). See Learning Objective 3.16.

Through the use of functional neuroimaging, researchers have been able to see the overlap that occurs in brain areas activated during visual mental imagery tasks as compared to actual tasks involving visual perception (Dijkstra et al., 2018; Fulford et al., 2018; Ganis et al., 2004; Winlove et al., 2018). During both types of tasks, activity is present in the frontal cortex (cognitive control), temporal lobes (memory), parietal lobes (attention and spatial memory), and occipital lobes (visual processing). However, the amount of activity in these areas differs between the two types of tasks. For example, activity in the visual cortex is stronger during perception than in imagery, suggesting sensory input activates this area more strongly than memory input. In other words, although very similar, mental imagery produces a weaker version of what we perceive by our senses (Pearson et al., 2015) (see **Figure 7.2**). Overall, it appears we can store information in multiple ways, including both a *depictive*, pictorial format and in a *propositional*, descriptive format (Pearson & Kosslyn, 2015). Furthermore, mental imagery can involve all of the senses and not all imagery is voluntary. Both internal associations and external stimuli can trigger mental imagery, even when unwanted, such as intrusive thoughts or imagery that can occur in individuals diagnosed with a psychological disorder such as an anxiety disorder, depression, or posttraumatic stress disorder (PTSD; Pearson et al., 2015; Pearson & Westbrook, 2015). See Learning Objectives 13.4, 13.6, 13.8.

Figure 7.2 Mental Imagery vs. Sensory Perception

Mental imagery (right) is weaker than normal perception (left). Mental imagery provides a weaker perceptual experience than sensory perception.

Source: Based on and adapted from Pearson et al. (2015). Photo courtesy of Noland White.

7.2 Concepts and Prototypes

7.2 Describe how concepts and prototypes influence our thinking.

💬 Images are not the only way we think, are they?

Mental images are only one form of mental representation. Another aspect of thought processes is the use of concepts. **Concepts** are ideas that represent a class or category of objects, events, or activities. People use concepts to think about objects or events without having to think about all the specific examples of the category. For example, a person can think about "fruit" without thinking about every kind of fruit in the world, which would take far more effort and time. This ability to think in terms of concepts allows us to communicate with each other: If I mention a bird to you, you know what I am referring to, even if we aren't actually thinking of the same *type* of bird. As you will see later in the

concepts
ideas that represent a class or category of objects, events, or activities.

Both of these animals are dogs. They both have fur, four legs, a tail—but the similarities end there. With so many variations in the animals we call "dogs," what is the prototype for "dog"?

text, concepts play an important role in the theory of cognitive development put forth by Jean Piaget. See Learning Objective 8.7.

Concepts not only contain the important features of the objects or events people want to think about, but they also allow the identification of new objects and events that may fit the concept. For example, dogs come in all shapes, sizes, colors, and lengths of fur. Yet most people have no trouble recognizing dogs as dogs, even though they may never before have seen that particular breed of dog. Friends of the author have a dog called a briard, which is a kind of sheepdog. In spite of the fact that this dog is easily the size of a small pony, the author had no trouble recognizing it as a dog, albeit a huge and extremely shaggy one.

Concepts can have very strict definitions, such as the concept of a square as a shape with four equal sides. Concepts defined by specific rules or features are called *formal concepts* and are quite rigid. To be a square, for example, an object must be a two-dimensional figure with four equal sides and four angles adding up to 360 degrees. Mathematics is full of formal concepts. For example, in geometry there are triangles, squares, rectangles, polygons, and lines. In psychology, there are double-blind experiments, sleep stages, and conditioned stimuli, to name a few. Each of these concepts must fit very specific features to be considered true examples.

💬 But what about things that don't easily fit the rules or features? What if a thing has some, but not all, features of a concept?

People are surrounded by objects, events, and activities that are not as clearly defined as formal concepts. What is a vehicle? Cars and trucks leap immediately to mind, but what about a bobsled or a raft? Those last two objects aren't quite as easy to classify as vehicles immediately, but they fit some of the rules for "vehicle." These are examples of *natural concepts*, concepts people form not as a result of a strict set of rules but rather as the result of experiences with these concepts in the real world (Ahn, 1998; Barton & Komatsu, 1989; Rosch, 1973). Formal concepts are well defined, but natural concepts are "fuzzy" (Hampton, 1998). Natural concepts are important in helping people understand their surroundings in a less structured manner than school-taught formal concepts, and they form the basis for interpreting those surroundings and the events that may occur in everyday life.

When someone says "fruit," what's the first image that comes to mind? More than likely, it's a specific kind of fruit like an apple, pear, or orange. It's less likely that someone's first impulse will be to say "guava" or "papaya" or even "banana," unless that person comes from a tropical area. In the United States, apples are a good example of a **prototype**, a concept that closely matches the defining characteristics of the concept (Mervis & Rosch, 1981; Rosch, 1977). Fruit is sweet, grows on trees, has seeds, and is usually round—all very applelike qualities. Coconuts are sweet and they also grow on trees, but many people in the Northern Hemisphere have never actually seen a coconut tree. They have more likely seen countless apple trees. So, people who have very different experiences with fruit, for instance, will have different prototypes, which are the most basic examples of concepts.

A duck-billed platypus is classified as a mammal yet shares features with birds, such as webbed feet and a bill, and it also lays eggs. The platypus is an example of a "fuzzy" natural concept.

💬 What about people who live in a tropical area? Would their prototype for fruit be different? And would people's prototypes vary in other cultures?

prototype
an example of a concept that closely matches the defining characteristics of the concept.

More than likely, prototypes develop according to the exposure a person has to objects in that category. So, someone who grew up in an area where there are many coconut trees might think of coconuts as more prototypical than apples, whereas someone growing up in the northwestern United States would more likely see apples as a prototypical fruit (Aitchison, 1992). Culture also matters in the formation of prototypes. Research on concept prototypes across various cultures found greater differences and variations in prototypes between cultures that were dissimilar, such as Taiwan and America, than between cultures that are more similar, such as Hispanic Americans and non–Hispanic Americans living in Florida (Lin et al., 1990; Lin & Schwanenflugel, 1995; Schwanenflugel & Rey, 1986).

How do prototypes affect thinking? People tend to look at potential examples of a concept and compare them to the prototype to see how well they match—which is why it takes most people much longer to think about olives and tomatoes as fruit because they aren't sweet, one of the major characteristics of the prototype of fruit (Rosch & Mervis, 1975). As the video *The Mind Is What the Brain Does* explains, we use a combination of cognitive processes including concepts, prototypes, and mental images to identify objects in our daily lives.

Watch The Mind Is What the Brain Does

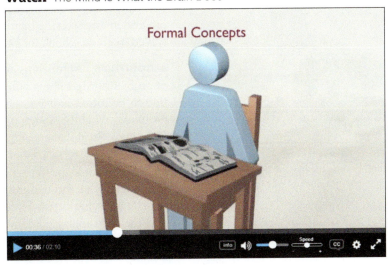

Watch the Video at MyLab Psychology

No matter what type, concepts are one of the ways people deal with all the information that bombards* their senses every day, allowing them to organize their perceptions of the world around them. This organization may take the form of *schemas*, mental generalizations about objects, places, events, and people (for example, one's schema for "library" would no doubt include books and bookshelves), or *scripts*, a kind of schema that involves a familiar sequence of activities (for example, "going to a movie" would include traveling there, getting the ticket, buying snacks, finding the right theater, etc.). Concepts not only help people think, but they also are an important tool in *problem solving*, a type of thinking that people engage in every day and in many different situations.

7.3 Problem-Solving and Decision-Making Strategies

7.3 Identify some methods that people use to solve problems and make decisions.

AP 5.I Identify problem-solving strategies as well as factors that influence their effectiveness.

💬 Problem solving is certainly a big part of any student's life. Is there any one "best" way to go about solving a problem?

Think about it as you read on and solve the following: Put a coin in a bottle and then cork the opening. How can you get the coin out of the bottle without pulling out the cork or breaking the bottle? (For the solution, see the section on Insight.)

As stated earlier, images and concepts are mental tools that can be used to solve problems and make decisions. For the preceding problem, you are probably trying to create an image of the bottle with a coin in it. **Problem solving** occurs when a goal must be reached by thinking and behaving in certain ways. Problems range from figuring out how to cut a recipe in half to understanding complex mathematical proofs to deciding what to major in at college. Problem solving is one aspect of **decision making**, or identifying, evaluating, and choosing among several alternatives. There are several different ways in which people can think in order to solve problems.

TRIAL AND ERROR (MECHANICAL SOLUTIONS) One method is to use **trial and error**, also known as a **mechanical solution**. Trial and error refers to trying one solution after another until finding one that works. For example, if Shelana has forgotten the PIN for her

problem solving
process of cognition that occurs when a goal must be reached by thinking and behaving in certain ways.

decision making
process of cognition that involves identifying, evaluating, and choosing among several alternatives.

trial and error (mechanical solution)
problem-solving method in which one possible solution after another is tried until a successful one is found.

---

*bombards: attacks again and again.

This child may try one piece after another until finding the piece that fits. This is an example of trial-and-error learning.

online banking Web site, she can try one combination after another until she finds the one that works, if she has only a few such PINs that she normally uses. Mechanical solutions can also involve solving by *rote*, or a learned set of rules. This is how word problems were solved in grade school, for example. One type of rote solution is to use an algorithm.

ALGORITHMS **Algorithms** are specific, step-by-step procedures for solving certain types of problems. Algorithms will always result in a correct solution if there is a correct solution to be found and you have enough time to find it. Mathematical formulas are algorithms. When librarians organize books on bookshelves, they also use an algorithm: Place books in alphabetical order within each category, for example. Many puzzles, like a Rubik's Cube®, have a set of steps that, if followed exactly, will always result in solving the puzzle. But algorithms aren't always practical to use. For example, if Shelana didn't have a clue what those four numbers might be, she *might* be able to figure out her forgotten PIN by trying *all possible combinations* of four digits, 0 through 9. She would eventually find the right four-digit combination—but it might take a very long while! Computers, however, can run searches like this one very quickly, so the systematic search algorithm is a useful part of some computer programs.

HEURISTICS Unfortunately, humans aren't as fast as computers and need some other way to narrow down the possible solutions to only a few. One way to do this is to use a heuristic. A **heuristic**, or "rule of thumb," is a simple rule that is intended to apply to many situations. Whereas an algorithm is very specific and will always lead to a solution, a heuristic is an educated guess based on prior experiences that helps narrow down the possible solutions for a problem. For example, if a student is typing a paper in a word-processing program and wants to know how to format the page, he or she could try to read an entire manual on the word-processing program. That would take a while. Instead, the student could use an Internet search engine or type "format" into the help feature's search program. Doing either action greatly reduces the amount of information the student will have to look at to get an answer. Using the help feature or clicking on the appropriate toolbar word will also work for similar problems.

REPRESENTATIVENESS HEURISTIC Will using a rule of thumb always work, like algorithms do? Using a heuristic is faster than using an algorithm in many cases, but unlike algorithms, heuristics will *not* always lead to the correct solution. What you gain in speed is sometimes lost in accuracy. For example, a **representativeness heuristic** is used for categorizing objects and simply assumes that any object (or person) that shares characteristics with the members of a particular category is also a member of that category. This is a handy tool when it comes to classifying plants but doesn't work as well when applied to people. The representativeness heuristic can cause errors due to ignoring base rates, the actual probability of a given event. Are all people with dark skin from Africa? Does everyone with red hair also have a bad temper? Are all blue-eyed blondes from Sweden? See the point? The representativeness heuristic can be used—or misused—to create and sustain stereotypes (Kahneman & Tversky, 1973; Kahneman et al., 1982).

AVAILABILITY HEURISTIC Another heuristic that can have undesired outcomes is the **availability heuristic**, which is based on our estimation of the frequency or likelihood of an event based on how easy it is to recall relevant information from memory or how easy it is for us to think of related examples (Tversky & Kahneman, 1973).

The availability heuristic impacts our judgment based on how easy it is to bring an example to mind, not the accuracy of what we recall. What are some areas of your life where the availability heuristic may have come into play? Perhaps there has been something on the news, Facebook, Twitter, or LinkedIn that impacted your beliefs or decisions about specific events. For example, what is the actual likelihood of being the victim of

algorithms
very specific, step-by-step procedures for solving certain types of problems.

heuristic
an educated guess based on prior experiences that helps narrow down the possible solutions for a problem. Also known as a "rule of thumb."

representativeness heuristic
assumption that any object (or person) sharing characteristics with the members of a particular category is also a member of that category.

availability heuristic
estimating the frequency or likelihood of an event based on how easy it is to recall relevant information from memory or how easy it is for us to think of related examples.

terrorism versus the emphasis we often see on terrorism in various media outlets? You might also easily recall a campus crime incident, a plane crash, or child abduction from the news or media, but how frequent are these events? Now, compare those to the likelihood of being in a car accident, something for which many of us are at much higher risk. The availability heuristic does not only apply to such extreme examples. What about choosing to not study for a given exam because you know that one person who had the same class and professor last semester did okay and they "never studied"? Can you think of other examples where you may have used the availability heuristic and it did not work in your favor?

WORKING BACKWARD A useful heuristic that *does* work much of the time is to *work backward from the goal*. For example, if you want to know the shortest way to get to the new coffee shop in town, you already know the goal, which is finding the coffee shop. There are probably several ways to get there from your house, and some are shorter than others. Assuming you have the address of the store, for many the best way to determine the shortest route is to look up the location of the store on an Internet map, a GPS, or a smartphone and compare the different routes by the means of travel (walking versus driving). People actually used to do this with a physical map and compare the routes manually! Think about it: Does technology help or hinder some aspects of problem solving? What are, if any, the benefits to using technology for solving some problems as compared to actively engaging in problem solving as a mental challenge?

Smartphones and other portable devices provide tools for easy navigation. How might the use or overuse of these tools affect our ability to navigate when we do not have access to them?

> What if my problem is writing a term paper? Starting at the end isn't going to help me much!

SUBGOALS Sometimes it's better to break a goal down into *subgoals* so that as each subgoal is achieved, the final solution is that much closer. Writing a term paper, for example, can seem overwhelming until it is broken down into steps: Choose a topic, research the topic, organize what has been gathered, write one section at a time, and so on. See Learning Objective PIA.7. Other examples of heuristics include making diagrams to help organize the information concerning the problem or testing possible solutions to the problem one by one and eliminating those that do not work.

> Sometimes I have to find answers to problems one step at a time, but in other cases the answer seems to just "pop" into my head all of a sudden. Why do some answers come so easily to mind?

INSIGHT When the solution to a problem seems to come suddenly to mind, it is called insight. Chapter Five contained a discussion of Köhler's (1925) work with Sultan the chimpanzee, which demonstrated that even some animals can solve problems by means of a sudden insight. See Learning Objective 5.11. In humans, insight often takes the form of an "aha!" moment—the solution seems to come in a flash. A person may realize that this problem is similar to another one that he or she already knows how to solve or might see that an object can be used for a different purpose than its original one, like using a dime as a screwdriver.

Remember the problem of the bottle discussed earlier in this chapter? The task was to get the coin out of the bottle without removing the cork or breaking the bottle. The answer is simple: *Push the cork into the bottle and shake out the coin. Aha!*

Insight is not really a magical process, although it can seem like magic. What usually happens is that the mind simply reorganizes a problem, sometimes while the person is thinking about something else (Durso et al., 1994).

functional fixedness
a block to problem solving that comes from thinking about objects in terms of only their typical functions.

mental set
the tendency for people to persist in using problem-solving patterns that have worked for them in the past.

AP 5.K Identify problem-solving strategies as well as factors that create bias and errors in thinking.

Figure 7.3 The String Problem

How do you tie the two strings together if you cannot reach them both at the same time?

Figure 7.4 The Dot Problem

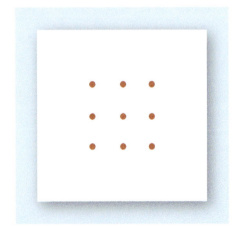

Can you draw four straight lines so that they pass through all nine dots *without lifting your pencil from the page and without touching any dot more than once?*

Here's a problem that can be solved with insight: Marsha and Marjorie were born on the same day of the same month of the same year to the same mother and the same father yet they are not twins. How is that possible? Think about it and then look for the answer in the section on Mental Sets.

In summary, thinking is a complex process involving the use of mental imagery and various types of concepts to organize the events of daily life. Problem solving is a special type of thinking that involves the use of many tools, such as trial-and-error thinking, algorithms, and heuristics, to solve different types of problems.

7.4 Problems with Problem Solving and Decision Making

7.4 Identify three common barriers to successful problem solving.

Using insight to solve a problem is not always foolproof. Sometimes a solution to a problem remains just "out of reach" because the elements of the problem are not arranged properly or because people get stuck in certain ways of thinking that act as barriers* to solving problems. Such ways of thinking occur more or less automatically, influencing attempts to solve problems without any conscious awareness of that influence. Here's a classic example:

Two strings are hanging from a ceiling but are too far apart to allow a person to hold one and walk to the other (see **Figure 7.3**). Nearby is a table with a pair of pliers on it. The goal is to tie the two pieces of string together. How? For the solution to this problem, read on.

People can become aware of automatic tendencies to try to solve problems in ways that are not going to lead to solutions and, in becoming aware, can abandon the "old" ways for more appropriate problem-solving methods. Three of the most common barriers to successful problem solving are functional fixedness, mental sets, and confirmation bias.

FUNCTIONAL FIXEDNESS One problem-solving difficulty involves thinking about objects only in terms of their typical uses, which is a phenomenon called **functional fixedness** (literally, "fixed on the function"). Have you ever searched high and low for a screwdriver to fix something around the house? All the while there are several objects close at hand that could be used to tighten a screw: a butter knife, a key, or even a dime in your pocket. Because the tendency is to think of those objects in terms of cooking, unlocking, and spending, we sometimes ignore the less obvious possible uses. The string problem introduced before is an example of functional fixedness. The pair of pliers is often seen as useless until the person realizes it can be used as a weight. (See answer in the section on Creativity.)

MENTAL SETS Functional fixedness is actually a kind of **mental set**, which is defined as the tendency for people to persist in using problem-solving patterns that have worked for them in the past. Solutions that have worked in the past tend to be the ones people try first, and people are often hesitant or even unable to think of other possibilities. Look at **Figure 7.4** and see if you can solve the dot problem.

People are taught from the earliest grades to stay within the lines, right? That tried-and-true method will not help in solving the dot problem. The solution involves drawing the lines beyond the actual dots, as seen in the solution in the section on Creativity.

Answer to insight problem: *Marsha and Marjorie are two of a set of triplets. Gotcha!*

---

*barrier: something that blocks one's path; an obstacle preventing a solution.

CONFIRMATION BIAS Another barrier to effective decision making or problem solving is **confirmation bias**, the tendency to search for evidence that fits one's beliefs while ignoring any evidence to the contrary. This is similar to a mental set, except that what is "set" is a belief rather than a method of solving problems. Believers in ESP tend to remember the few studies that seem to support their beliefs and psychic predictions that worked out while at the same time "forgetting" the cases in which studies found no proof or psychics made predictions that failed to come true. They remember only that which confirms their bias toward a belief in the existence of ESP.

Another example is that people who believe that they are good multitaskers and can safely drive a motor vehicle while talking or texting on their cell phones may tend to remember their own personal experiences, which may not include any vehicle accidents or "near-misses" (that they are aware of). Recent research on sensory processing in the brain has found that when faced with multiple sources of sensory information, we can actually become overloaded under high-demand situations and experience temporary blindness or deafness due to inattention. In one study, researchers found that when faced with a very demanding visual task, participants lost the ability to detect auditory information (Molloy et al., 2015).

While it might be tempting to think of one's self as a "supertasker," research suggests otherwise. When tested on driving simulators while having to perform successfully on two attention-demanding tasks, more than 97 percent of individuals are unable to do so without significant impacts on their performance. During the dual-task condition, only 2.5 percent of individuals were able to perform without problems (Watson & Strayer, 2010). Research also suggests the people that are most likely to talk on their cell phone while driving, as indicated by self-report, are actually the worst at multitasking when tested (Sanbonmatsu et al., 2013). It is estimated that at least 27 percent of all traffic crashes are caused by drivers using their cell phone and/or texting (National Safety Council, 2015).

The driver of this train was texting from his cell phone immediately before this crash that killed 25 people and injured more than 130 others.

confirmation bias
the tendency to search for evidence that fits one's beliefs while ignoring any evidence that does not fit those beliefs.

7.5 Creativity

7.5 Recall some characteristics of creative, divergent thinking.

AP 5.J List the characteristics of creative thought and creative thinkers.

> 💬 So far, we've only talked about logic and pretty straightforward thinking. How do people come up with totally new ideas, things no one has thought of before?

Not every problem can be answered by using information already at hand and the rules of logic in applying that information. Sometimes a problem requires coming up with entirely new ways of looking at the problem or unusual, inventive solutions. This kind of thinking is called **creativity**: solving problems by combining ideas or behavior in new ways (Csikszentmihalyi, 1996; pronounced chĭck-sĕnt-mē-HĪ-ē).

The logical method for problem solving that has been discussed so far is based on a type of thinking called **convergent thinking**. In convergent thinking, a problem is seen as having only one answer, and all lines of thinking will eventually lead to (converge on) that single answer by using previous knowledge and logic (Ciardiello, 1998). For example, the question "In what ways are a pencil and a pen alike?" can be answered by listing the features that the two items have in common: Both can be used to write, have similar shapes, and so on, in a simple comparison process. Convergent thinking works well for routine problem solving but may be of little use when a more creative solution is needed.

creativity
the process of solving problems by combining ideas or behavior in new ways.

convergent thinking
type of thinking in which a problem is seen as having only one answer, and all lines of thinking will eventually lead to that single answer, using previous knowledge and logic.

Solution to the String Problem

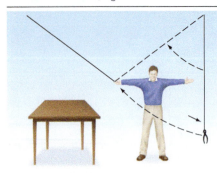

The solution to the string problem is to use the pliers as a pendulum to swing the second string closer to you.

Solution to the Dot Problem

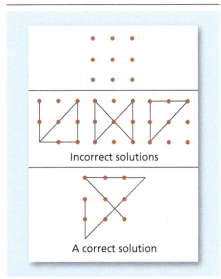

When people try to solve this problem, a mental set causes them to think of the dots as representing a box, and they try to draw the line while staying in the box. The only way to connect all nine dots without lifting the pencil from the paper is to draw the lines so they extend out of the box of dots—literally "thinking outside the box."

divergent thinking

type of thinking in which a person starts from one point and comes up with many different ideas or possibilities based on that point.

Divergent thinking is the reverse of convergent thinking. Here a person starts at one point and comes up with many different, or divergent, ideas or possibilities based on that point (Finke, 1995). For example, if someone were to ask the question, "What is a pencil used for?" the convergent answer would be "to write." But if the question is put this way: "How many different uses can you think of for a pencil?" the answers multiply: "writing, poking holes, a weight for the tail of a kite, a weapon." Divergent thinking has been attributed not only to creativity but also to intelligence (Guilford, 1967).

What are the characteristics of a creative, divergent thinker? Theorists in the field of creative thinking have found through examining the habits of highly creative people that the most productive periods of divergent thinking for those people tend to occur when they are doing some task or activity that is more or less automatic, such as walking or swimming (Csikszentmihalyi, 1996; Gardner, 1993a; Goleman, 1995). These automatic tasks take up some attention processes, leaving the remainder to devote to creative thinking. The fact that all of one's attention is not focused on the problem is actually a benefit, because divergent thinkers often make links and connections at a level of consciousness just below alert awareness, so that ideas can flow freely without being censored* by the higher mental processes (Goleman, 1995). In other words, having part of one's attention devoted to walking, for example, allows the rest of the mind to "sneak up on" more creative solutions and ideas.

Divergent thinkers will obviously be less prone to some of the barriers to problem solving, such as functional fixedness. For example, what would most people do if it suddenly started to rain while they are stuck in their office with no umbrella? How many people would think of using a see-through vinyl tote bag as a makeshift umbrella?

Creative, divergent thinking is often a neglected topic in the education of young people. Although some people are naturally more creative, it is possible to develop one's creative ability. The ability to be creative is important—coming up with topics for a research paper, for example, is something that many students have trouble doing. Cross-cultural research (Basadur et al., 2002; Colligan, 1983) has found that divergent thinking and problem-solving skills cannot be easily taught in the Japanese or Omaha Native American cultures, for example. In these cultures, creativity in many areas is not normally prized, and the preference is to hold to well-established cultural traditions, such as traditional dances that have not varied for centuries. See **Table 7.1** for some ways to become a more divergent thinker.

Table 7.1 Stimulating Divergent Thinking

Method	Strategy
Brainstorming	Generate as many ideas as possible in a short period of time without judging each idea's merits until all ideas are recorded.
Keeping a Journal	Carry a journal to write down ideas as they occur, or use a note-taking or voice-recording app on your cell phone to capture those same ideas and thoughts.
Freewriting	Write down or record everything that comes to mind about a topic without revising or proofreading until all of the information is written or recorded in some way. Organize it later.
Mind or Subject Mapping	Start with a central idea and draw a "map" with lines from the center to other related ideas, forming a visual representation of the concepts and their connections.

Many people have the idea that creative people are also a little different from other people. There are artists and musicians, for example, who actually encourage others

---

*censored: blocked from conscious awareness as unacceptable thoughts.

to see them as eccentric. But the fact is that creative people are actually pretty normal. According to Csikszentmihalyi (1997):

1. Creative people usually have a broad range of knowledge about a lot of subjects and are good at using mental imagery.
2. Creative people aren't afraid to be different—they are more open to new experiences than many people, and they tend to have more vivid dreams and daydreams than others do.
3. Creative people value their independence.
4. Creative people are often unconventional in their work, but not otherwise.

A DJ performing before an audience. What aspects of creativity apply to the work of a DJ?

Concept Map L.O. 7.1, 7.2, 7.3, 7.4, 7.5

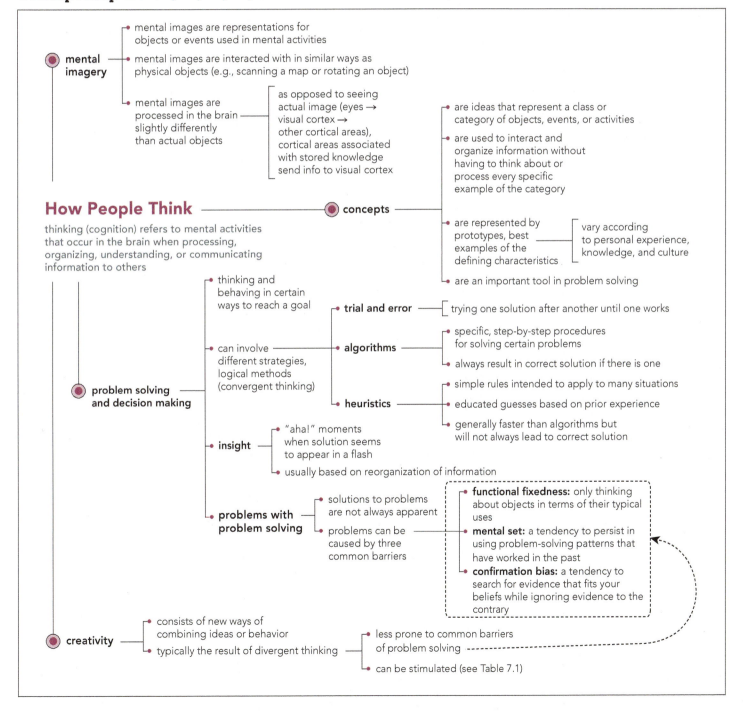

Practice Quiz — How much do you remember?

Pick the best answer.

1. What is thinking?
   a. simply and succinctly, our ability to remember
   b. all mental activity that is not involved with physical movements
   c. spontaneous, nondirected, and unconscious mental activity
   d. mental activity that involves processing, organizing, understanding, and communicating information
   e. all mental activity except memory

2. People in the United States often think of a sports car when asked to envision a fun, fast form of travel. In this example, a sports car would be considered a _____.
   a. fuzzy concept
   b. prototype
   c. mental image
   d. natural concept
   e. formal concept

3. While taking a shower, Jordan suddenly realizes the solution to a problem at work. When later asked how he solved this problem, Jordan said, "The answer just seemed to pop into my head." Jordan's experience is an example of _____.
   a. a heuristic
   b. trial and error
   c. a mechanical solution
   d. insight
   e. an algorithm

4. Julie leaves her office building only to find it is raining. She returns to her office and gets a trash bag out of the supply cabinet. Using a pair of scissors, she cuts the bag so that she can put her head and arms through the bag without getting wet. In using the trash bag as a makeshift rain jacket, Julie has overcome _____.
   a. confirmation fixedness
   b. confirmation bias
   c. functional fixedness
   d. creativity bias
   e. metacognition

5. Ed and Harry believe that ghosts are running rampant in a nearby town. When looking for information on the Internet, they ignore any sites that are skeptical of their beliefs and only visit sites that support their beliefs. This is an example of _____.
   a. functional fixedness
   b. confirmation bias
   c. confirmation fixedness
   d. creativity bias
   e. metacognition

6. Which of the following is the best way to encourage divergent, creative thinking?
   a. Force yourself to think of something new and creative.
   b. Go for a walk or engage in some other automatic activity.
   c. Stare at a blank sheet of paper until a new, innovative solution comes to mind.
   d. Engage in many activities simultaneously.
   e. Focus intently on following instructions precisely.

AP 5.L Define intelligence and list characteristics of how psychologists measure intelligence.

AP 5.N Compare and contrast historic and contemporary theories of intelligence.

AP 5.O Identify the contributions of key researchers in intelligence research and testing.

intelligence
the ability to learn from one's experiences, acquire knowledge, and use resources effectively in adapting to new situations or solving problems.

g factor
the ability to reason and solve problems, or general intelligence.

s factor
the ability to excel in certain areas, or specific intelligence.

7.6–7.10 Intelligence

What does it mean to be "smart"? Is this the same as being intelligent? It is likely the answer depends on the immediate task or context. What exactly do we mean by the term *intelligence*?

7.6 Theories of Intelligence

7.6 Compare and contrast different theories on the nature of intelligence.

Is intelligence merely a score on some test, or is it practical knowledge of how to get along in the world? Is it making good grades or being a financial or social success? Ask a dozen people and you will probably get a dozen different answers. Psychologists have come up with a workable definition that combines many of the ideas just mentioned: They define **intelligence** as the ability to learn from one's experiences, acquire knowledge, and use resources effectively in adapting to new situations or solving problems (Sternberg & Kaufman, 1998; Wechsler, 1975). These are the characteristics that individuals need in order to survive in their culture.

Although we have defined intelligence in a general way, there are differing opinions of the specific knowledge and abilities that make up the concept of intelligence. We will discuss several theories that offer different explanations of the nature and number of intelligence-related abilities.

SPEARMAN'S G FACTOR Charles Spearman (1904) saw intelligence as two different abilities. The ability to reason and solve problems was labeled **g factor** for *general intelligence*, whereas task-specific abilities in certain areas such as music, business, or art are labeled **s factor** for *specific intelligence*. A traditional IQ test would most likely measure g factor, but Spearman believed that superiority in one type of intelligence predicts superiority overall. Although his early research found some support for specific intelligences, other researchers (Guilford, 1967; Thurstone, 1938) felt that Spearman had oversimplified the concept of intelligence. Intelligence began to be viewed as composed of numerous factors. In fact, Guilford (1967) proposed that there were 120 types of intelligence.

GARDNER'S MULTIPLE INTELLIGENCES One of the later theorists to propose the existence of several kinds of intelligence is Howard Gardner (1993b, 1999a). Although many people use the terms *reason*, *logic*, and *knowledge* as if they are the same ability, Gardner believes that they are different aspects of intelligence, along with several other abilities. He originally listed seven different kinds of intelligence but later added an eighth type and then proposed a tentative ninth (Gardner, 1998, 1999b). The nine types of intelligence are described in the video *Theories of Intelligence: Gardner's Theory* and summarized in **Table 7.2**.

triarchic theory of intelligence

Sternberg's theory that there are three kinds of intelligence: analytical, creative, and practical.

Table 7.2 Gardner's Nine Intelligences

Type of Intelligence	Description	Sample Occupation
Verbal/linguistic	Ability to use language	Writers, speakers
Musical	Ability to compose and/or perform music	Musicians, even those who do not read musical notes but can perform and compose
Logical/mathematical	Ability to think logically and to solve mathematical problems	Scientists, engineers
Visual/spatial	Ability to understand how objects are oriented in space	Pilots, astronauts, artists, navigators
Movement	Ability to control one's body motions	Dancers, athletes
Interpersonal	Sensitivity to others and understanding motivation of others	Psychologists, managers
Intrapersonal	Understanding of one's emotions and how they guide actions	Various people-oriented careers
Naturalist	Ability to recognize the patterns found in nature	Farmers, landscapers, biologists, botanists
Existentialist (a candidate intelligence)	Ability to see the "big picture" of the human world by asking questions about life, death, and the ultimate reality of human existence	Various careers, philosophical thinkers

Source: Based on Gardner, 1998, 1999b.

The idea of multiple intelligences has great appeal, especially for educators. However, some argue that there are few scientific studies providing evidence for the concept of multiple intelligences (Waterhouse, 2006a, 2006b), while others claim that the evidence does exist (Gardner & Moran, 2006). Some critics propose that such intelligences are no more than different abilities and that those abilities are not necessarily the same thing as what is typically meant by *intelligence* (Hunt, 2001).

STERNBERG'S TRIARCHIC THEORY Robert Sternberg (1988a, 1997b) has theorized that there are three kinds of intelligence. Called the **triarchic theory of intelligence** (*triarchic* means three), this theory includes *analytical*, *creative*, and *practical intelligence*. **Analytical intelligence** refers to the ability to break problems down into component parts, or analysis, for problem solving. This is the type of intelligence that is measured by intelligence tests and academic achievement tests, or "book smarts" as some people like to call it. **Creative intelligence** is the ability to deal with new and different concepts and to come up with new ways of solving problems (divergent thinking, in other words); it also refers to the ability to automatically process certain aspects of information, which frees up cognitive resources to deal with novelty (Sternberg, 2005). **Practical intelligence** is best described as "street smarts," or the ability to use information to get along in life. People with a high degree of practical intelligence know how to be tactful, how to manipulate situations to their advantage, and how to use inside information to increase their odds of success.

How might these three types of intelligence be illustrated? All three might come into play when planning and completing an experiment. For example:

- *Analytical:* Being able to run a statistical analysis on data from the experiment.
- *Creative:* Being able to design the experiment in the first place.
- *Practical:* Being able to get funding for the experiment from donors.

Watch Theories of Intelligence: Gardner's Theory

Watch the Video at MyLab Psychology

analytical intelligence

the ability to break problems down into component parts, or analysis, for problem solving.

creative intelligence

the ability to deal with new and different concepts and to come up with new ways of solving problems.

practical intelligence

the ability to use information to get along in life and become successful.

Practical intelligence has become a topic of much interest and research. Sternberg (1996, 1997a, 1997b) has found that practical intelligence predicts success in life but has a surprisingly low relationship to academic (analytical) intelligence. However, when practical intelligence is taken into account or used to supplement standardized tests, studies have found that college, high school, and elementary school programs benefit in a variety of areas due to the diverse range of individuals being included (Sternberg, 2015).

CATTELL-HORN-CARROLL (CHC) THEORY Another influential theory of intelligence is actually based on the culmination of work from several theorists, Raymond Cattell, John Horn, and John Carroll (Flanagan & Dixon, 2013; McGrew, 2009; Schneider & McGrew, 2012). Interestingly, Cattell was a student of Charles Spearman and Horn was a student of Cattell (Schneider & McGrew, 2012). Raymond Cattell suggested intelligence was composed of *crystalized intelligence*, which represents acquired knowledge and skills, versus *fluid intelligence*, or problem solving and adaptability in unfamiliar situations. John Horn expanded on Cattell's work and added other abilities based on visual and auditory processing, memory, speed of processing, reaction time, quantitative skills, and reading-writing skills (Flanagan & Dixon, 2013). Based on an extensive factor analysis of data from more than 460 studies, John Carroll developed a three-tier hierarchical model of cognitive abilities that fit so well with the Cattell-Horn crystalized and fluid intelligence models that a new theory was suggested, the Cattell-Horn-Carroll (CHC) Theory of Intelligence (McGrew, 2009).

One component of the CHC framework is general intelligence, or *g*. It is also composed of 16 broad abilities including general brain-based factors comprising fluid reasoning, short-term memory, long-term storage and retrieval, processing speed, reaction and decision speed, and psychomotor speed (see **Figure 7.5**). Four abilities are based on Cattell's description of crystalized intelligence: comprehension-knowledge, domain-specific knowledge, reading and writing, and quantitative knowledge. Other abilities are tied to sensory systems and their respective primary and association areas of the cortex: visual processing, auditory processing, olfactory abilities, tactile abilities, kinesthetic abilities, and psychomotor abilities (Schneider & McGrew, 2012).

Figure 7.5 Cattell-Horn-Carroll (CHC) Theory of Intelligence

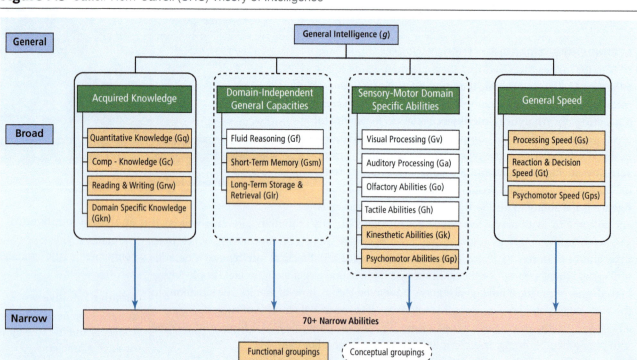

Source: Based on and adapted from Schneider & McGrew (2012, 2013).

Of all of the theories of intelligence, it has been suggested that the CHC theory is the most researched, empirically supported, and comprehensive (Flanagan & Dixon, 2013). In fact, many new assessments of intelligence and revisions of earlier assessments have been driven by the CHC theory (Keith & Reynolds, 2010).

NEUROSCIENCE THEORIES It is probably no surprise that the brain has been closely linked to intelligence. Not only have specific brain areas and brain functions been tied to differences in intellectual ability, but differing levels of specific cognitive abilities have also been a topic of study. With regard to brain area and function, some researchers have suggested that the frontal and parietal brain areas play the most important roles, and these areas are actually components of one of the leading neuroscience theories of intelligence, the *Parieto-Frontal Integration Theory*, or P-FIT (Haier, 2017; Jung & Haier, 2007). Researchers have expanded on P-FIT and suggested other areas such as the posterior cingulate cortex, insular cortex, and specific subcortical areas also play critical roles (Basten et al., 2015). See Learning Objectives 2.7, 2.8. For specific cognitive abilities, working memory has been tied to *fluid intelligence*, or the ability to adapt and deal with new problems or challenges the first time you encounter them, without having to depend on knowledge you already possess. Working memory in and of itself is a contributing factor to a variety of higher cognitive functions. See Learning Objective 6.4. When examined in relation to fluid intelligence, individual differences in working memory components such as capacity, attention control, and ability to retrieve items from long-term memory appear to be most influential, and that overall, the ability to reliably preserve relevant information for successful cognitive processing appears to be vital (Colom et al., 2015; Unsworth et al., 2014, 2015).

7.7 Measuring Intelligence

7.7 Compare and contrast some methods of measuring intelligence.

AP 5.L Define intelligence and list characteristics of how psychologists measure intelligence.

The history of intelligence testing spans the twentieth century and has at times been marked by controversies and misuse. A full history of how intelligence testing developed would take at least an entire chapter, so this section will discuss only some of the better-known forms of testing and how they came to be.

AP 5.O Identify the contributions of key researchers in intelligence research and testing.

💬 It doesn't sound like intelligence would be easy to measure on a test—how do IQ tests work, anyway?

The measurement of intelligence by some kind of test is a concept that is less than a century old. It began when educators in France realized that some students needed more help with learning than others did. They thought that if a way could be found to identify these students more in need, they could be given a different kind of education than the more capable students.

BINET'S MENTAL ABILITY TEST In those early days, a French psychologist named Alfred Binet was asked by the French Ministry of Education to design a formal test of intelligence that would help identify children who were unable to learn as quickly or as well as others so that they could be given remedial education. Eventually, he and colleague Théodore Simon came up with a test that distinguished not only between fast and slow learners but also between children of different age groups as well (Binet & Simon, 1916). They noticed that the fast learners seemed to give answers to questions that older children might give, whereas the slow learners gave answers that were more typical of a younger child. Binet decided that the key element to be tested was a child's *mental age*, or the average age at which children could successfully answer a particular level of questions.

intelligence quotient (IQ)
a number representing a measure of intelligence, resulting from the division of one's mental age by one's chronological age and then multiplying that quotient by 100.

STANFORD-BINET AND IQ Lewis Terman (1916), a researcher at Stanford University, adopted German psychologist William Stern's method for comparing mental age and *chronological age* (number of years since birth) for use with the translated and revised Binet test. Stern's (1912) formula was to divide the mental age (MA) by the chronological age (CA) and multiply the result by 100 to get rid of any decimal points. The resulting score is called an **intelligence quotient,** or **IQ.** (A *quotient* is a number that results from dividing one number by another.)

$$IQ = MA/CA \times 100$$

For example, if a child who is 10 years old takes the test and scores a mental age of 15 (is able to answer the level of questions typical of a 15-year-old), the IQ would look like this:

$$IQ = 15/10 \times 100 = 150$$

The quotient has the advantage of allowing testers to compare the intelligence levels of people of different age groups. While this method works well for children, it produces IQ scores that start to become meaningless as the person's chronological age passes 16 years. (Once a person becomes an adult, the idea of questions that are geared for a particular age group loses its power. For example, what kind of differences would there be between questions designed for a 30-year-old versus a 40-year-old?) Most intelligence tests today, such as the *Stanford-Binet Intelligence Scales, Fifth Edition* (SB5; Roid, 2003) and the Wechsler tests (see the following section), use age-group comparison norms instead. The SB5 is often used by educators to make decisions about the placement of students into special educational programs, both for those with disabilities and for those with exceptionalities. Many children are given this test in the second grade, or age 7 or 8. The SB5 yields an overall estimate of intelligence, verbal and nonverbal domain scores, all composed of five primary areas of cognitive ability—fluid reasoning, knowledge, quantitative processing, visual–spatial processing, and working memory (Roid, 2003). Test items vary by task and difficulty and are typically completed successfully at different ages. Test items include tasks such as inserting correct shapes into matching holes on a form board (age 2), digit reversal or being able to repeat four digits backward (age 9), and testing vocabulary by defining 20 words from a list (average adult; Roid, 2003).

THE WECHSLER TESTS Although the original Stanford-Binet Test is now in its fifth edition and includes different questions for people of different age groups, it is not the only IQ test that is popular today. David Wechsler was the first to devise a series of tests designed for specific age groups. Originally dissatisfied with the fact that the Stanford-Binet test was designed for children but being administered to adults, he developed an IQ test specifically for adults. He later designed tests specifically for older school-age children and preschool children, as well as those in the early grades. The Wechsler Adult Intelligence Scale (WAIS-IV; Wechsler, 2008), Wechsler Intelligence Scale for Children (WISC-V; Wechsler, 2014), and the Wechsler Preschool and Primary Scale of Intelligence (WPPSI-IV; Wechsler, 2012) are the three current versions of this test, and in the United States these tests are now used more frequently than the Stanford-Binet. In earlier editions, another way these tests differed from the Stanford-Binet was by having both a verbal and performance (nonverbal) scale, as well as providing an overall score of intelligence (the original Stanford-Binet was composed predominantly of verbal items). While still using both verbal and nonverbal items, the Wechsler tests now provide an overall score of intelligence and index scores related to cognitive domains. **Table 7.3** has sample items for each of the four index scales from the WAIS-IV.

AP 5.P Explain how psychologists design tests, including standardization strategies and other techniques to establish reliability and validity.

7.8 Test Construction: Good Test, Bad Test?

7.8 Identify ways to evaluate the quality of a test.

All tests are not equally good tests. Some tests may fail to actually test what they are designed for. Others may fail to give the same results on different occasions for the same person when that person has not changed. These tests would be considered invalid and unreliable, respectively.

Table 7.3 Simulated Sample Items from the Wechsler Adult Intelligence Scale (WAIS-IV)

Verbal Comprehension Index	
Similarities	In what way are a circle and a triangle alike? In what way are a saw and a hammer alike?
Vocabulary	What is a hippopotamus? What does "resemble" mean?
Information	What is steam made of? What is pepper? Who wrote *Tom Sawyer*?
Perceptual Reasoning Index	
Block Design	After looking at a pattern or design, try to arrange small cubes in the same pattern.
Matrix Reasoning	After looking at an incomplete matrix pattern or series, select an option that completes the matrix or series.
Visual Puzzles	Look at a completed puzzle and select three components from a set of options that would recreate the puzzle, all within a specified time limit.
Working Memory Index	
Digit Span	Recall lists of numbers, some lists forward and some lists in reverse order, and recall a mixed list of numbers in correct ascending order.
Arithmetic	Three women divided 18 golf balls equally among themselves. How many golf balls did each person receive? If two buttons cost $0.15, what will be the cost of a dozen buttons?
Processing Speed Index	
Symbol Search	Visually scan a group of symbols to identify specific target symbols, within a specified time limit.
Coding	Learn a different symbol for specific numbers and then fill in the blank under the number with the correct symbol. (This test is timed.)

Source: Simulated items and descriptions similar to those in the *Wechsler Adult Intelligence Scale* —Fourth Edition (2008).

RELIABILITY AND VALIDITY **Reliability** of a test refers to the test producing consistent results each time it is given to the same individual or group of people. For example, if Nicholas takes a personality test today and then again in a month or so, the results should be very similar if the personality test is reliable. Other tests might be easy to use and even reliable, but if they don't actually measure what they are supposed to measure, they are also useless. These tests are thought of as "invalid" (untrue) tests. **Validity** is the degree to which a test actually measures what it's supposed to measure. Another aspect of validity is the extent to which an obtained score accurately reflects the intended skill or outcome in real-life situations, or *ecological validity*, not just validity for the testing or assessment situation. For example, we hope that someone who passes his or her test for a driver's license will also be able to safely operate a motor vehicle when they are actually on the road. When evaluating a test, consider what a specific test score means and to what or to whom it is compared.

Take the hypothetical example of Professor Stumpwater, who—for reasons best known only to him—believes that intelligence is related to a person's golf scores. Let's say that he develops an adult intelligence test based on golf scores. What do we need to look at to determine if his test is a good one?

STANDARDIZATION OF TESTS First of all, we would want to look at how he tried to standardize his test. *Standardization* refers to the process of giving the test to a large group of people that represents the kind of people for whom the test is designed.

reliability
the tendency of a test to produce the same scores again and again each time it is given to the same people.

validity
the degree to which a test actually measures what it's supposed to measure.

One aspect of standardization is in the establishment of consistent and standard methods of test administration. All test subjects would take the test under the same conditions. In the professor's case, this would mean that he would have his sample members play the same number of rounds of golf on the same course under the same weather conditions, and so on. Another aspect addresses the comparison group whose scores will be used to compare individual test results. Standardization groups are chosen randomly from the population for whom the test is intended and, like all samples, must be representative of that population. See Learning Objectives 1.9 and 1.11. If a test is designed for children, for example, then a large sample of randomly selected children would be given the test.

NORMS The scores from the standardization group would be called the *norms*, the standards against which all others who take the test would be compared. Most tests of intelligence follow a *normal curve*, or a distribution in which the scores are the most frequent around the *mean*, or average, and become less and less frequent the farther from the mean they occur (see **Figure 7.6**). See Learning Objectives 1.12, 1.13, and 1.14.

AP 5.Q Interpret the meaning of scores in terms of the normal curve.

Figure 7.6 The Normal Curve

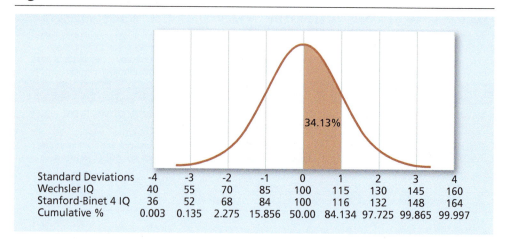

The percentages under each section of the normal curve represent the percentage of scores falling within that section for each *standard deviation (SD)* from the mean. Scores on intelligence tests are typically represented by the normal curve. The vertical lines each represent one standard deviation from the mean, which is always set at 100. For example, an IQ of 115 on the Wechsler represents one standard deviation above the mean, and the area under the curve indicates that 34.13 percent of the population falls between 100 and 115 on this test. See Learning Objectives 1.12, 1.13, and 1.14. Note: The figure shows the mean and standard deviation for the Stanford-Binet Fourth Edition (Stanford-Binet 4). The Stanford-Binet Fifth Edition was published in 2003 and now has a mean of 100 and a standard deviation of 15 for composite scores.

On the Wechsler IQ test, the percentages under each section of the normal curve represent the percentage of scores falling within that section for each *standard deviation (SD)* from the mean on the test. The standard deviation is the average variation of scores from the mean. See Learning Objective 1.14.

In the case of the professor's golf test, he might find that a certain golf score is the average, which he would interpret as average intelligence. People who scored extremely well on the golf test would be compared to the average, as well as people with unusually poor scores.

The normal curve allows IQ scores to be more accurately estimated than the old IQ scoring method formula devised by Stern. Test designers replaced the old ratio IQ of the earlier versions of IQ tests with **deviation IQ scores**, which are based on the normal curve distribution (Eysenck, 1994): IQ is assumed to be normally distributed with a mean IQ of 100 and a typical standard deviation of about 15 (the standard deviation can vary according to the particular test). An IQ of 130, for example, would be two standard deviations

deviation IQ scores

a type of intelligence measure that assumes that IQ is normally distributed around a mean of 100 with a standard deviation of about 15.

above the mean, whereas an IQ of 70 would be two standard deviations below the mean, and in each case the person's score is being compared to the population's average score.

With respect to validity and reliability, the professor's test fares poorly. If the results of the professor's test were compared with other established intelligence tests, there would probably be no relationship at all. Golf scores have nothing to do with intelligence, so the test is not a valid, or true, measure of intelligence.

On the other hand, his test might work well for some people and poorly for others on the question of reliability. Some people who are good and regular golfers tend to score about the same for each game that they play, so for them, the golf score IQ would be fairly reliable. But others, especially those who do not play golf or play infrequently, would have widely varying scores from game to game. For those people, the test would be very unreliable, and if a test is unreliable for some, it's not a good test.

A test can fail in validity but still be reliable. If for some reason Professor Stumpwater chose to use height as a measure of intelligence, an adult's score on Stumpwater's "test" would always be the same, as height does not change by very much after the late teens. But the opposite is not true. If a test is unreliable, how can it accurately measure what it is supposed to measure? For example, adult intelligence remains fairly constant. If a test meant to measure that intelligence gave different scores at different times, it's obviously not a valid measure of intelligence.

> Just because an IQ test gives the same score every time a person takes it doesn't mean that the score is actually measuring real intelligence, right?

That's right—think about the definition of intelligence for a moment: the ability to learn from one's experiences, acquire knowledge, and use resources effectively in adapting to new situations or solving problems. How can anyone define what "effective use of resources" might be? Does everyone have access to the same resources? Is everyone's "world" necessarily perceived as being the same? Intelligence tests are useful measuring devices but should not necessarily be assumed to be measures of all types of intelligent behavior, or even good measures for all groups of people, as the next section discusses.

IQ TESTS AND CULTURAL BIAS The problem with trying to measure intelligence with a test that is based on an understanding of the world and its resources is that not everyone comes from the same "world." People raised in a different culture, or even a different economic situation, from the one in which the designer of an IQ test is raised are not likely to perform well on such a test—not to mention the difficulties of taking a test that is written in an unfamiliar language or dialect. In the early days of immigration, people from non-English-speaking countries would score very poorly on intelligence tests, in some cases being denied entry to the United States on the basis of such tests (Allen, 2006).

It is very difficult to design an intelligence test that is completely free of *cultural bias*, a term referring to the tendency of IQ tests to reflect, in language, dialect, and content, the culture of the person or persons who designed the test. A person who comes from the same culture (or even socioeconomic background) as the test designer may have an unfair advantage over a person who is from a different cultural or socioeconomic background (Helms, 1992). If people raised in an Asian culture are given a test designed within a traditional Western culture, many items on the test might make no sense to them. For example, one kind of question might be: Which one of the five is least like the other four?

DOG—CAR—CAT—BIRD—FISH

The answer is supposed to be "car," which is the only one of the five that is not alive. But a Japanese child, living in a culture that relies on the sea for so much of its food and culture, might choose "fish," because none of the others are found in the ocean. That child's test score would be lower but not because the child is not intelligent.

AP 5.M Discuss how culture influences the definition of intelligence.

AP 5.T Debate the appropriate testing practices, particularly in relation to culture-fair test uses.

How might culture determine or influence how intelligence is defined?

In 1971, Adrian Dove designed an intelligence test to highlight the problem of cultural bias. Dove, an African American sociologist, created the Dove Counterbalance General Intelligence Test in an attempt to demonstrate that a significant language/dialect barrier exists among children of different backgrounds. Questions on this test were derived from African American culture in the southeastern United States during the 1960s and 1970s. Anyone not knowledgeable of this culture will probably score very poorly on this test, including African American people from other geographical regions. The point is simply this: Tests are created by people from a particular culture and background. Questions and answers that test creators might think are common knowledge may relate to their own experiences and not to people of other cultures, backgrounds, or socioeconomic levels.

Attempts have been made to create intelligence tests that are as free of cultural influences as is humanly possible. For example, to possibly avoid or limit the influence of language, or to accommodate someone with hearing impairments or low cognitive abilities, there are a variety of nonverbal assessments of intelligence available. Some of these are the *Beta-4*, the *Test of Nonverbal Intelligence, Fourth Edition* (TONI-4), the *Comprehensive Test of Nonverbal Intelligence, Second Edition* (CTONI-2), the *Leiter International Performance Scale, Third Edition* (Leiter-3), the *Naglieri Nonverbal Ability Test* (NNAT), the *Test of Nonverbal Intelligence, Fourth Edition* (TONI-4), the *Universal Nonverbal Intelligence Test - Second Edition* (UNIT2), and the *Wechsler Nonverbal Scale of Ability* (WNV).

Figure 7.7 Sample Test Item from Raven's Progressive Matrices

Facsimile of an item that may be found in Raven's Progressive Matrices. Which of the bottom images completes the pattern?

Many test designers have come to the conclusion that it may be impossible to create a test that is completely free of cultural bias (Carpenter et al., 1990). Instead, they are striving to create tests that are at least *culturally fair*. These tests use questions that do not create a disadvantage for people whose culture differs from that of the majority. Many items on a "culture-fair" test require the use of nonverbal abilities, such as rotating objects, rather than items about verbal knowledge that might be culturally specific. One example is Raven's Progressive Matrices, a test of abstract reasoning. The test consists of a series of items containing abstract patterns, either in a 2 × 2 or 2 × 3 matrix, from which test takers have to identify a missing portion that best completes a pattern (see **Figure 7.7**). However, although once believed to be largely culture free, or at least fair, even this test is not immune to the influence of culture, as age, generational cohort, and education appear to impact performance (Brouwers et al., 2009; Fox & Mitchum, 2013).

THINKING CRITICALLY 7.1

What kind of questions would you include on an intelligence test to minimize cultural bias?

💬 If intelligence tests are so flawed, why do people still use them?

USEFULNESS OF IQ TESTS IQ tests are generally valid for predicting academic success and job performance (Sackett et al., 2008). This may be truer for those who score at the higher and lower ends of the normal curve. (For those who score in the average range of IQ, the predictive value is less clear.) The kinds of tests students are given in school are often similar to intelligence tests, and so people who do well on IQ tests typically do well on other kinds of academically oriented tests as well, such as the SAT, the American College Test (ACT), the Graduate Record Exam (GRE), and actual college examinations. These achievement tests are very similar to IQ tests but are administered to groups of people rather than to individuals. However, research suggests skills in self-regulation or levels of motivation may impact IQ measures and raises concerns about situations or circumstances in which IQ scores may not be unbiased predictors of academic or job success (Duckworth et al., 2011; Duckworth & Seligman, 2005; Nisbett et al., 2012).

Intelligence testing also plays an important role in neuropsychology, where specially trained psychologists use intelligence tests and other forms of cognitive and behavioral testing to assess neurobehavioral disorders in which cognition and behavior are impaired as the result of brain injury or brain malfunction (National Academy of Neuropsychology, 2001). As part of their profession, neuropsychologists use intelligence testing in diagnosis (e.g., head injury, learning disabilities, neuropsychological disorders), tracking progress of individuals with such disorders, and in monitoring possible recovery. See Learning Objective A.5.

Neuropsychologists often work with individuals who have traumatic brain injury (TBI). Many traumatic brain injuries can also be permanent, impacting the day-to-day functioning of both individuals and their loved ones for the rest of their lives. Depending on the area or areas of the brain injured and the severity of the trauma, some possible outcomes might include difficulty thinking, speech disturbances, memory problems, reduced attention span, headaches, sleep disturbances, frustration, mood swings, and personality changes. Not only do these outcomes negatively impact formal tests of intelligence, the deficits from such injuries may also affect thinking, problem solving, and cognition in general.

Mild TBI, or concussion, is an impairment of brain function for minutes to hours following a head injury. Concussions may include a loss of consciousness for up to 30 minutes, "seeing stars," headache, dizziness, and sometimes nausea or vomiting (Blumenfeld, 2010; Ruff et al., 2009). Amnesia for the events immediately before or after the accident is also a primary symptom and more likely to be anterograde in nature. See Learning Objective 6.5 and 6.13.

The effects of repeated concussions and the long-term effects of head injuries in general are of particular interest to neuropsychologists and other health professionals because the potential issues (memory problems, changes in personality, etc.) may not be evident until many years later. American football is one sport in which athletes may have extended playing careers. The possibility of an increased risk for depression, dementia, or other neurological risks for these athletes after they have quit playing has spawned ongoing research with professional football players (Guskiewicz et al., 2007; Hazrati et al., 2013; G. Miller, 2009). Former players who had three or more concussions were three times more likely to have significant memory problems and five times more likely to be diagnosed with mild cognitive impairment, often a precursor to Alzheimer's disease. *Chronic traumatic encephalopathy* (CTE) is a progressive brain disease linked to repetitive TBIs. In a study of 66 brains examined from individuals that had participated in contact sports, 21 had brain changes and pathology consistent with CTE. Furthermore, of 198 brains from individuals that did not play contact sports, no CTE signs were detected, even in the brains of 33 individuals that suffered from a single TBI (Bieniek et al., 2015). Recent research suggests that the level of CTE pathology may be tied to the level of experience, with CTE-related changes noted in 87% of former football players (Mez et al., 2017). For those with CTE, former high school players had mild pathology, whereas the majority of former college, semiprofessional, Canadian Football League, and National Football League players had severe pathological changes (Mez et al., 2017).

AP 5.R Describe relevant labels related to intelligence testing.

AP 8.F Discuss the major diagnostic categories, including neurodevelopmental disorders, neurocognitive disorders, schizophrenia spectrum, and other psychotic disorders, and their corresponding symptoms.

7.9 Individual Differences in Intelligence

7.9 Define intellectual disability, giftedness, and emotional intelligence.

Another use of IQ tests is to help identify people who differ from those of average intelligence by a great degree. Although one such group is composed of those who are sometimes called "geniuses" (who fall at the extreme high end of the normal curve for intelligence), the other group is made up of people who, for various reasons, are considered intellectually disabled and whose IQ scores fall well below the mean on the normal curve.

INTELLECTUAL DISABILITY Intellectual disability (intellectual developmental disorder), formerly *mental retardation* or *developmentally delayed*, is a neurodevelopmental disorder and is defined in several ways. First, the person exhibits deficits in mental abilities, which is typically associated with an IQ score approximately two standard deviations below the mean on the normal curve, such as below 70 on a test with a mean of 100 and standard deviation of 15. Second, the person's *adaptive behavior* (skills that allow people to live independently, such as being able to work at a job, communicate well with others, and grooming skills such as being able to get dressed, eat, and bathe with little or no help) is severely below a level appropriate for the person's age. Finally, these limitations must begin in the developmental period. Intellectual disability occurs in about 1 percent of the population (American Psychiatric Association, 2013).

> 💬 So how would a professional go about deciding whether or not a child has an intellectual disability? Is the IQ test the primary method?

DIAGNOSIS Previous editions of the *Diagnostic and Statistical Manual of Mental Disorders (DSM)* relied heavily on IQ tests for determining the diagnosis and level of severity of *mental retardation*. Recognizing tests of IQ are less valid as one approaches the lower end of the IQ range, and the importance of adaptive living skills in multiple life areas, levels of severity are now based on the level of adaptive functioning and level of support the individual requires (American Psychiatric Association, 2013). Thus, a *Diagnostic and Statistical Manual of Mental Disorders, Fifth Edition (DSM-5*; American Psychiatric Association, 2013) diagnosis of intellectual disability is based on deficits in intellectual functioning, determined by standardized tests of intelligence and clinical assessment, which impact adaptive functioning across three domains. The domains include: conceptual (memory, reasoning, language, reading, writing, math, and other academic skills), social (empathy, social judgment, interpersonal communication, and other skills that impact the ability to make and maintain friendships), and practical (self-management skills that affect personal care, job responsibilities, school, money management, and other areas; American Psychiatric Association, 2013). Symptoms must begin during the developmental period.

Intellectual disability can vary from mild to profound. According to the *DSM-5* (American Psychiatric Association, 2013), individuals with mild intellectual disability may not be recognized as having deficits in the conceptual domain until they reach school age, where learning difficulties become apparent; as adults, they are likely to be fairly concrete thinkers. In the social domain, they are at risk of being manipulated, as social judgment and interactions are immature as compared to same-age peers. In the practical domain, they are capable of living independently with proper supports in place but will likely require assistance with more complex life skills such as health-care decisions, legal issues, or raising a family (American Psychiatric Association, 2013). This category makes up the vast majority of those with intellectual disabilities. Other classifications in order of severity are moderate, severe, and profound. Conceptually, individuals with

intellectual disability (intellectual developmental disorder)
condition in which a person's behavioral and cognitive skills exist at an earlier developmental stage than the skills of others who are the same chronological age; may also be referred to as developmentally delayed. This condition was formerly known as mental retardation.

profound intellectual disability have a very limited ability to learn beyond simple matching and sorting tasks and, socially, have very poor communication skills, although they may recognize and interact nonverbally with well-known family members and other caretakers. In the practical domain, they may be able to participate by watching or assisting but are likely totally dependent on others for all areas of their care (American Psychiatric Association, 2013). All of these skill deficits are likely compounded by multiple physical or sensory impairments.

CAUSES What causes intellectual disability? Unhealthy living conditions can affect brain development. Examples of such conditions are lead poisoning from eating paint chips (Lanphear et al., 2000), exposure to industrial chemicals like polychlorinated biphenyls (PCBs; Darvill et al., 2000), prenatal exposure to mercury (Grandjean et al., 1997), as well as other toxicants (Eriksson et al., 2001; Eskenazi et al., 1999; Schroeder, 2000). Deficits may also be attributed to factors resulting in inadequate brain development or other health risks associated with poverty. Examples include malnutrition, health consequences as the result of not having adequate access to health care, or lack of mental stimulation through typical cultural and educational experiences.

Some of the biological causes of intellectual disability include Down syndrome (see Learning Objective 8.3), fetal alcohol syndrome, and fragile X syndrome. *Fetal alcohol syndrome* is a condition that results from exposing a developing embryo to alcohol, and intelligence levels can range from below average to levels associated with intellectual disability (Olson & Burgess, 1997). In *fragile X syndrome*, an individual (more frequently a male) has a defect in a gene on the X chromosome of the 23rd pair, leading to a deficiency in a protein needed for brain development. Depending on the severity of the damage to this gene, symptoms of fragile X syndrome can range from mild to severe or profound intellectual disability, and it is the most common inherited cause of intellectual disability (Dykens et al., 1994; Knopik et al., 2017; Valverde et al., 2007).

There are many other causes of intellectual disability (Murphy et al., 1998). Lack of oxygen at birth, damage to the fetus in the womb from diseases, infections, or drug use by the mother, and even diseases and accidents during childhood can lead to intellectual disability.

One thing should always be remembered: Intellectual disability affects a person's *intellectual* capabilities and adaptive behaviors. Individuals with an intellectual disability are just as responsive to love and affection as anyone else and need to be loved and to have friends just as all people do. Intelligence is only one characteristic; warmth, friendliness, caring, and compassion also count for a great deal and should not be underrated.

GIFTEDNESS At the other end of the intelligence spectrum are those who fall on the upper end of the normal curve (see Figure 7.6), above an IQ of 130 (about 2 percent of the population). The term applied to these individuals is **gifted**, and if their IQ falls above 140 to 145 (less than half of 1 percent of the population), they are often referred to as highly advanced or *geniuses*.

> 💬 I've heard that geniuses are sometimes a little "nutty" and odd. Are geniuses, especially the really high-IQ ones, "not playing with a full deck," as the saying goes?

People have long held many false beliefs about people who are very, very intelligent. Such beliefs have included that gifted people are weird and socially awkward, physically weak, and more likely to suffer from mental illnesses. From these beliefs come the "mad scientist" of the cinema and the "evil geniuses" of literature.

gifted
the 2 percent of the population falling on the upper end of the normal curve and typically possessing an IQ of 130 or above.

Stanford University psychologist Lewis Terman is pictured at his desk in 1942. Terman spent a good portion of his career researching children with high IQ scores and was the first to use the term *gifted* to describe these children.

These beliefs were shattered by a groundbreaking study that was initiated in 1921 by Lewis M. Terman, the same individual responsible for the development of the Stanford-Binet Test. Terman (1925) selected 1,528 children to participate in a longitudinal study. See Learning Objective 8.1. These children, 857 boys and 671 girls, had IQs (as measured by the Stanford-Binet) ranging from 130 to 200. The early findings of this major study (Terman & Oden, 1947) demonstrated that the gifted were socially well adjusted and often skilled leaders. They were also above average in height, weight, and physical attractiveness, putting an end to the myth of the weakling genius. Terman was able to demonstrate not only that his gifted children were *not* more susceptible to mental illness than the general population, but he was also able to show that they were actually more resistant to mental illnesses than those of average intelligence. Only those with the highest IQs (180 and above) were found to have some social and behavioral adjustment problems *as children* (Janos, 1987).

Terman's "Termites," as they came to be called, were also typically successful as adults. They earned more academic degrees and had higher occupational and financial success than their average peers (at least, the men in the study had occupational success—women at this time did not typically have careers outside the home). Researchers Zuo and Cramond (2001) examined some of Terman's gifted people to see if their identity formation as adolescents was related to later occupational success. See Learning Objective 8.14. They found that most of the more successful "Termites" had in fact successfully achieved a consistent sense of self, whereas those who were less successful had not done so. For more on Terman's famous study, see *Classic Studies in Psychology*.

A book by Joan Freeman called *Gifted Children Grown Up* (Freeman, 2001) describes the results of a similar longitudinal study of 210 gifted and nongifted children in Great Britain. One of the more interesting findings from this study is that gifted children who are "pushed" to achieve at younger and younger ages, sitting for exams long before their peers would do so, often grow up to be disappointed, somewhat unhappy adults. Freeman points to differing life conditions for the gifted as a major factor in their success, adjustment, and well-being: Some lived in poverty and some in wealth, for example. Yet another longitudinal study (Torrance, 1993) found that in both gifted students and gifted adults, there is more to success in life than intelligence and high academic achievement. In that study, liking one's work, having a sense of purpose in life, a high energy level, and persistence were also very important factors. If the picture of the genius as mentally unstable is a myth, so, too, is the belief that being gifted will always lead to success, as even Terman found in his original study.

Classic Studies in Psychology
Terman's "Termites"

Terman's (1925) longitudinal study is still providing information today. Terman himself died in 1956, but several other researchers (including Robert Sears, one of the original Termites, who died in 1989) kept track of the remaining Termites over the years (Holahan & Sears, 1996).

As adults, the Termites were relatively successful, with a median income in the 1950s of $10,556, compared to the national median at that time of $5,800 a year. Most of them graduated from college, many earning advanced degrees. Their occupations included doctors, lawyers, business executives, university professors, scientists, and even one famous science fiction writer and an Oscar-winning director.

By 2000, only about 200 Termites were still living. Although the study was marred by several flaws, it still remains one of the most important and rich sources of data on an entire generation. Terman's study was actually the first truly longitudinal study (see Learning Objective 8.1) ever to be accomplished, and scientists have gotten data about the effects of phenomena such as World War II and the influence of personality traits on how long one lives from the questionnaires filled out by the participants over the years.

Terman and Oden (1959) compared the 100 most successful men in the group to the 100 least successful by defining "successful" as holding jobs that related to or used their intellectual skills. The more successful men earned more money, had careers with more prestige, and were healthier and less likely to be divorced or alcoholics than the less successful men. The IQ scores were relatively equal between the two groups, so the differences in success in life had to be caused by some other factor or factors. Terman and Oden found that the successful adults were different from the others in three ways: They were more goal oriented, more persistent in pursuing those goals, and were more self-confident than the less successful Termites.

What were the flaws in this study? Terman acquired his participants by getting recommendations from teachers and principals, not through random selection, so that there was room for bias in the pool of participants from the start. It is quite possible that the teachers and principals were less likely, especially in 1921, to recommend students who were "troublemakers" or different from the majority. Consequently, Terman's original group consisted of almost entirely White, urban, and middle-class children, with the majority (857 out of 1,528) being male. There were only two African Americans, six Japanese Americans, and one Native American.

Another flaw is the way Terman interfered in the lives of his "children." In any good research study, the investigator should avoid becoming personally involved in the lives of the participants in the study to reduce the possibility of biasing the results. Terman seemed to find it nearly impossible to remain objective (Leslie, 2000). He became like a surrogate father to many of them.

Flawed as it may have been, Terman's groundbreaking study did accomplish his original goal of putting to rest the myths that existed about genius in the early part of the twentieth century. Gifted children and adults are no more prone to mental illnesses or odd behavior than any other group, and they also have their share of failures as well as successes. Genius is obviously not the only factor that influences success in life—personality and experiences are strong factors as well. For example, the homes of the children in the top 2 percent of Terman's group had an average of 450 books in their libraries, a sign that the parents of these children valued books and learning, and these parents were also more likely to be teachers, professionals, doctors, and lawyers. The experiences of these gifted children growing up would have been vastly different from those in homes with less emphasis on reading and lower occupational levels for the parents.

Questions for Further Discussion

1. In Terman and Oden's 1959 study of the successful and unsuccessful Termites, what might be the problems associated with the definition of "successful" in the study?
2. Thinking back to the discussion of research ethics in Chapter One (see Learning Objective 1.17), what ethical violations may Terman have committed while involved in this study?
3. If gifted children thrive when growing up in more economically sound and educationally focused environments, what should the educational system strive to do to nourish the gifted? Should the government get involved in programs for the gifted?

EMOTIONAL INTELLIGENCE What about people who have a lot of "book smarts" but not much common sense? There are some people like that who never seem to get ahead in life in spite of having all of that so-called intelligence. It is true that not everyone who is intellectually able is going to be a success in life (Mehrabian, 2000). Sometimes the people who are most successful are those who didn't do all that well in the regular academic setting.

One explanation for why some people who do poorly in school succeed in life and why some who do well in school don't do so well in the "real" world is that success relies on a certain degree of **emotional intelligence**, the accurate awareness of and ability to manage one's own emotions to facilitate thinking and attain specific goals, and the ability to understand what others feel (Mayer & Salovey, 1997; Mayer, Salovey, et al., 2008).

The concept of emotional intelligence was first introduced by Peter Salovey and John Mayer (Salovey & Mayer, 1990) and later popularized by Dan Goleman (Goleman, 1995). And while Goleman originally suggested emotional intelligence was a more powerful influence on success in life than more traditional views of intelligence, his work and the work of others used the term in a variety of different ways than originally proposed, and claims by some were not backed by scientific evidence. For example, studies have been criticized for their lack of validity and, thus, their applicability (Antonakis, 2004). Furthermore, emotional intelligence is not the same as having high self-esteem or being optimistic. One who is emotionally intelligent possesses self-control of emotions such as anger, impulsiveness, and anxiety. Empathy, the ability to understand what others feel, is also a component, as are an awareness of one's own emotions, sensitivity, persistence even in the face of frustrations, and the ability to motivate oneself (Mayer & Salovey, 1997; Salovey & Mayer, 1990).

> That all sounds very nice, but how can anything like this be measured?

Is there research to support this idea? In one study, researchers asked 321 participants to read passages written by nonparticipants and try to guess what the nonparticipants were feeling while they were writing (Mayer & Geher, 1996). The assumption was that people who were good at connecting thoughts to feelings would also have a high degree of empathy and emotional intelligence. The participants who more correctly judged the writers' emotional experiences (assessed by both how well each participant's emotional judgments agreed with a group consensus and the nonparticipant's actual report of feelings) also scored higher on the empathy measure and lower on the defensiveness measure. These same participants also had higher SAT scores (self-reported), leading Mayer and colleagues to conclude not only that emotional intelligence is a valid and measurable concept but also that general intelligence and emotional intelligence may be related: Those who are high in emotional intelligence are also smarter in the traditional sense (Mayer et al., 2000). Another review found individuals with higher emotional intelligence tended to have better social relationships for both children and adults, better family and intimate relationships, were perceived more positively by others, had better academic achievement, were more successful at work, and experienced greater psychological well-being (Mayer, Roberts, et al., 2008).

Another example of research supporting the role of emotional intelligence in real-world settings has been in the field of health and medicine. In a sample of college students and an evaluation of their health behaviors, those with healthier behaviors tended to have higher levels of emotional intelligence (Espinosa & Kadic-Maglajlic, 2018). Studies have supported the fact that medical school students with higher emotional intelligence tended to perform better in courses related to patient relationships, or "bedside manners" (Libbrecht et al., 2014). In this sample of students, success appeared to be related more to the individual's ability to regulate their own emotions, as

emotional intelligence

the awareness of and ability to manage one's own emotions to facilitate thinking and attain goals, as well as the ability to understand emotions in others.

compared to their ability to understand the emotions of others. There has also been reported evidence for emotional intelligence being related to physician competence and areas of improved physician–patient interactions, including enhanced communication and more empathic and compassionate patient care (Arora et al., 2010). In a study of Japanese medical students, emotional intelligence was only weakly associated with empathy but evidenced a strong negative correlation with the *Big Five* personality dimension of neuroticism (Abe et al., 2018). See Learning Objectives 1.8, 12.10. This is slightly different than what has been observed in a study of medical students in the United States, where there were weaker negative associations with neuroticism, and may be tied to either cultural differences in personality and emotional intelligence or cultural influences when measuring emotional intelligence and empathy in different settings or countries (Bertram et al., 2016).

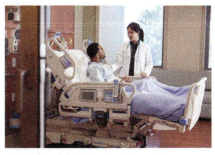

Emotional intelligence includes empathy, which is the ability to feel what others are feeling. This physician is not only able to listen to her patient's concerns but also is able to show by her facial expression, body language, and gestures that she understands how the patient feels.

7.10 The Nature/Nurture Issue Regarding Intelligence

7.10 Evaluate the influence of heredity and environment on the development of intelligence.

Are people born with all of the "smarts" they will ever have, or do experience and learning count for something in the development of intellect? The influence of nature (heredity or genes) and nurture (environment) on personality traits has long been debated in the field of human development, and intelligence is one of the traits that has been examined closely. See Learning Objective 8.2.

AP 2.A Discuss psychology's abiding interest in how heredity, environment, and evolution work together to shape behavior.

TWIN AND ADOPTION STUDIES The problem with trying to separate the role of genes from that of environment is that controlled, perfect experiments are neither practical nor ethical. Instead, researchers find out what they can from *natural experiments*, circumstances existing in nature that can be examined to understand some phenomenon. *Twin studies* are an example of such circumstances.

AP 5.T Debate the appropriate testing practices, particularly in relation to culture-fair test uses.

Identical twins are those who originally came from one fertilized egg and, therefore, share the same genetic inheritance. Any differences between them on a certain trait, then, should be caused by environmental factors. Fraternal twins come from two different eggs, each fertilized by a different sperm, and share only the amount of genetic material that any two siblings would share. See Learning Objective 8.3. By comparing the IQs of these two types of twins reared together (similar environments) and reared apart (different environments), as well as persons of other degrees of relatedness, researchers can get a general, if not exact, idea of how much influence heredity has over the trait of intelligence (see **Figure 7.8**). As can be easily seen from the chart, the greater the degree of genetic relatedness, the stronger the correlation is between the IQ scores of those persons. The fact that genetically identical twins show a correlation of 0.86 means that the environment must play a part in determining some aspects of intelligence as measured by IQ tests. If heredity alone were responsible, the correlation between genetically identical twins should be 1.00. At this time, researchers have determined that the estimated **heritability** (proportion of change in IQ within a population that is caused by hereditary factors) for intelligence is about .50 or 50 percent (Knopik et al., 2017; Plomin & DeFries, 1998; Plomin & Spinath, 2004). Furthermore, the impact of genetic factors increases with increasing age, but the set of genes or genetic factors remains the same. The effects of the same set of genes becomes larger with increasing age (Knopik et al., 2017; Plomin & Deary, 2015; Plomin et al., 2016; Posthuma et al., 2009).

heritability

degree to which the changes in some trait within a population can be considered to be due to genetic influences; the extent individual genetic differences affect individual differences in observed behavior; in IQ, proportion of change in IQ within a population that is caused by hereditary factors.

💬 Wait a minute—if identical twins have a correlation of .86, wouldn't that mean that intelligence is 86 percent inherited?

Figure 7.8 Correlations between IQ Scores of Persons with Various Relationships

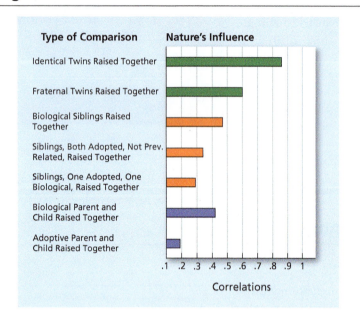
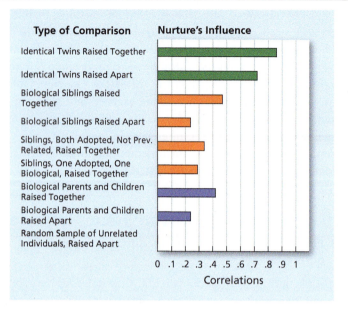

In the graph on the left, the degree of genetic relatedness seems to determine the agreement (correlation) between IQ scores of the various comparisons. For example, identical twins, who share 100 percent of their genes, are more similar in IQ than fraternal twins, who share only about 50 percent of their genes, even when raised in the same environment. In the graph on the right, identical twins are still more similar to each other in IQ than are other types of comparisons, but being raised in the same environment increases the similarity considerably.

Although the correlation between identical twins is higher than the estimated heritability of .50, that similarity is not entirely due to the twins' genetic similarity. Twins who are raised in the same household obviously share very similar environments as well. Even twins who are reared apart, as seen in adoption studies, are usually placed in homes that are similar in socioeconomic and ethnic background—more similar than one might think. So when twins who are genetically similar are raised in similar environments, their IQ scores are also going to be similar. However, similar environmental influences become less important over time (where genetic influences increase over time), accounting for only about 20 percent of the variance in intelligence by age 11 or 12 (Posthuma et al., 2009). In turn, environmental influences tend not to be a factor by adolescence, and with the increasing impact of genetic factors, it has been suggested that the heritability of intelligence might be as high as .91 or 91 percent by the age of 65 (Posthuma et al., 2009), while other research suggests it is closer to 80 percent at age 65, or may actually decline some in later life (Knopik et al., 2017).

One of the things that people need to understand about heritability is that estimates of heritability apply only to changes in IQ within a *group* of people, *not to the individual people themselves*. Each individual is far too different in experiences, education, and other nongenetic factors to predict exactly how a particular set of genes will interact with those factors in that one person. Only differences among people *in general* can be investigated for the influence of genes (Dickens & Flynn, 2001). Genes always interact with environmental factors, and in some cases extreme environments can modify even very heritable traits, as would happen in the case of a severely malnourished child's growth pattern. Enrichment, on the other hand, could have improved outcomes. Even a family's socioeconomic status is influenced by genetics, and a child's socioeconomic status during infancy through adolescence is positively correlated with his or her intelligence development (Trzaskowski et al., 2014; von Stumm & Plomin, 2015). Some observations suggest IQ scores are steadily increasing over time, from generation to generation, in modernized countries, a phenomenon called the *Flynn effect* (Flynn, 2009).

THINKING CRITICALLY 7.2

How might you determine whether or not flute-playing ability is a highly heritable trait? If you want to improve your flute playing and someone tells you that musical ability is heritable, should you stop practicing?

THE BELL CURVE AND MISINTERPRETATION OF STATISTICS One of the other factors that has been examined for possible heritable differences in performance on IQ tests is the concept of race. (The term *race* is used in most of these investigations as a way to group people with common skin colors or facial features, and one should always be mindful of how suspect that kind of classification is. Cultural background, educational experiences, and socioeconomic factors typically have far more to do with similarities in group performances than does the color of one's skin.) In 1994, Herrnstein and Murray published the controversial book *The Bell Curve*, in which they cite large numbers of statistical studies (never published in scientific journals prior to the book) that led them to make the claim that IQ is largely inherited. These authors go further by also implying that people from lower economic levels are poor because they are unintelligent.

AP 5.L Define intelligence and list characteristics of how psychologists measure intelligence.

In their book, Herrnstein and Murray made several statistical errors and ignored the effects of environment and culture. First, they assumed that IQ tests actually do measure intelligence. As discussed earlier, IQ tests are not free of cultural or socioeconomic bias. Furthermore, as the video *Intelligence Tests and Stereotypes* explains, just being aware of negative stereotypes can result in an individual scoring poorly on intelligence tests, a response called **stereotype threat** (Steele & Aronson, 1995). So all they really found was a correlation between race and *IQ*, not race and *intelligence*. Second, they assumed that intelligence itself is very heavily influenced by genetics, with a heritability factor of about .80. The current estimate of the heritability of intelligence is about .50 (Knopik et al., 2017; Plomin & DeFries, 1998; Plomin & Spinath, 2004).

Watch the **Video** at **MyLab Psychology**

Herrnstein and Murray also failed to understand that heritability only applies to differences that can be found *within* a group of people as opposed to those *between* groups of people or individuals (Gould, 1981). Heritability estimates can only be made truly from a group that was exposed to a similar environment.

One of their findings was that Japanese Americans are at the top of the IQ ladder, a finding that they attribute to racial and genetic characteristics. They seem to ignore the cultural influence of intense focus on education and achievement by Japanese-American parents (Neisser et al., 1996). Scientists (Beardsley, 1995; Kamin, 1995) have concluded that, despite the claims of *The Bell Curve*, there is no real scientific evidence for genetic differences in intelligence *between* different racial groups. A series of studies, using blood-group testing for racial grouping (different racial groups have different rates of certain blood groups, allowing a statistical estimation of ancestry), found no significant relationship between ethnicity and IQ (Neisser et al., 1996).

stereotype threat
condition in which being made aware of a negative performance stereotype interferes with the performance of someone that considers himself or herself part of that group.

Concept Map L.O. 7.6, 7.7, 7.8, 7.9, 7.10

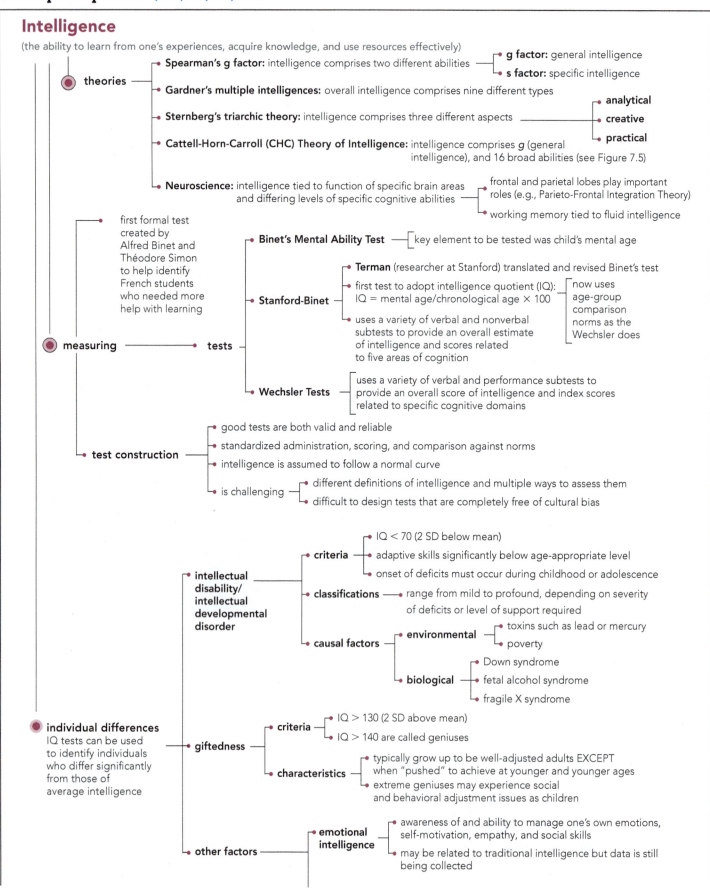

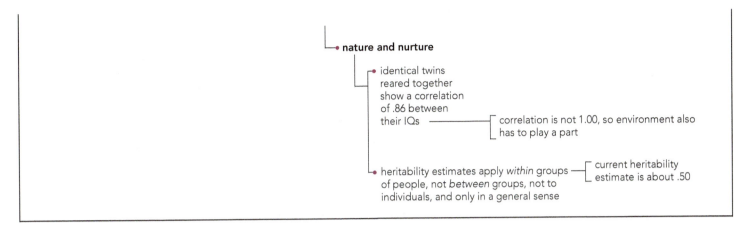

Practice Quiz — How much do you remember?

Pick the best answer.

1. In Gardner's view, effective counseling psychologists and managers would likely be high in _____ intelligence.
   a. verbal/linguistic
   b. interpersonal
   c. naturalist
   d. visual–spatial
   e. intrapersonal

2. According to Sternberg, intelligence comprises analytical, creative, and _____ aspects.
   a. scientific
   b. emotional
   c. artistic
   d. logical
   e. practical

3. Professor Snipes designed an IQ test. To validate this test, she should be careful to do which of the following?
   a. Give the test at least twice to the same group to ensure accuracy.
   b. Strive to make sure that the test measures what it is supposed to measure.
   c. Give the test at least twice to the same group in two different cultures and compare the results.
   d. Select only university professors to take the test so that they can critique the questions on the test.
   e. Select the people in the sample from the population of people for whom the test is designed.

4. In terms of differing cultures, what should be a realistic goal of every test designer?
   a. to create a test free of cultural bias
   b. to create a series of culture-varied tests
   c. to create a series of culture-specific tests
   d. to create a test with no questions involving culture
   e. to create a test that is culturally fair

5. In recent studies, what do some researchers argue is a more accurate means of gauging success in relationships and careers?
   a. annual income
   b. emotional intelligence
   c. intellectual intelligence
   d. stress surveys
   e. heredity studies

6. Which of the following would be an example of a stereotype threat?
   a. Malik, who believes that all tests are equal and that he can, and will, excel on them
   b. Joaquim, who believes IQ tests are unfair to Hispanics, something that his IQ score seems to reflect
   c. Doug, who believes he is not good at math
   d. Jasmine, who feels she must excel on her IQ test
   e. Tiana, who believes that all testing, no matter the type, is biased

7.11–7.14 Language

In Chapter Six we discussed how language can possibly affect our memory. For example, being asked "Did you see the car bump into the truck?" may prompt a slightly different memory than "Did you see the car smash into the truck?" In this section, we will examine language and how cognition can be affected by language.

7.11 The Levels of Language Analysis

7.11 Identify the different elements and structure of language.

Language is a system for combining symbols (such as words) so that an infinite* number of meaningful statements can be made for the purpose of communicating with others. Language allows people not only to communicate with one another but also to represent their own internal mental activity. In other words, language is a very important part of how people think.

language

a system for combining symbols (such as words) so that an unlimited number of meaningful statements can be made for the purpose of communicating with others.

___

*infinite: unlimited, without end.

The structures of languages all over the world share common characteristics. They consist of the sounds that exist within a language, word meanings, word order, the rules for making words into other words, the meanings of sentences and phrases, and the rules for practical communication with others.

GRAMMAR **Grammar** is the system of rules governing the structure and use of a language. According to famed linguist Noam Chomsky (Chomsky, 2006; Chomsky et al., 2002), humans have an innate ability to understand and produce language through a device he calls the *language acquisition device*, or *LAD*. He defined the LAD as an innate "program" that contained a *schema* for human language. The children matched the language they heard against this schema and, thus, language developed in a well-researched sequence (Chomsky, 1957, 1964, 1981, 1986). While humans may learn the *specific* language (English, Spanish, Mandarin, etc.) through the processes of imitation, reinforcement, and shaping (see Learning Objectives 5.5, 5.9, and 5.13), the complexities of the grammar of a language are, according to Chomsky, to some degree "wired in" to the developing brain. Recent research has supported Chomsky's ideas, with evidence of both hierarchical development of language comprehension and the underlying brain processes involved (Ding et al., 2015). See Learning Objective 2.9. The LAD "listens" to the language input of the infant's world and then begins to produce language sounds and eventually words and sentences in a pattern found across cultures. This pattern is discussed in greater detail in the next section. See Learning Objective 7.12. Grammar includes phonemes (the basic sounds of language), morphology (the study of the formation of words), rules for the order of words known as syntax, and pragmatics (the practical social expectations and uses of language).

PHONEMES **Phonemes** are the basic units of sound in a language. The *a* in the word *car* is a very different phoneme from the *a* in the word *day*, even though it is the same letter of the alphabet. The difference is in how we say the sound of the *a* in each word. Phonemes are more than just the different ways in which we pronounce single letters, too. *Th*, *sh*, and *au* are also phonemes. Phonemes for different languages are also different, and one of the biggest problems for people who are trying to learn another language is the inability to both hear and pronounce the phonemes of that other language. Although infants are born with the ability to recognize all phonemes (Werker & Lalonde, 1988), after about 9 months, that ability has deteriorated, and the infant recognizes only the phonemes of the language to which the infant is exposed (Boyson-Bardies et al., 1989).

MORPHEMES **Morphemes** are the smallest units of meaning within a language. For example, the word *playing* consists of two morphemes, *play* and *ing*.

SYNTAX **Syntax** is a system of rules for combining words and phrases to form grammatically correct sentences. Syntax is quite important, as just a simple mix-up can cause sentences to be completely misunderstood. For example, "John kidnapped the boy" has a different meaning from "John, the kidnapped boy," although all four words are the same (Lasnik, 1990). Another example of the importance of syntax can be found in the lobby of a Moscow hotel across from a monastery: "You are welcome to visit the cemetery where famous composers, artists, and writers are buried daily except Thursday." So if people want to watch famous composers, artists, and writers being buried, they should not go to this monastery on Thursday.

SEMANTICS **Semantics** are rules for determining the meaning of words and sentences. Sentences, for example, can have the same semantic meaning while having different syntax: "Johnny hit the ball" and "the ball was hit by Johnny."

PRAGMATICS The **pragmatics** of language has to do with the practical aspects of communicating with others, or the social "niceties" of language. Simply put, pragmatics involves knowing things like how to take turns in a conversation, the use of gestures to emphasize a point or indicate a need for more information, and the different ways in which one speaks to different people (Yule, 1996). For example, adults speak to small children differently than

---

AP 5.C Identify the contributions of key researchers in cognitive psychology.

---

grammar
the system of rules governing the structure and use of a language.

phonemes
the basic units of sound in language.

morphemes
the smallest units of meaning within a language.

syntax
the system of rules for combining words and phrases to form grammatically correct sentences.

semantics
the rules for determining the meaning of words and sentences.

pragmatics
aspects of language involving the practical ways of communicating with others, or the social "niceties" of language.

they do to other adults by using simpler words. Both adults and children use higher-pitched voices and many repeated phrases when talking to infants; such infant- or child-directed speech plays an important role in the development of language in children. Part of the pragmatics of language includes knowing just what rhythm and emphasis to use when communicating with others, called *intonation*. When speaking to infants, adults and children are changing the inflection when they use the higher pitch and stress certain words differently than others. Some languages, such as Japanese, are highly sensitive to intonation, meaning that changing the stress or pitch of certain words or syllables of a particular word can change its meaning entirely (Beckman & Pierrehumbert, 1986). For example, the Japanese name Yoshiko should be pronounced with the accent or stress on the first syllable: YO-she-koh. This pronunciation of the name means "woman-child." But if the stress is placed on the second syllable (yo-SHE-ko), the name means "woman who urinates."

Pragmatics involves the practical aspects of communicating. This young mother is talking and then pausing for the child's response. In this way, the child is learning about taking turns, an important aspect of language development. What kinds of games do adults play with children that also aid the development of language?

7.12 Development of Language

7.12 Explain how language develops.

The development of language is a very important milestone in the cognitive development of a child because language allows children to think in words rather than just images, to ask questions, to communicate their needs and wants to others, and to form concepts (L. Bloom, 1974; P. Bloom, 2000).

AP 5.S Synthesize how biological, cognitive, and cultural factors converge to facilitate acquisition, development, and use of language.

Language development in infancy is influenced by the language they hear, a style of speaking known as *child-directed speech* (also called *infant-directed speech, baby talk,* or *motherese*; the way adults and older children talk to infants and very young children, with higher-pitched, repetitious, sing-song speech patterns). Infants and toddlers attend more closely to this kind of speech, which creates a learning opportunity in the dialogue between caregiver and infant (Dominey & Dodane, 2004; Fernald, 1984, 1992; Küntay & Slobin, 2002). Furthermore, this kind of speech can be found in a variety of languages including English, German, Hebrew, Italian, Japanese, Korean, Sri Lankan Tamil, Tagalog, and Thai (Saint-Georges et al., 2013; Sulpizio et al., 2018). Interestingly, a recent fNIRS study found infants had greater activation in the prefrontal cortex in response to infant-directed speech produced by females as compared to males, implying infants may have a brain-based mechanism for both attention to, and preference for, "motherese" (Sulpizio et al., 2018). See Learning Objectives 2.5, 2.8. Researchers are also looking at infants' use of gestures and signs (Behne et al., 2005; Konishi et al., 2018; Lizskowski et al., 2006; Moll & Tomasello, 2007; Orr, 2018; Tomasello et al., 2007). Infants also seem to understand far more than they can produce, a phenomenon known as the *receptive-productive lag* (Stevenson et al., 1988). They may be able to only produce one or two words, but they understand much longer sentences from their parents and others.

There are several stages of language development that all children experience, no matter what culture they live in or what language they will learn to speak (Brown, 1973), as shown in **Table 7.4**.

Table 7.4 Stages of Language Development

1. **Cooing:** At around 2 months of age, babies begin to make vowel-like sounds.

2. **Babbling:** At about 6 months, infants add consonant sounds to the vowels to make a babbling sound, which at times can almost sound like real speech. Deaf children actually decrease their babbling after 6 months while increasing their use of primitive hand signs and gestures (Petitto & Marentette, 1991; Petitto et al., 2001).

3. **One-word speech:** Somewhere just before or around age 1, most children begin to say actual words. These words are typically nouns and may seem to represent an entire phrase of meaning. They are called *holophrases* (whole phrases in one word) for that reason. For example, a child might say "Milk!" and mean "I want some milk!" or "I drank my milk!"

4. **Telegraphic speech:** At around a year and a half, toddlers begin to string words together to form short, simple sentences using nouns, verbs, and adjectives. "Baby eat," "Mommy go," and "Doggie go bye-bye" are examples of telegraphic speech. Only the words that carry the meaning of the sentence are used.

5. **Whole sentences:** As children move through the preschool years, they learn to use grammatical terms and increase the number of words in their sentences, until by age 6 or so they are nearly as fluent as an adult, although the number of words they know is still limited when compared to adult vocabulary.

> **AP** 5.S Synthesize how biological, cognitive, and cultural factors converge to facilitate acquisition, development, and use of language.

> **AP** 6.I Identify the contributions of major researchers in the area of cognitive development in childhood.

7.13 The Relationship between Language and Thought

7.13 Evaluate whether or not language influences how people think.

As with the different views on the relative importance of nature and nurture, researchers have long debated the relationship between language and thought. Does language actually influence thought, or does thinking influence language?

TWO THEORIES ON THE RELATIONSHIP BETWEEN LANGUAGE AND THOUGHT Two very influential developmental psychologists, Jean Piaget and Lev Vygotsky, often debated the relationship of language and thought (Duncan, 1995). Piaget (1926, 1962) theorized that concepts preceded and aided the development of language. See Learning Objective 8.7. For example, a child would have to have a concept or mental schema for "mother" before being able to learn the word "mama." In a sense, concepts become the "pegs" upon which words are "hung." Piaget also noticed that preschool children seemed to spend a great deal of time talking to themselves—even when playing with another child. Each child would be talking about something totally unrelated to the speech of the other, in a process Piaget called *collective monologue*. Piaget believed that this kind of nonsocial speech was very egocentric (from the child's point of view only, with no regard for the listener) and that as the child became more socially involved and less egocentric, these nonsocial speech patterns would reduce.

Vygotsky, however, believed almost the opposite. He theorized that language actually helped develop concepts and that language could also help the child learn to control behavior—including social behavior (Vygotsky, 1934/1962, 1978, 1987). For Vygotsky, the word helped form the concept: Once a child had learned the word "mama," the various elements of "mama-ness"—*warm, soft, food, safety*, and so on—could come together around that word. Vygotsky also believed that the "egocentric" speech of the preschool child was actually a way for the child to form thoughts and control actions. This "private speech" was a way for children to plan their behavior and organize actions so that their goals could be obtained. Since socializing with other children would demand much more self-control and behavioral regulation on the part of the preschool child, Vygotsky believed that private speech would actually increase as children became more socially active in the preschool years. This was, of course, the opposite of Piaget's assumption, and the evidence seems to bear out Vygotsky's view: Children, especially bright children, do tend to use more private speech when learning how to socialize with other children or when working on a difficult task (Berk, 1992; Berk & Spuhl, 1995; Bivens & Berk, 1990).

LINGUISTIC RELATIVITY HYPOTHESIS The hypothesis that language shapes and influences thoughts was accepted by many theorists, with a few notable exceptions, such as Piaget. One of the best-known versions of this view is the Sapir-Whorf hypothesis (named for the two theorists who developed it, Edward Sapir and his student, Benjamin Lee Whorf). This hypothesis assumes that the thought processes and concepts within any culture are determined by the words of the culture (Sapir, 1921; Whorf, 1956). It has come to be known as the **linguistic relativity hypothesis**, meaning that thought processes and concepts are controlled by (relative to) language. That is, the words people use determine much of the way in which they think about the world around them.

One of the most famous examples used by Whorf to support this idea was that of the Inuits, Native Americans living in the Arctic. Supposedly, the Inuits have many more words for *snow* than do people in other cultures. One estimate was 23 different words, whereas other estimates have ranged in the hundreds. Unfortunately, this anecdotal evidence has turned out to be false, being more myth than reality (Pullum, 1991). In fact, English speakers also have many different words for snow (sleet, slush, powder, dusting, and yellow to name a few). Is there evidence for the linguistic relativity hypothesis? Neither Sapir nor Whorf provided any scientific studies that would support their proposition. There have been numerous studies by other researchers, however. For example, in

Breakfast in an Ethiopian restaurant. What does "breakfast" food mean to you?

linguistic relativity hypothesis

the theory that thought processes and concepts are controlled by language.

one study researchers assumed that a language's color names would influence the ability of the people who grew up with that language to distinguish among and perceive colors. The study found that basic color terms did directly influence color recognition memory (Lucy & Shweder, 1979). But an earlier series of studies of the perception of colors by Eleanor Rosch-Heider and others (Rosch-Heider, 1972; Rosch-Heider & Olivier, 1972) had already found just the opposite effect: Members of the Dani tribe, who have only two names for colors, were no different in their ability to perceive all of the colors than were the English speakers in the study. More recent studies (Davies et al., 1998a, 1998b; Laws et al., 1995; Pinker & Bloom, 1990) support Rosch-Heider's findings and the idea of a **cognitive universalism** (concepts are universal and influence the development of language) rather than linguistic relativity.

Other research suggests that although the linguistic relativity hypothesis may not work for fine perceptual discriminations such as those in the Rosch-Heider studies, it may be an appropriate explanation for concepts of a higher level. In one study, researchers showed pictures of two animals to preschool children (Gelman & Markman, 1986). The pictures were of a flamingo and a bat. The children were told that the flamingo feeds its baby mashed-up food but the bat feeds its baby milk. Then they were shown a picture of a blackbird (which looked more like the bat than the flamingo). Half of the children were told that the blackbird was a bird, while the other children were not. When asked how the blackbird fed its baby, the children who had been given the bird label were more likely to say that it fed its baby mashed-up food than were the children who were not given the label, indicating that the preschoolers were making inferences about feeding habits based on category membership rather than perceptual similarity—the word *bird* helped the children who were given that label to place the blackbird in its proper higher-level category.

Research continues in the investigation of relationships between language and thought and appears to support linguistic relativity and how language can shape our thoughts about space, time, colors, and objects (Boroditsky, 2001, Boroditsky, 2009). Even our reasoning can be impacted, including making important decisions on such topics as how to manage crime (Thibodeau & Boroditsky, 2013, Thibodeau & Boroditsky, 2015; Thibodeau et al., 2017). However, researchers do not always agree, and for some studies that offer support, there are others that reinterpret the data, fail to replicate, or offer critiques of the original studies, so findings are sometimes still in question (J. Y. Chen, 2007; January & Kako, 2007).

Psychologists cannot deny the influence of language on problem solving, cognition, and memory. Sometimes a problem can simply be worded differently to have the solution become obvious, and memory (see Learning Objective 6.5) is certainly stored in terms of the semantics of language. Language can definitely influence the perception of others as well—"computer geek" and "software engineer" might be used to describe the same person, but one phrase is obviously less flattering, and the image brought to mind is different for the two terms. In the end, trying to determine whether language influences thoughts or thoughts influence language may be like trying to determine which came first, the chicken or the egg.

cognitive universalism
theory that concepts are universal and influence the development of language.

7.14 Animal Studies in Language

7.14 Summarize the research on the ability of animals to communicate and use language.

> I've heard that chimpanzees can be taught to use sign language. Is this for real, or are the chimps just performing tricks like the animals in the circus or the zoo?

There are really two questions about animals and language. The first is "Can animals communicate?" and the second is "Can animals use language?" The answer to the first question is a definite "Yes." Animals communicate in many ways. They use sounds such as the rattle of a rattlesnake or the warning growl of an angry dog. There are also physical behaviors, such as the "dance" of honeybees that tells the other bees where a source of pollen is (Gould & Gould, 1994). But the answer to the second question is more complicated, because language is defined as the use of symbols, and symbols are things that stand for something else. Words are symbols, and gestures can be symbols. But the gestures used by animals are instinctual, meaning they are controlled by the animal's genetic makeup. The honeybee doing the "dance" is controlled completely by instinct, as is the growling dog. In human language, symbols are used quite deliberately and voluntarily, not by instinct, and abstract symbols have no meaning until people assign meaning to them. (Although Chomsky's innate language acquisition device might lead some to think that language for humans is instinctual, it should be noted that the infant's production of speech sounds becomes quite deliberate within a short period of time.)

Can animals be taught to use symbols that are abstract? There have been attempts to teach animals (primates and dolphins) how to use sign language (as animals lack the vocal structure to form spoken words), but many of these attempts were simply not "good science." The most successful of these experiments (which is not without its critics as well) has been with Kanzi, a bonobo chimpanzee trained to press abstract symbols on a computer keyboard (Savage-Rumbaugh & Lewin, 1994). Kanzi actually was not the original subject of the study—his mother, Matata, was the chimp being trained. She did not learn many of the symbols, but Kanzi watched his mother use the keyboard and appeared to learn how to use the symbols through that observation. One estimate suggested Kanzi could understand about 150 spoken English words. Trainers who speak to him are not in his view, so he is not responding to physical cues or symbols. He has managed to follow correctly complex instructions up to the level of a 2-year-old child (Savage-Rumbaugh et al., 1998). A later report suggested Kanzi and his half-sister Pan-Banisha eventually acquired a working vocabulary of 480 symbols and understood up to 2,000 English words (Roffman et al., 2012)! However, aside from anecdotal reports based on video recordings, little to no data have been offered in published studies. One published study with Kanzi does suggest he makes sounds that seem to have consistent meaning across different situations (Taglialatela et al., 2003). Nearly 100 videotaped hours of Kanzi engaged in day-to-day activities were analyzed for these sounds. The researchers were able to identify four sounds that seemed to represent banana, grapes, juice, and the word *yes*. (However, remember that four sounds do not come close to making an entire language.)

Other studies, with dolphins (Herman et al., 1993) and with parrots (Pepperberg, 1998, 2007), have also met with some success. Is it real language? The answer seems to be a qualified "yes." The qualification is that none of the animals that have achieved success so far can compare to the level of language development of a 3-year-old human child (Pinker, 1995). However, linguists still debate whether these animals are truly learning language if they are not also learning how to use syntax—combining words into grammatically correct sentences as well as being able to understand the differences between sentences such as "The girl kissed the boy" and "The boy kissed the girl." Combining different elements (e.g., words), which each have some meaning, to form more complex expressions that reflect the meaning of the different elements is referred to as *compositional syntax*.

As yet, there does not appear to be any widely accepted, conclusive evidence that wild animals have this kind of syntax or that any of the animals trained in language have been able to master this kind of syntax (Hurford, 2012).

There has been at least one report of non-human use of vocal compositional syntax in the lab, demonstrated by the type of notes produced by Japanese great tits, a type of perching bird, or "songbird." In this study, and consistent with previous research, Japanese great tits were found to respond to "ABC" calls by scanning the horizon (typically used in response to predators), and they approached the sound source in response to "D" calls (typically used to attract other members of the flock; Suzuki et al., 2016). Interestingly, when researchers combined the two into ABC-D calls, the birds both scanned their surroundings and approached the sound source. When the order was reversed to D-ABC calls, the birds reduced scanning and rarely approached the sound source. As indicated by the authors, it appears the birds perceived ABC-D calls as a single meaningful unit (Suzuki et al., 2016).

Concept Map L.O. 7.11, 7.12, 7.13, 7.14

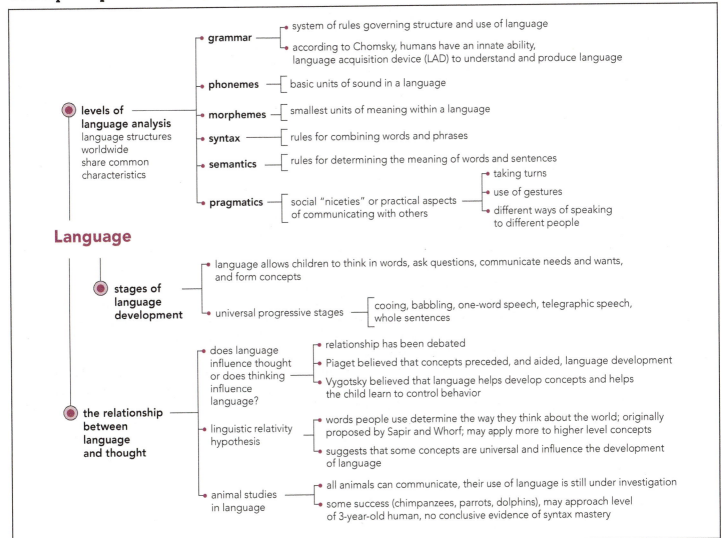

Practice Quiz — How much do you remember?

Pick the best answer.

1. The basic units of sound in a language are known as _____.
   a. syntax
   b. words
   c. grammar
   d. morphemes
   e. phonemes

2. According to Noam Chomsky, what is a language acquisition device?
   a. a digital audio player or recorder
   b. a biological element of the brain that allows us to learn language
   c. an environmental entity that allows people to learn foreign languages
   d. a part of the brain that develops during puberty that allows teens and adults to formulate questions and engage others
   e. a learning method that many can use to understand the language of infants and small children

3. Researchers believe that up to the age of _____, individuals possess the ability to understand phonemes of all languages.
   a. 7 years
   b. 16 years
   c. 3 months
   d. 2 years
   e. 9 months

4. _____ believed that language helps develop concepts, whereas _____ believed that concepts must be developed first if language is to follow.
   a. Piaget, Rosch-Heider
   b. Vygotsky, Piaget
   c. Sapir and Whorf, Vygotsky
   d. Chomsky, Sapir and Whorf
   e. Piaget, Vygotsky

5. "Mommy go bye-bye" is an example of _____.
   a. a holophrase
   b. a syntax anomaly
   c. babbling
   d. telegraphic speech
   e. cooing

APA Goal 2: Scientific Inquiry and Critical Thinking

A Cognitive Advantage for Bilingual Individuals?

Addresses APA Learning Objectives 2.1: Use scientific reasoning to interpret psychological phenomena; and 2.3: Engage in innovative and integrative thinking and problem solving.

In our growing, interconnected world, more and more of the population speaks more than one language (Bialystok et al., 2009). Individuals that speak a single language are *monolingual* and those that speak two are *bilingual.* Aside from enhanced communication, individuals who speak more than one language reportedly have greater cognitive reserves, are less prone to some age-related decreases in functioning, and are even less susceptible to some types of egocentric biases (Calvo et al., 2015; Rubio-Fernandez & Glucksberg, 2012).

Many studies suggest that bilingual people have other cognitive advantages as compared to monolingual people. The advantages stem from their ability to successfully manage the activities of more than one language, with some studies reporting changes in neuropsychological function and others reporting changes in the structure and connectivity of the brain (Hervais-Adelman et al., 2011; Kroll et al., 2014; Olulade et al., 2015; Pliatsikas et al., 2015). Those cognitive advantages extend beyond general language skills and are believed to result in better cognitive performance overall, and multiple enhanced executive functions, including better inhibitory control, better conflict monitoring, and more efficient mental set shifting (von Bastian et al., 2016).

However, despite many studies, over many years, not everyone agrees that bilingual individuals have such cognitive advantages. Some studies have failed to replicate previous results or reported either inconsistent or no benefits for those that are bilingual (Paap & Greenberg, 2013; von Bastian et al., 2016). Additionally, others cite poor methodology, small samples, and even publication bias for positive results related to the bilingual cognitive advantage (de Bruin et al., 2015; Paap, 2014; Paap et al., 2014). Some researchers suggest both the evidence for and against a bilingual advantage should be considered, and it is possible any differences are subtle or may only be evident at certain points in time for a given task and that only some individuals may demonstrate any such cognitive advantage (Blanco-Elorrieta & Pylkkanen, 2018; Incera, 2018).

APA Goal 2 A Cognitive Advantage for Bilingual Individuals?

Review the following table of variables. Compare and contrast the "Greater Support items" with the "Less Support" items regarding strengthening future research investigating the possible cognitive advantages that being bilingual might provide.

"Greater Support" Items	"Less Support" Items
Developing studies based on updated and revised theories	Developing studies based on older, existing theories
Using valid measures of executive function	Using novel measures for which validity has not yet been established
Better selection of bilingual groups for comparison	Selecting individuals for the bilingual group from a convenience sample
Matching study groups on socioeconomic and immigrant status	Comparing groups without regard to socioeconomic or immigrant status
Matching study groups on cultural status	Using study groups comprised of participants from a wide and varied collection of cultural backgrounds and experiences, not matched between conditions
Using assessments that have greater ecological validity, representative of real, everyday challenges and situations	Using laboratory measures that have little relation to tasks or challenges in everyday life.
Identification of specific bilingual experiences most relevant to enhancing executive functions	Using a single, non-specific measure of cognitive function
Using more than one assessment of a specific executive function	Using a single test of broad executive functions

Applying Psychology to Everyday Life
Recognizing Cognitive Biases

7.15 **Identify personal cognitive biases and determine how to prevent them from negatively impacting decision making.**

We discussed several different cognitive biases, heuristics, and other ways of thinking earlier in this chapter that can sometimes lead to errors of judgment or poor decisions. Some research suggests that simple awareness of cognitive biases is not enough, and while biases may be extremely resistant to change, focusing on behavior may be a solution. Can you think of some ways you can modify your own behavior or help yourself be less prone to the cognitive biases highlighted in this chapter? Watch the following video to see how cognitive biases have impacted other students and the steps they take now to avoid or minimize undesired consequences.

Applying Psychology to Everyday Life Recognizing Cognitive Biases

Watch the Video at MyLab Psychology

After watching the video, answer the following questions:

1. Identify two of the cognitive biases shared by students in the video.
2. How can you help yourself to be more aware of cognitive biases and less prone to their effects?

Chapter Summary

How People Think

- Thinking (cognition) is mental activity that occurs in the brain when information is being organized, stored, communicated, or processed.

7.1 Explain how mental images are involved in the process of thinking.

- Mental images represent objects or events and have a picture-like quality.

7.2 Describe how concepts and prototypes influence our thinking.

- Concepts are ideas that represent a class or category of events, objects, or activities.
- Prototypes are examples of a concept that more closely match the defining characteristics of that concept.

7.3 Identify some methods that people use to solve problems and make decisions.

- Problem solving consists of thinking and behaving in certain ways to reach a goal.
- Mechanical solutions include trial-and-error learning and rote solutions.
- Algorithms are a type of rote solution in which one follows step-by-step procedures for solving certain types of problems.
- A heuristic or "rule of thumb" is a strategy that narrows down the possible solutions for a problem.
- Insight is the sudden perception of a solution to a problem.

7.4 Identify three common barriers to successful problem solving.

- Functional fixedness is the tendency to perceive objects as having only the use for which they were originally intended and, therefore, failing to see them as possible tools for solving other problems.
- Mental set refers to the tendency to persist in using strategies that have worked in the past.
- Confirmation bias is the tendency to search for evidence that confirms one's beliefs, ignoring any evidence to the contrary.

7.5 Recall some characteristics of creative, divergent thinking.

- Divergent thinking involves coming up with as many different answers as possible. This is a kind of creativity (combining ideas or behavior in new ways).
- Creative people are usually good at mental imagery and have knowledge on a wide range of topics, are unafraid to be different, value their independence, and are often unconventional in their work but not in other areas.

Intelligence

7.6 Compare and contrast different theories on the nature of intelligence.

- Intelligence is the ability to understand the world, think rationally or logically, and use resources effectively when faced with challenges or problems.

- Spearman proposed general intelligence, or g factor, as the ability to reason and solve problems, whereas specific intelligence, or s factor, includes task-specific abilities in certain areas such as music, business, or art.
- Gardner proposed nine different types of intelligence, ranging from verbal, linguistic, and mathematical to interpersonal and intrapersonal intelligence.
- Sternberg proposed three types of intelligence: analytical, creative, and practical.
- The Cattell-Horn-Carroll (CHC) Theory of Intelligence includes general intelligence, or *g*, 16 broad abilities, and many narrow abilities within each broad area.
- Specific brain areas and brain functions have been tied to differences in intellectual ability, with some research indicating the frontal and parietal areas playing the most important roles.

7.7 Compare and contrast some methods of measuring intelligence.

- The Stanford-Binet Intelligence Test yields an IQ score that was once determined by dividing the mental age of the person by the chronological age and multiplying that quotient by 100, but now involves comparing a person's score to a standardized norm.
- The Wechsler Intelligence Tests yield four index scores derived from both verbal and nonverbal subtests and an overall score of intelligence.

7.8 Identify ways to evaluate the quality of a test.

- Standardization, validity, and reliability are all important factors in the construction of an intelligence test.
- Deviation IQs are based on the normal curve, defining different levels of intelligence based on the deviation of scores from a common mean.
- IQ tests are often criticized for being culturally biased.
- Neuropsychologists play an important role in the care of individuals with traumatic brain injury and other conditions in which brain functioning has been negatively impacted.
- Concussion, or mild traumatic brain injury, affects the lives of many athletes.

7.9 Define intellectual disability, giftedness, and emotional intelligence.

- Intellectual disability is a neurodevelopmental condition in which IQ falls below 70 and adaptive behavior across conceptual, social, and practical domains of life is severely deficient for a person of a particular chronological age. Symptoms must also first be present during the developmental period.
- The four levels of intellectual disability are mild, moderate, severe, and profound. These are determined by the level of adaptive functioning and level of supports the individual needs in their daily life.
- Causes of intellectual disability include deprived environments as well as chromosome and genetic disorders and dietary deficiencies.
- Gifted persons are defined as those having IQ scores at the upper end of the normal curve (130 or above).
- Emotional intelligence involves being able to reach goals and engage in productive thinking through accurate awareness and effective management of our own emotions. It also involves our ability to understand what others feel.
- Terman conducted a longitudinal study that demonstrated that gifted children grow up to be successful adults for the most part.
- Terman's study has been criticized for a lack of objectivity because Terman became too involved in the lives of several of his participants, even to the point of intervening on their behalf.

7.10 Evaluate the influence of heredity and environment on the development of intelligence.

- Stronger correlations are found between IQ scores as genetic relatedness increases. Heritability of IQ is estimated at .50.
- In 1994, Herrnstein and Murray published *The Bell Curve*, in which they made widely criticized claims about the heritability of intelligence.

Language

7.11 Identify the different elements and structure of language.

- Language is a system for combining symbols so that an infinite number of meaningful statements can be created and communicated to others.
- Grammar is the system of rules by which language is governed and includes the rules for using phonemes, morphemes, and syntax. Pragmatics refers to practical aspects of language.

7.12 Explain how language develops.

- The stages of language development are cooing, babbling, one-word speech (holophrases), telegraphic speech, and whole sentences.

7.13 Evaluate whether or not language influences how people think.

- Sapir and Whorf originally proposed that language controls and helps the development of thought processes and concepts, an idea that is known as the linguistic relativity hypothesis.
- Other researchers have found evidence that concepts are universal and directly influence the development of language, called the cognitive universalism viewpoint.

7.14 Summarize the research on the ability of animals to communicate and use language.

- Studies with chimpanzees, parrots, and dolphins have been somewhat successful in demonstrating that animals can develop a basic kind of language, including some abstract ideas.
- Controversy exists over the lack of evidence that animals can learn syntax, which some feel means that animals are not truly learning and using language.

Applying Psychology to Everyday Life: Recognizing Cognitive Biases

7.15 Identify personal cognitive biases and determine how to prevent them from negatively impacting decision making.

- There are many cognitive biases that can negatively affect the decisions we make. While increasing awareness might be able to help, the use of outside resources such as other people or checklists may be our best defense against making poor decisions.

Test Yourself: Preparing for the AP Exam

PART I: MULTIPLE-CHOICE QUESTIONS

Directions for Part I: Read each of the questions or incomplete sentences below. Then choose the response that best answers the question or completes the sentence.

1. Researchers have found that it takes _____ to view a mental image that is larger or covers more distance than a smaller or more compact one.
   a. the same amount of time
   b. about a third of the time
   c. less time
   d. half the time
   e. longer

2. Research suggests we engage mental images in our mind _____ the way we engage or interact with physical objects.
   a. a little like
   b. much like
   c. in a random but completely different fashion than
   d. not at all like
   e. in an orderly but completely different fashion than

3. Trial and error is sometimes referred to as a(n) _____.
   a. algorithm
   b. mechanical solution
   c. rule of thumb
   d. heuristic
   e. cognitive bias

4. Julie and Rette bought a new house with an unfinished basement. To determine how they want to finish it, they lay down tape on the floor showing where walls will go and rooms will be. This process of problem solving is known as _____.
   a. a mechanical solution
   b. working backward from the goal
   c. representativeness heuristic
   d. an algorithm
   e. trial and error

5. One day at work, Tatum's earring fell on the floor, and she was unable to find the back. To keep from losing her earring, Tatum reinserted it and used part of a pencil eraser to keep the earring in place. Using a pencil eraser as a temporary earring back showed that Tatum overcame _____.
   a. confirmation bias
   b. metacognition
   c. a mental set
   d. functional fixedness
   e. transformation bias

6. Which of the following questions would be more likely to produce divergent thinking?
   a. "What does a clothes hanger typically look like?"
   b. "How many uses can you think of for a clothes hanger?"
   c. "What is a clothes hanger typically made of?"
   d. "How do you spell clothes hanger?"
   e. "What is a clothes hanger?"

7. According to Sternberg, "book smarts" is another way of talking about which kind of intelligence?
   a. spatial
   b. analytical
   c. practical
   d. emotional
   e. creative

8. Which of the following tests came first?
   a. the Stanford-Binet
   b. the ACT
   c. the PPVT
   d. Binet's mental ability test
   e. the Wechsler tests

9. Dr. Stevenson gives all her classes 45 minutes to complete their psychology test regardless of if the class meets for 50 minutes, 75 minutes, or even 3 hours. Such a technique promotes test _____.
   a. reliability
   b. norms
   c. differentiation
   d. validity
   e. standardization

10. In contrast to comparing mental age to chronological age, most modern tests of intelligence use _____.
    a. emotional assessments
    b. quotients of intelligence
    c. Stern's formula
    d. creativity assessments
    e. age-group comparison norms

11. A realistic goal for all test developers is to _____ cultural bias in their intelligence tests.
    a. eliminate
    b. hide
    c. maximize
    d. minimize
    e. diversify

12. Dr. Garber works with children who have grown up in poor socio-economic conditions. Many of her clients come from homes that do not emphasize education or social involvement, and opportunities for advancement are practically nonexistent. Many are malnourished, have been exposed to a variety of environmental toxins, and have multiple infections without adequate or timely health care. What might these children be at risk for?
    a. genetic inhibition
    b. intellectual disability
    c. increased emotional intelligence
    d. organically induced deprivation
    e. color-deficient vision

13. Dr. Park has found that her patient, Ye-Jun, has a defect in a gene on the X chromosome of his 23rd pair, resulting in a deficiency of a protein needed for brain development. Ye-Jun most likely suffers from _____.
    a. Down syndrome
    b. fragile X syndrome
    c. fetal alcohol syndrome
    d. cretinism
    e. ASD

14. What does the Flynn effect theorize?
    a. Intelligence scores are meaningless and should be abandoned.
    b. Intelligence scores are identical across all cultures.
    c. Intelligence scores are decreasing due to an overreliance on technology.
    d. Intelligence scores are relatively stable in contrast to improvement in our educational system.
    e. Intelligence scores are steadily increasing in modernized countries.

15. Edward Sapir and Benjamin Whorf theorized that _____, a concept reflected in their linguistic relativity hypothesis.
    a. our ability to learn linguistics is based on the degree of relatedness of the individual teaching us
    b. language shapes thoughts
    c. thoughts shape language
    d. language and thought influence each other
    e. language and thought develop independently

PART II: FREE-RESPONSE QUESTION

Directions for Part II: Read the essay question that follows. Then respond to the question in a clear, concise essay. Do not simply list facts. Instead, present a thorough argument based on your critical consideration of the topic. Use of proper terminology is necessary.

Mike was driving his delivery truck when he experienced a flat tire. While changing the tire, he accidentally knocked all but one of the lug nuts he needed to reattach the spare tire into a storm drain. After he thought for a while, he removed one lug nut from each other wheel so he could use them to reattach the wheel with the spare tire, allowing him to drive to then nearest repair shop to replace the lost nuts.

Part A

Explain how each of the following terms helped Mike solve his problem:

- insight
- divergent thinking
- practical intelligence
- creative intelligence

Part B

Explain how each of the following terms may have presented an obstacle to Mike's solving his problem:

- mental set
- convergent thinking
- prototypes

Chapter 8
Development Across the Life Span

Ralf strm/EyeEm/Getty Images

In your words

How have you changed since your early teenage years? In what ways are you similar to other individuals of your age and in what ways are you different and unique?

After you have thought about these questions, watch the video to see how other students would answer them.

Watch the Video at MyLab Psychology

Why study human development?

Beginning to understand how we come to be the people we are is a critical step in understanding ourselves as we are today and who we may become as we grow older. From the moment of conception, each of us is headed down a pathway of change, influenced by our biology, environment, and social interactions, to a final destination that is the same for all of us. The twists and turns of the pathway are what make each of us unique individuals. In this chapter, we'll look at the influences that help determine our developmental pathway through life.

Learning Objectives

8.1 Compare and contrast the special research methods used to study development.

8.2 Explain the relationship between heredity and environmental factors in determining development.

8.3 Summarize the role of chromosomes and genes in determining the transmission of traits and the inheritance of disorders.

8.4 Explain the process of fertilization, including the twinning process.

8.5 Describe the three stages of prenatal development.

8.6 Describe the physical and sensory changes that take place in infancy and childhood.

8.7 Compare and contrast two theories of cognitive development, and define autism spectrum disorder.

8.8 Identify the development of personality, relationships, and self-concept in infancy and childhood.

8.9 Define gender, and discuss the development of gender roles.

8.10 Compare and contrast two theories of gender-role development.

8.11 Distinguish among the various sexual orientations.

8.12 Describe the physical changes of puberty.

8.13 Identify the cognitive and moral advances that occur in adolescence.

8.14 Describe how the adolescent search for personal identity influences relationships with others.

8.15 Identify the physical changes and health issues associated with adulthood.

8.16 Describe how memory abilities change during adulthood.

8.17 Apply Erikson's theory to some common psychosocial concerns of adulthood.

8.18 Compare and contrast four theories of why aging occurs.

8.19 Describe Kübler-Ross's theory of death and dying, and identify some criticisms of this theory.

8.20 Compare and contrast some cross-cultural differences in views of death and dying.

8.21 Describe the differences between the periods of adolescence and emerging adulthood.

8.1–8.3 Studying Human Development

What is development? In the context of life, **human development** is the scientific study of the changes that occur in people as they age, from conception until death. This chapter will touch on almost all of the topics covered in the other chapters of this text, such as personality, cognition, biological processes, and social interactions. But here, all of those topics will be studied in the context of changes that occur as a result of the process of human development.

8.1 Research Designs

8.1 Compare and contrast the special research methods used to study development.

As briefly discussed in Chapter One, research in human development is affected by the problem of age. In any experiment, the participants who are exposed to the independent variable (the variable in an experiment that is deliberately manipulated by the experimenter) should be randomly assigned to the different experimental conditions. The challenge in developmental research is that the age of the people in the study should always be an independent variable, but people cannot be randomly assigned to different age groups.

There are some special designs that are used in researching age-related changes: the **longitudinal design**, in which one group of people is followed and assessed at different times as the group ages; the **cross-sectional design**, in which several different age groups are studied at one time; and the **cross-sequential design**, which is a combination of the longitudinal and cross-sectional designs (Baltes et al., 1988; Schaie & Willis, 2010).

The longitudinal design has the advantage of looking at real age-related changes as those changes occur in the same individuals. Disadvantages of this method are the lengthy amount of time, money, and effort involved in following participants over the years, as well as the loss of participants when they move away, lose interest, or die. The cross-sectional design has the advantages of being quick, relatively inexpensive, and easier to accomplish than the longitudinal design. Its main disadvantage is that the study no longer compares an individual to that same individual as he or she ages; instead, individuals of different ages are being compared to one another. Differences between age groups are often a problem in developmental research. For example, if comparing the IQ scores of 30-year-olds to 80-year-olds to see how aging affects intelligence, questions arise concerning the differing educational experiences and opportunities those two age groups have had that might affect IQ scores, in addition to any effects of aging. This is known as the **cohort effect**, the particular impact on development that occurs when a group of people share a common time period or common life experience (for example, having been born in the same time period or having gone through a specific historical event together). **Table 8.1** shows a comparison between examples of a longitudinal design, a cross-sectional design, and a cross-sequential design.

In studying human development, developmental psychologists have outlined many theories of how these age-related changes occur. There are some areas of controversy, however, and one of these is the issue of nature versus nurture.

8.2 Nature and Nurture

8.2 Explain the relationship between heredity and environmental factors in determining development.

Nature refers to heredity, the influence of inherited characteristics on personality, physical growth, intellectual growth, and social interactions. **Nurture** refers to the influence of

---

human development
the scientific study of the changes that occur in people as they age from conception until death.

AP 1.F Differentiate types of research with regard to purpose, strengths, and weaknesses.

longitudinal design
research design in which one participant or group of participants is studied over a long period of time.

cross-sectional design
research design in which several different participant age-groups are studied at one particular point in time.

cross-sequential design
research design in which participants are first studied by means of a cross-sectional design but are also followed and assessed longitudinally.

cohort effect
the impact on development occurring when a group of people share a common time period or common life experience.

nature
the influence of our inherited characteristics on our personality, physical growth, intellectual growth, and social interactions.

nurture
the influence of the environment on personality, physical growth, intellectual growth, and social interactions.

AP 2.A Discuss psychology's abiding interest in how heredity, environment, and evolution work together to shape behavior.

Table 8.1 A Comparison of Three Developmental Research Designs

Cross-Sectional Design		
Different participants of various ages are compared at one point in time to determine age-related *differences*.	**Group One:** 20-year-old participants **Group Two:** 40-year-old participants **Group Three:** 60-year-old participants	Research done in 2020
Longitudinal Design		
The same participants are studied at various ages to determine age-related *changes*.	**Study One:** 20-year-old participants **Study Two:** Same participants at 40 years old **Study Three:** Same participants are now 60 years old	Research done in 1980 Research done in 2000 Research done in 2020
Cross-Sequential Design		
Different participants of various ages are compared at several points in time to determine both age-related *differences* and age-related *changes*.	**Study One:** *Group One*: 20-year-old participants *Group Two*: 40-year-old participants **Study Two:** *Group One*: Participants will be 25 years old *Group Two*: Participants will be 45 years old	Research done in 2020 Research to be done in 2025

the environment on all of those same things and includes parenting styles, physical surroundings, economic factors, and anything that can have an influence on development that does not come from within the person.

> 💬 So is a person like Hitler born that way, or did something happen to make him the person he was?

How much of a person's personality and behavior is determined by nature and how much is determined by nurture? This is a key question, and the answer is quite complicated. It is also quite important: Are people like Hitler or Nikolas Cruz (the 20-year-old who killed seventeen students and staff members and wounded seventeen more at Marjory Stoneman Douglas High School in Parkland, Florida, on February 14, 2018) the result of bad genes, bad parenting, or life-altering experiences in childhood? How much of Stephen Hawking's genius was due to his genetic inheritance? What part did the parenting choices of his family play? Or were his cognitive abilities the unique combination of both hereditary and environmental influences? After many years of scientific research, most developmental psychologists now agree that the last possibility is the most likely explanation for most of human development: All that people are and all that people become is the product of an interaction between nature and nurture (Davis et al., 2012; Insel & Wang, 2010; Polderman et al., 2015; Ridley, 1999; Sternberg & Grigorenko, 2006; Ursini et al., 2018). This does not mean that the nature versus nurture controversy no longer exists; for example, intelligence is still a "hot topic" with regard to how much is inherited and how much is learned. Some researchers and theorists assume a large genetic influence (Bouchard & Segal, 1985; Herrnstein & Murray, 1994; Jensen, 1969; Johnson et al., 2007; Kristensen & Bjerkedal, 2007), whereas many others believe that culture, economics, nutrition in early childhood, and educational opportunities have a greater impact (Gardner et al., 1996; Gould, 1996; Rose et al., 1984; Wahlsten, 1997).

Behavioral genetics is a field of study in which researchers try to determine how much of behavior is the result of genetic inheritance and how much is due to a person's experiences.

AP 6.B Discuss the interaction of nature and nurture (including cultural variations), specifically physical development, in the determination of behavior.

AP 6.F Discuss the interaction of nature and nurture (including cultural variations), specifically social development, in the determination of behavior.

Watch Family and Twin Studies

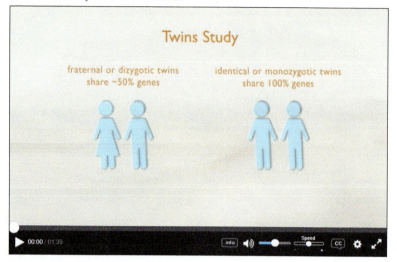

Watch the Video at MyLab Psychology

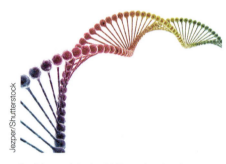

In this model of a DNA molecule, the two strands making up the sides of the "twisted ladder" are composed of sugars and phosphates. The "rungs" of the ladder that link the two strands are amines. Amines contain the genetic codes for building the proteins that make up organic life.

genetics
the science of inherited traits.

DNA (deoxyribonucleic acid)
special molecule that contains the genetic material of the organism.

gene
section of DNA having the same arrangement of chemical elements.

chromosome
tightly wound strand of genetic material or DNA.

dominant
referring to a gene that actively controls the expression of a trait.

recessive
referring to a gene that only influences the expression of a trait when paired with an identical gene.

As the video *Family and Twin Studies* explains, behavioral geneticists use a variety of methods to determine this, including family, twin, and adoption studies.

8.3 The Basic Building Blocks of Development

8.3 Summarize the role of chromosomes and genes in determining the transmission of traits and the inheritance of disorders.

Any study of the human life span must begin with looking at the complex material contained in the cells of the body that carries the instructions for life itself. After discussing the basic building blocks of life, we will discuss how the processes of conception and the development of the infant within the womb take place.

CHROMOSOMES, GENES, AND DNA **Genetics** is the science of heredity. Understanding how genes transmit human characteristics and traits involves defining a few basic terms.

DNA (deoxyribonucleic acid) is a very special kind of molecule (the smallest particle of a substance that still has all the properties of that substance). DNA consists of two very long sugar–phosphate strands, each linked together by certain chemical elements called *amines* or *bases* arranged in a particular pattern. The amines are organic structures that contain the genetic codes for building the proteins that make up organic life (hair coloring, muscle, and skin, for example) and that control the life of each cell. Each section of DNA containing a certain sequence (ordering) of these amines is called a **gene**. These genes are located on rod-shaped structures called **chromosomes**, which are found in the nucleus of a cell.

Humans have a total of 46 chromosomes in each cell of their bodies (with the exception of the egg and the sperm). Twenty-three of these chromosomes come from the mother's egg and the other 23 from the father's sperm. Most characteristics are determined by 22 such pairs, called the *autosomes*. The last (23rd) pair determines the sex of the person. The two chromosomes of this pair are called the *sex chromosomes*. Two X-shaped chromosomes indicate a female, while an X and a Y indicate a male.

The 46 chromosomes can be arranged in pairs, with one member of each pair coming from the mother and the other member from the father. Let's consider just one of these pairs for the moment.

In this particular pair of chromosomes, assume that there is a gene influencing hair color on each chromosome. The observable color of the person's hair will be determined by those two genes, one gene from each parent. If both genes influence brown hair, the person will obviously have brown hair, right? And if both influence blond hair, the person's hair will be blond.

💬 But what if one gene influences brown hair and the other blond hair?

The answer lies in the nature of each gene. Some genes that are more active in influencing a trait are called **dominant**. A dominant gene will always be expressed in the observable trait, in this case, hair color. For example, if Saida has a dominant gene for brown eyes, she will actually have brown eyes—even with only one brown-eye gene.

Some genes are less active in influencing the trait and will only be expressed in the observable trait if they are paired with another less active gene. These genes tend to recede, or fade, into the background when paired with a more dominant gene, so they are called **recessive**. Blond is the most recessive hair color and it will only show up as a trait if that person receives a blond-hair-color gene from each parent.

💬 What about red hair? And how come some people have a mixed hair color, like strawberry blond?

In reality, the patterns of genetic transmission of traits are usually more complicated. Almost all traits are influenced by more than one pair of genes in a process called *polygenic inheritance*. (*Polygenic* means "many genes.") Sometimes certain kinds of genes tend to group themselves with certain other genes, like the genes influencing blond hair and blue eyes. Other genes are so equally dominant or equally recessive that they combine their traits in the organism. For example, genes involved in blond hair and red hair are recessive. When a child inherits one of each from his or her parents, instead of one or the other influencing the child's hair color, the genes may blend together to form a strawberry-blond mix.

GENETIC AND CHROMOSOME PROBLEMS Some disorders, such as Huntington's disease (a breakdown in the neurons of the brain) and Marfan syndrome (a connective tissue disorder), are carried by dominant genes. In these disorders, only one parent needs to have the gene for the disorder to be passed on to offspring. Other genetically determined disorders are carried by recessive genes. Diseases carried by recessive genes are inherited when a child inherits two recessive genes, one from each parent. Examples of disorders inherited in this manner are cystic fibrosis (a disease of the respiratory and digestive tracts), sickle-cell anemia (a blood disorder), Tay-Sachs disease (a fatal neurological disorder), and phenylketonuria (PKU), in which an infant is born without the ability to break down phenylalanine, an amino acid controlling coloring of the skin and hair. If levels of phenylalanine build up, brain damage can

Figure 8.1 Dominant and Recessive Genes and PKU

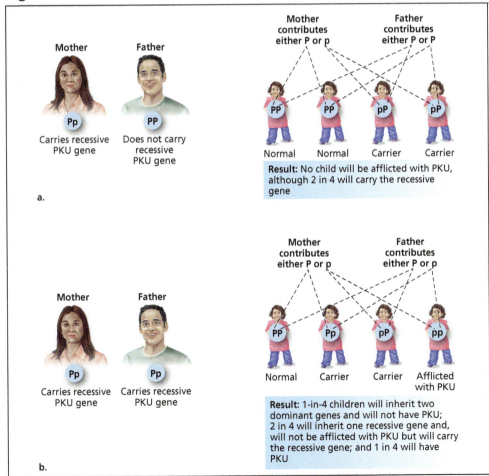

This figure shows the variation of one or two parents carrying recessive genes and the result of this in their offspring. (a) If only one parent carries the PKU gene, their children might be carriers but will not have PKU. (b) Only if both parents are carriers of PKU, will a child have the 1-in-4 possibility of having PKU.

occur; if untreated, it can result in severe intellectual disabilities. **Figure 8.1** on the previous page illustrates a typical pattern of inheritance for dominant and recessive genes using the example of PKU.

Sometimes the chromosome itself is the problem. Although each egg and each sperm is only supposed to have 23 chromosomes, in the formation of these cells a chromosome can end up in the wrong cell, leaving one cell with only 22 and the other with 24. If either of these cells survives to "mate," the missing or extra chromosome can cause mild to severe problems in development (American Academy of Pediatrics, 1995; Barnes & Carey, 2002; Centers for Disease Control and Prevention, 2018a; Gardner & Sutherland, 1996; Sing et al., 2018).

One example of a chromosome disorder is *Down syndrome*, a disorder in which there is an extra chromosome in what would normally be the 21st pair. Symptoms commonly include the physical characteristics of almond-shaped, wide-set eyes, intellectual disability, and the increased risk of organ failure later in life (Barnes & Carey, 2002; Hernandez & Fisher, 1996; Patel et al., 2015). Other chromosome disorders occur when there is an extra sex chromosome in the 23rd pair, such as *Klinefelter syndrome*, in which the 23rd set of sex chromosomes is XXY, with the extra X producing a male with reduced masculine characteristics, enlarged breasts, obesity, and excessive height (Bock, 1993; Frühmesser & Kotzot, 2011; Spaziani et al., 2018); and *Turner syndrome*, in which the 23rd pair is actually missing an X, so that the result is a lone X chromosome (Ranke & Saenger, 2001). These females tend to be very short, infertile, and sexually underdeveloped (American Academy of Pediatrics, 1995; Conway, 2018; Cramer et al., 2014; Hong et al., 2009; Rovet, 1993).

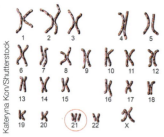

Down syndrome is a form of intellectual disability caused by an extra chromosome 21.

Concept Map L.O. 8.1, 8.2, 8.3

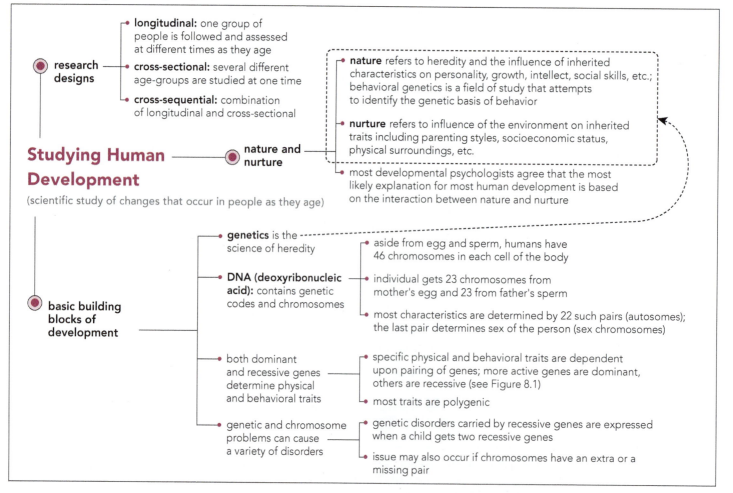

Practice Quiz — How much do you remember?

Pick the best answer.

1. In a _____ design, one group of people is followed and assessed at different times as the group ages.
   a. cross-sectional
   b. longitudinal
   c. cohort-sequential
   d. cross-longitudinal
   e. cross-sequential

2. The cognitive and social changes students go through because they are born and grow up in an age of smartphones would be referred to as a(n) _____.
   a. dominance effect
   b. cohort effect
   c. experimental group
   d. control group
   e. sequential effect

3. Kandi has naturally blond hair. Based on this information, what do we know about Kandi's parents?
   a. Each of her parents must have one dominant brown hair gene.
   b. Each of her parents must have one recessive blond hair gene.
   c. At least one of her parents has a recessive blond hair gene.
   d. Neither of her parents has a recessive blond hair gene.
   e. Neither of her parents has a recessive blue eye gene.

4. When sets of genes group together, the result can be multiple traits expressed as a single dominant trait. This is best explained by the process known as _____.
   a. recessive inheritance
   b. polygenic inheritance
   c. dominant inheritance
   d. amines
   e. single expression

5. Which of the following is a disorder resulting from recessive inheritance?
   a. Klinefelter syndrome
   b. cystic fibrosis
   c. Turner syndrome
   d. Down syndrome
   e. Trisomy 21

6. Which disorder is characterized by having only one X chromosome in the 23rd pairing?
   a. PKU
   b. Tay-Sachs disease
   c. Down syndrome
   d. Turner syndrome
   e. Klinefelter syndrome

8.4–8.5 Prenatal Development

From conception to the actual birth of the baby is a period of approximately 9 months, during which a single cell becomes a complete infant. It is also during this time that many things can have a positive or negative influence on the developing infant.

AP 6.A Explain the process of conception and gestation, including factors that influence successful pre-natal development.

ovum
the female sex cell, or egg.

sperm
the male sex cell.

fertilization
the union of the ovum and sperm.

zygote
cell resulting from the uniting of the ovum and sperm.

monozygotic twins
identical twins formed when one zygote splits into two separate masses of cells, each of which develops into a separate embryo.

8.4 Fertilization

8.4 Explain the process of fertilization, including the twinning process.

When an egg (also called an **ovum**) and a **sperm** unite in the process of **fertilization**, the resulting single cell will have a total of 46 chromosomes and is called a **zygote**. Normally, the zygote will begin to divide, first into two cells, then four, then eight, and so on, with each new cell also having 46 chromosomes, because the DNA molecules produce duplicates, or copies, of themselves before each division. (This division process is called *mitosis*.) Eventually, the mass of cells becomes a baby. See **Figure 8.2** for a closer look at what occurs once an egg is fertilized.

Sometimes this division process doesn't work exactly this way, and twins or multiples are the result.

There are actually two kinds of twins (see **Figure 8.3**). Twins who are commonly referred to as "identical" are **monozygotic twins**, meaning that the two babies come from one (mono) fertilized egg (zygote). Early in the division process, the mass of cells splits completely—no one knows exactly why—into two separate masses, each of which will develop into a separate infant. The infants will be the same sex and have identical features because they each possess the same set of 46 chromosomes. The other type of twin is more an accident of timing and is more common in women who are older and who are from certain ethnic groups (Allen & Parisi, 1990; Bonnelykke, 1990; Fuchs & D'Alton, 2018; Imaizumi, 1998). A woman's body may either release more than one egg at a time or release an egg in a later ovulation

Figure 8.2 Journey of a Fertilized Egg

Watch the Video at MyLab Psychology

Figure 8.3 Monozygotic and Dizygotic Twins

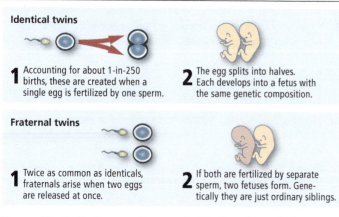

Because identical twins come from one fertilized egg (zygote), they are called monozygotic. Fraternal twins, who come from two different fertilized eggs, are called dizygotic.

dizygotic twins

often called fraternal twins, occurring when two individual eggs get fertilized by separate sperm, resulting in two zygotes in the uterus at the same time.

bioethics

the study of ethical and moral issues brought about by new advances in biology and medicine.

period after a woman has already conceived once. If two eggs are fertilized, the woman may give birth to fraternal or **dizygotic twins** (two zygotes) or possibly triplets or some other multiple number of babies (Bryan & Hallett, 2001; Fuchs & D'Alton, 2018). This is also more likely to happen to women who are taking fertility drugs to help them get pregnant.

Pregnancies involving multiple babies are often very high risk and can be associated with premature birth and low birth weight, both factors in possible long-term disabilities in both physical and cognitive areas. Some of the babies may not survive, or doctors might actually recommend selective termination of some of the babies to increase the chances of survival for the remaining infants (Drugan & Weissman, 2017; Qin et al., 2015; Wilkinson et al., 2015). This is a concern of an area called **bioethics**, the study of ethical and moral issues brought about by new advances in biology and medicine and how those advances should influence policies and practices (Kirsten, 2017; Muzur, 2014; Qin et al., 2015).

For developmental psychologists, twins provide an important way to look at the contribution of nature and nurture to human development. Researchers may seek out genetically identical twins who have been separated at birth, looking at all the ways those twins are alike in spite of being raised in different environments. It should be noted that the environments in which children are raised within a particular culture are not necessarily that different, so twin studies are not a perfect method. Researchers may also compare children who are adopted to their adoptive parents (an environmental influence) and to their biological parents (a genetic influence). See Learning Objective 12.13.

THINKING CRITICALLY 8.1

The time is coming when choosing the genetic traits of your child is going to be possible. What kinds of ethical and practical problems may arise from this development?

8.5 Three Stages of Development

8.5 Describe the three stages of prenatal development.

As you might imagine, the 9 months of a typical pregnancy involve a great many changes. While many people think in terms of trimesters (3-month periods), there are really three stages of pregnancy during which major aspects of development occur: the germinal period, the embryonic period, and the fetal period (see **Figure 8.4**).

Figure 8.4 Three Periods of Pregnancy

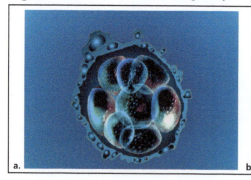
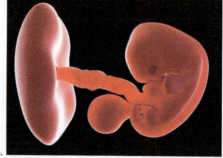
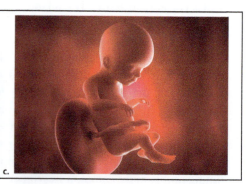

a.   b.   c.

The three periods of pregnancy are (a) the germinal period, lasting about 2 weeks, (b) the embryonic period, from about 2 to 8 weeks, and (c) the fetal period, which lasts from 8 weeks until the end of pregnancy.

Sources: (left) VEM/BSIP SA/Alamy Stock Photo; (center) Sebastian Kaulitzki/Science Photo Library/Alamy Stock Photo; (right) Sebastian Kaulitzki/Science Photo Library/Getty Images.

THE GERMINAL PERIOD Once fertilization has taken place, the zygote begins dividing and moving down to the *uterus*, the muscular organ that will contain and protect the developing organism. This process takes about a week, followed by about a week during which the mass of cells, now forming a hollow ball, firmly attaches itself to the wall of the uterus. This 2-week period is called the **germinal period** of pregnancy. The *placenta* also begins to form during this period. The placenta is a specialized organ that provides nourishment and filters away the developing baby's waste products. The *umbilical cord* also begins to develop at this time, connecting the organism to the placenta.

> How does a mass of cells become a baby, with eyes, nose, hands, feet, and so on? How do all those different things come from the same original single cell?

During the germinal period, the cells begin to differentiate, or develop into specialized cells, in preparation for becoming all the various kinds of cells that make up the human body—skin cells, heart cells, and so on. Perhaps the most important of these cells are the *stem cells*, which stay in a somewhat immature state until needed to produce more cells. Researchers are looking into ways to use stem cells found in the umbilical cord to grow new organs and tissues for transplant or to repair neurological damage (Canals et al., 2018; Chen & Ende, 2000; Ding et al., 2015; Holden & Vogel, 2002; Li et al., 2018; Lu & Ende, 1997). See Learning Objective 2.11.

THE EMBRYONIC PERIOD Once firmly attached to the uterus, the developing organism is called an **embryo**. The **embryonic period** will last from 2 weeks after conception to 8 weeks, and during this time the cells will continue to specialize and become the various organs and structures of a human infant. By the end of this period, the embryo is about 1 inch long and has primitive eyes, nose, lips, teeth, and little arms and legs, as well as a beating heart. Although no organ is fully developed or completely functional at this time, nearly all are "there."

CRITICAL PERIODS As soon as the embryo begins to receive nourishment from the mother through the placenta, it becomes vulnerable to hazards such as diseases of the mother, drugs, and other toxins that can pass from the mother through the placenta to the developing infant. Because of this direct connection between mother and embryo and the fact that all major organs are in the process of forming, we can clearly see the effects of **critical periods**, times during which some environmental influences can have an impact—often devastating—on the development of the infant. The structural development of the arms and legs, for example, is only affected during the time that these limbs are developing (3 to 8 weeks), whereas the heart's structure is most affected very early in this period (2 to 6 weeks). Other physical and structural problems can occur with the central nervous system (2 to 5 weeks), eyes (3 to 8 weeks), and the teeth and roof of the mouth (about 7 to 12 weeks).

PRENATAL HAZARDS: TERATOGENS Any substance such as a drug, chemical, virus, or other factor that can cause a birth defect is called a **teratogen**. Table 8.2 shows some common teratogens and their possible negative effects on the developing embryo.

One of the more common teratogens is alcohol. Consumption of alcohol during pregnancy, particularly during the critical embryonic period, can lead to one of several possible **fetal alcohol spectrum disorders (FASDs)**, in which a combination of physical, mental, and behavioral problems may be present. For example, the most severe FASD, *fetal alcohol syndrome* (FAS), includes a series of physical and mental defects including stunted growth, facial deformities, and brain damage (Andreu-Fernandez et al., 2019; Denny et al., 2017; Rangmar et al., 2015). Exposure to alcohol in early pregnancy is the leading known cause of intellectual disability (previously called mental retardation) in the Western hemisphere (Abel & Sokol, 1987; Caley et al., 2005). Globally, 8 out of every 1,000 children born

germinal period
first 2 weeks after fertilization, during which the zygote moves down to the uterus and begins to implant in the lining.

embryo
name for the developing organism from 2 weeks to 8 weeks after fertilization.

embryonic period
the period from 2 to 8 weeks after fertilization, during which the major organs and structures of the organism develop.

critical periods
times during which certain environmental influences can have an impact on the development of the infant.

teratogen
any factor that can cause a birth defect.

fetal alcohol spectrum disorders (FASDs)
a group of possible conditions caused by a mother consuming alcohol during pregnancy, in which a combination of physical, mental, and behavioral problems may be present

Table 8.2 Common Teratogens

Teratogenic Agent	Effect on Development
Measles, Mumps, and Rubella	Blindness, deafness, heart defects, brain damage
Marijuana	Irritability, nervousness, tremors; infant is easily disturbed, startled
Cocaine	Decreased height, low birth weight, respiratory problems, seizures, learning difficulties; infant is difficult to soothe
Alcohol	Fetal alcohol spectrum disorders (FASDs), e.g., fetal alcohol syndrome (intellectual disability, delayed growth, facial malformation), learning difficulties, smaller-than-normal heads
Nicotine	Miscarriage, low birth weight, stillbirth, short stature, intellectual disability, learning disabilities
Mercury	Intellectual disability, blindness
Vitamin A (high doses)	Facial, ear, central nervous system, and heart defects
Caffeine	Miscarriage, low birth weight
Toxoplasmosis	Brain swelling, spinal abnormalities, deafness, blindness, intellectual disability
High Water Temperatures	Increased chance of neural tube defects

Source: Based on March of Dimes Foundation (2006); Organization of Teratology Information Specialists (2017); Shepard & Lemire (2010).

have some degree of FASD, and one out of every 13 women who drank alcohol while pregnant has given birth to a child with a FASD (Lange et al., 2017). FASDs are extremely preventable, and no amount of alcohol is safe to drink while pregnant.

THE FETAL PERIOD: GROW, BABY, GROW The **fetal period** is a period of tremendous growth lasting from about 8 weeks after conception until birth. The length of the developing organism (now referred to as a **fetus**) increases by about 20 times, and its weight increases from about 1 ounce at 2 months to an average of a little over 7 pounds at birth. The organs, while accomplishing most of their differentiation in the embryonic period, continue to develop and become functional. At this time, teratogens will more likely affect the physical functioning (physiology) of the organs rather than their structure. The functioning of the central nervous system, for example, is vulnerable throughout the fetal period, as are the eyes and the external sexual organs.

The last few months continue the development of fat and the growth of the body, until about the end of the 38th week. At 38 weeks, the fetus is considered full term. Most babies are born between 38 and 40 weeks. Babies born before 38 weeks are called *preterm* or premature and may need life support to survive. If they are very premature, they may also experience problems later in life. This is especially true if the baby weighs less than 5½ pounds at birth. How early can an infant be born and still survive? The age of viability (the point at which it is possible for an infant to survive outside the womb) is between 22 and 26 weeks, with the odds of survival increasing from 10 percent at 22 weeks up to about 85 percent at 26 weeks (National Commission for the Protection of Human Subjects of Biomedical and Behavioral Research, 2006). Those odds will also increase if the infant is in a facility with advanced neonatal health care (Rysavy et al., 2015).

The most likely time for a *miscarriage*, or *spontaneous abortion*, is in the first 3 months, as the organs are forming and first becoming functional (Katz, 2007; Speroff et al., 1999). Some 15 to 20 percent of all pregnancies end in miscarriage, many so early that the mother may not have even known she was pregnant (American College of Obstetricians and Gynecologists, 2015; Doubilet et al., 2013; Hill, 1998; Medical Economics Staff, 1994; Nelson et al., 2015). When a miscarriage occurs, it is most likely caused by a genetic defect in the way the embryo or fetus is developing that will not allow the infant to survive. In other words, there isn't anything that the mother did wrong or that could have been done to prevent the miscarriage.

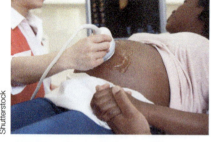

This pregnant woman is getting an ultrasound. Ultrasounds use high-frequency sound waves to create a picture, or sonogram, that allows doctors to see any physical deformities and make accurate measurements of gestational age without risk to the mother or the fetus.

fetal period
the time from about 8 weeks after conception until the birth of the baby.

fetus
name for the developing organism from 8 weeks after fertilization to the birth of the baby.

Concept Map L.O. 8.4, 8.5

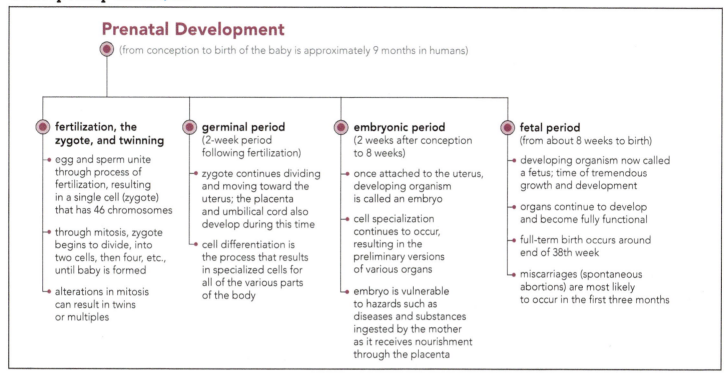

Practice Quiz — How much do you remember?

Pick the best answer.

1. The first 2 weeks of pregnancy are called the _____ period.
   a. placental
   b. embryonic
   c. germinal
   d. fetal
   e. latency

2. Which of the following does NOT happen in the germinal period?
   a. A dividing mass of cells travels to the uterus.
   b. A mass of cells form a hollow ball.
   c. Developing organs can be affected by toxins passing through the placenta.
   d. Cells begin to differentiate.
   e. Developing organism now called a fetus.

3. The period of pregnancy that contains the clearest examples of critical periods is the _____ period.
   a. fetal
   b. embryonic
   c. germinal
   d. gestational
   e. zygotic

4. Intellectual disability and blindness are possible outcomes of the effects of _____ on the developing baby.
   a. mercury
   b. alcohol
   c. caffeine
   d. cocaine
   e. nicotine

8.6–8.8 Infancy and Childhood Development

Infancy and early childhood are a time of rapid growth and development in the body, motor skills, cognitive abilities, and sensory systems.

8.6 Physical Development

8.6 Describe the physical and sensory changes that take place in infancy and childhood.

Immediately after birth, several things start to happen. The respiratory system begins to function, filling the lungs with air and putting oxygen into the blood. The blood now circulates only within the infant's system because the umbilical cord has been cut. Body temperature is now regulated by the infant's own activity and body fat (which acts as insulation) rather than by the amniotic fluid. The digestive system probably takes the longest to adjust to life outside the womb. This is another reason for the baby's excess body fat. It provides fuel until the infant is able to take in enough nourishment on its own. That is why most babies lose a little weight in the first week after birth.

💬 How much can babies really do? Aren't they pretty much unaware of what's going on around them at first?

Surprisingly, babies can do quite a lot more than you might think. Researchers have developed ways of studying what infants cannot tell us in words. Two common methods are the use of *preferential looking* and *habituation*. Preferential looking assumes that the longer an infant spends looking at a stimulus, the more the infant prefers that stimulus over others (Fantz, 1961). Habituation is the tendency for infants (and adults) to stop paying attention to a stimulus that does not change. See Learning Objective 3.3. By exposing the infant to an unchanging sound or picture, for example, researchers can wait for the infant to habituate (look away) and then change the stimulus. If the infant reacts (dishabituates), the infant is capable of detecting that change (Columbo & Mitchell, 2009).

REFLEXES Babies come into this world able to interact with it. Infants have a set of *innate* (existing from birth), involuntary behavior patterns called *reflexes*. Until a baby is capable of learning more complex means of interaction, reflexes help the infant survive. **Figure 8.5** shows five infant reflexes. Pediatricians use these and other reflexes to determine whether a newborn's nervous system is working properly.

Figure 8.5 Five Infant Reflexes

Shown here are (a) grasping reflex; (b) startle reflex (also known as the Moro reflex); (c) rooting reflex (when you touch a baby's cheek, it will turn toward your hand, open its mouth, and search for the nipple); (d) stepping reflex; and (e) sucking reflex. These infant reflexes can be used to check the health of an infant's nervous system. If a reflex is absent or abnormal, it may indicate brain damage or some other neurological problem.

Sources: (a) Tony Wear/Shutterstock; (b) Jules Selmes/Pearson Education Ltd; (c) Cathy Melloan/PhotoEdit; (d) Denise Hager/Catchlight Visual Services/Alamy Stock Photo; (e) Vlavetal/Shutterstock.

MOTOR DEVELOPMENT: FROM CRAWLING TO A BLUR OF MOTION Infants manage a tremendous amount of development in motor skills from birth to about 2 years of age. **Figure 8.6** shows some of the major physical milestones of infancy. When looking at the age ranges listed, remember that even these ranges are averages based on large samples of infants. An infant may reach these milestones earlier or later than the average and still be considered to be developing normally.

AP 6.C Discuss maturation of motor skills.

Figure 8.6 Six Motor Milestones

Shown here are (a) raising head and chest—2 to 4 months, (b) rolling over—2 to 5 months, (c) sitting up with support—4 to 6 months, (d) sitting up without support—6 to 7 months, (e) crawling—7 to 8 months, and (f) walking—8 to 18 months. The motor milestones develop as the infant gains greater voluntary control over the muscles in its body, typically from the top of the body downward. This pattern is seen in the early control of the neck muscles and the much later development of control of the legs and feet.

Sources: (a) Michael Pettigrew/Shutterstock; (b) Keisuke kai/123RF; (c) Tatiana Chekryzhova/123RF; (d) Samuel Borges Photography/Shutterstock; (e) Oksana Kuzmina/123RF; (f) Ivanko80/Shutterstock.

BRAIN DEVELOPMENT At birth, an infant's brain consists of more than 100 billion neurons. Rapid and extensive growth of these neurons occurs as the brain triples in weight from birth to age 3 years, with much of the increase caused by growth of new dendrites, axon terminals, and increasing numbers of synaptic connections (Nelson, 2011; Paredes et al., 2016). Surprisingly, the development of the infant brain after birth involves a necessary loss of neurons called *synaptic pruning*, as unused synaptic connections and nerve cells are cleared away to make way for functioning connections and cells (Couperus & Nelson, 2006; Graven & Browne, 2008; Kozberg et al., 2013; Zhan et al., 2014). This process is similar to weeding your garden—you take out the weeds to make room for the plants that you want.

BABY, CAN YOU SEE ME? BABY, CAN YOU HEAR ME? SENSORY DEVELOPMENT

💬 I've heard that babies can't see or hear very much at birth. Is that true?

Although most infant sensory abilities are fairly well developed at birth, some require a bit more time to reach "full power." The sense of touch is the most well developed, understandable when you realize how much skin-to-womb contact the baby has in the last months of pregnancy. The sense of smell is also highly developed. Breast-fed babies can actually tell the difference between their own mother's milk scent and another woman's milk scent within a few days after birth.

Taste is also nearly fully developed. At birth, infants show a preference for sweets (and human breast milk is very sweet) and by 4 months have developed a preference for salty tastes (which may come from exposure to the salty taste of their mother's skin). Sour and bitter, two other taste sensations, produce spitting up and the making of horrible faces (Ganchrow et al., 1983).

Hearing is functional before birth but may take a little while to reach its full potential after the baby is born. The fluids of the womb first must clear out of the auditory canals completely. From birth, newborns seem most responsive to high pitches, as in a woman's voice, and low pitches, as in a man's voice.

The least functional sense at birth is vision. The eye is quite a complex organ. See Learning Objective 3.4. The rods, which see in black and white and have little visual acuity, are fairly well developed at birth, but the cones, which see color and provide sharpness of vision, will take about another 6 months to fully develop. As a result, the newborn has relatively poor color perception when compared to sharply contrasting lights and darks until about 2 months of age (Adams, 1987) and has fairly "fuzzy" vision, much as a nearsighted person would have. The lens of the newborn stays fixed until the muscles that hold it in place mature. Until then the newborn is unable to shift what little focus it has from close to far. Thus, newborns actually have a fixed distance for clear vision of about 7–10 inches, which is the distance from the baby's face to the mother's face while nursing (Slater, 2000; von Hofsten et al., 2014).

Newborns also have visual preferences at birth, as discovered by researchers using preferential looking, measures of the time that infants spent looking at certain visual stimuli (Fantz, 1961). They found that infants prefer to look at complex patterns rather than simple ones, three dimensions rather than two, and that the most preferred visual stimulus was a human face. The fact that infants prefer human voices and human faces (DeCasper & Fifer, 1980; DeCasper & Spence, 1986; Fantz, 1964; Maurer & Young, 1983; Morii & Sakagami, 2015) makes it easier for them to form relationships with their caregivers and to develop language later on. Infants' preference for seeing things in three dimensions suggests that they possess depth perception. The following classic experiment provided evidence for that assumption.

Classic Studies in Psychology
The Visual Cliff

Eleanor Gibson and her fellow researcher, Michael Walk, wondered if infants could perceive the world in three dimensions, and so they devised a way to test babies for depth perception (Gibson & Walk, 1960). They built a special table (see **Figure 8.7**) that had a big drop on one side. The surface of the table on both the top and the drop to the floor were covered in a patterned tablecloth, so that the different size of the patterns would be a cue for depth (remember, in size constancy, if something looks smaller, people assume it is farther away from them). See Learning Objective 3.15. The whole table was then covered by a clear glass top, so that a baby could safely be placed on or crawl across the "deep" side.

The infants tested in this study ranged from 6 to 14 months in age. They were placed on the middle of the table and then encouraged (usually by their mothers) to crawl over either the shallow side or the deep side. Most babies—81 percent—refused to crawl over the deep side, even though they could touch it with their hands and feel that it was solid. They were upset and seemed fearful when encouraged to crawl across. Gibson and Walk interpreted this as a very early sign of the concept of depth perception.

Figure 8.7 The Visual Cliff Experiment

In the visual cliff experiment, the table has both a shallow and a "deep" side, with glass covering the entire table. When an infant looks down at the deep-appearing side, the squares in the design on the floor look smaller than the ones on the shallow side, forming a visual cue for depth. Notice that this little girl seems to be very reluctant to cross over the deep-appearing side of the table, gesturing to be picked up instead.

Source: Mark Richard/PhotoEdit.

Questions for Further Discussion

1. Does the fact that 19 percent of the infants did crawl over the deep side of the visual cliff necessarily mean that those infants could not perceive the depth?
2. What other factors might explain the willingness of the 19 percent to crawl over the deep side?
3. Are there any ethical concerns in this experiment?
4. Ducks aren't bothered by the visual cliff at all—why might that be?

8.7 Cognitive Development

8.7 Compare and contrast two theories of cognitive development, and define autism spectrum disorder.

AP 6.H Explain the maturation of cognitive abilities (Piaget's stages, Information process).

AP 6.I Identify the contributions of major researchers in the area of cognitive development in childhood.

By the time the average infant has reached the age of 1 year, it has tripled its birth weight and added about another foot to its height. The brain triples its weight in the first 2 years, reaching about 75 percent of its adult weight. By age 5, the brain is at 90 percent of its adult weight. This increase makes possible a tremendous amount of major advances in **cognitive development**, including the development of thinking, problem solving, and memory.

PIAGET'S THEORY: FOUR STAGES OF COGNITIVE DEVELOPMENT Early researcher Jean Piaget developed his theory of cognitive development from detailed observations of infants and children, most especially his own three children. Piaget believed that children form mental concepts or **schemas** (sometimes referred to as schemes) as they experience new situations and events. For example, if Sandy points to a picture of an apple and tells her child, "that's an apple," the child forms a schema for "apple" that looks something like that picture. Piaget also believed that children first try to understand new things in terms of schemas they already possess, a process called *assimilation*. The child might see an orange and say "apple" because both objects are round. When corrected, the child might alter the schema

cognitive development
the development of thinking, problem solving, and memory.

schema
a mental concept or framework that guides organization and interpretation of information, which forms and evolves through experiences with objects and events.

Watch Assimilation and Accommodation in Children

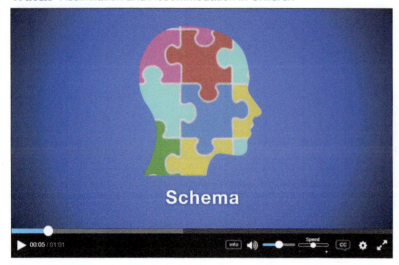

Watch the Video at MyLab Psychology

sensorimotor stage
Piaget's first stage of cognitive development, in which the infant uses its senses and motor abilities to interact with objects in the environment.

object permanence
the knowledge that an object exists even when it is not in sight.

for apple to include "round" and "red." The process of altering or adjusting old schemas to fit new information and experiences is *accommodation* (Piaget, 1952, 1962, 1983). Watch the video *Assimilation and Accommodation in Children* to learn more about these processes.

Piaget also proposed that there are four distinct stages of cognitive development that occur from infancy to adolescence, as shown in **Table 8.3** (Piaget, 1952, 1962, 1983).

THE SENSORIMOTOR STAGE The **sensorimotor stage** (birth to age 2) is the first of Piaget's stages. In this stage, infants use their senses and motor abilities to learn about the world around them. At first, infants only have the involuntary reflexes present at birth to interact with objects and people. As their sensory and motor development progresses, they begin to interact deliberately with objects by grasping, pushing, tasting, and so on. Infants move from simple repetitive actions, such as grabbing their toes, to complex patterns, such as trying to put a shape into a sorting box.

By the end of the sensorimotor stage, infants have fully developed a sense of **object permanence**, the knowledge that an object exists even when it is not in sight. For example, the game of "peek-a-boo" is important in teaching infants that Mommy's smiling face is always going to be behind her hands. This is a critical step in developing language (and eventually abstract thought), as words themselves are symbols of things that may not be present. Symbolic thought, which is the ability to represent objects in one's thoughts with symbols such as words, becomes possible by the end of this stage, with children at 2 years old capable of thinking in simple symbols and planning out actions.

💬 Why is it so easy for children to believe in Santa Claus and the Tooth Fairy when they're little?

Table 8.3 Piaget's Stages of Cognitive Development

Stage	Age	Cognitive Development
Sensorimotor	Birth to 2 years old	Children explore the world using their senses and ability to move. They develop object permanence and the understanding that concepts and mental images represent objects, people, and events.
Preoperational	2 to 7 years old	Young children can mentally represent and refer to objects and events with words or pictures, and they can pretend. However, they can't conserve, logically reason, or simultaneously consider many characteristics of an object.
Concrete Operations	7 to 12 years old	Children at this stage are able to conserve, reverse their thinking, and classify objects in terms of their many characteristics. They can also think logically and understand analogies but only about concrete events.
Formal Operations	12 years old to adulthood	People at this stage can use abstract reasoning about hypothetical events or situations, think about logical possibilities, use abstract analogies, and systematically examine and test hypotheses. Not everyone can eventually reason in all these ways.

Source: Based on Piaget, J. (1926). The language and thought of the child. New York: Harcourt Brace. Piaget, J. (1962). Play, dreams and imitation in childhood. New York: W. W. Norton. Piaget, J. (1983). Piaget's theory. In W. Kessen (Ed.), Handbook of child psychology: Volume 1. Theoretical models of human development (pp. 103–128). New York: Wiley.

THE PREOPERATIONAL STAGE The **preoperational stage** (ages 2–7) is a time of developing language and concepts. Children, who can now move freely about in their world, no longer have to rely only on senses and motor skills but now can ask questions and explore their surroundings more fully. Pretending and make-believe play become possible because children at this stage can understand, through symbolic thinking, that a line of wooden blocks can "stand in" for a train. They are limited, however, in several ways. They are not yet capable of logical thought—they can use simple mental concepts but are not able to use those concepts in a more rational, logical sense. They believe that everything is alive and has feelings just like their own, a quality called *animism*, so they might apologize to a chair for bumping it. They also tend to believe that what they see is literally true, so when children of this age see Santa Claus in a book, on television, or at the mall, Santa Claus becomes real to them. It doesn't occur to them to think about how Santa might get to every child's house in one night or why those toys he delivers are the same ones they saw in the store just last week.

Another limitation is **egocentrism**, the inability to see the world through anyone else's eyes but one's own. For the preoperational child, everyone else must see what the child sees, and what is important to the child must be important to everyone else. For example, 2-year-old Hiba, after climbing out of her crib for the third time, was told by her mother, "I don't want to see you in that living room again tonight!" Hiba's next appearance was made with her hands over her eyes—if she couldn't see her mother, her mother couldn't see *her*. Egocentrism is not the same as being egotistical or selfish—it would also be egocentric, but completely unselfish, if 4-year-old Jamal wants to give his grandmother an action figure for her birthday because that's what *he* would want.

Remember that children in this stage are also overwhelmed by appearances. A child who complains that his piece of pie is smaller than his brother's may be quite happy once his original piece is cut into two pieces—now he thinks he has "more" than his brother. He has focused only on the number of pieces, not the actual amount of the pie. Focusing only on one feature of some object rather than taking all features into consideration is called **centration**. In the coin example in **Figure 8.8**, children of this stage will focus (or center) on the *length* of the top line of coins only and ignore the *number* of coins. Centration is one of the reasons that children in this stage often fail to understand that changing the way something looks does not change its substance. The ability to understand that altering the appearance of something does not change its amount (as in the coin example), its volume, or its mass is called **conservation**.

preoperational stage
Piaget's second stage of cognitive development, in which the preschool child learns to use language as a means of exploring the world.

egocentrism
the inability to see the world through anyone else's eyes.

centration
in Piaget's theory, the tendency of a young child to focus only on one feature of an object while ignoring other relevant features.

conservation
in Piaget's theory, the ability to understand that simply changing the appearance of an object does not change the object's nature.

irreversibility
in Piaget's theory, the inability of the young child to mentally reverse an action.

Figure 8.8 Conservation Experiment

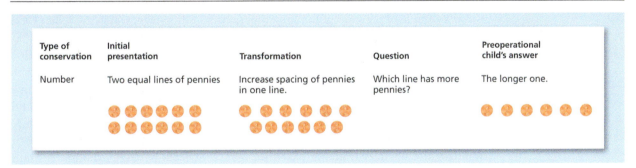

In this conservation task, pennies are laid out in two equal lines. When the pennies in the top line are spaced out, the child who cannot yet conserve will centrate on the top line and assume that there are actually more pennies in that line.

Preoperational children fail at conservation not only because they *centrate* (focus on just one feature, such as the number of pieces of pie) but also because they are unable to "mentally reverse" actions. This feature of preoperational thinking is called **irreversibility**.

Watch Conservation

Watch the Video at MyLab Psychology

For example, if a preoperational child sees liquid poured from a short, wide glass into a tall, thin glass, the child will assume that the second glass holds more liquid. This failure to "conserve" (save) the volume of liquid as it takes on a different shape in the tall, thin glass is not only caused by the child's centration on the height of the liquid in the second glass but also by the inability of the child to imagine pouring the liquid back into the first glass and having it be the same amount again. Similar "reasoning" causes children of this age to assume that a ball of clay, when rolled out into a "rope" of clay, is now greater in mass. Watch the video *Conservation* to see this in action.

CONCRETE OPERATIONS In the **concrete operations stage** (ages 7–12), children finally become capable of conservation and reversible thinking. Centration no longer occurs as children become capable of considering all the relevant features of any given object. They begin to think more logically about beliefs such as Santa Claus or the Tooth Fairy and to ask questions, eventually coming to their own more rational conclusions about these fantasies of early childhood. They are in school, learning all sorts of science and math, and are convinced that they know more than their parents at this point (an impression that will likely not change until early adulthood, when their parents seem to get smarter as they get older).

These concrete operational children, seen in a science class, have begun to think logically and are able to solve many kinds of problems that were not possible for them to solve while in the preoperational stage.

The major limitation of this stage is the inability to deal effectively with *abstract concepts*. Abstract concepts are those that do not have some physical, *concrete*, touchable reality. For example, "freedom" is an abstract concept. People can define it, they can get a good sense of what it means, but there is no "thing" that they can point to and say, "This is freedom." *Concrete concepts*, which are the kind of concepts understood by children of this age, are about objects, written rules, and real things. Children need to be able to see it, touch it, or at least "see" it in their heads to be able to understand it.

FORMAL OPERATIONS In the last of Piaget's stages, **formal operations** (age 12 to adulthood), abstract thinking becomes possible. Teenagers not only understand concepts that have no physical reality, but also they get deeply involved in hypothetical thinking, or thinking about possibilities and even impossibilities. "What if everyone just got along?" "If women were in charge of countries, would there be fewer wars?" For an example of the kind of thinking that occurs in this stage, watch the video *Formal Operational Thought*.

Piaget did not believe that everyone would necessarily reach formal operations, and studies show that only about half of all adults in the United States reach this stage (Sutherland, 1992). Adults who do not achieve formal operations tend to use a more practical, down-to-earth kind of intelligence that suits their particular lifestyle. Successful college students, however, need formal-operational thinking to succeed in their college careers, as most college classes require critical thinking, problem-solving abilities, and abstract thinking based on formal-operational skills (Bolton & Hattie, 2017; Powers, 1984).

Others have proposed another stage beyond formal operations, a relativistic thinking stage found in young adults, particularly those who have found their old ways of thinking in "black and white" terms challenged by the diversity they encounter in the college environment (LaBouvie-Vief, 1980, 1992; Perry, 1970). In this kind of thinking, young adults recognize

concrete operations stage
Piaget's third stage of cognitive development, in which the school-age child becomes capable of logical thought processes but is not yet capable of abstract thinking.

formal operations stage
Piaget's last stage of cognitive development, in which the adolescent becomes capable of abstract thinking.

that all problems cannot be solved with pure logic, and there can be multiple points of view for a single problem.

EVALUATING PIAGET'S THEORY Piaget saw children as active explorers of their surroundings, engaged in the discovery of the properties of objects and organisms within those surroundings. Educators have put Piaget's ideas into practice by allowing children to learn at their own pace, by "hands-on" experience with objects, and by teaching concepts that are at the appropriate cognitive level for those children (Brooks & Brooks, 1993). But Piaget's theory has also been criticized on several points. Some researchers believe that the idea of distinct stages of cognitive development is not completely correct and that changes in thought are more continuous and gradual rather than abruptly jumping from one stage to another (Courage & Howe, 2002; Feldman, 2003; Schwitzgebel, 1999; Siegler, 1996). Others point out that preschoolers are not as egocentric as Piaget seemed to believe (Flavell, 1999) and that object permanence exists much earlier than Piaget thought (Aguiar & Baillargeon, 2003; Baillargeon, 1986).

Watch Formal Operational Thought

Watch the Video at MyLab Psychology

VYGOTSKY'S THEORY: THE IMPORTANCE OF BEING THERE Russian psychologist Lev Vygotsky's pioneering work in developmental psychology has had a profound influence on school education in Russia, and interest in his theories continues to grow throughout the world (Bodrova & Leong, 1996; Duncan, 1995; Shabani, 2016). Vygotsky wrote about children's cognitive development but differed from Piaget in his emphasis on the role of others in cognitive development (Vygotsky, 1934/1962, 1978, 1987). Whereas Piaget stressed the importance of the child's interaction with objects as a primary factor in cognitive development, Vygotsky stressed the importance of social and cultural interactions with other people, typically more highly skilled children and adults. Vygotsky believed that children develop cognitively when someone else helps them by asking leading questions and providing examples of concepts in a process called **scaffolding**. In scaffolding, the more highly skilled person gives the learner more help at the beginning of the learning process and then begins to withdraw help as the learner's skills improve (Gonulal & Loewen, 2018; Rogoff, 1994).

Vygotsky also proposed that each developing child has a **zone of proximal development (ZPD)**, which is the difference between what a child can do alone versus what a child can do with the help of a teacher. For example, if Jenny can do fourth-grade math problems by herself but also can successfully work sixth-grade math problems with the help of a teacher, her ZPD is about 2 years: the difference between what she can do alone and what she can do with help. Suzi might be the same age as Jenny and just as skilled at working fourth-grade math problems (and might even score the same on a traditional IQ test), but if Suzi can only work up to fifth-grade math problems with the teacher's help, Suzi's ZPD is only about 1 year and is not as great as Jenny's. Both girls are smart, but Jenny could be seen as possessing a higher potential intelligence than Suzi. This might be a better way of thinking about intelligence: It isn't what you know (as measured by traditional tests), it's what you *can do*.

Other researchers have applied Vygotsky's social focus on learning to the development of a child's memory for personal (autobiographical) events, finding evidence that children learn the culturally determined structures and purposes of personal stories from the early conversations they have with their parents. This process begins with the parent telling the story to the very young child, followed by the child repeating elements of the

scaffolding

process in which a more skilled learner gives help to a less skilled learner, reducing the amount of help as the less skilled learner becomes more capable.

zone of proximal development (ZPD)

Vygotsky's concept of the difference between what a child can do alone and what that child can do with the help of a teacher.

This girl is helping her younger brother learn to read a book. Vygotsky's view of cognitive development states that the help of skilled others aids in making cognitive advances such as this one.

story as the child's verbal abilities grow. The child reaches the final stage at around age 5 or 6 when the child creates the personal story entirely—an excellent example of scaffolding (Fivush et al., 1996; Fivush & Nelson, 2004; Gonulal & Loewen, 2018; Nelson, 1993). Unlike Piaget, who saw a child's talking to himself or herself as egocentric, Vygotsky thought that private speech was a way for the child to "think out loud" and advance cognitively. As adults, we still do this when we talk to ourselves to help solve a particular problem. Vygotsky's ideas have been put into practice in education through the use of cooperative learning, in which children work together in groups to achieve a common goal, and in reciprocal teaching, in which teachers lead students through the basic strategies of reading until the students themselves become capable of teaching the strategies to others. Chapter Seven details the stages of language development in infancy and childhood. See Learning Objective 7.12.

AP 8.F Discuss the major diagnostic categories, neurodevelopmental disorders, neurocognitive disorders, schizophrenia spectrum, and other psychotic disorders, and their corresponding symptoms.

AUTISM SPECTRUM DISORDER Before leaving the topic of cognitive development in infancy, let's briefly discuss a topic that, thanks to inaccurate and false viral posts on various social media forums, is very misunderstood: the causes underlying autism spectrum disorder. Autism spectrum disorder (ASD) is a neurodevelopmental disorder that actually encompasses a whole range of previous disorders (with what may be an equally broad range of causes), which cause problems in thinking, feeling, language, and social skills in relating to others (American Psychiatric Association, 2013; Atladóttir et al., 2009; Johnson & Myers, 2007; Lai et al., 2015; Schuwerk et al., 2015).

Theory of mind is a term that refers to the ability to understand not only your own mental states, such as beliefs, intentions, and desires, but also to understand that other people have beliefs, intentions, and desires that may be different from yours (Baron-Cohen et al., 1985). Autism research suggests that one of the main problems for people with autism is that they do not possess a theory of mind, failing to understand that other people have their own points of view (Baron-Cohen et al., 1985; Kimhi, 2014; Korkmaz, 2011).

Research continues into the possible causes of ASD, with studies implicating genetic mutations, changes in certain areas of the brain, and even the possibility that a maternal grandmother's smoking during pregnancy could be related to her grandchild being at a higher risk for ASD (Cai et al., 2018; Chen et al., 2018; Golding et al., 2017). Despite such scholarly research, rumors and misinformation about a possible cause of autism have been circulating on the Internet for many years (Mitchell & Locke, 2015). The major source of misinformation began in 1998, when British gastroenterologist Dr. Andrew Wakefield published the results of two studies that seemed to link the MMR (measles, mumps, and rubella) vaccine to autism and bowel disease in children (Wakefield et al., 1998). Experts reviewed the quality of his research, and the studies were quickly denounced as inadequate and dangerous by autism specialists and others (Fitzpatrick, 2004; Judelsohn, 2007; Matthew & Dallery, 2007; Novella, 2007; Stratton et al., 2001a, 2001b). See Learning Objectives 1.8 and 1.9. Nevertheless, Wakefield's publication was followed by measles epidemics due to parents refusing the MMR inoculation for their children, as well as an anti-vaccination movement founded on nothing more than fear and lack of education about vaccination safety and importance (MacDougall & Monnais, 2018). The myth of a link persists, in spite of numerous studies that have consistently failed to show any link between the MMR vaccine and autism (Burns, 2010; Gilberg & Coleman, 2000; Jain et al., 2015; Johnson & Myers, 2007; Madsen et al., 2002; Mars et al., 1998; Taylor et al., 1999; Thompson et al., 2007). In 2004, the other authors listed on the study formally retracted the 1998 paper. In 2009, the final blow came to Wakefield's credibility when it was discovered that he had falsified his data, resulting in the revoking of his medical license in May of 2010 (Meikle & Bosley, 2010).

8.8 Psychosocial Development

8.8 Identify the development of personality, relationships, and self-concept in infancy and childhood.

The psychological and social development of infants and children involves the development of personality, relationships, and a sense of being male or female. Although these processes begin in infancy, they will continue, in many respects, well into adulthood.

> Why are some children negative and whiny while others are sweet and good natured?

TEMPERAMENT One of the first ways in which infants demonstrate that they have different personalities (i.e., the long-lasting characteristics that make each person different from others) is in their **temperament**, the behavioral and emotional characteristics that are fairly well established at birth. Researchers (Chess & Thomas, 1986; Thomas & Chess, 1977) have identified three basic temperament styles of infants:

1. **Easy:** "Easy" babies are regular in their schedules of waking, sleeping, and eating, and are adaptable to change. Easy babies are happy babies and when distressed are easily soothed.
2. **Difficult:** "Difficult" babies are almost the opposite of easy ones. Difficult babies tend to be irregular in their schedules and are very unhappy about change of any kind. They are loud, active, and tend to be crabby rather than happy.
3. **Slow to warm up:** This kind of temperament is associated with infants who are less grumpy, quieter, and more regular than difficult children but who are slow to adapt to change. If change is introduced gradually, these babies will "warm up" to new people and new situations.

Of course, not all babies will fall neatly into one of these three patterns—some children may be a mix of two or even all three patterns of behavior, as Chess and Thomas (1986) discovered. Even so, longitudinal research strongly suggests that these temperament styles last well into adulthood and are strongly influenced by heredity (Kagan, 1998; Kagan et al., 2007; Kopal-Sibley et al., 2018; Korn, 1984; Scarpa et al., 1995; Schwartz et al., 2010), although they are somewhat influenced by the environment in which the infant is raised. For example, a "difficult" infant who is raised by parents who are themselves very loud and active may not be perceived as difficult by the parents, whereas a child who is slow to warm up might be perceived as difficult if the parents themselves like lots of change and noise. The first infant is in a situation in which the "goodness of fit" of the infant's temperament to the parents' temperament is very close, but the parents of the second infant are a "poor fit" in temperament for that less active child (Chess & Thomas, 1986). A poor fit can make it difficult to form an attachment, the important psychosocial–emotional bond we will discuss next.

ATTACHMENT The emotional bond that forms between an infant and a primary caregiver is called **attachment**. Attachment is an extremely important development in the social and emotional life of the infant, usually forming within the first 6 months of the infant's life and showing up in a number of ways during the second 6 months, such as *stranger anxiety* (wariness of strangers) and *separation anxiety* (fear of being separated from the caregiver). Although attachment to the mother is usually the primary attachment, infants can attach to fathers and to other caregivers as well.

AP 6.D Describe the influence of temperament and other social factors on attachment and appropriate socialization.

temperament
the behavioral characteristics that are fairly well established at birth, such as "easy," "difficult," and "slow to warm up;" the enduring characteristics with which each person is born.

attachment
the emotional bond between an infant and the primary caregiver.

AP 6.E Identify the contributions of major researchers in developmental psychology in the area of social development in childhood.

ATTACHMENT STYLES Mary Ainsworth (Ainsworth, 1985; Ainsworth et al., 1978) devised a special experimental design to measure the attachment of an infant to the caregiver; she called it the "Strange Situation" (exposing an infant to a series of leave-takings and returns of the mother and a stranger). Through this measurement technique, Ainsworth and another colleague identified four attachment styles:

1. **Secure:** Infants labeled as secure were willing to get down from their mother's lap soon after entering the room with their mothers. They explored happily, looking back at their mothers and returning to them every now and then (sort of like "touching base"). When the stranger came in, these infants were wary but calm as long as their mother was nearby. When the mother left, the infants got upset. When the mother returned, the infants approached her, were easily soothed, and were glad to have her back.

2. **Avoidant:** In contrast, avoidant babies, although somewhat willing to explore, did not "touch base." They did not look at the stranger or the mother and reacted very little to her absence or her return, seeming to have no interest or concern.

3. **Ambivalent:** The word *ambivalent* means to have mixed feelings about something. Ambivalent babies in Ainsworth's study were clinging and unwilling to explore, very upset by the stranger regardless of the mother's presence, protested mightily when the mother left, and were hard to soothe. When the mother returned, these babies would demand to be picked up but at the same time push the mother away or kick her in a mixed reaction to her return.

4. **Disorganized–disoriented:** In subsequent studies, other researchers (Main & Hesse, 1990; Main & Solomon, 1990) found that some babies seemed unable to decide just how they should react to the mother's return. These disorganized–disoriented infants would approach her but with their eyes turned away from her, as if afraid to make eye contact. In general, these infants seemed fearful and showed a dazed and depressed look on their faces.

This toddler shows reluctance to explore her environment, instead clinging to her parent's leg. Such clinging behavior, if common, can be a sign of an ambivalent attachment.

It should come as no surprise that the mothers of each of the four types of infants also behaved differently from one another. Mothers of secure infants were loving, warm, sensitive to their infant's needs, and responsive to the infant's attempts at communication. Mothers of avoidant babies were unresponsive, insensitive, and coldly rejecting. Mothers of ambivalent babies tried to be responsive but were inconsistent and insensitive to the baby's actions, often talking to the infant about something totally unrelated to what the infant was doing at the time. Mothers of disorganized–disoriented babies were found to be abusive or neglectful in interactions with the infants.

Attachment is not necessarily the result of the behavior of the mother alone, however. The temperament of the infant may play an important part in determining the reactions of the mother (Goldsmith & Campos, 1982; Skolnick, 1986). For example, an infant with a difficult temperament is hard to soothe. A mother with this kind of infant might come to avoid unnecessary contact with the infant, as did the mothers of the avoidant babies in Ainsworth's studies.

Critics of Ainsworth's Strange Situation research focus on the artificial nature of the design and wonder if infants and mothers would behave differently in the more familiar surroundings of home, even though Ainsworth's experimental observers also observed the infants and mothers in the home prior to the Strange Situation setting (Ainsworth, 1985). Other research has found results supporting Ainsworth's findings in home-based assessments of attachment (Blanchard & Main, 1979). Other studies have also found support for the concept of attachment styles and relative stability of attachment throughout the life span (Lutkenhaus et al., 1985; Main & Cassidy, 1988;

Owen et al., 1984; Umemura et al., 2018; Wartner et al., 1994; Widom et al., 2018). Even adult relationships can be seen as influenced by the attachment style of the adult—those who are avoidant tend to have numerous shallow and brief relationships with different partners, whereas those who are ambivalent tend to have repeated breakups and makeups with the same person (Bartholomew, 1990; Frederick et al., 2016; Harms et al., 2016; Hazan & Shaver, 1987; Schroeder et al., 2014). Attachment style can also affect how people begin, maintain, and end non-romantic relationships in their broader social network (Gillath et al., 2017).

INFLUENCES ON ATTACHMENT As day care has become more widely acceptable and common, many parents have been concerned about the effect of day care on attachment. Researchers have concluded that while high-quality day care (i.e., consistent and educated caregivers, small child-to-caregiver ratio) is important, the quality of parenting received by infants and toddlers in the home has a greater impact on positive development (Belsky, 2005; Belsky & Johnson, 2005; Belsky et al., 2007).

Although there are some cultural differences in attachment—such as the finding that mothers in the United States tend to wait for a child to express a need before trying to fulfill that need, while Japanese mothers prefer to anticipate the child's needs (Rothbaum et al., 2000), attachment does not seem to suffer in spite of the differences in sensitivity. Evidence that similar attachment styles are found in other cultures demonstrates the need to consider attachment as an important first step in forming relationships with others, one that may set the stage for all relationships that follow (Agerup et al., 2015; Hu & Meng, 1996; Keromoian & Leiderman, 1986; Nievar et al., 2015; Posada et al., 2013; Stefanovic-Stanojevic et al., 2015; Zreik et al., 2017). Before leaving the topic of attachment, let's take a look at one of the first studies that examined the key factors necessary for attachment.

Classic Studies in Psychology
Harlow and Contact Comfort

AP 6.E Identify the contributions of major researchers in developmental psychology in the area of social development in childhood.

As psychologists began to study the development of attachment, they at first assumed that attachment to the mother occurred because the mother was associated with satisfaction of primary drives such as hunger and thirst. The mother is always present when the food (a primary reinforcer) is presented, so the mother becomes a secondary reinforcer capable of producing pleasurable feelings. See Learning Objective 5.5.

Psychologist Harry Harlow felt that attachment had to be influenced by more than just the provision of food. He conducted a number of studies of attachment using infant rhesus monkeys (Harlow, 1958). Noticing that the monkeys in his lab liked to cling to the soft cloth pad used to line their cages, Harlow designed a study to examine the importance of what he termed *contact comfort*, the seeming attachment of the monkeys to something soft to the touch.

He isolated eight baby rhesus monkeys shortly after their birth, placing each in a cage with two surrogate (substitute) "mothers." The surrogates were actually a block of wood covered in soft padding and terry cloth and a wire form, both heated from within. For half of the monkeys, the wire "mother" held the bottle from which they fed, while for the other half the soft "mother" held the bottle. Harlow then recorded the time each monkey spent with each "mother." If time spent with the surrogate is taken as an indicator of attachment, then learning theory would predict that the monkeys would spend more time with whichever surrogate was being used to feed them.

The results? Regardless of which surrogate was feeding them, all of the infant monkeys spent significantly more time with the soft, cloth-covered surrogate. In fact, all monkeys spent very little time with the wire surrogate, even if this was the one with the bottle. Harlow and his colleagues concluded that "contact comfort was an important basic affectional or love variable" (Harlow, 1958, p. 574).

Harlow's work represents one of the earliest investigations into the importance of touch in the attachment process and remains an important study in human development.

Questions for Further Discussion

1. Even though the cloth surrogate was warm and soft and seemed to provide contact comfort, do you think that the monkeys raised in this way would behave normally when placed into contact with other monkeys? How might they react?
2. What might be the implications of Harlow's work for human mothers who feed their infants with bottles rather than breastfeeding?

The wire surrogate "mother" provides the food for this infant rhesus monkey. But the infant spends all its time with the soft, cloth-covered surrogate. According to Harlow, this demonstrates the importance of contact comfort in attachment.

WHO AM I?: THE DEVELOPMENT OF THE SELF-CONCEPT Infants begin life without understanding that they are separate from their surroundings and also from the other people in their social world. The **self-concept** is the image you have of yourself, and it is based on your interactions with the important people in your life. As infants experience the world around them, they slowly learn to separate "me" from both physical surroundings and the other people in their world.

One way to demonstrate a child's growing awareness of self is known as the rouge test. A spot of red rouge or lipstick is put on the end of the child's nose and the child is then placed in front of a mirror. Infants from about 6 months to a little over a year will reach out to touch the image of the baby in the mirror, reacting as if to another child (Amsterdam, 1972; Courage & Howe, 2002). In fact, some infants crawl or walk to the other side of the mirror to look for the "other." But at about 15 to 18 months of age, the infant begins to touch his or her own nose when seeing the image in the mirror, indicating an awareness that the image in the mirror is the infant's own (Filippetti & Tsakiris, 2018; Nielsen et al., 2006). As the child grows, the self-concept grows to include gender ("I'm a boy" or "I'm a girl"), physical appearances ("I have brown hair and blue eyes"), and in middle childhood, personality traits and group memberships (Stipek et al., 1990).

💬 I've heard that you shouldn't pick up a baby every time it cries—that if you do, it might spoil the baby.

ERIKSON'S THEORY Unfortunately, a lot of people have not only heard this advice but also acted on it by frequently ignoring an infant's crying, which turns out to be a very bad thing for babies. When a baby under 6 months of age cries, it is an instinctive reaction meant to get the caregiver to tend to the baby's needs—hunger, thirst, pain, and even loneliness. Research has shown that babies whose cries are tended to consistently (that is, the infant is fed when hungry, changed when wet, and so on) in the early months are more securely attached at age 1 than those infants whose caregivers frequently allow the

self-concept
the image of oneself that develops from interactions with important significant people in one's life.

infants to cry when there is a need for attention—hunger, pain, or wetness, for example (Brazelton, 1992; Heinicke et al., 2000). Erik Erikson, a psychodynamic theorist who emphasized the importance of social relationships in the development of personality, would certainly disagree with letting a baby "cry it out," although allowing an infant who has been fed, changed, burped, and checked to cry on occasion will not damage attachment.

Erikson believed that development occurred in a series of eight stages, with the first four of these stages occurring in infancy and childhood (Erikson, 1950; Erikson & Erikson, 1997). See Learning Objective 12.4. Each of Erikson's stages is an emotional *crisis*, or a kind of turning point, in personality, and the crisis in each stage must be successfully met for normal, healthy psychological development.

Erikson focused on the relationship of the infant and the child to significant others in the immediate surroundings—parents and then later teachers and even peers. **Table 8.4** summarizes the conflict in each of Erikson's eight stages and some of the implications for future development (Erikson, 1950; Erikson & Erikson, 1997). For now, look at the first four stages in particular.

Table 8.4 Erikson's Psychosocial Stages of Development

Stage	Developmental Crisis	Successful Dealing with Crisis	Unsuccessful Dealing with Crisis
1. Infant Birth to 1 year old	Trust vs. Mistrust Infants learn a basic sense of trust dependent upon how their needs are met.	If babies' needs for food, comfort, and affection are met, they develop a sense of trust in people and expect those needs to be met in future.	If babies' needs for food, comfort, and affection are not met, they develop a sense of mistrust and do not expect their needs to be met in future.
2. Toddler 1 to 3 years old	Autonomy vs. Shame and Doubt Toddlers begin to understand that they can control their own actions.	Toddlers who are successful in controlling their own actions develop independence.	Toddlers whose attempts at being independent are blocked develop a sense of self-doubt and shame for failing.
3. Preschool Age 3 to 5 years old	Initiative vs. Guilt Preschool children learn to take responsibility for their own behavior as they develop self-control.	If preschoolers succeed in controlling their reactions and behavior, they feel capable and develop a sense of initiative.	If preschoolers fail in controlling their reactions and behavior, they feel irresponsible and anxious and develop a sense of guilt.
4. Elementary School Age 5 to 12 years old	Industry vs. Inferiority The school-aged child must learn new skills in both the academic world and the social world. They compare themselves to others to measure their success or failure.	When children feel they have succeeded at learning these skills, they develop a sense of industry, making them feel competent and improving their self-esteem.	When children fail or feel that they have failed in learning these skills, they feel inferior when compared to others.
5. Adolescence 13 to early 20s	Identity vs. Role Confusion Adolescents must decide who they are, what they believe, and what they want to be as an adult.	Adolescents who are able to define their values, goals, and beliefs will develop a stable sense of identity.	Adolescents who are unable to define themselves remain confused and may isolate themselves from others or try to be like everyone else instead of themselves.
6. Early Adulthood 20s and 30s	Intimacy vs. Isolation Young adults face the task of finding a person with whom they can share their identity in an ongoing, close, personal relationship.	Young adults who successfully find someone and share their identities will have a fulfilling relationship founded on psychological intimacy.	Young adults who are unable to find someone (often because they do not yet have a stable identity to share) will isolate themselves and may experience loneliness, even when involved in shallow relationships with others.
7. Middle Adulthood 40s and 50s	Generativity vs. Stagnation The focus of this task is to find a way to be a creative, productive person who is nurturing the next generation.	Adults who are able to focus on the next generation will be productive and creative, leaving a legacy for the future.	Adults who are unable to focus outside themselves will remain stagnated and self-centered, and feel that they have not made a difference.
8. Late Adulthood 60s and beyond	Ego Integrity vs. Despair The task in this stage involves coming to terms with the end of life, reaching a sense of wholeness and acceptance of life as it has been.	Older adults who are able to come to terms with their lives and the things they have done and left undone and are able to "let go" of regrets will have a sense of completion and will see death as simply the last stage of a full life.	Older adults who have not been able to achieve identity or intimacy or generativity, who cannot let go of their regrets, will feel a sense of having left things until too late and see death as coming too soon.

Source: Based on Erikson, E. H. (1950). Childhood and society. New York: Norton.

Concept Map L.O. 8.6, 8.7, 8.8

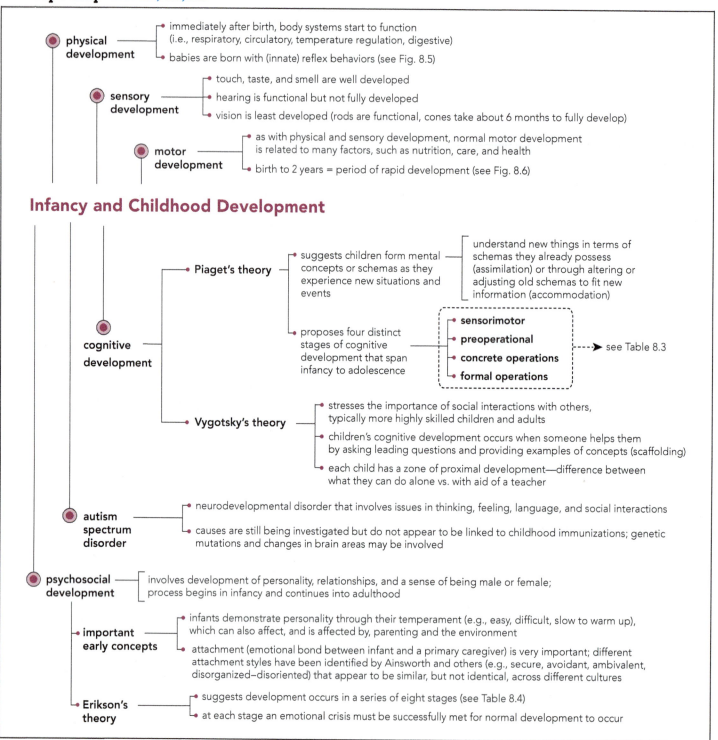

Practice Quiz — How much do you remember?

Pick the best answer.

1. One way researchers study newborn development involves measuring how long infants continue to focus upon a nonchanging stimulus. This technique is referred to as _____.
   a. a cross-sequential design
   b. a cross-sectional design
   c. adaptation
   d. habituation
   e. longitudinal study

2. In which of Piaget's stages would a child be who has just developed the ability to conserve?
   a. preoperational
   b. sensorimotor
   c. motor operations
   d. formal operations
   e. concrete operations

3. Vygotsky defines _____ as the process of helping less as the learner improves at a given task.
   a. metacognition
   b. metamemory
   c. habituation
   d. scaffolding
   e. zone of proximal development

4. What kind of attachment, according to Ainsworth, is shown by a baby who clings to his or her mother, gets upset when the mother leaves, and demands to be picked up but at the same time kicks and pushes her away?
   a. secure
   b. disorganized–disoriented
   c. frustrating
   d. ambivalent
   e. avoidant

5. Studies by Harry Harlow showed that the most important element to developing attachment is _____.
   a. sleep
   b. exercise
   c. feeding
   d. mental challenges
   e. physical contact

6. According to Erikson, which stage results in a sense of independence because of one's ability to control his or her own actions?
   a. trust versus mistrust
   b. identity versus role confusion
   c. autonomy versus shame and doubt
   d. initiative versus guilt
   e. generativity versus stagnation

APA Goal 2: Scientific Inquiry and Critical Thinking

The Facts About Immunizations

Addresses APA Learning Objectives 2.1: Use scientific reasoning to interpret psychological phenomena; 2.3: Engage in innovative and integrative thinking and problem-solving.

You'd think that by now, people would be well aware that immunizations do not cause autism or a host of other problems and that in fact immunization is a very good thing. Sadly, there is still a big problem with people failing to vaccinate their children against deadly diseases because they have been listening to the wrong people and reading the wrong information. In December of 2015, news outlets reported that an Australian elementary school (known for its tolerance of parents who do not want to vaccinate their children) had suffered an outbreak of chicken pox (Campbell, 2015). The school had only a 73 percent vaccination rate, compared to 92 percent in the surrounding community. At least 80 of the 320 students (roughly 25 percent) were affected, including some who had been vaccinated (they would get only mild cases of chicken pox, however). Because so many unvaccinated children attend the school, this particular population lost its "herd immunity"—the immunity a population gains over time as a significant majority of its members become immune to a particular disease (Plotkin et al., 2011). Herd immunity is being lost in many places around the globe: a polio outbreak in the Congo (Roberts, 2018), smaller measles outbreaks in 21 U.S. states (Centers for Disease Control and Prevention, 2018c), and also a measles outbreak across Europe (The Associated Press, 2018) all took place in 2018.

Why do parents fail to vaccinate? Primarily, it's a failure of critical thinking. Think back to the discussion of critical thinking in Chapter One of this text. See Learning Objective 1.5. The first criterion of critical thinking was "there are very few 'truths' that do not need to be subjected to testing." The link between vaccines and autism, for example, has been well studied and tested over many years, and the findings are clear: There is NO link (Burns, 2010; CDC, 2004, 2011, DeStefano et al., 2013; Gilberg & Coleman, 2000; Jain et al., 2015; Johnson & Myers, 2007; Madsen et al., 2002; Mars et al., 1998; Offit & Bell, 1998; Stratton et al., 2001a, 2001b; Taylor et al., 1999; Thompson et al., 2007; Institute of Medicine, 2012).

Unfortunately, the people involved in the antivaccination movement get their information not from scientifically rigorous studies but from anecdotes and Internet blogs. The second criterion of critical thinking was: All evidence is not equal in quality. Testimonials, anecdotes, and the ravings of people on the Internet are not good evidence.

Another problem is the number of celebrities who have joined the antivaccination movement. These people have no real expertise, but they do have the ability to reach a lot of people and—unfortunately—some people are very willing to believe their favorite celebrity despite the lack of any authority on the subject at hand. The third criterion is one that is often forgotten: Just because someone is considered to be an authority or to have a lot of expertise does not make everything that person claims automatically true, as the Wakefield disaster clearly demonstrated. The evidence is what is important, and in the case of immunizations, the evidence is clear: Vaccinate your children.

APA Goal 2 The Facts About Immunizations

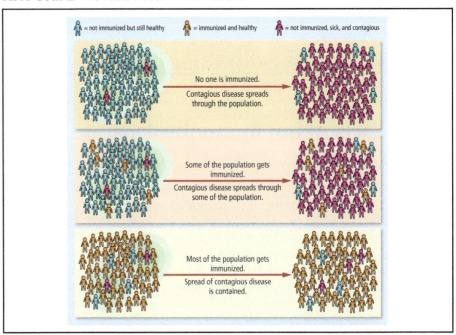

Herd immunity is a term that refers to the immunity of a population to a particular disease, typically because a majority of the population's members have acquired immunity through vaccination. As you can see from the diagram at the top, when a population does not have herd immunity, a disease carried by only a few people, or even one person, can spread throughout the whole population. This is what happened in the famous case of "Typhoid Mary," in which a woman who carried typhoid spread the disease to a large number of employees and their families. As more of a population gets immunized (middle diagram), the spread of disease begins to lessen. As most of the population gets immunized (bottom diagram), the spread of the disease is minimized—the "herd" is immune.

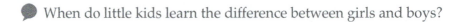

AP 6.P Describe how sex and gender influence socialization and other aspects of development.

8.9–8.11 Gender Development and Sexual Orientation

One important aspect of development that encompasses both physical and psychological changes is gender development, the growing sense of being male or female.

8.9 Gender Roles

8.9 Define gender, and discuss the development of gender roles.

💬 When do little kids learn the difference between girls and boys?

Whereas sex can be defined as the physical characteristics of being male or female, **gender** is defined as the psychological aspects of being male or female. The expectations of one's culture, the development of one's personality, and one's sense of identity are all affected by the concept of gender.

Gender roles are the culture's expectations for behavior of a person who is perceived as male or female, including attitudes, actions, and personality traits associated with a particular gender within that culture (Tobach, 2001; Unger, 1979). **Gender typing** is the process by which people learn their culture's preferences and expectations for male and female behavior. The process of developing a person's **gender identity** (a sense of being male or female) is influenced by both biological and environmental factors (in the form of parenting and other child-rearing behaviors), although which type of factor has greater influence is still controversial. Most researchers today would agree that biology has an important role in gender identity, at least in certain aspects of gender identity and behavior (Attia, 2017; Diamond et al., 2018 Diamond & Sigmundson, 1997; Money, 1994; Reiner, 1999, 2000). What are the biological influences on gender? Aside from the obvious external sexual characteristics of the genitals, there are also hormonal differences between men and women. Some researchers believe that exposure to these hormones during fetal development not only causes the formation of the sexual organs but also predisposes the infant to behavior that is typically associated with one gender or the other, although not necessarily to a certain gender identity (Berenbaum, 2018; Berenbaum & Beltz, 2016).

Environment must also play its part. Cultures that are more individualistic (those stressing independence and with loose ties among individuals) and have fairly high standards of living are becoming more nontraditional, especially for women in those cultures, whereas the more traditional views seem to be held by collectivistic cultures (those stressing interdependence and with strong ties among individuals, especially familial ties) that have less wealth, although even in the latter, women were more likely to be less traditional than men (Forbes et al., 2009; Gibbons et al., 1991; Li & Fung, 2015; Shafiro et al., 2003).

Gender identity is not always as straightforward as males who are masculine and females who are feminine. People's sense of gender identity does not always match their external appearance or even the sex chromosomes that determine whether they are male or female (Califia, 1997; Crawford & Unger, 2004; White, 2000). Such people are typically termed *transgender*. In today's culture, being transgender is only beginning to become part of accepted gender identity, with many transgender individuals facing mockery, discrimination, and abuse, resulting in increased risk of stress-induced problems such as eating disorders and suicide (Diemer et al., 2015; Gruskin et al., 2018; Haas et al., 2014). See Learning Objectives 13.4 and 13.11.

AP 6.B Discuss the interaction of nature and nurture (including cultural variations), specifically physical development, in the determination of behavior.

AP 6.F Discuss the interaction of nature and nurture (including cultural variations), specifically social development, in the determination of behavior.

gender
the psychological aspects of being male or female.

gender roles
the culture's expectations for male or female behavior, including attitudes, actions, and personality traits associated with being male or female in that culture.

gender typing
the process of acquiring gender-role characteristics.

gender identity
the individual's sense of being male or female.

8.10 Theories of Gender-Role Development

8.10 Compare and contrast two theories of gender-role development.

How do children acquire the knowledge of their society or culture's gender-role expectations? How does that knowledge lead to the development of a gender identity? Many modern theorists focus on learning and cognitive processes for the development of gender identity and behavior.

SOCIAL LEARNING THEORY Social learning theory, which emphasizes learning through observation and imitation of models, attributes* gender-role development to those processes. Children observe their same-sex parents behaving in certain ways and imitate that behavior. When the children imitate the appropriate gender behavior, they

---

*attributes: explains as a cause.

are reinforced with positive attention. Inappropriate gender behavior is either ignored or actively discouraged (Bussey & Bandura, 1999; Fagot & Hagan, 1991; Mischel, 1966; Wiggert et al., 2015).

GENDER SCHEMA THEORY A theory of gender-role development that combines social learning theory with cognitive development is called **gender schema theory** (Bem, 1987, 1993). In this theory based on the Piagetian concept of schemas, children develop a schema, or mental pattern, for being male or female in much the same way that they develop schemas for other concepts such as "dog," "bird," and "big."

In a similar manner, children develop a concept for "boy" and "girl." Once that schema is in place, children can identify themselves as "boy" or "girl" and will notice other members of that schema. They notice the behavior of other "boys" or "girls" and imitate that behavior. Rather than being simple imitation and reinforcement, as in social learning theory, children acquire their gender role behavior by organizing that behavior around the schema of "boy" or "girl." Evidence for this theory includes the finding that children can discriminate between male and female faces and voices before age 1 as well as preschool boys' refusal to wear pink or girls' sudden demands to wear only dresses (Martin, 2000; Halim et al., 2014), signs that the world is already being organized into those two concepts. The concept of **androgyny** (Bem, 1975, 1981) describes a gender role characteristic of people whose personalities reflect the characteristics of both males and females, regardless of physical sex. Androgynous people can make decisions based on the situation's demands rather than being masculine or feminine, which allows them to be more flexible in everyday behavior and career choices.

Concepts of gender play a large role in the search for identity, one of the primary task of the next stage of life: the teenage years.

8.11 Sexual Orientation

8.11 Distinguish among the various sexual orientations.

The term **sexual orientation** refers to a person's sexual attraction and affection for members of either the opposite or the same sex.

The most common sexual orientation is **heterosexual**, in which people are sexually attracted to members of the opposite physical sex, as in a man being attracted to a woman or vice versa. (The Greek word *hetero* means "other.") **Homosexual** orientation is sexual attraction to members of one's own sex. (The Greek word *homo* means "same.") A national survey estimates that about 1.8 percent of men and 1.5 percent of women aged 18 and older consider themselves gay or lesbian, meaning that their sexual orientations are exclusively or predominantly homosexual (Ward et al., 2014).

> If people have had homosexual as well as heterosexual experiences, does that make them bisexuals?

A person who is **bisexual** may be either male or female and is attracted to both sexes. In the same national survey, only 0.4 percent of the men and 0.9 percent of the women considered themselves predominantly bisexual (Ward et al., 2014). Many people experiment with alternative sexual behavior before deciding on their true sexual identity; one bisexual experience does not make a person bisexual any more than one homosexual experience makes a person homosexual.

There are also people who do not identify as heterosexual, homosexual, or bisexual but see themselves as *asexual*. Asexuality is a lack of sexual attraction to anyone, or a lack of interest in sexual activity (Prause & Graham, 2004).

Homosexuality is a sexual orientation that has faced discrimination and prejudice in many cultures.

gender schema theory
theory of gender identity acquisition in which a child develops a mental pattern, or schema, for being male or female and then organizes observed and learned behavior around that schema.

androgyny
characteristic of possessing the most positive personality characteristics of males and females regardless of actual sex.

sexual orientation
a person's sexual attraction to and affection for members of either the opposite or the same sex.

heterosexual
sexual attraction toward or sexual activity with members of the opposite sex.

homosexual
sexual attraction toward or sexual activity with members of the same sex.

bisexual
sexual attraction toward or sexual activity with both men and women.

Concept Map L.O. 8.9, 8.10, 8.11

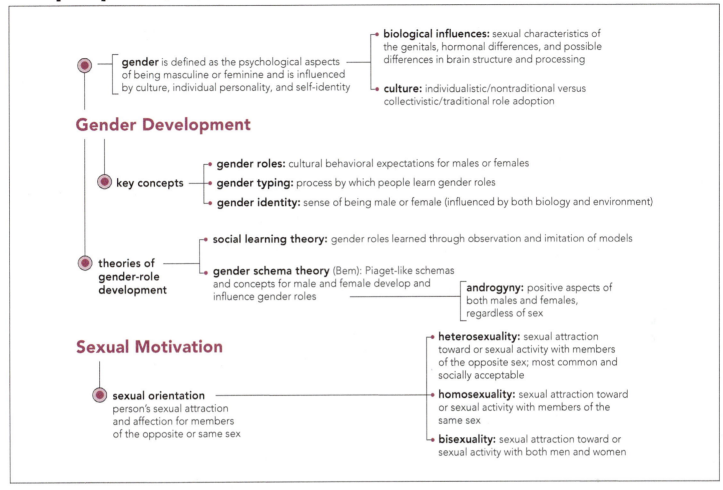

Practice Quiz How much do you remember?

Pick the best answer.

1. The process by which people learn their culture's preferences and expectations for the behaviors of females and males is called gender _____.
   a. identity
   b. role
   c. typing
   d. stereotyping
   e. differences

2. People whose sense of gender identity does not match what is expected for their biological sex are known as _____.
   a. intersex
   b. androgynous
   c. hermaphrodites
   d. bisexual
   e. transgender

3. Kira sees her mother mixing ingredients for a cake. Later, Kira takes a bowl and spoon out of the cabinet and pretends to mix some imaginary ingredients. Of which theory of gender development would this be a good example?
   a. psychoanalytic theory
   b. actualization theory
   c. gender schema theory
   d. gender-role theory
   e. social learning theory

4. Which theory of gender-role development places a heavy emphasis on the use of mental patterns?
   a. social learning theory
   b. psychoanalytic theory
   c. gender schema theory
   d. behavioral theory
   e. prototype theory

5. Micah is often perceived as strong and tough, but he also has been known to be sincere and loving. Mira is warm and kind but is also independent and assertive. Bem would classify such behavior as examples of _____.
   a. benevolent sexism
   b. positive stereotyping
   c. schema error
   d. negative stereotyping
   e. androgyny

AP 6.J Discuss maturational challenges in adolescence, including related family conflicts.

8.12–8.14 Adolescence

Adolescence is the period of life from about age 13 to the early 20s, during which a young person is no longer physically a child but is not yet an independent, self-supporting adult. Although in the past, adolescence was always defined as the "teens," from ages 13 to 19, adolescence isn't necessarily determined by chronological age. It also concerns how a person deals with life issues such as work, family, and relationships. So, although there is a clear age of onset, the end of adolescence may come earlier or later for different individuals.

8.12 Physical Development

8.12 Describe the physical changes of puberty.

Many adolescents feel that they are so unique, so special, that bad things just won't happen to them. This personal fable can cause some pretty risky behavior, like what this young man is doing.

💬 Isn't adolescence just the physical changes that happen to your body?

The clearest sign of the beginning of adolescence is the onset of **puberty**, the physical changes in both *primary sex characteristics* (growth of the actual sex organs such as the penis or the uterus) and *secondary sex characteristics* (changes in the body such as the development of breasts and body hair) that occur in the body as sexual development reaches its peak. Puberty occurs as the result of a complex series of glandular activities involving the pituitary, thyroid, adrenal, and sex glands (Grumbach & Kaplan, 1990; Grumbach & Styne, 1998). Puberty often begins about 2 years after the beginning of the *growth spurt*, the rapid period of growth that takes place at around age 10 for girls and around age 12 for boys.

In addition to an increase in height, physical characteristics related to being male or female undergo rapid and dramatic change. In fact, the rate of growth and development in puberty approaches that of development in the womb.

After about 4 years, the changes of puberty are relatively complete. The development of the brain, however, continues well into the early 20s. In particular, the prefrontal cortex of the brain, which is responsible in part for impulse control, decision making, and the organization and understanding of information, does not complete its development until about age 25 (Somerville et al., 2013). When the still-developing brain is paired with the adolescent's lack of life experience in making reasoned judgments, it becomes easy to understand why adolescents may engage in risky behavior even when they should know better (Romer et al., 2017).

8.13 Cognitive Development

8.13 Identify the cognitive and moral advances that occur in adolescence.

💬 If I'm remembering correctly, teenagers should be in Piaget's formal operations stage. So why don't many teenagers think just like adults?

The cognitive development of adolescents is less visible than the physical development but still represents a major change in the way adolescents think about themselves, their peers and relationships, and the world around them.

PIAGET'S FORMAL OPERATIONS REVISITED Adolescents, especially those who receive a formal high school education, may move into Piaget's final stage of formal operations,

adolescence
the period of life from about age 13 to the early 20s, during which a young person is no longer physically a child but is not yet an independent, self-supporting adult.

puberty
the physical changes that occur in the body as sexual development reaches its peak.

in which abstract thinking becomes possible. Teenagers begin to think about hypothetical situations, leading to a picture of what an "ideal" world would be like.

Piaget's theory has had a tremendous impact in the education of children and in stimulating research about children's cognitive development (Hopkins, 2011; Satterly, 1987). Children in different cultures usually come to understand the world in the way that Piaget described, although the age at which this understanding comes varies from one child to another.

Although headed into an adult style of thinking, adolescents are not yet completely free of egocentric thought. At this time in life, however, their egocentrism shows up in their preoccupation* with their own thoughts. They do a lot of introspection (turning inward) and may become convinced that their thoughts are as important to others as they are to themselves. Two ways in which this adolescent egocentrism emerges are the personal fable and the imaginary audience (Elkind, 1985; Galanaki, 2012; Lapsley et al., 1986; Potard et al., 2017; Rai et al., 2014; Vartanian, 2000).

In the **personal fable**, adolescents have spent so much time thinking about their own thoughts and feelings that they become convinced that they are special, one of a kind, and that no one else has ever had these thoughts and feelings before them. "You just don't understand me, I'm different from you" is a common feeling of teens. The personal fable is not without a dangerous side. Because they feel unique, teenagers may feel that they are somehow protected from the dangers of the world and so do not take the precautions that they should. This may result in an unwanted pregnancy, severe injury or death while racing in a car, drinking (or texting) and driving, and drug use, to name a few possibilities. "It can't happen to me, I'm special" is a risky but common thought.

The **imaginary audience** shows up as extreme self-consciousness in adolescents. They become convinced that *everyone is looking at them* and that they are always the center of everyone else's world, just as they are the center of their own. This explains the intense self-consciousness that many adolescents experience concerning what others think about how the adolescent looks or behaves.

MORAL DEVELOPMENT Another important aspect in the cognitive advances that occur in adolescence concerns the teenager's understanding of "right" and "wrong." Harvard University professor Lawrence Kohlberg was a developmental psychologist who, influenced by Piaget and others, outlined a theory of the development of moral thinking through looking at how people of various ages responded to stories about people caught up in moral dilemmas (see **Figure 8.9** for an example of a dilemma).

Kohlberg (1973) proposed three levels of moral development, or the knowledge of right and wrong behavior. These levels are summarized in **Table 8.5**, along with an example of each type of thinking. Although these stages are associated with certain age groups, adolescents and adults can be found at all three levels. For example, a juvenile delinquent tends to be preconventional in moral thinking.

Kohlberg's theory has been criticized as being male oriented and biased toward Western cultures, especially since he used only males in his studies (Gilligan, 1982; Snarey, 1985). Carol Gilligan (1982) proposed that men and women have different perspectives on morality: Men tend to judge as moral the actions that lead to a fair or just end, whereas women tend to judge as moral the actions that are nonviolent and hurt the fewest people. Earlier researchers did not find consistent support for gender

personal fable
type of thought common to adolescents in which young people believe themselves to be unique and protected from harm.

imaginary audience
type of thought common to adolescents in which young people believe that other people are just as concerned about the adolescent's thoughts and characteristics as they themselves are.

AP 6.N Identify the contributions of major researchers in the area of moral development.

AP 6.O Compare and contrast models of moral development.

Figure 8.9 Example of a Moral Dilemma

Example of a Moral Dilemma

The ant worked long and hard over the summer to gather food for himself and his family. The grasshopper, who preferred to play and be lazy all summer, laughed at the ant for working so hard. The ant said, "you will be sorry this winter when you have no food." Sure enough, when winter came the very sorry grasshopper, cold and hungry, came to the ant and begged for food and shelter. Should the ant give food and shelter to the grasshopper?

---

*preoccupation: extreme or excessive concern with something.

Table 8.5 Kohlberg's Three Levels of Morality

Level of Morality	How Rules Are Understood	Example
Preconventional morality (very young children)	Morality of an action is based on the consequences; actions that get rewarded are right and those that earn punishment are wrong.	A child who takes money from a parent's wallet and does not get caught does not see that action as wrong.
Conventional* morality (older children, adolescents, and most adults)	An action is morally right if it conforms to the rules of the society and wrong if it does not.	A child scolds a parent for littering because there is a sign saying not to do so.
Postconventional morality (about one fifth of the adult population)	Morality is now determined by the experiences and judgment of the person, even if that judgment disagrees with society's rules.	A husband helps his dying wife commit suicide to end her pain, even though society considers that action to be murder.

*The term *conventional* refers to general standards or norms of behavior for a particular society, which will differ from one social group or culture to another.

Source: Based on Kohlberg, L. (1969). Stage and sequence: the cognitive-developmental approach to socialization. In D. A. Goslin (Ed.), Handbook of socialization: Theory in research (pp. 347-480). Boston: Houghton-Mifflin.

differences in moral thinking (Walker, 1991), although more recent research suggests that males may be more willing than females to accept the idea of committing a harmful action when it is in the interest of the greater good (Friesdorf et al., 2015), a finding that seems to support Gilligan's proposal. Other research suggests that if measurements of empathy, a key component of moral behavior, are based on objective methods rather than self report, there are no appreciable gender differences (Baez et al., 2017). Another criticism is that Kohlberg's assessment of moral development involves asking people what they think should be done in hypothetical moral dilemmas. What people say they will do and what people actually do when faced with a real dilemma are often two different things.

8.14 Psychosocial Development

8.14 Describe how the adolescent search for personal identity influences relationships with others.

The development of personality and social relationships in adolescence primarily concerns the search for a consistent sense of self or personal identity.

identity versus role confusion

stage of personality development in which the adolescent must find a consistent sense of self.

ERIKSON'S IDENTITY VERSUS ROLE CONFUSION The psychosocial crisis that must be faced by the adolescent, according to Erikson, is that of **identity versus role confusion**. In this stage, the teenager must choose from among many options for values in life and beliefs concerning things such as political issues, career options, and marriage (Feldman, 2003). From those options, a consistent sense of self must be found. Erikson believed that teens who have successfully resolved the conflicts of the earlier four stages are much better "equipped" to resist peer pressure to engage in unhealthy or illegal activities and find their own identity during the adolescent years. Those teens who are not as successful come into the adolescent years with a lack of trust in others, feelings of guilt and shame, low self-esteem, and dependency on others. Peer pressure is quite effective on teenagers who desperately want to "fit in" and have an identity of a certain sort and who feel that others will not want to be with them unless they conform to the expectations and demands of the peer group. They play the part of the model child for the parents, the good student for the teachers, and the "cool" juvenile delinquent to their friends and will be confused about which of the many roles they play really represents their own identity.

Can you see the effects of peer pressure in this picture? Most young people start smoking because their friends talk them into doing so, thinking it will make them seem more grown-up. What are some other choices that adolescents may make due to peer pressure?

PARENT–TEEN CONFLICT Even for the majority of adolescents who end up successfully finding a consistent sense of self, there will be conflicts with parents. Many researchers believe that a certain amount of "rebellion" and conflict is a necessary step in breaking away from childhood dependence on the parents and becoming a self-sufficient* adult (Bengston,

*self-sufficient: able to function without outside aid; capable of providing for one's own needs.

1970; Lynott & Roberts, 1997). Although many people think that these conflicts are intense and concern very serious behavior, the reality is that most parent–teen conflict is over trivial issues—hair, clothing, taste in music, and so on. On the really big moral issues, most parents and teens would be quite surprised to realize that they agree (Giancola, 2006).

Concept Map L.O. 8.12, 8.13, 8.14

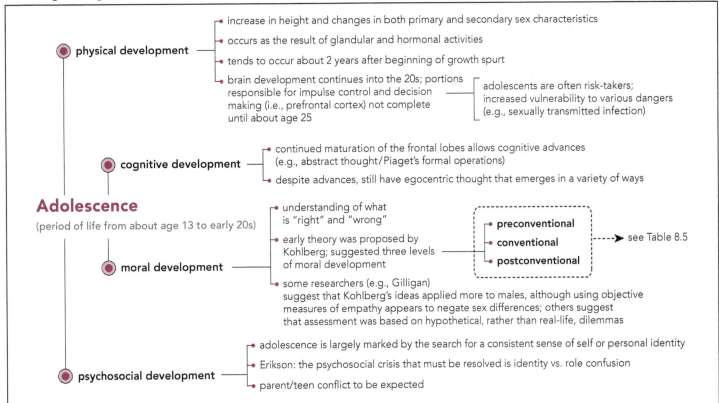

Practice Quiz How much do you remember?

Pick the best answer.

1. A change in the body of young boys such as the appearance and growth of body hair is considered as _____.
   a. the final stage of puberty
   b. a sign of emerging adulthood
   c. a sign of postconventional morality
   d. a primary sex characteristic
   e. a secondary sex characteristic

2. "It can't happen to me. I'm special" is a common attitude found in adolescents who have developed a(n) _____.
   a. self-concept
   b. puberty mindset
   c. preconventional morality
   d. imaginary audience
   e. personal fable

3. According to Kohlberg, about one fifth of the adult population is at the _____ level of morality.
   a. preconventional
   b. most basic
   c. preliminary
   d. conventional
   e. postconventional

4. According to Erikson, the task of the adolescent is to _____.
   a. find intimacy with another
   b. develop a sense of initiative
   c. find a consistent sense of self
   d. develop a sense of industry
   e. learn a basic sense of trust

5. If Tyra is going to argue and disagree with her parents, which of the following topics will she typically be arguing over?
   a. social values
   b. religious beliefs
   c. his taste in clothes
   d. political beliefs
   e. family values

8.15–8.20 Adulthood and Aging

 When exactly does adulthood begin?

Adulthood can be thought of as the period of life from the early 20s until old age and death. Exactly when adulthood begins is not always easy to determine. In some cultures, adulthood is reached soon after puberty (Bledsoe & Cohen, 1993; Ocholla-Ayayo et al., 1993). Some people feel that it begins after graduation from high school, whereas others would say adulthood doesn't begin until after graduation from college. Others define it as the point when a person becomes totally self-sufficient with a job and a home separate from his or her parents. In that case, some people are not adults until their late 30s.

Many developmental psychologists now talk about **emerging adulthood** as a time from late adolescence through the 20s and referring to mainly those in developed countries who are childless, do not live in their own home, may still be in the process of forming romantic relationships, and are not earning enough money to be independent (Arnett, 2000, 2013; Azmitia et al., 2008; Greeson, 2013; Nelson et al., 2008; Shulman et al., 2018). Decisions about identity, values, and the preparation for a career have begun to take longer and longer, and together with the downturn in the economy, many young people who would have been working and raising families a few decades ago now find that they cannot "leave the nest" so easily.

AP 6.L Predict the physical and cognitive challenges that emerge through the lifespan, including steps that can be taken to maximize function.

8.15 Physical Development: Use It or Lose It

8.15 Identify the physical changes and health issues associated with adulthood.

Adulthood can also be divided into at least three periods: young adulthood, middle age, and late adulthood.

PHYSICAL AGING Physical changes in young adulthood are relatively minimal. The good news is that the 20s are a time of peak physical health, sharp senses, fewer insecurities, and mature cognitive abilities. The bad news is that even in the early 20s, the signs of aging are already beginning. Oil glands in the neck and around the eyes begin to malfunction, contributing to wrinkles in those areas near the end of the 20s and beginning of the 30s. The 30s may not bring noticeable changes, but vision and hearing are beginning to decline, and by around age 40, bifocal lenses may become necessary as the lens of the eye hardens, becoming unable to change its shape to shift focus. Hearing loss may begin in the 40s and 50s but often does not become noticeable until the 60s or 70s, when hearing aids may become necessary.

Many people end up needing bifocals at some point in their 30s or 40s, as the lens hardens and loses its ability to visually accommodate to different distances of objects.

In the 40s, while most adults are able to experience some security and stability without the worries and concerns of adolescence and young adulthood, physical aging continues: Skin begins to show more wrinkles, hair turns gray (or falls out), vision and hearing decline further, and physical strength may begin to decline (Frontera et al., 1991). In the 50s, these changes continue. Throughout middle age, weight may increase as the rate at which the body functions slows down but eating increases and less time is spent exercising. Height begins to decrease, with about half an inch of height lost for every 10 years past age 40, although people with the bone-loss disease osteoporosis may lose up to 8 inches or more (Cummings & Melton, 2002). Although sexual functioning usually does not decline in middle age, opportunities for sexual activity may be fewer than in the days of young adulthood (Hodson & Skeen, 1994; Kalra et al., 2011; Williams, 1995). Children, mortgages, and career worries can put a damper on middle-age romance, as can various health factors and the medications associated with those factors (Steinke et al., 2018).

emerging adulthood

a time from late adolescence through the 20s referring to those who are childless, do not live in their own home, and are not earning enough money to be independent, mainly found in developed countries.

MENOPAUSE In a woman's 40s, the levels of the female hormone estrogen decline as the body's reproductive system prepares to cease that function. Some women begin to experience "hot flashes," a sudden sensation of heat and sweating that may keep them awake at night. Interestingly, in some cultures, particularly those in which the diet contains high amounts of soy products, hot flashes are almost nonexistent (Cassidy et al., 1994; Lock, 1994). However, one study suggests soy intake is not a primary factor (Gold et al., 2013). One study found that hot flashes may continue to occur for some women into their 70s and 80s (David et al., 2018). The changes that happen at this time are called the *climacteric*, and the period of 5 to 10 years over which these changes occur is called *perimenopause*. At an average age of 51, most women will cease ovulation altogether, ending their reproductive years. The cessation of ovulation and the menstrual cycle is called **menopause** (Mishell, 2001). Many women look forward to the freedom from monthly menstruation and fear of unplanned pregnancies (Adler et al., 2000; Hvas, 2001; Leon et al., 2007).

💬 Do men go through anything like menopause?

Men also go through a time of sexual changes, but it is much more gradual and less dramatic than menopause. In males, **andropause** (Carruthers, 2001; Renneboog, 2012; Rezaei et al., 2018) usually begins in the 40s with a decline in several hormones, primarily testosterone (the major male hormone). Physical symptoms are also less dramatic but no less troubling: fatigue, irritability, possible problems in sexual functioning, and reduced sperm count. Males, however, rarely lose all reproductive ability.

EFFECTS OF AGING ON HEALTH It is in middle age that many health problems first occur, although their true cause may have begun in the young adulthood years. Young adults may smoke, drink heavily, stay up late, and get dark tans, and the wear and tear that this lifestyle causes on their bodies will not become obvious until their 40s and 50s.

Some of the common health problems that may show up in middle age are high blood pressure, skin cancer, heart problems, arthritis, and obesity. High blood pressure can be caused by lifestyle factors such as obesity and stress but may also be related to hereditary factors (Rudd & Osterberg, 2002). Sleep problems, such as loud snoring and sleep apnea (in which breathing stops for 10 seconds or more), may also take their toll on physical health. There is some evidence that high blood pressure and apnea are linked, although the link very well may be the common factor of obesity (Nieto et al., 2000). In the United States, the five most frequent health-related causes of death in middle age (45 to 64 years of age) are heart disease, followed closely by cancer, unintentional injuries, chronic respiratory disease, and stroke for men (Centers for Disease Control [CDC], 2018b). For U.S. women in that age group, the results are slightly different: heart disease, followed closely by cancer, chronic lung disease, stroke, and Alzheimer's disease (CDC, 2018g). This is a change for both men and women, as cancer used to be the number one cause of death.

8.16 Cognitive Development

8.16 Describe how memory abilities change during adulthood.

During this time, intellectual abilities do not decline overall, although speed of processing (or reaction time) does slow down. Compared to a younger adult, a middle-aged person may take a little longer to solve a problem. However, a middle-aged person also has more life experience and knowledge to bring to bear on a problem, which counters the lack of speed (Bugaiska et al., 2007; Migo et al., 2014).

CHANGES IN MEMORY Changes in memory ability are probably the most noticeable changes in middle-aged cognition. People find themselves having a hard time recalling a particular word or someone's name. This difficulty in retrieval is probably not evidence of a physical decline (nor the beginning of Alzheimer's disease: See Learning Objective 6.13) but is more likely caused by the stresses a middle-aged person experiences and the sheer amount of information that a person of middle years must try to keep straight (Craik, 1994; Launer et al., 1995; Sands & Meredith, 1992; Sindi et al., 2017). Some studies suggest that thinking about the positive events of the past aids the formation of newer memories—the

AP 6.L Predict the physical and cognitive challenges that emerge through the lifespan, including steps that can be taken to maximize function.

menopause

the cessation of ovulation and menstrual cycles and the end of a woman's reproductive capability.

andropause

gradual changes in the sexual hormones and reproductive system of middle-aged males.

areas of the brain that are linked to processing emotional content seem to have a strong connection to the areas of the brain responsible for memory formation (Addis et al., 2010, 2014; Madore & Schacter, 2016). Think positively!

HOW TO KEEP YOUR BRAIN YOUNG People who exercise their mental abilities have been found to be less likely to develop memory problems and possibly affect the progression of more serious dementias, such as Alzheimer's, in old age (Ball et al., 2002; Colcombe et al., 2003; Dumas, 2017; Fiatarone, 1996). "Use it or lose it" is the phrase to remember. Working challenging crossword puzzles, for example, can be a major factor in maintaining a healthy level of cognitive functioning. Reading, having an active social life, going to plays, taking classes, and staying physically active can all have a positive impact on the continued well-being of the brain (Bosworth & Schaie, 1997; Cabeza et al., 2002; Hayes et al., 2015; Singh-Manoux et al., 2003).

8.17 Psychosocial Development

8.17 Apply Erikson's theory to some common psychosocial concerns of adulthood.

In adulthood, concerns involve career, relationships, family, and approaching old age. The late teens and early 20s may be college years for many, although other young people go to work directly from high school. The task of choosing and entering a career is very serious and a task that many young adults have difficulty accomplishing. A college student may change majors more than once during the first few years of college, and even after obtaining a bachelor's degree, many may either get a job in an unrelated field or go on to a different type of career choice in graduate school. Those who are working may also change careers several times (perhaps as many as five to seven times) and may experience periods of unemployment while between jobs.

ERIKSON'S INTIMACY VERSUS ISOLATION: FORMING RELATIONSHIPS Erikson saw the primary task in young adulthood to be that of finding a mate. True **intimacy** is an emotional and psychological closeness that is based on the ability to trust, share, and care (an ability developed during the earlier stages such as trust versus mistrust) while still maintaining one's sense of self. See Learning Objective 11.13. Young adults who have difficulty trusting others and who are unsure of their own identities may find isolation instead of intimacy—loneliness, shallow relationships with others, and even a fear of real intimacy. For example, many marriages end in divorce within a few years, with one partner leaving the relationship—and even the responsibilities of parenting—to explore personal concerns and those unfinished issues of identity.

ERIKSON'S GENERATIVITY VERSUS STAGNATION: PARENTING In middle adulthood, persons who have found intimacy can now turn their focus outward, toward others. Erikson saw this as parenting the next generation and helping them through their crises, a process he called **generativity**. Educators, supervisors, health-care professionals, doctors, and community volunteers might be examples of positions that allow a person to be generative.

Other ways of being generative include engaging in careers or some major life work that can become one's legacy to the generations to come. Those who are unable to focus outward and are still dealing with issues of intimacy or even identity are said to be *stagnated*. People who frequently hand the care of their children over to grandparents or other relatives so that they can go out and "have fun" may be unable to focus on anyone else's needs but their own.

> What kind of parent is the best parent—one who's really strict or one who's pretty easygoing?

Parenting children is a very important part of most people's middle adulthood. Diana Baumrind (1967) outlined three basic styles of parenting, each of which may be related to certain personality traits in the child raised by that style of parenting. The video *Parenting Styles* describes each of these parenting styles in more detail and explains why goodness of fit, or matching the parenting style to the child's needs, may be most important.

AP 6.E Identify the contributions of major researchers in developmental psychology in the area of social development in childhood.

AP 6.M Identify the contributions of key researchers in the area of adulthood and aging.

AP 6.K Characterize the development of decisions related to intimacy as people mature.

AP 6.G Explain how parenting styles influence development.

intimacy
an emotional and psychological closeness that is based on the ability to trust, share, and care, while still maintaining a sense of self.

generativity
providing guidance to one's children or the next generation, or contributing to the well-being of the next generation through career or volunteer work.

Authoritarian parenting tends to be overly concerned with rules. This type of parent is stern, rigid, controlling, and uncompromising,* demands perfection, and has a tendency to use physical punishment. Children raised in this way are often insecure, timid, withdrawn, and resentful. As teenagers, they will very often rebel against parental authority in very negative and self-destructive ways, such as delinquency (criminal acts committed by minor children), drug use, or premarital sex (Baumrind, 1991, 2005; Sleddens et al., 2011).

Permissive parenting occurs when parents put very few demands on their children for behavior. **Permissive neglectful** parents simply aren't involved with their children, ignoring them and allowing them to do whatever they want, until it interferes with what the parent wants. At that point, this relationship may become an abusive one. **Permissive indulgent** parents seem to be too involved with their children, allowing their "little angels" to behave in any way they wish, refusing to set limits on the child's behavior or to require any kind of obedience. Children from both kinds of permissive parenting tend to be selfish, immature, dependent, lacking in social skills, and unpopular with peers (Baumrind, 1991, 2005; Dwairy, 2004; Sleddens et al., 2011).

Authoritative parenting involves combining firm limits on behavior with love, warmth, affection, respect, and a willingness to listen to the child's point of view. Authoritative parents are more democratic, allowing the child to have some input into the formation of rules but still maintaining the role of final decision maker. Punishment tends to be nonphysical, such as restrictions, time-out, or loss of privileges. Authoritative parents set limits that are clear and understandable, and when a child crosses the limits, they allow an explanation and then agree upon the right way to handle the situation. Children raised in this style of parenting tend to be self-reliant and independent (Baumrind, 1991, 2005; Dwairy, 2004; Moran et al., 2018; Sleddens et al., 2011; Sorkhabi, 2005; Underwood et al., 2009).

Watch Parenting Styles

Watch the **Video** at **MyLab Psychology**

ERIKSON'S EGO INTEGRITY VERSUS DESPAIR: DEALING WITH MORTALITY As people enter the stage known as late adulthood, life becomes more urgent as the realities of physical aging and the approaching end of life become harder and harder to ignore. Erikson (1980) believed that at this time, people look back on the life they have lived in a process called a life review. In the life review people must deal with mistakes, regrets, and unfinished business. If people can look back and feel that their lives were relatively full and are able to come to terms with regrets and losses, then a feeling of **ego integrity** or wholeness results. Integrity is the final completion of the identity, or ego. If people have many regrets and lots of unfinished business, they feel despair, a sense of deep regret over things that will never be accomplished because time has run out.

8.18 Theories of Physical and Psychological Aging

8.18 Compare and contrast four theories of why aging occurs.

> 💬 Why do people age? What makes us go through so many physical changes?

There are a number of theories of why people physically age. Some theories of physical aging point to biological changes in cellular structure, whereas others focus on the influence of external stresses on body tissues and functioning.

---

*uncompromising: not making or accepting any viewpoint other than one's own, allowing no other viewpoints.

authoritarian parenting
style of parenting in which parent is rigid and overly strict, showing little warmth to the child.

permissive parenting
style of parenting in which parent makes few, if any, demands on a child's behavior.

permissive neglectful
permissive parenting in which parent is uninvolved with child or child's behavior.

permissive indulgent
permissive parenting in which parent is so involved that children are allowed to behave without set limits.

authoritative parenting
style of parenting in which parent combines warmth and affection with firm limits on a child's behavior.

ego integrity
sense of wholeness that comes from having lived a full life possessing the ability to let go of regrets; the final completion of the ego.

CELLULAR-CLOCK THEORY One of the biologically based theories is the *cellular-clock theory* (Hayflick, 1977). In this theory, cells are limited in the number of times they can reproduce to repair damage. Evidence for this theory is the existence of *telomeres,* structures on the ends of chromosomes that shorten each time a cell reproduces (Martin & Buckwalter, 2001). When telomeres are too short, cells cannot reproduce and damage accumulates, resulting in the effects of aging. (Sounds almost like what happens when the warranty is up on a car, doesn't it?)

WEAR-AND-TEAR THEORY The theory that points to outside influences such as stress, physical exertion, and bodily damage is known as the *wear-and-tear theory of aging*. In this theory, the body's organs and cell tissues simply wear out with repeated use and abuse. Damaged tissues accumulate and produce the effects of aging. *Collagen,* for example, is a natural elastic tissue that allows the skin to be flexible. As people age, the collagen "wears out," becoming less and less "stretchy" and allowing skin to sag and wrinkle (Cua et al., 1990; Kligman & Balin, 1989). (This process is not unlike what happens to the elastic in the waistband of one's underwear over time.)

FREE-RADICAL THEORY The *free-radical theory* is actually the latest version of the wear-and-tear theory in that it gives a biological explanation for the damage done to cells over time. *Free radicals* are oxygen molecules that have an unstable electron (negative particle). They bounce around the cell, stealing electrons from other molecules and increasing the damage to structures inside the cell. As people get older, more and more free radicals do more and more damage, producing the effects of aging (Hauck & Bartke, 2001; Knight, 1998: Zhang et al., 2016).

💬 I've heard that most older people just want to be left alone and have some peace and quiet. Is that true?

ACTIVITY THEORY Activity theory (Grotz et al., 2017; Havighurst et al., 1968) proposes that an elderly person adjusts more positively to aging when remaining active in some way. Even if a career must end, there are other ways to stay active and involved in life. Elderly people who volunteer at hospitals or schools, those who take up new hobbies or throw themselves full time into old ones, and those who maintain their friendships with others and continue to have social activities have been shown to be happier and live longer than those who withdraw themselves from activity. Contrary to the view of the elderly as voluntarily withdrawing from activities, the withdrawal of many elderly people is not voluntary at all; their lack of involvement is often because others simply stop inviting elderly people to social activities and including them in their lives.

8.19 Stages of Death and Dying

8.19 Describe Kübler-Ross's theory of death and dying, and identify some criticisms of this theory.

There are several ways of looking at the process of dying. One of the more well-known theories is that of Elisabeth Kübler-Ross (Kübler-Ross, 1997), who conducted extensive interviews with dying persons and their caregivers.

Elisabeth Kübler-Ross theorized that people go through five stages of reaction when faced with death (Backer et al., 1994; Kübler-Ross, 1997). These stages are *denial,* in which people refuse to believe that the diagnosis of death is real; *anger,* which is really anger at death itself and the feelings of helplessness to change things; *bargaining,* in which the dying person tries to make a deal with doctors or even with God; *depression,* which is sadness from losses already experienced (e.g., loss of a job or one's dignity) and those yet to come (e.g., not being able to see a child grow up); and finally *acceptance,* when the person has accepted the inevitable* and quietly awaits death.

Obviously, some people do not have time to go through all of these stages or even go through them in the listed order (Schneidman, 1983, 1994). Some theorists do not

One way to age successfully and maintain psychological health is to remain active and involved in life. This woman is volunteering with grade-school students as a teacher's aide. This not only allows her to feel useful but also helps her to stay mentally alert and socially involved.

activity theory

theory of adjustment to aging that assumes older people are happier if they remain active in some way, such as volunteering or developing a hobby.

---

*inevitable: something that cannot be avoided or escaped.

agree with the stage idea, seeing the process of dying as a series of ups and downs, with hope on the rise at times and then falling, to be replaced by a rise in despair or disbelief (Corr, 1993; Maciejewski et al., 2007; Schneidman, 1983, 1994; Weisman, 1972). Still others question the idea of common reactions among dying people, stating that the particular disease or condition and its treatment, the person's personality before the terminal diagnosis, and other life history factors make the process of dying unique and unpredictable (Kastenbaum & Costa, 1977; Zlatin, 1995). The danger in holding too strictly to a stage theory is that people may feel there is a "right" way to face death and a "wrong" way, when in fact each person's dying process is unique.

8.20 Death and Dying in Other Cultures

8.20 Compare and contrast some cross-cultural differences in views of death and dying.

Attitudes and rituals associated with death and the dying process vary from culture to culture. While Westerners see a person as either dead or alive, in some cultures a person who is still alive, is mourned as already dead. For example, in the Northern Cheyenne Native American tribe, death is considered only the end of the physical body, while the self and one's Cheyenne nature will persist. Death itself is a long process, with various aspects of one's spirit leaving at different times. The first such "leaving" results in changes in the behavior and the mental activity of the dying person, but the person may still be able to walk and communicate. The second leads to loss of the senses, then consciousness, and finally, breathing. The very last essence to leave is the life principle. This life principle stays in the skeleton until the bones begin to crumble into dust. Thus some Cheyenne believe that bones can become alive again (Strauss, 2004).

In Navajo culture, a person who has died is believed to be in the underworld. It is possible for a dead person to visit the living; this is a feared situation, so the living try to avoid looking at the dead, and only a few people are permitted to touch or handle the body. A dying person is usually taken to a place removed from others, with only one or two very close relatives staying—because to do so is to risk exposure to evil spirits. If a person dies in his or her own home, the home is destroyed. At the time of death, two men who are stripped down to only their moccasins and covered in ashes (to protect them from the evil spirits) prepare the body for burial. Two additional men dig the grave; only these four men will attend the burial, which is held as quickly as possible—usually the next day. The deceased is buried along with all of his or her belongings, the dirt is returned to the grave, and all footprints are swept away. Even the tools used to dig the grave are destroyed (Downs, 1984).

In contrast, in a wealthy Hindu family in India, the dying person is surrounded by family members, even while in the hospital. Many people will attend to the dying person, creating a nearly constant flow of visitors in and out of the room. Once the person has passed away, preparations for the funeral period—which can take nearly 2 weeks—are begun. The body is taken into the family home until the actual day of the funeral. During the funeral preparation period, visitors and family stream in and out of the deceased's home, and an abundance of food—all vegetarian at this time—is prepared and eaten. All but the very old and infirm are expected to sleep on mattresses placed on the floor, and the body of the deceased is also placed on the floor. The family members wash the body in preparation for wrapping and the trip to a crematorium, not a burial in the ground (Parkes et al., 1997). In Hinduism, it is believed that the dead person's soul will be reincarnated at either a higher level or a lower level of status, depending upon how the person lived his or her life.

The washed and wrapped body of a Hindu man is being carried to the crematorium by his family members.

THINKING CRITICALLY 8.2

What are your thoughts on the need for closure in dealing with someone's death? Do you think it is always necessary?

Concept Map L.O. 8.15, 8.16, 8.17, 8.18, 8.19, 8.20

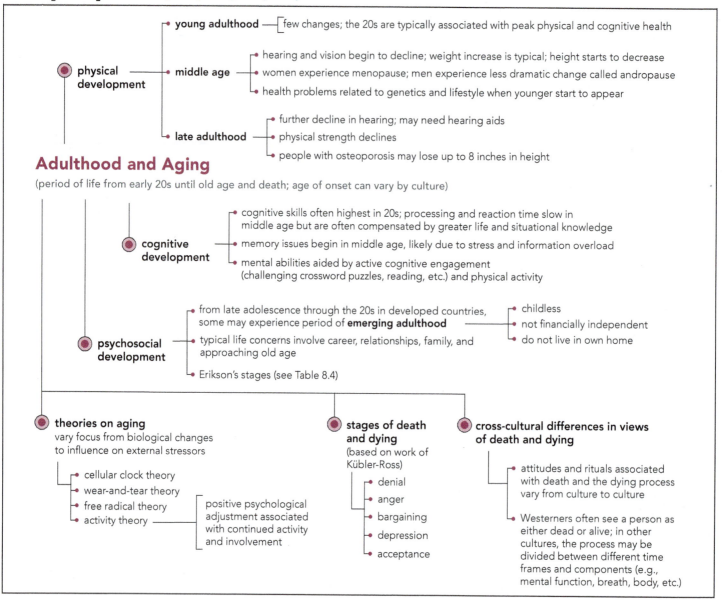

Practice Quiz   How much do you remember?

Pick the best answer.

1. As Daniel has gotten older, he finds that it is becoming more difficult to remember certain words or the name of a new acquaintance. What is the most likely explanation for this change in memory?
    a. heredity
    b. steroids
    c. stress
    d. the aging process
    e. Alzheimer's disease

2. According to Erikson, the primary task of early adulthood is _____.
    a. taking care of aging parents
    b. getting a job
    c. starting a career
    d. completing your education
    e. finding a mate

3. According to Baumrind, which type of parent would most likely say, "Because I said so" or "It's my way or the highway!"?
    a. permissive neglectful
    b. authoritative
    c. authoritarian
    d. permissive indulgent
    e. permissive authoritative

4. Which theory of aging is compared to the limited number of repairs you can have before your car's warranty runs out?
    a. ego theory
    b. cellular-clock theory
    c. wear-and-tear theory
    d. activity theory
    e. free-radical theory

5. According to research, the reason many older people are no longer involved in their community is because _____.
   a. they move away
   b. they do not wish to be involved
   c. they die
   d. they are not asked to take part
   e. they quite often are unable to take part

6. What stage might terminally ill patients be in if they refuse to write a last will and testament because they believe that in doing so, they are admitting they will die?
   a. resentful
   b. bargaining
   c. denial
   d. anger
   e. depression

Applying Psychology to Everyday Life

Not an Adolescent, but Not Yet an Adult?

8.21 Describe the differences between the periods of adolescence and emerging adulthood.

We like to think of the 20s as the period of young adulthood, but "adulting" may be more difficult for some. As discussed earlier, the term *emerging adulthood* refers to the period from the late teens into the late 20s but not to every twenty-something. While many in their 20s have jobs, live on their own, or even have families, there are many who still live in their parents' home, have no children, and while they may have a job, they don't make enough money to be able to live independently. In the following video, students share their thoughts on what it means to be an adult. Are any of their ideas consistent with your ideas? How do you see the definition of what it means to be an adult changing in the future?

Applying Psychology to Everyday Life Not an Adolescent, but Not Yet an Adult?

👁 **Watch** the **Video** at **MyLab Psychology**

After watching the video, answer the following questions:

1. As discussed in the video, people's definition of adulthood varies widely. What were two of the characteristics or examples of being an adult discussed in the video?

2. Do you consider yourself to be an adult? If so, why? If not, when will you be an adult, and what will determine that you've become an adult?

Chapter Summary

Studying Human Development

8.1 Compare and contrast the special research methods used to study development.

- Three special methods used in developmental research are the longitudinal design, the cross-sectional design, and the cross-sequential design.

8.2 Explain the relationship between heredity and environmental factors in determining development.

- Behavioral genetics is a field investigating the relative contributions to development of heredity (nature) and environment (nurture). Most developmental psychologists agree that development is a product of an interaction between nature and nurture.

8.3 Summarize the role of chromosomes and genes in determining the transmission of traits and the inheritance of disorders.

- Dominant genes determine the expression of a trait, whereas recessive gene traits are only expressed when paired with another recessive gene influencing the same trait. Almost all traits are the result of combinations of genes working together in a process called polygenic inheritance.
- Chromosome disorders include Down syndrome, Klinefelter syndrome, and Turner syndrome, whereas genetic disorders include PKU, cystic fibrosis, sickle-cell anemia, and Tay-Sachs disease.

Prenatal Development

8.4 Explain the process of fertilization, including the twinning process.

- The fertilized egg cell is called a zygote and divides into many cells, eventually forming the baby.
- Monozygotic twins are formed when the zygote splits into two separate masses of cells, each of which will develop into a baby identical to the other.
- Dizygotic twins are formed when the mother's body releases multiple eggs and at least two are fertilized or when another ovulation occurs even though the mother has already become pregnant.

8.5 Describe the three stages of prenatal development.

- The germinal period is the first 2 weeks of pregnancy in which the dividing mass of cells moves into the uterus.
- The embryonic period begins at 2 weeks after conception and ends at 8 weeks. The vital organs and structures of the baby form during this period, making it a critical one when teratogens may adversely affect the development of organs and structures.
- The fetal period is from the beginning of the 9th week until the birth of the baby. During the fetal period, tremendous growth occurs, length and weight increase, and organs continue to become fully functional.

Infancy and Childhood Development

8.6 Describe the physical and sensory changes that take place in infancy and childhood.

- Four critical areas of adjustment for the newborn are respiration, digestion, circulation, and temperature regulation.
- Infants are born with reflexes that help the infant survive until more complex learning is possible. These reflexes include sucking, rooting, Moro (startle), grasping, and stepping.
- The senses, except for vision, are fairly well developed at birth. Vision is blurry and lacking in full color perception until about 6 months of age. Gross and fine motor skills develop at a fast pace during infancy and early childhood.

8.7 Compare and contrast two theories of cognitive development, and define autism spectrum disorder.

- Piaget's stages include the sensorimotor stage of sensory and physical interaction with the world, preoperational thought in which language becomes a tool of exploration, concrete operations in which logical thought becomes possible, and formal operations in which abstract concepts are understood and hypothetical thinking develops.
- Vygotsky believed that children learn best when being helped by a more highly skilled peer or adult in a process called scaffolding. The zone of proximal development is the difference between the mental age of tasks the child performs without help and those the child can perform with help.
- Autism spectrum disorder (ASD) is a neurodevelopmental disorder, which involves impairments in thinking, feeling, language, and social skills in relating to others.
- Parents and others who fear immunizing their children against dangerous diseases have failed to understand the basic principles of critical thinking.

8.8 Identify the development of personality, relationships, and self-concept in infancy and childhood.

- The three basic infant temperaments are easy (regular, adaptable, and happy), difficult (irregular, nonadaptable, and irritable), and slow to warm up (need to adjust gradually to change).
- The four types of attachment are secure, avoidant (unattached), ambivalent (insecurely attached), and disorganized–disoriented (insecurely attached and sometimes abused or neglected).
- Harlow's classic research with infant rhesus monkeys demonstrated the importance of contact comfort in the attachment process, contradicting the earlier view that attachment was merely a function of associating the mother with the delivery of food.
- In trust versus mistrust, the infant must gain a sense of predictability and trust in caregivers or risk developing a mistrustful nature; in autonomy versus shame and doubt, the toddler needs to become physically independent.
- In initiative versus guilt, the preschool child is developing emotional and psychological independence; in industry versus inferiority, school-age children are gaining competence and developing self-esteem.

Gender Development and Sexual Orientation

8.9 Define gender, and discuss the development of gender roles.

- Gender is the psychological aspects of being male or female.
- Gender roles are the culture's expectations for male and female behavior and personality.
- Gender identity is a person's sense of being male or female.
- There are both biological and environmental influences on the formation of gender identity.

8.10 Compare and contrast two theories of gender-role development.

- Social learning theorists believe that gender identity is formed through reinforcement of appropriate gender behavior as well as imitation of gender models.
- Gender schema theorists believe that gender identity is a mental schema that develops gradually, influenced by growth of the brain and organization of observed male and female behavior around the schema.

8.11 Distinguish among the various sexual orientations.

- Sexual orientations include heterosexuality, homosexuality, bisexuality, and asexuality.

Adolescence

8.12 Describe the physical changes of puberty.

- Adolescence is the period of life from about age 13 to the early 20s during which physical development reaches completion.
- Puberty is a period of about 4 years during which the sexual organs and systems fully mature and during which secondary sex characteristics such as body hair, breasts, menstruation, deepening voices, and the growth spurt occur.

8.13 Identify the cognitive and moral advances that occur in adolescence.

- Adolescents engage in two kinds of egocentric thinking called the imaginary audience and the personal fable.
- Kohlberg proposed three levels of moral development: preconventional morality, conventional morality, and postconventional morality. Gilligan suggested that Kohlberg's ideas applied more to males.

8.14 Describe how the adolescent search for personal identity influences relationships with others.

- In Erikson's identity versus role confusion crisis, the job of the adolescent is to achieve a consistent sense of self from among all the roles, values, and futures open to him or her.

Adulthood and Aging

8.15 Identify the physical changes and health issues associated with adulthood.

- Adulthood begins in the early 20s and ends with death in old age. It can be divided into young adulthood, middle adulthood, and late adulthood.
- The 20s are the peak of physical health; in the 30s the signs of aging become more visible, and in the 40s visual problems may occur, weight may increase, strength may decrease, and height begins to decrease.
- Women experience a physical decline in the reproductive system called the climacteric, ending at about age 50 with menopause, when a woman's reproductive capabilities are at an end. Men go through andropause, a less dramatic change in testosterone and other male hormones, beginning in the 40s.
- Many health problems such as high blood pressure, skin cancers, and arthritis begin in middle age, with the most common causes of death in middle age being heart disease, cancer, and stroke.

8.16 Describe how memory abilities change during adulthood.

- Reaction times slow down, but intelligence and memory remain relatively stable.

8.17 Apply Erikson's theory to some common psychosocial concerns of adulthood.

- Erikson's crisis of young adulthood is intimacy versus isolation, in which the young adult must establish an intimate relationship, usually with a mate.
- The crisis of middle adulthood is generativity versus stagnation, in which the task of the middle-aged adult is to help the next generation through its crises, either by parenting, mentoring, or a career that leaves some legacy to the next generation.
- Baumrind proposed three parenting styles: authoritarian (rigid and uncompromising), authoritative (consistent and strict but warm and flexible), and permissive (either indifferent and unconcerned with the daily activities of the child or indulgent and unwilling to set limits on the child).
- Erikson's final crisis is integrity versus despair, in which an older adult must come to terms with mortality.

8.18 Compare and contrast four theories of why aging occurs.

- Research strongly indicates that remaining active and involved results in the most positive adjustment to aging; this is a component of activity theory.
- The cellular-clock theory is based on the idea that cells only have so many times that they can reproduce; once that limit is reached, damaged cells begin to accumulate.
- The wear-and-tear theory of physical aging states that as time goes by, repeated use and abuse of the body's tissues cause it to be unable to repair all the damage.
- The free-radical theory states that oxygen molecules with an unstable electron move around the cell, damaging cell structures as they go.

8.19 Describe Kübler-Ross's theory of death and dying, and identify some criticisms of this theory.

- The five stages of reaction to death and dying are denial, anger, bargaining, depression, and acceptance.

8.20 Compare and contrast some cross-cultural differences in views of death and dying.

- In Northern Cheyenne culture, death is seen as part of the process of the life cycle and takes place in three stages.

- In Navajo culture, the dead are believed to move to the underworld, and contact with the body is strictly limited for fear of luring evil spirits to the world of the living.
- In wealthy Hindu families, a dying person is surrounded by family and friends and then honored with a funeral process of nearly 2 weeks.

Applying Psychology to Everyday Life: Not an Adolescent, but Not Yet an Adult?

8.21 Describe the differences between the periods of adolescence and emerging adulthood.

- Emerging adulthood is a period from the late teen years to the late 20s during which many people cannot or do not yet live as fully independent adults.

Test Yourself: Preparing for the AP Exam

PART I: MULTIPLE-CHOICE QUESTIONS

Directions for Part I: Read each of the questions or incomplete sentences below. Then choose the response that best answers the question or completes the sentence.

Pick the best answer.

1. The thinking and attitudes of many who survived the Depression of the 1930s changed them for the rest of their lives. This would be an example of a _____.
   a. longitudinal group
   b. cultural group
   c. cohort effect
   d. cross-sequential group
   e. cross-cultural group

2. If a person has one gene influencing blue eyes but actually has brown eyes, blue eyes must be a _____ trait.
   a. sex-linked
   b. recessive
   c. dominant
   d. polygenic
   e. monogenic

3. Which of the following represents the fertilization process for monozygotic twins?
   a. One egg splits and is then fertilized by two different sperm.
   b. One egg is fertilized by one sperm and then splits.
   c. Two eggs are fertilized by two different sperm.
   d. One egg is fertilized by two different sperm.
   e. Two eggs are fertilized by the same sperm.

4. Dr. Baar measures how long baby Xena looks at a particular stimulus. The technique is known as _____.
   a. stimulus discrimination
   b. dishabituation
   c. habituation
   d. stimulus discrimination
   e. preferential looking

5. At what age can the typical infant roll over?
   a. 10 months
   b. 12 months
   c. 2 months
   d. 5 weeks
   e. 8 months

6. Studies of the infant brain show signs of what scientists call synaptic pruning. What occurs during this process?
   a. Old cells will not be removed until the infant's head circumference increases by 38%.
   b. New cells will not develop until the body makes sufficient physical space within the brain.
   c. Unused synaptic connections and nerve cells are cleared out to make way for new cells.
   d. The brain creates additional neural connections by removing parts of the surrounding bone.
   e. New cells work to "rewrite" old cells and ultimately change their functioning.

7. In which of Piaget's stages does the child become capable of abstract reasoning?
   a. postconventional operations
   b. concrete operations
   c. preoperational
   d. formal operations
   e. sensorimotor

8. In the Strange Situation, _____ babies would cry when their mother left the room but were happy upon her return.
   a. avoidant–ambivalent
   b. disorganized–disoriented
   c. secure
   d. avoidant
   e. ambivalent

9. What is the most likely explanation as to why teenagers and young adults may engage in risky and dangerous behavior?
   a. Such behavior is due to abstract egocentrism.
   b. Such behavior is due to the tremendous pressure applied by peers.
   c. Such behavior may be due to the incomplete development of the prefrontal cortex.
   d. Such behavior is actually hereditary.
   e. Such behavior may be due to unbalanced levels of hormones in the body.

10. What cognitive changes occurring during middle adulthood are the most noticeable?
    a. Response times get shorter.
    b. Hair begins to turn gray.
    c. Changes in memory begin to occur.
    d. Problem-solving skills diminish.
    e. Hearing begins to decline.

11. Independence and self-reliance in the teenage years are most likely due to _____ parenting.
    a. indulgent authoritarian
    b. permissive indulgent
    c. authoritative
    d. authoritarian
    e. permissive neglectful

12. The crisis of late adulthood, according to Erikson, is _____.
    a. industry versus inferiority
    b. identity versus role confusion
    c. integrity versus despair
    d. generativity versus stagnation
    e. intimacy versus isolation

13. Leo is worried that he is losing his mind because he finds himself angry at a friend who died in an automobile accident. Based on Kübler-Ross's research, what might you tell him?
    a. All anger should be suppressed.
    b. Anger of this type is self-destructive and unhealthy.
    c. Anger is a normal reaction to death and not a sign of mental illness.
    d. Anger is usually a mask to your true feelings of sadness.
    e. Anger towards a deceased individual is simply not normal and may require psychological counseling.

14. Chiara's mother wants her daughter to grow up to become a mother of a large family. Such an expectation for Chiara might be seen as an example of her gender _____.
    a. typing
    b. identity
    c. role
    d. constancy
    e. specificity

15. In social learning theory, gender identity results _____.
    a. when a child learns that they are either a girl or a boy
    b. from biological changes that occurred before birth
    c. from observation and imitation
    d. from unconscious forces
    e. from physical changes that occur during puberty

PART II: FREE-RESPONSE QUESTION

Directions for Part II: Read the essay question that follows. Then respond to the question in a clear, concise essay. Do not simply list facts. Instead, present a thorough argument based on your critical consideration of the topic. Use of proper terminology is necessary.

Mina is a developmental psychology researcher who wants to study the relationship between parenting style and children's behavior. She designs a study in which she administers a survey to parents asking about how they discipline their children and about how frequently they express affection to their children. She then measures how frequently the children copy the parents' modeled behavior in a laboratory task. Throughout the study, she looks for trends between how parents answered the survey and the children's behavior.

Part A
For each of the following terms, explain how Mina's study could be modified to incorporate that method into her design:

- longitudinal study
- cross-sectional study
- cross-sequential study

Part B
Explain how each of the following terms may influence the results of Mina's study:

- heredity
- attachment

Part C
Describe how parents who raise their children according to the following parenting styles might answer Mina's two survey questions:

- authoritarian parenting
- permissive-indulgent parenting

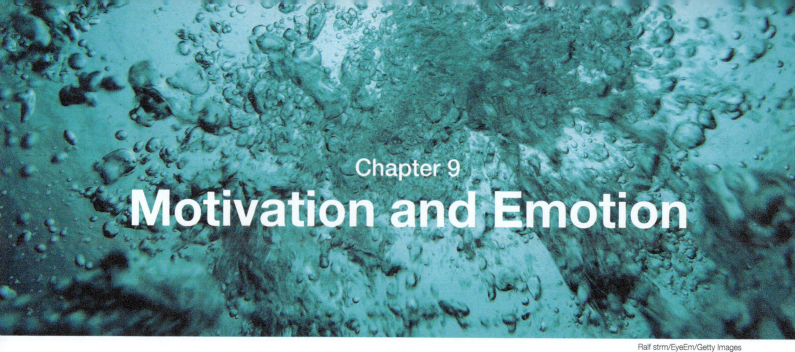

Chapter 9
Motivation and Emotion

Ralf strm/EyeEm/Getty Images

In your words

As a busy student, how do you stay motivated to succeed?

After you have thought about the question, watch the video to see how other students would answer it.

Watch the Video at MyLab Psychology

Why study motivation and emotion?

The study of motivation helps us understand not only why we do the things we do but also why our behaviors can change when our focus shifts or gets redirected. Emotions are a part of everything we do, affecting our relationships with others and our own health, as well as influencing important decisions. In this chapter, we will explore the motives behind our actions and the origins and influences of emotions.

Learning Objectives

9.1 Define motivation, and distinguish between intrinsic motivation and extrinsic motivation.

9.2 Identify the key elements of the early instinct and drive-reduction approaches to motivation.

9.3 Explain the characteristics of the three types of needs.

9.4 Identify the key elements of the arousal and incentive approaches to motivation.

9.5 Describe how Maslow's hierarchy of needs and self-determination theories explain motivation.

9.6 Identify the physical and social factors that influence hunger.

9.7 Recognize some of the factors that contribute to obesity.

9.8 Describe the three elements of emotion.

9.9 Distinguish among the common sense, James-Lange, Cannon-Bard, and facial feedback theories of emotion.

9.10 Identify the key elements in the cognitive arousal and cognitive-mediational theories of emotion.

9.11 Identify possible barriers, and benefits, to implementing a personal system to manage your time and tasks.

9.1–9.5 Understanding Motivation

Some people are content to sit and watch life pass them by, while others seem to need far more out of life. Some people want to do great things, while others are happy with more ordinary lives. What motivates people to do the things they do? What exactly is motivation?

9.1 Defining Motivation

9.1 Define motivation, and distinguish between intrinsic motivation and extrinsic motivation.

Motivation is the process by which activities are started, directed, and continued so that physical or psychological needs or wants are met (Petri, 1996). The word itself comes from the Latin word *movere*, which means "to move." Motivation is what "moves" people to do the things they do. For example, when a person is relaxing in front of the television and begins to feel hungry, the physical need for food might cause the person to get up, go into the kitchen, and search for something to eat. The physical need of hunger caused the action (getting up), directed it (going to the kitchen), and sustained the search (finding or preparing something to eat). Hunger is only one example, of course. Loneliness may lead to calling a friend or going to a place where there are people. The desire to get ahead in life motivates many people to go to college. Just getting out of bed in the morning is motivated by the need to keep a roof over one's head and food on the table by going to work.

There are different types of motivation. Sometimes people are driven to do something because of an external reward of some sort (or the avoidance of an unpleasant consequence, as when someone goes to work at a job to make money and avoid losing possessions such as a house or a car). See Learning Objective 5.5. In **extrinsic motivation**, a person performs an action because it leads to an outcome that is separate from the person (Lemos & Verissimo, 2014; Ryan & Deci, 2000). Other examples would be giving a child money for every A received on a report card, offering a bonus to an employee for increased performance, or tipping a server in a restaurant for good service. The child, employee, and server are motivated to work for the external or extrinsic rewards. In contrast, **intrinsic motivation** is the type of motivation in which a person performs an action because the act itself is fun, rewarding, challenging, or satisfying in some internal manner. Both outcome and level of effort can vary depending on the type of motivation. Psychologist Teresa Amabile (Amabile et al., 1976) found that children's creativity was affected by the kind of motivation for which they worked: Extrinsic motivation decreased the degree of creativity shown in an experimental group's artwork when compared to the creativity levels of the children in an intrinsically motivated control group.

9.2 Early Approaches to Understanding Motivation

9.2 Identify the key elements of the early instinct and drive-reduction approaches to motivation.

Researchers and theorists began the serious study of motivation almost as soon as psychology became its own recognized field of study. As is often the case when first examining a topic such as this, there were many different areas of focus in those early days. As the decades have gone by, some approaches have fallen out of favor, some have been modified, and newer approaches have been developed. Let's take a look at some of the earlier theories.

INSTINCTS AND THE EVOLUTIONARY APPROACH Early attempts to understand motivation focused on the biologically determined and innate patterns of behavior called **instincts** that exist in both people and animals. Just as animals are governed by their

---

AP 7.A Identify and apply basic motivational concepts to understand the behavior of humans and other animals.

motivation
the process by which activities are started, directed, and continued so that physical or psychological needs or wants are met.

extrinsic motivation
type of motivation in which a person performs an action because it leads to an outcome that is separate from or external to the person.

intrinsic motivation
type of motivation in which a person performs an action because the act itself is rewarding or satisfying in some internal manner.

instincts
the biologically determined and innate patterns of behavior that exist in both people and animals.

AP 7.B Compare and contrast motivational theories, including the strengths and weaknesses of each.

AP 2.A Discuss psychology's abiding interest in how heredity, environment, and evolution work together to shape behavior.

instincts to perform activities such as migrating, nest building, mating, and protecting their territory, evolutionary theorists proposed that human beings may also be governed by similar instincts (James, 1890; McDougall, 1908). For instance, according to these theorists, the human instinct to reproduce is responsible for sexual behavior, and the human instinct for territorial protection may be related to aggressive behavior.

William McDougall (1908) actually proposed a total of 18 instincts for humans, including curiosity, flight (running away), pugnacity (aggressiveness), and acquisition (gathering possessions). As the years progressed, psychologists added more and more instincts to the list until there were thousands of proposed instincts. However, none of these early theorists did much more than give names to these instincts. Although there were plenty of descriptions, such as "submissive people possess the instinct of submission," there was no attempt to explain why these instincts exist in humans, if they exist at all (Petri, 1996).

Instinct approaches have faded away because, although they could describe human behavior, they could not explain it. But these approaches did accomplish one important thing by forcing psychologists to realize that some human behavior is controlled by hereditary factors. This idea remains central in the study of human behavior today. For example, research on the genetics of both cognitive and behavioral traits suggests that hereditary factors can account for more than 50 percent of the variance in some aspects of human cognition, temperament, and personality; and much of this variance is due to the influence of multiple genes or hereditary factors, not just one (Kempf & Weinberger, 2009; Plomin et al., 1994; Plomin & Deary, 2015; Plomin & Spinath, 2004).

DRIVE-REDUCTION THEORY The next approach to understanding motivation focuses on the concepts of needs and drives. A **need** is a requirement of some material (such as food or water) that is essential for survival of the organism. When an organism has a need, it leads to a psychological tension as well as a physical arousal that motivates the organism to act in order to fulfill the need and reduce the tension. This tension is called a **drive** (Hull, 1943).

Drive-reduction theory proposes just this connection between internal physiological states and outward behavior. In this theory, there are two kinds of drives. **Primary drives** involve survival needs of the body such as hunger and thirst, whereas **acquired (secondary) drives** are learned through experience or conditioning such as the need for money or social approval or the need of recent former smokers to have something to put in their mouths. If this sounds familiar, it should. The concepts of primary and secondary reinforcers from Chapter Five are related to these drives. Primary reinforcers satisfy primary drives, and secondary reinforcers satisfy acquired, or secondary, drives. See Learning Objective 5.5.

This theory also includes the concept of **homeostasis**, or the tendency of the body to maintain a steady state. One could think of homeostasis as the body's version of a thermostat—thermostats keep the temperature of a house at a constant level, and homeostasis does the same thing for the body's functions. When there is a primary drive need, the body is in a state of imbalance. This stimulates behavior that brings the body back into balance, or homeostasis. For example, if Cade's body needs food, he feels hunger and the state of tension/arousal associated with that need. He will then seek to restore his homeostasis by eating something, which is the behavior stimulated to reduce the hunger drive (see **Figure 9.1**).

Although the drive-reduction theory works well to explain the actions people take to reduce

need
a requirement of some material (such as food or water) that is essential for survival of the organism.

drive
a psychological tension and physical arousal arising when there is a need that motivates the organism to act in order to fulfill the need and reduce the tension.

drive-reduction theory
approach to motivation that assumes behavior arises from internal drives to push the organism to satisfy physiological needs and reduce tension and arousal.

primary drives
those drives that involve needs of the body such as hunger and thirst.

acquired (secondary) drives
those drives that are learned through experience or conditioning, such as the need for money or social approval.

homeostasis
the tendency of the body to maintain a steady state.

AP 7.E Discuss the biological underpinnings of motivation, including needs, drives, and homeostasis.

Figure 9.1 Homeostasis

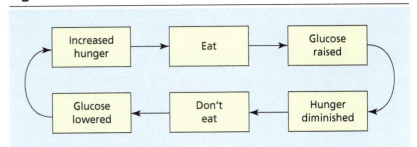

In homeostasis, the body maintains balance in its physical states. For example, this diagram shows how increased hunger (a state of imbalance) prompts a person to eat. Eating increases the level of glucose (blood sugar), causing the feelings of hunger to reduce. After a period without eating, the glucose levels become low enough to stimulate the hunger drive once again, and the entire cycle is repeated.

tension created by needs, it does not explain all human motivation. Why do people eat when they are not really hungry? People don't always seek to reduce their inner arousal either—sometimes they seek to increase it. Bungee-jumping, parachuting as recreation, rock climbing, and watching horror movies are all activities that increase the inner state of tension and arousal, and many people love doing these activities. Why? The answer is complex: There are different types of needs, different effects of arousal, different incentives, and different levels of importance attached to many forms of behavior. The following theories explore some of these factors in motivation.

9.3 Different Strokes for Different Folks: Psychological Needs

9.3 Explain the characteristics of the three types of needs.

Obviously, motivation is about needs. Drive-reduction theory talks about needs, and other theories of motivation include the concept of needs. In many of these theories, most needs are the result of some inner physical drive (such as hunger or thirst) that demands to be satisfied, but other theories examine our psychological needs.

MCCLELLAND'S THEORY: AFFILIATION, POWER, AND ACHIEVEMENT NEEDS Harvard University psychologist David C. McClelland (1961, 1987) proposed a theory of motivation that highlights the importance of three psychological needs not typically considered by the other theories: affiliation, power, and achievement.

According to McClelland, human beings have a psychological need for friendly social interactions and relationships with others. Called the **need for affiliation** (abbreviated as **nAff** in McClelland's writings), people high in this need seek to be liked by others and to be held in high regard by those around them. This makes high-affiliation people good team players, whereas a person high in achievement just might run over a few team members on the way to the top.

A second psychological need proposed by McClelland is the **need for power (nPow)**. Power is not about reaching a goal but about having control over other people. People high in this need would want to have influence over others and make an impact on them. They want their ideas to be the ones that are used, regardless of whether their ideas will lead to success. Status and prestige are important, so these people wear expensive clothes, live in expensive houses, drive fancy cars, and dine in the best restaurants. Whereas someone who is a high achiever may not need a lot of money to validate the achievement, someone who is high in the need for power typically sees the money (and cars, houses, jewelry, and other "toys") as the achievement—the one with the most toys wins.

The **need for achievement (nAch)** involves a strong desire to succeed in attaining goals, not only realistic ones but also challenging ones. People who are high in nAch look for careers and hobbies that allow others to evaluate them because these high achievers also need to have feedback about their performance in addition to the achievement of reaching the goal. Although many of these people do become wealthy, famous, and publicly successful, others fulfill their need to achieve in ways that lead only to their own personal success, not material riches—they just want the challenge. Achievement motivation appears to be strongly related to success in school, occupational success, and the quality and amount of what a person produces (Collins et al., 2004; Gillespie et al., 2002; Hoferichter et al., 2015; Spangler, 1992).

Many people are driven by a need to attain both realistic and challenging goals. These students seem eager to provide an answer to the teacher's question, and the teacher's positive feedback will help foster their need for achievement.

need for affiliation (nAff)
the need for friendly social interactions and relationships with others.

need for power (nPow)
the need to have control or influence over others.

need for achievement (nAch)
a need that involves a strong desire to succeed in attaining goals, not only realistic ones but also challenging ones.

THINKING CRITICALLY 9.1

How might the three types of needs discussed in this section relate to the goals of many politicians? Would some needs be more important than others?

> How do people get to be high achievers?

PERSONALITY AND nAch: CAROL DWECK'S SELF-THEORY OF MOTIVATION According to motivation and personality psychologist Carol Dweck (Dweck, 1999; Nussbaum & Dweck, 2008), the need for achievement is closely linked to personality factors, including a person's view of how *self* (the beliefs a person holds about his or her own abilities and relationships with others) can affect the individual's perception of the success or failure of his or her actions. This concept is related to the much older notion of *locus of control*, in which people who assume that they have control over what happens in their lives are considered to be *internal* in locus of control, and those who feel that their lives are controlled by powerful others, luck, or fate are considered to be *external* in locus of control (A. P. MacDonald, 1970; Rotter, 1966).

Dweck has amassed a large body of empirical research, particularly in the field of education, to support the idea that people's "theories" about their own selves can affect their level of achievement motivation and their willingness to keep trying to achieve success in the face of failure (Dweck, 1986; Dweck & Elliott, 1983; Dweck & Leggett, 1988; Elliott & Dweck, 1988; Yeager et al., 2014). According to this research, people can form one of two belief systems about intelligence, which in turn affects their motivation to achieve. Those who believe intelligence is fixed and unchangeable often demonstrate an external locus of control when faced with difficulty, leading them to give up easily or avoid situations in which they might fail—often ensuring their own failure in the process (Dweck & Molden, 2008). They are prone to developing learned helplessness, the tendency to stop trying to achieve a goal because past failure has led them to believe that they cannot succeed. See Learning Objective 5.12. Their goals involve trying to "look smart" and to outperform others ("See, at least I did better than she did"). For example, a student faced with a big exam may avoid coming to class that day, even though that might mean getting an even lower score on a makeup exam. This does not mean that students with this view of intelligence are always unsuccessful. In fact, Dweck's research (1999) suggests that students who have had a long history of successes may be most at risk for developing learned helplessness after a big failure precisely because their previous successes have led them to believe in their own fixed intelligence. For example, a child who had never earned anything less than an A in school who then receives his first C might become depressed and refuse to do any more homework, ensuring future failure.

The other type of person believes that intelligence is changeable and can be shaped by experiences and effort in small increases, or increments. These people also tend to show an internal locus of control, both in believing their own actions and efforts will improve their intelligence and in taking control or increasing their efforts when faced with challenges (Dweck & Molden, 2008). They work at developing new strategies and get involved in new tasks, with the goal of increasing their "smarts." They are motivated to master tasks and don't allow failure to destroy their confidence in themselves or prevent them from trying again and again, using new strategies each time.

Based on this and other research, Dweck recommends that parents and teachers praise efforts and the methods that children use to make those efforts, not just successes or ability. Instead of saying, "You're right, how smart you are," the parent or teacher should say something such as, "You are really thinking hard" or "That was a very clever way to think about this problem." In the past, teachers and parents have been told that praise is good and criticism is bad—it might damage a child's self-esteem. Dweck believes that constructive criticism, when linked with praise of effort and the use of strategies, will be a better influence on the child's self-esteem and willingness to challenge themselves than endless praise that can become meaningless when given indiscriminately (Gunderson et al., 2013).

AP 7.B Compare and contrast motivational theories, including the strengths and weaknesses of each.

9.4 Arousal and Incentive Approaches

9.4 Identify the key elements of the arousal and incentive approaches to motivation.

Another explanation for human motivation involves the recognition of yet another type of need, the need for stimulation. A **stimulus motive** is one that appears to be unlearned but causes an increase in stimulation. Examples would be curiosity, playing, and exploration. On the other hand, sometimes our motives for doing things involve the rewards or incentives we get when we act, such as eating food even when we are not hungry just because it tastes so good—an example of learned behavior.

AROUSAL THEORY In **arousal theory**, people are said to have an optimal level of tension that is best or ideal for them. In turn, individuals are motivated to engage in behaviors or seek out experiences that are consistent with that optimal level. Maintaining an optimal level of cognitive arousal, then, may involve reducing tension or creating it, see **Figure 9.2** (Hebb, 1955). For example, husbands or wives who are underaroused may pick a fight with their spouse. Students who experience test anxiety (a high level of arousal) may seek out ways to reduce that anxiety to improve their test performance. Students who are not anxious at all may not be motivated to study well, thus lowering their test performance. Many arousal theorists believe the optimal level of arousal for most people under normal circumstances is somewhere in the middle, neither too high nor too low.

stimulus motive
a motive that appears to be unlearned but causes an increase in stimulation, such as curiosity.

arousal theory
theory of motivation in which people are said to have an optimal (best or ideal) level of tension that they seek to maintain by increasing or decreasing stimulation.

sensation seeker
someone who needs more arousal than the average person.

💬 If people are supposed to be seeking a level of arousal somewhere around the middle, why do some people love to do things like bungee-jumping?

Even though the average person might require a moderate level of arousal to feel content, some people need less arousal and some need more. The person who needs more arousal is called a **sensation seeker** (Lauriola et al., 2014; Zuckerman, 1979, 1994). Sensation seekers seem to need more complex and varied sensory experiences than other people. For example, someone scoring higher in sensation seeking might endorse a statement such as "I prefer friends who are excitingly unpredictable," versus someone scoring lower in sensation seeking possibly endorsing statements like "Before I begin a complicated job, I make careful plans" (Zuckerman, 2002). The need does not always have to involve danger. For example, students who travel to other countries to study tend to score higher on scales of sensation seeking than students who stay at home (Schroth & McCormack, 2000). Sensation seeking may be related to temperament. See Learning Objective 8.8.

Figure 9.2 Arousal and Behavior

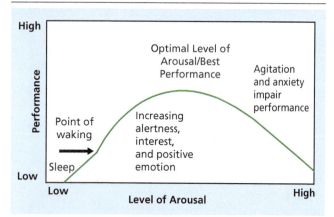

According to Hebb's (1955) conception of motivation and drive, individuals perform tasks best at an optimal level of cognitive arousal, often a somewhat moderate level. In turn, individuals may be motivated to engage in behaviors that are stimulating and at other times pursue less-stimulating circumstances.

Source: Based on Hebb, D. O. (1955). Drives and the CNS (Conceptual Nervous System). Psychological Review, 62, 243–254.

Is the tendency to be a sensation seeker something people have when they are born? Although it is tempting to think of 6-month-old children as having little in the way of experiences that could shape their personalities, the fact is that the first 6 months of life are full of experiences that might affect children's choices in the future. For example, a very young infant might, while being carried, stick a hand into some place that ends up causing pain. This experience might affect that infant's willingness in the future to put his or her hand in something else through the simple learning process of operant conditioning. See Learning Objective 5.5. In a longitudinal study taking place over about 4 years, researchers found that adolescents who played video games in which high risk taking is positively presented became more likely to engage in risky behavior and had increased scores on levels of sensation seeking (Hull et al., 2012).

The presence of other people may matter as well. Adolescents tend to make more risky decisions when in a group of peers than when alone, a phenomenon that is part of peer pressure (Albert et al., 2013; Chein et al., 2011; Smith et al., 2015; Willoughby et al., 2013). In one recent study (Silva et al., 2016), late-adolescent males (18 to 22 years of age) were given a battery of tests on decision making under three conditions: alone, in a group of four males of the same age, and in a group with three age-mates and one older male (25 to 30 years of age). When tested alone or in the group with the older male, the participants exhibited about the same level of risky behavior, but when tested in the group with same-age peers, they exhibited significantly greater risk taking. It would seem that the presence of just the one older male was enough to cancel out the risk-taking increase usually found in peer pressure situations.

INCENTIVE APPROACHES

> 💬 Last Thanksgiving, I had eaten about all I could. Then my aunt brought out a piece of her wonderful pumpkin pie and I couldn't resist—I ate it, even though I was not at all hungry. What makes us do things even when we don't have the drive or need to do them?

It's true that sometimes there is no physical need present, yet people still eat, drink, or react as if they did have a need. Even though that piece of pie was not necessary to reduce a hunger drive, it was very rewarding, wasn't it? And on past occasions, that pie was also delicious and rewarding, so there is anticipation of that reward now. The pie, in all its glorious promise of flavor and sweetness, becomes, in itself, an incentive to eat. **Incentives** are things that attract or lure people into action.

In **incentive approaches**, behavior is explained in terms of the external stimulus and its rewarding properties. These rewarding properties exist independently of any need or level of arousal and can cause people to act only upon the incentive. Thus, incentive theory is actually based, at least in part, on the principles of learning that were discussed in Chapter Five. See Learning Objective 5.5.

By itself, the incentive approach does not explain the motivation behind all behavior. Many theorists today see motivation as a result of both the "push" of internal needs or drives and the "pull" of a rewarding external stimulus. For example, sometimes a person may actually be hungry (the push) but choose to satisfy that drive by selecting a candy bar instead of a celery stick. The candy bar has more appeal to most people, and it therefore has more pull than the celery. (Frankly, to most people, just about anything has more pull than celery.)

incentives
things that attract or lure people into action.

incentive approaches
theories of motivation in which behavior is explained as a response to the external stimulus and its rewarding properties.

self-actualization
according to Maslow, the point that is seldom reached at which people have sufficiently satisfied the lower needs and achieved their full human potential.

9.5 Humanistic Approaches

9.5 Describe how Maslow's hierarchy of needs and self-determination theories explain motivation.

Some final approaches to the study of motivation are humanistic in nature. One of the classic humanistic approaches is that of Maslow, while a more modern approach is represented by the self-determination theory.

MASLOW'S HIERARCHY OF NEEDS The first humanistic theory is based on the work of Abraham Maslow (1943, 1987). As explained in the video *Maslow's Hierarchy of Needs*, Maslow proposed several levels of needs a person must strive to meet before achieving the highest level of personality fulfillment. According to Maslow, **self-actualization** is the point that is seldom reached—at which people have satisfied the lower needs and achieved their full human potential.

These needs include both fundamental deficiency needs, such as the need for food or water, and growth needs, such as the desire for having friends or feeling good about

AP 7.B Compare and contrast motivational theories, including the strengths and weaknesses of each.

AP 7.D Identify contributions of key researchers in the psychological field of motivation and emotion.

AP 7.J Identify the contributions of major researchers in personality theory.

Watch Maslow's Hierarchy of Needs

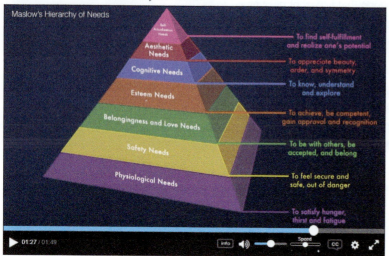

Watch the Video at MyLab Psychology

oneself (Maslow, 1971; Maslow & Lowery, 1998). For a person to achieve self-actualization, which is one of the highest levels of growth needs, the primary, fundamental needs must first be fulfilled. The Maslow's Hierarchy of Needs video shows the typical way to represent Maslow's series of needs as a pyramid with the most basic needs for survival at the bottom and the highest needs at the top. This type of ranking is called a hierarchy.* The only need higher than self-actualization is transcendence, a search for spiritual meaning beyond one's immediate self, that Maslow added many years after his original hierarchy was formulated.

People move up the pyramid as they go through life, gaining wisdom and the knowledge of how to handle many different situations. But a shift in life's circumstances can result in a shift down to a lower need. Moving up and down and then back up can occur frequently—even from one hour to the next. Times in a person's life in which self-actualization is achieved, at least temporarily, are called **peak experiences**. For Maslow, the process of growth and self-actualization is the striving to make peak experiences happen again and again.

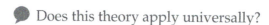 Does this theory apply universally?

Maslow's theory has had a powerful influence on the field of management (Heil et al., 1998) and has spawned new ideas and concepts of what might be an appropriate revised hierarchy. See Learning Objective A.7. In spite of this influence, Maslow's theory is not without its critics. There are several problems that others have highlighted, and the most serious is that there is little scientific support (Drenth et al., 1984). Like Sigmund Freud, Maslow developed his theory based on his personal observations of people rather than any empirically gathered observations or research. Although many people report that while they were starving, they could think of nothing but food, there is anecdotal evidence in the lives of many people, some of them quite well known, that the lower needs do not have to be satisfied before moving on to a higher need (Drenth et al., 1984). For example, artists and scientists throughout history have been known to deny their own physical needs while producing great works (a self-actualization need).

Maslow's work was also based on his studies of Americans. Cross-cultural research suggests that the order of needs on the hierarchy does not always hold true for other cultures, particularly those cultures with a stronger tendency than U.S. culture to avoid uncertainty, such as Greece and Japan. In those countries, security needs are much stronger than self-actualization needs in determining motivation (Hofstede, 1980; Hofstede et al., 2002). This means that people in those cultures value job security more than they value job satisfaction (holding an interesting or challenging job). In countries such as Sweden and Norway, which stress the quality of life as being of greater importance than what a person produces, social needs may be more important than self-actualization needs (Hofstede et al., 2002). See Learning Objective 12.15.

Other theorists (Alderfer, 1972; Kenrick et al., 2010) have developed and refined Maslow's hierarchy. Douglas Kenrick and colleagues have suggested a modification to Maslow's original hierarchy that encompasses aspects of evolutionary biology, anthropology, and psychology. Their modification incorporates dynamics between internal

peak experiences
according to Maslow, times in a person's life during which self-actualization is temporarily achieved.

---

*hierarchy: a graded or ranked series.

motives and environmental threats and opportunities (Kenrick et al., 2010). However, their revision has not been without critique and has spawned further contemplation. Some elements of Kenrick's theory have been challenged, including a questioning of its focus on evolutionary aspects instead of human cultural influences (Kesebir et al., 2010) and its removal of self-actualization from both the pinnacle of the pyramid and from the hierarchy altogether as a stand-alone motive (Peterson & Park, 2010). Just as there are many aspects to motivation, any revision or discussion of an appropriate hierarchy of needs will need to take into account a wide variety of opinions and viewpoints.

SELF-DETERMINATION THEORY (SDT) Another theory of motivation similar to Maslow's hierarchy of needs is the **self-determination theory (SDT)** of Richard Ryan and Edward Deci (Ryan & Deci, 2000). In this theory, three inborn and universal needs help people gain a complete sense of self and whole, healthy relationships with others. The three needs are *autonomy*, or the need to be in control of one's own behavior and goals (i.e., self-determination); *competence*, or the need to be able to master the challenging tasks of one's life; and *relatedness*, or the need to feel a sense of belonging, intimacy, and security in relationships with others. These needs are common in several theories of personality; the relatedness need is, of course, similar to Maslow's belongingness and love needs, and both autonomy and competence are important aspects of Erikson's theory of psychosocial personality development (Erikson, 1950, 1980). See Learning Objective 8.7. For more about this theory and how it compares to Maslow as well as life in today's world, watch the video *Self-Determination Theory*.

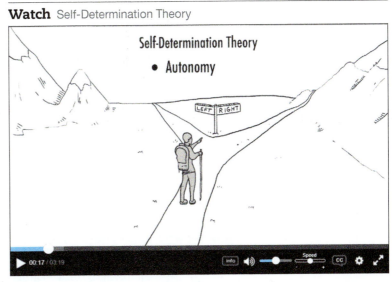

Watch Self-Determination Theory

Watch the Video at MyLab Psychology

Ryan, Deci, and their colleagues (Deci et al., 1994; Ryan & Deci, 2000) believe that satisfying these needs can best be accomplished if the person has a supportive environment in which to develop goals and relationships with others. Such satisfaction will not only foster healthy psychological growth but also increase the individual's intrinsic motivation, that is, focusing more on actions that are performed because they are internally rewarding or satisfying. Evidence suggests that intrinsic motivation is increased or enhanced when a person feels not only competence, through experiencing positive feedback from others and succeeding at what are perceived to be challenging tasks, but also a sense of autonomy or the knowledge that his or her actions are self-determined rather than controlled by others (deCharms, 1968; Deci & Ryan, 1985; Evans, 2015; Hancox et al., 2015; Ryan et al., 2012; Silva et al., 2014).

Previous research has found a negative impact on intrinsic motivation when an external reward is given for the performance (Deci et al., 1999), while other studies find negative effects only for tasks that are not interesting in and of themselves (Cameron et al., 2001). When the task itself is interesting to the person (as might be an assignment that an instructor or manager has explained in terms of its importance and future value), external rewards may increase intrinsic motivation, at least in the short term. The bulk of current research seems to support this latter idea (Evans, 2015; Rigby et al., 2014; Silva et al., 2014). Researchers in this field are also using techniques such as fMRI to examine the role of the brain, particularly the ventromedial prefrontal cortex, in intrinsic and extrinsic motivation (Marsden et al., 2014; Murayama et al., 2015). See Learning Objectives 2.5, 2.8.

self-determination theory (SDT)
theory of human motivation in which the social context of an action has an effect on the type of motivation existing for the action.

 But don't we sometimes do things for both kinds of motives?

There are usually elements of both intrinsic and extrinsic motives in many of the things people do. Most teachers, for example, work for money to pay bills (the extrinsic motive) but may also feel that they are helping young children become better adults in the future, which makes the teachers feel good about themselves (the intrinsic motive).

How universal are these three needs? Some cultures, such as the United States and Great Britain, are *individualistic*, stressing the needs of the individual over the group, independence, and self-reliance. Other cultures are collectivistic, such as those in Japan and China, and stress strong social ties, interdependence, and cooperation. Cross-cultural research indicates that even across such different cultures, the needs for autonomy, mastery, and belongingness are of similar importance (Chirkov, 2009; Chirkov et al., 2011; Ryan et al., 1999; Sheldon, 2012). The *APA Goal 2: Scientific Inquiry and Critical Thinking* feature looks at the effects of praise, a typical form of motivating achievement, across cultures.

Concept Map L.O. 9.1, 9.2, 9.3, 9.4, 9.5

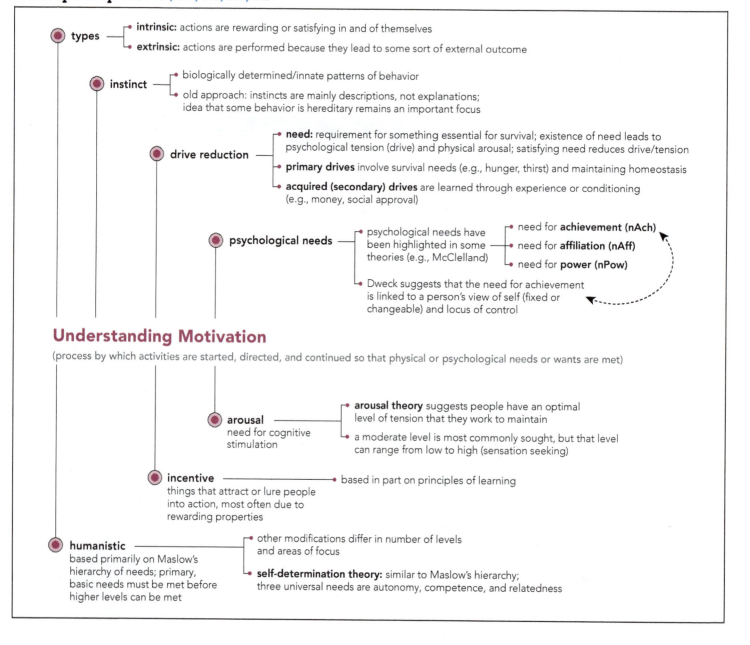

Practice Quiz — How much do you remember?

Pick the best answer.

1. If a person carries out a behavior to receive an outcome that is separate from the person, this is known as _____ motivation.
   a. instinctual
   b. evolutionary
   c. intrinsic
   d. extrinsic
   e. drive-reduction

2. What motivational theory relies heavily on the concept of homeostasis?
   a. McClelland's theory
   b. need for achievement theory
   c. drive-reduction theory
   d. need for affiliation theory
   e. instinctual theory

3. People high in the need for _____ want to be liked by others and are good team players.
   a. emotion
   b. power
   c. internal locus of control
   d. affiliation
   e. achievement

4. In terms of arousal theory, if individuals are currently bored or underaroused, they are likely to pursue activities to help them _____ their overall level of arousal.
   a. significantly decrease
   b. moderately decrease
   c. maintain
   d. maintain or decrease
   e. elevate

5. In Maslow's theory, how often do people reach a point of self-actualization?
   a. Most people reach a state of self-actualization before they reach adulthood.
   b. Seldom, although there are times in a person's life when he or she is self-actualized at least temporarily.
   c. Some people reach a state of self-actualization in late childhood.
   d. Most people reach a state of self-actualization as they finish adolescence.
   e. No one ever reaches the ultimate state. Our motivations express themselves in how we try to attain it.

6. In Ryan and Deci's self-determination theory, what is the key to achieving one's needs for autonomy, competence, and relatedness?
   a. support from others around you
   b. extrinsic motivation and an external locus of control
   c. an instinctual motivation
   d. a driving desire not to be a failure
   e. a motivation often driven by heredity

APA Goal 2: Scientific Inquiry and Critical Thinking

Cultural Differences in the Use of Praise as a Motivator

Addresses APA Learning Objective 2.5: Incorporate sociocultural factors in scientific inquiry.

In Western cultures, and particularly in the educational system of the United States, parents and teachers have been told to praise children's achievements rather than using too much negative feedback and criticism (Trumbull & Rothstein-Fisch, 2011). The thinking behind this focus on positive reinforcement is that praise will boost a student's self-esteem, while excessive criticism will most likely do damage. In the individualistic culture of the United States, this does appear to work very well. But when the students are from a different cultural background, such as the more collectivistic Asian and Latin cultures, the story is quite different. What works in one culture may not always work in another culture.

In collectivistic cultures, it is more desirable to promote the welfare of the group rather than the individual. Students from these cultures who are singled out to receive praise, particularly in front of other classmates, may feel very uncomfortable to be "elevated" above their classmates. Instead of having the effect of motivating them to succeed, such praise might backfire, leading the student to underachieve so as to keep a lower profile, so to speak (Geary, 2001; Markus & Kitayama, 1991; Rothstein-Fisch & Trumbull, 2008; Trumbull & Rothstein-Fisch, 2011).

One study found that Latina students who were taught English responded very negatively to the abundant praise given to them by their tutor, having been made uncomfortable by the positive reinforcement rather than bolstered by it (Geary, 2001; Trumbull & Rothstein-Fisch, 2011). Other research found that, when compared to Canadian students, Japanese students were more critical of their own performances and more responsive to negative feedback (Heine et al., 2001). Contrary to what typical learning theory would predict, the benefits of positive reinforcement are not always as expected when dealing with very different cultural expectations.

> **THINKING CRITICALLY 9.2**
>
> Would the cultural differences in the effects of praise be likely to affect areas of daily life other than educational situations?

AP 7.C Describe classic research findings in specific motivations.

9.6–9.7 What, Hungry Again? Why People Eat

Satisfying hunger is one of our most primary needs. The eating habits of people today have become a major concern and a frequent topic of news programs, talk shows, and scientific research. Countless pills, supplements, and treatments are available to "help" people eat less and others to eat more. Eating is not only a basic survival behavior that reduces a primary drive; it is also a form of entertainment for many, and the attractive presentations and social environment of many eating experiences are a powerful incentive.

9.6 Physiological and Social Components of Hunger

9.6 Identify the physical and social factors that influence hunger.

 Why do we eat? What causes us to feel hungry in the first place?

Several factors are involved in the hunger drive. Walter Cannon (Cannon & Washburn, 1912) believed that stomach contractions, or "hunger pangs," caused hunger and that the presence of food in the stomach would stop the contractions and appease the hunger drive. Oddly enough, having an empty stomach is not the deciding factor in many cases. Although the stomach does have sensory receptors that respond to the pressure of the stretching stomach muscles as food is piled in and that send signals to the brain indicating that the stomach is full (Geliebter, 1988), people who have had their stomachs removed still get hungry (Janowitz, 1967).

HORMONAL INFLUENCES One factor in hunger seems to be the insulin response that occurs after we begin to eat. **Insulin** and **glucagon** are hormones that are secreted by the pancreas to control the levels of fats, proteins, and carbohydrates in the whole body, including glucose (blood sugar). Insulin reduces the level of glucose in the bloodstream, for example, whereas glucagon increases the level. Insulin, normally released in greater amounts after eating has begun, causes a feeling of more hunger because of the drop in blood sugar levels. Carbohydrates, especially those that are simple or highly refined (such as table sugar, fruit drinks, white flour, and white bread or pasta), cause the insulin level to spike even more than other foods do because there is such a large amount of glucose released by these foods at one time. High blood sugar leads to more insulin released, which leads to a low blood sugar level, increased appetite, and the tendency to overeat.

insulin
a hormone secreted by the pancreas to control the levels of fats, proteins, and carbohydrates in the body by reducing the level of glucose in the bloodstream.

glucagon
hormone that is secreted by the pancreas to control the levels of fats, proteins, and carbohydrates in the body by increasing the level of glucose in the bloodstream.

That is the basic principle behind many of the diets that promote low carbohydrate intake. The proponents of these diets argue that if people control the carbohydrates, they can control the insulin reaction and prevent hunger cravings later on.

In recent years, a hormone called **leptin** has been identified as one of the factors that seems to control appetite. When released into the bloodstream, leptin signals the hypothalamus that the body has had enough food, reducing appetite and increasing the feeling of being full, or satiated. Genetic abnormalities in the receptors for leptin as well as leptin resistance may play an important role in obesity (Dubern & Clement, 2012; Pan et al., 2014).

THE ROLE OF THE HYPOTHALAMUS The stomach and the pancreas are only two of the body parts involved in hunger. In Chapter Two, the role of the hypothalamus in controlling many kinds of motivational stimuli, including hunger, was seen as a result of its influence on the pituitary. But the hypothalamus itself has different areas, controlled by the levels of glucose and insulin in the body, which appear to control eating behavior.

The *ventromedial hypothalamus (VMH)* may be involved in stopping the eating response when glucose levels go up (Neary et al., 2004). In one study, rats whose VMH areas (located toward the bottom and center of the hypothalamus) were damaged would no longer stop eating—they ate and ate until they were quite overweight (Hetherington & Ranson, 1940). However, they did not eat everything in sight. They actually got rather picky, only overeating on food that appealed to them (Ferguson & Keesey, 1975; Parkinson & Weingarten, 1990). In fact, if all the food available to them was unappealing, they did not become obese and in some cases even lost weight.

Another part of the hypothalamus, located on the side and called the *lateral hypothalamus (LH)*, seems to influence the onset of eating when insulin levels go up (Neary et al., 2004). Damage to this area caused rats to stop eating to the point of starvation. They would eat only if force-fed and still lost weight under those conditions (Anand & Brobeck, 1951; Hoebel & Teitelbaum, 1966). Both of these areas of the hypothalamus are involved in the production of orexin-A, a neuropeptide (a small, protein-like molecule that neurons use to communicate) involved in appetite control (Li et al., 2014; Messina et al., 2014).

WEIGHT SET POINT AND BASAL METABOLIC RATE Obviously, the role of the hypothalamus in eating behavior is complex. Some researchers (Leibel et al., 1995; Nisbett, 1972) believe that the hypothalamus affects the particular level of weight that the body tries to maintain, called the **weight set point**. Injury to the hypothalamus does raise or lower the weight set point rather dramatically, causing either drastic weight loss or weight gain.

Metabolism, the speed at which the body burns available energy, and exercise also play a part in the weight set point. Some people are no doubt genetically wired to have faster metabolisms, and those people can eat large amounts of food without gaining weight. Others have slower metabolisms and may eat a normal or even less-than-normal amount of food and still gain weight or have difficulty losing it (Bouchard et al., 1990; Higginson et al., 2016). (Some people swear they can gain weight just by *looking* at a piece of cake!) Regular, moderate exercise can help offset the slowing of metabolism and the increase in the weight set point that comes with it (Tremblay et al., 1999).

The rate at which the body burns energy when a person is resting is called the **basal metabolic rate (BMR)** and is directly tied to the set point. If a person's BMR decreases (as it does in adulthood and with decreased activity levels), that person's weight set point increases if the same number of calories is consumed. **Figure 9.3** shows the changes in BMR of a typical woman and man as age increases from 10 to 80 years. Notice that the BMR decreases more dramatically as the age of the person increases.

The rat on the left has reached a high level of obesity because its ventromedial hypothalamus has been deliberately damaged in the laboratory. The result is a rat that no longer receives signals of being satiated, and so the rat continues to eat and eat and eat.

leptin

a hormone that, when released into the bloodstream, signals the hypothalamus that the body has had enough food and reduces the appetite while increasing the feeling of being full.

weight set point

the particular level of weight that the body tries to maintain.

basal metabolic rate (BMR)

the rate at which the body burns energy when the organism is resting.

Figure 9.3 Average BMR for a Female and Male

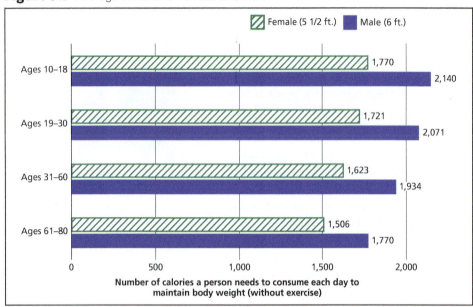

Adolescents typically have a very high BMR and activity level and, therefore, a lower weight set point, meaning they can eat far more than an adult of the same size and not gain weight. But when that adolescent becomes an adult, the BMR begins to decline. Adults should reduce the number of calories they consume and exercise more days than not, but the tendency is to eat more and move less as income levels and job demands increase. Even if the eating habits of the teenage years are simply maintained, excessive weight gain is not far behind. (In some people, the excessive weight gain may be mostly "behind.")

If you would like to calculate your own BMR, there are numerous Web sites that allow a person to enter data such as height, age, weight, and activity level. The BMR is then automatically calculated according to a standard formula. Simply type "basal metabolic rate calculator" into your favorite search engine to find these sites.

SOCIAL COMPONENTS OF HUNGER People often eat when they are not really hungry. There are all sorts of social cues that tell people to eat, such as the convention of eating breakfast, lunch, and dinner at certain times. A large part of that "convention" is actually the result of classical conditioning. See Learning Objective 5.2. The body becomes conditioned to respond with the hunger reflex at certain times of the day; through association with the act of eating, those times of the day have become conditioned stimuli for hunger. Sometimes a person who has just eaten a late breakfast will still "feel" hungry at noon, simply because the clock says it's time to eat. People also respond to the appeal of food. How many times has someone finished a huge meal only to be tempted by that luscious-looking cheesecake on the dessert cart?

Food can also be used in times of stress as a comforting routine, an immediate escape from whatever is unpleasant (Dallman et al., 2003). Rodin (Rodin, 1981, 1985) found that the insulin levels that create hunger may actually increase *before* food is eaten (similar to the way Pavlov's dogs began salivating before they received their food). Like getting hungry at a certain time of day, this physiological phenomenon may also be due to classical conditioning: In the past, eating foods with certain visual and sensory characteristics led to an insulin spike, and this pairing occurred so frequently that now just looking at or smelling the food produces the spike before the food is consumed (Stockhorst et al., 1999). This may explain why some people (who are called "externals" because of their tendency to focus on the external features of food rather than internal hunger) are far more responsive to these external signals—they produce far more insulin in response to the *anticipation* of eating than do nonexternals, or people who are less affected by external cues (Rodin, 1985).

Cultural factors and gender also play a part in determining hunger and eating habits. For example, studies have shown people in the United States are more likely to start eating for emotional reasons, such as depression, while in Japan eating is more likely a result of hunger signals or social demands, and this is particularly true for women in these cultures (Hawks et al., 2003; Levine et al., 2016). Both culture and gender must be taken into account when studying why and under what circumstances people eat.

9.7 Obesity

9.7 Recognize some of the factors that contribute to obesity.

Several maladaptive eating problems, including anorexia nervosa, bulimia nervosa, and binge-eating disorder, are classified as clinical (mental) disorders in the *Diagnostic and Statistical Manual of Mental Disorders, Fifth Edition*, or *DSM-5* (American Psychiatric Association, 2013), which is a listing of disorders and their symptoms used by psychological professionals to make a diagnosis. These disorders are discussed in a later chapter. See Learning Objective 13.11.

In this section, we look at the problem of obesity. Why are some people overweight to the point they are classified as being obese?

Several factors contribute to *obesity*, a condition in which the body weight of a person is 20 percent or more over the ideal body weight for that person's height. A significant factor in obesity is heredity. There appear to be several sets of genes, some on different chromosomes, that influence a person's likelihood of becoming obese (Barsh et al., 2000; Locke et al., 2015; Shungin et al., 2015). Genetic factors also appear to influence both brain structure and cognitive functions. BMI has been associated with differences in cortical thickness between the right and left prefrontal areas (L > R), increased size of the left amygdala, and reduction in areas surrounding the hippocampus on both sides (Vainik et al., 2018). See Learning Objectives 2.7, 2.8. Furthermore, BMI was also negatively correlated with a variety of cognitive tasks, including verbal memory and tests of executive function such as cognitive flexibility and ability to delay gratification (Vainik et al., 2018). Overall, the results support genetics likely predisposing some individuals to have heightened attention and responsivity to food cues, paired with lower ability to effect self-control and delay of gratification (Jansen et al., 2015; Vainik et al., 2018).

If there is a history of obesity in a particular family, each family member has a risk of becoming obese that is double or triple the risk of people who do not have a family history of obesity (Bouchard, 1997). Hormones also play a role, particularly leptin, which plays an important part in controlling appetite. Problems with leptin production or detection can lead to overeating (Friedman & Halaas, 1998), although this may not be the whole story. In a study in which leptin action was blocked in both obese and nonobese mice, there were no differences between the two groups in how much they ate or how much weight they gained, leading the researchers to conclude that impaired leptin activity may not be as important a cause of obesity as previously thought (Ottaway et al., 2015).

Certainly, another obesity factor is overeating. Around the world, as developing countries build stronger economies and their food supplies become stable, the rates of obesity increase dramatically and quickly, particularly among those with less education (Barsh et al., 2000; Kinge et al., 2015). Foods become more varied and enticing* as well, and an increase in variety is associated with an increase in eating beyond the physiological need to eat (Raynor & Epstein, 2001). In industrialized societies, when workers spend more hours in the workplace, there is less time available for preparing meals at home and more incentive to dine out (Chou et al., 2004). When the "dining out" choices include fast food and soft drinks, as is so often the case, obesity rates increase. For example, obesity rates are increasing in the United States, and in 2013–2016, approximately 36.6% of adults aged 20 and over consumed fast food on any given day (Fryar et al., 2018; Hales et al., 2017). The quality of the food we eat may also have an additional impact, with some research indicating that diets high in simple sugars and processed grains lend themselves to increased fat storage even when calories are kept low (Ebbeling et al., 2012).

---

*enticing: attractive, desirable.

In sum, as cultures become more industrialized and follow Western-culture lifestyles, negative aspects of those lifestyles, such as obesity, also increase. Over the last 20 years, rates of obesity in developing countries have tripled. Specifically, this is a trend in countries that have adopted the Western lifestyle of lower exercise rates and overeating—especially those foods that are cheap but high in fat and calories. In 2016, approximately 18 percent of children aged 5–19 worldwide were overweight, with rates ranging from 6.8 percent in India to 64.9 percent in Naru, the world's smallest republic; obesity rates ranged from 1 percent in Burkina Faso to 33.2 percent in Naru (World Health Organization, 2017).

Stress also contributes to obesity. One study found that female children of military personnel, for example, seem to be at a higher risk for eating disorders, including obesity, a risk that may be associated with higher rates of depression (Schvey et al., 2015). Related to stress is how much sleep we get, and sleep disturbances are also a factor in weight gain (Roane et al., 2015). See Chapter Four: *APA Goal 2: Scientific Inquiry and Critical Thinking: Weight Gain and Sleep.*

As mentioned earlier, metabolism slows down as people age. Aside from not changing the eating habits of their youth and lowering their intake, as they earn more income, people also often increase the amount of food they consume, thereby assuring a weight gain that may lead to obesity. The United States has one of the highest rates of obesity in the world: In 2015–2016, approximately 39.6 percent of adults aged 20 and over and 18.5 percent of youth aged 2–19 years were classified as obese (Hales et al., 2017; NCD Risk Factor Collaboration, 2017). Approximately only one half of the adult population in the United States engages in physical activity consistent with the most recent recommendations for adults, 150 to 300 minutes of moderate-to-vigorous physical activity a week (2018 Physical Activity Guidelines Advisory Committee, 2018). This report also indicates that 30 percent of the United States adult population does not engage in any moderate-to-vigorous activity, suggesting even modest increases in regular physical activity can prove beneficial. For many individuals, establishing healthier eating or exercise behaviors is key. And while behavioral change can be difficult, it is not always impossible. For some possible ways to manage your own eating and exercise behavior, review the strategies listed below.

- Pay attention to your food, especially to low-calorie or healthier food options, and when eating, just eat; turn the TV, tablet, and phone off (see Learning Objective 3.17).
- Be mindful of emotional triggers or eating when stressed or bored. Ask yourself if you are really hungry and perhaps wait a while (set a timer for 15–20 minutes) or find another way to cope with the emotions.
- Focus on food quality and eat real food; avoid processed or over-processed grains, starches, and concentrated sugars (white bread, white potatoes, table sugar, soft drinks).
- Be careful of sweet or salty foods and snacks.
- Stay hydrated; make sure you are getting enough water throughout the day through both beverages and food items.
- Exercise on a regular basis, and more days out of the week than not. Go for a walk, work out in a gym, or participate in sports with friends or family.
- Strive to reduce sedentary behavior and increase moderate-intensity physical activity; even small bouts of exercise add up and have cumulative positive health benefits.
- If you are already engaging in regular and substantial amounts of moderate or vigorous physical activity, you may benefit by doing more.

Concept Map L.O. 9.6, 9.7

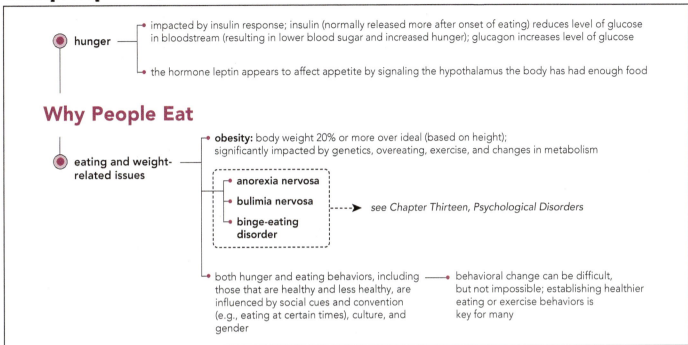

Practice Quiz — How much do you remember?

Pick the best answer.

1. Damage to the _____ in rats can cause them to starve to death, while damage to the _____ will cause them to eat and eat and eat.
   a. pancreas, stomach
   b. cingulate gyrus, corpus callosum
   c. ventromedial hypothalamus, lateral hypothalamus
   d. liver, kidneys
   e. lateral hypothalamus, ventromedial hypothalamus

2. In a study examining the influence of culture on individual eating habits, researchers found that women from the United States were more likely to eat in response to _____, whereas women from Japan were more likely to eat in response to _____.
   a. the smell of fresh food, the sight of fresh food.
   b. emotional cues, hunger signals or social demands
   c. being instructed that it was "mealtime," being told "you will not have another chance to eat today"
   d. stress, depression
   e. hunger signals or social demands, emotional cues

3. Hunter eats a late breakfast at 10:00 a.m., but finds he is hungry at 11:30 a.m., when he typically eats lunch. What best explains his hunger pains only 90 minutes after eating breakfast?
   a. classical conditioning
   b. heredity
   c. circadian cycles
   d. social pressure
   e. self-actualization

4. In cultures in which Western lifestyles of eating and exercising have been adopted, obesity rates have _____ over the last 20 years.
   a. doubled
   b. tripled
   c. remained relatively stable
   d. decreased slightly
   e. decreased significantly

9.8–9.10 Emotion

> What part does the way we feel about things play in all of our daily activities—what exactly causes feelings?

This chapter began with an overview of the motives that drive human behavior. But people do more than just behave—they experience feelings during every human action. Human beings are full of feelings, or emotions, and although emotions may be internal processes, there are outward physical signs of what people are feeling. This section of the

emotion

the "feeling" aspect of consciousness, characterized by a certain physical arousal, a certain behavior that reveals the emotion to the outside world, and an inner awareness of feelings.

chapter explores the world of human emotions and how those emotions are connected to both thinking and actions.

9.8 The Three Elements of Emotion

9.8 Describe the three elements of emotion.

The Latin root word *mot*, meaning "to move," is the source of both of the words we use in this chapter over and over again—*motive* and *emotion*. **Emotion** can be defined as the "feeling" aspect of consciousness, characterized by three elements: a certain physical arousal, a certain behavior that reveals the feeling to the outside world, and an inner awareness of the feeling.

THE PHYSIOLOGY OF EMOTION Physically, when a person experiences an emotion, an arousal is created by the sympathetic nervous system. See Learning Objective 2.12. The heart rate increases, breathing becomes more rapid, the pupils dilate, and the mouth may become dry. Think about the last time you were angry and then about the last time you were frightened. Weren't the physical symptoms pretty similar? Although facial expressions do differ among various emotional responses (Ekman, 1980; Ekman et al., 1969; Ekman & Friesen, 1978), emotions are difficult to distinguish from one another on the basis of physiological reactions alone. However, in the laboratory using devices to measure the heart rate, blood pressure, and skin temperature, researchers have found that different emotions may be associated with different physiological reactions: Sadness, anger, and fear are associated with greater increases in heart rate than is disgust; higher increases in skin conductance occur during disgust as compared to happiness; and anger is more often associated with vascular measures, such as higher diastolic blood pressure, as compared to fear (Larsen et al., 2008; Levenson, 1992; Levenson et al., 1992).

The polygraph test was originally designed as a kind of "lie detector" test in the early 1900s. The idea was that lying would produce different physiological reactions from telling the truth (Bell & Grubin, 2010; Iacono, 2001). This assumption has proven to be false: There is no specific, unique physiological reaction associated with lying versus telling the truth. There have been improvements added to the original polygraph test such as the use of questions about knowledge that only the police, the victim, and the suspect should know (Concealed Information Test, or CIT), but there is still a great deal of controversy over the validity of the results (Ben-Shakhar et al., 2015; Palmatier & Rovner, 2015; Vrij, 2015). While it may be a useful tool to convince suspects to confess to their crimes, it really only detects the physiological correlates of emotion in general, not lying in specific, and is not admissible as evidence of guilt or innocence in a courtroom in the United States.

Which parts of the brain are involved in various aspects of emotion? As discussed in Chapter Two, the *amygdala* is associated with fear-related emotions and memories, but it is also involved in pleasure-seeking behaviors (Fernando et al., 2013; Kim et al., 2017, Ritchey et al., 2011) and in the facial expressions of human emotions (Morris et al., 1998).

When portions of the amygdala are damaged in rats, the animals cannot be classically conditioned to fear new objects—they apparently cannot remember to be afraid (R. J. Davidson et al., 2000; Fanselow & Gale, 2003). In humans, damage to the amygdala has been associated with similar effects (LaBar et al., 1995) and with impairment of the ability to determine emotions from looking at the facial expressions of others (Adolphs & Tranel, 2003).

A lot of what we know about the amygdala's role in emotion comes from the work of Dr. Joseph LeDoux and his many colleagues and students. The amygdala is a complex structure with many different nuclei and subdivisions, whose roles

AP 7.F Compare and contrast major theories of emotion.

have been investigated primarily through studies of fear conditioning (LeDoux & Phelps, 2008). Fear conditioning has been very helpful in relating behaviors to brain function because it results in stereotypical autonomic and behavioral responses. It is basically a classical conditioning procedure in which an auditory stimulus (conditioned stimulus) is paired with foot shock (unconditioned stimulus) to elicit autonomic and behavioral conditioned responses (LeDoux, 1996; LeDoux & Phelps, 2008).

LeDoux's work has provided many insights into the brain's processing of emotional information and the role of the amygdala. Emotional stimuli travel to the amygdala by both a fast, crude "low road" (subcortical) and a slower but more involved cortical "high road" (LeDoux, 1996, 2007; LeDoux & Phelps, 2008) (see **Figure 9.4**). The direct route allows for quick responses to stimuli that are possibly dangerous, sometimes before we actually know what the stimuli are, but with the awareness provided by the indirect cortical route (specifically, processing by the prefrontal cortex), we can override the direct route and take control of our emotional responses (LeDoux, 1996; LeDoux & Phelps, 2008; Öhman, 2008).

LeDoux's work also provides a mechanism for understanding psychological disorders related to anxiety or fear. See Learning Objective 13.6. It is possible that the direct route may be the primary processing pathway for individuals with anxiety disorders and the indirect, cortical pathway is not able to override the processing initiated by the direct route. This would result in difficulty or inability to control our anxieties or the inability to extinguish fears we've already acquired (LeDoux, 1996; LeDoux & Phelps, 2008).

Besides the amygdala, other subcortical and cortical areas of the brain are involved in the processing of emotional information (Frank et al., 2014; Treadway et al., 2014). Research suggests that emotions may work differently depending on which side of the

Figure 9.4 The "Low Road" and "High Road"

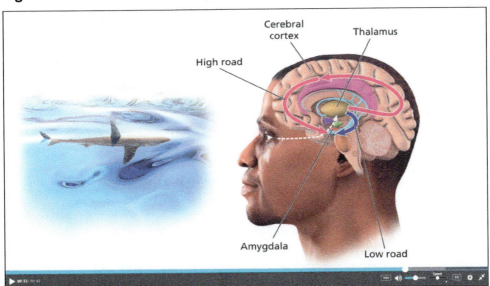

👁 Watch the Video at MyLab Psychology

When we are exposed to an emotion-provoking stimulus (such as a shark), the neural signals travel by two pathways to the amygdala. The "low road" is the pathway underneath the cortex and is a faster, simpler path, allowing for quick responses to the stimulus, sometimes before we are consciously aware of the nature of the stimulus. The "high road" uses cortical pathways and is slower and more complex, but it allows us to recognize the threat and, when needed, take more conscious control of our emotional responses. In this particular example, the low road shouts, "Danger!" and we react before the high road says, "It's a shark!"

brain is involved. One area of investigation has been the frontal lobes. Researchers have found that positive emotions are associated with the left frontal lobe of the brain, whereas negative feelings such as sadness, anxiety, and depression seem to be a function of the right frontal lobe (R. J. Davidson, 2003; Garland et al., 2015; Geschwind & Iacoboni, 2007; Heilman, 2002). In studies in which the electrical activity of the brain has been tracked using an electroencephalograph (see Learning Objective 2.5), left frontal lobe activation has been associated with pleasant emotions, while right frontal lobe activity has been associated with negative emotional states (R. J. Davidson, 2003). Furthermore, increased left frontal lobe activity has been found in individuals trained in meditation, and for the participants in this study, greater left frontal lobe activity was accompanied by a reduction in their anxiety as well as a boost in their immune system (Garland et al., 2015; R. J. Davidson et al., 2003).

The ability to interpret the facial expressions of others as a particular emotion also seems to be a function of one side of the brain more than the other. Researchers have found that when people are asked to identify the emotion on another person's face, the right hemisphere is more active than the left, particularly in women (Voyer & Rodgers, 2002). This difference begins weakly in childhood but increases in adulthood, with children being less able to identify negative emotions as well as they can positive emotions when compared to adults (Barth & Boles, 1999; Lane et al., 1995). This finding is consistent with early research that assigns the recognition of faces to the right hemisphere (Berent, 1977; Ellis, 1983).

Other types of emotional processing involve a variety of other brain areas. Have you ever been told to control your emotions? Different brain areas take primary roles based on the different ways you try to control your emotions, but there is a degree of overlap across several of the strategies. For example, some common strategies for regulating one's emotions include distraction, reappraisal, and controlling the influence of emotions on decision making. All three of these strategies take advantage of the lateral prefrontal cortex and anterior cingulate cortex and, as you might expect from the discussion before, the amygdala also comes into play (J. S. Beer, 2009).

However, distraction appears to be supported by activity in the anterior cingulate cortex, and reappraisal is supported by activity in the lateral orbitofrontal cortex; and both are accompanied by lower activity in the amygdala (J. S. Beer, 2009). Furthermore, distraction and reappraisal may engage more brain areas in general as compared to spontaneous control of emotions in decision making. Generally, brain areas associated with emotional control are the same brain areas responsible for control of nonemotional information (J. S. Beer, 2009; Buhle et al., 2014; Etkin et al., 2011).

AP 7.G Describe how cultural influences shape emotional expression, including variations in body language.

AP 2.A Discuss psychology's abiding interest in how heredity, environment, and evolution work together to shape behavior.

THE BEHAVIOR OF EMOTION: EMOTIONAL EXPRESSION How do people behave when in the grip of an emotion? There are facial expressions, body movements, and actions that indicate to others how a person feels. Frowns, smiles, and sad expressions combine with hand gestures, the turning of one's body, and spoken words to produce an understanding of emotion. People fight, run, kiss, and yell, along with countless other actions stemming from the emotions they feel.

Facial expressions can vary across different cultures, although some aspects of facial expression seem to be universal. (See **Figure 9.5** for some examples of universal facial expressions.) Charles Darwin (1898) was one of the first to theorize that emotions were a product of evolution and, therefore, universal—all human beings, no matter what their culture, would show the same facial expression because the facial muscles evolved to communicate specific information to onlookers. For example, an angry face would signal to onlookers that they should act submissively or expect a fight. Although Darwin's ideas were not in line with the behaviorist movement of the early and middle twentieth century, which promoted environment rather than heredity as the cause of behavior, other researchers have since found evidence that there is a universal nature to at least seven basic emotions, giving more support to the evolutionary perspective within psychology (Ekman, 1973; Ekman & Friesen, 1969, 1971). See Learning Objective 1.3. Even children who are blind from birth can produce the appropriate facial expressions for any given situation without ever having witnessed those expressions on others, which strongly supports the idea that emotional expressions have their basis in biology rather than in learning (Charlesworth & Kreutzer, 1973; Fulcher, 1942).

Figure 9.5 Facial Expressions of Emotions

Facial expressions appear to be universal. For example, these faces are consistently interpreted as showing (a) anger, (b) fear, (c) disgust, (d) happiness, (e) surprise, and (f) sadness by people of various cultures from all over the world. Although the situations that cause these emotions may differ from culture to culture, the expression of particular emotions remains strikingly the same.

Source: (a) Steve Photography/Shutterstock; (b) Denis Pepin/Shutterstock; (c) Platslee/Shutterstock; (d) Blend Images/Shutterstock; (e) Viorel Sima/Shutterstock; (f) Dundanim/Shutterstock.

In their research, Ekman and Friesen found that people of many different cultures (including Japanese, European, American, and the Fore tribe of New Guinea) can consistently recognize at least seven facial expressions: anger, fear, disgust, happiness, surprise, sadness, and contempt (Ekman & Friesen, 1969, 1971). Although the emotions and the related facial expressions appear to be universal, exactly when, where, and how an emotion is expressed may be determined by the culture. **Display rules** that can vary from culture to culture (Ekman, 1973; Ekman & Friesen, 1969) are learned ways of controlling displays of emotion in social settings. For example, Japanese people have strict social rules about showing emotion in public situations—they simply do not show emotion, remaining cool, calm, and collected, at least on the *outside*. But if in a more private situation, as a parent scolding a child within the home, the adult's facial expression would easily be recognized as "angry" by people of any culture. The emotion is universal and the way it is expressed on the face is universal, but whether it is expressed or displayed depends on the learned cultural rules for displaying emotion.

Display rules are different between cultures that are *individualistic* (placing the importance of the individual above the social group) and those that are *collectivistic* (placing

AP 2.B Identify key research contributions of scientists in the area of heredity and environment.

display rules

learned ways of controlling displays of emotion in social settings.

How might the display rules for this family differ if they were in a public place rather than at home?

the importance of the social group above that of the individual). Whereas the culture of the United States is individualistic, for example, the culture of Japan is collectivistic. At least part of the difference between the two types of display rules may be due to these cultural differences (Edelmann & Iwawaki, 1987; Hofstede, 1980; Hofstede et al., 2002). See Learning Objective 12.15.

Display rules are also different for males and females. Researchers looking at the display rules of boys and girls found that boys are reluctant to talk about feelings in a social setting, whereas girls are expected and encouraged to do so (Polce-Lynch et al., 1998). With adults, researchers looking at the expression of anger in the workplace found that women are generally less willing than men to express negative emotions, although factors such as status complicate the findings somewhat (Domagalski & Steelman, 2007). When adults do express anger, context and sex also have an impact on perceived abilities or effectiveness. In a study of emotional expression in attorneys, when both male and female attorneys gave closing arguments, either in a neutral or angry tone, both undergraduate and community samples rated male attorneys as more effective than female attorneys (Salerno et al., 2018).

Crying is also an emotional behavior—we cry for many different reasons such as being sad, grieving, angry, or even happy. While most of us don't like to cry, many people seem to think that "a good cry" can make them feel better. Researchers in one study examined the effects of crying on mood both immediately after participants watched two emotionally charged films and after a delay (Gračanin et al., 2015). They found a fascinating difference between the people who cried and those who did not: While the mood of those who did not cry was not affected immediately, those who cried experienced a slight dip in mood immediately but an increase in positive mood after a delay. This may explain why many people claim to feel "better" after crying.

SUBJECTIVE EXPERIENCE: LABELING EMOTION The third element of emotion is interpreting the subjective feeling by giving it a label: anger, fear, disgust, happiness, sadness, shame, interest, and so on. Another way of labeling this element is to call it the "cognitive element," because the labeling process is a matter of retrieving memories of previous similar experiences, perceiving the context of the emotion, and coming up with a solution—a label.

The label a person applies to a subjective feeling is at least in part a learned response influenced by their language and culture. Such labels may differ in people of different cultural backgrounds. For example, researchers in one study (J. L. Tsai et al., 2004) found that Chinese Americans who were still firmly rooted in their original Chinese culture were far more likely to use labels to describe their emotions that referred to bodily sensations (such as "dizzy") or social relationships (such as "friendship") than were more "Americanized" Chinese Americans and European Americans, who tended to use more directly emotional words (such as "liking" or "love").

In another study, even the subjective feeling of happiness showed cultural differences (Kitayama & Markus, 1994). In this study, Japanese students and students from the United States were found to associate a general positive emotional state with entirely different circumstances. In the case of the Japanese students, the positive state was more associated with friendly or socially engaged feelings. The students from the United States associated their positive emotional state more with feelings that were socially disengaged, such as pride. This finding is a further reflection of the differences between collectivistic and individualistic cultures. A major goal for psychologists engaged in cross-cultural research in emotions is to attempt to understand the meaning of other people's mental and emotional states without interpreting them incorrectly, or misleadingly, in the language or mindset of the researchers (Shweder et al., 2008).

9.9 Early Theories of Emotion

9.9 Distinguish among the common-sense, James-Lange, Cannon-Bard, and facial feedback theories of emotion.

> 💬 So which of the three elements is the most important?

In the early days of psychology, it was assumed that feeling a particular emotion led first to a physical reaction and then to a behavioral one. According to this viewpoint—we'll call it *the common-sense theory* of emotion—seeing a snarling dog in one's path causes the feeling of fear, which stimulates the body to arousal, followed by the behavioral act of running; that is, people are aroused because they are afraid (see **Figure 9.6**).

Figure 9.6 Common-Sense Theory of Emotion

	Stimulus	First response	Second response
Common sense theory "I'm shaking because I'm afraid."	Snarling dog	Conscious fear (FEAR)	ANS arousal

In the common-sense theory of emotion, a stimulus (snarling dog) leads to an emotion of fear, which then leads to bodily arousal (in this case, indicated by shaking) through the autonomic nervous system (ANS).

JAMES-LANGE THEORY OF EMOTION William James (1884, 1890, 1894), who was also the founder of the functionalist perspective in the early history of psychology, see Learning Objective 1.1, disagreed with the common-sense viewpoint. He believed that the order of the components of emotions was quite different. At nearly the same time, a physiologist and psychologist in Denmark, Carl Lange (1885), came up with an explanation of emotion so similar to that of James that the two names are used together to refer to the theory—the **James-Lange theory of emotion** (see **Figure 9.7**).

Figure 9.7 James-Lange Theory of Emotion

	Stimulus	First response	Second response
James-Lange theory "I'm afraid because I'm shaking."	Snarling dog	ANS arousal, changes in body	Conscious fear (FEAR)

In the James-Lange theory of emotion, a stimulus leads to bodily arousal first, which is then interpreted as an emotion.

In this theory, a stimulus of some sort (for example, the large snarling dog) produces a physiological reaction. This reaction, which is the arousal of the "fight-or-flight" sympathetic nervous system (wanting to run), produces bodily sensations such as increased heart rate, dry mouth, and rapid breathing. James and Lange believed that the physical arousal led to the labeling of the emotion (fear). Simply put, "I am afraid because I am aroused," "I am embarrassed because my face is red," "I am nervous because my stomach is fluttering," and "I am in love because my heart rate increases when I look at her (or him)."

AP 7.F Compare and contrast major theories of emotion.

AP 7.D Identify contributions of key researchers in the psychological field of motivation and emotion.

James-Lange theory of emotion
theory in which a physiological reaction leads to the labeling of an emotion.

What about people who have spinal cord injuries that prevent the sympathetic nervous system from functioning? Although James-Lange would predict that these people should show decreased emotion because the arousal that causes emotion is no longer there, this does not in fact happen. Several studies of people with spinal cord injuries report that these people are capable of experiencing the same emotions after their injury as before, sometimes even more intensely (Bermond et al., 1991; Chwalisz et al., 1988).

CANNON-BARD THEORY OF EMOTION Physiologists Walter Cannon (1927) and Philip Bard (1934) theorized that the emotion and the physiological arousal occur more or less at the same time. Cannon, an expert in sympathetic arousal mechanisms, did not feel that the physical changes caused by various emotions were distinct enough to allow them to be perceived as different emotions. Bard expanded on this idea by stating that the sensory information that comes into the brain is sent simultaneously (by the thalamus) to both the cortex and the organs of the sympathetic nervous system. The fear and the bodily reactions are, therefore, experienced at the same time—not one after the other. "I'm afraid and running and aroused!" (see **Figure 9.8**).

Figure 9.8 Cannon-Bard Theory of Emotion

| Stimulus | First response | Second response |

Cannon-Bard theory
"I'm shaking and feeling afraid at the same time."

Snarling dog — Subcortical brain activity — ANS arousal, changes in body / FEAR / Conscious fear

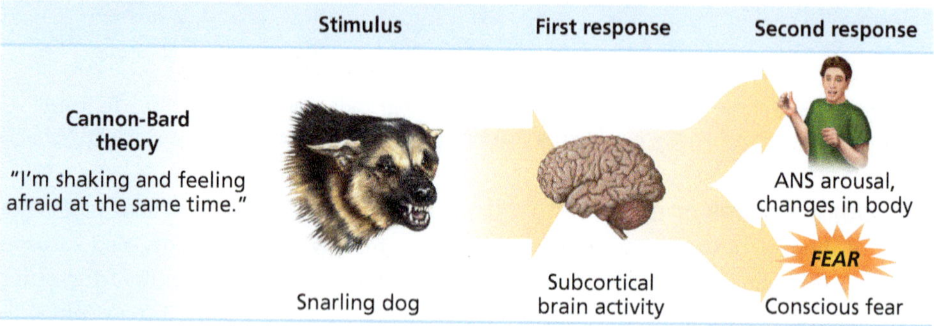

In the Cannon-Bard theory of emotion, a stimulus leads to activity in the brain, which then sends signals to arouse the body and interpret the emotion at the same time.

Cannon-Bard theory of emotion

theory in which the physiological reaction and the emotion are assumed to occur at the same time.

facial feedback hypothesis

theory of emotion that assumes that facial expressions provide feedback to the brain concerning the emotion being expressed, which in turn causes and intensifies the emotion.

This theory, known as the **Cannon-Bard theory of emotion**, also had its critics. Karl Lashley (1938) stated that the thalamus would have to be pretty sophisticated to make sense of all the possible human emotions and relay them to the proper areas of the cortex and body. It would seem that other areas of the brain must be involved in processing emotional reactions. The studies of people with spinal cord injuries, which appear to suggest that emotions can be experienced without feedback from the sympathetic organs to the cortex and were cited as a criticism of the James-Lange theory, seem at first to support the Cannon-Bard version of emotions: People do not need feedback from those organs to experience emotion. However, there is an alternate pathway that does provide feedback from these organs to the cortex; this is the *vagus nerve*, one of the cranial nerves (LeDoux, 1994). The existence of this feedback pathway makes the case for Cannon-Bard a little less convincing.

AP 2.B Identify key research contributions of scientists in the area of heredity and environment.

THE FACIAL FEEDBACK HYPOTHESIS: SMILE, YOU'LL FEEL BETTER In his 1898 book *The Expression of the Emotions in Man and Animals*, Charles Darwin stated that facial expressions evolved as a way of communicating intentions, such as threat or fear, and that these expressions are universal within a species rather than specific to a culture. He also believed (as in the James-Lange theory) that when such emotions are expressed freely on the face, the emotion itself intensifies—meaning that the more one smiles, the happier one feels.

Psychologists proposed a theory of emotion that was consistent with much of Darwin's original thinking. Called the **facial feedback hypothesis**, this explanation assumes that facial expressions provide feedback to the brain concerning the emotion being expressed, which in turn not only intensifies the emotion but also actually *causes* the emotion (Buck, 1980; Ekman, 1980; Ekman & Friesen, 1978; Keillor et al., 2002) (see **Figure 9.9**).

Figure 9.9 Facial Feedback Theory of Emotion

In the facial feedback theory of emotion, a stimulus such as this snarling dog causes arousal and a facial expression. The facial expression then provides feedback to the brain about the emotion. The brain then interprets the emotion and may also intensify it.

The facial feedback hypothesis assumes that changing your own facial expression can change the way you feel. Smiling makes people feel happy, and frowning makes people feel sad. This effect seems to have an impact on the people around us as well. Is it hard for you to stay in a bad mood when the people around you are smiling and laughing?

💬 Does that mean that I don't smile because I'm happy—I'm happy because I smile?

As the old song goes, "put on a happy face" and yes, you'll feel happier, according to the facial feedback hypothesis. Some studies cast some doubt on the validity of this hypothesis, however. If the facial feedback hypothesis is correct, then people who have facial paralysis on both sides of the face should be unable to experience emotions in a normal way. But a case study conducted on just such a person revealed that although she was unable to express emotions on her paralyzed face, she could respond emotionally to slides meant to stimulate emotional reactions, just as anyone else would (Keillor et al., 2002). A meta-analysis of numerous studies attempting to replicate an earlier experiment supporting this hypothesis failed to find similar results (Wagenmakers et al., 2016). Clearly, the question of how much the actual facial expression determines the emotional experience has yet to be fully answered.

cognitive arousal theory (two-factor theory)
theory of emotion in which both the physical arousal and the labeling of that arousal based on cues from the environment must occur before the emotion is experienced.

9.10 Cognitive Theories of Emotion

9.10 Identify the key elements in the cognitive arousal and cognitive-mediational theories of emotion.

AP 7.F Compare and contrast major theories of emotion.

The early theories talked about the emotion and the physical reaction, but what about the mental interpretation of those components?

COGNITIVE AROUSAL THEORY In their **cognitive arousal theory (two-factor theory)**, Schachter and Singer (1962) proposed that two things have to happen before emotion occurs: the physical arousal and a labeling of the arousal based on cues from the surrounding environment. These two things happen at the same time, resulting in the labeling of the emotion (see **Figure 9.10**).

AP 7.D Identify contributions of key researchers in the psychological field of motivation and emotion.

For example, if a person comes across a snarling dog while taking a walk, the physical arousal (heart racing, eyes opening wide) is accompanied by the thought (cognition) that this must be fear. Then and only then will the person experience the fear emotion. In other words, "I am aroused in the presence of a scary dog; therefore, I must be afraid." Evidence for this theory was found in what is now a classic experiment, described in the accompanying *Classic Studies in Psychology*.

Figure 9.10 Schachter-Singer Cognitive Arousal Theory of Emotion

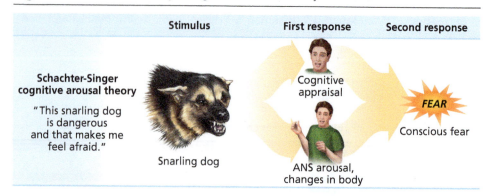

Schachter and Singer's cognitive arousal theory is similar to the James-Lange theory but adds the element of cognitive labeling of the arousal. In this theory, a stimulus leads to both bodily arousal and the labeling of that arousal (based on the surrounding context), which leads to the experience and labeling of the emotional reaction.

Classic Studies in Psychology
The Angry/Happy Man

In 1962, Stanley Schachter and Jerome Singer designed an experiment to test their theory that emotions are determined by an interaction between the physiological state of arousal and the label, or cognitive interpretation, that a person places on the arousal. Male student volunteers were told that they were going to answer a questionnaire about their reactions to a new vitamin called Suproxin. In reality, they were all injected with a drug called epinephrine, which causes physical arousal in the form of increased heart rate, rapid breathing, and a reddened face—all responses that happen during a strong emotional reaction.

Each student then participated in one of two conditions. In one condition, a confederate* posing as one of the participants started complaining about the experimenter, tearing up his questionnaire and storming out. In the other condition, there was one man who acted more like he was very happy, almost giddy, and playing with some of the objects in the room. The "angry" man and the "happy" man in both conditions deliberately behaved in the two different ways as part of the experiment.

After both conditions had played out, participants in each of the two conditions were asked to describe their own emotions. The participants who had been exposed to the "angry" man interpreted their arousal symptoms as anger, whereas those exposed to the "happy" man interpreted their arousal as happiness. In all cases, the actual cause of arousal was the epinephrine and the physical symptoms of arousal were identical. The only difference between the two groups of participants was their exposure to the two different contexts. Schachter and Singer's theory would have predicted exactly these results: Physiological arousal has to be interpreted cognitively before it is experienced as a specific emotion.

Although this classic experiment stimulated a lot of research, much of that research has failed to find much support for the cognitive arousal theory of emotion (Reisenzein, 1983, 1994). But this theory drew attention to the important role that cognition plays in determining emotions. The role of cognition in emotion has been revisited in some more modern theories of emotion, as you will see in the remainder of the chapter.

Questions for Further Discussion

1. According to Schachter and Singer's theory, for your first date with a person, should you choose a happy movie or a sad one?

---

*confederate: someone who is cooperating with another person on some task.

2. In this experiment, what was the independent variable manipulated by the experimenters? What was the dependent variable?

3. This experiment used deception, as the participants were not told the true nature of the injection they received. What kind of ethical problems might have arisen from this deception? What problems would the experimenters have had in getting this study approved by an ethics committee today?

LAZARUS AND THE COGNITIVE-MEDIATIONAL THEORY OF EMOTION As mentioned in the *Classic Studies in Psychology* section, Schachter and Singer's (1962) study stressed the importance of cognition, or thinking, in the determination of emotions. One of the more modern versions of cognitive emotion theories is Lazarus's **cognitive-mediational theory** of emotion (Lazarus, 1991). In this theory, the most important aspect of any emotional experience is how the person interprets, or appraises, the stimulus that causes the emotional reaction. To *mediate* means to "come between," and in this theory, the cognitive appraisal mediates by coming between the stimulus and the emotional response to that stimulus.

For example, remember the person who encountered a snarling dog while walking through the neighborhood? According to Lazarus, the appraisal of the situation would come *before* both the physical arousal and the experience of emotion. If the dog is behind a sturdy fence, the appraisal would be something like "no threat." The most likely emotion would be annoyance, and the physical arousal would be minimal. But if the dog is not confined, the appraisal would more likely be "danger—threatening animal!" which would be followed by an increase in arousal and the emotional experience of fear. In other words, it's the *interpretation* of the arousal that results in the emotion of fear, not the labeling as in the Schachter-Singer model, and the interpretation comes first (see **Figure 9.11**).

Figure 9.11 Lazarus's Cognitive-Mediational Theory of Emotion

	Stimulus	First response	Second response
Lazarus's cognitive-mediational theory "The snarling dog is dangerous and therefore I should feel afraid."		Appraisal of threat → FEAR	Bodily response

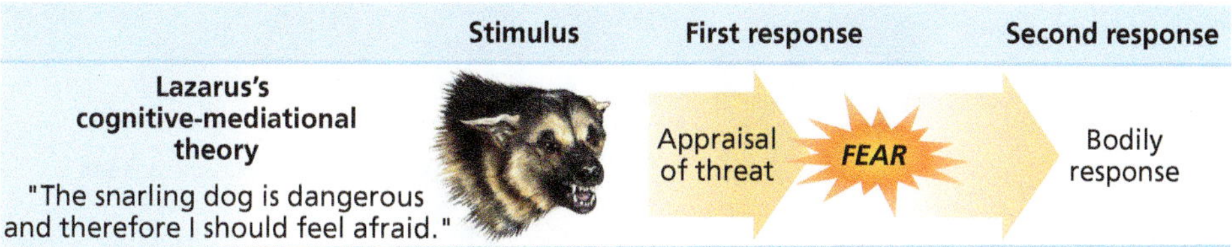

In Lazarus's cognitive-mediational theory of emotion, a stimulus causes an immediate appraisal (e.g., "The dog is snarling and not behind a fence, so this is dangerous."). The cognitive appraisal results in an emotional response, which is then followed by the appropriate bodily response.

Not everyone agrees with this theory, of course. Some researchers believe that emotional reactions to situations are so fast that they are almost instantaneous, which would leave little time for a cognitive appraisal to occur first (Zajonc, 1998). Others (Kihlstrom et al., 2000) have found that the human brain can respond to a physical threat before conscious thought enters the picture. And as addressed earlier, the amygdala can prompt emotional reactions before we are consciously aware of what we are responding to (LeDoux, 1996, 2007; LeDoux & Phelps, 2008).

💬 Which theory is right?

Human emotions are so incredibly complex that it might not be out of place to say that all of the theories are correct to at least some degree. In certain situations, the cognitive appraisal might have time to mediate the emotion that is experienced (such as falling in love), whereas in other situations, the need to act first and to think and feel later is more important (see **Figure 9.12**).

cognitive-mediational theory
theory of emotion in which a stimulus must be interpreted (appraised) by a person in order to result in a physical response and an emotional reaction.

Figure 9.12 Comparison of Theories of Emotion

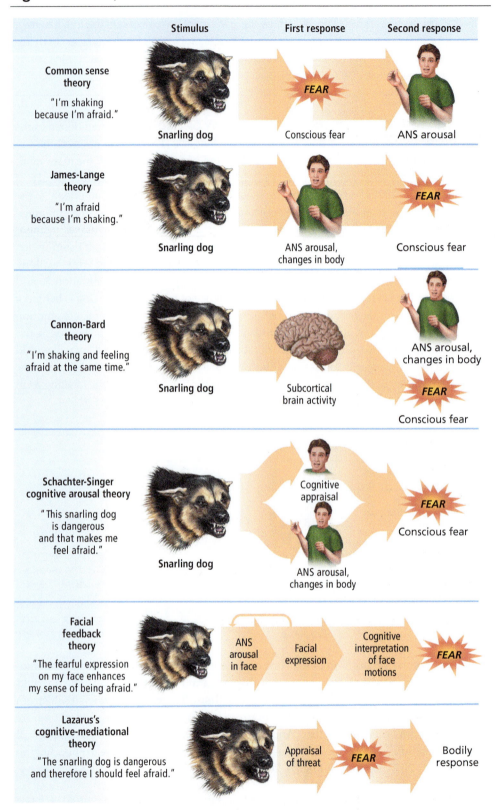

These figures represent the six different theories of emotion as discussed in the text.

THINKING CRITICALLY 9.3

Which of these theories of emotion do you feel is most correct? Why?

Concept Map L.O. 9.8, 9.9, 9.10

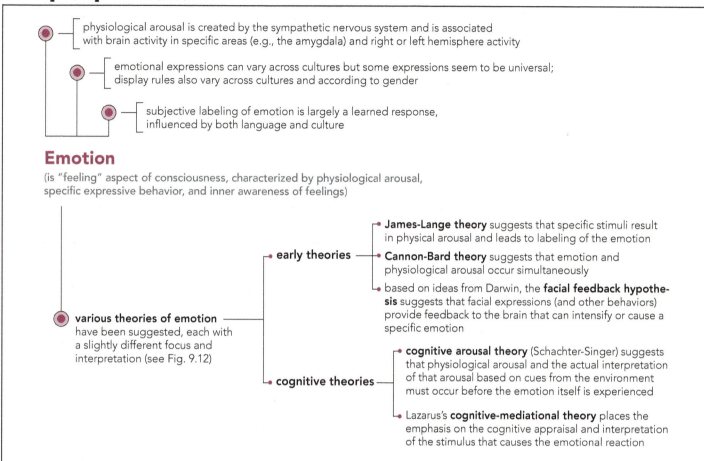

Practice Quiz   How much do you remember?

Pick the best answer.

1. Which of the following is NOT an element of emotion?
   a. physical arousal
   b. inner awareness
   c. behavioral reaction
   d. subjective experience
   e. objective experience

2. The phrase "I'm embarrassed because my face is red" is best explained by which theory of emotion?
   a. Cannon-Bard
   b. James-Lange
   c. cognitive-mediational theory
   d. common-sense theory of emotion
   e. Schachter-Singer

3. "I believe that emotions and physiological arousal tend to happen simultaneously." Which theorist would be responsible for making such a statement?
   a. Charles Darwin or Paul Ekman
   b. Stanley Schachter or Jerome Singer
   c. Walter Cannon or Philip Bard
   d. Sigmund Freud or Erik Erikson
   e. William James or Carl Lange

4. One day at school, someone collides with you in the hall and knocks you down, causing you to be angry. However, when playing football with friends, if you get knocked down, you do not express anger. What theory best explains how we label each situation and choose the appropriate emotion to show?
   a. facial feedback
   b. common sense
   c. James-Lange
   d. Cannon-Bard
   e. Schachter-Singer

5. In Schachter and Singer's classic study, participants who received epinephrine and were in the company of the "angry" research confederate interpreted their physiological arousal as _____, whereas those who were exposed to the "happy" confederate interpreted their arousal as _____.
   a. anger, happiness
   b. happiness, happiness
   c. anger, anger
   d. fear, suspicion
   e. happiness, anger

6. Sydney smiles wherever she goes. She smiles a lot in the classroom, which in turn prompts her fellow students to smile, making them feel happier too. This effect is best explained by which of the following theories of emotion?
   a. common sense
   b. facial feedback
   c. Schachter-Singer
   d. James-Lange
   e. cognitive-mediational

Applying Psychology to Everyday Life
What Is Holding You Back from Keeping Track?

9.11 Identify possible barriers, and benefits, to implementing a personal system to manage your time and tasks.

Now that we have discussed a variety of ways in which behavior gets initiated or maintained, what can you do to make sure you complete the tasks you need to finish or address the commitments you've made? As David Allen, the creator of the *Getting Things Done* approach stresses, "Your mind is for having ideas, not holding them" (Allen, 2018). If motivation is not enough to help you get things accomplished, what else can you do to ensure that you do what needs to be done? There are a variety of systems available to help you manage your time, tasks, and commitments. See Learning Objective PIA.2. If you have been avoiding implementing a time- or task-management system, what is holding you back? Watch the following video as students share the negative consequences of not using a task- or time-management system as well as some benefits they have experienced since implementing one.

Applying Psychology to Everyday Life What Is Holding You Back from Keeping Track?

Watch the Video at MyLab Psychology

After watching the video, answer the following questions:

1. Students in the video highlighted several benefits of effective time and task management. What were two of them?
2. Several of the students in the video shared the negative consequences of not effectively managing their time or tasks related to schoolwork. What are some other areas of your life in which ineffective time or task management can have negative outcomes, and what are the negative outcomes that could occur?

Chapter Summary

Understanding Motivation

9.1 Define motivation, and distinguish between intrinsic motivation and extrinsic motivation.

- Motivation is the process by which activities are started, directed, and sustained so that physical and psychological needs are fulfilled.
- Intrinsic motivation occurs when people act because the act itself is satisfying or rewarding, whereas extrinsic motivation occurs when people receive an external reward (such as money) for the act.

9.2 Identify the key elements of the early instinct and drive-reduction approaches to motivation.

- Instinct approaches proposed that some human actions may be motivated by instincts, which are innate patterns of behavior found in both people and animals.
- Drive-reduction approaches state that when an organism has a need (such as hunger), the need leads to psychological tension that motivates the organism to act, fulfilling the need and reducing the tension.
- Primary drives involve needs of the body, whereas acquired (secondary) drives are those learned through experience. Homeostasis is the tendency of the body to maintain a steady state.

9.3 Explain the characteristics of the three types of needs.

- The need for affiliation is the desire to have friendly social interactions and relationships with others as well as the desire to be held in high regard by others.
- The need for power concerns having control over others, influencing them, and having an impact on them. Status and prestige are important to people high in this need.
- The need for achievement is a strong desire to succeed in achieving one's goals, both realistic and challenging.
- The self-theory of emotion links the need for achievement to the concept of locus of control. A belief in control over one's life leads to more attempts to achieve, even in the face of failure. Those who believe that they have little control over what happens to them are more likely to develop learned helplessness.

9.4 Identify the key elements of the arousal and incentive approaches to motivation.

- In arousal theory, a person has an optimal level of arousal to maintain. People who need more arousal than others are called sensation seekers.
- In the incentive approach, an external stimulus may be so rewarding that it motivates a person to act toward that stimulus even in the absence of a drive.

9.5 Describe how Maslow's hierarchy of needs and self-determination theories explain motivation.

- Maslow proposed a hierarchy of needs, beginning with basic physiological needs and ending with transcendence needs. The more basic needs must be met before the higher needs can be fulfilled.
- Self-determination theory (SDT) is a model of motivation in which three basic needs are seen as necessary to an individual's successful development: autonomy, competence, and relatedness.

What, Hungry Again? Why People Eat

9.6 Identify the physical and social factors that influence hunger.

- The physiological components of hunger include signals from the stomach and the hypothalamus and the increased secretion of insulin.
- When the basal metabolic rate slows down, the weight set point increases and makes weight gain more likely.
- The social components of hunger include social cues for when meals are to be eaten, cultural customs and food preferences, and the use of food as a comfort device or as an escape from unpleasantness.
- Some people may be externals who respond to the anticipation of eating by producing an insulin response, increasing the risk of obesity.

9.7 Recognize some of the factors that contribute to obesity.

- There are genetic and hormonal factors that can influence obesity.
- Maladaptive eating may lead to obesity.
- Worldwide, approximately 18 percent of children and adolescents, and 39 percent of men and women are obese.

Emotion

9.8 Describe the three elements of emotion.

- Emotion is the "feeling" aspect of consciousness and includes physical, behavioral, and subjective (cognitive) elements.
- Physical arousal is tied to activation of the sympathetic nervous system.
- The amygdala plays a key role in emotional processing.

9.9 Distinguish among the common-sense, James-Lange, Cannon-Bard, and facial feedback theories of emotion.

- The common-sense theory of emotion states that an emotion is experienced first, leading to a physical reaction and then to a behavioral reaction.
- The James-Lange theory states that a stimulus creates a physiological response that then leads to the labeling of the emotion.
- The Cannon-Bard theory asserts that the physiological reaction and the emotion are simultaneous, as the thalamus sends sensory information to both the cortex of the brain and the organs of the sympathetic nervous system.
- In the facial feedback hypothesis, facial expressions provide feedback to the brain about the emotion being expressed on the face, intensifying the emotion.

9.10 Identify the key elements in the cognitive arousal and cognitive-mediational theories of emotion.

- In Schachter and Singer's cognitive arousal theory, both the physiological arousal and the actual interpretation of that arousal must occur before the emotion itself is experienced. This interpretation is based on cues from the environment.
- In the cognitive-mediational theory of emotion, the cognitive component of emotion (the interpretation) precedes both the physiological reaction and the emotion itself.

Applying Psychology to Everyday Life: What Is Holding You Back from Keeping Track?

9.11 Identify possible barriers, and benefits, to implementing a personal system to manage your time and tasks.

- Time- or task-management systems can help you keep track of commitments and accomplish specific tasks and general goals.
- Identifying past reasons for personally avoiding such structure may be useful when trying to implement a successful system.

Test Yourself: Preparing for the AP Exam

PART I: MULTIPLE-CHOICE QUESTIONS

Directions for Part I: Read each of the questions or incomplete sentences below. Then choose the response that best answers the question or completes the sentence.

1. Liam enjoys woodcarving. Although none of his teenage friends are interested, he often spends hours creating several different pieces. His enjoyment of the task is all his own, and he rarely shows others his work. Many would call his motivation _____ in nature.
   a. arousal
   b. drive-based
   c. extrinsic
   d. intrinsic
   e. instinctual

2. The approach to motivation that forced psychologists to consider the value of homeostasis in motivation was the _____ approach.
   a. incentive
   b. extrinsic
   c. arousal
   d. instinct
   e. drive-reduction

3. Motivational theories such as _____ are physical in terms of their needs, while _____ is based on psychological motives.
   a. the drive theory, McClelland's need theory
   b. the biological theory, the drive theory
   c. self-determination, the instinctual theory
   d. need for power, the drive theory
   e. the drive theory, the instinctual theory

4. An important component to Carol Dweck's theory of motivation is _____.
   a. the importance of heredity in biological motivations
   b. one's view of self
   c. an understanding of classical conditioning and its impact on motivation
   d. an understanding of emotions
   e. a moderately low level of arousal

5. According to the arousal theory, people are typically motivated towards the _____ point of arousal.
   a. highest
   b. optimal
   c. threshold
   d. quickest
   e. easiest

6. According to Maslow, what is meant by a peak experience?
   a. the point at which someone must descend back down the hierarchy to address a previous need which is no longer secure
   b. the point at which all physiological needs have been met
   c. the point at which someone reaches transcendence
   d. the point at which someone begins to work through the hierarchy
   e. that point, even for a moment, when someone reaches a state of self-actualization

7. Zayden believes he is in control of his own destiny. He feels he is secure in the friendships he has with others. However, he still feels the need to master many of the challenges in his own life and career. According to the self-determination theory, which stage is Zayden still working to complete?
   a. affiliation
   b. competence
   c. autonomy
   d. life review
   e. relatedness

8. Leptin is a hormone involved in _____.
   a. neurotransmissions
   b. digestion of fatty foods
   c. social bonding
   d. appetite control
   e. metabolism control

9. Since Amaia's family has a history of obesity, she has _____ risk of becoming obese compared to people without such a family history.
   a. the same
   b. five times the
   c. double or triple the
   d. slightly reduced
   e. greatly reduced

10. LeDoux's work on the physiology involving emotions has focused on what part of the brain?
    a. amygdala
    b. hypothalamus
    c. prefrontal cortex
    d. thalamus
    e. hippocampus

11. Research on facial expressions has taught us that some facial expressions are _____.
    a. inherent to a region and therefore mean different things in different countries
    b. largely unique to each individual
    c. learned
    d. inherent to a culture and therefore mean different things to different cultures
    e. universal

12. What is meant by a display rule?
    a. an understanding of how to hide emotions from others
    b. an understanding of when and under what conditions emotions and feelings may be displayed within a culture
    c. an understanding of how children are to act in the presence of adults
    d. an understanding of what behaviors can be expressed when someone is new to a situation
    e. an understanding of group conformity

13. What theory of emotion states that the emotion typically occurs before arousal and behavior?
    a. James and Lange's theory
    b. facial feedback theory
    c. Schachter and Singer's theory
    d. the original, or common-sense, theory
    e. Cannon and Bard's theory

14. Which theory of emotion relies heavily on cognition and labeling?
    a. Cannon and Bard's theory
    b. Schachter and Singer's theory
    c. facial feedback theory
    d. James and Lange's theory
    e. the original, or common-sense, theory

15. Amanda is a full-time student and heavily involved in various school and community activities. Constantly on the go, and despite her best intentions, she seems to regularly miss homework, assignment, and paper deadlines. Amanda might benefit from using a _____ resource to keep up with commitments.
    a. free-form and internal
    b. memory-based
    c. systematic and external
    d. systematic and mental
    e. location-specific

PART II: FREE-RESPONSE QUESTION

Directions for Part II: Read the essay question that follows. Then respond to the question in a clear, concise essay. Do not simply list facts. Instead, present a thorough argument based on your critical consideration of the topic. Use of proper terminology is necessary.

Your friend Devashish is afraid of snakes, but you have convinced him to go hiking in a forest near campus. About 30 minutes into the hike, you hear a commotion behind you, and when you turn around, Devashish is sitting next to the trail. He is flushed, and a tad embarrassed. He fell after mistaking a root for a snake. After getting up and brushing himself off, he starts laughing.

Part A
For each of the following terms, explain how it may have motivated Devashish to join you for your hike:

- need for affiliation
- arousal theory
- self-determination theory
- drive reduction theory

Part B
For each of the following theorists, explain Devashish's emotional response using their ideas:

- Joseph LeDoux
- Schacter and Singer
- James and Lange

Chapter 10
Stress and Health

Ralf strm/EyeEm/Getty Images

In your words

What are some common sources of stress in your life?

After you have thought about this question, watch the video to see how other students would answer it.

👁 **Watch** the **Video** at **MyLab Psychology**

Why study stress and health?

How are they related? Stress is not a rare experience but something that all people experience in varying degrees every day. This chapter will explore the sources of stress in daily life, the factors that can make the experience of stress easier or more difficult, and the ways that stress influences our physical and mental health. We'll finish by discussing various ways to cope with the stresses of everyday life as well as with the extraordinary experiences that arise in life that have the potential to induce stress.

Learning Objectives

10.1 Distinguish between distress and eustress.

10.2 Identify three types of external events that can cause stress.

10.3 Identify psychological factors in stress.

10.4 Describe the stages of the general adaptation syndrome.

10.5 Explain how the immune system is impacted by stress.

10.6 Describe the branch of psychology known as health psychology.

10.7 Summarize Lazarus's cognitive appraisal approach to stress.

10.8 Explain how personality types and attitudes can influence people's reaction to stress.

10.9 Identify social and cultural factors that influence stress reactions.

10.10 Distinguish between problem-focused and emotion-focused coping strategies to reduce stress.

10.11 Explain how a social-support system influences a person's ability to cope with stress.

10.12 Describe cultural differences in coping with stress.

10.13 Explain how religious beliefs can affect the ability to cope with stress.

10.14 Identify common sources of stress for college students, and describe healthy and effective strategies for coping with the effects.

AP 7.H Discuss theories of stress and the effects of stress on psychological and physical well-being.

10.1–10.3 Stress and Stressors

Life is really about change. Every day, each person faces some kind of challenge, big or small. Just deciding what to wear to work or school can be a challenge for some people, whereas others find the drive to the workplace or school the most challenging part of the day. There are decisions to be made and changes that will require that you adapt already-made plans. Sometimes there are actual threats to well-being—an accident, a fight with the boss, a failed exam, or the loss of a job, to name a few. All of these challenges, threats, and changes require people to respond in some way.

10.1 The Relationship Between Stress and Stressors

10.1 Distinguish between distress and eustress.

Stress is the term used to describe the physical, emotional, cognitive, and behavioral responses to events that are appraised* as threatening or challenging.

Stress can show itself in many ways. Physical problems can include unusual fatigue, sleeping problems, frequent colds, and even chest pains and nausea. People under stress may behave differently, too: pacing, eating too much, crying a lot, smoking and drinking more than usual, or physically striking out at others by hitting or throwing things. Emotionally, people under stress experience anxiety, depression, fear, and irritability, as well as anger and frustration. Mental symptoms of stress include problems in concentration, memory, and decision making, and people under stress often lose their sense of humor.

💬 **I feel like that most of the time!**

Most people experience some degree of stress on a daily basis, and students are even more likely to face situations and events that require them to make changes and adapt their behavior: Assigned readings, papers, studying for tests, juggling jobs, car problems, relationships, and dealing with deadlines are all examples of things that can cause a person to experience stress. Some people feel the effects of stress more than others because what is appraised as a threat by one person might be appraised as an opportunity by another. (For example, think of how you and your friends might respond differently to the opportunity to write a 10-page paper for extra credit in the last 3 weeks of the semester.) Stress-causing events are called **stressors**; they can come from within a person or from an external source and range from relatively mild to severe.

Events that can become stressors range from being stuck behind a person in the 10-items-or-less lane of the grocery store who has twice that amount to dealing with the rubble left after a tornado or a hurricane destroys one's home. Stressors can range from the deadly serious (hurricanes, fires, crashes, combat) to the merely irritating and annoying (delays, rude people, losing one's car keys). Stressors can even be imaginary, as when a couple puts off doing their income tax return, imagining that they will have to pay a huge tax bill, or when a parent imagines the worst happening to a teenage child who isn't yet home from an evening out.

Actually, there are two kinds of stressors: those that cause **distress**, which occurs when people experience unpleasant stressors, and those that cause *eustress*, which results from positive events that still make demands on a person to adapt or change. Marriage, a job promotion, and having a baby may all be positive events for most people, but they all require a great deal of change in people's habits, duties, and often lifestyle, thereby creating stress. Hans Selye (1936) originally coined the term *eustress* to describe the stress experienced when positive events require the body to adapt.

Taking a test is just one of many possible stressors in a student's life. What aspects of life have you found to be stressful? Do other students experience the same degree of stress in response to the same stressors?

stress
the term used to describe the physical, emotional, cognitive, and behavioral responses to events that are appraised as threatening or challenging.

stressors
events that cause a stress reaction.

distress
the effect of unpleasant and undesirable stressors.

---

*appraised: in this sense, evaluated or judged in terms of importance or significance.

In an update of Selye's original definition, researchers now define **eustress** as the optimal amount of stress that people need to promote health and well-being. The arousal theory, discussed in Chapter Nine, is based on the idea that a certain level of stress, or arousal, is actually necessary for people to feel content and function well (Zuckerman, 1994). See Learning Objective 9.4. That arousal can be viewed in terms of eustress. Many students are aware that experiencing a little anxiety or stress is helpful to them because it motivates them to study, for example. Without the arousal created by the impending exam, many students might not study very much or at all. In fact, as the video *Stress and Memory* describes, studies have shown that small amounts of stress may actually improve our memory. What about the student who is so stressed out that everything he's studied just flies right out of his head? Obviously, a high level of anxiety concerning an impending exam that actually interferes with the ability to study or to retrieve the information at exam time is distress. The difference is not only in the degree of anxiety but also in how the person interprets the exam situation. What is eustress for one person may be distress for another, and although both kinds of stress produce similar bodily reactions, a more positive interpretation of a stressor leads to more positive coping with that stressor (Fevre et al., 2006; Sarada & Ramkumar, 2014). A number of events, great and small, good and bad, can cause us to feel "stressed out." The next section looks at how life's big deals and little hassles contribute to our overall stress experience.

Watch Stress and Memory

Watch the Video at MyLab Psychology

10.2 Environmental Stressors: Life's Ups and Downs

10.2 Identify three types of external events that can cause stress.

From the annoyingly loud next-door neighbor to major life changes, good or bad, stress is a fact of life. Let's take a look at the various causes of stress in everyday life.

CATASTROPHES Losing one's home in a tornado is an example of a stressor called a **catastrophe**, an unpredictable event that happens on a large scale and creates tremendous amounts of stress and feelings of threat. Wars, hurricanes, floods, fires, airplane crashes, and other disasters are catastrophes.

The terrorist-driven destruction of the World Trade Center in New York City on September 11, 2001, is a prime example of a catastrophe. In one study, nearly 8 percent of the people living in the area near the attacks developed a severe stress disorder, and nearly 10 percent reported symptoms of depression even as late as 2 months after the attack (Galea et al., 2002). A study done 4 years later found a nearly 14 percent increase in stress disorders as well as continued persistence of previously diagnosed stress disorders (Pollack et al., 2006). See Learning Objective 13.7. In 2011, the Great East Japan Earthquake (GEJE) was not only one of the most massive earthquakes ever recorded in Japan, but it also triggered a tsunami that killed more than 18,000 people and destroyed homes and other buildings (Sakuma et al., 2015). In a study examining stress and depression in firefighters, hospital staff, and municipality workers 14 months after the GEJE, municipality workers and medical staff had more significant amounts of psychological stress, probable PTSD, and depression as compared to firefighters (Sakuma et al., 2015). Furthermore, work-related factors, specifically lack of rest and communication, were related to increased risk of depression and PTSD in both the municipality and medical workers (Sakuma et al., 2015). Other examples of catastrophes are the 2016 attacks

eustress
the effect of positive events, or the optimal amount of stress that people need to promote health and well-being.

catastrophe
an unpredictable, large-scale event that creates a tremendous need to adapt and adjust as well as overwhelming feelings of threat.

in Brussels, Orlando, Manchester, and Nice and, in 2018, the attacks in Parkland and Pittsburgh, the California wildfires, and Hurricane Michael.

Some research suggests that the impact of catastrophic events can affect not only the people who experience the events directly but also any unborn children whose mothers are involved in the events. The prenatal stress can not only have short-term consequences such as premature birth but also long-term effects such as lower-than-normal intelligence levels and poor health behavior in adult life (Cao-Lei et al., 2014; Eriksson et al., 2014; Raposa et al., 2014; Witt et al., 2014).

MAJOR LIFE CHANGES Thankfully, most people do not have to face the extreme stress of a catastrophe. But stress is present even in relatively ordinary life experiences and does not have to come from only negative events, such as job loss. Sometimes there are big events, such as marriage or going to college, that also require a person to make adjustments and changes—and adjustments and changes are really the core of stress, according to early researchers in the field (Holmes & Rahe, 1967).

THE SOCIAL READJUSTMENT RATING SCALE (SRRS) Thomas Holmes and Richard Rahe (1967) believed that any life event that required people to change, adapt, or adjust their lifestyles would result in stress. Like Selye, they assumed that both negative events (such as getting fired) and positive events (such as getting a promotion) demand that a person adjust in some way, and so both kinds of events are associated with stress. Using a sample of nearly 400 people, Holmes and Rahe devised a scale to measure the amount of stress in a person's life by having that person add up the total "life change units" associated with each major event in their **Social Readjustment Rating Scale** (**SRRS**; see **Table 10.1**).

Table 10.1 Sample Items from the Social Readjustment Rating Scale (SRRS)

Major Life Event	Life Change Units
Death of spouse	100
Divorce	75
Marital separation	65
Jail term	63
Death of a close family member	63
Personal injury or illness	53
Marriage	50
Dismissal from work	47
Marital reconciliation	45
Pregnancy	40
Death of close friend	37
Change to different line of work	36
Change in number of arguments with spouse	36
Major mortgage	31
Foreclosure of mortgage or loan	30
Begin or end school	26
Change in living conditions	25
Change in work hours or conditions	20
Change in residence/schools/recreation	19
Change in social activities	18
Small mortgage or loan	17
Vacation	13
Christmas	12
Minor violations of the law	11

Source: Based on Holmes, T. H., & Rahe, R. H. (1967). The Social Readjustment Rating Scale. Journal Of Psychosomatic Research II, 213–218.

Social Readjustment Rating Scale (SRRS)

assessment that measures the amount of stress in a person's life over a 1-year period resulting from major life events.

When an individual adds up the points for each event that has happened to him or her within the past 12 months (and counting points for repeat events as well), the resulting score can provide a good estimate of the degree of stress being experienced by that person. The researchers found that certain ranges of scores on the SRRS could be associated with increased risk of illness or accidents. (Note: Table 10.1 is not a complete listing of the original 43 events and associated life change units and should not be used to calculate a stress "score"! If you would like to calculate your SRRS score, try this free Web site: **mindtools.com/pages/article/newTCS_82.htm**.)

The risk of illness or accidents increases as the score increases. If a person's score is 300 or above, that person has a very high chance of becoming ill or having an accident in the near future (Holmes & Masuda, 1973). Illness includes not only physical conditions such as high blood pressure, ulcers, or migraine headaches but mental illness as well. In one study, researchers found that stressful life events of the kind listed in the SRRS were excellent predictors of the onset of episodes of major depression (Kendler & Prescott, 1999).

The SRRS was later revised (Miller & Rahe, 1997) to reflect changes in the ratings of the events in the 30 intervening years. Miller and Rahe found that overall stress associated with many of the items on the original list had increased by about 45 percent from the original 1967 ratings, citing changes in such issues as gender roles, economics, and social norms as possible reasons.

How can stress cause a person to have an accident? Many studies conducted on the relationship between stress and accidents in the workplace have shown that people under a lot of stress tend to be more distracted and less cautious and, therefore, place themselves at a greater risk for having an accident (Hansen, 1988; Sherry et al., 2003).

THE COLLEGE UNDERGRADUATE STRESS SCALE (CUSS) The SRRS, as it was originally designed, seems more appropriate for adults who are already established in their careers. There are versions of the SRRS that use as life events some of those things more likely to be experienced by college students. One of these more recent versions is the **College Undergraduate Stress Scale (CUSS**; Renner & Mackin, 1998). This scale is quite different from Holmes and Rahe's original scale because the stressful events listed and rated include those that would be more common or more likely to happen to a college student. Some of the higher-stress items on the CUSS include rape, a close friend's death, contracting a sexually transmitted disease, as well as final exam week and flunking a class. Some of the lower stress items include peer pressure, homesickness, falling asleep in class, pressure to make high grades, and dating concerns. **Table 10.2** lists some of the items from the CUSS.

> You mention that the CUSS has "falling asleep in class" as one of its items. How can falling asleep in class be stressful? It's what happens when the professor catches you that's stressful, isn't it?

Ah, but if you fall asleep in class, even if the professor doesn't catch on, you'll miss the lecture notes. You might then have to get the notes from a friend, take a photo of them or scan them, try to read your friend's handwriting, and so on—all stressful situations. Actually, all the events listed on both the SRRS and the CUSS are stressful not just because some of them are emotionally intense but also because there are so many little details, changes, adjustments, adaptations, frustrations, and delays that are caused by the events themselves. The death of a spouse, for example, rates 100 life change units because it requires the greatest amount of adjustment in a person's life. A lot of those adjustments are going to be the little details: planning the funeral, deciding what to do with the spouse's clothes and belongings, getting the notice in the obituaries, answering all of the condolence cards with a thank-you card, dealing with insurance and changing names on policies, and on and on and on. In other words, major life events create a whole host of hassles.

College Undergraduate Stress Scale (CUSS)
assessment that measures the amount of stress in a college student's life over a 1-year period resulting from major life events.

Table 10.2 College Undergraduate Stress Scale (CUSS)

Event	Rating
Being raped	100
Finding out that you are HIV-positive	100
Death of a close friend	97
Contracting a sexually transmitted infection (other than AIDS)	94
Concerns about being pregnant	91
Finals week	90
Oversleeping for an exam	89
Flunking a class	89
Having a boyfriend or girlfriend cheat on you	85
Financial difficulties	84
Writing a major term paper	83
Being caught cheating on a test	83
Two exams in one day	80
Getting married	76
Difficulties with parents	73
Talking in front of a class	72
Difficulties with a roommate	66
Job changes (applying, new job, work hassles)	65
A class you hate	62
Confrontations with professors	60
Maintaining a steady dating relationship	55
Commuting to campus or work, or both	54
Peer pressures	53
Being away from home for the first time	53
Getting straight A's	51
Fraternity or sorority rush	47
Falling asleep in class	40

Source: Renner, M. J., & Mackin, R. S. A life stress instrument for classroom use. Teaching of Psychology, 25(1), 46–48 © 1998 by SAGE Publications. Reprinted by Permission of SAGE Publications, Inc.

THINKING CRITICALLY 10.1

What aspects of college life do you think you will find most stressful? What might make those more stressful than others?

HASSLES Although it's easy to think about big disasters and major changes in life as sources of stress, the bulk of the stress we experience daily actually comes from little frustrations, delays, irritations, minor disagreements, and similar small aggravations. These daily annoyances are called **hassles** (Lazarus, 1993; Lazarus & Folkman, 1984). Experiencing major changes in one's life is like throwing a rock into a pond: There will be a big splash, but the rock itself is gone. What is left behind are all the ripples in the water that came from the impact of the rock. Those "ripples" are the hassles that arise from the big event.

Lazarus and Folkman (1984) developed a *hassles scale* that has items such as "misplacing or losing things" and "troublesome neighbors." A person taking the test for hassles would rate each item in the scale in terms of how much of a hassle that particular item was for the person. The ratings range between 0 (no hassle or didn't occur) to 3 (extremely severe hassle). Whereas the major life events of Holmes and Rahe's scale (1967) may have a long-term effect on a person's chronic physical and mental health, the

hassles
the daily annoyances of everyday life.

day-to-day minor annoyances, delays, and irritations that affect immediate health and well-being are far better predictors of short-term illnesses such as headaches, colds, backaches, and similar symptoms (Burks & Martin, 1985; DeLongis et al., 1988; Dunn et al., 2006). In one study, researchers found that among 261 participants who experienced headaches, scores on a scale measuring the number and severity of daily hassles were significantly better predictors of headaches than were scores on a life-events scale (Fernandez & Sheffield, 1996). The researchers also found that it was not so much the number of daily hassles that predicted headaches but rather the perceived severity of the hassles.

Research has indicated that hassles may also come from quite different sources depending on a person's developmental stage (Ellis et al., 2001). In this study, researchers surveyed 270 randomly selected people from ages 3 to 75. The participants were asked to check off a list of daily hassles and pleasures associated with having "bad days" and "good days," respectively, as well as ranking the hassles in terms of frequency and severity of impact. For children ages 3 to 5, getting teased was the biggest daily hassle. For children in the 6 to 10 age group, the biggest hassle was getting bad grades. Children 11 to 15 years old reported feeling pressured to use drugs, whereas older adolescents (ages 16 to 22) cited trouble at school or work. Adults found fighting among family members the greatest source of stress, whereas the elderly people in the study cited a lack of money.

In that same study, the researchers were somewhat surprised to find that elderly people were much more strongly affected by such hassles as going shopping, doctor's appointments, and bad weather than the children and younger adults were. It may be that while a young person may view going shopping as an opportunity to socialize, older adults find it threatening: Physically, they are less able to get to a place to shop and may have to rely on others to drive them and help them get around and, thus, may take much more time for shopping and doing errands than a younger person would. Mentally, shopping could be seen as threatening because of a lack of financial resources to pay for needed items. Even the need to make decisions might be seen as unpleasant to an older person.

10.3 Psychological Stressors: What, Me Worry?

10.3 Identify psychological factors in stress.

Although several specific stressors (such as marriage, car problems, etc.) have already been mentioned, the psychological reasons people find these events stressful fall into several categories.

PRESSURE When there are urgent demands or expectations for a person's behavior coming from an outside source, that person is experiencing **pressure**. Pressure occurs when people feel that they must work harder or faster or do more, as when meeting a deadline or studying for final exams.

Time pressure is one of the most common forms of pressure. Although some people claim to "work well under pressure," the truth is that pressure can have a negative impact on a person's ability to be creative. Psychologist Teresa Amabile has gathered research within actual work settings strongly indicating that when time pressure is applied to workers who are trying to come up with creative, innovative ideas, creativity levels decrease dramatically—even though the workers may think they have been quite productive because of the effort they have made (Amabile et al., 2002).

UNCONTROLLABILITY Another factor that increases a person's experience of stress is the degree of control that the person has over a particular event or situation. The less control a person has, the greater the degree of stress. Researchers in both clinical interviews and experimental studies have found that lack of control in a situation actually increases stress disorder symptoms (Breier et al., 1987; Henderson et al., 2012).

In studies carried out in a nursing home with the elderly residents as the participants, researchers Rodin and Langer (Langer & Rodin, 1976; Rodin & Langer, 1977) found that those residents who were given more control over their lives (e.g., being able to

pressure
the psychological experience produced by urgent demands or expectations for a person's behavior that come from an outside source.

choose activities and their timing) were more vigorous, active, and sociable than those in the control group. Employees at mental health clinics who have more input into and control over policy changes experience less stress than those who believe themselves to have little control (Johnson et al., 2006). A more recent study has reported that late-life workers in Europe and the United States who have voluntarily chosen part-time employment have less stress and anger than individuals still working full time, and individuals who have the choice to continue working, either full- or part-time, have an improved sense of well-being as compared to retirees (Nikolova & Graham, 2014).

The stress-increasing effects of lack of control explain the relationship between unpredictability and stress as well. When potentially stressful situations are unpredictable, as in police work, the degree of stress experienced is increased. An unpredictable situation is one that is not controllable, which may at least partially explain the increase in stress (Zucchi et al., 2009). In one study, rats were either given an electric shock after a warning tone or given a shock with no warning. The rats receiving the unpredictable shocks developed severe stomach ulcers (Weiss, 1972). There can also be an interaction between lack of control and unpredictability. In research with humans and the experience of electric shock that was either predictable or unpredictable and controllable or uncontrollable, individuals demonstrated the highest levels of anxiety during conditions where the electric shock was uncontrollable and unpredictable (Havranek et al., 2015). Furthermore, individuals with lower levels of self-reported anxiety prior to the tasks reported less anxiety as both predictable and unpredictable sessions progressed; in contrast, anxiety did not decrease within sessions for individuals with higher but still not clinical-level self-reported anxiety (Havranek et al., 2015).

FRUSTRATION **Frustration** occurs when people are blocked or prevented from achieving a desired goal or fulfilling a perceived need. As a stressor, frustration can be *external*, such as when a car breaks down, a desired job offer doesn't come through after all, or a theft results in the loss of one's belongings. Losses, rejections, failures, and delays are all sources of external frustration.

Obviously, some frustrations are minor and others are more serious. The seriousness of a frustration is affected by how important the goal or need actually is. A person who is delayed in traffic while driving to the mall to do some shopping just for fun will be less frustrated than a person who is trying to get to the mall before it closes to get that last-minute forgotten and important anniversary gift.

Internal frustrations, also known as *personal frustrations*, occur when the goal or need cannot be attained because of internal or personal characteristics. For example, someone who wants to be an astronaut might find that severe motion sickness prevents him or her from such a goal. If a man wants to be a professional basketball player but is only 5 feet tall and weighs only 85 pounds, he may find that he cannot achieve that goal because of his physical characteristics. A person wanting to be an engineer but who has no math skills would find it difficult to attain that goal.

When frustrated, people may use several typical responses. The first is *persistence*, or the continuation of efforts to get around whatever is causing the frustration. Persistence may involve making more intense efforts or changing the style of response. For example, anyone who has ever put coins into a vending machine only to find that the drink does not come out has probably (1) pushed the button again, more forcefully, and (2) pushed several other buttons in an effort to get some kind of response from the machine. If neither of these strategies works, many people may hit or kick the machine itself in an act of aggression.

Aggression, or action meant to harm or destroy, is unfortunately another typical reaction to frustration. Early psychologists in the field of behaviorism proposed a connection between frustration and aggression, calling it the *frustration–aggression hypothesis* (Dollard et al., 1939; Miller et al., 1941). See Learning Objective 11.15. Although they believed that some form of frustration nearly always precedes aggression, that does not mean that frustration *always* leads to aggression. In fact, aggression is a frequent and incessant response

frustration
the psychological experience produced by the blocking of a desired goal or fulfillment of a perceived need.

aggression
actions intended to harm physically or psychologically.

to frustration, but it is seldom the first response. In a reformulation of the frustration–aggression hypothesis, Berkowitz (1993) stated that frustration creates an internal "readiness to aggress" but that aggression will not follow unless certain external cues are also present. For example, if the human source of a person's frustration is far larger and stronger in appearance than the frustrated person, aggression is an unlikely outcome!

> Okay, so if the person who ticked you off is bigger than you—if aggression isn't possible—what can you do?

One could try to reason with the person who is the source of frustration. Reasoning with someone is a form of persistence. Trying to "get around" the problem is another way in which people can deal with frustration. Another possibility is to take out one's frustrations on less threatening, more available targets, in a process called **displaced aggression**. Anyone who has ever been frustrated by things that occurred at work or school and then later yelled at another person (such as a spouse, parent, child, etc.) has experienced displaced aggression. The person one really wants to strike out at is one's boss, the teacher, or whoever or whatever caused the frustration in the first place. That could be dangerous, so the aggression is reserved for another less threatening or weaker target. For example, unemployment and financial difficulties are extremely frustrating, as they block a person's ability to maintain a certain standard of living and acquire desired possessions. In one study, male unemployment and single parenthood were the two factors most highly correlated to rates of child abuse (Gillham et al., 1998). Among abusive men, being unemployed is also one of the factors correlated most highly with the murder of abused women, creating four times the risk of murder for women in abusive relationships (Campbell et al., 2003). Both studies are examples of displaced aggression toward the weaker targets of children and women. Such targets often become *scapegoats*, or habitual targets of displaced aggression. Scapegoats are often pets, children, spouses, and even minority groups (who are seen as having less power). See Learning Objective 11.10.

Another possible reaction to frustration is **escape** or **withdrawal**. Escape or withdrawal can take the form of leaving, dropping out of school, quitting a job, or ending a relationship. Some people manage a psychological escape or withdrawal into apathy (ceasing to care about or act upon the situation), fantasy (which is only a temporary escape), or the use of drugs. Obviously the latter reaction can lead to even more problems. Others resort to what they see as the final escape: suicide.

CONFLICT Whenever you find yourself torn between two or more competing and incompatible desires, goals, or actions, you are in conflict. There are different forms of conflict, depending upon the nature of the incompatible desires, goals, or actions.

APPROACH–APPROACH CONFLICT In an **approach–approach conflict**, a person experiences desire for two goals, each of which is attractive. Typically, this type of conflict, often called a "win–win situation," is relatively easy to resolve and does not involve a great deal of stress. Because both goals are desirable, the only stress involved is having to choose between them, acquiring one and losing the other. An example of this might be the need to choose between the chocolate cake or key lime pie for dessert or from among several good choices for a date to the prom. "Six on one hand, half a dozen on the other" is a phrase that sums up this conflict nicely.

AVOIDANCE–AVOIDANCE CONFLICT **Avoidance–avoidance conflicts** are much more stressful. In this conflict, the choice is between two or more goals or events that are unpleasant. This type of conflict is so common that there are numerous phrases to symbolize it, for example, "caught between a rock and a hard place," "between the devil and the deep blue sea," "out of the frying pan into the fire," and "lose–lose situation." People who are fearful of dental procedures might face the conflict of suffering the pain of a toothache or going to the dentist. Because neither alternative is pleasant, many people

displaced aggression
taking out one's frustrations on some less threatening or more available target.

escape or withdrawal
leaving the presence of a stressor, either literally or by a psychological withdrawal into fantasy, drug abuse, or apathy.

approach–approach conflict
conflict occurring when a person must choose between two desirable goals.

avoidance–avoidance conflict
conflict occurring when a person must choose between two undesirable goals.

avoid making a choice by delaying decisions (Tversky & Shafir, 1992). For example, given the choice of risky back surgery or living with the pain, some people would wait, hoping that the pain would go away on its own and relieve them of the need to make a choice.

APPROACH–AVOIDANCE CONFLICT **Approach–avoidance conflicts** are a bit different in that they only involve one goal or event. That goal or event may have both positive and negative aspects that make the goal appealing and yet unappealing at the same time. For example, marriage is a big decision to make for anyone and usually has both its attractive features, such as togetherness, sharing good times, and companionship, and also its negative aspects, such as disagreements, money issues, and mortgages. This is perhaps the most stressful of all of the types of conflict, causing many people to vacillate* or be unable to decide for or against the goal or event. The author of this text experienced a very stressful approach–avoidance conflict when deciding to write the book: On the one hand, there would be money, prestige, and the challenge of doing something new. On the other hand, a tremendous amount of effort and time would be required to write the text, which would take time and energy away from other areas of life. Another example is the offer of a promotion that would require a person to move to a city he or she doesn't like—more money and higher status but all the hassles of moving and living in a less-than-perfect place.

💬 What if I have to choose between two things, and each of them has good points and bad points?

MULTIPLE APPROACH–AVOIDANCE CONFLICTS When the choice is between two goals that have both positive and negative elements to each goal, it is called a **double approach–avoidance conflict**. For example, what if a person had the choice of buying a house out in the country or in the city? The house in the country has its attractions: privacy, fresh air, and quiet. But there would be a long commute to one's job in the city. A house in the city would make getting to work a lot easier, but then there are the negative aspects of pollution, noise, and crowded city streets. Each choice has both good and bad points. This type of conflict also tends to lead to vacillation. Other examples of this type of conflict might be trying to decide which of two people one wants to date or which of two majors one should choose.

It is fairly common to face **multiple approach–avoidance conflicts** in daily life. In a multiple approach–avoidance conflict, one would have more than two goals or options to consider, making the decision even more difficult and stressful. For many students, deciding on a specific school or a career is actually this type of conflict.

See **Table 10.3** for a summary of these four types of conflicts.

*vacillate: to go back and forth between one decision and another.

approach–avoidance conflict

conflict occurring when a person must choose or not choose a goal that has both positive and negative aspects.

double approach–avoidance conflict

conflict in which the person must decide between two goals, with each goal possessing both positive and negative aspects.

multiple approach–avoidance conflict

conflict in which the person must decide between more than two goals, with each goal possessing both positive and negative aspects.

Table 10.3 Different Forms of Conflict

Conflict Type	Definition	Example
Approach–approach	Must choose between two desirable goals.	You would like to go to both Italy and England, but you can only choose to go to one.
Avoidance–avoidance	Must choose between two undesirable goals.	You dislike both cleaning the bathroom and cleaning the kitchen but must choose one or the other.
Approach–avoidance	Must choose or not choose a goal that has both desirable and undesirable aspects.	You want to have a pet for the companionship but don't like the idea of cleaning up after it.
Multiple approach–avoidance	Must choose from among two or more goals, with each goal possessing both desirable and undesirable aspects.	You have to decide on a college. One close to home would be less expensive and closer to your friends but not as academically desirable. The one in another state would be academically challenging and would look much better when applying for jobs but is very expensive and far away from friends and family.

Concept Map L.O. 10.1, 10.2, 10.3

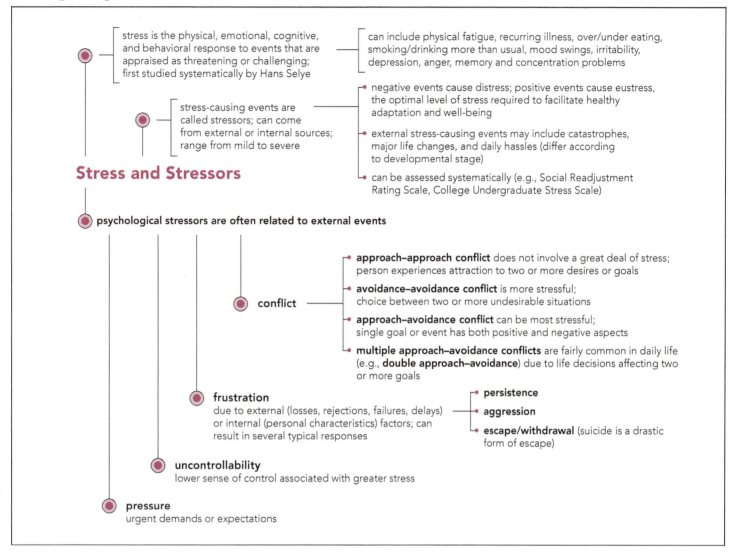

Practice Quiz   How much do you remember?

Pick the best answer.

1. Studies show that _____ is the optimal amount of stress that people need to positively promote their health and sense of well-being, which coincides with _____ theory.
   a. eustress, Maslow's
   b. arousal, eustress
   c. eustress, arousal
   d. intensity, cognitive consistency
   e. distress, biological instinct

2. What does the Social Readjustment Rating Scale (SRRS) use to determine its results?
   a. The SRRS looks exclusively at any catastrophes that a person has experienced.
   b. The SRRS records specific positive and negative life events to determine an individual's current level of stress.
   c. The SRRS asks users to subjectively rate their stress level.
   d. The SRRS examines diet and family history to determine one's overall health risks.
   e. The SRRS looks exclusively at subjective ratings of random situations in a person's life.

3. Who, if anyone, would consider going shopping as a daily hassle and therefore stressful?
   a. those in their 20s and 30s
   b. senior citizens
   c. Hassles are stressful at any age, and studies do not find shopping to be a stressor or hassle at any age.
   d. adolescents
   e. those in their late teens

4. A retail store has announced to its employees that half of them will be laid off after a 2-week, random review of their personnel records. No current performance appraisals or individual interviews are being held. Over the next 2 weeks, many of the employees are arguing, fighting, and doing a poor job of taking care of their customers. What aspects of stress most likely started these behaviors?
   a. pressure and frustration
   b. uncontrollability and conflict
   c. uncontrollability and frustration
   d. pressure and conflict
   e. daily hassles

5. Liza wants the lead singing part in the next school musical, but by all accounts, she is not musically gifted in any way and has a rather unpleasant singing voice. Liza may eventually realize her lack of singing ability is an _____ frustration.
   a. unacceptable
   b. internal
   c. extrinsic
   d. external
   e. secondary

6. Marriage is sometimes perceived as a unique stressor. On one hand, you have many good aspects such as finding that special someone, long-term commitment, and sometimes even combined incomes. On the other hand, there is a perceived loss of independence, a sense of finality, and the fear of "what if this isn't the right one?" Therefore, marriage may be seen as an example of a(n) _____ conflict.
   a. multiple avoidance–avoidance
   b. approach–avoidance
   c. approach–approach
   d. avoidance–avoidance
   e. multiple approach–approach

10.4–10.9 Physiological Factors: Stress and Health

Chapter Two discussed in detail the function of the *autonomic nervous system* (ANS), the part of the human nervous system that is responsible for automatic, involuntary, and life-sustaining activities. The ANS consists of two divisions, the *parasympathetic* and the *sympathetic*. It is the sympathetic nervous system (the "fight-or-flight" system, see Learning Objective 2.12), that reacts when the human body is subjected to stress: Heart rate increases, digestion slows or shuts down, and energy is sent to the muscles to help deal with whatever action the stressful situation requires. The parasympathetic system returns the body to normal, day-to-day functioning after the stress is ended. Both systems, including many neural structures in the limbic system (Gianaros & Wager, 2015; Seo et al., 2014), figure prominently in a classic theory of the body's physiological reactions to stress, the general adaptation syndrome.

10.4 The General Adaptation Syndrome

10.4 Describe the stages of the general adaptation syndrome.

Endocrinologist Hans Selye was the founder of the field of research concerning stress and its effects on the human body. He studied the sequence of physiological reactions that the body goes through when adapting to a stressor. This sequence (see **Figure 10.1**) is called the **general adaptation syndrome (GAS)** and consists of three stages (Selye, 1956):

- **Alarm:** When the body first reacts to a stressor, the sympathetic nervous system is activated. The adrenal glands release hormones that increase heart rate, blood pressure, and the supply of blood sugar, resulting in a burst of energy. Reactions such as fever, nausea, and headache are common.

- **Resistance:** As the stress continues, the body settles into sympathetic division activity, continuing to release the stress hormones that help the body fight off, or resist, the stressor. The early symptoms of alarm lessen and the person or animal may actually feel better. This stage will continue until the stressor ends or the organism has used up all of its resources. Researchers have found that one of the hormones released under stress, noradrenaline (norepinephrine), actually seems to affect the brain's processing of pain, so that when under stress a person may experience a kind of analgesia (insensitivity to pain) if, for example, the person hits an arm or a shin (Delaney et al., 2007).

- **Exhaustion:** When the body's resources are gone, exhaustion occurs. Exhaustion can lead to the formation of stress-related diseases (e.g., high blood pressure or a weakened immune system) or the death of the organism if outside help is unavailable (Stein-Behrens et al., 1994). When the stressor ends, the parasympathetic division activates and the body attempts to replenish its resources.

Figure 10.1 General Adaptation Syndrome

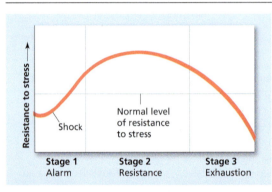

The graph shows the relationship of each of the three stages to the individual's ability to resist a stressor. In the alarm stage, resistance drops at first as the sympathetic system quickly activates. But resistance then rapidly increases as the body mobilizes its defense systems. In the resistance stage, the body is working at a much-increased level of resistance, using resources until the stress ends or the resources run out. In the exhaustion stage, the body is no longer able to resist, as resources have been depleted, and at this point disease and even death are possible.

AP 7.D Identify contributions of key researchers in the psychological field of motivation and emotion.

AP 7.H Discuss theories of stress and the effects of stress on psychological and physical well-being.

general adaptation syndrome (GAS)
the three stages of the body's physiological reaction to stress, including alarm, resistance, and exhaustion.

Alarm and resistance are stages that people experience many times throughout life, allowing people to adapt to life's demands (Selye, 1976). It is the prolonged secretion of the stress hormones during the exhaustion stage that can lead to the most harmful effects of stress. It was this aspect of Selye's work that convinced other researchers of the connection between stress and certain *diseases of adaptation* as Selye termed them, such as high blood pressure and peptic ulcers. And, while there certainly seems to be an association between stress and some disease processes (more on some of those in a moment), some research suggests long-term stress may not always be associated with blood pressure remaining chronically high and the relationship between psychological stress and risk for peptic ulcers is an ongoing area of investigation and debate (Levenstein et al., 2015; Steptoe & Kivimaki, 2013a).

10.5 The Immune System and Stress

10.5 Explain how the immune system is impacted by stress.

AP 7.H Discuss theories of stress and the effects of stress on psychological and physical well-being.

As Selye first discovered, the **immune system** (the system of cells, organs, and chemicals in the body that responds to attacks on the body from diseases and injuries) is affected by stress. The field of **psychoneuroimmunology** concerns the study of the effects of psychological factors such as stress, emotions, thinking, learning, and behavior on the immune system (Ader, 2003; Cohen & Herbert, 1996; Kiecolt-Glaser, 2009; Kiecolt-Glaser et al., 1995, 1996, 2002). Researchers in this field have found that stress triggers the same response in the immune system that infection triggers (Maier & Watkins, 1998). Certain enzymes and other chemicals (including antibodies) are created by immune cells when the immune cells, or white blood cells, encounter an infection in the body. The white blood cells surround the bacteria or other infectious material and release the chemicals and enzymes into the bloodstream. From there, these chemicals activate receptor sites on the *vagus nerve*, the longest nerve that connects the body to the brain. It is the activation of these receptor sites that signals the brain that the body is sick, causing the brain to respond by further activation of the immune system.

Stress activates this same system but starts in the brain rather than in the bloodstream. The same chemical changes that occur in the brain when it has been alerted by the vagus nerve to infection in the body occurred in laboratory animals when they were kept isolated from other animals or given electric shocks (Maier & Watkins, 1998). This has the effect of "priming" the immune system, allowing it to more successfully resist the effects of the stress, as in Selye's resistance stage of the GAS.

Hormones also play a part in helping the immune system fight the effects of stress. Researchers (Morgan et al., 2009) have found that a hormone called dehydroepiandrosterone (DHEA), known to provide antistress benefits in animals, also aids humans in stress toleration—perhaps by regulating the effects of stress on the hippocampus (part of the limbic system). See Learning Objective 2.7.

💬 So stress actually increases the activity of the immune system? But then how does stress end up causing those diseases, like high blood pressure?

The positive effects of stress on the immune system only seem to work when the stress is not a continual, chronic condition. As stress continues, the body's resources begin to fail in the exhaustion phase of the general adaptation to stress (Kiecolt-Glaser et al., 1987, 1995, 1996; Prigerson et al., 1997). In one study, college students who were undergoing a stressful series of exams were compared to a group of similar students relaxing during a time of no classes and no exams (Deinzer et al., 2000). The exam group tested significantly lower for immune system chemicals that help fight off disease than did the

immune system
the system of cells, organs, and chemicals of the body that responds to attacks from diseases, infections, and injuries.

psychoneuroimmunology
the study of the effects of psychological factors such as stress, emotions, thoughts, and behavior on the immune system.

relaxing control group, even as long as 14 days after the exams were over. The suppression of immune system functioning by stress apparently can continue even after the stress itself is over.

One reason that the early stress reaction is helpful but prolonged stress is not might be that the stress reaction, in evolutionary terms, is really only "designed" for a short-term response, such as running from a predator (Sapolsky, 2004). That level of intense bodily and hormonal activity isn't really meant to go on and on, as it does for human beings in the modern, stress-filled life we now know. Humans experience the stress reaction over prolonged periods of time and in situations that are not necessarily life-threatening, leading to a breakdown in the immune system (see **Figure 10.2**).

While it is clear that stress affects the immune system and overall health, exactly why this occurs has been a topic of research. The *inflammatory response* happens when the tissues of the body are injured in some way—bacterial infections, heat, toxic substances, physical injury, and so on. Damaged cells release chemicals that then cause the blood vessels to leak fluids into surrounding tissues, and this causes swelling or inflammation. Believe it or not, this inflammation is an important part of the immune system's response to invading substances, serving to block access to other body tissues. Researchers are now finding that inflammation may actually be the means through which stress can have its negative impact on health. One early study (Cohen et al., 1991) found that people under psychological stress are more likely to catch cold viruses than those who are not stressed. In later studies, it was suggested that prolonged stress can cause cortisol, which plays a role in controlling the inflammatory response, to become less effective (Cohen 2005; Cohen et al., 1999). This increases the inflammatory response, thus increasing the likelihood of getting a cold when exposed. In a more recent study (Cohen et al., 2012), the researchers found more evidence that prolonged stress was associated with a decrease in ability to regulate inflammation, and those higher levels of inflammation are associated with many diseases such as arthritis, heart disease, diabetes, and cancer (Hildreth, 2008; Pashkow, 2011; Rakoff-Nahoum, 2006). As we will see in the next section, although useful, Selye's GAS model is not the only way of conceptualizing and possibly understanding the impacts of short- and long-term stress.

Figure 10.2 Stress Duration and Illness

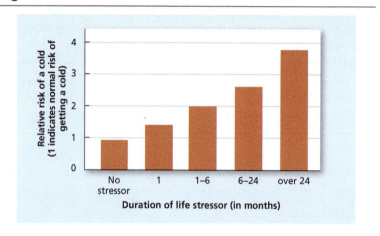

In this graph, the risk of getting a cold virus increases greatly as the months of exposure to a stressor increase. Although a stress reaction can be useful in its early phase, prolonged stress has a negative impact on the immune system, leaving the body vulnerable to illnesses such as a cold.

Source: Based on Cohen, S., Frank, E., Doyle, B. J., Skoner, D. P., Rabin, B. S., & Gwaltney, J. M. (1998). Types of stressors that increase susceptibility to the common cold. Health Psychology, 17, 214–223.

ALLOSTASIS AND ALLOSTATIC LOAD Selye's conceptualization of the body's reaction to stress was based on the idea of homeostasis, or maintaining a constant internal environment. This was an idea first put forth by the French scientist Claude Bernard in 1865, who believed maintaining a stable internal environment (*milieu intérieur*) was vital to complex organisms (Bernard, 1865/1949; Gross, 1998), and the idea of homeostasis, or coordination of physiological processes for maintaining steady states in the body, was first introduced by Walter Cannon in 1926 (Bernston et al., 2017; Cannon, 1929). It was also Walter Cannon who coined the idea of "fight or flight" (Cannon, 1915) and later developed an influential theory of emotion (Cannon, 1927). See Learning Objective 9.10.

Although useful, the concept of homeostasis does not adequately capture all of what has been discovered about the stress response, and the differential effects on the body during short- and long-term stress. Another way of looking at the body's dynamic responses to arousal and stress is the idea of *allostasis*, or "maintaining stability through change" to meet both perceived and anticipated demands (Sterling, 2004; Sterling & Eyer, 1988). Through allostasis, the body protects itself from both internal and external stress. This is accomplished by activation of the sympathetic nervous system (SNS), the *hypothalamic-pituitary-adrenal (HPA) axis*, and changes in metabolism, heart rate, blood pressure, and immune systems (McEwen, 1998). Activation of the SNS and HPA axis result in the release of stress hormones like adrenaline, cortisol, and glucocorticoids. However, prolonged exposure to elevated levels of these hormones and other stress mediators over weeks, months, or years may result in *allostatic load* or *allostatic overload*, resulting in wear and tear on the brain and body and subsequent decreased function and other pathological changes in the brain and body (McEwen, 1998, 2005).

Constant exposure to these stress mediators can have damaging effects on the brain and the brain's ability to interact successfully with the rest of the body. In turn, allostatic load or overload can lead to increased risk or vulnerability to stress-related brain, mental, and physical health conditions, and affect our ability to effectively respond to stressful experiences (McEwen & Gianaros, 2011; McEwen & McEwen, 2016; Russo et al., 2012). Through examining some of these changes, researchers hope to better identify the various active behaviors, hormonal changes, brain mechanisms, and molecular processes associated with *resilience*, or our capacity to avoid the negative biological, psychological, and social outcomes of stress (Cohen et al., 2019; McEwen et al., 2015; McEwen & Morrison, 2013; Russo et al., 2012).

HEART DISEASE Of course, anything that can weaken the immune system can have a negative effect on other bodily systems. Stress has been shown to put people at a higher risk of **coronary heart disease (CHD)**, the buildup of a waxy substance called plaque in the arteries of the heart. Stress can affect the release of immune system chemicals such as cytokines, small proteins involved in the inflammatory process (Frostegård, 2013; Tian et al., 2014). Stress also affects the functioning of the liver, which is not activated while the sympathetic nervous system is aroused and does not have a chance to clear the fat and cholesterol from the bloodstream. This can lead to clogged arteries and eventually the possibility of heart attacks or strokes. In one study, middle-aged men were questioned about stress, diet, and lifestyle factors and were examined for biological risk factors for heart disease: obesity, high blood sugar, high triglycerides (a type of fatty acid found in the blood), and low levels of HDL or "good" cholesterol (see **Figure 10.3**). Stress and the production of stress hormones were found to be strongly linked to all four biological risk factors: The more stress the men were exposed to in their work environment and home lives, the more likely they were to exhibit these risk factors (Brunner et al., 2002).

Other studies have produced similar findings. One study looked at the heart health of people who suffered acute stress reactions after the 9/11 terrorist attacks and found a 53 percent increase in heart ailments over the 3 years following the attacks

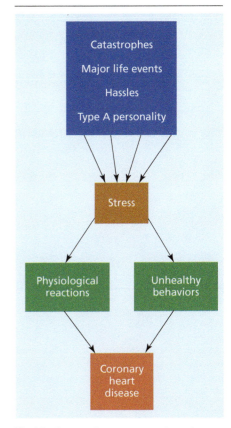

Figure 10.3 Stress and Coronary Heart Disease

The blue box on the top represents various sources of stress (Type A personality refers to someone who is ambitious, always working, and usually hostile). In addition to the physical reactions that accompany the stress reaction, an individual under stress may be more likely to engage in unhealthy behavior such as overeating, drinking alcohol or taking other kinds of drugs, avoiding exercise, and acting out in anger or frustration. This kind of behavior also contributes to an increased risk of coronary heart disease (CHD).

coronary heart disease (CHD)
the buildup of a waxy substance called plaque in the arteries of the heart.

(Holman et al., 2008), whereas another large-scale study found that work stress is highly associated with an increased risk of CHD due to negative effects of stress on the ANS and glandular activity (Chandola et al., 2008). While stress in and of and itself also continues to be investigated as a possible causal factor, exposure to chronic stress has been associated with diabetes and cardiovascular disease (Hackett & Steptoe, 2016; Kivimaki & Kawachi, 2015). Chronic sources of stress including work stress (such as high demands, low control, long work hours, and job insecurity), social isolation, and loneliness contribute to the development of CHD, and this may be due in part to metabolic dysfunction (Steptoe & Kivimaki, 2013b). Studies have shown a clear relationship between stress in the workplace and an increased risk of CHD as well as depression, sleep disturbances, and unhealthy habits such as a lack of physical activity—none of which are good for coronary health (Emeny et al., 2012, 2013). Prolonged stress is simply not good for the heart.

DIABETES Review the last paragraph, and it becomes obvious that weight problems may also become associated with stress. One chronic illness sometimes associated with excessive weight gain is *diabetes*, specifically **Type 2 diabetes**. (Type 1 diabetes is an autoimmune disorder associated with failure of the pancreas to secrete enough insulin, necessitating medication, and is usually diagnosed before the age of 40). Type 2 diabetes is associated with excessive weight gain and occurs when pancreas insulin levels become less efficient as the body size increases. Insulin resistance has been linked by research to higher levels of the immune system's cytokines. Stress, as mentioned earlier, can increase the release of these cytokines (Tian et al., 2014). Type 2 diabetes can respond favorably to proper diet, exercise, and weight loss but may also require medication. Typically, it is associated with older adults, but with the rise in obesity among children, more cases of Type 2 diabetes in children are now occurring.

While controllable, diabetes is a serious disorder that has now been associated with an increased risk of Alzheimer's disease, although memory loss appears to be slower for diabetic Alzheimer patients than for nondiabetic Alzheimer's patients (Sanz et al., 2009). Several ongoing longitudinal studies strongly suggest that Type 2 diabetes not only is associated with mental decline in middle-aged individuals (Nooyens et al., 2010), but there is also indication that stress can compound the risk of that mental decline (Reynolds et al., 2010).

Research has continued to link high levels of stress with increased risk of diabetes. A 35-year study in Sweden monitored the health and stress factors of 7,500 men who began the study with no history of diabetes or CHD (Novak et al., 2013). Those men who reported experiencing permanent stress, related to home life and/or work life, had a 45 percent higher chance of developing diabetes compared to men who reported no stress or only periodic stress. Another study found that high levels of stress in the workplace can accurately predict who will develop diabetes, particularly in those people who had low levels of social support (Toker et al., 2012). Overall, stress appears to increase the risk of diabetes in otherwise healthy individuals, and it is likely that both behavioral and biological factors are involved (Hackett & Steptoe, 2016).

CANCER Cancer is not one disease but rather a collection of diseases that can affect any part of the body. Unlike normal cells, which divide and reproduce according to genetic instructions and stop dividing according to those same instructions, cancer cells divide without stopping. The resulting tumors affect the normal functioning of the organs and systems they invade, causing them to fail, eventually killing the organism.

Although stress itself cannot directly give a person cancer, stress can have a suppressing effect on the immune system, making the unchecked growth of cancer more likely (Le et al., 2016). In particular, an immune-system cell called a **natural killer (NK) cell** has as its main functions the suppression of viruses and the destruction of tumor cells (Chan et al., 2014; Herberman & Ortaldo, 1981). Stress has been shown to depress the release of natural killer cells, making it more difficult for the body's systems to fight cancerous growths

Type 2 diabetes
disease typically occurring in middle adulthood when the body either becomes resistant to the effects of insulin or can no longer secrete enough insulin to maintain normal glucose levels.

natural killer (NK) cell
immune-system cell responsible for suppressing viruses and destroying tumor cells.

(Chan et al., 2014; Zorilla et al., 2001). The hormone adrenaline is released under stress and has been found to interfere with a protein that normally would suppress the growth of cancer cells (Sastry et al., 2007). In other research, stress has been linked to the release of hormones such as adrenaline and noradrenaline that, over time, can cause mistakes (such as damage to the telomeres, structures at the ends of chromosomes that control the number of times a cell can reproduce) in the instructions given by the genes to the cells of the body. As these mistakes "pile up" over the years, cells can begin to grow out of control, causing the growth of tumors and possibly cancer (Kiecolt-Glaser et al., 2002).

Stress may impact the effectiveness of cancer treatments as well. In one study of mice implanted with human prostate cancer cells, treatment with a drug to destroy the cancer cells and prevent growth of tumors was effective when the mice were kept calm and stress free but failed miserably when the mice were stressed (Hassan et al., 2013).

One possible bit of positive news: Unlike the research linking stress at work to heart disease and diabetes, one study has found that work-related stress does not appear to be linked to developing cancer of the colon, lungs, breasts, or prostate (Heikkila et al., 2013). While 5 percent of more than 100,000 participants in the 12 years over which the study took place developed some form of cancer, there was no association between job-related stress and risk of cancer.

OTHER HEALTH ISSUES Heart disease and cancer are not the only diseases affected by stress. Studies have shown that children in families experiencing ongoing stress are more likely to develop fevers with illness than are other children (Wyman et al., 2007). Oddly enough, this same study showed that in children, stress actually seems to improve the function of their natural killer cells, just the opposite effect that is seen in adults. Another longitudinal study's findings suggest that experiencing work-related stress in middle age may increase an individual's chances of developing both physical and mental disabilities in old age (Kulmala et al., 2013).

Reviews of research and scientific literature have found stress to be a contributing factor in other diseases and disorders, including depression and various infectious diseases (Cohen et al., 2007; Cohen et al., 2019). With regard to cancer, the data is less clear, but stress is believed to negatively influence its progression and recurrence (Cohen et al., 2007; Cohen et al., 2019). In all, experiencing stressful life events appears to predict both the severity and progression of numerous diseases and health issues (Cohen et al., 2019).

health psychology
area of psychology focusing on how physical activities, psychological traits, stress reactions, and social relationships affect overall health and rate of illnesses.

AP 7.H Discuss theories of stress and the effects of stress on psychological and physical well-being.

10.6 Health Psychology

10.6 Describe the branch of psychology known as *health psychology*.

In the last three decades, people have become more aware of health issues and their relationship to what we do, what we eat, who we see, and how we think. A branch of psychology has begun to explore these relationships. **Health psychology** focuses on how our physical activities, psychological traits, and social relationships affect our overall health and rate of illnesses. See Learning Objective A.6. Psychologists who specialize in this field are typically clinical or counseling psychologists and may work with medical doctors in a hospital or clinic setting, although there are health psychologists who are primarily engaged in teaching and research. Some health psychologists focus on health and wellness issues in the workplace or public health issues such as disease prevention through immunizations or nutrition education. Others are more concerned with health-care programs that service all levels of the socioeconomic

Watch Health Psychology

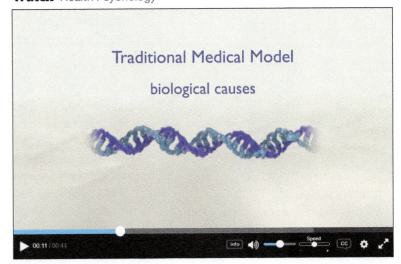

Watch the Video at MyLab Psychology

layers of society (Marks et al., 2005). These health psychologists examine specific groups and situations, such as protective factors against alcohol abuse in first- or second-generation immigrant adolescents (Laghi et al., 2019), the role of online support communities for individuals faced with a genetic illness (Smedley & Coulson, 2019), or how ethnicity and sexual orientation may impact one's experience of the health-care system (Ejaife & Ho, 2017). Still others focus on the effects of stress on cognitive functioning, such as memory and attention (Aggarwal et al., 2014; Bianchi et al., 2018; Munoz et al., 2015; Olver et al., 2015), or the effects of chronic pain on depression and physical disability (Costa et al., 2016). For more on the subject of health psychology, see the video *Health Psychology*.

Health psychologists seek to understand how thoughts and behavior (such as use of drugs, optimism, personality, or the type of food one eats) can affect a person's ability to fight off illnesses—or increase the likelihood of getting sick. They also want to know how factors like poverty, wealth, religion, social support, personality, and even one's ethnicity can affect health. *Clinical health psychology* is a subfield of health psychology focused on using the knowledge gained by researchers in the field to help promote healthy lifestyles, help people maintain their health, and also prevent or treat illnesses (Boll et al., 2002). Improving the health-care system is another goal of clinical health psychologists. Health psychology also has connections to *behavioral psychology*, a field combining both medicine and psychology as well as numerous other scientific fields related to health issues (Christensen & Nezu, 2013; Miller, 1983). In this age of a new and intense focus on health care, health psychology is destined to become a more important force in future research. One important area in which health psychologists may focus is on the psychological effects of alternative medicines, as illustrated by the *APA Goal 2: Scientific Inquiry and Critical Thinking* feature.

10.7 Cognitive Factors in Stress

10.7 Summarize Lazarus's cognitive appraisal approach to stress.

The physical effects of stress on the body and the immune system are only part of the picture of the influence of stress in daily life. Cognitive factors, such as how an individual interprets a stressful event, can also affect the impact of stress.

Cognitive psychologist Richard Lazarus developed a cognitive view of stress called the *cognitive–mediational theory* of emotions, in which the way people think about and appraise a stressor is a major factor in how stressful that particular stressor becomes (Lazarus, 1991, 1999; Lazarus & Folkman, 1984). See Learning Objective 9.10. According to Lazarus, there is a two-step process in assessing the degree of threat or harm of a stressor and how one should react to that stressor (see **Figure 10.4**).

The first step in appraising a stressor is called **primary appraisal**, which involves estimating the severity of the stressor and classifying it as a threat (something that could be harmful in the future), a challenge (something to be met and defeated), or a harm or loss that has already occurred. If the stressor is appraised as a threat, negative emotions may arise that inhibit the person's ability to cope with the threat. For example, a student who has not read the text or taken good notes will certainly appraise an upcoming exam as threatening. If the stressor is seen as a challenge, however, it is possible to plan to meet that challenge, which is a more positive and less stressful approach. For example, the student who has studied and read and feels prepared is much more likely to appraise the upcoming exam as an opportunity to do well.

Perceiving a stressor as a challenge instead of a threat makes coping with the stressor (or the harm it may already have caused) more likely to be successful. Whereas perceiving the stressor as an embarrassment, or imagining future failure or rejection, is more likely to lead to increased stress reactions, negative emotions, and an inability to cope well (Folkman, 1997; Lazarus, 1993). Think positively!

AP 7.F Compare and contrast major theories of emotion.

AP 7.H Discuss theories of stress and the effects of stress on psychological and physical well-being.

primary appraisal
the first step in assessing stress, which involves estimating the severity of a stressor and classifying it as either a threat or a challenge.

Figure 10.4 Responses to a Stressor

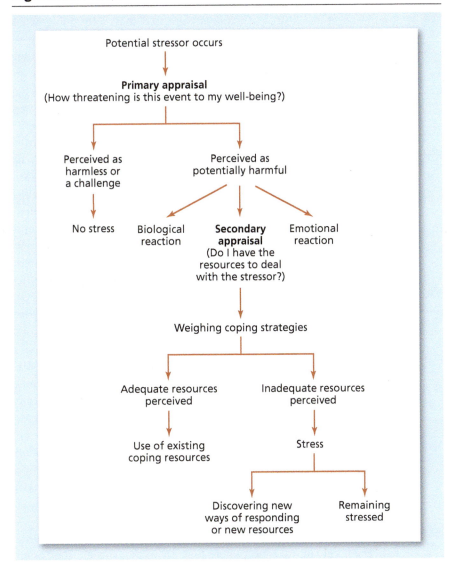

According to Lazarus's *cognitive appraisal approach*, there are two steps in cognitively determining the degree of stress created by a potential stressor. Primary appraisal involves determining if the potential stressor is a threat. If it is perceived as a threat, secondary appraisal occurs in addition to bodily and emotional reactions. Secondary appraisal involves determining the resources one has to deal with the stress. Inadequate resources lead to increased feelings of stress and the possibility of developing new resources to deal with it.

In **secondary appraisal**, people who have identified a threat or harmful effect must estimate the resources that they have available for coping with the stressor. Resources might include social support, money, time, energy, ability, or any number of potential resources, depending on the threat. If resources are perceived as adequate or abundant, the degree of stress will be considerably less than if resources are missing or lacking. Using the example of the student and the upcoming exam, a student who feels that she has the time to study and the ability to understand the material in that time will feel much less distress than the student who has little time to study and doesn't feel that she understood all the content of the lectures covered on the exam.

An addition to the cognitive appraisal approach is the *cognitive reappraisal approach* (Jamieson et al., 2012, 2013). Researchers have found that instructing participants

secondary appraisal
the second step in assessing a stressor, which involves estimating the resources available to the person for coping with the threat.

Figure 10.5 Arousal and Performance

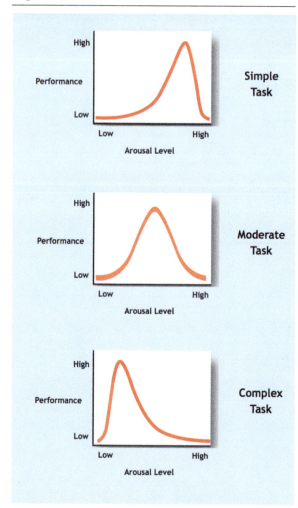

The optimal level of arousal for task performance depends on the difficulty of the task. We generally perform easy tasks well if we are at a high–moderate level of cognitive arousal, complete medium-complexity tasks at a moderate level of arousal, and accomplish complex tasks well if we are at a low–moderate level.

Source: Noland White

AP 7.B Compare and contrast motivational theories, including the strengths and weaknesses of each.

Yerkes-Dodson law
law stating that when tasks are simple, a higher level of arousal leads to better performance; when tasks are difficult, lower levels of arousal lead to better performance.

AP 7.H Discuss theories of stress and the effects of stress on psychological and physical well-being.

to reappraise their arousal while experiencing a stressor helped shift the negative effects of stress arousal to more positive effects. In one study (Jamieson et al., 2012), participants were told they were going to engage in a public-speaking task. Just before the task, participants were placed in three conditions: no instructions, a "placebo" instruction stating the best way of coping with stress was to ignore the source of stress, and an arousal-reappraisal condition in which they were given instructions that not only educated them about the reasons for physical arousal during stress but also encouraged them to interpret that arousal as a tool that would help them deal with the stress. For example, instead of seeing one's racing heartbeat as a sign of fear, one could interpret it as the heart supplying blood to organs and tissues in preparation for dealing with the demands of the situation or as a sign of excitement. The reappraisal participants were significantly less likely to look for cues of threat than were the other two groups. In a subsequent study (Jamieson et al., 2013), arousal reappraisal was found to help participants recover from stress as well, enabling them to return to normal physiological responses more quickly after stress when compared with participants who received no reappraisal instructions. Apparently, there's a big difference between feeling "excited" rather than "stressed."

How might appraisal and reappraisal impact everyday life? In general, an individual's performance on a task may suffer if the level of stress or arousal is too high (e.g., severe test anxiety) or if the level of arousal is too low (e.g., boredom). For many tasks, a moderate level of arousal seems to be best. See Learning Objective 9.4. However, the necessary level of arousal for a given task also depends on task difficulty: Easy tasks demand a somewhat "high–moderate" level of arousal for optimal performance, whereas difficult tasks require a "low–moderate" level. This relationship between task performance and arousal has been explained by the **Yerkes-Dodson law** (Teigen, 1994; Yerkes & Dodson, 1908), although Yerkes and Dodson formulated the law referring to stimulus intensity, not arousal level (Winton, 1987). Cognitive appraisal of a task can impact someone's experience of the task as being easy or difficult (see **Figure 10.5**).

For example, a sports psychologist might work with an athlete to help them get "in the zone" where they are in that specific zone of arousal (not too low and not too high) and state of mental focus to maximize their athletic skills and performance. See Learning Objective A.6. Social psychologists also examine the effect of the presence of other people on the facilitation or impairment of an individual's performance. See Learning Objective 11.2. Imagine someone in a classroom speaking to a classmate nearby. The act of speaking directly to another person is a fairly easy task for many people. However, ask that same individual to stand, turn, and address the entire classroom, and it is a different task altogether. All of a sudden, their arousal level spikes and many may find themselves unable to put words together well enough to form coherent sentences or to pronounce words correctly. In essence, they may become "tongue-tied;" because of the appraised difficulty of the oral presentation, their arousal level has gotten too high.

10.8 Personality Factors in Stress

10.8 Explain how personality types and attitudes can influence people's reaction to stress.

Of course, how one cognitively assesses a stressor has a lot to do with one's personality, the unique and relatively stable ways in which people think, feel, and interact with others. People with certain kinds of personality traits—such as aggressiveness or a naturally high level of anxiety, for example—seem to create more stress for themselves than may exist in the actual stressor. Even as long ago as the early 1930s, psychologists have had evidence that personality characteristics are a major factor in predicting health. A longitudinal study begun in 1932 (Lehr & Thomae, 1987) found that personality was almost as important to longevity* as were genetic, physical, or lifestyle factors. Other researchers have found that people who live to be very old—into their 90s and even over 100 years—tend to be relaxed, easygoing, cheerful, and active. People who have the opposite personality traits, such as aggressiveness, stubbornness, inflexibility, and tenseness, typically do not live as long as the *average* life expectancy (Levy et al., 2002).

PERSONALITY TYPES Those positive and negative traits just discussed are some of the factors associated with personality types that have been related to how people deal with stress and that may influence CHD. However, it should be noted that while personality is really far more complex than just a few "types," the following categories are simply handy, compact ways to refer to sets of associated traits. And as you will see, while there are limitations, many of the personality traits associated with these types do seem to be associated with stress and longevity.

TYPE A AND TYPE B In 1974, cardiologists Meyer Freidman and Ray Rosenman published a book titled *Type A Behavior and Your Heart*. The book was the result of studies spanning three decades of research into the influence of certain personality characteristics on CHD (Friedman & Kasanin, 1943; Friedman & Rosenman, 1959; Rosenman et al., 1975). Since then, numerous researchers have explored the link between what Friedman called Type A and Type B personalities.

Type A people are workaholics—they are very competitive, ambitious, hate to waste time, and are easily annoyed. They feel a constant sense of pressure and have a strong tendency to try to do several things at once. Often successful but frequently unsatisfied, they always seem to want to go faster and do more, and they get easily upset over small things. A typical Type A finds it difficult to relax and do nothing—Type A people take work with them on vacation, a laptop to the beach, and do business over the phone in the car.

In contrast, **Type B** people are not that competitive or driven, tend to be easygoing and slow to anger, and seem relaxed and at peace. Type B people are more likely to take a book to the beach to cover up their face than to actually read the book.

In 1961, the Western Collaborative Group Study (Rosenman et al., 1975) assessed 3,500 men and followed them for 8 years. For example, participants were asked to agree or disagree with statements such as "I can relax without guilt," in which strong agreement indicates a Type B personality. The results were that Type A men were three times more likely to develop heart disease than were Type B men.

The Framingham Heart Study found that the risk of CHD for women who work and are also Type A is four times that of Type B working women (Eaker & Castelli, 1988). Other research has narrowed the key factors in Type A personality and heart disease to one characteristic: hostility** (Fredrickson et al., 2000; Matthews et al., 2004; Williams, 1999; Williams et al., 1980). Williams and his colleagues used the Minnesota Multiphasic Personality Inventory, a personality test that looks for certain characteristics that include the level of hostility. See Learning Objective 12.14. In this study, 424 patients who had undergone exploratory surgery for CHD were examined, and the presence of heart disease was related both to being Type A and to being hostile, with hostility being the more significant factor in the hardening of the arteries to the heart (Williams, 2001; Williams et al., 1980).

Type A personality

person who is ambitious, time conscious, extremely hardworking, and tends to have high levels of hostility and anger as well as being easily annoyed.

Type B personality

person who is relaxed and laid-back, less driven and competitive than Type A, and slow to anger.

---

*longevity: how long people live.
**hostility: feelings of conflict, anger, and ill will that are long lasting.

Numerous studies support the link between hostility and increased risk of CHD. Anger and hostility appear to have harmful effects in both healthy individuals and those with existing CHD (Chida & Steptoe, 2009). In one study, people with any observed hostility, as assessed by a stressful interview, were significantly at greater risk for heart disease over ten years of follow up (Newman et al., 2011). Studies have also found that hostility in college-aged males and females was significantly related to increased risk of heart disease, particularly if levels of hostility rose in middle age (Brondolo et al., 2003; Siegler et al., 2003).

Even children may not escape the hostility–heart disease link. One study found that children and adolescents who scored high on assessments of hostility were more likely to show physical changes such as obesity, resistance to insulin, high blood pressure, and elevated levels of triglycerides 3 years after the initial measurements of hostility had been made (Raikkonen et al., 2003).

> 💬 What about people who don't blow their top but try to keep everything "in" instead? Wouldn't that be bad for a person's health?

TYPE C A third personality type was identified by researchers Temoshok and Dreher (1992) as being associated with a higher incidence of cancer. **Type C** people tend to be very pleasant and try to keep the peace but find it difficult to express emotions, especially negative ones. They tend to internalize their anger and often experience a sense of despair over the loss of a loved one or a loss of hope. They are often lonely. These personality characteristics are strongly associated with cancer, and people who have cancer and this personality type often have thicker cancerous tumors as well (Eysenck, 1994; Temoshok & Dreher, 1992). Just as the stress of hostility puts the cardiovascular systems of Type A people at greater risk, the internalized negative emotions of the Type C personality may increase the levels of harmful stress hormones, weaken the immune system, and slow recovery.

TYPE D Another set of personality characteristics has become a topic of interest to researchers and seems to characterize individuals who are prone to experience psychological distress. **Type D**, or "distressed" individuals are prone to chronic stress, tend to experience negative emotions such as anxiety and depression across multiple situations, and experience social inhibition due to fear of rejection or disapproval (Denollet, 2005; Denollet et al., 2010; Denollet et al., 1995; Denollet et al., 2018; Kupper & Denollet, 2018). This combination of characteristics occurs in approximately 25 percent of individuals with CHD and is both a risk factor for developing and a risk factor in the overall prognosis of CHD for these individuals (Kupper & Denollet, 2018).

THE HARDY PERSONALITY Not all Type A people are prone to heart disease. Some people actually seem to thrive on stress instead of letting stress wear them down. These people have what is called the **hardy personality**, a term first coined by psychologist Suzanne Kobasa (1979). Hardy people (call them "Type H") differ from ordinary, hostile Type A people and others who suffer more ill effects due to stress in three ways:

- Hardy people have a deep sense of *commitment* to their values, beliefs, sense of identity, work, and family life.
- Hardy people also feel that they are in *control* of their lives and what happens to them.
- Hardy people tend to interpret events in primary appraisal differently than people who are not hardy. When things go wrong, they do not see a frightening problem to be avoided but instead a *challenge* to be met and answered.

Why would those three characteristics (often known as the three "Cs" of hardiness) lessen the negative impact of stress? Commitment makes a person more willing to make sacrifices and deal with hardships than if commitment were lacking. Think about it: Have

---

Type C personality
pleasant but repressed person, who tends to internalize his or her anger and anxiety and who finds expressing emotions difficult.

Type D personality
"distressed" personality type; person who experiences negative emotions such as anger, sadness, and fear and tends not to share these emotions in social situations out of fear of rejection or disapproval.

hardy personality
a person who seems to thrive on stress but lacks the anger and hostility of the Type A personality.

you ever had a job that you hated? Every little frustration and every snag was very stressful, right? Now think about doing something you love to do. The frustrations and snags that inevitably come with any endeavor just don't seem quite as bad when you are doing something you really want to do, do they?

As for control, uncontrollability is one of the major factors cited as increasing stress, as was discussed earlier in this chapter. Seeing events as challenges rather than problems also changes the level of stress experienced, a difference similar to that felt when riding a roller coaster: If riding the coaster is your own idea, it's fun; if someone makes you ride it, it's not fun.

The tendency for hardiness may even have genetic roots. Researchers have recently found that there seems to be a biochemical link between feeling miserable and an increased risk of death and that there may be a genetic variation in some individuals that actually severs that link, making that individual more biologically resilient or hardy (Cole et al., 2010).

The four personality types discussed so far could be summed up this way: If life gives you lemons,

- Type A people get enraged and throw the lemons back, having a minor heart attack while doing so.
- Type B people gather all the lemons and make lemonade.
- Type C people don't say anything but fume inside where no one can see.
- Type D people will not let you know how they feel but will likely be both a bit stressed about getting the lemons and depressed in that they may not know what they will do with them.
- Type H people gather the lemons, make lemonade, sell it, turn it into a franchise business, and make millions. (Remember, laughing is good for you!)

A word of caution here: "personality type" theories have come under criticism in recent years. Many consider them to be too simplistic—many people would not fall easily into one type or another. More specifically, there have been questions raised about the validity of ongoing research related to Type A behavior and CHD. Researchers have suggested the continued negative and inconsistent findings in numerous epidemiological studies should raise concerns, including the possibility that Type A research may fall in the category of "zombie science" in that despite repeated negative findings, Type A research continues to be published (Charlton, 2008; Petticrew et al., 2016).

Despite the criticisms of particular personality type theories, some of the associated characteristics of type-based theories hold promise for both understanding some of the psychological determinants and impacts on individual health in the face of acute or chronic stress and in preventing or treating a variety of health disorders. Many of the characteristics of the Type A personality, for example, fit the description of a major personality trait called *neuroticism*, the tendency to worry, be moody, and be emotionally intense. See Learning Objective 12.10. Also, aspects of the Type D personality have overlap with symptoms of both anxiety and depression, aspects of several psychological disorders. See Learning Objectives 13.4, 13.6.

EXPLANATORY STYLE: OPTIMISTS AND PESSIMISTS In addition to personality there are other personal factors that have an influence on people's reactions to stressors. One of these factors is the attitude that people have toward the things that happen to them in life. **Optimists** are people who always tend to look for positive outcomes. *Pessimists* seem to expect the worst to happen. For an optimist, a glass is half full, whereas for a pessimist, the glass is half empty. Researchers have found that optimism is associated with longer life and increased immune-system functioning. Mayo Clinic researchers conducted a longitudinal study of optimists and pessimists (as assessed by a scale) over a period of 30 years (Maruta et al., 2002). The results for pessimists were not good: They had a much higher death rate

optimists

people who expect positive outcomes.

than the optimists, more problems with physical and emotional health, more pain, less ability to take part in social activities, and less energy than optimists. The optimists had a 50 percent lower risk of premature death and were calmer, more peaceful, and happier than the pessimists (Maruta et al., 2002). Other studies link being optimistic to higher levels of helper T cells (immune system cells that direct and increase the functioning of the immune system) and higher levels of natural killer cells, the body's antivirus and anticancer cells (Segerstrom et al., 1998; Segerstrom & Sephton, 2010; Sin et al., 2015). Martin Seligman is a social learning psychologist who developed the concept of *learned helplessness*, see Learning Objective 5.12, and began the positive psychology movement. Seligman (2002) has outlined four ways in which optimism may affect how long a person lives:

1. Optimists are less likely to develop learned helplessness, the tendency to stop trying to achieve a goal that has been blocked in the past.
2. Optimists are more likely than pessimists to take care of their health by preventive measures (such as going to the doctor regularly, eating right, and exercising) because they believe that their actions make a difference in what happens to them. (Remember, this is a characteristic of hardy people as well.)
3. Optimists are far less likely than pessimists to become depressed, and depression is associated with mortality because of the effect of depression on the immune system.
4. Optimists have more effectively functioning immune systems than pessimists do, perhaps because they experience less psychological stress.

Regular exercise—whether alone or in the company of family and friends—increases the functioning of the immune system and helps give people a sense of control over their health. Having a sense of control decreases feelings of stress, which also helps the immune system function well.

Seligman (1998) has also found that optimists are more successful in their life endeavors than pessimists are. Optimistic politicians win more elections, optimistic students get better grades, and optimistic athletes win more contests.

10.9 Social and Cultural Factors in Stress: People Who Need People

10.9 Identify social and cultural factors that influence stress reactions.

As stated earlier, much of the stress in everyday life comes from having to deal with other people and with the rules of social interaction. Overcrowding, for example, is a common source of stress. Overcrowding on our roadways, or traffic congestion, is one factor in aggressive driving behavior, which may escalate, or trigger in someone else, a disproportionate response or even *road rage* (AAA Foundation, 2009; Jeon et al., 2014). Road rage is a criminal act of assault by drivers against other drivers, which can result in serious injuries or even death. In 2014 in the United States, 78 percent of drivers surveyed reported engaging in at least one aggressive driving behavior, most commonly tailgating on purpose to get the driver of the car ahead to speed up or move over, yelling at another driver, honking their horn to show annoyance or anger, in the past year (AAA Foundation for Traffic Safety, 2016). In the same AAA survey, aggressive acts consistent with road rage were reported by a few, including 3.7 percent of drivers getting out of their vehicle to confront another driver and 2.8 percent of respondents intentionally bumping or ramming another vehicle in the past year.

Two of the more prominent social factors in creating stressful living conditions are both economically based—poverty and job stress—while the third factor we will discuss has to do with the culture within which we live, work, and play.

POVERTY Living in poverty is stressful for many reasons. Lack of sufficient money to provide the basic necessities of life can lead to many stressors for both adults and children: overcrowding, lack of medical care, increased rates of disabilities due to poor prenatal care, noisy environments, increased rates of illness (such as asthma in childhood), psychological problems, conduct problems and violence, and substance abuse (Aligne et al., 2000; Evans & Kim, 2013; Leroy & Symes, 2001; Park et al., 2002; Pryor et al., 2019; Schmitz et al., 2001; Wong et al., 2018).

JOB STRESS Even if a person has a job and is making an adequate salary, there are stresses associated with the workplace that add to daily stressors. Some of the typical sources of stress in the workplace include the workload, a lack of variety or meaningfulness in work, lack of control over decisions, long hours, poor physical work conditions, racism, sexism, and lack of job security (Murphy, 1995).

Stress at work can result in the same symptoms as stress from any other source: headaches, high blood pressure, indigestion, and other physical symptoms; anxiety, irritability, anger, depression, and other psychological symptoms; and behavioral symptoms such as overeating, drug use, poor job performance, or changes in family relationships (Anschuetz, 1999; Chandola et al., 2006).

Poverty can lead to many conditions that increase the degree of stress experienced by both adults and children. Approximately 34 percent of the people in this New York neighborhood live in poverty, as compared to 20 percent in the city overall and 12.3 percent in the United States as a whole. What type of stressors might the people in this neighborhood be at an increased risk of experiencing?

💬 There are times when I feel like I've just had it with school and all the work the teachers pile on—is that something like workplace stress?

One of the more serious effects of workplace stress is a condition called burnout. **Burnout** can be defined as negative changes in thoughts, emotions, and behavior as a result of prolonged stress or frustration, resulting in both mental and physical exhaustion (Bakker et al., 2014). In addition to exhaustion, symptoms of burnout are extreme dissatisfaction, pessimism, lowered job satisfaction, and a desire to quit. Although burnout is most commonly associated with job stress, students can also suffer from burnout when the stresses of life—term papers, exams, assignments, and the like—become overwhelming. The emotional exhaustion associated with burnout can be lessened when a person at risk of burnout is a member, within the work environment, of a social group that provides support and also the motivation to continue to perform despite being exhausted (Halbesleben & Bowler, 2007; Li et al., 2015).

HOW CULTURE AFFECTS STRESS When a person from one culture must live in another culture, that person may experience a great deal of stress. *Acculturation* means the process of adapting to a new or different culture, often the dominant culture (Sam & Berry, 2010; Sodowsky et al., 1991). The stress resulting from the need to change and adapt to the dominant or majority culture is called **acculturative stress** (Berry & Kim, 1988 Berry & Sam, 1997). Some of the more obvious sources of acculturative stress include dealing with prejudice and discrimination. Others may include learning how to navigate the educational system, developing proficiency in a new language, and finding employment (Sue & Sue, 2016).

The way in which a minority person chooses to enter into the majority culture can also have an impact on the degree of stress that person will experience (Berry & Kim, 1988; Ramos et al., 2015). One method is called *integration*, in which the individual tries to maintain a sense of the original cultural identity while also trying to form a positive relationship with members of the majority culture. For example, an integrated person will maintain a lot of original cultural traditions within the home and with immediate family members but will dress like the majority culture and adopt some of those characteristics as well. For people who choose integration, acculturative stress is usually low (Ramdhonee & Bhowon, 2012; Rudmin, 2003; Ward & Rana-Deuba, 1999).

AP 7.G Describe how cultural influences shape emotional expression, including variations in body language.

burnout

negative changes in thoughts, emotions, and behavior as a result of prolonged stress or frustration, leading to feelings of exhaustion.

acculturative stress

stress resulting from the need to change and adapt a person's ways to the majority culture.

In *assimilation*, the minority person gives up the old cultural identity and completely adopts the majority culture's ways. In the early days of the United States, many immigrants were assimilated into the mainstream American culture, even changing their names to sound more "American." Assimilation leads to moderate levels of stress, most likely due to the loss of cultural patterns and rejection by other members of the minority culture who have not chosen assimilation (LaFromboise et al., 1993; Lay & Nguyen, 1998; Rudmin, 2003).

Separation is a pattern in which the minority person rejects the majority culture's ways and tries to maintain the original cultural identity. Members of the minority culture refuse to learn the language of the dominant culture, and they live where others from their culture live, socializing only with others from their original culture. An example of this might be seen in many "Chinatown" areas across the United States, in which there are some residents who do not speak any English and who rarely go outside their neighborhood. Separation results in a fairly high degree of stress, and that stress will be even higher if the separation is forced (by discrimination from the majority group) rather than voluntary (self-imposed withdrawal from the majority culture).

The greatest acculturative stress will most likely be experienced by people who are *marginalized*, neither maintaining contact with their original culture nor joining the majority culture. Although it can be by choice, it is more likely the result of direct or indirect actions of the larger society. These people essentially live on the "margins" of both cultures without feeling or becoming part of either culture. Many Native Americans may feel marginalized, belonging neither to their original tribe of origin nor to the majority culture. Marginalized individuals do not have the security of the familiar culture of origin or the acceptance of the majority culture and may suffer a loss of identity and feel alienated from others (Roysircar-Sodowsky & Maestas, 2000; Rudmin, 2003). In addition to possible alienation, marginalized communities may not take advantage of support systems such as health-care centers (Montesanti et al., 2017). Overall, as the result of their marginalization, these individuals or communities may have restricted support systems to help them deal with both everyday stresses and major life changes.

Concept Map L.O. 10.4, 10.5, 10.6, 10.7, 10.8, 10.9

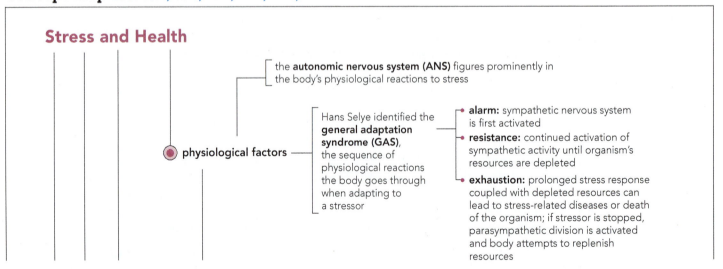

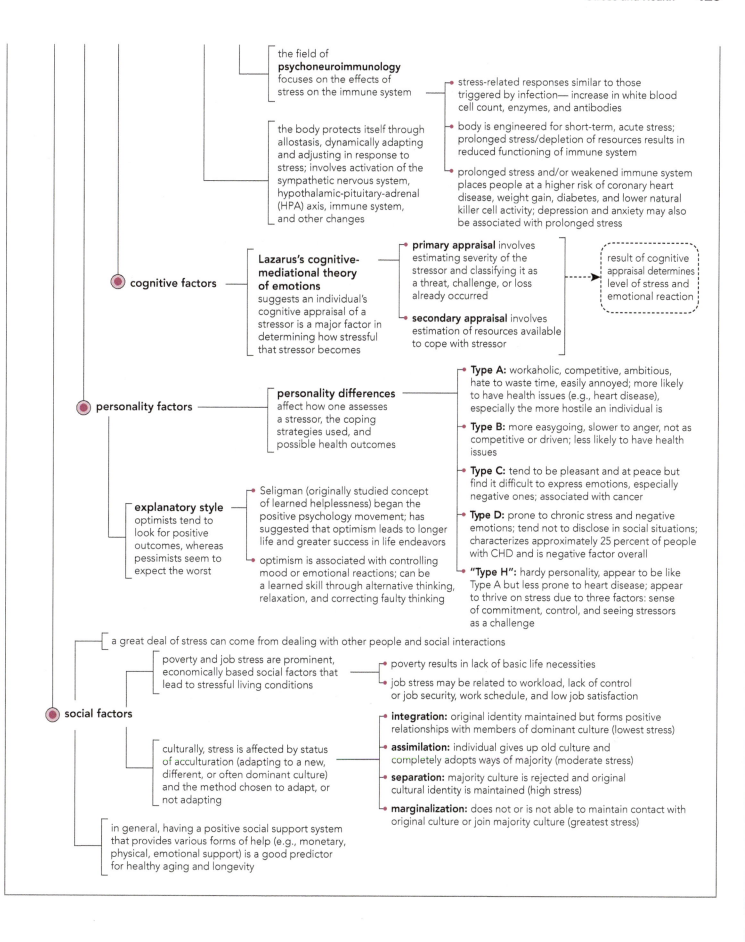

Practice Quiz — How much do you remember?

Pick the best answer.

1. Which stage of the general adaptation syndrome is accompanied by activation of the sympathetic nervous system?
   a. resistance
   b. alarm
   c. resolution
   d. exhaustion
   e. termination

2. According to Richard Lazarus, when someone asks himself or herself, "How can I deal with this potentially harmful stressor?" the individual is focused on a _____ appraisal.
   a. primary
   b. basic
   c. secondary
   d. tertiary
   e. minimal

3. Jon rushes to an appointment, arriving 20 minutes early, while Chazz arrives with only minutes to spare. Slightly annoyed when Jon points this out, Chazz replies very casually, "Hey, I'm here." We might assume Jon has more of a Type _____ personality, while Chazz is more Type _____.
   a. A, B
   b. B, C
   c. D, H
   d. A, C
   e. C, A

4. Danae feels as if she is in control of her life and is committed to her goals. What final aspect of hardiness does she need to possess to be considered a hardy personality?
   a. being concerned when faced with problems
   b. exhibiting callousness in the face of threat
   c. being able to contain her anger
   d. being self-conscious about her approaches
   e. seeing an event as a challenge rather than a problem

5. Brooke is a full-time college student who has not taken a semester off in 3 years. She increasingly finds herself fatigued and stressed by the seemingly never-ending stream of papers, exams, and group projects. It has gotten to the point where she lacks the energy to work on her projects and puts little effort into her studying, figuring "What's the point?" What might Brooke be experiencing?
   a. Brooke is simply stressed. Nothing more.
   b. Brooke is suffering from acculturative stress.
   c. Brooke appears to be an extreme optimist.
   d. Brooke is suffering from burnout.
   e. Brooke is suffering from eustress.

6. Alejandro moved from Nicaragua to the United States. He learned to speak and write English, changed his last name so that it would sound more "American," and no longer maintains any of his old culture's styles of dress or customs. Alejandro has used which method of entering the majority culture?
   a. integration
   b. assimilation
   c. accommodation
   d. separation
   e. marginalization

APA Goal 2: Scientific Inquiry and Critical Thinking

Homeopathy: An Illusion of Healing

Addresses APA Learning Objectives 2.1: Use scientific reasoning to interpret psychological phenomena; and 2.3: Engage in innovative and integrative thinking and problem solving.

In the late nineteenth century, conventional medicine still made use of extremely questionable—and often harmful—practices such as purging (giving the patient enemas and substances meant to induce diarrhea and vomiting), bloodletting, blistering, and leeching (Lilienfeld et al., 2014). It is no small wonder that many patients died. Into this arena came a doctor, Samuel Hahnemann, who truly wanted to find a safer way to treat his patients. The birth of the alternative medicine technique called **homeopathy**, the treatment of disease by introducing minute amounts of substances that would cause disease in larger doses, came from a series of events in Hahnemann's own experience. He took a dose of cinchona bark, used to treat malaria, and developed symptoms of malaria. From this one incident, he reasoned that if a substance causes a symptom of a disease in a healthy person, that substance can also be used to treat the same symptom in a sick person (Hahnemann, 1907; Hall, 2014). This was the first law of homeopathy, "like cures like." Notice that he is clearly making an assumption here based on one experience and no actual research whatsoever—remember the first criterion for critical thinking? "There are very few 'truths' that do not need to be subjected to testing." See Learning Objective 1.5.

homeopathy
the treatment of disease by introducing minute amounts of substances that would cause disease in larger doses.

His second law, the law of infinitesimals, came from the need to dilute his treatments to levels that would not actually cause symptoms, which he believed would make it not only safer but also more potent. Again, this was his belief, not a tested and carefully examined result of research. From these two laws the field of homeopathy was born, and even though famed nineteenth-century physician Oliver Wendell Holmes debunked the practice in the latter part of that century (Holmes, 1892), it is still going strong and has become big business.

There is ample evidence that homeopathy does not work (Ernst, 2002, 2012; Maddox et al., 1988; National Center for Complementary and Integrative Health [NCCIH], 2018; Sehon & Stanley, 2010; Shelton, 2004). The so-called substances that are supposed to effect a treatment are diluted to the extent that people using homeopathic remedies are simply using water, sugar pills, or glycerin—there is no effective medicine in these remedies at all.

And while there are studies out there that claim to have found support for the claims of homeopathy's effectiveness in treating diseases, systematic and scientific reviews of those studies have found numerous flaws in how that research was designed, conducted, and reported (Ernst, 2002, 2012). Plausible and likely explanations for their results were overlooked, such as the *placebo effect* (see Learning Objective 1.10), natural healing that has occurred as time has passed, the power of suggestion, and regression to the mean, which basically states that things tend to even out over the long run (see Learning Objective A.3). The fact is, people often don't look too closely at promised remedies for their ailments. That's really too bad, because a little critical thinking on their part could save them quite a bit of money.

THINKING CRITICALLY 10.2

Many people have tried some pretty wild things to address issues like acne, bad breath, hiccups, and other such maladies. What is the strangest thing you have ever tried to solve or cure such conditions? Did it work, and what prompted you to try it?

10.10–10.13 Coping with Stress

💬 I have exams and my job and my relationship to worry about, so I feel pretty stressed out—how do people deal with all the stress they face every day?

AP 7.H Discuss theories of stress and the effects of stress on psychological and physical well-being.

So far, this chapter has talked about what stress is and the factors that can magnify the effects of stress, as well as the effects of stress on a person's physical health. Effectively dealing with stress involves increased awareness so changes can be made in factors that are actually controllable.

10.10 Coping Strategies

10.10 Distinguish between problem-focused and emotion-focused coping strategies to reduce stress.

Coping strategies are actions that people can take to master, tolerate, reduce, or minimize the effects of stressors, and they can include both behavioral strategies and psychological strategies. While there are medications used for the treatment of stress-related problems, as well as nonmedical treatments such as hypnosis (see Learning Objective 4.9) and meditation (discussed later in this chapter), some ways of coping are healthier and more

coping strategies
actions that people can take to master, tolerate, reduce, or minimize the effects of stressors.

effective than others. For example, one avoidance strategy that tends to have a variety of negative effects is eating more food in general or eating more convenience food (i.e., fast food) or "comfort" foods (higher calories, higher carbohydrates, sometimes higher in fat). Research with college students supports increased emotional eating with higher levels of perceived stress (Deasy et al., 2014; Wilson et al., 2015). Obesity has a host of negative health effects, including increased risk of Type 2 diabetes, high levels of cholesterol and triglycerides in the blood, high blood pressure, CHD, and some types of cancer (National Heart, Lung, and Blood Institute, 2018). Other escape or avoidance strategies might include social isolation, problematic Internet use, and substance use (alcohol, tobacco, cannabis). So what are some healthier ways to cope with stress?

PROBLEM-FOCUSED COPING One type of coping strategy is to work on eliminating or changing the stressor itself. When people try to eliminate the source of a stress or reduce its impact through their own actions, it is called **problem-focused coping** (Folkman & Lazarus, 1980; Lazarus, 1993). For example, a student might have a problem understanding a particular professor. The professor is knowledgeable but has trouble explaining the concepts of the course in a way that this student can understand. Problem-focused coping might include talking to the professor after class, asking fellow students to clarify the concepts, getting a tutor, or forming a study group with other students who are also having difficulty to pool the group's resources.

EMOTION-FOCUSED COPING Problem-focused coping can work quite well but is not the only method people can use. Most people use both problem-focused coping and **emotion-focused coping** to successfully deal with controllable stressful events (Eschenbeck et al., 2008; Folkman & Lazarus, 1980; Lazarus, 1993; Stowell et al., 2001). Emotion-focused coping is a strategy that involves changing the way a person feels or emotionally reacts to a stressor. This reduces the emotional impact of the stressor and makes it possible to deal with the problem more effectively. For example, the student who is faced with a professor who isn't easy to understand might share his concerns with a friend, talking it through until calm enough to tackle the problem in a more direct manner. Emotion-focused coping also works for stressors that are uncontrollable and for which problem-focused coping is not possible. Someone using emotion-focused coping may decide to view the stressor as a challenge rather than a threat, decide that the problem is a minor one, write down concerns in a journal, or even ignore the problem altogether.

 Ignore it? But won't that just make matters worse?

True, ignoring a problem is not a good strategy when there is something a person can actively do about solving the problem. But when it is not possible to change or eliminate the stressor, or when worrying about the stressor can be a problem itself, ignoring the problem is not a bad idea. Researchers working with people who had suffered heart attacks found that those people who worried about a future attack were more likely to suffer from symptoms of severe stress, such as nightmares and poor sleep (both factors that increase the risk of a future heart attack), than were the people who tried to ignore their worries (Ginzburg et al., 2003). See Learning Objective 13.7.

Using humor can also be a form of emotion-focused coping. A study on the effects of laughter found that laughter actually boosted the action of the immune system by increasing the work of natural killer cells (cells that attack viruses in the body). In this study, participants were shown a humor video for 1 hour. Blood samples were taken 10 minutes before the viewing, 30 minutes into the viewing, 30 minutes after viewing, and 12 hours after viewing the humor video. There were significant increases in natural killer cell activity and nearly half a dozen other immune-system cells and systems, with some effects lasting the full 12 hours after the video ended (Berk et al., 2001).

problem-focused coping
coping strategies that try to eliminate the source of a stress or reduce its impact through direct actions.

emotion-focused coping
coping strategies that change the impact of a stressor by changing the emotional reaction to the stressor.

In another study, researchers found that laughing can not only significantly *increase* levels of health-protecting hormones, but also just *looking forward* to a positive and humorous laughing experience can significantly *decrease* levels of potentially damaging hormones (Berk et al., 2008; Svebak et al., 2010). Other studies have found that repetitive, joyous laughter causes the body to respond as if receiving moderate exercise, which enhances mood and immune system activity, lowers both bad cholesterol and blood pressure, raises good cholesterol, decreases stress hormones, and even improves short-term memory in the elderly (Bains et al., 2012; Berk et al., 2009).

Meditation is a series of mental exercises meant to refocus attention and achieve a trancelike state of consciousness. See Learning Objective 4.1. Meditation can produce a state of relaxation that can aid in coping with the physiological reactions to a stressful situation. When properly meditating, brain waves change to include more theta and alpha waves (indicating deep relaxation) but little to no delta waves, which would indicate deep sleep (Lagopoulos et al., 2009).

These people are practicing meditation. Meditation increases relaxation and helps lower blood pressure and muscle tension.

Have you ever found yourself staring out into space or at some little spot on the wall or table, only to realize that your mind has been a complete blank for the last several minutes?

The state just described is really nothing more than **concentrative meditation**, the form of meditation best known to the general public. In concentrative meditation, the goal is to focus the mind on some repetitive or unchanging stimulus (such as a spot or the sound of one's own heart beating) so that the mind can forget daily hassles and problems and the body can relax. In fact, Herbert Benson (Benson, 1975; Benson et al., 1974a, 1974b) found that meditation produces a state of relaxation in which blood pressure is lowered, alpha waves (brain waves associated with relaxation) are increased, and the amounts of melatonin secreted at night (the hormone that helps induce sleep) are increased.

Research shows that meditation is a good way to relax and lower blood pressure in adolescents and adults, men and women, and both Whites and African Americans (Barnes et al., 1997; Rainforth et al., 2007; Schneider et al., 1995; Wenneberg et al., 1997). Other research has suggested that meditation can reduce the levels of chronic pain (Brown & Jones, 2010; Kabat-Zinn et al., 1986), reduce the symptoms of anxiety, depression, and hostility (Kabat-Zinn et al., 1985), reduce the risk of heart disease (Schneider et al., 2012), and reduce stress levels in cancer patients (Speca et al., 2000). Reducing stress levels in cancer patients through meditation will increase the likelihood of recovery and reduce the incidence of recurrence.

In a form of concentrative meditation called **mindfulness meditation**, people deliberately and purposefully pay attention to the moment-by-moment "unfolding" of experience without judging or evaluating that experience (Hozel et al., 2011; Kabat-Zinn, 2003; Simkin & Black, 2014). Meditation in general and mindfulness meditation particularly has been found to help reduce stress, improve control of both emotions and cognitions, increase a sense of well-being, and improve emotional health (Creswell et al., 2014; Heppner & Shirk, 2018; Tang et al., 2015).

meditation

mental series of exercises meant to refocus attention and achieve a trancelike state of consciousness.

concentrative meditation

form of meditation in which a person focuses the mind on some repetitive or unchanging stimulus so that the mind can be cleared of disturbing thoughts and the body can experience relaxation.

mindfulness meditation

a form of concentrative meditation in which the person purposefully pays attention to the present moment, without judgment or evaluation.

Some people think that meditation is nothing more than sitting around doing nothing, or even just another form of sleep. But learning to "sit around and do nothing" actually takes some practice—it's not easy to be in one's own head without thinking of dozens of other things. Besides focusing on breath, or intentionally focusing and increasing awareness of various parts of the body through a body scan, mindfulness can also be experienced through other activities such as mindful eating (Heppner & Shirk, 2018). Meditation and

Watch Yoga and Meditation

Watch the Video at MyLab Psychology

activities involving meditative practices like yoga impact the body and brain in multiple ways. To learn more about meditation and changes in the brain, watch the video *Yoga and Meditation*.

Meditation isn't the only way to relax, as reading a good book, taking a warm bath, or simply resting also produce relaxation. There are a couple of techniques recommended by experts to promote stress relief (Anspaugh et al., 2011; Mayo Clinic, 2016). One method is *progressive muscle relaxation*, in which you focus on tensing and then relaxing each of your muscle groups, usually beginning with the feet and working your way up the body. The purpose of this exercise is to help people recognize the difference between tense muscles and relaxed ones—we are often tensed up without realizing it. Another method is *visualization*, in which you use your imagination to "go" to a calm, peaceful place or situation, using as many of your senses as you can.

10.11 How Social Support Affects Coping

10.11 Explain how a social-support system influences a person's ability to cope with stress.

> I hear the term "social-support system" all the time now. Exactly what is it?

A **social-support system** is the network of friends, family members, neighbors, coworkers, and others who can offer help to a person in need. That help can take the form of advice, physical or monetary support, information, emotional support, love and affection, or companionship. Research has consistently shown that having a good social-support system is of critical importance in a person's ability to cope with stressors: People with good social-support systems are less likely to die from illnesses or injuries than those without such support (Kulik & Mahler, 1989, 1993). Breast cancer patients who have good social support tend to be better able to deal with pain and other symptoms of their disease (Kroenke et al., 2012). A good social-support system also may promote better thinking: The more group ties a person has, the greater that person's cognitive health (Haslam et al., 2016).

Marriage, itself a form of social support, is a good predictor of healthy aging and longevity (Gardner & Oswald, 2004; Vaillant, 2002). Social support has been found to have a positive effect on the immune system (Holt-Lunstad et al., 2003); for example, it has been shown to improve the mental health and physical functioning of people who have *lupus*, a chronic inflammatory disease that can affect nearly any part of the body (Sutcliffe et al., 1999; M. M. Ward et al., 1999), as well as those with cancer and HIV (Carver & Antoni, 2004; Gonzalez et al., 2004). Thinking positively impacts health as well: In one recent study, people who experience warmer, more pleasant and upbeat emotions tend to have better health, and the researchers conclude that this connection is likely due to these people being able to make more social connections (Kok et al., 2013). The increased social-support network then has a positive effect on the health of these individuals.

Social support can make a stressor seem less threatening because people with such support know that there is help available. Having people to talk to about one's problems reduces the physical symptoms of stress—talking about frightening or frustrating events with others can help people think more realistically about the threat, for example, and talking with people who have had similar experiences can help put the event into perspective (Townsend et al., 2014). See Learning Objective 14.6. The negative emotions of loneliness and depression, which are less likely to occur with someone who has social support, can adversely affect one's ability to cope (Beehr et al., 2000; Weisse, 1992). The presence of multiple sources of support, such as friends, parents, and teachers, has been found to significantly decrease

social-support system
the network of family, friends, neighbors, coworkers, and others who can offer support, comfort, or aid to a person in need.

loneliness and social anxiety in adolescents (Cavanaugh & Buehler, 2016). Positive emotions, on the other hand, have a decidedly beneficial effect on health, helping people recover from stressful experiences more quickly and effectively (Tugade & Fredrickson, 2004). Positive emotions are more likely to occur in the presence of friends and family.

There is also a theory that gender makes a difference in coping with stress. While men are seen as dealing with stress by preparing to "fight or flee," women are more likely to resort to more socially oriented behavior. If there is an actual enemy, women may try to befriend that enemy and negate the threat, or if no actual enemy is available, they may seek out social support from family or friends (Taylor et al., 2000; Taylor, 2006). This *tend and befriend* theory may have a basis in a genetic difference between men and women. One study suggests that the *SRY* gene (a protein found only on the Y chromosome responsible for determining male sex characteristics) heightens sympathetic activity to stress, increasing the likelihood of the fight-or-flight response in males (Lee & Harley, 2012). The researchers believe that women use a different genetic mechanism in coping with stress. The Y chromosome and associated genes play a role in different behaviors. For example, *SRY* is also involved in the regulation of dopamine, and males appear to be more susceptible to a variety of behaviors and conditions that are related to dysfunction in brain areas that involve dopamine, including impulsive behavior, ADHD, autism spectrum disorder, and Parkinson's disease (Pinares-Garcia et al., 2018; Varshney & Nalvarte, 2017; Yang et al., 2017). As genetic research progresses, it will remain to be seen if this study's results will be supported.

10.12 How Culture Affects Coping

10.12 Describe cultural differences in coping with stress.

AP 7.G Describe how cultural influences shape emotional expression, including variations in body language.

Imagine this scene: You are driving out in the country when you come upon an elderly man working on a large wooden box, polishing it with great care. You stop to talk to the man and find out that the box is his own coffin, and he spends his days getting it ready, tending to it with great care. He isn't frightened of dying and doesn't feel strange about polishing his own coffin. How would you react?

If you were from the same rural area of Vietnam as the elderly man, you would probably think nothing strange is going on. For elderly people in the Vietnamese culture, thoughts of death and the things that go along with dying, such as a coffin, are not as stressful as they are to people from Western cultures. In fact, *stress* isn't all that common a term in Vietnamese society compared to Western societies (Phan & Silove, 1999).

Coping with stress in Vietnamese culture may include rituals, consulting a fortune-teller, or eating certain foods (Phan & Silove, 1999). In many Asian cultures, meditation is a common stress-relief tool, including the art of tai chi, a form of meditational exercise (Yip, 2002).

Other examples of cultural differences in coping: Thai children are twice as likely to use emotion-focused coping methods when facing powerful adults (doctors giving shots, angry teachers, etc.) than are children in the United States (McCarty et al., 1999). Adolescents in Northern Ireland, when compared to those in Colombia and Australia, tend to blame themselves when experiencing stress over social issues (e.g., fear of war, community violence) but also use more social/emotional support (Frydenberg et al., 2001). The Colombian youth used more problem-focused coping, as well as spiritual support and taking social action. Even within subcultures, there are different forms

These people visiting a Mexican cemetery are honoring their loved ones who have passed away. The Day of the Dead is not only a celebration of the lives of those who have passed on but also a celebration for the living, who use this holiday to gain a sense of control over one of life's most uncontrollable events—death itself. What rituals or ceremonies do people of other cultures use to cope with death?

of coping: In interviews with Asian American, African American, and Hispanic American people living in New York after the September 11 terrorist attacks, researchers found that while both African American and Hispanic American people reported using church attendance and other forms of religious coping, Asian Americans reported using acceptance of the event as something out of their control (Constantine et al., 2005; Kuo, 2011). Cultures also vary in how much they engage their social network to help them cope. In a study of African American, Latina, and White women who were victims of intimate partner violence, the use of social support varied by both the type of stress the individuals experienced, with greater social support used with symptoms of hyperarousal, and by ethnicity; Whites and Latinas were more likely to use social support to cope (Weiss et al., 2017).

Obviously, culture is an important factor in the kinds of coping strategies an individual may adopt and even in determining the degree of stress that is experienced. Mental health professionals should make an effort to include an assessment of a person's cultural background as well as immediate circumstances when dealing with adjustment problems due to stress.

10.13 How Religion Affects Coping

10.13 Explain how religious beliefs can affect the ability to cope with stress.

A belief in a higher power can be a source of great comfort in times of stress. There are several ways that religious beliefs can affect the degree of stress people experience and the ability to cope with that stress (Hill & Butter, 1995; Pargament, 1997).

First, most people who hold strong religious beliefs belong to a religious organization and attend regular religious functions, such as services at a synagogue, mosque, temple, or church. This membership can be a vital part of a person's social-support system. People do not feel alone in their struggle, both literally because of the people who surround them in their religious community and spiritually because of the intangible presence of their deity (Koenig et al., 1999).

Another way that religion helps people cope involves the rituals and rites that help people feel better about personal weaknesses, failures, or feelings of inadequacy (Koenig et al., 2001). These include rituals such as confession of sins or prayer services during times of stress. Religion can also increase the likelihood that a person will volunteer to help others, which may benefit both the person receiving the assistance and the individual doing the volunteering. For example, older adults who volunteer on a continuous basis report fewer cognitive complaints such as poorer memory or difficulty concentrating or making decisions than older adults who do not volunteer or those who only do so sporadically (Griep et al., 2017). Finally, religious beliefs can give meaning to things that otherwise seem to have no meaning or purpose, such as viewing death as a pathway to a paradise or the destruction of one's home in a natural disaster as a reminder to place less attachment on material things.

Many religions also encourage healthy behavior and eating habits—eating wisely; limiting or forgoing the use of alcohol, tobacco, and other drugs; and sanctioning monogamous relationships. Some research even suggests that people with religious commitments live longer than those who have no such beliefs, although this is correlational research (see Learning Objective 1.8) and should not be interpreted as concluding that religious belief causes longer life expectancies (Hummer et al., 1999; Koenig et al., 1999; Lambert et al., 2013; Strawbridge et al., 1997; Thoresen & Harris, 2002).

THINKING CRITICALLY 10.3

Are there particular situations in which you seek assistance in dealing with stress versus situations where you tackle things on your own? If so, what is different between those situations?

Concept Map L.O. 10.10, 10.11, 10.12, 10.13

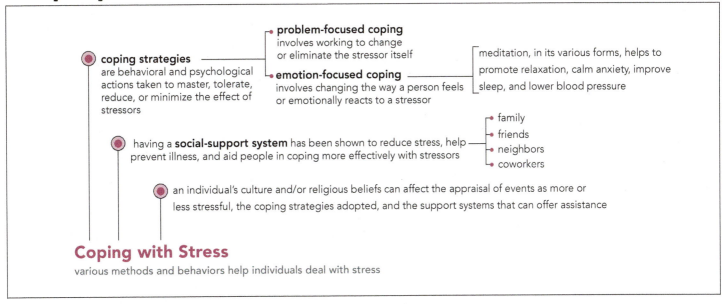

Coping with Stress
various methods and behaviors help individuals deal with stress

Practice Quiz   How much do you remember?

Pick the best answer.

1. Betsy explains that she ignores her problems when she feels she cannot control them or when she worries about them to the point of causing problems elsewhere in her life. What does the research say about using such an approach?
   a. This method can be somewhat harmful even if used only occasionally.
   b. This method is common in early childhood.
   c. This method is helpful only if you are a Type B personality.
   d. This method is fine when the stressor cannot be eliminated or worrying about the stressor causes problems.
   e. This method is dangerous, since a stressor really must be dealt with so as to feel better.

2. What does the research tell us about the effects of laughter on alleviating stress?
   a. Laughter in reality has little to no effect on one's overall stress level.
   b. Laughter has been shown to help the immune system.
   c. Laughter can alleviate immediate stress, but the effects last only a few minutes.
   d. Laughter can increase the negative psychological effects of distress.
   e. Laughter can actually have a negative effect on the body.

3. Simply put, what type of stress reduction is tai chi, the focusing of the mind on specific movements of the body?
   a. personality type
   b. meditation
   c. optimism
   d. problem-focused
   e. progressive muscle relaxation

4. Meditation, progressive muscle relaxation, and guided visualization are _____ coping strategies for stress.
   a. homeopathic
   b. very effective
   c. basically ineffective
   d. emotion-focused
   e. problem-focused

5. What effect, if any, does religion have on one's stress?
   a. Religion can help alleviate stress in young people but not in senior citizens.
   b. Religion can actually increase one's stress.
   c. Religion can help people effectively cope with stress in multiple ways.
   d. Religion can help alleviate stress in senior citizens but not young people.
   e. Religion has not been shown to affect one's stress.

Applying Psychology to Everyday Life

Coping with Stress in College

10.14 Identify common sources of stress for college students, and describe healthy and effective strategies for coping with the effects.

Stress is all around us, and sometimes we make more stress for ourselves by trying to fit too much into our days and nights. How aware are you of all the stressors in your life at any given moment or in any given day? Take a look at the following video. Do you experience any of the same stressors and have you ever used ineffective or unhealthy strategies to cope with them? What healthy coping strategies do you find most useful?

Applying Psychology to Everyday Life Coping with Stress in College

👁 Watch the Video at MyLab Psychology

After watching the video, answer the following questions:

1. What were three healthy strategies for effectively coping with stress highlighted by students in the video?
2. In addition to the strategies shared by the students in the video, what are some other healthy ways in which you effectively cope with stress?

Chapter Summary

Stress and Stressors

10.1 Distinguish between distress and eustress.
- Stress is the physical, emotional, and behavioral responses that occur when events are identified as threatening or challenging.
- Stress that has a negative impact is called "distress." Eustress is the optimal amount of stress that people need to function well.

10.2 Identify three types of external events that can cause stress.
- Catastrophes are events such as floods or crashes that can result in high levels of stress.
- Major life changes create stress by requiring adjustments. Major life changes have an impact on chronic health problems and risk of accidents.
- Hassles are the daily frustrations and irritations that have an impact on day-to-day health.

10.3 Identify psychological factors in stress.
- Four sources of stress are pressure, uncontrollability, frustration, and conflict.
- Frustration, which can be internal or external, may result in persistence, aggression, displaced aggression, or withdrawal.

Physiological Factors: Stress and Health

10.4 Describe the stages of the general adaptation syndrome.
- The autonomic nervous system consists of the sympathetic system, which responds to stressful events, and the parasympathetic system, which restores the body to normal functioning after the stress has ceased.
- The general adaptation syndrome is the body's reaction to stress and includes three stages of reaction: alarm, resistance, and exhaustion.

10.5 Explain how the immune system is impacted by stress.
- Stress causes the immune system to react as though an illness or invading organism has been detected, increasing the functioning of the immune system.
- As the stress continues or increases, the immune system can begin to fail.
- The body also protects itself through allostasis, dynamically adapting and adjusting in response to stress, through activation of the sympathetic nervous system (SNS), hypothalamic-pituitary-adrenal (HPA) axis, along with changes in heart rate, blood pressure, metabolism, and the immune system.

10.6 Describe the branch of psychology known as *health psychology*.
- Health psychology focuses on the impact of physical and social activities as well as psychological traits on health and rates of illness.
- Clinical health psychology is a subfield in which knowledge is gained by researchers to promote health and wellness.

10.7 Summarize Lazarus's cognitive appraisal approach to stress.
- The cognitive appraisal approach states that how people think about a stressor determines, at least in part, how stressful that stressor will become.
- The first step in appraising a stressor is called primary appraisal, in which the person determines whether an event is threatening, challenging, or of no consequence. Threatening events are more stressful than those seen as challenging.
- The second step is secondary appraisal, in which the person assesses the resources available to deal with the stressor, such as time, money, and social support.

10.8 Explain how personality types and attitudes can influence people's reaction to stress.
- Type A personalities are ambitious, time-conscious, hostile, and angry workaholics who are at increased risk of coronary heart disease (CHD), primarily due to their anger and hostility.
- Type B personalities are relaxed and easygoing and have one-third the risk of CHD as do Type A personalities if male and one-fourth the risk if female and working outside the home.
- Type C personalities are pleasant but repressed, internalizing their negative emotions.
- Type D personalities are distressed, and marked by negative emotions, which they tend not to disclose in social situations due to fear of rejection or disapproval.
- Hardy people are hard workers who lack the anger and hostility of the Type A personality, instead seeming to thrive on stress.
- Optimists look for positive outcomes and experience far less stress than pessimists, who take a more negative view.

10.9 Identify social and cultural factors that influence stress reactions.
- Several social factors can be a source of stress or increase the effects of stress: poverty, stresses on the job or in the workplace, and entering a majority culture that is different from one's culture of origin.
- Burnout is a condition that occurs when job stress is so great that the person develops negative thoughts, emotions, and behavior as well as an extreme dissatisfaction with the job and a desire to quit.
- The four methods of acculturation are integration, assimilation, separation, and marginalization.
- Social-support systems are important in helping people cope with stress.

Coping with Stress

10.10 Distinguish between problem-focused and emotion-focused coping strategies to reduce stress.
- Problem-focused coping is used when the problem can be eliminated or changed so that it is no longer stressful or so that the impact of the stressor is reduced.
- Emotion-focused coping is often used with problem-focused coping and involves changing one's emotional reactions to a stressor.
- Meditation can produce a state of relaxation and reduce the physical reactions common to stressful situations.
- Concentrative meditation involves focusing inward on some repetitive stimulus, such as one's breathing.

10.11 Explain how a social-support system influences a person's ability to cope with stress.
- A social-support system is the network of friends, family members, neighbors, coworkers, and others who can offer help to a person in need. Having a social-support system has been shown to reduce stress, help prevent illness, and aid people in coping more effectively with stressors.

10.12 Describe cultural differences in coping with stress.
- Different cultures perceive stressors differently, and coping strategies will also vary from culture to culture.

10.13 Explain how religious beliefs can affect the ability to cope with stress.
- People with religious beliefs also have been found to cope better with stressful events.

Applying Psychology to Everyday Life: Coping with Stress in College

10.14 Identify common sources of stress for college students, and describe healthy and effective strategies for coping with the effects.
- Stressors are the things in our lives that cause us to feel stress (that feeling we get when we experience events we see as challenging or threatening). College may present some unique challenges, and what is stressful for one student may not be stressful for another.
- Healthy and effective coping strategies likely entail being aware of the sources of stress and selecting strategies that work best for a given individual. Strategies may be emotion- or problem-focused and take advantage of both individual proactive behaviors (e.g., regular exercise, adequate sleep, healthy diet) and particular family, social, campus, or community resources for support.

Test Yourself: Preparing for the AP Exam

PART I: MULTIPLE-CHOICE QUESTIONS

Directions for Part I: Read each of the questions or incomplete sentences below. Then choose the response that best answers the question or completes the sentence.

1. Sam has a comprehensive final exam in three weeks that he is concerned about. His concerns prompt him to go ahead and start studying, and in doing so, he feels less worried as the exam approaches. In this example, the exam, Sam concerns, and his behavior may be seen as an example of _____.
   a. burnout
   b. depression
   c. denial
   d. distress
   e. eustress

2. Researchers today believe that eustress is based on _____ theory of motivation.
   a. Maslow's
   b. the arousal
   c. the need for power
   d. the biological
   e. the need for affiliation

3. In addition to being emotionally intense, many items on both the SRRS and CUSS are stressful because they _____.
   a. turn into catastrophes
   b. lead to mild stress disorder
   c. involve the most hassles
   d. cause heart disease
   e. involve money

4. Research suggests the number and perceived severity of daily hassles are strong predictors of _____.
   a. depression
   b. diabetes
   c. heart attacks
   d. headaches
   e. back pain

5. Based on previous research, who is more likely to experience lack of money as the biggest daily hassle in their life?
   a. adolescents
   b. children
   c. young adults
   d. college students
   e. elderly people

6. Brice was cut from his high school basketball team. He told his friends that he was cut because the coach did not like him, but his close friends know Brice was cut because he hardly ever practiced. In this situation, Brice's excuse is an example of a(n) _____ frustration, while the fact he despises practicing is an example of a(n) _____ frustration.
   a. external, personal
   b. internal, external
   c. personal, internal
   d. personal, external
   e. individual, social

7. Olya's husband comes home from work angry because of an argument he had with his boss. Subsequently, Olya's husband begins yelling at her for no apparent reason. Ultimately, Olya finds herself yelling at their youngest child for apparently no good reason other than being frustrated. Olya and her husband are displaying _____.
   a. withdrawal
   b. escape
   c. displaced aggression
   d. projection
   e. denial

8. Seth is trying to decide if he should go on spring break with his friends to Las Vegas or with his other friends to Miami Beach, both of which he has enjoyed going to in the past. Seth's situation is an example of a(n) _____ conflict.
   a. approach–avoidance
   b. avoidance–avoidance
   c. multiple approach–avoidance
   d. approach–approach
   e. multiple avoidance–avoidance

9. In which of Selye's stages of the general adaptation syndrome is death a possible outcome?
   a. reaction
   b. alarm
   c. exhaustion
   d. resistance
   e. resolution

10. According to Richard Lazarus, determining what can be done to deal with one's stress is an example of a _____ appraisal.
    a. formal
    b. tertiary
    c. secondary
    d. primary
    e. foundational

11. Penny rarely takes any work home, preferring to leave her work worries at the office. She is a bit carefree and not as ambitious as some of the other people in her office. Instead, Penny likes to have a lot of leisure time whenever possible. She is also easygoing and doesn't lose her temper often, preferring to avoid conflict. Which of the following statements about Jolene is most likely TRUE?
    a. She is a Type C personality.
    b. Penny's risk of cancer is high.
    c. She is a Type A personality.
    d. Penny's risk of coronary heart disease is high.
    e. She is a Type B personality.

12. Sumit seems to thrive on stress and feels very much in control of his life. He would probably be labeled a _____ personality.
    a. Type C
    b. Type A
    c. hardy
    d. Type B
    e. Type F

13. Bai has moved from China to the United States. While she dresses and acts like her American friends, she still has retained much of her cultural heritage and attends traditional Chinese dance classes on the weekends. This is an example of _____.
    a. integration
    b. minimalization
    c. marginalization
    d. assimilation
    e. separation

14. Trip is having trouble with psychology and statistics. He goes to the school's academic help center for tutoring and spends extra time working on problems at home. Trip's method of coping is _____.
    a. defensive focused
    b. internal
    c. problem focused
    d. emotion focused
    e. indirect

15. Which of the following people may have the greatest ability to cope with stress?
    a. Pearl, who has few friends and whose family lives far away from her
    b. Lexie, who has many contacts on social media but no real friends to speak of
    c. Emil, who works hard but doesn't have any apparent hobbies or other interests
    d. Mia, a very religious person who is involved in her community
    e. Bill, who is highly driven to succeed

PART II: FREE-RESPONSE QUESTION

Directions for Part II: Read the essay question that follows. Then respond to the question in a clear, concise essay. Do not simply list facts. Instead, present a thorough argument based on your critical consideration of the topic. Use of proper terminology is necessary.

Myron works for a video game development company. Whenever his team nears a product launch date, he and all the other developers have to work long hours of "crunch time" for weeks in order to make sure the game is ready for release.

Part A
For each of the following terms, explain how they relate to Myron's experience under "crunch time":

- distress
- pressure
- resistance phase of the general adaptation syndrome
- primary appraisal
- Yerkes-Dodson law

Part B
After getting passed over for a promotion, Myron is considering taking a new job. He likes the idea that the new job will pay more, but he would have to relocate his whole family to a new city if he accepts it. If he keeps his current job, he will continue to face the same stresses, but he will also get to stay in the area he knows well. For each of the following terms, explain how it might influence Myron's decision:

- frustration
- double approach-avoidance conflict

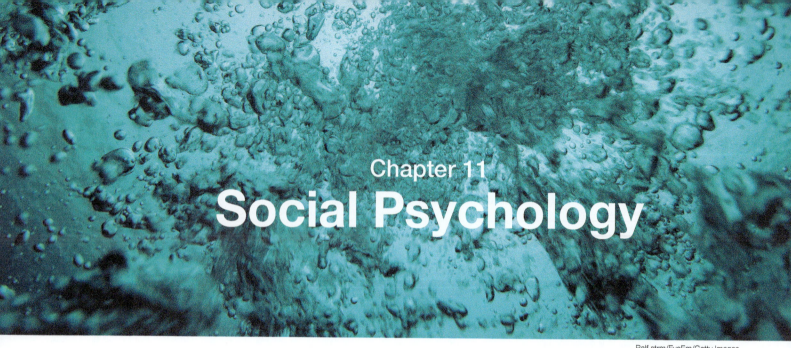

Ralf strm/EyeEm/Getty Images

Chapter 11
Social Psychology

In your words

How are your actions influenced by others? Are there certain actions or personal beliefs that you feel are consistent regardless of your social surroundings?

After you have thought about these questions, watch the video to see how other students would answer them.

Watch the Video at MyLab Psychology

Why study social psychology?

If people lived in total isolation from other people, there would be no reason to study the effect that other people have on the behavior of individuals and groups. But human beings are social creatures—we live with others, work with others, and play with others. The people who surround us all of our lives have an impact on our beliefs and values, decisions and assumptions, and the way we think about ourselves and about other people in general. Why are some people prejudiced toward certain other people? Why do we obey some people but not others? What causes us to like, to love, or to hate others? The answers to all these questions and many more can be found in the study of social psychology.

Learning Objectives

11.1 Identify factors that influence people or groups to conform to the actions of others.

11.2 Explain how our behavior is impacted by the presence of others.

11.3 Compare and contrast three compliance techniques.

11.4 Identify factors that make obedience more likely.

11.5 Identify the three components of an attitude and how attitudes are formed.

11.6 Describe how attitudes can be changed.

11.7 Explain how people react when attitudes differ from behavior.

11.8 Describe how people form impressions of others.

11.9 Describe the process of explaining one's own behavior and the behavior of others.

11.10 Distinguish between prejudice and discrimination.

11.11 Describe theories of how prejudice is learned and how it can be overcome.

11.12 Identify factors involved in interpersonal attraction.

11.13 Describe the different types of love outlined in Sternberg's theory.

11.14 Explain how aggressive behavior is determined by biology and learning.

11.15 Identify the factors influencing why people help others.

11.16 Identify everyday examples of group conformity and group identity.

11.1–11.4 Social Influence

social psychology

the scientific study of how a person's thoughts, feelings, and behavior influence and are influenced by social groups; area of psychology in which psychologists focus on how human behavior is affected by the presence of other people.

social influence

the process through which the real or implied presence of others can directly or indirectly influence the thoughts, feelings, and behavior of an individual.

Chapter One defined psychology as the scientific study of behavior and mental processes, including how people think and feel. The field of **social psychology** also looks at behavior and mental processes but includes the social world in which we exist, as we are surrounded by others to whom we are connected and by whom we are influenced in so many ways. It is the scientific study of how a person's behavior, thoughts, and feelings influence and are influenced by social groups.

Each of us lives in a world filled with other people. An infant is born into a world with adults who have an impact on the infant's actions, personality, and growth. Adults must interact with others on a daily basis. Such interactions provide ample opportunity for the presence of other people to directly or indirectly influence the behavior, feelings, and thoughts of each individual in a process called **social influence**. There are many forms of social influence. People can influence others to follow along with their own actions or thoughts, to agree to do things even when the person might prefer to do otherwise, and to be obedient to authorities.

AP 9.G Explain how individuals respond to the expectations of others, including groupthink, conformity, and obedience to authority.

11.1 Conformity

11.1 Identify factors that influence people or groups to conform to the actions of others.

Have you ever noticed someone looking up at something? Did the urge to look up to see what that person was looking at become so strong that you actually found yourself looking up? This common practical joke always works, even when people suspect that it's a joke. It clearly demonstrates the power of **conformity**: changing one's own behavior to more closely match the actions of others.

In 1936, social psychologist Muzafer Sherif conducted a study in which participants were shown into a darkened room and exposed to a single point of light. Under those conditions, a point of light will seem to move because of tiny, involuntary movements of the eye. See Learning Objective 3.3. The participants were not told of this effect and reported the light moved anywhere from a few inches to several feet. When a confederate (a person chosen by the experimenter to deliberately manipulate the situation) also gave estimates, the original participants began to make estimates of motion that were more and more similar to those of the confederate (Sherif, 1936). This early experiment on conformity has been criticized because the judgments being made were ambiguous* (i.e., the light wasn't really moving, so any estimate within reason would sound good). Would participants be so easily swayed if the judgments were more specifically measurable and certain?

AP 9.F Identify the contributions of key researchers in the areas of conformity, compliance, and obedience.

Solomon Asch (1951) conducted the first of his classic studies on conformity by having seven participants gather in a room. They were told that they were participating in an experiment on visual judgment. They were then shown a white card with only one line on it followed by another white card with three lines of varying lengths. The task was to determine which line on the second card was most similar to the line on the first card (see **Figure 11.1**).

In reality, only the next-to-the-last person in the group was a real participant. The others were all confederates who, after responding with the correct answer on a few trials, were instructed by the experimenter to start picking the same *incorrect* line from the comparison lines. Would the real participant, having heard the others pick what seemed to be the wrong answer, change to conform to the group's opinion? Surprisingly, the participants conformed to the group answer a little more than one third of the time. Asch

conformity

changing one's own behavior to match that of other people.

---

*ambiguous: having no clear interpretation or able to be interpreted in many ways rather than just one way.

Figure 11.1 Stimuli Used in Asch's Study

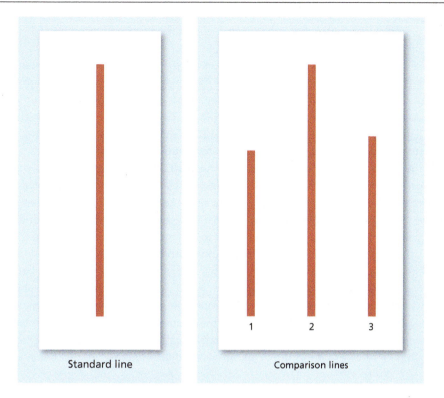

Participants in Asch's famous study on conformity were first shown the standard line. They were then shown the three comparison lines and asked to determine to which of the three the standard line was most similar. Which line would you pick? What if you were one of several people, and everyone who answered ahead of you chose line 3? How would that affect your answer?

Source: Based on Asch, S. E. (1956). Studies of independence and conformity: A minority of one against a unanimous majority. Psychological Monographs, 70 (Whole no. 416).

also found that the number of confederates mattered: Conformity increased with each new confederate until there were four confederates; more than that did not increase the participants' tendency to conform (Asch, 1951). Asch (1956) also found that conformity greatly decreased if there was just one confederate who gave the correct answer. Knowing that at least one other person agreed with them greatly reduced the pressure to conform. For more about this classic study, see the video *Conformity: The Asch Study*.

Subsequent research in the United States has found less conformity among participants, perhaps suggesting that the Asch conformity effect was due to the more conforming nature of people in the era and culture of the United States in the 1950s (Lalancette & Standing, 1990; Nicholson et al., 1985; Perrin & Spencer, 1980, 1981). In other cultures, however, studies have found conformity effects similar to those in Asch's study (Neto, 1995). Still others have found even greater effects of conformity in collectivist cultures, such as Hong Kong, Japan, and Zimbabwe (Bond & Smith, 1996; Kim & Markus, 1999). This cultural difference may exist only when face-to-face contact is a part of the task, however. One study found that when the Asch

Watch Conformity: The Asch Study

Watch the Video at MyLab Psychology

judgment task is presented in an online format (participants were in communication but not able to see each other), the cultural difference disappears (Cinnirella & Green, 2007).

 What about gender—are men or women more conforming?

Research shows that gender differences are practically nonexistent unless the situation involves behavior that is not private. If it is possible to give responses in private, conformity is no greater for women than for men, but if a public response is required, women tend to show more conformity than men (Eagly, 1987; Eagly et al., 2000; Eagly & Carli, 2007). This effect may be due to the socialization that women receive in being agreeable and supportive; however, the difference in conformity is quite small.

Why do people feel the need to conform at all? One factor at work is *normative social influence*, the need to act in ways that we feel will let us be liked and accepted by others (Hewlin, 2009; Kaplan & Miller, 1987). We use the behavior and attitudes of other people as our "measuring stick" of what is "normal." We then judge how we are doing against that "norm." Have you ever laughed at a joke you really didn't get because everyone else was laughing? That's an example of normative social influence. Another factor at work is *informational social influence*, in which we take our cues for how to behave from other people when we are in a situation that is not clear or is ambiguous (Isenberg, 1986). In this case, the behavior of the people around us provides us with information about how we should act, and so we conform to their actions. Another possible explanation for some conforming behavior may involve individuals confusing their own behavior with the behavior of others, resulting in a kind of "mental averaging" of that behavior (Kim & Hommel, 2015).

11.2 Group Behavior

11.2 Explain how our behavior is impacted by the presence of others.

Social influence is clearly seen in the behavior of people within a group, as Asch's classic study illustrated. But conformity is only one way in which a group can influence the behavior of an individual. Here are just a few others.

THE HAZARDS OF GROUPTHINK In February 2017, a 19-year-old college sophomore named Timothy Piazza fell headfirst down a flight of stairs after a night of heavy drinking during a fraternity initiation event and lost consciousness. One fraternity member initially tried to take him to the hospital, but others, including a fraternity leader, dismissed the idea and asked the person offering help to leave. The fraternity members tried to revive Mr. Piazza by slapping him and eventually carried him back upstairs. In all, about 20 fraternity members failed to get help (Ortiz & Lubell, 2017; Silva, 2017). Sometime after midnight, Mr. Piazza appeared to become responsive and went down to the basement. The members discovered him unresponsive around 10 a.m. and again tried to wake him by shaking him (Ortiz & Lubell, 2017). Finally at approximately 10:48 a.m., almost 12 hours after Mr. Piazza had fallen, someone called 911. Mr. Piazza died almost two days later as the result of multiple brain injuries that were reportedly possibly survivable had he received timely medical attention (Silva, 2017).

Why did almost 20 individuals come to the consensus to not seek aid? Why did no one stand up to the leaders of the fraternity and the rest of the group? This appears to be an example of the type of adverse outcome and, in this case, tragedy that can occur when members of a group engage in **groupthink**. Groupthink occurs when people within a group feel it is more important to maintain the group's cohesiveness than to consider the facts realistically (Hogg & Hains, 1998; Janis, 1972, 1982; Kamau & Harorimana, 2008; Schafer & Crichlow, 1996). Other examples include the sinking of the *Titanic* in 1912 (the group responsible for designing and building the ship assumed she was unsinkable

---

AP 9.G Explain how individuals respond to expectations of others, including groupthink, conformity, and obedience to authority.

AP 9.H Describe the structure and function of different kinds of group behavior.

AP 9.I Predict the impact of the presence of others on individual behavior.

groupthink
kind of thinking that occurs when people place more importance on maintaining group cohesiveness than on assessing the facts of the problem with which the group is concerned.

and did not even bother to include enough lifeboats on board for all the passengers), the *Challenger* disaster of 1986 in which the shuttle was known by a few to have structural issues and was not approved for the cold temperatures that day (but no one spoke up to delay the launch), and the decision to invade Iraq shortly after the terrorist attack on the World Trade Center in New York.

Why does groupthink happen? Social psychologist Irving Janis (1972, 1982), who originally gave this phenomenon its name, lists several "symptoms" of groupthink. For example, group members may come to feel that the group can do no wrong, is morally correct, and will always succeed, creating the illusion of invulnerability.* Group members also tend to hold stereotyped views of those who disagree with the group's opinions, causing members to think that those who oppose the group have no worthwhile opinions. They exert pressure on individual members to conform to group opinion, prevent those who might disagree from speaking up, and even censor themselves so that the group's mindset will not be disturbed in a "don't rock the boat" mentality. Self-appointed "mind guards" work to protect the leader of the group from contrary viewpoints. (See **Table 11.1**.)

Table 11.1 Characteristics of Groupthink

Characteristic	Description
Invulnerability	Members feel they cannot fail.
Rationalization	Members explain away warning signs and help each other rationalize their decision.
Lack of introspection	Members do not examine the ethical implications of their decision because they believe that they cannot make immoral choices.
Stereotyping	Members stereotype their enemies as weak, stupid, or unreasonable.
Pressure	Members pressure each other not to question the prevailing opinion.
Lack of disagreement	Members do not express opinions that differ from the group consensus.
Self-deception	Members share in the illusion that they all agree with the decision.
Insularity	Members prevent the group from hearing disruptive but potentially useful information from people who are outside the group.

Source: Based On Janis, I. (1972). Victims of groupthink. Boston: Houghton-Mifflin. Janis, I. (1982). Groupthink (2nd ed.). Boston: Houghton-Mifflin.

Several things can be done to minimize the possibility of groupthink (Hart, 1998; McCauley, 1998; Moorhead et al., 1998). For example, leaders should remain impartial, and the entire group should seek the opinions of people outside the group. Any voting should be done by secret ballots rather than by a show of hands, and it should be made clear that group members will be held responsible for decisions made by the group.

THINKING CRITICALLY 11.1

Can you think of a time when you conformed with the actions of a group of friends, even though you disagreed with their actions? Based on Asch's studies and studies on groupthink, what might have kept you from objecting?

GROUP POLARIZATION Once called the "risky shift" phenomenon, **group polarization** is the tendency for members involved in a group discussion to take somewhat more extreme positions and suggest riskier actions when compared to individuals who have not participated in a group discussion (Bossert & Schworm, 2008; Moscovici & Zavalloni, 1969). A good example of group polarization can occur when a jury tries to decide on punitive damages during a civil trial: Studies have found that if members of a jury individually

group polarization
the tendency for members involved in a group discussion to take somewhat more extreme positions and suggest riskier actions when compared to individuals who have not participated in a group discussion.

---
*invulnerability: quality of being unable to be attacked or harmed.

favored a relatively low amount of punitive damages before deliberation, after deliberation the amount usually lessened further. Similarly, if the individual jurors favored stiffer penalties, the deliberation process resulted in even higher penalties (MacCoun & Kerr, 1988). If information is provided in an online forum such as a social networking group, group polarization can become even more pronounced because group members are exposed to only the information fitting their worldview (Hansen et al., 2013). Group polarization is thought to be due to both normative social influence and informational social influence.

SOCIAL FACILITATION AND SOCIAL LOAFING Social influence can affect the success or failure of an individual's task performance within a group. The perceived difficulty of the task seems to determine the particular effect of the presence of others as well: If a task is perceived as easy, the presence of other people seems to improve performance. If the task is perceived as difficult, the presence of others actually has a negative effect on performance. The positive influence of others on performance is called **social facilitation**, whereas the negative influence is called **social impairment** (Aiello & Douthitt, 2001; Michaels et al., 1982; Zajonc, 1965).

In both social facilitation and social impairment, the presence of other people acts to increase arousal (Rosenbloom et al., 2007; Zajonc, 1965, 1968; Zajonc et al., 1970). Social facilitation occurs because the presence of others creates just enough increased arousal to improve performance. But the presence of others when the task is difficult produces too high a level of arousal, resulting in impaired performance. See Learning Objective 10.7.

Interestingly, people who are lazy tend not to do as well when other people are also working on the same task, but they can do quite well when working on their own. This phenomenon is called **social loafing** (Karau & Williams, 1993, 1997; Latané et al., 1979; Suleiman & Watson, 2008). The reason for this is that it is easier for a lazy person (a "loafer") to hide laziness when working in a group of people, because it is less likely that the individual will be evaluated alone. But when the social loafer is working alone, the focus of evaluation will be on that person only. In that case, the loafer works harder because there is no one else to whom the work can be shifted.

Social loafing depends heavily on the assumption that personal responsibility for a task is severely lessened when working with a group of other people. One study suggests that although Americans may readily make that assumption, Chinese people, who come from a more interdependent cultural viewpoint, tend to assume that each individual within the group is still nearly as responsible for the group's outcome as the group at large (Menon et al., 1999). Chinese people may, therefore, be less likely to exhibit social loafing than are people in the United States.

DEINDIVIDUATION Finally, when people are gathered in a group, there is often a tendency for each individual in the group to experience **deindividuation**, the lessening of their sense of personal identity and personal responsibility (Diener et al., 1980). This can result in a lack of self-control when in the group that would not be as likely to occur if the individual were acting alone. People in a crowd feel a degree of anonymity—being unknown and unidentified—and are more likely to act impulsively as a result. One only has to think about behavior of people in a riot or even the actions of groups like the Ku Klux Klan to see examples of deindividuation. The Stanford prison experiment, discussed later in this chapter, is a historical example of deindividuation in action (Zimbardo, 1970, 1971; Zimbardo et al., 2000). Players in online games often play anonymously, and research results suggest that this anonymity results in greater deindividuation, leading to increased cheating and other deviant behavior online (Chen & Wu, 2013). It also allows *trolling*, which is the posting of deliberately inflammatory comments in online communities (Buckels et al., 2014). This anonymity, and even a possible dissociation from offline identity, also appears to be a factor in individuals with higher online disinhibition who tend to cyber bully others for entertainment as they are not likely to be held responsible for their

social facilitation
the tendency for the presence of other people to have a positive impact on the performance of an easy task.

social impairment
the tendency for the presence of other people to have a negative impact on the performance of a difficult task.

social loafing
the tendency for people to put less effort into a simple task when working with others on that task.

deindividuation
the lessening of personal identity, self-restraint, and the sense of personal responsibility that can occur within a group.

actions (Suler, 2004; Tanrikulu & Erdur-Baker, 2019). In 2014, a harassment campaign against female gamers, and particularly a few female game developers, was begun using the Twitter hashtag #Gamergate (Chess & Shaw, 2015; Heron et al., 2014). The harassment included threats of rape and death by people hiding under the cloak of anonymity. According to a 2017 Pew Research Center survey, approximately 41 percent of American adults had been harassed online and 66 percent had witnessed harassing online behaviors directed at others (Pew Research Center, 2017).

11.3 Compliance

11.3 Compare and contrast three compliance techniques.

AP 9.G Explain how individuals respond to expectations of others, including groupthink, conformity, and obedience to authority.

> 💬 I have a friend who watches YouTube and Instagram celebrities hyping some beauty treatment or product and then buys stuff that isn't worth the money or that doesn't work like it's supposed to work. Why do people fall for pitches like that?

Marketing products is really very much a psychological process. In fact, the whole area of **consumer psychology** is devoted to figuring out how to get people to buy things that someone is selling. See Learning Objective A.7. But advertising, online videos, social media, and infomercials are not the only means by which people try to get others to do what they want them to do. **Compliance** occurs when people change their behavior as a result of another person or group asking or directing them to change. The person or group asking for the change in behavior typically doesn't have any real authority or power to command a change; when that authority does exist and behavior is changed as a result, it is called *obedience*, which is the topic of the next major section of this chapter.

A number of techniques that people use to get the compliance of others clearly shows the relationship of compliance to the world of marketing, as they refer to techniques that salespeople would commonly use. A common example of these techniques will also be apparent to anyone who has ever bought a car, as the video *Compliance Techniques* explains.

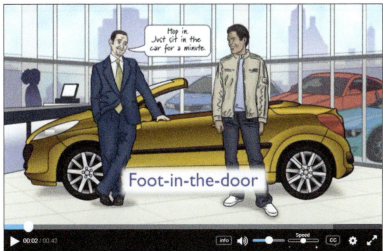

Watch Compliance Techniques

👁 Watch the Video at MyLab Psychology

FOOT-IN-THE-DOOR TECHNIQUE A neighbor asks you to keep an eye on his house while he is on vacation. It's a small request, so you agree. Later that day the neighbor asks if you would kindly water his plants while he's gone. This is a little bit more involved and requires more of your time and energy—will you do it? If you are like most people, you probably will comply with this second, larger request.

When compliance with a smaller request is followed by a larger request, people are quite likely to comply because they have already agreed to the smaller one and they want to behave consistently with their previous response (Cialdini et al., 1995; Dillard, 1990, 1991; Freedman & Fraser, 1966; Meineri & Guéguen, 2008). This is called the **foot-in-the-door technique** because the first small request acts as an opener.

DOOR-IN-THE-FACE TECHNIQUE Closely related to the foot-in-the-door technique is its opposite: the **door-in-the-face technique** (Cialdini et al., 1975). In this method, the larger request comes first, which is usually refused. This is followed by a second smaller and more reasonable request that often gets compliance. An example of this would be if the neighbor first asked you to take care of his dog and cat in your home. After you refused

consumer psychology
branch of psychology that studies the habits of consumers in the marketplace.

compliance
changing one's behavior as a result of other people directing or asking for the change.

foot-in-the-door technique
asking for a small commitment and, after gaining compliance, asking for a bigger commitment.

door-in-the-face technique
asking for a large commitment and being refused and then asking for a smaller commitment.

lowball technique
getting a commitment from a person and then raising the cost of that commitment.

obedience
changing one's behavior at the command of an authority figure.

to do so, the neighbor might ask if you would at least water his plants, which you would now be more likely to do.

LOWBALL TECHNIQUE Another compliance technique, also common in the world of sales, is called the **lowball technique** (Bator & Cialdini, 2006; Burger & Petty, 1981; Weyant, 1996). In this technique that is related to the foot-in-the-door technique, once a commitment is made, the cost of that commitment is increased. In the sense used here, *cost* does not necessarily mean money; *cost* can also mean time, effort, or other kinds of sacrifices. A common example of this is the way in which cellular, cable, or satellite TV companies will advertise low prices in order to get people to sign up for their particular service. Once the service is established, the consumer is often unpleasantly surprised by the number of additional fees, surcharges, and taxes added onto the bill. Another example will also be obvious to those who have bought a car. The commitment to buy the car at a given price is quickly followed by the addition of other costs: extended warranties, additional options, taxes and fees, and so on, causing the buyer to spend more money than originally intended.

CULTURAL DIFFERENCES IN COMPLIANCE Cultural differences exist in people's susceptibility to these techniques. For the foot-in-the door technique in particular, research has shown that people in individualistic cultures (such as the United States) are more likely to comply with the second request than are people in collectivistic cultures (such as Japan). The research suggests that people in collectivistic cultures are not as concerned with being consistent with previous behavior because they are less focused on their inner motivation than are people in individualistic cultures, who are more concerned with their inner motives and consistency (Cialdini et al., 1999; Petrova et al., 2007). See Learning Objective 12.13.

The concept of compliance, along with conformity, also figures heavily in cult behavior, and both concepts can interfere with thinking critically about cult activities. The *APA Goal 2: Scientific Inquiry and Critical Thinking* feature has more information about cults.

AP 9.G Explain how individuals respond to expectations of others, including groupthink, conformity, and obedience to authority.

11.4 Obedience

11.4 Identify factors that make obedience more likely.

There is a difference between the concepts of compliance, which is agreeing to change one's behavior because someone else asks for the change, and **obedience**, which is changing one's behavior at the direct order of an authority figure. A salesperson who wants a person to buy a car has no real power to force that person to buy, but an authority figure is a person with social power—such as a police officer, a teacher, or a work supervisor—who has the right to demand certain behavior from the people under the authority figure's command or supervision.

How far will people go in obeying the commands of an authority figure? What factors make obedience more or less likely? These are some of the questions that researchers have been investigating for many years. The answers to these questions became very important not only to researchers but also to people everywhere after the atrocities committed by the soldiers in Nazi Germany—soldiers who were "just following orders."

AP 9.F Identify the contributions of key researchers in the areas of conformity, compliance, and obedience.

MILGRAM'S SHOCKING RESEARCH In what is now a classic study, social psychologist Stanley Milgram set out to find answers to these questions. He was aware of Asch's studies of conformity and wondered how much impact social influence could have on a behavior that was more meaningful than judging the length of lines on cards. He designed what has become one of the most famous (even notorious*) experiments in the history of psychology.

---

*notorious: widely and unfavorably known.

Through ads placed in the local newspaper, Milgram recruited people who were told that they would be participating in an experiment to test the effects of punishment on learning behavior (Milgram, 1963, 1974). Although there were several different forms of this experiment with different participants, the basic premise was the same: The participants believed they had randomly been assigned to either the "teacher" role or the "learner" role, when in fact the learner was a confederate already aware of the situation. The task for the learner was a simple memory test for paired words.

The teacher was seated in front of a control panel of a shock generator through which shocks would seemingly be administered to the learner if and when the learner gave an incorrect answer. The level, or intensity, of the shocks changed as the experiment progressed (see **Figure 11.2**). For each mistake made by the learner, the teacher was instructed to increase the level of shock by 15 volts. The learner (who was not actually shocked) followed a carefully arranged script by pounding on the wall and playing a series of recorded audio responses (sounds of discomfort, asking for the experiment to end, screaming) or remained silent as if unconscious—or dead (see Figure 11.2 for samples similar to the scripted responses of the learner). As the teachers became reluctant to continue administering the shocks, the experimenter in his authoritative white lab coat said, for example, "The experiment requires you to continue" or "You must continue" and reminded the teacher that the experimenter would take full responsibility for the safety of the learner.

Figure 11.2 Milgram's Experiment

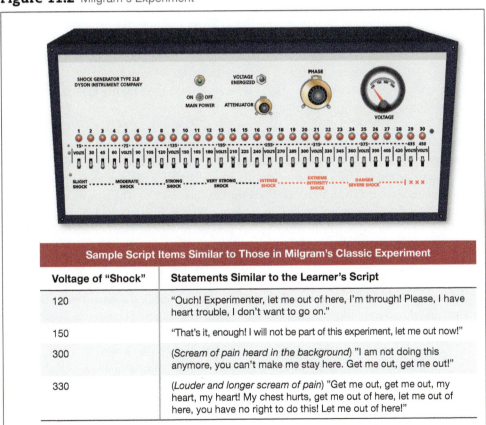

Sample Script Items Similar to Those in Milgram's Classic Experiment	
Voltage of "Shock"	**Statements Similar to the Learner's Script**
120	"Ouch! Experimenter, let me out of here, I'm through! Please, I have heart trouble, I don't want to go on."
150	"That's it, enough! I will not be part of this experiment, let me out now!"
300	(*Scream of pain heard in the background*) "I am not doing this anymore, you can't make me stay here. Get me out, get me out!"
330	(*Louder and longer scream of pain*) "Get me out, get me out, my heart, my heart! My chest hurts, get me out of here, let me out of here, you have no right to do this! Let me out of here!"

In Stanley Milgram's classic study on obedience, the participants were presented with a control panel like this one. Each participant ("teacher") was instructed to give electric shocks to another person (the "learner," who only pretended to be shocked by pounding on the wall and playing a recorded audiotape of grunts, protests, and screams). At what point do you think you would have refused to continue the experiment?

Source: Based on Milgram, S. (1963). Behavioral study of obedience. The Journal of Abnormal and Social Psychology, 67(4), 371-378. doi: 10.1037/h004052Ã; Milgram, S. (1974). Obedience to authority: An experimental view. New York: Harper & Row.

How many of the participants continued to administer what they believed were real shocks? Milgram surveyed psychiatrists, college students, and other adults prior to the experiments for their opinions on how far the participants would go in administering shocks. Everyone predicted that the participants would all refuse to go on at some point, with most believing that the majority of the participants would start refusing as soon as the learner protested—150 volts. None of those he surveyed believed that any participant would go all the way to the highest voltage.

So, were they right? Far from it—in the first set of experiments, 65 percent of the teachers went all the way through the experiment's final 450-volt shock level, although many were obviously uncomfortable and begged to be allowed to stop. Of those teachers who did protest and finally stopped, not one of them quit before reaching 300 volts! The control panel they interacted with was clearly labeled with both the voltage and a description ranging from "slight shock" at the lowest levels, to "danger severe shock," and finally "XXX," representing deadly, at the very highest level (see **Figure 11.2**).

> What happened? Were those people sadists? Why would they keep shocking someone like that?

No one was more stunned than Milgram himself. He had not believed his experiments would show such a huge effect of obedience to authority. These results do not appear to be some random "fluke" resulting from a large population of cruel people residing in the area. These experiments have been repeated at various times, in the United States and in other countries, and the percentage of participants who went all the way consistently remained between 61 and 66 percent (Blass, 1999; Burger, 2009; Doliński et al., 2017; Slater et al., 2006).

> That's incredible—I just don't believe that I could do something like that to someone else.

EVALUATION OF MILGRAM'S RESEARCH Researchers have looked for particular personality traits that might be associated with high levels of obedience but have not found any one trait or group of traits that consistently predicts who will obey and who will not in experiments similar to Milgram's original studies (Blass, 1991). The people who "went all the way" were not necessarily more dependent or susceptible to being controlled by others; they were simply people like most other people, caught in a situation of "obey or disobey" the authority. Some have suggested that Milgram's results may have been due to the same kind of foot-in-the-door technique of compliance as discussed earlier, with participants more likely to go on with each next demanding step of the experiment because they had already agreed to the smaller increments of shock (Gilbert, 1981). Gradually increasing the size of follow-up requests is helpful in changing behavior or attitudes, and participants may have actually come to see themselves as the type of person that follows the experimenter's instructions (Burger, 1999, 2009; Cialdini & Goldstein, 2004).

Milgram's research also raised a serious ethical question: How far should researchers be willing to go to answer a question of interest? Some have argued that the participants in Milgram's studies may have suffered damaged self-esteem and serious psychological stress from the realization that they were willing to administer shocks great enough to kill another person, just on the say-so of an experimenter (Baumrind, 1964). Milgram (1964) responded to the criticism by citing his follow-up study of the participants, in which he found that 84 percent of the participants were glad to have been a part of the experiment and only 1.3 percent said they were sorry they had been in the experiment. A follow-up psychiatric exam 1 year later also found no signs of harm or trauma in the participants. Even so, most psychologists do agree that under the current ethical rules that exist for such research, this exact study would never be allowed to happen today.

Some also believe deception research violates the participant's right to make an informed decision about agreeing or refusing to participate in a given experiment (Baumrind, 2015). See Learning Objective 1.11.

More recent criticisms of Milgram's study include inadequate debriefing of the participants, many of whom did not find out the learner was not actually shocked until six months to a year later (Griggs & Whitehead, 2015; Perry, 2013a, 2013b). It also appears that only some of the results of Milgram's 23 study variations were reported. If they had been reported collectively, they would result in an obedience rate to the highest voltage of only 43.6 percent and a disobedience rate of 56.4 percent (N. Haslam et al., 2014; Perry, 2015). The off-script prodding of the teachers by the experimenter during some of the studies and Milgram's selective editing of his film *Obedience* to downplay participants' resistance have also been examined (Griggs, 2017; Perry, 2015).

There have been attempts to replicate Milgram's study in recent years, although with a shock limit of only 150 volts (Burger, 2009; Doliński et al., 2017). In a 2009 study, the confederates asked to end the study at 150 volts and the participants were asked whether they should continue or not. Regardless of their answer, the study was ended at that point. The results showed that the participants were only slightly less likely to obey than those in Milgram's study. Results of a 2017 replication were also very similar to the original's (Doliński et al., 2017). Interestingly, in the 2017 replication, researchers attempted to examine if the sex of the "learner" had an impact on the level of shock participants would administer. And while participants appeared to be more likely to withdraw when the learner was female, the high rate of obedience overall prevented any conclusive results (Doliński et al., 2017).

Other research has suggested that these studies may not actually examine "obedience" as most often portrayed. A follow-up study to the 2009 replication (Burger et al., 2011) found none of the participants continued with the experiment when the highest of the four prompts the experimenter used was reached. This was the only prompt readily seen as an actual order, "You have no other choice, you must go on." The more the prompts came across as an order, the less likely the teachers "obeyed" (Burger et al., 2011). Furthermore, it has been suggested that instead of obedience, the outcomes of the Milgram paradigm may be more about social identity. The participants identified themselves more in line with the experimenter than the learner and acted in a way that demonstrated their commitment to the larger scientific process rather than to the ordinary community (Reicher et al., 2012). Instead of blindly following orders, the participants were actively working to reach a goal established by the leader or, in this case, the experimenter. In other words, what they were doing was a type of "engaged followership" with the experimenter and the scientific community at large (Griggs, 2017; S. A. Haslam et al., 2015). The people in this study and others may have obeyed because they came to believe that what they were doing was right—with help in developing that belief from the authority figure (Frimer et al., 2014; S. A. Haslam & Reicher, 2012b; Reicher et al., 2012). They were decent people who did something terrible because they believed they were doing the right thing in the long run. For a look at how obedience to an authority figure might work in a real-world situation, watch the video *Obedience to Authority*.

While people can recognize that otherwise good individuals can sometimes do bad things, they often do a poor job applying this information to themselves, even when made aware of these experiments. In the context of a hypothetical experiment, individuals will estimate their level of obedience as low (Grzyb & Doliński, 2017).

Watch Obedience to Authority

Watch the Video at MyLab Psychology

These observations, critiques, and possible reformulations will certainly offer psychologists points to consider in any possible future investigations of the complex topic of obedience. However, some have voiced the need for an extensive and critical examination of ethical justifications for any such manipulations or deception in psychological research (Baumrind, 2015; Nicholson, 2011).

Concept Map L.O. 11.1, 11.2, 11.3, 11.4

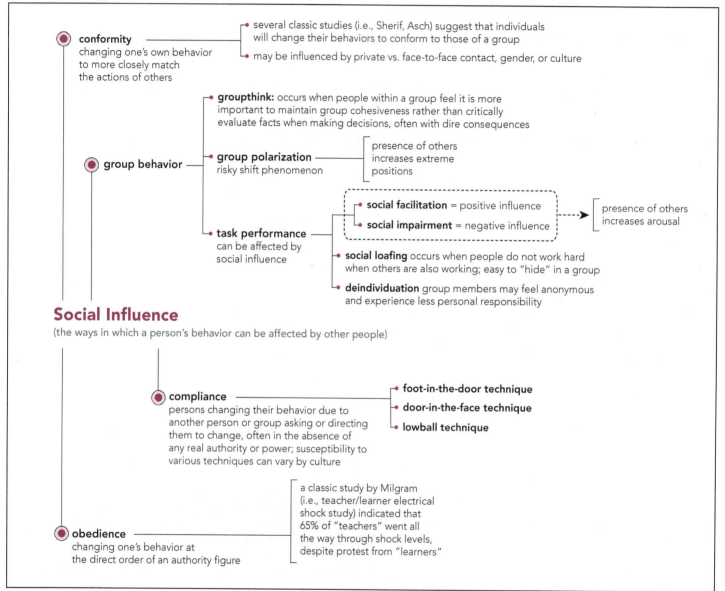

Practice Quiz — How much do you remember?

Pick the best answer.

1. In Asch's study, conformity decreased when _____.
   a. at least four confederates were present
   b. at least one confederate agreed with the participant
   c. the participant was a male
   d. a verbal response was required
   e. the participant had high self-esteem

2. One of the keys to deindividuation is _____.
   a. anonymity
   b. conformity
   c. group protection
   d. group polarization
   c. obedience

3. Which of the following would NOT be effective in minimizing groupthink?
   a. Tracy wants her team to openly vote by a show of hands either for or against her business plan.
   b. Diana reminds her team that everyone will be held responsible for the ultimate decision of her group.
   c. Kristina openly invites input from all team members.
   d. Whitney invites input from individuals not on the team but from outside the group.
   e. Ashley works hard to remain impartial to all ideas no matter what they are.

4. Lance needs just $20 more to go out with his friends. He asks his mother for $50, but she tells him he can have $30 instead. In the end, Lance ended up with $10 more than he originally planned. What technique did Lance use?
   a. foot-in-the-door technique
   b. door-in-the-face technique
   c. BOGO
   d. lowball technique
   e. planned obedience

5. According to reports of Stanley Milgram's original studies, the most often cited statistic is that _____ percent of "teachers" will deliver shocks up to the point of being lethal.
   a. less than 30
   b. 40
   c. 50
   d. 65
   e. 80

APA Goal 2: Scientific Inquiry and Critical Thinking

Cults and the Failure of Critical Thinking

Addresses APA Learning Objective 2.3: Engage in innovative and integrative thinking and problem-solving.

The term **cult** literally refers to any group of people with a particular religious or philosophical set of beliefs and identity. In the strictest sense of the word, the Roman Catholic Church and Protestantism are cults within the larger religion of Christianity. But most people associate the term *cult* with a negative connotation*: a group of people whose religious or philosophical beliefs and behavior are so different from that of mainstream organizations that they are viewed with suspicion and seen as existing on the fringes of socially acceptable behavior. Although many cults exist without much notice from more mainstream groups, at times members of cults have horrified the public with their actions, as was the case in 1997, when the followers of the Heaven's Gate cult, who believed that aliens in a spaceship were coming in the tail of the Hale-Bopp comet, committed suicide under the leadership of Marshall Applewhite. They believed that their souls would be taken up by the comet aliens. The splinter group calling itself ISIS in the Middle East is also an example of a cult, one that commits acts of extreme violence and destruction (Hassan, 2014).

Why would any person get so caught up in cult beliefs that suicide, and in some cases murder, becomes a desired behavior? What happened to their ability to think critically about ideas that, to those of us on the outside, seem obviously foolish and dangerous? The most likely targets of cult recruitment are people who are under a lot of stress, dissatisfied with their lives, unassertive, gullible, dependent, who feel a desire to belong to a group, and who are unrealistically idealistic ("We can solve all the world's problems if everyone will just love each other"; Langone, 1996). Young people rebelling against parental authority or trying to become independent of families are therefore prime targets.

Cult leaders have certain techniques for gaining compliance that are common to most cult organizations. The first step may be something called "love-bombing" by current cult members, who shower the recruits with affection and attention and claim to understand just how the potential cult members feel. Second, efforts are made to isolate the recruits from family and friends who might talk them out of joining. This is accomplished in part by keeping the recruits so busy with rigid rituals, ways of dress, meditations, and other activities that they do not allow the recruits time to think about what is happening. Third, cults also teach their members how to stop questioning thoughts or criticisms, which are typically seen as

cult
any group of people with a particular religious or philosophical set of beliefs and identity.

---
*connotation: the meaning of a word or concept that is more suggestive than directly stated.

sins or extremely undesirable behavior. In other words, cults promote a high degree of conformity and compliance (Singer & Lalich, 1995; Zimbardo & Hartley, 1985).

Commitments to the cult are small at first, such as attending a music concert or some other cult function. (Notice that this is the foot-in-the-door technique.) Eventually, a major step is requested by the cult, such as quitting one's job, turning over money or property to the cult, or similar commitments. Leaving a cult is quite difficult, as members of the cult in good standing will often track down a "deserter." Actress Leah Remini has written a detailed and frank account of her struggles with Scientology and the difficulties of leaving that organization (Remini, 2015).

Cults have existed all through recorded history and will probably continue to exist in the future. Most cults do not pose a physical threat to their members or others, but the examples of the followers of Jim Jones, Marshall Applewhite, David Koresh (the Waco, Texas, disaster in 1993), and ISIS clearly demonstrate that cults, like any group of people, can become deadly.

APA Goal 2 Cults and the Failure of Critical Thinking

Identify the method of persuasion used for each of the following possible statements from cult recruiters.

We're having a performance by some friends tonight, why don't you come? There will be some good food and it'll be fun!   ....

You are such a wonderful person, people in your life have not really appreciated you the way we do. We love you and will always be there for you.   ....

Let's start our day with some meditation. Then I have some clothes you can try out, and we'll go to a lecture later on. The day is just packed with things to do right here!   ....

> WORLD BANK
> Isolation from outsiders · Love-bombing · Foot-in-the-door

11.5–11.9 Social Cognition

social cognition
the mental processes that people use to make sense of the social world around them.

Social cognition focuses on the ways in which people think about other people and how those cognitions influence behavior toward those other people. In this section, we'll concentrate on how we perceive others and form our first impressions of them, as well as how we explain the behavior of others and ourselves.

AP 9.E Discuss attitude formation and change, including persuasion strategies and cognitive dissonance.

11.5 Attitudes

11.5 Identify the three components of an attitude and how attitudes are formed.

attitude
a tendency to respond positively or negatively toward a certain person, object, idea, or situation.

One area of social cognition concerns the formation and influence of attitudes on the behavior and perceptions of others. An **attitude** can be defined as a tendency to respond positively or negatively toward a certain idea, person, object, or situation (Triandis, 1971). This tendency, developed through people's experiences as they live and work with others, can affect the way they behave toward those ideas, people, objects, and situations and can include opinions, beliefs, and biases. In fact, attitudes influence the way people view these things *before* they've actually been exposed to them (Petty et al., 2003).

💬 What do you mean—how can an attitude have an effect on something that hasn't happened yet?

Attitudes are not something people have when they are born. They are learned through experiences and contact with others and even through direct instruction from parents, teachers, and other important people in a person's life. Because attitudes involve a positive or negative evaluation of things, it's possible to go into a new situation, meet a new person, or be exposed to a new idea with one's "mind already made up" to like or dislike, agree or disagree, and so on (Eagly & Chaiken, 1993; Petty et al., 2003; Petty & Briñol, 2015). For example, children are known for making up their minds about certain foods before ever tasting them, simply because the foods are "green." Those children may have tried a green food in the past and disliked it and now are predisposed* to dislike any green food whether they've tasted it or not.

THE ABC MODEL OF ATTITUDES Attitudes are actually made up of three different parts, or components, as shown in **Figure 11.3**. These components should not come as a surprise to anyone who has been reading the other chapters in this text because, throughout the text, references have been made to personality and traits being composed of the ways people think, feel, and act. By using certain terms to describe these three things, psychologists have come up with a handy way to describe the three components of attitudes (Eagly & Chaiken, 1993, 1998; Fazio & Olson, 2003).

AFFECTIVE COMPONENT The *affective component* of an attitude is the way a person feels toward the object, person, or situation. *Affect* is used in psychology to mean "emotions" or "feelings," so the affective component is the emotional component. For example, some people might feel that country music is fun and uplifting.

BEHAVIOR COMPONENT The *behavior component* of an attitude is the action a person takes in regard to the person, object, or situation. For example, a person who feels that country music is fun is likely to listen to a country music station, buy country music, or go to a country music concert.

Figure 11.3 Three Components of an Attitude

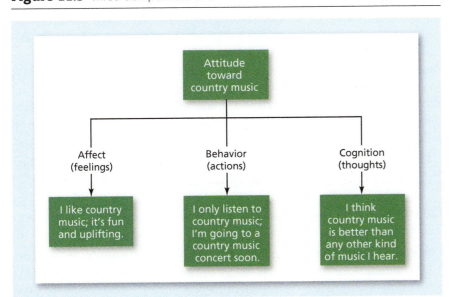

Attitudes consist of the way a person feels and thinks about something, as well as the way the person chooses to behave. If you like country music, you are also likely to think that country music is good music. You are also more likely to listen to this style of music, buy this type of music, and even go to a performance. Each of the three components influences the other two.

---

*predisposed: referring to a tendency to respond in a particular way based on previous experience.

COGNITIVE COMPONENT Finally, the *cognitive component* of an attitude is the way a person thinks about himself or herself, an object, or a situation. These thoughts, or cognitions, include beliefs and ideas about the focus of the attitude. For example, the country music lover might believe that country music is superior to other forms of music.

> 💬 So if you know what someone thinks or feels about something, you can predict what that person will do, right?

Oddly enough, attitudes turn out to be pretty poor predictors of actual behavior in a number of studies. The results of several decades of research indicate that what people say and what people do are often two very different things (van de Garde-Perik et al., 2008; Wicker, 1971). Surveys and studies have found that attitudes predict behavior only under certain conditions. For example, it can probably be assumed that younger women, or those in short-term or temporary relationships, may be more motivated to avoid an unplanned pregnancy as compared to older women in more stable relationships (Firman et al., 2018). However, in a survey of sexually active women in Britain, one in six 16–24-year-olds reported using either no or unreliable methods of birth control (Firman et al., 2018). And in a broad survey of 4,500 women ages 21 to 29 from nine countries in Europe and North and South America, 39.5 percent reported they had forgotten to take their birth control pill at least once in the last month, and 34.5 of those had forgotten at least once a week (Caetano et al., 2019).

Another factor in matching attitudes and behavior concerns how specific the attitude itself is. People may hold a general attitude about something without reflecting that attitude in their actual behavior. For example, doctors generally hold the attitude that people should do everything they can to protect their health and promote wellness, yet many doctors still smoke tobacco, fail to exercise, and often get too little sleep. But a very specific attitude, such as "exercise is important to my immediate health," will more likely be associated with the behavior of exercising (Ajzen, 2001; Ajzen & Fishbein, 2000). Even playing a simulation game in which players control a character within a fictional health care setting, making specific decisions about health behavior, has been shown to have a positive effect on attitudes toward health care in those players (Kaufman et al., 2015).

Some attitudes are stronger than others, and strong attitudes are more likely to predict behavior than weak ones. A person who quit smoking because of failing health might have a stronger attitude toward secondhand smoke than someone who quit smoking on a dare, for example. The importance, or salience*, of a particular attitude in a given situation also has an impact on behavior—the more important the attitude appears, the more likely the behavior will match the attitude. Someone who is antismoking might be more likely to confront a smoker breaking the rules in a hospital, for example, than they would a smoker outside the building (Eagly & Chaiken, 1998).

ATTITUDE FORMATION Attitude formation is the result of a number of different influences with only one thing in common: They are all forms of learning.

DIRECT CONTACT One way in which attitudes are formed is by direct contact with the person, idea, situation, or object that is the focus of the attitude. For example, a child who tries and dislikes brussels sprouts will form a negative attitude about brussels sprouts.

DIRECT INSTRUCTION Another way attitudes are formed is through direct instruction, either by parents or some other individual. Parents may tell their children that smoking cigarettes is dangerous and unhealthy, for example.

---

*salience: importance or having the quality of being obvious or easily seen.

INTERACTION WITH OTHERS Sometimes attitudes are formed because the person is around other people with that attitude. If a person's friends, for example, all hold the attitude that smoking is cool, that person is more likely to think that smoking is cool (Brenner, 2007; Eddy et al., 2000; Hill, 1990; Shean et al., 1994).

VICARIOUS CONDITIONING (OBSERVATIONAL LEARNING) Many attitudes are learned through the observation of other people's actions and reactions to various objects, people, or situations. Just as a child whose mother shows a fear of dogs may develop a similar fear, see Learning Objective 5.3, a child whose mother or father shows a positive attitude toward classical music may grow into an adult with a similarly positive attitude.

Attitudes are not only influenced by other people in a person's immediate world but also by the larger world of the educational system (many attitudes may be learned in school or through reading books) and the mass media of social networking sites, magazines, television, and the movies—a fact of which advertisers and marketing experts are well aware (Gresham & Shimp, 1985; MacKenzie et al., 1986; Visser & Mirabile, 2004).

11.6 Attitude Change: The Art of Persuasion

11.6 Describe how attitudes can be changed.

AP 9.E Discuss attitude formation and change, including persuasion strategies and cognitive dissonance.

💬 Sometimes people learn attitudes that aren't necessarily good ones, right? So can attitudes change?

Because attitudes are learned, they are also subject to change with new learning. The world is full of people, companies, and other organizations that want to change people's attitudes. It's all about the art of **persuasion**, the process by which one person tries to change the belief, opinion, position, or course of action of another person through argument, pleading, or explanation.

persuasion
the process by which one person tries to change the belief, opinion, position, or course of action of another person through argument, pleading, or explanation.

Persuasion is not a simple matter. Several factors become important in predicting how successful any persuasive effort at attitude change might be. These factors include the following:

- Source: The *communicator* is the person delivering the message. There is a strong tendency to give more weight to people who are perceived as experts as well as those who seem trustworthy, attractive, and similar to the person receiving the message (Eagly & Chaiken, 1975; O'Keefe, 2009; Petty & Cacioppo, 1986, 1996; Priester & Petty, 1995).

- Message: The actual message should be clear and well organized (Booth-Butterfield, 1996). It is usually more effective to present both sides of an argument to an audience that has not yet committed to one side or the other (Crowley & Hoyer, 1994; O'Keefe, 2009; Petty & Cacioppo, 1996; Petty et al., 2003). Messages directed at producing fear have been thought to be more effective if they produce only a moderate amount of fear and provide information about how to avoid the fear-provoking consequences (Kleinot & Rogers, 1982; Meyrick, 2001; Petty, 1995; Rogers & Mewborn, 1976). Research now suggests that fear messages with a higher amount of fear may be very effective when they not only provide information about how to avoid the consequences but also stress the severity of those consequences, particularly among women (Tannenbaum et al., 2015).

- Target Audience: The characteristics of the people who are the intended target of the message of persuasion are also important in determining the effectiveness of the message. The age of the audience members can be a factor, for example. Researchers have found that people who are in the young adult stage of the late teens to the

How the jurors in this courtroom interpret and process the information they are given will determine the outcome of the trial. Those who listen carefully to what is said by persons involved in the trial are using central-route processing. There may be some jurors, however, who are more affected by the appearance, dress, attractiveness, or tone of voice of the lawyers, defendant, and witnesses. When people are persuaded by factors other than the message itself, it is called peripheral-route processing.

elaboration likelihood model

model of persuasion stating that people will either elaborate on the persuasive message or fail to elaborate on it and that the future actions of those who do elaborate are more predictable than those who do not.

AP 9.E Discuss attitude formation and change, including persuasion strategies and cognitive dissonance.

AP 9.D Identify important figures and research in the areas of attitude formation and change.

AP 7.B Compare and contrast motivational theories, including the strengths and weaknesses of each.

central-route processing

type of information processing that involves attending to the content of the message itself.

peripheral-route processing

type of information processing that involves attending to factors not involved in the message, such as the appearance of the source of the message, the length of the message, and other noncontent factors.

cognitive dissonance

sense of discomfort or distress that occurs when a person's behavior does not correspond to that person's attitudes.

mid-20s are more susceptible to persuasion than older people (O'Keefe, 2009; Visser & Krosnick, 1998).

- **Medium:** The form through which a person receives a message is also important. For example, seeing and hearing a politician's speech on television may have a very different effect than simply reading about it in the newspaper or online. The visual impact of the television coverage is particularly important because it provides an opportunity for the source of the message to be seen as attractive, for example.

How easily influenced a person is will also be related to the way people tend to process information. In the **elaboration likelihood model** of persuasion (Briñol & Petty, 2015; Petty & Cacioppo, 1986), it is assumed that people either elaborate (add details and information) based on what they hear (the facts of the message), or they do not elaborate at all, preferring to pay attention to the surface characteristics of the message (length, who delivers it, how attractive the message deliverer is, etc.). Two types of processing are hypothesized in this model: **central-route processing**, in which people attend to the content of the message; and **peripheral-route processing**, a style of information processing that relies on peripheral cues (cues outside of the message content itself), such as the expertise of the message source, the length of the message, and other factors that have nothing to do with the message content. This style of processing causes people not to pay attention to the message itself but instead to base their decisions on those peripheral factors (Briñol & Petty, 2015; Petty & Cacioppo, 1986; Stiff & Mongeau, 2002). For example, one of the authors once participated on a jury panel in which one woman voted "guilty" because the defendant had "shifty eyes" and not because of any of the evidence presented.

> **THINKING CRITICALLY 11.2**

Imagine that you are asked to create a television commercial to sell a new product. Given what you know of the factors that effectively influence persuasion, how might you persuade a customer?

11.7 Cognitive Dissonance: When Attitudes and Behavior Clash

11.7 Explain how people react when attitudes differ from behavior.

> 💬 I once called a friend of mine on his behavior, telling him that what he said and what he did were two very different things, and he got really upset with me. Why?

When adults find themselves doing things or saying things that don't match their idea of themselves as smart, nice, or moral, for example, they experience an emotional discomfort (and physiological arousal) known as **cognitive dissonance** (Aronson, 1997; Festinger, 1957; Kelly et al., 1997). When people are confronted with the knowledge that something they have done or said was dumb, immoral, or illogical, they suffer an inconsistency in cognitions. For example, they may have a cognition that says "I'm pretty smart" but also the cognition "That was a dumb thing to do," which causes a dissonance. (*Dissonance* is a term referring to an inconsistency or lack of agreement.)

When people experience cognitive dissonance, the resulting tension and arousal are unpleasant, and their motivation is to change something so that the unpleasant feelings and tension are reduced or eliminated. There are three basic things that people can do to reduce cognitive dissonance:

1. Change their conflicting behavior to make it match their attitude.
2. Change their current conflicting cognition to justify their behavior.
3. Form new cognitions to justify their behavior.

For some examples of dissonance, take a look at the video *Cognitive Dissonance*.

In a classic experiment conducted at Stanford University by psychologist Leon Festinger and colleague James Carlsmith (1959), each male student volunteer was given an hour-long, very boring task of sorting wooden spools and turning wooden pegs. After the hour, the experimenters asked the participant to tell the female volunteer in the waiting room that the task was enjoyable. While half of the participants were paid only $1 to try to convince the waiting woman, the other participants were paid $20. (In the late 1950s, $20 was a considerable sum of money—the average income was $5,000, the average car cost $3,000, and gas was only 25 cents a gallon.)

At the time of this study, many researchers would have predicted that the more the participants were paid to lie, the more they would come to like the task, because they were getting more reinforcement ($20) for doing so. But what actually happened was that those participants who were paid only $1 for lying actually convinced themselves that the task was interesting and fun. The reason is cognitive dissonance: Participants who were paid only $1 experienced discomfort at thinking that they would lie to someone for only a dollar. Therefore, they must not be lying—the task really was pretty interesting, after all, and fun, too! Those who were paid more experienced no dissonance, because they knew exactly why they were lying—for lots of money—and the money was a sufficient amount to explain their behavior to their satisfaction. Although most people don't want to be thought of as liars, back then, getting paid enough money to fill the gas tank of one's car three or four times over was incentive enough to tell what probably seemed to be a harmless fib. Those who were paid only $1 had to change their attitude toward the task so that they would not really be lying and could maintain their self-image of honesty (see **Figure 11.4**).

There is evidence that cognitive dissonance occurs in children as young as 4 years of age, but the basic strategy for dealing with dissonance seems to be different for them than for older children and adults. Researchers compared the behavior of 4- and 6-year-old children by having them complete tasks to earn stickers (Benozio & Diesendruck, 2015). In one group, children of both ages had to work very hard to get stickers, while in another group, the tasks were very easy. The stickers they earned were also of two types, highly desirable (current cartoon characters) and unattractive (e.g., a plant sticker or a princess sticker for a boy). After earning 10 stickers each, the children were told they were going to play a game in which they had to decide how many stickers they wanted to give to a child they had seen in a video (a later variation had them giving stickers to a box to avoid possible social concerns). While both age groups gave away fewer of the attractive stickers, the 6-year-olds gave away far fewer unattractive stickers if they had been hard to get. This suggests that the older children changed their cognition, with effort changing the desirability of the stickers, like the adults in the classic Festinger and Carlsmith (1959) study. But the younger children gave away significantly more unattractive stickers that were hard to earn compared to those that were easily earned, suggesting that they chose to change their conflicting behavior rather than their cognition. It may be that changing one's cognitions requires a little more brain maturation than the younger children possessed.

College students experience cognitive dissonance in their daily lives. Experimental results suggest many students, for example, will not report seeing a classmate cheating on an exam unless there is a cost for remaining silent, such as

Watch Cognitive Dissonance

Watch the **Video** at **MyLab Psychology**

Figure 11.4 Cognitive Dissonance: Attitude Toward a Task

Inducement	Attitude
$1	+1.35
$20	−0.5
Control	−.45

*Based on a −5 to +5 scale, where −5 means "extremely boring" and +5 means "extremely interesting"

After completing a boring task, some participants were paid $1 and some $20 to convince another person waiting to do the same task that the task was interesting and fun. Surprisingly, the participants who were paid only $1 seemed to change their own attitude toward the task, rating it as interesting, whereas those who were paid $20 rated the task no differently than a control group did.

Source: Based on Festinger, L., & Carlsmith, J. (1959). $1/$20 experiment: Cognitive consequences of forced compliance. Journal of Abnormal and Social Psychology, 58(2), 203–210..

a lower grade for themselves (Yachison et al., 2018). Some of the ways students might rationalize a usually moral or honest classmate's behavior are by downplaying the seriousness of the act in light of the immediate circumstances, justifying the actions, blaming someone else, or thinking "it just happened" (Simola, 2017).

Cognitive dissonance theory has been challenged over the last 50 years by other possible explanations. Daryl Bem's *self-perception theory* says that instead of experiencing negative tension, people look at their own actions and then infer their attitudes from those actions (Bem, 1972). New research on dissonance still occurs, much of it focusing on finding the areas of the brain that seem to be involved when people are experiencing dissonance. These studies have found that the left frontal cortex (where language and much of our decision making occurs) is particularly active when people have made a decision that reduces dissonance and then acted upon that decision (Harmon-Jones, 2000, 2004, 2006; Harmon-Jones et al., 2008, 2011). Since reducing cognitive dissonance is mainly a function of people "talking" themselves into or out of a particular course of action, this neurological finding is not surprising. But researchers at Yale University have found surprising evidence for cognitive dissonance in both 4-year-old humans and capuchin monkeys—two groups that are not normally associated with having the developed higher-level mental abilities thought to be in use during the resolution of dissonance (Egan et al., 2007, 2010). Are monkeys and preschool humans more complex thinkers than we had assumed? Or are the cognitive processes used to resolve dissonance a lot simpler than previously indicated? Obviously, there are still questions to be answered with new research in cognitive dissonance.

11.8 Impression Formation

11.8 Describe how people form impressions of others.

When one person meets another for the first time, it is the first opportunity either person will have to make initial evaluations and judgments about the other. That first opportunity is a very important one in **impression formation**, the forming of the first knowledge a person has about another person. Impression formation includes assigning the other person to a number of categories and drawing conclusions about what that person is likely to do—it's really all about prediction. In a sense, when first meeting another person, the observer goes through a process of concept formation similar to that discussed in Chapter Seven. Impression formation is another kind of social cognition.

There is a *primacy effect* in impression formation: The first time people meet someone, they form an impression of that person, often based on physical appearance alone, that persists even though they may later have other contradictory information about that person (DeCoster & Claypool, 2004; Lorenzo et al., 2010; Luchins, 1957; Macrae & Quadflieg, 2010). So the old saying is pretty much on target: First impressions do count.

SOCIAL CATEGORIZATION One of the processes that occurs when people meet someone new is the assignment of that person to some kind of category or group. This assignment is usually based on characteristics the new person has in common with other people or groups with whom the perceiver has had prior experience. This **social categorization** is mostly automatic and occurs without conscious awareness of the process (Macrae & Bodenhausen, 2000; Vernon et al., 2014). Although this is a natural process (human beings are just born categorizers, see Learning Objective 7.2), sometimes it can cause problems. When the characteristics used to categorize the person are superficial*

---

impression formation
the forming of the first knowledge that a person has concerning another person.

social categorization
the assignment of a person one has just met to a category based on characteristics the new person has in common with other people with whom one has had experience in the past.

---

*superficial: on the surface.

ones that have become improperly attached to certain ideas, such as "red hair equals a bad temper," social categorization can result in a *stereotype*, a belief that a set of characteristics is shared by all members of a particular social category (Fiske, 1998). Social stereotypes (although not always negative) are very limiting, causing people to misjudge what others are like and often to treat them differently as a result. Add the process of stereotyping to the primacy effect and it becomes easy to see how important first impressions really are. That first impression not only has more importance than any other information gathered about a person later on but may include a stereotype that is resistant to change as well (Hall et al., 2013; Hilton & von Hipple, 1996; Hugenberg & Bodenhausen, 2003).

💬 It sounds as though we'd be better off if people didn't use social categorization.

Social categorization does have an important place in the perception of others. It allows people to access a great deal of information that can be useful about others, as well as helping people remember and organize information about the characteristics of others (Macrae & Bodenhausen, 2000). The way to avoid falling into the trap of negatively stereotyping someone is to be aware of existing stereotypes and apply a little critical thinking: "Okay, so he's a guy with a lot of piercings. That doesn't mean that he's overly aggressive—it just means he has a lot of piercings."

IMPLICIT PERSONALITY THEORIES The categories into which people place others are based on something called an **implicit personality theory**. Implicit personality theories are sets of assumptions formed in childhood about how different types of people, personality traits, and actions are all related (Dweck et al., 1995; Erdley & Dweck, 1993; Plaks et al., 2005). For example, many people have an implicit personality theory that includes the idea that happy people are also friendly people and people who are quiet are shy. Although these assumptions or beliefs are not necessarily true, they do serve the function of helping organize *schemas*, or mental patterns that represent (in this case) what a person believes about certain "types" of people. (See Learning Objective 8.7.) Of course, the schemas formed in this way can easily become stereotypes when people have limited experience with others who are different from them, especially in superficial ways such as skin color or other physical characteristics (Levy et al., 1998).

There is a test designed to measure the implicit attitudes that make up one's implicit personality theory, called the Implicit Association Test, or IAT (Greenwald & Banaji, 1995; Greenwald et al., 1998). The test, taken by computer, measures the degree of association between certain pairs of concepts. For example, you might see the word "pleasant" on one side of the computer screen and the word "unpleasant" on the other side. In the middle would be another word that may be associated with one or the other of the two categories. You would be asked to sort the word into the appropriate category by pressing certain keys as quickly as you can. The computer measures reaction times, and it is the difference in reaction times over a series of similar comparisons that reveals implicit attitudes (Nosek et al., 2007).

Some evidence suggests that implicit personality theories may differ from culture to culture as well as from individual to individual (Church et al., 2016). For example, one study found that Americans and Hong Kong Chinese people have different implicit personality theories about how much the personality of an individual is able to change. Whereas Americans assume that personality is relatively fixed and unchanging, Chinese people native to Hong Kong assume that personalities are more changeable (Chiu et al., 1997).

implicit personality theory
sets of assumptions about how different types of people, personality traits, and actions are related to each other.

AP 9.A Apply attribution theory to explain motives.

11.9 Attribution

11.9 Describe the process of explaining one's own behavior and the behavior of others.

Another aspect of social cognition is the need people seem to have to explain the behavior of other people. Have you ever watched someone who was doing something you didn't understand? Chances are you were going through a number of possible explanations in your head: "Maybe he's sick, or maybe he sees something I can't see," and so on. It seems to be human nature to want to know why people do the things they do so that we know how to behave toward them and whom we might want to use as role models. If no obvious answer is available, people tend to come up with their own reasons. People also need an explanation for their own behavior. This need is so great that if an explanation isn't obvious, it causes the distress known as cognitive dissonance. The process of explaining both one's own behavior and the behavior of other people is called **attribution**.

CAUSES OF BEHAVIOR **Attribution theory** was originally developed by social psychologist Fritz Heider (1958) as a way of not only explaining why things happen but also why people choose the particular explanations of behavior that they do. There are basically two kinds of explanations—those that involve an external cause and those that assume that causes are internal.

When the cause of behavior is assumed to be from external sources, such as the weather, traffic, educational opportunities, and so on, it is said to be a **situational cause**. The observed behavior is assumed to be caused by whatever situation exists for the person at that time. For example, if John is late, his lateness might be explained by heavy traffic or car problems.

On the other hand, if the cause of behavior is assumed to come from within the individual, it is called a **dispositional cause**. In this case, it is the person's internal personality characteristics that are seen as the cause of the observed behavior. Someone attributing John's behavior to a dispositional cause, for example, might assume that John was late because his personality includes being careless of his and other people's time.

There's also an emotional component to these kinds of attributions. When people are happy in a marriage, for example, researchers have found a tendency to attribute a spouse's behavior that has a positive effect to an internal cause ("He did it because he wanted me to feel good"). When the effect is negative, the behavior is attributed to an external cause ("She must have had a difficult day"). But if the marriage is an unhappy one, the opposite attributions occur: "He is only being nice because he wants something from me" or "She's being mean because it's her nature to be crabby" (Fincham et al., 2000; Karney & Bradbury, 2000).

FUNDAMENTAL ATTRIBUTION ERROR

💬 But what else determines which type of cause a person will use? For example, what determines how people explain the behavior of someone they don't already know or like?

The best-known attributional bias is the **fundamental attribution error**, which is the tendency for people observing someone else's actions to overestimate the influence of that person's internal characteristics on behavior and underestimate the influence of the situation. In explaining our own behavior, the tendency to use situational attributions instead of personal is called the *actor–observer* bias because we are the actor, not the observer. In other words, people tend to explain the actions of others based on what "kind" of person they are rather than looking for outside causes, such as social influences or situations (Blanchard-Fields et al., 2007; Harman, 1999; Jones & Harris, 1967; Leclerc & Hess, 2007; Weiner, 1985). For example, people hearing about Milgram's "shock" study tend to

---

attribution
the process of explaining one's own behavior and the behavior of others.

attribution theory
the theory of how people make attributions.

situational cause
cause of behavior attributed to external factors, such as delays, the action of others, or some other aspect of the situation.

dispositional cause
cause of behavior attributed to internal factors such as personality or character.

fundamental attribution error
the tendency to overestimate the influence of internal factors in determining behavior while underestimating situational factors.

assume that something is wrong with the "teachers" in the study rather than explaining their behavior within the circumstances of the situation.

> But why do we do that? Why not assume an external cause for everyone?

When people are the actors, they are very aware of the situational influences on their own behavior. For example, Tardy John was actually the one driving to work, and he knows that heavy traffic and a small accident made him late to work—he was *there*, after all. But an outside observer of John's behavior doesn't have the opportunity to see all of the possible situational influences and has only John himself in focus and, thus, assumes that John's tardiness is caused by some internal personality flaw.

Other research has shown that when students are given an opportunity to make attributions about cheating, they make the fundamental attribution error and actor–observer bias: If others are cheating, it's because they are not honest people, but if the students themselves are cheating, it is because of the situation (Bogle, 2000).

Can the tendency to make these errors be reduced? There are several strategies for making errors in attribution less likely. One is to notice how many other people are doing the same thing. As a college professor, the author often has students who come in late. When it is only one student and it happens frequently, the assumption is that the student is not very careful about time (dispositional cause). But when a large number of students come straggling in late, the assumption becomes "there must be a wreck on the bridge," which is a situational attribution. In other words, if a lot of people are doing it, it is probably caused by an outside factor.

Another trick is to think about what you would do in the same situation. If you think that you might behave in the same way, the cause of behavior is probably situational. People should also make the effort of looking for causes that might not be obvious. If John were to look particularly stressed out, for example, the assumption might be that something stressed him out, and that "something" might have been heavy traffic.

Although the fundamental attribution error has been found in American culture (Jones & Harris, 1967), would the same error occur in a culture very different from that of America's, such as Japan's? This is the question asked by researchers Masuda and Kitayama (2004), who had both American and Japanese participants ask a target person to read a prewritten attitudinal statement. The participants were then asked to give their opinion on the target's real attitude. American participants made the classic error, assuming that the target's attitude matched the reading. The Japanese participants, however, assumed that the person's attitude might be different from the statement—the person might have been under social obligation to write the piece. Japanese society is a collectivistic culture, and a Japanese person might expect to write a paper to please a teacher or employer even though the paper's contents do not necessarily express the writer's attitudes. A summary of the research in cross-cultural differences in attribution provides further support for the idea that the fundamental attribution error is not a universal one (Peng et al., 2000). The work of Miller (1984) and many other researchers (Blanchard-Fields et al., 2007; Cha & Nam, 1985; Choi & Nisbett, 1998; Choi et al., 1999; Choi et al., 2003; Lee et al., 1996; Morris & Peng, 1994; Morris et al., 1995; Norenzayan et al., 1999) strongly suggests that in more interdependent, collectivistic cultures found in China, Hong Kong, Japan, and Korea, people tend to assume that external situational factors are more responsible for the behavior of other people than internal dispositional factors—a finding that is exactly the reverse of the fundamental attribution error so common in the United States and other individualist Western cultures.

Even age is a factor in how likely someone is to fall prey to the fundamental attribution error. Several studies (Blanchard-Fields & Horhota, 2005; Follett & Hess, 2002; Leclerc & Hess, 2007) have found that older adults show a stronger bias toward attributing the actions of another to internal causes than do younger people. Some attributions even vary based on the degree of belief in a soul, which might cause people to be more prone to internal attribution (Li et al., 2012).

One study has found that attribution of motive may also create conflict between groups (Waytz et al., 2014). The study compared Israelis and Palestinians in the Middle East as well as Republicans and Democrats in the United States. Obviously, these groups continue to experience a great deal of animosity, conflict, and an unwillingness to shift from long-held beliefs. Over the course of five studies, in which participants were asked to rate the motives of others for engaging in conflict, researchers found that each side felt that their side was motivated by love more than hate but that the other side's motivating force was hate. Calling this idea *motive attribution asymmetry*, the researchers suggest that this is at least one reason compromise and negotiation are so difficult to obtain—if the other side hates you, you believe them to be unreasonable and negotiations impossible.

Concept Map L.O. 11.5, 11.6, 11.7, 11.8, 11.9

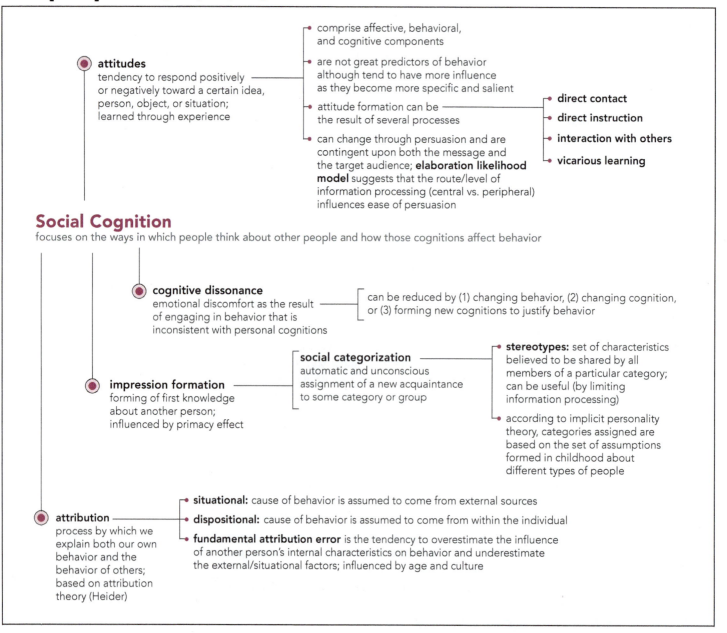

Practice Quiz   How much do you remember?

Pick the best answer.

1. Which of the following represents the affective component of an attitude?
   a. "I love to go to the clubs—it makes me so happy!"
   b. "It is interesting to watch people when I'm out at a club."
   c. "Tonight, we're going to that new club downtown."
   d. "I'm going to wear a new outfit to the club tonight."
   e. "I think a lot of cool people go to clubs."

2. Dani hates snakes, even though she has never been bitten by or close to one. She developed her feelings by seeing how scared her mother was when she came across them in the garden or even when watching a movie or television show in which there was a snake. Dani's attitude toward snakes was most likely acquired through _____.
   a. vicarious conditioning
   b. interaction with others
   c. direct instruction
   d. direct contact
   e. punishment

3. One of your friends tells you, "I didn't like the environmental-awareness presentation today. First of all, it was too long, not to mention the person that gave it was drinking out of a polystyrene cup and drove away in a huge SUV." What kind of processing might your friend be using?
   a. central-route processing
   b. cognitive-route processing
   c. peripheral-route processing
   d. active-modality processing
   e. visual-route processing

4. Mika thinks that everyone who smiles must always be happy, and those people who are quiet must be naturally shy. Such assumptions are the basis for _____.
   a. implicit personality theory
   b. stereotypes
   c. attribution theory
   d. attitudes
   e. dissonance theory

5. Noah almost always shows up late for work. His friends attribute this to Noah's laziness. This is an example of a _____ cause.
   a. dispositional
   b. situational
   c. dispensational
   d. superficial
   e. secondary

6. How might someone who unknowingly is committing the fundamental attribution error explain Stanley Milgram's obedience study?
   a. Subjects in that study must have been the kind of people who like to hurt others.
   b. Subjects in that study desired a high degree of positive reinforcement.
   c. Individuals in that study wanted to be part of Milgram's group.
   d. Subjects in that study were highly influenced by the power of Milgram and his team.
   e. Individuals in that study wanted to be good research subjects.

11.10–11.15 Social Interaction

Social influence and social cognition are two of three main areas included in the field of social psychology. The third major area has to do with social interactions with others, or the relationships between people, both casual and intimate. Social interactions include prejudice and discrimination, liking and loving, and aggression and prosocial behavior.

11.10 Prejudice and Discrimination

11.10 Distinguish between prejudice and discrimination.

We've seen how stereotypes, a set of characteristics that people believe is shared by all members of a particular social category or group, can be formed by using only superficial information about that person or group of people. When a person holds an unsupported and often negative stereotyped *attitude* about the members of a particular social group, it is called **prejudice**. The video *Are Stereotypes and Prejudices Inevitable?* explains the connection between stereotypes and prejudice.

When prejudicial attitudes cause members of a particular social group to be treated differently than others in situations that call for equal treatment, it is called **discrimination**. Prejudice is the attitude, and discrimination is the behavior that can result from that attitude. Although laws can be made to minimize

AP 9.J Describe processes that contribute to differential treatment of group members.

prejudice
negative attitude held by a person about the members of a particular social group.

discrimination
treating people differently because of prejudice toward the social group to which they belong.

Watch Are Stereotypes and Prejudices Inevitable?

Watch the Video at MyLab Psychology

The Black Lives Matter movement, begun in 2013, has become a force for advocating change, particularly in how Black men are viewed by the police but also in advocating for a change to discriminatory treatment of all people.

discriminatory behavior, it is not possible to have laws against holding certain attitudes. In other words, discrimination can be controlled and in some cases eliminated, but the prejudicial attitude that is responsible for the discrimination cannot be so easily controlled or eliminated.

TYPES OF PREJUDICE AND DISCRIMINATION There are many kinds of prejudice. There are also many kinds of discrimination that occur as a result of prejudice. There's ageism, or prejudicial attitudes toward the elderly or teenagers (among others); sexism; racism, or prejudice toward those from different ethnic groups; prejudice toward those from different religions, those from different economic levels, those who are overweight, those who are too thin, or those who have a different sexual orientation. Prejudice can also vary in terms of what type of people or groups make the most likely targets. In any society, there will always be **in-groups** and **out-groups**, or "us" versus "them." The in-group is all the people with whom a particular person identifies and the out-groups are everyone else (Brewer, 2001; Hewstone et al., 2002; Tajfel & Turner, 1986). An example of this can be found in the Black Lives Matter movement that began as a Twitter campaign in 2013 in response to the acquittal of George Zimmerman in the shooting death of Trayvon Martin (Day, 2015). The formation of in-groups and out-groups begins in childhood (Ruble et al., 2004) and continues as children become adults.

Once an in-group is established, prejudice toward and discriminatory treatment of the out-group or groups soon follow, causing stress and possible negative impact on the health of the out-group members (Brewer, 2001; Forsyth et al., 2014). Members of the out-groups are usually going to become stereotyped according to some superficial characteristic, such as skin color or hair color, and getting rid of a stereotype once formed is difficult at best (Cameron et al., 2001; Hamilton & Gifford, 1976). *Microaggressions*, the seemingly minor insults and negative exchanges that members of the dominant culture often use toward minorities, add to the discriminatory treatment. Microaggressions are not as blatant as someone using a racial or gender-biased epithet, but are more subtle statements that might repeat a stereotyped idea or that minimize the reality of discrimination (Sue, 2010). For example, a professional woman who is told by a supervisor that she needs to change her hairstyle because it is unprofessional may be seen as experiencing microaggression from the supervisor.

SCAPEGOATING Conflicts between groups are usually greater when there are other pressures or stresses going on, such as war, economic difficulties, or other misfortunes. When such pressures exist, the need to find a *scapegoat* becomes stronger. A scapegoat is a person or a group, typically a member or members of an out-group, who serves as the target for the frustrations and negative emotions of members of the in-group. (The term comes from the ancient Jewish tradition of sending a goat out into the wilderness with the symbolic sins of all the people on its head.)

Scapegoats are going to be the group of people with the least power, and the newest immigrants to any area are typically those who have the least power at that time. That is why many social psychologists believe that the rioting that took place in Los Angeles, California, in the spring of 1992 occurred in the areas it did. This was the time of the infamous Rodney King beating. Rodney King was an African American man who was dragged out of his car onto the street and severely beaten by four police officers. The beating was caught on tape by a bystander. At the trial, the officers were found not guilty of assault with a deadly weapon. This decision was followed by a series of violent riots (Knight, 1996).

The puzzling thing about these riots is that the greatest amount of rioting and violence did not take place in the neighborhoods of the mostly White police officers or in the African American neighborhoods. The rioting was greatest in the neighborhoods of the Asian Americans and Asians who were the most recent immigrants to the area. When a group has only recently moved into an area, as the Asians had, that group has the

in-groups
social groups with whom a person identifies; "us."

out-groups
social groups with whom a person does not identify; "them."

least social power and influence in that new area. The rioters took out their frustrations *not* on the people seen as directly responsible for those frustrations but on the group of people with the least power to resist (Chang, 2004; Kim & Kim, 1999). After the events of September 11, 2001, many Muslims living in predominantly non-Muslim countries may now be seen in a similar light, despite the fact that the atrocity was committed by one radical group.

11.11 How People Learn and Overcome Prejudice

11.11 Describe theories of how prejudice is learned and how it can be overcome.

As we will see in the *Classic Studies in Psychology* section, even children are, under the right circumstances, prone to developing prejudiced attitudes. Exposure to the attitudes of parents, teachers, other children, and the various forms of media are just a few ways in which children can learn and develop prejudice.

ORIGINS OF PREJUDICE Is all prejudice simply a matter of learning, or are other factors at work? Several theories have been proposed to explain the origins and the persistence of prejudice. In **social cognitive theory** (using cognitive processes in relation to understanding the social world), prejudice is seen as an attitude that is formed as other attitudes are formed, through direct instruction, modeling, and other social influences on learning.

REALISTIC CONFLICT THEORY The **realistic conflict theory** of prejudice states that increasing prejudice and discrimination are closely tied to an increasing degree of conflict between the in-group and the out-group when those groups are seeking a common resource such as land or available jobs (Horowitz, 1985; Taylor & Moghaddam, 1994). Because the examples of this from history and modern times are so numerous, it is possible to list only a few: the conflict between the early Crusaders and the Muslims, between the Jewish people and the Germans, the hatred between the Irish Catholics and the Irish Protestants, and the conflict between the native population of you-name-the-country and the colonists who want that land. The section that follows is a classic study that illustrates how easily in-groups and out-groups can be formed and how quickly prejudice and discrimination follow.

These Korean demonstrators were protesting the riots that followed the 1992 not-guilty verdict in the beating of Rodney King. The riots lasted 6 days, killing 42 people and damaging 700 buildings in mainly Korean and other Asian American neighborhoods. The Asian American population of Los Angeles, California, became scapegoats for aggression.

social cognitive theory

referring to the use of cognitive processes in relation to understanding the social world.

realistic conflict theory

theory stating that prejudice and discrimination will be increased between groups that are in conflict over a limited resource.

Classic Studies in Psychology

Brown Eyes, Blue Eyes

In a small town in Iowa in 1968, a few days after the assassination of Dr. Martin Luther King, Jr., a second-grade teacher named Jane Elliott tried to teach her students a lesson in prejudice and discrimination. She divided her students into two groups, those with blue eyes and those with brown eyes.

On the first day of the lesson, the blue-eyed children were given special privileges, such as extra time at recess and getting to leave first for lunch. She also told the blue-eyed children they were superior to the brown-eyed children, telling the brown-eyed children not to bother taking seconds at lunch because it would be wasted. She kept the blue-eyed children and the brown-eyed children apart (Peters, 1971).

Although Elliott tried to be critical of the brown-eyed out-group, she soon found that the blue-eyed children were also criticizing, belittling, and were quite vicious in their attacks on the brown-eyed children. By the end of the day, the blue-eyed children felt and acted superior, and the brown-eyed children were miserable. Even the lowered test scores of the brown-eyed children reflected their misery. Two days later, the brown-eyed children

Social comparison involves comparing yourself to others so that your self-esteem is protected. Through status updates, selfies and photos, "likes," and other feedback tools, social media provides multiple opportunities for social comparison.

became the favored group, and the effects from the first two days appeared again but in reverse this time: The blue-eyed children began to feel inferior, and their test scores dropped.

The fact that test scores reflected the treatment received by the out-group is a stunning one, raising questions about the effects of prejudice and discrimination on the education of children who are members of stereotyped out-groups. That the children were so willing to discriminate against their own classmates, some of whom were their close friends before the experiment, is also telling. In his book about this classroom experiment, *A Class Divided*, Peters (1971) reported that the students who were part of the original experiment, when reunited 15 years later to talk about the experience, said they believed that this early experience with prejudice and discrimination helped them become less prejudiced as young adults.

Questions for Further Discussion

1. Is there anything about this experiment you find disturbing?
2. How do you think adults might react in a similar experiment?
3. Are there any ethical concerns with what Elliott did in her classroom?
4. What kinds of changes might have occurred in the personalities and performances of the children if the experiment had continued for more than 2 days with each group?

AP 9.B Articulate the impact of social and cultural categories on self-concept and relations with others.

social identity theory
theory in which the formation of a person's identity within a particular social group is explained by social categorization, social identity, and social comparison.

social identity
the part of the self-concept including one's view of self as a member of a particular social category.

social comparison
the comparison of oneself to others in ways that raise one's self-esteem.

stereotype vulnerability
the effect that people's awareness of the stereotypes associated with their social group has on their behavior.

self-fulfilling prophecy
the tendency of one's expectations to affect one's behavior in such a way as to make the expectations more likely to occur.

AP 9.C Anticipate the impact of self-fulfilling prophecy on behavior.

SOCIAL IDENTITY THEORY In **social identity theory**, three processes are responsible for the formation of a person's identity within a particular social group and the attitudes, concepts, and behavior that go along with identification with that group (Tajfel & Turner, 1986; Richard et al., 2015). The first process is *social categorization*, as discussed earlier in this chapter. Just as people assign categories to others (such as Black, White, student, teacher, and so on) to help organize information about those others, people also assign themselves to social categories to help determine how they should behave. The second element of social identity theory is *identification*, or the formation of one's **social identity**. A social identity is the part of the self-concept that includes the view of oneself as a member of a particular social group within the social category—typically, the in-group. The third aspect of social identity theory is **social comparison**, Festinger's (1954) concept in which people compare themselves favorably to others to improve their own self-esteem: "Well, at least I'm better off than that person." Members of the out-group make handy comparisons. All three aspects of social identity form, at least in part, through interaction with a group, particularly a small group (Thomas et al., 2016).

With respect to prejudice, social identity theory helps explain why people feel the need to categorize or stereotype others, producing the in-group sense of "us versus them" that people adopt toward out-groups. Prejudice may result, at least in part, from the need to increase one's own self-esteem by looking down on others.

STEREOTYPE VULNERABILITY As discussed previously, stereotypes are the widespread beliefs a person has about members of another group. Not only do stereotypes affect the way people perceive other people, but they can also affect the way people see themselves and their performance (Snyder et al., 1977). **Stereotype vulnerability** refers to the effect that a person's knowledge of another's stereotyped opinions can have on that person's behavior (Osborne, 2007; Steele, 1992, 1997). Research has shown that when people are aware of stereotypes that are normally applied to their own group by others, they may feel anxious about behaving in ways that might support that stereotype. This fear results in anxiety and self-consciousness that have negative effects on their performance in a kind of **self-fulfilling prophecy**, or the effect that expectations can have on outcomes.

Stereotype vulnerability is highly related to *stereotype threat*, in which members of a stereotyped group are made anxious and wary of any situation in which their behavior might confirm a stereotype (Abdou et al., 2016; Hartley & Sutton, 2013; Hyde & Kling, 2001; Steele, 1999). See Learning Objective 7.10. In one study, researchers administered a difficult verbal test to both Caucasian and African American participants (Steele & Aronson, 1995). Half of the African American participants were asked to record their race on a demographic* question before the test, making them very aware of their minority status. Those participants showed a significant decrease in scores on the test when compared to the other participants, both African American and Caucasian, who did not answer such a demographic question. They had more incorrect answers, had slower response times, answered fewer questions, and demonstrated more anxiety when compared to the other participants (Steele & Aronson, 1995).

Similar effects of stereotype threat on performance have been found in women (Gonzales et al., 2002; Steele, 1997; Steele et al., 2002) and for athletes in academic settings (Yopyk & Prentice, 2005). A recent study did find that some people can overcome feelings of stereotype threat by identifying themselves with a different social identity, such as a woman who identifies herself with "college students" when taking a math exam rather than with "females," since the latter group is often stereotyped as being math deficient (Rydell & Boucher, 2010). This effect only held for those women with fairly high self-esteem, however.

OVERCOMING PREJUDICE The best weapon against prejudice is education: learning about people who are different from you in many ways. The best way to learn about others is to have direct contact with them and to have the opportunity to see them as people rather than "as outsiders or strangers." *Intergroup contact* is very common in college settings, for example, where students and faculty from many different backgrounds live, work, and study together. Because they go through many of the same experiences (midterms, finals, and so on), people from these diverse** backgrounds find common ground to start building friendships and knowledge of each other's cultural, ethnic, or religious differences.

Intergroup contact is one of the best ways to combat prejudice. When people have an opportunity to work together, as the students in this diverse classroom do, they get to know each other on common ground. Can you think of the first time you had direct contact with someone who was different from you? How did that contact change your viewpoint?

EQUAL STATUS CONTACT Contact between social groups can backfire under certain circumstances, however, as seen in a famous study (Sherif et al., 1961) called the "Robber's Cave." In this experiment conducted at a summer camp called Robber's Cave, 22 White, well-adjusted, 11- and 12-year-old boys were divided into two groups. The groups each lived in separate housing and were kept apart from each other for daily activities. During the second week, after in-group relationships had formed, the researchers scheduled highly competitive events pitting one group against the other. Intergroup conflict quickly occurred, with name-calling, fights, and hostility emerging between the two groups.

The third week involved making the two groups come together for pleasant, noncompetitive activities, in the hope that cooperation would be the result. Instead, the groups used the activities of the third week as opportunities for more hostility. It was only after several weeks of being forced to work together to resolve a series of crises (created deliberately by the experimenters) that the boys lost the hostility and formed friendships between the groups. When dealing with the crises, the boys were forced into a situation of **equal status contact**, in which they were all in the same situation with neither group holding power over the other. Equal status contact has been shown to reduce prejudice and discrimination, along with ongoing, positive cooperation. It appears that personal involvement with people from another group must be cooperative and occur when all groups are equal in terms of power or status

equal status contact

contact between groups in which the groups have equal status with neither group having power over the other.

---

*demographic: having to do with the statistical characteristics of a population.
**diverse: different, varied.

to have a positive effect on reducing prejudice (Pettigrew & Tropp, 2000; Robinson & Preston, 1976). And while some have called into question his research methodologies (Perry, 2014), Sherif's studies still serve as important resources in attempts to understand the collective nature of behavior, including how intergroup competition can lead to prejudice while cooperation can reduce it (Platow & Hunter, 2012; Reicher & Haslam, 2014).

THE "JIGSAW CLASSROOM" One possible way to help contact between people from different backgrounds occur in a collaborative fashion is to make success at a task dependent on the cooperation of each person in a group of people of mixed abilities or statuses. If each member of the group has information needed to solve the problem at hand, a situation is created in which people must depend on one another to meet their shared goals (Aronson et al., 1978). Ordinarily, school classrooms are not organized along these lines but are instead more competitive and therefore more likely to create conflict between people of different abilities and backgrounds.

In a "**jigsaw classroom**," students have to work together to reach a specific goal. Each student is given a "piece of the puzzle," or information that is necessary for solving the problem and reaching the goal (Aronson et al., 1978; Clarke, 1994). Students then share their information with other members of the group. Interaction among diverse students is increased, making it more likely that those students will come to see each other as partners and form friendly relationships rather than labeling others as members of an out-group and treating them differently. This technique works at the high school and college level as well as in the lower school grades (Johnson et al., 1991; Lord, 2001).

> **AP** 9.L Describe the variables that contribute to attraction.

11.12 Interpersonal Attraction

11.12 Identify factors involved in interpersonal attraction.

Prejudice pretty much explains why people don't like each other. What does psychology say about why people like someone else? There are some "rules" for those whom people like and find attractive. Liking or having the desire for a relationship with someone else is called **interpersonal attraction**, and there's a great deal of research on the subject. (Who wouldn't want to know the rules?) Several factors are involved in the attraction of one person to another, including both superficial physical characteristics, such as physical beauty and proximity, as well as elements of personality.

PHYSICAL ATTRACTIVENESS When people think about what attracts them to others, one of the topics that usually arises is the physical attractiveness of the other person. Some research suggests that physical beauty is one of the main factors that influence individuals' choices for selecting people they want to know better, although other factors may become more important in the later stages of relationships (Eagly et al., 1991; Feingold, 1992; White, 1980).

PROXIMITY—CLOSE TO YOU The closer together people are physically, such as working in the same office building or living in the same dorm, the more likely they are to form a relationship. *Proximity* refers to being physically near someone else. People choose friends and lovers from the pool of people available to them, and availability depends heavily on proximity.

One theory about why proximity is so important involves the idea of repeated exposure to new stimuli, sometimes called the *mere exposure effect*. The more people experience something, whether it is a song, a picture, or a person, the more they tend to like it. The phrase "it grew on me" refers to this reaction. When people are in physical proximity to each other, repeated exposure may increase their attraction to each other.

"jigsaw classroom"
educational technique in which each individual is given only part of the information needed to solve a problem, causing the separate individuals to be forced to work together to find the solution.

interpersonal attraction
liking or having the desire for a relationship with another person.

BIRDS OF A FEATHER—SIMILARITY Proximity does not guarantee attraction, just as physical attractiveness does not guarantee a long-term relationship. People tend to like being around others who are *similar* to them in some way. The more people find they have in common with others—such as attitudes, beliefs, and interests—the more they tend to be attracted to those others (Hartfield & Rapson, 1992; Moreland & Zajonc, 1982; Neimeyer & Mitchell, 1998). Similarity as a factor in relationships makes sense when seen in terms of validation of a person's beliefs and attitudes. When other people hold the same attitudes and beliefs and do the same kinds of actions, it makes a person's own concepts seem more correct or valid.

> Isn't there a saying about "opposites attract"? Aren't people sometimes attracted to people who are different instead of similar?

There is often a grain of truth in many old sayings, and "opposites attract" is no exception. Some people find that forming a relationship with another person who has *complementary* qualities (characteristics in the one person that fill a need in the other) can be very rewarding (Carson, 1969; Schmitt, 2002). Research does not support this view of attraction, however. It is similarity, not complementarity, that draws people together and helps them stay together (Bahns et al., 2017; Berscheid & Reis, 1998; McPherson et al., 2001).

RECIPROCITY OF LIKING Finally, people have a very strong tendency to like people who like them, a simple but powerful concept referred to as **reciprocity of liking**. In one experiment, researchers paired college students with other students (Curtis & Miller, 1986). Neither student in any of the pairs knew the other member. One member of each pair was randomly chosen to receive some information from the experimenters about how the other student in the pair felt about the first member. In some cases, target students were led to believe that the other students liked them and, in other cases, that the targets disliked them.

When the pairs of students were allowed to meet and talk with each other again, they were friendlier, disclosed more information about themselves, agreed with the other person more, and behaved in a warmer manner *if they had been told* that the other student liked them. The other students also came to like these students better, so liking produced more liking.

The only time that liking someone does not seem to make that person like the other in return is if a person suffers from feelings of low self-worth. In that case, finding out that someone likes you when you don't even like yourself makes you question his or her motives. This mistrust can cause you to act unfriendly to that person, which makes the person more likely to become unfriendly to you in a kind of self-fulfilling prophecy (Murray et al., 1998).

INTERPERSONAL RELATIONS ONLINE No discussion of friendships and "liking" can be complete without some mention of the growing importance of social networking online. For example, which social network sites a college student selects may be related to racial identity and ethnic identity (Duggan et al., 2015). In that study, Facebook seems to be the most widely used platform regardless of one's racial or ethnic identity at 71 percent reported use. But when looking at other online platforms, White students preferred the interest/hobby-sharing site Pinterest, while Hispanic and African-American students preferred the photo-sharing site Instagram (Duggan et al., 2015). In the United States overall, Facebook and YouTube are the most widely used, and among young adults 18 to 24 years old, 94 percent use YouTube, 80 percent use Facebook, 78 percent use Snapchat, 71 percent use Instagram, and 45 percent use Twitter (Smith & Anderson, 2018).

In China, the popular social networking site is Ozone, but Chinese users of this site spend less time on it, have fewer contacts, and seem to consider its use as less important

reciprocity of liking
tendency of people to like other people who like them in return.

when compared to users of Facebook in the United States (Jackson & Wang, 2013). When you consider the self-promotion focus of such social networking sites, it doesn't seem surprising that Chinese users, coming from a collectivistic cultural background that promotes connections with others over individual independence, would be less likely to use such a resource.

In another study, researchers found that young people who already experience positive social relationships use the online sites to enhance those same relationships, contrary to the stereotyped view that it would be the socially inept who would gravitate toward the anonymous nature of online networking (Mikami et al., 2010). Those who are less well-adjusted either did not use social networking sites or used them in more negative ways: excessive bad language, hostile remarks, aggressive gestures, or posting of unflattering or suggestive photographs.

There may also be gender differences in how people organize their social networking. In a recent study, researchers found that females have more "friends," do more buying and selling, and are more likely to "friend" people who make the request than males (Szell & Thurner, 2013). The study also found that females take fewer risks online than males. Males talk to larger groups of contacts and are less likely to "friend" other males than females. They respond very quickly to females requesting a friendship.

11.13 Love Is a Triangle—Robert Sternberg's Triangular Theory of Love

11.13 Describe the different types of love outlined in Sternberg's theory.

Dictionary definitions of love refer to a strong affection for another person due to kinship, personal ties, sexual attraction, admiration, or common interests.

💬 But those aren't all the same kind of relationships. We love family and friends differently, right?

Psychologists generally agree that there are different kinds of love. One psychologist, Robert Sternberg, outlined a theory of what he determined were the three main components of love and the different types of love that combinations of these three components can produce (Sternberg, 1986, 1988b, 1997a).

THE THREE COMPONENTS OF LOVE According to Sternberg, love consists of three basic components: intimacy, passion, and commitment.

Intimacy, in Sternberg's view, refers to the feelings of closeness that one has for another person or the sense of having close emotional ties to another. Intimacy in this sense is not physical but psychological. Friends have an intimate relationship because they disclose things to each other that most people might not know, they feel strong emotional ties to each other, and they enjoy the presence of the other person.

Passion is the physical aspect of love. Passion refers to the emotional and sexual arousal a person feels toward the other person. Passion is not simply sex; holding hands, loving looks, and hugs can all be forms of passion.

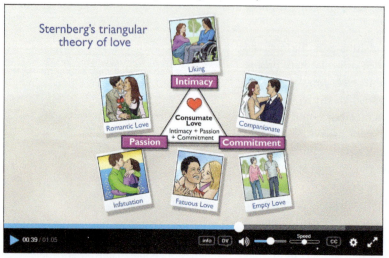

Watch Attraction: Sternberg's Triangular Theory

👁 Watch the Video at MyLab Psychology

Commitment involves the decisions one makes about a relationship. A short-term decision might be, "I think I'm in love." An example of a more long-term decision is, "I want to be with this person for the rest of my life."

THE LOVE TRIANGLES A love relationship between two people can involve one, two, or all three of these components in various combinations. The combinations can produce seven different forms of love, as can be seen in the video *Attraction: Sternberg's Triangular Theory*.

Two of the more familiar and more heavily researched forms of love from Sternberg's theory are romantic love and companionate love. When intimacy and passion are combined, the result is the more familiar **romantic love**, which is sometimes called passionate love by other researchers (Bartels & Zeki, 2000; Diamond, 2003; Hartfield, 1987). Romantic love is often the basis for a more lasting relationship. In many Western cultures, the ideal relationship begins with liking, then becomes romantic love as passion is added to the mix, and finally becomes a more enduring form of love as a commitment is made.

When intimacy and commitment are the main components of a relationship, it is called **companionate love**. In companionate love, people who like each other, feel emotionally close to each other, and understand one another's motives have made a commitment to live together, usually in a marriage relationship. Companionate love is often the binding tie that holds a marriage together through the years of parenting, paying bills, and lessening physical passion (Gottman & Krokoff, 1989; Steinberg & Silverberg, 1987). In many non-Western cultures, companionate love is seen as more sensible. Choices for a mate on the basis of compatibility are often made by parents or matchmakers rather than by the couple themselves (Duben & Behar, 1991; Hortaçsu, 1999; Jones, 1997; Thornton & Hui-Sheng, 1994).

Finally, when all three components of love are present, the couple has achieved *consummate love*, the ideal form of love that many people see as the ultimate goal. This is also the kind of love that may evolve into companionate love when the passion lessens during the middle years of a relationship's commitment.

11.14 Aggression

11.14 Explain how aggressive behavior is determined by biology and learning.

AP 9.K Describe the variables that contribute to altruism and aggression.

Unfortunately, violence toward others is another form of social interaction. When one person tries to harm another person deliberately, either physically or psychologically, psychologists call it *aggression*. One common cause of aggressive behavior is frustration, which occurs when a person is prevented from reaching some desired goal. The concept of aggression as a reaction to frustration is known as the *frustration–aggression hypothesis* (Berkowitz, 1993; Miller et al., 1941). Many sources of frustration can lead to aggressive behavior. Pain, for example, produces negative sensations that are often intense and uncontrollable, leading to frustration and often aggressive acts against the nearest available target (Berkowitz, 1993). Loud noises, excessive heat, the irritation of someone else's cigarette smoke, and even awful smells can lead people to act out in an aggressive manner (Anderson, 1987; Rotton & Frey, 1985; Rotton et al., 1979; Zillmann et al., 1981).

Frustration is not the only source of aggressive behavior. Many early researchers, including Sigmund Freud (1930), believed that aggression was a basic human instinct, part of our death instinct. Famed sociobiologist Konrad Lorenz (1966) saw aggression as an instinct for fighting to promote the survival of our species. In evolutionary terms, those early humans who were most successful in protecting their territory, resources, and offspring were probably more aggressive and so survived to pass on their genetic material (Buss, 2009b; Cosmides & Tooby, 2013). But if aggression is an instinct present

romantic love

type of love consisting of intimacy and passion.

companionate love

type of love consisting of intimacy and commitment.

in all humans, it should occur in far more similar patterns across cultures than it does. Instinctual behavior, as often seen in animals, is not modifiable by environmental influences. Modern approaches include explanations of aggression as a biological phenomenon or a learned behavior.

AGGRESSION AND BIOLOGY There is some evidence that human aggression has, at least partially, a genetic basis. Studies of twins reared together and reared apart have shown that if one identical twin has a violent temper, the identical sibling will most likely also have a violent temper. This agreement between twins' personalities happens more often with identical twins than with fraternal twins (Miles & Carey, 1997; Rowe et al., 1999). It may be that, in some people, a gene or more likely a complex combination of genes influences a susceptibility to aggressive responses under the right environmental conditions.

As discussed in Chapter Two, certain areas of the brain seem to control aggressive responses. The frontal lobes, amygdala, and other structures of the limbic system, see Learning Objective 2.7, have been shown to trigger aggressive responses when stimulated in both animals and humans (Adams, 1968; Albert & Richmond, 1977; LaBar et al., 1995; Scott et al., 1997; Yang et al., 2010). Charles Whitman, the Texas Tower sniper, who in 1966 killed his mother and his wife and then shot and killed 12 more people before finally being killed by law enforcement officers, left a note asking for an examination of his brain. An autopsy did reveal a tumor that was pressing into his amygdala (Lavergne, 1997).

There are also chemical influences on aggression. Testosterone, a male sex hormone, has been linked to higher levels of aggression in humans (Archer, 1991). This may help explain why violent criminals tend to be young, male, and muscular. They typically have high levels of testosterone and low levels of serotonin, another important chemical found in the brain (Alexander et al., 1986; Brown & Linnoila, 1990; Coccaro & Kavoussi, 1996; Dabbs et al., 2001; Robins, 1996). Dopamine, glutamate, GABA, and serotonin, neurotransmitters found in the brain, all appear to play a part in aggressive behavior (Coccaro et al., 2015; Narvaes & Martins de Almeida, 2014; Takahashi et al., 2015).

> Don't some people get pretty violent after drinking too much? Does alcohol do something to those brain chemicals?

Alcohol does have an impact on aggressive behavior. Psychologically, alcohol acts to release inhibitions, making people less likely to control their behavior even if they are not yet intoxicated. Biologically, alcohol affects the functioning of many neurotransmitters and in particular is associated with a decrease in serotonin (Virkkunen & Linnoila, 1996). See Learning Objective 2.3. In one study, volunteers were asked to administer electric shocks to an unseen "opponent" in a study reminiscent of Milgram's shock experiment. The actual responses to the shock were simulated by a computer, although the volunteers believed the responses were coming from a real person. The volunteers were told it was a test of reaction time and learning (Bushman, 1997). Volunteers participated both before consuming alcohol and after consuming alcohol. Participants were much more aggressive in administering stronger shocks after drinking. Other research has demonstrated that in intoxicated individuals, more aggression is observed in those who tend to ignore future consequences (Bushman et al., 2012).

SOCIAL LEARNING EXPLANATIONS FOR AGGRESSION Although frustration, genetics, body chemicals, and even the effects of drugs can be blamed for aggressive behavior to some degree, much of human aggression is also influenced by learning. The social learning theory explanation for aggression states that aggressive behavior is learned (in a process called observational learning) by watching aggressive models get reinforced for their aggressive behavior (Bandura, 1980; Bandura et al., 1961). See Learning Objective 5.13. Aggressive models can be parents, siblings, friends, or people on television or in computerized games.

THE POWER OF SOCIAL ROLES Some evidence suggests that even taking on a particular *social role*, such as that of a soldier, can lead to an increase in aggressive behavior. A **social role** is the pattern of behavior that is expected of a person who is in a particular social position. For example, "doctor" is a social role that implies wearing a white coat, asking certain types of questions, and writing prescriptions, among other things. A deeply disturbing experiment was conducted by famed social psychologist Philip Zimbardo at Stanford University in 1971. The Stanford prison experiment (SPE) was recorded from the beginning to its rather abrupt end. About 75 young men, most of whom were college students, volunteered to participate for 2 weeks. After completing a variety of assessments, 24 were selected as they were judged to be the most mentally and physically stable and mature and the least likely to be involved in antisocial behavior. The final sample consisted of 21: ten "prisoners" and eleven "guards" (Haney et al., 1973a; Haney et al., 1973b).

They were told that they would be randomly assigned the social role of either a guard or a prisoner in the experiment. The "guards" were given uniforms and instructions not to use violence but to maintain control of the "prison." The "prisoners" were booked at a real jail, blindfolded, and transported to the campus "prison," which was actually the basement of one of the campus buildings. On Day 2, the prisoners staged a revolt (not planned as part of the experiment), which was quickly crushed by the guards. About a third of the guards then became increasingly aggressive, using humiliation to control and punish the prisoners. For example, prisoners were forced to clean out toilet bowls with their bare hands. Even the "tough-but-fair" and friendly guards failed to intervene on behalf of the prisoners when the aggressive guards gave orders (Zimbardo, 1972). The staff observing the experiment had to release five of the prisoners who became so upset that they were physically ill. The entire experiment was canceled on the morning of the sixth day (Zimbardo, 2007).

The conclusions of Zimbardo and his colleagues highlighted the possible influence that a social role, such as that of "guard," can have on perfectly ordinary people. During the war in Iraq in 2003, an army reserve general was suspended from duty while an investigation into reported prisoner abuses was conducted. Between October and December 2003, investigators found numerous cases of cruel, humiliating, and other startling abuses of the Iraqi prisoners by the army military police stationed at the prison of Abu Ghraib (Hersh, 2004). Among the cruelties reported were pouring cold water on naked detainees, beating them with a broom handle or chair, threatening them with rape, and one case of actually carrying out the threat. How could any normal person have done such things? The "guards" in the Stanford prison study were reportedly normal people, but the effect of putting on the uniform and taking on the social role of guard apparently changed their behavior radically. If that is the case, is it possible that a similar factor was at work at Abu Ghraib?

There have been a variety of criticisms offered of both the study and its possible applications (Bartels, 2015; Bartels et al., 2016; Griggs, 2014; Griggs & Whitehead, 2015; S. A. Haslam & Reicher, 2012a). For one, it's possible the guards and prisoners might not have been as "normal" as they were assessed to be, and *participant selection bias* may have skewed the results. In a later study investigating characteristics of individuals volunteering to be in a prison study versus a nonspecific psychological study, individuals responding to the prison study ad were significantly higher on personality measures

AP 9.F Identify the contributions of key researchers in the areas of conformity, compliance, and obedience.

social role
the pattern of behavior that is expected of a person who is in a particular social position.

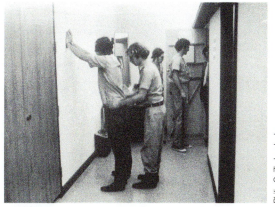

This photograph shows a "guard" searching a "prisoner" in Zimbardo's famous Stanford prison experiment. The students in the experiment became so deeply involved in their assigned roles that Zimbardo had to cancel the experiment on the sixth day—less than half the time originally scheduled for the study.

associated with dispositional aggression and lower in dispositional empathy and altruism (Carnahan & McFarland, 2007).

The study's *ecological validity*, or degree to which results can be applied to the real world, has been questioned (Bartels, 2015; Griggs, 2014). Dr. Zimbardo's dual role of researcher and prison superintendent could have had unintended consequences. Dr. Zimbardo was responsible for orienting the guards to their roles and positions, stressing he wanted the guards to maintain law and order without using violence but also wanted them to develop in the prisoners a mindset of powerlessness (Zimbardo, 2007). Lastly, it is likely that both the guards and prisoners acted as they believed they were expected to consistent with their surroundings, while responding to the *demand characteristics* of the experiment (Banuazizi & Movahedi, 1975; Reicher & Haslam, 2006).

There have been at least two partial replications of the SPE, attempting to control for some of its cautions and caveats. In the first, three experimental prison paradigms were used: standard, based on medium-security prisons in Australia; individualized, which emphasized inmates retaining self-respect; and participatory, where guards were trained to involve prisoners in decision making (Lovibond et al., 1979). There were few hostile actions between guards and prisoners in the participatory groups, and in the standard group, any underlying hostility was less extreme than that in the SPE (Lovibond et al., 1979). The researchers indicated their results supported the ideas put forth by the SPE, namely the influence of the situation (Lovibond et al., 1979).

A 2001 study, the British Broadcasting Corporation (BBC) prison study (BPS), sought to investigate interactions between groups with unequal power and privilege (Reicher & Haslam, 2006). The BPS was different in that the researchers avoided demand characteristics by not assuming any roles in the prison; it looked at interactions through the lens of *social identity theory* (SIT; S. A. Haslam & Reicher, 2012a; Reicher & Haslam, 2006). SIT suggests people only take on roles associated with group membership after they come to identify with that particular group (Tajfel & Turner, 1979). In the BPS, guards did not just adopt the role of "guard;" due to confusion about what a guard was supposed to do, they even had difficulty running the prison (Reicher & Haslam, 2006). The prisoners did not succumb to their assigned role and back down, and after a revolt, the guards and prisoners started to work collaboratively. That said, the BPS also had to be shut down early to avoid issues with those who didn't want to collaborate (S. A. Haslam & Reicher, 2012a; Reicher & Haslam, 2006). Findings from the BPS are supportive of SIT in that the behaviors adopted by both prisoners and guards were chosen by the individuals themselves, not in accordance with the roles assigned to them (Reicher & Haslam, 2006). Behaviors and actions came about as the result of a dynamic interaction between the individual, prior experiences, and a sense of shared social identity. Overall, it appears that any aggressive behavior between individuals in different social roles is based on a combination of individual predispositions, their situations, and the people with whom they interact in a given place (S. A. Haslam & Reicher, 2012a). To learn more about the SPE and BPS, visit **prisonexp.org/** and **bbcprisonstudy.org/**

> 💬 I've heard that violent television programs can cause children to become more aggressive. How true is that?

VIOLENCE IN THE MEDIA AND AGGRESSION Bandura's early study in which small children viewed a video of an aggressive model was one of the first attempts to investigate the effect of violence in the media on children's aggressive behavior (Bandura et al., 1963). See Learning Objective 5.13. Since then, researchers have examined the impact of television and other media violence on the aggressive behavior of children of various ages. The conclusions have all been similar: Children who are exposed to high levels of violent media are more aggressive than children who are not (Anderson et al., 2010; Baron & Reiss, 1985; Bushman & Huesmann, 2001, 2006; Centerwall, 1989; Geen & Thomas, 1986; Huesmann & Miller, 1994; Huesmann et al., 1997; Huesmann et al., 2003; Villani, 2001). These studies have found that there are several contributing factors involving the normal aggressive tendencies of the child, with more aggressive children preferring to watch more aggressive media, as well as the age at which exposure begins: The younger the child, the greater the impact. Parenting issues also have an influence, as the aggressive impact of television is lessened in homes where hostile behavior is not tolerated and punishment is not physical. Research has also demonstrated in a 1-year study of schoolchildren, parental monitoring of violent media decreased the likelihood of getting into a fight (Gentile & Bushman, 2012).

Violent video games have also come under fire as causing violent acting-out in children, especially young adolescents. The tragic shootings at schools all over the United States have, at least in part, been blamed on violent video games that the students seemed to be imitating. This was especially a concern in the Littleton, Colorado, shootings because the adolescent boys involved in those incidents had not only played a violent video game in which two shooters killed people who could not fight back but also had made a video of themselves in trench coats, shooting school athletes. This occurred less than a year before these same boys killed 13 of their fellow students at Columbine High School and wounded 23 others (Anderson & Dill, 2000). In one study, second-grade boys were allowed to play either an aggressive or a nonaggressive video game. After playing the game, the boys who had played the aggressive video game demonstrated more verbal and physical aggression both to objects around them and to their playmates while playing in a free period than did the boys who had played the nonaggressive video game (Irwin & Gross, 1995).

Adults are not immune to the effects of video games either. In a study with 211 university students aged 18 to 37, individuals who played a game with a sexualized female character were more likely to sexually harass women than those who played the same game with non-sexualized female characters (Burnay et al., 2019). The study was made up of an almost equivalent number of male and female participants, and both males and females sexually harassed a female partner more after playing the sexualized video game (Burnay et al., 2019).

In a large meta-analysis of research (a careful statistical analysis of a large number of studies on a particular topic, able to more accurately measure the sizes of research effects than any one smaller study can measure) into the connection between violent media and aggressive behavior in children, social psychologist Craig Anderson and colleagues found clear and consistent evidence that even short-term exposure to violent media significantly increases the likelihood that children will engage in both physical and verbal aggression as well as aggressive thoughts and emotions (Anderson et al., 2003). Even larger, more recent studies have provided additional support (Anderson et al., 2010; Bushman & Huesman, 2006). While it should be noted there are some researchers that do not agree, with some questioning the measures of aggression being used, the analysis procedures, or finding different outcomes (Adachi & Willoughby, 2011; Ferguson, 2015; Ferguson & Kilburn, 2010), evidence appears strong that playing violent video games correlates with increased aggression levels of the children who play them, both young children and adolescents (Anderson, 2003; Anderson & Bushman, 2001; Anderson et al., 2008; Bartlett et al., 2008; Ferguson et al., 2008; Przybylski et al., 2014). And while correlation does *not* prove causation, some researchers believe we may be able to infer causation based on examination of the observed risk factors, outcomes, experimental studies of violent media exposure, and the positive effects of preventative measures (Bushman et al., 2016; see Learning Objective 1.8).

When evaluating the science of violent media effects and individual application, consider the following five points highlighted by Dr. Brad Bushman (2018):

- There have been hundreds of studies, and although not all of the data show a link between violent media and aggression, much of it does.
- Exposure to violent media is not the only risk factor for aggressive behavior, but it is an important one.
- Concerns about exposure to violent media center around age-appropriate consumption; adults can choose to consume violent media if they want, children should not.
- Is there any psychological theory that predicts that observing violence in the home, school, or community can have a negative impact on children but observing it via a screen will not? The answer is no, there isn't one.
- The typical American child spends approximately 7.5 hours a day consuming media, more time than they do in school; is there anything anyone can do for that long every day without it affecting them?

11.15 Prosocial Behavior

11.15 Identify the factors influencing why people help others.

Another and far more pleasant form of human social interaction is **prosocial behavior**, or socially desirable behavior that benefits others rather than brings them harm.

ALTRUISM One form of prosocial behavior that almost always makes people feel good about other people is **altruism**, or helping someone in trouble with no expectation of reward and often without fear for one's own safety. Although no one is surprised by the behavior of a mother who enters a burning house to save her child, some people are often surprised when total strangers step in to help, risking their own lives for people they do not know.

Sociobiologists, scientists who study the evolutionary and genetic bases of social organizations in both animals and humans, see altruistic behavior as a way of preserving one's genetic material, even at the cost of one's own life. This is why the males of certain species of spiders, for example, seem to willingly become "dinner" for the female mates they have just fertilized, ensuring the continuation of their genes through the offspring she will produce (Koh, 1996). It also explains the mother or father who risks life and limb to save a child.

But why do people risk their own lives to help total strangers? One answer may lie in the structure of the brain. Using brain-imaging techniques, researchers have found evidence that a brain region known as the temporoparietal junction (TPJ) is larger in individuals who make altruistic choices, particularly in the right hemisphere (Morishima et al., 2012). This area was also more active during decision making that involved a greater cost of helping the individual.

More importantly, why do people sometimes refuse to help when their own lives are not at risk?

WHY PEOPLE WON'T HELP On March 13, 1964, at about 3:15 in the morning, Winston Mosely saw Catherine "Kitty" Genovese on the street near her apartment complex, stabbed her, left, and then came back nearly half an hour later to rape and stab her to death in a stairwell of the complex. Upon learning of the crime, a reporter for *The New York Times* wrote a story in which he claimed that at least 38 people heard or

---

AP 9.K Describe the variables that contribute to altruism and aggression.

prosocial behavior
socially desirable behavior that benefits others.

altruism
prosocial behavior that is done with no expectation of reward and may involve the risk of harm to oneself.

watched some part of the fatal attack from their apartment windows and that not one of these people called the police until after the attack was over (Delfiner, 2001; Gado, 2004; Rosenthal, 1964). This story outraged the public and has since become a symbol of bystander apathy.

In recent years, the truth of that fateful event has come to light, and the details may be more complex than originally reported. It appears there were errors in the original newspaper story and there is no evidence that 38 people watched the sequence of events that night and then stood by doing nothing during her murder (Levine, 2012; Manning et al., 2007). According to trial records, the two attacks occurred much closer in time than originally believed. At the first attack, a man shouted out his window "Leave that girl alone!" and Moseley fled. Another man supposedly called the police after that first attack, although there is no record of the call. The second attack took place in a stairwell of the apartment complex—a far more sheltered area in which there could have been only a few witnesses at most (Levine, 2012; Manning et al., 2007). One man, whose apartment door opened onto the stairwell where the second attack occurred, cracked open his apartment door, saw the attack—and closed the door (Cook, 2014). He called a friend who told him not to get involved and then called Kitty's neighbor Sophia Farrar. There are conflicting reports about whether Sophia called the police or the man did, but it was Sophia who went to Kitty Genovese's aid and held her until an ambulance arrived (Cook, 2014; Manning et al., 2007; Takooshian et al., 2005).

Fifty-three years later in March 2017, a 15-year-old Chicago girl was lured to a home where she was held prisoner and then gang-raped, beaten, and abused by as many as six young men before being found two days later, dazedly walking down a street near her home. Two boys, a 14-year-old and a 15-year-old, were arrested in connection with this horrible crime. The brutal attack was streamed as a live video on Facebook, where as many as forty people watched the attack. None of those people called the police (WLS-TV, Chicago, 2017). When other people are present at the scene or are assumed to be present, individuals are affected by two basic principles of social psychology: the bystander effect and diffusion of responsibility.

The **bystander effect** refers to the finding that the likelihood of a bystander (someone observing an event and close enough to offer help) to help someone in trouble decreases as the number of bystanders increases. If only one person is standing by, that person is far more likely to help than if there is another person, and the addition of each new bystander decreases the possibility of helping behavior even more (Darley & Latané, 1968; Eagly & Crowley, 1986; Latané & Darley, 1969).

Social psychologists Bibb Latané and John Darley conducted several classic experiments about the bystander effect. In one study, participants were filling out questionnaires in a room that began to fill with smoke. Some participants were alone in the room, whereas in another condition there were three participants in the room. In a third condition, one participant was in the room with two confederates of the experimenter, who were instructed to notice the smoke but ignore it afterward. In the "participant alone" condition, three fourths of the participants left the room to report the smoke. In the "three participants" condition, only a little more than one third of the participants reported the smoke, whereas only one tenth of the participants who were in the room with confederates did so (see **Figure 11.5**).

bystander effect
referring to the effect that the presence of other people has on the decision to help or not help, with help becoming less likely as the number of bystanders increases.

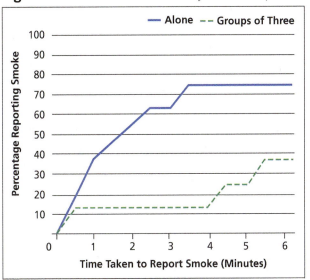

Figure 11.5 Elements Involved in Bystander Response

In a classic experiment, participants were filling out surveys as the room began to fill with smoke. As you can see in the accompanying graph, the time taken to report smoke and the percentage of people reporting smoke both depended on how many people were in the room at the time the smoke was observed. If a person was alone, he or she was far more likely to report the smoke and report it more quickly than when there were three people.

Source: Based On Latané, B., & Darley, J. M. (1969). Bystander "apathy" American Scientist, 57(2), 244–268.

💬 But why does the number of bystanders matter?

Diffusion of responsibility is the phenomenon in which a person fails to take responsibility for either action or inaction because of the presence of other people who are seen to share the responsibility (Leary & Forsyth, 1987). Diffusion of responsibility is a form of attribution in which people explain why they acted (or failed to act) as they did because of others. Contrary to popular belief, bystanders who fail to act do not typically do so out of apathy (a lack of caring about the victim) but instead may care quite deeply. They do not act because of diffusion of responsibility, among other concerns (Glassman & Hadad, 2008). "I was just following orders," "Other people were doing it," and "There were a lot of people there, and I thought one of them would do something" are all examples of statements made in such situations. Kitty Genovese and the 15-year-old girl from Chicago may not have received help because there were too many potential "helpers," and no one took the responsibility to intervene—they thought someone else was doing something about it, or the help came too late.

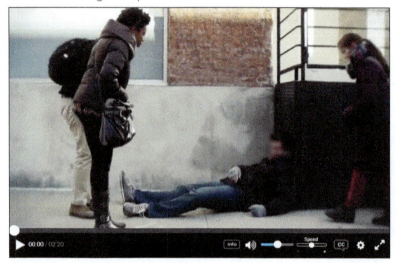

Watch Deciding to Help

👁 Watch the Video at MyLab Psychology

FIVE DECISION POINTS IN HELPING BEHAVIOR What kind of decision-making process do people go through before deciding to help? What are the requirements for deciding when help is needed? Darley and Latané (1968) identified several cognitive decision points that a bystander must face before helping someone in trouble. These decision points, which are discussed in the video *Deciding to Help* and outlined in **Table 11.2**, are still considered useful more than 40 years later.

Table 11.2 Help or Don't Help: Five Decision Points

Decision Point	Description	Factors Influencing Decision
Noticing	Realizing there is a situation that might be an emergency	Hearing a loud crash or a cry for help.
Defining an Emergency	Interpreting the cues as signaling an emergency	Loud crash is associated with a car accident; people are obviously hurt.
Taking Responsibility	Personally assuming the responsibility to act	A single bystander is much more likely to act than when others are present (Latané & Darley, 1969).
Planning a Course of Action	Deciding how to help and what skills might be needed	People who feel they have the necessary skills to help are more likely to help.
Taking Action	Actually helping	Costs of helping (e.g., danger to self) must not outweigh the rewards of helping.

diffusion of responsibility

occurring when a person fails to take responsibility for actions or for inaction because of the presence of other people who are seen to share the responsibility.

Aside from the factors listed in the table, there are other influences on the decision to help. For example, the more ambiguity* in a situation, the less likely it will be defined as an emergency. If other people are nearby, especially if the situation is ambiguous, bystanders may rely on the actions of the others to help determine if the situation is an emergency or not. Since all the bystanders may be doing this, it is very likely that the situation will be seen as a nonemergency because no one is moving to help.

---

*ambiguity: having the quality of being difficult to identify specific elements of the situation.

People in a good mood are generally more likely to help than people in a bad mood, but are not as likely to help if helping would destroy the good mood. Women are more likely to receive help than men if the bystander is male, but not if the bystander is female. Physically attractive people are more likely to be helped. Victims who look like "they deserve what is happening" are less likely to be helped. For example, a man lying on the side of the street who is dressed in shabby clothing and appears to be drunk will be passed by, but if he is dressed in a business suit, people are more likely to stop and help. Racial and ethnicity differences between victim and bystander also decrease the probability of helping (Richards & Lowe, 2003; Tukuitonga & Bindman, 2002). Social identity theory suggests that because people define themselves as part of a social group, an individual's behavior will be influenced by their group's norms and values; helping behavior may then be increased by promoting a sense of shared social identity (Levine, 2012). In other words, the bystander effect may be lessened if people do not encounter each other as strangers (Levine, 2012)

Concept Map L.O. 11.10, 11.11, 11.12, 11.13, 11.14, 11.15

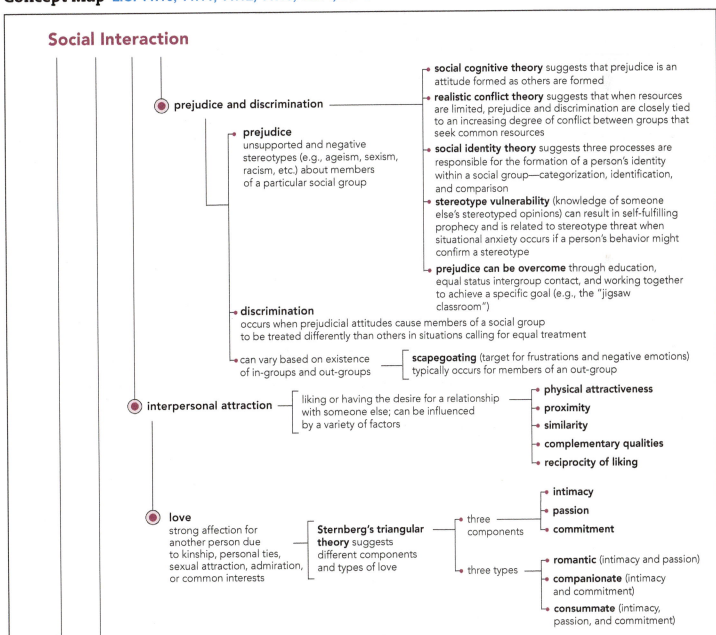

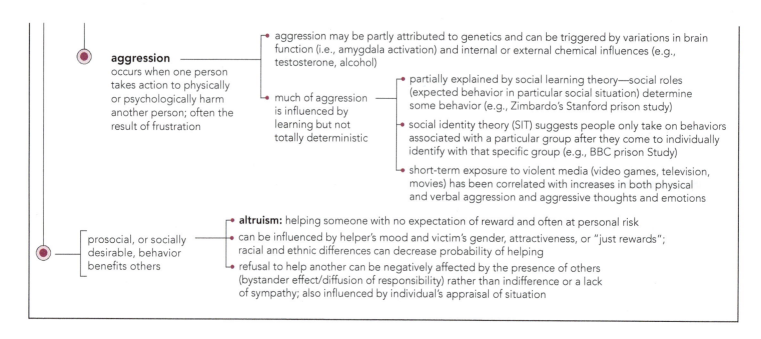

Practice Quiz — How much do you remember?

Pick the best answer.

1. Prejudice is about _____, while discrimination is about _____.
   a. behavior, attitudes
   b. attitudes, behavior
   c. perceptions, beliefs
   d. beliefs, perceptions
   e. race, gender

2. Ruby and Mary became friends while taking an evening class at the local community college. Ruby was later horrified to find out that Mary was actually a teacher at the college. Subsequently, Ruby stopped talking with Mary, thus ending their friendship. What theory of prejudice and discrimination might this be an example of?
   a. realistic conflict theory
   b. in-group/out-group theory
   c. stereotype vulnerability theory
   d. social cognitive theory
   e. scapegoating theory

3. What does the research say about the concept of opposites attract?
   a. Studies do not support this idea but instead offer the explanation of complementary qualities.
   b. Research notes that opposites attract but is unable to explain why this happens.
   c. Opposites attract is really more an example of proximity, although studies show that opposites can be and often are attracted to one another.
   d. While it goes against the concept of similarity, it is real, and research supports it.
   e. It only happens in a few cultures.

4. According to Robert Sternberg's three components of love, which component addresses the physical aspects?
   a. passion
   b. commitment
   c. intimacy
   d. concern
   e. infatuation

5. When people are unable to reach a goal, frustration may result, which can ultimately turn into _____.
   a. aggression
   b. confusion
   c. pain
   d. depression
   e. anxiety

6. Which of the following scenarios probably will NOT result in the bystander effect?
   a. You see someone pass out at a concert.
   b. You come across someone lying on a walking path while you are walking alone at your local nature center.
   c. You drive past an automobile accident where a crowd has gathered.
   d. You come across someone lying on a busy sidewalk in a large city.
   e. You witness a heated argument outside a crowded restaurant.

Applying Psychology to Everyday Life
Looking at Groups

11.16 Identify everyday examples of group conformity and group identity.

In this chapter, we discussed both how we conform to the groups we are in and how we sometimes see our group as the in-group and other groups as the out-group. In the following video, students share various things they have done to fit in with the people around them. In what ways have you changed your behavior, speech, or manner of dress to fit into a group?

Applying Psychology to Everyday Life: Looking at Groups

Watch the Video at MyLab Psychology

After watching the video, answer the following questions:

1. Identify two of the ways students in the video changed their behavior, speech, or dress to fit into a group.
2. In what ways have you changed your behavior, speech, or manner of dress to fit into a group? What social groups do you consider yourself to be a member of?

Chapter Summary

- Social psychology is the scientific study of how a person's thoughts, feelings, and behavior are influenced by the real, imagined, or implied presence of other people.

Social Influence

11.1 Identify factors that influence people or groups to conform to the actions of others.

- Asch used a set of comparison lines and a standard line to experiment with conformity, finding that subjects conformed to group opinion about one third of the time, with that number increasing as the number of confederates rose to four and decreasing if just one confederate gave the correct answer.
- Cross-cultural research has found that collectivistic cultures show more conformity than individualistic cultures. Gender differences do not exist in conformity unless the response is not private, in which case women are more conforming than men.

11.2 Explain how our behavior is impacted by the presence of others.

- Groupthink occurs when a decision-making group feels that it is more important to maintain group unanimity and cohesiveness than to consider the facts realistically. Minimizing groupthink involves holding group members responsible for the decisions made by the group.
- Group polarization occurs when members take somewhat more extreme positions and take greater risks as compared to those made by individuals.
- When the performance of an individual on a relatively easy task is improved by the presence of others, it is called social facilitation. When the performance of an individual on a relatively difficult task is negatively affected by the presence of others, it is called social impairment.
- When a person who is lazy is able to work in a group of people, that person often performs less well than if the person were working alone, in a phenomenon called social loafing.
- Deindividuation occurs when group members feel anonymous and personally less responsible for their actions.

11.3 Compare and contrast three compliance techniques.

- Compliance occurs when a person changes behavior as a result of another person asking or directing that person to change.
- Three common ways of getting compliance from others are the foot-in-the-door technique, the door-in-the-face technique, and the lowball technique.

11.4 Identify factors that make obedience more likely.

- Obedience involves changing one's behavior at the direct order of an authority figure.
- Milgram did experiments in which he found that up to 65 percent of people obeyed an authority figure even if they believed they were hurting, injuring, or possibly killing another person with electric shock.

Social Cognition

11.5 Identify the three components of an attitude and how attitudes are formed.

- Attitudes are tendencies to respond positively or negatively toward ideas, persons, objects, or situations.
- The three components of an attitude are the affective (emotional) component, the behavior component, and the cognitive component.
- Attitudes are often poor predictors of behavior unless the attitude is very specific or very strong.
- Direct contact with the person, situation, object, or idea can help form attitudes.
- Attitudes can be formed through direct instruction from parents or others.
- Interacting with other people who hold a certain attitude can help an individual form that attitude.
- Attitudes can also be formed through watching the actions and reactions of others to ideas, people, objects, and situations.

11.6 Describe how attitudes can be changed.

- Persuasion is the process by which one person tries to change the belief, opinion, position, or course of action of another person through argument, pleading, or explanation.
- The key elements in persuasion are the source of the message, the message itself, and the target audience.
- In the elaboration likelihood model, central-route processing involves attending to the content of the message itself, whereas peripheral-route processing involves attending to factors not involved in the message, such as the appearance of the source of the message, the length of the message, and other noncontent factors.

11.7 Explain how people react when attitudes differ from behavior.

- Cognitive dissonance is discomfort or distress that occurs when a person's actions do not match the person's attitudes.
- Cognitive dissonance is lessened by changing the conflicting behavior, changing the conflicting attitude, or forming a new attitude to justify the behavior.

11.8 Describe how people form impressions of others.

- Impression formation is the forming of the first knowledge a person has about another person.
- The primacy effect in impression formation means that the very first impression one has about a person tends to persist even in the face of evidence to the contrary.
- Impression formation is part of social cognition, or the mental processes that people use to make sense out of the world around them.
- Social categorization is a process of social cognition in which a person, upon meeting someone new, assigns that person to a category or group on the basis of characteristics the person has in common with other people or groups with whom the perceiver has prior experience.
- One form of a social category is the stereotype, in which the characteristics used to assign a person to a category are superficial and believed to be true of all members of the category.
- An implicit personality theory is a form of social cognition in which a person has sets of assumptions about different types of people, personality traits, and actions that are assumed to be related to each other.
- Schemas are mental patterns that represent what a person believes about certain types of people. Schemas can become stereotypes.

11.9 Describe the process of explaining one's own behavior and the behavior of others.

- Attribution is the process of explaining the behavior of others as well as one's own behavior.
- A situational cause is an explanation of behavior based on factors in the surrounding environment or situation.
- A dispositional cause is an explanation of behavior based on the internal personality characteristics of the person being observed.
- The fundamental attribution error is the tendency to overestimate the influence of internal factors on behavior while underestimating the influence of the situation.

Social Interaction

11.10 Distinguish between prejudice and discrimination.

- Prejudice is a negative attitude that a person holds about the members of a particular social group. Discrimination occurs when members of a social group are treated differently because of prejudice toward that group.
- There are many forms of prejudice, including ageism, sexism, racism, and prejudice toward those who are "too fat or too thin."
- In-groups are the people with whom a person identifies, whereas out-groups are everyone else at whom prejudice tends to be directed.
- Scapegoating refers to the tendency to direct prejudice and discrimination at out-group members who have little social power or influence. New immigrants are often the scapegoats for the frustration and anger of the in-group.

11.11 Describe theories of how prejudice is learned and how it can be overcome.

- Social cognitive theory views prejudice as an attitude acquired through direct instruction, modeling, and other social influences.
- Conflict between groups increases prejudice and discrimination according to realistic conflict theory.

- Social identity theory sees a person's formation of a social sense of self within a particular group as being due to three things: social categorization (which may involve the use of reference groups), social identity (the person's sense of belonging to a particular social group), and social comparison (in which people compare themselves to others to improve their own self-esteem).
- Stereotype vulnerability refers to the effect that a person's knowledge of the stereotypes that exist against his or her social group can have on that person's behavior.
- People who are aware of stereotypes may unintentionally come to behave in a way that makes the stereotype real in a self-fulfilling prophecy.
- Intergroup contact is more effective in reducing prejudice if the groups have equal status.
- Prejudice and discrimination can also be reduced when a superordinate goal that is large enough to override all other goals needs to be achieved by all groups.
- Prejudice and discrimination are reduced when people must work together to solve a problem because each person has an important key to solving the problem, creating a mutual interdependence. This technique used in education is called the "jigsaw classroom."

11.12 Identify factors involved in interpersonal attraction.

- Interpersonal attraction refers to liking or having the desire for a relationship with another person.
- People tend to form relationships with people who are in physical proximity to them.
- People are attracted to others who are similar to them in some way.
- People may also be attracted to people who are different from themselves, with the differences acting as a complementary support for areas in which each may be lacking.
- People tend to like other people who like them in return, a phenomenon called the reciprocity of liking.
- Use of a specific social networking site may be partially determined by racial identity and ethnic identity. The ways sites are used are influenced by both gender and the status of current social relationships.

11.13 Describe the different types of love outlined in Sternberg's theory.

- Love is a strong affection for another person due to kinship, personal ties, sexual attraction, admiration, or common interests.
- Sternberg states that the three components of love are intimacy, passion, and commitment.
- Romantic love is intimacy with passion, companionate love is intimacy with commitment, and consummate love contains all three components.

11.14 Explain how aggressive behavior is determined by biology and learning.

- Aggression is behavior intended to physically or psychologically harm. Frustration is a major source of aggression.
- Biological influences on aggression may include genetics, the amygdala and limbic system, and testosterone and serotonin levels.
- Social roles are powerful influences on the expression of aggression. Social learning theory states that aggression can be learned through direct reinforcement and through the imitation of successful aggression by a model.
- Studies have concluded that violent television, movies, and video games stimulate aggressive behavior, both by increasing aggressive tendencies and by providing models of aggressive behavior.

11.15 Identify the factors influencing why people help others.

- Prosocial behavior is behavior that is socially desirable and benefits others.
- Altruism is prosocial behavior in which a person helps someone else without expectation of reward or recognition, often without fear for his or her own safety.
- The bystander effect means that people are more likely to get help from others if there are one or only a few people nearby rather than a larger number. The more people nearby, the less likely it is that help will be offered.
- When others are present at a situation in which help could be offered, there is a diffusion of responsibility among all the bystanders, reducing the likelihood that any one person or persons will feel responsibility for helping.
- Researchers Latané and Darley found that people who were alone were more likely to help in an emergency than people who were with others.
- The five steps in making a decision to help are noticing, defining an emergency, taking responsibility, planning a course of action, and taking action.

Applying Psychology to Everyday Life: Looking at Groups

11.16 Identify everyday examples of group conformity and group identity.

- We are all influenced by other people in many ways; one of those ways is the pressure to conform to the behavior and appearance of the groups with which we identify.

Test Yourself: Preparing for the AP Exam

PART I: MULTIPLE-CHOICE QUESTIONS

Directions for Part I: Read each of the questions or incomplete sentences below. Then choose the response that best answers the question or completes the sentence.

1. Gordon admits that he conforms so as to be liked and accepted by others. This is known as _____.
   a. compliance
   b. informational social influence
   c. conforming conformity
   d. normative social influence
   e. obedience

2. Many businesses now require their employees to work in teams, believing that a group of four to five employees will accomplish more than four to five individuals working alone. This is an example of what concept?
   a. social laziness
   b. groupthink
   c. social facilitation
   d. social loafing
   e. social impairment

3. Yadira was approached by her neighbor, who asked her to adopt three kittens that were abandoned by their mother. While Yadira refused to take in three kittens, she did agree to adopt just one. What compliance technique did her neighbor use on Yadira?
   a. double foot-in-the-door
   b. FOMO
   c. door-in-the-face
   d. lowball
   e. foot-in-the-door

4. Follow-up studies to Stanley Milgram's research have suggested that a teacher's willingness to deliver potentially lethal shocks may be more a product of _____ than of obedience.
   a. deindividuation
   b. conformity
   c. sadism
   d. compliance
   e. social identity

5. The public-service messages that encourage parents to sit down with their children and talk frankly about drugs are promoting which method of attitude formation?
   a. observational learning
   b. direct instruction
   c. direct contact
   d. vicarious conditioning
   e. social contagion

6. Researchers have found that a _____ degree of fear in a message makes it more effective, particularly when it is combined with _____.
   a. maximum, information about how to prevent the fearful consequences
   b. moderate, information about how to prevent the fearful consequences
   c. minimum, threats
   d. moderate, threats
   e. minimum, humor

7. Sandy was a juror in the trial for a man accused of stealing guns from a sporting-goods store. The defendant was not very well spoken and came from a very poor background, but Sandy listened carefully to the evidence presented and made her decision based on that. Sandy was using _____ processing.
   a. visual-route
   b. central-route
   c. peripheral-route
   d. cognitive-route
   e. biased-route

8. If Jaime was experiencing a sense of cognitive dissonance between her attitude and behavior, which of the following would help her reduce that uncomfortable sensation?
   a. thinking constantly about the mismatch
   b. thinking constantly about the current behavior
   c. changing her behavior
   d. discussing the inconsistency with others
   e. maintaining her existing attitude

9. Misha goes to a job interview dressed in patched blue jeans, a torn T-shirt, and sandals. His hair is uncombed, and he hasn't shaved in a few days. Obviously, Misha knows nothing about _____.
   a. groupthink
   b. in-groups
   c. attitude formation
   d. impression formation
   e. cognitive dissonance

10. If behavior is assumed to be caused by external characteristics, this is known as _____.
    a. actor–observer bias
    b. a situational cause
    c. a dispositional cause
    d. a fundamental attribution error
    e. actor–bias

11. Bobby likes to "hang with the guys." These people with whom he identifies most strongly are called a(n) _____.
    a. "them" group
    b. "that" group
    c. in-group
    d. out-group
    e. referent group

12. The "Robber's Cave" experiment showed the value of _____ in combating prejudice.
    a. stereotyping vulnerability
    b. cognitive dissonance
    c. "jigsaw classrooms"
    d. equal-status contact
    e. subordinate goals

13. Katie and Jake met at work. At first they were just friends, but over time, they found themselves falling in love—or, as Katie tells her friends, "Jake just grew on me!" According to research in interpersonal attraction, the most likely explanation for their attraction is _____.
    a. reciprocity of liking
    b. physical attractiveness
    c. intellectual appeal
    d. fate
    e. mere exposure

14. Which of the following chemicals seems to be the most involved in aggression?
    a. oxytocin
    b. testosterone
    c. dopamine
    d. norepinephrine
    e. endorphins

15. To which two processes do some social psychologists attribute the phenomenon of people not helping someone they do not know?
    a. bystander effect and altruism
    b. bystander effect and diffusion of responsibility
    c. aggression and diffusion of responsibility
    d. bystander effect and aggression
    e. altruism and diffusion of responsibility

PART II: FREE-RESPONSE QUESTION

Directions for Part II: Read the essay question that follows. Then respond to the question in a clear, concise essay. Do not simply list facts. Instead, present a thorough argument based on your critical consideration of the topic. Use of proper terminology is necessary.

Karthik had his first appointment to meet his new counselor for 8:00am, the first appointment of the day. However, his counselor was running late, and after some time, Karthik thought, "My counselor must not be very professional to be late for this appointment." After waiting even longer, he began to lose his patience, but when his counselor arrived and explained she was delayed by a vehicle accident on her drive to the office, Karthik decided to forgive her.

Part A
For each of the following terms, explain Karthik's thinking and behavior:

- dispositional attribution
- situational attribution
- cognitive dissonance
- social role

Part B
For each of the following terms, explain how they might influence Karthik's attitude toward his counselor:

- prejudice
- impression formation
- reciprocity of liking

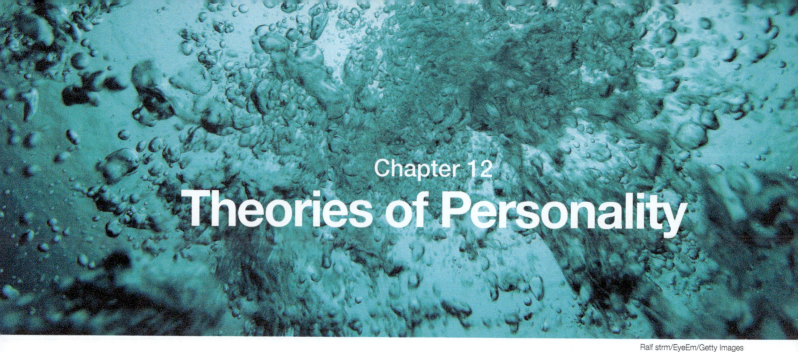

Chapter 12
Theories of Personality

Ralf strm/EyeEm/Getty Images

In your words

In what ways are you similar to and different from your siblings? How has your personality been shaped by your environment?

After you have thought about these questions, watch the video to see how other students would answer them.

Watch the Video at MyLab Psychology

Why study personality?

Personality is the sum total of who you are—your attitudes and reactions, both physical and emotional. It's what makes each person different from every other person in the world. How can any study of human behavior not include the study of who we are and how we got to be that way?

Learning Objectives

12.1 Define the term *personality* and identify several traditional perspectives in the study of personality.

12.2 Explain how the mind and personality are structured, according to Freud.

12.3 Distinguish among the five psychosexual stages of personality development.

12.4 Describe how the neo-Freudians modified Freud's theory.

12.5 Evaluate the influence of Freudian theory on modern personality theories.

12.6 Compare and contrast the learning theories of Bandura and Rotter.

12.7 Evaluate the strengths and limitations of the behavioral and social cognitive learning views of personality.

12.8 Describe how humanists such as Carl Rogers explain personality.

12.9 Evaluate the strengths and limitations of the humanistic view of personality.

12.10 Describe early attempts to use traits to conceptualize personality.

12.11 Identify the five trait dimensions of the five-factor model of personality.

12.12 Evaluate the strengths and limitations of the trait view of personality.

12.13 Explain how twin studies and adoption studies are used in the field of behavioral genetics.

12.14 Evaluate the role of neuroscience in the investigation of biological bases of personality.

12.15 Summarize current research on the heritability and neuroscience of personality.

12.16 Identify the advantages and disadvantages of using interviews, behavioral assessments, and personality inventories to measure personality.

12.17 Identify the advantages and disadvantages of using projective personality tests.

12.18 Identify ways in which you informally assess the personality of others.

12.1 Theories of Personality

12.1 Define the term *personality* and identify several traditional perspectives in the study of personality.

Personality is the unique way in which each individual thinks, acts, and feels throughout life. Personality should not be confused with **character**, which refers to value judgments made about a person's morals or ethical behavior; nor should it be confused with **temperament**, the biologically innate and enduring characteristics with which each person is born, such as irritability or adaptability. Both character and temperament are vital parts of personality, however. Every adult personality is a combination of temperaments and personal history of family, culture, and the time during which they grew up (Kagan, 2010).

Personality is an area of psychology in which there are several ways to explain the characteristic behavior of human beings. Despite the investigation of personality reaching back to at least the fourth century B.C.E. (Dumont, 2010), one reason no single explanation of personality exists is because personality is still difficult to measure precisely and scientifically, and different perspectives of personality have arisen. Overall these tend to examine the source of personality, such as individual behavioral tendencies or situational variables, both of which are influences that may be conscious or unconscious (Mischel & Shoda, 1995). Sources overlap and influence each other, such as the interaction of biological, developmental, social, and cultural factors. Some perspectives are influenced by early schools of thought in psychology such as structuralism, functionalism, Gestalt, learning, or the cognitive perspective. Theories or perspectives may also be influenced by newer ideas from evolution, social adaptation, motivation, and information processing (Buss, 2009a, 2011; Higgins & Scholer, 2010; McAdams & Olson, 2010; Mischel & Shoda, 1995). From a foundational aspect, we will focus on several traditional perspectives in personality:

- The *psychodynamic perspective* had its beginnings in the work of Sigmund Freud and still exists today. It focuses on the role of the unconscious mind in the development of personality. This perspective is also heavily focused on biological causes of personality differences.

- The *behavioral perspective* is based on the theories of learning as discussed in Chapter Five. This approach focuses on the effect of the environment on behavior and, as addressed here, includes aspects of social cognitive theory in that, interactions with others and personal thought processes also influence learning and personality.

- The *humanistic perspective* first arose as a reaction against the psychoanalytic and behaviorist perspectives and focuses on the role of each person's conscious life experiences and choices in personality development.

- The *trait perspective* differs from the other three in its basic goals: The psychodynamic, behaviorist, and humanistic perspectives all seek to explain the process that causes personality to form into its unique characteristics, whereas trait theorists are more concerned with the end result—the characteristics themselves. Although some trait theorists assume that traits are biologically determined, others make no such assumption.

personality
the unique and relatively stable ways in which people think, feel, and behave.

character
value judgments of a person's moral and ethical behavior.

AP 7.K Compare and contrast the psychoanalytic theories of personality with other theories of personality.

12.2–12.5 Psychodynamic Perspectives

Do you believe you are a different person now than you were at age 5 or 6? Do you believe things that happen to people early in their life impact who they are later in life? Have you ever said or done something and later wondered why you said or did what you did? If you said yes to any of these, you have embraced some of the ideas that were put forth by Sigmund Freud or by others that later expanded on, or modified, some of Freud's ideas about personality.

12.2 Freud's Conception of Personality

12.2 Explain how the mind and personality are structured, according to Freud.

It's hard to understand how Freud developed his ideas about personality unless we have some knowledge of the world in which he and his patients lived. He was born and raised in Europe during the Victorian Age, a time of sexual repression. People growing up in this period were told by their church that sex should take place only in the context of marriage and then only to make babies. To enjoy sexual intercourse was considered a sin. Men were understood to be unable to control their "animal" desires at times, and a good Victorian husband would father several children with his wife and then turn to a mistress for sexual comfort, leaving his virtuous* wife untouched. Women, especially those of the upper classes, were not supposed to have sexual urges. It is no wonder that many of Freud's patients were wealthy women with problems stemming from unfulfilled sexual desires or sexual repression. Freud's "obsession" with sexual explanations for abnormal behavior seems more understandable in light of his cultural background and that of his patients.

Freud came to believe there were layers of consciousness in the mind. His belief in the influence of the unconscious mind on conscious behavior, published in *The Psychopathology of Everyday Life* (Freud, 1901), shocked the Victorian world.

THE STRUCTURE OF THE MIND Freud believed that the mind was divided into three parts: the preconscious, conscious, and unconscious (Freud, 1900). While no one really disagreed with the idea of a conscious mind in which one's current awareness exists or even of a preconscious mind containing memories, information, and events of which one can easily become aware, the **unconscious mind** (also called "the unconscious") was the real departure for the professionals of Freud's day. Freud theorized that there is a part of the mind that remains hidden at all times, surfacing only in symbolic form in dreams and in some of the behavior people engage in without knowing why they have done so. Even when a person makes a determined effort to bring a memory out of the unconscious mind, it will not appear directly, according to Freud. Freud believed the unconscious mind was the most important determining factor in human behavior and personality.

FREUD'S DIVISIONS OF THE PERSONALITY Freud believed, based on observations of his patients, that personality itself could be divided into three parts, each existing at one or more levels of conscious awareness (see **Figure 12.1**). The way these three parts of the personality develop and interact with one another became the heart of his theory (Freud, 1923, 1933, 1940).

ID: IF IT FEELS GOOD, DO IT The first and most primitive part of the personality, present in the infant, is the **id**. *Id* is a Latin word that means "it." The id is a completely unconscious, pleasure-seeking, amoral part of the personality that exists at birth, containing all of the basic biological drives: hunger, thirst, self-preservation, and sex, for example.

💬 Wait a minute—Freud thought babies have sex drives?

Yes, Freud thought babies have sex drives, which shocked and outraged his colleagues and fellow Victorians. By "sex drive" he really meant "pleasure drive," the need to seek out pleasurable sensations. People do seem to be pleasure-seeking creatures,

AP 7.J Identify the contributions of major researchers in personality theory.

unconscious mind
level of the mind in which thoughts, feelings, memories, and other information are kept that are not easily or voluntarily brought into consciousness.

id
part of the personality present at birth and completely unconscious.

---
*virtuous: morally excellent.

Figure 12.1 Freud's Conception of the Personality

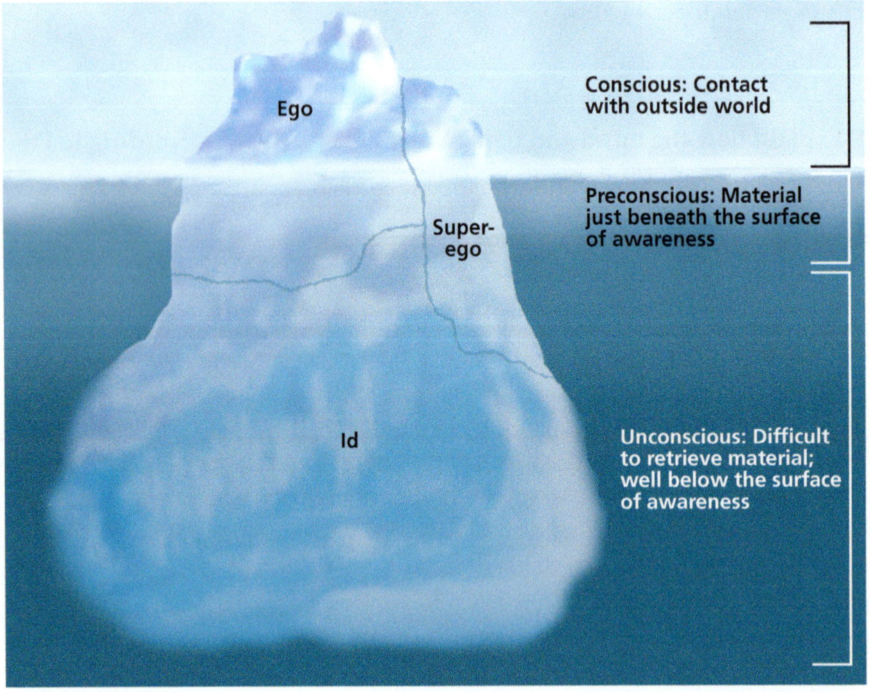

This iceberg represents the three levels of the mind. The part of the iceberg visible above the surface is the conscious mind. Just below the surface is the preconscious mind, everything that is not yet part of the conscious mind. Hidden deep below the surface is the unconscious mind, feelings, memories, thoughts, and urges that cannot be easily brought into consciousness. While two of the three parts of the personality (ego and superego) exist at all three levels of awareness, the id is completely in the unconscious mind.

and even infants seek pleasure from sucking and chewing on anything they can get into their mouths. In fact, thinking about what infants are like when they are just born provides a good picture of the id. Infants are demanding, irrational, illogical, and impulsive. They want their needs satisfied immediately, and they don't care about anyone else's needs or desires. (A word of caution: The fact that infant behavior seems to fit Freud's concept of the id is not proof that the id exists. It simply means that Freud came up with the concept of the id to fit what he already knew about infants.)

Freud called this need for satisfaction the **pleasure principle**, which can be defined as the desire for immediate gratification of needs with no regard for the consequences. The pleasure principle can be summed up simply as "if it feels good, do it."

EGO: THE EXECUTIVE DIRECTOR People normally try to satisfy an infant's needs as quickly as possible. Infants are fed when hungry, changed when wet, and tended to whenever they cry. But as infants begin to grow, adults start denying them their every wish. There will be things they cannot touch or hold, and they must learn to wait for certain things, such as food. Freud would say that reality has reared its ugly head, and the id simply cannot deal with the reality of having to wait or not getting what it wants. Worse still would be the possibility of punishment as a result of the id's unrestrained actions.

According to Freud, to deal with reality, a second part of the personality develops called the **ego**. The ego, from the Latin word for "I," is mostly conscious and is far more rational, logical, and cunning than the id. The ego works on the **reality principle**, which is the need to satisfy the demands of the id only in ways that will not lead to negative consequences. This means that sometimes the ego decides to deny the id its desires because the consequences would be painful or too unpleasant.

pleasure principle

principle by which the id functions; the desire for the immediate satisfaction of needs without regard for the consequences.

ego

part of the personality that develops out of a need to deal with reality; mostly conscious, rational, and logical.

reality principle

principle by which the ego functions; the satisfaction of the demands of the id only when negative consequences will not result.

For example, while an infant might reach out and take an object despite a parent's protests, a toddler with the developing ego will avoid taking the object when the parent says, "No!" to avoid punishment—but may go back for the object when the parent is not looking. A simpler way of stating the reality principle, then, is "if it feels good, do it, but only if you can get away with it."

> 💬 If everyone acted on the pleasure principle, the world would be pretty scary. How does knowing right from wrong come into Freud's theory?

SUPEREGO: THE MORAL WATCHDOG Freud called the third and final part of the personality, the moral center of personality, the **superego**. The superego (also Latin, meaning "over the self") develops as a preschool-aged child learns the rules, customs, and expectations of society. The superego contains the **conscience**, the part of the personality that makes people feel guilt, or *moral anxiety*, when they do the wrong thing. It is not until the conscience develops that children have a sense of right and wrong. (Note that the term *conscience* is a different word from *conscious*. They may look and sound similar, but they represent totally different concepts.)

THE ANGEL, THE DEVIL, AND ME: HOW THE THREE PARTS OF THE PERSONALITY WORK TOGETHER Anyone who has ever watched cartoons while growing up has probably seen these three parts of the personality shown in animated form—the id is usually a little devil, the superego an angel, and the ego is the person or animal caught in the middle, trying to decide what action to take. So the id makes demands, the superego puts restrictions on how those demands can be met, and the ego has to come up with a plan that will quiet the id but satisfy the superego. Sometimes the id or the superego does not get its way, resulting in a great deal of anxiety for the ego itself. This constant state of conflict is Freud's view of how personality works; it is only when the anxiety created by this conflict gets out of hand that disordered behavior arises. Note that despite the id being portrayed as the devil in the example, the id is not "evil"; it is concerned with survival and immediate gratification.

The **psychological defense mechanisms** are ways of dealing with anxiety through unconsciously distorting one's perception of reality. These defense mechanisms were mainly outlined and studied by Freud's daughter, Anna Freud, who was a psychoanalyst (Benjafield, 1996; A. Freud, 1946). In order for the three parts of the personality to function, the constant conflict among them must be managed, and Freud assumed the defense mechanisms were among the most important tools for dealing with the anxiety caused by this conflict. A list of the defense mechanisms, their definitions, and examples of each appears in **Table 12.1**.

superego
part of the personality that acts as a moral center.

conscience
part of the superego that produces guilt, depending on how acceptable behavior is.

psychological defense mechanisms
unconscious distortions of a person's perception of reality that reduce stress and anxiety.

psychosexual stages
five stages of personality development proposed by Freud and tied to the sexual development of the child.

fixation
disorder in which the person does not fully resolve the conflict in a particular psychosexual stage, resulting in personality traits and behavior associated with that earlier stage.

12.3 Stages of Personality Development

12.3 Distinguish among the five psychosexual stages of personality development.

AP 6.E Identify the contributions of major researchers in developmental psychology in the area of social development in childhood.

> 💬 So the id exists at birth, but the other two parts of the personality develop later—how much later? When is personality finished?

Freud believed that personality development occurs in a series of **psychosexual stages** that are determined by the developing sexuality of the child. At each stage, a different *erogenous zone*, or area of the body that produces pleasurable feelings, becomes important and can become the source of conflicts. Conflicts that are not fully resolved can result in **fixation**, or getting "stuck" to some degree in a stage of development.

Table 12.1 The Psychological Defense Mechanisms

Defense Mechanism and Definition	Example
Denial: refusal to recognize or acknowledge a threatening situation.	A mother refuses to acknowledge her son was killed during his recent military deployment.
Repression: "pushing" threatening or conflicting events or situations out of conscious memory.	Eli, who was sexually abused as a child, cannot remember the abuse at all.
Rationalization: making up acceptable excuses for unacceptable behavior.	"If I don't have breakfast, I can have that piece of cake later on without hurting my diet."
Projection: placing one's own unacceptable thoughts onto others, as if the thoughts belonged to them and not to oneself.	Ella is attracted to her sister's husband but denies this and believes the husband is attracted to her.
Reaction formation: forming an emotional reaction or attitude that is the opposite of one's threatening or unacceptable actual thoughts.	Jaden has negative prejudices toward other religions but goes out of his way to appear open-minded and accepting.
Displacement: expressing feelings that would be threatening if directed at the real target onto a less threatening substitute target.	Sandra gets reprimanded by her boss and goes home to angrily pick a fight with her husband.
Regression: falling back on childlike patterns as a way of coping with stressful situations.	Four-year-old Zachary starts wetting his bed after his parents bring home a new baby.
Identification: trying to become like someone else to deal with one's anxiety.	Amber really admires Kaylee, the most popular girl in school, and tries to copy her behavior and dress.
Compensation (substitution): trying to make up for areas in which a deficit is perceived by becoming superior in some other area.	José is not good at athletics, so he puts all of his energies into becoming an academic scholar.
Sublimation: turning socially unacceptable urges into socially acceptable behavior.	Angel, who is very aggressive, becomes a mixed martial arts fighter.

The child may grow into an adult but will still carry emotional and psychological "baggage" from that earlier fixated stage.

ORAL STAGE (FIRST 18 MONTHS) The first stage is called the **oral stage** because the erogenous zone is the mouth. The conflict that can arise here, according to Freud, will be over weaning (taking the mother's breast away from the child, who will now drink from a cup). Weaning that occurs too soon or too late can result in too little or too much satisfaction of the child's oral needs, resulting in the activities and personality traits associated with an orally fixated adult personality: overeating, drinking too much, chain smoking, talking too much, nail biting, gum chewing, and a tendency to be either too dependent and optimistic (when the oral needs are overindulged) or too aggressive and pessimistic (when the oral needs are denied).

ANAL STAGE (18 TO 36 MONTHS) As the child becomes a toddler, Freud believed that the erogenous zone moves from the mouth to the anus, because he also believed that children got a great deal of pleasure from both withholding and releasing their feces at will. This stage is, therefore, called the **anal stage**.

Obviously, Freud thought that the main area of conflict here is toilet training, the demand that the child use the toilet at a particular time and in a particular way. This invasion of reality is part of the process that stimulates the development of the ego during this stage. Fixation in the anal stage, from toilet training that is too harsh, can take one of two forms. The child who rebels openly will refuse to go in the toilet and, according to Freud, translate in the adult as an *anal expulsive personality*, someone who sees messiness as a statement of personal control and who is somewhat destructive and hostile. Some children, however, are terrified of making a mess and rebel passively—refusing to go at all or retaining the feces. No mess, no punishment. As adults, they are stingy, stubborn, and excessively neat. This type is called the *anal retentive personality*.

oral stage

the first stage in Freud's psychosexual stages, occurring in the first 18 months of life in which the mouth is the erogenous zone and weaning is the primary conflict.

anal stage

the second stage in Freud's psychosexual stages, occurring from about 18 to 36 months of age, in which the anus is the erogenous zone and toilet training is the source of conflict.

PHALLIC STAGE (3 TO 6 YEARS) As the child grows older, the erogenous zone shifts to the genitals. Children have discovered the differences between the sexes by now, and most have also engaged in perfectly normal self-stimulation of the genitals, or masturbation. One can only imagine the horror of the Victorian parent who discovered a child engaged in masturbation. People of that era believed masturbation led to all manner of evils, including mental illness.

This awakening of sexual curiosity and interest in the genitals is the beginning of what Freud termed the **phallic stage**. (The word *phallic* comes from the Greek word *phallos* and means "penis.") Freud believed that when boys realized that the little girl down the street had no penis, they developed a fear of losing the penis called *castration anxiety*, while girls developed *penis envy* because they were missing a penis. If this seems an odd focus on male anatomy, remember the era—the Western world at that time was very male oriented and male dominated. Fortunately, nearly all psychoanalysts have long since abandoned the concept of penis envy (Horney, 1939; Horney, 1967/1973; Slipp, 1993). The conflict in the phallic stage centers on the awakening sexual feelings of the child. Freud essentially believed boys develop both sexual attraction to their mothers and jealousy of their fathers during this stage, a phenomenon called the **Oedipus complex**. (Oedipus was a king in a Greek tragedy who unknowingly killed his father and married his mother.)

The sexual attraction is not that of an adult male for a female but more of a sexual curiosity that becomes mixed up with the boy's feelings of love and affection for his mother. Of course, his jealousy of his father leads to feelings of anxiety and fears that his father, a powerful authority figure, might get angry and do something terrible—remember that castration anxiety? To deal with this anxiety, two things must occur by the time the phallic stage ends. The boy will *repress* his sexual feelings for his mother and *identify* with his father. (*Identification* is one of the defense mechanisms used to combat anxiety.) The boy tries to be just like his father in every way, taking on the father's behavior, mannerisms, values, and moral beliefs as his own, so that Daddy won't be able to get angry with the boy. Girls go through a similar process called the **Electra complex** with their father as the target of their affections and their mother as the rival. The result of identification is the development of the superego, the internalized moral values of the same-sex parent. Of note, while Freud referred to the Oedipal conflict or complex when referring to either boys or girls, it was Carl Jung who gave the female variant of this conflict the name *Electra complex* (Jung, 1915).

What happens when things go wrong? If a child does not have a same-sex parent with whom to identify, or if the opposite-sex parent encourages the sexual attraction, fixation can occur. Fixation in the phallic stage usually involves immature sexual attitudes as an adult. People who are fixated in this stage, according to Freud, will often exhibit promiscuous* sexual behavior and be very vain. The vanity is seen as a cover-up for feelings of low self-worth arising from the failure to resolve the complex, and the lack of moral sexual behavior stems from the failure of identification and the inadequate formation of the superego. Additionally, men with this fixation may be "mama's boys" who never quite grow up, and women with this fixation may look for much older father figures to marry.

LATENCY STAGE (6 YEARS TO PUBERTY) Remember, by the end of the phallic stage, children have pushed their sexual feelings for the opposite sex into the unconscious in another defensive reaction: repression. From age 6 to the onset of puberty, children will remain in this stage of hidden, or *latent*, sexual feelings, so this stage is called **latency**.

phallic stage
the third stage in Freud's psychosexual stages, occurring from about 3 to 6 years of age, in which the child discovers sexual feelings.

Oedipus complex/Electra complex
situation occurring in the phallic stage in which a child develops a sexual attraction to the opposite-sex parent and jealousy of the same-sex parent. Males develop an Oedipus complex whereas females develop an Electra complex.

latency
the fourth stage in Freud's psychosexual stages, occurring during the school years, in which the sexual feelings of the child are repressed while the child develops in other ways.

---

*promiscuous: having sexual relations with more than one partner.

In this stage, children grow and develop intellectually, physically, and socially but not sexually. This is the age at which boys play only with boys, girls play only with girls, and each thinks the opposite sex is pretty awful.

GENITAL STAGE (PUBERTY ON) When puberty does begin, the sexual feelings that were once repressed can no longer be ignored. Bodies are changing and sexual urges are once more allowed into consciousness, but these urges will no longer have the parents as their targets. Instead, the focus of sexual curiosity and attraction will become other adolescents, celebrities, and other objects of adoration. Since Freud tied personality development into sexual development, the **genital stage** represented the final process in Freud's personality theory, as well as the entry into adult social and sexual behavior. Table 12.2 summarizes the stages of the psychosexual theory of personality development.

genital stage
the final stage in Freud's psychosexual stages; from puberty on, sexual urges are allowed back into consciousness and the individual moves toward adult social and sexual behavior.

Table 12.2 Freud's Psychosexual Stages

Stage	Age	Focus of Pleasure	Focus of Conflicts	Difficulties at this Stage Affect Later …
Oral	Birth to 1 or 1½ years old	Oral activities (such as sucking, feeding, and making noises with the mouth)	Weaning	• Ability to form interpersonal attachments • Basic feelings about the world • Tendency to use oral forms of aggression, such as sarcasm • Optimism or pessimism • Tendency to take charge or be passive
Anal	1 or 1½ to 3 years old	Bowel and bladder control	Toilet training	• Sense of competence and control • Stubbornness or willingness to go along with others • Neatness or messiness • Punctuality or tardiness
Phallic	3 to 6 years old	Genitals	Sexual awareness	• Development of conscience through identification with same-sex parent • Pride or humility
Latency	6 years old to puberty	Social skills (such as the ability to make friends) and intellectual skills; dormant period in terms of psychosexual development	School, play, same-sex friendships	• Ability to get along with others
Genital	Puberty to death	Sexual behavior	Sexual relationship with partner	• Immature love or indiscriminate hate • Uncontrollable working or inability to work

Note: Freud thought that the way a person finds pleasure or is prevented from satisfying urges for pleasure at each stage affects personality. Thus, like Erikson's stage model described in Chapter Eight, see Learning Objective 8.8, Freud's model argues that the way a person deals with particular psychological challenges has long-term effects on personality.

AP 7.J Identify the contributions of major researchers in personality theory.

psychoanalysis
an insight therapy based on the theory of Freud, emphasizing the revealing of unconscious conflicts; Freud's term for both the theory of personality and the therapy based on it.

12.4 The Neo-Freudians

12.4 Describe how the neo-Freudians modified Freud's theory.

At first, Freud's ideas were met with resistance and ridicule by the growing community of doctors and psychologists. Eventually, a number of early psychoanalysts, objecting to Freud's emphasis on biology and particularly on sexuality, broke away from a strict interpretation of psychoanalytic theory, instead altering the focus of **psychoanalysis** (the term Freud applied to both his explanation of the workings of the unconscious mind and the development of personality and the therapy he based on that theory) to the impact of the social environment. See Learning Objective 1.2. At the same time, they retained many of Freud's original concepts such as the id, ego, superego, and defense mechanisms. These early psychoanalysts became the **neo-Freudians**, or "new" Freudian psychoanalysts. This section briefly covers some of the more famous neo-Freudians.

JUNG Carl Gustav Jung ("YOONG") disagreed with Freud about the nature of the unconscious mind. Jung believed the unconscious held much more than personal fears, urges, and memories. He believed there was not only a **personal unconscious**, as described by Freud, but a **collective unconscious** (Jung, 1933).

According to Jung, the collective unconscious contains a kind of "species" memory, memories of ancient fears and themes that seem to occur in many folktales and cultures. These collective, universal human memories were called **archetypes** by Jung. There are many archetypes, but two of the more well known are the *anima/animus* (the feminine side of a man/the masculine side of a woman) and the *shadow* (the dark side of personality, called the "devil" in Western cultures). The side of one's personality shown to the world is termed the *persona*.

ADLER Alfred Adler was also in disagreement with Freud over the importance of sexuality in personality development. Adler (1954) developed the theory that as young, helpless children, people all develop feelings of inferiority when comparing themselves to the more powerful, superior adults in their world. The driving force behind all human endeavors, emotions, and thoughts for Adler was not the seeking of pleasure but the seeking of superiority. The defense mechanism of *compensation*, in which people try to overcome feelings of inferiority in one area of life by striving to be superior in another area, figured prominently in Adler's theory (see Table 12.1).

Adler (1954) also developed a theory that the birth order of a child affected personality. Firstborn children with younger siblings feel inferior once those younger siblings get all the attention and often overcompensate by becoming overachievers. Middle children have it slightly easier, getting to feel superior over the dethroned older child while dominating younger siblings. They tend to be very competitive. Younger children are supposedly pampered and protected but feel inferior because they are not allowed the freedom and responsibility of the older children.

Although some researchers have found evidence to support Adler's birth order theory (Stein, 2001; Sulloway, 1996), and some have even linked birth order to career choices (Leong et al., 2001; Watkins & Savickas, 1990), other researchers point to sloppy methodology and the bias of researchers toward the birth order idea (Beer & Horn, 2001; Freese et al., 1999; Ioannidis, 1998). In what has been referred to as the most thorough study of birth order and personality to date, evidence strongly suggests birth order has very little to no significant impact on personality development and only a tiny influence on the development of our intellect (Damian & Roberts, 2015; Rohrer et al., 2015).

HORNEY Karen Horney (horn-EYE) disagreed with Freudian views about the differences between males and females and most notably with the concept of penis envy. She countered with her own concept of "womb envy," stating that men felt the need to compensate for their lack of child-bearing ability by striving for success in other areas (Burger, 1997).

Rather than focusing on sexuality, Horney focused on the **basic anxiety** created in a child born into a world so much bigger and more powerful than the child. While people whose parents gave them love, affection, and security would overcome

neo-Freudians
followers of Freud who developed their own competing psychodynamic theories.

personal unconscious
Jung's name for the unconscious mind as described by Freud.

collective unconscious
Jung's name for the memories shared by all members of the human species.

archetypes
Jung's collective, universal human memories.

basic anxiety
anxiety created when a child is born into the bigger and more powerful world of older children and adults.

Of the three ways children deal with anxiety according to Horney, which way do you think this child might be using?

this anxiety, others with less secure upbringings would develop **neurotic personalities** and maladaptive ways of dealing with relationships. Some children, according to Horney, try to deal with their anxiety by moving toward people, becoming dependent and clingy. Others move against people, becoming aggressive, demanding, and cruel. A third way of coping would be to move away from people by withdrawing from personal relationships.

ERIKSON Erik Erikson (1950, 1959, 1982) was an art teacher who became a psychoanalyst by studying with Anna Freud. He also broke away from Freud's emphasis on sex, preferring instead to emphasize the social relationships that are important at every stage of life. Erikson's eight psychosocial stages are discussed in detail in Chapter Eight. See Learning Objective 8.8.

💬 It sounds as if all of these theorists became famous by ditching some of Freud's original ideas. Is Freud even worth studying anymore?

12.5 Current Thoughts on Freud and the Psychodynamic Perspective

12.5 Evaluate the influence of Freudian theory on modern personality theories.

Although Freud's original psychoanalytic theory seems less relevant in today's sexually saturated world, many of his concepts have remained useful and still form a basis for many modern personality theories as well as the psychodynamic perspective. The idea of the defense mechanisms has had some research support and has remained useful in clinical psychology as a way of describing people's defensive behavior and irrational thinking. The concept of an unconscious mind also has some research support.

> **THINKING CRITICALLY 12.1**
>
> What aspects of psychodynamic theory do you think still have relevance in today's world? Was there one neo-Freudian whose theory appealed to you, and if so, why?

As strange as the idea of an unconscious mind that guides behavior must have seemed to Freud's contemporaries, modern researchers have had to admit that there are influences on human behavior that exist outside of normal conscious awareness. In fact, in addition to Systems 1 and 2, a "Type 3" process for unconscious thought has been proposed (Dijksterhuis & Strick, 2016). See Chapter Seven. And, while researchers have found evidence of unconscious processing through studies of brain activation, subliminal perception, implicit memory, and implicit and associative learning (Creswell et al., 2013; Koizumi et al., 2016; Victor et al., 2017), see Learning Objective 6.5, others still question the impact of unconscious processes and some of the approaches and methodologies used (Newell & Shanks, 2014; Vadillo et al., 2016).

This might be a good time to point out a very important fact about Freud's theory: He did no experiments to arrive at his conclusions about personality. His theory is based on his own observations (case studies) of numerous patients. Basing his suppositions on his patients' detailed memories of their childhoods and life experiences, he interpreted their behavior and reminiscences to develop his theory of psychoanalysis. He felt free to interpret what his patients told him of their childhoods as fantasy or fact, depending on how well those memories fit in with his developing theory.

neurotic personalities

personalities typified by maladaptive ways of dealing with relationships in Horney's theory.

For example, many of Freud's patients told him that they were sexually abused by fathers, brothers, and other close family members. Freud was apparently unable to accept these memories as real and decided that they were fantasies, making them the basis of the Oedipal conflict. He actually revised his original perceptions of his patients' memories of abuse as real in the face of both public and professional criticism from his German colleagues (Masson, 1984).

Freud based much of his diagnoses of patients' problems on the interpretations of dreams (see Learning Objective 4.7) and the results of the patient's free association (talking about anything without fear of negative feedback). These "sources" of information are often criticized as too ambiguous and without scientific support for the validity of his interpretations. The very ambiguity of these sources of information allowed Freud to fit the patient's words and recollections to his own preferred interpretation as well as increased the possibility that his own suggestions and interpretations, if conveyed to the patient, might alter the actual memories of the patient, who would no doubt be in a very suggestible state of mind during therapy (Grünbaum, 1984).

Another criticism of Freud's theory concerns the people upon whose dreams, recollections, and comments the theory of psychoanalysis was based. Freud's clients were almost all wealthy Austrian women living in the Victorian era of sexual repression. Critics state that basing his theory on observations made with such a demographically limited group of clients promoted his emphasis on sexuality as the root of all problems in personality, as women of that social class and era were often sexually frustrated. Freud rarely had clients who did not fit this description, and so his theory is biased in terms of sexual frustrations (Robinson, 1993). From a broader perspective, Freud's theory is based on conflict and the idea that humans are driven by forces they cannot control (McAdams & Pals, 2006). The family is seen as a primary source of disruption, even possibly leading to psychopathology (Giordano, 2011). Both of these ideas are tied to traditional Western thought and may be in stark contrast to other cultures' perspectives.

Although most professionals today view Freud's theory with a great deal of skepticism, his influence on the modern world cannot be ignored. Freudian concepts have had an impact on literature, movies, and even children's cartoons. People who have never taken a course in psychology are familiar with some of Freud's most basic concepts, such as the defense mechanisms. He was also one of the first theorists to emphasize the importance of childhood experiences on personality development—in spite of the fact that he did not work extensively with children.

It has only been in the last several decades that people have had the necessary tools to examine the concepts of the unconscious mind. One can only wonder how Freud might have changed his theory in light of what is known about the workings of the human brain and the changes in society that exist today.

Concept Map L.O. 12.1, 12.2, 12.3, 12.4, 12.5

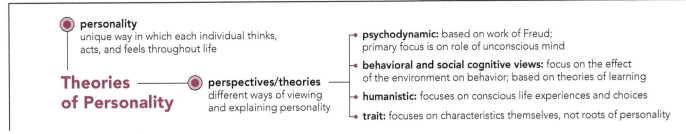

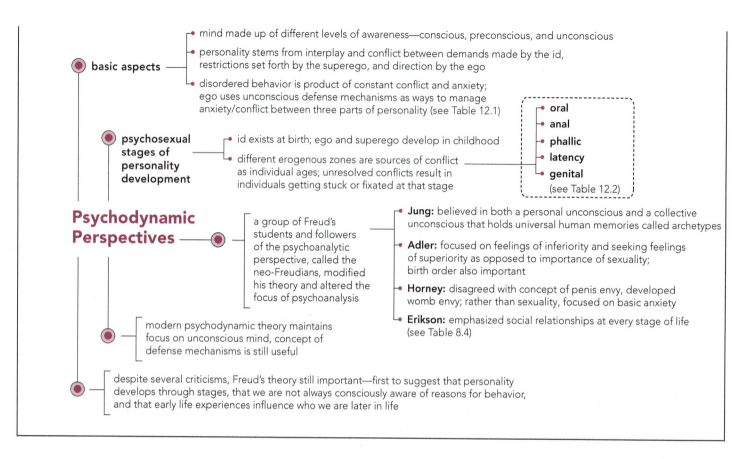

Practice Quiz — How much do you remember?

Pick the best answer.

1. If you are asked to describe your best friends by explaining how they act, what they typically feel, and what they think about, you would be describing their _____.
   a. mood
   b. character
   c. personality
   d. temperament
   e. affect

2. According to Freud, the _____ mind was the most important determining factor in human behavior and personality.
   a. external
   b. conscious
   c. conscience
   d. preconscious
   e. unconscious

3. According to Freud, which part of the personality is totally buried within each individual?
   a. conscience
   b. ego
   c. superego
   d. id
   e. ego-ideal

4. The awakening of sexual curiosity and interest in the genitals is the beginning of what Freud termed the _____ stage.
   a. latency
   b. anal
   c. phallic
   d. oral
   e. genital

5. Many of Gabriel's friends like to dress up on Halloween as devils, vampires, and zombies. According to Carl Jung's theory, what archetype is being expressed?
   a. shadow
   b. hero
   c. persona
   d. animus
   e. anima

6. Which neo-Freudian believed personality was mostly a product of dealing with anxieties during childhood?
   a. Alfred Adler
   b. Erich Fromm
   c. Erik Erikson
   d. Carl Jung
   e. Karen Horney

AP 7.L Compare and contrast the behaviorist and social cognitive theories of personality with other theories of personality.

12.6–12.7 The Behavioral and Social Cognitive View of Personality

At the time Freud's theory was shocking the Western world, another psychological perspective was also making its influence known. In Chapter Five, the theories of classical and operant conditioning were discussed in some detail. *Behaviorists* (researchers who use the principles of conditioning to explain the actions and reactions of both animals and humans) and *social cognitive theorists* (researchers who emphasize the influence of social and cognitive factors on learning) have a very different view of personality.

12.6 Learning Theories

12.6 Compare and contrast the learning theories of Bandura and Rotter.

For the behaviorist, personality is nothing more than a set of learned responses or **habits** (DeGrandpre, 2000; Dollard & Miller, 1950). In the strictest traditional view of Watson and Skinner, everything a person or animal does is a response to some stimulus that has been either conditioned, or reinforced in some way. And while Skinner rejected mental processes such as the way we think and feel as causal factors in and of themselves, and by themselves, he did not deny they existed. Skinner simply believed mental processes could not sufficiently explain why we do the things we do because they could not be validated objectively by others, and they should be operationalized behaviorally in order for them to be studied objectively and scientifically (Skinner, 1953, 1974).

💬 So how does a pattern of rewarding certain behavior end up becoming part of some kind of personality pattern?

Think about how a traditional behaviorist might explain a shy personality. Beginning in childhood, a person might be exposed to a parent with a rather harsh discipline style (stimulus). Avoiding the attention of that parent would result in fewer punishments and scoldings, so that avoidance response is negatively reinforced—the "bad thing" or punishment is avoided by keeping out of sight and quiet. Later, that child might generalize that avoidance response to other authority figures and adults, such as teachers. In this way, a pattern (habit) of shyness would develop.

Of course, many learning theorists today do not use only classical and operant conditioning to explain the development of the behavior patterns referred to as personality. **Social cognitive learning theorists**, who emphasize the importance of both the influences of other people's behavior and of a person's own expectancies on learning, hold that observational learning, modeling, and other cognitive learning techniques can lead to the formation of patterns of personality. See Learning Objective 5.12.

One of the more well-researched learning theories that includes the concept of cognitive processes as influences on behavior is the social cognitive theory of Albert Bandura. In the **social cognitive view**, behavior is governed not just by the influence of external stimuli and response patterns but also by cognitive processes such as anticipating, judging, and memory as well as learning through the imitation of models. In fact, you might remember Bandura's work with observation learning and imitation of models from his Bobo doll study. See Learning Objective 5.12.

BANDURA'S RECIPROCAL DETERMINISM AND SELF-EFFICACY Bandura (1989) believes three factors influence one another in determining the patterns of behavior that make up personality: the environment, the behavior itself, and personal or cognitive factors the person brings into the situation from earlier experiences (see **Figure 12.2**). These three factors each affect the other two in a reciprocal, or give-and-take, relationship. Bandura calls this relationship **reciprocal determinism**.

Take a look at Figure 12.2. The environment includes the actual physical surroundings, the other people who may or may not be present, and the potential for reinforcement in those surroundings.

AP 7.J Identify the contributions of major researchers in personality theory.

habits
in behaviorism, sets of well-learned responses that have become automatic.

social cognitive learning theorists
theorists who emphasize the importance of both the influences of other people's behavior and of a person's own expectancies on learning.

social cognitive view
learning theory that includes cognitive processes such as anticipating, judging, memory, and imitation of models.

reciprocal determinism
Bandura's explanation of how the factors of environment, personal characteristics, and behavior can interact to determine future behavior.

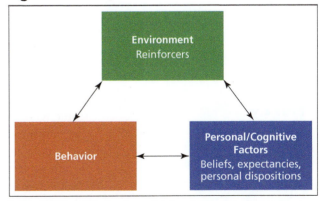

Figure 12.2 Reciprocal Determinism

In Bandura's model of reciprocal determinism, three factors influence behavior: the environment, which consists of the physical surroundings and the potential for reinforcement; the person (personal/cognitive characteristics that have been rewarded in the past); and the behavior itself, which may or may not be reinforced at this particular time and place.

The intensity and frequency of the behavior will not only be influenced by the environment but will also have an impact on that environment. The person brings into the situation previously reinforced responses (personality, in other words) and mental processes such as thinking and anticipating.

Here's how this might work: Richard walks into a classroom filled with other students, but no teacher is present at this time. (This is the *environment*.) Part of Richard's *personal* characteristics includes the desire to have attention from other people by talking loudly and telling jokes, which has been very rewarding to him in the past (past reinforcements are part of his cognitive processes, or expectancies of future rewards for his behavior). Also in the past, he has found that he gets more attention when an authority figure is not present. His *behavior* will most likely be to start talking and telling jokes, which will continue if he gets the reaction he expects from his fellow students. If the teacher walks in (the *environment* changes), his behavior will change. If the other students don't laugh, his behavior will change. In the future, Richard might be less likely to behave in the same way because his expectations for reward (a cognitive element of his *personal* variables) are different.

One of the more important personal variables Bandura talks about is **self-efficacy**, a person's expectancy of how effective his or her efforts to accomplish a goal will be in any particular circumstance (Bandura, 1998). (Self-efficacy is not the same concept as *self-esteem*, which is the positive values a person places on his or her sense of worth.)

People's sense of self-efficacy can be high or low, depending on what has happened in similar circumstances in the past (success or failure), what other people tell them about their competence, and their own assessment of their abilities. For example, if Fiona has an opportunity to write an extra-credit paper to improve her grade in psychology, she will be more likely to do so if her self-efficacy is high: She has gotten good grades on such papers in the past, her teachers have told her that she writes well, and she knows she can write a good paper. According to Bandura, people high in self-efficacy are more persistent and expect to succeed, whereas people low in self-efficacy expect to fail and tend to avoid challenges (Bandura, 1998).

ROTTER'S SOCIAL LEARNING THEORY: EXPECTANCIES Julian Rotter (1966, 1978, 1981, 1990) devised a theory based on a basic principle of motivation derived from Thorndike's law of effect: People are motivated to seek reinforcement and avoid punishment. He viewed personality as a relatively stable set of *potential* responses to various situations. If in the past a certain way of responding led to a reinforcing or pleasurable consequence, that way of responding would become a pattern of responding, or part of the "personality" as learning theorists see it.

One very important pattern of responding in Rotter's view became his concept of **locus of control**, the tendency for people to assume they either have control or do not have control over events and consequences in their lives. See Learning Objective 9.3. People who assume their own actions and decisions directly affect the consequences they experience are said to be *internal* in locus of control, whereas people who assume their lives are more controlled by powerful others, luck, or fate are *external* in locus of control (MacDonald, 1970; Rotter, 1966; see **Table 12.3**). Rotter associated people high in internal locus of control with the personality characteristics of high achievement motivation (the will to succeed in any attempted task). Those who give up too quickly or who attribute events in their lives to external causes can fall into patterns of learned helplessness and depression (Abramson et al., 1978, 1980; Gong-Guy & Hammen, 1980).

Locus of control and its impact has been studied in many different areas, ranging from Internet use to health care. In a study of mainly female college undergraduates in

---

AP 7.A Identify and apply basic motivational concepts to understand the behavior of humans and other animals.

self-efficacy
individual's expectancy of how effective his or her efforts to accomplish a goal will be in any particular circumstance.

locus of control
the tendency for people to assume that they either have control or do not have control over events and consequences in their lives.

Table 12.3 Locus of Control

Internal	External
Becoming a success is a matter of hard work; luck has little or nothing to do with it.	Most of the time I can't understand why politicians behave the way they do.
There is a direct connection between how hard I study and the grades I get.	Sometimes I feel like I don't have enough control over the direction my life is taking.
Trusting fate has never turned out as well for me as making a decision to take a definite course of action.	Getting a good job depends mainly on being in the right place at the right time.

China, students who were lonelier and unhappier and had an external locus of control engaged in more frequent online social interactions (Ye & Lin, 2015). As the researchers emphasized, the findings suggest all three of these variables may be targets for interventions aimed at reducing problematic Internet use, at least for college students in China.

Like Bandura, Rotter Rotter (1978, 1981) also believed an interaction of factors would determine the behavioral patterns that become a personality for an individual. For Rotter, there are two key factors influencing a person's decision to act in a certain way given a particular situation: expectancy and reinforcement value. **Expectancy** is fairly similar to Bandura's concept of self-efficacy in that it refers to the person's subjective feeling that a particular behavior will lead to a reinforcing consequence. A high expectancy for success is similar to a high sense of self-efficacy and is also based on past experiences with successes and failures. *Reinforcement value* refers to an individual's preference for a particular reinforcer over all other possible reinforcing consequences. Things or circumstances particularly appealing to us have a higher reinforcement value than other possible reinforcers.

12.7 Current Thoughts on the Behavioral and Social Cognitive Learning Views

12.7 Evaluate the strengths and limitations of the behavioral and social cognitive learning views of personality.

Behaviorism as an explanation of the formation of personality has its limitations. The classic theory does not take mental processes into account when explaining behavior, nor does it give weight to social influences on learning. The social cognitive view of personality, unlike traditional behaviorism, includes social and mental processes and their influence on behavior. Unlike psychoanalysis, the concepts in this theory can and have been tested under scientific conditions (Backenstrass et al., 2008; Bandura, 1965; Catanzaro et al., 2000; DeGrandpre, 2000; Domjan et al., 2000; Skinner, 1989). Some of this research has investigated how people's expectancies can influence their control of their own negative moods. Although some critics think human personality and behavior are too complex to explain as the result of cognitions and external stimuli interacting, others point out that this viewpoint has enabled the development of therapies based on learning theory that have become effective in changing undesirable behavior. See Learning Objective 14.4. However, concepts are not always interpreted or experienced in the same fashion by all people, and overgeneralization might lead to errors. For example, when examining locus of control, some individuals may be more likely to endorse an external locus of control as the result of their particular life experiences, including those who are female, of a low socioeconomic status, or from an ethnic minority (Sue & Sue, 2016). The experience of control in these individuals' lives is likely not the same as for those who are not a member of any of these groups (Sue & Sue, 2016).

expectancy
a person's subjective feeling that a particular behavior will lead to a reinforcing consequence.

Concept Map L.O. 12.6, 12.7

Behavioral and Social Cognitive Learning Perspectives

- for behaviorists, personality is a set of learned responses and habits, gained through classical and operant conditioning
- social cognitive learning theorists emphasize both the influences of other people's behavior and of a person's own expectancies on learning; observational learning, modeling, and other cognitive learning techniques influence personality
  - **Bandura:** concept of self-efficacy; believed three factors were important: the environment, the behavior itself, and personal or cognitive experiences from earlier experiences; each affect the other two in a reciprocal way—reciprocal determinism (see Figure 12.2)
    - in Bandura's **social cognitive view**, both learning (individual and through imitation of models) and cognitive processes (such as anticipation, judgment, and memory) are important
  - **Rotter:** theory based on principles of motivation derived from Thorndike's law of effect; personality is set of potential responses to various situations, including one's locus of control (internal vs. external), sense of expectancy, and preference for particular reinforcers.

Practice Quiz   How much do you remember?

Pick the best answer.

1. According to behavioral theory, personality primarily consists of _____.
   a. biologically driven traits
   b. social influence
   c. unconscious forces
   d. personal choices
   e. learned responses

2. Albert Bandura considers _____ as a person's expectancy of how effective his or her efforts to accomplish a goal will be in any particular circumstance.
   a. self-image
   b. locus of control
   c. self-esteem
   d. self-awareness
   e. self-efficacy

3. You have walked in late to class, and your psychology professor is explaining how one personality theorist sees personality as a relatively stable set of potential responses to various situations. You know immediately that your professor is talking about the theories of _____.
   a. Albert Bandura
   b. B. F. Skinner
   c. Julian Rotter
   d. John Watson
   e. Carl Rogers

4. Genevieve appreciates compliments about her new photography business but really values constructive criticism, as she can then address particular issues. According to Julian Rotter, Genevieve has a(n) _____.
   a. real self
   b. strong self-concept
   c. external locus of control
   d. internal locus of control
   e. outward focus

AP 7.M Compare and contrast humanistic theories of personality with other theories of personality.

12.8–12.9 The Third Force: Humanism and Personality

As first discussed in Chapter One, in the middle of the twentieth century, the pessimism of Freudian psychodynamic theory with its emphasis on conflict and animalistic needs, together with the emphasis of behaviorism on external control of behavior, gave rise to a third force in psychology: the *humanistic perspective*.

AP 7.J Identify the contributions of major researchers in personality theory.

humanistic perspective
the "third force" in psychology that focuses on those aspects of personality that make people uniquely human, such as subjective feelings and freedom of choice.

12.8 Carl Rogers and the Humanistic Perspective

12.8 Describe how humanists such as Carl Rogers explain personality.

The **humanistic perspective**, led by psychologists such as Carl Rogers and Abraham Maslow, wanted psychology to focus on the things that make people uniquely human, such as subjective emotions and the freedom to choose one's own destiny. As Maslow's theory was discussed more fully in Chapter Nine, in this chapter the discussion of the humanistic view of personality will focus on the theory of Carl Rogers. A brief overview of the humanistic perspective is also offered in the video *Humanistic Personality Theory*.

Both Maslow and Rogers (1961) believed human beings are always striving to fulfill their innate capacities and capabilities and to become everything their genetic potential will allow them to become. This striving for fulfillment is called the **self-actualizing tendency**. An important tool in human self-actualization is the development of an image of oneself, or the **self-concept**. The self-concept is based on what people are told by others and how the sense of **self** is reflected in the words and actions of important people in one's life such as parents, siblings, coworkers, friends, and teachers.

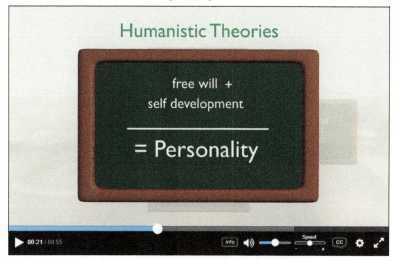

Watch Humanistic Personality Theory

Watch the Video at MyLab Psychology

REAL AND IDEAL SELF Two important components of the self-concept are the *real self* (one's actual perception of characteristics, traits, and abilities that form the basis of the striving for self-actualization) and the *ideal self* (the perception of what one should be or would like to be). The ideal self primarily comes from important, significant others in a person's life, especially our parents when we are children. Rogers believed that when the real self and the ideal self are very close or similar to each other, people feel competent and capable, but when there is a mismatch between the real self and ideal self, anxiety and neurotic behavior can be the result (see **Figure 12.3**).

The two halves of the self are more likely to match if they aren't that far apart at the start. When a person has a realistic view of the real self, and the ideal self is something that is actually attainable, there usually isn't a problem of a mismatch. It is when a person's view of self is distorted or the ideal self is impossible to attain that problems arise. Once again, how the important people (who can be either good or bad influences) in a person's life react to the person can greatly impact the degree of agreement, or congruence, between real and ideal selves. However, as an individual develops, they look less to others for approval and disapproval and more within themselves to decide if they are living in a way that is satisfying to them (Rogers, 1951, 1961).

CONDITIONAL AND UNCONDITIONAL POSITIVE REGARD Rogers defined **positive regard** as warmth, affection, love, and respect that come from the significant others (parents, admired adults, friends, and teachers) in people's experience. Positive regard is vital to people's ability to cope with stress and to strive to achieve self-actualization. Rogers believed that **unconditional positive regard**, or love, affection, and respect with no strings attached, is necessary for people to be able to explore fully all that they can achieve and become. Unfortunately, some parents, spouses, and friends give **conditional positive regard**, which is love, affection, respect, and warmth that depend, or seem to depend, on doing what those people want.

Here is an example: As a freshman, Sasha was thinking about becoming a math teacher, a computer programmer, or an elementary school teacher. Karen, also a freshman, already knew she was going to be a doctor. Whereas Sasha's parents had told her that what she wanted to become was up to her and that they would love her no matter what, Karen's parents had made it very clear to her as a small child that they expected her to become a doctor. She was under the very strong impression that if she tried to choose any other career, she would lose her parents' love and respect. Sasha's parents were giving her unconditional positive regard, but Karen's parents (whether they intended to or not) were giving her conditional positive regard. Karen was obviously not as free as Sasha to explore her potential and abilities.

self-actualizing tendency
the striving to fulfill one's innate capacities and capabilities.

self-concept
the image of oneself that develops from interactions with important significant people in one's life.

self
an individual's awareness of his or her own personal characteristics and level of functioning.

positive regard
warmth, affection, love, and respect that come from significant others in one's life.

unconditional positive regard
positive regard that is given without conditions or strings attached; in person-centered therapy, referring to the warm, respectful, and accepting atmosphere created by the therapist for the client.

conditional positive regard
positive regard that is given only when the person is doing what the providers of positive regard wish.

Figure 12.3 Real and Ideal Selves

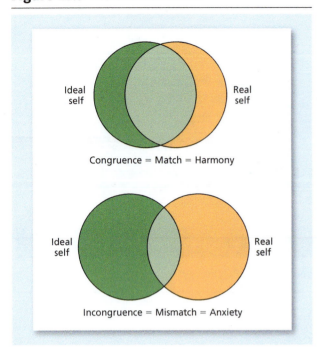

According to Rogers, the self-concept includes the real self and the ideal self. The real self is a person's actual perception of traits and abilities, whereas the ideal self is the perception of what a person would like to be or thinks he or she should be. When the ideal self and the real self are very similar (matching), the person experiences harmony and contentment. When there is a mismatch between the two selves, the person experiences anxiety and may engage in neurotic behavior.

These proud parents are giving their daughter unconditional positive regard.

For Rogers, a person who is in the process of self-actualizing, actively exploring potentials and abilities and experiencing a match between the real self and ideal self, is a **fully functioning person**. Fully functioning people are in touch with their own feelings and abilities and are able to trust their innermost urges and intuitions (Rogers, 1961). To become fully functioning, a person needs unconditional positive regard. In Rogers's view, Karen would not have been a fully functioning person.

💬 What kind of people are considered to be fully functioning? Is it the same thing as being self-actualized?

Although the two concepts are highly related, there are some subtle differences. Self-actualization is a goal that people are always striving to reach, according to Maslow (1987). See Learning Objective 9.5. In Rogers's view, only a fully functioning person is capable of reaching the goal of self-actualization. To be fully functioning is a necessary step in the process of self-actualization. Maslow (1987) listed several people who he considered to be self-actualized people: Albert Einstein, Mahatma Gandhi, and Eleanor Roosevelt, for example. These were people who Maslow found to have the self-actualized qualities of being creative, autonomous, and unprejudiced. In Rogers's view, these same people would be seen as having trusted their true feelings and innermost needs rather than just going along with the crowd.

12.9 Current Thoughts on the Humanistic View of Personality

12.9 Evaluate the strengths and limitations of the humanistic view of personality.

Humanistic views of personality paint a very rosy picture. Some critics believe the picture is a little too rosy, ignoring the more negative aspects of human nature. For example, would humanistic theory easily explain the development of sociopathic personalities who have no conscience or moral nature? Or could a humanist explain the motivation behind terrorism?

Some aspects of humanistic theory are difficult to test scientifically, and it has been suggested this viewpoint could be considered more a philosophical view of human behavior than a psychological explanation. Despite the challenges, how people view themselves continues to be central to many aspects of psychology and the study of personality (Leary & Toner, 2015). Overall, humanistic theory's greatest impact has been in the development of therapies designed to promote self-growth and to help people better understand themselves and others. For example, when viewed through the lens of psychotherapy and therapist variables, there appears to be a consistent relationship between Rogers's ideas of unconditional positive regard and the level of therapist empathy perceived by clients, positively contributing to improvements in clients' self-evaluation and improving clients' relationships with others (Watson et al., 2014). See Learning Objective 14.3.

Some of the premises of positive psychology have their roots in humanistic psychology. The term "positive psychology" was first used by Maslow in 1954 when he stressed the need for psychology to focus on human potential rather than on problems (Maslow, 1954). And some have pointed out that related views go back to the work of William James and beyond (Froh, 2004; Taylor, 2001). However, the field of positive psychology itself has emerged more recently; it strives to understand how human beings prosper during difficult times and focuses on the science of subjective, individual, and group factors that foster positive experiences (Seligman & Csikszentmihalyi, 2000). There has been debate between the two fields, primarily on the choice of research approaches and some philosophical nuances, but nonetheless, positive psychology shares many facets with the humanistic perspective and other areas in psychology in its focus on human potential, identification of strengths, and the positive aspects of what it means to be a human (Mahoney, 2005; Seligman, 2005; Snyder & Lopez, 2005; Waterman, 2013).

fully functioning person
a person who is in touch with and trusting of the deepest, innermost urges and feelings.

Concept Map L.O. 12.8, 12.9

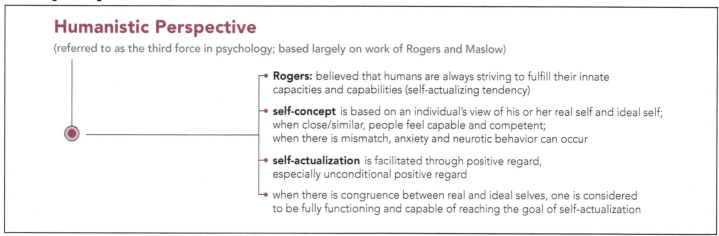

Practice Quiz — How much do you remember?

Pick the best answer.

1. In Rogers's viewpoint, what is the striving to fulfill innate capacities and needs called?
   a. self-concept
   b. ideal self
   c. functioning fully
   d. real self
   e. self-actualizing tendency

2. What did Carl Rogers mean by the term "fully functioning person"?
   a. someone who has discovered his or her self-efficacy
   b. someone who is working to discover his or her ideal self
   c. someone who has discovered his or her locus of control
   d. someone who is working to discover his or her real self
   e. someone who is experiencing a match between his or her real and ideal self and who is also trusting of his or her innermost intuitions and urges

3. Which of the following statements concerning the self-concept is false?
   a. It is based on what people are told by others.
   b. It is a reflection of the sense of self in the words and actions of others.
   c. It is formed based solely on what a person believes about himself or herself.
   d. It is an important tool in human self-actualization.
   e. It is the image one has of himself or herself.

4. Yadira's parents told her that they expected her to become a doctor like her father and grandfather before her. They told her that if she chose any other career, they would no longer support her or respect her choice. According to Rogers, Yadira's parents were giving her _____ regard.
   a. conditional negative
   b. vicarious
   c. unconditional positive
   d. unconditional negative
   e. conditional positive

AP 7.O Compare and contrast trait theories of personality with other theories of personality.

12.10–12.12 Trait Theories: Who Are You?

The theories discussed so far attempt to explain how personality develops or how factors within or external to the individual influence personality. These theories may also provide psychologists and other professionals with hints as to how personality may be changed. However, not all personality theories have the same goals.

12.10 Allport and Cattell: Early Attempts to List and Describe Traits

12.10 Describe early attempts to use traits to conceptualize personality.

Trait theories are less concerned with the explanation for personality development and changing personality than they are with describing personality and predicting behavior based on that description. A **trait** is a consistent, enduring way of thinking, feeling, or behaving, and trait theories attempt to describe personality in terms of a person's traits. The video *Trait Theories of Personality* describes this perspective in more detail.

ALLPORT One of the earliest attempts to list and describe the traits that make up personality can be found in the work of Gordon Allport (Allport & Odbert, 1936). Allport and his colleague H. S. Odbert literally scanned the dictionary for words that could be traits, finding about 18,000, then paring that down to 200 traits after eliminating synonyms. Allport believed (with no scientific evidence, however) these traits were wired into the nervous system to guide one's behavior across many different situations and that each person's "constellation" of traits was unique. (In spite of Allport's lack of evidence, behavioral geneticists have found support for the heritability of personality traits, and these findings are discussed in the next section of this chapter.)

CATTELL AND THE 16PF Two hundred traits is still a very large number of descriptors. How might an employer be able to judge the personality of a potential employee by looking at a list of 200 traits? A more compact way of describing personality was needed. Raymond Cattell (1990) defined two types of traits as *surface traits* and *source traits*. **Surface traits** are like those found by Allport, representing the personality characteristics easily seen by other people. **Source traits** are those more basic traits that underlie the surface traits. For example, shyness, being quiet, and disliking crowds might all be surface traits related to the more basic source trait of **introversion**, a tendency to withdraw from excessive stimulation.

Using a statistical technique that looks for groupings and commonalities in numerical data called *factor analysis*, Cattell identified 16 source traits (Cattell, 1950, 1966). Although he later determined that there might be another 7 source traits to make a total of 23 (Cattell & Kline, 1977), he developed his assessment questionnaire, *The Sixteen Personality Factor (16PF) Questionnaire* (Cattell, 1995), based on just 16 source traits. These 16 source traits are seen as trait dimensions, or continuums, in which there are two opposite traits at each end with a range of possible degrees for each trait measurable along the dimension. For example, someone scoring near the "reserved" end of the "reserved/outgoing" dimension would be more introverted than someone scoring in the middle or at the opposite end.

trait theories
theories that endeavor to describe the characteristics that make up human personality in an effort to predict future behavior.

trait
a consistent, enduring way of thinking, feeling, or behaving.

surface traits
aspects of personality that can easily be seen by other people in the outward actions of a person.

source traits
the more basic traits that underlie the surface traits, forming the core of personality.

introversion
dimension of personality in which people tend to withdraw from excessive stimulation.

Watch Trait Theories of Personality

Watch the Video at MyLab Psychology

The personality profiles of individuals working in various occupations may be characterized by using such tools as Cattell's 16PF self-report inventory. For example, airline pilots versus writers. Airline pilots, when compared to writers, tend to be more conscientious, relaxed, self-assured, and far less sensitive. Writers, on the other hand, were more imaginative and better able to think abstractly. Based on Cattell (1973).

12.11 Modern Trait Theories: The Big Five

12.11 Identify the five trait dimensions of the five-factor model of personality.

AP 7.J Identify the contributions of major researchers in personality theory

Sixteen factors are still quite a lot to discuss when talking about someone's personality. Later, researchers attempted to reduce the number of trait dimensions to a more manageable number, with several groups of researchers arriving at more or less the same five trait dimensions (Botwin & Buss, 1989; Jang et al., 1998; McCrae & Costa, 1996). These five dimensions have become known as the **five-factor model**, or the **Big Five** (see **Table 12.4**), and represent the core description of human personality—that is, the only dimensions necessary to understand what makes us tick.

Table 12.4 The Big Five

High Scorer Characteristics	Factor (Ocean)	Low Scorer Characteristics
Creative, artistic, curious, imaginative, nonconforming	Openness (O)	Conventional, down-to-earth, uncreative, conservative, resistant to change
Organized, reliable, neat, ambitious	Conscientiousness (C)	Unreliable, lazy, careless, negligent, spontaneous
Talkative, optimistic, sociable, affectionate	Extraversion (E)	Reserved, comfortable being alone, stays in the background
Good-natured, trusting, helpful	Agreeableness (A)	Rude, uncooperative, irritable, aggressive, competitive
Worrying, insecure, anxious, temperamental	Neuroticism (N)	Calm, secure, relaxed, stable

Source: Based on McCrae, R. R., Piedmont, R. L., & Costa, P T.. Jr. (1990, August). The CPI and the five-factor model: Rational and empirical analyses. Paper presented at the annual convention of the American Psychological Association. Boston.

As shown in the table, these five trait dimensions can be remembered by using the acronym OCEAN, in which each of the letters is the first letter of one of the five dimensions of personality.

- **Openness** can best be described as a person's willingness to try new things and be open to new experiences. People who try to maintain the status quo and who don't like to change things would score low on openness.
- **Conscientiousness** refers to a person's organization and motivation, with people who score high in this dimension being those who are careful about being places on time and careful with belongings as well. Someone scoring low on this dimension,

five-factor model (Big Five)

model of personality traits that describes five basic trait dimensions.

for example, might always be late to important social events or borrow belongings and fail to return them or return them in poor condition.

- **Extraversion** is a term first used by Carl Jung (1933), who believed that all people could be divided into two personality types: **extraverts** and **introverts**. Extraverts are outgoing and sociable, whereas introverts are more solitary and dislike being the center of attention.
- **Agreeableness** refers to the basic emotional style of a person, who may be easygoing, friendly, and pleasant (at the high end of the scale) or grumpy, crabby, and hard to get along with (at the low end).
- **Neuroticism** refers to emotional instability or stability. People who are excessive worriers, overanxious, and moody would score high on this dimension, whereas those who are more even-tempered and calm would score low.

Robert McCrae and Paul Costa proposed that these five traits are not interdependent. In other words, knowing someone's score on extraversion would not give any information about scores on the other four dimensions, allowing for a tremendous amount of variety in personality descriptions.

Beyond descriptions of personality, there is also a good deal of support for the predictive power of the five-factor model. These traits predict many different outcomes in life such as how we feel about ourselves, our physical and mental health, success in school and work, and various aspects of social behavior (Ozer & Benet-Martinez, 2006). The five-factor model has even been used for *geographical psychology* or looking at how local environments and regions, such as the neighborhood, city, or state you live in, might affect individual behavior (Rentfrow & Jokela, 2016). For example, when examined at a state level, higher levels of neuroticism are associated with lower rates of formal volunteering among college students. In turn, lower state rates of neuroticism were associated with higher rates of college students volunteering (McCann, 2017). Aspects of the five-factor model have also been linked to cognition. In older adults, openness is positively related to an individual's general level of cognitive ability. It is also positively related to verbal ability, episodic memory, and fluid intelligence (Curtis et al., 2015). In contrast, individuals lower in conscientiousness but higher in neuroticism appear to be at greater risk for Alzheimer's disease (Terracciano et al., 2014).

12.12 Current Thoughts on the Trait Perspective

12.12 Evaluate the strengths and limitations of the trait view of personality.

Some theorists have cautioned that personality traits will not always be expressed in the same way across different situations. Walter Mischel, a social cognitive theorist, has emphasized that there is a **trait–situation interaction** in which the particular circumstances of any given situation are assumed to influence the way in which a trait is expressed (Mischel & Shoda, 1995). An outgoing extravert, for example, might laugh, talk to strangers, and tell jokes at a party. That same person, if at a funeral, would still talk and be open, but the jokes and laughter would be less likely to occur. However, the five-factor model provides a dimensional approach to classifying personality structure (as opposed to a categorical approach), which is consistent with possible alternative approaches to diagnosing personality disorders discussed in the most recent edition of the *Diagnostic and Statistical Manual of Mental Disorders* (*DSM-5*; American Psychiatric Association, 2013). See Learning Objective 13.3.

The components of the five-factor model are the topic of many studies. For example, openness has been linked to intellect as a related trait, leading some five-factor researchers to use the label *Openness/Intellect* to recognize both subfactors (Allen & DeYoung, 2016). Both appear to be related to cognitive exploration, with individuals

extraverts
people who are outgoing and sociable.

introverts
people who prefer solitude and dislike being the center of attention.

trait–situation interaction
the assumption that the particular circumstances of any given situation will influence the way in which a trait is expressed.

higher in *Openness/Intellect* displaying a greater ability and tendency to pursue, understand, and make use of information than those lower in the construct (DeYoung et al., 2014). When examined further as a compound trait, *Openness* appears to be associated with verbal intelligence, and *Intellect* appears to be associated with general intelligence, nonverbal intelligence, and verbal intelligence (DeYoung et al., 2014). See Learning Objective 7.6.

While traits are influential, they are not absolute determinants of all human behavior. From both an evolutionary and cross-cultural perspective, persistent, heritable traits, or basic tendencies, impact an individual's *characteristic adaptations* such as motives, goals, plans, skills, interests, attributes, and relationships (Buss, 2009a; Church, 2010; Costa et al., 2018; McAdams & Pals, 2006). Furthermore, an individual's self-concept (self-esteem, self-knowledge, life story, or narrative) is a subcomponent of these characteristic adaptations (Costa et al., 2018). Situational and external influences such as cultural norms, life events, and social interactions can impact characteristic adaptations in profound ways (Church, 2010; Costa et al., 2018; McAdams & Pals, 2006).

AP 2.C Predict how traits and behavior can be selected for their adaptive value.

Although regional variations exist, cross-cultural research from 56 countries has found evidence of these five trait dimensions in all primary cultural regions of the world (Schmitt et al., 2007). Furthermore, it appears these dimensions are evident or recognizable not only in most languages and cultures, they are also consistent when assessed by either self-ratings or observers (Allik et al., 2013; McCrae & Terracciano, 2005). Looking across cultures, there appears to be a reasonably consistent course of development of the five-factor traits as one gets older. In general, both *Extraversion* and *Neuroticism* tend to decline over the lifespan while *Agreeableness* and *Conscientiousness* tend to increase; *Openness* typically rises in adolescence and declines in later adulthood (Costa et al., 2018). This cultural commonality raises the question of the origins of the Big Five trait dimensions: Are child-rearing practices across all those cultures similar enough to result in these five aspects of personality, or could these five dimensions have a genetic component that transcends cultural differences? The next section will discuss the evidence for a genetic basis of the Big Five.

Concept Map L.O. 12.10, 12.11, 12.12

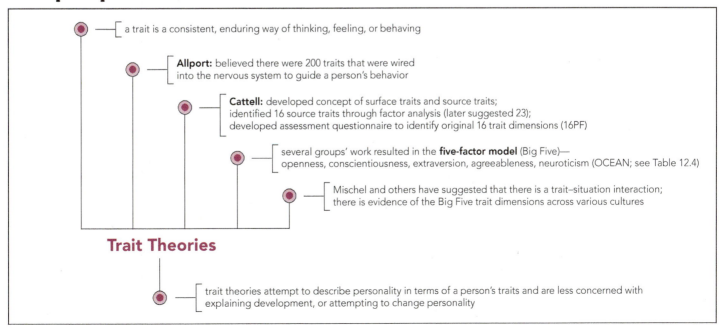

Practice Quiz — How much do you remember?

Pick the best answer.

1. Trait theories are less concerned with _____ and more concerned with _____.
   a. predicting behavior, changing personality
   b. predicting personality, changing personality
   c. describing personality, explaining personality development
   d. changing personality, predicting personality
   e. predicting behavior, explaining personality development

2. Colleagues at work are asked to describe you to the new manager. Most likely, the traits they will use in their description are examples of _____ traits.
   a. common
   b. cardinal
   c. surface
   d. source
   e. innate

3. Cattell's research and use of factor analysis essentially scaled down many, many different ways of describing aspects of personality into _____ source traits.
   a. 10
   b. 5
   c. 2
   d. 16
   e. 8

4. In the Big Five theory of personality, "E" stands for _____.
   a. energy
   b. external
   c. empathy
   d. extraversion
   e. empathy

AP 7.I Describe and compare research methods that psychologists use to investigate personality

12.13–12.15 Personality: Genetics, Neuroscience, and Culture

💬 What about genetics? How much of our personality is inherited?

When was the last time you were around a lot of family members other than your own? Was it a reunion? Or maybe when meeting your significant other's family for the first time? Did you notice any commonalities in the way different family members interacted, spoke, or behaved? This section will explore the "nature" side of personality, or the degree that some of our personality is linked to our parents and close relations.

AP 2.A Discuss psychology's abiding interest in how heredity, environment, and evolution work together to shape behavior.

12.13 The Biology of Personality: Behavioral Genetics

12.13 Explain how twin studies and adoption studies are used in the field of behavioral genetics.

The field of **behavioral genetics** is devoted to the study of just how much of an individual's personality is due to inherited traits. Animal breeders have known for a long time that selective breeding of certain animals with specific desirable traits can produce changes not only in size, fur color, and other physical characteristics but also in the temperament of the animals (Isabel, 2003; Trut, 1999). As stated earlier in this chapter, temperament consists of the characteristics with which each person is born and is therefore determined by biology to a great degree. If the temperaments of animals can be influenced by manipulating patterns of genetic inheritance, then it is only one small step to assume that at least those personality characteristics related to temperament in human beings may also be influenced by heredity.

Animal breeders have an advantage over those who are studying the influence of genes in human behavior. Those who breed animals can control the mating of certain animals and the conditions under which those animals are raised. Human research cannot ethically or practically develop that degree of control and so must fall back on the accidental "experiments" of nature and opportunity, studies of twins and adopted persons.

behavioral genetics
field of study devoted to discovering the genetic bases for personality characteristics.

TWIN STUDIES The difference between monozygotic (identical) and dizygotic (fraternal) twins was discussed in Chapter Eight. See Learning Objective 8.4. As discussed previously, identical twins share 100 percent of their genetic material, having come from one fertilized egg originally, whereas fraternal twins share only about 50 percent of their genetic material, as any other pair of siblings would. By comparing identical twins to fraternal twins, especially when twins can be found who were not raised in the same environment, researchers can begin to find evidence of possible genetic influences on various traits, including personality (see **Figure 12.4**).

Figure 12.4 Personalities of Identical and Fraternal Twins

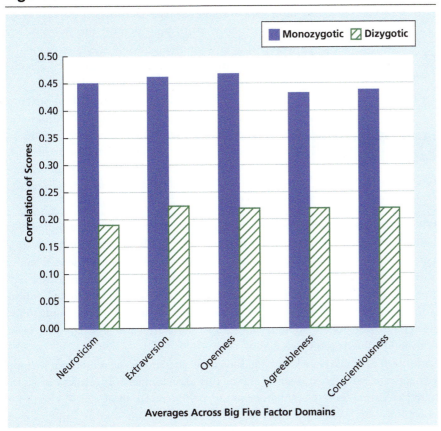

Identical and fraternal twins differ in the way they express the Big Five personality factors. In a 2010 study, data from 696 twin pairs suggest identical twins have a correlation of about 45 percent for self-ratings across each of the Big Five factor domains, whereas fraternal twins have a correlation of about 22 percent. These findings give support to the idea that some aspects of personality are genetically based.

Source: Based On Kandler, C., Riemann, R., Spinath, F. M., & Angleitner, A. (2010). Sources of variance in personality facets: A multiple-rater twin study of self-peer, peer-peer, and self-self (dis)agreement. Journal of Personality, 78(5), 1565-1594. doi: 10.1111/j.1467-6494.2010.00661.x

Many people have heard the story of the "Jim" twins, James Arthur Springer and James Edward Lewis, identical twins separated just after birth. At age 39, Springer and Lewis were the first set of twins studied by University of Minnesota psychologist Thomas Bouchard, who examined the differences and similarities between identical and fraternal twins raised apart from each other (Bouchard et al., 1990).

The two Jims were remarkably similar. They shared interests in mechanical drawing and carpentry, they smoked and drank the same amount, and they even both divorced women named Linda before marrying women named Betty. It is easy to attribute these similarities to their shared genetics. But Springer and Lewis were both raised in Ohio by parents from relatively similar socioeconomic backgrounds—how much of their similarity to each other might be due to those conditions? Furthermore, how much of any environmental influence on their personality was mediated genetically?

Watch Behavioral Genetics and Heritability

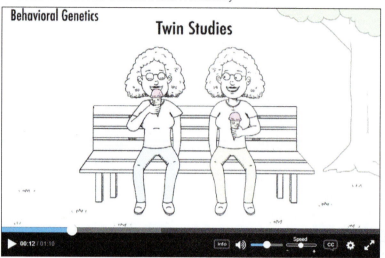

Watch the Video at MyLab Psychology

The results of the Minnesota twin study have revealed that identical twins are more similar than fraternal twins or unrelated people in intelligence, leadership abilities, the tendency to follow rules, and the tendency to uphold traditional cultural expectations (Bouchard, 1997; Finkel & McGue, 1997). They are also more alike with regard to nurturance,* empathy,** assertiveness (Neale et al., 1986), and aggressiveness (Miles & Carey, 1997). This similarity appears to hold even if the twins are raised in separate environments. While the environment has a significant impact, even if shared, genetics account for most of the similarity among siblings (Knopik et al., 2017; Plomin et al., 2016; Polderman et al., 2015). Furthermore, the genetics of a child's parents, even those not inherited, can impact the family and child's environment, a term referred to as *genetic nurture*. Genetic nurture appears to affect outcomes such as a child's years of educational attainment (Kong et al., 2018). To learn more, watch the video *Behavioral Genetics and Heritability*.

ADOPTION STUDIES Another tool of behavioral geneticists is to study adopted children and their adoptive and birth families. If studying genetically identical twins raised in different environments can help investigators understand the genetic influences on personality, then studying *unrelated* people who are raised in the *same* environment should help investigators discover the influence of environment. By comparing adopted children to their adoptive parents and siblings and, if possible, to their biological parents who have not raised them, researchers can uncover some of the shared and nonshared environmental and genetic influences on personality.

Adoption studies have confirmed what twin studies have shown: Genetic influences account for a great deal of personality development, regardless of shared or nonshared environments (Hershberger et al., 1995; Knopik et al., 2017; Loehlin et al., 1985; Loehlin et al., 1998; Plomin et al., 2016). Through this kind of study, for example, a genetic basis has been suggested for anxiety-related shyness, or inhibition, and aggression, namely aggressive antisocial behavior (Burt & Neiderhiser, 2009; Knopik et al., 2017; Trzaskowski et al., 2012), both of which are related to a variety of psychological disorders. See Chapter Thirteen.

12.14 The Biology of Personality: Neuroscience

12.14 Evaluate the role of neuroscience in the investigation of biological bases of personality.

In 1796, Dr. Franz Joseph Gall, a German physician, developed a theory of personality traits based on the shape of a person's skull. This theory became very popular in the nineteenth century and was known as *phrenology*. Gall believed that certain areas of the brain were responsible for certain aspects of personality and that the skull itself would bulge out according to which of these traits were dominant (Finger, 1994; Simpson, 2005). As psychology became a scientific area of its own, nonscience-based ideas such as phrenology were soon relegated to the realm of pseudoscience.

---

*nurturance: affectionate care and attention.
**empathy: the ability to understand the feelings of others.

Fast forward to modern methods of research. While the brain may not cause the skull to bulge, it does appear specific areas of the brain are related to aspects of personality. In addition to genetics, ongoing research using various modern neuroscience methods has resulted in the field of *personality neuroscience*. Personality neuroscience rests on the idea that aspects of our personality must be related to consistent patterns of functioning in the brain (Allen & DeYoung, 2016; DeYoung, 2010). Among various other methods, personality neuroscience uses both structural and functional neuroimaging methods to explore the biological bases of personality. See Learning Objective 2.5.

For example, researchers believe they have evidence for possible biological foundations of the Big Five: extraversion, neuroticism, agreeableness, conscientiousness, and openness (Allen & DeYoung, 2016; DeYoung et al., 2010).

- *Extraversion* has been associated with a higher volume in the medial orbitofrontal cortex (underside of the frontal lobe, directly above the eyes). This area of the brain is associated with recognizing the value of rewarding information. Given its role in processing emotionally relevant information, the amygdala also appears to be associated with the trait of extraversion (Allen & DeYoung, 2016; Cremers et al., 2011).

- *Neuroticism* has been associated with lower brain volume in several areas responding to threat, punishment, and negative emotions. Reduced volumes were found in the dorsomedial prefrontal cortex (toward the top and middle of the prefrontal cortex) and in the left posterior hippocampus of those with neuroticism. It has also been associated with higher brain volume in the middle cingulate cortex (cortical component of the limbic system), linked with error detection and response to pain. Other brain structures, including the amygdala, have been implicated and other measures such as cortical thickness are being explored (Holmes et al., 2012).

- *Agreeableness* has been correlated with areas of the brain associated with the intentions of actions and mental states of others, with the area of the posterior cingulate cortex showing a greater volume in individuals high in that trait and a lesser volume in the left superior temporal sulcus.

- *Conscientiousness* seems to be associated with the left lateral prefrontal cortex, an area located on the side of the frontal lobes involved in planning, working memory, and voluntary control of behavior.

- Findings for the fifth of the Big Five traits, *openness*, have been mixed. Research about its association with brain volume has been inconsistent, but it's still being investigated along with the role of white matter integrity and of specific neurotransmitters including both dopamine and serotonin (Allen & DeYoung, 2016).

The advances in personality neuroscience, coupled with better understanding of brain function and brain processes, have also led to new and revised theories of personality. For example, the *Cybernetic Big Five Theory (CB5T*; DeYoung, 2015) looks at personality through traits that are related to variations in brain structure and also through *characteristic adaptations*, or how someone's life circumstances influence their individual goals, strategies, and personal interpretations (DeYoung, 2015).

Despite the advances offered through personality neuroscience, some researchers urge caution. Some studies have been with small samples. To counterbalance this, researchers need to take advantage of meta-analysis techniques to attempt to synthesize the results of hundreds of smaller studies as well as conduct studies with larger sample sizes (Yarkoni, 2015). Additional studies and meta-analyses will continue to help us understand the links between personality and the physical structure and functioning of the brain.

> **AP** 2.A Discuss psychology's abiding interest in how heredity, environment, and evolution work together to shape behavior.

12.15 Current Thoughts on the Heritability and Neuroscience of Personality

12.15 Summarize current research on the heritability and neuroscience of personality.

One important aspect of genetic studies is the concept of *heritability*, or how much some trait within a population can be attributed to genetic influences, and the extent individual genetic variation impacts differences in observed behavior. See Learning Objectives 7.10 and 8.3. Several studies have found that the five personality factors of the five-factor model have nearly a 50 percent rate of heritability across several cultures (Bouchard, 1994; Herbst et al., 2000; Knopik et al., 2017; Jang et al., 1996; Loehlin, 1992; Loehlin et al., 1998). Personality's relationship to psychopathology, or traits related to the development of psychopathology, are also being investigated via genetic techniques (Mann et al., 2015; Plomin & Spinath, 2004). Together with the results of the Minnesota twin study and other research (Lubinski, 2000; Lykken & Tellegen, 1996; Plomin, 1994), the studies of genetics and personality seem to indicate that variations in personality traits are about 30 to 50 percent inherited (Plomin et al., 2016). This also means that environmental influences apparently account for about half of the variation in personality traits as well. At present, there are twin studies taking place all over the world, including twin registries in Texas, California, Massachusetts, Denmark, Finland, Italy, Sri Lanka, Sweden, Vietnam, and many other locations.

Aspects of personality are also being investigated through methods associated with personality neuroscience. While still a relatively new area, personality neuroscience is based on the idea that all persistent aspects of an individual's personality must be based on consistent functioning of specific brain areas (Allen & DeYoung, 2016; DeYoung, 2010). The five-factor model has served as a foundation for much of this research and for new theories informed by personality neuroscience, including the *CB5T* (DeYoung, 2015).

Lastly, although the five factors have been found across several cultures, this does not mean that different cultures do not have an impact on personality. For more on this topic, see the *Classic Studies in Psychology* section that follows.

> **AP** 7.N Speculate how cultural context can facilitate or constrain personality development, especially as it relates to self-concept.

Classic Studies in Psychology

Geert Hofstede's Four Dimensions of Cultural Personality

In the early 1980s, organizational management specialist Geert Hofstede conducted a massive study into the work-related values of employees of IBM, a multinational corporation (Hofstede, 1980; Hofstede et al., 2002). The study surveyed workers in 64 countries across the world. Hofstede analyzed the data collected from this survey and found four basic dimensions of personality along which cultures differed.

1. **Individualism/collectivism:** *Individualistic cultures* tend to have loose ties between individuals, with people tending to look after themselves and their immediate families only. Members of such cultures have friends based on shared activities and interests and may belong to many different loosely organized social groups. Autonomy,* change, youth, security of the individual, and equality are all highly valued. In contrast, in a *collectivistic culture*, people are from birth deeply tied into very strong in-groups, typically extended families that include grandparents, aunts and uncles, and cousins.

---

*autonomy: the quality of being self-directed or self-controlled.

Loyalty to the family is highly stressed, and the care of the family is placed before the care of the individual. Group membership is limited to only a few permanent groups that have tremendous influence over the individual. The values of this kind of culture are duty, order, tradition, respect for the elderly, group security, and respect for the group status and hierarchy.* Whereas the United States and Great Britain are examples of individualistic cultures, Japan, China, Korea, Mexico, and Central America are much more collectivistic.

2. **Power distance:** This dimension refers to the degree to which the less powerful members of a culture accept and even expect that the power within the culture is held in the hands of a select few rather than being more evenly distributed. Countries such as the Philippines, Mexico, many Arab countries, and India were found to be high in such expectations, whereas countries such as Austria, Sweden, Australia, Great Britain, and the United States were low in power distance.

3. **Masculinity/femininity:** Referring to how a culture distributes the roles played by men and women within the culture, this dimension varies more for the men within a culture than for the women. "Masculine" cultures are assertive and competitive, although more so for men than for women, and "feminine" cultures are more modest and caring. Both men and women in "feminine" countries have similar, caring values, but in "masculine" countries, the women are not quite as assertive and competitive as the men, leading to a greater difference between the sexes in masculine countries. Japan, Austria, Venezuela, Italy, Switzerland, Mexico, Ireland, Jamaica, the United States, Great Britain, and Germany were found to be masculine countries, whereas Sweden, Norway, the Netherlands, Denmark, Costa Rica, Yugoslavia, Finland, Chile, Portugal, Thailand, and Guatemala were ranked as more feminine.

4. **Uncertainty avoidance:** Some cultures are more tolerant of uncertainty, ambiguity,** and unstructured situations. Cultures that do not tolerate such uncertainty and lack of structure tend to have strict rules and laws, with lots of security and safety measures, and tend toward a philosophical/religious belief of One Truth (and "we have it!"). Cultures that are more accepting of uncertainty are more tolerant of different opinions and have fewer rules. They tend to allow many different religious beliefs to exist side by side and are less anxious and emotional than people in uncertainty-avoiding countries. Uncertainty-avoiding countries include Greece, Portugal, Guatemala, Uruguay, Belgium, El Salvador, Japan, Yugoslavia, and Peru, whereas those that are more tolerant of uncertainty include Singapore, Jamaica, Denmark, Sweden, Hong Kong, Ireland, Great Britain, Malaysia, India, Philippines, the United States, Canada, and Indonesia.

Note that the Big Five personality dimensions of Costa and McCrae (2000) are not necessarily in competition with Hofstede's dimensions. Hofstede's dimensions are cultural personality traits, whereas those of the Big Five refer to individuals.

Questions for Further Discussion

1. Was your own culture listed for any of these dimensions? If so, do you agree with the personality dimension assigned to your culture?
2. If your culture was not listed for a personality dimension, where do you think your culture would fall on that dimension?

---

*hierarchy: in this sense, a body of persons in authority over others.
**ambiguity: the quality of being uncertain and indistinct.

Concept Map L.O. 12.13, 12.14, 12.15

Personality: Genetics, Neuroscience, and Culture

- behavioral genetics studies how much of an individual's personality is due to inherited traits
- identical twins are more similar than fraternal twins or unrelated people in many facets of personality
- adoption studies of twins have confirmed that genetic influences account for a great deal of personality development, regardless of shared or nonshared environments
- the field of personality neuroscience is investigating the possible relationship between various aspects of personality and specific areas of brain functioning
- personality factors of the five-factor model have nearly a 50 percent rate of heritability across cultures; variations in personality are about 25 to 50 percent inherited

Practice Quiz — How much do you remember?

Pick the best answer.

1. What is a major shortcoming in the field of behavioral genetics in terms of its studies on human personality traits?
   a. Behavioral geneticists conduct their studies by looking at single individuals over a long period of time, thus slowing the rate at which they can gather data.
   b. Behavioral geneticists are unable to conduct studies on animals, only on humans.
   c. Behavioral geneticists are unable to scientifically validate anything.
   d. Behavioral geneticists are unable to conduct controlled research studies on human subjects.
   e. Behavioral geneticists conduct their studies by looking at survey data.

2. Which of the following traits or characteristics was NOT found to be more similar in identical twins when compared to fraternal twins in the Minnesota twin study?
   a. leadership
   b. tendency to divorce
   c. intelligence
   d. empathy
   e. tendency to follow rules

3. Personality neuroscience is based on the premise that persistent variations in dimensional aspects of personality must be based on _____ patterns of functioning in the brain.
   a. variable
   b. random
   c. infrequent
   d. consistent
   e. spontaneous

4. What, if anything, have adoption studies taught us regarding the relationship between heredity and personality?
   a. Adoption studies have resulted in conflicting findings, with some strongly supporting the influence of heredity on personality while others suggest that heredity has no influence whatsoever.
   b. Adoption studies are no longer used.
   c. Adoption studies are a new area of study and have yet to offer any information on the effects of heredity on personality.
   d. Adoption studies have not supported many behavioral genetics studies, thus questioning the idea that personality can be influenced by genetics.
   e. Adoption studies have confirmed that personality can be strongly influenced by genetics.

5. Several studies have found nearly a _____ percent rate of heritability across several cultures with respect to the five-factor model of personality.
   a. 30
   b. 20
   c. 50
   d. 40
   e. 99

AP 7.N Speculate how cultural context can facilitate or constrain personality development, especially as it relates to self-concept.

APA Goal 2: Scientific Inquiry and Critical Thinking

Personality, Family, and Culture

Addresses APA Learning Objective 2.5: Incorporate sociocultural factors in scientific inquiry.

Imagine this: You and your family immigrated to the United States when you were very young. Your life, as much as you can remember, has been in the United States. You speak

English as your primary language, although your mother and father work hard to maintain the family's cultural heritage and still speak their native language at home. Your mother and father have worked hard to create a safe home, valuing hard work, dedication, and self-reliance.

You are now starting college, and money is tight. Although you have saved money, your family has limited resources to assist you with the newfound challenges of paying for tuition, books, and supplies, all while balancing the demands of home, your part-time job, and keeping your grades up. In short, times are tough.

Your college has started a food pantry for students in need. Although it took a while, you decided to stop by to look at the offerings. The pantry has both prepared and fresh foods, including fruit and vegetables. Although your individual personality acknowledges that external assistance is sometimes necessary, your father and mother would never visit the food pantry, much less accept anything from one.

What challenges might this present to your sense of self?

How might you resolve any conflicts?

This Critical Thinking feature was based in part on the experiences of an actual college student. To learn more about campus food pantries and how some college students are using them, read or listen to the story on NPR, *Campus Food Pantries For Hungry Students On The Rise*, **http://n.pr/1R56pSw**.

APA Goal 2 Personality, Family, and Culture

Answer the following questions about campus food pantries.

1. Do you know whether there is a food pantry available on your campus?
   - Yes
   - No

2. How would you find out, or identify additional resources?

3. Have you experienced any of the following culturally challenging issues so far in your college experience?
   - Veteran returning to school
   - Working while in school
   - Parenting while in school
   - Increase or decrease in diversity
   - Different ethnic environment
   - Differences in socioeconomic status
   - Challenges related to sexual orientation

12.16–12.17 Assessment of Personality

💬 **With all the different theories of personality, how do people find out what kind of personality they have?**

The methods for measuring or assessing personality vary according to the theory of personality used to develop those methods, as one might expect. However, many psychological professionals doing a personality assessment on a client do not necessarily tie themselves down to one theoretical viewpoint only, preferring to take a more *eclectic* view of personality. The eclectic view is a way of choosing the parts of different theories that seem to best fit a particular situation rather than using only one theory to explain a phenomenon. In fact, looking at behavior from multiple perspectives can often bring insights

AP 7.I Describe and compare research methods that psychologists use to investigate personality.

AP 7.P Identify frequently used assessment strategies, and evaluate test quality based on reliability and validity of the instruments.

into a person's behavior that would not easily come from taking only one perspective. Many professionals will not only use several different perspectives but also several of the assessment techniques that follow. Even so, certain methods are more commonly used by certain kinds of theorists, as can be seen in **Table 12.5**.

Table 12.5 Who Uses What Method?

Type of Assessment	Most Likely Used by...
Interviews	Psychoanalysts, humanistic therapists

Projective Tests
  Rorschach
  Thematic Apperception Test
	Psychoanalysts

Behavioral Assessments
  Direct observation
  Rating scales
  Frequency counts
	Behavioral and social cognitive therapists

Personality Inventories
  Sixteen Personality Factor Questionnaire (16PF)
  Neuroticism/Extraversion/Openness Personality Inventory (NEO-PI-3)
  Eysenck Personality Questionnaire (EPQ)
  Keirsey Temperament Sorter II
  California Psychological Inventory (CPI)
  Minnesota Multiphasic Personality Inventory, Version II, Restructured Form (MMPI-2-RF)
	Trait theorists

Personality assessments may also differ in the purposes for which they are conducted. For example, sometimes a researcher may administer a personality test of some sort to participants in a research study so that the participants may be classified according to certain personality traits. There are tests available to people who simply want to learn more about their own personalities. Finally, clinical and counseling psychologists, psychiatrists, and other psychological professionals use these personality assessment tools in the diagnosis of disorders of personality. See Learning Objective 13.12.

12.16 Interviews, Behavioral Assessments, and Personality Inventories

12.16 Identify the advantages and disadvantages of using interviews, behavioral assessments, and personality inventories to measure personality.

As covered in the last section, the methods for measuring or assessing personality vary according to the theory of personality used to develop those methods. They also vary according to their response format and the type of data they provide. We will first examine a variety of methods that provide test takers a more structured response format, with the aim of getting data that are more objective.

BEHAVIORAL ASSESSMENTS Behaviorists do not typically want to "look into the mind." Because behaviorists assume personality is merely habitually learned responses to stimuli in the environment, the preferred method for a behaviorist would be to watch that behavior unfold in the real world.

In **direct observation**, the psychologist observes the client engaging in ordinary, everyday behavior, preferably in the natural setting of home, school, or workplace, for example. A therapist who goes to the classroom and observes that tantrum behavior only happens when a child is asked to do something involving fine motor abilities (like drawing or writing) might be able to conclude that the child has difficulty with those skills and throws a tantrum to avoid the task.

direct observation
assessment in which the professional observes the client engaged in ordinary, day-to-day behavior in either a clinical or natural setting.

Other methods often used by behavioral therapists and other assessors are rating scales and frequency counts. In a **rating scale**, a numerical rating is assigned, either by the assessor or by the client, for specific behaviors (Nadeau et al., 2001). In a **frequency count**, the assessor literally counts the frequency of certain behaviors within a specified time limit. Educators make use of both rating scales and frequency counts to diagnose behavioral problems such as attention-deficit/hyperactivity disorder (ADHD) and aspects of personality such as social-skill level through the various grade levels.

INTERVIEWS Some therapists ask questions and note down the answers in a survey process called an **interview**. See Learning Objective 1.7. This type of interview, unlike a job interview, may be *unstructured* and flow naturally from the beginning dialogue between the client and the psychologist. Other professionals may use a *semistructured* interview, which has specific questions, and, based on the individual's responses, guidance for follow-up items, similar to a decision tree or flow diagram.

> So an interview is a kind of self-report process?

Yes. When psychologists interview clients, clients must report on their innermost feelings, urges, and concerns—all things that only they can directly know.

PERSONALITY INVENTORIES Trait theorists are typically more interested in personality descriptions. They tend to use an assessment known as a **personality inventory**, a questionnaire that has a standard list of questions and only requires certain specific answers, such as "yes," "no," and "can't decide." The standard nature of the questions (everyone gets the same list) and the lack of open-ended answers make these assessments far more objective and reliable than projective tests (a more subjective form of assessment discussed in a later section of this chapter), although they are still a form of self-report (Garb et al., 1998).

THE MMPI-2-RF By far the most common personality inventory is the *Minnesota Multiphasic Personality Inventory, Version II, Restructured Form (MMPI-2-RF)*, which specifically tests for abnormal behavior and thinking patterns in personality and psychopathology (Ben-Porath & Tellegen, 2011; Butcher & Rouse, 1996; Butcher et al., 2000, 2001). The current questionnaire consists of 338 statements such as "I am often very tense" or "I believe I am being plotted against." The person taking the test must answer "true," "false," or "cannot say." The MMPI-2-RF has 12 higher-order and clinical scales, 10 validity scales, and numerous scales for specific problems (e.g., family problems, aggression, anxiety, etc.). Each scale tests for a particular kind of behavior or way of thinking. The thinking and behavior patterns include relatively mild personality problems such as excessive worrying and shyness as well as more serious disorders such as schizophrenia and depression. See Learning Objectives 13.4 and 13.14.

Besides assessment of personality or psychopathology, the MMPI-2-RF is also useful for other purposes. In addition to being a valuable tool for mental health settings, it has also been used for vocational guidance and job screening. For specific jobs in high-risk settings, something more involved than simply providing a resume and job application and possibly participating in an interview is likely to be required to identify the most successful applicants. For example, in conjunction with other requirements of the application process, research has supported the use of the MMPI-2-RF in screening potential police officers (Tarescavage et al., 2015). It is also being used in medical settings to help predict treatment effectiveness and outcomes for specific disorders and interventions (Block et al., 2017; Tarescavage et al., 2018).

> How can you tell if a person is telling the truth on a personality inventory?

rating scale
assessment in which a numerical value is assigned to specific behavior that is listed in the scale.

frequency count
assessment in which the frequency of a particular behavior is counted.

interview
method of personality assessment in which the professional asks questions of the client and allows the client to answer, either in a structured or unstructured fashion.

personality inventory
paper-and-pencil or computerized test that consists of statements that require a specific, standardized response from the person taking the test.

Validity scales, which are built into any well-designed psychological inventory, are intended to indicate whether a person taking the inventory is responding honestly. Responses to certain items on the test will indicate if people are trying to make themselves look better or worse than they are, for example, and certain items are repeated throughout the test in a slightly different form, so that anyone trying to "fake" the test will have difficulty responding to those items consistently (Butcher et al., 2001). For example, if one of the statements is "I am always happy" and a person responds "true" to that statement, the suspicion would be that this person is trying to look better than he or she really is. If several of the validity scale questions are answered in this way, the conclusion is that the person is not being honest. In fact, some validity scales are so good that even experts have a hard time pretending to have symptoms of specific disorders. For example, a group of mental health professionals, with both expertise and significant experience in assessing and treating major depression, were unable to successfully fake major depression on the MMPI-2 (Bagby et al., 2000). The validity scales of the MMPI-2-RF have recently been demonstrated to have utility in identifying individuals with true chronic pain versus those who were malingering (Aguerrevere et al., 2018).

OTHER COMMON INVENTORIES Another common personality inventory is Cattell's 16PF, described earlier in this chapter. Costa and McCrae have further revised their *Revised Neuroticism/Extraversion/Openness Personality Inventory (NEO-PI-R)*, which is based on the five-factor model of personality traits and still being published. The newest version is the NEO-PI-3, which has been made easier to read for use with adolescents and has new norms (McCrae et al., 2005; McCrae, Martin, et al., 2005).

Another inventory in common use is the *Myers-Briggs Type Indicator (MBTI)*, which is based on the ideas of Carl Jung and looks at four personality dimensions: the *sensing/intuition* (S/N) dimension, the *thinking/feeling* (T/F) dimension, the *introversion/extraversion* (I/E) dimension, and the *perceiving/judging* (P/J) dimension. These four dimensions can differ for each individual, resulting in 16 (4 × 4) possible personality types: ISTJ, ISTP, ISFP, ISFJ, and so on (Briggs & Myers, 1998). The Myers-Briggs is often used to assess personality to help people know the kinds of careers for which they may best be suited. However, despite the widespread use of the MBTI in business and vocational counseling, it has some significant limitations. There appears to be little relationship between the MBTI and other more established assessments of personality and vocational measures (Hunsley et al., 2015). The assessment has been questioned for both its validity and its reliability, and it has been suggested that more robust assessments be used, especially in employee selection and assignment situations (Hunsley et al., 2015; Pittenger, 2005). See Learning Objective 7.8.

Other common personality tests include the Eysenck Personality Questionnaire (Eysenck & Eysenck, 1993), the Keirsey Temperament Sorter II (Keirsey, 1998), and the California Psychological Inventory (Gough, 1995).

EVALUATING BEHAVIORAL ASSESSMENTS, INTERVIEWS, AND PERSONALITY INVENTORIES We have discussed a variety of structured assessment techniques aimed at providing objective responses and data. Each of these has advantages and disadvantages. For example, the same problems that exist with self-report data (such as surveys) exist with interviews. Clients can lie, distort the truth, misremember, or give what they think is a socially acceptable answer instead of true information. Interviewers themselves can be biased, interpreting what the client says in light of their own belief systems or prejudices. Freud certainly did this when he refused to believe that his patients had actually been sexually molested as children, preferring to interpret that information as a fantasy instead of reality (Russell, 1986).

Another problem with interviews is something called the **halo effect**, which is a tendency to form a favorable or unfavorable impression of someone at the first meeting, so that all of a person's comments and behavior after that first impression will be interpreted to agree with the impression—positively or negatively. The halo effect can happen in any social situation, including interviews between a psychological professional and a client. First impressions really do count, and people who make a good first impression

AP 9.A Apply attribution theory to explain motives.

halo effect

tendency of an interviewer to allow positive characteristics of a client to influence the assessments of the client's behavior and statements.

because of clothing, personal appearance, or some other irrelevant* characteristic will seem to have a "halo" hanging over their heads—they can do no wrong after that (Lance et al., 1994; Thorndike, 1920). And of course, as we discussed in Chapter Eleven, negative first impressions are hard to change. See Learning Objective 11.8.

Problems with behavioral assessments can include the observer effect (when a person's behavior is affected by being watched) and observer bias, which can be controlled by having multiple observers and correlating their observations with each other. See Learning Objective 1.7. As with any kind of observational method, there is no control over the external environment. A person observing a client for a particular behavior may not see that behavior occur within the observation time—much as some car problems never seem to show up when the mechanic is examining the car.

The advantage of personality inventories over interviews and projective tests (discussed in the next section) is that inventories are standardized (i.e., everyone gets exactly the same questions and the answers are scored in exactly the same way). In fact, responses to inventories are often scored on a computer. Observer bias and bias of interpretation are typically not possible. Across different scoring programs, though, there may be some variability in the diagnostic suggestions provided by the computerized scoring (Pant et al., 2014). In general, the validity and reliability of personality inventories are generally recognized as being greatly superior to those of projective tests (Anastasi & Urbina, 1997; Lilienfeld et al., 2000; Wood et al., 2010).

There are some problems, however. The validity scales, for example, are a good check against cheating, but they are not perfect. Some people are still able to modify their response patterns and respond in what they feel are more socially appropriate ways (Anastasi & Urbina, 1997; Hicklin & Widiger, 2000). Despite the best intentions of the test creators, individual responses to specific questions may also vary, as questions may be interpreted in different ways by different individuals (Lilienfeld et al., 2015a), and are very likely to be subject to cultural influences (Kagan, 2010). Other problems have to do with human nature itself: Some people may develop a habit of picking a particular answer rather than carefully considering the statement, whereas others may simply grow tired of responding to all those statements and start picking answers at random.

THINKING CRITICALLY 12.2

Should employers require prospective employees to take a personality test? Why or why not? Would such a requirement make more sense in certain professions, and, if so, what professions might those be?

12.17 Projective Tests

12.17 Identify the advantages and disadvantages of using projective personality tests.

Have you ever tried to see "shapes" in the clouds? You might see a house where another person might see the same cloud as a horse. The cloud isn't really either of those things but can be *interpreted* as one or the other, depending on the person doing the interpretation. That makes a cloud an ambiguous stimulus—one that is capable of being interpreted in more than one way.

In just this way, psychoanalysts (and a few other psychologists) show their clients ambiguous visual stimuli and ask the clients to tell them what they see. The hope is that the client will project unconscious concerns onto the visual stimulus, revealing them to the examiner. Tests using this method are called **projective tests**. Such tests are performance based

projective tests

personality assessments that present ambiguous visual stimuli to the client and ask the client to respond with whatever comes to mind.

---

*irrelevant: not applying to the case or example at hand.

Figure 12.5 Rorschach Inkblot Example

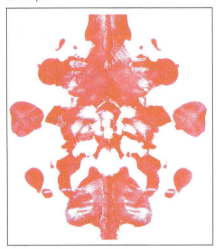

A facsimile of a Rorschach inkblot. A person being tested is asked to tell the interviewer what he or she sees in an inkblot similar to the one shown. Answers are neither right nor wrong but may reveal unconscious concerns. What do you see in this inkblot?

Source: Noland White

Rorschach inkblot test

projective test that uses 10 inkblots as the ambiguous stimuli.

Thematic Apperception Test (TAT)

projective test that uses 20 pictures of people in ambiguous situations as the visual stimuli.

Figure 12.6 TAT Example

A sample from the Thematic Apperception Test (TAT). When you look at this picture, what story does it suggest to you? Who is the person? Why is he climbing a rope?

Source: Bill Aron/PhotoEdit

and can be used to explore a client's personality or used as a diagnostic tool to uncover problems in personality. To learn more about this approach, watch the video *Projective Tests*.

Watch Projective Tests

👁 Watch the Video at MyLab Psychology

THE RORSCHACH INKBLOTS One of the more well-known projective tests is the **Rorschach inkblot test**, developed in 1921 by Swiss psychiatrist Hermann Rorschach (ROR-shok). There are 10 inkblots, 5 in black ink on a white background and 5 in colored inks on a white background (see **Figure 12.5** for an image similar to a Rorschach-type inkblot).

People being tested are asked to look at each inkblot and simply say whatever it might look like to them. Using predetermined categories and responses commonly given by people to each picture (Exner, 1980), psychologists score responses on key factors, such as reference to color, shape, figures seen in the blot, and response to the whole or to details.

Rorschach tested thousands of inkblots until he narrowed them down to the 10 in use today. They are still used to describe personality, diagnose mental disorders, and predict behavior (Watkins et al., 1995; Weiner, 1997). However, along with the use of other projective techniques in general, their use is controversial given questions about some scoring methods and overall validity (Lilienfeld et al., 2000).

THE TAT First developed in 1935 by psychologist Henry Murray and his colleagues (Morgan & Murray, 1935), the **Thematic Apperception Test (TAT)** consists of 20 pictures, all black and white, that are shown to a client. The client is asked to tell a story about the person or people in the picture, who are all deliberately drawn in ambiguous situations (see **Figure 12.6**). Again, the story developed by the client is interpreted by the psychoanalyst, who looks for revealing statements and projection of the client's own problems onto the people in the pictures.

These are only two of the more well-known projective tests. Other types of projective tests include the Sentence Completion test, Draw-A-Person, and House-Tree-Person. In the Sentence Completion test, the client is given a series of sentence beginnings, such as "I wish my mother …" or "Almost every day I feel …" and asked to finish the sentence, whereas in the Draw-A-Person and House-Tree-Person tests, the client is asked to draw the named items.

💬 But how can anyone know if the interpretation is correct? Isn't there a lot of room for error?

PROBLEMS WITH PROJECTIVE TESTS Projective tests are by their nature very **subjective** (valid only within the person's own perception), and interpreting the answers of clients is almost an art. It is certainly not a science and is not known for its accuracy. Problems lie in the areas of reliability and validity. In Chapter Seven, *reliability* was defined as the tendency of a test to give the same score every time it is administered to the same person or group of people, and *validity* was defined as the ability of the test to measure what it is intended to measure. See Learning Objective 7.8. Projective tests, with no standard grading scales, have both low reliability and low validity (Gittelman-Klein, 1978; Lilienfeld, 1999; Lilienfeld et al., 2000; Wood et al., 1996). A person's answers to the Rorschach, for example, might be quite different from one day to the next, depending on the person's mood and what scary movie might have been on television the previous night.

Projective tests may sound somewhat outdated, but many psychologists and psychiatrists still use this type of testing (McGrath & Carroll, 2012). Some psychologists believe the latest versions of these tests and others like them still have practical use and some validity (Choca, 2013; Meyer & Kurtz, 2006; Weiner, 2013), especially when a client's answers on these tests are used as a starting point for digging deeper into the client's recollections, concerns, and anxieties.

subjective

referring to concepts and impressions that are only valid within a particular person's perception and may be influenced by biases, prejudice, and personal experiences.

Concept Map L.O. 12.16, 12.17

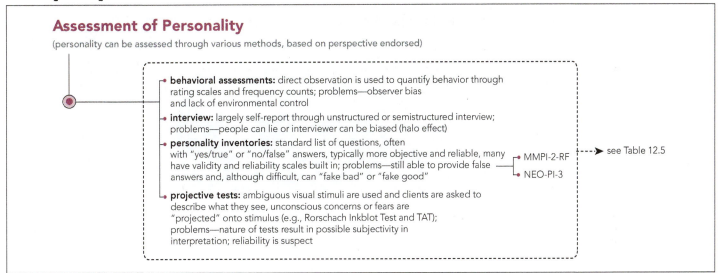

Practice Quiz   How much do you remember?

Pick the best answer.

1. Which of the following is an example of a halo effect?
    a. Jordan tends to distrust all instructors, regardless of if they are new or if he has had them for multiple classes.
    b. Cade unknowingly tends to rate his new client's behavior slightly higher during testing after noticing the client is wearing a class ring from his own alma mater.
    c. Yvonne provided her diagnosis only after conducting her own assessment and compiling information from two of her professional colleagues.
    d. Nicole always seems to like the last person she interviews for a job because she remembers the most about them.
    e. Camille likes pink because her mother likes pink.

2. Frequency counts and rating scales are especially helpful in assessing _____.
    a. personal values
    b. internal thought processes
    c. observable behaviors
    d. self-efficacy
    e. attitudes

3. Which of the following personality assessments might be best suited for objectively identifying abnormal patterns of behavior or thinking?
    a. TAT
    b. direct observation
    c. MBTI
    d. personal interview
    e. MMPI-2-RF

4. What is the function of a validity scale?
    a. to offer a diagnosis of abnormal behavior plus a positive therapeutic treatment
    b. to help better explain the results of a personality test
    c. to determine how a subject really feels
    d. to determine if a person is giving an accurate response
    e. to see how consistent scores are from assessment to assessment

Applying Psychology to Everyday Life
Informally Assessing Personality

12.18 Identify ways in which you informally assess the personality of others.

This chapter has highlighted several methods for assessing personality, and the results of those assessments may be used by psychology professionals to assist with diagnosis or treatment decisions. They may also be used in research, employee selection for a given job, and a variety of other areas. Most of us assess the personality characteristics of others on a daily basis. What are some of the behaviors or attitudes you find most informative when you see them in others and in your experience, which of these appear to have the highest validity and reliability for the characteristic you are evaluating? Watch the following video to see what some students find most informative when informally assessing others' personality traits.

Applying Psychology to Everyday Life Informally Assessing Personality

👁 Watch the Video at MyLab Psychology

After watching the video, answer the following questions:

1. As discussed in the video, we often observe people's surface traits and behaviors to informally assess their personalities, at least during initial encounters. What were two behaviors students in the video used to assess the personalities of those around them?
2. What are some of the behaviors or attitudes you find most informative when assessing the personality characteristics of others?

Chapter Summary

Theories of Personality

12.1 Define the term *personality* and identify several traditional perspectives in the study of personality.

- Personality is the unique way individuals think, feel, and act. It is different from character and temperament but includes those aspects.
- Four traditional perspectives in the study of personality are the psychodynamic, behavioral (including social cognitive theory), humanistic, and trait perspectives.

Psychodynamic Perspectives

12.2 Explain how the mind and personality are structured, according to Freud.

- The three divisions of the mind are the conscious, preconscious, and unconscious. The unconscious can be revealed in dreams.
- The three parts of the personality are the id, ego, and superego.
- The id works on the pleasure principle and the ego works on the reality principle.

- The superego is the moral center of personality, containing the conscience, and is the source of moral anxiety.
- The conflicts between the demands of the id and the rules and restrictions of the superego lead to anxiety for the ego, which uses defense mechanisms to deal with that anxiety.

12.3 Distinguish among the five psychosexual stages of personality development.

- The personality develops in a series of psychosexual stages: oral (id dominates), anal (ego develops), phallic (superego develops), latency (period of sexual repression), and genital (sexual feelings reawaken with appropriate targets).
- The Oedipus and Electra complexes (sexual "crushes" on the opposite-sex parent) create anxiety in the phallic stage, which is resolved through identification with the same-sex parent.
- Fixation occurs when conflicts are not fully resolved during a stage, resulting in adult personality characteristics reflecting childhood inadequacies.

12.4 Describe how the neo-Freudians modified Freud's theory.

- The neo-Freudians changed the focus of psychoanalysis to fit their own interpretation of the personality, leading to the more modern version known as the psychodynamic perspective.
- Jung developed a theory of a collective unconscious.
- Adler proposed feelings of inferiority as the driving force behind personality and developed birth order theory.
- Horney developed a theory based on basic anxiety and rejected the concept of penis envy.
- Erikson developed a theory based on social rather than sexual relationships, covering the entire life span.

12.5 Evaluate the influence of Freudian theory on modern personality theories.

- Current research has found support for the defense mechanisms and the concept of an unconscious mind that can influence conscious behavior, but other concepts cannot be scientifically researched.

The Behavioral and Social Cognitive View of Personality

12.6 Compare and contrast the learning theories of Bandura and Rotter.

- Behaviorists define personality as a set of learned responses or habits.
- The social cognitive view of personality includes the concept of reciprocal determinism, in which the environment, characteristics of the person, and the behavior itself all interact.
- Self-efficacy is a characteristic in which a person perceives a behavior as more or less effective based on previous experiences, the opinions of others, and perceived personal competencies.
- Locus of control is a determinant of personality in which one either assumes that one's actions directly affect events and reinforcements one experiences or that such events and reinforcements are the results of luck, fate, or powerful others.
- Personality, in the form of potential behavior patterns, is also determined by an interaction between one's expectancies for success and the perceived value of the potential reinforcement.

12.7 Evaluate the strengths and limitations of the behavioral and social cognitive learning views of personality.

- Traditional behavioral personality theory has scientific support but is criticized as being too simplistic.
- The social cognitive theory of Bandura and social learning theory of Rotter account for the influences of individual cognitive processes and social influences on personality.

The Third Force: Humanism and Personality

12.8 Describe how humanists such as Carl Rogers explain personality.

- Humanism developed as a reaction against the negativity of psychoanalysis and the deterministic nature of behaviorism.
- Carl Rogers proposed that self-actualization depends on proper development of the self-concept.
- The self-concept includes the real self and the ideal self. When these two components do not match or agree, anxiety and disordered behavior result.
- Unconditional positive regard from important others in a person's life helps the formation of the self-concept and the congruity of the real and ideal selves, leading to a fully functioning person.

12.9 Evaluate the strengths and limitations of the humanistic view of personality.

- Some aspects of humanistic theory are not easy to evaluate through research.
- Despite noted challenges, humanistic theory approaches have been effective in therapy situations. The theory has also led to therapies promoting self-growth and increased understanding of self and others.

Trait Theories: Who Are You?

12.10 Describe early attempts to use traits to conceptualize personality.

- Trait theorists describe personality traits in order to predict behavior.
- Allport first developed a list of about 200 traits and believed that these traits were part of the nervous system.
- Cattell reduced the number of traits to between 16 and 23 with a computer method called factor analysis.

12.11 Identify the five trait dimensions of the five-factor model of personality.

- Several researchers have arrived at five trait dimensions that have research support across cultures, called the Big Five or five-factor model. The five factors are openness, conscientiousness, extraversion, agreeableness, and neuroticism.
- Traits may be used to predict a variety of life outcomes, including occupations, success in school and work, physical health, and mental health.
- Specific traits appear to be related to different aspects of cognition and intelligence.

12.12 Evaluate the strengths and limitations of the trait view of personality.
- Some researchers believe the expression of some traits will differ based on situation or context.
- Factors continue to be researched. For example, some five-factor researchers use the label *Openness/Intellect* to recognize potentially different aspects of cognition and intelligence.

Personality: Genetics, Neuroscience, and Culture

12.13 Explain how twin studies and adoption studies are used in the field of behavioral genetics.
- Behavioral genetics is a field of study of the relationship between heredity and personality.
- Studies with both identical and fraternal twins, either raised together or raised apart, assist researchers in investigating the role of genetics and environment on the development of personality.
- Adoption studies of twins or non-twin siblings also provide valuable information.

12.14 Evaluate the role of neuroscience in the investigation of biological bases of personality.
- Personality neuroscience is a growing area of research, and brain structure differences associated with aspects of the Big Five dimensions of personality have been identified using both structural and functional neuroimaging methods.

12.15 Summarize current research on the heritability and neuroscience of personality.
- Studies of twins and adopted children have found support for a genetic influence on many personality traits, including intelligence, leadership abilities, traditionalism, nurturance, empathy, assertiveness, neuroticism, and extraversion.
- Cross-cultural research has found support for the five-factor model of personality traits in a number of different cultures.
- Future research will explore the degree to which child-rearing practices and heredity may influence the five personality factors.
- Personality neuroscience continues to inform the study of personality, linking individual difference, both positive and negative, with various brain areas and informing new theories of personality.

Assessment of Personality

12.16 Identify the advantages and disadvantages of using interviews, behavioral assessments, and personality inventories to measure personality.
- Interviews are used primarily by psychoanalysts and humanists and can include structured or unstructured interviews. Disadvantages of interviews can include the halo effect and bias of the interpretation on the part of the interviewer.
- Behavioral assessments are primarily used by behaviorists and include direct observation of behavior, rating scales of specific behavior, and frequency counts of behavior. Behavioral assessments have the disadvantage of the observer effect, which causes an observed person's behavior to change, and observer bias on the part of the person doing the assessment.
- Personality inventories are typically developed by trait theorists and provide a detailed description of certain personality traits. The NEO-PI-3 is based on the five-factor model, whereas the MMPI-2-RF is designed to detect abnormal personality.
- Personality inventories include validity scales to prevent minimization or exaggeration of symptoms, or "faking bad," but such measures are not perfect.

12.17 Identify the advantages and disadvantages of using projective personality tests.
- Projective tests are based on the defense mechanism of projection and are used by psychoanalysts. Projective tests include the Rorschach inkblot test and the Thematic Apperception Test.
- Projective tests can be useful in finding starting points to open a dialogue between therapist and client but have been criticized for being low in reliability and validity.

Applying Psychology to Everyday Life: Informally Assessing Personality

12.18 Identify ways in which you informally assess the personality of others.
- Personal experience and reactions to social interactions with others often serve as informal methods for assessing the personality of others.

Test Yourself: Preparing for the AP Exam

PART I: MULTIPLE-CHOICE QUESTIONS

Directions for Part I: Read each of the questions or incomplete sentences below. Then choose the response that best answers the question or completes the sentence.

1. According to Freud, the _____ works off of the pleasure principle, while the _____ is often perceived as the executive director of your personality.
   a. superego, ego
   b. superego, id
   c. ego, superego
   d. id, ego
   e. conscious mind, preconscious

2. Four-year-old Tyler has watched his father as he has mowed the lawn. This year, Tyler has asked for a lawn mower of his own for his birthday. Freud would say that Tyler is beginning the process of _____ as a way of resolving his Oedipal conflict.
   a. denial
   b. sublimation
   c. compensation
   d. identification
   e. reactance

3. Your professor explains how all females have an inner masculine side that adds to their personality. This concept is known as a(n) _____.
   a. source trait
   b. anima
   c. animus
   d. shadow
   e. persona

4. According to Adler, the defense mechanism of _____ is important in our personality development, as we attempt to overcome feelings of inferiority.
   a. identification
   b. rationalization
   c. denial
   d. sublimation
   e. compensation

5. Grace believes that fate will help her find the right man with whom to live her life. According to Rotter, she has a(n) _____.
   a. internal locus of control
   b. perceived sense of control
   c. high self-esteem
   d. external locus of control
   e. strong self-efficacy

6. What is a primary advantage of the social cognitive view of personality over the psychodynamic view?
   a. The social cognitive view tries to explain how people become the people they are.
   b. The social cognitive view stresses the importance of early childhood in personality development.
   c. The social cognitive view has concepts that can be tested scientifically.
   d. The social cognitive view is fully able to explain all the complexities of human behavior.
   e. The social cognitive view can explain personality characteristics present at birth.

7. An old motto of the U.S. Army was, "Be all you can be." This concept fits well with Carl Rogers's theory of _____.
   a. the real versus the ideal self
   b. ego ideal
   c. empathy
   d. unconditional positive regard
   e. self-actualizing tendency

8. According to Rogers, a mismatch between the real and ideal self _____.
   a. causes an increase in unconditional positive regard
   b. causes an increase in congruence
   c. typically motivates individuals to close the gap
   d. causes people to better understand their unconscious motives
   e. can result in anxiety and neurotic behavior

9. Dr. Huff is constantly late for meetings. She often arrives to her classes 5 to 10 minutes late and leaves students waiting at her door during office hours for up to 30 minutes. Using the five-factor model, which dimension would show a very low score for Dr. Huff?
   a. self-sufficiency
   b. neuroticism
   c. openness
   d. agreeableness
   e. conscientiousness

10. To explain an individual's personality, trait theorists would look to _____.
    a. early childhood emotional traumas
    b. the early experiences of rewards and punishments for certain behavior
    c. the kind of love, warmth, and affection given to the person by his or her parents
    d. the constellation of personality characteristics possessed by the person
    e. projective assessments

11. Personality neuroscience is an emerging field offering evidence of a possible relationship between various aspects of personality and _____.
    a. the structure and function of individual neurons
    b. neuroticism
    c. involvement in the field of neuroscience as a profession
    d. skull shape and size
    e. brain structure and function

12. Studies of the heritability of personality traits have found _____.
    a. strong evidence that personality is passed on exclusively by genetics
    b. little evidence to support the belief that personality can be passed on by genetics
    c. evidence to support the belief that personality can be passed on by genetics but only in highly developed countries
    d. strong evidence to support the belief that some personality traits can be passed on by genetics
    e. strong evidence that no aspects of personality are passed on by genetics

13. Which type of assessment would be the most reliable?
    a. observational study
    b. Internet survey
    c. projective test
    d. subjective test
    e. personality inventory

14. The _____ is based on the five-factor model, while _____ is based on the work of Raymond Cattell.
    a. 16PF, MMPI-2-RF
    b. MBTI, NEO-PI-3
    c. NEO-PI-3, 16PF
    d. MMPI-2-RF, MBTI
    e. CPI, TAT

15. As examples of what might be required as parts of specific projective tests, the _____ asks clients to look at a picture and tell a story while the _____ asks clients to report everything they see in an ambiguous figure.
    a. Rorschach, Thematic Apperception Test
    b. Rorschach, MMPI-2-RF
    c. MMPI-2-RF, Thematic Apperception Test
    d. MMPI-2-RF, NEO-PI-3
    e. Thematic Apperception Test, Rorschach

Part II: Free-Response Question

Directions for Part II: Read the essay question that follows. Then, respond to the question in a clear, concise essay. Do not simply list facts. Instead, present a thorough argument based on your critical consideration of the topic. Use of proper terminology is necessary.

Marta is an industrial-organizational psychologist who works for a major technology company. In her job, she conducts personality assessment for prospective employees for the company. As a global company, they hire people from all over the world.

Part A
Explain how each of the following terms would affect how Marta conducts personality assessments:
- normative sample
- culture-fair
- validity scale
- trait-situation interaction

Part B
Explain how Marta might administer each of the following kinds of assessments:
- personality inventory
- projective test
- direct observation

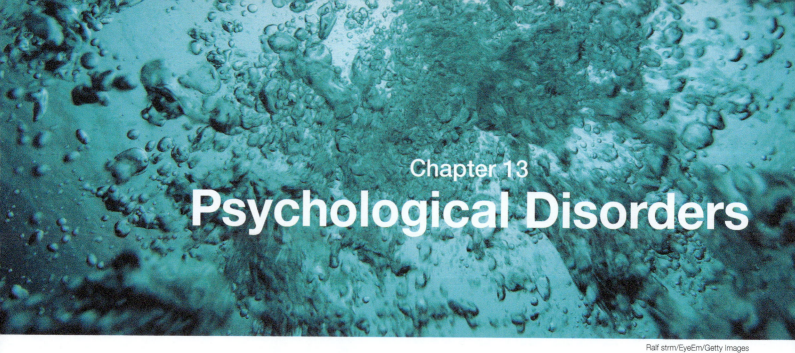

Chapter 13
Psychological Disorders

Ralf strm/EyeEm/Getty Images

In your words

Have you ever questioned if someone's way of thinking or acting was normal? How do you know if a behavior is normal or abnormal?

After you have thought about these questions, watch the video to see how other students would answer them.

Watch the Video at MyLab Psychology

Why study abnormal behavior and mental processes?

Because it is all around us, which raises many questions: How should one react? What should be done to help? What kind of person develops a mental illness? Could this happen to someone close to you? The key to answering these questions is to develop an understanding of just what is meant by abnormal behavior and thinking and the different ways in which thinking and behavior can depart from the "normal" path.

Learning Objectives

13.1 Explain how our definition of abnormal behavior and thinking has changed over time.

13.2 Identify models used to explain psychological disorders.

13.3 Describe how psychological disorders are diagnosed and classified.

13.4 Describe different disorders of mood, including major depressive disorder and bipolar disorders.

13.5 Compare and contrast potential explanations for depression and other disorders of mood.

13.6 Identify different types of anxiety disorders and their symptoms.

13.7 Describe obsessive-compulsive disorder and stress-related disorders.

13.8 Identify potential causes of anxiety, trauma, and stress disorders.

13.9 Differentiate among dissociative amnesia, dissociative fugue, and dissociative identity disorder.

13.10 Summarize explanations for dissociative disorders.

13.11 Identify the symptoms and risk factors associated with anorexia nervosa, bulimia nervosa, and binge-eating disorder.

13.12 Classify different types of personality disorders.

13.13 Identify potential causes of personality disorders.

13.14 Distinguish between the positive and negative symptoms of schizophrenia.

13.15 Evaluate the biological and environmental influences on schizophrenia.

13.16 Identify some ways to overcome test anxiety.

13.1–13.3 What Is Abnormality?

💬 I've heard people call the different things other people do "crazy" or "weird." How do psychologists decide when people are really mentally ill and not just a little odd?

Exactly what is meant by the term *abnormal behavior*? When is thinking or a mental process *maladaptive*? Abnormal or maladaptive as compared to what? Who gets to decide what is normal and what is not? Has the term always meant what it means now?

> **AP** 8.B Describe contemporary and historical conceptions of what constitutes psychological disorders.

13.1 Changing Conceptions of Abnormality

13.1 Explain how our definition of abnormal behavior and thinking has changed over time.

The study of abnormal behavior and psychological dysfunction is called **psychopathology**. Defining abnormality is a complicated process, and our view of what is abnormal has changed significantly over time.

A VERY BRIEF HISTORY OF PSYCHOLOGICAL DISORDERS Dating from as early as 3000 B.C.E, archaeologists have found human skulls with small holes cut into them, holes made while the person was still alive. Many of the holes show evidence of healing, meaning that the person survived the process. Although *trephining*, or cutting holes into the skull of a living person, is still done today to relieve pressure of fluids on the brain, in ancient times the reason may have had more to do with releasing the "demons" possessing the poor victim (Gross, 1999).

A Greek physician named Hippocrates (460–377 B.C.E.) challenged that belief with his assertion that illnesses of both the body and the mind were the result of imbalances in the body's vital fluids, or *humors*. Although he was not correct, his was the first recorded attempt to explain abnormal thinking or behavior as due to some biological process.

Moving forward in time, people of the Middle Ages believed in spirit possession as one cause of abnormality. The treatment of choice was a religious one: *exorcism*, or the formal casting out of the demon through a religious ritual (Lewis, 1995). During the Renaissance, belief in demonic possession (in which the possessed person was seen as a victim) gave way to a belief in witchcraft, and mentally ill persons were most likely called witches and put to death.

Fast forward to the present day, where psychological disorders are often viewed from a *medical model*, in that they can be diagnosed according to various symptoms and have an *etiology,** *course*, and *prognosis* (Kihlstrom, 2002b). In turn, psychological disorders can be treated, and like many physical ailments, some may be "cured," whereas other psychological disorders will require lifelong attention. And while numerous perspectives in psychology are not medical in nature, the idea of diagnosis and treatment of symptoms bridges many of them. This chapter will focus on the types of psychological disorders and some of their possible causes whereas we will focus more on psychological treatment and therapies in the next chapter, see Chapter Fourteen: Psychological Therapies.

HOW CAN WE DEFINE WHAT IS ABNORMAL? Defining abnormal behavior, abnormal thinking, or abnormality is not as simple as it might seem at first. The easy way out is to

These human skull casts show signs of trephining, a process in which holes were cut into the skulls of a living person, perhaps to release "demons" that were making the person's behavior or thinking odd or disturbed. Some who were treated in this way must have survived, as some of the holes show evidence of healing.

psychopathology
the study of abnormal behavior and psychological dysfunction.

---
*etiology: the origin, cause, or set of causes for a disorder.

say that abnormal behavior is behavior that is not normal, abnormal thinking is thinking that is not normal, but what does that mean? It's complicated, as you'll see by considering different criteria for determining abnormality.

STATISTICAL OR SOCIAL NORM DEVIANCE One way to define *normal* and *abnormal* is to use a statistical definition. Frequently occurring behavior would be considered normal, and behavior that is rare would be abnormal. Or how much behavior or thinking deviates from the norms of a society. For example, refusing to wear clothing in a society that does not permit nudity would likely be rare and be seen as abnormal. But deviance (variation) from social norms is not always labeled as negative or abnormal. For instance, a person who decides to become a monk and live in a monastery in the United States would be exhibiting unusual behavior, and certainly not what the society considers a standard behavior, but it wouldn't be a sign of abnormality. What is considered abnormal also depends on the setting or situation and the country in which a behavior occurs. For example, how might individuals in different countries rate the appropriateness of such behaviors as eating in an elevator, flirting at a funeral, or singing on a city sidewalk? For such behaviors, research suggests individuals are more restrained in some countries as compared to others and even in some states than others in the United States (Gelfand et al., 2017; Gelfand et al., 2011; Harrington & Gelfand, 2014).

The **situational context** (the social or environmental setting of a person's behavior) can also make a difference in how behavior or thinking is labeled. For example, if a man comes to a therapist complaining of people listening in on his phone conversations and spying on all his activities, the therapist's first thought might be that the man is suffering from thoughts of persecution. But if the man then explains that he is in a witness protection program, the complaints take on an entirely different and quite understandable tone.

SUBJECTIVE DISCOMFORT One sign of abnormality is when the person experiences a great deal of **subjective discomfort**, or emotional distress while engaging in a particular behavior or thought process. A woman who suffers from a fear of going outside her house, for example, would experience a great deal of anxiety when trying to leave home and distress over being unable to leave. However, all thoughts or behavior that might be considered abnormal do not necessarily create subjective discomfort in the person having them or committing the act—a serial killer, for example, does not experience emotional distress after taking someone's life, and some forms of disordered behavior involve showing no emotions at all.

INABILITY TO FUNCTION NORMALLY Thinking or behavior that does not allow a person to fit into society or function normally can also be labeled abnormal. These may be termed **maladaptive**, meaning that the person finds it hard to adapt to the demands of day-to-day living. Maladaptive thinking or behavior may initially help a person cope but has harmful or damaging effects. For example, a woman who cuts herself to relieve anxiety does experience initial relief but is harmed by the action. Maladaptive thinking and behavior are key elements in the definition of abnormality.

situational context
the social or environmental setting of a person's behavior.

subjective discomfort
emotional distress or emotional pain.

maladaptive
anything that does not allow a person to function within or adapt to the stresses and everyday demands of life.

Have you ever questioned if someone was talking to themselves and then discovered they were on the phone? What are some other public behaviors that may vary by context or situation?

THINKING CRITICALLY 13.1

In today's growing technological age, can you think of any new criteria that should be considered in defining abnormal behavior or thinking?

 So how do psychologists decide what is abnormal?

A WORKING DEFINITION OF ABNORMALITY To get a clear picture of abnormality, it is often necessary to take all of the factors just discussed into account. Psychologists and other psychological professionals must consider several different criteria when determining whether psychological functioning or behavior is abnormal (at least two of these criteria must be met to form a diagnosis of abnormality):

1. Is the thinking or behavior unusual, such as experiencing severe panic when faced with a stranger or being severely depressed in the absence of any stressful life situations?
2. Does the thinking or behavior go against social norms? (And keep in mind that social norms change over time—e.g., homosexuality was once considered a psychological disorder rather than a variation in sexual orientation.)
3. Does the behavior or psychological function cause the person significant subjective discomfort?
4. Is the thought process or behavior maladaptive, or does it result in an inability to function?
5. Does the thought process or behavior cause the person to be dangerous to self or others, as in the case of someone who tries to commit suicide or who attacks other people without reason?

Abnormal thinking or behavior that includes at least two of these five criteria is perhaps best classified by the term **psychological disorder**, which is defined as any pattern of behavior or psychological functioning that causes people significant distress, causes them to harm themselves or others, or harms their ability to function in daily life.

Before moving on, it is important to clarify how the term *abnormality* is different from the term *insanity*. Only psychological professionals can diagnose disorders and determine the best course of treatment for someone who suffers from mental illness. Lawyers and judges are sometimes charged with determining how the law should address crimes committed under the influence of mental illness. Psychologists and psychiatrists determine whether certain thinking or behavior is abnormal, but they do not decide whether a certain person is insane. In the United States, *insanity* is not a psychological term; it is a legal term used to argue that a mentally ill person who has committed a crime should not be held responsible for his or her actions because that person was unable to understand the difference between right and wrong at the time of the offense. This argument is called the *insanity defense*.

13.2 Models of Abnormality

13.2 Identify models used to explain psychological disorders.

 What causes psychological disorders?

Recognition of abnormal behavior and thinking depends on the "lens," or perspective, from which it is viewed. Different perspectives determine how the disordered behavior or thinking is explained. And, as we will see in Chapter Fourteen, those same perspectives influence how psychological disorders are treated.

THE BIOLOGICAL MODEL The **biological model** proposes that psychological disorders have a biological or medical cause (Gamwell & Tomes, 1995). This model explains disorders such as anxiety, depression, and schizophrenia as caused by faulty neurotransmitter systems, genetic problems, brain damage and dysfunction, or some combination of those causes. For example, as you may recall from the discussion of trait theory and the five-factor theory of personality traits, see Learning Objectives 12.10, 12.11, a growing body of evidence suggests that basic personality traits are as much influenced by genetic inheritance as they are by experience and upbringing, even across cultures (Bouchard, 1994; Herbst et al., 2000; Jang et al., 1996; Knopik et al., 2017; Loehlin, 1992; Loehlin et al., 1998; Plomin et al., 2016). One of the Big Five factors was neuroticism, for example, and it is easy to see how someone who scores high in neuroticism would be at greater risk for anxiety-based disorders.

THE PSYCHOLOGICAL MODELS Although biological explanations of psychological disorders are influential, they are not the only ways or even the first ways in which disorders are explained. Several different theories of personality were discussed in Chapter Twelve. These theories of personality can be used to describe and explain the formation of not only personality but disordered thinking, behavior, and abnormal personality.

PSYCHODYNAMIC VIEW: HIDING PROBLEMS For instance, the psychodynamic model, based on the work of Freud and his followers, see Learning Objectives 12.3, 12.4, explains disordered thinking and behavior as the result of repressing one's threatening thoughts, memories, and concerns in the unconscious mind (Carducci, 1998). These repressed thoughts and urges try to resurface, and disordered functioning develops as a way of keeping the thoughts repressed. According to this view, a woman who has unacceptable thoughts of sleeping with her brother-in-law might feel "dirty" and be compelled to wash her hands every time those thoughts threaten to become conscious, ridding herself symbolically of the "dirty" thoughts.

BEHAVIORISM: LEARNING PROBLEMS Behaviorists, who define personality as a set of learned responses, have no trouble explaining disordered behavior as being learned just like normal behavior (Skinner, 1971; Watson, 1913). For example, when Emma was a small child, a spider dropped onto her leg, causing her to scream and react with fear. Her mother made a big fuss over her, giving her lots of attention. Each time Emma saw a spider after this, she screamed again, drawing attention to herself. Behaviorists would say that Emma's fear of the spider was classically conditioned, and her screaming reaction was positively reinforced by all the attention. See Learning Objectives 5.2 and 5.5.

COGNITIVE PERSPECTIVE: THINKING PROBLEMS **Cognitive psychologists**, who study the way people think, remember, and mentally organize information, see maladaptive functioning as resulting from illogical thinking patterns (Mora, 1985). A cognitive psychologist might explain Emma's fear of spiders as distorted thinking: "All spiders are vicious and will bite me, and I will die!" Emma's particular thinking patterns put her at a higher risk of depression and anxiety than those of a person who thinks more logically.

THE SOCIOCULTURAL PERSPECTIVE What's normal in one culture may be abnormal in another culture. In the **sociocultural perspective** of abnormality, abnormal thinking or behavior (as well as normal) is shaped within the context of social interactions, family influences, the social group to which one belongs, and the culture within which the family and social group exist. In particular, cultural differences in abnormal thoughts or actions must be addressed when psychological professionals are attempting to assess and treat members of a culture different from that of the professional. **Cultural relativity** is a term that refers to the need to consider the unique characteristics of the culture in which the person with a disorder was nurtured to be able to correctly diagnose and treat the disorder (Castillo, 1997). For example, in most traditional Asian cultures, mental illness is often seen as a shameful thing that brings embarrassment not only to the individual experiencing the issues but also to one's family (Iwamasa, 2003). Traditional Asian cultures also have a more holistic view of the mind and body, with less separation between what may be defined as a mental condition versus what may be interpreted or expressed

cognitive psychologists
psychologists who study the way people think, remember, and mentally organize information.

sociocultural perspective
perspective that focuses on the relationship between social behavior and culture; in psychopathology, perspective in which abnormal thinking and behavior (as well as normal) is seen as the product of learning and shaping within the context of the family, the social group to which one belongs, and the culture within which the family and social group exist.

cultural relativity
the need to consider the unique characteristics of the culture in which behavior takes place.

as a physical condition. In turn, many Asian people suffering from disorders that would be labelled as depression or even schizophrenia may report bodily symptoms rather than emotional or mental ones (Fedoroff & McFarlane, 1998; Iwamasa, 2003; Sue & Sue, 2016). And while that may be the case for some Asian individuals, in the case of depression, expression of depressive symptoms can also vary by ethnicity (Kalibatseva & Leong, 2011; Kim et al., 2015). For example, the results of one study provided evidence of different clusters of depressive symptoms among Chinese Americans, more likely to report *somatic*, or physical symptoms like headaches and insomnia, Japanese Americans, more likely to experience interpersonal issues, and European Americans, more likely to experience depressed mood and hopelessness (Marsella et al., 1973). Appetite was also different between the groups, with European American individuals reporting the urge to eat more frequently whereas Chinese and Japanese American individuals more frequently reported having a poor appetite, further highlighting how the experience of depression may vary between different ethnic groups (Kalibatseva & Leong, 2011; Marsella et al., 1973).

The conceptualization of culture and its influences on psychological function and disorders has been explained by three concepts: **cultural syndromes**, *cultural idioms of distress*, and *cultural explanations or perceived cause* (American Psychiatric Association, 2013). Cultural syndromes may or may not be recognized as an illness within the culture but are nonetheless recognizable as a distinct set of symptoms or characteristics of distress. Cultural idioms of distress refer to terms or phrases used to describe suffering or distress within a given cultural context. And cultural explanations or perceived cause are culturally defined ways of explaining the source or cause of symptoms or illness (American Psychiatric Association, 2013).

A migrant farming background has been found to be related to increased symptoms of anxiety and depression among college students of Mexican heritage when compared to those without a migrant background.

It is important to consider other background and influential factors such as socioeconomic status and education level. Another area of awareness should be primary language and, if applicable, degree of acculturation (adapting to or merging with another culture). Psychosocial functioning has been part of the diagnostic process for some time now, but traditionally, greater attention has been paid to specifically identifying symptoms of pathology rather than focusing on the environmental factors that influence an individual's overall level of functioning (Ro & Clark, 2009). In one study, college students of Mexican heritage with migrant farming backgrounds reported more symptoms of anxiety and depression as compared to nonmigrant college students of Mexican heritage (Mejía & McCarthy, 2010). The nature of migrant farming poses different stressors than those faced by nonmigrant families. An individual's pre- and current immigration status and responses to respective immigration policies can also have differential impacts on mental health. For example, Latino/a immigrants may experience mental health issues related to pre-immigration trauma and discrimination and stress related to both immigration policies and the immigration process (Torres et al., 2018).

BIOPSYCHOSOCIAL PERSPECTIVE: ALL OF THE ABOVE In recent years, the biological, psychological, and sociocultural influences on abnormality are no longer seen as independent causes. Instead, these influences interact with one another to cause the various forms of disorders. For example, a person may have a genetically inherited tendency for a type of disorder, such as anxiety, but may not develop a full-blown disorder unless the family and social environments produce the right stressors at the right time in development. We will see later how this idea specifically applies to a theory of schizophrenia. How accepting a particular culture is of a specific disorder will also play a part in determining the exact degree and form that disorder might take. This is known as the **biopsychosocial model** of disorder, which has become a very influential way to view the connection between mind and body.

cultural syndromes

sets of particular symptoms of distress found in particular cultures, which may or may not be recognized as an illness within the culture.

biopsychosocial model

perspective in which abnormal behavior is seen as the result of the combined and interacting forces of biological, psychological, social, and cultural influences.

13.3 Diagnosing and Classifying Disorders

13.3 Describe how psychological disorders are diagnosed and classified.

Have you ever asked a young child, or remember from being one yourself, "What's wrong?" when she or he reported not feeling well? If so, you likely received a variety of answers describing their tummy ache, ouchie, or booboo. And in turn, you may have not known exactly what was wrong due to differences in their descriptive language and yours, especially when you could not see where or why they were hurting. The same applies to understanding and treating psychological disorders. Having a common set of terms and systematic way of describing psychological and behavioral symptoms is vital to not only correct identification and diagnosis but also in communication among and between psychological professionals and other health-care providers.

AP 8.A Recognize the use of the most recent version of the Diagnostic and Statistical Manual (DSM) published by the American Psychiatric Association as the primary reference for making diagnostic judgments.

THE DSM-5 One international resource is the World Health Organization's (WHO's) *International Classification of Diseases* (ICD), currently in its tenth edition. In the United States, the prevalent resource to help psychological professionals diagnose psychological disorders has been the *Diagnostic and Statistical Manual of Mental Disorders* (DSM), first published in 1952. The *DSM* has been revised multiple times as our knowledge and ways of thinking about psychological disorders have changed. The most recent version, which was released in 2013, is the *Diagnostic and Statistical Manual of Mental Disorders, Fifth Edition* (*DSM-5*; American Psychiatric Association, 2013). It includes changes in the organization of disorders, modifications in terminology used to describe disorders and their symptoms, and a discussion of the possibility of dimensional assessments for some disorders in future versions of the manual. The *DSM* has been useful in providing clinicians with descriptions and criteria for diagnosing mental disorders. To learn more about the development and role of the DSM, watch the video *Diagnosing and Classifying Disorders: The DSM*.

Watch Diagnosing and Classifying Disorders: The DSM

Watch the **Video** at **MyLab Psychology**

The *DSM-5* describes about 250 different psychological disorders. Each disorder is described in terms of its symptoms, the typical path the disorder takes as it progresses, and a checklist of specific criteria that must be met in order for the diagnosis of that disorder to be made. Whereas previous editions of the manual divided disorders and relevant facts about the person being diagnosed along five different categories, or axes, the *DSM-5* uses a single axis for all disorders, with provisions for also noting significant and relevant facts about the individual (American Psychiatric Association, 2013).

A few of the 20 categories of disorders that can be diagnosed include depressive disorders, anxiety disorders, schizophrenia spectrum and other psychotic disorders, feeding and eating disorders, and neurodevelopmental disorders such as ADHD (American Psychiatric Association, 2013). Other categories include personality disorders, intellectual disability, trauma- and stressor-related disorders, and obsessive-compulsive and related disorders.

While the diagnosis of psychological disorders into categories, based on signs and symptoms, has been the prevalent approach for many years, it is not the only way to think about psychological disorders. Continuing advances in neuroimaging, genetics, and cognitive science have led the National Institute of Mental Health (NIMH) to call for a change in the way we think about and study disorders through the launch of their

Research Domain Criteria (RDoC) project. This project promotes research that incorporates all of these advances, and other types of information, to provide a knowledge base for a new system of classifying psychological disorders (Insel, 2013). The RDoC research matrix is a framework consisting of several domains, each containing certain measurable and related ideas or constructs. For example, one domain is "negative valence systems" and contains the constructs fear, anxiety, and loss, among others. The purpose of the matrix is to provide a means by which disorders may be better conceptualized and measured, based on more modern research approaches in genetics and neuroscience in addition to those of the behavioral sciences (Cuthbert, 2014; Insel & Cuthbert, 2015; see **Figure 13.1**).

Figure 13.1 RDoC Research Matrix Example

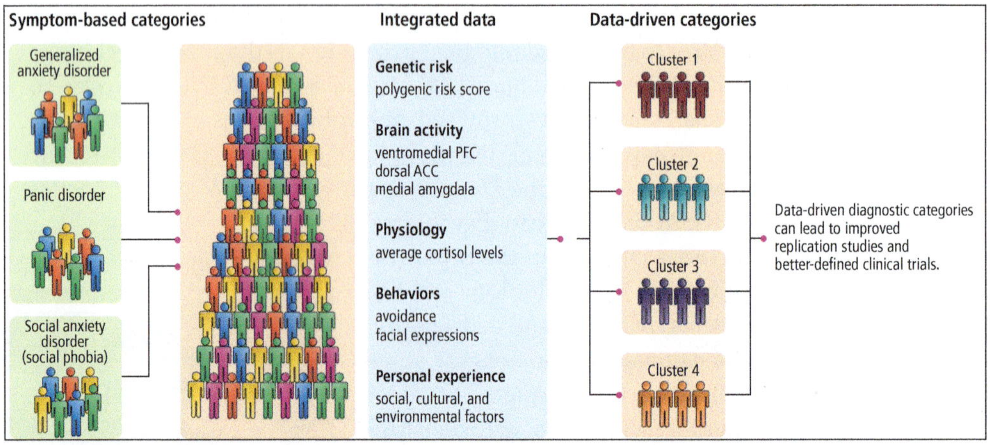

Hypothetical application of the RDoC approach. Individuals with a variety of symptom-based anxiety disorders are examined with different methods, and across different areas of investigation, to identify specific data-based clusters and categories for diagnosis.

Source: Based on and adapted from Insel & Cuthbert, 2015, and information from the RDoC Matrix, http://www.nimh.nih.gov/research-priorities/rdoc/constructs/rdoc-matrix.shtml

HOW COMMON ARE PSYCHOLOGICAL DISORDERS?

> That sounds like a lot of possible disorders, but most people don't get these problems, right?

Actually, psychological disorders are more common than most people might think. Estimates of prevalence can vary based on the survey methodology, the groups used, and the questions being asked. For example, different analyses of data from the same survey suggest that anywhere from 26.2 to 32.4 percent of American adults over age 18 suffer from a mental disorder (Harvard Medical School, 2007; Kessler et al., 2005). Data from the *National Survey on Drug Use and Health* (NSDUH) reveals about 46.6 million American adults over age 18, or 18.9 percent, experienced some kind of mental illness in 2017 (excluding developmental and substance use disorders). Fortunately, the same survey revealed only about 4.5 percent of American adults had a serious mental disorder (Substance Abuse and Mental Health Services Administration [SAMHSA], 2018). Overall, it appears that more than 1 in 5 American adults experience a psychological disorder in any given year.

Psychological disorders do not impact everyone in an equal fashion, as different rates of diagnoses are seen across sex, age, and race/ethnicity. **Figure 13.2** has prevalence data for mental illness among American adults in 2017 (SAMHSA, 2018). Globally, prevalence rates for various disorders also differ by the resources available. (Scott et al., 2018; see **Figure 13.3** for lifetime prevalence rates of mental illness by country income level).

Figure 13.2 Past Year Prevalence of Mental Illness in the United States (2017)

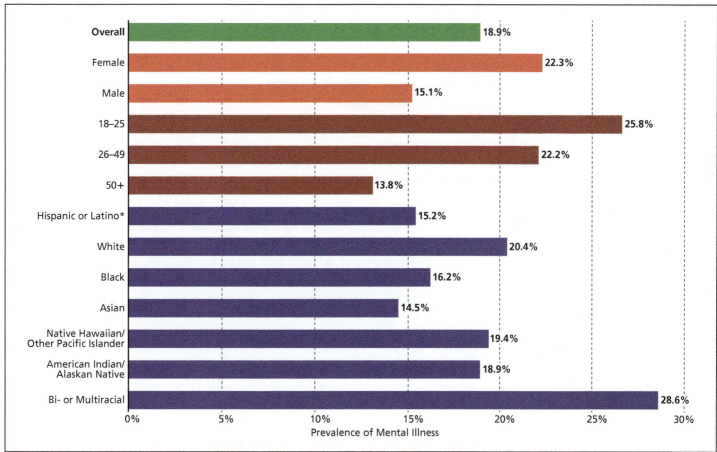

*All other race/ethnicity groups are non-Hispanic or Latino

Source: Based on and adapted from National Institute of Mental Health (2019) and the 2017 National Survey on Drug Use and Health (SAMHSA, 2018).

Worldwide, prevalence of mental disorders in a given year is 20 percent, with lifetime estimates up to 36 percent (Kessler et al., 2009; Steel et al., 2014), and only a small minority number of people get treatment; even less get high-quality treatment (World Health Organization, 2016a). Furthermore, it is quite common for people to suffer from more than one mental disorder at a time, such as a person with depression who also has a substance-abuse disorder or a person with an anxiety disorder who also suffers from sleep disorders. For example, in 2017, of the 18.7 million American adults who had a substance use disorder in the past year, approximately 45.6 percent met criteria for another psychological disorder (SAMHSA, 2018). **Table 13.1** has percentages of selected psychological disorders in the United States. Please note the most recent *National Survey on Drug Use and Health* data does not provide prevalence information for all of the different disorders.

Figure 13.3 Lifetime Prevalence Rates of Mental Disorders by Country Income Level

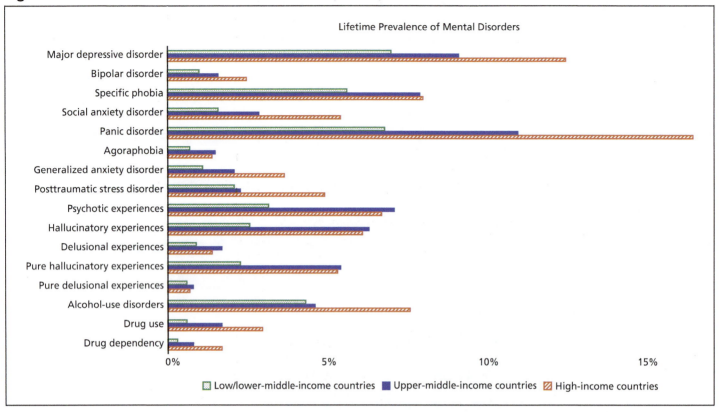

Low-/lower-middle-income countries (Colombia, Iraq, Nigeria, Peru), upper-middle-income countries (Brazil, Lebanon, Mexico, Romania), high-income countries (Belgium, France, Germany, Italy, New Zealand, Portugal, Spain, Netherlands, United States).

Source: Data presented comes from the WHO World Mental Health Surveys (Scott et al., 2018).

Table 13.1 Yearly Occurrence of Psychological Disorders in the United States

Category of Disorder	Specific Disorder	Percentage of U.S. Population and Number Affected*
Bipolar and Depressive disorders	All types	9.7% or 31.7 million
	Major depressive disorder	6.8% or 22.2 million
	Persistent depressive disorder (dysthymia)	1.5% or 4.9 million
	Bipolar disorder	2.8% or 9.2 million
Anxiety, Obsessive-Compulsive, and Trauma-Related disorders	All types	19.1% or 62.5 million
	Specific phobia	9.1% or 29.8 million
	Social anxiety disorder (social phobia)	7.1% or 23.2 million
	Panic disorder	2.7% or 8.8 million
	Agoraphobia	0.9% or 2.9 million
	Generalized anxiety disorder	2.7% or 8.8 million
	Obsessive-compulsive disorder	1.2% or 3.9 million
	Posttraumatic stress disorder	3.6% or 11.8 million
Schizophrenia	All types	0.25 to 0.64% or 817,900 to 2.1 million

*Percentage of adults over age 18 affected annually and approximate number within the population based on estimated 2018 United States Census data.

Source: Based on National Institute of Mental Health (2018) and National Comorbidity Study (Harvard Medical School, 2007). Table uses terminology from both the *DSM-IV* and *DSM-5* (American Psychiatric Association, 2000, 2013).

💬 What about college students? How common are psychological disorders for them?

Based on a sample of over 155,000 students from 196 campuses in the United States, approximately 36 percent of college students had been diagnosed with a mental health condition in their lifetime (Lipson et al., 2018). Worldwide estimates from almost 14,000 students enrolled at 19 colleges, across 8 countries, indicated 35 percent reported having a disorder in their lifetime and 31 percent had experienced a significant issue in the previous 12 months (Auerbach et al., 2018). About a third of these students will receive treatment, and there is an increase overall in services being offered by many college counseling centers (Lipson et al., 2018). See Learning Objective 14.4.

THE PROS AND CONS OF LABELS With its lists of disorders and their corresponding symptoms, the *DSM-5* helps psychological professionals diagnose patients and provide those patients with labels that explain their conditions. In the world of psychological diagnosis and treatment, labels like *depression*, *anxiety*, and *schizophrenia* can be very helpful: They make up a common language in the mental health community, allowing psychological professionals to communicate with each other clearly and efficiently. Labels establish distinct diagnostic categories that all professionals recognize and understand, and they can help patients receive effective treatment.

AP 8.E Identify the positive and negative consequences of diagnostic labels.

However, labels can also be dangerous—or, at the very least, overly prejudicial. In 1972, researcher David Rosenhan asked healthy participants to enter psychiatric hospitals and complain that they were hearing voices. All of the participants, whom Rosenhan called "pseudopatients," were admitted into the hospitals and diagnosed with either schizophrenia or manic depression (now called bipolar disorder). Once the pseudopatients were admitted, they stopped pretending to be ill and acted as they normally would, but the hospital staff's interpretation of the pseudopatients' normal behavior was skewed by the label of mental illness. For example, hospital workers described one pseudopatient's relatively normal relationships with family and friends as evidence of a psychological disorder, and another pseudopatient's note-taking habits were considered to be a pathological behavior. The pseudopatients had been diagnosed and labeled, and those labels stuck, even when actual symptoms of mental illness disappeared. Rosenhan concluded that psychological labels are long-lasting and powerful, affecting not only how other people see mental patients but how patients see themselves (Rosenhan, 1973).

Overall, labels can be time-saving and even lifesaving tools, but they can also bias us, affect our judgment, and give us preconceived notions that may very well turn out to be false. But just to be clear, the diagnostic labels listed in the *DSM-5* are intended to help both psychologists and patients, and they do help. As you read on, remember the power that labels have to shape our perceptions of reality.

Before describing the various categories and types of disorders, here is a word of caution: It's very easy to see oneself in these disorders. Medical students often become convinced that they have every one of the symptoms for some rare, exotic disease they have been studying. Psychology students studying abnormal behavior can also become convinced that they have some mental disorder, a problem that can be called "psychology student's syndrome." The problem is that so many psychological disorders are really ordinary variations in human behavior taken to an extreme. For example, some people are natural-born worriers. They look for things that can go wrong around every corner. That doesn't make them disordered—it makes them pessimistic worriers. Remember, it doesn't become a disorder until the worrying causes them significant distress, causes them to harm themselves or others, or harms their ability to function in everyday life. So if you start "seeing" yourself or even your friends and family in any of the following discussions, don't panic—all of you are *probably* okay.

Concept Map L.O. 13.1, 13.2, 13.3

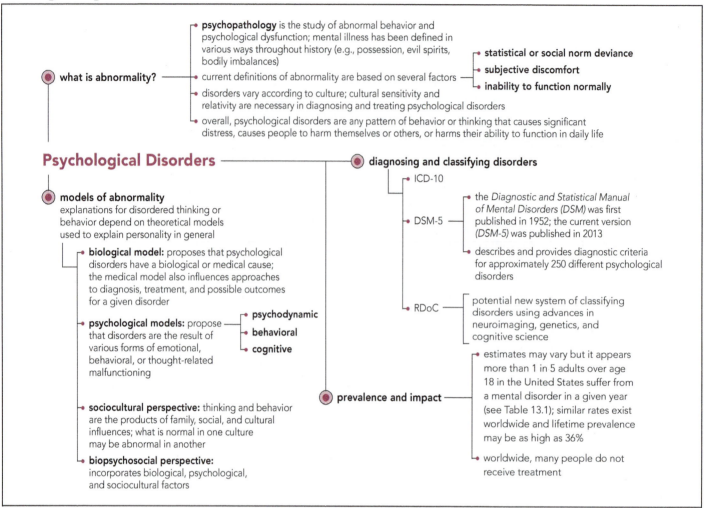

Practice Quiz   How much do you remember?

Pick the best answer.

1. How would the Greek physician Hippocrates have typically dealt with someone suffering from mental illness?
   a. He would have made a hole in the patient's skull to release the pressure, a process known today as trephining.
   b. He would have focused on correcting the imbalance of bodily fluids, or humors.
   c. He would have used an early form of functional behavior analysis.
   d. He would have tried to understand the person's unconscious and the forces at work there.
   e. He would have had someone conduct the religious ritual known as an exorcism.

2. Kay has just been fired from her new job for consistently arriving 2 hours late for work. Kay tries to explain that she must often drive back home to ensure that all the doors are locked and that no appliances have been left on. Kay's condition is abnormal according to the _____ definition.
   a. situational context
   b. maladaptive
   c. social deviance
   d. subjective discomfort
   e. danger to self or others

3. In the United States, "insanity" is a term typically used by _____.
   a. psychologists
   b. health-care professionals
   c. psychiatrists
   d. the social work system
   e. the legal system

4. Ernie became widowed after nearly 40 years of marriage. He has convinced himself that no one will ever love him again. His irrational thinking has caused him to suffer from depression, and he rarely leaves his house. What perspective might best explain his behavior?
   a. psychodynamic
   b. cognitive
   c. biological
   d. sociocultural
   e. behavioral

5. Which of the following concepts is NOT specifically associated with the *DSM-5* examination of culture-related disorders?
   a. cultural syndrome
   b. suffering or distress within a given cultural context
   c. cultural idioms of distress
   d. cultural explanations or perceived cause
   e. cultural binding

13.4–13.5 Disorders of Mood: The Effect of Affect

AP 8.G Discuss the major diagnostic categories, including anxiety disorders, bipolar and related disorders, depressive disorders, obsessive-compulsive and related disorders, and their corresponding symptoms.

When was the last time you felt down and sad? Or maybe a period of excitement or jubilation? Did these come about as the result of normal, day-to-day events or circumstances and change accordingly? Imagine how the experience of such feelings would impact your life if they lasted for much longer periods of time, were much more persistent across life events, and if you were unable to identify the source or cause for such emotions. That is often the case when someone experiences a disordered mood.

13.4 Major Depressive Disorder and Bipolar Disorders

13.4 Describe different disorders of mood, including major depressive disorder and bipolar disorders.

In psychological terms, the word **affect** is used to mean "emotion" or "mood." **Mood disorders** are disturbances in emotion and are also referred to as affective disorders. Although the range of human emotions runs from deep, intense sadness and despair to extreme happiness and elation, under normal circumstances people stay in between those extremes—neither too sad nor too happy but content (see **Figure 13.4**). When stress or some other factor pushes a person to one extreme or the other, mood disorders can result. Mood disorders can be relatively mild or moderate (straying only a short distance from the "average"), or they can be extreme (existing at either end of the full range). While we will examine disorders of mood together here, note that in the *DSM-5*, disorders of mood can be found under "Bipolar and Related Disorders" or "Depressive Disorders."

affect
in psychology, a term indicating "emotion" or "mood."

mood disorders
disorders in which mood is severely disturbed.

major depressive disorder
severe depression that comes on suddenly and seems to have no external cause, or is too severe for current circumstances.

Figure 13.4 The Range of Emotions

| Extreme sadness | Mild sadness | Normal emotions | Mild elation | Extreme elation |

Most people experience a range of emotions over the course of a day or several days, such as mild sadness, calm contentment, or mild elation and happiness. A person with a disorder of mood experiences emotions that are extreme and therefore abnormal.

MAJOR DEPRESSIVE DISORDER When a deeply depressed mood comes on fairly suddenly and either seems to be too severe for the circumstances or exists without any external cause for sadness, it is called **major depressive disorder**. Major depression would fall at the far extreme of sadness on Figure 13.4. People suffering from major depressive disorder are depressed for most of every day, take little or no pleasure in any activities, feel tired, have trouble sleeping or sleep too much, experience changes in appetite and significant weight changes, experience excessive guilt or feelings of worthlessness, and have trouble concentrating. Some people with this disorder also suffer from delusional thinking and may experience hallucinations. Most of these symptoms occur on a daily basis, lasting for the better part of the day (American Psychiatric Association, 2013). To learn more about mood disorders, watch the video *Mood Disorder: Depressive Disorder*.

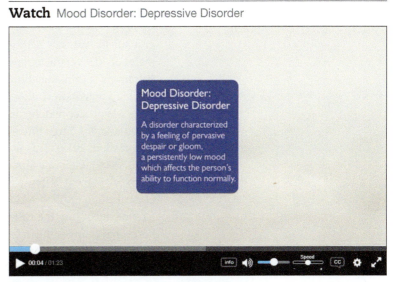

Watch Mood Disorder: Depressive Disorder

Mood Disorder: Depressive Disorder
A disorder characterized by a feeling of pervasive despair or gloom, a persistently low mood which affects the person's ability to function normally.

Watch the Video at MyLab Psychology

Some people with depression may have thoughts of death or suicide, including suicide attempts. Death by suicide is the most serious negative outcome for the person with depression. It is now the second leading cause of death among young people from 15 to 34 years of age in the United States, and more than 90 percent of suicides are associated with a psychological disorder, with depression being the most likely cause (Centers for Disease Control and Prevention, 2015e; Hyman & Cohen, 2013). Just as with depression, the rates of suicide are not the same for all people. In the United States, suicide rates vary between males and females, and by race/ethnicity (see **Figure 13.5**).

Figure 13.5 Suicide Rates in the United States

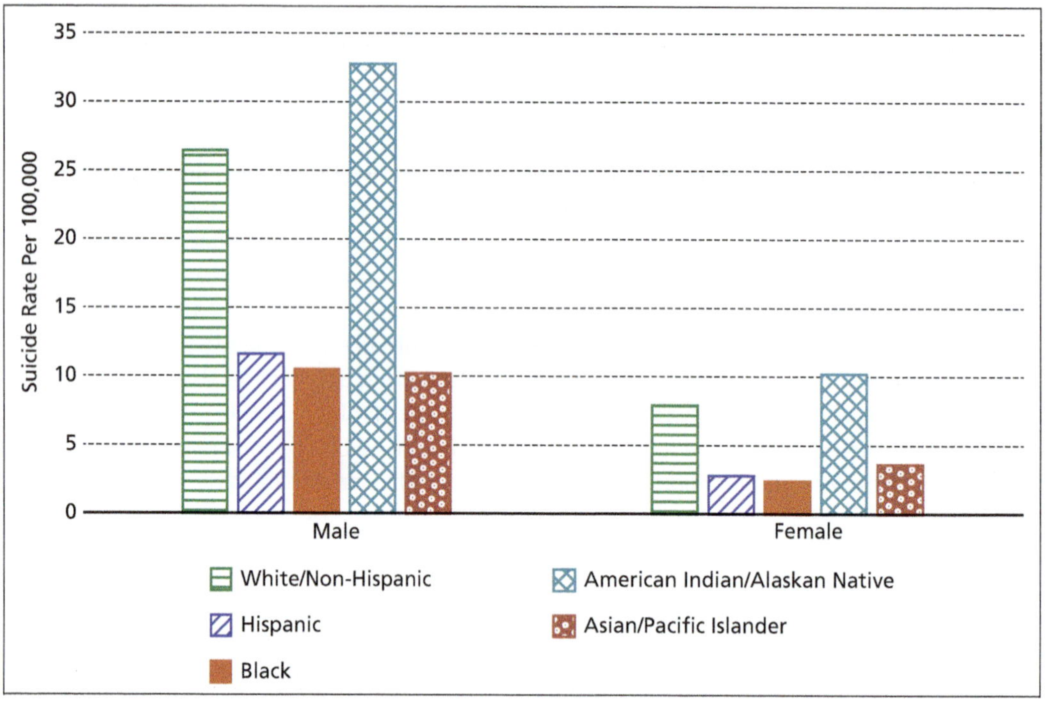

[Bar chart showing suicide rates per 100,000 by sex and race/ethnicity. Categories: White/Non-Hispanic, Hispanic, Black, American Indian/Alaskan Native, Asian/Pacific Islander. Male rates are substantially higher than female rates across all groups, with American Indian/Alaskan Native males showing the highest rate (~33) followed by White/Non-Hispanic males (~26).]

In the United States, suicide rates vary between males and females and by race/ethnicity.

Source: Data from National Institute of Mental Health (2018)

Among adolescents in the United States, increases in both depressive symptoms and suicide from 2010 to 2015 have been associated with increased screen time, or use of electronic devices, social media, and reading news on the Internet, and less face-to-face social interaction, print media use, engagement in sports or exercise, and attendance of religious services (Twenge et al., 2017). Global estimates from the World Health Organization suggest suicide rates in 2016 were approximately 10.6 per 100,000 population and higher in males at 10.9 versus females at 9.4 (World Health Organization, 2018). If you or someone you know is thinking about suicide, confidential assistance is available from the National Suicide Prevention Lifeline, 1-800-273-TALK (8255), **suicidepreventionlifeline.org.**

Major depressive disorder is the most common of the diagnosed disorders of mood and is 1.5 to 3 times more likely in women than it is in men (American Psychiatric Association, 2013). This is true even across various cultures (Kessler et al., 2012; Seedat et al., 2009). Global estimates suggest 4.4 percent of the population were depressed in 2015; 5.1 percent of females were depressed versus 3.6 percent of males (World Health Organization, 2017a). Many possible explanations have been proposed for this sex difference, including the different hormonal structure of the female system (menstruation, hormonal changes during and after pregnancy, menopause, etc.) and different social roles played by women in the culture (Blehar & Oren, 1997). Research has found little support for hormonal influences in general, instead finding that the role of hormones and other biological factors in depression is unclear. Furthermore, studies have found that the degree of differences between male and female rates of depression is decreasing and is nonexistent in college students and single adults, leading some to conclude that gender roles and social factors such as marital status, career type, and number of children may have more importance in creating the sex difference than biological differences do (McGrath et al., 1992; Nolen-Hoeksema, 1990; Seedat et al., 2009; Weissman & Klerman, 1977). Women also tend to ruminate, or repeatedly focus on negative emotions, more than men, and this may also be a contributing factor for reported differences in prevalence rates for both depression and anxiety (Krueger & Eaton, 2015; Nolen-Hoeksema, 2012).

Prevalence of depression also varies by ethnicity. For example, while Asian Americans are less likely to be diagnosed with any mental disorder, estimates from community samples suggest as many as 26.9 percent to 35.6 percent of Asian Americans may have depressive symptoms (Kim et al., 2015). Furthermore, prevalence rates among Asian Americans may be impacted by both ethnicity and place of birth. For example, some studies have found higher rates of depression among Korean and Filipino subgroups and higher rates for Chinese Americans born in the United States as compared to Chinese Americans not born in the United States (Kalibatseva & Leong, 2011; Kim et al., 2015).

Some people believe that depression symptoms worsen or that they only get depressed at certain times of the year. For them, their depression seems to set in during the fall and winter months and goes away with the coming of spring and summer. In the *DSM-5*, this pattern of depressive episodes is referred to as *major depressive disorder with a seasonal pattern* (American Psychiatric Association, 2013). These kinds of seasonal mood changes, sometimes referred to as *seasonal affective disorder (SAD)*, are reportedly due to the body's reaction to low levels of light present in the winter months (Partonen & Lonnqvist, 1998). Research with mice has demonstrated how light can impact mood-related behaviors and learning (Fernandez et al., 2018; LeGates et al., 2012) and at least one recent neuroimaging study with humans provides support for areas of the visual cortex, frontal lobe, and limbic areas being affected by exposure to light (Sanes et al., 2019). As you may remember, areas of the frontal lobes and limbic system structures are associated with regulation of mood. See Learning Objectives 2.7 and 2.8.

Despite the experimental evidence of exposure to light affecting areas of the brain related to mood, cognition, and mood-related behaviors and the wide use and acceptance of SAD as an actual disorder or type of depression, some researchers suggest there may not be a valid category of major depression that varies by season and raise questions about the continued use of this diagnosis (Traffanstedt et al., 2016). Likewise, evidence for mild depression varying by season was not found in a recent study examining the effects of season, latitude of residence, or number of daylight hours on the prevalence of mild forms of depression (LoBello & Mehta, 2019). Some researchers suggest that instead of a disorder, SAD may be a measure of severity of depressive symptoms, with perceived worsening during winter months (Winthorst et al., 2017). Also, of concern for some researchers is the use of the terms in general describing seasonal variation in depression, which provide a basis for the possibly erroneous belief that changes in mood and season are causally linked (LoBello & Mehta, 2019; Traffanstedt et al., 2016). In other words, be mindful of assuming causation versus correlation; just because someone is depressed in winter does not mean they are depressed as a result of winter.

BIPOLAR DISORDERS Major depressive disorder is sometimes referred to as a *unipolar disorder* because the emotional problem exists at only one end, or "pole," of the emotional range. When a person experiences periods of mood that can range from severe depression to **manic** episodes (excessive excitement, energy, and elation), that person is said to suffer from a type of **bipolar disorder** (American Psychiatric Association, 2013). However, while an individual may experience periods of mood at the two extremes, in some instances the individual may only experience mood that spans from normal to manic and may or may not experience episodes of depression, called *bipolar I disorder*.

manic
having the quality of excessive excitement, energy, and elation or irritability.

bipolar disorder
periods of mood that may range from normal to manic, with or without episodes of depression (bipolar I disorder), or spans of normal mood interspersed with episodes of major depression and episodes of hypomania (bipolar II disorder).

Demi Lovato has been very public about her ongoing challenges associated with bipolar disorder and has been an advocate for mental health. Other artists and world figures have been diagnosed or are believed to have had symptoms of bipolar disorder, including Kurt Cobain, Carrie Fisher, Catherine Zeta-Jones, Winston Churchill, and Vincent Van Gogh.

In the manic episodes, the person is extremely happy or euphoric* without any real cause to be so happy. Restlessness, irritability, an inability to sit still or remain inactive, and seemingly unlimited energy are also common. The person may seem silly to others and can become aggressive when not allowed to carry out the grand (and sometimes delusional) plans that may occur in mania. Speech may be rapid and jump from one topic to another. Oddly, people in the manic state are often very creative until their lack of organization renders their attempts at being creative useless (Blumer, 2002; McDermott, 2001; Rothenberg, 2001). In *bipolar II disorder*, spans of normal mood are interspersed with episodes of major depression and episodes of *hypomania*, a level of mood that is elevated but at a level below or less severe than full mania (American Psychiatric Association, 2013).

💬 That sounds almost like a description of an overactive child—can't sit still, can't concentrate—are the two disorders related?

The answer to that question is actually part of an ongoing controversy. There does seem to be a connection between attention-deficit/hyperactivity disorder (ADHD) and the onset of bipolar disorder in adolescence (Carlson et al., 1998), but only a small percentage of children with ADHD go on to develop bipolar disorder. A recent investigation examining two decades of data from a Canadian cohort found no significant differences in lifetime occurrences of ADHD between children of parents with bipolar disorder, those at a higher risk of developing bipolar disorder, and the control group (Duffy et al., 2018). Other researchers have found evidence of significantly higher rates of ADHD among relatives of individuals with bipolar disorder and a higher prevalence of bipolar disorder among relatives of individuals with ADHD (Faraone et al., 2012). However, when children have bipolar disorder alone versus ADHD alone, their relatives are more likely to have the respective disorder, and if children have both disorders, their relatives are more likely to have both disorders, indicating bipolar plus ADHD may actually be a distinct disorder (Biederman et al., 2013). The symptoms of bipolar disorder include irrational thinking and other manic symptoms that are not present in ADHD (Geller et al., 1998).

Confusion between the two disorders arises because hyperactivity (excessive movement and an inability to concentrate) is a symptom of both disorders. In one study, researchers compared children diagnosed with both bipolar disorder and ADHD to children diagnosed with ADHD only on measures of academic performance and a series of neurological tests (Henin et al., 2007). They found that the two groups responded in very similar ways, showing the same deficits in information-processing abilities, with only one exception: The children with both disorders performed more poorly on one measure of processing speed when compared to children with only ADHD. The researchers concluded that the neurological deficits often observed in children with bipolar disorder are more likely to be due to the ADHD than to the bipolar disorder itself. Children with bipolar disorder also seem to suffer from far more severe emotional and behavioral problems than those with ADHD (Ferguson-Noyes, 2005; McDougall, 2009) and children with bipolar disorder may have more impaired sleep than children with ADHD (Faedda et al., 2016).

13.5 Causes of Disordered Mood

13.5 Compare and contrast potential explanations for depression and other disorders of mood.

Explanations of depression and other disorders of mood come from the perspectives of behavioral, cognitive, and biological theories as well as genetics.

---

*euphoric: having a feeling of vigor, well-being, or high spirits.

Behavioral theorists link depression to learned helplessness (Seligman, 1975, 1989), whereas cognitive theorists point to distortions of thinking such as blowing negative events out of proportion and minimizing positive, good events (Beck, 1976, 1984). See Learning Objectives 5.12, 14.5. In the cognitive view, depressed people continually have negative, self-defeating thoughts about themselves, which depress them further in a downward spiral of despair. Learned helplessness has been linked to an increase in such self-defeating thinking and depression in studies with people who have experienced uncontrollable, painful events (Abramson et al., 1978, 1980). In contrast, researchers have found that when therapists focus on helping clients change their way of thinking, depression improves significantly when compared to therapy that focuses only on changing behavior; these results lend support to the cognitive explanation of distorted thinking as the source of depression (Strunk et al., 2010).

This link does not necessarily mean that negative thoughts *cause* depression; it may be that depression increases the likelihood of negative thoughts (Gotlib et al., 2001). There is also an interaction between people's thoughts, behaviors, and symptoms with their culture or social environment. One study found that when comparing adolescents who were depressed to those who were not, the depressed group faced risk factors specifically associated with the social environment, such as being female or a member of an ethnic minority, living in poverty, regular use of drugs (including tobacco and alcohol), and engaging in delinquent behavior (Costello et al., 2008). In contrast, those in the nondepressed group of adolescents were more likely to come from two-parent households; had higher self-esteem; and felt connected to parents, peers, and school. Clearly, learned helplessness in the face of discrimination, prejudice, and poverty may be associated with depression in adolescents. In a recent meta-analysis, perceptions of racial/ethnic discrimination were associated with more depressive symptoms in Latino, Asian, and African American adolescents (Benner et al., 2018). Adults are also susceptible to discrimination. In a study of Black, Guyanese, Hispanic, and White adults, the experience of racial discrimination was significantly associated with symptoms of depression (Hosler et al., 2018).

Biological explanations of disordered mood focus on the effects of brain chemicals such as serotonin, norepinephrine, and dopamine; drugs used to treat depression and mania typically affect the levels of these three neurotransmitters, either alone or in combination (Cohen, 1997; Cummings & Coffey, 1994; Ruhe et al., 2007; Stahl, 2013, 2017). And as with other psychological disorders, neuroimaging continues to provide information regarding possible brain areas associated with mood. Gray matter loss has been found in individuals with a history of neglect or physical, emotional, or sexual abuse in brain areas associated with mood, regulation of emotional behaviors, and attention (Lim et al., 2014). One recent investigation across different psychological disorders found variations in gray matter loss in several brain regions. Think back to the coverage of different brain areas in Chapter Two. In addition to the reductions found in the dorsal anterior cingulate and bilateral insular cortex across disorders, there was greater loss in the hippocampus and amygdala in depressed individuals (Goodkind, et al., 2015). Another investigation has found that baseline thickness of cortical gray matter in the right medial orbitofrontal and right precentral areas of the frontal lobe, the left anterior cingulate, and bilateral areas of insular cortex predicted future onset of major depression in a group of 33 adolescent females (Foland-Ross et al., 2015). For subcortical structures, researchers have found smaller volumes in the caudate, part of the basal ganglia, for individuals with major depressive disorder (MDD) and bipolar disorder (BD) as compared to controls, but individuals with MDD had greater volume in the ventral diencephalon, an area that includes the hypothalamus, than both controls and individuals with BD (Sacchet et al., 2015). Functional neuroimaging has also found dysfunction in many of these brain areas, with some being more active and others less active as compared to controls, and to complicate it even further, the direction of altered activity may be different in youth than in adults with depression (Miller et al., 2015; Su et al., 2014).

Genes also play a part in these disorders. The fact that the more severe mood disorders are not a reaction to some outside source of stress or anxiety but rather seem to come from within the person's own body, together with the tendency of mood disorders to appear in genetically related individuals at a higher rate, suggests rather strongly that inheritance may play a significant part in these disorders (Barondes, 1998; Farmer, 1996). It is possible that some mood disorders share a common gene, but actual rates vary. For example, genetic risks are higher in bipolar disorder as compared to unipolar depression (Hyman & Cohen, 2013; McMahon et al., 2010). More than 65 percent of people with bipolar disorder have at least one close relative with either bipolar disorder or major depression (Craddock et al., 2005; National Institute of Mental Health Genetics Workgroup, 1998; Sullivan et al., 2000). Twin studies have shown that if one identical twin has either major depression or bipolar disorder, the chances that the other twin will also develop a mood disorder are about 40 to 70 percent (Muller-Oerlinghausen et al., 2002).

Concept Map L.O. 13.4, 13.5

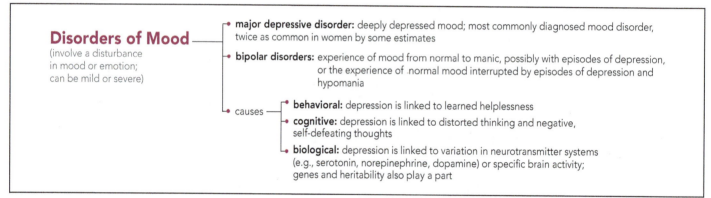

Practice Quiz — How much do you remember?

Pick the best answer.

1. Filip finds himself feeling depressed most of the day. He is constantly tired yet he sleeps very little. He has feelings of worthlessness that have come on suddenly and seemingly have no basis in reality. What might Filip be diagnosed with?
   a. bipolar disorder
   b. major depressive disorder
   c. acute depressive disorder
   d. seasonal affective disorder
   e. hypomania

2. Studies have suggested the increased rates of major depressive disorder in women may have a basis in _____.
   a. place of birth
   b. gender roles, social factors, and emotional processing
   c. hormonal differences
   d. heredity
   e. biological differences

3. What disorder seems to hold an association with bipolar disorder?
   a. persistent depressive disorder (dysthymia)
   b. major depressive disorder with a seasonal pattern
   c. cyclothymia
   d. phobic disorder
   e. ADHD

4. Biological explanations of disordered mood have focused on the effects of several different brain chemicals, and medications used to treat these disorders are designed to work on these various neurotransmitter systems. Which of the following is NOT one of the chemicals that has been implicated in mood disorders?
   a. serotonin
   b. 5-HT
   c. dopamine
   d. norepinephrine
   e. melatonin

AP 8.G Discuss the major diagnostic categories, including anxiety disorders, bipolar and related disorders, depressive disorders, obsessive-compulsive and related disorders, and their corresponding symptoms.

13.6–13.8 Disorders of Anxiety, Trauma, and Stress: What, Me Worry?

In this section, we will examine disorders in which the most dominant symptom is excessive or unrealistic **anxiety**. In addition to anxiety disorders, we will also address disorders that many people associate with anxiety symptoms, including obsessive-compulsive disorder, posttraumatic stress disorder, and acute stress disorders. These were classified as anxiety disorders in previous editions of the *DSM*. However, they now fall under different categories in the *DSM-5*. Obsessive-compulsive disorder now falls in the category of "Obsessive-Compulsive and Related Disorders," while posttraumatic stress disorder and acute stress disorder are found under "Trauma- and Stressor-Related Disorders" (American Psychiatric Association, 2013).

13.6 Anxiety Disorders

13.6 Identify different types of anxiety disorders and their symptoms.

The category of **anxiety disorders** includes disorders in which the most dominant symptom is excessive or unrealistic anxiety. Anxiety can take very specific forms, such as a fear of a specific object, or it can be a very general emotion, such as that experienced by someone who is worried and doesn't know why. Global estimates suggest 3.6 percent of the population experienced an anxiety disorder in 2015, and just as it was with depression, they appear to be more common among females at 4.6 percent versus males at 2.6 percent (World Health Organization, 2017a).

💬 But doesn't everybody have anxiety sometimes? What makes it a disorder?

Everyone does have anxiety, and some people have a great deal of anxiety at times. When talking about anxiety disorders, the anxiety is either excessive—greater than it should be given the circumstances—or unrealistic. If final exams are coming up and a student hasn't studied enough, that student's anxiety is understandable and realistic. But a student who has studied, has done well in all the exams, and is very prepared and still worries *excessively* about passing is showing an unrealistic amount of anxiety. For more about test anxiety, see the *Applying Psychology to Everyday Life* section in this chapter. **Free-floating anxiety** is the term given to anxiety that seems to be unrelated to any realistic and specific, known factor, and it is often a symptom of an anxiety disorder (Freud, 1977).

PHOBIC DISORDERS: WHEN FEARS GET OUT OF HAND One of the more specific anxiety disorders is a **phobia**, an irrational, persistent fear of something. The "something" might be an object or a situation or may involve social interactions. For example, many people would feel fear if they suddenly came upon a live snake as they were walking and would take steps to avoid the snake. Although those same people would not necessarily avoid a *picture* of a snake in a book, a person with a phobia of snakes would. Avoiding a live snake is rational; avoiding a picture of a snake is not.

SOCIAL ANXIETY DISORDER (SOCIAL PHOBIA) **Social anxiety disorder** (also called *social phobia*) involves a fear of interacting with others or being in a social situation and is one of the most common phobias people experience (Kessler et al., 2012). People with social anxiety disorder are afraid of being evaluated in some negative way by others, so they tend to avoid situations that could lead to something embarrassing or humiliating. They are very self-conscious as a result. Common types of social phobia are stage fright, fear of public speaking, and fear of urinating in a public restroom. Not surprisingly, people with social phobias often have a history of being shy as children (Sternberger et al., 1995).

SPECIFIC PHOBIAS A **specific phobia** is an irrational fear of some object or specific situation, such as a fear of dogs (*cynophobia*) or a fear of being in small, enclosed spaces (**claustrophobia**). Other specific phobias include:

- a fear of injections or hypodermic needles (*trypanophobia*)
- fear of dental work (*odontophobia*)

anxiety
the anticipation of some future threat, often associated with worry, vigilance, and muscle tension; anxiety is different from, but typically related to, the emotion of fear and the physiological consequences of sympathetic activation (the fight-or-flight response).

anxiety disorders
class of disorders in which the primary symptom is excessive or unrealistic anxiety.

free-floating anxiety
anxiety that is unrelated to any specific and known cause.

phobia
an irrational, persistent fear of an object, situation, or social activity.

social anxiety disorder (social phobia)
fear of interacting with others or being in social situations that might lead to a negative evaluation.

specific phobia
fear of objects or specific situations or events.

claustrophobia
fear of being in a small, enclosed space.

Many people get nervous when they have to speak in front of an audience. Fear of public speaking is a common social phobia. Can you remember a time when you experienced a fear like this?

- fear of blood (*hematophobia*)
- fear of washing and bathing (*ablutophobia*)
- fear of heights (**acrophobia**)
- fear of thunder (*tonitrophobia*)
- fear of spiders (*arachnophobia*)

AGORAPHOBIA A third type of phobia is **agoraphobia**, a Greek name that literally means "fear of the marketplace." It is the fear of being in a place or situation from which escape is difficult or impossible if something should go wrong (American Psychiatric Association, 2013). Furthermore, the anxiety is present in more than one situation. Someone is diagnosed with agoraphobia if they feel anxiety in at least two of five possible situations such as using public transportation like a bus or plane, being out in an open space such as on a bridge or in a parking lot, being in an enclosed space such as a grocery store or movie theatre, standing in line or being in a crowd like at a concert, or being out of the home alone (American Psychiatric Association, 2013).

> 💬 If a person has agoraphobia, it might be difficult to even go to work or to the store, right?

Exactly. People with specific phobias can usually avoid the object or situation without too much difficulty, and people with social phobias may simply avoid jobs and situations that involve meeting people face to face. But people with agoraphobia cannot avoid their phobia's source because it is simply being outside in the real world. A severe case of agoraphobia can make a person's home a prison, leaving the person trapped inside unable to go to work, shop, or engage in any kind of activity that requires going out of the home.

PANIC DISORDER Fourteen-year-old Dariya was sitting in science class watching a film. All of a sudden, she started feeling really strange. Her ears seemed to be stuffed with cotton and her vision was very dim. She was cold, had broken out in a sweat, and felt extremely afraid for no good reason. Her heart was racing, and she immediately became convinced she was dying. A friend sitting near her saw how pale she had become and tried to ask her what was wrong, but Dariya couldn't speak. She was in a state of panic and couldn't move.

Dariya's symptoms are the classic symptoms of a **panic attack**, a sudden onset of extreme panic with various physical symptoms: racing heart, rapid breathing, a sensation of being "out of one's body," dulled hearing and vision, sweating, and dry mouth (Kumar & Oakley-Browne, 2002). Many people who have a panic attack think they are having a heart attack and can experience pain as well as panic, but the symptoms are caused by the panic, not by any actual physical disorder. Psychologically, the person having a panic attack is in a state of terror, thinking that this is it, death is happening, and many people may feel a need to escape. The attack happens without warning and quite suddenly. Although some panic attacks can last as long as half an hour, some last only a few minutes, with most attacks peaking within 10 to 15 minutes.

Having a panic attack is not that unusual, especially for adolescent girls and young adult women (Eaton et al., 1994; Hayward et al., 1989, 2000; Kessler et al., 2007). Researchers have also found evidence that cigarette smoking greatly increases the risk of panic attacks in adolescence, young adulthood, and middle adulthood (Bakhshaie et al., 2016; Johnson et al., 2000; Zvolensky et al., 2003). Regardless, it is only when panic attacks occur more than once or repeatedly and cause persistent worry or changes in behavior that they become a **panic disorder**. Many people try to figure out what triggers a panic attack and then do their best to avoid the situation if possible. If driving a car sets off an

Anxiety disorders affect children and adults.

acrophobia
fear of heights.

agoraphobia
fear of being in a place or situation from which escape is difficult or impossible.

panic attack
sudden onset of intense panic in which multiple physical symptoms of stress occur, often with feelings that one is dying.

panic disorder
disorder in which panic attacks occur more than once or repeatedly, and cause persistent worry or changes in behavior.

attack, they don't drive. If being in a crowd sets off an attack, they don't go where crowds are. Watch the video *Panic Attacks Impair Daily Functioning* to learn more about the symptoms and effects of a panic attack.

GENERALIZED ANXIETY DISORDER

💬 What about people who are just worriers? Can that become a disorder?

Remember free-floating anxiety? That's the kind of anxiety that has no known specific source and may be experienced by people with **generalized anxiety disorder**, in which excessive anxiety and worries (apprehensive expectations) occur more days than not for at least six months. People with this disorder may also experience anxiety about a number of events or activities (such as work or school performance). These feelings of anxiety have no particular source that can be pinpointed, nor can the person control the feelings even if an effort is made to do so.

People with this disorder aren't just plain worriers (Ruscio et al., 2001). They worry *excessively* about money, their children, their lives, their friends, the dog, as well as things no one else would see as a reason to worry. They feel tense, edgy, get tired easily, and may have trouble concentrating. They have muscle aches, they experience sleeping problems, and they are often irritable—all signs of stress. Generalized anxiety disorder is often found occurring with other anxiety disorders and depression. For a listing of anxiety disorders and their symptoms, see **Table 13.2**.

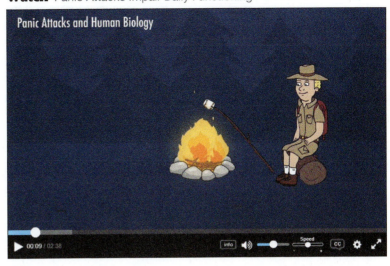

Watch Panic Attacks Impair Daily Functioning

Watch the Video at MyLab Psychology

generalized anxiety disorder
disorder in which a person has feelings of dread and impending doom along with physical symptoms of stress, which lasts 6 months or more.

Table 13.2 Anxiety Disorders and Their Symptoms

Anxiety Disorder	Definition	Examples/Symptoms
Social Anxiety Disorder	Fear of interacting with others or being in social situations that might lead to a negative evaluation	Stage fright, fear of public speaking, fear of urinating in public, fear of eating with other people
Specific Phobias	Fear of objects or specific situations or events	Fears of animals, the natural environment such as thunderstorms, blood injections/injury, specific situations such as flying
Agoraphobia	Fear of being in a place or situation from which escape is difficult or impossible	Using public transportation, open spaces, enclosed spaces, being in a crowd
Panic Disorder	Disorder in which panic attacks occur more than once or repeatedly and cause persistent worry or changes in behavior	Various physical symptoms: racing heart, dizziness, rapid breathing, dulled senses, along with uncontrollable feelings of terror
Generalized Anxiety Disorder	Disorder in which a person has feelings of dread and impending doom along with physical symptoms of stress, which lasts 6 months or more	Tendency to worry about situations, people, or objects that are not really problems, tension, muscle aches, sleeping problems, problems concentrating

13.7 Other Disorders Related to Anxiety

13.7 Describe obsessive-compulsive disorder and stress-related disorders.

As discussed earlier, despite anxiety being a common symptom, the following disorders are no longer classified as anxiety disorders in the *DSM-5*. *Obsessive-compulsive disorder* now falls in the category of "Obsessive-Compulsive and Related Disorders," while *post-traumatic stress disorder* and *acute stress disorder* are found under "Trauma- and Stressor-Related Disorders" (American Psychiatric Association, 2013).

obsessive-compulsive disorder

disorder in which intruding, recurring thoughts or obsessions create anxiety that is relieved by performing a repetitive, ritualistic behavior or mental act (compulsion).

acute stress disorder (ASD)

a disorder resulting from exposure to a major stressor, with symptoms of anxiety, dissociation, recurring nightmares, sleep disturbances, problems in concentration, and moments in which people seem to "relive" the event in dreams and flashbacks for as long as 1 month following the event.

posttraumatic stress disorder (PTSD)

a disorder resulting from exposure to a major stressor, with symptoms of anxiety, dissociation, nightmares, poor sleep, reliving the event, and concentration problems, lasting for more than 1 month; symptoms may appear immediately, or not occur until 6 months or later after the traumatic event.

AP 8.H Discuss the major diagnostic categories, including dissociative disorders, somatic symptom and related disorders, and trauma- and stressor-related disorders and their corresponding symptoms.

What stressors and types of trauma might refugees fleeing war-torn countries experience?

OBSESSIVE-COMPULSIVE DISORDER Sometimes people get a thought running through their head that just won't go away, like when a song gets stuck in one's mind. If that particular thought causes a lot of anxiety, it can become the basis for an **obsessive-compulsive disorder**, or OCD. OCD is a disorder in which intruding* thoughts that occur again and again (obsessions, such as a fear that germs are on one's hands) are followed by some repetitive, ritualistic behavior or mental acts (compulsions, such as repeated hand washing, counting, etc.). The compulsions are meant to lower the anxiety caused by the thought (Soomro, 2001).

💬 I knew someone who had just had a baby, and she spent the first few nights home with the baby checking it to see if it was breathing—is that an obsessive-compulsive disorder?

No, many parents check their baby's breathing often at first. Everyone has a little obsessive thinking on occasion or some small ritual that makes them feel better. The difference is whether a person *likes* to perform the ritual (but doesn't *have* to) or feels *compelled* to perform the ritual and feels extreme anxiety if unable to do so. You may wash your hands a time or two after picking up garbage, but it is entirely different if you *must* wash them a *thousand times* to prevent getting sick. The distress caused by a failure or an inability to successfully complete the compulsion is a defining feature of OCD.

ACUTE STRESS DISORDER (ASD) AND POSTTRAUMATIC STRESS DISORDER (PTSD) Both general and specific stressors were discussed in Chapter Ten: Stress and Health. Two trauma- and stressor-related disorders—*acute stress disorder* and *posttraumatic stress disorder*—are related to exposure to significant and traumatic stressors. The trauma, severe stress, and anxiety such as that experienced by people after 9/11, Hurricane Katrina, the April 2013 Boston Marathon bombings, the 2015 terrorist attacks in Paris and the earthquake in Nepal, the 2016 attacks in Brussels, Orlando, Manchester, and Nice, the 2018 attacks in Parkland and Pittsburgh, the California wildfires, and Hurricane Michael can lead to **acute stress disorder (ASD)**. The symptoms of ASD often occur immediately after the traumatic event and include anxiety, dissociative symptoms (such as emotional numbness/lack of responsiveness, not being aware of surroundings, dissociative amnesia), recurring nightmares, sleep disturbances, problems in concentration, and moments in which people seem to "relive" the event in dreams and flashbacks for as long as 1 month following the event. In a study of children and adolescents exposed to a single-event trauma (medical emergency, dog attack, assault, serious accidental injury, or motor vehicle collision) seen in emergency departments in England, 13.2 percent of them met criteria for ASD two weeks after the traumatic event (Meiser-Stedman et al., 2017).

When the symptoms associated with ASD last for more than 1 month, the disorder is then called **posttraumatic stress disorder (PTSD)**. But not everyone who experiences ASD will go on to meet criteria for PTSD, and not everyone who does not initially meet criteria for ASD will be in the clear. In the same study (Meiser-Stedman et al., 2017) of youth diagnosed with ASD at two weeks, the probability of having PTSD when assessed again 9 weeks after their traumatic event was only 48 percent. However, 30 percent of youth diagnosed with PTSD at week 9 had not met criteria for ASD when assessed at week 2 (Meiser-Stedman et al., 2017). Furthermore, none of the youth in this study were offered any psychological or psychiatric support following their traumatic events, speaking to the potential for significant recovery from acute stress events in the first few months following trauma (Meiser-Stedman et al., 2017). Whereas the onset of ASD often occurs immediately after the traumatic event, the symptoms of PTSD may not occur until 6 months or later after the event (American Psychiatric Association, 2013). Treatment of these stress

---

*intruding: forcing one's way in; referring to something undesirable that enters awareness.

disorders may involve psychotherapy and the use of drugs to control anxiety. See Learning Objectives 14.10, 14.13. The video *PTSD: The Memories We Don't Want* describes PTSD in more detail.

Watch PTSD: The Memories We Don't Want

Watch the Video at MyLab Psychology

Researchers have found that women have almost twice the risk of developing PTSD as do men and that the likelihood increases if the traumatic experience took place before the woman was 15 years old (Breslau et al., 1997, 1999). However, female and male veterans tend to have similar symptoms of PTSD, at least for military-related stressors (King et al., 2013). Children may also suffer different effects from stress than adults. Severe PTSD has been linked to a decrease in the size of the hippocampus in children with the disorder (Carrion et al., 2007). The hippocampus is important in the formation of new long-term declarative memories (see Learning Objectives 2.7, 6.5, and 6.12), and this may have a detrimental effect on learning and the effectiveness of treatments for these children. Changes in the connections between different brain areas, especially those involved in regulating fear, also likely impair possible recovery efforts (Keding & Herringa, 2015). Specifically, hyperreactivity in the amygdala in response to threat appears to be associated with ongoing symptoms of trauma, and lack of sustained activity in the ventral anterior cingulate cortex related to threat (indicating habituation, or reduced activity in response to threat) appears to predict later PTSD symptoms (Stevens et al., 2017).

Some life experiences lend themselves to people experiencing traumatic events. For example, the rate of PTSD (self-reported) among combat-exposed military personnel has tripled since 2001 (Smith et al., 2008). One study of older veterans over a 7-year period (Yaffe et al., 2010) found that those with PTSD were also more likely to develop dementia (10.6 percent risk) when compared to those without PTSD (only 6.6 percent risk). Increased levels of stress can make things worse. The risk of developing dementia appears to be more than 75 percent higher for veterans that were prisoners of war (POWs) than veterans that were not (Meziab et al., 2014).

Last, individuals with ASD and PTSD likely perceive the world around them differently. A study of assault and motor vehicle accident survivors treated in a South London, UK, emergency room suggested individuals with ASD or PTSD were more likely to identify trauma-related pictures than neutral pictures, as compared to trauma survivors not diagnosed with ASD or PTSD. Furthermore, such preferential processing of trauma-related information may be more strongly primed in individuals with PTSD (Kleim et al., 2012) and is supported by fMRI studies demonstrating heightened brain processing in areas linked with associative learning and priming in individuals with PTSD (Sartory et al., 2013). See Learning Objective 6.5.

13.8 Causes of Anxiety, Trauma, and Stress Disorders

13.8 Identify potential causes of anxiety, trauma, and stress disorders.

Different perspectives on how personality develops offer different explanations for these disorders. For example, the psychodynamic model sees anxiety as a kind of danger signal that repressed urges or conflicts are threatening to surface (Freud, 1977). A phobia is seen as a kind of displacement, in which the phobic object is actually only a symbol of whatever the person has buried deep in his or her unconscious mind—the true source of the fear. A fear of knives might mean a fear of one's own aggressive tendencies, or a fear of heights may hide a suicidal desire to jump.

BEHAVIORAL AND COGNITIVE FACTORS Behaviorists believe anxious behavioral reactions are learned. They see phobias, for example, as nothing more than classically conditioned fear responses, as was the case with "Little Albert" (Rachman, 1990; Watson & Rayner, 1920). See Learning Objective 5.3. Others could be established through operant conditioning, or observation or modeling. For example, if a spider were to drop on your kitchen table as a child, how would the individuals around you behave? Cognitive psychologists see anxiety disorders as the result of illogical, irrational thought processes. One way in which people with anxiety disorders show irrational thinking (Beck, 1976, 1984) is through **magnification**, or the tendency to "make mountains out of molehills" by interpreting situations as being far more harmful, dangerous, or embarrassing than they actually are. In panic disorder, for example, a person might interpret a racing heartbeat as a sign of a heart attack instead of just a momentary arousal.

Cognitive-behavioral psychologists may see anxiety as related to another distorted thought process called **all-or-nothing thinking**, in which a person believes his or her performance must be perfect or the result will be a total failure. **Overgeneralization** (a single negative event interpreted as a never-ending pattern of defeat), jumping to conclusions without facts to support that conclusion, and **minimization** (giving little or no emphasis to one's successes or positive events and traits) are other examples of irrational thinking. In a recent study with firefighters, a profession with repeated exposure to trauma, research suggested cognitive flexibility in regulating emotions according to the demands of particular situations can protect someone from developing PTSD symptoms (Levy-Gigi et al., 2016). Overall, for many of the anxiety disorders, psychological approaches are the treatment of choice.

BIOLOGICAL FACTORS Growing evidence exists that biological factors contribute to anxiety disorders. While many anxiety disorders are not typically treated with psychotropic medications, medication may be useful for severe cases, or used in combination with psychotherapy (Preston et al., 2017). When medications are used for anxiety, they tend to act on several key neurotransmitter systems, with some impacting GABA and others influencing serotonin or norepinephrine (Preston et al., 2017; Stahl, 2017). See Learning Objective 14.10. Several disorders, including generalized anxiety disorder, panic disorders, phobias, and OCD, tend to run in families, pointing to a genetic basis for these disorders. Furthermore, genetic factors in PTSD seem to influence both the risk of developing the disorder and the likelihood individuals may be involved in potentially dangerous situations (Hyman & Cohen, 2013). Functional neuroimaging studies, see Learning Objective 2.5, have revealed that the amygdala, an area of the limbic system, is more active in phobic people responding to pictures of spiders than in nonphobic people (LeDoux, 2003; Rauch et al., 2003) and more active in individuals with PTSD and social anxiety disorder, suggesting excessive conditioning and exaggerated responses to stimuli that would typically elicit minimal fear-related responses (Hyman & Cohen, 2013). See Learning Objectives 2.7, 6.12, and 9.8. Structural neuroimaging studies have also been helpful, see Learning Objective 2.5, in that specific brain areas have been associated with a variety of anxiety disorders, namely reductions of gray matter in the parts of the right ventral anterior cingulate gyrus (at the bottom and front of the right cingulate gyrus) and left inferior frontal gyrus (Shang et al., 2014). In a study of individuals across six different psychological disorders, reductions in gray matter were found in the dorsal anterior (at the top and front) cingulate gyrus and both the left and right insula (Goodkind et al., 2015).

CULTURAL VARIATIONS Anxiety disorders are found around the world, although the particular form the disorder takes might be different in various cultures. For example, in some Latin American cultures, anxiety can take the form of *ataque de nervios*, or "attack of nerves," in which the person may have fits of crying, shout uncontrollably, experience sensations of heat, and become very aggressive, either verbally or physically. These attacks usually come after some stressful event such as the death of a loved one (American Psychiatric Association, 2013). Several syndromes that are essentially types of phobias are specific to

magnification
the tendency to interpret situations as far more dangerous, harmful, or important than they actually are.

all-or-nothing thinking
the tendency to believe that one's performance must be perfect or the result will be a total failure.

overgeneralization
distortion of thinking in which a person draws sweeping conclusions based on only one incident or event and applies those conclusions to events that are unrelated to the original; the tendency to interpret a single negative event as a neverending pattern of defeat and failure.

minimization
the tendency to give little or no importance to one's successes or positive events and traits.

certain cultures. For example, *koro*, found primarily in China and a few other South Asian and East Asian countries, involves a fear that one's genitals are shrinking (Pfeiffer, 1982), and *taijin kyofusho* (TKS), found primarily in Japan, involves excessive fear and anxiety, but in this case it is the fear that one will do something in public that is socially inappropriate or embarrassing, such as blushing, staring, or having an offensive body odor (Kirmayer, 1991). Panic disorder occurs at similar rates in adolescents and adults in the United States and parts of Europe but is found less often in Asian, African, and Latin American countries. Within the United States, American Indians have significantly higher rates, whereas Latinos, African Americans, Caribbean Blacks, and Asian Americans have significantly lower rates as compared to non-Latino Whites (American Psychiatric Association, 2013).

Concept Map L.O. 13.6, 13.7, 13.8

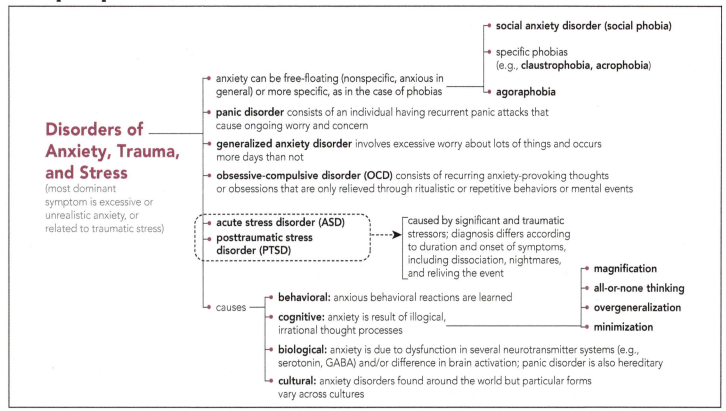

Practice Quiz   How much do you remember?

Pick the best answer.

1. Who is most likely to be diagnosed with a phobic disorder?
   a. Bayli, who is afraid of snakes after nearly being bitten while running
   b. Celine, who is fearful of snakes after watching a documentary on poisonous snakes found in her region
   c. Jade, who is morbidly afraid of snakes and refuses to even look at a picture of a snake
   d. Both Bayli's and Celine's behavior would qualify as a phobic disorder.
   e. Both Celine's and Jade's behavior would qualify as a phobic disorder.

2. Nayeli has recently given birth to her first child. She mentions that she often goes into her baby's bedroom to check if he is still breathing. Would this qualify as obsessive-compulsive disorder (OCD)?
   a. If Nayeli continues to carry out this behavior for more than 1 or 2 days, this would qualify as OCD.
   b. If Nayeli continues to carry out this behavior for more than 72 hours, this would qualify as OCD.
   c. If Nayeli and her husband both carry out this behavior, then it would qualify as OCD.
   d. If Nayeli enjoys frequently checking to see that her baby is breathing, then this would qualify as OCD.
   e. As long as Nayeli is not compelled to check on her baby and does not suffer from severe anxiety if she is unable to do so, then this is not OCD.

3. Sandy took part in the April 2013 Boston Marathon, where two bombs were detonated near the finish line, killing three spectators. For approximately 2 weeks after the marathon, Sandy was unable to sleep or concentrate and often found herself reliving the moment she heard the bombs explode. What disorder might Sandy be diagnosed with?
   a. generalized anxiety disorder
   b. acute stress disorder
   c. posttraumatic stress disorder
   d. panic disorder
   e. phobic disorder

4. Melanie has just received an exam grade in her psychology class. She earned a grade of 89 percent, which is a B. All of her work during the semester thus far has earned A grades, and she is very upset about the exam score. "This is the worst thing that could possibly have happened," she laments to her best friend, Keesha, who just rolls her eyes. A cognitive psychologist would suggest that Melanie is employing the cognitive distortion called _____.
   a. all-or-nothing thinking
   b. minimization
   c. magnification
   d. overgeneralization
   e. mind reading

AP 8.H Discuss the major diagnostic categories, including dissociative disorders, somatic symptom and related disorders, and trauma- and stressor-related disorders and their corresponding symptoms.

13.9–13.10 Dissociative Disorders: Altered Identities

Just as there is sometimes overlap of symptoms between different diagnoses, various disorders can be related to similar circumstances or phenomena. As already discussed, exposure to trauma is a key component to ASD and PTSD, and both may include symptoms of dissociation. Dissociation plays a more prominent role in the dissociative disorders, where the dissociative symptoms encompass many aspects of everyday life and not just memories of the traumatic events themselves or the time around them (American Psychiatric Association, 2013).

13.9 Types of Dissociative Disorders

13.9 Differentiate among dissociative amnesia, dissociative fugue, and dissociative identity disorder.

Dissociative disorders involve a break, or dissociation, in consciousness, memory, or a person's sense of identity. This "split" is easier to understand when thinking about how people sometimes drive somewhere and then wonder how they got there—they don't remember the trip at all. This sort of "automatic pilot" driving happens when the route is familiar and frequently traveled. One part of the conscious mind was thinking about work, school, or whatever was uppermost in the mind, while lower centers of consciousness were driving the car, stopping at signs and lights, and turning when needed. This split in conscious attention is very similar to what happens in dissociative disorders. The difference is that in these disorders, the dissociation is much more pronounced and involuntary. Dissociative symptoms can be present not only in dissociative disorders but in others as well, including PTSD and *borderline personality disorder*. See Learning Objective 13.13. A recent meta-analysis suggests dissociative symptoms are most prevalent in dissociative disorders, PTSD, borderline personality disorder, and conversion disorder but may also occur less frequently in substance-related disorders, schizophrenia, anxiety disorders, OCD, and mood disorders (Lyssenko et al., 2018).

DISSOCIATIVE AMNESIA AND FUGUE: WHO AM I AND HOW DID I GET HERE? In *dissociative amnesia*, the individual cannot remember personal information such as one's own name or specific personal events—the kind of information contained in episodic long-term memory. See Learning Objective 6.5. Dissociative amnesia may sound like retrograde amnesia, but it differs in its cause. In retrograde amnesia, the memory loss is typically caused by a physical injury, such as a blow to the head. In dissociative amnesia, the cause is psychological rather than physical. The "blow" is a mental one, not a physical one. The reported memory loss is usually associated with a stressful or emotionally traumatic experience, such as rape or childhood abuse (Chu et al., 1999; Kirby et al., 1993) and cannot be easily

dissociative disorders
disorders in which there is a break in conscious awareness, memory, the sense of identity, or some combination.

explained by simple forgetfulness. It can be a loss of memory for only one small segment of time, or it can involve a total loss of one's past personal memories. For example, a soldier might be able to remember being in combat but cannot remember witnessing a friend get killed, or a person might forget his or her entire life. These memories usually resurface, sometimes quickly and sometimes after a long delay. Dissociative amnesia can occur with or without *fugue*. The Latin word *fugere* means "flight" and is the word from which the term *fugue* is taken. A *dissociative fugue* occurs when a person suddenly travels away from home (the flight) and afterward cannot remember the trip or even personal information such as identity. The individual may become confused about identity, sometimes even taking on a whole new identity in the new place (Nijenhuis, 2000). Such flights usually take place after an emotional trauma and are more common in times of disasters or war.

DISSOCIATIVE IDENTITY DISORDER: HOW MANY AM I? Perhaps the most controversial dissociative disorder is **dissociative identity disorder (DID)**, formerly known as multiple personality disorder. In this disorder, a person seems to experience at least two or more distinct personalities existing in one body. There may be a "core" personality, who usually knows nothing about the other personalities and is the one who experiences "blackouts" or losses of memory and time. Fugues are common in dissociative identity disorder, with the core personality experiencing unsettling moments of "awakening" in an unfamiliar place or with people who call the person by another name (Kluft, 1984).

With the publication of several famous books and movies made from those books, dissociative identity disorder became well known to the public. Throughout the 1980s, psychological professionals began to diagnose this condition at an alarming rate—"multiple personality," as it was then known, had become the "fad" disorder of the late twentieth century, according to some researchers (Aldridge-Morris, 1989; Boor, 1982; Cormier & Thelen, 1998; Showalter, 1997). Although the diagnosis of dissociative identity disorder has been a point of controversy and scrutiny, with many professionals doubting the validity of previous diagnoses, some believe it does exist.

Some research suggests DID is not only a valid diagnostic category, it may co-occur in other disorders, such as individuals with *borderline personality disorder*, and may possibly be characterized by specific variations in brain functioning (Dorahy et al., 2014; Ross et al., 2014; Schlumpf et al., 2014). Dissociative symptoms and features can also be found in other cultures. The trancelike state known as *amok* in which a person suddenly becomes highly agitated and violent (found in Southeast Asia and Pacific Island cultures) is usually associated with no memory for the period during which the "trance" lasts (Hagan et al., 2015; Suryani & Jensen, 1993). However, despite their occurrence, in some cultures dissociative symptoms in and of themselves are not always perceived as a source of stress or a problem (van Duijl et al., 2010).

13.10 Causes of Dissociative Disorders

13.10 Summarize explanations for dissociative disorders.

Overall, there are two primary models of dissociation and dissociative disorders. In the older posttraumatic model, the core aspects of DID are the result of trauma, although trauma does not always cause dissociation, and the symptoms of DID serve to regulate the fear response and are discovered by the therapist (Dalenberg et al., 2012; Lilienfeld & Lynn, 2015; Lowenstein, 2018; Lynn et al., 2014). According to the *sociocognitive model*, in people with coexisting or ambiguous psychological symptoms, DID may be unintentionally constructed by therapist cuing, media influences, and sociocultural expectations about what DID is supposed to be like (Lilienfeld & Lynn, 2015; Lynn et al., 2014). Psychology professionals need to remain mindful of many potentially contributing and influential factors, including client suggestibility, proneness to fantasy, cognitive distortions, and co-occurring disorders (Lynn et al., 2014).

dissociative identity disorder (DID)
disorder occurring when a person seems to have two or more distinct personalities within one body.

Psychodynamic theory sees the repression of threatening or unacceptable thoughts and behavior as a defense mechanism at the heart of all disorders, and the dissociative disorders in particular seem to have a large element of repression—motivated forgetting—in them. For example, having a history of neglect or physical or sexual abuse in childhood is common in DID (Lowenstein, 2018), with approximately 90% of individuals diagnosed in the United States, Canada, and Europe having a history of neglect or childhood abuse (American Psychiatric Association, 2013). In the psychodynamic view, loss of memory or disconnecting one's awareness from a stressful or traumatic event is adaptive in that it reduces the emotional pain (Dorahy, 2001).

Cognitive and behavioral explanations for dissociative disorders are connected: The person may feel guilt, shame, or anxiety when thinking about disturbing experiences or thoughts and start to avoid thinking about them. This "thought avoidance" is negatively reinforced by the reduction of the anxiety and unpleasant feelings and eventually will become a habit of "not thinking about" these things. This is similar to what many people do when faced with something unpleasant, such as an injection or a painful procedure such as having a root canal. They "think about something else." In doing that, they are deliberately not thinking about what is happening to them at the moment, and the experience of pain is decreased. People with dissociative disorders may simply be better at doing this sort of "not thinking" than other people are.

Also, consider the positive reinforcement possibilities for a person with a dissociative disorder: attention from others and help from professionals. Shaping may also play a role in the development of some cases of dissociative identity disorder. The therapist may unintentionally pay more attention to a client who talks about "feeling like someone else," which may encourage the client to report more such feelings and even elaborate on them.

There are also some possible biological sources for dissociations. Researchers have found that people with *depersonalization/derealization disorder* (a dissociative disorder in which people feel detached and disconnected from themselves, their bodies, and their surroundings) have lower brain activity in the areas responsible for their sense of body awareness than do people without the disorder (Simeon et al., 2000). For individuals with PTSD experiencing dissociations, it has been suggested they too may have lower activity in areas associated with awareness of body states, coupled with lower activation in the amygdala but higher activation in medial prefrontal areas, resulting in an overall emotional "overmodulation" that results in dissociative symptoms (Lanius et al., 2012; Lanius et al., 2010). Others have found evidence that people with dissociative identity disorders show significant differences in brain activity, as evidenced by PET and fMRI, when different "personalities" are present (Reinders et al., 2001; Schlumpf et al., 2014; Tsai et al., 1999). It is also possible individuals with DID may be more elaborative when forming memories and are better at memory recall as a result (García-Campayo et al., 2009).

Concept Map L.O. 13.9, 13.10

Dissociative Disorders (involve a dissociation in consciousness, memory, or sense of identity, often associated with extreme stress or trauma)

- **dissociative amnesia:** one cannot remember personal information; may involve a dissociative fugue in that the person takes a sudden trip and also cannot remember the trip
- **dissociative identity disorder:** person seems to experience at least two or more distinct personalities; validity of actual disorder has been topic of debate
- causes
  - **psychodynamic:** repressed thoughts and behavior is primary defense mechanism and reduces emotional pain
  - **cognitive and behavioral:** trauma-related thought avoidance is negatively reinforced by reduction in anxiety and emotional pain
  - **biological:** support for brain activity differences in body awareness has been found in individuals with depersonalization/derealization disorder

Practice Quiz   How much do you remember?

Pick the best answer.

1. What is the major difference between dissociative amnesia and retrograde amnesia?
   a. Individuals with retrograde amnesia cannot form new memories for information or events following some psychological event.
   b. Retrograde amnesia patients often suffer from some form of physical brain trauma.
   c. Individuals suffering from dissociative amnesia often have a history of memory loss that seems to be hereditary.
   d. Retrograde amnesia patients often have suffered from painful psychological trauma.
   e. Those suffering from dissociative amnesia have prior damage to the brain, which in turn causes memory loss.

2. Tim wakes up on a cot in a homeless shelter in another town. He doesn't know where he is or how he got there, and he's confused when people say he has been calling himself Danny. This is most likely an episode of dissociative _____.
   a. amnesia
   b. amnesia with fugue
   c. multiple personality
   d. identity disorder
   e. anxiety

3. Dr. Spiegelman believes that Dina's dissociation disorder may be due to her apparent enhanced ability to think about things other than those associated with her traumatic childhood. What psychological perspective is Dr. Spiegelman applying?
   a. psychodynamic perspective
   b. evolutionary perspective
   c. biological perspective
   d. cognitive/behavioral perspective
   e. sociocultural perspective

4. Dissociative symptoms and features can be found in many different cultures. For example, in Southeast Asian and Pacific Islander cultures, people sometimes experience a trancelike state called _____ that is associated with increased agitation and violent tendencies.
   a. TKS
   b. *susto*
   c. *koro*
   d. *amok*
   e. *ataque de nervios*

13.11 Eating Disorders

Thus far we have talked about disorders that have primarily focused on mood, anxiety, stress, and trauma. We will now shift to disorders of a slightly different type: eating disorders.

> **AP** 8.I Discuss the major diagnostic categories, including feeding and eating disorders, personality disorders, and their corresponding symptoms.

13.11 Eating Disorders

13.11 Identify the symptoms and risk factors associated with anorexia nervosa, bulimia nervosa, and binge-eating disorder.

There are a variety of disorders that relate to the intake of food, or in some cases nonnutritive substances, or in the elimination of bodily waste. These are found in the *DSM-5* under "Feeding and Eating Disorders."

TYPES OF EATING DISORDERS We will specifically examine three eating disorders: *anorexia nervosa, bulimia nervosa,* and *binge-eating disorder.*

ANOREXIA NERVOSA **Anorexia nervosa**, often called **anorexia**, is a condition in which a person (typically young and female) reduces eating to the point that their body weight is significantly low, or less than minimally expected. For adults, this is likely a body mass index (BMI; weight in kilograms/height in meters^2) less than 18.5 (American Psychiatric Association, 2013). Hormone secretion becomes abnormal, especially in the thyroid and adrenal glands. The heart muscles become weak and heart rhythms may alter. Other physical effects of anorexia may include diarrhea, loss of muscle tissue, loss of sleep, low blood pressure, and lack of menstruation in females. If the weight loss due to anorexia is severe (40 percent or more below expected normal weight), dehydration, severe chemical imbalances, and possibly organ damage may result.

Some individuals with anorexia will eat in front of others (whereas individuals with bulimia tend to binge eat as secretly as possible) but then force themselves to throw up or take large doses of laxatives. They are often obsessed with exercising and with food—cooking elaborate meals for others while eating nothing themselves. They have extremely distorted body images, seeing fat where others see only skin and bones.

anorexia nervosa (anorexia)
a condition in which a person reduces eating to the point that their body weight is significantly low, or less than minimally expected. In adults, this is likely associated with a BMI less than 18.5.

BULIMIA NERVOSA **Bulimia nervosa**, often called **bulimia**, is a condition in which a person develops a cycle of "bingeing," or overeating enormous amounts of food at one sitting, and then using inappropriate methods for avoiding weight gain (American Psychiatric Association, 2013). Most individuals with bulimia engage in "purging" behaviors, such as deliberately vomiting after the binge or misuse of laxatives, but some may not, using other inappropriate methods to avoid weight gain such as fasting the day or two after the binge or engaging in excessive exercise (American Psychiatric Association, 2013). There are some similarities to anorexia: The victims are usually female, are obsessed with their appearance, diet excessively, and believe themselves to be fat even when they are quite obviously not fat. But individuals with bulimia are typically a little older than individuals with anorexia at the onset of the disorder—early 20s rather than early puberty. Individuals with bulimia often maintain a normal weight, making the disorder difficult to detect. The most obvious difference between the two conditions is that the individual with bulimia will eat, and eat to excess, bingeing on huge amounts of food—an average of 3,600 calories in less than two hours, roughly equivalent to the total calories needed for an average women over two days (Keel, 2018a). A typical binge may include a gallon of ice cream, a package of cookies, and a gallon of milk—all consumed as quickly as possible.

💬 But wait a minute—if individuals with bulimia are so concerned about gaining weight, why do they binge at all?

The binge itself may be prompted by an anxious or depressed mood, social stressors, feelings about body weight or image, or intense hunger after attempts to diet. The binge continues due to a lack of or impairment in self-control once the binge begins. The individual is unable to control when to stop eating or how much to eat. Eating one cookie while trying to control weight can lead to a binge—after all, since the diet is completely blown, why not go all out? This kind of thought process is another example of the cognitive distortion of all-or-nothing thinking.

One might think that bulimia is not as damaging to the health as anorexia. After all, the individual with bulimia is in no danger of starving to death. But bulimia comes with many serious health consequences: severe tooth decay and erosion of the lining of the esophagus from the acidity of the vomiting, enlarged salivary glands, potassium, calcium, and sodium imbalances that can be very dangerous, damage to the intestinal tract from overuse of laxatives, heart problems, fatigue, and seizures (Berg, 1999).

BINGE-EATING DISORDER **Binge-eating disorder** also involves uncontrolled binge eating but differs from bulimia primarily in that individuals with binge-eating disorder do not purge or use other inappropriate methods for avoiding weight gain (American Psychiatric Association, 2013). Lifetime prevalence estimates for anorexia nervosa, bulimia nervosa, and binge eating disorder are 1.75 to 3 times higher in females than for males (Hudson et al., 2007). However, when examining binge eating occurring at least twice weekly for at least 3 months, but not meeting criteria for a diagnosis, researchers found males had a lifetime prevalence rate 3 times higher than females (Hudson et al., 2007). Examined globally, data from the WHO World Mental Health (WMH) Survey Initiative reveals lifetime prevalence estimates average 1.9 percent for binge-eating disorder (Kessler et al., 2018).

CAUSES OF EATING DISORDERS The causes of anorexia, bulimia, and binge-eating disorder are not yet fully understood, but the greatest risk factor appears to be someone being an adolescent or young adult female (Keel & Forney, 2013). Increased sensitivity to food and its reward value may play a role in bulimia and binge-eating disorder, while fear and anxiety may become associated with food in anorexia nervosa, with altered activity or functioning of associated brain structures in each (Attia, 2018; Friedrich et al., 2013; Frank et al., 2018; Kaye et al., 2009; Kaye et al., 2013). Research continues to investigate genetic components for eating disorders, as they account for 40 to 60 percent of the risk for anorexia, bulimia, and binge-eating disorder, and although several genes have been implicated, the exact ones

bulimia nervosa (bulimia)
a condition in which a person develops a cycle of "bingeing," or overeating enormous amounts of food at one sitting, and then using unhealthy methods to avoid weight gain.

binge-eating disorder
a condition in which a person overeats, or binges on, enormous amounts of food at one sitting, but unlike bulimia nervosa, the individual does not then purge or use other unhealthy methods to avoid weight gain.

to focus on have not yet been identified (Culbert et al., 2015; Knopik et al., 2017; Trace et al., 2013; Wade et al., 2013). Individuals with a history of neglect or abuse (emotional, physical, or sexual) may also have an increased risk of having an eating disorder, particularly for those who are genetically vulnerable (Culbert et al., 2015; Nemeroff, 2016).

Although many researchers have believed eating disorders, especially anorexia, are cultural syndromes that only show up in cultures obsessed with being thin (as many Western cultures are), eating disorders are also found in non-Western cultures (Culbert et al., 2015; Keel, 2018b; Keel & Klump, 2003; Miller & Pumariega, 1999). What differs between Western and non-Western cultures is the rate at which such disorders appear, at least historically. For example, Chinese and Chinese American women were previously found to be far less likely to suffer from eating disorders than non-Hispanic White women (Pan, 2000). Why wouldn't Chinese American women be more likely to have eating disorders after being exposed to the Western cultural obsession with thinness? Pan (2000) suggested that whatever Chinese cultural factors "protect" Chinese women from developing eating disorders may also still have a powerful influence on Chinese American women. And while the prevalence of eating disorders is increasing in general in Asian countries, it cannot be assumed that exposure to Western ideals is all powerful. Various Asian societies respond differentially to Western influences and despite the exposure, many have not incorporated Western ideals of beauty (Pike & Dunne, 2015). Overall, researchers have suggested that for some eating disorders, particularly anorexia nervosa, there may be genetic influences but the actual expression or occurrence is culture-bound. In contrast, bulimia nervosa appears to be culture-bound and tied to Western influences on thinness and weight, with an excessive and improper influence of shape or weight on an individual's self-evaluation (Culbert et al., 2015; Keel, 2018a, 2018b; Keel & Klump, 2003).

One challenge with studying eating disorders in other cultures is that the behavior of starving oneself may be seen in other cultures as having an entirely different purpose than in Western cultures. One key component of anorexia, for example, is a fear of being fat, a fear that is missing in many other cultures. Yet women in those cultures have starved themselves for other socially recognized reasons: religious fasting or unusual ideas about nutrition (Castillo, 1997). Likewise, many of the measures used to classify eating disorders are based on Western models and have not been fully validated with non-Western populations (Pike & Dunne, 2015).

Eating disorders impact a diverse range of people. Among women in the United States, 12-month and lifetime prevalence rates for anorexia, bulimia, and binge-eating disorders are comparable for White, Latina, Asian, and African American women (Marques et al., 2011). Furthermore, prevalence rates for White females and males were not higher than for the other ethnic groups. In one study, Non-Latino White and African American females were more likely to be diagnosed with an eating disorder than eight other ethnic groups (Assari & DeFreitas, 2018). Binge-eating disorder appears to occur at about the same rates in both males and females, but at greater rates in Latinos and African Americans (Marques et al., 2011). In another U.S. study, body weight and frequency of binge eating was higher in Black participants as compared to White participants, but dieting, binge eating, and obesity occurred at an earlier age for White than Black and Hispanic participants with binge eating disorder (Lydecker & Grilo, 2016).

As noted, eating disorders are present in males, and as compared to females, adolescent males may be more likely to be diagnosed with an eating disorder other than anorexia or bulimia (Kinasz et al., 2016). However, when they do meet criteria, they are more likely to be diagnosed with anorexia than with bulimia, and they may be more likely to have had a previous diagnosis of ADHD (Welch et al., 2015). There is also a high rate of eating disorders among transgender individuals (Diemer et al., 2015; Haas et al., 2014). If clinicians and doctors are not aware that these disorders can affect more than the typical White, young, middle-class to upper-middle-class woman, important signs and symptoms of eating disorders in non-White or non-Western people may allow these disorders to go untreated until it is too late. Overall, as a result of weight loss and malnutrition, the estimated mortality rate in anorexia is highest among all of the eating disorders and much higher than for any other psychological disorder (Arcelus et al., 2011; Mehler, 2018).

> **THINKING CRITICALLY 13.2**
>
> How might the proliferation of various media and the Internet affect the development of eating disorders in cultures not previously impacted by them?

Concept Map L.O. 13.11

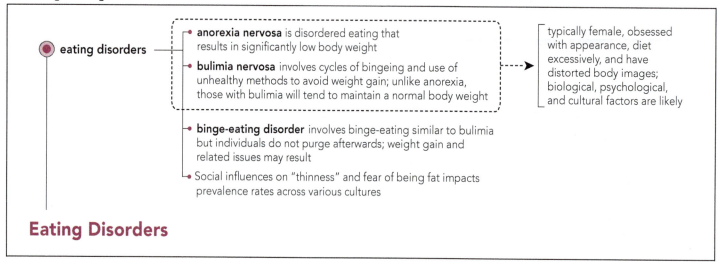

Eating Disorders

Practice Quiz — How much do you remember?

Pick the best answer.

1. Reagan has been diagnosed with anorexia nervosa. Which of the following may accurately describe Reagan?
   a. Reagan is young and female.
   b. Reagan has a greatly distorted body image.
   c. Reagan likely has a BMI less than 18.5.
   d. Reagan has significantly low body weight.
   e. All of these are likely accurate descriptions of Reagan.

2. Researchers believe that 40 to 60 percent of the risk for anorexia, bulimia, and binge-eating disorder is due to _____ factors.
   a. psychological
   b. genetic
   c. hormonal
   d. environmental
   e. sociocultural

3. Which of the following characteristics best describes differences between bulimia nervosa and anorexia nervosa?
   a. Individuals with anorexia do not have as severe health risks as individuals with bulimia have.
   b. Individuals with bulimia may have a normal body weight, whereas those with anorexia tend to be severely under their expected body weight.
   c. Anorexia tends to occur in early adulthood, while bulimia often starts in early adolescence.
   d. Individuals with anorexia have been known to binge like those with bulimia on occasion.
   e. Anorexia tends to occur in late adulthood, while bulimia often starts in early adulthood.

AP 8.I Discuss the major diagnostic categories, including feeding and eating disorders, personality disorders, and their corresponding symptoms.

13.12–13.13 Personality Disorders: I'm Okay, It's Everyone Else Who's Weird

Personality disorders are a little different from other psychological disorders in that the disorder does not affect merely one aspect of the person's life, such as a higher-than-normal level of anxiety or a set of distorted beliefs, but instead affects the entire life adjustment of the person. The disorder is the personality itself, not one aspect of it. However, despite personality disorders affecting the entire person, current research suggests they are not always lifelong in nature as once believed.

13.12 Categories of Personality Disorders

13.12 Classify different types of personality disorders.

In **personality disorder**, a person has an excessively rigid, maladaptive pattern of behavior and ways of relating to others (American Psychiatric Association, 2013). This rigidity and the inability to adapt to social demands and life changes make it very difficult for the individual with a personality disorder to fit in with others or have relatively normal social relationships. The *DSM-5* lists 10 primary types of personality disorder across three basic categories (American Psychiatric Association, 2013): those in which the people are seen as odd or eccentric by others (Paranoid, Schizoid, Schizotypal), those in which the behavior of the person is very dramatic, emotional, or erratic (Antisocial, Borderline, Histrionic, Narcissistic), and those in which the main emotion is anxiety or fearfulness (Avoidant, Dependent, Obsessive-Compulsive). These categories are labeled Cluster A, Cluster B, and Cluster C, respectively.

PARANOID PERSONALITY DISORDER In **paranoid personality disorder**, people believe everyone is out to get them; they are not the easiest people to get along with due to their distrust of others. People with a paranoid personality disorder, who are most often male, are suspicious, interpreting the motives of others as having some hidden agenda or ill intent. They may continuously question the behavior and loyalty of friends, if they have them, and interpret otherwise innocent remarks to be demeaning or threatening. The paranoid individual is likely to carry grudges and not forgive any perceived trespasses. If they are in a romantic relationship, they are more likely to suspect their partner of being unfaithful, and if they have other close ties, they are probably with those who have similar paranoid beliefs (American Psychiatric Association, 2013).

ANTISOCIAL PERSONALITY DISORDER One of the most well researched of the personality disorders is **antisocial personality disorder (ASPD)**. People with ASPD are literally "against society." The antisocial person may habitually break the law, disobey rules, tell lies, and use other people without worrying about their rights or feelings. The person with ASPD may be irritable or aggressive. These individuals may not keep promises or other obligations and are consistently irresponsible. They may also seem indifferent or able to rationalize taking advantage of or hurting others. Typically they borrow money or belongings and don't bother to repay the debt or return the items, are impulsive, don't keep their commitments either socially or in their jobs, and tend to be very selfish, self-centered, and manipulative. There is a definite gender difference in ASPD, with many more males diagnosed with this disorder than females (American Psychiatric Association, 2013).

BORDERLINE PERSONALITY DISORDER People with **borderline personality disorder (BLPD)** have relationships with other people that are intense and relatively unstable. They are impulsive, have an unstable sense of self, and are intensely fearful of abandonment. Life goals, career choices, friendships, and even sexual behavior may change quickly and dramatically. Close personal and romantic relationships are marked by extreme swings from idealization to demonization. Periods of depression are not unusual, and some may engage in excessive spending, drug abuse, or suicidal behavior (suicide attempts may be part of a pattern of manipulation used against others in a relationship). Emotions are often inappropriate and excessive, with a pattern of self-destructiveness, chronic loneliness, and disruptive anger in close relationships (American Psychiatric Association, 2013). The frequency of this disorder in women is nearly three times greater than in men (American Psychiatric Association, 2013).

DEPENDENT PERSONALITY DISORDER People with **dependent personality disorder** need constant attention and someone to take care of them. They are often passive and rely on others, or possibly just a single individual like a parent or partner, to assume responsibility for many areas of their life. They may need someone else to tell them what to wear, who to be friends with, or where to go to school. They have little faith in being able to do things themselves and may be fearful of doing them too well out of fear of abandonment (American Psychiatric Association, 2013).

personality disorders
disorders in which a person adopts a persistent, rigid, and maladaptive pattern of behavior that interferes with normal social interactions.

paranoid personality disorder
personality disorder in which a person exhibits pervasive and widespread distrust and suspiciousness of others.

antisocial personality disorder (ASPD)
disorder in which a person uses other people without worrying about their rights or feelings and often behaves in an impulsive or reckless manner without regard for the consequences of that behavior.

borderline personality disorder (BLPD)
maladaptive personality pattern in which the person is moody, unstable, lacks a clear sense of identity, and often clings to others with a pattern of self-destructiveness, chronic loneliness, and disruptive anger in close relationships.

dependent personality disorder
personality disorder in which the person is clingy, submissive, fearful of separation, requires constant reassurance, feels helpless when alone, and has others assume responsibility for most areas of life.

13.13 Causes of Personality Disorders

13.13 Identify potential causes of personality disorders.

Cognitive-behavioral theorists talk about how specific behavior can be learned over time through the processes of reinforcement, shaping, and modeling. More cognitive explanations involve the belief systems formed by the personality disordered persons, such as the paranoia, extreme self-importance, and fear of being unable to cope by oneself of the paranoid, narcissistic, and dependent personalities, for example.

There is some evidence of genetic factors in personality disorders (Reichborn-Kjennerud, 2008). Close biological relatives of people with disorders such as antisocial, schizotypal, and borderline are more likely to have these disorders than those who are not related (American Psychiatric Association, 2013; Kendler et al., 2006; Reichborn-Kjennerud et al., 2007; Torgersen et al., 2008). Adoption studies of children whose biological parents had antisocial personality disorder show an increased risk for that disorder in those children, even though they are raised in a different environment by different people (American Psychiatric Association, 2013). A longitudinal study has linked the temperaments of children at age 3 to antisocial tendencies in adulthood, finding that those children with lower fearfulness and inhibitions were more likely to show antisocial personality characteristics in a follow-up study at age 28 (Glenn et al., 2007).

Other causes of personality disorders have been suggested. Antisocial personalities are emotionally unresponsive to stressful or threatening situations when compared to others, which may be one reason that they are not afraid of getting caught (Arnett et al., 1997; Blair et al., 1995; Lykken, 1995). This unresponsiveness seems to be linked to lower than normal levels of stress hormones in antisocial persons (Fairchild et al., 2008; Lykken, 1995).

Disturbances in family relationships and communication have also been linked to personality disorders and, in particular, to antisocial personality disorder (Benjamin, 2005; Livesley, 1995). Childhood abuse, neglect, overly strict parenting, overprotective parenting, and parental rejection have all been put forth as possible causes, making the picture of the development of personality disorders a complicated one. It is safe to say that many of the same factors (genetics, social relationships, and parenting) that help create ordinary personalities also create disordered personalities.

Concept Map L.O. 13.12, 13.13

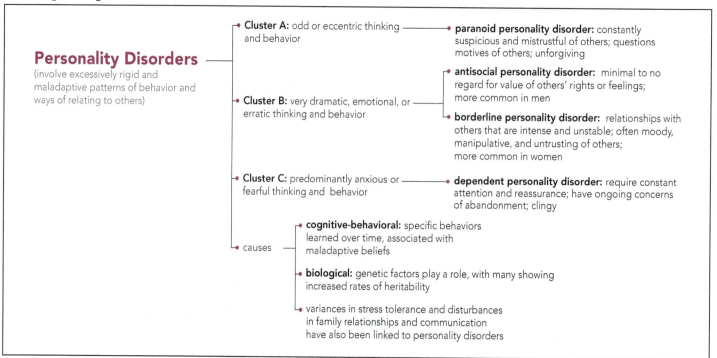

Practice Quiz   How much do you remember?

Pick the best answer.

1. Which of the following is NOT an accurate portrayal of antisocial personality disorder?
   a. People with this disorder are consistently irresponsible and don't keep commitments.
   b. Most people with this disorder are female.
   c. Most people with this disorder are male.
   d. People with this disorder suffer little or no guilt for their criminal acts.
   e. People with this disorder tell lies and use other people.

2. What is the most prominent feature of paranoid personality disorder that makes it sometimes difficult for individuals with this disorder to establish close and long-lasting relationships?
   a. extreme fluctuations in mood
   b. difficulties with interpreting social cues
   c. overreliance on support from other people
   d. ever-present distrust and suspiciousness of others
   e. being selfish and self-centered

3. Robyn has a difficult time making decisions, often relying on her mother to tell her what, when, and how to do things. This stems solely from Robyn's difficulty making decisions and acting independently, not from her mother. Assuming this pattern characterizes many areas of her life, what might best represent Robyn's pattern of thoughts and behavior?
   a. narcissistic personality disorder
   b. dependent personality disorder
   c. borderline personality disorder
   d. antisocial personality disorder
   e. histrionic personality disorder

4. Due to the types and degree of emotions often experienced by people with borderline personality disorder, their personal relationships are often characterized by _____.
   a. periods of domestic bliss
   b. long periods of boredom
   c. long-term stability
   d. intense emotions, impulsivity, and relative instability
   e. deep, genuine commitment

13.14–13.15 Schizophrenia: Altered Reality

> **AP 8.F** Discuss the major diagnostic categories, including neurodevelopmental disorders, neurocognitive disorders, schizophrenia spectrum, and other psychotic disorders, and their corresponding symptoms.

Once known as *dementia praecox*, a Latin-based term meaning "out of one's mind before one's time," schizophrenia was renamed by Eugen Bleuler, a Swiss psychiatrist, to better illustrate the division (*schizo-*) within the brain (*phren*) among thoughts, feelings, and behavior that seems to take place in people with this disorder (Bleuler, 1911; Möller & Hell, 2002). Because the term literally means "split mind," it has often been confused with dissociative identity disorder, which was at one time called "split personality."

13.14 Symptoms of Schizophrenia

13.14 Distinguish between the positive and negative symptoms of schizophrenia.

Today, **schizophrenia** is described as a long-lasting **psychotic** disorder (involving a severe break with reality), in which there is an inability to distinguish what is real from fantasy as well as disturbances in thinking, emotions, behavior, and perception. The disorder typically arises in the late teens or early 20s, affects both males and females, and is consistent across cultures.

Schizophrenia includes several different kinds of symptoms. Disorders in thinking are a common symptom and are called **delusions**. Although delusions are not prominent in everyone with schizophrenia, they are the symptom that most people associate with this disorder. Delusions are false beliefs about the world that the person holds and that tend to remain fixed and unshakable even in the face of evidence that disproves the delusions. Common schizophrenic delusions include *delusions of persecution*, in which people believe that others are trying to hurt them in some way; *delusions of reference*, in which people believe that other people, television characters, and even books are specifically talking to them; *delusions of influence*, in which people believe that they are being controlled by external forces, such as the devil, aliens, or cosmic forces; and *delusions of grandeur* (or *grandiose delusions*), in which people are convinced that they are powerful people who can save the world or have a special mission (American Psychiatric Association, 2013).

schizophrenia
severe disorder in which the person suffers from disordered thinking, bizarre behavior, hallucinations, and inability to distinguish between fantasy and reality.

psychotic
refers to an individual's inability to separate what is real and what is fantasy.

delusions
false beliefs held by a person who refuses to accept evidence of their falseness.

Delusional thinking alone is not enough to merit a diagnosis of schizophrenia, as other symptoms must be present (American Psychiatric Association, 2013). Speech disturbances are common: People with schizophrenia will make up words, repeat words or sentences persistently, string words together on the basis of sounds (called *clanging*, such as "come into house, louse, mouse, mouse and cheese, please, sneeze"), and experience sudden interruptions in speech or thought. Thoughts are significantly disturbed as well, with individuals with schizophrenia having a hard time linking their thoughts together in a logical fashion, and in advanced schizophrenia, they may express themselves in a meaningless and jumbled mixture of words and phrases sometimes referred to as a *word salad*. Attention is also a problem for many people with schizophrenia. They seem to have trouble "screening out" information and stimulation that they don't really need, causing them to be unable to focus on information that is relevant (Asarnow et al., 1991; Luck & Gold, 2008).

People with schizophrenia may also have **hallucinations**, in which they hear voices or see things or people that are not really there. Hearing voices is actually more common and one of the key symptoms in making a diagnosis of schizophrenia (Kuhn & Nasar, 2001; Nasar, 1998). Hallucinations involving touch, smell, and taste are less common but also possible. Emotional disturbances are also a key feature of schizophrenia. **Flat affect** is a condition in which the person shows little or no emotion. Emotions can also be excessive and/or inappropriate—a person might laugh when it would be more appropriate to cry or show sorrow, for example. The person's behavior may also become disorganized and extremely odd. The person may not respond to the outside world and either doesn't move at all, maintaining often odd-looking postures for hours on end, or moves about wildly in great agitation. Both extremes, either wildly excessive movement or total lack thereof, are referred to as **catatonia**. Interestingly, data from the WHO World Mental Health surveys indicate various symptoms related to schizophrenia, and other related diagnoses, are not persistent, with only 32.2 percent of individuals reporting a single psychotic experience in their lifetime and 64 percent reporting no more than five lifetime occurrences (McGrath et al., 2018). Watch the video *Living with a Disorder: Schizophrenia* for an interview with a person experiencing schizophrenia.

hallucinations
false sensory perceptions, such as hearing voices that do not really exist.

flat affect
a lack of emotional responsiveness.

catatonia
disturbed behavior ranging from statue-like immobility to bursts of energetic, frantic movement and talking.

positive symptoms
symptoms of schizophrenia that are excesses of behavior or occur in addition to normal behavior; hallucinations, delusions, and distorted thinking.

negative symptoms
symptoms of schizophrenia that are less than normal behavior or an absence of normal behavior; poor attention, flat affect, and poor speech production.

Watch Living with a Disorder: Schizophrenia

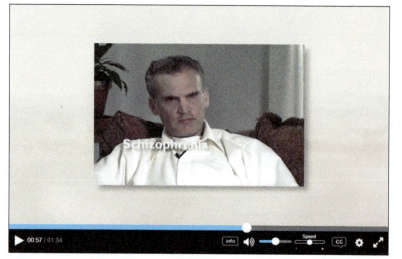

Watch the Video at MyLab Psychology

Another way of describing symptoms in schizophrenia is to group them by the way they relate to normal functioning. **Positive symptoms** appear to reflect an excess or distortion of normal functions, such as hallucinations and delusions. **Negative symptoms** appear to reflect a decrease of normal functions, such as poor attention or lack of affect (American Psychiatric Association, 2013). According to the American Psychiatric Association (2013), at least two or more of the following symptoms must be present frequently for at least 1 month to diagnose schizophrenia: delusions, hallucinations, disorganized speech, negative symptoms, and grossly disorganized or catatonic behavior, and at least one of the two symptoms has to be delusions, hallucinations, or disorganized speech. The video *Positive and Negative Symptoms of Schizophrenia* summarizes the key positive and negative symptoms of the disorder.

13.15 Causes of Schizophrenia

13.15 Evaluate the biological and environmental influences on schizophrenia.

When trying to explain the cause or causes of schizophrenia, biological models and theories prevail, as it appears to be most likely caused by a combination of genetic and environmental factors. This is captured by the neurodevelopmental model, or neurodevelopmental hypothesis, of schizophrenia (Rapoport et al., 2005; Rapoport et al., 2012). Biological explanations of schizophrenia have generated a significant amount of research pointing to genetic origins, prenatal influences such as the mother experiencing viral infections during pregnancy, inflammation in the brain, chemical influences (dopamine, GABA, glutamate, and other neurotransmitters), and brain structural defects (frontal lobe defects, deterioration of neurons, and reduction in white matter integrity) as the causes of schizophrenia (Birnbaum & Weinberger, 2017; Brown & Derkits, 2010; Cardno & Gottesman, 2000; Gottesman & Shields, 1982; Grace, 2016; Harrison, 1999; Kety et al., 1994; Nestor et al., 2008; Rijsdijk et al., 2011; Söderlund et al., 2009). Dopamine was first suspected when amphetamine users began to show schizophrenia-like psychotic symptoms. One of

Watch Positive and Negative Symptoms of Schizophrenia

Watch the **Video** at **MyLab Psychology**

the side effects of amphetamine usage is to increase the release of dopamine in the brain. Drugs used to treat schizophrenia decrease the activity of dopamine in areas of the brain responsible for some of the positive symptoms. However, it is not that simple. The prefrontal cortex (an area of the brain involved in planning and organization of information) of people with schizophrenia has been shown to produce lower levels of dopamine than normal (Harrison, 1999), resulting in attention deficits (Luck & Gold, 2008) and poor organization of thought, negative symptoms of the disorder.

Further support for a biological explanation of schizophrenia comes from studies of the incidence of the disorder across different cultures. If schizophrenia were caused mainly by environmental factors, the expectation would be that rates of schizophrenia would vary widely from culture to culture. There is some variation for immigrants and children of immigrants, but about 7 to 8 individuals out of 1,000 will develop schizophrenia in their lifetime, regardless of the culture (Saha et al., 2005). Based on data from the WHO's World Mental Health Surveys, it appears that approximately 5.8 percent of individuals have had one or more psychotic experiences in their lifetime and approximately 2 percent have had them in the last year (McGrath et al., 2018).

Family, twin, and adoption studies have provided strong evidence that genes are a major means of transmitting schizophrenia. The highest risk for developing schizophrenia if one has a blood relative with the disorder is faced by monozygotic (identical) twins, who share 100 percent of their genetic material, with a risk factor of about 50 percent (Cardno & Gottesman, 2000; Gottesman & Shields, 1976, 1982; Gottesman et al., 1987). Dizygotic twins, who share about 50 percent of their genetic material, have about a 17 percent risk, the same as a child with one parent with schizophrenia. As genetic relatedness decreases, so does the risk (see **Figure 13.6**). Twin studies are not perfect tools, however; identical twins share the same womb but are not necessarily exposed to the same exact prenatal or postnatal environments, causing some to urge caution in interpreting the 50 percent figure; and even twins reared apart are often raised in similar childhood environments (Davis et al., 1995).

Adoption studies also support the genetic basis of schizophrenia (Sullivan, 2005; Tienari et al., 2004). In one study, the biological and adoptive relatives of adoptees with schizophrenia were compared to a control group of adoptees without schizophrenia but from similar backgrounds and conditions (Kety et al., 1994). The adoptees with schizophrenia had relatives with schizophrenia but *only among their biological relatives*. When the prevalence of schizophrenia was compared between the biological relatives of the adoptees with schizophrenia and the biological relatives of the control group, the rate of the disorder in the relatives of the group with schizophrenia was 10 times higher than in the

Figure 13.6 Genetics and Schizophrenia

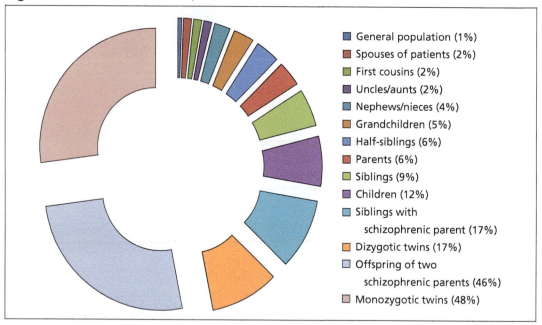

This chart shows a definite pattern: The greater the degree of genetic relatedness, the higher the risk of schizophrenia in individuals related to each other. The only individual to carry a risk even close to that of identical twins (who share 100 percent of their genes) is a person who is the child of two parents with schizophrenia.

Source: Based On Gottesman, I. I. (1991). Schizophrenia genesis: The origins of madness. New York: Freeman

control group (Kety et al., 1994). Research has found a strong genetic risk associated with a gene that plays a role in synaptic pruning during development. In individuals with schizophrenia that have this gene, this process appears to go awry during adolescence, leading to the removal of too many connections between neurons (Sekar et al., 2016). As you can imagine, it is unlikely that a single gene causes schizophrenia; many, possibly over a thousand, genetic variants may actually contribute to the diagnosis (Birnbaum & Weinberger, 2017; Knopik et al., 2017). For example, one recent investigation has identified 237 genes that are expressed differently between individuals with and without schizophrenia (Jaffe et al., 2018).

> There's something I don't understand. If one identical twin has the gene and the disorder, shouldn't the other one always have it, too? Why is the rate only 50 percent?

If schizophrenia were entirely controlled by genes, identical twins would indeed both have the disorder at a risk of 100 percent, not merely 50 percent. Obviously, there is some influence of environment on the development of schizophrenia. One model that has been proposed is the **stress-vulnerability model**, which assumes that persons with the genetic "markers" for schizophrenia have a physical vulnerability to the disorder but will not develop schizophrenia unless they are exposed to environmental or emotional stress at critical times in development (Harrison, 1999; Weinberger, 1987). That would explain why only one twin out of a pair might develop the disorder when both carry the genetic markers for schizophrenia—the life stresses for the affected twin were different from those of the one who remained healthy. The immune system is activated during stress, and one study has found that in recent-onset schizophrenia (the early stages of the disorder), the brain's immune system secretes high levels of an inflammation-fighting substance, indicating a possible infection (Söderlund et al., 2009). Overall, despite the

stress-vulnerability model

explanation of disorder that assumes a biological sensitivity, or vulnerability, to a certain disorder will result in the development of that disorder under the right conditions of environmental or emotional stress.

diagnosis most often occurring in late adolescence or early adulthood, it appears the genetic and epigenetic influences on the brain that lead to the diagnosis of schizophrenia occur primarily during early brain development (Birnbaum & Weinberger, 2017; Jaffe et al., 2018).

Both structural and functional neuroimaging have provided information about how schizophrenia affects the brain or how the brain operates in an individual with schizophrenia. In one study, researchers using *diffusion tensor imaging* (DTI), see Learning Objective 2.5, in addition to other neurological testing, found that, when compared to healthy control participants, participants with schizophrenia showed structural differences in two particular areas of the brain (Nestor et al., 2008). Specifically, a white matter tract called the cingulum bundle (CB) that lies under the cingulate gyrus and links part of the limbic system and another that links the frontal lobe to the temporal lobe were found to have significantly less myelin coating on the axons of the neurons within the bundle. This makes these areas of the brain less efficient in sending neural messages to other cells, resulting in decreased memory and decision-making ability. Examination of differences in functional connectivity between brain areas is providing new information about schizophrenia and its symptoms (Schilbach et al., 2016; Shaffer et al., 2015). For example, an overview of both behavioral and neuroimaging studies suggests individuals with schizophrenia may have impairments in some aspects of social emotional responses and social interactions, while some social processes are seemingly normal (Green et al., 2015). Neuroimaging studies are also being used to help delineate possible brain connectivity differences between disorders. The results of one recent study supported abnormalities in white matter connectivity in schizophrenia, but not in bipolar disorder, as compared to controls (Tonnesen et al., 2018). Measuring cortical thickness and tracking changes in the volume of gray matter and white matter is also providing valuable information about the abnormal patterns of brain development in schizophrenia and other disorders (Gogtay et al., 2008; Gogtay & Thompson, 2010; Goldman et al., 2009; Goodkind et al., 2015).

Concept Map L.O. 13.14, 13.15

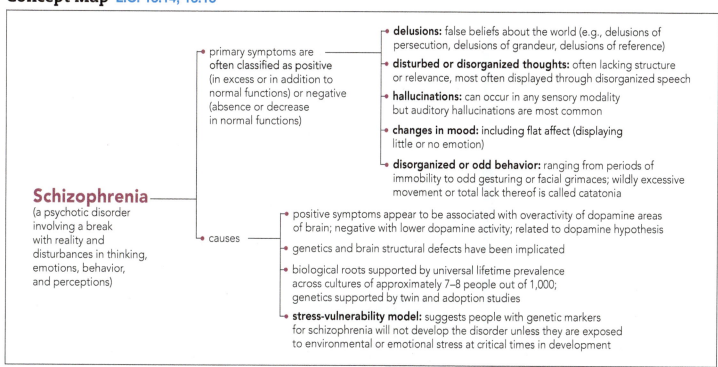

Practice Quiz — How much do you remember?

Pick the best answer.

1. Marty believes that characters in a popular science fiction show are secretly sending him messages. This would be an example of a delusion of _____.
   a. persecution
   b. reference
   c. grandeur
   d. influence
   e. hallucination

2. Nico has suffered from schizophrenia for many years and now resides in a group treatment facility. One day a nurse approaches him and quietly tells him that his sister, who has been fighting cancer for many months, died that morning. Nico has no appreciable facial reaction, and in a very monotone voice says, "Okay." The nurse is not surprised by Nico's lack of response to the awful news, because she knows that _____ is one symptom often seen in those suffering from schizophrenia.
   a. clang associations
   b. perseveration
   c. echolalia
   d. flat affect
   e. rumination

3. Dr. Hahn has several patients with schizophrenia who appear to exhibit excessive or distorted characteristics in relation to what one might consider normal functioning. Specific symptoms include varied hallucinations and multiple delusions. According to the *DSM-5*, these are referred to as _____.
   a. flat affect
   b. positive symptoms
   c. catatonia
   d. negative symptoms
   e. clanging

4. Neuroimaging studies examining potential causes of schizophrenia have discovered that an area of the brain called the _____ appears to have significantly less myelin coating on the axons of its neurons in people with schizophrenia compared to those without the condition.
   a. lateral geniculate nucleus of the thalamus
   b. cingulum bundle
   c. striate nuclei
   d. putamen
   e. arcuate fasciculus

APA Goal 2: Scientific Inquiry and Critical Thinking

Learning More: Psychological Disorders

Addresses APA Learning Objective 2.2: Demonstrate psychology information literacy.

We have covered several areas of research that have prompted various levels of controversy, and for various reasons. You have read about the possible comorbidity of ADHD and bipolar disorders in children. You have also read about genetics research in psychological disorders. How might this knowledge impact your personal behavior or thinking about the disorders themselves or the people they affect? While these topics can certainly raise multiple ethical questions, consider each of them from a psychological information and literacy perspective.

What information would you want to know as the parent of a child with ADHD or bipolar disorder? If you are the spouse or partner of someone with a psychological disorder, how might the knowledge of genetic contributions impact decisions to have children, or what might you want to be mindful of in the children you already have?

Several research studies have been cited and summarized in this chapter. If you wanted to look beyond your text, what sources of information would be most useful to you in trying to learn more about a possible disorder or the contribution of genetics? Where would you find or obtain those sources? What would you look for in each? What are some characteristics of objective data, as opposed to personal reports? Do you know how to interpret a graph or chart? How do you determine if the information is relevant? Can it be generalized to your current situation?

THINKING CRITICALLY 13.3

After reviewing the questions raised in the last paragraph above, identify at least two information sources you would pursue and what data you would want to get from them.

Applying Psychology to Everyday Life

Taking the Worry Out of Exams

13.16 **Identify some ways to overcome test anxiety.**

While not a clinical disorder, test anxiety has caused countless students considerable stress and agony over the years. Remember "psychology student's syndrome"? You may not really have any of the psychological disorders we've discussed in this chapter, but chances are good that you *have* experienced test anxiety a time or two. It is often easier to address milder forms of anxiety *before* they escalate to a more serious disorder.

If you suffer from test anxiety, or know someone who does, what steps can be taken to avoid or minimize its negative impacts? Watch the following and compare your responses to those of the students in the video.

Applying Psychology to Everyday Life Taking the Worry Out of Exams

Watch the **Video** at **MyLab Psychology**

After watching the video, answer the following questions:

1. Students in the video highlighted several strategies for dealing with test anxiety. What were two of them?
2. Other than those mentioned in the video, what are some ways you prevent or minimize the negative impacts of test anxiety?

Chapter Summary

What Is Abnormality?

13.1 Explain how our definition of abnormal behavior and thinking has changed over time.

- Psychopathology is the study of abnormal behavior and psychological dysfunction.
- In ancient times, holes were cut in an ill person's head to let out evil spirits in a process called trephining. Hippocrates believed that mental illness came from an imbalance in the body's four humors, whereas in the early Renaissance period the mentally ill were labeled as witches.
- Abnormality can be characterized as thinking or behavior that is statistically rare, deviant from social norms, causes subjective discomfort, does not allow day-to-day functioning, or causes a person to be dangerous to self or others.
- In the United States, *insanity* is a legal term, not a psychological term.

13.2 Identify models used to explain psychological disorders.

- In biological models of abnormality, the assumption is that mental illnesses are caused by chemical or structural malfunctions in the nervous system.

- Psychodynamic theorists assume that abnormal thinking and behavior stem from repressed conflicts and urges that are fighting to become conscious.
- Behaviorists see abnormal behavior or thinking as learned.
- Cognitive theorists see abnormal behavior as coming from irrational beliefs and illogical patterns of thought.
- The sociocultural perspective conceptualizes all thinking and behavior as the product of learning and shaping of behavior within the context of family, social group, and culture.
- Cultural relativity refers to the need to consider the norms and customs of another culture when diagnosing a person from that culture with a disorder.
- The biopsychosocial model views abnormal thinking and behavior as the sum result of biological, psychological, social, and cultural influences.

13.3 Describe how psychological disorders are diagnosed and classified.

- *The Diagnostic and Statistical Manual of Mental Disorders, Fifth Edition (DSM-5)* is a manual of psychological disorders and their symptoms.
- More than one fifth of all adults over age 18 suffer from a mental disorder in any given year.
- Diagnoses provide a common language for health-care providers, but they may also predispose providers to think about their patients in particular ways.
- In contrast to categorical approaches to diagnosis, research is building related to dimensional assessment of psychopathology across brain, behavior, cognitive, and genetic factors.

Disorders of Mood: The Effect of Affect

13.4 Describe different disorders of mood, including major depressive disorder and bipolar disorders.

- Mood disorders, also called affective disorders, are severe disturbances in emotion.
- Major depressive disorder has a fairly sudden onset of extreme sadness and despair, typically with no obvious external cause. It is the most common of the mood disorders and is more common in women than in men.
- Bipolar disorders are characterized by shifts in mood that may range from normal to manic, with or without episodes of depression (bipolar I disorder) or spans of normal mood interspersed with episodes of major depression and hypomania (bipolar II disorder).

13.5 Compare and contrast potential explanations for depression and other disorders of mood.

- Learning theories link depression to learned helplessness.
- Cognitive theories see depression as the result of distorted, illogical thinking.
- Biological explanations of mood disorders look at the function of serotonin, norepinephrine, and dopamine systems in the brain.
- Mood disorders are more likely to appear in genetically related people, with higher rates of risk for closer genetic relatives.

Disorders of Anxiety, Trauma, and Stress: What, Me Worry?

13.6 Identify different types of anxiety disorders and their symptoms.

- Anxiety disorders are all disorders in which the most dominant symptom is excessive and unrealistic anxiety.
- Phobias are irrational, persistent fears. Three types of phobias are social anxiety disorder (social phobia), specific phobias, and agoraphobia.
- Panic disorder is the sudden and recurrent onset of intense panic for no apparent reason, with all the physical symptoms that can occur in sympathetic nervous system arousal.
- Generalized anxiety disorder is a condition of intense and unrealistic anxiety that lasts 6 months or more.

13.7 Describe obsessive-compulsive disorder and stress-related disorders.

- Obsessive-compulsive disorder consists of an obsessive, recurring thought that creates anxiety and a compulsive, ritualistic, and repetitive behavior or mental action that reduces that anxiety.
- Significant and traumatic stressors can lead to acute stress disorder or posttraumatic stress disorder. The diagnosis differs according to duration and onset but includes symptoms of anxiety, dissociation, nightmares, and reliving the event.

13.8 Identify potential causes of anxiety, trauma, and stress disorders.

- Psychodynamic explanations of anxiety and related disorders point to repressed urges and desires that are trying to come into consciousness, creating anxiety that is controlled by the abnormal behavior.
- Behaviorists state that disordered behavior is learned through both operant conditioning and classical conditioning techniques.
- Cognitive psychologists believe that excessive anxiety comes from illogical, irrational thought processes.
- Biological explanations of anxiety-related disorders include neurotransmitter dysfunction in the nervous system, in particular serotonin, GABA, and norepinephrine, and brain areas such as the amygdala, parts of the frontal lobe, and insula.
- Genetic transmission may be responsible for anxiety-related disorders among related persons.

Dissociative Disorders: Altered Identities

13.9 Differentiate among dissociative amnesia, dissociative fugue, and dissociative identity disorder.

- Dissociative disorders involve a break in consciousness, memory, or both. These disorders include dissociative amnesia, with or without fugue, and dissociative identity disorder.

13.10 Summarize explanations for dissociative disorders.

- Psychodynamic explanations point to repression of memories, seeing dissociation as a defense mechanism against anxiety.
- Cognitive and behavioral explanations see dissociative disorders as a kind of avoidance learning. Biological explanations point to lower-than-normal activity levels in the areas of the brain responsible for body awareness.

Eating Disorders

13.11 Identify the symptoms and risk factors associated with anorexia nervosa, bulimia nervosa, and binge-eating disorder.

- Maladaptive eating problems include anorexia nervosa, bulimia nervosa, and binge-eating disorder.
- Genetics, increased sensitivity to the rewarding value of food, or food-related anxiety, altered brain function, and being female contribute to the risk of being diagnosed with an eating disorder.

Personality Disorders: I'm Okay, It's Everyone Else Who's Weird

13.12 Classify different types of personality disorders.

- Personality disorders are extremely rigid, maladaptive patterns of behavior that prevent a person from having normal social interactions and relationships.
- The *DSM-5* lists 10 primary types of personality disorders across three broad categories.
- In paranoid personality disorder, individuals are constantly suspicious and mistrustful of others.
- In antisocial personality disorder, a person consistently violates the rights of others.
- In borderline personality disorder, a person is moody, unstable in relationships, and suffers from problems with identity.
- In dependent personality disorder, individuals require constant attention and reassurance and have ongoing concerns of abandonment.

13.13 Identify potential causes of personality disorders.

- Cognitive-learning theorists see personality disorders as a set of learned behavior that has become maladaptive—bad habits learned early on in life. Belief systems of the personality-disordered person are seen as illogical.
- Biological relatives of people with personality disorders are more likely to develop similar disorders, supporting a genetic basis for such disorders.
- Biological explanations look at the lower-than-normal stress hormones in antisocial personality disordered persons as responsible for their low responsiveness to threatening stimuli.
- Other possible causes of personality disorders may include disturbances in family communications and relationships, childhood abuse, neglect, overly strict parenting, overprotective parenting, and parental rejection.

Schizophrenia: Altered Reality

13.14 Distinguish between the positive and negative symptoms of schizophrenia.

- Schizophrenia is a split among thoughts, emotions, and behavior. It is a long-lasting psychotic disorder in which reality and fantasy become confused.
- Symptoms of schizophrenia include delusions (false beliefs about the world), hallucinations, emotional disturbances, attentional difficulties, disturbed speech, and disordered thinking.
- Positive symptoms are excesses of behavior associated with increased dopamine activity in some parts of the brain, whereas negative symptoms are deficits in behavior associated with decreased dopamine activity in other parts of the brain.

13.15 Evaluate the biological and environmental influences on schizophrenia.

- Biological explanations for schizophrenia focus on dopamine, structural defects in the brain, and genetic influences. Rates of risk of developing schizophrenia increase drastically as genetic relatedness increases, with the highest risk faced by an identical twin whose twin sibling has schizophrenia.

Applying Psychology to Everyday Life: Taking the Worry Out of Exams

13.16 Identify some ways to overcome test anxiety.

- Test anxiety is the personal experience of possible negative consequences or poor outcomes on an exam or evaluation.
- Some ways to deal with test anxiety are to find an internal motivation, develop strategies for studying and controlling your emotional reactions, and focus on the positive rather than the negative.

Test Yourself: Preparing for the AP Exam

PART I: MULTIPLE-CHOICE QUESTIONS

Directions for Part I: Read each of the questions or incomplete sentences below. Then choose the response that best answers the question or completes the sentence

Pick the best answer.

1. In 1972, a jet carrying a rugby team from Peru crashed high in the snow-covered Andes Mountains. Many of the players survived for more than 2 months by eating the remains of those who died. Psychologists justified their cannibalism because that was the only way they could have survived so long without food. By what definition might their behavior best be classified?
   a. statistical
   b. normative
   c. subjective discomfort
   d. maladaptive
   e. situational context

2. Which of the following is an example of cultural relativity?
   a. Dr. Han believes that the voices his patient is hearing stem from a biological instead of a psychological cause.
   b. Dr. Roland uses a behavioral approach to treat all his clients who are younger than age 10.
   c. While Dr. Howard believes that hypnosis is the best way to understand all disorders, his approach is not shared by his colleagues.
   d. While Dr. Gambon knows that his patient, Aki, believes her anxiety has a biological explanation, in learning more about her family of origin, he suspects it has a psychological cause.
   e. Dr. Jarvie uses cognitive behavioral techniques for any disorder he is qualified to treat.

3. How many axes does the *DSM-5* use to aid mental health professionals in making a diagnosis?
   a. five
   b. one
   c. two
   d. four
   e. ten

4. Which type of depression is the most common type of mood disorder?
   a. bipolar disorder
   b. mania
   c. dysthymia
   d. major depressive disorder
   e. major depressive disorder with a seasonal pattern

5. Behavioral theorists link depression to _____, whereas social cognitive theorists point to _____.
   a. distortions in thinking, learned helplessness
   b. magnification, minimization
   c. biological abnormalities, distortions in thinking
   d. unconscious forces, learned helplessness
   e. learned helplessness, distortions in thinking

6. *Trypanophobia*, also known as a fear of receiving an injection, is an example of _____.
   a. obsession
   b. compulsion
   c. social phobia
   d. anxiety attack
   e. specific phobia

7. Sage hates to go to restaurants for fear that she will be seated in the far back of the restaurant and be unable to get out in case of an emergency. This may be a symptom of _____.
   a. social phobia
   b. claustrophobia
   c. specific phobia
   d. agoraphobia
   e. ablutophobia

8. Val experienced a sudden attack of intense fear when she was boarding a plane with her friends to fly to Mexico for spring break. Val's heart raced, she became dizzy, and she was certain she would die in a plane crash if she boarded the plane. Subsequently she did not go on her trip, and the plane arrived safely in Mexico 3 hours later. Val experienced _____.
   a. a depressive episode
   b. a panic attack
   c. agoraphobia
   d. panic disorder
   e. a fugue state

9. Survivors of natural disasters like Hurricane Michael in 2018 may experience higher incidences of _____.
   a. bipolar disorder
   b. posttraumatic stress disorder
   c. schizophrenia
   d. personality disorders
   e. ADHD

10. Dr. Tyson has been meeting with 9-year-old Noel, whose family lost everything in a tornado. In her initial visit, Noel was diagnosed with acute stress disorder. During a 2-month follow-up with Dr. Tyson, Noel is still exhibiting many of the same symptoms. What should Dr. Tyson do?
    a. Dr. Tyson should tell Noel she is cured so as to speed her recovery.
    b. Dr. Tyson will revise Noel's diagnosis from ASD to posttraumatic stress disorder.
    c. Dr. Tyson will revise Noel's diagnosis from ASD to generalized anxiety disorder.
    d. Dr. Tyson will continue treatment for acute stress disorder for at least 6 months.
    e. Dr. Tyson should refer Noel to another professional.

11. Individuals with bulimia often rationalize that since they have had a single treat, their diet is ruined and therefore they might as well go ahead and eat excessively. Such irrational thinking is an example of the cognitive distortion known as _____.
    a. overgeneralization
    b. all-or-nothing thinking
    c. minimization
    d. magnification
    e. mind reading

12. Binge-eating disorder is different from bulimia in that individuals with binge-eating disorder _____.
    a. typically eat much smaller portions before purging the food
    b. do not typically purge the food they eat
    c. often resort to anorexic methods to rid themselves of the food they have eaten
    d. only purge their food after several binge sessions
    e. are significantly below normal weight

13. At most times, Emory appears to be a fairly pessimistic person. It seems no matter the circumstance, someone always does her wrong. Even during otherwise seemingly kind gestures, she "just knows" the other person must have some hidden agenda. She can tell you, in explicit detail, about every perceived trespass or wrongdoing going back to, at least, middle school. What personality disorder best describes Emory's thinking and behavior?
    a. antisocial personality disorder
    b. paranoid personality disorder
    c. borderline personality disorder
    d. schizotypal personality disorder
    e. dependent personality disorder

14. Darryl has been diagnosed with schizophrenia. He rarely smiles and often shows little emotion in any situation. Psychologists refer to this characteristic as _____.
    a. negative symptoms
    b. flat affect
    c. catatonia
    d. positive symptoms
    e. clanging

15. Dysfunction in what neurotransmitter system was first believed to be the cause of schizophrenia?
    a. GABA
    b. serotonin
    c. norepinephrine
    d. epinephrine
    e. dopamine

PART II: FREE-RESPONSE QUESTION

Directions for Part II: Read the essay question that follows. Then respond to the question in a clear, concise essay. Do not simply list facts. Instead, present a thorough argument based on your critical consideration of the topic. Use of proper terminology is necessary.

Mia, a young woman from Puerto Rico, works as a simulated patient actor. She helps train medical students and resident doctors by presenting specific patterns of symptoms that the trainees should identify to arrive at a proper diagnosis.

Part A

For each of the following terms, describe the pattern of behavior Mia would show in order to present the illness:

- panic disorder
- major depressive disorder
- specific phobia
- generalized anxiety disorder
- acute stress disorder

Part B

Sometimes the trainees find it difficult to diagnose the simulated patient Mia is portraying. For each of the following terms, explain how it might complicate diagnosis of her symptoms:

- cultural syndrome
- ataque de nervios

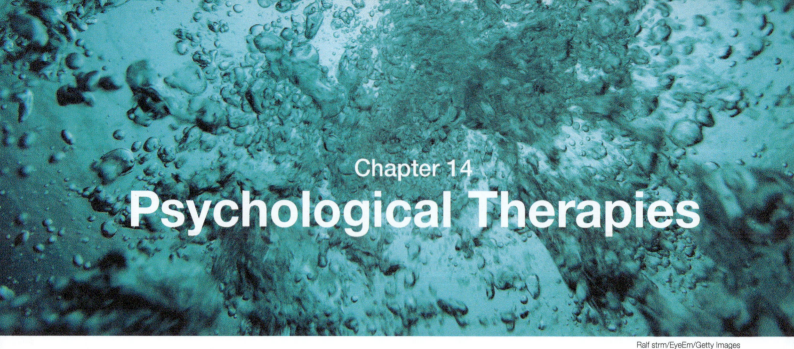

Chapter 14
Psychological Therapies

In your words

What information might be most useful for someone interested in pursuing a particular therapy or treatment for a psychological disorder?

After you have thought about the question, watch the video to see how other students would answer it.

Watch the Video at MyLab Psychology

Why study therapies for psychological disorders?

There are almost as many therapy methods as there are disorders. Correctly matching the type of therapy to the disorder can mean the difference between a cure and a crisis. It is important to know the choices available for treatment and how they relate to the different kinds of disorders so that an informed decision can be made and the best possible outcome can be achieved for mental health and wellness.

Learning Objectives

14.1 Describe how the treatment of psychological disorders has changed throughout history.

14.2 Describe the basic elements of Freud's psychoanalysis and psychodynamic approaches today.

14.3 Identify the basic elements of the humanistic therapies known as person-centered therapy and Gestalt therapy.

14.4 Explain how behavior therapists use classical and operant conditioning to treat disordered behavior.

14.5 Summarize the goals and basic elements of cognitive and cognitive-behavioral therapies.

14.6 Compare and contrast different forms of group therapy.

14.7 Identify the advantages and disadvantages of group therapy.

14.8 Summarize the research on the effectiveness of psychotherapy.

14.9 Identify factors that influence the effectiveness of therapy.

14.10 Categorize types of drugs used to treat psychological disorders.

14.11 Explain how electroconvulsive therapy and psychosurgery are used to treat psychological disorders.

14.12 Identify some of the newer technologies being used to treat psychological disorders.

14.13 Describe how regular physical exercise and spending time in nature may benefit mental health.

14.14 Describe strategies for reducing stigma associated with mental illness or seeking help for a psychological disorder.

14.1 Treatment of Psychological Disorders: Past to Present

14.1 Describe how the treatment of psychological disorders has changed throughout history.

As discussed in Chapter Thirteen, although psychological or social causes might have been identified for some disorders, until the late 1700s, people suffering severe mental illnesses were sometimes thought to be possessed by demons or evil spirits, and the "treatments" to rid the person of these spirits were severe and deadly. Even within the last 200 years, a period of supposedly more "enlightened" awareness, the mentally ill did not always receive humane* treatment.

> I've seen movies about mental hospitals, and they didn't look like great places to be in—how bad was it back then? What did people do with relatives who were ill that way?

The first truly organized effort to do something with mentally ill persons began in England in the middle of the sixteenth century. Bethlehem Hospital in London (later known as "Bedlam") was converted into an asylum (a word meaning "place of safety") for the mentally ill. In reality, the first asylums were little more than prisons where the mentally ill were chained to their beds. "Treatments" consisted of bloodletting (which often led to death or the need for lifelong care), beatings, ice baths in which the person was submerged until passing out or suffering a seizure, and induced vomiting in a kind of spiritual cleansing (Hunt, 1993). This cleansing or purging was meant to rid the body of physical impurities so the person's mind and soul could function more perfectly.

It was not until 1793 that efforts were made to treat the mentally ill with kindness and guidance—known as "moral treatment"—rather than beating them or subjecting them to the harsh physical purging that had been commonplace. It was at this time that Philippe Pinel prompted the unlocking of patient chains at La Bicêtre Asylum in Paris, France, beginning the movement of humane treatment of the mentally ill (Brigham, 1844; Curtis, 1993).

Today, we can group the primary approaches to **therapy** (treatment methods aimed at making people feel better and function more effectively) into two broad categories. One category is based primarily in psychological theory and techniques; people tell the therapist about their problems, and the therapist listens and tries to help them understand those problems or assists them in changing the behaviors related to the problem. The other category uses medical interventions to bring the symptoms under control. Although we can separate treatments into these two larger categories, in actual practice, many effective treatment strategies or treatment plans combine facets of both. Just as there is no one single "cause" of a disorder (Maxmen et al., 2009), different psychological treatments are often used in tandem or combined with biomedical interventions. Furthermore, many psychology professionals do not limit themselves to a single technique and are **eclectic**, using more than one treatment approach or technique to best meet the needs of the people with whom they are working. The fields of clinical psychology and counseling psychology are diverse, and professionals have a wide variety of educational and training experiences. See Learning Objective A.5.

Psychotherapy typically involves an individual, couple, or small group of individuals working directly with a therapist and discussing their concerns or problems. Psychotherapy is an interpersonal intervention, with the therapist and client working together in a manner that is intended to be therapeutic, or that helps the client to be healthier (Wampold, 2010). The goal of most psychotherapy is to help both mentally healthy and psychologically disordered persons understand themselves better (Goin, 2005; Wolberg, 1977).

AP 8.J Describe the central characteristics of psychotherapeutic intervention.

therapy
treatment methods aimed at making people feel better and function more effectively.

eclectic
approach to therapy that results from combining elements of several different approaches or techniques.

psychotherapy
therapy for mental disorders in which a person with a problem talks with a psychological professional.

---

*humane: marked by compassion, sympathy, or consideration for humans (and animals).

Because understanding one's motives and actions is called *insight*, therapies aimed mainly at this goal are called **insight therapies**. A therapy directed more at changing behavior than providing insights into the reasons for that behavior is called **action therapy**. Many psychological professionals use a combination of insight and action therapeutic* methods.

The other main type of therapy uses some biological treatment in the form of a medical procedure to bring about changes in the person's disordered behavior. **Biomedical therapies** include the use of drugs, surgical methods, electric shock treatments, and noninvasive stimulation techniques. It is important to understand that biomedical therapy often eliminates or alleviates the symptoms of a disorder, while psychotherapy addresses issues associated with the disorder and, when used together, these two types of therapy facilitate** each other (Maxmen et al., 2009). For example, when medications are needed, individuals taking the proper medications are going to benefit more from psychotherapy, as their symptoms will be better controlled. Furthermore, psychotherapy, not medication, is going to help them better understand what the symptoms of their disorder are and facilitate adjustment, other coping strategies, and proactive ways of addressing the disorder or its related outcomes (Maxmen et al., 2009). Information and education regarding the efficacy and benefits of psychotherapy are important, especially given the decline in psychological well-being and rise in psychological distress, in particular for those of low socioeconomic status (Goldman et al., 2018), accompanied by trends toward decreasing numbers of individuals seeing or talking to mental health professionals, declines in the use of psychotherapy, alone or in combination with medication, and a rise in medication being used as a standalone treatment (Cohen & Zammitti, 2016; Gaudiano & Ellenberg, 2014).

The National Institute of Mental Health's (NIMH) Research Domain Criteria (RDoC) project was introduced in Chapter Thirteen. See Learning Objective 13.3. Goals of the RDoC project are consistent with attempts to classify psychological disorders along dimensions of brain, cognitive, and behavioral functioning. Instead of simply identifying someone with depression as having a "mental disorder," a psychological professional might be able to better understand the respective cluster of symptoms and features as a subset of disrupted functions and be better able to identify more effective treatment strategies (Insel & Cuthbert, 2015). There are also attempts to identify common factors that bridge a variety of diagnoses. Such "transdiagnostic" factors may include internalizing versus externalizing types of symptoms or brain areas shared by a variety of disorders (Goodkind et al., 2015; Krueger & Eaton, 2015). Overall, these approaches have a lot of potential to improve both diagnostic and treatment approaches in the future.

insight therapies

therapies in which the main goal is helping people to gain insight with respect to their behavior, thoughts, and feelings.

action therapy

therapy in which the main goal is to change disordered or inappropriate behavior directly.

biomedical therapies

therapies that directly affect the biological functioning of the body and brain; therapies for mental disorders in which a person with a problem is treated with biological or medical methods to relieve symptoms.

Concept Map L.O. 14.1

Treatment of Psychological Disorders

- **early interventions**
  - historically, psychological or social causes identified for some disorders; for others, individuals with mental illness were believed to be possessed by demons or evil spirits
  - organized treatment began in England around the middle 1500s
  - Pinel started the "moral treatment" movement in France
- **modern treatments**
  - **psychotherapy:** based on psychological techniques, individuals talk about their problems and the therapist assists them in understanding and changing behavior
    - insight therapies
    - action therapies
  - **biomedical therapy:** uses medical interventions to bring symptoms under control

---

*therapeutic: providing or assisting in a cure.
**facilitate: to assist, make possible, or make easier.

Practice Quiz — How much do you remember?

Pick the best answer.

1. One of the first therapists to begin a movement toward the humane treatment of patients was _____.
   a. Robert Fleury
   b. Philippe Pinel
   c. Josef Breuer
   d. Sigmund Freud
   e. Alfred Adler

2. Psychotherapies that attempt to increase the understanding of a client's motives are known as _____ therapies.
   a. psychoanalytic
   b. insight
   c. action
   d. biomedical
   e. activation

3. Jim has decided to seek psychotherapy for some personal difficulties he has been having. While on the telephone with one possible clinician, he asks her to describe the kind of treatment approach she uses with clients. "I don't limit myself to a single theory or approach," the therapist answers. "Instead I operate in a(n) _____ fashion, integrating various treatment approaches based on the specific needs of each client."
   a. atheoretical
   b. eclectic
   c. Gestalt
   d. supratheoretical
   e. accommodating

4. Which of the following is *not* one of the main types of therapy noted by your text that helps people improve their overall functioning?
   a. insight therapy
   b. regressive therapy
   c. action therapy
   d. biomedical therapy
   e. combined psychotherapy and biomedical therapy

AP 8.L Describe major treatment orientations used in therapy and how those orientations influence therapeutic planning.

14.2–14.3 Insight Therapies: Psychodynamic and Humanistic Approaches

We'll begin our discussion of psychotherapy with two types of insight therapies: psychodynamic therapy and humanistic therapy. While these approaches use different methods, they both strive to gain an understanding of one's motives and actions.

AP 8.K Identify the contributions of major figures in psychological treatment.

14.2 Psychotherapy Begins: Freud's Psychoanalysis

14.2 Describe the basic elements of Freud's psychoanalysis and psychodynamic approaches today.

💬 So what exactly happens in psychoanalysis? I've heard lots of stories about it, but what's it really like?

In a sense, Freud took the sixteenth-century method of physical cleansing to a different level. Instead of a physical purge, cleansing for Freud meant removing all the "impurities" of the unconscious mind that he believed were responsible for his patients' psychological and nervous disorders. (Freud was a medical doctor and referred to the people who came to him for help as "patients.") The impurities of the unconscious mind were considered to be disturbing thoughts, socially unacceptable desires, and immoral urges that originated in the id, the part of the personality that is itself unconscious and driven by basic needs for survival and pleasure. See Learning Objective 12.1.

PSYCHOANALYSIS Freud believed that his patients used these unconscious thoughts to prevent anxiety, and as such, the thoughts would not be easily brought into conscious awareness. Freud designed a therapy technique to help his patients feel more relaxed, open, and able to explore their innermost feelings without fear of embarrassment or rejection. This method was called *psychoanalysis*, and it is an insight therapy that emphasizes revealing the unconscious conflicts, urges, and desires that are assumed to cause disordered emotions and behavior (Freud, 1904a, 1904b; Mitchell & Black, 1996). This is the original reason for the couch in Freud's version of psychoanalysis; people lying on the couch were more relaxed and would, Freud thought, feel more dependent and childlike, making it easier for them to "get at" those early childhood memories. An additional plus was that he could sit behind the patients at the head of the couch and take notes. Without the patients being able to see his reactions to what they said, they remained unaffected by his reactions.

Freud also made use of two techniques to try to reveal the repressed information in his patients' unconscious minds. These techniques were the interpretation of dreams and allowing patients to talk freely about anything that came to mind.

DREAM INTERPRETATION *Dream interpretation*, or the analysis of the elements within a patient's reported dream, formed a large part of Freud's psychoanalytic method. See Learning Objective 4.7. Freud believed repressed material often surfaced in dreams, although in symbolic form. The *manifest content* of the dream was the actual dream and its events, but the **latent content** was the hidden, symbolic meaning of those events that would, if correctly interpreted, reveal the unconscious conflicts that were creating the nervous disorder (Freud, 1900).

FREE ASSOCIATION The other technique for revealing the unconscious mind was a method originally devised by Freud's coworker, Josef Breuer (Breuer & Freud, 1895). Breuer encouraged his patients to freely say whatever came into their minds without fear of being negatively evaluated or condemned. As the patients talked, they began to reveal things that were loosely associated with their flow of ideas, often revealing what Breuer felt were hidden, unconscious concerns. Freud adopted this method of **free association**, believing that repressed impulses and other material were trying to "break free" into consciousness and would eventually surface using this technique.

RESISTANCE AND TRANSFERENCE Other components of Freud's original psychoanalytic method were **resistance** (the point at which the patient becomes unwilling to talk about certain topics) and **transference** (when the therapist becomes a symbol of a parental authority figure from the past). Therapists can also experience *countertransference*, in which the therapist has a transference reaction to the patient. This reaction might not always be to the benefit of the patient. As in all of the therapeutic approaches, peer and professional supervision helps therapists recognize potential issues in providing effective therapy.

EVALUATION OF PSYCHOANALYSIS AND PSYCHODYNAMIC APPROACHES Freud's original theory, on which he based his interpretations of his patients' revelations, has been criticized as having several flaws, which were discussed in Chapter Twelve. These included the lack of scientific research to support his claims, his unwillingness to believe some of the things revealed by his patients when those revelations did not fit into his view of the world, and his almost obsessive need to assume that problems with sex and sexuality were at the heart of nearly every nervous disorder.

Few psychoanalysts today still use Freud's original methods, which could take years to produce results. The couch is gone, and the *client* (a term used to support the active role of the person seeking help and to avoid implying "sickness," as might result when using the term *patient*) may sit face to face with the therapist. The client may also stand or walk about. Rather than remaining quiet until the client says something revealing, the modern psychoanalyst is far more **directive**, asking questions, suggesting helpful behavior, and giving opinions and interpretations earlier in the relationship, which helps speed up the therapeutic process. Today's psychoanalysts also focus

latent content
the symbolic or hidden meaning of dreams.

free association
psychoanalytic technique in which a patient was encouraged to talk about anything that came to mind without fear of negative evaluations.

resistance
occurring when a patient becomes reluctant to talk about a certain topic, by either changing the subject or becoming silent.

transference
in psychoanalysis, the tendency for a patient or client to project positive or negative feelings for important people from the past onto the therapist.

directive
therapy in which the therapist actively gives interpretations of a client's statements and may suggest certain behavior or actions.

AP 8.Q Compare and contrast different treatment methods.

Psychotherapy often takes place one on one, with a client and therapist exploring various issues together to achieve deeper insights or to change undesirable behavior.

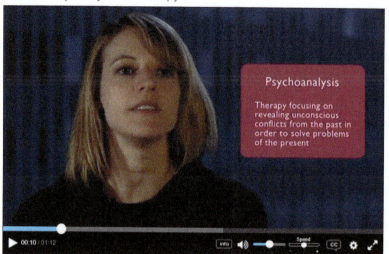

Watch Psychodynamic Therapy

Watch the Video at MyLab Psychology

less on the id as the motivator of behavior, instead looking more at the ego or sense of self as the motivating force behind all actions, and some more on basic relationship issues, including the relationship between the therapist and client (McWilliams, 2016; Prochaska & Norcross, 2014). Some psychoanalysts also focus on the process of transference more than on other typical aspects of traditional psychoanalysis, leading to the more method called **psychodynamic therapy**. Psychodynamic therapy is typically shorter in duration than traditional psychoanalysis. Watch the video *Psychodynamic Therapy* to learn more about the history and practice of this therapy.

Even so, all of the psychodynamic techniques require the client to be fairly intelligent and verbally able to express his or her ideas, feelings, and thoughts effectively. People who are extremely withdrawn or who suffer from the more severe psychotic disorders are not good candidates for this form of psychotherapy. People who have nonpsychotic adjustment disorders, such as anxiety, *somatic symptom and related disorders* (experiencing physical symptoms such as pain or fatigue accompanied by psychological distress about the physical symptoms or disruption in daily life [American Psychiatric Association, 2013]), or dissociative disorders, are more likely to benefit from psychodynamic therapy.

Interpersonal psychotherapy (IPT) is a psychotherapy developed to address depression. It is an insight therapy focusing on relationships of the individual with others and the interplay between mood and the events of everyday life (Bleiberg & Markowitcz, 2014). It is based on the interpersonal theories of Adolph Meyer and Harry Stack Sullivan along with the attachment theory of John Bowlby and focuses on interpersonal relationships and functioning (Bleiberg & Markowitcz, 2014). It is one of the few theories derived from psychodynamic thinking that does have some research support for its effectiveness in treating depression, particularly when combined with medication (Mufson et al., 2004; Reynolds et al., 1999). Given the prevalence of interpersonal issues and depression in eating disorders, IPT has been used with anorexia nervosa (AN), bulimia nervosa (BN), and binge-eating disorder (BED), although research to date suggests it appears to be a better option and has greater efficacy for BN and BED than for AN (Wilfley & Eichen, 2017). See Learning Objective 13.11. Despite its origins, IPT is not considered to be a psychodynamic therapy, as it combines aspects of humanistic and cognitive-behavioral therapies, making it truly eclectic.

14.3 Humanistic Therapy: To Err Is Human

14.3 Identify the basic elements of the humanistic therapies known as person-centered therapy and Gestalt therapy.

Unlike psychodynamic therapists, humanistic theorists do not focus on unconscious, hidden conflicts. Instead, humanists focus on conscious, subjective experiences of emotion and people's sense of self as well as the more immediate experiences in their daily lives rather than early childhood experiences of the distant past (Cain & Seeman, 2001; Rowan, 2001; Schneider et al., 2001). See Learning Objective 1.3. Humanistic therapy emphasizes the importance of the choices made by individuals and the potential to change one's behavior. The two most common therapy styles based on humanistic theory are Carl Rogers's person-centered therapy and Fritz Perls's Gestalt therapy; both are primarily insight therapies.

psychodynamic therapy
a newer and more general term for therapies based on psychoanalysis with an emphasis on transference, shorter treatment times, and a more direct therapeutic approach.

interpersonal psychotherapy (IPT)
form of therapy for depression that incorporates multiple approaches and focuses on interpersonal problems.

TELL ME MORE: ROGERS'S PERSON-CENTERED THERAPY Chapter Twelve discussed the basic elements of Rogers's theory of personality, which emphasizes the sense of self (Rogers, 1961). To sum it up quickly, Rogers proposed that everyone has a *real self* (how people see their actual traits and abilities) and an *ideal self* (how people think they should be). The more closely the real and ideal selves match up, the happier and more well-adjusted the person. To have these two self-concepts match, people need to receive *unconditional positive regard*, which is love, warmth, respect, and affection without any conditions attached. If people think there are conditions put on the love and affection they receive, their ideal selves will be determined by those conditions and become more difficult to achieve, resulting in a mismatch of selves and unhappiness.

> So the key to getting over unhappiness would be to get the real and ideal selves closer together? How does a therapist do that?

Rogers believed the goal of the therapist should be to provide the unconditional positive regard that has been absent from the troubled person's life and to help the person recognize the discrepancies between the real and ideal selves. He also believed the person would actually have to do most of the work, talking out problems and concerns in an atmosphere of warmth and acceptance from the therapist, so he originally called the people in this therapy relationship "clients" instead of "patients," to put the therapeutic relationship on a more equal footing. As a result, Rogers's therapy is very **nondirective** because the person actually does all the real work, with the therapist merely acting as a sounding board. However, therapists may help individuals redirect or reallocate their attention to focus on feelings not fully processed previously, assisting the client by serving as an auxiliary information processor (Anderson, 1974; Prochaska & Norcross, 2014). Later, the term *client* was changed to the even more neutral term *person*. His therapy is now called **person-centered therapy** because the person is truly the center of the process.

BASIC ELEMENTS Rogers (1961) saw three key elements as being necessary in any successful person–therapist relationship.

- **Authenticity** The therapist must show **authenticity** in a genuine, open, and honest response to the individual. It is easier for some professionals to "hide" behind the role of the therapist, as was often the case in psychoanalysis. In person-centered therapy, the therapist has to be able to tolerate a person's differences without being judgmental.
- **Unconditional Positive Regard** Another key element of person-centered therapy is the warm, accepting, completely uncritical atmosphere that the therapist must create for the people they work with. Having respect for an individual and their feelings, values, and goals, even if they are different from those of the therapist, is called **unconditional positive regard**.
- **Empathy** Last, the therapist needs to be able to see the world through the eyes of the person with whom they are working. The therapist has to be able to acknowledge what people are feeling and experiencing by using a kind of understanding called **empathy**. This involves listening carefully and closely to what individuals are saying and trying to feel what they feel. Therapists must also avoid getting their own feelings mixed up with their clients' feelings (e.g., countertransference).

A person-centered therapist typically responds in a way that seeks clarification and demonstrates attempts to understand the experience of the individual. **Reflection** refers to a technique therapists use to allow clients to continue to talk and have insights without

AP 8.K Identify the contributions of major figures in psychological treatment.

nondirective
therapy style in which the therapist remains relatively neutral and does not interpret or take direct actions with regard to the client, instead remaining a calm, nonjudgmental listener while the client talks.

person-centered therapy
a nondirective insight therapy based on the work of Carl Rogers in which the client does much of the talking and the therapist listens.

authenticity
the genuine, open, and honest response of the therapist to the client.

unconditional positive regard
positive regard that is given without conditions or strings attached; in person-centered therapy, referring to the warm, respectful, and accepting atmosphere created by the therapist for the client.

empathy
the ability of the therapist to understand the feelings of the client.

reflection
therapy technique in which the therapist restates what the client says rather than interpreting those statements.

A Rogerian person-centered therapist listens with calm acceptance to anything the client says. A sense of empathy with the client's feelings is also important.

the interference of the therapist's interpretations and possible biases. Reflection is literally a kind of mirroring of clients' statements. Here's an example from one of Rogers's own therapy sessions with a client (Meador & Rogers, 1984, p. 143):

CLIENT: I just ain't no good to nobody, never was, and never will be.
ROGERS: Feeling that now, hmm? That you're just no good to yourself, no good to anybody. Never will be any good to anybody. Just that you're completely worthless, huh?—Those really are lousy feelings. Just feel that you're no good at all, hmm?
CLIENT: Yeah.

MOTIVATIONAL INTERVIEWING A variation of person-centered therapy is *motivational interviewing*, or MI (Miller & Rollnick, 2002), which has been described by Hal Arkowitz and William R. Miller as "client-centered therapy with a twist" (p. 4). In contrast to person-centered therapy, MI has specific goals: to reduce ambivalence about change and to increase intrinsic motivation to bring that change about (Arkowitz & Miller, 2008). As originally conceived, the four principles of MI were to express empathy, develop discrepancy between the client's present behaviors and values, roll with resistance, and support the client's self-efficacy (Miller & Rollnick, 2002). While still true to its foundations, MI has recently been updated and now consists of four broad processes: *engaging* with the client to develop a therapeutic working alliance, *focusing* on the goals and direction of counseling, *evoking* and eliciting the client's motivation to change, and when the client is ready to change, *planning* how to implement change (Miller & Arkowitz, 2015; Miller & Rollnick, 2013). The idea of resistance has been recast, with a focus on differentiating *sustain talk*, conversations reinforcing no change, from *change talk*, conversations leading to improvement (Corbett, 2016; Miller & Rollnick, 2013). Although it was originally developed and validated as effective for addictive disorders, it has also been useful in the treatment of anxiety and mood disorders (Arkowitz & Miller, 2008; Barlow et al., 2013), with applications to both health and mental health increasing (Corbett, 2016).

GESTALT THERAPY Another therapy based on humanistic ideas is called **Gestalt therapy**. The founder of this therapeutic method is Fritz Perls, who believed that people's problems often stemmed from hiding important parts of their feelings from themselves. If some part of a person's personality, for example, is in conflict with what society says is acceptable, the person might hide that aspect behind a false "mask" of socially acceptable behavior. As happens in Rogers's theory when the real and ideal selves do not match, in Gestalt theory the person experiences unhappiness and maladjustment when the inner self does not match the mask (Perls, 1951, 1969).

> That sounds pretty much like the same thing, only with slightly different words. How is Gestalt therapy different from person-centered therapy?

The two therapy types are similar because they are both based in humanism. But whereas person-centered therapy is nondirective, allowing the client to talk out concerns and eventually come to insights with only minimal guidance from the therapist, Gestalt therapists are very directive, often confronting clients about the statements they have made. This means that a Gestalt therapist does more than simply reflect back clients' statements; instead, a Gestalt therapist actually leads clients through a number of planned experiences, with the goal of helping clients to become more aware of their own feelings and take responsibility for their own choices in life, both now and in the past. These experiences might include a dialogue that clients have with their own conflicting feelings in which clients actually argue both sides of those feelings. Clients may talk with

Gestalt therapy
form of directive insight therapy in which the therapist helps clients to accept all parts of their feelings and subjective experiences, using leading questions and planned experiences such as role-playing.

an empty chair to reveal their true feelings toward the person represented by the chair or take on the role of a parent or other person with whom they have a conflict so that the clients can see things from the other person's point of view. The Gestalt therapist pays attention to body language as well as to the events going on in the client's life at the time of therapy. Unlike psychoanalysis, which focuses on the *hidden past*, Gestalt therapy focuses on the *denied past*. Gestalt therapists do not talk about the unconscious mind. They believe everything is conscious but that it is possible for some people to simply refuse to "own up" to having certain feelings or to deal with past issues. By looking at the body language, feelings both stated and unstated, and the events in the life of the client, the therapist gets a *gestalt*—a whole picture—of the client.

In Gestalt therapy, it is not unusual to find a client talking to an empty chair. The chair represents some person from the past with whom the client has unresolved issues; this is the opportunity to deal with those issues.

EVALUATION OF THE HUMANISTIC THERAPIES Humanistic therapies have been used to treat psychological disorders, help people make career choices, deal with workplace problems, and counsel married couples. Person-centered therapy in particular can be a very "hands-off" form of therapy because it is so nondirective: Most often, there's nothing the therapist says that the client has not already said, so the therapist runs a lower risk of misinterpretation. However, omission or not reflecting some things back might be a source of error.

AP 8.Q Compare and contrast different treatment methods.

As noted in Chapter Twelve, how people view themselves is central to many approaches in psychology (Leary & Toner, 2015). Many therapeutic approaches benefit from humanistic influences, namely the importance of the client–therapist relationship, including Rogers's concepts of unconditional positive regard and how much empathy clients perceive in the therapist (Angus et al., 2014; Goldfried, 2007; Watson et al., 2014). Humanistic therapies have some of the same drawbacks as Freudian psychoanalysis and other forms of modern psychodynamic therapy. Much of the research on this approach, at least the earlier studies, relied heavily on case studies. Also, people must be intelligent, verbal, and able to express their thoughts, feelings, and experiences in a logical manner. This makes humanistic therapies a somewhat less practical choice for treating a disorder like schizophrenia, at least as a first line of treatment. However, the data from a collection of studies are promising and suggest humanistic therapy approaches may be beneficial for individuals with schizophrenia and other psychotic disorders (Elliott et al., 2013). Furthermore, humanistic approaches are associated with large pre–post client changes that are maintained for a significant period of time, appear to be statistically equivalent to other approaches for some conditions, and have demonstrated positive effects for some in particular, such as moderate depression, perinatal depression, and interpersonal and relationship problems (Angus et al., 2014; Elliott et al., 2013).

Concept Map L.O. 14.2, 14.3

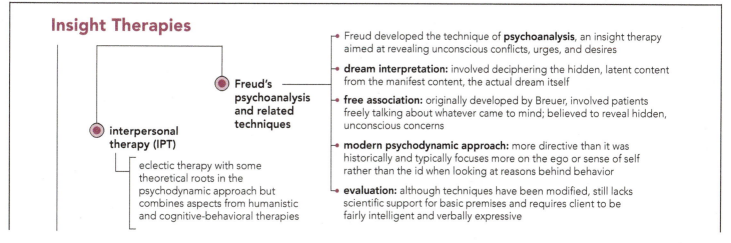

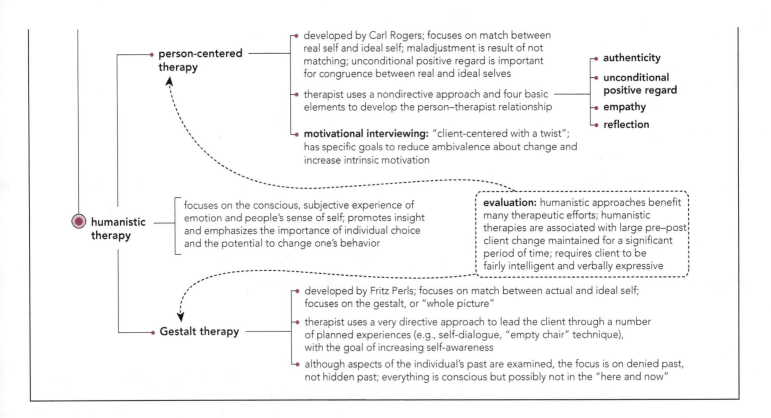

Practice Quiz — How much do you remember?

Pick the best answer.

1. Although the term may apply to many therapies, "transference" is typically associated with _____ therapies.
   a. behavioral
   b. cognitive
   c. humanistic
   d. biomedical
   e. psychodynamic

2. Motivational interviewing is an alternative therapy to what therapeutic approach?
   a. psychodynamic therapy
   b. group therapy
   c. Gestalt therapy
   d. person-centered therapy
   e. behavior therapy

3. Dr. Farmer is directive in his approach with clients. He pays close attention to body language and often focuses on a client's denied past. What type of therapeutic approach is Dr. Farmer using?
   a. humanistic approach
   b. Gestalt approach
   c. behavioral approach
   d. group approach
   e. psychodynamic approach

4. In which of the following cases would a humanistic approach probably be least effective as the first choice of treatment?
   a. Jean, a homemaker who is experiencing relationship issues in her marriage
   b. Mandy, a corporate executive who suffers from marked delusions and active auditory hallucinations
   c. Wendy, a professional musician who feels worthless and suffers from moderate depression
   d. Louise, a university professor who has feelings of inadequacy
   e. Dina, a high school senior who is experiencing mild depression

AP 8.L Describe major treatment orientations used in therapy and how those orientations influence therapeutic planning.

14.4–14.5 Action Therapies: Behavior Therapies and Cognitive Therapies

While insight therapies strive to understand the motives behind one's behavior, action therapies are focused on changing the behavior itself. In behavior therapies, the goal is to change behavior through the use of learning techniques, while cognitive therapies strive to change maladaptive thoughts.

14.4 Behavior Therapies: Learning One's Way to Better Behavior

14.4 Explain how behavior therapists use classical and operant conditioning to treat disordered behavior.

AP 8.K Identify the contributions of major figures in psychological treatment.

> 💬 The last chapter talked about how behaviorists have a very different way of looking at abnormality—it's all learned. So do behaviorists do any kind of therapy?

That's right—the basic concept behind behaviorism is that all behavior, whether "normal" or "abnormal," is learned through the same processes of classical and operant conditioning. Unlike the psychodynamic and humanistic therapies, **behavior therapies** are action based rather than insight based. Their aim is to change behavior through the use of the same kinds of learning techniques that people (and animals) use to learn any new responses. The abnormal or undesirable behavior is not seen as a symptom of anything else but rather is the problem itself. Learning created the problem, and new learning can correct it (Onken et al., 1997; Skinner, 1974; Sloan & Mizes, 1999).

THERAPIES BASED ON CLASSICAL CONDITIONING Classical conditioning is the learning of involuntary responses by pairing a stimulus that normally causes a particular response with a new, neutral stimulus. After enough pairings, the new stimulus will also cause the response to occur. See Learning Objectives 5.2 and 5.3. Through classical conditioning, old and undesirable automatic responses can be replaced by desirable ones. There are several techniques that have been developed using this type of learning to treat disorders such as phobias, anxiety disorders, and obsessive-compulsive disorder.

Using learning techniques to change undesirable behavior and increase desirable behavior has a long history (Hughes, 1993; Lovaas, 1987; Lovaas et al., 1966). Originally called *behavior modification*, the more recent adaptation of these techniques is *applied behavior analysis*. The newer approach highlights the need for a *functional analysis*, systematically determining the reasons for and consequences influencing the behavior to be modified, which is then followed by the use of conditioning techniques to modify the behavior. Watch the video *Behavioral Therapy* to learn more about the use of these techniques.

Watch Behavioral Therapy

👁 Watch the Video at MyLab Psychology

SYSTEMATIC DESENSITIZATION **Systematic desensitization**, in which a therapist guides the client through a series of steps meant to reduce fear and anxiety, is normally used to treat phobic disorders and consists of a three-step process (Wolpe, 1958). First, the client must learn to relax through deep muscle relaxation training. Next, the client and the therapist construct a list, beginning with the object or situation that causes the least fear to the client, eventually working up to the object or situation that produces the greatest degree of fear. Finally, under the guidance of the therapist, the client begins with the first item on the list that causes minimal fear and looks at it, thinks about it, or actually confronts it, all while remaining in a relaxed state. By pairing the old conditioned stimulus (the fear object) with a new relaxation response that is incompatible* with the emotions and physical arousal associated with fear, the person's fear is reduced and relieved. The person then proceeds to the next item on the list of fears (called a *hierarchy of fears*) until the phobia is gone (see **Table 14.1**).

behavior therapies
action therapies based on the principles of classical and operant conditioning and aimed at changing disordered behavior without concern for the original causes of such behavior.

systematic desensitization
behavior technique used to treat phobias, in which a client is asked to make a list of ordered fears and taught to relax while concentrating on those fears.

---

*incompatible: referring to two or more things that cannot exist together or at the same time.

Table 14.1 Fear Hierarchy

Situation	Fear Level
Being bitten by a rabbit	100
Petting a rabbit on the head	90
Petting a rabbit on the back	80
Holding a rabbit	70
Touching a rabbit held by someone else	60
Seeing someone I trust hold a rabbit	50
Being in a room with a rabbit	40
Thinking about petting a rabbit	30
Looking at pictures of rabbits	20
Watching the movie *Hop*	10

Items are ranked by level of fear from most fearful, Fear = 100, to least fearful, Fear = 0.

EXPOSURE THERAPIES Behavioral techniques that introduce the client to situations, under carefully controlled conditions, which are related to their anxieties or fears are called **exposure therapies**. Exposure can be accomplished through a variety of routes and is intended to promote new learning. It can be *in vivo* ("in life"), where the client is exposed to the actual anxiety-related stimulus; *imaginal*, where the client visualizes or imagines the stimulus; and even *virtual*, where virtual reality (VR) technology is used (Barlow et al., 2015; Najavits & Anderson, 2015). For example, if Chang-sun has social phobia (fairly rare for South Korean males at a lifetime prevalence of only about 0.4 percent; Cho et al., 2015), for in vivo exposure he might have to attend a social event; for imaginal exposure he might be asked to visualize himself attending a social event; and for virtual exposure, Chang-sun might experience a social event, such as attending a dinner party, through VR technology.

Exposure methods can introduce the feared stimulus gradually or quite suddenly. A gradual, or *graded*, exposure involves the client and therapist developing a fear hierarchy as in systematic desensitization: Exposure begins at the least feared event and progresses through to the most feared, similar to desensitization. If the exposure is rapid and intense, it begins with the most feared event and is called **flooding** (Gelder, 1976; Olsen, 1975). Flooding is used under very controlled conditions and, like graded exposure, produces extinction of the conditioned fear response by preventing an escape or avoidance response (e.g., Chang-sun would not be allowed to leave the party).

A primary exposure-based treatment for PTSD is *prolonged exposure* (PE), which involves both exposure and components of *cognitive-behavioral therapy*. See Learning Objective 14.5. The approach involves four primary components: education about PTSD and common trauma reactions, learning to breathe in a relaxing and calming way, repeated *in vivo* exposure to safe activities, objects, situations, or places that are causing the person anxiety, and repeated, prolonged imaginal exposure to memories associated with the trauma (Foa et al., 2007). As with many other treatments for trauma, a primary goal of treatment is to help individuals approach memories and stimuli they fear or avoid to overcome their anxiety and to process the emotions associated with the trauma (Foa et al., 2007; Ruzek et al., 2014). Preliminary research suggests PE and successful remission of PTSD may lead to changes in brain structures associated with the positive changes, such as the anterior cingulate cortex (Helpman et al., 2016).

exposure therapies
behavioral techniques that expose individuals to anxiety- or fear-related stimuli, under carefully controlled conditions, to promote new learning.

flooding
technique for treating phobias and other stress disorders in which the person is rapidly and intensely exposed to the fear-provoking situation or object and prevented from making the usual avoidance or escape response.

Eye-movement desensitization and reprocessing, or EMDR, is another therapy sometimes used in the treatment of PTSD and other trauma-related disorders. As originally formulated, it involves very brief and repeated imaginal flooding, cognitive reprocessing and desensitization of the fearful event, and rapid eye movements or other bilateral stimulation (Shapiro, 2001, 2012). However, it remains a somewhat controversial therapy for some, as it evolved from the founder's personal observation, not psychological theory or modification of techniques for other disorders, and research has suggested the eye movements or other bilateral stimulation serve little to no purpose (Lilienfeld et al., 2015b; Monson et al., 2014). The actual effects of eye movements in EMDR are still unknown but are purported to have additive effects to the treatment (Solomon & Shapiro, 2008). The results from one recent meta-analysis support the use of eye movements, especially by trained individuals using manualized, standardized EMDR treatment approaches (Lee & Cuijpers, 2013). However, in contrast, results from a recent laboratory study suggest the type of eye movements used in EMDR might have adverse effects in some situations in that they may make some individuals more susceptible to misinformation or false memories (Houben et al., 2018). See Learning Objective 6.9.

Some published treatment guidelines provide conditional recommendations for EMDR in the treatment of PTSD in adults (American Psychological Association, 2017), while others provide strong recommendations for its use in PTSD (Department of Veterans Affairs Department of Defense, 2017). Overall, when EMDR is compared to other therapies, such as PE, there does not appear to be any differences in treatment outcomes or the length of treatment for PTSD (Najavits & Anderson, 2015).

Exposure therapy eventually results in extinction of the conditioned fear. While *in vivo* and imaginal approaches are useful, VR technology has the potential to offer unique advantages. Using VR likely ensures the person being treated cannot avoid exposure, as the sight and sound of the animal, open spaces, or whatever the phobia involves is always right in front of him or her. For example, one study examined the use of exposure therapy using VR technology with a specific phobia of small animals, namely spiders and cockroaches (Botella et al., 2016). Participants wore VR goggles and were able to interact with the spiders or cockroaches virtually. The control group participants were exposed to real spiders or cockroaches. After the VR and *in vivo* exposure treatments, both conditions resulted in significant improvements (Botella et al., 2016). There has also been preliminary research with VR paired with an automated virtual coach, as opposed to clients working with a real therapist, for treating acrophobia (Freeman et al., 2018).

Posttraumatic stress disorder (PTSD) is another mental health issue in which VR technology is being investigated. Cases of this disorder are rising (and with the tragic world events discussed in Chapter Thirteen and other such stressors, psychologists expect the number of PTSD cases to continue to rise), and traditional treatments are not always effective. Although still a relatively new area of research, evidence suggests VR psychotherapy may be as effective as traditional exposure methods in the treatment of PTSD and may especially be appealing for clients who do not want to pursue traditional exposure methods or techniques (Goncalves et al., 2012; Motraghi et al., 2014). Overall, it appears VR-enhanced interventions appear to be as effective as traditional in vivo or imaginal approaches, at least in the treatment of anxiety, depression, PTSD, and social anxiety, but are not more effective than traditional approaches (Chesham et al., 2018; Fodor et al., 2018; Reger et al., 2016).

Exposure and response prevention (EX/RP), or exposure and ritual prevention, is one of the most effective strategies for treating OCD (Bornheimer, 2015; Fisher & Wells, 2005; Lilienfeld et al., 2013; Strauss et al., 2015). Grounded in behavioral theory and the core component of exposure, like PE, it also has features of *cognitive-behavioral therapy*. See Learning Objective 14.5. In short, it encourages individuals with OCD to gradually and regularly expose themselves to the things that trigger their obsessive thoughts but not to engage in their

VR psychotherapy has been effective for many soldiers experiencing symptoms of PTSD.

typical compulsive act or process (Strauss et al., 2015). In addition to adults with OCD, it has also been demonstrated to be effective with youth (Kircanski & Peris, 2015).

AVERSION THERAPY Another way to use classical conditioning is to reduce the frequency of undesirable behaviors, such as smoking or overeating, by teaching the client to pair an aversive (unpleasant) stimulus with the stimulus that results in the undesirable response in a process called **aversion therapy**. For example, someone who wants to stop smoking might go to a therapist who uses a *rapid-smoking* technique, in which the client is allowed to smoke but must take a puff on the cigarette every 5 or 6 seconds. As nicotine is a poison, such rapid smoking produces nausea and dizziness, both unpleasant effects.

THERAPIES BASED ON OPERANT CONDITIONING Operant conditioning techniques include reinforcement, extinction, shaping, and modeling to change the frequency of voluntary behavior. See Learning Objectives 5.8, 5.9, 5.13, and 5.14. In the treatment of psychological disorders, the goal is to reduce the frequency of undesirable behavior and increase the frequency of desirable responses.

One of the advantages of using operant conditioning to treat a problem behavior is that results are usually quickly obtained rather than gained through years of more insight-oriented forms of therapy. When bringing the behavior under control (rather than finding out why it occurs in the first place) is the goal, operant and other behavioral techniques are very practical. There's an old joke about a man whose fear of things hiding under his bed is cured by a behavioral therapist in one night. The therapist simply cut the legs off the bed.

MODELING Modeling, or learning through the observation and imitation of a model, is discussed in Chapter Five. The use of modeling as a therapy is based on the work of Albert Bandura, which states that a person with specific fears or someone who needs to develop social skills can learn to do so by watching someone else (the model) confront those fears or demonstrate the needed social skills (Bandura et al., 1969). In **participant modeling**, a model demonstrates the desired behavior in a step-by-step, gradual process. The client is encouraged by the therapist to imitate the model in the same gradual, step-by-step manner (Bandura, 1986; Bandura et al., 1974). The model can be a person actually present in the same room with the client or someone viewed on video. For example, a model might first approach a dog, then touch the dog, then pet the dog, and finally hug the dog. A child (or adult) who fears dogs would watch this process and then be encouraged to repeat the steps that the model demonstrated.

Behavioral therapists can give parents or others advice and demonstrations on how to carry out behavioral techniques. Once a person knows what to do, modeling is a fairly easy technique. Modeling has been effective in helping children with dental fears (Klorman et al., 1980; Ollendick & King, 1998), social withdrawal (O'Connor, 1972), phobias (Hintze, 2002), and while interacting with LEGO© play materials, to facilitate improved social skills in children with autism spectrum disorder (LeGoff, 2004). Researchers are also investigating how modeling can impact drug responses in both positive and negative ways. Viewing another person have favorable effects can increase the placebo effect of medication and seeing a model report unwanted side effects can increase an individual's experience of negative effects (Faasse et al., 2018; Faasse & Petrie, 2016). As with other behavioral techniques, modeling can be combined with other interventions. For example, when addressing specific phobias in children, modeling may be combined with *cognitive behavioral therapy* (CBT; see Learning Objective 14.5), systematic desensitization, reinforced practice, and other techniques in the treatment strategy called *One-Session Treatment* (Davis et al., 2018).

USING REINFORCEMENT *Reinforcement* is the strengthening of a response by following it with some pleasurable consequence (positive reinforcement) or the removal of an unpleasant stimulus (negative reinforcement). Reinforcement of both types can form the basis for treatment of people with behavioral problems.

aversion therapy
form of behavioral therapy in which an undesirable behavior is paired with an aversive stimulus to reduce the frequency of the behavior.

modeling
learning through the observation and imitation of others.

participant modeling
technique in which a model demonstrates the desired behavior in a step-by-step, gradual process while the client is encouraged to imitate the model.

In a *token economy*, objects known as *tokens* can be traded for food, candy, treats, or special privileges. Clients earn tokens for behaving correctly or accomplishing behavioral goals and can later exchange those tokens for things that they want. They may also lose tokens for inappropriate behavior. This trading system is a token economy. See Learning Objective 5.9. Token economies have also been used successfully in modifying the behavior of relatively disturbed persons in mental institutions, such as people with schizophrenia or depressed persons (Dickerson et al., 1994; Glynn, 1990; McMonagle & Sultana, 2002). As with modeling, tokens are also used in other settings and in combination with other treatments. For example, CBT and a token economy are used to decrease problem behaviors such as impulsiveness, hyperactivity, disorganization, and disobeying rules in children with attention-deficit/hyperactivity disorder (ADHD; Coelho et al., 2015).

Another method based on the use of reinforcement involves making a **contingency contract** with the client (Salend, 1987). This contract is a formal agreement between therapist and client (or teacher and student, or parent and child) in which both parties' responsibilities and goals are clearly stated. Such contracts are useful in treating specific problems such as drug addiction (Talbott & Crosby, 2001), educational problems (Evans & Meyer, 1985; Evans et al., 1989), and eating disorders (Brubaker & Leddy, 2003). Monetary contingency contracts may be useful in weight-loss programs (Sykes-Muskett et al., 2015). Because the stated tasks, penalties, and reinforcements are clearly stated and consistent, both parties are always aware of the consequences of acting or failing to act within the specifications of the contract, making this form of behavioral treatment fairly effective. Consistency is one of the most effective tools in using both rewards and punishments to mold behavior. See Learning Objectives 5.6, 5.7.

Token economies can be useful for encouraging and maintaining a variety of desired behaviors. When positive behaviors are demonstrated, individuals earn tokens, such as these stars, which can later be exchanged for desired items or privileges, which serve as reinforcers for the positive behaviors.

USING EXTINCTION *Extinction* involves the removal of a reinforcer to reduce the frequency of a particular response. In modifying behavior, operant extinction often involves removing one's attention from the person when that person is engaging in an inappropriate or undesirable behavior. With children, this removal of attention may be a form of **time-out**, in which the child is removed from the situation that provides reinforcement (Kazdin, 1980). In adults, a simple refusal by the other persons in the room to acknowledge the behavior is often successful in reducing the frequency of that behavior.

BEHAVIORAL ACTIVATION *Behavioral activation* is an operant-based intervention that has been used successfully with depression. Individuals with depression may limit their involvement with others or the typical activities they would normally engage in. This avoidant behavior limits their opportunities to be positively reinforced through social activities or pleasant experiences. Behavioral activation involves reintroducing individuals to their regular environments and routines as one way to increase opportunities for positive reinforcement (Dimidjian et al., 2006; Ekers et al., 2014; Forman, n.d.). Therapists work with their clients to schedule activities through daily activity monitoring, activity scheduling, and a variety of other ways to restore an environment that increases the likelihood of activation behavior, decreases avoidant and depressive behavior, and increases positive reinforcement (Craighead et al., 2015; Manos et al., 2010; Puspitasari et al., 2013).

EVALUATION OF BEHAVIOR THERAPIES Behavior therapies may be more effective than other forms of therapy in treating specific behavioral problems, such as bed-wetting, overeating, drug addictions, and phobic reactions (Burgio, 1998; Wetherell, 2002).

Some problems do not respond as well overall to behavioral treatments, although improvement of specific symptoms can be achieved (Glynn, 1990; McMonagle & Sultana, 2002). While EX/RP is often a successful treatment for OCD, some associated cognitive

contingency contract
a formal, written agreement between the therapist and client (or teacher and student) in which goals for behavioral change, reinforcements, and penalties are clearly stated.

time-out
an extinction process in which a person is removed from the situation that provides reinforcement for undesirable behavior, usually by being placed in a quiet corner or room away from possible attention and reinforcement opportunities.

AP 8.Q Compare and contrast different treatment methods.

"Heather has left my text message unread for over an hour … I must have done something to tick her off …"

How many times have you jumped to a conclusion without first examining the actual evidence, or getting the whole story?

AP 8.K Identify the contributions of major figures in psychological treatment.

symptoms, such as deficits in executive functioning, may interfere with the use of this approach (Snyder et al., 2015). Bringing symptoms under control is an important step in allowing a person to function normally in the social world, and behavior therapies are a relatively quick and efficient way to eliminate or greatly reduce such symptoms. However, some behavioral paradigms are not simple to establish or continually implement, and steps have to be taken so adaptive behaviors can be maintained and generalized to other situations and environments, such as the family and the individual's culture (Prochaska & Norcross, 2014). Others are easier to implement and may in fact not require extensive training to be successful. For example, behavioral activation is an effective intervention for depression that is relatively simple to implement, even by nonspecialists, and it has been shown to be either comparable or superior to antidepressant medication in the short term and superior to cognitive therapies (Craighead et al., 2015; Dimidjian et al., 2006; Ekers et al., 2014). Furthermore, EX/RP for OCD, PE for PTSD, and other exposure-based approaches may possibly be enhanced, such as by using two fear-provoking stimuli at the same time to facilitate learning during exposure (Culver et al., 2015).

14.5 Cognitive Therapies: Thinking Is Believing

14.5 Summarize the goals and basic elements of cognitive and cognitive-behavioral therapies.

Cognitive therapy (Beck, 1979; Freeman et al., 1989) was developed by Aaron T. Beck and is focused on helping people change their ways of thinking. Rather than focusing on the behavior itself, the cognitive therapist focuses on the distorted thinking and unrealistic beliefs that lead to maladaptive behavior (Hollon & Beck, 1994), especially those distortions relating to depression (Abela & D'Allesandro, 2002; McGinn, 2000). The goal is to help clients test in a more objective, scientific way the truth of their beliefs and assumptions as well as their attributions concerning both their own behavior and the behavior of others in their lives. See Learning Objective 11.9. Then they can recognize thoughts that are distorted and negative and replace them with more positive, helpful thoughts. Because the focus is on changing thoughts rather than gaining deep insights into their causes, this kind of therapy is primarily an action therapy.

BECK'S COGNITIVE THERAPY

 What are these unrealistic beliefs?

Cognitive therapy focuses on the distortions of thinking. Here are some of the more common distortions in thought that can create negative feelings and unrealistic beliefs:

- **Arbitrary inference:** This refers to "jumping to conclusions" without any evidence. Arbitrary means to decide something based on nothing more than personal whims. Example: "Suzy canceled our lunch date—I'll bet she's seeing someone else!"

- **Selective thinking:** In selective thinking, the person focuses only on one aspect of a situation, leaving out other relevant facts that might make things seem less negative. Example: Peter's teacher praised his paper but made one comment about needing to check his punctuation. Peter assumes his paper is lousy and the teacher really didn't like it, ignoring the other praise and positive comments.

- **Overgeneralization:** With overgeneralization, a person draws a sweeping conclusion from one incident and then assumes the conclusion applies to areas of life that have nothing to do with the original event. Example: "I got yelled at by my boss. My boyfriend is going to break up with me and kick me out of the apartment—I'll end up living in a van down by the river."

cognitive therapy

therapy in which the focus is on helping clients recognize distortions in their thinking and replacing distorted, unrealistic beliefs with more realistic, helpful thoughts.

- **Magnification and minimization:** With magnification and minimization, a person blows bad things out of proportion while not emphasizing good things. Example: A student who has received good grades on every other exam believes the C she got on the last quiz means she's not going to succeed in school.
- **Personalization:** In personalization, an individual takes responsibility or blame for events that are not really connected to the individual. Example: When Sandy's husband comes home in a bad mood because of something that happened at work, she immediately assumes he is angry with her.

A cognitive therapist tries to get clients to look at their beliefs and test them to see how accurate they really are. The first step is to identify an illogical or unrealistic belief, which the therapist and client do in their initial talks. Then the client is guided by the therapist through a process of asking questions about that belief, such as "When did this belief of mine begin?" or "What is the evidence for this belief?"

COGNITIVE-BEHAVIORAL THERAPY (CBT)

💬 Don't those questions sound like critical thinking, which was discussed in Chapter One?

Cognitive therapy really is critical thinking applied to one's own thoughts and beliefs. Just as cognitive psychology grew out of behaviorism, see Learning Objectives 1.3 and 1.4, therapies using cognitive methods have behavioral elements within them as well, leading to the term **cognitive-behavioral therapy (CBT)**. To learn more about how CBT works, watch the video *Cognitive-Behavioral Therapy*.

CBT focuses on the present rather than the past (like behaviorism), but also assumes that people interact with the world with more than simple, automatic reactions to external stimuli. People observe the world and the people in the world around them, make assumptions and inferences* based on those observations or cognitions, and then decide how to respond (Rachman & Hodgson, 1980). CBT also assumes that disorders come from illogical, irrational cognitions and that changing the thinking patterns to more rational, logical ones will relieve the symptoms of the disorder, making it an action therapy. CBT has three basic elements: Cognitions affect behavior, cognitions can be changed, behavior change can result from cognitive change (Dobson & Block, 1988). Cognitive-behavioral therapists may also use any of the tools behavioral therapists use to help clients alter their actions. The three basic goals of any cognitive-behavioral therapy follow.

Watch Cognitive-Behavioral Therapy

👁 Watch the Video at MyLab Psychology

cognitive-behavioral therapy (CBT)
action therapy in which the goal is to help clients overcome problems by learning to think more rationally and logically, which in turn will impact their behavior.

1. Relieve the symptoms and help clients resolve the problems.
2. Help clients develop strategies to cope with future problems.
3. Help clients change the way they think from irrational, self-defeating thoughts to more rational, self-helping, positive thoughts.

---

*inferences: conclusions drawn from observations and facts.

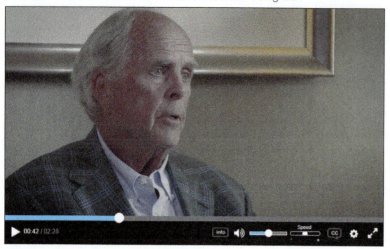

Watch Effective Treatment of Panic Disorder Using CBT

Watch the Video at MyLab Psychology

To learn more about CBT and how it is used with a specific disorder, watch the video *Effective Treatment of Panic Disorder Using CBT*.

ELLIS AND RATIONAL EMOTIVE BEHAVIOR THERAPY (REBT) Albert Ellis proposed a version of CBT called **rational emotive behavior therapy (REBT)**, in which clients are taught a way to challenge their own irrational beliefs with more rational, helpful statements (Ellis, 1997, 1998). Here are some examples of irrational beliefs:

- Everyone should love and approve of me (if they don't, I am awful and unlovable).
- When things do not go the way I wanted and planned, it is terrible, and I am, of course, going to get very disturbed. I can't stand it!

💬 But I've felt that way at times. Why are these statements so irrational?

Notice that these statements have one thing in common: It's either all or nothing. Can a person really expect the love and affection of every single person? Is it realistic to expect things to work as planned every time? Rational emotive behavioral therapy is about challenging these types of "my way or nothing" statements, helping people realize that life can be good without being "perfect." In REBT, therapists take a very directive role, challenging the client when the client makes statements like those listed earlier, assigning homework, using behavioral techniques to modify behavior, and arguing with clients about the rationality of their statements.

AP 8.Q Compare and contrast different treatment methods.

EVALUATION OF COGNITIVE AND COGNITIVE-BEHAVIORAL THERAPIES Cognitive and cognitive-behavioral therapies are less expensive than typical insight therapy because they are comparatively short-term therapies. As in behavior therapy, clients do not have to dig too deep for the hidden sources of their problems. Instead, cognitive-based therapies get right to the problems themselves, helping clients deal with their symptoms more directly. In fact, one of the criticisms of these therapies as well as behavior therapies is that they treat the symptom, not the cause. However, it should be noted that in the cognitive viewpoint, the maladaptive thoughts are seen as the cause of the problems, not merely the symptoms. There is also an element of potential bias because of the therapist's opinions as to which thoughts are rational and which are not (Westen, 2005).

Nevertheless, cognitive and cognitive-behavioral therapies have considerable success in treating many types of disorders, including insomnia, depression, stress disorders, eating disorders, anxiety disorders, personality disorders, and even—in addition to other forms of therapy—some types of schizophrenia (Craske & Barlow, 2014; Fairburn, 2018; Hay, 2013; Heimberg & Magee, 2014; Meichenbaum, 1996; Savard et al., 2014; Tarrier & Taylor, 2014; Trauer et al., 2015; Young et al., 2014). As an offshoot of behaviorism, the learning principles that are the basis of cognitive-behavioral therapies are considered empirically sound (Barlow et al., 2015; Masters et al., 1987). For a summary of the various types of psychotherapies discussed up to this point, see **Table 14.2**.

rational emotive behavior therapy (REBT)
cognitive behavioral therapy in which clients are directly challenged in their irrational beliefs and helped to restructure their thinking into more rational belief statements.

Table 14.2 Characteristics of Psychotherapies

Type of Therapy (Key People)	Goal	Methods
Psychodynamic therapy (Freud)	Insight	Aims to reveal unconscious conflicts through dream interpretation, free association, resistance and transference
Humanistic therapy Person-centered therapy (Rogers)	Insight	Nondirective therapy; client does most of the talking; key elements are authenticity, unconditional positive regard, and empathy
Gestalt therapy (Perls)		Directive therapy; therapist uses leading questions and role playing to help client accept all parts of their feelings and experiences
Behavior therapy (Watson, Jones, Skinner, Bandura)	Action	Based on principles of classical and operant conditioning; aimed at changing behavior without concern for causes of behavior
Cognitive therapy (Beck) CBT (various professionals)	Action	Aims to help clients overcome problems by learning to think more rationally and logically
REBT (Ellis)		Clients are challenged in their irrational beliefs and helped to restructure their thinking

Concept Map L.O. 14.4, 14.5

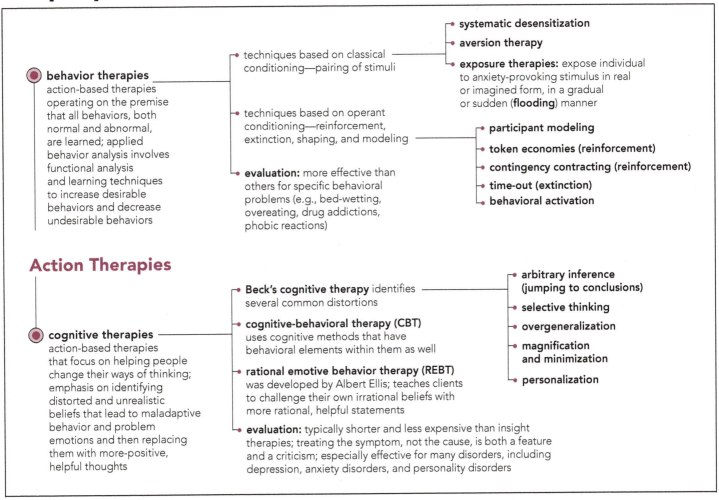

Practice Quiz — How much do you remember?

Pick the best answer.

1. Behavior-based therapies are _____ based, while psychodynamic and humanistic therapies are _____ based.
   a. insight, action
   b. action, insight
   c. medically, action
   d. rationale, medically
   e. personality, family

2. Dr. Kalua works with clients to help them learn deep relaxation. Next, he has them list their fears from least to most anxiety provoking. Finally, Dr. Kalua slowly exposes his clients to each of their fears and assists them in gaining control of their anxiety. His approach is best known as _____.
   a. aversion therapy
   b. flooding
   c. fear therapy
   d. systematic desensitization
   e. shaping

3. Dr. Kelly uses exposure-based therapies to treat many of her patients. Client A is actually confronted with the situation that causes her anxiety, while Client B is asked to think about and visualize the frightening situation. Client A's treatment method would be described as _____, while client B's treatment method is _____.
   a. virtual, in vivo
   b. systematic, in vivo
   c. imaginal, virtual
   d. in vivo, imaginal
   e. modern, historic

4. Which of the following therapies has been successful across multiple settings in the establishment of desirable behaviors and modification of problem behaviors?
   a. flooding
   b. diversion therapy
   c. aversion therapy
   d. systematic desensitization
   e. token economies

5. Bryn's therapist tells her that she is applying arbitrary inference to her thinking, which ultimately is causing her to be depressed. Which of the following is an example of arbitrary inference?
   a. Bryn maximizes the bad things she experiences while minimizing the good aspects of life.
   b. Bryn tends to jump to conclusions with little or no evidence to support her beliefs.
   c. Bryn tends to overgeneralize a single bad event and assume all things about her life are failing.
   d. Bryn focuses strictly on a single negative event while ignoring less negative aspects.
   e. Bryn tends to label herself negatively after a single negative event.

14.6–14.7 Group Therapies: Not Just for the Shy

An alternative to individual therapy, in which the client and the therapist have a private, one-on-one session, is **group therapy**, in which a group of clients with similar problems gathers together to discuss their problems under the guidance of a single therapist (Yalom, 1995; Yalom & Leszcz, 2005). Group members learn through interpersonal relationships, insight, and feedback as the group is a reflection of the members' broader life and relationships outside of the group (Goldberg & Hoyt, 2015; Yalom & Leszcz, 2005).

14.6 Types of Group Therapies

14.6 Compare and contrast different forms of group therapy.

Group therapy can be accomplished in several ways. The therapist may use either an insight- or action-oriented style. And while person-centered, Gestalt, and behavior therapies seem to work better in group settings (Andrews, 1989), effective group cognitive behavioral therapy (CBT-G) and group interpersonal therapy (IPT-G) strategies have been developed (Yalom & Leszcz, 2005). In addition to the variations in the style of therapy, the group structure can also vary. There may be small groups formed of related persons or other groups of unrelated persons that meet without the benefit of a therapist. Their goal is to share their problems and provide social and emotional support for each other.

FAMILY COUNSELING One form of group therapy is **family counseling** or **family therapy**, in which all of the members of a family who are experiencing some type of problem—marital problems, problems in child discipline, or sibling rivalry, for example—are seen by the therapist as a group. The therapist may also meet with one or more family members individually at times, but the real work in opening the lines of communication among family members is accomplished in the group setting (Frankel & Piercy, 1990; Pinsof & Wynne, 1995). The family members may include grandparents,

---

In family therapy, a therapist will often meet with the entire family in the effort to identify what aspects of the family dynamic are contributing to a problem, such as conflict between different family members.

group therapy
form of therapy or treatment during which a small group of clients with similar concerns meet together with a therapist to address their issues.

family counseling (family therapy)
a form of group therapy in which family members meet together with a counselor or therapist to resolve problems that affect the entire family.

aunts and uncles, and in-laws as well as the core family. This is because family therapy focuses on the family as a whole unit or system of interacting "parts." No one person is seen as "the problem" because all members of the family system are part of the problem: They are experiencing it, rewarding it, or by their actions or inactions causing it to occur in the first place.

The goal in family therapy, then, is to discover the unhealthy ways in which family members interact and communicate with one another and change those ways to healthier, more productive means of interaction. Family therapists work not only with families but also with couples who are in a committed relationship, with the goal of improving communication, helping the couple to learn better ways of solving their problems and disagreements, and increasing feelings of intimacy and emotional closeness (Christensen et al., 1995; Heavey et al., 1993).

SELF-HELP GROUPS Many people may feel that a therapist who has never had, for example, a drug problem would be unable to truly understand their situation; and they may also feel that someone who has experienced addiction and beaten it is more capable of providing real help. Therapists are also often in short supply, and they charge a fee for leading group-therapy sessions. These are reasons some people choose to meet with others who have problems similar to their own, with no therapist in charge. Called **self-help groups** or **support groups**, these groups are usually formed around a particular problem. Some examples of self-help groups are Alcoholics Anonymous, Overeaters Anonymous, and Narcotics Anonymous, all of which have groups meeting all over the country at almost any time of the day or night. There are countless smaller support groups for nearly every condition imaginable, including anxiety, phobias, having a parent with dementia, having difficult children, depression, and dealing with stress—to name just a few. The advantages of self-help groups are that they are free and provide the social and emotional support that a group session can provide (Bussa & Kaufman, 2000). Self-help groups do not have leaders but instead have people who volunteer monthly or weekly to lead individual meetings. So the person who is in charge of organizing the meetings is also a member of the group, with the same problem as all the other members.

In self-help groups, the person or persons leading a group are not specialists or therapists but just members of the group. They often have the same problem as all of the other people in the room, which is the strength of this type of program—people may be more likely to trust and open up to someone who has struggled as they have.

14.7 Evaluation of Group Therapy

14.7 Identify the advantages and disadvantages of group therapy.

AP 8.Q Compare and contrast different treatment methods.

Group therapy can provide help to people who might be unable to afford individual psychotherapy. Because the therapist can see several clients at one time, this type of therapy is usually less expensive than individual therapy. It also allows an opportunity for both the therapist and the person to see how that person interacts with others.

Another advantage of group therapy is that it offers social and emotional support from people who have problems similar or nearly identical to one's own. This advantage is an important one; studies have shown that breast cancer patients who were part of a group-therapy process had much higher survival and recovery rates than those who received only individual therapy or no psychotherapy (Fawzy et al., 1993; Spiegel et al., 1989). Another study found that adolescent girls in Africa, suffering from depression due to the stresses of the war in Uganda, experienced significant reductions in depression when treated with group therapy (Bolton et al., 2007). Group therapy and family-based therapy are often primary treatment strategies for individuals with anorexia nervosa (AN; Hay, 2013). In particular, family therapy for adolescents with AN is an effective treatment; for adolescents with bulimia nervosa (BN) and adults with an eating disorder, other treatments, including CBT, appear to be better options (Grange & Eisler, 2018).

self-help groups (support groups)
a group composed of people who have similar problems and who meet together without a therapist or counselor for the purpose of discussion, problem solving, and social and emotional support.

Group therapy is not appropriate for all situations, and there can be disadvantages. Clients must share the therapist's time during the session. People who are not comfortable in social situations or who have trouble speaking in front of others may not find group therapy as helpful as those who are more verbal and social by nature. In addition, since the therapist is no longer the only person to whom secrets and fears are revealed, some people may be reluctant to speak freely. However, while an extremely shy person may initially have great difficulty speaking up in a group setting, cognitive-behavioral group therapy can be effective for social anxiety disorder (Heimberg & Becker, 2002; Heimberg & Magee, 2014). People with psychiatric disorders involving paranoia that is not well controlled, such as schizophrenia, may not be able to tolerate group-therapy settings. A survey and comparison of the effectiveness of both individual and group therapy found that group therapy is only effective if it is long term, and that it is more effective when used to promote skilled social interactions rather than as an attempt to decrease the more bizarre symptoms of delusions and hallucinations (Evans et al., 2000). It is also important to note that group therapy can be used in combination with individual and biomedical therapies.

Concept Map L.O. 14.6, 14.7

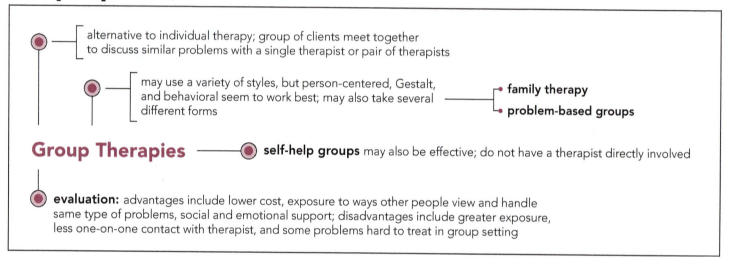

Practice Quiz — How much do you remember?

Pick the best answer.

1. Which of the following may be an effective option for some concerns if there isn't a therapist available in your local community?
   a. family therapy
   b. psychodynamic therapy
   c. group therapy
   d. self-help group
   e. behavior therapy

2. Which of the following is *not* a noted advantage of group psychotherapy?
   a. Group therapy is less expensive than individual psychotherapy.
   b. Group therapy offers emotional support from people facing similar challenges.
   c. Group therapy offers social support from people facing similar challenges.
   d. Group therapy is appropriate for anyone, so it is more "available" to those with personal struggles.
   e. Group therapy can be used in conjunction with individual and biomedical therapies.

3. Laurel runs a weekly meeting of Alcoholics Anonymous, and several dozen members come every week. In addition, each week some new members show up to see what the group is all about, and some members who were there the previous week do not return. Which of the following is most likely true about Laurel?
   a. Laurel has probably never experienced a substance-related problem herself.
   b. Laurel has likely experienced some problems with alcohol in her past and is probably not a professional therapist.
   c. Laurel is probably a licensed psychologist.
   d. Laurel is probably a licensed psychiatrist.
   e. Laurel is probably a licensed counselor.

4. Penny and Leonard, along with their children Parker and Paisley, are all seeing a psychologist to help work through some difficulties that have been occurring in their home. From time to time, their therapist opts to work with one of them instead of all four at once. This group of individuals is receiving _____ therapy.
   a. psychodynamic
   b. family
   c. group
   d. self-help group
   e. behavioral

14.8–14.9 Does Psychotherapy Really Work?

> AP 8.M Summarize effectiveness of specific treatments used to address specific problems.

💬 There sure are a lot of psychotherapies, but do any of them really work?

In the 1950s, Hans Eysenck conducted one of the earliest studies of the effectiveness of therapy. His conclusion: People receiving psychotherapy did not recover at any higher rate than those who had no psychotherapy and the passage of time alone could account for all recovery. Since that time, researchers have continued to investigate the overall effectiveness of psychotherapy, seemingly necessary components, and the opinion of individuals who have been in therapy.

14.8 Studies of Effectiveness

14.8 Summarize the research on the effectiveness of psychotherapy.

Eysenck's classic survey created a major controversy within the world of clinical and counseling psychology. Other researchers began their own studies to find evidence that would contradict Eysenck's findings. One such effort reviewed studies that the researchers considered to be well controlled and concluded that the psychotherapies did not differ from one another in effectiveness (Luborsky et al., 1975). Of course, that can mean either that the psychotherapies were all equally effective or that they were all equally ineffective. (Reminder—many psychological professionals take an eclectic approach, using more than one psychotherapy technique.)

Studies that do not use empirical procedures but instead try to determine if the clients who have been helped by the therapy in general are plagued by problems such as experimenter bias (the therapist expects the therapy to work and is the one assessing the progress of the client), the inaccuracies of self-report information, and placebo-effect expectations cited by Shapiro and Shapiro (Seligman, 1995; Shapiro & Shapiro, 1997; Wampold, 1997). See Learning Objectives 1.5, 1.10.

Surveys have shown that people who have received psychotherapy believe they have been helped more often than not (*Consumer Reports*, 1995; Hunsley et al., 2014; Kotkin et al., 1996). The *Consumer Reports* research was a survey of the magazine's readers in which those who had been or were currently clients in psychotherapy rated the effectiveness of the therapy they received. Here are the findings from a summary of this and several other similar surveys (Lambert & Ogles, 2004; Seligman, 1995; Thase, 1999):

- An estimated 75 to 90 percent of people feel that psychotherapy has helped them.
- The longer a person stays in therapy, the greater the improvement.

Other studies have found that some psychotherapies are more effective for certain types of disorders (Clarkin et al., 2007; Hollon et al., 2002) but that no one psychotherapy is the most effective or works for every type of problem. Overall, the evidence for psychotherapy is strong, and data support its efficacy with different age groups, across a broad range of disorders, and with clients from a variety of backgrounds and orientations (American Psychological Association, 2013; Campbell et al., 2013; Chorpita et al., 2011).

Watch Finding a Therapist if You Need One

Watch the Video at MyLab Psychology

AP 8.Q Compare and contrast different treatment methods.

therapeutic alliance
the relationship between therapist and client that develops as a warm, caring, accepting relationship characterized by empathy, mutual respect, and understanding.

evidence-based treatment
also called empirically supported treatment, refers to interventions, strategies, or techniques that have been found to produce therapeutic and desired changes during controlled research studies.

14.9 Characteristics of Effective Therapy

14.9 Identify factors that influence the effectiveness of therapy.

💬 So, how does a person with a problem know what kind of therapist to go to? How do you pick a good one?

It can sometimes be hard to determine if you or someone you know needs professional help and, if so, where to find it. The video *Finding a Therapist if You Need One* offers some advice.

COMMON FACTORS APPROACH The *common factors approach* in psychotherapy is a modern approach to eclecticism and focuses on those factors common to successful outcomes from different forms of therapy (Norcross, 2005). These factors are seen as the source of the success rather than specific differences among therapies. The most important common factor of a successful psychotherapy may be the relationship between the client and the therapist, known as the **therapeutic alliance**. This relationship should be caring, warm, and accepting, and characterized by empathy, mutual respect, and understanding. Therapy should also offer clients a *protected setting* in which to release emotions and reveal private thoughts and concerns and should help clients understand why they feel the way they do and provide them with ways to feel better. Other common factors in therapy effectiveness are *opportunity for catharsis* (relieving pent-up emotions), *learning and practice of new behaviors*, and *positive experiences* for the client (Norcross, 2005).

EVIDENCE-BASED TREATMENT An ongoing area of research in psychology is related to identifying those treatments and other aspects of treatment that work best for specific disorders. As scientists, psychologists and other mental health professionals serve their clients best by being familiar with and using those treatments that work the best as evidenced by studies using systematic research designs and not by relying solely on personal experience or intuition (David et al., 2018; Lilienfeld et al., 2014). Some treatments may not only be ineffective for certain disorders, they may even prove to be dangerous or harmful (David et al., 2018; Lilienfeld et al., 2014). Especially in light of managed health care and tight budgets, clients benefit through *evidence-based practice*. Empirically supported or **evidence-based treatment** (EBT) refers to techniques or interventions that have produced desired outcomes or therapeutic change in controlled studies (Barlow et al., 2013; David et al., 2018; Kazdin, 2008). Evidence-based practice includes systematic reviews of relevant and valid information that ranges from assessment to intervention (American Psychological Association, 2005, 2013; Hunsley & Mash, 2008; Kazdin, 2008; Nathan & Gorman, 2015). Some examples of evidence-based, or empirically supported, treatments are exposure therapies, cognitive-behavioral therapy, and cognitive processing for PTSD (Ehlers et al., 2010; Hajcak & Starr, n.d.; Najavits & Anderson, 2015; Monson et al., 2014), cognitive-behavioral treatment for panic disorder with agoraphobia (Barlow et al., 2015; Craske & Barlow, 2014), cognitive-behavioral individual and group therapy for social anxiety disorder (Heimberg & Magee, 2014), cognitive therapy, behavior therapy, and interpersonal psychotherapy for depression. For additional information, Division 12 of the American Psychological Association maintains an excellent resource on research-supported treatments for a variety of diagnoses, **div12.org/diagnoses/**.

NEUROIMAGING OF PSYCHOTHERAPY A growing body of research is focused on the potential uses of neuroimaging in evaluating psychological treatments. These studies are looking at the structural and functional changes that occur as the result of treatment, those that occur during treatment, and the potential identification of personalized treatment options for someone with a given disorder. While it will be quite some time before such approaches may be feasible and broadly available for individual consumers, if ever, it is still an exciting area of investigation and one that will likely improve treatment options for many. Broadly speaking, there is support for psychotherapy altering activity in brain areas associated with negative emotion, emotion regulation, fear, and reward (Fournier & Price, 2014). Novel targets are also being revealed. In one study, researchers were able to assess brain changes linked with positive treatment outcomes associated with prolonged exposure in the treatment of PTSD. By using fMRI with individuals who received treatment, and later using concurrent TMS-fMRI with healthy subjects, researchers were able to demonstrate that following prolonged exposure and during deliberate emotion regulation, activity is impacted in the prefrontal cortex, which in turn affects activity in the ventromedial cortex (Fonzo et al., 2017). Of note, these are not only areas of the brain that have not previously been highlighted but are also functionally different than areas commonly identified in previous studies of changes in brain activity associated with psychotherapy. Instead of prominent changes in limbic regions, the most noticeable changes appear to be prefrontal, possibly leading to new ways of understanding how exposure therapy or new simulation-based strategies work (Fonzo et al., 2017). Neuroimaging has also been used to illustrate how individuals with major depressive disorder respond to either psychological or pharmacological treatment based on pretreatment brain activity. In one study, depressed individuals with hypometabolism in the insula responded best with cognitive-behavioral therapy, while individuals with hypermetabolism in the insula responded best to antidepressant medication (McGrath et al., 2013). Watch the video *Assessing Treatment Effectiveness* to learn more about how advances in neuroscience help psychologists better understand treatment effectiveness.

Watch Assessing Treatment Effectiveness

Watch the Video at MyLab Psychology

TELEPSYCHOLOGY Although psychotherapy is usually accomplished by the client or clients speaking face to face with the therapist, other modalities of therapy or counseling are available using various forms of telecommunication technology. *Telepsychology* refers to the use of email, phone, text, chat, mobile devices, interactive videoconferencing, the Internet, or similar types of technology to provide psychological services (Joint Task Force for the Development of Telepsychology Guidelines for Psychologists, 2013). Telepsychology options can be used to supplement traditional in-person psychological services, or used independently (Joint Task Force for the Development of Telepsychology Guidelines for Psychologists, 2013). *Distance counseling, online counseling, cybertherapy, Internet-based therapy, online therapy*, and *web therapy* are other terms referring to similar or related services. Although telepsychology may offer advantages including lower or minimal cost, availability of therapy opportunities for those unable to get to a therapist easily (such as people living in a remote or rural area), access to support groups online, and relative anonymity for some modalities, there are risks.

Just as with face-to-face interventions, clients need to make sure the therapist has appropriate training and credentials in psychotherapy. Therapists should also have training and experience with distance counseling and be able to address the relative risks and benefits of distance counseling, including what steps to take when the counselor is not available (American Counseling Association, 2014; Jencius, 2015). The web and other forms of technology can offer other challenges as well. Clients and counselors alike should be mindful of the prevalence of social media and avoid "personal virtual relationships" (American Counseling Association, 2014; Jencius, 2015; Kaplan, 2016). Just as counselors and clients avoid multiple relationships to maintain professional boundaries, with the widespread use of social media, even greater attention is likely required to avoid the blurring of any personal and professional boundaries (Kaplan, 2016).

CULTURAL, ETHNIC, AND GENDER CONCERNS IN PSYCHOTHERAPY Consider the following situation (adapted from Wedding, 2004).

> K. is a 24-year-old Korean American. She lived with her parents, who were both born and reared in Korea before moving to the United States as adults. She came to a therapist because she was depressed and unhappy with her lack of independence. Her father was angry about her plans to marry a non-Korean. Her therapist immediately began assertiveness training and role playing to prepare K. to deal with her father. The therapist was disappointed when K. failed to keep her second appointment.

This example of an actual case demonstrates a problem that exists in the therapist–client relationship for many clients when the ethnicity or culture of the client is different from that of the therapist. This cultural difference makes it difficult for therapists to understand the exact nature of their clients' problems and for clients to benefit from therapies that do not match their needs (Matsumoto, 1994; Moffic, 2003; Wedding, 2004). The values of different cultures and ethnic groups are not universally the same. How, for example, could a female therapist who is White, from an upper-middle-class family, and well educated understand the problems of a Latino adolescent boy from a poor family living in substandard housing if she did not acknowledge the differences between them? What if a young Black lesbian was the therapist for a recently divorced, middle-aged Native American male who uses a wheelchair? In these cases, the economic backgrounds, sex, ethnicity, sexual orientation, ability, and life experiences of the clients and therapists are all vastly different.

In the case of K., for example, the therapist mistakenly assumed that the key to improving K.'s situation was to make her more assertive and independent from her family, particularly her father. This Western idea runs counter to Korean cultural values. Korean culture stresses interdependence, not independence. The family comes first, obedience to one's elders is highly valued, and "doing one's own thing" is not acceptable. K.'s real problem may have been her feelings of guilt about her situation and her father's anger. She may have wanted help in dealing with her family situation and her feelings about that situation, not help in becoming more independent.

For therapy to be effective, the client must continue in treatment until a successful outcome is reached. K. never came back after the first session. One of the problems that can occur when the culture or ethnic backgrounds of the client and therapist are mismatched, as in K.'s case, is that the therapist may project his or her values onto the client, failing to achieve true empathy with the client's feelings or even to realize what the client's true feelings are, thus causing the client to drop out of therapy. Studies of such situations have found that members of minority racial or ethnic groups drop out of therapy at a significantly higher rate than the majority-group clients (Brown et al., 2003; Cooper et al., 2003; Flaherty & Adams, 1998; Fortuna et al., 2010; Sue, 1977, 1992; Sue et al., 1994; Vail, 1976; Vernon & Roberts, 1982). Time in therapy and more sessions are typically associated with better treatment outcomes (Hansen, 2002). When the ethnicity of the therapist and client are matched, some studies indicate longer engagement and

---

AP 8.N Discuss how cultural and ethnic context influence choice and success of treatment (e.g., factors that lead to premature termination of treatment).

retention, but overall treatment outcomes do not appear to be impacted in some studies; whereas in other studies, ethnicity matching appears to have a significant positive effect (Cabral & Smith, 2011; Lau & Zane, 2000; Meyer & Zane, 2013).

Traditional forms of psychotherapy, developed mainly in Western, individualistic cultures, may need to be modified to fit the more collectivistic, interdependent cultures. For example, Japanese psychologist Dr. Shigeru Iwakabe has pointed out that the typical "talking cure" practiced by many psychotherapists—including psychodynamic and humanistic therapists—may have to be altered to a nontalking cure and the use of nonverbal tasks (like drawing) due to the reluctance of many traditional Japanese people to talk openly about private concerns (Iwakabe, 2008).

How might the establishment of an effective therapeutic relationship be impacted when the client and therapist are from different ethnic or cultural backgrounds?

> 💬 Are differences in gender that important? For example, do women prefer female therapists, but men would rather talk to another man?

Research on gender and therapist–client relationships varies. When talking about White, middle-class clients, it seems that both men and women prefer a female therapist (Jones et al., 1987). But African American clients were more likely to drop out of therapy if the therapist was the *same* sex as the client (Vail, 1976); male Asian clients seemed to prefer a male therapist; and female Asian clients stayed in therapy equally long with either male or female therapists (Flaherty & Adams, 1998; Flaskerud, 1991).

Multiple barriers to effective psychotherapy exist when the culture or ethnic backgrounds of client and therapist are different (Sue & Sue, 2016):

- **Culture-bound values.** Including being individual centered versus other (or others) centered, verbal/emotional/behavioral expressiveness, communication patterns from client to counselor, insight, self-disclosure, scientific empiricism, and distinctions between mental and physical functioning (Sue & Sue, 2016). Differing cultural values can cause therapists to fail at forming an empathetic relationship (Sattler, 1977; Wedding, 2004).

- **Class-bound values.** Social class, including impact of poverty and therapeutic class bias, adherence to time schedules, ambiguous approach to problems, looking for long-range goals (Sue & Sue, 2016). Clients from impoverished backgrounds may have values and experiences that the therapist cannot understand (Wedding, 2004).

- **Language.** Use of standard English, emphasis on verbal communication (Sue & Sue, 2016). Speaking different languages becomes a problem in understanding what both client and therapist are saying and in psychological testing (Betancourt & Jacobs, 2000; Lewis, 1996).

- **"American" cultural assumptions.** Particular values differ, and "American" values cannot be assumed. Differences can occur as related to identity, relationships, role of the family (individualism versus collectivism, nuclear family versus extended family), relationships with nature, time orientation, relationships with others, and activity (doing versus being; Sue & Sue, 2016).

- **Communication style.** Both verbal and nonverbal communication can differ between cultures and ethnicities. *Communication style* has a huge impact on what is actually said, referring to things like the physical distance between the client and therapist, the use of gestures, eye contact, and the use of personal space (Sue & Sue, 2016). People in some cultures are content with long periods of silence whereas others are not, direct eye contact is desirable in some cultures and offensive in others, and even facial expressions of emotion vary. For example, smiling to express happiness may be commonplace in U.S. society, whereas in some Chinese and Japanese individuals, restraint of facial expressions may be more common (Sue & Sue, 2016).

The American Psychiatric Association (2013) has included information for psychology professionals concerning cultural issues and culture syndromes. See Learning Objective 13.2. All therapists need to make an effort to become aware of cultural differences, syndromes, and possible gender issues. Sociopolitical issues should also be examined. For example, therapists need to be mindful of their assumptions and biases, some of which may be sincerely denied but possibly expressed nonverbally such as if a White therapist in training distanced themselves from an African American client by leaning away or crossing his or her legs or arms during an animated, emotional discussion (Sue & Sue, 2016). There is great value in learning characteristics about different groups, but in doing so, therapists need to remain mindful of not using that information to overgeneralize and stereotype the people with whom they are working (Sue & Sue, 2016).

THINKING CRITICALLY 14.1

Which of the forms of psychotherapy discussed so far would probably work best for a client who has commitment issues in relationships? Why?

Concept Map L.O. 14.8, 14.9

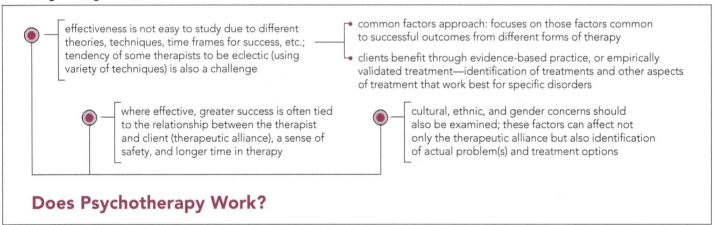

Does Psychotherapy Work?

- effectiveness is not easy to study due to different theories, techniques, time frames for success, etc.; tendency of some therapists to be eclectic (using variety of techniques) is also a challenge
- where effective, greater success is often tied to the relationship between the therapist and client (therapeutic alliance), a sense of safety, and longer time in therapy
- common factors approach: focuses on those factors common to successful outcomes from different forms of therapy
- clients benefit through evidence-based practice, or empirically validated treatment—identification of treatments and other aspects of treatment that work best for specific disorders
- cultural, ethnic, and gender concerns should also be examined; these factors can affect not only the therapeutic alliance but also identification of actual problem(s) and treatment options

Practice Quiz   How much do you remember?

Pick the best answer.

1. Dr. Briscoe is trying to establish what is known as a therapeutic alliance with her clients. What specifically should she do to accomplish this goal?
   a. She should work to better understand the disorder that she is treating.
   b. She should openly consult with others on all cases to ensure quality therapeutic treatment.
   c. She should be more confrontational in her approach so as to make clients aware of their difficulties.
   d. She should be more empathetic and caring when working with her clients.
   e. She should study different cultures for other examples of the symptoms her clients experience.

2. Research shows that African American clients prefer a therapist _____ while Asian men prefer a _____ therapist.
   a. of the same sex, female
   b. of the opposite sex, male
   c. of the opposite sex, female
   d. of the same sex, male
   e. who is male, female

3. What do studies show about the overall effectiveness of telepsychology?
   a. It is a fad, and studies indicate that telepsychology is relatively ineffective.
   b. Telepsychology can be effective for people who otherwise might be unable to get to a therapist.
   c. Telepsychology cannot be used to supplement in-person services.
   d. There currently are not enough studies to indicate whether telepsychology is or is not effective.
   e. Studies indicate that many clients who use online chat as part of their telepsychology often stop showing up after 1 or 2 sessions.

4. _____ treatment refers to techniques or interventions that have produced desired outcomes or therapeutic change in controlled studies.
   a. Client-friendly
   b. Cost-friendly
   c. Evidence-based
   d. Clinically valid
   e. Insurance-approved

APA Goal 2: Scientific Inquiry and Critical Thinking

Does It Work? Psychological Treatment

Addresses APA Learning Objective 2.4: Interpret, design, and conduct basic psychological research.

Now that you have learned about a variety of treatment options for psychological disorders, how would you design an experiment to study the effects of Treatments A and B for Disorder X?

There are numerous problems with studying the effectiveness of psychotherapy. Controlled studies can be done using an experimental group of people who receive a particular psychotherapy and a comparison group of people who are put on a waiting list, but this is less than ideal. The comparison group is not getting the attention from the therapist, for one thing, and so there would be no placebo-effect expectations about getting better because of therapy (Shapiro & Shapiro, 1997). Also, not all therapies take the same amount of time to be effective. For example, psychoanalysis, even in its short form, takes longer than a behavioral therapy. In a short-term study, behavioral therapy would obviously look more effective. Action therapies such as behavior therapy measure the success of the therapy differently than do insight therapies; in a behavioral therapy the reduction of the undesired behavior is easy to objectively measure, but gaining insights and feelings of control, self-worth, self-esteem, and so on are not as easily evaluated (Shadish et al., 2002).

Let's assume your research hypothesis is something like, "Treatment A will be more effective than Treatment B for Disorder X, and both Treatment A and B will be more effective than no treatment for Disorder X." How would you evaluate these treatments? What kind of research methods would you use to be able to speak to cause-and-effect relationships? How are you going to operationalize the treatments and their effects? What data will you need to confirm your hypothesis?

For example, let's assume Treatment A consists of ten 50-minute sessions of one-on-one cognitive-behavioral therapy with a psychologist. Treatment B consists of ten Internet-based, self-study modules based on cognitive-behavioral therapy, each requiring approximately 45 minutes to complete. Although progression through the sessions will be monitored by a psychologist, there will not be any direct interaction with a psychology professional.

Based on the information presented, what data do you need and how will you collect it? You will likely want to make sure you have individuals that have similar symptoms of Disorder X, and if possible, do not have any other disorders. What do you need to keep in mind as you populate your treatment groups and a comparison group? Preferably, these groups need to be close to identical in terms of demographics, including age, level of education, socioeconomic status, gender, and so on. Will you randomly assign individuals to each of the three groups? Where will you get your participants? How many individuals do you need in each group? Ideally, you would have 30 or more people in each group. Groups should contain approximately the same amount of people. See Learning Objectives 1.11, 1.15.

Assume you find that either Treatment A or Treatment B has a positive effect on the symptoms of Disorder X. Following the study, how do you accommodate the individuals that were in the comparison group? One way is to offer treatment to the people in the comparison group at the conclusion of the original study. What if the hypothesis is confirmed and Treatment A is more effective than Treatment B? Which treatment do you offer to the comparison group, or do you give them a choice? In this case, you may want to offer both and allow them to choose, explaining the benefits of each and letting the individuals decide which they prefer.

Regardless of the outcomes of the study, how might you share the results with other psychology professionals? How might you share the information with the public? With students taking an introduction to general psychology class? Would the manner in which you share the information differ based on the hypothesis being confirmed versus some other finding or combination of findings?

THINKING CRITICALLY 14.2

After reviewing the questions raised above, describe how you would share the results of Treatment A versus Treatment B with students who are not psychology majors. What would be the most relevant points you would share?

14.10–14.12 Biomedical Therapies

AP 8.P Summarize effectiveness of specific treatments used to address specific problems from a biological perspective.

AP 8.Q Compare and contrast different treatment methods.

Just as a therapist trained in psychoanalysis is more likely to use that technique, a therapist whose perspective on personality and behavior is biological will most likely turn to medical techniques to manage disordered behavior. Even psychotherapists who are not primarily biological in orientation may combine psychotherapy with medical treatments that are supervised by a medical doctor working with the psychologist. As medical doctors, psychiatrists are almost inevitably biological in perspective and thus use **biomedical therapies** (directly affecting the biological functioning of the body and brain) in addition to any psychotherapy technique they may favor. The biomedical therapies fall into several approaches and may consist of drug therapy, shock therapy, surgical treatments, or noninvasive stimulation techniques.

14.10 Psychopharmacology

AP 2.H Discuss the influence of drugs on neurotransmitters.

14.10 Categorize types of drugs used to treat psychological disorders.

The use of drugs to control or relieve the symptoms of a psychological disorder is called **psychopharmacology**. Although these drugs are sometimes used alone, they are more often combined with some form of psychotherapy and are more effective as a result (Cuijpers et al., 2014; Guidi et al., 2016; Kearney & Silverman, 1998; Keller et al., 2000). There are four basic categories of drugs used to treat psychotic disorders, anxiety disorders, the manic phase of mood disorders, and depression.

ANTIPSYCHOTIC DRUGS Drugs used to treat psychotic symptoms, such as hallucinations, delusions, and bizarre behavior, are called **antipsychotic drugs**. These drugs can be classified into two categories, the classical first-generation, or *typical antipsychotics*, and newer second-generation *atypical antipsychotics*. The first of the typical antipsychotics to be developed was *chlorpromazine*. The first-generation antipsychotics caused "neurolepsis," or psychomotor slowing and reduced emotionality, and thus were referred to as *neuroleptics* due to the neurological side effects they produced (Advokat et al., 2019; Preston et al., 2017; Stahl, 2013).

Typical antipsychotic drugs work by blocking certain dopamine receptors in the brain, namely the D2 receptor, thereby serving as a dopamine antagonist and reducing the effect of dopamine in synaptic transmission (Advokat et al., 2019; Preston

biomedical therapies
therapies that directly affect the biological functioning of the body and brain; therapies for mental disorders in which a person with a problem is treated with biological or medical methods to relieve symptoms.

psychopharmacology
the use of drugs to control or relieve the symptoms of psychological disorders.

antipsychotic drugs
drugs used to treat psychotic symptoms such as delusions, hallucinations, and other bizarre behavior.

et al., 2017; Stahl, 2013). Remember, an *agonist* facilitates effects whereas an *antagonist* blocks or reduces them (see **Figure 14.1**, Learning Objective 2.3). However, because they block more pathways in the dopamine system than are involved in psychosis, with prolonged use they tend to cause problems. Such problems include movement disorders similar to those in Parkinson's disease, sometimes called *extrapyramidal symptoms*, and others such as *tardive dyskinesia*. Tardive dyskinesia is a syndrome caused by long-term treatment and can even persist when typical antipsychotic medications are no longer being used. The syndrome is characterized by the person making facial and tongue movements such as repeatedly sticking their tongue out, grimacing, or constant chewing, or causing repetitive involuntary jerks or dance-like movements of the arms and legs (Advokat et al., 2019; Preston et al., 2017; Stahl, 2013).

The atypical antipsychotics may also suppress dopamine but to a much greater degree in the one dopamine pathway that seems to cause psychotic problems. These drugs also block or partially block certain serotonin receptors, resulting in fewer negative side effects and occasionally some improvement in the negative symptoms of schizophrenia (Advokat et al., 2019; Preston et al., 2017; Stahl, 2013). Despite their effectiveness, the atypical antipsychotics may also have unwanted side effects, such as weight gain, diabetes, blood lipid level changes, or changes in the electrical rhythms of the heart (Advokat et al., 2019; Stahl, 2017). One of these, clozapine, can cause a potentially fatal reduction in the white blood cells of the body's immune system in a very small percentage of people. For this reason, the blood of patients on clozapine is closely monitored, and it is not considered to be a first choice when selecting treatment options but is used more often when other antipsychotic drugs are ineffective (Preston et al., 2017; Stahl, 2013, 2017).

Newer classes of atypical antipsychotics include *partial dopamine agonists* that affect the release of dopamine rather than blocking its receptors in the brain and other agents that have agonistic or antagonistic properties for dopamine and serotonin (Stahl, 2013). Drugs are also being investigated that are linked to the actions of *glutamate*. See Learning Objective 2.3.

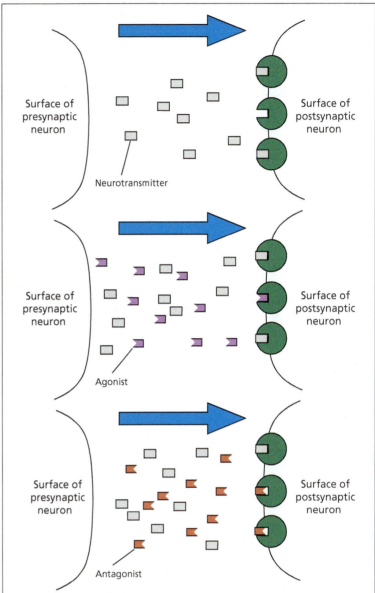

Figure 14.1 Agonistic and Antagonistic Effects of Drugs

Some drugs yield their agonistic or antagonistic effects by binding to postsynaptic receptors to either open or block ion channels.

💬 How long do people generally have to take these antipsychotic medications?

In some cases, a person might have a psychotic episode that lasts only a few months or a few years and may need drug treatment only for that time. But in most cases, especially in schizophrenia that starts in adolescence or young adulthood, the medication must be taken for the rest of the person's life. Long-term use of antipsychotics, particularly the older typical drugs, has been associated with a decrease in cognitive functioning such as impaired memory and sedation, possibly due to the chemical actions of the drugs themselves. The hope for newer atypical antipsychotics is that they will not only produce fewer negative side effects but also have less impact on the cognitive processes of those persons taking these drugs (Advokat et al., 2019; Preston et al., 2017; Stahl, 2013). Overall, antipsychotic drugs remain an important and empirically supported treatment for schizophrenia (Abbas & Lieberman, 2015).

ANTIANXIETY DRUGS The traditional **antianxiety drugs** are the minor tranquilizers or *benzodiazepines* such as Xanax, Ativan, and Valium. All of these drugs have a sedative effect and, in the right dose, can start to relieve symptoms of anxiety within 20 to 30 minutes of taking the drug by mouth (Preston et al., 2017). Although many side effects are possible, the main concern in using these drugs is their potential for addiction as well as abuse in the form of taking larger doses to "escape" (National Institute on Drug Abuse [NIDA], 2002). Other drugs used to treat anxiety include *antihistamines*, including Benadryl and Vistaril, *atypical benzodiazepines* such as Ambien and Lunesta, and other unique antianxiety drugs, including Buspar (Preston et al., 2017; Stahl, 2017).

MOOD-STABILIZING DRUGS For many years, the treatment of choice for bipolar disorder and episodes of mania has been *lithium*, a metallic chemical element that in its salt form (lithium carbonate) evens out both the highs and the lows of bipolar disorder. It is generally recommended that treatment with lithium continue at maintenance levels in people with recurring bipolar disorder. Lithium affects the way sodium ions in neuron and muscle cells are transported, although it is not clear exactly how this affects mood. Side effects typically disappear quickly, although the use of lithium has been associated with weight gain. Diet needs to be controlled when taking lithium because lowered levels of sodium in the diet can cause lithium to build up to toxic levels, as can any substance that removes water from the body such as the caffeine in sodas, tea, and coffee.

Anticonvulsant drugs, normally used to treat seizure disorders, have also been used to treat mania. Examples are carbamazepine, valproic acid (Depakote), and lamotrigine. These drugs can be as effective in controlling mood swings as lithium and can also be used in combination with lithium treatments (Bowden et al., 2000; Thase & Sachs, 2000). Some atypical antipsychotics work as mood stabilizers and may be used alone or in conjunction with anticonvulsant medications (Advokat et al., 2019; Preston et al., 2017; Stahl, 2013, 2017).

ANTIDEPRESSANT DRUGS As is so often the case in scientific discoveries, the first types of drugs used in the treatment of depression were originally developed to treat other disorders. Iproniazid, for example, was used to treat tuberculosis symptoms in the early 1950s and was found to have a positive effect on mood, becoming the first modern **antidepressant** (López-Muñoz & Alamo, 2009). This drug became the first of the *monoamine oxidase inhibitors* (MAOIs), a class of antidepressants that blocks the activity of an enzyme called monoamine oxidase. Monoamine oxidase is the brain's "cleanup worker" because its primary function is to break down the neurotransmitters norepinephrine, serotonin, and dopamine—the three neurotransmitters most involved in control of mood. Under normal circumstances, the excess neurotransmitters are broken down *after* they have done their "job" in mood control. In depression, these neurotransmitters need more time to do their job, and the MAOIs allow them that time by inhibiting the enzyme's action.

Some common MAOIs in use today are isocarboxazid (Marplan), phenelzine sulfate (Nardil), and tranylcypromine sulfate (Parnate). These drugs can produce some unwanted side effects, although in most cases the side effects decrease or disappear with

antianxiety drugs
drugs used to treat and calm anxiety reactions, typically minor tranquilizers.

antidepressant
drugs used to treat depression and anxiety.

continued treatment: weight gain, constipation, dry mouth, dizziness, headache, drowsiness or insomnia, and sexual arousal disorders are possible. People taking MAOIs in general should also be careful about eating certain smoked, fermented, or pickled foods; drinking certain beverages; or taking some other medications due to a risk of severe high blood pressure in combination with consumption of these items, although there are a couple of MAOIs that do not require any dietary restrictions (Stahl, 2013). And while these precautions are very important, certain drug–drug interactions may be more common and sometimes even lethal, so individuals taking MAOIs should work closely with their health-care professionals to monitor adverse drug interactions (Advokat et al., 2019; Preston et al., 2017; Stahl, 2013).

The second category of antidepressant drug to be developed is called the *tricyclic antidepressants*. These drugs were discovered in the course of developing treatments for schizophrenia (López-Muñoz & Alamo, 2009). Tricyclics, so called because of their molecular structure consisting of three rings (cycles), increase the activity of serotonin and norepinephrine in the nervous system by inhibiting their reuptake into the synaptic vesicles of the neurons. See Learning Objective 2.3. Some common tricyclics are imipramine (Tofranil), desipramine (Norpramin, Pertofrane), amitriptyline (Elavil), and doxepin (Sinequan, Adapin). Side effects of these drugs, which may also decrease over the course of treatment, are very similar to those of the MAOIs but can also include skin rashes, blurred vision, lowered blood pressure, and weight gain (Advokat et al., 2019; Preston et al., 2017; Stahl, 2013).

The effect of the MAOIs and the tricyclics on the action of the three critical neurotransmitters led researchers to try to develop drugs that would more specifically target the critical neural activity involved in depression with fewer negative side effects. This led to the development of the *selective serotonin reuptake inhibitors* (SSRIs), drugs that inhibit the reuptake process of only serotonin (see **Figure 14.2**). This causes fewer side effects while still providing effective antidepressant action, making these drugs relatively safe when compared to the older antidepressants. But like the other two classes of antidepressants, the SSRIs may take from 2 to 6 weeks to produce effects. Some of the better-known SSRIs are fluoxetine (Prozac), sertraline (Zoloft), and paroxetine (Paxil). Other classes of antidepressants have been or are being investigated, including *serotonin-norepinephrine reuptake inhibitors* (SNRIs), *serotonin partial agonist/reuptake inhibitors* (SPARIs), *norepinephrine-dopamine reuptake inhibitors* (NDRIs), *selective norepinephrine reuptake inhibitors* (NRIs), and *serotonin antagonist/reuptake inhibitors* (SARIs).

As with many types of medication, sometimes medications from different classes, or that have a different mechanism of function, will be combined to augment or facilitate each other or to manage unwanted side effects. Different drugs can also be used for a variety of purposes. For example, bupropion (Wellbutrin) is an NDRI and is commonly used as an antidepressant by itself or to augment SSRIs (Preston et al., 2017; Stahl, 2017). It may also be used to help people quit smoking by managing nicotine cravings, treat ADHD, or manage sexual dysfunctions (Preston et al., 2017; Stahl, 2017).

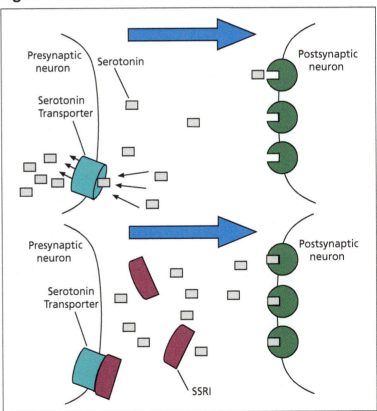

Figure 14.2 How SSRIs Work

Selective serotonin reuptake inhibitors (SSRIs) prevent the reuptake of serotonin into the presynaptic neuron, prolonging the time serotonin remains in the synapse and resulting in an overall agonistic effect.

There is also research examining the potential use of subanesthetic doses of *ketamine* as an antidepressant due to its apparent ability to have immediate antidepressant effects and reduction of suicidal thoughts (Stahl, 2013, 2007). The effects are not permanent, but its effects can come on within a few hours and last for several days and up to a week in some individuals (DiazGranados et al., 2010a; DiazGranados et al., 2010b; Zarate et al., 2006; Zarate et al., 2012). In addition to rapid effects, it appears to also facilitate synaptogenesis and reverse some of the neuronal effects of chronic stress (Duman & Aghajanian, 2012). Drugs that act like ketamine are being investigated for potential use as antidepressants. Ketamine itself is an anesthetic, sometimes abused due to its dissociative and hallucinogenic effects (e.g., "Special K" or "K") or used in cases of sexual assault.

Concerns have arisen that children and teenagers taking newer antidepressant medications may have an increased risk of suicide versus those not receiving treatment. Recent meta-analyses have provided conflicting information, with some data suggesting an increased risk for suicide while other data do not support an increased risk (Gibbons et al., 2012; Hetrick et al., 2012). Another important factor is efficacy, and particularly efficacy of antidepressant medications for depression in children and adolescents. One recent meta-analysis provided evidence suggesting the risk of suicidality was more pronounced with particular antidepressants, and fluoxetine (Prozac) may be the only antidepressant that might actually work in children and adolescents to reduce the symptoms of depression (Cipriani et al., 2016). Regardless, caution is urged, especially in children and teens being treated with newer antidepressant medications.

With regard to other uses for antidepressant medication, in the last several years the use of the benzodiazepines to treat anxiety has declined, and physicians and therapists have begun to prescribe antidepressant drugs to treat anxiety and related disorders such as panic disorder, obsessive-compulsive disorder, and posttraumatic stress disorder. Although the antidepressants take from 3 to 5 weeks to show any effect, they are not as subject to abuse as the minor tranquilizers and have fewer of the same side effects. Overall, the use of antidepressant drugs for depression in adults (Cipriani et al., 2016; Prendes-Alvarez et al., 2015), SSRIs for panic disorder and SSRIs and SNRIs for social anxiety disorder, and buspirone and antidepressants for generalized anxiety disorder (Kimmel et al., 2015) are empirically supported treatments. And while the search for effective pharmacological treatments for anorexia nervosa continues, SSRIs and other antidepressants are proving useful in the treatment of bulimia nervosa (Mayer, 2018; Preston et al., 2017; Stahl, 2017).

> **THINKING CRITICALLY 14.3**
>
> At what age do you think children and/or teenagers should be able to decide if they will take medications to treat abnormal psychological functioning or behavior?

AP 8.Q Compare and contrast different treatment methods.

Overall, many psychological professionals today believe combining psychotherapy with medical therapies—particularly drug therapy—is a more effective approach to treating many disorders. For example, the treatment of bulimia can involve many of the same measures taken to treat anorexia (such as interpersonal therapy, cognitive-behavioral therapy, group therapy, or family-based therapy), but as noted above, the use of antidepressant medications can be helpful, especially those that affect serotonin levels such as SSRIs (Mayer, 2018; Mitchell et al., 2013). A person dealing with major depressive disorder may be given an antidepressant drug to alleviate symptoms but may also still need to talk about what it's like to deal with their symptoms and with needing the medication. Psychotherapy combined with antidepressant medication therapy is more effective in treating major depressive disorder than medication therapy alone and possibly better than psychotherapy alone (Craighead & Dunlop, 2014).

However, cognitive-behavioral therapy in combination with drug therapy may not be more effective, as it may have a larger impact than some other approaches, leaving less room for improvement (Craighead & Dunlop, 2014). Individuals with such disorders as schizophrenia also benefit from combined approaches, with strategies ranging from family- and community support-based programs to individual or group-based cognitive-behavioral therapy proving to be valuable conjunctive therapies to psychopharmacological treatment (Stahl, 2013). However, at least for individuals with major depressive disorder, combined treatment should not be the default, as some individuals may respond effectively to only one treatment modality, and there are increased monetary costs for combined treatments (Craighead & Dunlop, 2014). **Table 14.3** lists several drugs and their side effects.

Table 14.3 Types of Drugs Used in Psychopharmacology

Classification	Treatment Areas	Side Effects	Examples
Antipsychotic: Typical antipsychotic	Positive (excessive) symptoms such as delusions or hallucinations	Motor problems, tardive dyskinesia	chlorpromazine (Thorazine), haloperidol (Haldol), loxapine (Loxitane)
Antipsychotic: Atypical antipsychotic	Positive and some negative symptoms of psychoses	Fewer than typical antipsychotic; clozapine may cause serious blood disorder	aripiprazole (Abilify), clozapine (Clozaril), lurasidone (Latuda), olanzapine (Zyprexa), quetiapine (Seroquel), risperidone (Risperdal)
Antianxiety: Benzodiazepines	Symptoms of anxiety and phobic reactions	Slight sedative effect; potential for physical dependence	alprazolam (Xanax), clonazepam (Klonopin), diazepam (Valium), lorazepam (Ativan)
Antianxiety: Atypical and nonbenzodiazepines, other agents	Symptoms of anxiety	Sedation, blurred vision, dizziness, nausea	buspirone (Buspar), eszopiclone (Lunesta), hydroxine (Atarax, Vistaril), zaleplon (Sonata), zolpidem (Ambien)
Mood stabilizers/bipolar medications	Manic behavior or bipolar depression	Potential for toxic buildup	lithium; some anticonvulsant drugs (carbamazepine/Tegretol, divalproex/Depakote, lamotrigine/Lamictal), some atypical antipsychotics
Antidepressants: MAOIs	Depression	Weight gain, constipation, dry mouth, dizziness, headache, drowsiness, insomnia, some sexual arousal disorders	isocarboxazid (Marplan), phenelzine (Nardil), tranylcypromine (Parnate)
Antidepressants: Tricyclics	Depression	Skin rashes, blurred vision, lowered blood pressure, weight loss	amitriptyline (Elavil), clomipramine (Anafranil), desipramine (Norpramin), imipramine (Tofranil), nortriptyline (Pamelor)
Antidepressants: SSRIs	Depression	Nausea, nervousness, insomnia, diarrhea, rash, agitation, some sexual arousal problems	citalopram (Celexa), escitalopram (Lexapro), fluoxetine (Prozac), paroxetine (Paxil), sertraline (Zoloft)
Antidepressants: Atypical, SNRIs, NRIs	Depression	Anxiety, insomnia, nausea, headache, sedation, dizziness, weight gain	bupropion (Wellbutrin), duloxetine (Cymbalta), mirtazapine (Remeron), venflaxine (Effexor)

14.11 ECT and Psychosurgery

14.11 Explain how electroconvulsive therapy and psychosurgery are used to treat psychological disorders.

As addressed at the beginning of the chapter, psychological disorders have been treated in a variety of ways, via a variety of medical means, and some treatments have been better options than others. Unfortunately, some methods were used indiscriminately, were ineffective, or caused more harm than good. That has changed, and current alternative biomedical options are effective options when other strategies have not been successful, and they are sometimes the best option.

ELECTROCONVULSIVE THERAPY Many people are—well—*shocked* to discover that **electroconvulsive therapy (ECT)** is still in use to treat cases of severe depression. ECT involves the delivery of an electric shock to either one side or both sides of a person's head, resulting in a seizure or convulsion of the body and the release of a flood of neurotransmitters in the brain (American Psychiatric Association [APA] Committee on Electroconvulsive Therapy, 2001). The result is an almost immediate improvement in mood, and ECT is used not only in severe cases of depression that have not responded to drug treatments or psychotherapy or where the side effects of medication are not acceptable but also in the treatment of several other severe disorders, such as schizophrenia and severe mania, that are not responding to alternate treatments (APA Committee on Electroconvulsive Therapy, 2001; Pompili et al., 2013; Preston et al., 2017; Stahl, 2013).

In the 1930s, doctors actually were researching the possible uses of inducing seizures in treating schizophrenia, although the seizures were induced through means of a drug (camphor) in those early experiments. It was Italian researchers Cerletti and Bini who first used electricity to induce a seizure in a man with schizophrenia, who fully recovered after only 11 such treatments (Endler, 1988; Fink, 1984; Shorter, 1997). Soon doctors were using ECT on every kind of severe mental disorder. In those early days, no anesthesia was used because the shock was severe enough to result in a loss of consciousness (most of the time). Broken bones, bitten tongues, and fractured teeth were not untypical "side effects."

Today's ECT is far more controlled and humane. It is only used to treat severe disorders, and written and informed consent is required in most states. ECT has been found most useful for severe depression that has not responded to medications or psychotherapy and in cases where suicide is a real possibility or has already been attempted. ECT works more quickly than antidepressant medications, so it can play an important role in helping prevent suicide attempts (APA Committee on Electroconvulsive Therapy, 2001). Although relationships to clinical symptoms are not yet clear, it has also been shown to increase the volume of gray matter and increase cortical thickness in some areas of the brain, including the hippocampus and amygdala, areas involved in emotion and memory (Bouckaert et al., 2015; Sartorius et al., 2015). See Learning Objective 2.7. Despite the results and these findings, ECT should not be considered a "cure." It is a way to get a person suffering from severe depression into a state of mind that is more receptive to other forms of therapy or psychotherapy. Relapse is very possible in individuals receiving ECT, and maintenance or continuation therapies are an important treatment strategy to pursue (Nordenskjold et al., 2011; Petrides et al., 2011; Preston et al., 2017; Stahl, 2013).

> What are some of the side effects? Wasn't there something from an earlier chapter about this therapy affecting memory?

ECT does have several negative side effects, some of which last longer than others. Memory is definitely affected, as ECT disrupts the consolidation process and prevents the formation of long-term memories. See Learning Objective 6.12. This causes both retrograde amnesia, the loss of memories for events that happen close to the time of the treatment, and anterograde amnesia, the rapid forgetting of new material (APA Committee on Electroconvulsive Therapy, 2001; Lisanby et al., 2000; Weiner, 2000). The retrograde effects can extend to several months before and a few weeks after treatment, and the older memories may return with time, whereas the anterograde amnesia is more temporary, clearing up in a few weeks after treatment. When ECT is used today,

---

electroconvulsive therapy (ECT)
form of biomedical therapy to treat severe depression in which electrodes are placed on either one or both sides of a person's head and an electric current is passed through the electrodes that is strong enough to cause a seizure or convulsion.

every effort is made to reduce as many side effects as possible. The modern patient is given muscle relaxants to reduce the effects of the convulsion as well as a very short-term anesthetic. There are even ECT approaches that use *ultrabrief* pulses, which appear to have fewer cognitive side effects but not the same level of therapeutic results as other methods (Tor et al., 2015). Despite its efficacy, the utilization of ECT in general is not uniform. In the United States, racial differences in the use of ECT appear to be present, with African Americans with depression less likely to pursue or receive ECT treatment as compared to White Americans, and the overall use of ECT in general appears to be declining (Case et al., 2013; Case et al., 2012). Besides lack of availability for a treatment with demonstrated efficacy, declines are of concern as use of ECT may result in up to 46 percent fewer readmissions within 30 days of discharge, which benefits both the individuals receiving treatment and the institutions offering ECT (Slade et al., 2017). To learn more about the use of ECT as a treatment for depression, watch the video *Electroconvulsive Therapy*.

PSYCHOSURGERY Just as surgery involves cutting into the body, **psychosurgery** involves cutting into the brain to remove or destroy brain tissue for the purpose of relieving symptoms of mental disorders. One of the earliest and best-known psychosurgical techniques is the **prefrontal lobotomy**, in which the connections of the prefrontal cortex to other areas of the brain are severed. The lobotomy was developed in 1935 by Portuguese neurologist Dr. Antonio Egas Moniz, who was awarded the Nobel Prize in medicine for his contribution to psychosurgery (Cosgrove & Rauch, 1995; Freeman & Watts, 1937). Walter Freeman and James W. Watts modified Moniz's technique and developed a procedure called the *transorbital lobotomy*, during which an instrument resembling an ice pick, called a leucotome, was inserted through the back of the eye socket and into the brain to sever the brain fibers. It was this technique that became widely used, and unfortunately sometimes overused, in the pursuit of relief for so many people suffering from mental illness.

💬 But I thought lobotomies left most people worse off than before—didn't it take away their emotions or something?

Although it is true that some of the early lobotomy patients did seem less agitated, anxious, and delusional, it is also true that some early patients did not survive the surgery (about 6 percent died), and others were left with negative changes in personality: apathy, lack of emotional response, intellectual dullness, and childishness, to name a few. Fortunately, the development of antipsychotic drugs, beginning with chlorpromazine, together with the results of long-term studies that highlighted serious side effects of lobotomies, led to the discontinuation of lobotomies as a psychosurgical technique (Cosgrove & Rauch, 1995; Swayze, 1995).

💬 Are there any psychosurgical techniques in use today since the lobotomy is no longer used?

The lobotomy is gone, but there is a different and more modern technique called **bilateral anterior cingulotomy**, in which magnetic resonance imaging, see Learning

psychosurgery

surgery performed on brain tissue to relieve or control severe psychological disorders.

prefrontal lobotomy

psychosurgery in which the connections of the prefrontal cortex to other areas of the brain are severed.

bilateral anterior cingulotomy

psychosurgical technique in which an electrode wire is inserted into the anterior cingulate gyrus, with the guidance of magnetic resonance imaging, to destroy a very small portion of that brain area with electric current.

Watch What Is Psychosurgery?

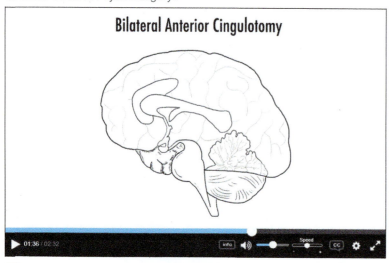

Watch the Video at MyLab Psychology

Objective 2.5, is used to guide an electrode to a specific area of the brain called the cingulate gyrus. This area connects the frontal lobes to the limbic system, which controls emotional reactions. By running a current through the electrode, a very small and specific area of brain cells can be destroyed. This process is called *lesioning*. See Learning Objective 2.4. Cingulotomies are relatively rare and only used as a last resort, but they have been shown to be effective in some cases of major depressive disorder and obsessive-compulsive disorder that have not responded to any other therapy techniques (Nuttin et al., 2014). Because this is deliberate brain damage and quite permanent, all other possible treatments must be exhausted before it will be performed and, unlike the early days of lobotomies, it can be performed only with the patient's full and informed consent (Nuttin et al., 2014). Given that not all individuals respond positively to this invasive procedure, current research efforts are ongoing to better predict who will respond to this treatment versus those that may not (Banks et al., 2015). To learn more about the different forms of psychosurgery, watch the video *What Is Psychosurgery?*

14.12 Emerging Techniques

14.12 Identify some of the newer technologies being used to treat psychological disorders.

Some newer noninvasive techniques for effecting changes in the brain were discussed in Chapter Two, including repetitive transcranial magnetic stimulation (rTMS), in which magnetic pulses are applied to the cortex, and transcranial direct current stimulation (tDCS), which uses scalp electrodes to pass very-low-amplitude direct currents to the brain. These new and exciting noninvasive brain stimulation (NIBS) strategies are being evaluated as possible treatment options for a variety of psychological and medical disorders or in assisting researchers to better understand the brain mechanisms underlying them or treatment for them, including adult ADHD, substance use disorders, PTSD, depression, and stroke, along with many others (Allenby et al., 2018; D'Agata et al., 2016; Kelly et al., 2017; Kozel et al., 2018; Meille et al., 2017; Trojak et al., 2017; Wang et al., 2017). See Learning Objective 2.4.

Another technique highlighted in Chapter Two is deep brain stimulation (DBS). And while rTMS and tDCS are noninvasive, DBS is not and is used when other approaches have failed. DBS is being evaluated as a treatment modality for both depression and OCD (Denys et al., 2010; Holtzheimer et al., 2012), with some evidence that DBS may also improve some neuropsychological functions in depressed individuals (Moreines et al., 2014). As noted in Chapter Thirteen, anorexia nervosa (AN) has the greatest risk of death of all the psychological disorders. See Learning Objective 13.11. Exciting research is investigating the use of DBS for individuals with chronic AN who have not responded well to other treatments (such as supportive clinical management, interpersonal therapy, cognitive-behavioral therapy, group therapy, family-based therapy, or drug therapy), with initial results suggesting some individuals have improved body mass index (BMI), mood, and anxiety symptoms after DBS treatment (Lee et al., 2018; Lipsman et al., 2013). Pilot studies and initial investigations are also examining the potential use of DBS in chronic obesity (Lee et al., 2018; Val-Laillet et al., 2015; Whiting et al., 2013).

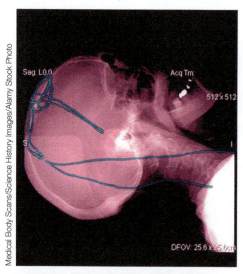

Deep brain stimulation (DBS) is an invasive procedure, and sometimes used when all other treatment options have failed. It involves the implantation of a pulse generator, a device that will send electric stimulation to specific areas of the brain.

Concept Map L.O. 14.10, 14.11, 14.12

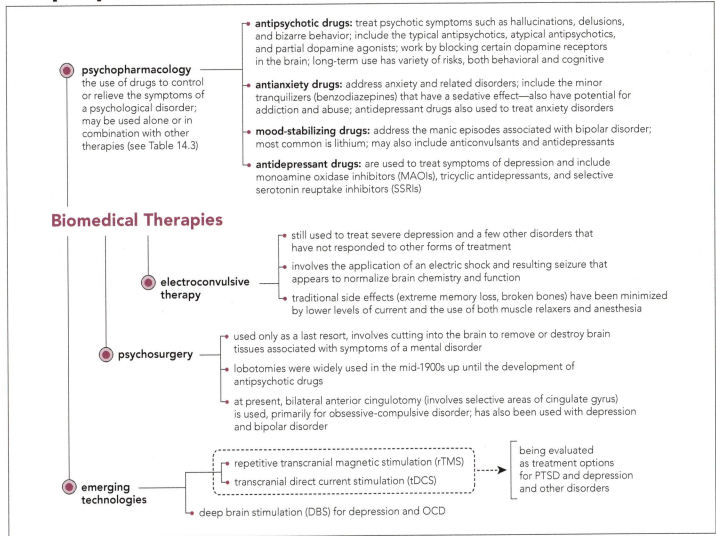

Practice Quiz How much do you remember?

Pick the best answer.

1. Why are antidepressants taking the place of many antianxiety drugs in the treatment of anxiety disorders?
   a. Antidepressants are more cost effective.
   b. Antianxiety drugs may be addictive and have more side effects.
   c. Antianxiety drugs are actually no longer available.
   d. Antianxiety drugs are becoming less effective.
   e. Antianxiety drugs were never effective.

2. Prolonged use of antipsychotic medication can lead to a side effect called _____, which is characterized by involuntary facial and tongue movements (e.g., grimacing, constant chewing), or repetitive involuntary jerks or dance-like movements of the arms and legs.
   a. agranulocytosis
   b. tardive dyskinesia
   c. neuromalignant disorder
   d. synesthesia
   e. akinesia

3. Today's electroconvulsive shock therapy is often quite useful in the treatment of _____.
   a. dissociative identity disorder
   b. bipolar I disorder
   c. schizophrenia
   d. mild anxiety
   e. severe depression

4. A new therapeutic technique known as deep brain stimulation (DBS) is showing promise in the treatment of _____.
   a. mania
   b. anorexia nervosa where other treatments have failed
   c. phobias
   d. personality disorders
   e. hypomania

AP 8.0 Describe prevention strategies that build resilience and promote competence.

14.13 Lifestyle Factors: Fostering Resilience

14.13 Describe how regular physical exercise and spending time in nature may benefit mental health.

In this chapter, we have covered several approaches to therapy, with some highlighting one-to-one interactions with a therapist, others working in a group, and still others that include the use of medication in treating psychological disorders. We have also discussed the overall efficacy of psychotherapy and various interventions. But beyond reactionary approaches and formal psychotherapeutic interventions, what might we do as individuals to foster positive mental health?

Individuals can take a proactive role in promoting positive mental health and overall *resiliency*, our ability to adapt to challenges in a healthy manner and bounce back when life seems to be trying to knock us down. One primary way to build resiliency is for people to take care of both their minds and their bodies. In general, it is important to get enough sleep (8–9 hours a night), eat a healthy diet, and exercise on a regular basis (several times a week). Also, as highlighted in Chapters 3, 7, 10, and 13, our attention to the immediate situation, overall level of physical activity, and surroundings, culture, and the environment in which we grow up can significantly impact the way we perceive the world around us, the way we think, and the way we feel. How might we take advantage of this knowledge?

Attention that is caught by some prominent aspect of a stimulus is called *involuntary attention*. In contrast, voluntary attention, or directed or *focused attention*, refers to our ability to actively concentrate on specific information while not being distracted by other stimuli or data. These two different types of attention have been compared to bottom-up and top-down processing, respectively (S. Kaplan & Berman, 2010). See Learning Objective 3.16. As with many cognitive skills, ability to maintain active focus is limited by many different factors and is subject to fatigue. When people experience attentional fatigue, they are more likely to make poor decisions and have lower levels of self-control (Ohly et al., 2016). These abilities might recover if time is spent immersed in nature, allowing attention to be captured by the environment itself in a bottom-up fashion (R. Kaplan & Kaplan, 1989; S. Kaplan, 1995; S. Kaplan & Berman, 2010).

Attention restoration theory (ART) suggests interactions with nature restore directed attention, and some studies have demonstrated improved performance on objective measures of attention after exposure to natural environments (Berman et al., 2008; S. Kaplan, 1995; Ohly et al., 2016). Beyond potentially changing the way people view and experience the world around them, time in nature has been demonstrated to impact the way people both think and feel, and it is a primary component of some types of therapy, such as *adventure therapy* (Berman et al., 2012; Gass et al., 2012; Gillis et al., 2016; Russell et al., 2017). Research suggests taking walks in a natural environment is more beneficial for both cognition and mood as compared to walking in an urban environment (Bratman et al., 2015a). Even brief nature experiences such as a 90-minute walk have been demonstrated to reduce self-reports of cognitive *rumination*—obsessional or repetitive thinking that is most often negative—and measured brain activity in areas associated with rumination (Bratman et al., 2015b). Research with high school students suggests attentional capabilities improved when students were able to view natural scenes such as trees and shrubs during breaks, and studies with both college students and older adults suggest viewing pictures of nature can be restorative (Felsten, 2009; Gamble et al., 2014; Li & Sullivan, 2016).

What else can benefit positive mental health? Engaging in regular physical activity. Even relatively small amounts of exercise can have positive benefits. Results from a recent study support more active individuals in general as being less likely to develop depression, and protective effects may be evident within the first hour of exercise in a given week (Harvey et al., 2018). For overall physical health, recent guidelines suggest American adults should get at least 150 minutes of moderate-intensity aerobic exercise each week, preferably spread over several days, and should engage in whole-body muscle-strengthening activities at least two days of the week (U.S. Department of Health and Human Services, 2018). And consistent with the information presented above, there may be additional benefits to overall well-being if some of the exercise is in a natural setting (Lawton et al., 2017; Passmore & Howell, 2014).

In sum, here are some research-based suggestions for fostering resiliency and positive mental health:

- Get enough sleep (8–9 hours a night).
- Try to eat a healthy diet.
- Make an effort to regularly spend time outdoors and experience nature.
- Take study breaks outside or, at minimum, in locations where you can see plants, trees, and grass.
- Make time for exercise and have exercise as part of your regular routine. Even small amounts add up.
- If you can exercise daily, do so, if not, get at least 2.5 hours of aerobic exercise spread over several days of the week and engage in muscle-building activities at least twice a week.
- If you don't like exercising by yourself, do so with family or friends, or join a league or community group.

For additional tips and strategies on building resilience, see the American Psychological Association's web site, *The Road to Resilience*, **apa.org/helpcenter/road-resilience.aspx**

Concept Map L.O. 14.13

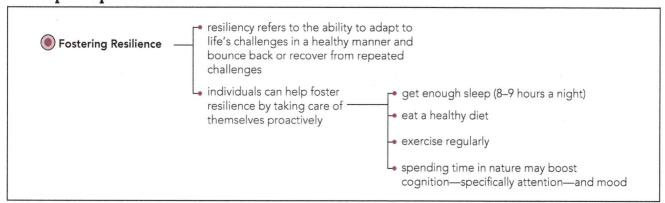

Practice Quiz How much do you remember?

Pick the best answer.

1. What are some basic proactive strategies for taking care of your mental and physical health?
   a. Conserve energy by camping out on the couch and soothe stress by bingeing on comfort foods and Netflix.
   b. Get enough sleep, exercise on a regular basis, and eat a healthy diet.
   c. Work as hard and as fast as you can throughout the school term and recuperate during breaks.
   d. Sleep when you can during the week and longer on the weekends, and eat what is fast and convenient.
   e. Ignore anything that causes distress and socially isolate yourself.

2. Ari and Lake have stressful lives and are trying to get it all done. They don't like to exercise and have hectic schedules. They are physically and mentally fatigued and want to create downtime and start a fitness routine. Based on the information in this section, how might they maximize their efforts?
   a. Find or create opportunities to take breaks or exercise outdoors—do so together if it will help them keep their commitments.
   b. Find a secluded, windowless room in which to take 16-minute breaks every 6 hours they are on campus.
   c. Join a competitive midnight Wii Bowling league.
   d. Have a goal of 90 minutes of high-intensity indoor aerobics every weekday and create downtime by playing Fortnite all weekend.
   e. Join an international, interpretive dance competition league.

Applying Psychology to Everyday Life

How to Help Others: Reducing the Stigma of Seeking Help

14.14 Describe strategies for reducing stigma associated with mental illness or seeking help for a psychological disorder.

The number of college students seeking treatment for mental health issues is increasing, and though some data suggests it is decreasing for some disorders (Lipson et al., 2018), both personal and perceived stigma surrounding mental health conditions and treatment may prevent students from seeking help. Stigma can prevent people from getting the care they need in a variety of ways (Corrigan et al., 2014), but it can be combatted with education, reliable information, experience, and compassion. Imagine you or someone you know is interested in seeking help for a known or possible psychological disorder. How might you assist them to find the help they are looking for? What resources might you be able to tell them about? Watch the following video, and compare your responses to those of the students featured.

Applying Psychology to Everyday Life How to Help Others: Reducing the Stigma of Seeking Help

Watch the Video at MyLab Psychology

After watching the video, answer the following questions:

1. As discussed by students in the video, there are a variety of ways you might assist someone seeking help for a known or possible psychological disorder. What are two things you can do if you find yourself in this situation?

2. Have you ever been told or exposed to stigmatizing information about mental illness? Visit two or more of the sites listed in this **Applying Psychology to Everyday Life** section and share two additional strategies for reducing stigma associated with mental illness or with seeking help for a psychological disorder.

For more information on combatting stigma, there are a variety of useful Web sites, including those hosted by the National Alliance on Mental Illness (NAMI), American Psychological Association (APA), and the Association for Psychological Science (APS). See the URLs below or perform a web search for "overcoming stigma of mental illness."

- https://www.nami.org/stigma
- https://www.nami.org/Get-Involved/StigmaFree/StigmaFree-Community/StigmaFree-on-Campus
- https://www.nami.org/Find-Support/Teens-Young-Adults/Managing-a-Mental-Health-Condition-in-College

- https://www.nami.org/collegeguide/download
- https://www.apa.org/advocacy/higher-education/mental-health/index.aspx
- https://www.psychologicalscience.org/news/releases/stigma-as-a-barrier-to-mental-health-care.html
- http://stampoutstigma.com/
- https://cdn.ymaws.com/www.psichi.org/resource/resmgr/eye_pdf/HelpHelpedMe_Spring2018.pdf
- https://psychsessionspodcast.libsyn.com/sb03-psi-chi-and-the-help-helped-me-initiative
- On Twitter: #CureStigma, #Help_HelpedMe, #StampOutStigma

Chapter Summary

Treatment of Psychological Disorders: Past to Present

14.1 Describe how the treatment of psychological disorders has changed throughout history.

- Mentally ill people began to be confined to institutions called asylums in the mid-1500s. Treatments were harsh and often damaging.
- Philippe Pinel became famous for demanding that the mentally ill be treated with kindness, personally unlocking the chains of inmates at Bicêtre Asylum in Paris, France.
- Psychotherapy involves a person talking to a psychological professional about the person's problems.
- Psychotherapy for the purpose of gaining understanding into one's motives and actions is called insight therapy, whereas psychotherapy aimed at changing disordered behavior directly is called action therapy.
- Biomedical therapy uses a medical procedure to bring about changes in behavior.

Insight Therapies: Psychodynamic and Humanistic Approaches

14.2 Describe the basic elements of Freud's psychoanalysis and psychodynamic approaches today.

- Sigmund Freud developed a treatment called psychoanalysis that focused on releasing a person's hidden, repressed urges and concerns from the unconscious mind.
- Psychoanalysis uses interpretation of dreams, free association, positive and negative transference, and resistance to help patients reveal their unconscious concerns.
- Freud's original therapy technique is criticized for its lack of scientific research and his own personal biases that caused him to misinterpret much of what his patients revealed.
- Modern psychodynamic therapists have modified the technique so that it takes less time and is much more direct, and they do not focus on the id and sexuality as Freud did.

14.3 Identify the basic elements of the humanistic therapies known as person-centered therapy and Gestalt therapy.

- Humanistic therapies focus on the conscious mind and subjective experiences to help clients gain insights.
- Person-centered therapy is very nondirective, allowing the client to talk through problems and concerns while the therapist provides a supportive background.
- The three basic elements of person-centered therapy are authenticity of the therapist in the client's perception, unconditional positive regard given to the client by the therapist, and the empathy of the therapist for the client.
- Gestalt therapy is more directive, helping clients become aware of their feelings and take responsibility for their choices in life.
- Gestalt therapists try to help clients deal with things in their past that they have denied and will use body language and other nonverbal cues to understand what clients are really saying.
- Humanistic therapies are also not based in experimental research and work best with intelligent, highly verbal persons.

Action Therapies: Behavior Therapies and Cognitive Therapies

14.4 Explain how behavior therapists use classical and operant conditioning to treat disordered behavior.

- Behavior therapies are action therapies that do not look at thought processes but instead focus on changing the abnormal or disordered behavior itself through classical or operant conditioning.
- Classical conditioning techniques for changing behavior include systematic desensitization, aversion therapy, and various exposure therapies.
- Virtual reality therapy is a computer-based simulation of environments that can be used to treat disorders such as phobias and PTSD.
- Therapies based on operant conditioning include modeling, reinforcement and the use of token economies, extinction, and behavioral activation.

- Behavior therapies can be effective in treating specific problems, such as bed wetting, drug addictions, and phobias, and can help improve some of the more troubling behavioral symptoms associated with more severe disorders.

14.5 Summarize the goals and basic elements of cognitive and cognitive-behavioral therapies.

- Cognitive therapy is oriented toward teaching clients how their thinking may be distorted and helping clients see how inaccurate some of their beliefs may be.
- Some of the cognitive distortions in thinking include arbitrary inference, selective thinking, overgeneralization, magnification and minimization, and personalization.
- Cognitive-behavioral therapies are action therapies that work at changing a person's illogical or distorted thinking.
- The three goals of cognitive-behavioral therapies are to relieve the symptoms and solve the problems, to develop strategies for solving future problems, and to help change irrational, distorted thinking.
- Rational emotive behavior therapy is a directive therapy in which the therapist challenges clients' irrational beliefs, often arguing with clients and even assigning them homework.
- Although CBT has seemed successful in treating depression, stress disorders, and anxiety, it is criticized for focusing on the symptoms and not the causes of disordered behavior.

Group Therapies: Not Just for the Shy

14.6 Compare and contrast different forms of group therapy.

- Group therapy can be accomplished using many styles of psychotherapy and may involve treating people who are all part of the same family, as in family counseling.
- Group therapy can also be accomplished without the aid of a trained therapist in the form of self-help or support groups composed of other people who have the same or similar problems.
- Group therapy may be useful to persons who cannot afford individual therapy; participants may also obtain a great deal of social and emotional support from other group members.

14.7 Identify the advantages and disadvantages of group therapy.

- Group therapy has the advantages of low cost, exposure to other people with similar problems, social interaction with others, and social and emotional support from people with similar disorders or problems. It has also been demonstrated to be very effective for people with social anxiety.
- Disadvantages of group therapy can include the need to share the therapist's time with others in the group, the lack of a private setting in which to reveal concerns, and the inability of people with severe disorders to tolerate being in a group.

Does Psychotherapy Really Work?

14.8 Summarize the research on the effectiveness of psychotherapy.

- Eysenck's early survey of client improvement seemed to suggest that clients would improve as time passed, with or without therapy.
- Surveys of people who have received therapy suggest that psychotherapy is more effective than no treatment at all.
- Surveys reveal that 75 to 90 percent of people who receive therapy report improvement, the longer a person stays in therapy the better the improvement, and psychotherapy works as well alone as with drugs.
- Some types of psychotherapy are more effective for certain types of problems, and no one psychotherapy method is effective for all problems.

14.9 Identify factors that influence the effectiveness of therapy.

- Effective therapy should be matched to the particular client and the particular problem, there should exist a therapeutic alliance between therapist and client, and a protected setting in which clients can release emotions and reveal private thoughts is essential.
- Treatment approaches that have the greatest research support are referred to as evidence-based or empirically supported treatments.
- Neuroimaging is being used to potentially identify the mechanisms and outcomes of effective treatment.
- Telepsychology, including therapy or other psychological services, involves services offered remotely or via the Internet. Clients need to make sure remote therapists have appropriate training and credentials in psychotherapy and specific experience and training in distance counseling.
- When the culture, ethnic group, or gender of the therapist and the client differs, misunderstandings and misinterpretations can occur due to differences in cultural/ethnic values, socioeconomic differences, gender roles, and beliefs.
- Barriers to effective psychotherapy exist when the backgrounds of client and therapist differ and include language, cultural values, social class, and nonverbal communication.

Biomedical Therapies

14.10 Categorize types of drugs used to treat psychological disorders.

- Biomedical therapies include the use of drugs, induced convulsions, and surgery to relieve or control the symptoms of mental disorders.
- Antipsychotic drugs are used to control delusions, hallucinations, and bizarre behavior and include the typical antipsychotics, atypical antipsychotics, and partial dopamine agonists.
- Antianxiety drugs are used to treat anxiety and related disorders and include the benzodiazepines and certain antidepressant drugs.
- Antimanic drugs are used to treat bipolar disorder and include lithium and certain anticonvulsant and antipsychotic drugs.
- Antidepressant drugs are used in the treatment of depression and include monoamine oxidase inhibitors (MAOIs), tricyclic antidepressants, and selective serotonin reuptake inhibitors (SSRIs).

14.11 Explain how electroconvulsive therapy and psychosurgery are used to treat psychological disorders.

- Electroconvulsive therapy, or ECT, is used to treat severe depression, bipolar disorder, and schizophrenia and involves the use of a muscle relaxant, a short-term anesthetic, and induction of a seizure under controlled conditions.
- One of the earliest psychosurgeries was the prefrontal lobotomy, in which the front part of the frontal lobe was cut away from the back part of the brain, producing effects ranging from a disappearance of symptoms to a lack of emotional response and dulling of mental functions.
- Modern psychosurgery includes the bilateral anterior cingulotomy, used to treat major depression, bipolar disorders, and certain forms of obsessive-compulsive disorder that have not responded to other forms of treatment.

14.12 Identify some of the newer technologies being used to treat psychological disorders.

- Emerging technologies for treatment of psychological disorders include repetitive transcranial magnetic stimulation (rTMS), transcranial direct current stimulation (tDCS), and deep brain stimulation (DBS).

Lifestyle Factors: Fostering Resilience

14.13 Describe how regular physical exercise and spending time in nature may benefit mental health.

- Individuals with and without psychological disorders benefit from proactive, healthy strategies for taking care of their physical and mental health; getting enough sleep, eating a healthy diet, engaging in regular exercise, and spending time in nature can boost resiliency.

Applying Psychology to Everyday Life: How to Help Others: Reducing the Stigma of Seeking Help

14.14 Describe strategies for reducing stigma associated with mental illness or seeking help for a psychological disorder.

- Reducing stigma associated with mental illness and seeking treatment is beneficial for individuals both with and without psychological disorders. Education, reliable information, personal experience, and compassion can all help reduce this stigma.

Test Yourself: Preparing for the AP Exam

PART I: MULTIPLE-CHOICE QUESTIONS

Directions for Part I: Read each of the questions or incomplete sentences below. Then choose the response that best answers the question or completes the sentence.

Pick the best answer.

1. Clarke is going to a therapist to gain a better understanding of why he has self-destructive relationships with all his friends. This type of therapy is known as _____ therapy.
   a. biomedical
   b. insight
   c. action
   d. behavioral
   e. drama

2. Through _____, person-centered therapists convey they are trying to understand the experience of the person with whom they are working.
   a. authenticity
   b. conditional regard
   c. unconditional positive regard
   d. reflection and shaping
   e. empathy and reflection

3. What differentiates motivational interviewing from person-centered therapy?
   a. Motivational interviewing is a behavioral therapeutic technique, while person-centered therapy is biomedical.
   b. Motivational interviewing has specific goals of reducing ambivalence about change and increasing intrinsic motivation to bring changes about, while traditional person-centered therapy does not.
   c. Motivational interviewing focuses on unconscious motives, while traditional person-centered therapy focuses on the self.
   d. Motivational interviewing allows the client to talk about anything he or she wishes, while traditional person-centered therapy is more direct.
   e. Motivational interviewing is a psychodynamic technique, while person-centered therapy is humanistic.

4. Which of the following clients would probably get the least benefit from a humanistic therapy?
   a. Ansel, who is bright but confused about self-image
   b. Artis, who is very talkative and open in discussing feelings
   c. Asher, who has a hard time putting thoughts and feelings into words in a logical manner
   d. Anita, who enjoys exploring the inner workings of the mind
   e. Avery, who is sixteen and does not know what she wants to do with her life

5. To overcome her fear of balloons, because of the loud sound they might suddenly make should they pop, Gerry must sit in a room filled with balloons while the therapist pops each one. After a while, Gerry realizes that her fear is unjustified and even begins to pop balloons herself. This technique is known as _____.
   a. systematic desensitization
   b. aversion therapy
   c. flooding
   d. extinction
   e. time-out

6. Jake's son Otis was afraid of dogs. Jake took Otis to a therapist to help him overcome his fear but was surprised when the therapist brought a dog into the room. At first Otis was asked to watch from across the room as the therapist showed him how to approach and pet the dog and not grab its tail. Eventually, Otis was asked to come over and mimic the behavior he had observed. After just a few sessions, Otis was no longer fearful of dogs. What technique did the therapist use with Otis?
   a. virtual exposure
   b. participant modeling
   c. aversion therapy
   d. flooding
   e. imaginal exposure

7. For both children and adults, and for many undesirable behaviors, the use of _____ or some form of "time-out" can be quite effective.
   a. arbitrary inference
   b. extinction
   c. negative reinforcement
   d. positive reinforcement
   e. magnification

8. Dimitri's wife comes home angry from her job, and he immediately assumes that he has done something wrong. Such irrational thinking is an example of _____.
   a. selective thinking
   b. overgeneralization
   c. personalization
   d. arbitrary inference
   e. catastrophizing

9. Which therapy style requires the therapist to actively confront a client's irrational beliefs?
   a. person-centered
   b. cognitive restructuring
   c. frontal lobotomy
   d. rational emotive behavior therapy (REBT)
   e. motivational interviewing

10. Family therapy is a form of group therapy in which _____.
    a. nonprofessionals lead a selected group of family members with similar concerns
    b. the entire family participates, as no one person is seen as the problem
    c. psychology professionals treat their own family members
    d. family members meet to single out the individual who is causing problems in the family dynamic
    e. family members take turns role-playing the therapist

11. Both therapists and clients play significant roles in therapy. In order for psychotherapy to be the most effective, _____.
    a. therapists should choose one style of therapy and apply it to every one of their clients
    b. the therapist must be empathetic, and provide a protected setting for clients to reveal their feelings and private thoughts
    c. the therapist should maintain physical and emotional distance from the client, who should only say what he or she thinks the therapist wants to hear
    d. both clients and therapists should avoid openness and warmth in their relationship
    e. therapists should be extremely selective in whom they choose to work with, even if it means some clients do not receive treatment

12. With regard to treatment of psychological disorders, many psychological professionals believe medications work best in combination with _____.
    a. electroconvulsive therapy
    b. psychotherapy
    c. deep brain stimulation
    d. psychosurgery
    e. a wide variety of other medications

13. Typical antipsychotic drugs work by blocking what neurotransmitter?
    a. norepinephrine
    b. epinephrine
    c. serotonin
    d. dopamine
    e. glycine

14. In bilateral anterior cingulotomy, _____.
    a. the front of the brain is cut away from the back
    b. a thin wire electrode is used to destroy a small area of brain tissue
    c. a drug is injected into the brain to destroy a large area of brain tissue
    d. an electric shock is used to stimulate certain areas of the brain
    e. the corpus callosum is severed

15. In the context of positive mental health, which of the following are general strategies highlighted in the text?
    a. eating what you can, when you can, and sleeping 7 to 8 hours a night
    b. extreme exercise and socially isolating yourself from people that might have psychological disorders
    c. spending most of your time indoors and working as much as possible
    d. practicing yoga and eating a high-fiber diet
    e. caring for your mind and body by getting enough sleep and exercising on a regular basis, preferably outdoors

PART II: FREE-RESPONSE QUESTION

Directions for Part II: Read the essay question that follows. Then respond to the question in a clear, concise essay. Do not simply list facts. Instead, present a thorough argument based on your critical consideration of the topic. Use of proper terminology is necessary.

Hyun is a psychiatrist with an eclectic approach. She specializes in delivering many different forms of mental health treatment to her patients.

Part A
Explain how Hyun would use her training in the following techniques to treat someone dealing with major depressive disorder:

- person-centered therapy
- rational emotive behavior therapy
- electroconvulsive therapy

Part B
Explain how Hyun would use her training in the following techniques to treat someone dealing with panic disorder and comorbid agoraphobia:

- psychopharmacology
- exposure therapy

Part C
Explain how Hyun would use her training in the following techniques to treat someone dealing with a substance abuse disorder:

- aversive therapy
- group therapy

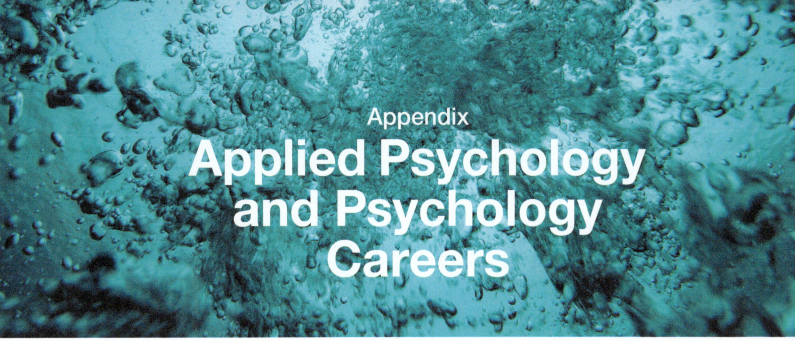

Appendix
Applied Psychology and Psychology Careers

Ralf strm/EyeEm/Getty Images

Why study applied psychology?

Many different kinds of psychologists study or work in many different fields. Whereas early psychologists were still discovering the processes that govern the human mind, today's psychologists are more often applying information and principles gained from research to people in the real world. Why study careers in psychology? With so many different areas of focus, a career in psychology can be varied and exciting. There is much more to psychology than helping people who have mental health problems.

Professor John Gambon of Ozarks Technical and Community College in Springfield, Missouri, begins his class like any other. After a few minutes, two students rush in and each throw two water balloons at the professor. As they run out, they yell something about fried eggs. Professor Gambon, soaked from the balloons, asks his students to write down everything they just saw, including what was said. After a few minutes, he gathers up the paperwork and invites his two balloon-throwing accomplices back into the room.

As he reads the papers of his students, many realize they made mistakes in identifying the perpetrators. Quite often, students mismatch hair color, height, facial features, and even the clothes each was wearing. What's more, nearly 90 percent claim they heard the two men yell, "That was for last Friday!" When students are shown the truth, many are shocked at their overall inaccuracy at identifying the two men.

Work such as this is not new to Professor Gambon. He has worked as a consultant in several trials where the issue of accurately identifying someone has been brought into question. His cases include several homicides, assault, breaking and entering, and armed robbery.

His demonstrations show the overall unreliability of eyewitness identification, as outlined by psychologist Elizabeth Loftus. See Learning Objective 6.7. The kind of issues that influence an eyewitness's accuracy include the presence of a weapon (people tend to look at a weapon more than the physical attributes of the assailant), time of day, fatigue, and the amount of time between the crime and when they are required to recall it. Clearly, there are flaws inherent in eyewitness identification.

Forensic psychology is just one of many areas in which psychological principles can be applied to issues and concerns of everyday life. This appendix will look at several areas of applied psychology as well as the types of careers open to someone who studies psychology today.

Learning Objectives

A.1 Define applied psychology.

A.2 Describe different types of psychological professionals, and identify their educational background and training.

A.3 List the kinds of careers available to someone with a master's degree in psychology.

A.4 List the kinds of careers available to someone with a bachelor's degree in psychology.

A.5 Describe some areas of specialization in psychology.

A.6 Describe how psychology interacts with other career fields.

A.7 Explain the fields of industrial-organizational (I-O) psychology and human factors psychology.

A.8 Describe how the I-O field has evolved throughout its history.

A.1 What Is Applied Psychology?

A.1 Define applied psychology.

The term **applied psychology** refers to using findings from psychological research to solve real-world problems. The psychological professional, who might be a psychiatrist, a psychologist, or even a psychiatric social worker (as described later in this appendix), may do testing or use some other type of assessment and then describe a plan of action intended to solve whatever problem is of concern. As is evident in the opening comments about John Gambon, you can see that his training in psychology and his specialized knowledge enabled him to testify in court as an expert witness. This is a practical application of psychological tools to a real problem—the professional literally "applies" psychology.

> 💬 It seems to me that psychology could be useful in a lot of different areas, not just education. In fact, wasn't that what all those Applying Psychology sections at the end of each chapter were about?

Every chapter in this text ends with some application of psychology to the real world. The field of applied psychology isn't just one field but rather a lot of different areas that all share the common goal of using psychology in a practical way. A large number of areas can be considered applied psychology, including one of the broadest areas of psychology: clinical and counseling psychology. For example, health psychologists examine the effects of stress on physical as well as mental health; educational and school psychologists look for ways to improve student learning and apply the findings to the classroom; sports psychologists help athletes prepare themselves mentally for competition; human factors psychologists deal with the way people and machines interact; forensic psychologists deal with psychological issues within the legal system; and industrial-organizational (I-O) psychologists deal with the work environment. In addition, environmental psychologists examine the interaction of people with their surroundings at work, in social settings, and in schools, homes, and other buildings. Those surroundings include not just the physical structures but also the particular population of people who live, work, and play in those surroundings. Other psychologists look at the factors that influence people to buy certain products, analyze the best ways to market a product, and examine the buying habits of the typical consumer.

This appendix includes information on the different roles of psychological professionals and the type of education required for many professions, along with a brief overview of many of the specialized areas in psychology. The remainder of this appendix briefly explores how psychology can be used in practical ways in several different areas of life: the environment, law, education, the military, sports, and the world of work.

applied psychology
the use of psychological concepts in solving real-world problems.

Practice Quiz — How much do you remember?

Pick the best answer.

1. The term _____ psychology refers to using findings from psychological research to solve real-world problems.
   a. academic
   b. applied
   c. practical
   d. pragmatic
   e. basic

2. Which of the following types of psychologists might be most interested in dealing with the work environment?
   a. a psychiatric social worker
   b. a health psychologist
   c. a vocational psychologist
   d. an industrial-organizational psychologist
   e. a clinical psychologist

3. Heidi has designed a new type of gearshift to be used in automobiles with an automatic transmission. Before she proposes it to the major car manufacturers, she wants to make sure that it will be more advantageous for people who drive such cars. With which of the following types of psychologists would Heidi most want to consult about her design?
   a. a human-factors psychologist
   b. a machinery psychologist
   c. an environmental psychologist
   d. an industrial-organizational psychologist
   e. a sports psychologist

A.2–A.6 Psychology as a Career

When most people think of psychology as a potential career, they assume certain things about the profession: For example, to help people with their problems, one has to be a psychologist, all psychologists are doctors, and all psychologists counsel mentally ill people. None of these assumptions are completely true.

A.2 Types of Psychological Professionals

A.2 Describe different types of psychological professionals and identify their educational background and training.

Several types of professionals work in psychology. These professionals have different training with different focuses and may have different goals.

PSYCHIATRIC SOCIAL WORKERS A *psychiatric social worker* is trained in the area of social work and usually has a master of social work (M.S.W.) degree and may be licensed in the state in which he or she works as a licensed clinical social worker (LCSW). These professionals focus more on the social conditions that can have an impact on mental disorders, such as poverty, overcrowding, stress, and drug abuse. They may administer psychotherapy (talking with clients about their problems) and often work in a clinical setting where other types of psychological professionals are available.

PSYCHIATRISTS A *psychiatrist* has a medical doctorate or a doctor of osteopathic medicine (M.D. or D.O.) degree and is a physician who specializes in the diagnosis and treatment of psychological disorders. Like any other medical doctor who may specialize in emergency medicine, treating the diseases of the elderly, treating infants and children, or any other special area of medicine, psychiatrists write prescriptions and perform medical procedures on their patients. They simply have special training in the diagnosis and treatment of disorders that are considered to be mental disorders such as schizophrenia, depression, or extreme anxiety. Because they are medical doctors, they tend to have a biopsychological perspective on the causes of and treatments for such disorders.

PSYCHOLOGISTS A *psychologist* doesn't have a medical degree but instead undergoes intense academic training, learning about many different areas of psychology before choosing an area in which to specialize. Psychologists typically have either a doctor of philosophy (Ph.D.) or doctor of psychology (Psy.D.) degree. (People who hold a master of science or M.S. degree are not usually called psychologists except in a few states. They can be called therapists or counselors, or they may be teachers or researchers.)

 What's the difference between a Ph.D. and a Psy.D.?

Psychologists specialize in many different areas and work in many different settings.

The Ph.D. is a type of degree that usually indicates the highest degree of learning available in almost any subject area—psychology, the study of languages, education, philosophy, the sciences, and many others. It is typically very research oriented, and earning the degree usually requires a previous master's degree, in addition to coursework for the doctorate itself, as well as a dissertation—a scholarly work of research in the area of focus as long as a book that may even be published as a book.

The Psy.D. is a type of degree developed in the late 1970s that focuses less on research and more on the practical application of psychological principles (Peterson, 1976, 1982). In addition to academic coursework such as that required for the Ph.D., this degree may require a major paper instead of a dissertation, with the difference being that the paper is not a report of research designed and conducted by the student but is rather a large-scale term paper. Each year of a Psy.D. program will also require the student to participate in a *practicum*, an actual experience with observing and eventually conducting therapy and treatments under supervision.

Unlike psychiatrists, psychologists typically cannot prescribe medicines or perform medical procedures. Some states are seeking legislative changes to allow psychologists to prescribe psychotropic medications if they receive special education in the use of prescription drugs. Such privileges were first pursued by the U.S. military. The reasoning behind this move, for which the American Psychological Association has been lobbying since 1984, involves both cost and the delay in receiving mental health services. If a person sees a psychologist and then has to go to a psychiatrist for medical prescriptions, the cost can be prohibitive. There are also fewer psychiatrists in some states than in others, causing long waits for mental health services from those doctors—delays that can sometimes lead to an increase in suicide rates for patients who are not getting the help they need. Although some psychologists in the military or Indian Health Service can already prescribe, as of May 2019, only five states and one territory (New Mexico, Louisiana, Illinois, Iowa, Idaho, and Guam) have successfully afforded prescription privileges to psychologists.

Some psychologists provide counseling or therapy and use a variety of techniques and approaches. See Learning Objectives 14.2–14.7. However, many psychologists do no counseling at all. There are psychologists who only engage in assessment, those who teach at colleges or universities, those who do only research in those same institutions or for industries, and those who do a combination of teaching and research (and some that do a combination of teaching, research, and counseling or clinical practice). Other psychologists are involved in designing equipment and workplaces, developing educational methods, or working as consultants to businesses and the court system. In the United States, the number of active psychologists has been stable from 2007 to 2014 with an approximate mean number of 84,000 active psychologists in the workforce (American Psychological Association, 2018b). However, this appears to be increasing as annual numbers were over 90,000 in 2015 through 2017 (American Psychological Association, 2018b, 2018c; see **Figure A.1**). The psychology workforce also appears to be getting more youthful with more young women and more young psychologists

Figure A.1 Number of Active Psychologists in the United States

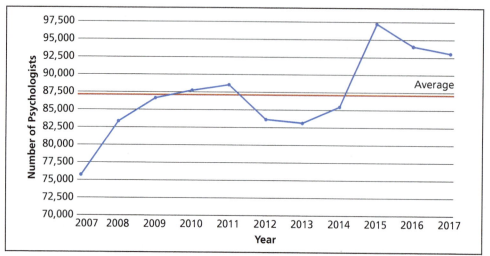

This graph shows the approximate number of active psychologists in the United States from 2007 to 2017.

Source: Data from American Psychological Association, 2018b, 2018c.

from racial/ethnic minority groups entering the workforce, although the percentage of psychologists from racial/ethnic minority groups is not as high as that of the U.S. population (American Psychological Association, 2018b). For more information about possible career pathways in psychology, visit the American Psychological Association's *Demographics of the U.S. Psychology Workforce* interactive data tool, **apa.org/workforce/data-tools/demographics**.

Although becoming a psychologist requires a doctorate degree of some kind, many career fields can benefit from a 4-year college degree in psychology as the basis of that career or going on to obtain a master's degree in psychology.

A.3 Careers with a Master's Degree in Psychology

A.3 List the kinds of careers available to someone with a master's degree in psychology.

While individuals earning a master's degree in psychology are not typically able to engage in the same level of independent research or practice of psychology as someone with a doctoral degree, they can still work in a variety of areas, both within and beyond the field of psychology. They may work directly under the supervision of a doctoral psychologist if engaged in clinical, counseling, or school psychology or in assessment. Others work outside of the field in jobs requiring research or analysis skills and work in health, industry, or government areas.

For those interested in counseling or providing therapy, many states allow individuals with master's degrees and prerequisite training and supervision experiences to become licensed to provide unsupervised counseling and therapy. Titles may vary by state, but some of the areas and titles associated with licensed master's-level work include licensed marriage and family therapist (LMFT), licensed professional counselor (LPC), licensed mental health counselor (LMHC), or licensed clinical social worker (LCSW). These individuals may work in a larger organization or independently in private practice. Beyond these areas, some individuals with a master's degree in psychology become certified or licensed to serve as school counselors at various levels and may work in an elementary, middle, or high school.

A.4 Careers with a Bachelor's Degree in Psychology

A.4 List the kinds of careers available to someone with a bachelor's degree in psychology.

Although people earning only the baccalaureate (bachelor's) degree in psychology cannot be called psychologists or provide therapy in a private practice, many career fields are open to such a person. More than 1 million bachelor's degrees in psychology have been awarded since 1970, and since 2000 the number has increased each year (Landrum, 2009; Snyder & Dillow, 2010). Approximately 1.2 to 1.6 million students take introductory psychology each year and over 117,000 bachelor's degrees in psychology were awarded in the 2014–2015 academic year (Gurung et al., 2016; National Center for Education Statistics, 2017; see **Figure A.2**). A bachelor's degree in psychology can be highly flexible and adaptable to many different kinds of careers (Dunn & Halonen, 2017; Landrum, 2009; Landrum & Davis, 2014; Schwartz, 2000). In 2017, approximately 3.5 million people in the United States held a bachelor's degree in psychology (American Psychological Association, 2018a). While surveys by both the American Psychological Association and others reveal many may work in health-related or social fields, individuals with a bachelor's degree in psychology may be employed in research development or research management, administration, business, education and teaching, professional services, sales, or management (Dunn & Halonen, 2017; Grocer & Kohout, 1997; Landrum, 2009). As compared to some majors, psychology students tend to show better reasoning skills as a result of their understanding of

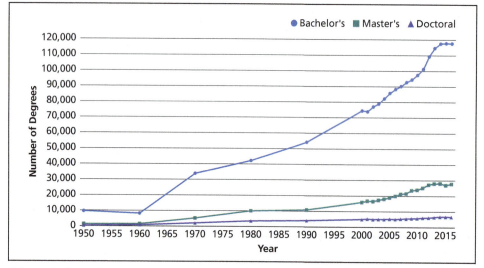

Figure A.2 Number of Psychology Degrees Awarded Annually in the United States

This graph shows the number of bachelor's, master's, and doctoral psychology degrees awarded annually in the United States from 1950 to 2015.

Source: Data from National Center for Education Statistics, 2017.

research methods and statistics (Dunn & Halonen, 2017).

Other possible careers include marketing researcher, social worker, and communications specialist (Dunn & Halonen, 2017; Landrum & Davis, 2014; Schwartz, 2000). With its emphasis on critical thinking and empirical observation, psychology trains people for a variety of potential workplace environments and requirements. Psychology is an excellent major even if you intend to do graduate work in some other career: Business, law, child care, teaching, and management are only a few of the areas that relate to psychology. In 2017, 30 percent of individuals who held a bachelor's degree in psychology obtained higher degrees in other areas of study (American Psychological Association, 2018a). For more information about possible career pathways in psychology, visit the American Psychological Association's *Degree Pathways in Psychology* interactive data tool, **apa.org/workforce/data-tools/degrees-pathways**.

AP 1.E Distinguish the different domains of psychology.

A.5 Areas of Specialization

A.5 Describe some areas of specialization in psychology.

> You said that some psychologists teach or do research. What kind of research do they do?

Psychologists may focus their energies in many different areas. They conduct experiments, surveys, observations, and so on to gather more information for their particular field of interest, to find support for current theories, or to develop new ones. Let's look at some of the areas in which psychologists may specialize.

CLINICAL PSYCHOLOGY Even though not all psychologists do counseling or therapy, many psychologists do. **Clinical psychology** is the most similar of the areas to psychiatry in that professionals with this focus traditionally work with individuals with more serious forms of mental illness. It is also the area of specialization with the largest number of psychologists. Approximately 45 percent of surveyed psychologists who are currently providing health services identified clinical psychology as their primary specialty area, and an additional 16 percent identified *clinical child and adolescent psychology* as their specialty area (American Psychological Association, 2016).

Clinical psychologists, like psychiatrists, diagnose and treat psychological disorders in people. However, the clinical psychologist cannot prescribe drugs or medical therapies (with the exceptions discussed earlier, of course) but instead relies on listening or observing the client's problems, possibly administering psychological tests, and then providing explanations for the client's behavior and feelings or directing the client in specific actions to make positive changes in his or her life.

COUNSELING PSYCHOLOGY **Counseling psychology** is similar to clinical psychology in that this type of psychologist diagnoses and treats problems. The difference is that a counseling psychologist usually works with relatively healthy people who have less

clinical psychology
area of psychology in which the psychologists diagnose and treat people with psychological disorders that may range from mild to severe.

counseling psychology
area of psychology in which the psychologists help people with problems of adjustment.

severe forms of mental illness or problems such as adjustment to college, marriage, family life, work problems, and so on. See Learning Objective 1.4. Counseling psychologists make up approximately 9 percent of psychologists currently providing health services (American Psychological Association, 2016).

DEVELOPMENTAL PSYCHOLOGY Developmental psychology is an area that focuses on the study of change, or development. Developmental psychologists are interested in changes in the way people think, in how people relate to others, and in the ways people feel over the entire span of life. These psychologists work in academic settings such as colleges and universities and may do research in various areas of development. They do not provide therapy. See Learning Objective 8.1.

EXPERIMENTAL PSYCHOLOGY Experimental psychology encompasses several different areas such as learning, memory, thinking, perception, motivation, and language. The focus of these psychologists, however, is on doing research and conducting studies and experiments with both people and animals in these various areas. They tend to work in academic settings, especially in large universities. See Learning Objective 1.4.

SOCIAL PSYCHOLOGY Social psychology is an area that focuses on how human behavior is affected by the presence of other people. For example, social psychologists explore areas such as prejudice, attitude change, aggressive behavior, and interpersonal attraction. Although most social psychologists work in academic settings teaching and doing research, some work in federal agencies and big business doing practical (applied) research. In fact, many social psychologists are experimental psychologists who perform their experiments in real-world settings rather than the laboratory to preserve the natural reactions of people. When people are in an artificial setting, they often behave in self-conscious ways, which is not the behavior the researcher wishes to study. See Learning Objective 11.1.

PERSONALITY PSYCHOLOGY Personality psychology focuses on the differences in personality among people. These psychologists may look at the influence of heredity on personality. They study the ways in which people are both alike and different. They look at the development of personality and do personality assessment. They may be involved in forming new theories of how personality works or develops. Personality psychologists work in academic settings, doing research and teaching. See Learning Objective 12.1.

PHYSIOLOGICAL PSYCHOLOGY Physiological psychology is an area that focuses on the study of the biological bases of behavior. Many professionals now refer to this area as *behavioral neuroscience* or *biopsychology*. Physiological psychologists study the brain, nervous system, and the influence of the body's chemicals, such as hormones and the chemicals in the brain, on human behavior. They study the effects of drug use and possible genetic influences on some kinds of abnormal and normal human behavior, such as schizophrenia or aspects of intelligence. Most physiological psychologists, like experimental psychologists, work in an academic setting. See Learning Objective 2.1.

NEUROPSYCHOLOGY Neuropsychology is an area within the field of psychology in which professionals explore the relationships between the brain systems and behavior. Neuropsychologists may be engaged in research or more focused on the assessment, diagnosis, treatment, and/or rehabilitation of individuals with various neurological, medical, neurodevelopmental, or psychiatric conditions (National Academy of Neuropsychology, 2001). See Learning Objective 7.8.

COMPARATIVE PSYCHOLOGY Comparative psychology is an area that focuses exclusively on animals and animal behavior. By comparing and contrasting animal behavior with what is already known about human behavior, comparative psychologists can contribute to the understanding of human behavior. Research in animal behavior also helps

developmental psychology
area of psychology in which the psychologists study the changes in the way people think, relate to others, and feel as they age.

experimental psychology
area of psychology in which the psychologists primarily do research and experiments in the areas of learning, memory, thinking, perception, motivation, and language.

personality psychology
area of psychology in which the psychologists study the differences in personality among people.

physiological psychology
area of psychology in which the psychologists study the biological bases of behavior.

neuropsychology
area of psychology in which psychologists specialize in the research or clinical implications of brain–behavior relationships.

comparative psychology
area of psychology in which the psychologists study animals and their behavior for the purpose of comparing and contrasting it to human behavior.

people learn how to treat animals more humanely and coexist with the animals in a common environment. Comparative psychologists might work in animal laboratories in a university or may do observation and studies of animals in the animals' natural habitats.

Psychologists in these areas may do research directed at discovering basic principles of human behavior (basic research), or they may engage in research designed to find solutions to practical problems of the here and now (applied research). See Learning Objective 1.4. There are many other areas in which psychologists may specialize that focus almost exclusively on applied research. These areas are those most often associated with applied psychology.

AP 1.E Distinguish the different domains of psychology.

A.6 Psychology Beyond the Classroom

A.6 Describe how psychology interacts with other career fields.

Individuals working in psychology can serve in important roles in many different fields. Some are extensions of the areas of specialization just covered. Other fields are also well suited due to the general and sometimes specific skills psychology professionals can provide.

PSYCHOLOGY AND HEALTH Health psychology focuses on the relationship of human behavior patterns and stress reactions to physical health with the goal of improving and helping maintain good health while preventing and treating illness. For example, a health psychologist might design a program to help people lose weight or stop smoking. Stress-management techniques are also a major focus of this area. Health psychologists may work in hospitals, clinics, medical schools, health agencies, academic settings, or private practice.

In one study (Kerwin et al., 2010), researchers found an association between obesity in older women and a decline in memory functioning in those women. This finding was particularly true for women carrying the excess weight around their hips (pear shapes) and less so for women carrying the excess weight around their waists (apple shapes). The study controlled for other health variables such as diabetes, heart disease, and stroke. This is a good example of the kind of research that health psychologists conduct. Other areas studied by health psychologists include the influence of optimistic attitudes on the progress of disease, the link between mental distress and health, and the promotion of wellness and hope in an effort to prevent illness. See Learning Objectives 10.5, 10.6.

PSYCHOLOGY AND EDUCATION Educational psychology is concerned with the study of human learning. As educational psychologists come to understand some of the basic aspects of learning, they develop methods and materials for aiding the process of learning. For example, educational psychologists helped design the phonics method of teaching children to read. This type of psychologist may have a doctorate of education (Ed.D.) rather than a Ph.D. and typically works in academic settings.

What types of research might an educational psychologist conduct? The February 2019 issue of *Journal of Educational Psychology* included articles on the impact of study strategies, the types of questions that are most beneficial for students, how to best use audio and visual cues in multimedia learning resources, and how automaticity in word recognition is related to reading ability—just to name a few.

School psychology is related to but not at all the same as educational psychology. Whereas educational psychologists may do research and develop new learning techniques, school psychologists may take the results of that research or those methods and apply them in the actual school system. School psychologists work directly with children in the school setting. They do testing and other forms of assessment to place children in special programs or to diagnose educational problems such as dyslexia or attention-deficit/hyperactivity disorder. They may act as consultants to teachers, parents, and educational administrators. Counseling students is actually a relatively small part of the job of a school psychologist, although counseling takes a much bigger role when tragedies strike a school. When traumatic events such as the unexpected and tragic death of

health psychology

area of psychology focusing on how physical activities, psychological traits, stress reactions, and social relationships affect overall health and rate of illnesses.

educational psychology

area of psychology in which the psychologists are concerned with the study of human learning and development of new learning techniques.

school psychology

area of psychology in which the psychologists work directly in the schools, doing assessments, educational placement, and diagnosing educational problems.

School psychologists often work with teachers to help families better understand their student's learning or mental health needs.

a classmate or even larger-scale tragedies such as the numerous school massacres of the past three decades take place, school psychologists are often called on to offer help and counseling to students.

PSYCHOLOGY AND SPORTS Sports psychology is a relatively new and fast-growing field in which the main focus is on helping athletes and others involved in sports activities prepare mentally rather than just physically for participation in sports. The idea behind this field is that a superior physical performance is not enough to guarantee success; rather, the mind must be prepared for the activity by setting clear short-term goals, holding positive thoughts, using visualization of the goal, stopping negative thoughts, and other techniques based primarily in the cognitive perspective. For example, a sports psychologist might have a golfer who has been having trouble with the accuracy of his drives perform visualization exercises, mentally seeing himself hit the ball down the fairway again and again. Sports psychologists work in athletic organizations and may have a private practice or do consulting work.

PSYCHOLOGY AND THE MILITARY Within the military, psychologists work in a variety of areas ranging from assessment, teaching, management, and research to the provision of mental health services. The variety of psychologists in this field may include clinical, counseling, experimental, I-O, or human factors, among others, and may reflect any specialty area in the field of psychology. In short, they apply psychological skills to human issues in military environments, working with both military personnel and their families (American Psychological Association, Division 19, 2019). One poignant example, the rise of suicides in the armed forces associated with the conflicts in Iraq and Afghanistan, has placed demands on both the military and military families at a level not seen before (Berman et al., 2010). Researchers are working with military personnel to try to determine how to possibly identify individuals who think about suicide, referred to as suicidal ideation (SI), but do not attempt suicide from those with SI who do attempt suicide (Naifeh et al., 2018).

PSYCHOLOGY AND THE LAW Psychologists have often been involved in the world of legal matters in various ways. Social psychologists often do research in the area of criminal behavior and may consult with attorneys or other agents of the court system on such topics as witness credibility, jury selection, and the kind of influences that exist for decision-making processes. Developmental psychologists may become involved in determining the accuracy of and influences on the testimony of children and adolescents as well as the needs of children caught up in a custody battle between divorced or divorcing parents. Cognitive psychologists may become expert witnesses on the accuracy of memory and eyewitness testimony or ways to determine the truth or falsehood of statements made by witnesses or defendants. Clinical psychologists may deliver their services directly to incarcerated prisoners or may conduct assessments of intelligence and/or mental status to determine whether a person charged with a crime should stand trial.

All of the forms of psychological involvement in legal matters mentioned here can be considered as part of the growing field of **forensic psychology**. Forensic psychology is the practice of psychology related to the legal system, and it involves examining criminal evidence and aiding law enforcement investigations into criminal activities. Some forensic psychologists provide information and advice to officials in the legal system, such as lawyers or judges; some act as expert witnesses (like Professor John Gambon in the opening story); some actually diagnose and treat criminals within the prison system; and others may administer psychological tests to criminal defendants. Forensic psychologists may aid either the prosecution or the defense in a trial by helping determine which potential jurors would be the best or worst choices. This type of professional may do consulting work in addition to maintaining a regular private practice in clinical or counseling psychology or may work entirely within the justice system as a police psychologist or a full-time jury expert, for example.

sports psychology
area of psychology in which the psychologists help athletes and others prepare themselves mentally for participation in sports activities.

forensic psychology
area of psychology concerned with people in the legal system, including psychological assessment of criminals, jury selection, and expert witnessing.

PSYCHOLOGY AND THE COMMUNITY Community psychology is an area that focuses on both individuals and their community. But instead of focusing on the individual, this field is often concerned with an ecological perspective, examining issues at various interconnected levels, including the individual, group, neighborhood, and society. It is an area that focuses on promoting health and preventing common societal issues across all levels. Community psychology aims to understand human behavior in context and recognizes the role of human diversity in promoting change. Advocacy is a key role for individuals in this area as they work to promote social justice, or practices and policies that directly impact aspects of life such as equal opportunity for all people, prevention of violence, and active citizenship. Community psychologists are involved in a variety of life activities and may be engaged in promoting mental health, physical health, educational interventions, or work policies.

PSYCHOLOGY AND THE ENVIRONMENT Another broad area in which psychological principles can be applied to solve practical problems is the area of managing the environment. **Environmental psychology** is an area that focuses on the relationship between human behavior and the environment in which the behavior takes place such as an office, store, school, dormitory, or hospital. Because the concern of researchers in this field deals directly with behavior in a particular setting, research is always conducted in that setting rather than in a laboratory. Environmental psychologists may work with other professionals, such as urban or city planners, economists, engineers, and architects, helping those professionals plan the most efficient buildings, parks, housing developments, or plants.

community psychology
area of psychology in which psychologists serve at various levels including individual, group, and community, focusing on promoting social welfare and preventing social problems.

environmental psychology
area of psychology in which the focus is on how people interact with and are affected by their physical environments.

Practice Quiz   How much do you remember?

Pick the best answer.

1. Dr. Mori works at a hospital and is regularly called to the emergency room to assist with patients who are having acute mental health crises. She often prescribes psychotropic medications to help these patients get stabilized. Which of the following degrees has Dr. Mori most likely earned?
   a. M.D.
   b. Ed.D.
   c. Ph.D.
   d. M.S.W.
   e. Psy.D.

2. Aisha has earned a master's degree but decided not to pursue her doctorate. She does, however, want to provide counseling and therapy to clients but does not want to be supervised for her entire career. After several years of training and appropriate supervision, she has achieved a degree that, in her state, will allow her to have this career. Which of the following would NOT likely be a title that Aisha may now hold?
   a. LMHC (licensed mental health counselor)
   b. LCP (licensed children's psychologist)
   c. LCSW (licensed clinical social worker)
   d. LMFT (licensed marriage and family therapist)
   e. LPC (licensed professional counselor)

3. _____ psychologists are primarily interested in changes in the way people think, in how people relate to others, and in the ways people feel over the entire span of life. They often work in academic settings such as colleges and universities and may do research in various areas. They do not generally provide therapy.
   a. Environmental
   b. Counseling
   c. Developmental
   d. Forensic
   e. Sociocultural

4. Dr. Cone has spent her entire career working with chimpanzees, studying the ways that their behavioral profiles are both similar to and different from those of human beings. Dr. Cone is probably a _____ psychologist.
   a. physiological
   b. forensic
   c. comparative
   d. zoological
   e. developmental

A.7–A.8 Psychology and Work

Work is a tremendous part of many people's lives. People often spend more time at work than they do with their families or in social activities. One of the largest branches of applied psychology focuses on how psychology can help people in management, productivity, morale*, and many other areas of the world of work.

---

*morale: a sense of common purpose, enthusiasm, confidence, and loyalty.

A.7 What Are Industrial-Organizational Psychology and Human Factors Psychology?

A.7 Explain the fields of industrial-organizational (I-O) psychology and human factors psychology.

AP 1.E Distinguish the different domains of psychology.

Industrial-organizational (I-O) psychology is concerned with the relationships between people and their work environments. I-O psychologists may help in personnel selection, administer job performance assessments, design work schedules that help workers adjust to new time periods of work hours with less difficulty, or design new work areas to increase morale and productivity. Psychologists in this field may study the behavior of entire organizations. They are often hired by corporations and businesses to deal with the hiring and assessment of employees. They may research and develop ways for workers to be more efficient and productive. They may work in business, government agencies, and academic settings. Table A.1 briefly lists some of the areas of specialization.

Table A.1 Areas in I-O Psychology

Areas in Industry	Areas In Organizations
Job analysis	Social behavior of work teams
Job evaluation and compensation	Job satisfaction
Characteristics critical to effective management	Personality characteristics critical to job performance
Personnel recruiting, selection, and placement	Relationships between management and workers
Occupational training	Leadership characteristics and training
Examination of working conditions	Consumer psychology
Interviewing and testing	Motivational concerns
Performance appraisal and feedback	Conflict management

A specific kind of I-O specialist, called a *human factors engineer*, focuses on ergonomics, or designing machines, furniture, and other devices people have to use so that those devices are the most practical, comfortable, and logical for human use. **Human factors psychology** consists of these researchers and designers who study the way humans and machines interact with each other. They may work directly in the companies involved in the design of appliances, airplane controls, and the operation of computers or other mechanical devices. For example, recall the iPhone commercial about how your thumb can reach all parts of the screen. Or have you ever seen an ergonomic chair? Most likely, a human factors engineer was involved in the design or testing of these products.

Psychologists working in I-O settings apply psychological principles and theories to the workplace. For example, Maslow's humanistic theory and hierarchy of needs (see Learning Objective 9.4) has had a powerful influence on the field of management (Heil et al., 1998). Douglas McGregor, in his explanations of two different styles of management (McGregor, 1960), relates the older and less productive "Theory X" (workers are unmotivated and need to be managed and directed) to Maslow's lower needs and the newer, more productive style of management called "Theory Y" (workers want to work and want that work to be meaningful) to the higher needs.

A.8 The History of Industrial-Organizational Psychology and the Field Today

A.8 Describe how the I-O field has evolved throughout its history.

Industrial-organizational psychology got its start near the beginning of the twentieth century with the work of Walter D. Scott, a former student of famed physiologist and founder of the first psychological laboratory Wilhelm Wundt. Scott applied psychological

industrial-organizational (I-O) psychology

area of psychology concerned with the relationships between people and their work environment.

human factors psychology

area of industrial-organizational psychology concerned with the study of the way humans and machines interact with each other.

principles to hiring, management, and advertising techniques (Schultz & Schultz, 2004). He also wrote one of the first books about the application of psychology to industry and advertising, called *The Theory and Practice of Advertising* (Scott, 1908). Another early figure in the newly developing field of industrial-organizational psychology was Hugo Münsterberg, a psychologist also trained by Wundt, who conducted research on such varied topics as the power of prayer and eyewitness testimony (Hothersall, 1995). Münsterberg wrote a book about eyewitness testimony called *On the Witness Stand* (1908) and later wrote *Psychology and Industrial Efficiency* (1913).

The I-O field became important during World War I when the army needed a way to test the intelligence of potential recruits. Psychologist Robert Yerkes, who would later become known for his groundbreaking research in comparative psychology while working with the great apes, developed the Army Alpha and Army Beta tests. The Army Alpha test was used with applicants who were able to read, whereas the Army Beta test was administered to applicants who were illiterate (McGuire, 1994; Yerkes, 1921).

In the mid-1920s, a series of studies conducted by Elton Mayo for the Western Electric Company (Franke & Kaul, 1978; Parsons, 1992; Roethlisberger & Dickson, 1939) broadened the field. These were the first studies to view the workplace as a social system rather than as just a production line. Instead of treating workers as simply other pieces of equipment, these studies suggested that allowing workers some input into the decision-making process not only improved worker morale but also reduced workers' resistance to changes in the workplace. These studies led the way for others to examine how management of employees and production could be improved. For example, the Society for Industrial and Organizational Psychology's (SIOP) 2019 annual list of top 10 workplace trends include artificial intelligence (AI) and machine learning. As both AI and machine learning help organizations to become more efficient and gain new insights from big data, I-O psychologists can help with interpreting the results and assist business leaders in gauging their employee's reactions to their new AI "coworkers" (Society for Industrial and Organizational Psychology [SIOP], 2019). Management theories and strategies may also be applied to other kinds of settings such as schools, colleges, and universities. Yet another setting I-O psychologists are currently involved in is working with NASA for the planned trip to Mars (Avolio, 2017; Novotney, 2013, March). I-O psychologists are researching ways to improve team selection and training for the astronauts who will have to endure a longer and further space voyage than anyone ever has, a trip that will take close to 3 years. Promotion of resiliency, adaptability, and group cohesion are some of the areas being investigated, especially in light of the lack of privacy and cramped quarters in which they will be living.

Practice Quiz   How much do you remember?

Pick the best answer.

1. Dr. Dickson is an industrial-organizational psychologist who has just been hired by a major electronics production company. His job there will include many different responsibilities. Which of the following is NOT likely to be high on his list of responsibilities?
    a. design work schedules to help maximize productivity
    b. helping select personnel
    c. designing new work areas to increase morale and productivity
    d. administering job performance assessments
    e. helping workers visualize their performance

2. Which of the following would a human factors psychologist have the most input in designing?
    a. a study tips resource for students with ADHD
    b. a set of maps that will show college students the closest stores that offer various products
    c. a new smartphone application that allows you to track your spending
    d. a new ergonomic chair that reduces muscle fatigue in the legs and back
    e. a book of recipes for single parents who do not have a lot of time to cook

3. One of the earliest industrial-organizational psychologists, _____, was a student of famed researcher Wilhelm Wundt and wrote a book entitled *The Theory and Practice of Advertising*.
    a. William James
    b. Elton Mayo
    c. Walter D. Scott
    d. Keith Engelhorn
    e. Robert Yerkes

Chapter Summary

What Is Applied Psychology?

A.1 Define applied psychology.

- Applied psychology refers to using psychological principles and research to solve problems in the real world.

Psychology as a Career

A.2 Describe different types of psychological professionals, and identify their educational background and training.

- Different types of psychological professionals vary by level of education and training. Examples include psychiatrists, psychiatric social workers, and psychologists.
- Psychologists hold either a Ph.D. or Psy.D. degree.

A.3 List the kinds of careers available to someone with a master's degree in psychology.

- Individuals with a master's degree may work under the supervision of a doctoral-level psychology professional, practice independently if licensed, or work in private or educational settings.

A.4 List the kinds of careers available to someone with a bachelor's degree in psychology.

- Education, statistical consulting, administration and other business occupations, as well as health services are examples of careers a person with a bachelor's degree in psychology might enter.

A.5 Describe some areas of specialization in psychology.

- Areas of specialization include clinical and counseling psychology, developmental, experimental, social, personality, and physiological psychology, neuropsychology, and comparative psychology.

A.6 Describe how psychology interacts with other career fields.

- Health psychology is an area in which the goal is to discover relationships between human behavior, including stress factors, and physical health, with the intention of preventing and treating ill health.
- Educational psychologists study the processes of human learning to develop new techniques and methods, whereas school psychologists apply those methods in the school, administer assessments, recommend placement, and provide counseling and diagnosis of educational problems.
- Sports psychologists help athletes prepare themselves mentally for participation in sports.
- Psychologists working in the military represent almost all subfields of psychology and work with both military personnel and their families in military environments.
- Psychologists may act as expert witnesses for legal matters, help in jury selection, provide clinical services to defendants or prisoners, or produce personality profiles of various types of criminals in the field of forensic psychology.
- Community psychologists help solve social issues and work to promote health for individuals and for the larger community in which people live.
- Environmental psychology looks at the relationship between human behavior and the physical environment in which that behavior takes place.

Psychology and Work

A.7 Explain the fields of industrial-organizational (I-O) psychology and human factors psychology.

- Industrial-organizational psychology is concerned with how people function in and are affected by their work environments.
- Human factors is a type of I-O psychology in which the focus is on the way humans and machines interact with each other, designing or helping design the machines used by people in various science and industrial settings.

A.8 Describe how the I-O field has evolved throughout its history.

- The I-O field began in the twentieth century with the application of psychological principles to hiring, management, and advertising.

Test Yourself

Pick the best answer.

1. Which of the following professionals has a medical degree?
    a. licensed professional counselor
    b. counseling psychologist
    c. clinical psychologist
    d. psychiatrist
    e. psychiatric social worker

2. Rachel has always wanted to be a psychologist. She wants to pursue doctoral-level training, but she is not interested in conducting scientific research or in becoming a medical doctor. What type of degree would be best for Rachel to pursue?
    a. Ph.D.
    b. master's degree in social work
    c. Psy.D.
    d. D.O.
    e. master's degree in psychology

3. Tomasz and his sister Kinga are both psychology majors about to graduate with their bachelor's degrees. Kinga plans to pursue graduate study in psychology while Tomasz wants to go into business for himself or pursue a graduate degree in management. Which of the following assets and skills will assist Tomasz in his pursuits?
    a. emphasis on empirical evidence
    b. quantitative skills
    c. all of these
    d. observation skills
    e. critical thinking

4. Dr. Pham conducts scientific studies on topics such as the power of prejudice, attitude change, aggressive behavior, and interpersonal attraction in teenagers. Dr. Pham's area of specialization is most likely in _____ psychology.
   a. human-factors
   b. personality
   c. comparative
   d. developmental
   e. social

5. Dr. Robinson is a(n) _____ psychologist who conducts experiments using animals as his subjects. His focus of study includes animal learning, memory, and even language.
   a. biological
   b. developmental
   c. comparative
   d. social
   e. comparative

6. What type of psychologist would be most likely to put together an antibullying program for middle school students?
   a. forensic
   b. human-factors
   c. clinical
   d. clinical
   e. educational

7. In working with a professional athlete, to what aspects of performance might a sports psychologist likely pay particular attention?
   a. equipment selection
   b. strength and agility training
   c. perception and problem solving
   d. focus and relaxation
   e. memory and motivation

8. Dr. Smith studies the topic of crowding. She often wonders why people can feel crowded in an elevator that has 8 to 10 people in it but not at a large sporting event where more than 2,000 people are present. What is Dr. Smith's specialty?
   a. developmental psychology
   b. comparative psychology
   c. environmental psychology
   d. physiological psychology
   e. social psychology

9. Which type of psychologist is most concerned with maximizing job satisfaction in night-shift employees?
   a. human-factors
   b. forensic
   c. environmental
   d. clinical
   e. industrial-organizational

10. Gina is working to redesign the controls for a new type of plane so that pilots can tell the difference between instruments in the dark just by the way each control feels. Gina is probably a(n) _____ psychologist.
    a. industrial-organizational
    b. military
    c. social
    d. human factors
    e. experimental

Glossary

absolute threshold the lowest level of stimulation that a person can consciously detect 50 percent of the time the stimulation is present.

accommodation as a monocular cue of depth perception; the brain's use of information about the changing thickness of the lens of the eye in response to looking at objects that are close or far away.

acculturative stress stress resulting from the need to change and adapt a person's ways to the majority culture.

acquired (secondary) drives those drives that are learned through experience or conditioning, such as the need for money or social approval.

acrophobia fear of heights.

action potential the release of the neural impulse, consisting of a reversal of the electrical charge within the axon.

action therapy therapy in which the main goal is to change disordered or inappropriate behavior directly.

activation-information-mode model (AIM) revised version of the activation-synthesis explanation of dreams in which information that is accessed during waking hours can have an influence on the synthesis of dreams.

activation-synthesis hypothesis premise that states that dreams are created by the higher centers of the cortex to explain the activation by the brain stem of cortical cells during REM sleep periods.

activity theory theory of adjustment to aging that assumes older people are happier if they remain active in some way, such as volunteering or developing a hobby.

acute stress disorder (ASD) a disorder resulting from exposure to a major stressor, with symptoms of anxiety, dissociation, recurring nightmares, sleep disturbances, problems in concentration, and moments in which people seem to "relive" the event in dreams and flashbacks for as long as 1 month following the event.

adaptive theory theory of sleep proposing that animals and humans evolved sleep patterns to avoid predators by sleeping when predators are most active.

adolescence the period of life from about age 13 to the early 20s, during which a young person is no longer physically a child but is not yet an independent, self-supporting adult.

adrenal glands endocrine glands located on top of each kidney that secrete more than 30 different hormones to deal with stress, regulate salt intake, and provide a secondary source of sex hormones affecting the sexual changes that occur during adolescence.

aerial (atmospheric) perspective monocular depth perception cue; the haziness that surrounds objects that are farther away from the viewer, causing the distance to be perceived as greater.

affect in psychology, a term indicating "emotion" or "mood."

afferent (sensory) neuron a neuron that carries information from the senses to the central nervous system.

afterimages images that occur when a visual sensation persists for a brief time even after the original stimulus is removed.

aggression actions intended to harm physically or psychologically.

agonists chemical substances that mimic or enhance the effects of a neurotransmitter on the receptor sites of the next cell, increasing or decreasing the activity of that cell.

agoraphobia fear of being in a place or situation from which escape is difficult or impossible.

alcohol the chemical resulting from fermentation or distillation of various kinds of vegetable matter.

algorithms very specific, step-by-step procedures for solving certain types of problems.

all-or-none referring to the fact that a neuron either fires completely or does not fire at all.

all-or-nothing thinking the tendency to believe that one's performance must be perfect or the result will be a total failure.

alpha waves brain waves that indicate a state of relaxation or light sleep.

altered state of consciousness state in which there is a shift in the quality or pattern of mental activity as compared to waking consciousness.

altruism prosocial behavior that is done with no expectation of reward and may involve the risk of harm to oneself.

amphetamines stimulants that are synthesized (made) in laboratories rather than being found in nature.

amygdala brain structure located near the hippocampus, responsible for fear responses and memory of fear.

anal stage the second stage in Freud's psychosexual stages, occurring from about 18–36 months of age, in which the anus is the erogenous zone and toilet training is the source of conflict.

analytical intelligence the ability to break problems down into component parts, or analysis, for problem solving.

androgyny characteristic of possessing the most positive personality characteristics of males and females regardless of actual sex.

andropause gradual changes in the sexual hormones and reproductive system of middle-aged males.

anorexia nervosa (anorexia) a condition in which a person reduces eating to the point that their body weight is significantly low, or less than minimally expected. In adults, this is likely associated with a BMI less than 18.5.

antagonists chemical substances that block or reduce a cell's response to the action of other chemicals or neurotransmitters.

anterograde amnesia loss of memory from the point of injury or trauma forward, or the inability to form new long-term memories.

antianxiety drugs drugs used to treat and calm anxiety reactions, typically minor tranquilizers.

antidepressant drugs drugs used to treat depression and anxiety.

antipsychotic drugs drugs used to treat psychotic symptoms such as delusions, hallucinations, and other bizarre behavior.

antisocial personality disorder (ASPD) disorder in which a person uses other people without worrying about their rights or feelings and often behaves in an impulsive or reckless manner without regard for the consequences of that behavior.

anxiety the anticipation of some future threat, often associated with worry, vigilance, and muscle tension; anxiety is different from, but typically related to, the emotion of fear and the physiological consequences of sympathetic activation (the fight or flight response).

anxiety disorders class of disorders in which the primary symptom is excessive or unrealistic anxiety.

applied behavior analysis (ABA) modern term for a form of functional analysis and behavior modification that uses a variety of behavioral techniques to mold a desired behavior or response.

applied psychology the use of psychological concepts in solving real-world problems.

applied research research focused on finding practical solutions to real-world problems.

approach–approach conflict conflict occurring when a person must choose between two desirable goals.

approach–avoidance conflict conflict occurring when a person must choose or not choose a goal that has both positive and negative aspects.

archetypes Jung's collective, universal human memories.

arousal theory theory of motivation in which people are said to have an optimal (best or ideal) level of tension that they seek to maintain by increasing or decreasing stimulation.

association areas areas within each lobe of the cortex responsible for the coordination and interpretation of information, as well as higher mental processing.

attachment the emotional bond between an infant and the primary caregiver.

attitude a tendency to respond positively or negatively toward a certain person, object, idea, or situation.

attribution the process of explaining one's own behavior and the behavior of others.

attribution theory the theory of how people make attributions.

auditory canal short tunnel that runs from the pinna to the eardrum.

auditory nerve bundle of axons from the hair cells in the inner ear.

authenticity the genuine, open, and honest response of the therapist to the client.

authoritarian parenting style of parenting in which parent is rigid and overly strict, showing little warmth to the child.

authoritative parenting style of parenting in which parent combines warmth and affection with firm limits on a child's behavior.

autobiographical memory the memory for events and facts related to one's personal life story.

automatic encoding tendency of certain kinds of information to enter long-term memory with little or no effortful encoding.

autonomic nervous system (ANS) division of the PNS consisting of nerves that control all of the involuntary muscles, organs, and glands.

availability heuristic estimating the frequency or likelihood of an event based on how easy it is to recall relevant information from memory or how easy it is for us to think of related examples.

aversion therapy form of behavioral therapy in which an undesirable behavior is paired with an aversive stimulus to reduce the frequency of the behavior.

avoidance–avoidance conflict conflict occurring when a person must choose between two undesirable goals.

axon tubelike structure of a neuron that carries the neural message from the cell body to the axon terminals for communication with other cells.

axon terminals enlarged ends of axonal branches of the neuron, specialized for communication between cells.

barbiturates depressant drugs that have a sedative effect.

basal metabolic rate (BMR) the rate at which the body burns energy when the organism is resting.

basic anxiety anxiety created when a child is born into the bigger and more powerful world of older children and adults.

basic research research focused on adding information to the scientific knowledge base.

behavioral genetics field of study devoted to discovering the genetic bases for personality characteristics.

behaviorism the science of behavior that focuses on observable behavior only.

behavior modification or applied behavior analysis the use of learning techniques to modify or change undesirable behavior and increase desirable behavior.

behavior therapies action therapies based on the principles of classical and operant conditioning and aimed at changing disordered behavior without concern for the original causes of such behavior.

benzodiazepines drugs that lower anxiety and reduce stress.

beta waves smaller and faster brain waves, typically indicating mental activity.

bilateral anterior cingulotomy psychosurgical technique in which an electrode wire is inserted into the anterior cingulate gyrus, with the guidance of magnetic resonance imaging, to destroy a very small portion of that brain area with electric current.

bimodal condition in which a distribution has two modes.

bimodal distribution frequency distribution in which there are two high points rather than one.

binge-eating disorder a condition in which a person overeats, or binges, on enormous amounts of food at one sitting, but unlike bulimia nervosa, the individual does not then purge or use other unhealthy methods to avoid weight gain.

binocular cues cues for perceiving depth based on both eyes.

binocular disparity binocular depth perception cue; the difference in images between the two eyes, which is greater for objects that are close and smaller for distant objects.

bioethics the study of ethical and moral issues brought about by new advances in biology and medicine.

biofeedback using feedback about biological conditions to bring involuntary responses, such as blood pressure and relaxation, under voluntary control.

biological model model of explaining thinking or behavior as caused by biological changes in the chemical, structural, or genetic systems of the body.

biological preparedness referring to the tendency of animals to learn certain associations, such as taste and nausea, with only one or few pairings due to the survival value of the learning.

biological psychology or behavioral neuroscience branch of neuroscience that focuses on the biological bases of psychological processes, behavior, and learning.

biomedical therapies therapies that directly affect the biological functioning of the body and brain; therapies for mental disorders in which a person with a problem is treated with biological or medical methods to relieve symptoms.

biopsychological perspective perspective that attributes human and animal behavior to biological events occurring in the body, such as genetic influences, hormones, and the activity of the nervous system.

biopsychosocial model perspective in which abnormal thinking or behavior is seen as the result of the combined and interacting forces of biological, psychological, social, and cultural influences.

bipolar disorder periods of mood that may range from normal to manic, with or without episodes of depression (bipolar I disorder), or spans of normal mood interspersed with episodes of major depression and episodes of hypomania (bipolar II disorder).

bisexual sexual attraction toward, or sexual activity with, both men and women.

blind spot area in the retina where the axons of the retinal ganglion cells exit the eye to form the optic nerve; insensitive to light.

borderline personality disorder (BLPD) maladaptive personality pattern in which the person is moody, unstable, lacks a clear sense of identity, and often clings to others with a pattern of self-destructiveness, chronic loneliness, and disruptive anger in close relationships.

bottom-up processing the analysis of the smaller features to build up to a complete perception.

brightness constancy the tendency to perceive the apparent brightness of an object as the same even when the light conditions change.

Broca's aphasia condition resulting from damage to Broca's area, causing the affected person to be unable to speak fluently, to mispronounce words, and to speak haltingly.

bulimia nervosa (bulimia) a condition in which a person develops a cycle of "bingeing," or overeating enormous amounts of food at one sitting, and then using unhealthy methods to avoid weight gain.

burnout negative changes in thoughts, emotions, and behavior as a result of prolonged stress or frustration, leading to feelings of exhaustion.

bystander effect referring to the effect that the presence of other people has on the decision to help or not help, with help becoming less likely as the number of bystanders increases.

caffeine a mild stimulant found in coffee, tea, and several other plant-based substances.

Cannon–Bard theory of emotion theory in which the physiological reaction and the emotion are assumed to occur at the same time.

case study study of one individual in great detail.

catastrophe an unpredictable, large-scale event that creates a tremendous need to adapt and adjust as well as overwhelming feelings of threat.

catatonia disturbed behavior ranging from statue-like immobility to bursts of energetic, frantic movement and talking.

central nervous system (CNS) part of the nervous system consisting of the brain and spinal cord.

central-route processing type of information processing that involves attending to the content of the message itself.

centration in Piaget's theory, the tendency of a young child to focus only on one feature of an object while ignoring other relevant features.

cerebellum part of the lower brain located behind the pons that controls and coordinates involuntary, rapid, fine motor movement and may have some cognitive functions.

cerebral hemispheres the two sections of the cortex on the left and right sides of the brain.

cerebrum the upper part of the brain consisting of the two hemispheres and the structures that connect them.

character value judgments of a person's moral and ethical behavior.

chromosome tightly wound strand of genetic material or DNA.

circadian rhythm a cycle of bodily rhythm that occurs over a 24-hour period.

classical conditioning learning to make an involuntary response to a stimulus other than the original, natural stimulus that normally produces the response.

claustrophobia fear of being in a small, enclosed space.

clinical psychology area of psychology in which the psychologists diagnose and treat people with psychological disorders that may range from mild to severe.

closure a Gestalt principle of perception; the tendency to complete figures that are incomplete.

cocaine a natural drug derived from the leaves of the coca plant.

cochlea snail-shaped structure of the inner ear that is filled with fluid.

cognitive arousal theory (two-factor theory) theory of emotion in which both the physical arousal and the labeling of that arousal based on cues from the environment must occur before the emotion is experienced.

cognitive–behavioral therapy (CBT) action therapy in which the goal is to help clients overcome problems by learning to think more rationally and logically, which in turn will impact their behavior.

cognitive development the development of thinking, problem solving, and memory.

cognitive dissonance sense of discomfort or distress that occurs when a person's behavior does not correspond to that person's attitudes.

cognitive-mediational theory theory of emotion in which a stimulus must be interpreted (appraised) by a person in order to result in a physical response and an emotional reaction.

cognitive neuroscience study of the physical changes in the brain and nervous system during thinking.

cognitive perspective modern perspective in psychology that focuses on memory, intelligence, perception, problem solving, and learning.

cognitive perspective in classical conditioning, modern theory in which conditioning is seen to occur because the conditioned stimulus provides information or an expectancy about the coming of the unconditioned stimulus.

cognitive psychologists psychologists who study the way people think, remember, and mentally organize information.

cognitive therapy therapy in which the focus is on helping clients recognize distortions in their thinking and replacing distorted, unrealistic beliefs with more realistic, helpful thoughts.

cognitive universalism theory that concepts are universal and influence the development of language.

cohort effect the impact on development occurring when a group of people share a common time period or common life experience.

collective unconscious Jung's name for the memories shared by all members of the human species.

College Undergraduate Stress Scale (CUSS) assessment that measures the amount of stress in a college student's life over a 1-year period resulting from major life events.

community psychology area of psychology in which psychologists serve at various levels including individual, group, and community, focusing on promoting social welfare and preventing social problems.

companionate love type of love consisting of intimacy and commitment.

comparative psychology area of psychology in which the psychologists study animals and their behavior for the purpose of comparing and contrasting it to human behavior.

compliance changing one's behavior as a result of other people directing or asking for the change.

computed tomography (CT) brain-imaging method using computer-controlled X-rays of the brain.

concentrative meditation form of meditation in which a person focuses the mind on some repetitive or unchanging stimulus so that the mind can be cleared of disturbing thoughts and the body can experience relaxation.

concept map an organized visual representation of knowledge consisting of concepts and their relationships to other concepts.

concepts ideas that represent a class or category of objects, events, or activities.

concrete operations stage Piaget's third stage of cognitive development, in which the school-age child becomes capable of logical thought processes but is not yet capable of abstract thinking.

conditional positive regard positive regard that is given only when the person is doing what the providers of positive regard wish.

conditioned emotional response (CER) emotional response that has become classically conditioned to occur to learned stimuli, such as a fear of dogs or the emotional reaction that occurs when seeing an attractive person.

conditioned response (CR) in classical conditioning, a learned response to a conditioned stimulus.

conditioned stimulus (CS) in classical conditioning, a previously neutral stimulus that becomes able to produce a conditioned response after pairing with an unconditioned stimulus.

conditioned taste aversion development of a nausea or aversive response to a particular taste because that taste was followed by a nausea reaction, occurring after only one association.

cones visual sensory receptors found at the back of the retina, responsible for color vision and sharpness of vision.

confirmation bias the tendency to search for evidence that fits one's beliefs while ignoring any evidence that does not fit those beliefs.

conformity changing one's own behavior to match that of other people.

conscience part of the superego that produces guilt, depending on how acceptable behavior is.

consciousness a person's awareness of everything that is going on around him or her at any given time.

conservation in Piaget's theory, the ability to understand that simply changing the appearance of an object does not change the object's nature.

consolidation the changes that take place in the structure and functioning of neurons when a memory is formed.

constructive processing referring to the retrieval of memories in which those memories are altered, revised, or influenced by newer information.

consumer psychology branch of psychology that studies the habits of consumers in the marketplace.

contiguity a Gestalt principle of perception; the tendency to perceive two things that happen close together in time as being related.

contingency contract a formal, written agreement between the therapist and client (or teacher and student) in which goals for behavioral change, reinforcements, and penalties are clearly stated.

continuity a Gestalt principle of perception; the tendency to perceive things as simply as possible with a continuous pattern rather than with a complex, broken-up pattern.

continuous reinforcement the reinforcement of each and every correct response.

control group participants in an experiment who are not subjected to the independent variable and who may receive a placebo treatment.

convergence binocular depth perception cue; the rotation of the two eyes in their sockets to focus on a single object, resulting in greater convergence for closer objects and lesser convergence if objects are distant.

convergent thinking type of thinking in which a problem is seen as having only one answer, and all lines of thinking will eventually lead to that single answer, using previous knowledge and logic.

coping strategies actions that people can take to master, tolerate, reduce, or minimize the effects of stressors.

coronary heart disease (CHD) the buildup of a waxy substance called plaque in the arteries of the heart.

corpus callosum thick band of neurons that connects the right and left cerebral hemispheres.

correlation a measure of the relationship between two variables.

correlation coefficient a number that represents the strength and direction of a relationship existing between two variables; number derived from the formula for measuring a correlation.

cortex outermost covering of the brain consisting of densely packed neurons, responsible for higher thought processes and interpretation of sensory input.

counseling psychology area of psychology in which the psychologists help people with problems of adjustment.

creative intelligence the ability to deal with new and different concepts and to come up with new ways of solving problems.

creativity the process of solving problems by combining ideas or behavior in new ways.

critical periods times during which certain environmental influences can have an impact on the development of the infant.

critical thinking making reasoned judgments about claims.

cross-sectional design research design in which several different participant age groups are studied at one particular point in time.

cross-sequential design research design in which participants are first studied by means of a cross-sectional design but are also followed and assessed longitudinally.

cult any group of people with a particular religious or philosophical set of beliefs and identity.

cultural relativity the need to consider the unique characteristics of the culture in which behavior takes place.

cultural syndromes sets of particular symptoms of distress found in particular cultures, which may or may not be recognized as an illness within the culture.

curve of forgetting a graph showing a distinct pattern in which forgetting is very fast within the first hour after learning a list and then tapers off gradually.

dark adaptation the recovery of the eye's sensitivity to visual stimuli in darkness after exposure to bright lights.

decay loss of memory due to the passage of time, during which the memory trace is not used.

decision making process of cognition that involves identifying, evaluating, and choosing among several alternatives.

declarative (explicit) memory type of long-term memory containing information that is conscious and known.

deindividuation the lessening of personal identity, self-restraint, and the sense of personal responsibility that can occur within a group.

delta waves long, slow brain waves that indicate the deepest stage of sleep.

delusions false beliefs held by a person who refuses to accept evidence of their falseness.

dendrites branchlike structures of a neuron that receive messages from other neurons.

dependent personality disorder personality disorder in which the person is clingy, submissive, fearful of separation, requires constant reassurance, feels helpless when alone, and has others assume responsibility for most areas of life.

dependent variable variable in an experiment that represents the measurable response or behavior of the participants in the experiment.

depressants drugs that decrease the functioning of the nervous system.

depth perception the ability to perceive the world in three dimensions.

descriptive statistics a way of organizing numbers and summarizing them so that patterns can be determined.

developmental psychology area of psychology in which the psychologists study the changes in the way people think, relate to others, and feel as they age.

deviation IQ scores a type of intelligence measure that assumes that IQ is normally distributed around a mean of 100 with a standard deviation of about 15.

diffusion process of molecules moving from areas of high concentration to areas of low concentration.

diffusion of responsibility occurs when a person fails to take responsibility for actions or for inaction because of the presence of other people who are seen to share the responsibility.

directive therapy in which the therapist actively gives interpretations of a client's statements and may suggest certain behavior or actions.

direct observation assessment in which the professional observes the client engaged in ordinary, day-to-day behavior in either a clinical or natural setting.

discrimination treating people differently because of prejudice toward the social group to which they belong.

discriminative stimulus any stimulus, such as a stop sign or a doorknob, that provides the organism with a cue for making a certain response in order to obtain reinforcement.

displaced aggression taking out one's frustrations on some less threatening or more available target.

display rules learned ways of controlling displays of emotion in social settings.

dispositional cause cause of behavior attributed to internal factors such as personality or character.

dissociation divided state of conscious awareness.

dissociative disorders disorders in which there is a break in conscious awareness, memory, the sense of identity, or some combination.

dissociative identity disorder (DID) disorder occurring when a person seems to have two or more distinct personalities within one body.

distress the effect of unpleasant and undesirable stressors.

distributed practice spacing the study of material to be remembered by including breaks between study periods.

disuse another name for decay, assuming that memories that are not used will eventually decay and disappear.

divergent thinking type of thinking in which a person starts from one point and comes up with many different ideas or possibilities based on that point.

dizygotic twins often called fraternal twins, occurring when two individual eggs get fertilized by separate sperm, resulting in two zygotes in the uterus at the same time.

DNA (deoxyribonucleic acid) special molecule that contains the genetic material of the organism.

dominant referring to a gene that actively controls the expression of a trait.

door-in-the-face technique asking for a large commitment and being refused and then asking for a smaller commitment.

double approach–avoidance conflict conflict in which the person must decide between two goals, with each goal possessing both positive and negative aspects.

double-blind study study in which neither the experimenter nor the participants know if the participants are in the experimental or the control group.

drive a state of psychological tension and physical arousal that arises when there is a need.

drive-reduction theory approach to motivation that assumes behavior arises from internal drives to push the organism to satisfy physiological needs and reduce tension and arousal.

drug tolerance the decrease of the response to a drug over repeated uses, leading to the need for higher doses of drug to achieve the same effect.

echoic memory auditory sensory memory, lasting only 2 to 4 seconds.

eclectic approach to therapy that results from combining elements of several different approaches or techniques.

educational psychology area of psychology in which the psychologists are concerned with the study of human learning and development of new learning techniques.

efferent (motor) neuron a neuron that carries messages from the central nervous system to the muscles of the body.

ego part of the personality that develops out of a need to deal with reality; mostly conscious, rational, and logical.

egocentrism the inability to see the world through anyone else's eyes.

ego integrity sense of wholeness that comes from having lived a full life, possessing the ability to let go of regrets; the final completion of the ego.

eidetic imagery the ability to access a visual memory for 30 seconds or more.

elaboration likelihood model model of persuasion stating that people will either elaborate on the persuasive message or fail to elaborate on it and that the future actions of those who do elaborate are more predictable than those who do not.

elaborative rehearsal a way of increasing the number of retrieval cues for information by connecting new information with something that is already well known.

Electra complex see Oedipus complex.

electroconvulsive therapy (ECT) form of biomedical therapy to treat severe depression in which electrodes are placed on either one or both sides of a person's head and an electric current is passed through the electrodes that is strong enough to cause a seizure or convulsion.

electroencephalogram (EEG) a recording of the electrical activity of large groups of cortical neurons just below the skull, most often using scalp electrodes.

embryo name for the developing organism from 2 weeks to 8 weeks after fertilization.

embryonic period the period from 2 to 8 weeks after fertilization, during which the major organs and structures of the organism develop.

emerging adulthood a time from late adolescence through the 20s referring to those who are childless, do not live in their own home, and are not earning enough money to be independent, mainly found in developed countries.

emotion the "feeling" aspect of consciousness, characterized by a certain physical arousal, a certain behavior that reveals the emotion to the outside world, and an inner awareness of feelings.

emotional intelligence the awareness of and ability to manage one's own emotions to facilitate thinking and attain goals, as well as the ability to understand emotions in others.

emotion-focused coping coping strategies that change the impact of a stressor by changing the emotional reaction to the stressor.

empathy the ability of the therapist to understand the feelings of the client.

encoding the set of mental operations that people perform on sensory information to convert that information into a form that is usable in the brain's storage systems.

encoding failure failure to process information into memory.

encoding specificity the tendency for memory of information to be improved if related information (such as surroundings or physiological state) that is available when the memory is first formed is also available when the memory is being retrieved.

endocrine glands glands that secrete chemicals called hormones directly into the bloodstream.

environmental psychology area of psychology in which the focus is on how people interact with and are affected by their physical environments.

enzymatic degradation process by which the structure of a neurotransmitter is altered so it can no longer act on a receptor.

epigenetics the interaction between genes and environmental factors that influence gene activity; environmental factors include diet, life experiences, and physical surroundings.

episodic memory type of declarative memory containing personal information not readily available to others, such as daily activities and events.

equal status contact contact between groups in which the groups have equal status with neither group having power over the other.

escape or withdrawal leaving the presence of a stressor, either literally or by a psychological withdrawal into fantasy, drug abuse, or apathy.

eustress the effect of positive events, or the optimal amount of stress that people need to promote health and well-being.

evidence-based treatment also called empirically supported treatment; refers to interventions, strategies, or techniques that have been found to produce therapeutic and desired changes during controlled research studies.

evolutionary perspective perspective that focuses on the biological bases of universal mental characteristics that all humans share.

excitatory synapse synapse at which a neurotransmitter causes the receiving cell to fire.

expectancy a person's subjective feeling that a particular behavior will lead to a reinforcing consequence.

experiment a deliberate manipulation of a variable to see if corresponding changes in behavior result, allowing the determination of cause-and-effect relationships.

experimental group participants in an experiment who are subjected to the independent variable.

experimental psychology area of psychology in which the psychologists primarily do research and experiments in the areas of learning, memory, thinking, perception, motivation, and language.

experimenter effect tendency of the experimenter's expectations for a study to unintentionally influence the results of the study.

exposure therapies behavioral techniques that expose individuals to anxiety- or fear-related stimuli under carefully controlled conditions to promote new learning.

extinction the disappearance or weakening of a learned response following the removal or absence of the unconditioned stimulus (in classical conditioning) or the removal of a reinforcer (in operant conditioning).

extraverts people who are outgoing and sociable.

extrinsic motivation type of motivation in which a person performs an action because it leads to an outcome that is separate from or external to the person.

facial feedback hypothesis theory of emotion that assumes that facial expressions provide feedback to the brain concerning the emotion being expressed, which in turn causes and intensifies the emotion.

family counseling (family therapy) a form of group therapy in which family members meet together with a counselor or therapist to resolve problems that affect the entire family.

fertilization the union of the ovum and sperm.

fetal alcohol spectrum disorders (FASDs) a group of possible conditions caused by a mother consuming alcohol during pregnancy, in which a combination of physical, mental, and behavioral problems may be present.

fetal period the time from about 8 weeks after conception until the birth of the baby.

fetus name for the developing organism from 8 weeks after fertilization to the birth of the baby.

figure–ground relationship the tendency to perceive objects, or figures, as existing on a background.

five-factor model (Big Five) model of personality traits that describes five basic trait dimensions.

fixation disorder in which the person does not fully resolve the conflict in a particular psychosexual stage, resulting in personality traits and behavior associated with that earlier stage.

fixed interval schedule of reinforcement schedule of reinforcement in which the interval of time that must pass before reinforcement becomes possible is always the same.

fixed ratio schedule of reinforcement schedule of reinforcement in which the number of responses required for reinforcement is always the same.

flashbulb memories type of automatic encoding that occurs because an unexpected event has strong emotional associations for the person remembering it.

flat affect a lack of emotional responsiveness.

flooding technique for treating phobias and other stress disorders in which the person is rapidly and intensely exposed to the fear-provoking situation or object and prevented from making the usual avoidance or escape response.

foot-in-the-door technique asking for a small commitment and, after gaining compliance, asking for a bigger commitment.

forensic psychology area of psychology concerned with people in the legal system, including psychological assessment of criminals, jury selection, and expert witnessing.

formal operations stage Piaget's last stage of cognitive development, in which the adolescent becomes capable of abstract thinking.

free association psychoanalytic technique in which a patient was encouraged to talk about anything that came to mind without fear of negative evaluations.

free-floating anxiety anxiety that is unrelated to any specific and known cause.

frequency count assessment in which the frequency of a particular behavior is counted.

frequency distribution a table or graph that shows how often different numbers or scores appear in a particular set of scores.

frequency theory theory of pitch that states that pitch is related to the speed of vibrations in the basilar membrane.

frontal lobes areas of the brain located in the front and top, responsible for higher mental processes and decision making as well as the production of fluent speech.

frustration the psychological experience produced by the blocking of a desired goal or fulfillment of a perceived need.

fully functioning person a person who is in touch with and trusting of the deepest, innermost urges and feelings.

functional fixedness a block to problem solving that comes from thinking about objects in terms of only their typical functions.

functionalism early perspective in psychology associated with William James, in which the focus of study is how the mind allows people to adapt, live, work, and play.

functional magnetic resonance imaging (fMRI) MRI-based brain-imaging method that allows for functional examination of brain areas through changes in brain oxygenation.

fundamental attribution error the tendency to overestimate the influence of internal factors in determining behavior while underestimating situational factors.

gender the psychological aspects of being masculine or feminine.

gender identity the individual's sense of being masculine or feminine.

gender roles the culture's expectations for male or female behavior, including attitudes, actions, and personality traits associated with being male or female in that culture.

gender schema theory theory of gender-role development in which a child develops a mental pattern or framework, or schema, for being male or female and then organizes observed and learned behavior around that schema.

gender typing the process of acquiring gender-role characteristics.

gene section of DNA having the same arrangement of chemical elements.

general adaptation syndrome (GAS) the three stages of the body's physiological reaction to stress, including alarm, resistance, and exhaustion.

generalized anxiety disorder disorder in which a person has feelings of dread and impending doom along with physical symptoms of stress, which lasts 6 months or more.

generativity providing guidance to one's children or the next generation, or contributing to the well-being of the next generation through career or volunteer work.

genetics the science of inherited traits.

genital stage the final stage in Freud's psychosexual stages; from puberty on, sexual urges are allowed back into consciousness and the individual moves toward adult social and sexual behavior.

germinal period first 2 weeks after fertilization, during which the zygote moves down to the uterus and begins to implant in the lining.

Gestalt psychology early perspective in psychology focusing on perception and sensation, particularly the perception of patterns and whole figures.

Gestalt therapy form of directive insight therapy in which the therapist helps clients accept all parts of their feelings and subjective experiences, using leading questions and planned experiences such as role-playing.

g factor the ability to reason and solve problems, or general intelligence.

gifted the 2 percent of the population falling on the upper end of the normal curve and typically possessing an IQ of 130 or above.

glial cells cells that provide support for the neurons to grow on and around, deliver nutrients to neurons, produce myelin to coat axons, clean up waste products and dead neurons, influence information processing, and, during prenatal development, influence the generation of new neurons.

glucagon hormone that is secreted by the pancreas to control the levels of fats, proteins, and carbohydrates in the body by increasing the level of glucose in the bloodstream.

gonads sex glands; secrete hormones that regulate sexual development and behavior as well as reproduction.

grammar the system of rules governing the structure and use of a language.

group polarization the tendency for members involved in a group discussion to take somewhat more extreme positions and suggest riskier actions when compared to individuals who have not participated in a group discussion.

group therapy form of therapy or treatment during which a small group of clients with similar concerns meet together with a therapist to address their issues.

groupthink kind of thinking that occurs when people place more importance on maintaining group cohesiveness than on assessing the facts of the problem with which the group is concerned.

gustation the sensation of a taste.

habits in behaviorism, sets of well-learned responses that have become automatic.

habituation tendency of the brain to stop attending to constant, unchanging information.

hallucinations false sensory perceptions, such as hearing voices that do not really exist.

hallucinogenics drugs including hallucinogens and marijuana that produce hallucinations or increased feelings of relaxation and intoxication.

hallucinogens drugs that cause false sensory messages, altering the perception of reality.

halo effect tendency of an interviewer to allow positive characteristics of a client to influence the assessments of the client's behavior and statements.

hardy personality a person who seems to thrive on stress but lacks the anger and hostility of the Type A personality.

hassles the daily annoyances of everyday life.

health psychology area of psychology focusing on how physical activities, psychological traits, stress reactions, and social relationships affect overall health and rates of illnesses.

heritability degree to which the changes in some trait within a population can be considered to be due to genetic influences; the extent to which individual genetic differences affect individual differences in observed behavior; in IQ, the proportion of change in IQ within a population that is caused by hereditary factors.

heroin narcotic drug derived from opium that is extremely addictive.

hertz (Hz) cycles or waves per second; a measurement of frequency.

heterosexual sexual attraction toward, or sexual activity with, members of the opposite sex.

heuristic an educated guess based on prior experiences that helps narrow down the possible solutions for a problem. Also known as a "rule of thumb."

higher-order conditioning occurs when a strong conditioned stimulus is paired with a neutral stimulus, causing the neutral stimulus to become a second conditioned stimulus.

hindsight bias the tendency to falsely believe, through revision of older memories to include newer information, that one could have correctly predicted the outcome of an event.

hippocampus curved structure located within each temporal lobe, responsible for the formation of long-term declarative memories.

histogram a bar graph showing a frequency distribution.

homeopathy the treatment of disease by introducing minute amounts of substances that would cause disease in larger doses.

homeostasis the tendency of the body to maintain a steady state.

homosexual sexual attraction toward, or sexual activity with, members of the same sex.

hormones chemicals released into the bloodstream by endocrine glands.

human development the scientific study of the changes that occur in people as they age from conception until death.

human factors psychology area of industrial-organizational psychology concerned with the study of the way humans and machines interact with each other.

humanistic perspective the "third force" in psychology that focuses on those aspects of personality that make people uniquely human, such as subjective feelings and freedom of choice.

hypnosis state of consciousness in which the person is especially susceptible to suggestion.

hypothalamus small structure in the brain located below the thalamus and directly above the pituitary gland, responsible for motivational behavior such as sleep, hunger, thirst, and sex.

hypothesis tentative explanation of a phenomenon based on observations.

iconic memory visual sensory memory, lasting only a fraction of a second.

identity versus role confusion stage of personality development in which the adolescent must find a consistent sense of self.

id part of the personality present at birth and completely unconscious.

imaginary audience type of thought common to adolescents in which young people believe that other people are just as concerned about the adolescent's thoughts and characteristics as they are themselves.

immune system the system of cells, organs, and chemicals of the body that responds to attacks from diseases, infections, and injuries.

implicit personality theory sets of assumptions about how different types of people, personality traits, and actions are related to each other.

impression formation the forming of the first knowledge that a person has concerning another person.

incentive approaches theories of motivation in which behavior is explained as a response to the external stimulus and its rewarding properties.

incentives things that attract or lure people into action.

independent variable variable in an experiment that is manipulated by the experimenter.

industrial-organizational (I-O) psychology area of psychology concerned with the relationships between people and their work environment.

infantile amnesia the inability to retrieve memories from much before age 3.

inferential statistics statistical analysis of two or more sets of numerical data to reduce the possibility of error in measurement and to determine if the differences between the data sets are greater than chance variation would predict.

information-processing model model of memory that assumes the processing of information for memory storage is similar to the way a computer processes memory in a series of three stages.

in-groups social groups with whom a person identifies; "us."

inhibitory synapse synapse at which a neurotransmitter causes the receiving cell to stop firing.

insight the sudden perception of relationships among various parts of a problem, allowing the solution to the problem to come quickly.

insight therapies therapies in which the main goal is helping people gain insight with respect to their behavior, thoughts, and feelings.

insomnia the inability to get to sleep, stay asleep, or get quality sleep.

instinctive drift tendency for an animal's behavior to revert to genetically controlled patterns.

instincts the biologically determined and innate patterns of behavior that exist in both people and animals.

insulin a hormone secreted by the pancreas to control the levels of fats, proteins, and carbohydrates in the body by reducing the level of glucose in the bloodstream.

intellectual disability (intellectual developmental disorder) condition in which a person's behavioral and cognitive skills exist at an earlier developmental stage than the skills of others who are the same chronological age; may also be referred to as developmentally delayed. This condition was formerly known as mental retardation.

intelligence the ability to learn from one's experiences, acquire knowledge, and use resources effectively in adapting to new situations or solving problems.

intelligence quotient (IQ) a number representing a measure of intelligence, resulting from the division of one's mental age by one's chronological age and then multiplying that quotient by 100.

interneuron a neuron found in the center of the spinal cord that receives information from the afferent neurons and sends commands to the muscles through the efferent neurons. Interneurons also make up the bulk of the neurons in the brain.

interpersonal attraction liking or having the desire for a relationship with another person.

interpersonal psychotherapy (IPT) form of therapy for depression that incorporates multiple approaches and focuses on interpersonal problems.

interview method of personality assessment in which the professional asks questions of the client and allows the client to answer in either a structured or unstructured fashion.

intimacy an emotional and psychological closeness that is based on the ability to trust, share, and care, while still maintaining a sense of self.

intrinsic motivation type of motivation in which a person performs an action because the act itself is rewarding or satisfying in some internal manner.

introversion dimension of personality in which people tend to withdraw from excessive stimulation.

introverts people who prefer solitude and dislike being the center of attention.

irreversibility in Piaget's theory, the inability of the young child to mentally reverse an action.

James-Lange theory of emotion theory in which a physiological reaction leads to the labeling of an emotion.

"jigsaw classroom" educational technique in which each individual is given only part of the information needed to solve a problem, causing the separate individuals to be forced to work together to find the solution.

just noticeable difference (JND or the difference threshold) the smallest difference between two stimuli that is detectable 50 percent of the time.

kinesthesia the awareness of body movement.

language a system for combining symbols (such as words) so that an unlimited number of meaningful statements can be made for the purpose of communicating with others.

latency the fourth stage in Freud's psychosexual stages, occurring during the school years, in which the sexual feelings of the child are repressed while the child develops in other ways.

latent content the symbolic or hidden meaning of dreams.

latent learning learning that remains hidden until its application becomes useful.

law of effect law stating that if an action is followed by a pleasurable consequence, it will tend to be repeated, and if followed by an unpleasant consequence, it will tend not to be repeated.

learned helplessness the tendency to fail to act to escape from a situation because of a history of repeated failures in the past.

learning any relatively permanent change in behavior brought about by experience or practice.

learning/performance distinction referring to the observation that learning can take place without actual performance of the learned behavior.

leptin a hormone that, when released into the bloodstream, signals the hypothalamus that the body has had enough food and reduces the appetite while increasing the feeling of being full.

lesioning insertion of a thin, insulated electrode into the brain through which an electrical current is sent, destroying the brain cells at the tip of the wire.

levels-of-processing model model of memory that assumes information that is more "deeply processed," or processed according to its meaning rather than just the sound or physical characteristics of the word or words, will be remembered more efficiently and for a longer period of time.

light adaptation the recovery of the eye's sensitivity to visual stimuli in light after exposure to darkness.

limbic system a group of several brain structures located primarily under the cortex and involved in learning, emotion, memory, and motivation.

linear perspective monocular depth perception cue; the tendency for parallel lines to appear to converge on each other.

linguistic relativity hypothesis the theory that thought processes and concepts are controlled by language.

locus of control the tendency for people to assume that they either have control or do not have control over events and consequences in their lives.

longitudinal design research design in which one participant or group of participants is studied over a long period of time.

long-term memory (LTM) the system of memory into which all the information is placed to be kept more or less permanently.

lowball technique getting a commitment from a person and then raising the cost of that commitment.

LSD (lysergic acid diethylamide) powerful synthetic hallucinogen.

magnetic resonance imaging (MRI) brain-imaging method using radio waves and magnetic fields of the body to produce detailed images of the brain.

magnification the tendency to interpret situations as far more dangerous, harmful, or important than they actually are.

maintenance rehearsal practice of saying some information to be remembered over and over in one's head in order to maintain it in short-term memory.

major depressive disorder severe depression that comes on suddenly and seems to have no external cause, or is too severe for current circumstances.

maladaptive anything that does not allow a person to function within or adapt to the stresses and everyday demands of life.

manic having the quality of excessive excitement, energy, and elation or irritability.

marijuana mild hallucinogen (also known as "pot" or "weed") derived from the leaves and flowers of a particular type of hemp plant.

MDMA (ecstasy or X) designer drug that can have both stimulant and hallucinatory effects.

mean the arithmetic average of a distribution of numbers.

measure of central tendency numbers that best represent the most typical score of a frequency distribution.

measures of variability measurement of the degree of differences within a distribution or how the scores are spread out.

median the middle score in an ordered distribution of scores, or the mean of the two middle numbers; the 50th percentile.

meditation mental series of exercises meant to refocus attention and achieve a trancelike state of consciousness.

medulla the first large swelling at the top of the spinal cord, forming the lowest part of the brain, which is responsible for life-sustaining functions such as breathing, swallowing, and heart rate.

memory an active system that receives information from the senses, puts that information into a usable form, and organizes it as it stores it away, and then retrieves the information from storage.

memory trace physical change in the brain that occurs when a memory is formed.

menopause the cessation of ovulation and menstrual cycles and the end of a woman's reproductive capability.

mental images mental representations that stand for objects or events and have a picture-like quality.

mental set the tendency for people to persist in using problem-solving patterns that have worked for them in the past.

microsleeps brief sidesteps into sleep lasting only a few seconds.

mindfulness meditation a form of concentrative meditation in which the person purposefully pays attention to the present moment, without judgment or evaluation.

minimization the tendency to give little or no importance to one's successes or positive events and traits.

mirror neurons neurons that fire when an animal or person performs an action and also when an animal or person observes that same action being performed by another.

misinformation effect the tendency of misleading information presented after an event to alter the memories of the event itself.

mode the most frequent score in a distribution of scores.

modeling learning through the observation and imitation of others.

monocular cues (pictorial depth cues) cues for perceiving depth based on one eye only.

monozygotic twins identical twins formed when one zygote splits into two separate masses of cells, each of which develops into a separate embryo.

mood disorders disorders in which mood is severely disturbed.

morphemes the smallest units of meaning within a language.

morphine narcotic drug derived from opium, used to treat severe pain.

motion parallax monocular depth perception cue; the perception of motion of objects in which close objects appear to move more quickly than objects that are farther away.

motivation the process by which activities are started, directed, and continued so that physical or psychological needs or wants are met.

motor cortex rear section of the frontal lobe, responsible for sending motor commands to the muscles of the somatic nervous system.

motor pathway nerves coming from the CNS to the voluntary muscles, consisting of efferent neurons.

mnemonic a strategy or trick for aiding memory.

Müller-Lyer illusion illusion of line length that is distorted by inward-turning or outward-turning corners on the ends of the lines, causing lines of equal length to appear to be different.

multiple approach–avoidance conflict conflict in which the person must decide between more than two goals, with each goal possessing both positive and negative aspects.

myelin fatty substances produced by certain glial cells that coat the axons of neurons to insulate, protect, and speed up the neural impulse.

narcolepsy sleep disorder in which a person falls immediately into REM sleep during the day without warning.

natural killer (NK) cell immune-system cell responsible for suppressing viruses and destroying tumor cells.

nature the influence of our inherited characteristics on our personality, physical growth, intellectual growth, and social interactions.

near-infrared spectroscopy (NIRS) a functional brain imaging method that measures brain activity by using infrared light to determine changes in blood oxygen levels in the brain.

need a requirement of some material (such as food or water) that is essential for survival of the organism.

need for achievement (nAch) a need that involves a strong desire to succeed in attaining goals, not only realistic ones but also challenging ones.

need for affiliation (nAff) the need for friendly social interactions and relationships with others.

need for power (nPow) the need to have control or influence over others.

negatively skewed a distribution of scores in which scores are concentrated in the high end of the distribution.

negative reinforcement the reinforcement of a response by the removal, escape from, or avoidance of an unpleasant stimulus.

negative symptoms symptoms of schizophrenia that are less than normal behavior or an absence of normal behavior; poor attention, flat affect, and poor speech production.

neo-Freudians followers of Freud who developed their own competing psychodynamic theories.

nerves bundles of axons coated in myelin that travel together through the body.

nervous system an extensive network of specialized cells that carries information to and from all parts of the body.

neurofeedback form of biofeedback using brain-scanning devices to provide feedback about brain activity in an effort to modify behavior.

neurogenesis the formation of new neurons; occurs primarily during prenatal development but may also occur at lesser levels in some brain areas during adulthood.

neuron the basic cell that makes up the nervous system and that receives and sends messages within that system.

neuroplasticity the ability within the brain to constantly change both the structure and function of many cells in response to experience or trauma.

neuropsychology area of psychology in which psychologists specialize in the research or clinical implications of brain–behavior relationships.

neuroscience a branch of the life sciences that deals with the structure and function of neurons, nerves, and nervous tissue.

neurotic personalities personalities typified by maladaptive ways of dealing with relationships in Horney's theory.

neurotransmitter chemical found in the synaptic vesicles that, when released, has an effect on the next cell.

neutral stimulus (NS) in classical conditioning, a stimulus that has no effect on the desired response prior to conditioning.

nicotine the stimulant found in tobacco.

nightmares bad dreams occurring during REM sleep.

night terrors relatively rare disorder in which the person experiences extreme fear and screams or runs around during deep sleep without waking fully.

nondeclarative (implicit) memory type of long-term memory including memory for skills, procedures, habits, and conditioned responses. These memories are not conscious but are implied to exist because they affect conscious behavior.

nondirective therapy style in which the therapist remains relatively neutral and does not interpret or take direct actions with regard to the client, instead remaining a calm, nonjudgmental listener while the client talks.

non-REM (NREM) sleep any of the stages of sleep that do not include REM.

normal curve a special frequency polygon, shaped like a bell, in which the scores are symmetrically distributed around the mean, and the mean, median, and mode are all located on the same point on the curve, with scores decreasing as the curve extends from the mean.

nurture the influence of the environment on personality, physical growth, intellectual growth, and social interactions.

obedience changing one's behavior at the command of an authority figure.

objective introspection the process of examining and measuring one's own thoughts and mental activities.

object permanence the knowledge that an object exists even when it is not in sight.

observational learning learning new behavior by watching a model perform that behavior.

observer bias tendency of observers to see what they expect to see.

observer effect tendency of people or animals to behave differently from normal when they know they are being observed.

obsessive-compulsive disorder disorder in which intruding, recurring thoughts or obsessions create anxiety that is relieved by performing a repetitive, ritualistic behavior or mental act (compulsion).

occipital lobe section of the brain located at the rear and bottom of each cerebral hemisphere containing the primary visual centers of the brain.

Oedipus complex/Electra complex situation occurring in the phallic stage in which a child develops a sexual attraction to the opposite-sex parent and jealousy of the same-sex parent. Males develop an Oedipus complex, whereas females develop an Electra complex.

olfaction (olfactory sense) the sensation of smell.

olfactory bulbs two bulb-like projections of the brain located just above the sinus cavity and just below the frontal lobes that receive information from the olfactory receptor cells.

operant any behavior that is voluntary and not elicited by specific stimuli.

operant conditioning the learning of voluntary behavior through the effects of pleasant and unpleasant consequences to responses.

operationalization specific description of a variable of interest that allows it to be measured.

opiates a class of opium-related drugs that suppress the sensation of pain by binding to and stimulating the nervous system's natural receptor sites for endorphins.

opioids synthetic drugs that mimic the pain-reducing effects of opiates and their addictive properties.

opium substance derived from the opium poppy from which all narcotic drugs are derived.

opponent-process theory theory of color vision that proposes visual neurons (or groups of neurons) are stimulated by light of one color and inhibited by light of another color.

optimists people who expect positive outcomes.

oral stage the first stage in Freud's psychosexual stages, occurring in the first 18 months of life, in which the mouth is the erogenous zone and weaning is the primary conflict.

out-groups social groups with whom a person does not identify; "them."

ovaries the female gonads or sex glands.

overgeneralization distortion of thinking in which a person draws sweeping conclusions based on only one incident or event and applies those conclusions to events that are unrelated to the original; the tendency to interpret a single negative event as a never-ending pattern of defeat and failure.

overlap (interposition) monocular depth perception cue; the assumption that an object that appears to be blocking part of another object is in front of the second object and closer to the viewer.

ovum the female sex cell, or egg.

oxytocin hormone released by the posterior pituitary gland that is involved in reproductive and parental behaviors.

pancreas endocrine gland; controls the levels of sugar in the blood.

panic attack sudden onset of intense panic in which multiple physical symptoms of stress occur, often with feelings that one is dying.

panic disorder disorder in which panic attacks occur more than once or repeatedly and cause persistent worry or changes in behavior.

parallel distributed processing (PDP) model a model of memory in which memory processes are proposed to take place at the same time over a large network of neural connections.

paranoid personality disorder personality disorder in which a person exhibits pervasive and widespread distrust and suspiciousness of others.

parasympathetic division (eat-drink-and-rest system) also called the parasympathetic nervous system, part of the ANS that restores the body to normal functioning after arousal and is responsible for the day-to-day functioning of the organs and glands.

parietal lobes sections of the brain located at the top and back of each cerebral hemisphere containing the centers for touch, temperature, and body position.

partial reinforcement effect the tendency for a response that is reinforced after some, but not all, correct responses to be very resistant to extinction.

participant modeling technique in which a model demonstrates the desired behavior in a step-by-step, gradual process while the client is encouraged to imitate the model.

participant observation a naturalistic observation in which the observer becomes a participant in the group being observed.

PCP synthesized drug now used as an animal tranquilizer that can cause stimulant, depressant, narcotic, or hallucinogenic effects.

peak experiences according to Maslow, times in a person's life during which self-actualization is temporarily achieved.

perception the method by which the sensations experienced at any given moment are interpreted and organized in some meaningful fashion.

perceptual set (perceptual expectancy) the tendency to perceive things a certain way because previous experiences or expectations influence those perceptions.

peripheral nervous system (PNS) all nerves and neurons that are not contained in the brain and spinal cord but that run through the body itself.

peripheral-route processing type of information processing that involves attending to factors not involved in the message, such as the appearance of the source of the message, the length of the message, and other non-content factors.

permissive indulgent permissive parenting in which parent is so involved that children are allowed to behave without set limits.

permissive neglectful permissive parenting in which parent is uninvolved with child or child's behavior.

permissive parenting style of parenting in which parent makes few, if any, demands on a child's behavior.

personal fable type of thought common to adolescents in which young people believe themselves to be unique and protected from harm.

personality the unique and relatively stable ways in which people think, feel, and behave.

personality disorders disorders in which a person adopts a persistent, rigid, and maladaptive pattern of behavior that interferes with normal social interactions.

personality inventory paper-and-pencil or computerized test that consists of statements that require a specific, standardized response from the person taking the test.

personality psychology area of psychology in which the psychologists study the differences in personality among people.

personal unconscious Jung's name for the unconscious mind as described by Freud.

person-centered therapy a nondirective insight therapy based on the work of Carl Rogers in which the client does much of the talking and the therapist listens.

persuasion the process by which one person tries to change the belief, opinion, position, or course of action of another person through argument, pleading, or explanation.

phallic stage the third stage in Freud's psychosexual stages, occurring from about 3 to 6 years of age, in which the child discovers sexual feelings.

phobia an irrational, persistent fear of an object, situation, or social activity.

phonemes the basic units of sound in language.

physical dependence condition occurring when a person's body becomes unable to function normally without a particular drug.

physiological psychology area of psychology in which the psychologists study the biological bases of behavior.

pineal gland endocrine gland located near the base of the cerebrum; secretes melatonin.

pinna the visible part of the ear.

pitch psychological experience of sound that corresponds to the frequency of the sound waves; higher frequencies are perceived as higher pitches.

pituitary gland gland located in the brain that secretes human growth hormone and influences all other hormone-secreting glands (also known as the master gland).

placebo effect the phenomenon in which the expectations of the participants in a study can influence their behavior.

place theory theory of pitch that states that different pitches are experienced by the stimulation of hair cells in different locations on the organ of Corti.

plagiarism the copying of someone else's exact words (or a close imitation of the words) and presenting them as your own.

pleasure principle principle by which the id functions; the desire for the immediate satisfaction of needs without regard for the consequences.

polygon line graph showing a frequency distribution.

pons the larger swelling above the medulla that relays information from the cortex to the cerebellum, and that plays a part in sleep, dreaming, left–right body coordination, and arousal.

population the entire group of people or animals in which the researcher is interested.

positively skewed a distribution of scores in which scores are concentrated in the low end of the distribution.

positive regard warmth, affection, love, and respect that come from significant others in one's life.

positive reinforcement the reinforcement of a response by the addition or experiencing of a pleasurable stimulus.

positive symptoms symptoms of schizophrenia that are excesses of behavior or occur in addition to normal behavior; hallucinations, delusions, and distorted thinking.

positron emission tomography (PET) brain-imaging method in which a radioactive sugar is injected into the subject and a computer compiles a color-coded image of the activity of the brain.

posttraumatic stress disorder (PTSD) a disorder resulting from exposure to a major stressor, with symptoms of anxiety, dissociation, nightmares, poor sleep, reliving the event, and concentration problems, lasting for more than 1 month; symptoms may appear immediately or not occur until 6 months or later after the traumatic event.

practical intelligence the ability to use information to get along in life and become successful.

pragmatics aspects of language involving the practical ways of communicating with others, or the social "niceties" of language.

prefrontal lobotomy psychosurgery in which the connections of the prefrontal cortex to other areas of the brain are severed.

prejudice negative attitude held by a person about the members of a particular social group.

preoperational stage Piaget's second stage of cognitive development, in which the preschool child learns to use language as a means of exploring the world.

pressure the psychological experience produced by urgent demands or expectations for a person's behavior that come from an outside source.

primacy effect tendency to remember information at the beginning of a body of information better than the information that follows.

primary appraisal the first step in assessing stress, which involves estimating the severity of a stressor and classifying it as either a threat or a challenge.

primary drives those drives that involve needs of the body such as hunger and thirst.

primary reinforcer any reinforcer that is naturally reinforcing by meeting a basic biological need, such as hunger, thirst, or touch.

proactive interference memory problem that occurs when older information prevents or interferes with the learning or retrieval of newer information.

problem-focused coping coping strategies that try to eliminate the source of a stress or reduce its impact through direct actions.

problem solving process of cognition that occurs when a goal must be reached by thinking and behaving in certain ways.

projective tests personality assessments that present ambiguous visual stimuli to the client and ask the client to respond with whatever comes to mind.

proprioception awareness of where the body and body parts are located in relation to each other in space and to the ground.

prosocial behavior socially desirable behavior that benefits others.

prototype an example of a concept that closely matches the defining characteristics of the concept.

proximity a Gestalt principle of perception; the tendency to perceive objects that are close to each other as part of the same grouping; physical or geographical nearness.

psychiatric social worker a social worker with some training in therapy methods who focuses on the environmental conditions that can have an impact on mental disorders, such as poverty, overcrowding, stress, and drug abuse.

psychiatrist a physician who specializes in the diagnosis and treatment of psychological disorders.

psychoactive drugs chemical substances that alter thinking, perception, and memory.

psychoanalysis an insight therapy based on the theory of Freud, emphasizing the revealing of unconscious conflicts; Freud's term for both the theory of personality and the therapy based on it.

psychodynamic perspective modern version of psychoanalysis that is more focused on the development of a sense of self and the discovery of motivations behind a person's behavior other than sexual motivations.

psychodynamic therapy a newer and more general term for therapies based on psychoanalysis with an emphasis on transference, shorter treatment times, and a more direct therapeutic approach.

psychological defense mechanisms unconscious distortions of a person's perception of reality that reduce stress and anxiety.

psychological dependence the belief that a drug is needed to continue a feeling of emotional or psychological well-being.

psychological disorder any pattern of behavior or thinking that causes people significant distress, causes them to harm others, or harms their ability to function in daily life.

psychologist a professional with an academic degree and specialized training in one or more areas of psychology.

psychology scientific study of behavior and mental processes.

psychoneuroimmunology the study of the effects of psychological factors such as stress, emotions, thoughts, and behavior on the immune system.

psychopathology the study of abnormal behavior and psychological dysfunction.

psychopharmacology the use of drugs to control or relieve the symptoms of psychological disorders.

psychosexual stages five stages of personality development proposed by Freud and tied to the sexual development of the child.

psychosurgery surgery performed on brain tissue to relieve or control severe psychological disorders.

psychotherapy therapy for mental disorders in which a person with a problem talks with a psychological professional.

psychotic refers to an individual's inability to separate what is real and what is fantasy.

puberty the physical changes that occur in the body as sexual development reaches its peak.

punishment any event or object that, when following a response, makes that response less likely to happen again.

punishment by application the punishment of a response by the addition or experiencing of an unpleasant stimulus.

punishment by removal the punishment of a response by the removal of a pleasurable stimulus.

random assignment process of assigning participants to the experimental or control groups randomly, so that each participant has an equal chance of being in either group.

range the difference between the highest and lowest scores in a distribution.

rapid eye movement (REM) sleep stage of sleep in which the eyes move rapidly under the eyelids and the person is typically experiencing a dream.

rating scale assessment in which a numerical value is assigned to specific behavior that is listed in the scale.

rational emotive behavior therapy (REBT) cognitive behavioral therapy in which clients are directly challenged in their irrational beliefs and helped to restructure their thinking into more rational belief statements.

realistic conflict theory theory stating that prejudice and discrimination will be increased between groups that are in conflict over a limited resource.

reality principle principle by which the ego functions; the satisfaction of the demands of the id only when negative consequences will not result.

recall type of memory retrieval in which the information to be retrieved must be "pulled" from memory with very few external cues.

recency effect tendency to remember information at the end of a body of information better than the information that precedes it.

receptor sites three-dimensional proteins on the surface of the dendrites or certain cells of the muscles and glands, which are shaped to fit only certain neurotransmitters.

recessive referring to a gene that only influences the expression of a trait when paired with an identical gene.

reciprocal determinism Bandura's explanation of how the factors of environment, personal characteristics, and behavior can interact to determine future behavior.

reciprocity of liking tendency of people to like other people who like them in return.

recognition the ability to match a piece of information or a stimulus to a stored image or fact.

reflection therapy technique in which the therapist restates what the client says rather than interpreting those statements.

reflex an involuntary response, one that is not under personal control or choice.

reflex arc the connection of the afferent neurons to the interneurons to the efferent neurons, resulting in a reflex action.

reinforcement any event or stimulus that, when following a response, increases the probability that the response will occur again.

reinforcers any events or objects that, when following a response, increase the likelihood of that response occurring again.

relative size monocular depth perception cue; perception that occurs when objects that a person expects to be of a certain size appear to be small and are, therefore, assumed to be much farther away.

reliability the tendency of a test to produce the same scores again and again each time it is given to the same people.

REM behavior disorder a rare disorder in which the mechanism that blocks the movement of the voluntary muscles fails, allowing the person to thrash around and even get up and act out nightmares.

REM rebound increased amounts of REM sleep after being deprived of REM sleep on earlier nights.

replicate in research, repeating a study or experiment to see if the same results will be obtained in an effort to demonstrate reliability of results.

representativeness heuristic assumption that any object (or person) sharing characteristics with the members of a particular category is also a member of that category.

representative sample randomly selected sample of participants from a larger population of participants.

resistance occurring when a patient becomes reluctant to talk about a certain topic by either changing the subject or becoming silent.

resting potential the state of the neuron when not firing a neural impulse.

restorative theory theory of sleep proposing that sleep is necessary to the physical health of the body and serves to replenish chemicals and repair cellular damage.

reticular formation (RF) an area of neurons running through the middle of the medulla and the pons and slightly beyond that is responsible for general attention, alertness, and arousal.

retrieval getting information that is in storage into a form that can be used.

retroactive interference memory problem that occurs when newer information prevents or interferes with the retrieval of older information.

retrograde amnesia loss of memory from the point of some injury or trauma backward, or loss of memory for the past.

reuptake process by which neurotransmitters are taken back into the synaptic vesicles.

reversible figures visual illusions in which the figure and ground can be reversed.

rods visual sensory receptors found at the back of the retina, responsible for noncolor sensitivity to low levels of light.

romantic love type of love consisting of intimacy and passion.

Rorschach inkblot test projective test that uses 10 inkblots as the ambiguous stimuli.

sample group of subjects selected from a larger population of subjects, usually selected randomly.

scaffolding process in which a more skilled learner gives help to a less skilled learner, reducing the amount of help as the less skilled learner becomes more capable.

schema a mental concept or framework that guides organization and interpretation of information, which forms and evolves through experiences with objects and events.

schizophrenia severe disorder in which the person suffers from disordered thinking, bizarre behavior, hallucinations, and inability to distinguish between fantasy and reality.

school psychology area of psychology in which the psychologists work directly in the schools, doing assessments, educational placement, and diagnosing educational problems.

scientific approach system of gathering data so that bias and error in measurement are reduced.

secondary appraisal the second step in assessing a stressor, which involves estimating the resources available to the person for coping with the threat.

secondary reinforcer any reinforcer that becomes reinforcing after being paired with a primary reinforcer, such as praise, tokens, or gold stars.

selective attention the ability to focus on only one stimulus from among all sensory input.

self an individual's awareness of his or her own personal characteristics and level of functioning.

self-actualization according to Maslow, the point that is seldom reached at which people have sufficiently satisfied the lower needs and achieved their full human potential.

self-actualizing tendency the striving to fulfill one's innate capacities and capabilities.

self-concept the image of oneself that develops from interactions with important significant people in one's life.

self-determination theory (SDT) theory of human motivation in which the social context of an action has an effect on the type of motivation existing for the action.

self-efficacy individual's expectancy of how effective his or her efforts to accomplish a goal will be in any particular circumstance.

self-fulfilling prophecy the tendency of one's expectations to affect one's behavior in such a way as to make the expectations more likely to occur.

self-help groups (support groups) a group composed of people who have similar problems and who meet together without a therapist or counselor for the purpose of discussion, problem solving, and social and emotional support.

semantic memory type of declarative memory containing general knowledge, such as knowledge of language and information learned in formal education.

semantic network model model of memory organization that assumes information is stored in the brain in a connected fashion, with concepts that are related stored physically closer to each other than concepts that are not highly related.

semantics the rules for determining the meaning of words and sentences.

sensation the process that occurs when special receptors in the sense organs are activated, allowing various forms of outside stimuli to become neural signals in the brain.

sensation seeker someone who needs more arousal than the average person.

sensorimotor stage Piaget's first stage of cognitive development, in which the infant uses its senses and motor abilities to interact with objects in the environment.

sensory adaptation tendency of sensory receptor cells to become less responsive to a stimulus that is unchanging.

sensory conflict theory an explanation of motion sickness in which the information from the eyes conflicts with the information from the vestibular senses, resulting in dizziness, nausea, and other physical discomfort.

sensory memory the very first system in memory, in which raw information from the senses is held for a very brief period of time.

sensory pathway nerves coming from the sensory organs to the CNS consisting of afferent neurons.

serial position effect tendency of information at the beginning and end of a body of information to be remembered more accurately than information in the middle of the body of information.

sexual orientation a person's sexual attraction to and affection for members of either the opposite or the same sex.

s factor the ability to excel in certain areas, or specific intelligence.

shape constancy the tendency to interpret the shape of an object as being constant, even when its shape changes on the retina.

shaping the reinforcement of simple steps in behavior through successive approximations that lead to a desired, more complex behavior.

short-term memory (STM) the memory system in which information is held for brief periods of time while being used.

signal detection theory provides a method for assessing the accuracy of judgments or decisions under uncertain conditions; used in perception research and other areas. An individual's correct "hits" and rejections are compared against their "misses" and "false alarms."

significant difference a difference between groups of numerical data that is considered large enough to be due to factors other than chance variation.

similarity a Gestalt principle of perception; the tendency to perceive things that look similar to each other as being part of the same group.

single-blind study study in which the participants do not know if they are in the experimental or the control group.

situational cause cause of behavior attributed to external factors, such as delays, the action of others, or some other aspect of the situation.

situational context the social or environmental setting of a person's behavior.

size constancy the tendency to interpret an object as always being the same actual size, regardless of its distance.

skewed distribution frequency distribution in which most of the scores fall to one side or the other of the distribution.

sleep apnea disorder in which the person stops breathing for 10 seconds or more.

sleep deprivation any significant loss of sleep, resulting in problems in concentration and irritability.

sleep paralysis the inability of the voluntary muscles to move during REM sleep.

sleepwalking (somnambulism) occurring during deep sleep, an episode of moving around or walking around in one's sleep.

social anxiety disorder (social phobia) fear of interacting with others or being in social situations that might lead to a negative evaluation.

social categorization the assignment of a person one has just met to a category based on characteristics the new person has in common with other people with whom one has had experience in the past.

social cognition the mental processes that people use to make sense of the social world around them.

social cognitive learning theorists theorists who emphasize the importance of both the influences of other people's behavior and of a person's own expectancies on learning.

social cognitive theory referring to the use of cognitive processes in relation to understanding the social world.

social cognitive theory of hypnosis theory that assumes that people who are hypnotized are not in an altered state but are merely playing the role expected of them in the situation.

social cognitive view learning theory that includes cognitive processes such as anticipating, judging, memory, and imitation of models.

social comparison the comparison of oneself to others in ways that raise one's self-esteem.

social facilitation the tendency for the presence of other people to have a positive impact on the performance of an easy task.

social identity the part of the self-concept including one's view of self as a member of a particular social category.

social identity theory theory in which the formation of a person's identity within a particular social group is explained by social categorization, social identity, and social comparison.

social impairment the tendency for the presence of other people to have a negative impact on the performance of a difficult task.

social influence the process through which the real or implied presence of others can directly or indirectly influence the thoughts, feelings, and behavior of an individual.

social loafing the tendency for people to put less effort into a simple task when working with others on that task.

social psychology the scientific study of how a person's thoughts, feelings, and behavior influence and are influenced by social groups; area of psychology in which psychologists focus on how human behavior is affected by the presence of other people.

Social Readjustment Rating Scale (SRRS) assessment that measures the amount of stress resulting from major life events over a 1-year period in a person's life.

social role the pattern of behavior that is expected of a person who is in a particular social position.

social-support system the network of family, friends, neighbors, coworkers, and others who can offer support, comfort, or aid to a person in need.

sociocultural perspective perspective that focuses on the influence of social interactions, society, and culture on an individual's thinking and behavior; in psychopathology, approach that examines the impact of social interactions, community, and culture on a person's thinking, behavior, and emotions.

soma the cell body of the neuron responsible for maintaining the life of the cell.

somatic nervous system division of the PNS consisting of nerves that carry information from the senses to the CNS and from the CNS to the voluntary muscles of the body.

somatosensory cortex area of cortex at the front of the parietal lobes responsible for processing information from the skin and internal body receptors for touch, temperature, and body position.

somesthetic senses the body senses consisting of the skin senses, the kinesthetic and proprioceptive senses, and the vestibular senses.

source traits the more basic traits that underlie the surface traits, forming the core of personality.

spatial neglect condition produced most often by damage to the parietal lobe association areas of the right hemisphere, resulting in an inability to recognize objects or body parts in the left visual field.

specific phobia fear of objects or specific situations or events.

sperm the male sex cell.

spinal cord a long bundle of neurons that carries messages between the body and the brain and is responsible for very fast, lifesaving reflexes.

spontaneous recovery the reappearance of a learned response after extinction has occurred.

sports psychology area of psychology in which the psychologists help athletes and others prepare themselves mentally for participation in sports activities.

standard deviation the square root of the average squared deviations from the mean of scores in a distribution; a measure of variability.

statistically significant referring to differences in data sets that are larger than chance variation would predict.

statistics branch of mathematics concerned with the collection and interpretation of numerical data.

stem cells special cells found in all the tissues of the body that are capable of becoming other cell types when those cells need to be replaced due to damage or wear and tear.

stereotype threat condition in which being made aware of a negative performance stereotype interferes with the performance of someone that considers himself or herself part of that group.

stereotype vulnerability the effect that people's awareness of the stereotypes associated with their social group has on their behavior.

stimulants drugs that increase the functioning of the nervous system.

stimulatory hallucinogenics drugs that produce a mixture of psychomotor stimulant and hallucinogenic effects.

stimulus discrimination the tendency to stop making a generalized response to a stimulus that is similar to the original conditioned stimulus because the similar stimulus is never paired with the unconditioned stimulus.

stimulus generalization the tendency to respond to a stimulus that is only similar to the original conditioned stimulus with the conditioned response.

stimulus motive a motive that appears to be unlearned but causes an increase in stimulation, such as curiosity.

storage holding on to information for some period of time.

stress the term used to describe the physical, emotional, cognitive, and behavioral responses to events that are appraised as threatening or challenging.

stressors events that cause a stress reaction.

stress-vulnerability model explanation of disorder that assumes a biological sensitivity, or vulnerability, to a certain disorder will result in the development of that disorder under the right conditions of environmental or emotional stress.

structuralism early perspective in psychology associated with Wilhelm Wundt and Edward Titchener, in which the focus of study is the structure or basic elements of the mind.

subjective referring to concepts and impressions that are only valid within a particular person's perception and may be influenced by biases, prejudice, and personal experiences.

subjective discomfort emotional distress or emotional pain.

superego part of the personality that acts as a moral center.

surface traits aspects of personality that can easily be seen by other people in the outward actions of a person.

sympathetic division (fight-or-flight system) also called the sympathetic nervous system (SNS), part of the ANS that is responsible for reacting to stressful events and bodily arousal.

synapse (synaptic gap) microscopic fluid-filled space between the axon terminal of one cell and the dendrites or soma of the next cell.

synaptic vesicles saclike structures found inside the synaptic knob containing chemicals.

synesthesia condition in which the signals from the various sensory organs are processed differently, resulting in the sense information being interpreted as more than one sensation.

syntax the system of rules for combining words and phrases to form grammatically correct sentences.

systematic desensitization behavior technique used to treat phobias, in which a client is asked to make a list of ordered fears and taught to relax while concentrating on those fears.

temperament the behavioral characteristics that are fairly well established at birth, such as "easy," "difficult," and "slow to warm up"; the enduring characteristics with which each person is born.

temporal lobes areas of the cortex located along the side of the brain, starting just behind the temples, containing the neurons responsible for the sense of hearing and meaningful speech.

teratogen any factor that can cause a birth defect.

testes (testicles) the male gonads or sex glands.

texture gradient monocular depth perception cue; the tendency for textured surfaces to appear to become smaller and finer as distance from the viewer increases.

thalamus part of the limbic system located in the center of the brain, this structure relays sensory information from the lower part of the brain to the proper areas of the cortex and processes some sensory information before sending it to its proper area.

Thematic Apperception Test (TAT) projective test that uses 20 pictures of people in ambiguous situations as the visual stimuli.

therapeutic alliance the relationship between therapist and client that develops as a warm, caring, accepting relationship characterized by empathy, mutual respect, and understanding.

theory a general explanation of a set of observations or facts.

therapy treatment methods aimed at making people feel better and function more effectively.

theta waves brain waves indicating the early stages of sleep.

thinking (cognition) mental activity that goes on in the brain when a person is organizing and attempting to understand information and communicating information to others.

thyroid gland endocrine gland found in the neck; regulates metabolism.

time-out an extinction process in which a person is removed from the situation that provides reinforcement for undesirable behavior, usually by being placed in a quiet corner or room away from possible attention and reinforcement opportunities.

token economy the use of objects called tokens to reinforce behavior in which the tokens can be accumulated and exchanged for desired items or privileges.

top-down processing the use of preexisting knowledge to organize individual features into a unified whole.

trait a consistent, enduring way of thinking, feeling, or behaving.

trait–situation interaction the assumption that the particular circumstances of any given situation will influence the way in which a trait is expressed.

trait theories theories that endeavor to describe the characteristics that make up human personality in an effort to predict future behavior.

transduction the process of converting outside stimuli, such as light, into neural activity.

transference in psychoanalysis, the tendency for a patient or client to project positive or negative feelings for important people from the past onto the therapist.

trial and error (mechanical solution) problem-solving method in which one possible solution after another is tried until a successful one is found.

triarchic theory of intelligence Sternberg's theory that there are three kinds of intelligence: analytical, creative, and practical.

trichromatic theory theory of color vision that proposes three types of cones: red, blue, and green.

***t*-test** type of inferential statistical analysis typically used when two means are compared to see if they are significantly different.

Type 2 diabetes disease typically occurring in middle adulthood when the body either becomes resistant to the effects of insulin or can no longer secrete enough insulin to maintain normal glucose levels.

Type A personality person who is ambitious, time conscious, extremely hardworking, and tends to have high levels of hostility and anger as well as being easily annoyed.

Type B personality person who is relaxed and laid back, less driven and competitive than Type A, and slow to anger.

Type C personality pleasant but repressed person, who tends to internalize his or her anger and anxiety and who finds expressing emotions difficult.

Type D personality "distressed" personality type; person who experiences negative emotions such as anger, sadness, and fear and tends not to share these emotions in social situations out of fear of rejection or disapproval.

unconditional positive regard positive regard that is given without conditions or strings attached; in person-centered therapy, referring to the warm, respectful, and accepting atmosphere created by the therapist for the client.

unconditioned response (UCR) in classical conditioning, an involuntary and unlearned response to a naturally occurring or unconditioned stimulus.

unconditioned stimulus (UCS) in classical conditioning, a naturally occurring stimulus that leads to an involuntary and unlearned response.

unconscious mind level of the mind in which thoughts, feelings, memories, and other information are kept that are not easily or voluntarily brought into consciousness.

validity the degree to which a test actually measures what it's supposed to measure.

variable interval schedule of reinforcement schedule of reinforcement in which the interval of time that must pass before reinforcement becomes possible is different for each trial or event.

variable ratio schedule of reinforcement schedule of reinforcement in which the number of responses required for reinforcement is different for each trial or event.

vestibular sense the awareness of the balance, position, and movement of the head and body through space in relation to gravity's pull.

vicarious conditioning classical conditioning of an involuntary response or emotion by watching the reaction of another person.

visual accommodation the change in the thickness of the lens as the eye focuses on objects that are far away or close.

volley principle theory of pitch that states that frequencies from about 400 Hz to 4,000 Hz cause the hair cells (auditory neurons) to fire in a volley pattern, or take turns in firing.

waking consciousness state in which thoughts, feelings, and sensations are clear and organized and the person feels alert.

weight set point the particular level of weight that the body tries to maintain.

Wernicke's aphasia condition resulting from damage to Wernicke's area, causing the affected person to be unable to understand or produce meaningful language.

withdrawal physical symptoms that can include nausea, pain, tremors, crankiness, and high blood pressure, resulting from a lack of an addictive drug in the body systems.

working memory an active system that processes the information in short-term memory.

Yerkes-Dodson law law stating that when tasks are simple, a higher level of arousal leads to better performance; when tasks are difficult, lower levels of arousal lead to better performance.

zone of proximal development (ZPD) Vygotsky's concept of the difference between what a child can do alone and what that child can do with the help of a teacher.

z score a statistical measure that indicates how far away from the mean a particular score is in terms of the number of standard deviations that exist between the mean and that score.

zygote cell resulting from the uniting of the ovum and sperm.

References

2018 Physical Activity Guidelines Advisory Committee. (2018). *Physical activity guidelines advisory committee scientific report.* Washington, DC: U.S. Department of Health and Human Services Retrieved from https://health.gov/paguidelines/second-edition/report/pdf/PAG_Advisory_Committee_Report.pdf

AAA Foundation. (2009, April). Aggressive driving: Research update. Retrieved from https://www.aaafoundation.org/sites/default/files/Aggressive Driving Research Update 2009.pdf

AAA Foundation for Traffic Safety. (2016). *Prevalence of self-reported aggressive driving behavior: United States, 2014.* Retrieved from Washington, DC: https://exchange.aaa.com/wp-content/uploads/2017/05/Aggressive-Driving-REPORT.pdf

Abad, V. C., & Guilleminault, C. (2017). New developments in the management of narcolepsy. *Nature and Science of Sleep, 9:* 39–57. DOI: https://doi.org/10.2147/NSS>S103467

Abadinsky, H. (1989). *Drug abuse: An introduction.* Chicago: Nelson-Hall Series in Law, Crime, and Justice.

Abbas, A. I., & Lieberman, J. A. (2015). Pharmacological treatments for schizophrenia. In P. E. Nathan & J. M. Gorman (Eds.), *A guide to treatments that work* (4th ed., pp. 175–215). New York, NY: Oxford University Press.

Abbott, L., Nadler, J., & Rude, R. K. (1994). Magnesium deficiency in alcoholism: Possible contribution to osteoporosis and cardiovascular disease in alcoholics. *Alcoholism, Clinical & Experimental Research, 18*(5), 1076–1082.

Abdou, C. M., Fingerhut, A. W., Jackson, J. S., & Wheaton, F. (2016). Healthcare stereotype threat in older adults in the health and retirement study. *American Journal of Preventive Medicine, 50*(2), 191–198. doi: 10.1016/j.amepre.2015.07.034

Abe, K., Niwa, M., Fujisaki, K., & Suzuki, Y. (2018). Associations between emotional intelligence, empathy and personality in Japanese medical students. *BMC Medical Education, 18*(1), 47. doi:10.1186/s12909-018-1165-7

Abel, E. L., & Sokol, R. J. (1987). Incidence of fetal alcohol syndrome and economic impact of FAS-related anomalies: Drug alcohol syndrome and economic impact of FAS-related anomalies. *Drug and Alcohol Dependency, 19*(1), 51–70.

Abel, G. G., & Osborn, C. A. (1992). The paraphilias: The extent and nature of sexually deviant and criminal behavior. In J. M. W. Bradford (Ed.), *Psychiatric Clinics of North America, 15*(3) (pp. 675–687). Philadelphia: W. B. Saunders Company.

Abela, J. R. Z., & D'Allesandro, D. U. (2002). Beck's cognitive theory of depression: The diathesis-stress and causal mediation components. *British Journal of Clinical Psychology, 41,* 111–128.

Abramson, L. Y., Garber, J., & Seligman, M. E. P. (1980). Learned helplessness in humans: An attributional analysis. In J. Garber & M. E. P. Seligman (Eds.), *Human Helplessness* (pp. 3–34). New York: Academic Press.

Abramson, L. Y., Seligman, M. E. P., & Teasdale, J. D. (1978). Learned helplessness in humans: Critique and reformulation. *Journal of Abnormal Psychology, 87,* 49–74.

Acheson, D. J., MacDonald, M. C., & Postle, B. R. (2010). The interaction of concreteness and phonological similarity in verbal working memory. *Journal of Experimental Psychology: Learning, Memory and Cognition, 36*(1), 17–36.

Adachi, P. J. C., & Willoughby, T. (2011). The effect of video game competition and violence on aggressive behavior: Which characteristic has the greatest influence? *Psychology of Violence, 1*(4), 259–274. doi: 10.1037/a0024908

Adam, K. (1980). Sleep as a restorative process and a theory to explain why. *Progressive Brain Research, 53,* 289–305.

Adamaszek, M., D'Agata, F., Ferrucci, R., Habas, C., Keulen, S., Kirkby, K. C.,… Verhoeven, J. (2017). Consensus paper: Cerebellum and emotion. *Cerebellum, 16*(2), 552–576. doi:10.1007/s12311-016-0815-8

Adams, D. B. (1968). The activity of single cells in the midbrain and hypothalamus of the cat during affective defense behavior. *Archives Italiennes de Biologie, 106,* 243–269.

Adams, R. J. (1987). An evaluation of colour preferences in early infancy. *Infant Behaviour and Development, 10,* 143–150.

Addis, D. R., Giovanello, K. S., Vu, M. A., & Schacter, D. L. (2014). Age-related changes in prefrontal and hippocampal contributions to relational encoding. *NeuroImage, 84,* 19–26.

Addis, D. R., Leclerc, C. M., Muscatell, K., & Kensinger, E. A. (2010). There are age-related changes in neural connectivity during the encoding of positive, but not negative, information. *Cortex, 46,* 9.

Ader, R. (2003). Conditioned immunomodulation: Research needs and directions. *Brain, Behavior, and Immunity, 17*(1), 51–57.

Adler, A. (1954). *Understanding human nature.* New York: Greenburg Publisher.

Adler, S. R., Fosket, J. R., Kagawa-Singer, M., McGraw, S. A., Wong-Kim, E., Gold, E., & Sternfeld, B. (2000). Conceptualizing menopause and midlife: Chinese American and Chinese women in the U.S. *Maturitas, 35*(1), 11–23.

Adolphs, R., Gosselin, F., Buchanan, T. W., Tranel, D., Schyns, P., & Damasio, A. R. (2005). A mechanism for impaired fear recognition after amygdala damage. *Nature, 433,* 68–72.

Adolphs, R., & Tranel, D. (2003). Amygdala damage impairs emotion recognition from scenes only when they contain facial expressions. *Neuropsychologia, 41,* 1281–1289.

Advokat, C. D., Comaty, J. E., & Julien, R. M. (2019). *Julien's primer of drug action: A comprehensive guide to the actions, uses, and side effects of psychoactive drugs* (14th ed.). New York, NY: Worth Publishers.

Afifi, T. O., Mota, N. P., Dasiewicz, P., MacMillan, H. L., & Sareen, J. (2012). Physical punishment and mental disorders: Results from a nationally representative US sample. *Pediatrics, 130*(2), 184–192. doi: 10.1542/peds.2011-2947

Afifi, T. O., Mota, N., Sareen, J., & MacMillan, H. L. (2017). The relationships between harsh physical punishment and child maltreatment in childhood and intimate partner violence in adulthood. *BMC Public Health, 17:* 493. DOI: https://doi.org/10.1186/s12889-017-4359-8

Agerup, T., Lydersen, S., Wallander, J., & Sund, A. M. (2015). Associations between parental attachment and course of depression between adolescence and young adulthood. *Child Psychiatry and Human Development, 46,* 632–642.

Aggarwal, N. T., Wilson, R. S., Beck, T. L., Rajan, K. B., de Leon, C. F. M., Evans, D. A., & Everson-Rose, S. A. (2014). Perceived stress and change in cognitive function among adults aged 65 and older. *Psychosomatic Medicine, 76,* 80–85.

Agresti, A., & Finlay, B. (1997). *Statistical methods for the social sciences.* Upper Saddle River, New Jersey: Prentice Hall.

Aguerrevere, L. E., Calamia, M. R., Greve, K. W., Bianchini, K. J., Curtis, K. L., & Ramirez, V. (2018). Clusters of financially incentivized chronic pain patients using the Minnesota Multiphasic Personality Inventory-2 Restructured Form (MMPI-2-RF). *Psychological Assessment, 30*(5), 634–644. doi: 10.1037/pas0000509

Aguiar, A., & Baillargeon, R. (2003). Perseverative responding in a violation-of-expectation task in 6.5-month-old infants. *Cognition, 88*(3), 277–316.

Aguilar, D. D., Giuffreda, A., & Lodge, D. J. (2018). Adolescent synthetic cannabinoid exposure produces enduring changes in dopamine neuron activity in a rodent model of schizophrenia susceptibility. *International Journal of Neuropsychopharmacology, 21*(4): 393–403. DOI: https://doi.org/10.1093/ijnp/pyy003

Ahlskog, J. E. (2003). Slowing Parkinson's disease progression: Recent dopamine agonist trials. *Neurology, 60*(3), 381–389.

Ahn, W. (1998). Why are different features central for natural kinds and artifacts? The role of causal status in determining feature centrality. *Cognition, 69,* 135–178.

Aiello, J. R., & Douthitt, E. A. (2001). Social facilitation from Triplett to electronic performance monitoring. *Group Dynamics: Theory, Research, and Practice, 5*(3), 163–180.

Ainsworth, M. D. S. (1985). Attachments across the life span. *Bulletin of the New York Academy of Medicine, 61,* 792–812.

Ainsworth, M. D. S., Blehar, M. C., Waters, E., & Wall, S. (1978). *Patterns of attachment: A study of the strange situation.* Hillsdale, NJ: Erlbaum.

Aitchison, J. (1992). Good birds, better birds, and amazing birds: The development of prototypes. In P. J. Arnaud & H. Béjoint (Eds.), *Vocabulary and applied linguistics* (pp. 71–84). London: Macmillan.

Ajzen, I. (2001). Nature and operation of attitudes. *Annual Review of Psychology, 52,* 27–58.

Ajzen, I., & Fishbein, M. (2000). Attitudes and the attitude–behavior relation: Reasoned and automatic processes. In W. Stroebe & M. Hewstone (Eds.), *European review of social psychology* (pp. 1–33). New York: John Wiley & Sons.

Åkerstedt, T., Ghilotti, F., Grotta, A., Zhao, H., Adami, H-O., Trolle-Lagerros, Y., & Bellocco, R. (2018). Sleep duration and mortality—Does weekend sleep matter? *Journal of Sleep Research,* e12712 DOI: 10.1111/jsr.12712

Åkerstedt, T., Hallvig, D., Nund, A., Fors, C., Schwarz, J., & Kecklund, G. (2013). Having to stop driving at night because of dangerous sleepiness—awareness, physiology and behavior. *Journal of Sleep Research, 22*(4), 380–388.

Akil, M., Kolachana, B. S., Rothmond, D. A., Hyde, T. M., Weinberger, D. R., & Kleinman, J. E. (2003). Catechol-o-methyltransferase genotype and dopamine regulation in the human brain. *Journal of Neuroscience, 23*(6), 2008–2013.

Albert, D. J., & Richmond, S. E. (1977). Reactivity and aggression in the rat: Induction by alpha–adrenergic blocking agents injected ventral to anterior septum but not into lateral septum. *Journal of Comparative and Physiological Psychology, 91,* 886–896 [DBA] *Physiology and Behavior, 20,* 755–761.

Albert, D., Chein, J., & Steinberg, L. (2013). The teenage brain: Peer influences on adolescent decision making. *Current Directions in Psychological Science, 22,* 114–120.

Alderfer, C. P. (1972). *Existence, relatedness and growth: Human needs in organisational settings*. New York: Free Press.

Aldridge-Morris, R. (1989). *Multiple personality: An exercise in deception*. Hillsdale, NJ: Erlbaum.

Alexander, G., DeLong, M. R., & Strick, P. L. (1986). Parallel organization of functionally segregated circuits linking basal ganglia and cortex. *Annual Review of Neuroscience, 9*, 357–381.

Algoe, S. B., Kurtz, L. E., & Grewen, K. (2017). Oxytocin and social bonds: The role of oxytocin in perceptions of romantic partners' bonding behavior. *Psychological Science, 28*(12), 1763–1772. doi:10.1177/0956797617716922

Alibiglou, L., Videnovic, A., Planetta, P. J., Vaillancourt, D. E., & MacKinnon, C. D. (2016). Subliminal gait initiation deficitys in rapid eye movement sleep behavior disorder: a harbinger of freezing of gait? *Movement Disorders, 31*(11): 1711–1719. DOI: https://doi.org/10.1002/mds.26465

Aligne, C. A., Auinger, P., Byrd, R. S., & Weitzman, M. (2000). Risk factors for pediatric asthma contributions of poverty, race, and urban residence. *American Journal of Respiratory Critical Care Medicine, 162*(3), 873–877.

Alkon, D. (1989). Memory storage and neural systems. *Scientific American, 261*(1), 42–50.

Allen, D. (2018). Getting Things Done® - David Allen's GTD® Methodology. Retrieved from https://gettingthingsdone.com/

Allen, D. (2001). *Getting things done: the art of stress-free productivity*. New York: Viking Adult.

Allen, D. (2008). *Making it all work*. New York: Viking Adult.

Allen, D., Williams, M., & Wallace, M. (2018). *Getting things done for teens: Take control of your life in a distracting world*. New York, NY: Penguin Books.

Allen, F. (1994). *Secret formula*. New York: HarperCollins.

Allen, G. E. (2006). *Intelligence tests and immigration to the United States, 1900–1940*. Hoboken, NJ: John Wiley and Sons.

Allen, G., & Parisi, P. (1990). Trends in monozygotic and dizygotic twinning rates by maternal age and parity. Further analysis of Italian data, 1949–1985, and rediscussion of U.S. data, 1964–1985. *Acta Genetic Medicine & Gemellology, 39*, 317–328.

Allen, J. J., Anderson, C. A., & Bushman, B. J. (2018). The General Aggression Model. *Current Opinion in Psychology, 19*, 75–80. http://doi.org/10.1016/j.copsyc.2017.03.034

Allen, T. A., & DeYoung, C. G. (2016). Personality neuroscience and the Five Factor Model. In T. A. Widiger (Ed.), Oxford Handbook of the Five Factor Model. New York, NY: Oxford University Press. doi: 10.1093/oxfordhb/9780199352487.013.26

Allenby, C., Falcone, M., Bernardo, L., Wileyto, E. P., Rostain, A., Ramsay, J. R.,... Loughead, J. (2018). Transcranial direct current brain stimulation decreases impulsivity in ADHD. *Brain Stimulation*. doi:10.1016/j.brs.2018.04.016

Allik, J., Realo, A., & McCrae, R. R. (2013). Universality of the five-factor model of personality. In T. A. Widiger & P. T. Costa (Eds.), *Personality disorders and the five-factor model of personality* (3rd ed., pp. 61–74). Washington, DC: American Psychological Association.

Alloway, T. P., Rajendran, G., & Archibald, L. (2009). Working memory in children with developmental disorders. *Journal of Learning Disabilities, 42*(4), 372–382.

Alloy, L. B., & Clements, C. M. (1998). Hopelessness theory of depression: Tests of the symptom component. *Cognitive Therapy and Research, 22*, 303–335.

Allport, G. W., & Odbert, H. S. (1936). Trait names: A psycho-lexical study. *Psychological Monographs, 47*(1), i.

Alm, H., & Nilsson, L. (1995). The effects of a mobile telephone conversation on driver behaviour in a car following situation. *Accident Analysis and Prevention, 27*(5), 707–715.

Almasy, S. (2016). Muhammad ali: Boxing legend, activist and 'the greatest' to a world of fans, from http://www.cnn.com/2016/06/04/world/muhammad-ali-obituary/

Alz.org®: Alzheimer's Association. (2018). Alzheimer's myths. Retrieved from http://www.alz.org/alzheimers_disease_myths_about_alzheimers.asp

Alzheimer's Association. (2010). Alzheimer's disease facts and figures. *Alzheimer's & Dementia, 6*, 4–54.

Alzheimer's Association. (2018). 2018 Alzheimer's disease facts and figures. *Alzheimer's & Dementia, 14*(3): 367-429. Retrieved on August 17, 2018 at https://www.alz.org/media/HomeOffice/Facts%20and%20Figures/facts-and-figures.pdf

Amabile, T., DeJong, W., & Lepper, M. R. (1976). Effects of externally imposed deadlines on subsequent intrinsic motivation. *Journal of Personality and Social Psychology, 34*, 92–98.

Amabile, T., Hadley, C. N., & Kramer, S. J. (2002). Creativity under the gun. *Harvard Business Review, 80*(8), 52–60.

Amabile, T. M., Hennessey, B. A., & Grossman, B. S. (1986). Social influences on creativity: The effects of contracted-for reward. *Journal of Personality and Social Psychology, 50*(1), 14–23.

Amaral, D. G., & Strick, P. L. (2013). The organization of the central nervous system. In E. R. Kandel, J. H. Schwartz, T. M. Jessell, S. A. Siegelbaum, & A. J. Hudspeth (Eds.), *Principles of neural science* (5th ed., pp. 337–355). USA: McGraw-Hill.

Amariglio, R. E., Donohue, M. C., Marshall, G. A., Rentz, D. M., Salmon, D. P., Ferris, S. H.,... Alzheimer's Disease Cooperative Study. (2015). Tracking early decline in cognitive function in older individuals at risk for Alzheimer disease dementia: The Alzheimer's disease cooperative study cognitive function instrument. *JAMA Neurology, 72*(4), 446–454. doi: 10.1001/jamaneurol.2014.3375

Amat, J., Aleksejev, R. M., Paul, E., Watkins, L. R., & Maier, S. F. (2010). Behavioral control over shock blocks behavioral and neurochemical effects of later social defeat. *Neuroscience, 165*(4), 1031–1038. doi: 10.1016/j.neuroscience.2009.11.005

Amat, J., Baratta, M. V., Paul, E., Bland, S. T., Watkins, L. R., & Maier, S. F. (2005). Medial prefrontal cortex determines how stressor controllability affects behavior and dorsal raphe nucleus. *Nature Neuroscience, 8*(3), 365–371.

American Academy of Pediatrics. (1995). Health supervision for children with Turner syndrome. *Pediatrics, 96*(6), 1166–1173.

American College of Obstetricians and Gynecologists. (2015). Early pregnancy loss. Practice Bulletin No. 150. *Obstetrics & Gynecoology, 125*: 1258–1267. Retrieved on September 12, 2018 at http://www.acog.org/Resources-And-Publications/Practice-Bulletins/Committee-on-Practice-Bulletins-Gynecology/Early-Pregnancy-Loss

American Counseling Association. (2014). 2014 ACA code of ethics. Retrieved from http://www.counseling.org/docs/ethics/2014-aca-code-of-ethics.pdf

American Psychiatric Association. (2000). *Diagnostic and statistical manual of mental disorders* (4th ed., Text Revision). Washington, DC: Author.

American Psychiatric Association. (2013). *Diagnostic and statistical manual of mental disorders* (5th ed.). Washington, DC: Author.

American Psychiatric Association Committee on Electroconvulsive Therapy. (2001). *The practice of electroconvulsive therapy: Recommendations for treatment, training, and privileging* (2nd ed.). Washington, DC: Author.

American Psychological Association. (2002). Ethical principles of psychologists and code of conduct. *American Psychologist, 57*, 1060–1073.

American Psychological Association. (2005). Policy statement on evidence-based practice in psychology. Retrieved September 22, 2010, from http://www.apa.org/practice/guidelines/evidence-based.pdf

American Psychological Association. (2013). Recognition of psychotherapy effectiveness. *Psychotherapy, 50*(1), 102–109. doi: 10.1037/a0030276

American Psychological Association. (2014). How many psychology doctorates are awarded by U.S. institutions? News from APA's Center for Workforce Studies. *Monitor on Psychology, 45*(7), 13.

American Psychological Association. (2016). Psychology Master's and Doctoral Degrees Awarded by Broad Field, Subfield, Institution Type and State (2004–2013): Findings from the Integrated Postsecondary Education Data System. Washington, DC: Author

American Psychological Association. (2018a). Degree pathways in psychology [interactive data tool]. Retrieved from https://www.apa.org/workforce/data-tools/degrees-pathways

American Psychological Association. (2018b). *Demographics of the U.S. Psychology workforce: Findings from the 2007–16 American Community Survey*. Washington, DC.: Author Retrieved from https://www.apa.org/workforce/publications/16-demographics/report.pdf

American Psychological Association. (2018c). Demographics of U.S. Psychology workforce. [interactive data tool]. Retrieved from https://www.apa.org/workforce/data-tools/demographics

American Psychological Association, Division 19. (2019). Society for Military Psychology. Retrieved from https://www.apa.org/about/division/div19

Amsterdam, B. (1972). Mirror self-image reactions before age two. *Developmental Psychobiology, 5*(4), 297–305. doi:10.1002/dev.420050403

Anand, B. K., & Brobeck, J. R. (1951). Hypothalamic control of food intake in rats and cats. *Yale Journal of Biological Medicine, 24*, 123–146.

Anastasi, A., & Urbina, S. (1997). *Psychological testing* (7th ed.). Upper Saddle River, NJ: Prentice-Hall.

Anderson, C. A. (1987). Temperature and aggression: Effects on quarterly, yearly, and city rates of violent and nonviolent crime. *Journal of Personality and Social Psychology, 52*(6), 1161–1173.

Anderson, C. A. (2003). Video games and aggressive behavior. In D. Ravitch & J. P. Viteritti (Eds.), *Kid stuff: Marketing sex and violence to America's children* (p. 157). Baltimore/London: The Johns Hopkins University Press.

Anderson, C. A., Berkowitz, L., Donnerstein, E., Huesmann, L. R., Johnson, J. D., Linz, D.,... Wartella, E. (2003). The influence of media violence on youth. *Psychological Science in the Public Interest, 4*(3), 81–110.

Anderson, C. A., & Bushman, B. J. (2001). Effects of violent video games on aggressive behavior, aggressive cognition, aggressive affect, physiological arousal, and prosocial behavior: A meta–analytic review of the scientific literature. *Psych Science, 12*(5), 353–359.

Anderson, C. A., Bushman, B. J., Donnerstein, E., Hummer, T. A., & Warburton, W. (2015). SPSSI research summary on media violence. *Analyses of Social Issues and Public Policy, 15*(1), 4–19.

Anderson, C. A., & Dill, K. E. (2000). Video games and aggressive thoughts, feelings, and behavior in the laboratory and in life. *Journal of Personality and Social Psychology, 78*(4), 772–790.

Anderson, C. A., Sakamoto, A., Gentile, D., Ihori, N., Shibuya, A., Yukawa, S.,... Kobayashi, K. (2008). Longitudinal effects of violent video games on aggression in Japan and the United States. *Pediatrics, 122*(5), e1067–e1072.

Anderson, C. A., Shibuya, A., Ihori, N., Swing, E. L., Bushman, B. J., Sakamoto, A.,... Saleem, M. (2010). Violent video game effects on aggression, empathy, and prosocial behavior in Eastern and Western countries: A meta-analytic review. *Psychological Bulletin, 136*(2), 151–173. doi: 10.1037/a0018251

Anderson, L. W., Krathwohl, D. R., Airasian, P. W., Cruikshank, K. A., Mayer, R. E., Pintrich, P. R., Raths, J., & Wittrock, M. C. (Eds.). (2001). *A taxonomy for learning, teaching, and assessing—A revision of Bloom's Taxonomy of Educational Objectives*. New York: Addison Wesley Longman.

Anderson, M. C., & Neely, J. H. (1996). Interference and inhibition in memory retrieval. In E. L. Bjork & R. A. Bjork (Eds.). *Handbook of perception and cognition, Memory* (2nd ed.), 237–313. San Diego, CA: Academic Press.

Anderson, W. (1974). Personal growth and client-centered therapy: An information processing view. In D. Wexler & L. Rice (Eds.), *Innovations in client-centered therapy* (pp. 21–48). New York, NY: Wiley.

Andreu-Fernandez, V., Bastons-Compta, A., Navarro-Tapia, E., Sailer, S., & Garcia-Algar, O. (2019). Serum concentrations of IGF-I/IGF-II as biomarkers of alcohol damage during foetal development and diagnostic markers of Foetal Alcohol Syndrome. *Scientific Reports, 9*(1), 1562. doi: 10.1038/s41598-018-38041-0

Andrews, J. D. W. (1989). Integrating visions of reality: Interpersonal diagnosis and the existential vision. *American Psychologist, 44*, 803–817.

Angus, L., Watson, J. C., Elliott, R., Schneider, K., & Timulak, L. (2014). Humanistic psychotherapy research 1990–2015: From methodological innovation to evidence-supported treatment outcomes and beyond. *Psychotherapy Research, 25*(3), 330–347. doi: 10.1080/10503307.2014.989290

Anschuetz, B. L. (1999). The high cost of caring: Coping with workplace stress. *The Journal, the Newsletter of the Ontario Association of Children's Aid Societies, 43*(3), 1–63.

Anspaugh, D., Hamrick, M., & Rosato, F. (2011). Coping with and managing stress. In D. Anspaugh, M. Hamrick, and F. Rosato (Eds.), *Wellness: Concepts and applications* (8th ed., pp. 307–340). New York: McGraw-Hill.

Antonakis, J. (2004). On why "emotional intelligence" will not predict leadership effectiveness beyond IQ or the "Big Five": An extension and rejoinder. *Organizational Analysis, 12*(2), 171–182.

Antuono, P. G., Jones, J. L., Wang, Y., & Li, S. (2001). Decreased glutamate [plus] glutamine in Alzheimer's disease detected in vivo with (1)H-MRS at 0.5 T. *Neurology, 56*(6), 737–742.

Apps, M. A. J., Lesage, E., & Ramnani, N. (2015). Vicarious reinforcement learning signals when instructing others. *The Journal of Neuroscience, 35*(7), 2904–2913.

Arcelus, J., Mitchell, A. J., Wales, J., & Nielsen, S. (2011). Mortality rates in patients with anorexia nervosa and other eating disorders: A meta-analysis of 36 studies. *Archives of General Psychiatry, 68*(7), 724–731. doi: 10.1001/archgenpsychiatry.2011.74

Archer, J. (1991). The influence of testosterone on human aggression. *British Journal of Psychology, 82*, 1–28.

Arkowitz, H., & Miller, W. R. (2008). Learning, applying, and extending motivational interviewing. In H. Arkowitcz, H. A. Westra, W. R. Miller, & S. Rollnick (Eds.). *Motivational interviewing in the treatment of psychological disorders* (pp. 1–25). New York: Guilford Press.

Armstrong, R. (1997). When drugs are used for rape. *Journal of Emergency Nursing, 23*(4), 378–381.

Arnett, J. J. (2000). Emerging adulthood. A theory of development from the late teens through the twenties. *American Psychologist, 55*(5), 469–480.

Arnett, J. J. (2013). The evidence of Generation We and against Generation Me. *Emerging Adulthood, 1*(1), 5–10.

Arnett, P. A., Smith, S. S., & Newman, J. P. (1997). Approach and avoidance motivation in psychopathic criminal offenders during passive avoidance. *Journal of Personality and Social Psychology, 72*(6), 1413–1428.

Arns, M., de Ridder, S., Strehl, U., Breteler, M., & Coenen, A. (2009). Efficacy of neurofeedback treatment in ADHD: The effects on inattention, impulsivity and hyperactivity: A meta-analysis. *Clinical EEG and Neuroscience, 40*(3), 180–189.

Arns, M., van der Heijden, K. B., Arnold, L. E., & Kenemans, J. L. (2013). Geographic variation in the prevalence of attention-deficit/hyperactivity disorder: The sunny perspective. *Biological Psychiatry* (74(8): 585–590). doi: 10.1016/j.biopsych.2013.02.010

Aron, A., Aron, E., & Coups, E. (2005). *Statistics for the behavioral and social sciences: Brief course*. (4th ed.). Upper Saddle River, NJ: Prentice-Hall.

Aronson, E. (1997). Back to the future. Retrospective review of Leon Festinger's—A theory of cognitive dissonance. *American Journal of Psychology, 110*, 127–137.

Aronson, E., Blaney, N., Stephan, C., Sikes, J., & Snapp, M. (1978). *The jigsaw classroom*. Beverly Hills, CA: Sage.

Arora, S., Ashrafian, H., Davis, R., Athanasiou, T., Darzi, A., & Sevdalis, N. (2010). Emotional intelligence in medicine: A systematic review through the context of the ACGME competencies. *Medical Education, 44*(8), 749–764. doi: 10.1111/j.1365-2923.2010.03709.x

Arulpragasam, A. R., Cooper, J. A., Nuutinen, M. R., & Treadway, M. T. (2018). Corticoinsular circuits encode subjective value expectation and violation for effortful goal-directed behavior. *Proceedings of the National Academy of Sciences, 115*(22): E5233-E5242. DOI: https://doi.org/10.1073/pnas.1800444115

Asarnow, L. D., McGlinchey, E., & Harvey, A. G. (2015). Evidence for a possible link between bedtime and change in body mass index. *Sleep, 38*(10), 1523–1527.

Asarnow, R. F., Granholm, E., & Sherman, T. (1991). Span of apprehension in schizophrenia. In H. A. Nasrallah (Ed.), *Handbook of Schizophrenia*, Vol. 5. In S. R. Steinhauer, J. H. Gruzelie, & J. Zubin (Eds.), *Neuropsychology, psychophysiology and information processing* (pp. 335–370). Amsterdam: Elsevier.

Asch, S. E. (1951). Effects of group pressure upon the modification and distortion of judgement. In H. Guetzkow (Ed.), *Groups, leadership and men*. Pittsburgh: Carnegie Press.

Asch, S. E. (1956). Studies of independence and conformity: A minority of one against a unanimous majority. *Psychological Monographs, 70* (Whole no. 416).

Aserinsky, E., & Kleitman, N. (1953). Regularly occurring periods of eye motility, and concomitant phenomena, during sleep. *Science, 118*, 273–274.

Ash, M. G. (1998). *Gestalt psychology in German culture, 1890–1967: Holism and the quest for objectivity*. Cambridge: Cambridge University Press.

Asp, E., & Tranel, D. (2013). False tagging theory. In D. T. Stuss & R. T. Knight (Eds.), *Principles of frontal lobe function* (pp. 383–416). New York, NY: Oxford University Press.

Assari, S., & DeFreitas, M. R. (2018). Ethnic variations in psychosocial and health correlates of eating disorders. *Healthcare (Basel), 6*(2). doi:10.3390/healthcare6020038

Atkinson, R. C., & Shiffrin, R. M. (1968). Human memory: A proposed system and its control processes. In K. W. Spence & J. T. Spence (Eds.). *The psychology of learning and motivation* (Vol. 2, pp. 89–105). New York: Academic Press.

Atladóttir, H. O., Pedersen, M. G., Thorsen, C., Mortensen, P. B., Deleuran, B., Eaton, W. W., & Parner, E. T. (2009). Association of family history of autoimmune diseases and autism spectrum disorders. *Pediatrics, 124*(2), 687–694.

Aton, S., Seibt, J., Dumoulin, M., Jha, S. K., Steinmetz, N., Coleman, T., ... Frank, M. G. (2009). Mechanisms of sleep-dependent consolidation of cortical plasticity. *Neuron, 61*(3), 454–466.

Attia, E. (2018). Anorexia nervosa. In W. S. Agras & A. Robinson (Eds.), *The Oxford handbook of eating disorders* (2nd ed., pp. 176–181). New York, NY: Oxford University Press.

Attia, N. A. (2017). Clinical approach for evaluation and management of disorders of sex development. *Journal of Current Medical Research and Opinion, 1*(3). DOI: https://doi.org/10.15520/jcmro.v1i3.18

Auerbach, R. P., Mortier, P., Bruffaerts, R., Alonso, J., Benjet, C., Cuijpers, P.,... Kessler, R. C. (2018). WHO world mental health surveys international college student project: Prevalence and distribution of mental disorders. *Journal of Abnormal Psychology, 127*(7), 623–638. doi:10.1037/abn0000362

Avolio, B. J. (2017). The practice and science connection: Let's not obsess over minding the gap. *Industrial and Organizational Psychology, 10*(04), 558–569. doi:10.1017/iop.2017.56

Axelrod, V., Schwarzkopf, D. S., Gilaie-Dotan, S., & Rees, G. (2017). Perceptual similarity and the neural correlates of geometrical illusions in human brain structure. *Scientific Reports, 7*, 39968. doi:10.1038/srep39968

Azmitia, M., Syed, M., & Radmacher, K. (2008). On the intersection of personal and social identities: Introduction and evidence from a longitudinal study of emerging adults. In M. Azmitia, M. Syed, & K. Radmacher (Eds.), *The intersections of personal and social identities. New Directions for Child and Adolescent Development, 120*, 1–16. San Francisco: Jossey-Bass.

Babiloni, C., Vecchio, F., Buffo, P., Buttiglione, M., Cibelli, G., & Rossini, P. M. (2010). Cortical responses to consciousness of schematic emotional facial expressions: A high-resolution EEG study. *Human Brain Mapping, 8*, 8.

Backenstrass, M., Pfeiffer, N., Schwarz, T., Catanzaro, S. J., & Mearns, J. (2008). Reliability and validity of the German version of the Generalized Expectancies for Negative Mood Regulation (NMR) Scale. *Diagnostica, 54*, 43–51.

Backer, B., Hannon, R., & Russell, N. (1994). *Death and dying: Understanding and care* (2nd ed.). Albany, NY: Delmar.

Baddeley, A. D. (1986). *Working memory*. London/New York: Oxford University Press.

Baddeley, A. D. (1988). Cognitive psychology and human memory. *Trends in Neurosciences, 11*, 176–181.

Baddeley, A. D. (1996). Exploring the central executive. *Quarterly Journal of Experimental Psychology, 49A*, 5–28.

Baddeley, A. D. (2003). Working memory: Looking back and looking visual forward. *Nature Reviews Neuroscience, 4*(10), 829–839.

Baddeley, A. D. (2012). Working memory: Theories, models, and controversies. *Annual Review of Psychology, 63*(1), 1–29. doi: 10.1146/annurev-psych-120710-100422

Baddeley, A. D., & Hitch, G. (1974). Working memory. In G. A. Bower (Ed.), *The psychology of learning and motivation, 8* (pp. 47–89). New York: Academic Press.

Baddeley, A. D., & Larson, J. D. (2007). The phonological loop unmasked? A comment on the evidence for a "perceptual-gestural" alternative. *Quarterly Journal of Experimental Psychology, 60*(4), 497–504.

Baehr, E. K., Revelle, W., & Eastman, C. I. (2000). Individual difference in the phase amplitude of the human circadian temperature rhythm: With an emphasis on morningness-eveningness. *Journal of Sleep Research, 9*, 117–127.

Baer, D. M., Wolf, M. M., & Risley, T. R. (1968). Some current dimensions of applied behavior analysis. *Journal of Applied Behavior Analysis, 1*, 91–97.

Baez, S., Flichtentrei, D., Prats, M., Mastandueno, R., García, A. M., Cetkovich, M., & Ibáñez, A. (2017) Men, women...who cares? A population-based study on sex differences and gender roles in empathy and moral cognition. *PLoS ONE 12*(6): e0179336. https://doi.org/10.1371/journal.pone.0179336

Bagby, R. M., Nicholson, R. A., Buis, T., & Bacchiochi, J. R. (2000). Can the MMPI-2 validity scales detect depression feigned by experts? *Assessment, 7*(1), 55–62.

Bahns, A. J., Crandall, C. S., Gillath, O., & Preacher, K. J. (2017). Similarity in relationships as niche construction: Choice, stability, and influence within dyads in a free choice environment. *Journal of Personality and Social Psychology, 112*(2), 329–355. doi:10.1037/pspp0000088

Bahrick, H. (1984). Fifty years of second language attrition: Implications for programmatic research. *Modern Language Journal, 68*, 105–118.

Bahrick, H. P., Hall, L. K., & Berger, S. A. (1996, September). Accuracy and distortion in memory for high school grades. *Psychological Science, 7*, 265–271.

Baillargeon, R. (1986). Representing the existence and the location of hidden objects: Object permanence in 6- and 8-month-old infants. *Cognition, 23*, 21–41.

Bains, G. S., Berk, L., Deshpande, P., Pawar, P., Daher, N., Lohman, E., ... Schwab, E. (2012). Effectiveness of humor on short term memory function in elderly subjects. *The Journal of the Federation of American Societies for Experimental Biology, 26*, lb834.

Bakhshaie, J., Zvolensky, M. J., & Goodwin, R. D. (2016). Cigarette smoking and the onset and persistence of panic attacks during mid-adulthood in the United States: 1994–2005. *Journal of Clinical Psychiatry, 77*(1), e21–24. doi: 10.4088/JCP.14m09290

Bakker, A. B., Demerouti, E., & Sanz-Vergel, A. I. (2014). Burnout and work engagement: The JD-R approach. *Annual Review of Organizational Psychology and Organizational Behavior, 1*, 389–411.

Ball, K., Berch, D. B., Helmers, K. F., Jobe, J. B., Leveck, M. D., Marsiske, M., ... Willis, S. L. (2002). Advanced Cognitive Training for Independent and Vital Elderly Study Group. Effects of cognitive training interventions with older adults: A randomized controlled trial. *Journal of the American Medical Association, 288*, 2271–2281.

Ball, T. M., Stein, M. B., & Paulus, M. P. (2014). Toward the application of functional neuroimaging to individualized treatment for anxiety and depression. *Depression and Anxiety, 31*(11), 920–933. doi: 10.1002/da.22299

Baltes, P. B., Reese, H. W., & Nesselroade, J. R. (1988). *Introduction to research methods, life-span developmental psychology*. Hillsdale, NJ: Lawrence Erlbaum

Bandura, A. (1965). Influence of models' reinforcement contingencies on the acquisition of imitative responses. *Journal of Social Psychology, 1*, 589–595.

Bandura, A. (1980). The social learning theory of aggression. In R. A. Falk & S. S. Kim (Eds.), *The war system: An interdisciplinary approach* (p. 146). Boulder, CO: Westview Press.

Bandura, A. (1986). *Social foundations of thought and action: A social cognitive theory*. Englewood Cliffs, NJ: Prentice Hall.

Bandura, A. (1989). Human agency in social cognitive theory. *American Psychologist, 44*, 1175–1184.

Bandura, A. (1998). Exploration of fortuitous determinants of life paths. *Psychological Inquiry, 9*, 95–99.

Bandura, A., Blanchard, E. B., & Ritter, B. (1969). Relative efficacy of desensitization and modeling approaches for inducing behavioral, affective, and attitudinal changes. *Journal of Personality and Social Psychology, 13*, 173–199.

Bandura, A., Jeffrey, R. W., & Wright, C. L. (1974). Efficacy of participant modeling as a function of response induction aids. *Journal of Abnormal Psychology, 83*, 56–64.

Bandura, A., & Rosenthal, T. L. (1966). Vicarious classical conditioning as a functioning of arousal level. *Journal of Personality and Social Psychology, 3*, 54–62.

Bandura, A., Ross, D., & Ross, S. A. (1961). Transmission of aggression through imitation of aggressive models. *Journal of Abnormal and Social Psychology, 63*, 575–582.

Bandura, A., Ross, D., & Ross, S. A. (1963). Imitation of film-mediated aggressive models. *Journal of Abnormal and Social Psychology, 66*, 3–11.

Banerjee, A., & Chaudhury, S. (2010). Statistics without tears: Populations and samples. *Industrial Psychiatry Journal, 19*(1), 60–65.

Banks, G. P., Mikell, C. B., Youngerman, B. E., Henriques, B., Kelly, K. M., Chan, A. K.,... Sheth, S. A. (2015). Neuroanatomical characteristics associated with response to dorsal anterior cingulotomy for obsessive-compulsive disorder. *JAMA Psychiatry, 72*(2), 127–135. doi: 10.1001/jamapsychiatry.2014.2216

Banuazizi, A., & Movahedi, S. (1975). Interpersonal dynamics in a simulated prison: A methodological analysis. *American Psychologist, 30*(2), 152–160. doi:10.1037/h0076835

Bard, P. (1934). On emotional expression after decortication with some remark on certain theoretical views. *Psychological Review, 41*, 309–329, 424–449.

Bargh, J. A., Chen, M., & Burrows, L. (1996). Automaticity of social behavior: Direct effects of trait construct and stereotype activation on action. *Journal of Personality & Social Psychology, 71*(2), 230–244.

Bargh, J. A., Schwader, K. L., Hailey, S. E., Dyer, R. L., & Boothby, E. J. (2012). Automaticity in social-cognitive processes. *Trends in Cognitive Sciences, 16*(12), 593–605.

Barkley, R. A. (2015). *Attention-deficit hyperactivity disorder: A handbook for diagnosis and treatment* (4th ed.). New York: Guilford Press.

Barkley, R. A. (2017). *When an adult you love has ADHD: Professional advice for parents, partners, and siblings*. Washington, DC: American Psychological Association.

Barlow, D. H., Bullis, J. R., Comer, J. S., & Ametaj, A. A. (2013). Evidence-based psychological treatments: An update and a way forward. *Annual Review of Clinical Psychology, 9*, 1–27. doi: 10.1146/annurev-clinpsy-050212-185629

Barlow, D. H., Conklin, L. R., & Bentley, K. H. (2015). Psychological treatments for panic disorders, phobia, and social and generalized anxiety disorders. In P. E. Nathan & J. M. Gorman (Eds.), *A guide to treatments that work* (4th ed., pp. 409–461). New York, NY: Oxford University Press.

Barnes, A. M., & Carey, J. C. (2002, January). Common problems of babies with trisomy 18 or 13. Rochester, NY, *Support Organization for Trisomy 18, 13, and Related Disorders*, January 11, New York: Soft Publications.

Barnes, V., Schneider, R., Alexander, C., & Staggers, F. (1997). Stress, stress reduction, and hypertension in African Americans: An updated review. *Journal of the National Medical Association, 89*(7), 464–476.

Barnyard, P., & Grayson, A. (1996). *Introducing psychological research*. London: MacMillan Press.

Baron, J. N., & Reiss, P. C. (1985). Same time, next year: Aggregate analyses of the mass media and violent behavior. *American Sociological Review, 50*, 347–363.

Baron-Cohen, S., Leslie, A. M., & Frith, U. (1985). Does the autistic child have a "theory of mind"? *Cognition, 21*(1), 3744.

Barondes, S. H. (1998). *Mood genes: Hunting for origins of mania and depression*. New York: W. H. Freeman.

Barsalou, L. W. (1992). *Cognitive psychology: An overview for cognitive scientists*. Hillsdale, NJ: Lawrence Erlbaum.

Barsh, G. S., Farooqi, I. S., & O'Rahilly, S. (2000). Genetics of body-weight regulation. *Nature, 404*, 644–651.

Bartels, A., & Zeki, S. (2000). The neural basis of romantic love. *NeuroReport, 11*, 3829–3834.

Bartels, J. M. (2015). The Stanford prison experiment in introductory psychology textbooks: A content analysis. *Psychology Learning & Teaching, 14*(1), 36–50. doi:10.1177/1475725714568007

Bartels, J. M., Milovich, M. M., & Moussier, S. (2016). Coverage of the Stanford prison experiment in introductory psychology courses. *Teaching of Psychology, 43*(2), 136–141. doi:10.1177/0098628316636290

Barth, J. M., & Boles, D. B. (1999, September,). *Positive relations between emotion recognition skills and right hemisphere processing*. Paper presented at the 11th Annual Convention of the American Psychological Society, Denver, CO.

Bartholomew, K. (1990). Avoidance of intimacy: An attachment perspective. *Journal of Social and Personal Relationships, 7*, 147–178.

Bartlett, C., Harris, R., & Bruey, C. (2008). The effect of the amount of blood in a violent video game on aggression, hostility, and arousal. *Journal of Experimental Social Psychology, 44*(3), 539–546.

Bartlett, F. C. (1932). *Remembering: A study in experimental ad social psychology*. Cambridge, UK: Cambridge University Press.

Bartlett, N. R. (1965). Dark and light adaptation. In C. H. Graham (Ed.), *Vision and visual perception* (185–207). New York: John Wiley & Sons

Bartol, T. M., Bromer, C., Kinney, J., Chirillo, M. A., Bourne, J. N., Harris, K. M., & Sejnowski, T. J. (2015). Nanoconnectomic upper bound on the variability of synaptic plasticity. *elife, 4*. doi: 10.7554/eLife.10778

Barton, M. E., & Komatsu, L. K. (1989). Defining features of natural kinds and artifacts. *Journal of Psycholinguistic Research, 18*, 433–447.

Bartoshuk, L. M. (1993). The biological basis for food perception and acceptance. *Food Quality and Preference, 4*(1/2), 21–32.

Bartoshuk, L. M., Duffy, V. B., & Miller, I. J. (1994). Ptc/prop tasting: Anatomy, psychophysics, and sex effects. *Physiology and Behavior, 56*(6), 1165–1171. doi:https://doi.org/10.1016/0031-9384(94)90361-1

Bartoshuk, L. M., Duffy, V. B., Hayes, J. E., Moskowitz, H. R., & Snyder, D. J. (2006). Psychophysics of sweet and fat perception in obesity: Problems, solutions and new perspectives. *Philosophical transactions of the Royal Society of London. Series B, Biological Sciences, 361*(1471), 1137–1148.

Bartoshuk, L. M., Fast, K., & Snyder, D. J. (2005). Differences in our sensory worlds. *Current Directions in Psychological Science, 14*(3), 122–125.

Bartz, J. A., Lydon, J. E., Kolevzon, A., Zaki, J., Hollander, E., Ludwig, N., & Bolger, N. (2015). Differential effects of oxytocin on agency and communion for anxiously and avoidantly attached individuals. *Psychological Science, 26*(8), 1177–1186. doi: 10.1177/0956797615580279

Bartz, J. A., Zaki, J., Bolger, N., Hollander, E., Ludwig, N. N., Kolevzon, A., & Ochsner, K. N. (2010). Oxytocin selectively improves empathic accuracy. *Psychological Science, 21*(10), 1426–1428. doi: 10.1177/0956797610383439

Bartz, J. A., Zaki, J., Bolger, N., & Ochsner, K. N. (2011). Social effects of oxytocin in humans: Context and person matter. *Trends in Cognitive Sciences, 15*(7), 301–309. doi: 10.1016/j.tics.2011.05.002

Basadur, M., Pringle, P., & Kirkland, D. (2002). Crossing cultures: Training effects on the divergent thinking attitudes of Spanish-speaking South American managers. *Creativity Research Journal, 14*(3, 4), 395–408.

Basten, U., Hilger, K., & Fiebach, C. J. (2015). Where smart brains are different: A quantitative meta-analysis of functional and structural brain imaging studies on intelligence. *Intelligence, 51*, 10–27. doi: 10.1016/j.intell.2015.04.009

Bastidas, J., Athauda, G., De La Cruz, G., Chan, W. M., Golshani, R., Berrocal, Y.,... Pearse, D. D. (2017). Human schwann cells exhibit long-term cell survival, are not tumorigenic and promote repair when transplanted into the contused spinal cord. *Glia, 65*(8), 1278–1301. doi:10.1002/glia.23161

Bastien, C. H., Morin, C. M., Ouellet, M., Blais, F. C., Bouchard, S. (2004). Cognitive-behavioral therapy for insomnia: Comparison of individual therapy, group therapy, and telephone consultations. *Journal of Consulting and Clinical Psychology, 72*(4), 653–659.

Bateman, R. J., Xiong, C., Benzinger, T. L., Fagan, A. M., Goate, A., Fox, N. C.,... Dominantly Inherited Alzheimer Network. (2012). Clinical and biomarker changes in dominantly inherited Alzheimer's disease. *New England Journal of Medicine, 367*(9), 795–804. doi: 10.1056/NEJMoa1202753

Bator, R. J., & Cialdini, R. B. (2006). The nature of consistency motivation: Consistency, aconsistency, and anticonsistency in a dissonance paradigm. *Social Influence, 1,* 208–233.

Baumann, O., Borra, R. J., Bower, J. M., Cullen, K. E., Habas, C., Ivry, R. B.,... Sokolov, A. A. (2015). Consensus paper: The role of the cerebellum in perceptual processes. *Cerebellum (London, England), 14*(2), 197–220. doi: 10.1007/s12311-014-0627-7

Baumeister, D., Tojo, L. M., & Tracy, D. K. (2015). Legal highs: Staying on top of the flood of novel psychoactive substances. *Therapeutic Advances in Psychopharmacology, 5*(2), 97–132.

Baumgart, M., Snyder, H. M., Carrillo, M. C., Fazio, S., Kim, H., & Johns, H. (2015). Summary of the evidence on modifiable risk factors for cognitive decline and dementia: A population-based perspective. *Alzheimer's & Dementia, 11*(6), 718–726.

Baumrind, D. (1964). Some thoughts on ethics of research: After reading Milgram's "Behavioral Study of Obedience." *American Psychologist, 19,* 421–423.

Baumrind, D. (1967). Child care practices anteceding three patterns of preschool behavior. *Genetic Psychology Monograph, 75,* 43–88.

Baumrind, D. (1991). The influence of parenting style on adolescent competence and substance abuse. *Journal of Early Adolescence, 11*(1), 56–95.

Baumrind, D. (1997). Necessary distinctions. *Psychological Inquiry, 8,* 176–182.

Baumrind, D. (2005). Patterns of parental authority and adolescent autonomy. In J. Smetana (Ed.), *New directions for child development: Changes in parental authority during adolescence* (pp. 61–69). San Francisco: Jossey-Bass.

Baumrind, D. (2015). When subjects become objects: The lies behind the Milgram legend. *Theory & Psychology, 25*(5), 690–696. doi:10.1177/0959354315592062

Bayliss, D. M., Baddeley, J. C., & Gunn, D. M. (2005). The relationship between short-term memory and working memory: Complex span made simple? *Memory, 13*(3–4), 414–421.

Beardsley, T. (1995, January). For whom the bell curve really tolls. *Scientific American,* 14–17.

Beauchamp, G. K., & Mennella, J. A. (2011). Flavor perception in human infants: Development and functional significance. *Digestion, 83* (Suppl 1), 1–6. doi: 10.1159/000323397

Bechtel, W., & Abrahamsen, A. (2002). *Connectionism and the mind: Parallel processing, dynamics, and evolution in networks* (2nd ed.). Oxford, UK: Basil Blackwell.

Beck, A. T. (1976). *Cognitive therapy and the emotional disorders.* New York: International Universities Press.

Beck, A. T. (1979). *Cognitive therapy and the emotional disorders.* New York: Penguin Books.

Beck, A. T. (1984). Cognitive approaches to stress. In C. Lehrer & R. L. Woolfolk (Eds.), *Clinical guide to stress management,* pp. 255–305. New York: Guilford Press.

Beck, H. P., & Irons, G. (2011). Finding Little Albert: A seven-year search for psychology's lost boy. *The Psychologist, 25,* 180–181.

Beck, H. P., Levinson, S., & Irons, G. (2009). Finding Little Albert: A journey to John B. Watson's infant laboratory. *American Psychologist, 64*(7), 605–614. doi: 10.1037/a0017234

Beckman, M., & Pierrehumbert, J. (1986). Intonational structure in English and Japanese. *Phonology Year Book III,* 15–70.

Beehr, T. A., Jex, S. M., Stacy, B. A., & Murray, M. A. (2000). Work stressors and coworker support as predictors of individual strain and job performance. *Journal of Organizational Behavior, 21*(4), 391–405.

Beer, J. M., & Horn, J. M. (2001). The influence of rearing order on personality development within two adoption cohorts. *Journal of Personality, 68,* 789–819.

Beer, J. S. (2009). The neural basis of emotion regulation: Making emotion work for you and not against you. In M. S. Gazzaniga (Ed.), *The Cognitive Neurosciences* (pp. 961–972). Cambridge, MA: The MIT Press.

Behne, T., Carpenter, M., & Tomasello, M. (2005). One-year-olds comprehend the communicative intentions behind gestures in a hiding game. *Developmental Science, 8,* 492–499.

Békésy, G. V. (1960). *Experiments in Hearing* (E. G. Wever, Trans.). New York: McGraw-Hill Book Company.

Bell, B. G., & Grubin, D. (2010). Functional magnetic resonance imaging may promote theoretical understanding of the polygraph test. *Journal of Forensic Psychiatry and Psychology, 21*(1), 52–65.

Belsky, J. (2005). Differential susceptibility to rearing influence: An evolutionary hypothesis and some evidence. In B. Ellis & D. Bjorklund (Eds.), *Origins of the social mind: Evolutionary psychology and child development* (pp. 139–163). New York: Guilford.

Belsky, J., & Johnson, C. D. (2005). Developmental outcome of children in day care. In J. Murph, S. D. Palmer, & D. Glassy (Eds.), *Health in child care: A manual for health professionals* (4th ed., pp. 81–95). Elks Grove Village, IL: American Academy of Pediatrics.

Belsky, J., Vandell, D., Burchinal, M., Clarke-Stewart, K. A., McCartney, K., Owen, M., & NICHD Early Child Care Research Network. (2007). Are there long-term effects of early child care? *Child Development, 78,* 681–701.

Bem, D. J. (1972). Self-perception theory. In L. Berkowitz (Ed.), *Advances in experimental social psychology* (Vol. 6, pp. 1–62). New York: Academic Press.

Bem, S. L. (1975). Sex role adaptability: The consequence of psychological androgyny. *Journal of Personality and Social Psychology, 31,* 634–643.

Bem, S. L. (1981). Gender schema theory: A cognitive account of sex typing. *Psychological Review, 88,* 354–364.

Bem, S. L. (1987). Gender schema theory and the romantic tradition. In P. Shaver & C. Hendrick (Eds.), *Review of personality and social psychology* (Vol. 7, pp. 251–271). Newbury Park, CA: Sage.

Bem, S. L. (1993). Is there a place in psychology for a feminist analysis of the social context? *Feminism & Psychology, 3,* 247–251.

Bengston, V. L. (1970). The generation gap. *Youth and Society, 2,* 7–32.

Benjafield, J. J. G. (1996). *A history of psychology.* Boston: Allyn and Bacon.

Benjamin, S. L. (2005). An interpersonal theory of personality disorders. In J. F. Clarkin & M. F. Lenzenweger (Eds.), *Major theories of personality disorder,* 157–230. New York: Guilford Press.

Benner, A. D., Wang, Y., Shen, Y., Boyle, A. E., Polk, R., & Cheng, Y.-P. (2018). Racial/ethnic discrimination and well-being during adolescence: A meta-analytic review. *American Psychologist, 73*(7), 855–883. doi:10.1037/amp0000204

Benozio, A., & Diesendruck, G. (2015). From effort to value: Preschool children's alternative to effort justification. Psychological Science, 26(9), 1423–1429. doi: 10.1177/0956797615589585

Ben-Porath, Y. S., & Tellegen, A. (2011). *Mmpi-2-RF (Minnesota Multiphasic Personality Inventory-2 Restructured Form): Manual for administration, scoring, and interpretation.* Minneapolis: University of Minnesota Press.

Ben-Shakhar, G., Garner, M., Iacono, W., Meijer, E., & Verschuere, B. (2015). Preliminary process theory does not validate the comparison question test: A comment on Palmatier and Rovner (2015). *International Journal of Psychophysiology, 95*(1),16–19.

Benson, H. (1975). *The relaxation response.* New York: Morrow.

Benson, H., Beary, J., & Carol, M. (1974a). The relaxation response. *Psychiatry, 37,* 37–46.

Benson, H., Rosner, B. A., Marzetta, B. R., & Klemchuk, H. M. (1974b). Decreased blood pressure in pharmacologically treated hypertensive patients who regularly elicited the relaxation response. *Lancet, 1*(7852), 289–291.

Benton, D., & Parker P. (1998). Breakfast, blood glucose and cognition. *American Journal of Clinical Nutrition, 67*(4), 772S–778S.

Berenbaum, S. A. (2018). Beyond pink and blue: The complexity of early androgen effects on gender development. *Child Development Perspectives, 12*(1), 58-64. doi:10.1111/cdep.12261

Berenbaum, S. A., & Beltz, A. M. (2016). How early hormones shape gender development. *Current Opinion in Behavioral Sciences, 7,* 53–60. doi:10.1016/j.cobeha.2015.11.011

Berent, S. (1977). Functional asymmetry of the human brain in the recognition of faces. *Neuropsychologia, 15,* 829–831.

Berg, F. (1999). Health risks associated with weight loss and obesity treatment programs. *Journal of Social Issues, 55*(2), 277–297.

Bergmann, O., Liebl, J., Bernard, S., Alkass, K., Yeung, M. S., Steier, P.,... Frisen, J. (2012). The age of olfactory bulb neurons in humans. *Neuron, 74*(4), 634–639. doi: 10.1016/j.neuron.2012.03.030

Berk, L., Prowse, M., Petrofsky, J. S., Batt, J., Laymon, M., Bains, G., ... Berk, D. (2009, May). *Laughercise: Health benefits similar of exercise lowers cholesterol and systolic blood pressure.* Presented at the Association for Psychological Science 21st Annual Convention, San Francisco, CA.

Berk, L. E. (1992). Children's private speech: An overview of theory and the status of research. In R. M. Diaz & L. E. Berk (Eds.), *Private speech: From social interaction to self-regulation* (pp. 17–53). Hillsdale, NJ: Erlbaum.

Berk, L. E., & Spuhl, S. T. (1995). Maternal interaction, private speech, and task performance in preschool children. *Early Childhood Research Quarterly, 10,* 145–169.

Berk, L. S., Felten, D. L., Tan, S. A., Bittman, B. B., & Westengard, J. (2001). Modulation of neuroimmune parameters during the eustress of humor-associated mirthful laughter. *Alternative Therapy Health Medicines, 7*(2), 62–72, 74–76.

Berk L. S., Tan, S. A., & Berk, D. (2008, April). *Cortisol and catecholamine stress hormone decrease is associated with the behavior of perceptual anticipation of mirthful laughter.* Presented at the 121st Annual Meeting of the American Physiological Society, San Diego, CA.

Berke, J., & Gould, S. (2019). This map shows every US state where pot is legal, from https://www.businessinsider.com/legal-marijuana-states-2018-1

Berkowitz, L. (1993). *Aggression: Its causes, consequences and control.* New York: McGraw-Hill.

Berlin, L. J., Ispa, J. M., Fine, M. A., Malone, P. S., Brooks-Gunn, J., Brady-Smith, C., ... Bai, Y. (2009). Correlates and consequences of spanking and verbal punishment for low-income white, African American, and Mexican American toddlers. *Child Development, 80*(5), 1403–1420.

Berman, A., Bradley, J. C., Carroll, B., Certain, R. D., Gabrelcik, J. C., Green, R.,... & Werbel, A. (2010). *The challenge and the promise: Strengthening the force, preventing suicide and saving lives. Final report of the Department of Defense task force on the prevention of suicide by members of the armed forces,* pp. 41–44. Washington, DC.

Berman, M. G., Jonides, J., & Kaplan, S. (2008). The cognitive benefits of interacting with nature. *Psychological Science, 19*(12), 1207–1212. doi:10.1111/j.1467-9280.2008.02225.x

Berman, M. G., Kross, E., Krpan, K. M., Askren, M. K., Burson, A., Deldin, P. J.,... Jonides, J. (2012). Interacting with nature improves cognition and affect for individuals with depression. *Journal of Affective Disorders, 140*(3), 300–305. doi:10.1016/j.jad.2012.03.012

Bermond, B., Nieuwenhuyse, B., Fasotti, L., & Schuerman, J. (1991). Spinal cord lesions, peripheral feedback, and intensities of emotional feelings. *Cognition and Emotion, 5,* 201–220.

Bernard, C. (1865/1949). *An introduction to the study of experimental medicine* (H. C. Greene, Trans.). United States of America: Henry Schuman, Inc.

Bernat, E., Shevrin, H., & Snodgrass, M. (2001). Subliminal visual oddball stimuli evoke a P300 component. *Clinical Neurophysiology, 112,* 159–171.

Bernston, G. G., Cacioppo, J. T., & Bosch, J. A. (2017). From homeostasis to allodynamic regulation. In J. T. Cacioppo, L. G. Tassinary, & G. G. Berntson (Eds.), *Handbook of psychophysiology* (pp. 401–426). United Kingdom: Cambridge University Press.

Berry, J. A., Cervantes-Sandoval, I., Chakraborty, M., & Davis, R. L. (2015). Sleep facilitates memory by blocking dopamine neuron-mediated forgetting. *Cell, 161*(7), 1656–1667.

Berry, J. W., & Kim, U. (1988). Acculturation and mental health. In P. R. Dasen, J. W. Berry, & N. Sartorius (Eds.), *Health and cross-cultural psychology: Toward applications* (pp. 207–236). Newbury Park, CA: Sage.

Berry, J. W., & Sam, D. L. (1997). Acculturation and adaptation. In J. W. Berry, M. H. Segall, & C. Kagitcibasi (Eds.), *Handbook of cross-cultural psychology, Vol. 3: Social behaviour and applications* (2nd ed., pp. 291–326). Boston: Allyn & Bacon.

Berscheid, E., & Reis, H. T. (1998). Attraction and close relationships. In D. T. Gilbert & S. T. Fiske & G. Lindzey (Eds.), *The handbook of social psychology,* Vol. 2 (4th ed., pp. 193–281), New York: McGraw-Hill.

Berteretche, M. V., Dalix, A. M., Cesar d'Ornano, A. M., Bellisle, F., Khayat, D., & Faurion, A. (2004). Decreased taste sensitivity in cancer patients under chemotherapy. *Supportive Care in Cancer, 12*(8), 571–576.

Berthiller, J., Straif, K., Boniol, M., Voirin, N., Behnaim-Luzon, V., Ayoub, W. B., ... Sasco, A. J. (2008). Cannabis smoking and risk of lung cancer in men: A pooled analysis of three studies in Maghreb. *Journal of Thoracic Oncology, 3*(12), 1398–1403.

Bertram, K., Randazzo, J., Alabi, N., Levenson, J., Doucette, J. T., & Barbosa, P. (2016). Strong correlations between empathy, emotional intelligence, and personality traits among podiatric medical students: A cross-sectional study. *Education for Health (Abingdon), 29*(3), 186–194. doi:10.4103/1357-6283.204224

Bertram, L., & Tanzi, R. E. (2005). The genetic epidemiology of neurodegenerative disease. *The Journal of Clinical Investigation, 115*(6), 1449–1457.

Betancourt, J. R., & Jacobs, E. A. (2000). Language barriers to informed consent and confidentiality: The impact on women's health. *Journal of American Medical Women's Association, 55,* 294–295.

Beyer, B. K. (1995). *Critical thinking.* Bloomington, IN: Phi Delta Kappa Educational Foundation.

Beyreuther, K., Biesalski, H. K., Fernstrom, J. D., Grimm, P., Hammes, W. P., Heinemann, U., ... Walker, R. (2007). Consensus meeting: Monosodium glutamate, an update. *European Journal of Clinical Nutrition, 61,* 304–313.

Bialystok, E., Craik, F. I., Green, D. W., & Gollan, T. H. (2009). Bilingual minds. *Psychological Science in the Public Interest, 10*(3), 89–129. doi: 10.1177/1529100610387084

Bianchi, R., Laurent, E., Schonfeld, I. S., Bietti, L. M., & Mayor, E. (2018). Memory bias toward emotional information in burnout and depression. *Journal of Health Psychology,* 1359105318765621. doi:10.1177/1359105318765621

Biederman, J., Faraone, S. V., Petty, C., Martelon, M., Woodworth, K. Y., & Wozniak, J. (2013). Further evidence that pediatric-onset bipolar disorder comorbid with ADHD represents a distinct subtype: Results from a large controlled family study. *Journal of Psychiatric Research, 47*(1), 15–22. doi:10.1016/j.jpsychires.2012.08.002

Biello, St. M., Bonsall, D. R., Atkinson, L. A., Molyneux, P. C., Harrington, M. E., & Lall, G. S. (2018). Alterations in glutamatergic signaling contribute to the decline of circadian photoentrainment in aged mice. *Neurobiology of Aging, 66:* 75-84. DOI: https://doi.org/10.1016/j.neurobiolaging.2018.02.013

Bieniek, K. F., Ross, O. A., Cormier, K. A., Walton, R. L., Soto-Ortolaza, A., Johnston, A. E.,... Dickson, D. W. (2015). Chronic traumatic encephalopathy pathology in a neurodegenerative disorders brain bank. *Acta Neuropathol, 130*(6), 877–889. doi: 10.1007/s00401-015-1502-4

Binder, J. R., Desai, R. H., Graves, W. W., & Conant, L. L. (2009). Where is the semantic system? A critical review and meta-analysis of 120 functional neuroimaging studies. *Cerebral Cortex, 19*(12), 2767–2796.

Binet, A., & Simon, T. (1916). *The development of intelligence in children.* Baltimore: Williams & Wilkins.

Bird, C. M., Keidel, J. L., Ing, L. P., Horner, A. J., & Burgess, N. (2015). Consolidation of complex events via reinstatement in posterior cingulate cortex. *Journal of Neuroscience, 35*(43), 14426–14434.

Birks, J., & Evans, J. G. (2009). Ginkgo biloba for cognitive impairment and dementia. *The Cochrane Database of Systematic Reviews 1,* CD003120. doi: 10.1002/14651858 .CD003120.pub2

Birnbaum, R., & Weinberger, D. R. (2017). Genetic insights into the neurodevelopmental origins of schizophrenia. *Nature Reviews: Neuroscience, 18*(12), 727–740. doi:10.1038/nrn.2017.125

Bivens, J. A., & Berk, L. E. (1990). A longitudinal study of the development of elementary school children's private speech. *Merill-Palmer Quarterly, 36,* 443–463.

Bjork, R. A., & Bjork, E. L. (1992). A new theory of disuse and an old theory of stimulus fluctuation. In A. Healy, S. Kosslyn, & R. Shiffrin (Eds.), *From learning processes to cognitive processes: Essays in honor of William K. Estes* (Vol. 2, pp. 35–67). Hillsdale, NJ: Erlbaum.

Bjork, R. A., & Whitten, W. B. (1974). Recency-sensitive retrieval processes in long-term free recall. *Cognitive Psychology, 6,* 173–189.

Blackmon, L. R., Batton, D. G., Bell, E. F., Engle, W. A., Kanto, W. P., Martin, G. I., ... Lemons, J. A. (Committee on Fetus and Newborn). (2003). *Apnea, sudden infant death syndrome, and home monitoring. Pediatrics, 111*(4), 914–917.

Blair, R. J. R., Sellars, C., Strickland, I., Clark, F., Williams, A. O., Smith, M., & Jones, L. (1995). Emotion attributions in the psychopath. *Personality and Individual Differences, 19*(4), 431–437.

Blanchard, M., & Main, M. (1979). Avoidance of the attachment figure and social-emotional adjustment in day-care infants. *Developmental Psychology, 15,* 445–446.

Blanchard-Fields, F., Chen, Y., Horhota, M., & Wang, M. (2007). Cultural differences in the relationship between aging and the correspondence bias. *Journals of Gerontology Series B: Psychological Sciences and Social Sciences, 62*(6), 362–365.

Blanchard-Fields, F., & Horhota, M. (2005). Age differences in the correspondence bias: When a plausible explanation matters. *Journals of Gerontology Series B: Psychological Sciences and Social Sciences, 60*(5), 259–267.

Blanco-Elorrieta, E., & Pylkkanen, L. (2018). Ecological validity in bilingualism research and the bilingual advantage. *Trends in Cognitive Sciences, 22*(12), 1117–1126. doi:10.1016/j.tics.2018.10.001

Blass, T. (1991). Understanding behavior in the Milgram obedience experiment: The role of personality, situations, and their interactions. *Journal of Personality and Social Psychology, 60,* 398–413.

Blass, T. (1999). The Milgram paradigm after 35 years: Some things we now know about obedience to authority. *Journal of Applied Social Psychology, 25,* 955–978.

Bledsoe, C. H., & Cohen, B. (1993). *Social dynamics of adolescent fertility in sub-Saharan Africa.* Washington, DC: National Academy Press.

Blehar, M. C., & Oren, D. A. (1997). Gender differences in depression. *Medscape General Medicine, 1*(2). Retrieved June 27, 2004, from http://www.medscape.com/viewarticle/719236

Bleiberg, K. L., & Markowitz, J. C. (2014). Interpersonal therapy for depression. In D. H. Barlow (Ed.), *Clinical handbook of psychological disorders: A step-by-step treatment manual* (5th ed., pp. 332–352). New York: The Guilford Press.

Bleuler, E. (1911, reissued 1950). *Dementia praecox or the group of schizophrenias.* New York: International Universities Press.

Block, A. R., Marek, R. J., Ben-Porath, Y. S., & Kukal, D. (2017). Associations between pre-implant psychosocial factors and spinal cord stimulation outcome: Evaluation using the MMPI-2-RF. *Assessment, 24*(1), 60–70. doi: 10.1177/1073191115601518

Block, N. (2005). Two neural correlates of consciousness. *Trends in Cognitive Sciences, 9,* 41–89.

Bloom, B. S. (Ed.). (1956) *Taxonomy of educational objectives, the classification of educational goals—Handbook I: Cognitive domain.* New York: McKay.

Bloom, L. (1974). Talking, understanding and thinking. In R. Schiefelbusch & L. L. Lloyd (Eds.), *Language perspectives: Acquisition, retardation and intervention.* New York: Macmillan.

Bloom, P. (2000). *How children learn the meaning of words.* Cambridge, MA: MIT Press.

Blum, K., Chen, A. L., Giordano, J., Borsten, J., Chen, T. J., Hauser, M., ... Barh, D. (2012). The addictive brain: All roads lead to dopamine. *Journal of Psychoactive Drugs, 44*(2), 134–143. doi: 10.1080/02791072.2012.685407

Blumenfeld, H. (2010). *Neuroanatomy through clinical cases* (2nd ed.). Sunderland, MA: Sinauer Associates, Inc.

Blumer, D. (2002). The illness of Vincent van Gogh. *American Journal of Psychiatry, 159*(4), 519–526.

Bock, R. (1993, August). *Understanding Klinefelter syndrome: A guide for XXY males and their families.* NIH Publication No. 93-3202. National Institutes of Health, Office of Research Reporting. Washington, DC: Retrieved August 10, 2010, from http://www.nichd.nih.gov/publications/pubs/klinefelter.cfm

Bodrova, E., & Leong, D. J. (1996). *Tools of the mind: The Vygotskian approach to early childhood education.* Englewood Cliffs, NJ: Prentice Hall.

Boes, A. D., Uitermarkt, B. D., Albazron, F. M., Lan, M. J., Liston, C., Pascual-Leone, A.,... Fox, M. D. (2018). Rostral anterior cingulate cortex is a structural correlate of repetitive tms treatment response in depression. *Brain Stimul, 11*(3), 575–581. doi:10.1016/j.brs.2018.01.029

Bogdanov, M., & Schwabe, L. (2016). Transcranial stimulation of the dorsolateral prefrontal cortex prevents stress-induced working memory deficits. *Journal of Neuroscience, 36*(4), 1429–1437. doi:10.1523/JNEUROSCI.3687-15.2016

Bogle, K. D. (2000). Effect of perspective, type of student, and gender on the attribution of cheating. *Proceedings of the Oklahoma Academy of Science, 80,* 91–97.

Boll, T. J., Johnson, S. B., Perry, N., & Roszensky, R. H. (2002). Handbook of Clinical Health Psychology. Washington, DC: American Psychological Association.

Bolton, P., Bass, J., Betancourt, T., Speelman, L., Onyango, G., Clougherty, K. F., ... Verdeli, H. (2007). Interventions for depression symptoms among adolescent survivors of war and displacement in northern Uganda. *Journal of Medical Association, 298*, 519–527.

Bolton, S., & Hattie, J. (2017). Cognitive and brain development: executive function, Piaget, and the prefrontal cortex. *Archives of Psychology, 1*(3). Retrieved on September 14, 2018 from https://archivesofpsychology.org/index.php/aop/article/view/30

Bond, R. A., & Smith, P. B. (1996). Culture and conformity: A meta-analysis of studies using Asch's (1952, 1956) line judgment task. *Psychological Bulletin, 119*, 111–137.

Bondarenko, L. A. (2004). Role of methionine in nocturnal melatonin peak in the pineal gland. *Bulletin of Experimental Biological Medicine, 137*(5), 431–432.

Bonnelykke, B. (1990). Maternal age and parity as predictors of human twinning. *Acta Genetic Medicine & Gemellology, 39*, 329–334.

Boor, M. (1982). The multiple personality epidemic: Additional cases and inferences regarding diagnosis, etiology, dynamics, and treatment. *Journal of Nervous and Mental Disease, 170*, 302–304.

Booth-Butterfield, S. (1996). Message characteristics. *Steve's primer of practical persuasion and influence*. Retrieved August 2, 2004, from http://www.austincc.edu/colangelo/1311/persuasivecharacteristics.htm

Bor, D., Rothen, N., Schwartzman, D. J., Clayton, S., & Seth, A. K. (2014). Adults can be trained to acquire synesthetic experiences. *Scientific Reports, 4*, 7089. doi:10.1038/srep07089

Borgelt, L. M., Franson, K. L., Nussbaum, A. M., & Wang, G. S. (February 2013). The pharmacologic and clinical effects of medical cannabis. *Pharmacotherapy (Review) 33*(2), 195–209. doi: 10.1002/phar.1187

Borges, M. A., Stepnowsky, M. A., & Holt, L. H. (1977). Recall and recognition of words and pictures by adults and children. *Bulletin of the Psychonomic Society, 9*, 113–114.

Bornheimer, L. A. (2015). Exposure and response prevention as an evidence-based treatment for obsessive–compulsive disorder: Considerations for social work practice. *Clinical Social Work Journal, 43*(1), 38–49.

Boroditsky, L. (2001). Does language shape thought? Mandarin and English speakers' conceptions of time. *Cognitive Psychology, 43*(1), 1–22.

Boroditsky, L. (2009). How does our language shape the way we think? In M. Brockman (Ed.), *What's next? Dispatches on the future of science* (pp. 116–129). New York: Vintage.

Bossert, W., & Schworm, W. (2008). A class of two-group polarization measures. *Journal of Public Economic Theory, Association for Public Economic Theory, 10*(6), 1169–1187.

Bosworth, H. B., & Schaie, K. W. (1997). The relationship of social environment, social networks, and health outcomes in the Seattle Longitudinal Study: Two analytical approaches. *Journals of Gerontology Series B: Psychological Sciences and Social Sciences, 52*(5), 197–205.

Botella, C., Perez-Ara, M. A., Breton-Lopez, J., Quero, S., Garcia-Palacios, A., & Banos, R. M. (2016). In vivo versus augmented reality exposure in the treatment of small animal phobia: A randomized controlled trial. *PLoS ONE, 11*(2), e0148237. doi: 10.1371/journal.pone.0148237

Botwin, M. D., & Buss, D. M. (1989). The structure of act data: Is the Five-Factor Model of personality recaptured? *Journal of Personality and Social Psychology, 56*, 988–1001.

Bouchard, C., Tremblay, A., Nadeau, A., Dussault, J., Despres, J. P., Theriault, G., ... Fournier, G. (1990). Long-term exercise training with constant energy intake. 1: Effect on body composition and selected metabolic variables. *International Journal on Obesity, 14*(1), 57–73.

Bouchard, T. (1994). Genes, environment, and personality. *Science, 264*, 1700–1701.

Bouchard, T. J., Jr. (1997). Whenever the twain shall meet. *The Science, 37*(5), 52–57.

Bouchard, T. J., & Segal, N. L. (1985). Environment and IQ. In B. B. Wolman (Ed.), *Handbook of intelligence: Theories, measurements, and applications* (pp. 391–464). New York: John Wiley.

Bouckaert, F., De Winter, F. L., Emsell, L., Dols, A., Rhebergen, D., Wampers, M., ... Vandenbulcke, M. (2015). Grey matter volume increase following electroconvulsive therapy in patients with late life depression: A longitudinal MRI study. *Journal of Psychiatry & Neuroscience, 40*(5), 140322. doi: 10.1503/jpn.140322

Boutwell, B. B., Franklin, C. A., Barnes, J. C., & Beaver, K. M. (2011). College students more likely to be lawbreakers if spanked as children. *Aggressive Behavior, 37*(6), 559.

Bowden, C. L., Calabrese, J. R., McElroy, S. L., Gyulai, L., Wassef, A., Petty, F., ... Wozniak, P. J. (2000). For the Divalproex Maintenance Study Group. A randomized, placebo-controlled 12-month trial of divalproex and lithium in treatment of outpatients with bipolar I disorder. *Archives of General Psychiatry, 57*(5), 481–489.

Bowers, K. S., & Woody, E. Z. (1996). Hypnotic amnesia and the paradox of intentional forgetting. *Journal of Abnormal Psychology, 105*, 381–390.

Bowman, E. S. (1996). Delayed memories of child abuse: Part II: An overview of research findings relevant to understanding their reliability and suggestibility. *Dissociation: Progress in the Dissociative Disorders, 9*, 232–243.

Boxer, P., Groves, C. L., & Docherty, M. (2015). Video games do indeed influence children and adolescents' aggression, prosocial behavior, and academic performance: A clearer reading of Ferguson. *Perspectives on Psychological Science, 10*(5), 671–673. doi: 10.1177/1745691615592239

Boyd, C. H., & Peeler, C. M. (May, 2004). *Highlighting vs note taking: A comparison of students' performance on tests*. Poster presented at 16th Annual Convention of the American Psychological Society, Chicago, IL, USA.

Boyd, L. A., & Winstein, C. J. (2004). Cerebellar stroke impairs temporal but not spatial accuracy during implicit motor learning. *Neurorehabilitation and Neural Repair, 18*(3), 134–143.

Boyson-Bardies, B., deHalle, P., Sagart, L., & Durand, C. (1989). A cross-linguistic investigation of vowel formats in babbling. *Journal of Child Language, 16*, 1–17.

Bratman, G. N., Daily, G. C., Levy, B. J., & Gross, J. J. (2015a). The benefits of nature experience: Improved affect and cognition. *Landscape and Urban Planning, 138*, 41–50. doi:10.1016/j.landurbplan.2015.02.005

Bratman, G. N., Hamilton, J. P., Hahn, K. S., Daily, G. C., & Gross, J. J. (2015b). Nature experience reduces rumination and subgenual prefrontal cortex activation. *Proceedings of the National Academy of Sciences of the United States of America, 112*(28), 8567–8572. doi:10.1073/pnas.1510459112

Braun, S. R. (1996). *Buzz: the science and lore of alcohol and caffeine*. New York: Oxford University Press.

Brazelton, T. B. (1992). *Touchpoints: Your child's emotional and behavioral development*. Reading, MA: Addison-Wesley.

Brecher, M., Wang, B. W., Wong, H., & Morgan, J. P. (1988). Phencyclidine and violence: Clinical and legal issues. *Journal of Clinical Psychopharmacology, 8*, 397–401.

Breedlove, S. M. (2010). Minireview: Organizational hypothesis: Instances of the fingerpost. *Endocrinology, 151*(9), 4116–4122. doi: 10.1210/en.2010-0041

Breier, A., Albus, M., Pickar, D., Zahn, T. P., Wolkowitz, O. M., & Paul, S. M. (1987). Controllable and uncontrollable stress in humans: Alterations in mood, neuroendocrine and psychophysiological function. *American Journal of Psychiatry, 144*, 1419–1425.

Breland, K., & Breland, M. (1961). The misbehavior of organisms. *American Psychologist, 16*, 681–684.

Bremmer, J. D. (2005). *Brain imaging handbook*. New York: W. W. Norton.

Bremner, A. J., Doherty, M. J., Caparos, S., de Fockert, J., Linnell, K. J., & Davidoff, J. (2016). Effects of culture and the urban environment on the development of the ebbinghaus illusion. *Child Development, 87*(3), 962–981. doi:10.1111/cdev.12511

Brennan, J. F. (2002). *History and systems of psychology* (6th ed.). Upper Saddle River, NJ: Prentice Hall.

Brenner, J. (2007, August). Parental impact on attitude formation—A siblings study on worries about immigration. *Ruhr Economic Paper No. 22*. Retrieved from Social Science Research Network (SSR) at http://ssrn.com/abstract=1012110

Breslau, N., Chilcoat, H. D., Kessler, R. C., Peterson, E. L., & Lucia, V. C. (1999). Vulnerability to assaultive violence: Further specification of the sex difference in posttraumatic stress disorder. *Psychological Medicine, 29*, 813–821.

Breslau, N., Davis, G. C., Andreski, P., & Peterson, E. L. (1997). Sex differences in posttraumatic stress disorder. *Archives of General Psychiatry, 54*(11), 1044–1048.

Breslow, R. A., Dong, C., & White, A. (2015). Prevalence of alcohol-interactive prescription medication use among current drinkers: United States, 1999 to 2010. *Alcoholism, Clinical and Experimental Research, 39*(2), 371–379.

Breuer, J., & Freud, S. (1895). *Studies on hysteria (cathartic method). Special Edition, 2*, 1–309.

Brewer, M. B. (2001). Ingroup identification and intergroup conflict: When does in-group love become outgroup hate? In R. D. Ashmore, L. Jussim, & D. Wilder (Eds.), *Social identity, intergroup conflict, and conflict reduction*. New York: Oxford University Press.

Brick, J. (2003). The characteristics of alcohol: Chemistry, use and abuse. In J. Brick (Ed.), *Handbook of the medical consequences of alcohol and drug abuse* (pp. 1–11). New York: Haworth Medical Press.

Briem, V., & Hedman, L. R. (1995). Behavioural effects of mobile telephone use during simulated driving. *Ergonomics, 38*, 2536–2562.

Briggs, K. C., & Myers, I. B. (1998). *The Myers-Briggs Type Indicator-Form M*. Palo Alto, CA: Consulting Psychologists Press.

Brigham, A. (1844). Asylums exclusively for the incurably insane. Classic article in *The American Journal of Psychiatry, 151*, 50–70.

Bright, S. (2013, April). *Not for human consumption: New and emerging drugs in Australia*. Prevention Research, Melbourne: Australian Drug Foundation.

Briñol, P., & Petty, R. E. (2015). Elaboration and validation processes: Implications for mass media attitude change. *Media Psychology, 18*, 267–291.

Broadbent, D. (1958). *Perception and communication*. Elmsford, NY: Pergamon.

Brodrick, J., & Mitchell, B. G. (2015). Hallucinogen persisting perception disorder and risk of suicide. *Journal of Pharmacy Practice, 29*(4), 431–434. Published online before print January 27. doi: 10.1177/0897190014566314.

Brondolo, E., Rieppi, R., Erickson, S. A., Bagiella, E., Shapiro, P. A., McKinley, P., & Sloan, R. P. (2003). Hostility, interpersonal interactions, and ambulatory blood pressure. *Psychosomatic Medicine, 65*, 1003–1011.

Bronfenbrenner, U. (1979). *The ecology of human development: Experiments by nature and design*. Cambridge, MA: Harvard University Press.

Bronkhorst, A. W. (2000). The cocktail party phenomenon: A review on speech intelligibility in multiple-talker conditions. *Acta Acustica united with Acustica, 86*, 117–128. Retrieved from http://eaa-fenestra.org/products/acta-acustica/most-cited/acta_86_2000_Bronkhorst.pdf

Brooks, J. G., & Brooks, M. G. (1993). *In search of understanding: The case for constructivist classrooms*. Alexandria, VA: The Association for Supervision and Curriculum Development.

Brooks, J. L. (2015). Traditional and new principles of perceptual grouping. In J. Wagemans (Ed.), *The Oxford handbook of perceptual organization* (pp. 57–87). Oxford, UK: Oxford University Press.

Brouwers, S. A., Van de Vijver, F. J. R., & Van Hemert, D. A. (2009). Variation in Raven's Progressive Matrices scores across time and place. *Learning and Individual Differences, 19*(3), 330–338. doi: 10.1016/j.lindif.2008.10.006

Brown, A. S., & Derkits, E. J. (2010). Prenatal infection and schizophrenia: A review of epidemiologic and translational studies. *The American Journal of Psychiatry, 167*(3), 261–280. doi: 10.1176/appi.ajp.2009.09030361

Brown, C., Taylor, J., Green, A., Lee, B. E., Thomas, S. B., & Ford, A. (2003). *Managing depression in African Americans: Consumer and provider perspectives*. (Final Report to Funders). Pittsburgh: Mental Health Association of Allegheny County.

Brown, C. A., & Jones, A. K. P. (2010). Meditation experience predicts less negative appraisal of pain: Electrophysiological evidence for the involvement of anticipatory neural responses. *Pain*. doi: 10.1016/j.pain.2010.04.017

Brown, G., Lawrence, T. B., & Robinson, S. L. (2005). Territoriality in management organizations. *Academy of Management Review, 30*(3), 577–594.

Brown, G. L., & Linnoila, M. I. (1990). CSF serotonin metabolite (5–HIAA) studies in depression, impulsivity, and violence. *Journal of Clinical Psychiatry, 51*(4), 31–43.

Brown, J. (1958). Some tests of the decay theory of immediate memory. *Quarterly Journal of Experimental Psychology, 10*, 12–21.

Brown, P. K., & Wald, G. (1964). Visual pigments in single rods and cones of the human retina. *Science, 144*, 45.

Brown, R. (1973). *A first language: The early stages*. Cambridge, MA: Harvard University Press.

Brown, R., & McNeill, D. (1966). The "tip of the tongue" phenomenon. *Journal of Verbal Learning & Verbal Behavior, 5*(4), 325–337.

Browne, D. (2004). Do dolphins know their own minds? *Biology & Philosophy, 19*, 633–653.

Browne, M. N., & Keeley, S. M. (2009). *Asking the right questions: A guide to critical thinking* (9th ed.). Upper Saddle River, NJ: Pearson Prentice-Hall.

Broyles, S. (2006). Subliminal advertising and the perpetual popularity of playing to people's paranoia. *Journal of Consumer Affairs, 40*(2), 392–406.

Brubaker, D. A., & Leddy, J. J. (2003). Behavioral contracting in the treatment of eating disorders. *The Physician and Sportsmedicine, 31*(9), 15–26.

Brugger, S. P., & Howes, O. D. (2017). Heterogeneity and homogeneity of regional brain structure in schizophrenia: A meta-analysis. *JAMA Psychiatry, 74*(11), 1104–1111. doi:10.1001/jamapsychiatry.2017.2663

Brunner, E. J., Hemingway, H., Walker, B., Page, M., Clarke, P., Juneja, M., ... Marmot, M. G. (2002). Adrenocortical, autonomic and inflammatory causes of the metabolic syndrome: Nested case-control study. *Circulation, 106*, 2659–2665.

Bryan, J., & Freed, F. (1982). Corporal punishment: Normative data and sociological and psychological correlates in a community college population. *Journal of Youth and Adolescence, 11*(2), 77–87.

Buccino, G., Binkofski, F., & Riggio, L. (2004). The mirror neuron system and action recognition. *Brain and Language, 89*(2), 370–376.

Buccino, G., Binkofski, F., Fink, G. R., Fadiga, L., Fogassi, L., Gallese, V., ... Freund, H. J. (2001). Action observation activates premotor and parietal areas in a somatotopic manner: An fMRI study. *European Journal of Neuroscience, 13*(2), 400–404.

Bucher, B. D., & Lovaas, O. I. (1967). Use of aversive stimulation in behavior modification. In M. R. Jones (Ed.), *Miami Symposium on the Prediction of Behavior 1967: Aversive Stimulation*, 77–145. Coral Gables: University of Miami Press.

Buck, L. B., & Bargmann, C. I. (2013). Smell and taste: The chemical senses. In E. R. Kandel, J. H. Schwartz, T. M. Jessell, S. A. Siegelbaum, & A. J. Hudspeth (Eds.), *Principles of neural science* (5th ed., pp. 712–735). New York: McGraw-Hill.

Buck, R. (1980). Nonverbal behavior and the theory of emotion: The facial feedback hypothesis. *Journal of Personality and Social Psychology, 38*, 811–824.

Buckels, E. E., Trapnell, P. D., & Paulhus, D. L. (2014). Trolls just want to have fun. *Personality and Individual Differences, 67*, 97–102.

Bugaiska, A., Clarys, D., Jarry, C., Taconnat, L., Tapia, G., Vanneste, S., & Isingring, M. (2007). The effect of aging in recollective experience: The processing speed and executive functioning hypothesis. *Consciousness and Cognition, 16*(4), 797–808.

Buhle, J. T., Silvers, J. A., Wager, T. D., Lopez, R., Onyemekwu, C., Kober, H., ... Ochsner, K. N. (2014). Cognitive reappraisal of emotion: A meta-analysis of human neuroimaging studies. *Cerebral Cortex, 24*(11), 2981–2993.

Bullock, T. H., Bennett, M. V., Johnston, D., Josephson, R., Marder, E., & Fields, R. D. (2005). Neuroscience. The neuron doctrine, redux. *Science, 310*(5749), 791–793.

Burger, J. M. (1997). *The psychoanalytic approach: Neo-Freudian theory, application, and assessment*. Personality (4th ed.). Pacific Grove, CA: Brooks/Cole.

Burger, J. M. (1999). The foot-in-the-door compliance procedure: A multiple-process analysis and review. *Personality and Social Psychology Review, 3*(4), 303–325. doi: 10.1207/s15327957pspr0304_2

Burger, J. M. (2009). Replicating Milgram: Would people still obey today? *American Psychologist, 64*(1), 1–11. doi: 10.1037/a0010932

Burger, J. M., Girgis, Z. M., & Manning, C. C. (2011). In their own words: Explaining obedience to authority through an examination of participants' comments. *Social Psychological and Personality Science, 2*, 460–466. doi: 10.1177/1948550610397632

Burger, J. M., & Petty, R. E. (1981). The low-ball compliance technique: Task or person commitment? *Journal of Personality and Social Psychology, 40*, 492–500.

Burgio, K. L. (1998). Behavioral vs. drug treatment for urge urinary incontinence in older women: A randomized controlled trial. *Journal of the American Medical Association, 280*, 1995–2000.

Burguière, E., Monteiro, P., Guoping, F., & Graybiel, A. M. (2013). Optogenetic stimulation of lateral orbitofronto-striatal pathway suppresses compulsive behaviors. *Science, 340*(6137), 1243–1246. doi: 10.1126/science.1232380

Burke, D. M., MacKay, D. G., Worthley, J. S., & Wade, E. (1991). On the tip of the tongue: What causes word finding failures in young and older adults. *Journal of Memory and Language, 30*, 542–579.

Burks, N., & Martin, B. (1985). Everyday problems and life change events: Ongoing versus acute sources of stress. *Journal of Human Stress, 11*, 27–35.

Burnay, J., Bushman, B. J., & Laroi, F. (2019). Effects of sexualized video games on online sexual harassment. *Aggressive Behavior, 45*(2), 214–223. doi:10.1002/ab.21811

Burns, J. F. (2010, May 24). British medical council bars doctor who linked vaccine with autism. *New York Times*.

Burt, S. A., & Neiderhiser, J. M. (2009). Aggressive versus nonaggressive antisocial behavior: Distinctive etiological moderation by age. *Developmental Psychology, 45*(4), 1164–1176. doi: 10.1037/a0016130

Bush, G., Frazier, J. A., Rauch, S. L., Seidman, L. J., Whalen, P. J., Jenike, M. A., ... Biederman, J. (1999). Anterior cingulate cortex dysfunction in attention-deficit/hyperactivity disorder revealed by fMRI and the Counting Stroop. *Biological Psychiatry, 45*(12), 1542–1552.

Bush, G., Spencer, T. J., Holmes, J., Shin, L. M., Valera, E. M., Seidman, L. J., Biederman, J. (2008). Functional magnetic resonance imaging of methylphenidate and placebo in attention-deficit/hyperactivity disorder during the Multi-Source Interference Task. *Archives of General Psychiatry, 65*(1), 102–114.

Bushey, D., Tononi, G., & Cirelli, C. (2011). Sleep and synaptic homeostasis: Structural evidence in Drosophila. *Science, 332*(6037), 1576–1581.

Bushman, B. J. (1997). Effects of alcohol on human aggression: Validity of proposed explanations. In M. Galanter (Ed.), *Recent developments in alcoholism. Vol. 1: Alcohol and violence—Epidemiology, neurobiology, psychology, family issues* (pp. 227–243). New York: Plenum Press.

Bushman, B. J. (2018). Teaching students about violent media effects. *Teaching of Psychology, 45*(2), 200–206. doi:10.1177/0098628318762936

Bushman, B. J., Giancola, P. R., Parrott, D. J., & Roth, R. M. (2012). Failure to consider future consequences increases the effects of alcohol on aggression. *Journal of Experimental Social Psychology, 48*(2), 591–595. doi:10.1016/j.jesp.2011.11.013

Bushman, B. J., & Huesmann, L. R. (2001). Effects of televised violence on aggression. In D. G. Singer & J. L. Singer (Eds.), *Handbook of children and the media* (Ch. 11, pp. 223–254). Thousand Oaks, CA: Sage.

Bushman, B. J., & Huesmann, L. R. (2006). Short-term and long-term effects of violent media on aggression in children and adults. *Archives of Pediatrics & Adolescent Medicine, 160*, 348–352. doi: 10.1001/archpedi.160.4.348

Bushman, B. J., Newman, K., Calvert, S. L., Downey, G., Dredze, M., Gottfredson, M.,... Webster, D. W. (2016). Youth violence: What we know and what we need to know. *American Psychologist, 71*(1), 17–39. doi: 10.1037/a0039687

Buss, D. M. (2009a). How can evolutionary psychology successfully explain personality and individual differences? *Perspectives on Psychological Science, 4*(4), 359–366. doi: 10.1111/j.1745-6924.2009.01138.x

Buss, D. M. (2009b). The multiple adaptive problems solved by human aggression. *Behavioral and Brain Sciences, 32*, 271–272.

Buss, D. M. (2011). Personality and the adaptive landscape: The role of individual differences in creating and solving social adaptive problems. In D. M. Buss & P. H. Hawley (Eds.), *The evolution of personality and individual differences*. New York: Oxford University Press.

Buss, D. M., Larsen, R. J., Westen, D., & Semmelroth, J. (1992). Sex differences in jealousy: Evolution, physiology, and psychology. *Psychological Science, 3*, 251–255.

Bussa, B., & Kaufman, C. (2000). What can self-help do? *The Journal of the California Alliance of the Mentally Ill, 2*(2), 34–45.

Bussey, K., & Bandura, A. (1999). Social cognitive theory of gender development and differentiation. *Psychological Review, 106*(4), 676–713.

Butcher, J. N., Graham, J. R., Ben-Poarth, Y. S., Tellegen, A., Dahlstrom, W. G., & Kaemmer, B. (2001). *Minnesota Multiphasic Personality Inventory-2. Manual for administration, scoring, and interpretation* (Rev. ed.). Minneapolis, MN: University of Minnesota Press.

Butcher, J. N., & Rouse, S. V. (1996). Personality: Individual differences and clinical assessment. *Annual Review of Psychology, 47*, 87–111.

Butcher, J. N., Rouse, S. V., & Perry, J. N. (2000). Empirical description of psychopathology in therapy clients: Correlates of MMPI-2 scales. In J. N. Butcher (Ed.), *Basic sources on the MMPI-2* (pp. 487–500). Minneapolis, MN: University of Minnesota Press.

Cabeza, R., Anderson, N. D., Locantore, J. K., & McIntosh, A. R. (2002). Aging gracefully: Compensatory brain activity in high-performing older adults. *NeuroImage, 17*(3), 1394–1402.

Cabeza, R., & Nyberg, L. (2000). Imaging cognition II: An empirical review of 275 PET and fMRI studies. *Journal of Cognitive Neuroscience, 12*(1), 1–47.

Cabral, R. R., & Smith, T. B. (2011). Racial/ethnic matching of clients and therapists in mental health services: A meta-analytic review of preferences, perceptions, and outcomes. *Journal of Counseling Psychology, 58*(4), 537–554. doi:10.1037/a0025266

Cacioppo, J. T. (2013). Psychological science in the 21st century. *Teaching of Psychology, 40*, 304–309.

Caetano, C., Peers, T., Papadopoulos, L., Wiggers, K., Engler, Y., & Grant, H. (2019). Millennials and contraception: Why do they forget? An international survey exploring the impact of lifestyles and stress levels on adherence to a daily contraceptive regimen. *European Journal of Contraception and Reproductive Health Care*, 1–9. doi:10.1080/13625187.2018.1563065

Cai, Y., Tang, X., Chen, X., Li, X. Wang, Y. Bao, X.,… & Fan, X. (2018). Liver X receptor β regulates the development of the dentate gyrus and autistic-like behavior in the mouse. *Proceedings of the National Academy of Sciences, 115*(12): E2725–E2733. DOI: https://doi.org/10.1073/pnas.1800184115

Cain, D., & Seeman, J. (Eds.). (2001). *Humanistic psychotherapies: Handbook of research and practice*. Washington, DC: APA Publications.

Cain, M. S., & Mitroff, S. R. (2011). Distractor filtering in media multitaskers. *Perception, 40*(10), 1183-1192. doi:10.1068/p7017

Caird, J. K., Simmons, S. M., Wiley, K., Johnston, K. A., & Horrey, W. J. (2018). Does talking on a cell phone, with a passenger, or dialing affect driving performance? And updated systematic review and meta-analysis of experimental studies. *Human Factors: The Journal of the Human Factors and Ergonomics Society, 60*(1): 101. DOI: http://dx.doi.org/10.1177/0018720817748145

Cairney, S. A., á Váli Guttesen, A., El Marj, N., & Staresina, B. P. (2018). Memory consolidation is linked to spindle-mediated information processing during sleep. *Current Biology, 28*(6): 948–954. DOI: http://dx.doi.org/10.1016/j.cub.2018.01.087

Cajal, S. R. y. (1995). *Histology of the nervous system of man and vertebrates* (translated from the French by Neely Swanson and Larry W. Swanson ed.). New York, NY: Oxford University Press.

Caldji, C., Tannenbaum, B., Sharma, S., Francis, D., Plotsky, P. M., & Meaney, M. J. (1998). Maternal care during infancy regulates the development of neural systems mediating the expression of fearfulness in the rat. *Proceedings of the National Academy of Sciences of the United States of America, 95*, 5335–5340.

Caley, L. M., Kramer, C., & Robinson, L. K. (2005). Fetal alcohol spectrum disorder. *The Journal of School Nursing, 21*(3), 139–146.

Califia, P. (1997). *Sex changes: The politics of transgenderism*. San Francisco: Cleis Press.

Calvo, N., Garcia, A. M., Manoiloff, L., & Ibanez, A. (2015). Bilingualism and cognitive reserve: A critical overview and a plea for methodological innovations. *Frontiers in Aging Neuroscience, 7*, 1–17. doi: 10.3389/fnagi.2015.00249

Camacho, E. M., Verstappen, S. M., Chipping, J., & Symmons, D. P. (2013). Learned helplessness predicts functional disability, pain and fatigue in patients with recent-onset inflammatory polyarthritis. *Rheumatology (Oxford), 52*(7), 1233–1238. doi: 10.1093/rheumatology/kes434

Cameron, J. A., Alvarez, J. M., Ruble, D. N., & Fuligni, A. J. (2001). Children's lay theories about ingroups and outgroups: Reconceptualizing research on prejudice. *Personality and Social Psychology Review, 5*, 118–128.

Cameron, J., Banko, K. M., & Pierce, W. D. (2001). Pervasive negative effects of rewards on intrinsic motivation: The myth continues. *The Behavior Analyst, 24*, 1–44.

Cami, J., Farre, M., Mas, M., Roset, P. N., Poudevida, S., Mas, A., … de la Torre, R. (2000). Human pharmacology of 3,4-methylenedioxymethamphetamine ("ecstasy"): Psychomotor performance and subjective effects. *Journal of Clinical Psychopharmacology, 20*, 455–466.

Campbell, A. (2015). 80 children get chicken pox at school with low vaccination rate. Huffpost Healthy Living, 12/10/2015. Retrieved from http://www.huffingtonpost.com/entry/chicken-pox-low-vaccination-outbreak_5669d5d4e4b0f290e5227559

Campbell, J. C., Webster, D., Koziol-McLain, J., Block, C., Campbell, D., Curry, M. A.,… Laughon, K. (2003). Risk factors for femicide in abusive relationships: Results from a multisite case control study. *American Journal of Public Health, 93*(7), 1089–1097.

Campbell, L. F., Norcross, J. C., Vasquez, M. J. T., & Kaslow, N. J. (2013). Recognition of psychotherapy effectiveness: The APA resolution. *Psychotherapy, 50*(1), 98–101. doi: 10.1037/a0031817

Canals, L., Ginisty, A., Quist, E., Timmerman, R., Fritze, J., Miskinyte, G.,… & Ahlenius, H. (2018). Rapid and efficient induction of functional astrocytes from human pluripotent stem cells. *Nature Methods, 15*: 693–696. DOI: http://dx.doi.org/10.1038/s41592-018-0103-2

Cannon, W. B. (1915). *Bodily changes in pain, hunger, fear and rage: An account of recent researches into the function of emotional excitement*. New York, NY: D. Appleton and Company.

Cannon, W. B. (1927). The James-Lange theory of emotion: A critical examination and an alternative theory. *American Journal of Psychology, 39*, 10–124.

Cannon, W. B. (1929). Organization for physiological homeostasis. *Physiological Reviews, 9*(3), 399–431.

Cannon, W. B., & Washburn, A. L. (1912). An explanation of hunger. *American Journal of Physiology, 29*, 444–454.

Cao-Lei, L., Massart, R., Suderman, M. J., Machnes, Z., Elgbeili, G., Laplante, D. P., & King, S. (2014). DNA methylation signatures triggered by prenatal maternal stress exposure to a natural disaster: Project Ice Storm. *PLoS ONE, 9*, e107653.

Caparos, S., Ahmed, L., Bremner, A. J., de Fockert, J. W., Linnell, K. J., & Davidoff, J. (2012). Exposure to an urban environment alters the local bias of a remote culture. *Cognition, 122*(1), 80–85. doi:10.1016/j.cognition.2011.08.013

Cardinali, D. P., Scacchi Bernasconi, P. A., Reynoso, R., Reyes Toso, C. F., & Scacchi, P. (2013). Melatonin may curtail the metabolic syndrome: Studies on initial and fully established fructose-induced metabolic syndrome in rats. *International Journal of Molecular Sciences, 14*(2), 2502–2514.

Cardno, A. G., & Gottesman, I. I. (2000). Twin studies of schizophrenia: From bow-and-arrow concordances to Star Wars Mx and functional genomics. *American Journal of Medical Genetics, 97*(1), 12–17. doi: 10.1002/(SICI)1096-8628(200021)97:1<12::AID-AJMG3>3.0.CO;2-U [pii]

Carducci, B. (1998). *The psychology of personality*. Pacific Grove, CA: Brooks/Cole Publishing Co.

Carlsen, A. (2013, March 18). Some people really can taste the rainbow [Web log post]. Retrieved from http://www.npr.org/blogs/thesalt/2013/03/12/174132392/synesthetes-really-can-taste-the-rainbow

Carlson, G. A., Jensen, P. S., & Nottelmann, E. D. (Eds.). (1998). Current issues in childhood bipolarity [Special issue]. *Journal of Affective Disorders, 51*, 1–5.

Carnahan, T., & McFarland, S. (2007). Revisiting the Stanford prison experiment: Could participant self-selection have led to the cruelty?*Personality & Social Psychology Bulletin, 33*(5), 603–614. doi:10.1177/0146167206292689

Carnot, M. J., Dunn, B., Cañas, A. J., Graham, P., & Muldoon, J. (2001). Concept Maps vs. Web Pages for Information Searching and Browsing. Manuscript in preparation. Institute for Human and Machine Cognition.

Carpenter, P. A., Just, M. A., & Shell, P. (1990). What one intelligence test measures: A theoretical account of the processing in the Raven Progressive Matrices test. *Psychological Review, 97*(3), 404–431.

Carr, E. G., & Lovaas, O. I. (1983). Contingent electric shock as a treatment for severe behavior problems. In S. Axelrod & J. Apsche (Eds.), *The effects of punishment on human behavior* (pp. 221–245). New York: Academic Press.

Carrion, V. G., Weems, C. F., & Reiss, A. L. (2007). Stress predicts brain changes in children: A pilot longitudinal study on youth stress, posttraumatic stress disorder, and the hippocampus. *Pediatrics, 119*(3), 509–516.

Carruthers, M. (2001). A multifactorial approach to understanding andropause. *Journal of Sexual and Reproductive Medicine, 1*, 69–74.

Carskadon, M. A., & Dement, W. C. (2005). Normal human sleep overview. In M. H. Kryger, T. Roth, & W. C. Dement (Eds.), *Principles and practice of sleep medicine* (4th ed., pp. 13–23). Philadelphia: Elsevier/Saunders.

Carskadon, M. A., & Dement, W. C. (2011). Normal human sleep: An overview. In M. H. Kryger, T. Roth, & W. C. Dement (Eds.), *Principles and practice of sleep medicine*, pp. 16–26. St. Louis, MO: Elsevier Saunders.

Carson, R. C. (1969). *Interaction concepts of personality*. Chicago: Aldine.

Carter, C., Bishop, J., & Kravits, S. L. (2005). *Keys to success: Building successful intelligence for college, career, and life* (5th ed.). Englewood Cliffs, NJ: Prentice Hall.

Carver, C. S., & Antoni, M. H. (2004). Finding benefit in breast cancer during the year after diagnosis predicts better adjustment 5 to 8 years after diagnosis. *Health Psychology, 26*, 595–598.

Carver, L. J., & Bauer, P. J. (2001). The dawning of a past: The emergence of long-term explicit memory in infancy. *Journal of Experimental Psychology: General, 130*, 726–745.

Case, B. G., Bertollo, D. N., Laska, E. M., Price, L. H., Siegel, C. E., Olfson, M., & Marcus, S. C. (2013). Declining use of electroconvulsive therapy in United States general hospitals. *Biological Psychiatry, 73*(2), 119–126. doi: 10.1016/j.biopsych.2012.09.005

Case, B. G., Bertollo, D. N., Laska, E. M., Siegel, C. E., Wanderling, J. A., & Olfson, M. (2012). Racial differences in the availability and use of electroconvulsive therapy for recurrent major depression. *Journal of Affective Disorders, 136*(3), 359–365. doi: 10.1016/j.jad.2011.11.026

Cassidy, A., Bingham, S., & Setchell, K. D. R. (1994). Biological effects of a diet of soy protein rich in isoflavones on the menstrual cycle of premenopausal women. *American Journal of Clinical Nutrition, 60*, 333–340.

Castellanos, F. X., & Proal, E. (2012). Large-scale brain systems in ADHD: Beyond the prefrontal-striatal model. *Trends in Cognitive Sciences, 16*(1), 17–26. doi:10.1016/j.tics.2011.11.007

Castillo, R. J. (1997). Eating disorders. In R. J. Castillo (Ed.), *Culture and mental illness: A client-centered approach* (p. 152). Pacific Grove, CA: Brooks/Cole.

Catanzaro, S. J., Wasch, H. H., Kirsch, I., & Mearns, J. (2000). Coping-related expectancies and dispositions as prospective predictors of coping responses and symptoms: Distinguishing mood regulation expectancies, dispositional coping, and optimism. *Journal of Personality, 68*, 757–788.

Cattell, R. B. (1950). *Personality: A systematic, theoretical, and factual study.* New York: McGraw-Hill.

Cattell, R. B. (1973). *Personality and mood by questionnaire.* San Francisco: Jossey-Bass.

Cattell, R. B. (1990). Advances in Cattellian personality theory. In L. A. Pervin (Ed.), *Handbook of personality: Theory and research* (pp. 101–110). New York: Guilford.

Cattell, R. B. (Ed.). (1966). *Handbook of multivariate experimental psychology.* Chicago: Rand McNally.

Cattell, R. B., & Cattell, H. E. P. (1995). Personality structure and the new fifth edition of the 16PF. *Educational and Psychological Measurement, 55*(6), 926–937. doi:10.1177/0013164495055006002

Cattell, R. B., & Kline, P. (1977). *The scientific analysis of personality and motivation.* New York: Academic Press.

Cavanaugh, A. M., & Buehler, C. (2016). Adolescent loneliness and social anxiety: The role of multiple sources of support. *Journal of Social and Personal Relationships, 33*(2), 149–170.

Cave, K. R., & Kim, M. (1999). Top-down and bottom-up attentional control: On the nature of interference from a salient distractor. *Perception & Psychophysics, 61,* 1009–1023.

Centers for Disease Control and Prevention (CDC). (2004). *Parents' guide to childhood immunization.* Atlanta, GA: U.S. Department of Health and Human Services, Public Health Service.

Centers for Disease Control and Prevention (CDC). (2010). *How tobacco smoke causes disease: The biology and behavioral basis for smoking-attributable disease: A report of the Surgeon General.* Retrieved from https://www.cdc.gov/tobacco/data_statistics/sgr/2010/index.htm

Centers for Disease Control and Prevention (CDC). (2011). Vaccines & immunizations: Some common misconceptions. Retrieved April 26, 2013, from http://www.cdc.gov/vaccines/vac-gen/6mishome.htm

Centers for Disease Control and Prevention (CDC). (2011a). FastStats: Alcohol use. Retrieved from the Internet March 27, 2013, from http://www.cdc.gov/nchs/fastats/alcohol.htm

Centers for Disease Control and Prevention (CDC). (2013). HIV basics: HIV transmission. Divisions of HIV/AIDS Prevention. Retrieved from http://www.cdc.gov/hiv/basics/transmission.html

Centers for Disease Control and Prevention (CDC). (2015a). Fact sheets: Alcohol use and your health. Atlanta, GA: CDC. Retrieved from http://www.cdc.gov/alcohol/fact-sheets/alcohol-use.htm

Centers for Disease Control and Prevention (CDC). (2015b). Smoking & tobacco use: Current cigarette smoking among adults in the United States. Office on Smoking and Health, National Center for Chronic Disease Prevention and Health Promotion. Atlanta, GA, CDC. Retrieved from http://www.cdc.gov/tobacco/data_statistics/fact_sheets/adult_data/cig_smoking/index.htm#national

Centers for Disease Control and Prevention (CDC). (2015c). *Vital signs: Today's heroin epidemic.* Atlanta, GA: CDC. Retrieved from http://www.cdc.gov/vitalsigns/heroin/

Centers for Disease Control and Prevention (CDC). (2015d). Injury prevention & control: Motor vehicle safety: Distracted driving. Retrieved from http://www.cdc.gov/motorvehiclesafety/distracted_driving/

Centers for Disease Control and Prevention (CDC). (2015e). *Suicide: Facts at a glance.* Retrieved from http://www.cdc.gov/violenceprevention/pdf/suicide-datasheet-a.pdf

Centers for Disease Control and Prevention (CDC). (2018a). Facts about Down syndrome. Retrieved September 11, 2018, from https://www.cdc.gov/ncbddd/birthdefects/downsyndrome.html

Centers for Disease Control and Prevention (CDC). (2018b). *Leading causes of death in males United States, 2015 (Current Listing).* Atlanta, GA: U.S. Department of Health and Human Services, Public Health Service.

Centers for Disease Control and Prevention (CDC). (2018c). Measles cases and outbreaks. Atlanta, Georgia. Retrieved from https://www.cdc.gov/measles/cases-outbreaks.html

Centers for Disease Control and Prevention. (2018d). Opioid basis: Understanding the epidemic, from https://www.cdc.gov/drugoverdose/epidemic/index.html

Centers for Disease Control and Prevention (CDC). (2018e). *Leading causes of death in females United States, 2015 (Current Listing).* Atlanta, GA: U.S. Department of Health and Human Services, Public Health Service.

Centerwall, B. S. (1989). Exposure to television as a risk factor for violence. *American Journal of Epidemiology, 129,* 643–652.

Cepeda, N. J., Pashler, H., Vul, E., Wixted, J. T., & Rohrer, D. (2006). Distributed practice in verbal recall tasks: A review and quantitative synthesis. *Psychological Bulletin, 132,* 354–380.

Cerdá, M., Sarvet, A. L., Wall, M., Feng, T., Keyes, K. M., Galea, S., & Hasin, D. S. (2018). Medical marijuana laws and adolescent use of marijuana and other substance: Alcohol, cigarettes, prescription drugs, and other illicit drugs. *Drug and Alcohol Dependence, 183*(1): 62–68. DOI: https://doi.org/10.1016/j.drugalcdep.2017.10.021

Cermak, L., & Craik, F. (1979). *Levels of processing in human memory.* Hillsdale, NJ: Erlbaum.

Cha, J. H., & Nam, K. D. (1985). A test of Kelley's cube theory of attribution: A cross-cultural replication of McArthur's study. *Korean Social Science Journal, 12,* 151–180.

Chahua, M., Sanchez-Niubo, A., Torrens, M., Sordo, L., Bravo, M. J., Brugal, M. T., & Domingo-Salvany, A. (2015). Quality of life in a community sample of young cocaine and/or heroin users: The role of mental disorders. *Quality of Life Research: An International Journal of Quality of Life Aspects of Treatment, Care, and Rehabilitation, 24*(9), 2129–2137.

Chan, C. J., Smyth, M. J., & Martinet, L. (2014). Molecular mechanisms of natural killer cell activation in response to cellular stress. *Cell Death and Differentiation, 21,* 5–14.

Chandola, T., Britton, A., Brunner, E., Hemingway, H., Malik, M., Kumari, M., Badrick, E., Kivimaki, M., & Marmot, M. (2008). Work stress and coronary heart disease: What are the mechanisms? *European Heart Journal.* doi:10.1093/eurheartj/ehm584

Chandola, T., Brunner, E., & Marmot, M. (2006). Chronic stress at work and the metabolic syndrome: Prospective study. *British Medical Journal, 332,* 521–525.

Chang, A.-M., Aeschbach, D., Duffy, J. F., & Czeisler, C. A. (2015). Evening use of light-emitting eReaders negatively affects sleep, circadian timing, and next-morning alertness. *Proceedings of the National Academy of Sciences of the United States of America, 112*(4), 1232–1237.

Chang, E. (2004). As Los Angeles burned, Korean America was born: Community in the twenty-first century. *Amerasia Journal, 30*(1), vii–ix.

Charlesworth, W. R., & Kreutzer, M. A. (1973). Facial expression of infants and children. In P. Ekman (Ed.), *Darwin and facial expression: A century of research in review.* New York: Academic.

Charlton, B. G. (2008). Zombie science: A sinister consequence of evaluating scientific theories purely on the basis of enlightened self-interest. *Medical Hypotheses, 71*(3), 327–329. doi:10.1016/j.mehy.2008.05.018

Chee, M. W. L., & Choo, W. C. (2004, April 24–May 1). Functional imaging of working memory following 24 hours of total sleep deprivation. *Program and abstracts of the 56th Annual Meeting of the American Academy of Neurology.* San Francisco.

Chein, J., Albert, D., O'Brien, L., Uckert, K., & Steinberg, L. (2011). Peers increase adolescent risk taking by enhancing activity in the brain's reward circuitry. *Developmental Science, 14,* F1–F10.

Chen, J. Y. (2007). Do Chinese and English speakers think about time differently? Failure of replicating Boroditsky (2001). *Cognition, 104*(2), 427–436.

Chen, L. Y., Rex, C. S., Sanaiha, Y., Lynch, G., & Gall, C. M. (2010). Learning induces neurotrophin signaling at hippocampal synapses. *Proceedings of the National Academy of Sciences, USA, 107*(15), 7030–7035.

Chen, R., & Ende, N. (2000). The potential for the use of mononuclear cells from human umbilical cord blood in the treatment of amyotrophic lateral sclerosis in SOD1 mice. *Journal of Medicine, 31,* 21–31.

Chen, S., Fragoza, R., Klei, L., Liu, Y., Wang, J., Roeder, K. Devlin, B., & Yu, H. (2018). An interactome perturbation framework prioritizes damaging missense mutations for developmental disorders. *Nature Genetics, 50:* 1032-1040. DOI: http://dx.doi.org/10.1038/s41588-018-0130-z

Chen, V. H. H., & Wu, Y. (2013). Group identification as a mediator of the effect of players' anonymity on cheating in online games. *Behaviour & Information Technology, 34*(7), 658–667. doi: 10.1080/0144929X.2013.843721

Chen, Y., Huang, X., Zhang, Y.-W., Rockenstein, E., Bu, G., Golde, T. E., Masliah, E., & Xu, H. (2012). Alzheimer's β-Secretase (BACE1) regulates the cAMP/PKA/CREB pathway independently of β-Amyloid. *Journal of Neuroscience, 32*(33), 11390. doi: 10.1523/JNEUROSCI.0757-12.2012

Cherry, E. C. (1953). Some experiments on the recognition of speech, with one and with two ears. *Journal of the Acoustical Society of America, 25*(5), 975–979.

Cheryan, S., Plaut, V. C., Handron, C., & Hudson, L. (2013). The stereotypical computer scientist: Gendered media representations as a barrier to inclusion for women. *Sex Roles: A Journal of Research, 69,* 58–71.

Cheryan, S., Plaut, V., Davis, P., & Steele, C. (2009). Ambient belonging: How stereotypical cues impact gender participation in computer science. *Journal of Personality and Social Psychology, 97*(6), 1045–1060.

Cheryan, S., Siy, J. O., Vichayapai, M., Drury, B. J., & Kim, S. (2011). Do female and male role models who embody STEM stereotypes hinder women's anticipated success in STEM? *Social Psychological and Personality Science, 2,* 656–664.

Chesham, R. K., Malouff, J. M., & Schutte, N. S. (2018). Meta-analysis of the efficacy of virtual reality exposure therapy for social anxiety. *Behaviour Change, 35*(03), 152–166. doi:10.1017/bec.2018.15

Chess, S., & Shaw, A. (2015). A conspiracy of fishes, or, How we learned to stop worrying about #GamerGate and embrace hegemonic masculinity. *Journal of Broadcasting & Electronic Media, 59*(1), 208–220.

Chess, S., & Thomas, A. (1986). *Temperament in clinical practice.* New York: Guilford Press.

Chida, Y., & Steptoe, A. (2009). The association of anger and hostility with future coronary heart disease: A meta-analytic review of prospective evidence. *Journal of the American College of Cardiology, 53*(11), 936–946. doi:10.1016/j.jacc.2008.11.044

Chirkov, V. I. (2009). A cross-cultural analysis of autonomy in education: A self-determination theory perspective. *Theory and Research in Education, 7*(2), 253–262.

Chirkov, V. I., Lebedeva, N. M., Molodtsova, I., & Tatarko, A. (2011). Social capital, motivational autonomy, and health behavior: A comparative study of Canadian and Russian youth. In D. Chadee & A. Kosti (Eds.), *Social psychological dynamics* (pp. 211–241). Trinidad: University of West Indies Press.

Chiu, C., Hong, Y., & Dweck, C. S. (1997). Lay dispositionism and implicit theories of personality. *Journal of Personality and Social Psychology, 73*, 19–30.

Cho, M. J., Seong, S. J., Park, J. E., Chung, I. W., Lee, Y. M., Bae, A.,… Hong, J. P. (2015). Prevalence and correlates of dsm-iv mental disorders in South Korean adults: The Korean epidemiologic catchment area study 2011. *Psychiatry Investigation, 12*(2), 164–170. doi:10.4306/pi.2015.12.2.164

Choca, J. P. (2013). *The Rorschach inkblot test: An interpretive guide for clinicians.* Washington, DC, US: American Psychological Association.

Choi, I., & Nisbett, R. E. (1998). Situational salience and cultural differences in the correspondence bias and in the actor–observer bias. *Personality and Social Psychology Bulletin, 24*, 949–960.

Choi, I., Dalal, R., Kim-Prieto, C., & Park, H. (2003). Culture and judgement of causal relevance. *Journal of Personality and Social Psychology, 84*(1), 46–59. doi:10.1037/0022-3514.84.1.46

Choi, I., Nisbett, R. E., & Norenzayan, A. (1999). Causal attribution across cultures: Variation and universality. *Psychological Bulletin, 125*, 47–63.

Chomsky, N. (1957). *Syntactic structures.* The Hague: Mouton.

Chomsky, N. (1964). *Current issues in linguistic theory.* The Hague: Mouton.

Chomsky, N. (1981). Principles and parameters in syntactic theory. In N. Hornstein & D. Lightfoot (Eds.), *Explanation in linguistics: The logical problem of language acquisition*, 32–75. London: Longman.

Chomsky, N. (1986). *Knowledge of language: Its nature, origin and use.* New York: Praeger.

Chomsky, N. (2006). *Language and mind* (3rd ed.). New York: Cambridge University Press.

Chomsky, N., Belletti, A., & Rizzi, L. (2002). *On nature and language.* New York: Cambridge University Press.

Chorpita, B. F., Daleiden, E. L., Ebesutani, C., Young, J., Becker, K. D., Nakamura, B. J.,… Starace, N. (2011). Evidence-based treatments for children and adolescents: An updated review of indicators of efficacy and effectiveness. *Clinical Psychology Science and Practice, 18*, 154–172. doi: 10.1111/j.1468-2850.2011.01247.x

Chou, S. Y., Grossman, M., & Saffer, H. (2004). An economic analysis of adult obesity: Results from the behavioral risk factor surveillance system. *Journal of Health Economics, 23*, 565–587.

Christensen, A. J., & Nezu, A. M. (2013). Behavioral medicine and clinical health psychology: Introduction to the special issue. *Journal of Consulting and Clinical Psychology, 81*(2), 193–195.

Christensen, A., Jacobson, N. S., & Babcock, J. C. (1995). Integrative behavioral couple therapy. In N. S. Jacobson & A. S. Gurman (Eds.), *Clinical handbook of couple therapy* (pp. 31–64). New York: Norton.

Chu, J. A., Frey, L. M., Ganzel, B. L., & Matthews, J. A. (1999). Memories of childhood abuse: Dissociation, amnesia, and corroboration. *American Journal of Psychiatry, 156*, 749–755.

Church, A. T., Katigbak, M. S., Ortiz, F. A., Del Prado, A. M., De Jesús Vargas-Flores, J., Ibáñez-Reyes, J.,… Cabrera, H. F. (2016). Investigating implicit trait theories across cultures. *Journal of Cross-Cultural Psychology, 36*(4), 476–496. doi:10.1177/0022022105275963

Church, A. T. (2010). Current perspectives in the study of personality across cultures. *Perspectives on Psychological Science, 5*(4), 441–449. doi: 10.1177/1745691610375559

Chwalisz, K., Diener, E., & Gallagher, D. (1988). Autonomic arousal feedback and emotional experience: Evidence from the spinal cord injured. *Journal of Personality and Social Psychology, 54*, 820–828.

Cialdini, R. B., & Goldstein, N. J. (2004). Social influence: Compliance and conformity. *Annual Review of Psychology, 55*, 591–621. doi: 10.1146/annurev.psych.55.090902.142015

Cialdini, R. B., Trost, M. R., & Newsom, J. T. (1995). Preference for consistency: The development of a valid measure and the discovery of surprising behavioral implications. *Journal of Personality and Social Psychology, 69*, 318–328.

Cialdini, R., Vincent, J., Lewis, S., Catalan, J., Wheeler, D., & Darby, B. (1975). Reciprocal concessions procedure for inducing compliance: The door–in–the–face technique. *Journal of Personality and Social Psychology, 31*, 206–215.

Cialdini, R., Wosinska, W., Barrett, D., Butner, J., & Gornik–Durose, M. (1999). Compliance with a request in two cultures: The differential influence of social proof and commitment/consistency on collectivists and individualists. *Personality and Social Psychology Bulletin, 25*, 1242–1253.

Ciardiello, A. (1998). Did you ask a good question today? Alternative cognitive and metacognitive strategies. *Journal of Adolescent & Adult Literacy, 42*, 210–219.

Cinnirella, M., & Green, B. (2007). Does "cyber-conformity" vary cross-culturally? Exploring the effect of culture and communication medium on social conformity. *Computers in Human Behavior, 23*(4), 2011–2025.

Cipriani, A., Zhou, X., Del Giovane, C., Hetrick, S. E., Qin, B., Whittington, C.,… Xie, P. (2016). Comparative efficacy and tolerability of antidepressants for major depressive disorder in children and adolescents: A network meta-analysis. *The Lancet, 388*(10047), 881–890. doi:10.1016/s0140-6736(16)30385-3

Cirelli, C. (2012). Brain plasticity, sleep and aging. *Gerontology, 58*: 441–445.

Clancy, S. A., McNally, R. J., Schacter, D. L., Lenzenweger, M. F., & Pitman, R. K. (2002). Memory distortion in people reporting abduction by aliens. *Journal of Abnormal Psychology, 111*(3), 455–461.

Clarke, J. (1994). Pieces of the puzzle: The jigsaw method. In S. Sharan (Ed.), *Handbook of cooperative learning methods* (pp. 34–50). Westport, CT: Greenwood Press.

Clarkin, J. F., Levy, K. N., Lenzenweger, M. F., & Kernberg, O. F. (2007). Evaluating three treatments for borderline personality disorder: A multiwave study. *American Journal of Psychiatry, 164*(6), 922–928.

Coccaro, E. F., & Kavoussi, R. J. (1996). Neurotransmitter correlates of impulsive aggression. In D. M. Stoff & R. B. Cairns (Eds.), *Aggression and violence* (pp. 67–86). Mahwah, NJ: Lawrence Erlbaum.

Coccaro, E. F., Fanning, J. R., Phan, K. L., & Lee, R. (2015). Serotonin and impulsive aggression. *CNS Spectrums, 20*(3), 295–302. doi:10.1017/S1092852915000310

Coelho, L. F., Barbosa, D. L., Rizzutti, S., Muszkat, M., Bueno, O. F., & Miranda, M. C. (2015). Use of cognitive behavioral therapy and token economy to alleviate dysfunctional behavior in children with attention-deficit hyperactivity disorder. *Frontiers in Psychiatry, 6*, 167. doi:10.3389/fpsyt.2015.00167

Cohen, L. J. (1997). Rational drug use in the treatment of depression. *Pharmacotherapy, 17*, 45–61.

Cohen, N. J., Eichenbaum, R., Decedo, J. C., & Corkin, S. (1985). Preserved learning capacity in amnesia: Evidence for multiple memory systems. In L. S. Squire & N. Butters (Eds.), *Neuropsychology of memory*, pp. 83–103. New York: Guilford Press.

Cohen, R. A., & Zammitti, E. P. (2016). *Access to care among adults aged 18–64 with serious psychological distress: Early release of estimates from the national health interview survey, 2012–september 2015.* Retrieved from https://www.cdc.gov/nchs/data/nhis/earlyrelease/er_spd_access_2015_f_auer.pdf

Cohen, S. (2005). Keynote presentation at the eight international congress of behavioral medicine: The Pittsburgh common cold studies: Psychosocial predictors of susceptibility to respiratory infectious illness. *International Journal of Behavioral Medicine, 12*(3), 123–131. doi:10.1207/s15327558ijbm1203_1

Cohen, S., Doyle, W. J., & Skoner, D. P. (1999). Psychological stress, cytokine production, and severity of upper respiratory illness. *Psychosomatic Medicine, 61*(2), 175–180.

Cohen, S., & Herbert, T. B. (1996). Health psychology: Psychological factors and physical disease from the perspective of human psychoneuroimmunology. *Annual Review of Psychology, 47*, 113–142.

Cohen, S., Frank, E., Doyle, B. J., Skoner, D. P., Rabin, B. S., & Gwaltney, J. M. (1998). Types of stressors that increase susceptibility to the common cold. *Health Psychology, 17*, 214–223.

Cohen, S., Janicki-Deverts, D., Doyle, W. J., Miller, G. E., Frank, E. Rabin, B. S., & Turner, R. B. (2012). Chronic stress, glucocorticoid receptor resistance, inflammation, and disease risk. *Proceedings of the National Academy of Sciences of the United States of America, 109*(16), 5995–5999.

Cohen, S., Janicki-Deverts, D., & Miller, G. E. (2007). Psychological stress and disease. *Journal of the American Medical Association, 298*(14), 1685–1687. doi:10.1001/jama.298.14.1685

Cohen, S., Murphy, M. L. M., & Prather, A. A. (2019). Ten surprising facts about stressful life events and disease risk. *Annual Review of Psychology, 70*, 7.1–7.21. doi:10.1146/annurev-psych-010418-102857

Cohen, S., Tyrrell, D. A., & Smith, A. P. (1991). Psychological stress and susceptibility to the common cold. *New England Journal of Medicine, 325*, 606–612.

Colcombe, S. J., Erickson, K. I., Raz, N., Webb, A. G., Cohen, N. J., McAuley, E., & Kramer, A. F. (2003). Aerobic fitness reduces brain tissue loss in aging humans. *Journal of Gerontology Series A: Biological Sciences and Medical Sciences, 58*, 176–180.

Cole, S. W., Arevalo, J. M. G., Takahashi, R., Sloan, E. K., Lutgendorf, S. K., Sood, A. K., Sheridan, J. F., & Seeman, T. E. (2010). Computational identification of gene-social environment interaction oat the human IL6 locus. *Proceedings of the National Academy of Sciences of the United States of America.* Retrieved September 27, 2010, from http://www.pnas.org/content/107/12/5681.full.

Colligan, J. (1983). Musical creativity and social rules in four cultures. *Creative Child and Adult Quarterly, 8*, 39–44.

Collin, S. H. P., Milivojevic, B., & Doeller, C. F. (2015). Memory hierarchies map onto the hippocampal long axis in humans. *Nature Neuroscience, 18*, 1562–1564.

Collins, A. M., & Loftus, E. F. (1975). A spreading activation theory of semantic processing. *Psychological Review, 82*, 407–428.

Collins, A. M., & Quillian, M. R. (1969). Retrieval time from semantic memory. *Journal of Verbal Learning and Verbal Behaviour, 8*, 240–247.

Collins, C. J., Hanges, P. J., & Locke, E. A. (2004). The relationship of achievement motivation to entrepreneurial behavior: A meta-analysis. *Human Performance, 17*(1), 95–117.

Colom, R., Privado, J., García, L. F., Estrada, E., Cuevas, L., & Shih, P-C. (2015). Fluid intelligence and working memory capacity: Is the time for working on intelligence problems relevant for explaining their large relationship? *Personality and Individual Differences, 79*, 75–80. doi: 10.1016/j.paid.2015.01.051

Colom, R., Shih, P. C., Flores-Mendoza, C., & Quiroga, M. A. (2006). The real relationship between short-term memory and working memory. *Memory, 14*(7), 804–813.

Columbo, J., & Mitchell, D. W. (2009). Infant visual habituation. *Neurobiology of Learning and Memory, 92*(2), 225–234.

Committee on Animal Research and Ethics. (2012). Research with animals in psychology. Retrieved October 12, 2012, from www.apa.org/science/animal2.html

Common Sense Media, Inc. (2015). The Common Sense Census: Media Use by Tweens and Teens. Page 15. Retrieved on July 17, 2018 at https://www.commonsensemedia.org/sites/default/files/uploads/research/census_executivesummary.pdf

Cone-Wesson, B. (2005). Prenatal alcohol and cocaine exposure: Influences on cognition, speech, language, and hearing. *Journal of Communication Disorders, 38*(4), 279–302.

Connor, S., Tenorio, G., Clandinin, M. T., & Sauv, Y. (2012). DHA supplementation enhances high-frequency, stimulation-induced synaptic transmission in mouse hippocampus. *Applied Physiology, Nutrition, and Metabolism, 37*(5), 880–887. doi: 10.1139/h2012-062

Conrad, R., & Hull, A. J. (1964). Information, acoustic confusion, and memory span. *British Journal of Psychology, 55*, 429–432.

Constantine, M. G., Alleyne, V. L., Caldwell, L. D., McRae, M. B., & Suzuki, M. B. (2005). Coping responses of Asian, Black, and Latino/Latina New York City residents following the September 11, 2001 terrorist attacks against the United States. *Cultural Diversity & Ethnic Minority, 11*, 293–308.

Consumer Reports. (1995, November). Mental health: Does psychotherapy help? 734–739.

Conway, G. (2018). Transition of care from childhood to adulthood: Turner syndrome. In M. Polak and P. Touraine (eds), *Transition of Care: From Childhood to Adulthood in Endocrinology, Gynecology, and Diabetes*, pp. 34-35. Basel, Switzerland: Karger Publishers.

Conway, M. A., Cohen, G., & Stanhope, N. (1992). Very long-term memory for knowledge acquired at school and university. *Applied Cognitive Psychology, 6*, 467–482.

Cook, K. (2014). *Kitty Genovese: The murder, the bystanders, the crime that changed America.* New York: W. W. Norton & Co.

Cook, M., & Mineka, S. (1989). Observational conditioning of fear to fear-relevant versus fear-irrelevant stimuli in rhesus monkeys. *Journal of Abnormal Psychology, 98*(4), 448–459.

Coolidge, F. L. (2006). *Dream interpretation as a psychotherapeutic technique.* London: Radcliffe.

Cooper, C., Li, R., Lyketsos, C., & Livingston, G. (2013). Treatment for mild cognitive impairment: Systematic review. *The British Journal of Psychiatry, 203*(4), 255–264.

Cooper, L. A., Gonzales, J. J., Gallo, J. J., Rost, K. M., Meredith, L. S., Rubenstein, L. V., Wang, N. Y., & Ford, D. E. (2003). The acceptability of treatment for depression among African-American, Hispanic, and White primary care patients. *Medical Care, 41*(4), 479–489.

Corballis, M. C. (2009). The evolution and genetics of cerebral asymmetry. *Philosophical Transactions of the Royal Society B: Biological Sciences, 364*(1519), 867–879. doi: 10.1098/rstb.2008.0232

Corbett, G. (2016). Motivational interviewing. In I. Marini & M. A. Stebnicki (Eds.), *The professional counselor's desk reference* (2nd ed., pp. 235–239). New York: Springer Publishing.

Corbetta, M., Kincade, M. J., Lewis, C., Snyder, A. Z., & Sapir, A. (2005). Neural basis and recovery of spatial attention deficits in spatial neglect. *Nature Neuroscience, 8*, 1603–1610.

Cormier, J. F., & Thelen, M. H. (1998). Professional skepticism of multiple personality disorder. *Professional Psychology: Research and Practice, 29*, 163–167.

Corr, C. A. (1993). Coping with dying: Lessons that we should and should not learn from the work of Elisabeth Kübler-Ross. *Death Studies, 17*, 69–83.

Corrigan, P. W., Druss, B. G., & Perlick, D. A. (2014). The impact of mental illness stigma on seeking and participating in mental health care. *Psychological Science in the Public Interest, 15*(2), 37–70. doi:10.1177/1529100614531398

Cosgrove, G. R., & Rauch, S. L. (1995). Psychosurgery. *Neurosurgery Clinics of North America, 6*, 167–176.

Cosmides, L., & Tooby, J. (2013). Evolutionary psychology: New perspectives on cognition and motivation. *Annual Review of Psychology, 64*, 201–229.

Costa, J., Pinto-Gouveia, J., & Maroco, J. (2016). Chronic pain experience on depression and physical disability: The importance of acceptance and mindfulness-based processes in a sample with rheumatoid arthritis. *Journal of Health Psychology*, 1359105316649785. doi:10.1177/1359105316649785

Costa, P. T., Jr., & McCrae, R. R. (2000). The Revised NEO Personality Inventory (NEO PI-R). In S. R. Briggs, J. Cheek & E. M. Donahue (Eds.), *Handbook of personality inventories*, pp. 410–413. New York: Plenum.

Costa, P. T., Jr., McCrae, R. R., & Lockenhoff, C. E. (2018). Personality across the life span. *Annual Review of Psychology*. doi: 10.1146/annurev-psych-010418-103244

Costello, D. M., Swendsen, J., Rose, J. S., & Dierker, L. C. (2008). Risk and protective factors associated with trajectories of depressed mood from adolescence to early adulthood. *Journal of Consulting and Clinical Psychology, 76*(2), 173–183.

Couperus, J. W., & Nelson, C. A. (2006). Early brain development and plasticity. In K. McCartney & D. Phillips (Eds.), *The Blackwell handbook of early childhood development* (pp. 85–105). Oxford, UK: Blackwell Press.

Courage, M. L., & Howe, M. L. (2002). From infant to child: The dynamics of cognitive change in the second year of life. *Psychological Bulletin, 128*, 250–277.

Cowan, N. (1988). Evolving conceptions of memory storage, selective attention, and their mutual constraints within the human information processing system. *Psychological Bulletin, 104*, 163–191.

Cowan, N. (2001). The magical number 4 in short-term memory: A reconsideration of mental storage capacity. *Behavioral and Brain Sciences, 24*, 97–185.

Cowan, N., Elliott, E. M., Saults, J. S., Morey, C. C., Mattox, S., Hismjatullina, A., & Conway, A. R. A. (2005). On the capacity of attention: Its estimation and its role in working memory and cognitive aptitudes. *Cognitive Psychology, 51*(1), 42–100.

Cowings, P. S., Toscano, W. B., Reschke, M. F., & Tsehay, A. (2018). Psychophysiological assessment and correction of spatial disorientation during simulated orion spacecraft re-entry. *International Journal of Psychophysiology*. doi:10.1016/.ijpsycho.2018.03.001

Craddock, N., O'Donovan, M. C., & Owen, M. J. (2005). The genetics of schizophrenia and bipolar disorder: Dissecting psychosis. *Journal of Medical Genetics, 42*, 288–299.

Craighead, W. E., & Dunlop, B. W. (2014). Combination psychotherapy and antidepressant medication treatment for depression: For whom, when, and how. *Annual Review of Psychology, 65*, 267–300. doi: 10.1146/annurev.psych.121208.131653

Craighead, W. E., Johnson, B. N., Carey, S., & Dunlop, B. W. (2015). Psychosocial treatments for major depressive disorder. In P. E. Nathan & J. M. Gorman (Eds.), *A guide to treatments that work* (4th ed., pp. 381–408). New York, NY: Oxford University Press.

Craik, F. I. M. (1970). The fate of primary memory items in free recall. *Journal of Verbal Learning and Verbal Behavior, 9*, 143–148.

Craik, F. I. M. (1994). Memory changes in normal aging. *Current Directions in Psychological Science, 3*(5), 155–158.

Craik, F. I. M., & Lockhart, R. S. (1972). Levels of processing. A framework for memory research. *Journal of Verbal Learning and Verbal Behaviour, 11*, 671–684.

Craik, F. I. M., & Tulving, E. (1975). Depth of processing and the retention of words in episodic memory. *Journal of Experimental Psychology: General, 104*, 268–294.

Cramer, J. W., Bartz, P. J., Simpson, P. M., & Zangwill, S. D. (2014). The spectrum of congenital heart disease and outcomes after surgical repair among children with Turner syndrome: A single-center review. *Pediatric Cardiology, 35*, 253.

Craske, M.G., & Barlow, D.H. (2014). Panic disorder and agoraphobia. In D. H. Barlow (Ed.), *Clinical handbook of psychological disorders: A step-by-step treatment manual* (5th ed., pp. 1–61). New York, NY: The Guilford Press.

Crawford, M., & Unger, R. (2004). *Women and gender: A feminist psychology* (4th ed.). Boston: McGraw-Hill.

Creed, M., Pascoli, V. J., & Lüscher, C. (2015). Refining deep brain stimulation to emulate optogenetic treatment of synaptic pathology. *Science, 347*(6222), 659–664. doi: 10.1126/science.1260776

Cremers, H., van Tol, M. J., Roelofs, K., Aleman, A., Zitman, F. G., van Buchem, M. A., ... van der Wee, N. J. (2011). Extraversion is linked to volume of the orbitofrontal cortex and amygdala. *PLoS ONE, 6*(12), e28421. doi: 10.1371/journal.pone.0028421

Creswell, J. D., Bursley, J. K., & Satpute, A. B. (2013). Neural reactivation links unconscious thought to decision-making performance. *Social Cognitive and Affective Neuroscience, 8*(8), 863–869. doi: 10.1093/scan/nst004

Creswell, J. D., Pacilio, L. E., Lindsay, E. K., & Brown, K. W. (2014). Brief mindfulness meditation training alters psychological and neuroendocrine responses to social evaluative stress. *Psychoneuroendocrinology, 44*, 1–12.

Crick, F., & Koch, C. (1990). Towards a neurobiological theory of consciousness. *Seminars in the Neurosciences, 2*, 263–275.

Crick, F., & Koch, C. (2003). A framework for consciousness. *Nature Neuroscience, 6*, 119–127.

Critchfield, T. S., Haley, R., Sabo, B., Colbert, J., & Macropoulis, G. (2003). A half century of scalloping in the work habits of the United States Congress. *Journal of Applied Behavior Analysis, 36*(4), 465–486.

Crowley, A. E., & Hoyer, W. D. (1994). An integrative framework for understanding two-sided persuasion. *Journal of Consumer Research, 20*, 561–574.

Csikszentmihalyi, M. (1996). *Creativity: Flow and the psychology of discovery and invention.* New York: Harper Perennial.

Csikszentmihalyi, M. (1997). *Finding flow: The psychology of engagement with everyday life.* New York: Basic Books.

Cua, A. B., Wilhelm, K. P., & Maibach, H. I. (1990). Elastic properties of human skin: Relation to age, sex and anatomical region. *Archives of Dermatology Research, 282*, 283–288.

Cuellar, N. G., Whisenant, D., & Stantoon, M. P. (2015). Hypnic jerks: A scoping literature review. *Sleep Medicine Clinics, 10*(3), 393–401.

Cuijpers, P., Sijbrandij, M., Koole, S. L., Andersson, G., Beekman, A. T., & Reynolds, C. F., 3rd. (2014). Adding psychotherapy to antidepressant medication in depression and anxiety disorders: A meta-analysis. *World Psychiatry, 13*(1), 56–67. doi:10.1002/wps.20089

Culbert, K. M., Racine, S. E., & Klump, K. L. (2015). Research review: What we have learned about the causes of eating disorders - a synthesis of sociocultural, psychological, and biological research. *Journal of Child Psychology and Psychiatry and Allied Disciplines, 56*(11), 1141–1164. doi:10.1111/jcpp.12441

Culver, N. C., Vervliet, B., & Craske, M. G. (2015). Compound extinction: Using the Rescorla-Wagner model to maximize exposure therapy effects for anxiety disorders. *Clinical Psychological Science, 3*(3), 335–348. doi: 10.1177/2167702614542103

Cummings, J. L., & Coffey C. E. (1994). Neurobiological basis of behavior. In C. E. Coffey & J. L. Cummings (Eds.), *Textbook of geriatric neuropsychiatry* (pp. 72–96). Washington, DC: American Psychiatric Press.

Cummings, S. R., & Melton, L. J., III. (2002). Epidemiology and outcomes of osteoporotic fractures. *Lancet, 359*(9319), 1761–1767.

Curtis, R. C., & Miller, K. (1986). Believing another likes or dislikes you: Behaviors making the beliefs come true. *Journal of Personality and Social Psychology, 51*, 284–290.

Curtis, R. G., Windsor, T. D., & Soubelet, A. (2015). The relationship between Big-5 personality traits and cognitive ability in older adults—A review. *Aging, Neuropsychology, and Cognition: A Journal on Normal and Dysfunctional Development, 22*(1), 42–71. doi: 10.1080/13825585.2014.888392

Curtis, R. H. (1993). *Great lives: Medicine*. New York: Charles Scribner's Sons Books for Young Readers.

Cuthbert, B. N. (2014). The RDoC framework: Facilitating transition from icd/dsm to dimensional approaches that integrate neuroscience and psychopathology. *World Psychiatry, 13*(1), 23–35. doi: http://doi.org/10.1002/wps.20087

Czeisler, C. A. (1995). The effect of light on the human circadian pacemaker. In D. J. Chadwick & K. Ackrill (Eds.), *Circadian clocks and their adjustment* (pp. 254–302). West Sussex, England: John Wiley & Sons.

Czeisler, C. A., Moore-Ede, M. C., & Coleman, R. M. (1982). Rotating shift work schedules that disrupt sleep are improved by applying circadian principles. *Science, 217*, 460–463.

Czeisler, C. A., Weitzman, E. D., Moore-Ede, M. C., Zimmerman, J. C., & Knauer, R. S. (1980). Human sleep: Its duration and organization depend on its circadian phase. *Science, 210*, 1264–1267.

Dabbs, J. M., Jr., Bernieri, F. J., Strong, R. K., Campo, R., & Milun, R. (2001). Going on stage: Testosterone in greetings and meetings. *Journal of Research in Personality, 35*, 27–40.

D'Agata, F., Peila, E., Cicerale, A., Caglio, M. M., Caroppo, P., Vighetti, S.,... Massazza, G. (2016). Cognitive and neurophysiological effects of non-invasive brain stimulation in stroke patients after motor rehabilitation. *Frontiers in Behavioral Neuroscience, 10*, 135. doi:10.3389/fnbeh.2016.00135

Dahl, R. E., & Lewin, D. S. (2002). Pathways to adolescent health: Sleep regulation and behavior. *Journal of Adolescent Health, 31*, 175–184.

Daiello, L. A., Gongvatana, A., Dunsiger, S., Cohen, R. A., & Ott, B. R. (2014). Association of fish oil supplement use with preservation of brain volume and cognitive function. *Alzheimer's & Dementia, 11*(2), 226–235.

Dalenberg, C. J. (1996). Accuracy, timing and circumstances of disclosure in therapy of recovered and continuous memories of abuse. *The Journal of Psychiatry and Law, 24*(2), 229–275.

Dalenberg, C. J., Brand, B. L., Gleaves, D. H., Dorahy, M. J., Loewenstein, R. J., Cardena, E.,... Spiegel, D. (2012). Evaluation of the evidence for the trauma and fantasy models of dissociation. *Psychological Bulletin, 138*(3), 550–588. doi:10.1037/a0027447

Dallman, M., Pecoraro, N., Akana, S., la Fleur, S. E., Gomez, F., Houshyar, H., Bell, M. E., Bhatnagar, S., Laugero, K. D., & Manalo, S. (2003). Chronic stress and obesity: A new view of "comfort food." *Proceedings of the National Academy of Sciences, USA, 100*(20), 11696–11701.

Daly, M., Wilson, M., & Weghorst, S. J. (1982). Male sexual jealousy. *Ethology and Sociobiology, 3*, 11–27.

Damasio, H., Grabowski, T., Frank, R., Galaburda, A. M., & Damasion, A. R. (1994). The return of Phineas Gage: Clues about the brain from the skull of a famous patient. *Science, 264*, 1102–1105.

Damian, R. I., & Roberts, B. W. (2015). Settling the debate on birth order and personality. *Proceedings of the National Academy of Sciences of the United States of America, 112*(46), 14119–14120. doi: 10.1073/pnas.1519064112

Dani, J., Burrill, C., & Demmig-Adams, B. (2005). The remarkable role of nutrition in learning and behavior. *Nutrition & Food Science, 35*(4), 258–263.

Darley, J. M., & Latané, B. (1968). Bystander intervention in emergencies: Diffusion of responsibility. *Journal of Personality and Social Psychology, 8*, 377–383.

Darvill, T., Lonky, E., Reihman, J., Stewart, P., & Pagano, J. (2000). Prenatal exposure to PCBs and infant performance on the Fagan test of infant intelligence. *Neurotoxicology, 21*(6), 1029–1038.

Darwin, C. (1859). *The origin of species by means of natural selection*. London: John Murray.

Darwin, C. (1898). *The expression of the emotions in man and animals*. New York: D. Appleton.

Daum, I., & Schugens, M. M. (1996). On the cerebellum and classical conditioning. *Current Directions in Psychological Science, 5*, 58–61.

David, D., Lynn, S. J., & Montgomery, G. H. (2018). An introduction to the science and practice of evidence-based psychotherapy: A framework for evaluation and a way forward. In D. David, S. J. Lynn, & G. H. Montgomery (Eds.), *Evidence-based psychotherapy: The state of the science and practice* (pp. 1–10). Hoboken, NJ: John WIley & Sons, Inc.

David, P. S., Kling, J. M., Vegunta, S., Faubion, S. S., Kapoor, E., Mara, K. C., Schroeder, D. R., Hilsaca, K. F., & Kuhle, C. L. (2018). Vasomotor symptoms in women over 60: Results from the Data Registry on Experiences of Aging, Menopause, and Sexuality (DREAMS). *Menopause, 25*(10): 1105-1109. DOI: https://doi.org/10.1097/GME.0000000000001126

Davidson, R. J. (2003). Affective neuroscience and psychophysiology: Toward a synthesis. *Psychophysiology, 40*(5), 655–665.

Davidson, R. J., Kabat-Zinn, J., Schumacher, J., Rosenkranz, M., Muller, D., Santorelli, S.,... Sheridan, J. (2003). Alterations in brain and immune function produced by mindfulness meditation. *Psychosomatic Medicine, 65*, 564–570.

Davidson, R. J., Putman, K. M., & Larson, C. L. (2000). Dysfunction in the neural circuitry of emotion regulation—A possible prelude to violence. *Science, 289*, 591–594.

Davies, I. R. L., Laws, G., Corbett, G. G., & Jerrett, D. J. (1998a). Cross-cultural differences in colour vision: Acquired "colour blindness" in Africa. *Personality and Individual Differences, 25*, 1153–1162.

Davies, I. R. L., Sowden, P., Jerrett, D. T., Jerrett, T., & Corbett, G. G. (1998b). A cross-cultural study of English and Setswana speakers on a colour triads task: A test of the Sapir-Whorf hypothesis. *British Journal of Psychology, 89*, 1–15.

Davis, C. J., Harding, J. W., & Wright, J. W. (2003). REM sleep deprivation induced deficits in the latency-to-peak induction and maintenance of longterm potentiation within the CA1 region of hippocampus. *Brain Research, 973*, 293–297.

Davis, J. O., Phelps, J. A., & Bracha, H. S. (1995). Prenatal development of monozygotic twins and concordance for schizophrenia. *Schizophrenia Bulletin, 21*, 357–366.

Davis, K. F., Parker, K. P., & Montgomery, G. (2004). Sleep in infants and young children: Part 1: Normal sleep. *Journal of Pediatric Healthcare, 18*(2), 65–71.

Davis, O. S. P., Haworth, C. M. A., Lewis, C. M., & Plomin, R. (2012). Visual analysis of geocoded twin data puts nature and nurture on the map. *Molecular Psychiatry, 17*, 867–874. doi: 10.1038/mp.2012.68

Davis, T. E., Ollendick, T. H., & Ost, L. G. (2018). One-session treatment of phobias in children: Recent developments and a systematic review. *Annual Review of Clinical Psychology*. doi:10.1146/annurev-clinpsy-050718-095608

Day, E. (2015). #BlackLivesMatter: The birth of a new civil rights movement. The Guardian, Sunday July 19, 2015. Retrieved from http://www.theguardian.com/world/2015/jul/19/blacklivesmatter-birth-civil-rights-movement

de Bruin, A., Treccani, B., & Della Sala, S. (2015). Cognitive advantage in bilingualism: An example of publication bias? *Psychological Science, 26*(1), 99–107. doi: 10.1177/0956797614557866

De Camp, J. E. (1917). The influence of color on apparent weight. A preliminary study. *Journal of Experimental Psychology: General, 2*(5), 347–370. doi:dx.doi.org/10.1037/h0075903

de Mooij, S. M. M., Henson, R. N. A., Waldorp, L. J., Cam, C. A. N., & Kievit, R. A. (2018). Age differentiation within grey matter, white matter and between memory and white matter in an adult lifespan cohort. *Journal of Neuroscience*. doi:10.1523/JNEUROSCI.1627-17.2018

De Valois, R. L., & De Valois, K. K. (1993). A multi-stage color model. *Vision Research, 33*(8), 1053–1065.

Dean, G., & Kelly, I. W. (2000). Does astrology work? Astrology and skepticism 1975–2000. In P. Kurtz (Ed.), *Skepticism: A 25 Year Retrospective* (pp. 191–207). Amherst, NY: Prometheus Books.

Deasy, C., Coughlan, B., Pironom, J., Jourdan, D., & Mannix-McNamara, P. (2014). Psychological distress and coping amongst higher education students: A mixed method enquiry. *PLoS ONE, 9*(12), e115193. doi:10.1371/journal.pone.0115193

Dêbiec, J., Díaz-Mataix, L., Bush, D. E. A., Doyère, V., & LeDoux, J. E. (2010). The amygdala encodes specific sensory features of an aversive reinforcer. *Nature Neuroscience, 13*, 536–537.

DeCasper, A. J., & Fifer, W. P. (1980). Of human bonding: Newborns prefer their mothers' voices. *Science, 208*, 1174–1176.

DeCasper, A. J., & Spence, M. J. (1986). Prenatal maternal speech influence on newborns' perception of sounds. *Infant Behaviour and Development, 9*, 133–150.

deCharms, R. (1968). *Personal causation*. New York: Academic Press.

Deci, E. L., & Ryan, R. M. (1985). *Intrinsic motivation and self-determination in human behavior*. New York: Plenum.

Deci, E. L., Eghrari, H., Patrick, B. C., & Leone, D. R. (1994). Facilitating internalization: The self-determination theory perspective. *Journal of Personality, 62*, 119–142.

Deci, E. L., Koestner, R., & Ryan, R. M. (1999). A meta-analytic review of experiments examining the effects of extrinsic rewards on intrinsic motivation. *Psychological Bulletin, 125*, 627–668.

DeCoster, J., & Claypool, H. M. (2004). A meta-analysis of priming effects on impression formation supporting a general model of informational biases. *Personality and Social Psychology Review, 8*(1), 2–27.

Defenderfer, J., Kerr-German, A., Hedrick, M., & Buss, A. T. (2017). Investigating the role of temporal lobe activation in speech perception accuracy with normal hearing adults: An event-related fNIRS study. *Neuropsychologia, 106*, 31–41. doi:10.1016/j.neuropsychologia.2017.09.004

Deger, M., Helias, M., Rotter, S., & Diesmann, M. (2012). Spike-timing dependence of structural plasticity explains cooperative synapse formation in the neocortex. *PLoS Computational Biology, 8*(9), e1002689. doi: 10.1371/journal.pcbi.1002689

DeGrandpre, R. J. (2000). A science of meaning: Can behaviorism bring meaning to psychological science? *American Psychologist, 55*, 721–739.

Deinzer, R., Kleineidam, C. H., Winkler, R., Idel, H., & Bachg, D. (2000). Prolonged reduction of salivary immunoglobulin A (sIgA) after a major academic exam. *International Journal of Psychophysiology, 37*, 219–232.

Delagrange, P., & Guardiola-Lemaitre, B. (1997). Melatonin, its receptors, and relationships with biological rhythm disorders. *Cliinnical Neuropharmacology, 20*, 482–510.

Delaney, A. J., Crane, J. W., & Sah, P. (2007). Noradrenaline modulates transmission at a central synapse by a presynaptic mechanism. *Neuron, 56*(6), 880–892.

Delfiner, R. (2001, November 16). Kitty left at death's door. *New York Post*.

DeLongis, A., Lazarus, R. S., & Folkman, S. (1988). The impact of daily stress on health and mood: Psychological and social resources as mediators. *Journal of Personality and Social Psychology, 54*(3), 486–495.

Dement, W. C. (1960). The effect of dream deprivation. *Science, 131*, 1705–1707.

Dement, W. C., Henry, P., Cohen, H., & Ferguson, J. (1969). Studies on the effect of REM deprivation in humans and animals. In K. H. Pribram (Ed.), *Mood, states, and mind*. Baltimore: Penguin.

Dempster, F. N., & Farris, R. (1990). The spacing effect: Research and practice. *Journal of Research and Development in Education 23*(2), 97–101.

Deng, L. X., Deng, P., Ruan, Y., Xu, Z. C., Liu, N. K., Wen, X.,... Xu, X. M. (2013). A novel growth-promoting pathway formed by GDNF-overexpressing Schwann cells promotes propriospinal axonal regeneration, synapse formation, and partial recovery of function after spinal cord injury. *The Journal of Neuroscience, 33*(13), 5655–5667. doi: 10.1523/jneurosci.2973-12.2013

Deng, L. X., Walker, C., & Xu, X. M. (2015). Schwann cell transplantation and descending propriospinal regeneration after spinal cord injury. *Brain Research, 1619*, 104–114. doi:10.1016/j.brainres.2014.09.038

Dennett, D. C. (1991). *Consciousness explained*. New York: Little, Brown.

Dennis, C. V., Suh, L. S., Rodriguez, M. L., Kril, J. J., & Sutherland, G. T. (2016). Human adult neurogenesis across the ages: An immunohistochemical study. *Neuropathology and Applied Neurobiology, 42*(7), 621–638. doi:10.1111/nan.12337

Denny, L., Coles, S., & Blitz, R. (2017). Fetal alcohol syndrome and fetal alcohol spectrum disorders. American Family Physician, 96(8), 515–522.

Denollet, J. (2005). Ds14: Standard assessment of negative affectivity, social inhibition, and Type D personality. *Psychosomatic Medicine, 67*(1), 89–97. doi:10.1097/01.psy.0000149256.81953.49

Denollet, J., Schiffer, A. A., & Spek, V. (2010). A general propensity to psychological distress affects cardiovascular outcomes: Evidence from research on the type d (distressed) personality profile. *Circulation: Cardiovascular Quality and Outcomes, 3*(5), 546–557. doi:10.1161/CIRCOUTCOMES.109.934406

Denollet, J., Sys, S. U., & Brutsaert, D. L. (1995). Personality and mortality after myocardial infarction. *Psychosomatic Medicine, 57*(6), 582–591.

Denollet, J., van Felius, R. A., Lodder, P., Mommersteeg, P. M., Goovaerts, I., Possemiers, N.,... Van Craenenbroeck, E. M. (2018). Predictive value of Type D personality for impaired endothelial function in patients with coronary artery disease. *International Journal of Cardiology, 259*, 205–210. doi:10.1016/j.ijcard.2018.02.064

Denys, D., Mantione, M., Figee, M., van den Munckhof, P., Koerselman, F., Westenberg, H.,... Schuurman, R. (2010). Deep brain stimulation of the nucleus accumbens for treatment-refractory obsessive-compulsive disorder. *Archives of General Psychiatry, 67*(10), 1061–1068. doi: 10.1001/archgenpsychiatry.2010.122

Department of Veterans Affairs Department of Defense. (2017). *Va/dod clinical practice guideline for the management of posttraumatic stress disorder and acute stress disorder*. Retrieved from https://www.healthquality.va.gov/guidelines/MH/ptsd/VADoDPTSDCPGFinal012418.pdf

Deregowski, J. B. (1969). Perception of the two-pronged trident by two- and three-dimensional perceivers. *Journal of Experimental Psychology, 82*, 9–13.

DeStefano, F., Price, C. S., & Weintraub, E. S. (2013). Increasing exposure to antibody-stimulating proteins and polysaccharides in vaccines is not associated with risk of autism. *The Journal of Pediatrics, 163*(2), 561-567. doi:10.1016/j.jpeds.2013.02.001

Devitt, A. L., & Schacter, D. L. (2018). An optimistic outlook creates a rosy past: The impact of episodic simulation on subsequent memory. *Psychological Science, 29*(6): 936-946. DOI: https://doi.org/10.1177%2F0956797617753936

DeYoung, C. G. (2010). Personality neuroscience and the biology of traits. *Social and Personality Psychology Compass, 4*(12), 1165–1180. doi: 10.1111/j.1751-9004.2010.00327.x

DeYoung, C. G. (2015). Cybernetic Big Five theory. *Journal of Research in Personality, 56*, 33–58. doi: 10.1016/j.jrp.2014.07.004

DeYoung, C. G., Hirsh, J. B., Shane, M. S., Papademetris, X., Rajeevan, N., & Gray, J. R. (2010). Testing predictions from personality neuroscience: Brain structure and the Big Five. *Psychological Science, 21*(6), 820–828. doi: 10.1177/0956797610370159

DeYoung, C. G., Quilty, L. C., Peterson, J. B., & Gray, J. R. (2014). Openness to experience, intellect, and cognitive ability. *Journal of Personality Assessment, 96*(1), 46–52. doi: 10.1080/00223891.2013.806327

Diamond, D. A., Swartz, J., Tishelman, A., Johnson, J., & Chan, Y-M. (2018). Management of pediatric patients with DSD and ambiguous genitalia: Balancing the child's moral claims to self-determination with parental values and preferences. *Journal of Pediatric Urology*, available online June 1, 2018. DOI: https://doi.org/10.1016/j.jpurol.2018.04.029

Diamond, L. M. (2003). What does sexual orientation orient? A biobehavioral model distinguishing romantic love and sexual desire. *Psychological Review, 110*, 173–192.

Diamond, M., & Sigmundson, H. K. (1997). Sex reassignment at birth. Long-term review and clinical implications. *Archives of Pediatric Adolescent Medicine, 151*(3), 298–304.

DiazGranados, N., Ibrahim, L. A., Brutsche, N. E., Ameli, R., Henter, I. D., Luckenbaugh, D. A.,... Zarate, C. A., Jr. (2010a). Rapid resolution of suicidal ideation after a single infusion of an N-methyl-D-aspartate antagonist in patients with treatment-resistant major depressive disorder. *The Journal of Clinical Psychiatry, 71*(12), 1605–1611. doi: 10.4088/JCP.09m05327blu

DiazGranados, N., Ibrahim, L., Brutsche, N. E., Newberg, A., Kronstein, P., Khalife, S.,... Zarate, C. A., Jr. (2010b). A randomized add-on trial of an N-methyl-D-aspartate antagonist in treatment-resistant bipolar depression. *Archives of General Psychiatry, 67*(8), 793–802. doi: 10.1001/archgenpsychiatry.2010.90

Dickens, W. T., & Flynn, J. R. (2001 April). Heritability estimates vs. large environmental effects: The IQ paradox resolved. *Psychological Review, 108*(2), 346–369.

Dickerson, F., Ringel, N., Parente, F., & Boronow, J. (1994). Seclusion and restraint, assaultiveness, and patient performance in a token economy. *Hospital and Community Psychiatry, 45*, 168–170.

Dickinson, T. (2015). Exploring the drugs/violence nexus among active offenders: Contributions from the St. Louis School. *Criminal Justice Review, 40*(1), 67–86.

Diener, E., Lusk, R., DeFour, D., & Flax, R. (1980). Deindividuation: Effects of group size, density, number of observers, and group member similarity on self-consciousness and disinhibited behavior. *Journal of Personality and Social Psychology, 39*, 449–459.

Digdon, N. (2017). The Little Albert controversy: Intuition, confirmation bias, and logic. *History of Psychology*. doi: 10.1037/hop0000055

Digdon, N., Powell, R. A., & Harris, B. (2014). Little Albert's alleged neurological impairment: Watson, Rayner, and historical revision. *History of Psychology, 17*(4), 312–324. doi: 10.1037/a0037325

Dijksterhuis, A., & Strick, M. (2016). A case for thinking without consciousness. *Perspectives on Psychological Science, 11*(1), 117–132. doi: 10.1177/1745691615615317

Dijkstra, N., Mostert, P., Lange, F. P., Bosch, S., & van Gerven, M. A. (2018). Differential temporal dynamics during visual imagery and perception. *elife, 7*. doi: 10.7554/eLife.33904

Dillard, J. (1990). Self-inference and the foot-in-the-door technique: Quantity of behavior and attitudinal mediation. *Human Communication Research, 16*, 422–447.

Dillard, J. (1991). The current status of research on sequential–request compliance techniques. *Personality and Social Psychology Bulletin, 17*, 282–288.

Dima, D. C., Perry, G., Messaritaki, E., Zhang, J., & Singh, K. D. (2018). Spatiotemporal dynamics in human visual cortex rapidly encode the emotional content of faces. *Human Brain Mapping*. doi:10.1002/hbm.24226

Dimidjian, S., Hollon, S. D., Dobson, K. S., Schmaling, K. B., Kohlenberg, R. J., Addis, M. E.,... Jacobson, N. S. (2006). Randomized trial of behavioral activation, cognitive therapy, and antidepressant medication in the acute treatment of adults with major depression. *Journal of Consulting and Clinical Psychology, 74*(4), 658–670. doi: 10.1037/0022-006X.74.4.658

Ding, D. C., Chang, Y. H., Shyu, W. C., & Lin, S. Z. (2015). Human umbilical cord mesenchymal stem cells: A new era for stem cell therapy. *Cell Transplantaton, 14*(3), 339–347.

Ding, F., O'Donnell, J., Xu, Q., Kang, N., Goldman, N., & Nedergaard, M. (2016). Changes in the composition of brain interstitial ions control the sleep–wake cycle. *Science, 352*(6285): 550–555. doi: 10.1126/science.aad4821.

Ding, M., Bhupathiraju, S. N., Chen, M., van Dam, R. M., & Hu, F. B. (2014). Caffeinated and decaffeinated coffee consumption and risk of Type 2 diabetes: A systematic review and a dose-response meta-analysis. *Diabetes Care, 37*(2), 569–586.

Ding, M., Satija, A., Bhupathiraju, S. N., Hu, Y., Sun, Q., Han, J., Lopez-Garcia, E., Willett, W., van Dam, R. M., & Hu, F. B. (2015). Association of coffee consumption with total and cause-specific mortality in three large prospective cohorts. *Circulation National Heart Association, 132*, 2305–2315.

Ding, N., Melloni, L., Zhang, H., Tian, X., & Poeppel, D. (2015). Cortical tracking of hierarchical linguistic structures in connected speech. *Nature Neuroscience, 19*(1), 158–164. doi: 10.1038/nn.4186

Dinges, D. F. (1995). An overview of sleepiness and accidents. *Journal of Sleep Research, 4*(2), 4–14.

Dobson, K. S., & Block, L. (1988). Historical and philosophical bases of the cognitive-behavioral therapies. In K. S. Dobson (Ed.), *Handbook of cognitive-behavioral therapies* (pp. 3–38). New York: Guilford Press.

Dolcos, F., LaBar, K. S., Cabeza, R., & Purves, D. (2005). Remembering one year later: Role of the amygdala and the medial temporal lobe memory system in retrieving emotional memories. *Proceedings of the National Academy of Sciences, USA*. doi: 10.1073/pnas.0409848102

Doliński, D., Grzyb, T., Folwarczny, M., Grzybała, P., Krzyszycha, K., Martynowska, K., & Trojanowski, J. (2017). Would you deliver an electric shock in 2015? Obedience in the experimental paradigm developed by Stanley Milgram in the 50 years following the original studies. *Social Psychological and Personality Science, 8*(8), 927–933. doi:10.1177/1948550617693060

Dollard, J., Doob, L. W., Miller, N. E., Mowrer, O. H., & Sears, R. R. (1939). *Frustration and aggression*. New Haven, CT: Yale University Press.

Dollard, J., & Miller, N. F. (1950). *Personality and psychotherapy*. New York: McGraw-Hill.

Domagalski, T. A., & Steelman, L. A. (2007). The impact of gender and organizational status on workplace anger expression. *Management Communication Quarterly, 20*(3), 297–315.

Domhoff, G. W. (1996). *Finding meaning in dreams: A quantitative approach*. New York: Plenum Publishing.

Domhoff, G. W. (2005). The content of dreams: Methodologic and theoretical implications. In M. Kryger, T. Roth, & W. Dement (Eds.), *Principles and practices of sleep medicine* (4th ed., pp. 522–534). Philadelphia: Saunders.

Domhoff, G. W., & Schneider, A. (2008). Similarities and differences in dream content at the cross-cultural, gender, and individual levels. *Consciousness and Cognition, 17*, 1257–1265.

Dominey, P. F., & Dodane, C. (2004). Indeterminacy in language acquisition: The role of child-directed speech and joint attention. *Journal of Neurolinguistics, 17*(2–3), 121–145.

Domjan, M., Cusato, B., & Villarreal, R. (2000). Pavlovian feed-forward mechanisms in the control of social behavior. *Behavioral and Brain Sciences, 23*, 235–282.

Donaldson, Z. R., & Young, L. J. (2008). Oxytocin, vasopressin, and the neurogenetics of sociality. *Science, 322*(5903), 900–904. doi: 10.1126/science.1158668

Donnelly, W. T., Bartlett, D., & Leiter, J. C. (2016). Serotonin in the solitary tract nucleus shortens the laryngeal chemoreflex in anesthetized neonatal rats. *Experimental-Physiology, 101*(7): 946–961. DOI: 10.1113/EP085716

Donohue, S. E., James, B., Eslick, A. N., & Mitroff, S. R. (2012). Cognitive pitfall! Videogame players are not immune to dual-task costs. *Attention, Perception, & Psychophysics, 74*(5), 803–809. doi: 10.3758/s13414-012-0323-y

Donovan, J. J., & Radosevich, D. R. (1999). A meta-analytic review of the distribution of practice effect: Now you see it, now you don't. *Journal of Applied Psychology, 84*, 795–805.

Dorahy, M. J. (2001). Dissociative identity disorder and memory dysfunction: The current state of experimental research and its future directions. *Clinical Psychology Review, 21*(5), 771–795.

Dorahy, M. J., Brand, B. L., Sar, V., Kruger, C., Stavropoulos, P., Martinez-Taboas, A.,... Middleton, W. (2014). Dissociative identity disorder: An empirical overview. *Australian and New Zealand Journal of Psychiatry, 48*(5), 402–417. doi: 10.1177/0004867414527523

Doron, K. W., Bassett, D. S., & Gazzaniga, M. S. (2012). Dynamic network structure of interhemispheric coordination. *Proceedings of the National Academy of Sciences of the United States of America, 109*(46), 18661–18668. doi:10.1073/pnas.1216402109

Doubilet, P. M., Benson, C. B., Bourne, T., & Blaivas, M. (2013). Diagnostic criteria for nonviable pregnancy early in the first trimester. *The New England Journal of Medicine, 369*(15),1443–1451.

Dove, A. (1971). The "Chitling" Test. In L. R. Aiken Jr. (Ed.), *Psychological and educational testings*. Boston: Allyn and Bacon.

Downs, J. F. (1984). *The Navajo*. Prospect Heights, IL: Waveland Press, International.

Drenth, P. J., Thierry, H., Willems, P. J., & de Wolff, C. J. (1984). *Handbook of work and organizational psychology*. Chichester, England: John Wiley and Sons.

Druckman, D., & Bjork, R. A. (Eds.). (1994). *Learning, remembering, believing: Enhancing human performance*. (Study conducted by the National Research Council). Washington, DC: National Academy Press.

Drugan, A., & Weissman, A. (2017). Multi-fetal pregnancy reduction (MFPR) to twins or singleton – medical justification and ethical slippery slope. *Journal of Perinatal Medicine, 45*(2): 181–184. DOI: https://10.1515/jpm-2016-005

Du, L., Shan, L., Wang, B., Li, H., Xu, Z., Staal, W. G., & Jia, F. (2015). A pilot study on the combination of applied behavior analysis and bumetanide treatment for children with autism. *Journal of Child and Adolescent Psychopharmacology, 25*(7), 585–588.

Duben, A., & Behar, C. (1991). *Istanbul households: Marriage, family and fertility 1880–1940*. Cambridge, NY: Cambridge University Press.

Dubern, B., & Clement, K. (2012). Leptin and leptin receptor-related monogenic obesity. *Biochimie, 94*(10), 2111–2115.

Dubowitz, H., & Bennett, S. (2007). Physical abuse and neglect of children. *Lancet, 369*(9576), 1891–1899.

Duckworth, A. L., Quinn, P. D., Lynam, D. R., Loeber, R., & Stouthamer-Loeber, M. (2011). Role of test motivation in intelligence testing. *Proceedings of the National Academy of Sciences, 108*(19), 7716–7720. doi: 10.1073/pnas.1018601108

Duckworth, A. L., & Seligman, M. E. P. (2005). Self-discipline outdoes IQ in predicting academic performance of adolescents. *Psychological Science, 16*(12), 939–944. doi: 10.1111/j.1467-9280.2005.01641.x

Dudai, Y. (2004). The neurobiology of consolidations, or, how stable is the engram? *Annual Review of Psychology, 55*, 51–86.

Duffy, A., Goodday, S., Keown-Stoneman, C., & Grof, P. (2018). The emergent course of bipolar disorder: Observations over two decades from the Canadian high-risk offspring cohort. *American Journal of Psychiatry*, appiajp201818040461. doi:10.1176/appi.ajp.2018.18040461

Duggan, M., Ellilson, N. B., Lampe, C., Lenhart, A., & Madden, M. (2015). Demographics of key social networking platforms. Pew Research Center: Social Media Update 2014. Retrieved from http://www.pewinternet.org/2015/01/09/demographics-of-key-social-networking-platforms-2/

Duker, P. C., & Seys, D. M. (1996). Long-term use of electrical aversion treatment with self-injurious behaviors. *Research in Developmental Disabilities, 17*, 293–301.

Duman, R. S., & Aghajanian, G. K. (2012). Synaptic dysfunction in depression: Potential therapeutic targets. *Science, 338*(6103), 68–72. doi: 10.1126/science.1222939

Dumas, J. A. (2017). Strategies for preventing cognitive decline in healthy older adults. *The Canadian Journal of Psychiatry, 62*(11): 754–760. DOI: https://doi.org/10.1177%2F0706743717720691

Dumont, F. (2010). *A history of personality psychology*. New York: Cambridge University Press.

Duncan, R. M. (1995). Piaget and Vygotsky revisited: Dialogue or assimilation? *Developmental Review, 15*, 458–472.

Dunn, D. S., & Halonen, J. S. (2017). *The psychology major's companion: Everything you need to know to get you where you want to go*. New York, NY: Worth Publishers.

Dunn, J. C., Whelton, W. J., & Sharpe, D. (2006). Maladaptive perfectionism, hassles, coping, and psychological distress in university professors. *Journal of Counseling Psychology, 53*(4), 511–523.

Durrant, J., & Ensom, R. (2012). Physical punishment of children: Lessons from 20 years of research. *Canadian Medical Association Journal, 184*(12), 1373–1377. doi: 10.1503/cmaj.101314

Durrant, M. (Ed.). (1993). *Aristotle's De anima in focus*. London: Routledge.

Durso, F., Rea, C., & Dayton, T. (1994). Graph-theoretic confirmation of restructuring during insight. *Psychological Science, 5*, 94–98.

Dwairy, M. (2004). Parenting styles and mental health of Palestinian-Arab adolescents in Israel. *Transcultural Psychiatry, 41*(2), 233–252.

Dweck, C. (1986). Motivational processes affecting learning. *American Psychologist, 41*(10), 1040–1048.

Dweck, C., & Elliott, E. (1983). Achievement motivation. In P. Mussen (Ed.), *Handbook of child psychology: Vol. 4. Socialization, personality, and social development* (pp. 643–691). New York: Wiley.

Dweck, C. S. (1999). *Self-theories: Their role in motivation, personality and development*. Philadelphia: Psychology Press.

Dweck, C. S., & Leggett, E. L. (1988). A social-cognitive approach to motivation and personality. *Psychological Review, 95*, 256–273.

Dweck, C. S., & Molden, D. C. (2008). Self-theories: The construction of free will. In J. Baer, J. C. Kaufman, & R. F. Baumeister (Eds.), *Are we free? Psychology and free will* (pp. 44–64). New York: Oxford University Press.

Dweck, C. S., Chiu, C., & Hong, Y. (1995). Implicit theories and their role in judgments and reactions: A world from two perspectives. *Psychological Inquiry, 6*, 267–285.

Dykens, E. M., Hodapp, R. M., & Leckman, J. F. (1994). *Behavior and development in fragile X syndrome*. Thousand Oaks, CA: Sage.

Eagleman, D. M. (2001). Visual illusions and neurobiology. *Nature reviews: Neuroscience, 2*(12), 920–926.

Eagly, A. H. (1987). *Sex difference in social behavior: A social-role interpretation*. Hillsdale, NJ: Lawrence Erlbaum.

Eagly, A. H., Ashmore, R. D., Makhijani, M. G., & Longo, L. C. (1991). What is beautiful is good, but...: A meta-analytic review of the physical attractiveness stereotype. *Psychological Bulletin, 110*, 109–128.

Eagly, A. H., & Carli, L. L. (2007). *Through the labyrinth: The truth about how women become leaders*. Boston: Harvard Business School Press.

Eagly, A. H., & Chaiken, S. (1975). An attribution analysis of the effect of communicator characteristics on opinion change: The case of communicator attractiveness. *Journal of Personality and Social Psychology, 37*, 136–144.

Eagly, A. H., & Chaiken, S. (1993). *The psychology of attitudes*. Fort Worth, TX: Harcourt Brace.

Eagly, A. H., & Chaiken, S. (1998). Attitude structure and function. In D. T. Gilbert, S. T. Fiske, & G. Lindzey (Eds.), *The handbook of social psychology* (4th ed., pp. 269–322). New York: McGraw-Hill.

Eagly, A. H., & Crowley, M. (1986). Gender and helping behavior: A meta-analytic review of the social psychological literature. *Psychological Bulletin, 100*, 283–308.

Eagly, A. H., Wood, W., & Diekman, A. B. (2000). Social role theory of sex differences and similarities: A current appraisal. In T. Eckes & H. M. Trautner (Eds.), *The developmental social psychology of gender* (pp. 123–174). Mahwah, NJ: Lawrence Erlbaum.

Eaker, E. D., & Castelli, W. P. (1988). Type A behavior and mortality from coronary disease in the Framingham Study. *New England Journal of Medicine, 319*, 1480–1481.

Eastern Virginia Medical School (2009, May 5). Texting while driving can be deadly, study shows. *ScienceDaily*. Retrieved May 5, 2010, from http://www.sciencedaily.com/releases/2009/05/090504094434.htm

Eaton, W. W., Kessler, R. C., Wittchen, H. U., & Magee, W. J. (1994). Panic and panic disorder in the United States. *American Journal of Psychiatry, 151*(3), 413–420.

Ebbeling, C. B., Swain, J. F., Feldman, H. A., Wong, W. W., Hachey, D. L., Garcia-Lago, E., & Ludwig, D. S. (2012). Effects of dietary composition on energy expenditure during weight-loss maintenance. *JAMA, 307*(24), 2627–2634. doi:10.1001/jama.2012.6607

Ebbinghaus, H. (1885). *Memory: A contribution to experimental psychology*. New York: Dover Publications.

Ebbinghaus, H. (1913). *Memory: A contribution to experimental psychology*. New York: Teachers College Press. (Translated from the 1885 German original.)

Eddy, J., Fitzhugh, E., & Wang, M. (2000). Smoking acquisition: Peer influence and self-selection. *Psychological Reports, 86*, 1241–1246.

Edelmann, R. J., & Iwawaki, S. (1987). Self-reported expression of embarrassment in five European cultures. *Psychologia: An International Journal of Psychology, 30*, 205–216.

Edlund, J. E., Heider, J. D., Scherer, C. R., Farc, M.-M., & Sagarin, B. J. (2006). Sex differences in jealousy in response to actual infidelity. *Evolutionary Psychology, 4*, 462–470.

Edwards, C., Mukherjee, S., Simpson, L., Palmer, L. J., Almeida, O. P., & Hillman, D. R. (2015). Depressive symptoms before and after treatment of obstructive sleep apnea in men and women. *Journal of Clinical Sleep Medicine,* 11(9), 1029–1038. doi: 10.5664/jcsm.5020

Egan, L. C., Bloom, P., & Santos, L. R. (2010). Choice-induced preferences in the absence of choice: Evidence from a blind two choice paradigm with young children and capuchin monkeys. *Journal of Experimental Social Psychology, 46*(1), 204–207.

Egan, L. C., Santos, L. R., & Bloom, P. (2007). The origins of cognitive dissonance. Evidence from children and monkeys. *Psychological Science, 18*(11), 978–983.

Ehlers, A., Bisson, J., Clark, D. M., Creamer, M., Pilling, S., Richards, D., Schnurr, P. P., Turner, S., & Yule, W. (2010). Do all psychological treatments really work the same in posttraumatic stress disorder? *Clinical Psychology Review, 30*(2), 269–276.

Eich, E., & Metcalfe, J. (1989). Mood dependent memory for internal vs. external events. *Journal of Experimental Psychology: Learning, Memory and Cognition, 15*, 443–455.

Eiden, R. D., McAuliffe, S., Kachadourian, L., Coles, C., Colder, C., & Schuetze, P. (2009). Effects of prenatal cocaine exposure on infant reactivity and regulation. *Neurotoxicology and Teratology, 31*, 60–68.

Ejaife, O. L., & Ho, I. K. (2017). Healthcare experiences of a black lesbian in the United States. *Journal of Health Psychology*, 1359105317690036. doi:10.1177/1359105317690036

Ekers, D., Webster, L., Van Straten, A., Cuijpers, P., Richards, D., & Gilbody, S. (2014). Behavioural activation for depression; an update of meta-analysis of effectiveness and sub group analysis. *PLoS ONE, 9*(6), e100100. doi: 10.1371/journal.pone.0100100

Ekman, P. (1973). Darwin and cross-cultural studies of facial expression. In P. Ekman (Ed.), *Darwin and facial expression: A century of research in review*. New York: Academic Press.

Ekman, P. (1980). Asymmetry in facial expression. *Science, 209*, 833–834.

Ekman, P., & Friesen, W. (1969). The repertoire of nonverbal behavior: Categories, origins, usage, and coding. *Semiotica, 1*, 49–98.

Ekman, P., & Friesen, W. (1971). Constants across cultures in the face and emotion. *Journal of Personality and Social Psychology, 17*(2), 124–129.

Ekman, P., & Friesen, W. V. (1978). *The facial action coding system*. Palo Alto, CA: Consulting Psychologists Press.

Ekman, P., Sorensen, E. R., & Friesen, W. V. (1969). Pan-cultural elements in facial displays of emotion. *Science, 164*, 86–88.

Elkind, D. (1985). Egocentrism redux. *Developmental Review, 5*, 218–226.

Ellenbogen, J. M., Payne, J. D., & Stickgold, R. (2006). The role of sleep in declarative memory consolidation: Passive, permissive, active or none? *Current Opinions in Neurobiology, 16*, 716–722.

Elliott, E., & Dweck, C. (1988). Goals: An approach to motivation and achievement. *Journal of Personality and Social Psychology, 54*, 5–12.

Elliott, R., Greenberg, L. S., Watson, J., Timulak, L., & Freire, E. (2013). Research on humanistic-experiential psychotherapies. In M. J. Lambert (Ed.), *Bergin & Garfield's handbook of psychotherapy and behavior change* (6th ed., pp. 495–538). New York: Wiley.

Ellis, A. (1997). *The practice of rational emotive behavior therapy*. New York: Springer.

Ellis, A. (1998). *The Albert Ellis reader: A guide to well-being using rational emotive behavior therapy*. Secaucus, NJ: Carol Publishing Group.

Ellis, H. D. (1983). The role of the right hemisphere in face perception. In A. W. Young (Ed.), *Functions of the right cerebral hemisphere* (pp. 33–64). London: Academic Press.

Ellis, J. G., & Barclay, N. L. (2014). Cognitive behavior therapy for insomnia: State of the science or a stated science? *Sleep Medicine, 15*(8), 849–850.

Ellis, L. K., Gay, P. E., & Paige, E. (2001). *Daily pleasures and hassles across the lifespan*. Poster presented at the September annual meeting of the American Psychological Association, San Francisco, CA.

Elmenhorst, D., Kroll, T., Matusch, A., & Bauer, A. (2012). Sleep deprivation increases cerebral serotonin 2a receptor binding in humans. *Sleep, 35*(12), 1615–1623. doi: 10.5665/sleep.2230

Emeny, R. T., Lacruz, M-E., Baumert, J., Zierer, A., von Eisenhart Rothe, A., Autenrieth, C., Herder, C.,... Ladwig, K-H. (2012). Job strain associated CRP is mediated by leisure time physical activity: Results from the MONICA/KORA study. *Brain, Behavior, and Immunity, 26*, 1077–1084.

Emeny, R. T., Zierer, A., Lacruz, M-E., Baumert, J., Herder, C., Gornitzka, G.,... Ladwig, K-H. (2013). Job strain–associated inflammatory burden and long-term risk of coronary events: Findings from the MONICA/KORA Augsburg case-cohort study. *Psychosomatic Medicine, 75*(3), 317–325.

Endler, N. S. (1988). The origins of electroconvulsive therapy (ECT). *Convulsive Therapy, 4*, 5–23.

Engle, R. W. (2018). Working memory and executive attention: A revisit. *Perspectives on Psychological Science, 13*(2): 190-193. DOI: https://doi.org/10.1177%2F1745691617720478

Engle, R. W., & Kane, M. J. (2004). Executive attention, working memory capacity, and a two-factor theory of cognitive control. *The Psychology of Learning and Motivation, 44*, 145–199.

Enns, J. T., & Coren, S. (1995). The box alignment illusion: An orientation illusion induced by pictorial depth. *Perception & Psychophysics, 57*, 1163–1174.

Ephraim, P. L., Wegener, S. T., MacKenzie, E. J., Dillingham, T. R., & Pezzin, L. E. (2005). Phantom pain, residual limb pain and back pain in persons with limb loss: Results of a national survey. *Archives of Physical Medicine and Rehabilitation, 86*, 1910–1919.

Epping-Jordan, M., Waltkins, S. S., Koob, G. F., & Markou, A. (1998). Dramatic decreases in brain reward function during nicotine withdrawal. *Nature, 393*, 76–79.

Erdley, C. A., & Dweck, C. S. (1993). Children's implicit personality theories as predictors of their social judgments. *Child Development, 64*, 863–878.

Erikson, E. H. (1950). *Childhood and society*. New York: Norton.

Erikson, E. H. (1959). Growth and crises of the healthy personality. *Psychological Issues, 1*, 50–100.

Erikson, E. H. (1980). Elements of a psychoanalytic theory of psychosocial development. In S. Greenspan & G. Pollock (Eds.), *The course of life* (Vol. 1, pp. 11–61). Washington, DC: U.S. Dept. of Health and Human Services.

Erikson, E. H. (1982). *The life cycle completed*. New York: Norton.

Erikson, E. H., & Erikson, J. M. (1997). *The life cycle completed*. New York: Norton.

Eriksson, M., Räikkönen, K., & Eriksson, J. G. (2014). Early life stress and later health outcomes—findings from the Helsinki Birth Cohort Study. *American Journal of Human Biology, 26*, 111–116.

Eriksson, P., Ankarberg, E., Viberg, H., & Fredriksson, A. (2001). The developing cholinergic system as target for environmental toxicants, nicotine and polychlorinated biphenyls (PCBs): Implications for neurotoxicological processes in mice. *Neurotoxicity Research, 3*(1), 37–51.

Eriksson, P. S., Perfilieva, E., Bjork-Eriksson, T., Alborn, A. M., Nordborg, C., Peterson, D. A., & Gage, F. H. (1998). Neurogenesis in the adult human hippocampus. *Nature Medicine, 4*(11), 1313–1317. doi:10.1038/3305

Ernst, A., & Frisen, J. (2015). Adult neurogenesis in humans—common and unique traits in mammals. *PLoS Biology, 13*(1), e1002045. doi: 10.1371/journal.pbio.1002045

Ernst, A., Alkass, K., Bernard, S., Salehpour, M., Perl, S., Tisdale, J.,... Frisen, J. (2014). Neurogenesis in the striatum of the adult human brain. *Cell, 156*(5), 1072–1083. doi: 10.1016/j.cell.2014.01.044

Ernst, E. (2002). A systematic review of systematic reviews of homeopathy. *British Journal of Clinical Pharmacology, 54*, 577–582.

Ernst, E. (2012). Homeopathy: A critique of current clinical research. *Skeptical Inquirer, 36*(6). Retrieved from http://www.csicop.org/si/show/homeopathy_a_critique_of_current_clinical_research/

Eschenbeck, H., Kohlmann, C.-W., & Lohaus, A. (2008). Gender differences in coping strategies in children and adolescents. *Journal of Individual Differences, 28*(1), 18–26.

Eskenazi, B., Bradman, A., & Castorina, R. (1999). Exposures of children to organophosphate pesticides and their potential adverse health effects. *Environmental Health Perspectives, 107*(Suppl. 3), 409–419.

Espinosa, A., & Kadic-Maglajlic, S. (2018). The mediating role of health consciousness in the relation between emotional intelligence and health behaviors. *Frontiers in Psychology, 9*, 2161. doi:10.3389/fpsyg.2018.02161

Etkin, A., Egner, T., & Kalisch, R. (2011). Emotional processing in anterior cingulate and medial prefrontal cortex. *Trends in Cognitive Sciences, 15*(2), 85–93.

European Monitoring Centre for Drugs and Drug Addiction (EMCDDA). (2015). *New psychoactive substances in Europe—An update from the EU Early Warning System*. Lisbon: Author.

Evans, D., Hodgkinson, B., O'Donnell, A., Nicholson, J., & Walsh, K. (2000). The effectiveness of individual therapy and group therapy in the treatment of schizophrenia. *Best Practice, 5*(3), 1–54.

Evans, G. W., & Kim, P. (2013). Childhood poverty, chronic stress, self-regulation, and coping. *Child Development Perspectives, 7*(1), 43–48.

Evans, I. M., & Meyer, L. H. (1985). *An educative approach to behavior problems: A practical decision model for interventions with severely handicapped learners*. Baltimore: Paul H. Brookes.

Evans, P. (2015). Self-determination theory: An approach to motivation in music education. *Musicae Scientiae, 19*(1), 65–83.

Evans, W. H., Evans, S. S., & Schmid, R. E. (1989). *Behavior and instructional management: An ecological approach*. Boston: Allyn and Bacon.

Everson, S. (1995). Psychology. In J. Barnes (Ed.), *The Cambridge companion to Aristotle* (pp. 168–194). Cambridge, England: Cambridge University Press.

Ewbank, M. P., Passamonti, L., Hagan, C. C., Goodyer, I. M., Calder, A. J., & Fairchild, G. (2018). Psychopathic traits influence amygdala-anterior cingulate cortex connectivity during facial emotion processing. *Social Cognitive and Affective Neuroscience, 13*(5): 525–534. DOI: https://doi.org/10.1093/scan/nsy019

Exner, J. E. (1980). But it's only an inkblot. *Journal of Personality Assessment, 44*, 562–577.

Eysenck, H. J. (1994). *Test your IQ*. Toronto: Penguin Books.

Eysenck, H. J., & Eysenck, S. B. G. (1993). *Eysenck personality questionnaire* (Rev. ed.). London: Hodder & Stoughton Educational.

Faasse, K., & Petrie, K. J. (2016). From me to you. *Current Directions in Psychological Science, 25*(6), 438–443. doi:10.1177/0963721416657316

Faasse, K., Parkes, B., Kearney, J., & Petrie, K. J. (2018). The influence of social modeling, gender, and empathy on treatment side effects. *Annals of Behavioral Medicine, 52*(7), 560–570. doi:10.1093/abm/kax025

Faedda, G. L., Ohashi, K., Hernandez, M., McGreenery, C. E., Grant, M. C., Baroni, A.,... Teicher, M. H. (2016). Actigraph measures discriminate pediatric bipolar disorder from attention-deficit/hyperactivity disorder and typically developing controls. *Journal of Child Psychology and Psychiatry, 57*(6), 706–716. doi:10.1111/jcpp.12520

Fagot, B. I., & Hagan, R. (1991). Observations of parent reactions to sex-stereotyped behaviours: Age and sex effects. *Child Development, 62,* 617–628.

Fairburn, C. G. (2018). Cognitive behavior therapy and eating disorders. In W. S. Agras & A. Robinson (Eds.), *The Oxford handbook of eating disorders* (2nd ed., pp. 284–289). New York, NY: Oxford University Press.

Fairchild, G., Van Goozen, S. H., Stollery, S. J., & Goodyer, I. M. (2008). Fear conditioning and affective modulation of the startle reflex in male adolescents with early-onset or adolescence-onset conduct disorder and healthy control subjects. *Biological Psychiatry 63*(3), 279–285.

Fan, Q., Davis, N., Anderson, A. W., & Cutting, L. E. (2014). Thalamo-cortical connectivity: What can diffusion tractography tell us about reading difficulties in children? *Brain Connectivity, 4*(6), 428–439. doi: 10.1089/brain.2013.0203

Fanselow, M. S., & Gale, G. D. (2003). The amygdala, fear, and memory. *Annals of the New York Academy of Sciences, 985,* 125–134.

Fantz, R. L. (1961). The origin of form perception. *Scientific American, 204,* 66–72.

Fantz, R. L. (1964). Visual experience in infants: Decreased attention to familiar patterns relative to novel ones. *Science, 146,* 668–670.

Faraone, S. V., Biederman, J., & Wozniak, J. (2012). Examining the comorbidity between attention deficit hyperactivity disorder and bipolar I disorder: A meta-analysis of family genetic studies. *The American Journal of Psychiatry, 169*(12), 1256–1266. doi: 10.1176/appi.ajp.2012.12010087

Farmer, A. E. (1996). The genetics of depressive disorders. *International Review of Psychiatry, 8*(4), 369–372.

Farmer, L. M., Le, B. N., & Nelson, D. J. (2013). CLC-3 chloride channels moderate long-term potentiation at Schaffer collateral-CA1 synapses. *The Journal of Physiology, 591*(Pt 4), 1001–1015. doi: 10.1113/jphysiol.2012.243485

Farthing, W. (1992). *The psychology of consciousness.* Upper Saddle River, NJ: Prentice-Hall.

Fawzy, F. I., Fawzy, N. W., Hyun, C. S., Elashoff, R., Guthrie, D., Fahey, J. L., & Morton, D. L. (1993). Malignant melanoma effects of an early structured psychiatric intervention, coping, and affective state on recurrence and survival 6 years later. *Archives of General Psychiatry, 50*(9), 681–689.

Fazel-Rezai, R., & Peters, J. F. (2005). P300 wave feature extraction: Preliminary results, in *Proceedings of the 18th Annual Canadian Conference on Electrical and Computer Engineering (CCECE '05,* pp. 390–393). Saskatoon, Saskatchewan, Canada.

Fazio, R. H., & Olson, M. A. (2003). Attitudes: Foundations, functions, and consequences. In M. A. Hogg & J. Cooper (Eds.), *The Handbook of Social Psychology* (pp. 139–160). London: Sage.

Fechner, G. T. (1860). *Elemente der Psykophysik.* Leipzig: Breitkopf und Härtel.

Fedoroff, I. C., & McFarlane, T. (1998). Cultural aspects of eating disorders. In S. S. Kazarian & D. R. Evans (Eds.), *Cultural clinical psychology: Theory, research and practice* (pp. 152–176). New York: Oxford University Press.

Feingold, A. (1992). Good-looking people are not what we think. *Psychological Bulletin, 111,* 304–341.

Feldman, D. H. (2003). Cognitive development in childhood. In R. M. Lerner, M. A. Easterbrooks, J. Mistry, and I. B. Weiner. (Eds.), *Handbook of psychology: Developmental psychology* (Vol. 6, pp. 195–201). New York: Wiley.

Feliciano, E. M. C., Quante, M., Rifas-Shiman, S. L., Redline, S., Oken, E., & Taveras, E. M. (2018). Objective sleep characteristics and cardiometabolic health in young adolescents. *Pediatrics,* June 14. Epub ahead of publication.

Felsten, G. (2009). Where to take a study break on the college campus: An attention restoration theory perspective. *Journal of Environmental Psychology, 29*(1), 160–167. doi:10.1016/j.jenvp.2008.11.006

Ferenczi, E. A., Zalocusky, K. A., Liston, C., Grosenick, L., Warden, M. R., Amatya, D.,... Deisseroth, K. (2016). Prefrontal cortical regulation of brainwide circuit dynamics and reward-related behavior. *Science, 351*(6268). doi: 10.1126/science.aac9698

Ferguson, C. J. (2015). Do Angry Birds make for angry children? A meta-analysis of video game influences on children's and adolescents' aggression, mental health, prosocial behavior, and academic performance. *Perspectives on Psychological Science, 10*(5), 646–666. doi: 10.1177/1745691615592234

Ferguson, C. J., & Kilburn, J. (2010). Much ado about nothing: The misestimation and overinterpretation of violent video game effects in Eastern and Western nations: Comment on Anderson et al. (2010). *Psychological Bulletin, 136*(2), 174–178; discussion 182–177. doi: 10.1037/a0018566

Ferguson, C. J., Rueda, S., Cruz, A., Ferguson, D., & Fritz, S. (2008). Violent video games and aggression: Causal relationship or byproduct of family violence and intrinsic violence motivation? *Criminal Justice and Behavior, 35*(3), 311–332.

Ferguson, J. N., Aldag, J. M., Insel, T. R., & Young, L. J. (2001). Oxytocin in the medial amygdala is essential for social recognition in the mouse. *The Journal of Neuroscience, 21*(20), 8278–8285.

Ferguson, N. B., & Keesey, R. E. (1975). Effect of a quinine-adulterated diet upon body weight maintenance in male rats with ventromedial hypothalamic lesions. *Journal of Comparative Physiological Psychology, 89*(5), 478–488.

Ferguson-Noyes, N. (2005). Bipolar disorder in children. *Advanced Nurse Practitioner, 13,* 35.

Fernald, A. (1984). The perceptual and affective salience of mothers' speech to infants. In L. Feagans, C. Garvey, & R. Golinkoff (Eds.), *The origins and growth of communication,* 5–29. Norwood, NJ: Ablex.

Fernald, A. (1992) Human maternal vocalizations to infants as biologically relevant signals: An evolutionary perspective. In J. H. Barkow, L. Cosmides, & J. Tooby (Eds.), *The adapted mind: Evolutionary psychology and the generation of culture,* 391–448. New York: Oxford University Press.

Fernandez, D. C., Fogerson, P. M., Lazzerini Ospri, L., Thomsen, M. B., Layne, R. M., Severin, D.,... Hattar, S. (2018). Light affects mood and learning through distinct retina-brain pathways. *Cell, 175*(1), 71–84.e18. doi:https://doi.org/10.1016/j.cell.2018.08.004

Fernandez, E., & Sheffield, J. (1996). Relative contributions of life events versus daily hassles to the frequency and intensity of headaches. *Headache, 36*(10), 595–602.

Fernando, A. B., Murray, J. E., & Milton, A. L. (2013). The amygdala: Securing pleasure and avoiding pain. *Frontiers in Behavioral Neuroscience, 7,* 190. doi: 10.3389/fnbeh.2013.00190

Feroah, T. R., Sleeper, T., Brozoski, D., Forder, J., Rice, T. B., & Forster, H. V. (2004). *Circadian slow wave sleep and movement behavior are under genetic control in inbred strains of rat.* Paper presented at the American Physiological Society Annual Conference, April 17–21, 2004, Washington, DC.

Ferrari, M., & Quaresima, V. (2012). A brief review on the history of human functional near-infrared spectroscopy (fNIRS) development and fields of application. *NeuroImage, 63*(2), 921–935. doi:10.1016/j.neuroimage.2012.03.049

Festinger, L. (1954). A theory of social comparison processes. *Human Relations, 7,* 117–140.

Festinger, L. (1957). *A theory of cognitive dissonance.* Stanford, CA: Stanford University Press.

Festinger, L., & Carlsmith, J. (1959). $1/$20 experiment: Cognitive consequences of forced compliance. *Journal of Abnormal and Social Psychology, 58*(2), 203–210.

Fevre, M. L., Kolt, G. S., & Matheny, J. (2006). Eustress, distress and their interpretation in primary and secondary occupational stress management interventions: Which way first? *Journal of Managerial Psychology, 21*(6), 547–565.

Fiatarone, M. (1996). Physical activity and functional independence in aging. *Research Quarterly for Exercise & Sport, 67,* 70–75.

Fibel, B., & Hale, W. (1978). The generalized expectancy for success scale: A new measure. *Journal of Consulting and Clinical Psychology, 46,* 924–931.

Fields, R. D. (2014). Neuroscience. Myelin—more than insulation. *Science, 344*(6181), 264–266. doi: 10.1126/science.1253851

Filippetti, M. L., & Tsakiris, M. (2018). Just before I recognize myself: The role of featural and multisensory cues leading up to explicit mirror self-recognition. *Infancy, 23*(4): 577–590. DOI: https://doi.org/10.1111/infa.12236

Fincham, F. D., Harold, G. T., & Gano-Phillips, S. (2000). The longitudinal association between attributions and marital satisfaction: Direction of effects and role of efficacy expectations. *Journal of Family Psychology, 14,* 267–285.

Finger, S. (1994). *Origins of neuroscience: A history of explorations into brain function.* New York: Oxford University Press.

Fink, M. (1984). Meduna and the origins of convulsive therapy. *American Journal of Psychiatry, 141,* 1034–1041.

Finke, C., Esfahani, N. E., & Ploner, C. J. (2012). Preservation of musical memory in an amnesic professional cellist. *Current Biology, 22*(15), R59.

Finke, R. (1995). Creative realism. In S. Smith, T. Ward & R. Finke (Eds.), *The creative cognition approach* (pp. 301–326). Cambridge, MA.: Cambridge University Press.

Finkel, D., & McGue, M. (1997). Sex differences and nonadditivity in heritability of the Multidimensional Personality Questionnaire scales. *Journal of Personality and Social Psychology, 72,* 929–938.

Finkelhor, D., Shattuck, A., Turner, H. A., & Hamby, S. L. (2014). The lifetime prevalence of child sexual abuse and sexual assault assessed in late adolescence. *Journal of Adolescent Health, 55*(3), 329–333. DOI: https://doi.org/10.1016/j.jadohealth.2013.12.026

Finkelstein, J. D. (2017). The Ψ-File: A review of the psychological literature regarding false memories of alien abduction. *New School Psychology Bulletin, 14*(1): 37–44.

Fioriti, L., Myers, C., Huang, Y. Y., Li, X., Stephan, J. S., Trifilieff, P.,... Kandel, E. R. (2015). The persistence of hippocampal-based memory requires protein synthesis mediated by the prion-like protein cpeb3. *Neuron, 86*(6), 1433–1448. doi: 10.1016/j.neuron.2015.05.021

Firman, N., Palmer, M. J., Timaeus, I. M., & Wellings, K. (2018). Contraceptive method use among women and its association with age, relationship status and duration: Findings from the third British National Survey of Sexual Attitudes and Lifestyles (Natsal-3). *BMJ Sex Reprod Health.* doi:10.1136/bmjsrh-2017-200037

Fischl, B., Liu, A., & Dale, A. M. (2001). Automated manifold surgery: Constructing geometrically accurate and topologically correct models of the human cerebral cortex. *IEEE Transactions on Medical Imaging, 20,* 70–80.

Fisher, P. L., & Wells, A. (2005). How effective are cognitive and behavioral treatments for obsessive–compulsive disorder? A clinical significance analysis. *Behaviour Research and Therapy, 43*(12), 1543–1558. doi: http://dx.doi.org/10.1016/j.brat.2004.11.007

Fishman, I., Keown, C. L., Lincoln, A. J., Pineda, J. A., & Muller, R. A. (2014). Atypical cross talk between mentalizing and mirror neuron networks in autism spectrum disorder. *JAMA Psychiatry, 71*(7), 751–760. doi:10.1001/jamapsychiatry.2014.83

Fiske, S. T. (1998). Stereotyping, prejudice, and discrimination. In D. T. Gilbert & S. T. Fiske (Eds.), *The handbook of social psychology* (4th ed., Vol. 2, pp. 357–411). New York: McGraw-Hill.

Fitzpatrick, M. (2004). *MMR and autism*. New York: Routledge.

Fivush, R., & Nelson, K. (2004). Culture and language in the emergence of autobiographical memory. *Psychological Science, 15*(9), 573.

Fivush, R., Haden, C., & Reese, E. (1996). Remembering, recounting, and reminiscing: The development of autobiographical memory in social context. In D. C. Rubin (Ed.), *Remembering our past: Studies in autobiographical memory* (pp. 341–359). New York: Cambridge University Press.

Flaherty, J. A., & Adams, S. A. (1998). Therapist–patient race and sex matching: Predictors of treatment duration. *Psychiatric Times, 15*(1), 1–4.

Flanagan, D. P., & Dixon, S. G. (2013). The Cattell-Horn-Carroll theory of cognitive abilities. In C. R. Reynolds, K. J. Vannest, & E. Fletcher-Janzen (Eds.), *Encyclopedia of special education* (pp. 368–382). Hoboken, NJ: John Wiley & Sons.

Flaskerud, J. H. (1991). Effects of an Asian client–therapist language, ethnicity and gender match on utilization and outcome of therapy. *Community Mental Health Journal, 27*, 31–42.

Flavell, J. H. (1999). Cognitive development: Children's knowledge about the mind. *Annual Review of Psychology, 50*, 21–45.

Fleming, M. F., & Barry, K. L. (1992). Clinical overview of alcohol and drug disorders. In M. F. Fleming & K. L. Barry (Eds.), *Addictive disorders*, 3–21. St. Louis: Mosby Year Book.

Flemons, W. W. (2002). Obstructive sleep apnea. *New England Journal of Medicine, 347*, 498–504.

Flinker, A., Korzeniewska, A., Shestyuk, A. Y., Franaszczuk, P. J., Dronkers, N. F., Knight, R. T., & Crone, N. E. (2015). Redefining the role of Broca's area in speech. *Proceedings of the National Academy of Sciences of the United States of America, 112*(9), 2871–2875. doi: 10.1073/pnas.1414491112

Flint, J., & Munafò, M. (2014). Schizophrenia: Genesis of a complex disease. *Nature, 511*, 412–413. doi: 10.1038/nature13645

Flor, H., Elbert, T., Knecht, S., Wienbruch, C., Pantev, C., Birbaumer, N.,... Taub, E. (1995). Phantom-limb pain as a perceptual correlate of cortical reorganization following arm amputation. *Nature, 375*(6531), 482–484. doi: 10.1038/375482a0

Floresco, S. B. (2015). The nucleus accumbens: An interface between cognition, emotion, and action. *Annual Review of Psychology, 66*, 25–52. doi: 10.1146/annurev-psych-010213-115159

Flynn, J. R. (2009). *What is intelligence? Beyond the Flynn effect*. New York: Cambridge University Press.

Foa, E. B., Hembree, E. A., & Rothbaum, B. O. (2007). *Prolonged exposure therapy for PTSD: Emotional processing of traumatic experiences, therapist guide*. New York: Oxford University Press.

Fodor, L. A., Cotet, C. D., Cuijpers, P., Szamoskozi, S., David, D., & Cristea, I. A. (2018). The effectiveness of virtual reality based interventions for symptoms of anxiety and depression: A meta-analysis. *Scientific Reports, 8*(1), 10323. doi:10.1038/s41598-018-28113-6

Foland-Ross, L. C., Sacchet, M. D., Prasad, G., Gilbert, B., Thompson, P. M., & Gotlib, I. H. (2015). Cortical thickness predicts the first onset of major depression in adolescence. *International Journal of Developmental Science, 46*, 125–131. doi: 10.1016/j.ijdevneu.2015.07.007

Folkard, S., & Tucker, P. (2003). Shift work, safety, and productivity. *Medicine, 53*, 95–101.

Folkard, S., Arendt, J., & Clark, M. (1993). Can melatonin improve shift workers' tolerance of the night shift? Some preliminary findings. *Chronobiology International: The Journal of Biological and Medical Rhythm Research, 10*(5), 315–320.

Folkard, S., Lombardi, D. A., & Spencer, M. B. (2006). Estimating the circadian rhythm in the risk of occupational injuries and accidents. *Chronobiology International: The Journal of Biological and Medical Rhythm Research, 23*(6), 1181–1192.

Folkard, S., Lombardi, D. A., & Tucker, P. (2005). Shiftwork: Safety, sleepiness, and sleep. *Industrial Health, 43*(1), 20–23.

Folkman, S. (1997). Positive psychological states and coping with severe stress. *Social Science and Medicine, 45*, 1207–1221.

Folkman, S., & Lazarus, R. S. (1980). An analysis of coping in a middle-aged community sample. *Journal of Health and Social Behavior, 21*(3), 219–239.

Follett, K. J., & Hess, T. M. (2002). Aging, cognitive complexity, and the fundamental attribution error. *Journals of Gerontology Series B: Psychological Sciences and Social Sciences, 57*, 312–323.

Fonzo, G. A., Goodkind, M. S., Oathes, D. J., Zaiko, Y. V., Harvey, M., Peng, K. K.,... Etkin, A. (2017). Selective effects of psychotherapy on frontopolar cortical function in PTSD. *American Journal of Psychiatry, 174*(12), 1175–1184. doi:10.1176/appi.ajp.2017.16091073

Forman, E. (n.d.). Behavioral activation for depression. Retrieved from http://www.div12.org/psychological-treatments/disorders/depression/behavioral-activation-for-depression/

Forrest, J. S., & Kendell, S. F. (2018). Phencyclidine (PCP)-related psychiatric disorders. *Medscape: Drugs & Disease—Psychiatry*. Retrieved on August 2, 2018 at https://emedicine.medscape.com/article/290476-overview

Forseth, K. J., Kadipasaoglu, C. M., Conner, C. R., Hickok, G., Knight, R. T., & Tandon, N. (2018). A lexical semantic hub for heteromodal naming in middle fusiform gyrus. *Brain A Journal of Neurology, 141*(7): 2112-2126. DOI: https://doi.org/10.1093/brain/awy120

Forsyth, J., Schoenthaler, A., Chaplin, W. F., Ogedegbe, G., & Ravenell, J. (2014). Perceived discrimination and medication adherence in black hypertensive patients: The role of stress and depression. *Psychosomatic Medicine, 76*, 229–236.

Fortuna, L. R., Alegria, M., & Gao, S. (2010). Retention in depression treatment among ethnic and racial minority groups in the United States. *Depression and Anxiety, 27*(5), 485–494. doi: *10.1002/da.20685 Fortune*. (2013). Best companies to work for 2013. Retrieved May 30, 2013, from http://money.cnn.com/magazines/fortune/best-companies/

Foulkes, D. (1982). *Children's dreams*. New York: Wiley.

Foulkes, D., & Schmidt, M. (1983). Temporal sequence and unit comparison composition in dream reports from different stages of sleep. *Sleep, 6*, 265–280.

Fournier, J. C., & Price, R. B. (2014). Psychotherapy and neuroimaging. *Focus (Am Psychiatr Publ), 12*(3), 290–298. doi: 10.1176/appi.focus.12.3.290

Fox, M. C., & Mitchum, A. L. (2013). A knowledge-based theory of rising scores on "culture-free" tests. *Journal of Experimental Psychology: General, 142*(3), 979–1000. doi: 10.1037/a0030155

Frank, D. W., Dewitt, M., Hudgens-Haney, M., Schaeffer, D. J., Ball, B. H., Schwarz, N. F., Hussein, A. A., Smart, L. M., & Sabatinelli, D. (2014). Emotion regulation: Quantitative meta-analysis of functional activation and deactivation. *Neuroscience and Biobehavioral Reviews, 45*, 202–211.

Frank, G. K. W., DeGuzman, M. C., Shott, M. E., Laudenslager, M. L., Rossi, B., & Pryor, T. (2018). Association of brain reward learning response with harm avoidance, weight gain, and hypothalamic effective connectivity in adolescent anorexia nervosa. *JAMA Psychiatry, 75*(10), 1071–1080. doi:10.1001/jamapsychiatry.2018.2151

Frank, M. G., & Benington, J. (2006). The role of sleep in brain plasticity: Dream or reality? *The Neuroscientist, 12*: 477–488.

Franke, R. H., & Kaul, J. D. (1978). The Hawthorne experiments: First statistical interpretation. *American Sociological Review, 43*, 623–643.

Frankel, B. R., & Piercy, F. P. (1990). The relationship among selected supervisor, therapist, and client behaviors. *Journal of Marital and Family Therapy, 16*, 407–421.

Frankenhuis, W. E., & Nettle, D. (2018). Open science is liberating and can foster creativity. *Perspectives on Psychological Science, 13*(4): 439-447. DOI: https://doi.org/10.1177/1745691618767878

Franzen, K. F., Willig, J., Talavera, S. C., Meusel, M., Sayk, F., Reppel, M., Dalhoff, K., Mortensen, K., & Droemann. (2018). E-cigarettes and cigarettes worsen peripheral and central hemodynamics as well as arterial stiffness: A randomized, double-blinded pilot study. *Vascular Medicine*. Published online at journals.sagepub.com/http://dx.doi.org/10.1177/1358863X18779694

Franzmeier, N., Duering, M., Weiner, M., Dichgans, M., Ewers, M., & Alzheimer's Disease Neuroimaging Initiative. (2017). Left frontal cortex connectivity underlies cognitive reserve in prodromal alzheimer disease. *Neurology, 88*(11), 1054–1061. doi:10.1212/WNL.0000000000003711

Franzmeier, N., Duzel, E., Jessen, F., Buerger, K., Levin, J., Duering, M.,... Ewers, M. (2018). Left frontal hub connectivity delays cognitive impairment in autosomal-dominant and sporadic alzheimer's disease. *Brain, 141*(4), 1186–1200. doi:10.1093/brain/awy008

Frederick, D. A., Sandhu, G., Morse, P. J., & Swami, V. (2016). Correlates of appearance and weight satisfaction in a U. S. National sample: Personality, attachment style, television viewing, self-esteem, and life satisfaction. *Body Image, 17*: 191–203. DOI: 10.1016/j.bodyim.2016.04.001

Fredrickson, B. L., Maynard, K. E., Helms, M. J., Haney, T. L., Siegler, I. C., & Barefoot, J. C. (2000). Hostility predicts magnitude and duration of blood pressure response to anger. *Journal of Behavioral Medicine, 23*, 229–243.

Freedman, J., & Fraser, S. (1966). Compliance without pressure: The foot-in-the-door technique. *Journal of Personality and Social Psychology, 4*, 195–202.

Freeman, A., Simon, K. M., Beutler, L. E., & Arkowitz, H. (Eds.). (1989). *Comprehensive handbook of cognitive therapy*. New York: Plenum Press.

Freeman, D., Haselton, P., Freeman, J., Spanlang, B., Kishore, S., Albery, E.,... Nickless, A. (2018). Automated psychological therapy using immersive virtual reality for treatment of fear of heights: A single-blind, parallel-group, randomised controlled trial. *The Lancet Psychiatry, 5*(8), 625–632. doi:10.1016/s2215-0366(18)30226-8

Freeman, J. (2001). *Gifted children grown up*. London: David Fulton.

Freeman, W., & Watts, J. W. (1937). Prefrontal lobotomy in the treatment of mental disorders. *Southern Medical Journal, 30*, 23–31.

Freese, J., Powell, B., & Steelman, L. C. (1999). Rebel without a cause or effect: Birth order and social attitudes. *American Sociological Review, 64*, 207–231.

Frenda, S. J., Patihis, L., Loftus, E. F., Lewis, H. C., & Fenn, K. M. (2014). Sleep deprivation and false memories. *Psychological Science, 25*(9), 1674–1681.

Freud, A. (1946). *The ego and the mechanisms of defense. American Edition*, New York: I.U.P.

Freud, S. (1900). *The interpretation of dreams. S.E., 4–5.* (cf. J. Crick, Trans., 1999). London: Oxford University Press.

Freud, S. (1901). *The psychopathology of everyday life. S.E., 6,* 1–290.

Freud, S. (1904a). *Psychopathology of everyday life*. New York: Macmillan; London: Fisher Unwin.

Freud, S. (1904b). Freud's psycho-analytic procedure. *S.E., 7,* 249–254.

Freud, S. (1923). The ego and the id. *S.E., 19,* 12–66.

Freud, S. (1930). *Civilization and its discontents*. New York: Jonathon Cape and Co.

Freud, S. (1933). *New introductory lectures on psycho-analysis*. London: Hogarth.

Freud, S. (1940). Splitting of the ego in the process of defence. *International Journal of Psychoanalysis, 22,* 65 [1938], S.E., 23, 275–278.

Freud, S. (1977). *Inhibitions, symptoms and anxiety. Standard edition of the complete works of Sigmund Freud*. New York: W. W. Norton.

Freud, S., Strachey, J., & Riviere, J. (1990). *The ego and the id (The standard edition of the complete psychological works of Sigmund Freud)*. New York: W. W. Norton and Company.

Fridlund, A. J., Beck, H. P., Goldie, W. D., & Irons, G. (2012). Little Albert: A neurologically impaired child. *History of Psychology, 15*(4), 302–327.

Friederich, H.-C., Wu, M., Simon, J. J., & Herzog, W. (2013). Neurocircuit function in eating disorders. *International Journal of Eating Disorders, 46*(5), 425–432. doi: 10.1002/eat.22099

Friedman, J. M., & Halaas, J. L. (1998). Leptin and the regulation of body weight in mammals. *Nature, 395,* 763.

Friedman, M., & Kasanin, J. D. (1943). Hypertension in only one of identical twins. *Archives of Internal Medicine, 72,* 767–774.

Friedman, M., & Rosenman, R. H. (1959). Association of specific behavior pattern with blood and cardiovascular findings. *Journal of the American Medical Association, 169,* 1286–1296.

Friesdorf, R., Conway, P., & Gawronski, B. (2015). Gender differences in responses to moral dilemmas: A process dissociation analysis. *Personality and Social Psychology Bulletin, 41*(5), 696–713.

Frimer, J. A., Gaucher, D., & Schaefer, N. K. (2014). Political conservatives' affinity for obedience to authority is loyal, not blind. *Personality and Social Psychology Bulletin, 40*(9), 1205–1214. doi: 10.1177/0146167214538672

Froh, J. J. (2004). The history of positive psychology: Truth be told. *NYS Psychologist, 16*(3), 18–20.

Frontera, W. R., Hughes, V. A., Lutz, K. J., & Evans, W. J. (1991). A cross-sectional study of muscle strength and mass in 45- to 78-year-old men and women. *Journal of Applied Physiology, 71,* 644–650.

Frostegård, J. (2013). Immunity, atherosclerosis and cardiovascular disease. *BMC Medicine, 11,* 117. doi: 10.1186/1741-7015-11-117

Frühmesser, A., & Kotzot, D. (2011). Chromosomal variants in Klinefelter syndrome. *Sexual Development, 5*(3), 109–123.

Fryar, C. D., Hughes, J. P., Herrick, K. A., & Ahluwalia, N. (2018). *Fast food consumption among adults in the United States, 2013–2016. NCHS data brief, no 322.* Retrieved from Hyattsville, MD: https://www.cdc.gov/nchs/data/databriefs/db322-h.pdf

Frydenberg, E., Lewis, R., Ardila, R., Cairns, E., & Kennedy, G. (2001). Adolescent concern with social issues: An exploratory comparison between Australian, Colombian and North Irish students. *Journal of Peace Psychology, 7,* 59–76.

Fuchs, K. M., & D'Alton, M. E. (2018). 158-Chorionicity of multiple gestations. In J. A. Copel, M. E. D'Alton, …& B. Tutscheck (eds), *Obstetric Imaging: Fetal Diagnosis and Care, 2e,* pp. 639–641.e1. Amsterdam, The Netherlands: Elsevier.

Fuentes, A., & Desrocher, M. (2013). The effects of gender on the retrieval of episodic and semantic components of autobiographical memory. *Memory, 21*(6), 619–632. DOI: https://doi.org/10.1080/09658211.2012.744423

Fulcher, J. S. (1942). "Voluntary" facial expression in blind and seeing children. *Archives of Psychology, 38,* 1–49.

Fulford, D., Woolley, J. D., & Vinogradov, S. (2017). Prefrontal cortical dysfunction in schizophrenia: Clinical implications and novel treatment development. In B. L. Miller & J. L. Cummings (Eds.), *The human frontal lobes* (3rd ed., pp. 437–469). New York: The Guilford Press.

Fulford, J., Milton, F., Salas, D., Smith, A., Simler, A., Winlove, C., & Zeman, A. (2018). The neural correlates of visual imagery vividness - An fMRI study and literature review. *Cortex, 105,* 26–40. doi:10.1016/j.cortex.2017.09.014

Furumoto, L. (1980). Mary Whiton Calkins (1863–1930). *Psychology of Women Quarterly, 5*(1): 55–68. DOI: https://doi.org/10.1111/j.1471-6402.1981.tb01033.x

Furumoto, L. (1991). From "paired associates" to a psychology of self: The intellectual odyssey of Mary Whiton Calkins. In A. Kimble, M. Wertheimer, & C. White (Ed.), *Portraits of pioneers in psychology* (pp. 57–72). Washington, DC: American Psychological Association.

Gable, R. S. (2004). Acute toxic effects of club drugs. *Journal of Psychoactive Drugs, 36*(1), 303–313.

Gado, M. (2004). A cry in the night: The Kitty Genovese murder. *Court TV's Crime Library: Criminal Minds and Methods.* Retrieved August 2, 2004, from www.crimelibrary.com/serial_killers/predators/kitty_genovese/1.html?sect=2

Galanaki, E. P. (2012). The imaginary audience and the personal fable: A test of Elkind's theory of adolescent egocentrism. *PSYCH, 3*(6), 457–466.

Galante, M., & Zeveloff, J. (2012). Harvard is investigating 125 undergrads in massive cheating scandal. *Business Insider,* August 30. Retrieved from http://www.businessinsider.com/harvard-cheating-scandal-2012-8

Gale, J. T., Shields, D. C., Ishizawa, Y., & Eskkandar, E. N. (2016). Reward and reinforcement activity in the nucleus accumbens during learning. *Frontiers of Behavioral Neuroscience, 15*(1), 114.

Galea, S., Resnick, H., Kilpatrick, D., Bucuvalas, M., Gold, J., & Vlahov, D. (2002, March 28). Psychological sequelae of the September 11 terrorist attacks in New York City. *New England Journal of Medicine, 346*(13), 982–987.

Gallistel, C. R., & Matzel, L. D. (2013). The neuroscience of learning: Beyond the Hebbian synapse. *Annual Review of Psychology, 64,* 169–200.

Gamble, K. R., Howard, J. H., Jr., & Howard, D. V. (2014). Not just scenery: Viewing nature pictures improves executive attention in older adults. *Experimental Aging Research, 40*(5), 513–530. doi:10.1080/0361073X.2014.956618

Gamwell, L., & Tomes, N. (1995). *Madness in America: Cultural and medical perspectives of mental illness before 1914*. Ithaca, NY: Cornell University Press.

Ganchrow, J. R., Steiner, J. E., & Munif, D. (1983). Neonatal facial expressions in response to different qualities and intensities of gustatory stimuli. *Infant Behavior Development, 6,* 473–478.

Gandhi, A. V., Mosser, E. A., Oikonomou, G., & Prober, D. A. (2015). Melatonin is required for the circadian regulation of sleep. *Neuron, 85,* 1193–1199.

Ganis, G., Thompson, W. L., & Kosslyn, S. M. (2004). Brain areas underlying visual mental imagery and visual perception: An fMRI study. *Cognitive Brain Research, 20*(2), 226–241.

Garb, H. N., Florio, C. M., & Grove, W. M. (1998). The validity of the Rorschach and the Minnesota Multiphasic Personality Inventory: Results from metaanalyses. *Psychological Science, 9,* 402–404.

Garcia, J., & Koelling, R. A. (1966). Relation of cue to consequence in avoidance learning. *Psychonomic Science, 4,* 123.

Garcia, J., Brett, L. P., & Rusiniak, K. W. (1989). Limits of Darwinian conditioning. In S. B. Klein & R. R. Mowrer (Eds.), *Contemporary learning theories: Instrumental conditioning theory and the impact of biological constraints on learning* (pp. 237–275). Hillsdale, NJ: Erlbaum.

García-Campayo, J., Fayed, N., Serrano-Blanco, A., & Roca, M. (2009). Brain dysfunction behind functional symptoms: Neuroimaging and somatoform, conversive, and dissociative disorders. *Current Opinion in Psychiatry, 22*(2), 224–231.

Gardner, E. L. (2011). Addiction and brain reward and antireward pathways. *Advances in Psychosomatic Medicine, 30,* 22–60. doi: 10.1159/000324065

Gardner, E. P., & Johnson, K. O. (2013). Sensory coding. In E. R. Kandel, J. H. Schwartz, T. M. Jessell, S. A. Siegelbaum, & A. J. Hudspeth (Eds.), *Principles of neural science* (5th ed., pp. 449–474). New York: McGraw-Hill.

Gardner, H. (1993a). *Creating minds: An anatomy of creativity seen through the lives of Freud, Einstein, Picasso, Stravinsky, Eliot, Graham, and Ghandi*. New York: Basic Books.

Gardner, H. (1993b). *Multiple intelligences: The theory in practice*. New York: Basic Books.

Gardner, H. (1998). Are there additional intelligences? The case for naturalist, spiritual, and existential intelligences. In J. Kane (Ed.), *Education, information, and transformation* (pp. 111–131). Upper Saddle River, NJ: Merrill-Prentice Hall.

Gardner, H. (1999a). *Intelligence reframed: Multiple intelligences for the 21st century*. New York: Basic Books.

Gardner, H. (1999b, February). Who owns intelligence? *Atlantic Monthly,* 67–76.

Gardner, H., & Moran, S. (2006). The science in multiple intelligences: A response to Lynn Waterhouse. *Educational Psychologist, 41,* 227–232.

Gardner, H., Kornhaber, M. L., & Wake, W. K. (1996). *Intelligence: Multiple perspectives*. Orlando, FL: Harcourt Brace & Co.

Gardner, J., & Oswald, A. J. (2004). How is mortality affected by money, marriage, and stress? *Journal of Health Economics, 23*(6), 1181–1207.

Gardner, R. J. M., & Sutherland, G. R. (1996). Chromosome abnormalities and genetic counseling. *Oxford Monographics on Medical Genetics No. 29*. New York: Oxford University Press.

Garland, E. L., Geschwind, N., Peeters, F., & Wichers, M. (2015). Mindfulness training promotes upward spirals of positive affect and cognition: Multilevel and autoregressive latent trajectory modeling analyses. *Frontiers in Psychology, 6,* 15.

Gass, M. A., Gillis, H. L. L., & Russell, K. C. (2012). *Adventure therapy: Theory, research, and practice*. New York, New York: Routledge.

Gaudiano, B. A., & Ellenberg, S. (2014). Psychotherapy in decline: What steps are needed to promote evidence-based practice? *Clinical Practice, 11*(4), 385–388.

Gautschi, O. P., Corniola, M. V., Smoll, N. R., Joswig, H., Schaller, K., Hildebrandt, G., & Stienen, M. N. (2016). Sex differences in subjective and objective measures of pain, functional impairment, and health-related quality of life in patients with lumbar degenerative disc disease. *Pain, 157*(5), 1065–1071. doi:0.1097/j.pain.0000000000000480

Gazzaley, A. G., Lee, T. G., & D'Esposito, M. (2018). The frontal lobes and cognitive control. In B. L. Miller & J. L. Cummings (Eds.), *The human frontal lobes* (3rd ed., pp. 103–123). New York, NY: The Guilford Press.

Gazzaniga, M. S. (2006). *The ethical brain: The science of our moral dilemmas*. New York: HarperCollins.

Gazzaniga, M. S. (2009). *Human: The science behind what makes us unique*. New York: Harper Perennial.

Gazzaniga, M. S. (2015). *Tales from boths sides of the brain*. New York: Harper Collins.

Gazzaniga, M. S. (2018). *The consciousness instinct: Unraveling the mystery of how the brain makes the mind*. New York: Farrar, Straus and Giroux.

Geary, D. C. (2000). Evolution and proximate expression of human paternal investment. *Psychological Bulletin, 126*, 55–77.

Geary, J. P. (2001). *Bridging culture through school counseling: Theoretical understanding and practical solutions* (Unpublished master's thesis). California State University, Northridge.

Geen, R. G., & Thomas, S. L. (1986). The immediate effects of media violence on behavior. *Journal of Social Issues, 42*, 7–27.

Geier, J., Bernáth, L., Hudák, M., & Sára, L. (2008). Straightness as the main factor of the Hermann grid illusion. *Perception, 37*(5), 651–665.

Gelder, M. (1976). Flooding. In T. Thompson & W. Dockens (Eds.), *Applications of behavior modification* (pp. 250–298). New York: Academic Press.

Gelfand, M. J., Harrington, J. R., & Jackson, J. C. (2017). The strength of social norms across human groups. *Perspectives on Psychological Science, 12*(5), 800–809. doi:10.1177/1745691617708631

Gelfand, M. J., Raver, J. L., Nishii, L., Leslie, L. M., Lun, J., Lim, B. C.,... Yamaguchi, S. (2011). Differences between tight and loose cultures: A 33-nation study. *Science, 332*(6033), 1100–1104. doi:10.1126/science.1197754

Geliebter, A. (1988). Gastric distension and gastric capacity in relation to food intake in humans. *Physiological Behavior, 44*, 665–668.

Geller, A. I., Shehab, N., Weidle, N. J., Lovegrove, M. C., Wolpert, B. J., Timbo, B. B., Mozersky, R. P., & Budnitz, D. S. (2015). Emergency department visits for adverse events related to dietary supplements. *New England Journal of Medicine, 373*, 1531–1540.

Geller, B., Williams, M., Zimerman, B., Frazier, J., Beringer, L., & Warner, K. L. (1998). Prepubertal and early adolescent bipolarity differentiate from ADHD by manic symptoms, grandiose delusions, ultra-rapid or ultradian cycling. *Journal of Affective Disorders, 51*(2), 81–91.

Gelman, S. A., & Markman, E. M. (1986). Categories and induction in young children. *Cognition, 23*, 183–209.

Gentile, D. A. (2015). What is a good skeptic to do? The case for skepticism in the media violence discussion. *Perspectives on Psychological Science, 10*(5), 674–676. doi: 10.1177/1745691615592238

Gentile, D. A., & Bushman, B. J. (2012). Reassessing media violence effects using a risk and resilience approach to understanding aggression. *Psychology of Popular Media Culture, 1*(3), 138–151. doi: 10.1037/a0028481

Gershoff, E. T. (2000). The short- and long-term effects of corporal punishment on children: A meta-analytical review. In D. Elliman & M. A. Lynch, *The physical punishment of children* (pp. 196–198).

Gershoff, E. T. (2002). Corporal punishment by parents: Effects on children and links to physical abuse. *Child Law Practice, 21*(10), 154–157.

Gershoff, E. T. (2010). More harm than good: A summary of scientific research on the intended and unintended effects of corporal punishment on children. *Law and Contemporary Problems, 73*(31), 31–56.

Gershoff, E. T., & Grogan-Kaylor, A. (2016). Spanking and child outcomes: Old controversies and new meta-analyses. *Journal of Family Psychology, 30*(4): 453–469. DOI: 10.1037/fam0000191

Gershoff, E. T., Sattler, K. M. P., & Ansari, A. (2017). Strengthening causal estimates for links between spanking and children's externalizing behavior problems. *Psychological Science, 29*(1): 110–120. DOI: 10.1177/0956797617729816

Geschwind, D. H., & Iacoboni, M. (2007). Structural and functional asymmetries of the frontal lobes. In B. L. Miller & J. K. Cummings (Eds.), *The human frontal lobes* (2nd ed., pp. 68–91). New York: Guilford Press.

Ghaziri, J., Tucholka, A., Larue, V., Blanchette-Sylvestre, M., Reyburn, G., Gilbert, G.,... Beauregard, M. (2013). Neurofeedback training induces changes in white and gray matter. *Clinical EEG and Neuroscience, 44*(4), 265–272. doi: 10.1177/1550059413476031

Giachero, M., Calfa, G. D., & Molina, V. A. (2015). Hippocampal dendritic spines remodeling and fear memory are modulated by gabaergic signaling within the basolateral amygdala complex. *Hippocampus, 25*(5), 545–555. doi: 10.1002/hipo.22409

Gianaros, P. J., & Wager, T. D. (2015). Brain-body pathways linking psychological stress and physical health. *Current Directions in Psychological Science, 24*, 313–321.

Giancola, F. (2006). The generation gap: More myth than reality. *Human Resource Planning, 29*(4), 32–37.

Gibbons, R. D., Brown, C. H., Hur, K., Davis, J., & Mann, J. J. (2012). Suicidal thoughts and behavior with antidepressant treatment: Reanalysis of the randomized placebo-controlled studies of fluoxetine and venlafaxine. *Archives of General Psychiatry, 69*(6), 580–587. doi: 10.1001/archgenpsychiatry.2011.2048

Gibson, E. J., & Walk, R. D. (1960). The "visual cliff." *Scientific American, 202*, 67–71.

Gilberg, C., & Coleman, M. (2000). *The biology of the autistic syndromes* (3rd ed.). London: Mac Keith Press.

Gilbert, S. J. (1981). Another look at the Milgram obedience studies: The role of the graduated series of shocks. *Personality and Social Psychology Bulletin, 7*(4), 690–695.

Gill, S. T. (1991). Carrying the war into the never-never land of psi. *Skeptical Inquirer, 15*(1), 269–273.

Gillath, O., Karantzas, G. C., & Selcuk, E. (2017). A net of friends: investigating friendship by integrating attachment theory and social network analysis. *Personality and Social Psychology Bulletin, 43*(11): 1546–1565. DOI: http://dx.doi.org/10.1177/0146167217719731

Gillen-O'Neel, C., Huynh, V. W., & Fuligni, A. J. (2012). To study or to sleep? The academic costs of extra studying at the expense of sleep. *Child Development, 84*(1), 133–142.

Gillespie, M. A., Kim, B. H., Manheim, L. J., Yoo, T., Oswald, F. L., & Schmitt, N. (2002, June). The development and validation of biographical data and situational judgment tests in the prediction of college student success. Presented in A. M. Ryan (Chair), *Beyond g: Expanding thinking on predictors of college success*. Symposium conducted at the 14th Annual Convention of the American Psychological Society, New Orleans, LA.

Gillham, B., Tanner, G., Cheyne, B., Freeman, I., Rooney, M., & Lambie, A. (1998). Unemployment rates, single parent density, and indices of child poverty: Their relationship to different categories of child abuse and neglect. *Child Abuse and Neglect, 22*(2), 79–90.

Gilligan, C. (1982). *In a different voice: Psychological theory and women's development*. Cambridge, MA: Harvard University Press.

Gillis Jr, H. L., Speelman, E., Linville, N., Bailey, E., Kalle, A., Oglesbee, N., . . . Jensen, J. (2016). Meta-analysis of treatment outcomes measured by the Y-OQ and Y-OQ-sr comparing wilderness and non-wilderness treatment programs. *Child & Youth Care Forum, 45*(6), 851–863. doi:10.1007/s10566-016-9360-3

Gillund, G., & Shiffrin, R. M. (1984). A retrieval model for both recognition and recall. *Psychological Review, 91*, 1–67.

Gilmour, J., & Skuse, D. (1999). A case-comparison study of the characteristics of children with a short stature syndrome induced by stress (hyperphagic short stature) and a consecutive series of unaffected "stressed" children. *Journal of Child Psychology and Psychiatry and Allied Disciplines, 40*(6), 969–978.

Ginzburg, K., Solomon, Z., Koifman, B., Keren, G., Roth, A., Kriwisky, M.,... Bleich, A. (2003). Trajectories of post-traumatic stress disorder following myocardial infarction: A prospective study. *Journal of Clinical Psychiatry, 64*(10), 1217–1223.

Giordano, P. J. (2011). Culture and theories of personality: Western, confucian, and buddhist perspectives. In K. D. Keith (Ed.), *Cross-cultural psychology: Contemporary themes and perspectives* (pp. 423–444). Hoboken, NJ: Wiley-Blackwell.

Girden, E., & Culler, E. (1937) *Journal of Comparative Psychology, 23*(2), 261–274.

Gittelman-Klein, R. (1978). Validity in projective tests for psychodiagnosis in children. In R. L. Spitzer & D. F. Klein (Eds.), *Critical issues in psychiatric diagnosis* (pp. 141–166). New York: Raven Press.

Glangetas, C., Fois, G. R., Jalabert, M., Lecca, S., Valentinova, K., Meye, F. J.,... Georges, F. (2015). Ventral subiculum stimulation promotes persistent hyperactivity of dopamine neurons and facilitates behavioral effects of cocaine. *Cell Symposia: Aging and Metabolism Cell Reports, 13*(10), 2287–2296.

Glassman, W. E., & Hadad, M. (2008). Chapter eight: Perspectives on social behaviour, altruism and bystander behavior. In William E. Glassman & Marilyn Hadad (Eds.), *Approaches to Psychology* (pp. 399–401). London: Open University Press.

Glenn, A. L., Raine, A., Mednick, S. A., & Venables, P. (2007). Early temperamental and psychophysiological precursors of adult psychopathic personality. *Journal of Abnormal Psychology, 116*(3), 508–518.

Gluckman, M. L. (2006). Psychoanalytic and psychodynamic education in the 21st century. *Journal of American Academy of Psychoanalysis, 34*, 215–222.

Glynn, S. M. (1990). Token economy approaches for psychiatric patients: Progress and pitfalls over 25 years. *Behavior Modification, 14*, 383–407.

Godden, D. R., & Baddeley, A. D. (1975). Context-dependent memory in two natural environments: On land and underwater. *British Journal of Psychology, 66*, 325–331.

Gogtay, N., & Thompson, P. M. (2010). Mapping gray matter development: Implications for typical development and vulnerability to psychopathology. *Brain and Cognition, 72*(1), 6–15.

Gogtay, N., Lu, A., Leow, A. D., Klunder, A. D., Lee, A. D., Chavez, A.,... Thompson, P. M. (2008). Three-dimensional brain growth abnormalities in childhood-onset schizophrenia visualized by using tensor-based morphometry. *Proceedings of the National Academy of Sciences, USA, 105*(41), 15979–15984.

Goin, M. K. (2005). Practical psychotherapy: A current perspective on the psychotherapies. *Psychiatric Services, 56*(3), 255–257.

Gold, E. B., Leung, K., Crawford, S. L., Huang, M. H., Waetjen, L. E., & Greendale, G. A. (2013). Phytoestrogen and fiber intakes in relation to incident vasomotor symptoms: Results from the Study of Women's Health Across the Nation. *Menopause, 20*(3), 305–314. doi: 10.1097/GME.0b013e31826d2f43

Goldberg, S. B., & Hoyt, W. T. (2015). Group as social microcosm: Within-group interpersonal style is congruent with outside group relational tendencies. *Psychotherapy (Chic), 52*(2), 195–204. doi:10.1037/a0038808

Goldfried, M. R. (2007). What has psychotherapy inherited from Carl Rogers? *Psychotherapy: Theory, Research, Practice, Training, 44*(3), 249–252. doi: 10.1037/0033-3204.44.3.249

Golding, J., Ellis, G., Gregory, S., Birmingham, K. Iles-Caven, Y., Rai, D., & Pembrey, M. (2017). Grand-maternal smoking in pregnancy and grandchild's autistic traits and diagnosed autism. *Scientific Reports, 7*: 46179. DOI: http://dx.doi.org/10.1038/srep46179

Goldman, A. L., Pezawas, L., Mattay, V. S., Fischl, B., Verchinski, B. A., Chen, Q., Weinberger, D. R., & Meyer-Lindenberg, A. (2009). Widespread reductions of cortical thickness in schizophrenia and spectrum disorders and evidence of heritability. *Archives of General Psychiatry, 66*(5), 467–477.

Goldman, N., Glei, D. A., & Weinstein, M. (2018). Declining mental health among disadvantaged Americans. *Proceedings of the National Academy of Sciences of the United States of America, 115*(28), 7290–7295. doi:10.1073/pnas.1722023115

Goldman-Rakic, P. S. (1998). The prefrontal landscape: Implications of functional architecture for understanding human mentation and the central executive. In A. C. Roberts, T. W. Robbins, & L. Weiskrantz (Eds.), *The prefrontal cortex: Executive and cognitive functions* (pp. 87–102). Oxford, UK: Oxford University Press.

Goldsmith, H. H., & Campos, J. (1982). Toward a theory of infant temperament. In R. Emde & R. Harmon (Eds.), *The development of attachment and affiliative systems: Psychobiological aspects* (pp. 161–193). New York: Plenum Press.

Goleman, D. (1982). Staying up: The rebellion against sleep's gentle tyranny. *Psychology Today, 3*, 24–35.

Goleman, D. (1995). *Emotional intelligence: Why it can matter more than IQ.* New York: Bantam Books.

Gomes, T., Tadrous, M. Mamdani, M. M., Patterson, J. M., & Juurlink, D. N. (2018). The burden of opioid-related mortality in the United States. *JAMA Network Open, 1*(2): e180217. DOI: https://doi.org/10.1001/jamanetworkopen.2018.0217

Goncalves, R., Pedrozo, A. L., Coutinho, E. S., Figueira, I., & Ventura, P. (2012). Efficacy of virtual reality exposure therapy in the treatment of PTSD: A systematic review. *PLoS ONE, 7*(12), e48469. doi: 10.1371/journal.pone.0048469

Gong, Q., Hu, X., Pettersson-Yeo, W., Xu, X., Lui, S., Crossley, N.,… Mechelli, A. (2017). Network-level dysconnectivity in drug-naive first-episode psychosis: Dissociating transdiagnostic and diagnosis-specific alterations. *Neuropsychopharmacology, 42*(4), 933–940. doi:10.1038/npp.2016.247

Gong-Guy, E., & Hammen, C. (1980). Causal perceptions of stressful events in depressed and nondepressed outpatients. *Journal of Abnormal Psychology, 89*, 662–669.

Gonsalves, B., Reber, P. J., Gitelman, D. R., Parrish, T. B., Mesulam, M. M., & Paller, K. A. (2004). Neural evidence that vivid imagining can lead to false remembering. *Psychological Science, 15*, 655–660.

Gonulal, T., & Loewen, S. (2018). Scaffolding technique. *The TESOL Encyclopedia of English Language Teaching, Wiley Online Library*. Retrieved on September 14, 2018 from https://doi.org/10.1002/9781118784235.eelt0180

Gonzales, P. M., Blanton, H., & Williams, K. J. (2002). The effects of stereotype threat and double–minority status on the test performance of Latino women. *Personality and Social Psychology Bulletin, 28*(5), 659–670.

Gonzalez, J. S., Penedo, F. J., Antoni, M. H., Durán, R. E., Fernandez, M. I., McPherson-Baker, S.,… Schneiderman, N. (2004). Social support, positive states of mind, and HIV treatment adherence in men and women living with HIV/AIDS. *Health Psychology, 23*(4), 413–418.

Goodglass, H., Kaplan, E., & Barresi, B. (2001). *The assessment of aphasia and related disorders* (3rd ed.). Baltimore: Lippincott, Williams & Wilkins.

Goodkind, M., Eickhoff, S. B., Oathes, D. J., Jiang, Y., Chang, A., Jones-Hagata, L. B.,… Etkin, A. (2015). Identification of a common neurobiological substrate for mental illness. *JAMA Psychiatry, 72*(4), 305–315. doi: 10.1001/jamapsychiatry.2014.2206

Goodman, E. S. (1980). Margaret Floy Washburn (1871–1939) first woman Ph.D. in psychology. *Psychology of Women Quarterly, 5*, 69–80.

Goossens, L., van Roekel, E., Verhagen, M., Cacioppo, J. T., Cacioppo, S., Maes, M., & Boomsma, D. I. (2015). The genetics of loneliness: Linking evolutionary theory to genome-wide genetics, epigenetics, and social science. *Perspectives on Psychological Science, 10*(2), 213–226. doi: 10.1177/1745691614564878

Gordon, A. J., Conley. J. W., Gordon, J. M. (2013). Medical consequences of marijuana use: A review of current literature. *Current Psychiatry Reports (Review) 15*(12), 419. doi: 10.1007/s11920-013-0419-7

Gorelick, D. A., Levin, K. H., Copersino, M. L., Heishman, S. J., Boggs, D. L., & Kelly, D. L. (2012). Diagnostic Criteria for Cannabis Withdrawal Syndrome. *Drug and Alcohol Dependency, 123*(1–3): 141–147. doi:10.1016/j.drugalcdep.2011.11.007.

Gosselin, R. E., Smith, R. P., Hodge, H. C., & Braddock, J. E. (1984). *Clinical toxicology of commercial products* (5th ed.). Sydney, Australia: Williams & Wilkins.

Gotlib, I. H., Sivers, H., Canli, T., Kasch, K. L., & Gabrieli, J. D. E. (2001, November). Neural activation in depression in response to emotional stimuli. In I. H. Gotlib (Chair), *New directions in the neurobiology of affective disorders*. Symposium conducted at the annual meeting of the Society for Research in Psychopathology, Madison, WI.

Gottesman, I. I. (1991). *Schizophrenia genesis: The origins of madness.* New York: Freeman.

Gottesman, I. I., & Shields, J. (1976). A critical review of recent adoption, twin and family studies of schizophrenia: Behavioural genetics perspectives. *Schizophrenia Bulletin, 2*, 360–401.

Gottesman, I. I., McGuffin, P., & Farmer, A. E. (1987). Clinical genetics as clues to the "Real" genetics of schizophrenia (A decade of modest gains while playing for time). *Schizophrenia Bulletin, 13*, 23–47.

Gottesman, I., & Shields, J. (1982). *Schizophrenia: The epigenetic puzzle.* New York: Cambridge University Press.

Gottman, J. M., & Krokoff, L. J. (1989). Marital interaction and satisfaction: A longitudinal view. *Journal of Consulting and Clinical Psychology, 57*, 47–52.

Gotz, M., Sirko, S., Beckers, J., & Irmler, M. (2015). Reactive astrocytes as neural stem or progenitor cells: In vivo lineage, in vitro potential, and genome-wide expression analysis. *Glia, 63*(8), 1452–1468. doi: 10.1002/glia.22850

Gough, H. G. (1995). *California Psychological Inventory* (3rd ed.). Palo Alto, CA: Consulting Psychologist-Press.

Gould, J. L., & Gould, C. G. (1994). *The animal mind.* New York: Scientific American Library.

Gould, S. J. (1981). *The mismeasure of man.* New York: Norton.

Gould, S. J. (1996). *The mismeasure of man.* New York: W. W. Norton.

Gračanin, A., Vingerhoets, A. J. J. M., Kardum, I., Zupčić, M., Šantek, M., & Šimić, M. (2015). Why crying does and sometimes does not seem to alleviate mood: A quasi-experimental study. *Motivation and Emotion, 39*(6), 953–960. doi: 10.1007/s11031-015-9507-9.

Grace, A. A. (2016). Dysregulation of the dopamine system in the pathophysiology of schizophrenia and depression. *Nature Reviews: Neuroscience, 17*(8), 524–532. doi:10.1038/nrn.2016.57

Grandjean, P., Weihe, P., White, R. F., Debes, F., Araki, S., Yokoyama, K., Murata, K., Sorensen, N., Dahl, R., & Jorgensen, P. J. (1997). Cognitive deficit in 7-year-old children with prenatal exposure to methylmercury. *Neurotoxicology and Teratology, 19*(6), 417–428.

Grange, D. L., & Eisler, I. (2018). Family therapy and eating disorders. In W. S. Agras & A. Robinson (Eds.), *The Oxford handbook of eating disorders* (2nd ed., pp. 296–301). New York, NY: Oxford University Press.

Graven, S. N., & Browne, J. V. (2008). Sleep and brain development: The critical role of sleep in fetal and early neonatal brain development. *Newborn & Infant Nursing Review, 8*, 173–179.

Green, D. M., & Swets, J. A. (1966). *Signal detection theory and psychophysics.* New York: Wiley.

Green, M. F., Horan, W. P., & Lee, J. (2015). Social cognition in schizophrenia. *Nature Reviews: Neuroscience, 16*(10), 620–631. doi:10.1038/nrn4005

Greenwald, A. G., & Banaji, M. R. (1995). Implicit social cognition: Attitudes, self-esteem, and stereotypes. *Psychological Review, 102*, 4–27.

Greenwald, A. G., McGhee, D. E., & Schwartz, J. K. L. (1998). Measuring individual differences in implicit cognition: The Implicit Association Test. *Journal of Personality and Social Psychology, 74*, 1464–1480.

Greer, G. R., Grob, C. S., & Halberstadt, A. L. (2014). PTSD symptom reports of patients evaluated for the New Mexico medical cannabis program. *Journal of Psychoactive Drugs, 46*(1), 73. doi: 10.1080/02791072.2013.873843

Greeson, J. (2013). Foster youth & the transition to adulthood: The theoretical & conceptual basis for natural mentoring. *Emerging Adulthood, 1*(1), 40–51.

Gregory, R. L. (1990). *Eye and brain, the psychology of seeing.* Princeton, NJ: Princeton University Press.

Gresham, L. G., & Shimp, T. A. (1985). Attitude toward the advertisement and brand attitudes: A classical conditioning prospective. *Journal of Advertising, 14*(1), 10–17, 49.

Griep, Y., Hanson, L. M., Vantilborgh, T., Janssens, L., Jones, S. K., & Hyde, M. (2017). Can volunteering in later life reduce the risk of dementia? A 5-year longitudinal study among volunteering and non-volunteering retired seniors. *PLoS ONE, 12*(3), e0173885. doi:10.1371/journal.pone.0173885

Griggs, E. M., Young, E. J., Rumbaugh, G., & Miller, C. A. (2013). MicroRNA-182 regulates amygdala-dependent memory formation. *Journal of Neuroscience, 33*(4), 1734. doi: 10.1523/JNEUROSCI.2873-12.2013

Griggs, R. A. (2014). Coverage of the Stanford prison experiment in introductory psychology textbooks. *Teaching of Psychology, 41*(3), 195–203. doi:10.1177/0098628314537968

Griggs, R. A. (2015). Coverage of the Phineas Gage story in introductory psychology textbooks: Was Gage no longer Gage? *Teaching of Psychology, 42*(3), 195–202. doi: 10.1177/0098628315587614

Griggs, R. A. (2015). Psychology's lost boy: Will the real Little Albert please stand up? *Teaching of Psychology, 42*(1), 14–18. doi: 10.1177/0098628314562668

Griggs, R. A. (2017). Milgram's obedience study: A contentious classic reinterpreted. *Teaching of Psychology, 44*(1), 32–37. doi:10.1177/0098628316677644

Griggs, R. A., & Whitehead, G. I. (2015). Coverage of Milgram's obedience experiments in social psychology textbooks: Where have all the criticisms gone? *Teaching of Psychology, 42*(4), 315–322. doi:10.1177/0098628315603065

Grimbos, T., Dawood, K., Burriss, R. P., Zucker, K. J., & Puts, D. A. (2010). Sexual orientation and the second to fourth finger length ratio: A meta-analysis in men and women. *Behavioral Neuroscience, 124*(2), 278–287. doi: 10.1037/a0018764

Grocer, S., & Kohout, J. (1997). *The 1995 APA survey of 1992 baccalaureate recipients.* Washington, DC: American Psychological Association.

Gross, C. G. (1998). Claude Bernard and the constancy of the internal environment. *The Neuroscientist, 4*, 380–385.

Gross, C. G. (1999). A hole in the head. *The Neuroscientist, 5*, 263–269.

Grotz, C., Matharan, F., Amieva, H., Pérès, K., Laberon, S., Vonthron, A-M., Dartigues, J-F., Adam, S., & Letenneur, L. (2017). Psychological transition and adjustment processes related to retirement: Influence on cognitive functioning. *Aging & Mental Health, 21*(12): 1310–1316. DOI: https://doi.org/10.1080/13607863.2016.1220920

Groves, C. L., Prot, S., & Anderson, C. A. (in press). Violent media use and violent outcomes. In David Faust, Kyle Faust, and Marc Potenza (Eds.), *How Digital Technology Use Can Help or Harm: Recent Developments, Treatment Considerations and Clinical Applications*. Oxford University Press.

Grumbach, M. M., & Kaplan, S. L. (1990). The neuroendocrinology of human puberty: An ontogenetic perspective. In M. M. Grumbach, P. C. Sizonenko, & M. L. Aubert (Eds.), *Control of the onset of puberty* (pp. 1–6). Baltimore: Williams & Wilkins.

Grumbach, M. M., & Styne, D. M. (1998). Puberty: Ontogeny, neuroendocrinology, physiology, and disorders. In J. D. Wilson, D. W. Foster, H. M. Kronenberg, & P. R. Larsen (Eds.), *Williams textbook of endocrinology* (9th ed. pp. 1509–1625). Philadelphia: W. B. Saunders.

Grünbaum, A. (1984). *The foundations of psychoanalysis: A philosophical critique*. Berkeley, CA: University of California Press.

Grzyb, T., & Dolinski, D. (2017). Beliefs about obedience levels in studies conducted within the Milgram paradigm: Better than average effect and comparisons of typical behaviors by residents of various nations. *Frontiers in Psychology, 8*, 1632. doi:10.3389/fpsyg.2017.01632

Guar, A., Dominguez, K., Kalish, M., Rivera-Hernandez, D., Donohoe, M., & Mitchell, C. (2008, February). *Practice of offering a child pre-masticated food: An unrecognized possible risk factor for HIV transmission*. Paper presented at the 15th Conference on Retroviruses and Opportunistic Infections, Boston, MA.

Guidi, J., Tomba, E., & Fava, G. A. (2016). The sequential integration of pharmacotherapy and psychotherapy in the treatment of major depressive disorder: A meta-analysis of the sequential model and a critical review of the literature. *American Journal of Psychiatry, 173*(2), 128–137. doi:10.1176/appi.ajp.2015.15040476

Guilford, J. P. (1967). *The nature of human intelligence*. New York: McGraw-Hill.

Gunderson, E. A., Gripshover, S. J., Romero, C., Dweck, C. S., Goldin-Meadow, S., & Levine, S. C. (2013). Parent praise to 1- to 3-year-olds predicts children's motivational frameworks 5 years later. *Child Development*, ePub ahead of print, 84(5), 1526–1541. doi: 10.1111/cdev.12064

Gurung, R. A. (2003). Pedagogical aids and student performance. *Teaching of Psychology, 30*, 92–95.

Gurung, R. A. (2004). Pedagogical aids: Learning enhancers or dangerous detours? *Teaching of Psychology, 31*(3), 164–166.

Gurung, R. A., Hackathorn, J., Enns, C., Frantz, S., Cacioppo, J. T., Loop, T., & Freeman, J. E. (2016). Strengthening introductory psychology: A new model for teaching the introductory course. *American Psychologist, 71*(2), 112–124. doi:10.1037/a0040012

Guskiewicz, K. M., Marshall, S. W., Bailes, J., McCrea, M., Harding, H. P., Jr., Matthews, A., … Cantu, R. C. (2007). Recurrent concussion and risk of depression in retired professional football players. *Medicine and Science in Sports and Exercise, 39*(6), 903–909.

Guthrie, R. V. (2004). *Even the rat was white: A historical view of psychology*. Boston: Allyn & Bacon.

Haass, C., Lemere, C. A., Capell, A., Citron, M., Seubert, P., Schenk, D.,… Selkoe, D. J. (1995). The Swedish mutation causes early-onset Alzheimer's disease by β-secretase cleavage within the secretory pathway. *Nature Medicine, 1*, 1291–1296. doi:10.1038/nm1295-1291

Haber, R. N. (1979). Twenty years of haunting eidetic imagery: Where's the ghost? *The Behavioral and Brain Sciences, 2*, 583–619.

Hackett, R. A., & Steptoe, A. (2016). Psychosocial factors in diabetes and cardiovascular risk. *Current Cardiology Reports, 18*(10), 95. doi:10.1007/s11886-016-0771-4

Hafri, A., Trueswell, J. C., & Epstein, R. A. (2017). Neural representations of observed actions generalize across static and dynamic visual input. *The Journal of Neuroscience*. doi:10.1523/JNEUROSCI.2496-16.2017

Hagan, C. R., Podlogar, M. C., & Joiner, T. E. (2015). Murder-suicide: Bridging the gap between mass murder, amok, and suicide. *Journal of Aggression, Conflict and Peace Research, 7*(3), 179–186.

Hahn, J., Wang, X., & Margeta, M. (2015). Astrocytes increase the activity of synaptic glun2b nmda receptors. *Frontiers in Cellular Neuroscience, 9*, 117. doi: 10.3389/fncel.2015.00117

Hahnemann, S. (1907). Indications of the homeopathic employment of medicines in ordinary practice. Hufeland's Journal (Journal der praktischen Azneikunde und Wundarzneykuns), Tome II, Parts 3 and 4.

Haier, R. J. (2017). *The neuroscience of intelligence*. New York, NY: Cambridge University Press.

Hajcak, G., & Starr, L. (n.d.). Posttraumatic stress disorder. Retrieved from http://www.div12.org/psychological-treatments/disorders/post-traumatic-stress-disorder/

Haj-Dahmane, S., & Shen, R.-Y. (2014). Chronic stress impairs α1-adrenoceptor-induced endocannabinoid-dependent synaptic plasticity in the dorsal raphe nucleus. *Journal of Neuroscience, 34*(44), 14560. doi: 10.1523/JNEUROSCI.1310-14.2014

Halbesleben, J. R. B., & Bowler, W. M. (2007). Emotional exhaustion and job performance: The mediating role of motivation. *Journal of Applied Psychology, 91*, 93–106.

Hales, C. M., Carroll, M. D., Fryar, C. D., & Ogden, C. L. (2017). *Prevalence of obesity among adults and youth: United States, 2015–2016. NCHS data brief, no 288*. Retrieved from *Hyattsville, MD:* https://www.cdc.gov/nchs/products/databriefs/db288.htm

Halim, M. L. D., Walsh, A. S., Tamis-LeMonda, C. S., Zosuls, K. M., & Ruble, D. N. (2018). The roles of self-socialization and parent socialization in toddlers' gender-typed appearance. *Archives of Sexual Behavior*, 1–9. DOI: https://doi.org/10.1007/s10508-018-1263-y

Halim, M. L., Ruble, D. N., Tamis-LeMonda, C. S., Zosuls, K. M., Lurye, L. E., & Greulich, F. K. (2014). Pink frilly dresses and the avoidance of all things "girly": Children's appearance rigidity and cognitive theories of gender development. *Developmental Psychology, 50*(4), 1091–1101.

Hall, A. P., & Henry, J. A. (2006). Acute toxic effects of 'Ecstasy' (MDMA) and related compounds: Overview of pathophysiology and clinical management. *British Journal of Anaesthesia, 96*(6), 678–685.

Hall, C. (1966). Studies of dreams collected in the laboratory and at home. *Institute of Dream Research Monograph Series* (No. 1). Santa Cruz, CA: Privately printed.

Hall, C. S. (1953). A cognitive theory of dreams. The Journal of General Psychology, 49, 273–282. Abridged version in M. F. DeMartino (Ed.). (1959). *Dreams and personality dynamics* (pp. 123–134). Springfield, IL: Charles C. Thomas.

Hall, H. (2014). An intro to homeopathy. *Skeptical Inquirer, 38*(5), 54–58. Retrieved from http://www.csicop.org/si/show/an_introduction_to_homeopathy/

Hall, J. A., Pennington, N., & Lueders, A. (2013). Impression management and formation on Facebook: A lens model approach. *New Media & Society, 16*(6), 958. doi: 10.1177/1461444813495166

Hall, W., & Degenhardt, L. (2009). Adverse health effects of non-medical cannabis use. *Lancet, 374*, 1383–1391.

Hamilton, D. L., & Gifford, R. K. (1976). Illusory correlation in interpersonal perception: A cognitive basis of stereotypic judgments. *Journal of Experimental Social Psychology, 12*, 392–407.

Hampton, J. A. (1998). Similarity-based categorization and fuzziness of natural categories. *Cognition, 65*, 137–165.

Hancox, J., Ntoumanis, N., Thogersen-Ntoumani, C., & Quested, E. (2015). Self-determination theory. In *Essentials of motivation & behaviour change* (pp. 68–85). Brussels: EuropeActive.

Handel, S. (1989). *Listening: An introduction to the perception of auditory events*. Cambridge, MA: MIT Press.

Haney, C., Banks, C., & Zimbardo, P. (1973a). Interpersonal dynamics in a simulated prison. *International Journal of Criminology and Penology, 1*, 69–97.

Haney, C., Banks, C., & Zimbardo, P. (1973b). A study of prisoners and guards in a simulated prison. *Naval Research Reviews, 9*, 1–17.

Hansen, C. P. (1988). Personality characteristics of the accident involved employee. *Journal of Business and Psychology, 2*(4), 346–365.

Hansen, N. B. (2002). The psychotherapy dose-response effect and its implications for treatment delivery services. *Clinical Psychology: Science and Practice, 9*(3), 329–343. doi:10.1093/clipsy.9.3.329

Hansen, P. G., Hendricks, V. F., & Rendsvig, R. K. (2013). Infostorms. *Metaphilosophy, 44*(3), 301. doi: 10.1111/meta.12028

Harlow, H. F. (1958). The nature of love. *American Psychologist, 13*, 573–685.

Harlow, J. M. (1848). Passage of an iron rod through the head. *Boston Medical and Surgical Journal, 39*, 389–393.

Harlow, J. M. (1868). Recovery from the passage of an iron bar through the head. *Publications of the Massachusetts Medical Society, 2*, 327–347.

Harman, G. (1999). Moral philosophy meets social psychology: Virtue ethics and the fundamental attribution error. *Proceedings of the Aristotelian Society, 1998–99, 99*, 315–331.

Harmon-Jones, E. (2000). Cognitive dissonance and experienced negative affect: Evidence that dissonance increases experienced negative affect even in the absence of aversive consequences. *Personality and Social Psychology Bulletin, 26*, 1490–1501.

Harmon-Jones, E. (2004). Insights on asymmetrical frontal brain activity gleaned from research on anger and cognitive dissonance. *Biological Psychology, 67*, 51–76.

Harmon-Jones, E. (2006). Integrating cognitive dissonance theory with neurocognitive models of control. *Psychophysiology, 43*, S16.

Harmon-Jones, E., Harmon-Jones, C., Fearn, M., Sigelman, J. D., & Johnson, P. (2008). Action orientation, relative left frontal cortical activation, and spreading of alternatives: A test of the action-based model of dissonance. *Journal of Personality and Social Psychology, 94*(1), 1–15.

Harmon-Jones, E., Harmon-Jones, C., Serra, R., & Gable, P. A. (2011). The effect of commitment on relative left frontal cortical activity: Tests of the action-based model of dissonance. *Personality and Social Psychology Bulletin, 37*(3), 395–408. doi: 10.1177/0146167210397059

Harms, P. D., Bai, Y., & Han, G. H. (2016). How leader and follower attachment styles are mediated by trust. *Human Relations, 69*(9): 1853–1876. DOI: 10.1177/0018726716628968

Harrington, J. R., & Gelfand, M. J. (2014). Tightness-looseness across the 50 United States. *Proceedings of the National Academy of Sciences of the United States of America, 111*(22), 7990–7995. doi:10.1073/pnas.1317937111

Harris, B. (2011). Letting go of Little Albert: Disciplinary memory, history, and the uses of myth. *Journal of the History of the Behavioral Sciences, 47*(1), 1–17. doi: 10.1002/jhbs.20470

Harrison, P. J. (1999). The neuropathology of schizophrenia: A critical review of the data and their interpretation. *Brain, 122*, 593–624.

Hart, P. (1998). Preventing groupthink revisited: Evaluating and reforming groups in government. *Organizational Behavior & Human Decision Processes, 73*(2–3), 306–326.

Hartfield, E. (1987). Passionate and companionate love. In R. J. Sternberg & M. L. Barnes (Eds.), *The psychology of love* (pp. 191–217). New Haven, CT: Yale University Press.

Hartfield, E., & Rapson, R. L. (1992). Similarity and attraction in intimate relationships. *Communication Monographs, 59*, 209–212.

Hartley, B. L., & Sutton, R. M. (2013). A stereotype threat account of boys' academic underachievement. *Child Development, 84*(5), 1716–1733. doi: 10.1111/cdev.12079

Harvard Medical School. (2007). National Comorbidity Survey (NSC). Data Table 2: 12-month prevalence of DSM-IV/WMH-CIDI disorders by sex and cohort. Retrieved from https://www.hcp.med.harvard.edu/ncs/index.php

Harvard Medical School, Department of Health Care Policy. (2007). *National comorbidity survey: 12-month prevalence of DSM-IV/WMH-CICI disorders by sex and cohort.* Retrieved from http://www.hcp.med.harvard.edu/ncs/ftpdir/NCS-R_12-month_Prevalence_Estimates.pdf

Harvey, A. R., Lovett, S. J., Majda, B. T., Yoon, J. H., Wheeler, L. P. G., & Hodgetts, S. I. (2015). Neurotrophic factors for spinal cord repair: Which, where, how and when to apply, and for what period of time? *Brain Research, 1619*, 36–71. doi: http://dx.doi.org/10.1016/j.brainres.2014.10.049

Harvey, S. B., Overland, S., Hatch, S. L., Wessely, S., Mykletun, A., & Hotopf, M. (2018). Exercise and the prevention of depression: Results of the HUNT Cohort Study. *American Journal of Psychiatry, 175*(1), 28–36. doi:10.1176/appi.ajp.2017.16111223

Hasin, D. S., Kerridge, B. T., Saha, T. D., Huang, B., Pickering, R., Smith, S. M., Jung, J., Zhang, H., & Grant, B. F. (2016). Prevalence and correlates of DSM-5 cannabis use disorder, 2012–2013: Findings from the National Epidemiologic Survey on Alcohol and Related Conditions-III. *American Journal of Psychiatry, 173*(6): 588–599. DOI: 10.1176/appi.ajp.2015.15070907

Hasin, D. S., Wall, M., Keyes, K. M., Cerdá, M., Schulenberg, J., O'Malley, P. M.,... Feng, T. (2015). Medical marijuana laws and adolescent marijuana use in the USA from 1991 to 2014: Results from annual, repeated cross-sectional surveys. *The Lancet, 2*(7), 601–608. doi: 10.1016/S2215-0366(15)00217-5

Haslam, C., Cruwys, T., Milne, M., Kan, C. H., & Haslam, S. A. (2016). Group ties protect cognitive health by promoting social identification and social support. *Journal of Aging and Health, 28*(2), 244–266.

Haslam, N., Loughnan, S., & Perry, G. (2014). Meta-Milgram: An empirical synthesis of the obedience experiments. *PLoS ONE, 9*(4), e93927. doi:10.1371/journal.pone.0093927

Haslam, S. A., & Reicher, S. (2012a). Tyranny: Revisiting Zimbardo's Stanford prison experiment. In J. Smith & S. Haslam (Eds.), *Social psychology: Revisiting the classic studies* (pp. 126–141). Los Angeles, CA: SAGE.

Haslam, S. A., & Reicher, S. D. (2012b). Contesting the "nature" of conformity: What Milgram and Zimbardo's studies really show. *Public Library of Science (PLoS) Biology, 10*(11), e1001426. doi: 10.1370/journal.pbio.1001426

Haslam, S. A., Reicher, S. D., Millard, K., & McDonald, R. (2015). 'Happy to have been of service': The Yale archive as a window into the engaged followership of participants in Milgram's 'obedience' experiments. *British Journal of Social Psychology, 54*(1), 55–83. doi:10.1111/bjso.12074

Hassan, S. (2014). ISIS is a cult that uses terrorism: A fresh new strategy. The WorldPost: The Huffington Post, October 21, 2014. Retrieved from http://www.huffingtonpost.com/steven-hassan/isis-is-a-cult-that-uses-_b_6023890.html

Hassan, S., Karpova, Y., Baiz, D., Yancey, D., Pullikuth, A., Flores, A., ... & Kulik, G. (2013). Behavioral stress accelerates prostate cancer development in mice. *Journal of Clinical Investigation, 123*(2), 874–886. doi:10.1172/JCI63324

Hauck, S. J., & Bartke, A. (2001). Free radical defenses in the liver and kidney of human growth hormone transgenic mice. *Journal of Gerontology and Biological Science, 56*, 153–162.

Havighurst R. J., Neugarten B. L., & Tobin S. N. S. (1968). Disengagement and patterns of aging. In B. L. Neugarten (Ed.), *Middle age and aging: A reader in social psychology* (pp. 161–172). Chicago: University of Chicago Press.

Havranek, M. M., Bolliger, B., Roos, S., Pryce, C. R., Quednow, B. B., & Seifritz, E. (2015). Uncontrollable and unpredictable stress interacts with subclinical depression and anxiety scores in determining anxiety response. *Stress, 19*(1), 53–62. doi:10.3109/10253890.2015.1117449

Hawks, S. R., Madanat, H. N., Merrill, R. M., Goudy, M. B., & Miyagawa, T. (2003). A cross-cultural analysis of "motivation for eating" as a potential factor in the emergence of global obesity: Japan and the United States. *Health Promotion International, 18*(2), 153–162.

Hay, P. (2013). A systematic review of evidence for psychological treatments in eating disorders: 2005–2012. *International Journal of Eating Disorders, 46*(5), 462–469. doi: 10.1002/eat.22103

Hayes, J. P., Bigler, E. D., & Verfaellie, M. (2016). Traumatic brain injury as a disorder of brain connectivity. *Journal of the International Neuropsychological Society, 22* (Special Issue 02), 120–137. doi: doi:10.1017/S1355617715000740

Hayes, S. M., Alosco, M. L., Hayes, J. P., Cadden, M., Peterson, K. M., Allsup, K.,... Verfaellie, M. (2015). Physical activity is positively associated with episodic memory in aging. *Journal of the International Neuropsychological Society, 21*(10), 780.

Hayflick, L. (1977). The cellular basis for biological aging. In C. E. Finch & L. Hayflick (Eds.), *Handbook of biology of aging* (p. 159). New York: Van Nostrand Reinhold.

Hayward, C., Killen, J. D., & Taylor, C. B. (1989). Panic attacks in young adolescents. *American Journal of Psychiatry, 146*(8), 1061–1062.

Hayward, C., Killen, J. D., Kraemer, H. C., & Taylor, C. B. (2000). Predictors of panic attacks in adolescents. *Journal of the American Academy of Child and Adolescent Psychiatry, 39*(2), 207–214.

Hazan, C., & Shaver, P. (1987). Romantic love conceptualized as an attachment process. *Journal of Personality and Social Psychology, 52*, 511–524.

Hazrati, L. N., Tartaglia, M. C., Diamandis, P., Davis, K. D., Green, R. E., Wennberg, R.,... Tator, C. H. (2013). Absence of chronic traumatic encephalopathy in retired football players with multiple concussions and neurological symptomatology. *Frontiers in Human Neuroscience, 7*, 222. doi: 10.3389/fnhum.2013.00222

He, J., McCarley, J. S., Crager, K. Jadliwala, M., Hua, L., & Huang, S. (2018). Does wearable device bring distraction closer to drivers? Comparing smartphones and Google Glass. *Applied Ergonomics, 70*: 156 DOI: 10.1016/j.apergo.2018.02.022

Heavey, C. L., Layne, C., & Christensen, A. (1993). Gender and conflict structure in marital interaction: A replication and extension. *Journal of Consulting and Clinical Psychology, 61*, 16–27.

Hebb, D. O. (1955). Drives and the CNS (Conceptual Nervous System). *Psychological Review, 62*, 243–254.

Hecker, T., Hermenau, K., Isele, D., & Elbert, T. (2014). Corporal punishment and children's externalizing problems: A cross-sectional study of Tanzanian primary school–aged children. *Child Abuse & Neglect, 38*(5), 884–892.

Heider, F. (1958). *The psychology of interpersonal relations.* New York: John Wiley & Sons.

Heikkila, K., Nyberg, S. T., Theorell, T., Fransson, E. I., Alfredsson, L., Bjorner, J. B.,... Kivimaki, M. (2013). Work stress and risk of cancer: Meta-analysis of 5700 incident cancer events in 116,000 European men and women. *BMJ, 346*(Feb07 1), f165. doi: 10.1136/bmj.f165

Heil, G., Maslow, A., & Stephens, D. (1998). *Maslow on management.* New York: John Wiley and Sons.

Heilman, K. M. (2002). *Matter of mind: A neurologist's view of brain-behavior relationships.* New York: Oxford University Press.

Heilman, K. M., Watson, R., & Valenstein, E. (1993). Neglect and related disorders. In K. Heilman & E. Valenstein (Eds.), *Clinical neuropsychology.* New York: Oxford University Press.

Heimberg, R. G., & Becker, R. E. (2002). *Cognitive-behavioral group therapy for social phobia: Basic mechanisms and clinical strategies.* New York: Guilford Press.

Heimberg, R. G., & Magee, L. (2014). Social anxiety disorder. In D. H. Barlow (Ed.), *Clinical handbook of psychological disorders: A step-by-step treatment manual* (5th ed., pp. 114–154). New York, NY: The Guilford Press.

Heimer, L. (1995). *The human brain and spinal cord: Functional neuroanatomy and dissection guide.* New York, NY: Springer-Verlag.

Heine, S., Kitayama, S., & Lehman. D. (2001). Cultural differences in self-evaluation: Japanese readily accept negative self-relevant information. *Journal of Cross-Cultural Psychology, 32*(4), 434–443.

Heinicke, C. M., Goorsky, M., Moscov, S., Dudley, K., Gordon, J., Schneider, C., & Guthrie, D. (2000). Relationship-based intervention with at-risk mothers: Factors affecting variations in outcome. *Infant Mental Health Journal, 21*, 133–155.

Heinrich, B. (2000). Testing insight in ravens. In C. Heyes & L. Huber (Eds.), *The evolution of cognition*, 289–305. Cambridge, MA: MIT Press.

Helms, J. E. (1992). Why is there no study of cultural equivalence in standardized cognitive ability testing? *American Psychologist, 47*(9), 1083–1101.

Helpman, L., Papini, S., Chhetry, B. T., Shvil, E., Rubin, M., Sullivan, G. M.,... Neria, Y. (2016). PTSD remission after prolonged exposure treatment is associated with anterior cingulate cortex thinning and volume reduction. *Depression and Anxiety*, n/a-n/a. doi: 10.1002/da.22471

Henderson, C. & McClelland, J. L. (2011). A PDP model of the simultaneous perception of multiple objects. *Connection Science, 23*, 161–172.

Henderson, R. K., Snyder, H. R., Gupta, T., & Banich, M. T. (2012). When does stress help or harm? The effects of stress controllability and subjective stress response on Stroop performance. *Frontiers in Psychology, 3*, 179.

Henin, A., Mick, E., Biederman, J., Fried, R., Wozniak, J., Faraone, S. V.,... Doyle, A. E. (2007). Can bipolar disorder-specific neuropsychological impairments in children be identified? *Journal of Consulting and Clinical Psychology, 75*(2), 210–220.

Heppner, W. L., & Shirk, S. D. (2018). Mindful moments: A review of brief, low-intensity mindfulness meditation and induced mindful states. *Social and Personality Psychology Compass, 12*(12). doi:10.1111/spc3.12424

Herberman, R. B., & Ortaldo, J. R. (1981). Natural killer cells: Their role in defenses against disease. *Science, 214,* 24–30.

Herbst, J. H., Zonderman, A. B., McCrae, R. R., & Costa, P. T., Jr. (2000). Do the dimensions of the Temperament and Character Inventory map a simple genetic architecture? Evidence from molecular genetics and factor analysis. *American Journal of Psychiatry, 157,* 1285–1290.

Herlitz, A., Nilsson, L., & Bäckman, L. (1997). Gender differences in episodic memory. *Memory & Cognition, 25*(6): 801–811.

Herman, L. M., Pack, A. A., & Morrell-Samuels, P. (1993). Representational and conceptual skills of dolphins. In H. L. Roitblatt, L. M. Herman, & P. E. Nachtigall (Eds.), *Language and communication: Comparative perspectives.* Hillsdale, NJ: Erlbaum.

Hernandez, D., & Fisher, E. M. (1996). Down syndrome genetics: Unravelling a multifactorial disorder. *Human Molecular Genetics, 5,* 1411–1416.

Heron, M. J., Belford, P., & Goker, A. (2014). Sexism in the circuitry. *ACM SIGCAS Computers and Society: Association for Computing Machinery, 44*(4), 18–29.

Herrnstein, R. J., & Murray, C. (1994). *The bell curve: The reshaping of American life by differences in intelligence.* New York: Free Press.

Hersh, S. M. (2004, May 10). Annals of national security: Torture at Abu Ghraib. *The New Yorker.*

Hershberger, S. L., Plomin, R., & Pedersen, N. L. (1995, October). Traits and metatraits: Their reliability, stability, and shared genetic influence. *Journal of Personality and Social Psychology, 69*(4), 673–685.

Hervais-Adelman, A. G., Moser-Mercer, B., & Golestani, N. (2011). Executive control of language in the bilingual brain: Integrating the evidence from neuroimaging to neuropsychology. *Frontiers in Psychology, 2,* 234. doi: 10.3389/fpsyg.2011.00234

Herxheimer, A., & Petrie, K. J. (2001). Melatonin for preventing and treating jet lag. *Cocharane Database of Systematic Reviews* (1), CD 001520.

Heslegrave, R. J., & Rhodes. W. (1997). Impact of varying shift schedules on the performance and sleep in air traffic controllers. *Sleep Research, 26,* 198.

Hetherington, A. W., & Ranson, S. W. (1940). Hypothalamic legions and adiposity in rats. *Anatomical Records, 78,* 149–172.

Hetrick, S. E., McKenzie, J. E., Cox, G. R., Simmons, M. B., & Merry, S. N. (2012). Newer generation antidepressants for depressive disorders in children and adolescents. *Cochrane Database of Systematic Reviews (Online), 11,* CD004851. doi: 10.1002/14651858.CD004851.pub3

Hewlin, P. F. (2009). Wearing the cloak: Antecedents and consequences of creating facades of conformity. *Journal of Applied Psychology, 94*(3), 727–741.

Hewstone, M., Rubin, M., & Willis, H. (2002). Intergroup bias. *Annual Review of Psychology, 53,* 575–604.

Heyes, C. M. (1998). Theory of mind in nonhuman primates. *Behavior and Brain Science, 21,* 101–148.

Hicklin, J., & Widiger, T. A. (2000). Convergent validity of alternative MMPI-2 personality disorder scales. *Journal of Personality Assessment, 75*(3), 502–518.

Higgins, E. T., & Scholer, A. A. (2010). When is personality revealed? A motivated cognition approach. In O. P. John, R. W. Robins, & L. A. Pervin (Eds.), *Handbook of personality: Theory and research* (pp. 182–207). New York: Guilford Press.

Higginson, A. D., McNamara, J. M., & Houston, A. I. (2016). Fatness and fitness: Exposing the logic of evolutionary explanations for obesity. *Proceedings of Biological Sciences, 283*(1822), 20152443.

Hildreth, C. J. (2008). Inflammation and diabetes. *The Journal of the American Medical Association, 300*(21), 2476.

Hilgard E. R. (1965). *Hypnotic susceptibility.* New York: Harcourt, Brace & World.

Hilgard, E. R. (1991). A neodissociation interpretation of hypnosis. In S. J. Lynn & J. W. Rhue (Eds.), *Theories of hypnosis* (pp. 83–104). New York: Guilford Press.

Hilgard, E. R., & Hilgard, J. R. (1994). *Hypnosis in the relief of pain* (Rev. ed.). New York: Brunner/Mazel.

Hill, D. (1990). Causes of smoking in children. In B. Durston & K. Jamrozik, *Smoking and health 1990—The global war. Proceedings of the 7th World Conference on Smoking and Health,* 1–5 April. Perth: Health Department of Western Australia, 205–209.

Hill, E. S., Vasireddi, S. K., Wang, J., Bruno, A. M., & Frost, W. N. (2015). Memory formation in tritonia via recruitment of variably committed neurons. *Current Biology, 25*(22), 2879–2888.

Hill, J. A. (1998). Miscarriage risk factors and causes: What we know now. *OBG Management, 10,* 58–68.

Hill, P. C., & Butter E. M. (1995). The role of religion in promoting physical health. *Journal of Psychology and Christianity, 14*(2), 141–155.

Hilton, J. L., & von Hipple, W. (1996). Stereotypes. *Annual Review of Psychology, 47,* 237–271.

Hines, T. (2003). *Pseudoscience and the paranormal: A critical examination of the evidence.* Amherst, NY: Prometheus.

Hintze, J. M. (2002). Interventions for fears and anxiety problems. In M. R. Shinn, H. R. Walker, & G. Stoner (Eds.), *Interventions for academic and behavior problems II: Preventive and remedial approaches* (pp. 939–954). Bethesda, MD: National Association of School Psychologists.

Hirshkowitz, M., Whiton, K., Albert, S. M., Alessi, C., Bruni, O., DonCarlos, L.,... Hillard, P. J. A. (2015). National Sleep Foundation's sleep time duration recommendations: Methodology and results summary. *Sleep Health: Journal of the National Sleep Foundation, 1*(1), 40–43. Available at http://www.sleephealthjournal.org/article/S2352-7218%2815%2900015-7/abstract

Hirst, W., & Phelps, E. A. (2016). Flashbulb memories. *Current Directions in Psychological Science, 25*(1), 36–41.

Hirtz, R., Weiss, T., Huonker, R., & Witte, O. W. (2018). Impact of transcranial direct current stimulation on structural plasticity of the somatosensory system. *Journal of Neuroscience Research.* doi:10.1002/jnr.24258

Hirvonen, J., Goodwin, R. S., Li, C.-T., Terry, G. E., Zoghbi, S. S., Morse, C.,... Innis, R. B. (2011). Reversible and regionally selective downregulation of brain cannabinoid CB1 receptors in chronic daily cannabis smokers. *Molecular Psychiatry, 17*(6), 642–649. doi: 10.1038/mp.2011.82

Hobson, J. A. (1988). *The dreaming brain.* New York: Basic Books.

Hobson, J. A., & McCarley, R. (1977). The brain as a dream state generator: An activation-synthesis hypothesis of the dream process. *American Journal of Psychiatry, 134,* 1335–1348.

Hobson, J. A., Pace-Schott, E., & Stickgold, R. (2000). Dreaming and the brain: Towards a cognitive neuroscience of conscious states. *Behavioral and Brain Sciences, 23*(6), 793–1121.

Hoche, F., Guell, X., Sherman, J. C., Vangel, M. G., & Schmahmann, J. D. (2016). Cerebellar contribution to social cognition. *Cerebellum, 15*(6), 732–743. doi:10.1007/s12311-015-0746-9

Hochman, J. (1994). Buried memories challenge the law. *National Law Journal, 1,* 17–18.

Hodges, J. R. (1994). Retrograde amnesia. In A. Baddeley, B. A. Wilson, & F. Watts (Eds.), *Handbook of memory disorders* (pp. 81–107). New York: Wiley.

Hodgson, B. (2001). *In the arms of Morpheus: The tragic history of laudanum, morphine, and patent medicines.* New York: Firefly Books.

Hodson, D. S., & Skeen, P. (1994). Sexuality and aging: The hammerlock of myths. *The Journal of Applied Gerontology, 13,* 219–235.

Hoebel, B. G., & Teitelbaum, P. (1966). Weight regulation in normal and hypothalamic hyperphagic rats. *Journal of Comparative Physiological Psychology, 61,* 189–193.

Hoeft, F., Gabrieli, J. D. E., Whitfield-Gabrieli, S., Haas, B. W., Bammer, R., Menon, V., & Spiegel, D. (2012). Functional brain basis of hypnotizability. *Archives of General Psychiatry, 69*(10), 1064.

Hoferichter, F., Raufelder, D., & Eid, M. (2015). Socio-motivational moderators—two sides of the same coin? Testing the potential buffering role of socio-motivational relationships on achievement drive and test anxiety among German and Canadian secondary school students. *Frontiers in Psychology, 6,* 1675.

Hoffrage, U., Hertwig, R., & Gigerenzer, G. (2000). Hindsight bias: A by-product of knowledge updating? *Journal of Experimental Psychology: Learning, Memory, and Cognition, 26,* 566–581.

Hofstede, G. H. (1980). *Culture's consequences, international differences in work-related values.* Beverly Hills, CA: Sage.

Hofstede, G. J., Pedersen, P. B., & Hofstede, G. H. (2002). *Exploring culture: Exercises, stories, and synthetic cultures.* Yarmouth, ME: Intercultural Press.

Hogg, M. A., & Hains, S. C. (1998). Friendship and group identification: A new look at the role of cohesiveness in groupthink. *European Journal of Social Psychology, 28*(1), 323–341.

Holahan, C. K., & Sears, R. R. (1996). *The gifted group at later maturity.* Stanford, CA: Stanford University Press.

Holden, C., & Vogel, G. (2002). Plasticity: Time for a reappraisal? *Science, 296,* 2126–2129.

Hollon, S. D., & Beck, A. T. (1994). Cognitive and cognitive-behavioral therapies. In A. E. Bergin & S. L. Garfield (Eds.), *Handbook of psychotherapy and behavior change* (4th ed., p. 428). Chichester, UK: John Wiley & Sons.

Hollon, S. D., These, M., & Markowitz, J. (2002). Treatment and prevention of depression. *Psychological Science in the Public Interest, 3,* 39–77.

Holman, E. A., Silver, R. C., Poulin, M., Andersen, J., Gil-Rivas, V., & McIntosh, D. N. (2008). Terrorism, acute stress, and cardiovascular health: A 3-year national study following the September 11th attacks. *Archives of General Psychiatry, 65,* 73–80.

Holm-Denoma, J. M., Joiner, T. E., Vohs, K. D., & Heatherton, T. F. (2008). The "freshman fifteen" (the "freshman five" actually): Predictors and possible explanations. *Health Psychology, 27*(1), S3–9. doi: 10.1037/0278-6133.27.1.S3

Holmes, A. J., Lee, P. H., Hollinshead, M. O., Bakst, L., Roffman, J. L., Smoller, J. W., & Buckner, R. L. (2012). Individual differences in amygdala-medial prefrontal anatomy link negative affect, impaired social functioning, and polygenic depression risk. *Journal of Neuroscience, 32*(50), 18087–18100. doi: 10.1523/JNEUROSCI.2531-12.2012

Holmes, O. W. (1892). Preface to "Homeopathy and its Kindred Delusions." Medical Essays, vol. X of The Standard Edition of The Works of Oliver Wendell Holmes, xiii, pp. 6–70. Boston: Houghton Mifflin.

Holmes, T. H., & Masuda, M. (1973). Psychosomatic syndrome: When mothers-in-law or other disasters visit, a person can develop a bad, bad cold. *Psychology Today, 5*(11), 71–72, 106.

Holmes, T. H., & Rahe, R. H. (1967). The Social Readjustment Rating Scale. *Journal of Psychosomatic Research II*, 213–218.

Holroyd, J. (1996). Hypnosis treatment of clinical pain: Understanding why hypnosis is useful. *International Journal of Clinical and Experimental Hypnosis, 44*, 33–51.

Holt-Lunstad, J., Uchino, B. N., Smith, T. W., Cerny, C. B., & Nealey-Moore, J. B. (2003). Social relationships and ambulatory blood pressure: Structural and qualitative predictors of cardiovascular function during everyday social interactions. *Health Psychology, 22*, 388–397.

Holtzheimer, P. E., Kelley, M. E., Gross, R. E., Filkowski, M. M., Garlow, S. J., Barrocas, A.,... Mayberg, H. S. (2012). Subcallosal cingulate deep brain stimulation for treatment-resistant unipolar and bipolar depression. *Archives of General Psychiatry, 69*(2), 150–158. doi: 10.1001/archgenpsychiatry.2011.1456

Hong, D., Scaletta-Kent, J., & Kesler, S. (2009). Cognitive profile of Turner syndrome. *Developmental Disabilities Research Reviews, 15*(4), 270–278. doi: 10.1002/ddrr.79

Hood, D. C. (1998). Lower-level visual processing and models of light adaptation. *Annual Review of Psychology, 49*, 503–535.

Hopfinger, J. B., Buonocore, M. H., & Mangun, G. R. (2000). The neural mechanisms of top-down attentional control. *Nature Neuroscience, 3*, 284–291.

Hopkins, J. R. (2011). The enduring influence of Jean Piaget. *Observer, 24*(10), 35–36. Retrieved from http://www.psychologicalscience.org/index.php/publications/observer/2011/december-11/jean-piaget.html

Horikawa, T., Tamaki, M., Miyawaki, Y., & Kamitani, Y. (2013). Neural decoding of visual imagery during sleep. *Science, 340*(6132), 639–642.

Horne, J. A., & Staff, C. H. (1983). Exercise and sleep: Body heating effects. *Sleep, 6*, 36–46.

Horney, K. (1939). *New ways in psychoanalysis*. New York: W. W. Norton.

Horney, K. (1967/1973). *Feminine psychology*. New York: W. W. Norton.

Hornung, J. P. (2012). Raphe nuclei. In J. K. Mai & G. Paxinos (Eds.), *The human nervous system* (pp. 642–685). London, UK: Academic Press.

Horowitz, D. L. (1985). *Ethnic groups in conflict*. Berkeley: University of California Press.

Hortaçsu, N. (1999). The first year of family and couple initiated marriages of a Turkish sample: A longitudinal investigation. *International Journal of Psychology, 34*(1), 29–41.

Hosler, A. S., Kammer, J. R., & Cong, X. (2018). Everyday discrimination experience and depressive symptoms in urban black, guyanese, hispanic, and white adults. *Journal of the American Psychiatric Nurses Association*, 1078390318814620. doi:10.1177/1078390318814620

Hothersall, D. (1995). *History of psychology*. New York: McGraw-Hill, Inc.

Houben, S. T. L., Otgaar, H., Roelofs, J., & Merckelbach, H. (2018). Lateral eye movements increase false memory rates. *Clinical Psychological Science, 6*(4), 610–616. doi:10.1177/2167702618757658

Hovland, C. I. (1937). The generalization of conditioned responses. I. The sensory generalization of conditioned responses with varying frequencies of tone. *Journal of General Psychology, 17*, 125–148.

Hozel, B., Lazar, S., Gard, T., Schulman-Olivier, Z., Vago, R., & Ott, U. (2011). How does mindfulness meditation work? Proposing mechanisms of action from a conceptual and neural perspective. *Perspectives on Psychological Science 6*(6), 537–559.

Hsu, B., Cumming, R. G., Waite, L. M., Blyth, F. M., Naganathan, V., Couteur, D. G. L.,... Handelsman, D. J. (2015). Longitudinal relationships between reproductive hormones and cognitive decline in older men: The Concord Health and Ageing in Men project. *The Journal of Clinical Endocrinology & Metabolism, 100*(6), 2223–2230. doi: doi:10.1210/jc.2015-1016

Hu, P., & Meng, Z. (August, 1996). *An examination of infant–mother attachment in China*. Poster session presented at the meeting of the International Society for the Study of Behavioral Development, Quebec City, Quebec, Canada.

Hu, S., & Stern, R. M. (1999). Retention of adaptation to motion sickness eliciting stimulation. *Aviation, Space, and Environmental Medicine, 70*, 766–768.

Huang, J. Y., & Bargh, J. A. (2014). The selfish goal: Autonomously operating motivational structures as the proximate cause of human judgment and behavior. *Behavioral and Brain Sciences, 37*(2), 121–135.

Huang, Y., Li, Y., Chen, J., Zhou, H., & Tan, S. (2015). Electrical stimulation elicits neural stem cells activation: New perspectives in CNS repair. *Frontiers in Human Neuroscience, 9*, 586. doi: 10.3389/fnhum.2015.00586

Hubbard, E. M., & Ramachandran, V. S. (2005). Neurocognitive mechanisms of synesthesia. *Neuron, 48*(3), 509–520. doi: 10.1016/j.neuron.2005.10.012

Hubel, D. H., & Wiesel, T. N. (1959). Receptive fields of single neurons in the cat's striate cortex. *The Journal of Physiology, 148*, 574–591.

Hudson, J. I., Hiripi, E., Pope, H. G., Jr., & Kessler, R. C. (2007). The prevalence and correlates of eating disorders in the national comorbidity survey replication. *Biological Psychiatry, 61*(3), 348–358. doi:10.1016/j.biopsych.2006.03.040

Huesmann, L. R., & Eron, L. (1986). *Television and the aggressive child: A cross-national comparison*. Hillsdale, NJ: Erlbaum.

Huesmann, L. R., & Miller, L. S. (1994). Long-term effects of repeated exposure to media violence in childhood. In L. R. Huesmann (Ed.), *Aggressive behavior: Current perspectives* (pp. 153–183). New York: Plenum Press.

Huesmann, L. R., Moise, J. F., & Podolski, C. L. (1997). The effects of media violence on the development of antisocial behavior. In D. M. Stoff, J. Breiling, & J. D. Maser (Eds.), *Handbook of antisocial behavior* (pp. 181–193). New York: John Wiley.

Huesmann, L. R., Moise-Titus, J., Podolski, C. L., & Eron, L. D. (2003). Longitudinal relations between children's exposure to TV violence and their aggressive and violent behavior in young adulthood: 1977–1992. *Developmental Psychology, 39*(2), 201–221.

Hugenberg, K., & Bodenhausen, G. V. (2003). Facing prejudice: Implicit prejudice and the perception of facial threat. *Psychological Science, 14*, 640–643.

Hughes, J. (1993). Behavior therapy. In T. R. Kratochwill & R. J. Morris (Eds.), *Handbook of psychotherapy with children and adolescents* (pp. 185–220). Boston: Allyn and Bacon.

Hughes, S. M., Harrison, M. A., & Gallup, G. G., Jr. (2007). Sex differences in romantic kissing among college students: An evolutionary perspective. *Evolutionary Psychology, 5*(3), 612–631.

Hull, C. L. (1943). *Principles of behavior*. New York: Appleton-Century.

Hull, J. G., Draghici, A. M., & Sargent, J. D. (2012). A longitudinal study of risk-glorifying video games and reckless driving. *Psychology of Popular Media Culture, 1*(4), 244–253. doi: 10.1037/a0029510

Hummer, R. A., Rogers, R. G., Nam, C. B., & Ellison, C. G. (1999). Religious involvement and U.S. adult mortality. *Demography, 36*(2), 273–285.

Hunsley, J., & Mash, E. J. (2008). Developing criteria for evidence-based assessment: An introduction to assessments that work. In J. Hunsley & E. J. Mash (Eds.), *A guide to assessments that work* (3rd ed.). pp. 3–14. New York: Guilford Press.

Hunsley, J., Elliott, K., & Therrien, Z. (2014). The efficacy and effectiveness of psychological treatments for mood, anxiety, and related disorders. *Canadian Psychology, 55*(3), 161–176.

Hunsley, J., Lee, C. M., Wood, J. M., & Taylor, W. (2015). Controversial and questionable assessment techniques. In S. O. Lilienfeld, S. J. Lynn, & J. M. Lohr (Eds.), *Science and pseudoscience in clinical psychology* (2nd ed., pp. 42–82). New York, NY: The Guilford Press.

Hunt, E. (2001). Multiple views of multiple intelligence. [Review of Intelligence reframed: Multiple intelligence in the 21st century.] *Contemporary Psychology, 46*, 5–7.

Hunt, M. (1993). *The story of psychology*. New York: Doubleday.

Hurford, J. R. (2012). *The origins of grammar: Language in the light of evolution*. New York, NY: Oxford University Press.

Hurley, D. (1989). The search for cocaine's methadone. *Psychology Today, 23*(7/8), 54.

Hurley, S., & Nudds, M. (Eds.). (2006). *Rational animals?* Oxford, UK: Oxford University Press.

Hurvich, L. M., & Jameson, D. (1957). An opponent-process theory of color vision. *Psychological Review, 64*, 384–404.

Hvas, L. (2001). Positive aspects of menopause: A qualitative study. *Maturitas 39*(1), 11–17.

Hyde, J. S., & Kling, K. C. (2001). Women, motivation, and achievement. *Psychology of Women Quarterly, 25*, 264–378.

Hygge, S. A., & Öhman, A. (1976). The relation of vicarious to direct instigation and conditioning of electrodermal responses. *Scandanavian Journal of Psychology, 17*(1), 217–222.

Hyman, I. E., Gilstrap, L. L., Decker, K., & Wilkinson, C. (1998). Manipulating remember and know judgements of autobiographical memories. *Applied Cognitive Psychology, 12*, 371–386

Hyman, I. E., Jr. (1993). Imagery, reconstructive memory, and discovery. In B. Roskos-Ewoldsen, M. J. Intons-Peterson, & R. E. Anderson (Eds.), *Imagery, creativity, and discovery: A cognitive perspective* (pp. 99–121). The Netherlands: Elsevier Science.

Hyman, I. E., Jr., & Loftus, E. F. (1998). Errors in autobiographical memories. *Clinical Psychology Review, 18*, 933–947.

Hyman, I. E., Jr., & Loftus, E. F. (2002). False childhood memories and eyewitness memory errors. In M. L. Eisen, J. A. Quas, & G. S. Goodman (Eds.), *Memory and suggestibility in the forensic interview* (pp. 63–84). Mahwah, NJ: Erlbaum.

Hyman, S. E., & Cohen, J. D. (2013). Disorders of mood and anxiety. In E. R. Kandel, J. H. Schwartz, T. M. Jessell, S. A. Siegelbaum, & A. J. Hudspeth (Eds.), *Principles of neural science* (5th ed., pp. 1402–1424). USA: McGraw-Hill.

Iacoboni, M., Woods, R. P., Brass, M., Bekkering, H., Mazziotta, J. C., & Rizzolatti, G. (1999). Cortical mechanisms of human imitation. *Science, 286*, 2526–2528.

Iacono, W. G. (2001). Forensic "lie detection": Procedures without scientific basis. *Journal of Forensic Psychology Practice, 1*(1), 75–86.

Iber, C., Ancoli-Israel, S., Chesson Jr., A. L., & Quan, S. F. (2007). *The AASM Manual for the scoring of sleep and associated events: Rules, terminology and technical specifications*. Westchester, IL: American Academy of Sleep Medicine.

Imaizumi, Y. (1998). A comparative study of twinning and triplet rates in 17 countries, 1972-1996. *Acta Genetic Medicine & Gemellology, 47*, 101–114.

Inagaki, R. K. (2018). Opioids and social connection. *Current Directions in Psychological Science, 27*(2): 85–90. DOI: https://doi.org/10.1177/0963721417735531

Incera, S. (2018). Measuring the timing of the bilingual advantage. *Frontiers in Psychology, 9*, 1983. doi:10.3389/fpsyg.2018.01983

Insel, T. R. (2013, Apr. 25). Transforming diagnosis. Retrieved from http://www.nimh.nih.gov/about/director/2013/transforming-diagnosis.shtml

Insel, T. R., & Cuthbert, B. N. (2015). Brain disorders? Precisely. *Science, 348*(6234), 499–500.

Insel, T. R., & Wang, P. S. (2010). Rethinking mental illness. *The Journal of the American Medical Association, 303*(19). 1970–1971.

Institute of Medicine. (2012). *Adverse effects of vaccines: Evidence and causality*. Washington, DC: The National Academies Press.

Ioannidis, J. P. A. (1998, January 28). Effect of the statistical significance of results on the time to completion and publication of randomized efficacy trials. *Journal of the American Medical Association, 279*, 281–286.

Irwin, A. R., & Gross, A. M. (1995). Cognitive tempo, violent video games, and aggressive behavior in young boys. *Journal of Family Violence, 10*(3), 337–350.

Irwin, M., Cole, J., & Nicassio, P. (2006). Comparative meta-analysis of behavioral intervention for insomnia and their efficacy in middle aged adults and in older adults 55+ years of age. *Health Psychology, 25*, 3–14.

Isabel, J. (2003). *Genetics: An introduction for dog breeders.* Loveland, CO: Alpine.

Isenberg, D. J. (1986). Group polarization: A critical review and meta-analysis. *Journal of Personality and Social Psychology, 50*(6), 1141–1151.

Iwakabe, S. (2008). Psychotherapy integration in Japan. *Journal of Psychotherapy Integration, 18*(1), 103–125.

Iwamasa, G. Y. (2003). Recommendations for the treatment of Asian American/Pacific Islander populations. *Psychological Treatment of Ethnic Minority Populations* (pp. 8–12). Washington, DC: Association of Black Psychologists.

Iwamoto, E. T., & Martin, W. (1988). A critique of drug self-administration as a method for predicting abuse potential of drugs. *National Institute on Drug Abuse Research Monograph, 1046*, 81457–81465.

Izard, C. (1988). Emotion-cognition relationships and human development. In C. Izard, J. Kagan, & R. Zajonc (Eds.), *Emotions, cognition, and behavior.* New York: Cambridge University Press.

Jackson, L. A., & Wang, J.-L. (2013). Cultural differences in social networking site use: A comparative study of China and the United States. *Computers in Human Behavior, 29*(3), 910. doi: 10.1016/j.chb.2012.11.024

Jackson, M. L., Gunzelmann, G., Whitney, P., Hinson, J. M., Belenky, G., Rabat, A., & Van Dongen, H. P. (2013). Deconstructing and reconstructing cognitive performance in sleep deprivation. *Sleep Medicine Reviews, 17*(3), 215–225. doi: 10.1016/j.smrv.2012.06.007

Jackson, T., Iezzi, T., Gunderson, J., Fritch, A., & Nagasaka, T. (2002). Gender differences in pain perception: The mediating role of self-efficacy beliefs. *Sex Roles, 47*, 561–568.

Jacobson, S. G., Cideciyan A. V., Regunath, G., Rodriguez, F. J., Vandenburgh, K., Sheffield, V. C., & Stone, E. M. (1995). Night blindness in Sorsby's fundus dystrophy reversed by vitamin A. *Nature Genetics, 11*, 27–32.

Jafarpour, A., Penny, W., Barnes, G., Knight, R. T., & Duzel, E. (2017). Working memory replay prioritizes weakly attended events. *eNeuro, 4*(4): 0171. DOI: https://doi.org/10.1523/ENEURO.0171-17.2017

Jaffe, A. E., Straub, R. E., Shin, J. H., Tao, R., Gao, Y., Collado-Torres, L.,... Weinberger, D. R. (2018). Developmental and genetic regulation of the human cortex transcriptome illuminate schizophrenia pathogenesis. *Nature Neuroscience, 21*(8), 1117–1125. doi:10.1038/s41593-018-0197-y

Jain, A., Marshall, J., Buikema, A., Bancroft, T., Kelly J. P., & Newschaffer, C. J. (2015). Autism occurrence by MMR vaccine status among US children with older siblings with and without autism. *Journal of the American Medical Association, 313*(15): 1534–1540. DOI: http://dx.doi.org/10.1001/jama.2015.3077

Jamal, A., Homa, D. M., O'Connor, E., Babb, S. D., Caraballo, R. S., Singh, T.,... King, R. A. (2015). Current cigarette smoking among adults—United States, 2005–2014. *Centers for Disease Control and Prevention: Morbidity and mortality weekly report (MMWR), 64*(44), 1233–1240.

James, D. (2015). Tjukurpa time. In A. McGrath & M. A. Jebb (Eds.), *Long history, deep time: Deepening histories of place* (pp. 33–46). Australian National University Press.

James, W. (1884). What is an emotion? *Mind, 9*, 188–205.

James, W. (1890). *Principles of psychology.* New York: Henry Holt.

James, W. (1890, 2002). *The principles of psychology* (Vols. 1 and 2). Cambridge, MA: Harvard University Press.

James, W. (1894). The physical basis of emotion. *Psychological Review, 1*, 516–529.

Jameson, M., Diehl, R., & Danso, H. (2007). Stereotype threat impacts college athletes' academic performance. *Current Research in Social Psychology, 12*(5), 68–79

Jamieson, G. A., Kittenis, M. D., Tivadar, R. I., & Evans, I. D. (2017). Inhibition of retrieval in hypnotic amnesia: Dissociation by upper-alpha gating. *Neuroscience of Consciousness, 2017*(1): nix005. DOI: https://doi.org/10.1093/nc/nix005

Jamieson, J. P., Nock, M. K., & Mendes, W. B. (2012). Mind over matter: Reappraising arousal improves cardiovascular and cognitive responses to stress. *Journal of Experimental Psychology: General, 141*(3), 417–422.

Jamieson, J. P., Nock, M. K., & Mendes, W. B. (2013). Changing the conceptualization of stress in social anxiety disorder: Affective and physiological consequences. *Clinical Psychological Science, 1*, 363–374.

Jang, K. L., Livesley, W. J., & Vernon, P. A. (1996). Heritability of the Big Five personality dimensions and their facets: A twin study. *Journal of Personality, 64*, 577–591.

Jang, K. L., McCrae, R. R., Angleitner, A., Riemann, R., & Livesley, W. J. (1998). Heritability of facet-level traits in a cross-cultural twin sample: Support for a hierarchical model of personality. *Journal of Personality and Social Psychology, 74*, 1556–1565.

Janis, I. (1972). *Victims of groupthink.* Boston: Houghton-Mifflin.

Janis, I. (1982). *Groupthink* (2nd ed.). Boston: Houghton-Mifflin.

Janos, P. M. (1987). A fifty-year follow-up of Terman's youngest college students and IQ-matched agemates. *Gifted Child Quarterly, 31*, 55–58.

Janowitz, H. D. (1967). Role of gastrointestinal tract in the regulation of food intake. In C. F. Code (Ed.), *Handbook of physiology: Alimentary canal,* Section 6, Volume 1. Washington, DC: American Physiological Society.

Jansen, A., Houben, K., & Roefs, A. (2015). A cognitive profile of obesity and its translation into new interventions. *Frontiers in Psychology, 6*, 1807. doi:10.3389/fpsyg.2015.01807

January, D., & Kako, E. (2007). Re-evaluating evidence for linguistic relativity: Reply to Boroditsky (2001). *Cognition, 104*(2), 417–426.

Jehn, K., Northcraft, G., & Neale, M. (1999). Why differences make a difference: A field study of diversity, conflict, and performance in workgroups. *Administrative Science Quarterly, 44*, 741–763.

Jencius, M. (2015). Technology, social media, and online counseling. In B. Herlihy & G. Corey (Eds.), *ACA ethical standards casebook* (7th ed., pp. 245–258). Alexandria, VA: American Counseling Association.

Jensen, A. R. (1969). How much can we boost IQ and scholastic achievement? *Harvard Educational Review, 39*, 1–123.

Jensen, M. P., Gertz, K. J., Kupper, A. E., Braden, A. L., Howe, J. D., Hakimian, S., & Sherlin, L. H. (2013). Steps toward developing an EEG biofeedback treatment for chronic pain. *Applied Psychophysiology and Biofeedback.* doi: 10.1007/s10484-013-9214-9

Jeon, M., Walker, B. N., & Gable, T. M. (2014). Anger effects on driver situation awareness and driving performance. *MIT Press Journals: Presence, 23*(1), 71–89.

Jiang, H., White, M. P., Greicius, M. D., Waelde, L. C., & Spiegel, D. (2016). Brain activity and functional connectivity associated with hypnosis. *Cerebral Cortex, 27*(8): 4083-4093. DOI: https://doi.org/10.1093/cercor/bhw220

Johnson, C. P., & Myers, S. M. (Council on Children with Disabilities). (2007). Identification and evaluation of children with autism spectrum disorders. *Pediatrics, 120*(5), 1183–1215.

Johnson, D., Johnson, R., & Smith, K. (1991). *Active learning: Cooperation in the college classroom.* Edna, MN: Interaction Book Company.

Johnson, J., Cohen, P., Pine, D. S., Klein, D. F., Kasen, S., & Brook, J. S. (2000). Association between cigarette smoking and anxiety disorders during adolescence and early adulthood. *Journal of the American Medical Association, 284*(18), 2348–2351.

Johnson, M. E., Brems, C., Mills, M. E., Neal, D. B., & Houlihan, J. L. (2006). Moderating effects of control on the relationship between stress and change. *Administration and Policy in Mental Health and Mental Health Services Research, 33*(4), 499–503.

Johnson, R. M., Fairman, B., Gilreath, T., Xuan, Z., Rothman, E. F., Parnham, T. C., & Furr-Holden, D. M. (2015). Past 15-year trends in adolescent marijuana use: Differences by race/ethnicity and sex. *Drug and Alcohol Dependence,* doi: 10.1016/j.drugalcdep.2015.08.025

Johnson, W., Bouchard, T. J., Jr., McGue, M., Segal, N. L., Tellegen, A., Keyes, M., & Gottesman, I. I. (2007). Genetic and environmental influences on the Verbal-Perceptual-Image Rotation (VPR) model of the structure of mental abilities in the Minnesota Study of Twins Reared Apart. *Intelligence, 35*(6), 542–562.

Johnston, L. D., O'Malley, P. M., Bachman, J. G., Schulenberg, J. E. (2007). *Monitoring the Future national survey results on drug use, 1975–2006: Vol. 1. Secondary school students 2006.* Bethesda, MD: National Institute on Drug Abuse; September 2007.

Johnston, L., O'Malley, P., Miech, R., Bachman, J., & Schulenberg, J. (2017). *Monitoring the Future national survey results on drug use, 1975–2016: Overview, key findings on adolescent drug use.* Ann Arbor: Institute for Social Research, The University of Michigan.

Joint Task Force for the Development of Telepsychology Guidelines for Psychologists. (2013). Guidelines for the practice of telepsychology. *American Psychologist, 68*(9), 791–800. doi: 10.1037/a0035001

Jones, E. E., & Harris, V. A. (1967). The attribution of attitudes. *Journal of Experimental Social Psychology, 3*, 1–24.

Jones, E. J., Krupnick, J. L., & Kerig, P. K. (1987). Some gender effects in a brief psychotherapy. *Psychotherapy, 24*, 336–352.

Jones, G. W. (1997). Modernization and divorce: Contrasting trends in Islamic Southeast Asia and the West. *Population and Development Review, 23*(1), 95–113.

Jones, M. C. (1924). A laboratory study of fear: The case of Peter. *Pedagogical Seminary, 31*, 308–315.

Jones, M. K., & Menzies, R. G. (1995). The etiology of fear of spiders. *Anxiety, Stress and Coping, 8*, 227–234.

Josephson Institute Center for Youth Ethics. (2012). *The ethics of American youth: 2012.* Retrieved from https://charactercounts.org/programs/reportcard/2012/installment_report_card_honesty-integrity.html

Jovasevic, V., Corcoran, K. A., Leaderbrand, K., Yamawaki, N., Guedea, A. L., Chen, H. J., ... Radulovic, J. (2015). GABAergic mechanisms regulated by miR-33 encode state-dependent fear. *Nature Neuroscience, 18*: 1265-1271. DOI: http://dx.doi.org/10.1038/nn.4084

Judelsohn, R. G. (2007, November/December). Vaccine safety: Vaccines are one of public health's great accomplishments. *Skeptical Inquirer, 31*(6), 32–35. Retrieved June 13, 2010, from http://www.csicop.org/si/show/vaccine_safety_vaccines_are_one_of_public_healthrsquos_great_accomplishment/

Julien, R. M., Advokat, C. D., & Comaty, J. E. (2011). *A primer of drug action: A comprehensive guide to the actions, uses, and side effects of psychoactive drugs* (12th ed.). New York: Worth Publishers.

Junco, R., & Cotton, S. R. (2012). No A 4 U: The relationship between multitasking and academic performance. *Computers & Education, 59*, 505–514.

Jung, C. (1933). *Modern man in search of a soul.* New York: Harcourt Brace.

Jung, C. G. (1915). *The theory of psychoanalysis.* New York: Journal of Nervous and Mental Disease Pub. Co.

Jung, R. E., & Haier, R. J. (2007). The parieto-frontal integration theory (P-FIT) of intelligence: Converging neuroimaging evidence. *Behavioral and Brain Sciences, 30*(2), 135–154; discussion 154–187. doi: 10.1017/S0140525X07001185

Kaas, J. H., & Bowes, C. (2014). Plasticity of sensory and motor systems after injury in mature primates. In M. S. Gazzaniga & G. R. Mangun (Eds.), *The cognitive neurosciences* (5th ed., pp. 103–118). Cambridge, MA: The MIT Press.

Kabat-Zinn, J. (2003). Mindfulness-based interventions in context: Past, present, and future. *Clinical Psychology: Science and Practice, 10*(2), 144–156. doi:10.1093/clipsy.bpg016

Kabat-Zinn, J., Lipworth, L., & Burney, R. (1985). The clinical use of mindfulness meditation for the self-regulation of chronic pain. *Journal of Behavioral Medicine, 8*, 163–190.

Kabat-Zinn, J., Lipworth, L., Burney, R., & Sellers, W. (1986). Four year follow-up of a meditation-based program for the self regulation of chronic pain: Treatment outcomes and compliance. *Clinical Journal of Pain, 2*, 159–173.

Kable, J. A., Coles, C. D., Lynch, M. E., & Platzman, K. (2008). Physiological responses to social and cognitive challenges in 8-year-olds with a history of prenatal cocaine exposure. *Developmental Psychobiology, 50*(3), 251–265.

Kagan, J. (1998). *Galen's prophecy: Temperament in human nature.* New York: Basic Books.

Kagan, J. (2010). *The temperamental thread.* New York: Dana Press.

Kagan, J., Snidman, N., Kahn, V., & Towsley, S. (2007). The preservation of two infant temperaments into adolescence. *SRCD Monographs, 72*(2), 76–80.

Kahan, M., & Sutton, N. (1998). Overview: Methadone treatment for the opioid-dependent patient. In B. Brands & J. Brands (Eds.), *Methadone maintenance: A physician's guide to treatment* (pp. 1–15). Toronto, ON: Addiction Research Foundation.

Kahneman, D. (2011). *Thinking, fast and slow.* New York, NY: Farrar, Straus and Giroux.

Kahneman, D., & Tversky, A. (1973). On the psychology of prediction. *Psychological Review, 80*, 237–251.

Kahneman, D., Slovic, P., & Tversky, A. (1982). *Judgment under uncertainty: Heuristics and biases.* New York: Cambridge University Press.

Kail, R., & Hall, L. K. (2001). Distinguishing short-term memory from working memory. *Memory & Cognition, 29*(1), 1–9.

Kakko, J., Svanborg, K. D., Kreek, M. J., & Heilig, M. (2003). 1-year retention and social function after buprenorphine-associated relapse prevention treatment for heroin dependence in Sweden: A randomised, placebo-controlled trial. *Lancet, 361*, 662–668.

Kales, A., Soldatos, C., Bixler, E., Ladda, R. L., Charney, D. S., Weber, G., & Schweitzer, P. K. (1980). Hereditary factors in sleepwalking and night terrors. *British Journal of Psychiatry, 137*, 111–118.

Kalibatseva, Z., & Leong, F. T. (2011). Depression among Asian Americans: Review and recommendations. *Depression Research and Treatment, 2011*, 320902. doi:10.1155/2011/320902

Kalra, G., Subramanyam, A., & Pinto, C. (2011). Sexuality: desire, activity and intimacy in the elderly. *Indian Journal of Psychiatry, 53*(4), 300–306.

Kamau, C., & Harorimana, D. (2008). Does knowledge sharing and withholding of information in organizational committees affect quality of group decision making? *Proceedings of the 9th European Conference on Knowledge Management* (pp. 341–348). Reading, PA: Academic.

Kamin, L. J. (1995, February). Behind the curve. *Scientific American*, 99–103.

Kandel, E. R. (2012). The molecular biology of memory: cAMP, PKA, CRE, CREB-1, CREB-2, and CPEB. *Molecular Brain, 5*(14). doi: 10.1186/1756-6606-5-14

Kandel, E. R., & Schwartz, J. H. (1982). Molecular biology of learning: Modulation of transmitter release. *Science, 218*, 433–443.

Kandel, E. R., & Siegelbaum, S. A. (2013). Cellular mechanisms of implicit memory storage and the biological basis of individuality. In E. R. Kandel, J. H. Schwartz, T. M. Jessell, S. A. Siegelbaum, & A. J. Hudspeth (Eds.), *Principles of neural science* (5th ed., pp. 1461–1486). USA: McGraw-Hill.

Kandler, C., Riemann, R., Spinath, F. M., & Angleitner, A. (2010). Sources of variance in personality facets: A multiple-rater twin study of self–peer, peer–peer, and self–self (dis)agreement. *Journal of Personality, 78*(5), 1565–1594. doi: 10.1111/j.1467-6494.2010.00661.x

Kanno, H., Pearse, D. D., Ozawa, H., Itoi, E., & Bunge, M. B. (2015). Schwann cell transplantation for spinal cord injury repair: Its significant therapeutic potential and prospectus. *Reviews in the Neurosciences, 26*(2), 121–128. doi:10.1515/revneuro-2014-0068

Kanno, H., Pressman, Y., Moody, A., Berg, R., Muir, E. M., Rogers, J. H.,... Bunge, M. B. (2014). Combination of engineered schwann cell grafts to secrete neurotrophin and chondroitinase promotes axonal regeneration and locomotion after spinal cord injury. *Journal of Neuroscience, 34*(5), 1838–1855. doi:10.1523/JNEUROSCI.2661-13.2014

Kaplan, D. M. (2016). Raising the bar: New concepts in the 2014 ACA code of ethics. In I. Marini & M. A. Stebnicki (Eds.), *The professional counselor's desk reference* (2nd ed., pp. 37–42). New York: Springer Publishing.

Kaplan, M. F., & Miller, C. E. (1987). Group decision making and normative versus informational influence: Effects of type of issue and assigned decision rule. *Journal of Personality and Social Psychology, 53*(2), 306–313.

Kaplan, R., & Kaplan, S. (1989). *The experience of nature: A psychological perspective.* New York, New York: Cambridge University Press.

Kaplan, S. (1995). The restorative benefits of nature: Toward an integrative framework. *Journal of Environmental Psychology, 15*(3), 169–182. doi:10.1016/0272-4944(95)90001-2

Kaplan, S., & Berman, M. G. (2010). Directed attention as a common resource for executive functioning and self-regulation. *Perspectives on Psychological Science, 5*(1), 43–57. doi:10.1177/1745691609356784

Karantzoulis, S., & Galvin, J. E. (2011). Distinguishing Alzheimer's disease from other major forms of dementia. *Expert Review of Neurotherapeutics, 11*(11), 1579–1591.

Karau, S. J., & Williams, K. D. (1993). Social loafing: A meta-analytic review and theoretical integration. *Journal of Personality and Social Psychology, 65*, 681–706.

Karau, S. J., & Williams, K. D. (1997). The effects of group cohesiveness on social loafing and social compensation. *Group Dynamics: Theory, Research and Practice, 1*, 156–168.

Karl, A., Birbaumer, N., Lutzenberger, W., Cohen, L. G., & Flor, H. (2001). Reorganization of motor and somatosensory cortex in upper extremity amputees with phantom limb pain. *The Journal of Neuroscience, 21*(10), 3609–3618.

Karney, B. R., & Bradbury, T. N. (2000). Attributions in marriage: State or trait? A growth curve analysis. *Journal of Personality and Social Psychology, 78*, 295–309.

Karpicke, J. D. (2012). Retrieval-based learning: Active retrieval promotes meaningful learning. *Current Directions in Psychological Science, 21*(3), 157–163. doi: 10.1177/0963721412443552

Karpicke, J. D., & Blunt, J. R. (2011). Retrieval practice produces more learning than elaborative studying with concept mapping. *Science*, doi: 10.1126scoemce/1199327.

Kastenbaum, R., & Costa, P. T., Jr. (1977). Psychological perspective on death. *Annual Review of Psychology, 28*, 225–249.

Katz, V. L. (2007). Spontaneous and recurrent abortion: Etiology, diagnosis, treatment. In V. L. Katz, G. M. Lentz, R. A. Lobo, & D. M. Gershenson (Eds.), *Comprehensive Gynecology* (5th ed). Philadelphia: Mosby Elsevier

Kaufman, G., Flanagan, M., Seidman, M., & Wien, S. (2015). "Replay health": An experiential role-playing sport for modeling healthcare decisions, policies, and outcomes. *Games for Health Journal, 4*(4), 295–304. doi: 10.1089/g4h.2014.0134

Kaye, W. H., Fudge, J. L., & Paulus, M. (2009). New insights into symptoms and neurocircuit function of anorexia nervosa. *Nature Reviews Neuroscience, 10*(8), 573–584. doi: 10.1038/nrn2682

Kaye, W. H., Wierenga, C. E., Bailer, U. F., Simmons, A. N., & Bischoff-Grethe, A. (2013). Nothing tastes as good as skinny feels: The neurobiology of anorexia nervosa. *Trends in Neurosciences, 36*(2), 110–120. doi:10.1016/j.tins.2013.01.003

Kazdin, A. E. (1980). Acceptability of time out from reinforcement procedures for disruptive behavior. *Behavior Therapy, 11*(3), 329–344.

Kazdin, A. E. (2008). Evidence-based treatment and practice: New opportunities to bridge clinical research and practice, enhance the knowledge base, and improve patient care. *American Psychologist, 63*(3), 146–159. doi: 10.1037/0003-066x.63.3.146

Kearney, C. A., & Silverman, W. K. (1998). A critical review of pharmacotherapy for youth with anxiety disorders: Things are not as they seem. *Journal of Anxiety Disorders, 12*, 83–102.

Keding, T. J., & Herringa, R. J. (2015). Abnormal structure of fear circuitry in pediatric post-traumatic stress disorder. *Neuropsychopharmacology, 40*(3), 537–545. doi: 10.1038/npp.2014.239

Keel, P. K. (2018a). Bulimia nervosa. In W. S. Agras & A. Robinson (Eds.), *The Oxford handbook of eating disorders* (2nd ed., pp. 187–191). New York, NY: Oxford University Press.

Keel, P. K. (2018b). Epidemilogy and course of eating disorders. In W. S. Agras & A. Robinson (Eds.), *The Oxford handbook of eating disorders* (2nd ed., pp. 34–43). New York, NY: Oxford University Press.

Keel, P. K., & Forney, K. J. (2013). Psychosocial risk factors for eating disorders. *The International Journal of Eating Disorders, 46*(5), 433–439. doi: 10.1002/eat.22094

Keel, P. K., & Klump, K. L. (2003). Are eating disorders culture-bound syndromes? Implications for conceptualizing their etiology. *Psychological Bulletin, 129*(5), 747–769. doi:10.1037/0033-2909.129.5.747

Keillor, J., Barrett, A., Crucian, G., Kortenkamp, S., & Heilman, K. (2002). Emotional experience and perception in the absence of facial feedback. *Journal of the International Neuropsychological Society, 8*(1), 130–135.

Keirsey, D. (1998). *Please understand me II: Temperament character intelligence.* Del Mar, CA: Prometheus Nemesis Book Company.

Keith, T. Z., & Reynolds, M. R. (2010). Cattell-Horn-Carroll abilities and cognitive tests: What we've learned from 20 years of research. *Psychology in the Schools.* doi: 10.1002/pits.20496

Keller, C. J., Huang, Y., Herrero, J. L., Fini, M. E., Du, V., Lado, F. A., ... Mehta, A. D. (2018). Induction and quantification of excitability changes in human cortical networks. *Journal of Neuroscience, 38*(23), 5384–5398. doi:10.1523/JNEUROSCI.1088-17.2018

Keller, M. B., McCullough, J. P., Klein, D. N., Arnow, B., Dunner, D., Gelenberg, A.,... & Zajecka, J. (2000). A comparison of nefazodone, the cognitive behavioral-analysis system of psychotherapy, and their combination for the treatment of chronic depression. *New England Journal of Medicine, 342*(20), 1462–1470.

Kellermann, T., Regenbogen, C., De Vos, M., Mößnang, C., Finkelmeyer, A., & Habel, U. (2012). Effective connectivity of the human cerebellum during visual attention. *The Journal of Neuroscience, 32*(33), 11453–11460. doi: 10.1523/jneurosci.0678-12.2012

Kelly, I. (1980). The scientific case against astrology. *Mercury, 10*(13), 135.

Kelly, J. A., McAuliffe, T. L., Sikkema, K. J., Murphy, D. A., Somlai, A. M., Mulry, G.,... Fernandez, M. I. (1997). Reduction in risk behavior among adults with severe mental illness who learned to advocate for HIV prevention. *Psychiatric Services, 48*(10), 1283–1288.

Kelly, M. S., Oliveira-Maia, A. J., Bernstein, M., Stern, A. P., Press, D. Z., Pascual-Leone, A., & Boes, A. D. (2017). Initial response to transcranial magnetic stimulation treatment for depression predicts subsequent response. *Journal of Neuropsychiatry and Clinical Neurosciences, 29*(2), 179–182. doi:10.1176/appi.neuropsych.16100181

Kempf, L., & Weinberger, D. R. (2009). Molecular genetics and bioinformatics: An outline for neuropsychological genetics. In T. E. Goldberg & D. R. Weinberger (Eds.), *The genetics of cognitive neuroscience* (pp. 3–26). Cambridge, MA: MIT Press.

Kendler, K. S. (1985). Diagnostic approaches to schizotypal personality disorders: A historical perspective. *Schizophrenia Bulletin, 11*, 538–553.

Kendler, K. S., & Prescott, C. A. (1999). A population-based twin study of lifetime major depression in men and women. *Archives of General Psychiatry, 56*(1), 39–44.

Kendler, K. S., Czajkowski, N., Tambs, K., Torgersen, S., Aggen, S. H., Neale, M. C., & Reichborn-Kjennerud, T. (2006). Dimensional representations of DSM-IV cluster A personality disorders in a population-based sample of Norwegian twins: A multivariate study. *Psychological Medicine, 36*(11), 1583–1591. doi: 10.1017/s0033291706008609

Kenett, Y. N., Levi, E., Anaki, D., & Faust, M. (2017). The semantic distance task: Quantifying semantic distance with semantic network path length. *Journal of Experimental Psychology: Learning, Memory, and Cognition, 43*(9), 1470–1489. DOI: http://dx.doi.org/10.1037/xlm0000391

Kenny, A. (1968). Mind and body, In *Descartes: A study of his philosophy* (p. 279). New York: Random House.

Kenny, A. (1994). Descartes to Kant. In A. Kenny (Ed.), *The Oxford history of western philosophy* (pp. 107–192). Oxford, England: Oxford University Press.

Kenrick, D. T., Griskevicius, V., Neuberg, S. L., & Schaller, M. (2010). Renovating the pyramid of needs: Contemporary extensions built upon ancient foundations. *Perspectives on Psychological Science, 5*(3), 292–314.

Kensinger, E. A., Shearer, D. K., Locascio, J. J., Growdon, J. H., & Corkin, S. (2003). Working memory in mild Alzheimer's disease and early Parkinson's disease. *Neuropsychology, 17*(2), 230–239.

Keromoian, R., & Leiderman, P. H. (1986). Infant attachment to mother and child caretaker in an East African community. *International Journal of Behavioral Development, 9*, 455–469.

Kerr-German, A. N., & Buss, A. T. (under review). Dimensional attention as a neural mechanism for selectivity and flexibility in 3.5- and 4.5-year-olds.

Kersten, A. W., & Earles, J. L. (2016). Feelings of familiarity and false memory for specific associations resulting from mugshot exposure. *Memory & Cognition, 45*(1): 93. DOI: http://dx.doi.org/10.3758/s13421-016-0642-7

Kerwin, D. R., Zhang, Y., Kotchen, J. M., Espeland, M. A., Van Horn, L., McTigue, K. M.,... Hoffmann, R. (2010). The cross-sectional relationship between body mass index, waist–hip ratio, and cognitive performance in postmenopausal women enrolled in the women's health initiative. *Journal of the American Geriatric Society, 58*, 1427–1432. [Article first published online July 14, 2010]. doi: 10.1111/j.1532-5415.2010.02969.x

Kesebir, S., Graham, J., & Oishi, S. (2010). A theory of human needs should be human-centered, not animal-centered. *Perspectives on Psychological Science, 5*(3), 315–319.

Kessler, R. C., Aguilar-Gaxiola, S., Alonso, J., Chatterji, S., Lee, S., Ormel, J., ... Wang, P. S. (2009). The global burden of mental disorders: An update from the WHO world mental health (WMH) surveys. *Epidemiologia e Psichiatria Sociale, 18*(1), 22–33.

Kessler, R. C., Chiu, W. T., Demler, O., & Walters, E. E. (2005). Prevalence, severity, and comorbidity of twelve-month DSM-IV disorders in the national comorbidity survey replication (NCS-R). *Archives of General Psychiatry, 62*(6), 617–627. doi: 10.1001/archpsyc.62.6.617

Kessler, R. C., Chiu, W. T., Jin, R., Ruscio, A. M., Shear, K., & Walters, E. E. (2007). The epidemiology of panic attacks, panic disorder, and agoraphobia in the National Comorbidity Survey replication. *Archives of General Psychiatry, 63*(4), 415–424. doi: 10.1001/archpsyc.63.4.415

Kessler, R. C., Hudson, J. I., Shahly, V., Kiejna, A., & Cardoso, G. (2018). Bulimia nervosa and binge-eating disorder. In K. Scott, P. De Jonge, D. Stein, & R. Kessler (Eds.), *Mental disorders around the world: Facts and figures from the WHO world mental health surveys* (pp. 263–285). Cambridge: Cambridge University Press.

Kessler, R. C., Petukhova, M., Sampson, N. A., Zaslavsky, A. M., & Wittchen, H. U. (2012). Twelve-month and lifetime prevalence and lifetime morbid risk of anxiety and mood disorders in the United States. *International Journal of Methods in Psychiatric Research, 21*(3), 169–184. doi: 10.1002/mpr.1359

Kettenmann, H., & Ransom, B. R. (Eds.). (2013). *Neuroglia*. New York, NY: Oxford University Press.

Kety, S. S., Wender, P. H., Jacobsen, B., Ingaham, L. J., Jansson, L., Faber, B., & Kinney, D. K. (1994). Mental illness in the biological and adoptive relatives of schizophrenic adoptees. *Archives of General Psychiatry, 51*, 442–455.

Khademi, J., Björkqvist, K., Österman, K., & Söderberg, P. (2018). The relationship between physical punishment at home and victimization from peer aggression at school in adolescents in Iran and Finland: a mediator-moderator analysis. *European Journal of Social Science Education and Research, 12*(1): 8–14. DOI: https://doi.org/10.26417/ejser.v12i1.p8-14

Kiecolt-Glaser, J. K. (2009). Psychoneuroimmunology: Psychology's gateway to the biomedical future. *Perspectives on Psychological Science, 4*(4), 367.

Kiecolt-Glaser, J. K., Fisher, L. D., Ogrocki, P., Stout, J. C., Speicher, C. E., & Glaser, R. (1987). Marital quality, marital disruption, and immune function. *Psychosomatic Medicine, 49*, 13–34.

Kiecolt-Glaser, J. K., Glaser, R., Gravenstein, S., Malarkey, W. B., & Sheridan, J. (1996). Chronic stress alters the immune response to influenza virus vaccine in older adults. *Proceedings of the National Academy of Sciences, USA, 93*(7), 3043–3047.

Kiecolt-Glaser, J. K., Marucha, P. T., Malarkey, W. B., & Marcado, A. M. (1995). Slowing of wound healing by psychological stress. *Lancet, 346*, 1194–1196.

Kiecolt-Glaser, J. K., McGuire, L., Robles, T., & Glaser, R. (2002). Psychoneuroimmunology: Psychological influences on immune function and health. *Journal of Consulting and Clinical Psychology, 70*, 537–547.

Kielar, A., Deschamps, T., Jokel, R., & Meltzer, J. A. (2018). Abnormal language-related oscillatory responses in primary progressive aphasia. *NeuroImage: Clinical, 18*, 560–574. doi:10.1016/j.nicl.2018.02.028

Kihlstrom, J. F. (1985). Hypnosis. *Annual Review of Psychology, 36*, 385–418.

Kihlstrom, J. F. (2002a). Memory, autobiography, history. *Proteus: A Journal of Ideas, 19*(2), 1–6.

Kihlstrom, J. F. (2002b). To honor Kraepelin...: From symptoms to pathology in the diagnosis of mental illness. In L. E. Beutler & M. L. Malik (Eds.), *Rethinking the DSM: A psychological perspective* (pp. 279–303). Washington, DC: American Psychological Association.

Kihlstrom, J. F. (2018). Hypnosis: Applications. In J. F. Kihlstrom (Ed.), *Reference module in neuroscience and biobehavioral psychology*, pp. 1–5. Amsterdam, The Netherlands: Elsevier.

Kihlstrom, J. F., Mulvaney, S., Tobias, B., & Tobis, I. (2000). The emotional unconscious. In E. Eich, J. Kihlstrom, G. Bower, J. Forgas, & P. Niedenthal (Eds.), *Cognition and emotion* (pp. 30–86). New York: Oxford University Press.

Kilner, J. M., & Lemon, R. N. (2013). What we know currently about mirror neurons. *Current Biology, 23*(23), R1057–1062. doi:10.1016/j.cub.2013.10.051

Kilner, J. M., Neal, A., Weiskopf, N., Friston, K. J., & Frith, C. D. (2009). Evidence of mirror neurons in human inferior frontal gyrus. *The Journal of Neuroscience, 29*(32), 10153–10159. doi: 10.1523/JNEUROSCI.2668-09.2009

Kim, C. E., Shin, S., Lee, H-W., Lim, J., Lee, J., Shin, A., & Kang, D. (2018). Association between sleep duration and metabolic syndrome: A cross-sectional study. *BMC Public Health, 18*: 720. DOI: https://doi.org/10.1186/s12889-018-5557-8

Kim, D., & Hommel, B. (2015). An event-based account of conformity. *Psychological Science, 26*(4), 484. doi: 10.1177/0956797614568319

Kim, H. J., Park, E., Storr, C. L., Tran, K., & Juon, H. S. (2015). Depression among Asian-American adults in the community: Systematic review and meta-analysis. *PLoS ONE, 10*(6), e0127760. doi:10.1371/journal.pone.0127760

Kim, H., & Markus, H. R. (1999). Deviance or uniqueness, harmony or conformity? A cultural analysis. *Journal of Personality and Social Psychology, 77*, 785–800.

Kim, J., Zhang, X., Muralidhar, S., LeBlanc, S.A., & Tonegawa, S. (2017). Basolateral to central amygdala neural circuits for appetitive behaviors. *Neuron, 93*(6), 1464–1479 e1465. doi: 10.1016/j.neuron.2017.02.034

Kim, K. C., & Kim, S. (1999). The multiracial nature of Los Angeles unrest in 1992. In Kwang Chung Kim (Ed.), *Koreans in the Hood: Conflict with African Americans* (pp. 17–38). Baltimore, MD: Johns Hopkins University Press.

Kimhi, Y. (2014). Theory of mind abilities and deficits in autism spectrum disorders. *Topics in Language Disorders, 34*(4), 329–343.

Kimmel, R. J., Roy-Byrne, P. P., & Cowley, D. S. (2015). Pharmacological treatments for panic disorder, generalized anxiety disorder, specific phobia, and social anxiety disorder. In P. E. Nathan & J. M. Gorman (Eds.), *A guide to treatments that work* (4th ed., pp. 463–505). New York, NY: Oxford University Press.

Kimura, R., Mactavish, E., Yang, J., Westaway, D., & Jhamandas, J. H. (2012). Beta amyloid-induced depression of hippocampal long-term potentiation is mediated through the amylin receptor. *Journal of Neuroscience, 32*(48), 17401–17406. doi: 10.1523/%u200BJNEUROSCI.3028-12.2012

Kinasz, K., Accurso, E. C., Kass, A. E., & Le Grange, D. (2016). Does sex matter in the clinical presentation of eating disorders in youth? *Journal of Adolescent Health, 58*(4), 410–416. doi:10.1016/j.jadohealth.2015.11.005

King, J.-R., Pescetelli, N., & Dehaene, S. (2016). Brain mechanisms underlying the brief maintenance of seen and unseen sensory information. *Neuron, 92*(5), 1122–1134. doi:10.1016/j.neuron.2016.10.051

King, M. W., Street, A. E., Gradus, J. L., Vogt, D. S., & Resick, P. A. (2013). Gender differences in posttraumatic stress symptoms among OEF/OIF veterans: An item response theory analysis. *Journal of Traumatic Stress, 26*(2), 175–183. doi: 10.1002/jts.21802

Kinge, J. M., Strand, B. H., Vollset, S. E., & Skirbekk, V. (2015). Educational inequalities in obesity and gross domestic product: Evidence from 70 countries. *Journal of Epidemiology and Community Health, 69*(12), 1141–1146. doi:10.1136/jech-2014-205353

Kirby, J. S., Chu, J. A., & Dill, D. L. (1993). Correlates of dissociative symptomatology in patients with physical and sexual abuse histories. *Comprehensive Psychiatry, 34*, 250–263.

Kircanski, K., & Peris, T. S. (2015). Exposure and response prevention process predicts treatment outcome in youth with OCD. *Journal of Abnormal Child Psychology, 43*(3), 543–552. doi: 10.1007/s10802-014-9917-2

Kirmayer, L. J. (1991). The place of culture in psychiatric nosology: *Taijin kyofusho* and the DSM-III-TR. *Journal of Nervous and Mental Disease, 179*, 19–28.

Kirsch, I. (2000). The response set theory of hypnosis. *American Journal of Clinical Hypnosis, 42*(3/42), 4, 274–292.

Kirsch, I., & Lynn, S. J. (1995). The altered state of hypnosis: Changes in the theoretical landscape. *American Psychologist, 50*, 846–858.

Kirsten, J. (2017). Top 15 bioethical issues in biological advancements. *Bio Explorer*, November 20. Retrieved on September 11, 2018 at https://www.bioexplorer.net/bioethical-issues.html/

Kitamura, T., Saitoh, Y., Takashima, N., Murayama, A., Niibori, Y., Ageta, H.,... Inokuchi, K. (2009). Adult neurogenesis modulates the hippocampus-dependent period of associative fear memory. *Cell, 139*(4), 814–827.

Kitayama, S., & Markus, H. R. (1994). Introduction to cultural psychology and emotion research. In S. Kitayama & H. R. Markus (Eds.), *Emotion and culture: Empirical studies of mutual influence* (pp. 1–22). Washington, DC: American Psychological Association.

Kivimaki, M., & Kawachi, I. (2015). Work stress as a risk factor for cardiovascular disease. *Current Cardiology Reports, 17*(9), 630. doi:10.1007/s11886-015-0630-8

Klaver, C. C., Wolfs, R. C., Vingerling, J. R., Hofman, A., & de Jong, P. T. (1998). Age-specific prevalence and causes of blindness and visual impairment in an older population: The Rotterdam Study. *Archives of Ophthalmology, 116*, 653–658.

Kleim, B., Ehring, T., & Ehlers, A. (2012). Perceptual processing advantages for trauma-related visual cues in post-traumatic stress disorder. *Psychological Medicine, 42*(1), 173–181. doi: 10.1017/s0033291711001048

Klein, N., & Kemper, K. J. (2016). Integrative approaches to caring for children with autism. Current Problems in Pediatric and Adolescent Health Care, E-pub ahead of print. doi: 10.1016/j.cppeds.2015.12.004

Klein, S. B., & Mowrer, R. R. (1989). *Contemporary learning theories: Pavlovian conditioning and the status of traditional learning theory.* Hillsdale, NJ: Lawrence Erlbaum.

Kleinot, M. C., & Rogers, R. W. (1982). Identifying effective components of alcohol misuse prevention programs. *Journal of Studies on Alcohol, 43*, 802–811.

Kligman, A. M., & Balin, A. K. (1989). Aging of human skin. In A. K. Balin & A. M. Kligman (Eds.), *Aging and the skin* (pp. 1–42). New York: Raven Press.

Klorman, R., Hilpert, P. L., Michael, R., LaGana, C., & Sveen, O. B. (1980). Effects of coping and mastery modeling on experienced and inexperienced pedodontic patients' disruptiveness. *Behavior Therapy, 11*, 156–168.

Kluft, R. P. (1984). Introduction to multiple personality disorder. *Psychiatric Annals, 14*, 19–24.

Klüver, H., & Bucy, P. C. (1939). Preliminary analysis of functions of the temporal lobes in monkeys. *Archives of Neurological Psychiatry, 42*, 979–1000.

Knecht, S., Dräger, B., Deppe, M., Bobe, L., Lohmann, H., Flöel, A.,... Henningsen, H. (2000). Handedness and hemispheric language dominance in healthy humans. *Brain, 123*(12), 2512–2518. doi: 10.1093/brain/123.12.2512

Knight, A. (1996). *The life of the law: The people and cases that have shaped our society, from King Alfred to Rodney King.* New York: Crown Publishing Group.

Knight, J. A. (1998). Free radicals: Their history and current status in aging and disease. *Annals of Clinical and Laboratory Science, 28*, 331–346.

Knoth, R., Singec, I., Ditter, M., Pantazis, G., Capetian, P., Meyer, R. P.,... Kempermann, G. (2010). Murine features of neurogenesis in the human hippocampus across the lifespan from 0 to 100 years. *PLoS ONE, 5*(1), e8809. doi:10.1371/journal.pone.0008809

Kobasa, S. (1979). Stressful life events, personality, and health: An inquiry into hardiness. *Journal of Personality and Social Psychology, 37*(1), 1–11.

Koberda, J. L. (2015). Application of Z-score LORETA neuro-feedback in therapy of epilepsy. *Journal of Neurology and Neurobiology, 1*(1), e101.

Koch, C., & Mormann, F. (2010). The neurobiology of consciousness. In G. Mashour (Ed.), *Consciousness, awareness, and anesthesia* (pp. 24–46). New York: Cambridge University Press.

Koenig, H. G., Hays, J. C., Larson, D. B., George, L. K., Cohen, H. J., McCullough, M. E.,... Blazer, D. G. (1999). Does religious attendance prolong survival? A six-year follow-up study of 3,968 older adults. *Journal of Gerontology, 54A*, M370–M377.

Koenig, H. G., McCullough, M. E., & Larson, D. B. (2001). *Handbook of religion and health.* Oxford, UK: Oxford University Press.

Koester, J., & Siegelbaum, S. A. (2013). Membrane potential and the passive electrical properties of the neuron. In E. R. Kandel, J. H. Schwartz, T. M. Jessell, S. A. Siegelbaum, & A. J. Hudspeth (Eds.), *Principles of neural science* (5th ed., pp. 148–171), New York: McGraw-Hill.

Koh, J. K. (1996). A guide to common Singapore spiders. *BP Guide to Nature* series. Singapore: Singapore Science Center.

Kohl, S., Schonherr, D. M., Luigjes, J., Denys, D., Mueller, U. J., Lenartz, D.,... Kuhn, J. (2014). Deep brain stimulation for treatment-refractory obsessive compulsive disorder: A systematic review. *BMC Psychiatry, 14*, 214. doi:10.1186/s12888-014-0214-y

Kohlberg, L. (1969). Stage and sequence: The cognitive-developmental approach to socialization. In D. A. Goslin (Ed.), Handbook of socialization: Theory in research (pp. 347–480). Boston: Houghton-Mifflin.

Kohlberg, L. (1973). Continuities in childhood and adult moral development revisited. In P. Baltes & K. W. Schaie (Eds.), *Life-span development psychology: Personality and socialization.* San Diego, CA: Academic Press.

Köhler, W. (1925, 1992). *Gestalt psychology: An introduction to new concepts in modern psychology (reissue).* New York: Liveright.

Koizumi, A., Amano, K., Cortese, A., Shibata, K., Yoshida, W., Seymour, B., … Lau, H. (2016). Fear reduction without fear through reinforcement of neural activity that bypasses conscious exposure. *Nature Human Behaviour, 1*(1), 0006. doi: 10.1038/s41562-016-0006

Kok, B. E., Coffey, K. A., Cohn, M. A., Catalino, L. I., Vacharkulksemsuk, T., Algoe, S. B.,... Fredrickson, B. L. (2013). How positive emotions build physical health: Perceived positive social connections account for the upward spiral between positive emotions and vagal tone. *Psychological Science, 24*(5), ePub ahead of print. doi: 10.1177/0956797612470827

Kolodny, A., Courtwright, D. T., Hwang, C. S., Kreiner, P., Eadie, J. L., Clark, T. W., & Alexander, G. C. (2015). The prescription opioid and heroin crisis: A public health approach to an epidemic of addiction. *Annual Review of Public Health, 36:* 559–574. DOI: https://doi.org/10.1146/annurev-publhealth-031914-122957

Kompanje, E. J. (2008). "The devil lay upon her and held her down." Hypnagogic hallucinations and sleep paralysis described by the Dutch physician Isbrand van Diemerbroeck (1609–1674). *Journal of Sleep Research, 17*(4), 464–467.

Kong, A., Thorleifsson, G., Frigge, M.L., Vilhjalmsson, B.J., Young, A.I., Thorgeirsson, T.E.,... Stefansson, K. (2018). The nature of nurture: Effects of parental genotypes. *Science, 359*(6374), 424–428. doi: 10.1126/science.aan6877

Konishi, H., Karsten, A., & Vallotton, C. D. (2018). Toddlers' use of gesture and speech in service of emotion regulation during distressing routines. *Infant Mental Health Journal, 39*(6), 730–750. doi:10.1002/imhj.21740

Konowal, N. M., Van Dongen, H. P. A., Powell, J. W., Mallis, M. M., & Dinges, D. F. (1999). Determinants of microsleeps during experimental sleep deprivation. *Sleep, 22*(Suppl. 1), 328.

Konrad, K., Di Martino, A., & Aoki, Y. (2018). Brain volumes and intrinsic brain connectivity in ADHD. In T. Banaschewski, D. Coghill, & A. Zuddas (Eds.), *Oxford textbook of attention deficit hyperactivity disorder* (pp. 57–63): Oxford University Press.

Koob, G. F., & Le Moal, M. (2005). Plasticity of reward neurocircuitry and the 'dark side' of drug addiction. *Nature Neuroscience, 8*(11), 1442–1444.

Koob, G.F., & Volkow, N.D. (2016). Neurobiology of addiction: A neurocircuitry analysis. *The Lancet Psychiatry, 3*(8), 760–773. doi: 10.1016/s2215-0366(16)00104-8

Kopal-Sibley, D. C., Olino, T., Durbin, E., Dyson, M. W., & Klein, D. N. (2018). The stability of temperament from early childhood to early adolescence: A multimethod, multi-informant examination. *European Journal of Personality, 32*(2): 128–145. DOI: https://doi.org/10.1002/per.2151

Korkmaz, B. (2011). Theory of mind and neurodevelopmental disorders of childhood. *Pediatric Research, 69*, 101R–108R.

Korn, S. (1984). Continuities and discontinuities in difficult/easy temperament: Infancy to young adulthood. *Merrill Palmer Quarterly, 30*, 189–199.

Korneev, S. A., Vavoulis, D. V., Naskar, S., Dyakonova, V. E., Kemenes, I., & Kemenes, G. (2018). A CREB2-targeting microRNA is required for long-term memory after single-trial learning. *Scientific Reports, 8*(1): 3950. DOI: https://doi.org/10.1016/j.beproc.2017.12.018

Kosslyn, S. M. (1983). Mental imagery. In Z. Rubin (Ed.), *The psychology of being human.* New York: Harper & Row.

Kosslyn, S. M., Alpert, N. M., Thompson, W. L., Maljkovic, V., Weise, S. B., Chabris, C. F.,... Buonano, F. S. (1993). Visual mental imagery activates topographically organized visual cortex: PET investigations. *Journal of Cognitive Neuroscience, 5*, 263–287.

Kosslyn, S. M., Ball, T. M., & Reiser, B. J. (1978). Visual images preserve metric spatial information: Evidence from studies of image scanning. *Journal of Experimental Psychology: Human Perception and Performance, 4*, 47–60.

Kosslyn, S. M., Ganis, G., & Thompson, W. L. (2001). Neural foundations of imagery. *Nature Reviews Neuroscience, 2*, 635–642.

Kosslyn, S. M., Pascual-Leone, A., Felician, O., Camposano, S., Keenan, J. P., Thompson, W. L.,... Alpert, N. M. (1999). The role of area 17 in visual imagery: Convergent evidence from PET and rTMS. *Science 284*, 167–170.

Kotkin, M., Daviet, C., & Gurin, J. (1996). The *Consumer Reports* mental health survey. *American Psychologist, 51*(10), 1080–1082.

Kovacs, K., Lajtha, A., & Sershen, H. (2010). Effect of nicotine and cocaine on neurofilaments and receptors in whole brain tissue and synaptoneurosome preparations. *Brain Research Bulletin, 82*(1–2), 109–117.

Kozberg, M., Chen, B. R., De Leo, S. E., Bouchard, M. B., & Hillman, E. M. C. (2013). Resolving the transition from negative to positive blood oxygen level-dependent responses in the developing brain. *Proceedings of the National Academy of Sciences of the United States of America (PNAS)*. Published online ahead of print, February 20, 2013. doi: 10.1073/pnas.1212785110

Kozel, F. A., Motes, M. A., Didehbani, N., DeLaRosa, B., Bass, C., Schraufnagel, C. D.,... Hart, J., Jr. (2018). Repetitive TMS to augment cognitive processing therapy in combat veterans of recent conflicts with PTSD: A randomized clinical trial. *Journal of Affective Disorders, 229*, 506–514. doi:10.1016/j.jad.2017.12.046

Koziol, L. F., Budding, D., Andreasen, N., D'Arrigo, S., Bulgheroni, S., Imamizu, H.,... Yamazaki, T. (2014). Consensus paper: The cerebellum's role in movement and cognition. *Cerebellum, 13*(1), 151–177. doi:10.1007/s12311-013-0511-x

Kraha, A., & Boals, A. (2014). Why so negative? Positive flashbulb memories for a personal event. *Memory, 22*(4), 442–449.

Kratofil, P. H., Baberg, H. T., & Dimsdale, J. E. (1996). Self-mutilation and severe self-injurious behavior associated with amphetamine psychosis. *General Hospital Psychiatry, 18*, 117–120.

Kriegstein, A., & Alvarez-Buylla, A. (2009). The glial nature of embryonic and adult neural stem cells. *Annual Review of Neuroscience, 32*(1), 149–184.

Kristensen, P., & Bjerkedal, T. (2007). Explaining the relation between birth order and intelligence. *Science, 316*(5832), 1717.

Kroenke, C. H., Quesenberry, C., Kwan, M. L., Sweeney, C., Castillo, A., & Caan, B. J. (2012). Social networks, social support, and burden in relationships, and mortality after breast cancer diagnosis in the Life After Breast Cancer Epidemiology (LACE) study. *Breast Cancer Research and Treatment, 137*(1), 261. doi: 10.1007/s10549-012-2253-8

Kroll, J. F., Bobb, S. C., & Hoshino, N. (2014). Two languages in mind: Bilingualism as a tool to investigate language, cognition, and the brain. *Current Directions in Psychological Science, 23*(3), 159–163. doi: 10.1177/0963721414528511

Krueger, R. F., & Eaton, N. R. (2015). Transdiagnostic factors of mental disorders. *World Psychiatry, 14*(1), 27–29. doi: http://doi.org/10.1002/wps.20175

Krüttner, S., Stepien, B., Noordermeer, J. N., Mommaas, M. A., Mechtler, K., Dickson, B. J., & Keleman, K. (2012). Drosophila CPEB Orb2A mediates memory independent of its RNA-binding domain. *Neuron, 76*(2), 383. doi: 10.1016/j.neuron.2012.08.028

Kryger, M., Lavie, P., & Rosen, R. (1999). Recognition and diagnosis of insomnia. *Sleep, 22*, S421–S426.

Kübler-Ross, E. (1997). *The wheel of life: A memoir of living and dying.* New York: Touchstone.

Kuhl, B. A., Dudukovic, N. M., Kahn, I., & Wagner, A. D. (2007). Decreased demands on cognitive control reveal the neural processing benefits of forgetting. *Nature Neuroscience, 10*(7), 908–914.

Kuhn, H. W., & Nasar, S. (Eds.). (2001). *The essential John Nash.* Princeton, NJ: Princeton University Press.

Kukula, K. C., Jackowich, R. A., & Wassersug, R. J. (2014). Eroticization as a factor influencing erectile dysfunction treatment effectiveness. *International Journal of Impotence Research, 26*(1), 1–6. doi: 10.1038/ijir.2013.29

Kulik, J. A., & Mahler, H. I. M. (1989). Social support and recovery from surgery. *Health Psychology, 8*, 221–238.

Kulik, J. A., & Mahler, H. I. M. (1993). Emotional support as a moderator of adjustment and compliance after coronary bypass surgery: A longitudinal study. *Journal of Behavioral Medicine, 16*, 45–63.

Kulmala, J., von Bonsdorff, M. B., Stenholm, S., Tormakangas, T., von Bonsdorff, M. E., Nygard, C-H.,... Rantanen, T. (2013). Perceived stress symptoms in midlife predict disability in old age: A 28-year prospective cohort study. *The Journals of Gerontology Series A: Biological Sciences and Medical Sciences*, doi: 10.1093/Gerona/gls339

Kumar, S., & Oakley-Browne, M. (2002). Panic disorder. *Clinical Evidence, 7*, 906–912.

Küntay, A., & Slobin, D. I. (2002). Putting interaction back into child language: Examples from Turkish. *Psychology of Language and Communication, 6*, 5–14.

Kuo, B. C. H. (2011). Culture's consequences on coping: Theories, evidences, and dimensionalities. *Journal of Cross-Cultural Psychology, 42*, 1084. doi: 10.1177/0022022110381126

Kupfer, D. J., & Reynolds, C. F., III. (1997). Management of insomnia. *New England Journal of Medicine, 336*(5), 341–346.

Kupper, N., & Denollet, J. (2018). Type D personality as a risk factor in coronary heart disease: A review of current evidence. *Current Cardiology Reports, 20*(11), 104. doi:10.1007/s11886-018-1048-x

Kurdziel, L., Duclos, K., & Spencer, R. M. C. (2013). Sleep spindles in midday naps enhance learning in preschool children. *Proceedings of the National Academy of Sciences, 110*(43), 17267–17272.

Kuriki, I., Ashida, H., Murakami, I., & Kitaoka, A. (2008). Functional brain imaging of the Rotating Snakes illusion by fMRI. *Journal of Vision, 8*(10), 16.1–10.

Kustermann, T., Popov, T., Miller, G. A., & Rockstroh, B. (2018). Verbal working memory-related neural network communication in schizophrenia. *Psychophysiology*, e13088. doi:10.1111/psyp.13088

Kvavilashvili, L., Mirani, J., Schlagman, S., Foley, K., & Dornbrot, D. E. (2009). Consistency of flashbulb memories of September 11 over long delays: Implications for consolidation and wrong time slice hypotheses. *Journal of Memory and Language, 61*(4), 556–572.

LaBar, K. S., LeDoux, J. E., Spencer, D. D., & Phelps, E. A. (1995). Impaired fear conditioning following unilateral temporal lobectomy to humans. *Journal of Neuroscience, 15*, 6846–6855.

LaBerge, D. (1980). Unitization and automaticity in perception. In J. H. Flowers (Ed.), *Nebraska Symposium on Motivation* (pp. 53–71). Lincoln: University of Nebraska Press.

Labkovsky, E., & Rosenfeld, J. P. (2014). A novel dual probe complex trial protocol for detection of concealed information. *Psychophysiology, 51*(11), 1122–1130. doi: 10.1111/psyp.12258

Labouvie-Vief, G. (1980). Beyond formal operations: Uses and limits of pure logic in lifespan development. *Human Development, 23*, 114–146.

Labouvie-Vief, G. (1992). A neo-Piagetian perspective on adult cognitive development. In R. Sternberg & C. Berg (Eds.), *Intellectual development* (pp. 197–228). Cambridge, UK: Cambridge University Press.

Lacayo, A. (1995). Neurologic and psychiatric complications of cocaine abuse. *Neuropsychiatry, Neuropsychology, and Behavioral Neurology, 8*(1), 53–60.

LaFromboise, T., Coleman, H. L. K., & Gerton J. (1993). Psychological impact of biculturalism: Evidence and theory. *Psychological Bulletin, 114*, 395–412.

Laghi, F., Bianchi, D., Lonigro, A., Pompili, S., & Baiocco, R. (2019). Emotion regulation and alcohol abuse in second-generation immigrant adolescents: The protective role of cognitive reappraisal. *Journal of Health Psychology*, 1359105318820715. doi:10.1177/1359105318820715

Lagopoulos, J., Xu, J., Rasmussen, I., Vik, A., Malhi, G. S., Eliassen, C. F.,... Ellingsen, Ø. (2009). Increased theta and alpha EEG activity during nondirective meditation. *The Journal of Alternative and Complementary Medicine, 15*(11), 1187.

Lai, M.-C., Lombardo, M. V., Auveung, B., Chakrabarti, B., & Baron-Cohen, S. (2015). Sex/gender differences and autism: Setting the scene for future research. Journal of the American Academy of Child & Adolescent Psychiatry, 54, 11–24.

Lal, S. (2002). Giving children security: Mamie Phipps Clark and the radicalization of child psychology. *American Psychologist, 57*(1), 20–28.

Lalancette, M.-F., & Standing, L. G. (1990). Asch fails again. *Social Behavior and Personality, 18*(1), 7–12.

Lambert, M. J., & Ogles, B. M. (2004). The efficacy and effectiveness of psychotherapy. In M. J. Lambert (Ed.), *Handbook of psychotherapy and behavior change* (5th ed.) (pp. 139–193). New York: Wiley.

Lambert, N., Fincham, F. D., Dewall, N. C., Pond, R., & Beach, S. R. (2013). Shifting toward cooperative tendencies and forgiveness: How partner-focused prayer transforms motivation. *Personal Relationships, 20*(1), 184. doi: 10.1111/j.1475-6811.2012.01411.x

Lana-Peixoto, Marco A. (2014). Complex visual hallucinations in mentally healthy people. *Arquivos de Neuro-Psiquiatria, 72*(5), 331–332. https://dx.doi.org/10.1590/0004-282X20140050.

Lance, C. J., LaPointe, J. A., & Fisicaro, S. (1994). Tests of three causal models of halo rater error. *Organizational Behavior and Human Decision Performance, 57*, 83–96.

Landrum, R. E. (2009). *Finding jobs with a psychology bachelor's degree.* Washington, DC: American Psychological Association.

Landrum, R. E., & Davis, S. F. (2014). *The psychology major: Career options and strategies for success* (5th ed). Upper Saddle River, NJ: Prentice Hall.

Lane, R. D., Kivley, L. S., DuBois, M. A. Shamasundara, P., & Schwartz, G. E. (1995). Levels of emotional awareness and the degree of right hemisphere dominance in the perception of facial emotion. *Neuropsychologia, 33*, 525–538.

Laney, C., & Loftus, E. F. (2013). Recent advances in false memory research. *South African Journal of Psychology, 43*(2), 137–146.

Lange, C. (1885). The emotions. Reprinted in C. G. Lange & W. James (Eds.), *The emotions.* New York: Harner.

Lange, S., Probst, C., Gmel, G., Rehm, J., Burd, L., & Popova, S. (2017). Global prevalence of fetal alcohol spectrum disorder among children and youth: A systematic review and meta-analysis. *JAMA Pediatrics, 171*(10): 948-956. DOI: http://dx.doi.org/10.1001/jamapediatrics.2017.1919

Langer, E. J., & Rodin, J. (1976). The effects of enhanced personal responsibility for the aged: A field experiment in an institutional setting. *Journal of Personality and Social Psychology, 34*, 191–198.

Langone, M. (1996). Clinical update on cults. *Psychiatric Times, 13*(7), 1–3.

Lanius, R. A., Brand, B., Vermetten, E., Frewen, P. A., & Spiegel, D. (2012). The dissociative subtype of posttraumatic stress disorder: Rationale, clinical and neurobiological evidence, and implications. *Depression and Anxiety, 29*(8), 701–708. doi:10.1002/da.21889

Lanius, R. A., Vermetten, E., Loewenstein, R. J., Brand, B., Schmahl, C., Bremner, J. D., & Spiegel, D. (2010). Emotion modulation in PTSD: Clinical and neurobiological evidence for a dissociative subtype. *American Journal of Psychiatry, 167*(6), 640–647. doi:10.1176/appi.ajp.2009.09081168

Lanphear, B. P., Dietrich, K., Auinger, P., & Cox, C. (2000). Cognitive deficits associated with blood lead concentrations <10 micrograms/dL in U.S. children and adolescents. *Public Health Reports, 115*(6), 521–529.

Lapsley, D. K., Milstead, M., Quintana, S. M., Flannery, D., & Buss, R. R. (1986). Adolescent egocentrism and formal operations: Tests of a theoretical assumption. *Developmental Psychology, 22*, 800–807.

Larsen, J. T., Berntson, G. G., Poehlmann, K. M., Ito, T. A., & Cacioppo, J. T. (2008). The psychophysiology of emotion. In M. Lewis, J. M. Haviland-Jones, & L. F. Barrett (Eds.), *Handbook of emotions* (3rd ed., pp. 180–195). New York: Guilford Press.

Larzelere, R. (1986). Moderate spanking: Model or deterrent of children's aggression in the family? *Journal of Family Violence, 1*(1), 27–36.

Lashley, K. S. (1938). The thalamus and emotion. *The Psychological Review, 45*, 21–61.

Lasnik, H. (1990). Metrics and morphophonemics in early English verse. *University of Connecticut Working Papers in Linguistics* (Vol. 3, pp. 29–40). Storrs: University of Connecticut.

Latané, B., & Darley, J. M. (1969). Bystander "apathy." *American Scientist, 57*(2), 244–268.

Latané, B., Williams, K., & Harkins, S. (1979). Many hands make light the work: The causes and consequences of social loafing. *Journal of Personality & Social Psychology, 37*(6), 822–832.

Lau, A., & Zane, N. (2000). Examining the effects of ethnic-specific services: An analysis of cost-utilization and treatment outcome for Asian American clients. *Journal of Community Psychology, 28*(1), 63–77.

Launer, L., Masaki, K., Petrovitch, H., Foley, D., & Havlik, R. (1995). The association between midlife blood pressure levels and late-life cognitive function. *Journal of the American Medical Association, 272*(23), 1846–1851.

Lauriola, M., Panno, A., Levin, I. P., & Lejuez, C. W. (2014). Individual differences in risky decision making: A meta-analysis of sensation seeking and impulsivity with the balloon alalogue risk task. *Journal of Behavioral Decision Making, 27*(1), 20–36.

Lavergne, G. M. (1997). *A sniper in the tower: The true story of the Texas Tower massacre*. New York: Bantam.

Laviolette, S. R., Lauzon, N. M., Bishop, S. F., Sun, N., & Tan, H. (2008). Dopamine signaling through D1-like versus D2-like receptors in the nucleus accumbens core versus shell differentially modulates nicotine reward sensitivity. *Journal of Neuroscience*, August 6, *28*(32), 8025–8033.

Laws, G., Davies, I., & Andrews, C. (1995). Linguistic structure and nonlinguistic cognition: English and Russian blues compared. *Language and Cognitive Processes, 10*, 59–94.

Laws, K. R., & Kokkalis, J. (2007). Ecstasy (MDMA) and memory function: A meta-analytic update. *Human Psychopharmacology: Clinical and Experimental, 22*(6), 381–388. doi: 10.1002/hup.857

Laws, K. R., Sweetnam, H., & Kondel, T. K. (2012). Is ginkgo biloba a cognitive enhancer in healthy individuals? A meta-analysis. *Human Psychopharmacology: Clinical and Experimental, 27*(6), 527–533.

Lawton, E., Brymer, E., Clough, P., & Denovan, A. (2017). The relationship between the physical activity environment, nature relatedness, anxiety, and the psychological well-being benefits of regular exercisers. *Frontiers in Psychology, 8*, 1058. doi:10.3389/fpsyg.2017.01058

Laxpati, N. G., Kasoff, W. S., & Gross, R. E. (2014). Deep brain stimulation for the treatment of epilepsy: Circuits, targets, and trials. *Neurotherapeutics, 11*(3), 508–526. doi:10.1007/s13311-014-0279-9

Lay, C., & Nguyen, T. T. I. (1998). The role of acculturation-related and acculturation non-specific daily hassles: Vietnamese-Canadian students and psychological distress. *Canadian Journal of Behavioural Science, 30*(3), 172–181.

Lazarus, R. S. (1991). *Emotion and adaptation*. New York: Oxford University Press.

Lazarus, R. S. (1993). From psychological stress to the emotions: A history of changing outlooks. *Annual Review of Psychology, 44*, 1–22.

Lazarus, R. S. (1999). *Stress and emotion: A new synthesis*. New York: Springer.

Lazarus, R. S., & Folkman, S. (1984). *Stress, appraisal and coping*. New York: Springer.

Le, C. P., Nowell, C. J., Kim-Fuchs, C., Botteri, E., Hiller, J. G., Ismail, H.,... Sloan, E. K. (2016). Chronic stress in mice remodels lymph vasculature to promote tumor cell dissemination. *Nature Communications, 7*, Article 10634. doi: 10.1038/ncomms10634

Leary, M. R., & Forsyth, D. R. (1987). Attributions of responsibility for collective endeavors. *Review of Personality and Social Psychology, 8*, 167–188.

Leary, M. R., & Toner, K. (2015). Self-processes in the construction and maintenance of personality. In M. Mikulincer & P. R. Shaver (Eds.), *APA handbook of personality and social psychology, Vol. 4: Personality processes and individual differences* (pp. 447–467). Washington, DC: American Psychological Association.

Leask, J., Haber, R. N., & Haber, R. B. (1969). Eidetic imagery in children: II. Longitudinal and experimental results. *Psychonomic Monograph Supplements, 3*, 25–48.

Leccese, A. P., Pennings, E. J. M., & De Wolff, F. A. (2000). *Combined use of alcohol and psychotropic drugs. A review of the literature*. Leiden, The Netherlands: Academisch Ziekenhuis Leiden (AZL).

Leclerc, C. M., & Hess, T. M. (2007). Age differences in the bases for social judgments: Tests of a social expertise perspective. *Experimental Aging Research, 33*(1), 95–120.

LeDoux, J. E. (1994). Emotion, memory and the brain. *Scientific American, 270*, 32–39.

LeDoux, J. E. (1996). *The emotional brain: The mysterious underpinnings of emotional life*. New York: Simon & Schuster.

LeDoux, J. E. (2003). The emotional brain, fear, and the amygdala. *Cellular and Molecular Neurobiology, 23*(4–5), 727–738.

LeDoux, J. E. (2007). The amygdala. *Current Biology, 17*(20), R868–R874.

LeDoux, J. E., & Damasio, A. R. (2013). Emotions and feelings. In E. R. Kandel, J. H. Schwartz, T. M. Jessell, S. A. Siegelbaum, & A. J. Hudspeth (Eds.), *Principles of neural science* (5th ed., pp. 1079–1094). New York: McGraw-Hill.

LeDoux, J. E., & Phelps, E. A. (2008). Emotional networks in the brain. In M. Lewis, J. M. Haviland-Jones, & L. F. Barrett (Eds.), *Handbook of emotions* (3rd ed., pp. 159–179). New York: Guilford Press.

Lee, C. W., & Cuijpers, P. (2013). A meta-analysis of the contribution of eye movements in processing emotional memories. *Journal of Behavior Therapy and Experimental Psychiatry, 44*(2), 231–239. doi:10.1016/j.jbtep.2012.11.001

Lee, D. J., Elias, G. J. B., & Lozano, A. M. (2018). Neuromodulation for the treatment of eating disorders and obesity. *Therapeutic Advances in Psychopharmacology, 8*(2), 73–92. doi:10.1177/2045125317743435

Lee, F., Hallahan, M., & Herzog, T. (1996). Explaining real life events: How culture and domain shape attributions. *Personality and Social Psychology Bulletin, 22*, 732–741.

Lee, J., & Harley, V. R. (2012). The male fight-flight response: A result of SRY regulation of catecholamines? *Bioessays, 34*(6), 454–457.

Lee, M., & Shlain, B. (1986). *Acid dreams: The complete social history of LSD: The CIA, the sixties, and beyond*. New York: Grove Press.

Lee, S. J., Altschul, I., & Gershoff, E. T. (2013). Does warmth moderate longitudinal associations between maternal spanking and child aggression in early childhood? *Developmental Psychology, 49*(11), 2017–2028.

Lefevre, A., Richard, N., Jazayeri, M., Beuriat, P. A., Fieux, S., Zimmer, L., . . . Sirigu, A. (2017). Oxytocin and serotonin brain mechanisms in the nonhuman primate. *Journal of Neuroscience, 37*(28), 6741–6750. doi: 10.1523/JNEUROSCI.0659-17.2017

Lega, B., Germi, J., & Rugg, M. D. (2017). Modulation of oscillatory power and connectivity in the human posterior cingulate cortex supports the encoding and retrieval of episodic memories. *Journal of Cognitive Neuroscience, 29*(8), 1415–1432. DOI: https://doi.org/10.1162/jocn_a_01133

LeGates, T. A., Altimus, C. M., Wang, H., Lee, H. K., Yang, S., Zhao, H.,... Hattar, S. (2012). Aberrant light directly impairs mood and learning through melanopsin-expressing neurons. *Nature, 491*(7425), 594–598. doi:10.1038/nature11673

LeGoff, D. B. (2004). Use of Lego© as a therapeutic medium for improving social competence. *Journal of Autism and Developmental Disorders, 34*(5), 557–571.

Lehnert, B. (2007). Joint wave-particle properties of the individual photon. *Progress in Physics, 4*(10), 104–108.

Lehr, U., & Thomae, H. (1987). *Patterns of psychological aging. Results from the Bonne Aging Longitudinal Study (BOLSA)*. Stuttgart, Germany: Enke.

Leib, R., Mawase, F., Karniel, A., Donchin, O., Rothwell, J., Nisky, I., & Davare, M. (2016). Stimulation of PPC affects the mapping between motion and force signals for stiffness perception but not motion control. *Journal of Neuroscience, 36*(41), 10545–10559. doi:10.1523/JNEUROSCI.1178-16.2016

Leibel, R. L., Rosenbaum, M., & Hirsch, J. (1995). Changes in energy expenditure resulting from altered body weight. *The New England Journal of Medicine, 332*, 621–628.

Lemos, M. S., & Verissimo, L. (2014). The relationships between intrinsic motivation, extrinsic motivation, and achievement, along elementary school. *Procedia: Social and Behavioral Sciences, 112*, 930–938.

Leon, P., Chedraui, P., Hidalgo, L., & Ortiz, F. (2007). Perceptions and attitudes toward the menopause among middle-aged women from Guayaquil, Ecuador. *Maturitas, 57*(3), 233–238.

Leong, A. T. L., Dong, C. M., Gao, P. P., Chan, R. W., To, A., Sanes, D. H., & Wu, E. X. (2018). Optogenetic auditory fMRI reveals the effects of visual cortical inputs on auditory midbrain response. *Scientific Reports, 8*(1), 8736. doi:10.1038/s41598-018-26568-1

Leong, F. T. L., Hartung, P. J., Goh, D., & Gaylor, M. (2001). Appraising birth order in career assessment: Linkages to Holland's and Super's models. *Journal of Career Assessment, 9*, 25–39.

LePort, A. K., Mattfeld, A. T., Dickinson-Anson, H., Fallon, J. H., Stark, C. E., Kruggel, F.,... McGaugh, J. L. (2012). Behavioral and neuroanatomical investigation of Highly Superior Autobiographical Memory (HSAM). *Neurobiology of Learning and Memory, 98*(1), 78. doi: 10.1016/j.nlm.2012.05.002

Lerner, A. G., Gelkopf, M., Skladman, I., Oyffe, I., Finkel, B., Sigal, M., & Weizman, A. (2002). Flashback and hallucinogen persisting perception disorder: Clinical aspects and pharmacological treatment approach. *The Israel Journal of Psychiatry and Related Sciences, 39*(2), 92–99.

Leroy, C., & Symes, B. (2001). Teachers' perspectives on the family backgrounds of children at risk. *McGill Journal of Education, 36*(1), 45–60.

Leslie, M. (2000, July/August). The vexing legacy of Louis Terman. *Stanford Magazine*. Retrieved August 12, 2010, from http://www.stanfordalumni.org/news/magazine/2000/julaug/articles/terman.html

Levenson, R. W. (1992). Autonomic nervous system differences among emotions. *Psychological Sciences, 3*, 23–27.

Levenson, R. W., Ekman, P., Heider, K., & Friesen, W. V. (1992). Emotion and autonomic nervous system activity in the Minangkabau of West Sumatra. *Journal of Personality and Social Psychology, 62*, 972–988.

Levenstein, S., Rosenstock, S., Jacobsen, R. K., & Jorgensen, T. (2015). Psychological stress increases risk for peptic ulcer, regardless of helicobacter pylori infection or use of nonsteroidal anti-inflammatory drugs. *Clinical Gastroenterology and Hepatology, 13*(3), 498–506 e491. doi:10.1016/j.cgh.2014.07.052

Levesque, R. J. R. (2014). Opiates. In R. J. R. Levesque (Ed.), *Encyclopedia of Adolescence* (p. 1941). New York: Springer.

Levine, C. S., Miyamoto, Y., Markus, H. R., Rigotti, A., Boylan, J. M., Park, J.,... Ryff, C. D. (2016). Culture and healthy eating: The role of independence and interdependence in the United States and Japan. *Personality & Social Psychology Bulletin, 42*(10), 1335–1348. doi:10.1177/0146167216658645

Levine, M. (2012). Helping in emergencies: Revisiting Latané and Darley's bystander studies. In J. Smith & S. Haslam (Eds.), *Social psychology: Revisiting the classic studies* (pp. 192–208). Los Angeles, CA: SAGE.

Levy, B. R., Slade, M. D., Kunkel, S. R., & Kasl, S. V. (2002). Longevity increased by positive self-perceptions of aging. *Journal of Personality and Social Psychology, 83*, 261–269.

Levy, S. R., Stroessner, S. J., & Dweck, C. S. (1998). Stereotype formation and endorsement: The role of implicit theories. *Journal of Personality and Social Psychology, 74*(6), 1421–1436. http://dx.doi.org/10.1037/0022-3514.74.6.1421

Levy-Gigi, E., Bonanno, G. A., Shapiro, A. R., Richter-Levin, G., Keri, S., & Sheppes, G. (2016). Emotion regulatory flexibility sheds light on the elusive relationship between repeated traumatic exposure and posttraumatic stress disorder symptoms. *Clinical Psychological Science, 4*(1), 28–39. doi: 10.1177/2167702615577783

Lewis, C. P., Nakonezny, P. A., Blacker, C. J., Vande Voort, J. L., Port, J. D., Worrell, G. A.,... Croarkin, P. E. (2018). Cortical inhibitory markers of lifetime suicidal behavior in depressed adolescents. *Neuropsychopharmacology*. doi:10.1038/s41386-018-0040-x

Lewis, D. K. (1996, June). A cross-cultural model for psychotherapy: Working with the African-American client. *Perspectives on Multiculturalism and Cultural Diversity, VI*(2).

Lewis, D. M., Russell, E. M., Al-Shawaf, L., & Buss, D. M. (2015). Lumbar curvature: A previously undiscovered standard of attractiveness. *Evolution and Human Behavior, 36*(5), 345–350. doi: 10.1016/j.evolhumbehav.2015.01.007

Lewis, J. R. (1995). *Encyclopedia of afterlife beliefs and phenomenon*. Detroit, MI: Visible Ink Press.

Lewis, P. A., Knoblich, G., & Poe, G. (2018). How memory replay in sleep boosts creative problem-solving. *Trends in Cognitive Sciences, 22*(6): 491. DOI: 10.1016/j.tics.2018.03.009

Lewis, R. W., Fugl-Meyer, K. S., Corona, G., Hayes, R. D., Laumann, E. O., Moreira, E. D., Jr.,... Segraves, T. (2010). Definitions/epidemiology/risk factors for sexual dysfunction. *The Journal of Sexual Medicine, 7*(4pt2), 1598–1607. doi: 10.1111/j.1743-6109.2010.01778.x

Li, D., & Sullivan, W. C. (2016). Impact of views to school landscapes on recovery from stress and mental fatigue. *Landscape and Urban Planning, 148*, 149–158. doi:10.1016/j.landurbplan.2015.12.015

Li, J., Hu, Z., & de Lecea, L. (2014). The hypcretins/orexins: Integrators of multiple psychological functions. *British Journal of Pharmacology, 171*(2), 332–350.

Li, L., Ruan, H., & Yuan, W.-J. (2015). The relationship between social support and burnout among ICU nurses in Shanghai: A cross-sectional study. *Chinese Nursing Research, 2*(2–3), 45–50.

Li, Y. J., Johnson, K. A., Cohen, A. B., Williams, M. J., Knowles, E. D., & Chen, Z. (2012). Fundamental(ist) attribution error: Protestants are dispositionally focused. *Journal of Personality and Social Psychology, 102*(2), 281–290. doi:10.1037/a0026294

Li, Z., Qian, P., Shao, W., Shi, H., He, X. C., Gogol, M.,... & Li, L. (2018). Suppression of m6a reader Ythdf2 promotes hematopoietic stem cell expansion. *Cell Research, 28*: 904–917. DOI: http://dx.doi.org/10.1038/s41422-018-0072-0

Libbrecht, N., Lievens, F., Carette, B., & Cote, S. (2014). Emotional intelligence predicts success in medical school. *Emotion, 14*(1), 64–73. doi: 10.1037/a0034392

Liechti, M. E., & Vollenweider, F. X. (2001). Which neuroreceptors mediate the subjective effects of MDMA in humans? A summary of mechanistic studies. *Human Psychopharmacology, 16*: 589–598.

Light, K. R, Kolata, S., Wass, C., Denman-Brice, A., Zagalsky, R., & Matzel, L. D. (2010). Working memory training promotes general cognitive abilities in genetically heterogeneous mice. *Current Biology, 20*(8), 777–782.

Lilienfeld, S. O. (1999). Projective measures of personality and psychopathology: How well do they work? *Skeptical Inquirer, 23*(5), 32–39.

Lilienfeld, S. O., & Lynn, S. J. (2015). Dissociative identity disorder. *Science and pseudoscience in clinical psychology* (2nd ed., pp. 113–152). New York, NY: The Guilford Press.

Lilienfeld, S. O., Lynn, S. J., & Lohr, J. M. (2004). Science and pseudoscience in clinical psychology: Initial thoughts, reflections, and considerations. In S. O. Lilienfeld, S. J. Lynn, & J. M. Lohr (Eds.), *Science and pseudoscience in clinical psychology* (p. 2). New York: Guilford Press.

Lilienfeld, S. O., Lynn, S. J., & Lohr, J. M. (2015b). *Science and pseudoscience in clinical psychology* (2nd ed.). New York: The Guilford Press.

Lilienfeld, S. O., Ritschel, L. A., Lynn, S. J., Cautin, R. L., & Latzman, R. D. (2013). Why many clinical psychologists are resistant to evidence-based practice: Root causes and constructive remedies. *Clinical Psychology Review, 33*(7), 883–900. doi: 10.1016/j.cpr.2012.09.008

Lilienfeld, S. O., Ritschel, L. A., Lynn, S. J., Cautin, R. L., & Latzman, R. D. (2014). Why ineffective psychotherapies appear to work: A taxonomy of causes of spurious therapeutic effectiveness. *Perspectives on Psychological Science, 9*(4), 355–387. doi:10.1177/1745691614535216

Lilienfeld, S. O., Sauvigné, K. C., Lynn, S. J., Cautin, R. L., Latzman, R. D., & Waldman, I. D. (2015a). Fifty psychological and psychiatric terms to avoid: A list of inaccurate, misleading, misused, ambiguous, and logically confused words and phrases. *Frontiers in Psychology, 6*, 1100. doi: 10:3389/fpsyg.2015.01100

Lilienfeld, S. O., Wood, J. M., & Garb, H. N. (2000). The scientific status of projective techniques. *Psychological Science in the Public Interest, 1*(2), 27–66. doi: 10.1111/1529-1006.002

Lim, J., Choo, W. C., & Chee, M. W. L. (2007). Reproducibility of changes in behavior and fMRI activation associated with sleep deprivation in a working memory task. *Sleep, 30*, 61–70.

Lim, L., Radua, J., & Rubia, K. (2014). Gray matter abnormalities in childhood maltreatment: A voxel-wise meta-analysis. *American Journal of Psychiatry, 171*(8), 854–863. doi: http://dx.doi.org/10.1176/appi.ajp.2014.13101427

Lim, M. M., & Young, L. J. (2006). Neuropeptidergic regulation of affiliative behavior and social bonding in animals. *Hormones and Behavior, 50*(4), 506–517. doi: 10.1016/j.yhbeh.2006.06.028

Lim, Y. Y., Ellis, K. A., Pietrzak, R. H., Ames, D., Darby, D., Harrington, K.,... Maruff, P. (2012). Stronger effect of amyloid load than APOE genotype on cognitive decline in healthy older adults. *Neurology, 79*(16), 1645. doi: 10.1212/WNL.0b013e31826e9ae6

Lin, C. S., Lyons, J. L., & Berkowitz, F. (2007). Somatotopic identification of language-SMA in language processing via fMRI. *Journal of Scientific and Practical Computing 1*(2), 3–8.

Lin, P. J., & Schwanenflugel, P. J. (1995). Cultural familiarity and language factors in the structure of category knowledge. *Journal of Cross-Cultural Psychology, 26*, 153–168.

Lin, P. J., Schwanenflugel, P. J., & Wisenbaker, J. M. (1990). Category typicality, cultural familiarity, and the development of category knowledge. *Developmental Psychology, 26*, 805–813.

Lindemann, B. (1996). Taste reception. *Physiological Review, 76*, 719–766.

Lipsman, N., Woodside, D. B., Giacobbe, P., Hamani, C., Carter, J. C., Norwood, S. J.,... Lozano, A. M. (2013). Subcallosal cingulate deep brain stimulation for treatment-refractory anorexia nervosa: A phase 1 pilot trial. *Lancet, 381*(9875), 1361–1370. doi: 10.1016/s0140-6736(12)62188-6

Lipson, S. K., Lattie, E. G., & Eisenberg, D. (2018). Increased rates of mental health service utilization by U.S. College students: 10-year population-level trends (2007–2017). *Psychiatric Services*, appips201800332. doi:10.1176/appi.ps.201800332

Lisanby, S. H., Maddox, J. H., Prudic, J., Devanand, D. P., & Sackeim, H. A. (2000). The effects of electroconvulsive therapy on memory of autobiographical and public events. *Archives of General Psychiatry, 57*, 581–590.

Liu, S., Athey, A., Killgore, W., Gehrels, J., Alfonso-Miller, P., & Grandner, M. (2018). 0964 Sleep paralysis and hypnogogic/hypnopompic hallucinations: Prevalence in student athletes and relationship to depressive symptoms. *Sleep, 41*(1): A358.

Livesley, J. W. (Ed.). (1995). *The DSM-IV Personality disorders*. New York: Guilford Press.

Lizskowski, U., Carpenter, M., Striano, T., & Tomasello, M. (2006). 12- and 18-month-olds point to provide information for others. *Journal of Cognition and Development, 7*, 173–187.

LoBello, S. G., & Mehta, S. (2019). No evidence of seasonal variation in mild forms of depression. *Journal of Behavior Therapy and Experimental Psychiatry, 62*, 72–79. doi:10.1016/j.jbtep.2018.09.003

Lo Bue, A., Salvaggio, A., Insalaco, G., & Marrone, O. (2014). Extreme REM rebound during continuous positive airway pressure titration for obstructive sleep apnea in a depressed patient. *Case Reports in Medicine, 2014*, 292181. doi: 10.1155/2014/292181

Lock, M. (1994). Menopause in cultural context. *Experimental Gerontology, 29*(3–4), 307–317.

Locke, A. E., Kahali, B., Berndt, S. I., Justice, A. E., Pers, T. H., Day, F. R.,... Speliotes, E. K. (2015). Genetic studies of body mass index yield new insights for obesity biology. *Nature, 518*(7538), 197–206. doi:10.1038/nature14177

Loehlin, J. C. (1992). *Genes and environment in personality development*. Newbury Park, CA: Sage.

Loehlin, J. C., McCrae, R. R., Costa, P. T., Jr., & John, O. P. (1998). Heritabilities of common and measure-specific components of the Big Five personality factors. *Journal of Research in Personality, 32*, 431–453.

Loehlin, J. C., Willerman, L., & Horn, J. M. (1985). Personality resemblances in adoptive families when the children are late-adolescent or adult. *Journal of Personality and Social Psychology, 48*, 376–392.

Loftus, E. (1975). Leading questions and the eyewitness report. *Cognitive Psychology, 7*, 560–572.

Loftus, E. (1987, June 29). Trials of an expert witness. *Newsweek, 109*: 10–11.

Loftus, E. F., & Loftus, G. R. (1980). On the permanence of stored information in the human brain. *American Psychologist, 35,* 409–420.

Loftus, E. F., Miller, D. G., & Burns H. J. (1978). Semantic integration of verbal information into a visual memory. *Journal of Experimental Psychology: Human Learning, 4,* 19–31.

Lombardi, C., Rocchi, R., Montagna, P., Silani, V., & Parati, G. (2009). Obstructive sleep apnea syndrome: A cause of acute delirium. *Journal of Clinical Sleep Medicine, 5*(6): 569–570.

Lopez-Quintero, C., Hasin, D. S., de Los Cobos, J. P., Pines, A., Wang, S., Grant, B. F., & Blanco, C. (2011). Probability and predictors of remission from life-time nicotine, alcohol, cannabis or cocaine dependence: Results from the National Epidemiologic Survey on Alcohol and Related Conditions. Addiction, *106*(3), 657–669. doi: 10.1111/j.1360-0443.2010.03194.x

Lopez-Quintero, C., Perez de los Cobos, J., Hasin, D.S., Okuda, M., Wang, S., Grant, B.F., & Blanco, C. (2011). Probability and predictors of transition from first use to dependence on nicotine, alcohol, cannabis, and cocaine: Results of the National Epidemiologic Survey on Alcohol and Related Conditions (NESARC). *Drug and Alcohol Dependence, 115*(1–2), 120–130. doi: 10.1016/j.drugalcdep.2010.11.004.

López-Muñoz, F., & Alamo, C. (2009). Monoaminergic neurotransmission: The history of the discovery of antidepressants from 1950s until today. *Current Pharmaceutical Design, 15,* 1563–1586.

Lord, T. R. (2001). 101 reasons for using cooperative learning in biology teaching. *The American Biology Teacher, 63*(1), 30–38.

Lorenz, K. (1966). *On Aggression.* (Marjorie Kerr Wilson, Trans.) New York: Harcourt, Brace & World, Inc.

Lorenzo, G. L., Biesanz, J. C., & Human, L. J. (2010). What is beautiful is good and more accurately understood: Physical attractiveness and accuracy in first impressions of personality. *Psychological Science, 21,* 1777–1782.

Lovaas, O. I. (1964). Cue properties of words: The control of operant responding by rate and content of verbal operants. *Child Development, 35,* 245–256.

Lovaas, O. I. (1987). Behavioral treatment and normal educational and intellectual functioning in young autistic children. *Journal of Consulting and Clinical Psychology, 55,* 3–9.

Lovaas, O. I., Berberich, J. P., Perloff, B. F., & Schaffer, B. (1966). Acquisition of imitative speech by schizophrenic children. *Science, 151,* 705–707.

Lovibond, S. H., Mithiran, & Adams, W. G. (1979). The effects of three experimental prison environments on the behaviour of non-convict volunteer subjects. *Australian Psychologist, 14*(3), 273–287. doi:10.1080/00050067908254355

Lowenstein, R. L. (2018). Dissociation debates: Everything you know is wrong. *Dialogues in Clinical Neuroscience, 20,* 229–242.

Lu, S., & Ende, N. (1997). Potential for clinical use of viable pluripotent progenitor cells in blood bank stored human umbilical cord blood. *Life Sciences, 61,* 1113–1123.

Lu, Y., Rosenfeld, J. P., Deng, X., Zhang, E., Zheng, H., Yan, G.,... Hayat, S. Z. (2018). Inferior detection of information from collaborative versus individual crimes based on a p300 concealed information test. *Psychophysiology, 55*(4). doi:10.1111/psyp.13021

Lubinski, D. (2000). Scientific and social significance of assessing individual differences: "Sinking shafts at a few critical points." *Annual Review of Psychology, 51,* 405–444.

Luborsky, L., Singer, B., & Luborsky, L. (1975). Comparative studies of psychotherapies: Is it true that "everyone has won and all must have prizes"? *Archives of General Psychiatry, 32,* 995–1008.

Luchins, A. S. (1957). Primacy-recency in impression formation. In C. Hovland (Ed.), *The order of presentation in persuasion* (pp. 33–40, 55–61). New Haven, CT: Yale University Press.

Luck, S. J., & Gold, J. M. (2008). The construct of attention in schizophrenia. *Biological Psychiatry, 64*(1), 34–39.

Lucy, J. A., & Shweder, R. A. (1979). Whorf and his critics: Linguistic and nonlinguistic influences on color memory. *American Anthropologist, 81,* 581–615.

Luria, A. R. (1965). Two kinds of motor perseveration in massive injury of the frontal lobes. *Brain, 88,* 1–10.

Luria, A. R. (1968). *The mind of a mnemonist.* New York: Basic Books.

Lutkenhaus, P., Grossmann, K. E., & Grossman, K. (1985). Infant–mother attachment at twelve months and style of interaction with a stranger at the age of three years. *Child Development, 56,* 1538–1542.

Lutz, P. E., Tanti, A., Gasecka, A., Barnett-Burns, S., Kim, J. J., Zhou, Y.,... Turecki, G. (2017). Association of a history of child abuse with impaired myelination in the anterior cingulate cortex: Convergent epigenetic, transcriptional, and morphological evidence. *American Journal of Psychiatry, 174*(12), 1185–1194. doi:10.1176/appi.ajp.2017.16111286

Ly, M., Adluru, N., Destiche, D. J., Lu, S. Y., Oh, J. M., Hoscheidt, S. M.,... Bendlin, B. B. (2016). Fornix microstructure and memory performance is associated with altered neural connectivity during episodic recognition. *Journal of the International Neuropsychological Society, 22*(Special Issue 02), 191–204. doi: doi:10.1017/S1355617715001216

Lydecker, J. A., & Grilo, C. M. (2016). Different yet similar: Examining race and ethnicity in treatment-seeking adults with binge eating disorder. *Journal of Consulting and Clinical Psychology, 84*(1), 88–94. doi:0.1037/ccp0000048

Lykken, D. T. (1995). *The antisocial personalities.* Hillsdale, NJ: Laurence Erlbaum.

Lykken, D. T., & Tellegen, A. (1996). Happiness is a stochastic phenomenon. *Psychological Science, 7,* 186–189.

Lynn, S. J., Kirsch, I., & Hallquist, M. N. (2012). Social cognitive theories of hypnosis. *The Oxford Handbook of Hypnosis.* 111–139. DOI: 10.1093/oxfordhb/9780198570097.013.0005

Lynn, S. J., Laurence, J. R., & Kirsch, I. (2015). Hypnosis, suggestion, and suggestibility: An integrative model. *The American Journal of Clinical Hypnosis, 57*(3), 314–329.

Lynn, S. J., Lilienfeld, S. O., Merckelbach, H., Giesbrecht, T., McNally, R. J., Loftus, E. F.,... Malaktaris, A. (2014). The trauma model of dissociation: Inconvenient truths and stubborn fictions. Comment on Dalenberg et al. (2012). *Psychological Bulletin, 140*(3), 896–910. doi:10.1037/a0035570

Lynott, P. P., & Roberts, R. (1997). The developmental stake hypothesis and changing perceptions of intergenerational relations, 1971–1985. *The Gerontologist, 37,* 394–405.

Lyssenko, L., Schmahl, C., Bockhacker, L., Vonderlin, R., Bohus, M., & Kleindienst, N. (2018). Dissociation in psychiatric disorders: A meta-analysis of studies using the dissociative experiences scale. *American Journal of Psychiatry, 175*(1), 37–46. doi:10.1176/appi.ajp.2017.17010025

Lyznicki, J. M., Doege, T. C., Davis, R. M., & Williams, M. A. (Council on Scientific Affairs, American Medical Association). (1998). Sleepiness, driving, and motor-vehicle crashes. *Journal of the American Medical Association, 279*(23), 1908–1913.

Ma, J., Han, Y., Grogan-Kaylor, A., Delva, J., & Castillo, M. (2012). Corporal punishment and youth externalizing behavior in Santiago, Chile. *Child Abuse & Neglect, 36*(6), 481–490. doi: 10.1016/j.chiabu.2012.03.006

MacCoun, R. J., & Kerr, N. L. (1988). Asymmetric influence in mock jury deliberation: Jurors' bias for leniency. *Journal of Personality and Social Psychology, 54,* 21–33.

MacDonald, A. P. (1970). Internal-external locus of control and the practice of birth control. *Psychological Reports, 27,* 206.

MacDonald, D., Kabani, N., Avis, D., & Evens, A. C. (2000). Automated 3D extraction of inner and outer surfaces of cerebral cortex from MRI. *NeuroImage, 12,* 340–356.

MacDougall, H., & Monnais, L. (2018). Vacinating in the age of apathy: Measles vaccination in Canada, 1963–1998. *Canadian Medical Association Journal, 190*(13): E399. DOI: http://dx.doi.org/10.1503/cmaj.171238

Maciejewski, P. K., Zhang, B., Block, S. D., & Prigerson, H. G. (2007). An empirical examination of the stage theory of grief. *The Journal of the American Medical Association, 297*(7), 716–723. doi:10.1001/jama.297.7.716

Mack, J. E. (1994). *Abduction.* New York: Scribner.

MacKenzie, M. J., Nicklas, E., Waldfogel, J., & Brooks-Gunn, Jeanne. (2012). Corporal punishment and child behavioral and cognitive outcomes through 5 years-of-age: Evidence from a contemporary urban birth cohort study. *Infant and Child Development, 21*(1): 3–33. DOI: https://doi.org/10.1002/icd.758

MacKenzie, S. B., Lutz, R. J., & Belch, G. E. (1986, May). The role of attitude toward the ad as a mediator of advertising effectiveness: A test of competing explanations. *Journal of Marketing Research, 23,* 130–143.

Macknik, S. L., & Martinez-Conde, S. (2009). Real magic: Future studies of magic should be grounded in neuroscience. *Nature reviews: Neuroscience, 10*(3), 241–241.

Macknik, S. L., King, M., Randi, J., Robbins, A., Teller, Thompson, J., & Martinez-Conde, S. (2008). Attention and awareness in stage magic: Turning tricks into research. *Nature Reviews: Neuroscience, 9*(11), 871–879.

MacLeod, C. M. (1998). Directed forgetting. In J. M. Golding & C. M. MacLeod (Eds.), *Intentional forgetting: Interdisciplinary approaches* (pp. 1–57). Mahwah, NJ: Erlbaum.

Macmillan, M. (2000). *An odd kind of fame: Stories of Phineas Gage.* Cambridge, MA: The MIT Press.

Macmillan, M., & Lena, M. L. (2010). Rehabilitating Phineas Gage. *Neuropsychological Rehabilitation, 20*(5), 641–658. doi: 10.1080/09602011003760527

Macmillan, N. A., & Creelman, C. D. (1991). *Detection theory: A user's guide.* Cambridge, UK; New York: Cambridge University Press.

Macquet, P., & Franck, G. (1996). Functional neuroanatomy of human rapid eye movement sleep and dreaming. *Nature, 383,* 163–166.

Macrae, C. N., & Bodenhausen, G. V. (2000). Social cognition: Thinking categorically about others. *Annual Review of Psychology, 51,* 93–120.

Macrae, C. N., & Quadflieg, S. (2010). Perceiving people. In S. Fiske, D. T. Gilbert, & G. Lindzey (Eds.), *The handbook of social psychology* (5th ed., pp. 428–463). New York: McGraw-Hill.

Maddox, J., Randi, J., & Stewart, W. W. (1988). "High-dilution" experiments a delusion. *Nature, 334*(6181), 368.

Madore, K. P., & Schacter, D. L. (2016). Remembering the past and imagining the future: Selective effects of an episodic specificity induction on detail generation. *The Quarterly Journal of Experimental Psychology, 69,* 285–298. doi: 10.1080/17470218.2014.999097

Madras, B. K. (2014). Dopamine challenge reveals neuroadaptive changes in marijuana abusers. *Proceedings of the National Academy of Sciences, 111*(33), 11915–11916. doi: 10.1073/pnas.1412314111

Madsen, K. M., Hviid, A., Vestergaard, M., Schendel, D., Wohlfahrt, J., Thorsen, P.,... Melbye, M. (2002). A population-based study of measles, mumps, rubella vaccine and autism. *New England Journal of Medicine, 347,* 1477–1482.

Maggioni, E., Crespo-Facorro, B., Nenadic, I., Benedetti, F., Gaser, C., Sauer, H.,... group, E. (2017). Common and distinct structural features of schizophrenia and bipolar disorder: The european network on psychosis, affective disorders and cognitive trajectory (enpact) study. *PLoS ONE, 12*(11), e0188000. doi:10.1371/journal.pone.0188000

Mahoney, M. J. (2005). Constructivism and positive psychology. In C. R. Snyder & S. J. Lopez (Eds.), *Handbook of positive psychology* (pp. 745–750). New York: Oxford University Press.

Mahowald, M. W., & Schenck, C. H. (1996). NREM sleep parasomnias. *Neurologic Clinics, 14*, 675–696.

Mahowald, M. W., Schenck, C. H., & Bornemann, M. A. (2005). Sleep-related violence. *Current Neurology and Neuroscience Reports, 5*, 153–158.

Mahr, I., Bambico, F. R., Mechawar, N., & Nobrega, J. N. (2013). Stress, serotonin, and hippocampal neurogenesis in relation to depression and antidepressant effects. *Neuroscience and Biobehavioral Reviews, 38*, 173–192. doi: 10.1016/j.neubiorev.2013.11.009

Maier, S. F., & Watkins, L. R. (1998). Cytokines for psychologists: Implications of bidirectional immune-to-brain communication for understanding behavior, mood, and cognition. *Psychological Review, 105*, 83–107.

Maier, S. F., & Watkins, L. R. (2005). Stressor controllability and learned helplessness: The roles of the dorsal raphe nucleus, serotonin, and corticotropin-releasing factor. *Neuroscience & Biobehavioral Reviews, 29*(4–5), 829–841.

Maier, S. F., Amat, J., Baratta, M. V., Paul, E., & Watkins, L. R. (2006). Behavioral control, the medial prefrontal cortex, and resilience. *Dialogues in Clinical Neuroscience, 8*(4), 397–406.

Main, M., & Cassidy, J. (1988). Categories of response to reunion with the parent at age 6: Predictable from infant attachment classifications and stable over a 1 month period. *Developmental Psychology, 24*, 415–426.

Main, M., & Hesse, E. (1990). Parents' unresolved traumatic experiences are related to infant disorganized attachment status; Is frightened and/or frightening parental behaviour the linking mechanism? In M. T. Greenberg, D. Cicchetti, & E. M. Cummings (Eds.), *Attachment in the preschool years: Theory, research and intervention* (pp. 161–182). Chicago: University of Chicago Press.

Main, M., & Solomon, J. (1990). Procedures for identifying infants as disorganized/disoriented during the Ainsworth Strange Situation. In M. T. Greenberg, D. Cicchetti, & E. M. Cummings (Eds.), *Attachment in the preschool years: Theory, research and intervention* (pp. 121–160). Chicago: University of Chicago Press.

Maitland, S. B., Herlitz, A., Nyberg, L., Backman, L., & Nilsson, L. G. (2004). Selective sex differences in declarative memory. *Memory & Cognition, 32*: 1160–1169.

Makin, T. R., Scholz, J., Henderson Slater, D., Johansen-Berg, H., & Tracey, I. (2015). Reassessing cortical reorganization in the primary sensorimotor cortex following arm amputation. *Brain, 138*(Pt 8), 2140–2146. doi: 10.1093/brain/awv161

Mancuso, C., Siciliano, R., Barone, E., & Preziosi, P. (2012). Natural substance and Alzheimer's disease: From preclinical studies to evidence-based medicine. *Biochimica et Biophysica Acta (BBA), 1822*(5), 616–624.

Mander, B. A., Winer, J. R., & Walker, M. P. (2017). Sleep and human aging. *Neuron, 94*(1): 19-36. DOI: https://doi.org/10.1016/j.neuron.2017.02.004

Mandler, G. (1967). Organization and memory. In K. W. Spence & J. T. Spence (Eds.), *The psychology of learning and motivation* (Vol. 1, pp. 327–372). New York: Academic Press.

Mann, F. D., Briley, D. A., Tucker-Drob, E. M., & Harden, K. P. (2015). A behavioral genetic analysis of callous-unemotional traits and Big Five personality in adolescence. *Journal of Abnormal Psychology, 124*(4), 982–993. doi:10.1037/abn0000099

Manning, R., Levine, M., & Collins, A. (2007). The Kitty Genovese murder and the social psychology of helping: The parable of the 38 witnesses. *American Psychologist, 62*(6), 555–562. doi:10.1037/0003-066X.62.6.555

Manos, R. C., Kanter, J. W., & Busch, A. M. (2010). A critical review of assessment strategies to measure the behavioral activation model of depression. *Clinical Psychology Review, 30*(5), 547–561. doi: 10.1016/j.cpr.2010.03.008

Manusov, V., & Patterson, M. L. (Eds.). (2006). *The Sage handbook of nonverbal communication*. Thousand Oaks, CA: Sage.

Maquet, P., Schwartz, S., Passingham, R., & Frith, C. (2003). Sleep-related consolidation of a visuomotor skill: Brain mechanisms as assessed by functional magnetic resonance imaging. *The Journal of Neuroscience, 23*(4), 1432.

March of Dimes Foundation. (2006). March of Dimes Global Report on Birth Defects. Retrieved on March 29, 2017 from http://www.marchofdimes.org/materials/global-report-on-birth-defects-the-hidden-toll-of-dying-and-disabled-children-full-report.pdf.

Marcus, G. F. (2001). *The algebraic mind: Integrating connectionism and cognitive science (learning, development, and conceptual change)*. Cambridge, MA: MIT Press.

Maren, S., & Fanselow, M. S. (1996). The amygdala and fear conditioning: Has the nut been cracked? *Neuron, 16*, 237–240.

Margolin, S., & Kubic, L. S. (1944). An apparatus for the use of breath sounds as a hypnogogic stimulus. *American Journal of Psychiatry, 100*, 610.

Marks, D. F., Murray, M., Evans, B., Willig, C., Sykes, C. M., & Woodall, C. (2005). *Health Psychology: Theory, research & practice* (pp. 3–25). London: Sage.

Markus, H. R., & Kitayama, S. (1991). Culture and the self: Implications for cognition, emotion, and motivation. *Psychological Review, 98*, 224–253.

Marques, L., Alegria, M., Becker, A. E., Chen, C. N., Fang, A., Chosak, A., & Diniz, J. B. (2011). Comparative prevalence, correlates of impairment, and service utilization for eating disorders across US ethnic groups: Implications for reducing ethnic disparities in health care access for eating disorders. *International Journal of Eating Disorders, 44*(5), 412–420. doi:10.1002/eat.20787

Mars, A. E., Mauk, J. E., & Dowrick, P. (1998). Symptoms of pervasive developmental disorders as observed in prediagnostic home videos of infants and toddlers. *Journal of Pediatrics, 132*, 500–504.

Marsden, K. E., Ma, W. J., Deci, E. L., Ryan, R. M., & Chiu, P. H. (2014). Diminished neural responses predict enhanced intrinsic motivation and sensitivity to external incentive. *Cognitive, Affective, Behavioral Neuroscience, 15*, 276–286. doi: 10.3758/s13415-014-0324-5

Marsella, A. J., Kinzie, D., & Gordon, P. (1973). Ethnic variations in the expression of depression. *4*(4), 435–458. doi:10.1177/002202217300400405

Martin, C. L. (2000). Cognitive theories of gender development. In T. Eckes & H. M. Trautner (Eds.), *The developmental social psychology of gender* (pp. 91–121). Mahwah, NJ: Lawrence Erlbaum.

Martin, J. A., & Buckwalter, J. J. (2001). Telomere erosion and senescence in human articular cartilage chondrocytes. *Journal of Gerontology and Biological Science, 56*(4), 172–179.

Martin, L. (2004). Can sleepwalking be a murder defense? Retrieved October 19, 2004, from http://www.lakesidepress.com/pulmonary/Sleep/sleep-murder.htm

Martín, R., Bajo-Grañeras, R., Moratalla, R., Perea, G., & Araque, A. (2015). Circuit-specific signaling in astrocyte-neuron networks in basal ganglia pathways. *Science, 349*(6249), 730–734. doi: 10.1126/science.aaa7945

Martinussen, R., Hayden J., Hogg-Johnson, S., & Tannock, R. (2005). A meta-analysis of working memory components in children with Attention-Deficit/Hyperactivity Disorder. *Journal of the American Academy of Child & Adolescent Psychiatry, 44*(4), 377–384.

Martyn, A. C., De Jaeger, X., Magalhaes, A. C., Kesarwani, R., Goncalves, D. F., Raulic, S.,... Prado, V. F. (2012). Elimination of the vesicular acetylcholine transporter in the forebrain causes hyperactivity and deficits in spatial memory and long-term potentiation. *Proceedings of the National Academy of Sciences, 109*(43), 17651–17656. doi: 10.1073/pnas.1215381109

Maruta, T., Colligan, R. C., Malinchoc, M., & Offord, K. P. (2002, August). Optimism-pessimism assessed in the 1960s and self-reported health status 30 years later. *Mayo Clinic Proceedings, 77*, 748–753.

Maslow, A. (1943). A theory of human motivation. *Psychological Review, 50*, 370–396.

Maslow, A. (1971). *The farther reaches of human nature*. New York: Viking Press.

Maslow, A. (1987). *Motivation and personality* (3rd ed.). New York: Harper & Row.

Maslow, A. H. (1954). *Motivation and personality*. New York: Harper & Row.

Maslow, A., & Lowery, R. (Ed.). (1998). *Toward a psychology of being* (3rd ed.). New York: Wiley & Sons.

Mason, I., Grimaldi, D., Malkani, R. G., Reid, K. J., & Zee, P. C. (2018). 0117 Impact of light exposure during sleep on cardiometabolic function. *Sleep, 41*(1): A46. DOI: https://doi.org/10.1093/sleep/zsy061.116

Massaro, D. W., & Cowan, N. (1993). Information processing models: Microscopes of the mind. *Annual Review of Psychology, 44*, 383–426.

Masson, J. M. (1984). *The assault on truth: Freud's suppression of the seduction theory*. New York: Farrar, Straus & Giroux.

Master, A., Cheryan, S., & Meltzoff, A. N. (2015). Computing whether she belongs: Stereotypes undermine girls' interest and sense of belonging in computer science. *Journal of Educational Psychology, 108*(3), 424–437. doi: 10.1037/edu0000061

Masters, J. C., Burish, T. G., Holton, S. D., & Rimm, D. C. (1987). *Behavior therapy: Techniques and empirical finding*. San Diego, CA: Harcourt Brace Jovanovich.

Masters, W. H., & Johnson, V. E. (1970). *Human sexual inadequacy*. Boston: Little, Brown.

Masuda, T., & Kitayama, S. (2004). Perceiver-induced constraint and attitude attribution in Japan and the U.S.: A case for the cultural dependence of the correspondence bias. *Journal of Experimental Social Psychology, 40*, 409–416.

Matsumoto, D. (1994). *People: Psychology from a cultural perspective*. Pacific Grove, CA: Brooks-Cole.

Matthew, N., & Dallery, J. (2007). Mercury rising: Exploring the vaccine–autism myth. *Skeptic, 13*(3). Retrieved May 3, 2010, from http://www.skeptic.com/eskeptic/07-06-20/#feature

Matthews, K. A., Dahl, R. E., Owens, J. F., Lee, L., & Hall, M. (2012). Sleep duration and insulin resistance in healthy black and white adolescents. *Sleep, 35*(10), 1353–1358.

Matthews, K. A., Gump, B. B., Harris, K. F., Haney, T. L., & Barefoot, J. C. (2004). Hostile behaviors predict cardiovascular mortality among men enrolled in the Multiple Risk Factor Intervention trial. *Circulation, 109*, 66–70.

Maurer, D., & Young, R. (1983). Newborns' following of natural and distorted arrangements of facial features. *Infant Behaviour and Development, 6*, 127–131.

Maxmen, J. S., Ward, N. G., & Kilgus, M. D. (2009). *Essential psychopathology and its treatment*. New York: W. W. Norton.

Mayer, B. (2014). How much nicotine kills a human? Tracing back the generally accepted lethal dose to dubious self-experiments in the nineteenth century. *Archives of Toxicology, 88*(1), 5–7.

Mayer, J. D., & Geher, G. (1996). Emotional intelligence and the identification of emotion. *Intelligence, 22*, 89–113.

Mayer, J. D., & Salovey, P. (1997). What is emotional intelligence? In P. Salovey & D. Sluyter (Eds.), *Emotional development and emotional intelligence: Educational implications* (pp. 3–31). New York: Basic Books.

Mayer, J. D., Roberts, R. D., & Barsade, S. G. (2008). Human abilities: Emotional intelligence. *Annual Review of Psychology, 59*(1), 507–536. doi: 10.1146/annurev.psych.59.103006.093646

Mayer, J. D., Salovey, P., & Caruso, D. R. (2000). Models of emotional intelligence. In R. J. Sternberg (Ed.), *Handbook of human intelligence* (2nd ed., pp. 396–420). New York: Cambridge University Press.

Mayer, J. D., Salovey, P., & Caruso, D. R. (2008). Emotional intelligence: New ability or eclectic traits? *American Psychologist, 63*(6), 503–517. doi: 10.1037/0003-066x.63.6.503

Mayer, L. E. S. (2018). Psychopharmacological treatment of anorexia nervosa and bulimia nervosa. In W. S. Agras & A. Robinson (Eds.), *The Oxford handbook of eating disorders* (2nd ed., pp. 302–307). New York, NY: Oxford University Press.

Mayo Clinic. (2016). Healthy lifestyle: Stress management. Mayo Foundation for Medical Education and Research. Retrieved from http://www.mayoclinic.org/healthy-lifestyle/stress-management/in-depth/relaxation-technique/art-20045368?pg=2

Mayo Clinic Staff. (2014). Diseases and conditions: Insomnia (web page). Mayo Foundation for Medical Education and Research. Retrieved from http://www.mayoclinic.org/diseases-conditions/insomnia/basics/definition/con-20024293

Mazzoni, G. A. L., Loftus, E. F., & Kirsch, I. (2001). Changing beliefs about implausible autobiographical events: A little plausibility goes a long way. *Journal of Experimental Psychology: Applied, 7*(1), 51–59.

McAdams, D. P., & Olson, B. D. (2010). Personality development: Continuity and change over the life course. *Annual Review of Psychology, 61*, 517–542. doi: 10.1146/annurev.psych.093008.100507

McAdams, D. P., & Pals, J. L. (2006). A new Big Five: Fundamental principles for an integrative science of personality. *American Psychologist, 61*(3), 204–217. doi: 10.1037/0003-066X.61.3.204

McCann, S. J. H. (2017). Higher USA state resident neuroticism is associated with lower state volunteering rates. *Personality and Social Psychology Bulletin, 43*(12), 1659–1674. doi: 10.1177/0146167217724802

McCann, S. J. H., & Stewin, L. L. (1988). Worry, anxiety, and preferred length of sleep. *Journal of Genetic Psychology, 149*, 413–418.

McCarty, C. A., Weisz, J. R., Wanitromanee, K., Eastman, K. L., Suwanlert, S., Chaiyasit, W., & Band, E. B. (1999). Culture, coping, and context: Primary and secondary control among Thai and American youth. *Journal of Child Psychology and Psychiatry, 40*, 809–818.

McCauley, C. (1998). Group dynamics in Janis's theory of groupthink: Backward and forward. *Organizational Behavior & Human Decision Processes, 73*(2–3), 142–162.

McClelland, D. C. (1961). *The achieving society*. Princeton, NJ: Van Nostrand.

McClelland, D. C. (1987). *Human motivation*. Cambridge, MA: Cambridge University Press.

McClelland, J. L., & Rumelhart, D. E. (1988). *Explorations in parallel distributed processing*. Cambridge, MA: MIT Press.

McCormick, D. A., & Westbrook, G. L. (2013). Sleep and dreaming. In E. R. Kandel, J. H. Schwartz, T. M. Jessell, S. A. Siegelbaum & A. J. Hudspeth (Eds.), Principles of neural science (5th ed., pp. 1140–1158). New York: McGraw Hill

McCrae, R. R., & Costa, P. T. (1990). *Personality in adulthood*. New York: Guilford Press.

McCrae, R. R., & Costa, P. T., Jr. (1996). Toward a new generation of personality theories: Theoretical contexts for the five-factor model. In J. S. Wiggins (Ed.), *The five-factor model of personality: Theoretical perspectives* (pp. 51–87). New York: Guilford.

McCrae, R. R., & Terracciano, A. (2005). Universal features of personality traits from the observer's perspective: Data from 50 cultures. *Journal of Personality and Social Psychology, 88*(3), 547–561. doi: 10.1037/0022-3514.88.3.547

McCrae, R. R., Costa Jr., P. T., & Martin, T. A. (2005). The NEO-PI-3: A more readable revised NEO Personality Inventory. *Journal of Personality Assessment, 84*(3), 261–270. doi: 10.1207/s15327752jpa8403_05

McCrae, R. R., Martin, T. A., & Costa, P. T., Jr. (2005). Age trends and age norms for the NEO Personality Inventory-3 in adolescents and adults. *Assessment, 12*(4), 363–373. doi: 10.1177/1073191105279724

McCrae, R. R., Piedmont, R. L., & Costa, P T.. Jr. (1990, August). The CPI and the five-factor model: Rational and empirical analyses. Paper presented at the annual convention of the American Psychological Association. Boston.

McDaniel, M. A., Howard, D. C., & Einstein, G. O. (2009). The read-recite-review study strategy: Effective and portable. *Psychological Science, 20*(4), 516–522.

McDermott, J. F. (2001). Emily Dickinson revisited: A study of periodicity in her work. *American Journal of Psychiatry, 158*(5), 686–690.

McDonald, G. P., O'Connell, M., & Suls, J. (2015). Cancer control falls squarely within the province of the psychological sciences. *American Psychologist, 70*, 61–74.

McDonald, W. M., Meeks, T. W., Carpenter, L. L., McCall, W. V., & Zorumski, C. F. (2017). Electroconvulsive therapy and other neuromodulation therapies. In A. F. Schatzberg & C. B. Nemeroff (Eds.), The American Psychiatric Association Publishing Textbook of Psychopharmacology. Arlington, VA: American Psychiatric Association Publishing. Retrieved from https://psychiatryonline.org/doi/abs/10.1176/appi.books.9781615371624.as45. doi:10.1176/appi.books.9781615371624.as45

McDougall, T. (2009). Nursing children and adolescents with bipolar disorder. *Journal of Child and Adolescent Psychiatric Nursing, 22*, 33–39.

McDougall, W. (1908). *An introduction to social psychology*. London: Methuen & Co.

McEwen, B. S. (1998). Protective and damaging effects of stress mediators. *The New England Journal of Medicine, 338*(3), 171–179.

McEwen, B. S. (2000). The neurobiology of stress: From serendipity to clinical relevance. *Brain Research, 886*, 172–189.

McEwen, B. S. (2005). Stressed or stressed out: What is the difference? *Journal of Psychiatry and Neuroscience, 30*(5), 315–318.

McEwen, B. S., & Gianaros, P. J. (2011). Stress- and allostasis-induced brain plasticity. *Annual Review of Medicine, 62*, 431–445. doi:10.1146/annurev-med-052209-100430

McEwen, B. S., & McEwen, C. A. (2016). Response to Jerome Kagan's essay on stress (2016). *Perspectives on Psychological Science, 11*(4), 451–455. doi:10.1177/1745691616646635

McEwen, B. S., & Morrison, J. H. (2013). The brain on stress: Vulnerability and plasticity of the prefrontal cortex over the life course. *Neuron, 79*(1), 16–29. doi:10.1016/j.neuron.2013.06.028

McEwen, B. S., Gray, J., & Nasca, C. (2015). Recognizing resilience: Learning from the effects of stress on the brain. *Neurobiol Stress, 1*, 1–11. doi:10.1016/j.ynstr.2014.09.001

McGaugh, J. L. (2004). The amygdala modulates the consolidation of memories of emotionally arousing experiences, *Annual Review Neuroscience, 27*, 1–28.

McGinn, L. K. (2000). Cognitive behavioral therapy of depression: Theory, treatment, and empirical status. *American Journal of Psychotherapy, 54*, 254–260.

McGrath, C. L., Kelley, M. E., Holtzheimer, P. E., Dunlop, B. W., Craighead, W. E., Franco, A. R.,… Mayberg, H. S. (2013). Toward a neuroimaging treatment selection biomarker for major depressive disorder. *JAMA Psychiatry, 70*(8), 821–829. doi: 10.1001/jamapsychiatry.2013.143

McGrath, E., Keita, G. P., Strickland, B. R., & Russo, N. F. (1992). *Women and depression: Risk factors and treatment issues*. Washington, DC: American Psychological Association.

McGrath, J. J., Saha, S., Lim, C. C. W., Gureje, O., & Florescu, S. (2018). Psychotic experiences. In K. Scott, P. De Jonge, D. Stein, & R. Kessler (Eds.), *Mental disorders around the world: Facts and figures from the WHO world mental health surveys* (pp. 286–296). Cambridge: Cambridge University Press.

McGrath, R. E., & Carroll, E. J. (2012). The current status of 'projective' 'tests'. In H. Cooper, P. M. Camic, D. L. Long, A. T. Panter, D. Rindskopf & K. J. Sher (Eds.), *APA handbook of research methods in psychology, Vol 1: Foundations, planning, measures, and psychometrics* (pp. 329–348). Washington, DC: American Psychological Association.

McGraw, K. (2016). Gender differences among military combatants: Does social support, ostracism, and pain perception influence psychological health? *Military Medicine, 181*(1 Suppl), 80–85. doi:10.7205/MILMED-D-15-00254

McGregor, D. (1960). *The human side of enterprise*. New York: McGraw-Hill.

McGrew, K. S. (2009). CHC theory and the human cognitive abilities project: Standing on the shoulders of the giants of psychometric intelligence research. *Intelligence, 37*(1), 1–10. doi: 10.1016/j.intell.2008.08.004

McGuire, F. (1994). Army alpha and beta tests of intelligence. In R. J. Sternberg (Ed.), *Encyclopedia of intelligence* (Vol. 1, pp. 125–129.) New York: Macmillan.

McIver, D. J., Hawkins, J. B., Chunara, R., Chatterjee, A. K., Bhandari, A., Fitzgerald, T. P.,… Brownstein, J. S. (2015). Characterizing sleep issues using Twitter. *Journal of Medical Internet Research, 17*(6), e140. doi: 10.2196/jmir.4476

McLaughlin, A. C., & McGill, A. E. (2017). Explicitly teaching critical thinking skills in a history course. *Science & Education, 26*(1–2): 93–105. DOI: 10.1007/s11191-017-9878-2

McLaughlin, S. K., & Margolskee, R. F. (1994). Vertebrate taste transduction. *American Scientist, 82*, 538–545.

McMahon, F. J., Akula, N., Schulze, T. G., Muglia, P., Tozzi, F., Detera-Wadleigh, S. D.,… Rietschel, M. (2010). Meta-analysis of genome-wide association data identifies a risk locus for major mood disorders on 3p21.1. *Nature Genetics, 42*(2), 128–131. doi: 10.1038/ng.523

McMillan, H. L., Boyle, M. H., Wong, M. Y., Duku, E. K., Fleming, J. E., & Walsh, C. A. (1999). Slapping and spanking in childhood and its association with lifetime prevalence of psychiatric disorders in a general population sample. *Canadian Medical Association Journal, 161*, 805–809.

McMonagle, T., & Sultana, A. (2002). Token economy for schizophrenia (Cochrane Review). In *The Cochrane Library, Issue 2*. Oxford: Update Software.

McPherson, J. M., Smith-Lovin, L., Cook, J. M. (2001). Birds of a feather: Homophily in social networks. *Annual Review of Sociology 27*, 415–444.

McWilliams, N. (2016). Psychoanalysis. In I. Marini & M. A. Stebnicki (Eds.), *The professional counselor's desk reference* (2nd ed., pp. 185–189). New York: Springer Publishing.

Meador, B. D., & Rogers, C. R. (1984). Person-centered therapy. In R. J. Corsini (Ed.), *Current psychotherapies* (3rd ed., pp. 142–195). Itasca, IL: Peacock.

Mease, R. A., Metz, M., & Groh, A. (2016). Cortical sensory responses are enhanced by the higher-order thalamus. *Cell Reports, 14*(1): 208–215. DOI: http://dx.doi.org/10.1016/j.celrep.2015.12.026

Medical Economics Staff. (1994). *PDR family guide to women's health & prescription drugs*. Montvale, NJ: Medical Economics Company.

Meeter, M., Murre, J. M. J., Janssen, S. M. J., Birkenhager, T., & vanden Broek, W. W. (2011). Retrograde amnesia after electroconvulsive therapy: A temporary effect? *Journal of Affective Disorders, 132*(1–2), 216–222.

Mehler, P. S. (2018). Medical complications of anorexia nervosa. In W. S. Agras & A. Robinson (Eds.), *The Oxford handbook of eating disorders* (2nd ed., pp. 214–218). New York, NY: Oxford University Press.

Mehrabian, A. (2000). Beyond IQ: Broad-based measurement of individual success potential or "emotional intelligence." *Genetic, Social, and General Psychology Monographs, 126*, 133–239.

Meichenbaum, D. (1996). Stress inoculation training for coping with stressors. *The Clinical Psychologist, 49*, 4–7.

Meikle, J., & Boseley, S. (2010, May 24). MMR row doctor Andrew Wakefield struck off register. *The Guardian* (London). Retrieved April 26, 2013, from http://www.guardian.co.uk/society/2010/may/24/mmr-doctor-andrew-wakefield-struck-off

Meille, V., Verges, B., Lalanne, L., Jonval, L., Duvillard, L., Chavet-Gelinier, J. C.,... Trojak, B. (2017). Effects of transcranial magnetic stimulation on the hypothalamic-pituitary axis in depression: Results of a pilot study. *Journal of Neuropsychiatry and Clinical Neurosciences, 29*(1), 70–73. doi:10.1176/appi.neuropsych.16010013

Meineri, S., & Guéguen N. (2008). An application of the foot-in-the-door strategy in the environmental field. *European Journal of Social Sciences, 7*, 71–74.

Meiser-Stedman, R., McKinnon, A., Dixon, C., Boyle, A., Smith, P., & Dalgleish, T. (2017). Acute stress disorder and the transition to posttraumatic stress disorder in children and adolescents: Prevalence, course, prognosis, diagnostic suitability, and risk markers. *Depression and Anxiety, 34*(4), 348–355. doi:10.1002/da.22602

Mejía, O. L., & McCarthy, C. J. (2010). Acculturative stress, depression, and anxiety in migrant farmwork college students of Mexican heritage. *International Journal of Stress Management, 17*(1), 1–20.

Melzack, R., & Wall, P. D. (1965). Pain mechanisms: A new theory. *Science, 150*, 971–979.

Melzack, R., & Wall, P. D. (1996). *The challenge of pain.* London: Penguin Books.

Mendez, M. F., & Fras, I. A. (2011). The false memory syndrome: Experimental studies and comparison to confabulations. *Medical Hypotheses, 76*(4), 492–496. doi: 10.1016/j.mehy.2010.110.33

Mennella, J. A., & Trabulsi, J. C. (2012). Complementary foods and flavor experiences: Setting the foundation. *Ann Nutr Metab, 60 Suppl 2*, 40–50. doi: 10.1159/000335337

Menon, T., Morris, M., Chiu, C. Y., & Hong, Y. I. (1999). Culture and the construal of agency: Attribution to individual versus group dispositions. *Journal of Personality and Social Psychology, 76*, 701–727.

Merikle, M. P. (2000). Subliminal perception. In A. E. Kazdin (Ed.), *Encyclopedia of Psychology* (Vol. 7, pp. 497–499). New York: Oxford University Press.

Mervis, C. B., & Rosch, E. (1981). Categorization of natural objects. *Annual Review of Psychology, 32*, 89–115.

Mesgarani, N., & Chang, E. F. (2012). Selective cortical representation of attended speaker in multi-talker speech perception. *Nature, 485*, 233–236. doi: 10.1038/nature11020

Messina, G., Dalia, C., Tafuri, D., Monda, V., Palmieri, F., Dato, A.,... Monda, M. (2014). Orexin-A controls sympathetic activity and eating behavior. *Frontiers in Psychology, 5*, 997.

Mesulam, M. M., Thompson, C. K., Weintraub, S., & Rogalski, E. J. (2015). The Wernicke conundrum and the anatomy of language comprehension in primary progressive aphasia. *Brain, 138*(Pt 8), 2423–2437. doi:10.1093/brain/awv154

Meyer, G. J., & Kurtz, J. E. (2006). Advancing personality assessment terminology: Time to retire 'objective' and 'projective' as personality test descriptors. *Journal of Personality Assessment, 87*(3), 223–225. doi: 10.1207/s15327752jpa8703_01

Meyer, J. S. (2013). 3,4-methylenedioxymethamphetamine (MDMA): Current perspectives. *Substance Abuse Rehabilitation, 4*, 83–99. doi: 10.2147/SAR.S37258

Meyer, O. L., & Zane, N. (2013). The influence of race and ethnicity in clients' experiences of mental health treatment. *Journal of Community Psychology, 41*(7), 884–901. doi:10.1002/jcop.21580

Meyrick, J. (2001). Forget the blood and gore: An alternative message strategy to help adolescents avoid cigarette smoking. *Health Education, 101*(3), 99–107.

Mez, J., Daneshvar, D. H., Kiernan, P. T., Abdolmohammadi, B., Alvarez, V. E., Huber, B. R.,... McKee, A. C. (2017). Clinicopathological evaluation of chronic traumatic encephalopathy in players of American football. *JAMA, 318*(4), 360–370. doi:10.1001/jama.2017.8334

Meziab, O., Kirby, K. A., Williams, B., Yaffe, K., Byers, A. L., & Barnes, D. E. (2014). Prisoner of war status, posttraumatic stress disorder, and dementia in older veterans. *Alzheimer's & Dementia, 10*(3 Suppl), S236–241. doi: 10.1016/j.jalz.2014.04.004

Michaels, J. W., Blommel, J. M., Brocato, R. M., Linkous, R. A., & Rowe, J. S. (1982). Social facilitation and inhibition in a natural setting. *Replications in Social Psychology, 2*, 21–24.

Michalski, D., Kohout, J., Wicherski, M., & Hart, B. (2011). 2009 Doctorate Employment Survey (Table 3). Washington, DC: American Psychological Association. Retrieved from https://www.apa.org/workforce/publications/09-doc-empl/report.pdf

Michelini, G., Kitsune, V., Vainieri, I., Hosang, G. M., Brandeis, D., Asherson, P., & Kuntsi, J. (2018). Shared and disorder-specific event-related brain oscillatory markers of attentional dysfunction in ADHD and bipolar disorder. *Brain Topography.* doi:10.1007/s10548-018-0625-z

Micoulaud-Franchi, J. A., Lanteaume, L., Pallanca, O., Vion-Dury, J., & Bartolomei, F. (2014). Biofeedback and drug-resistant epilepsy: Back to an earlier treatment? *Revue Neurologique, 170*(3), 187–196.

Migo, E. M., Quamme, J. R., Holmes, S., Bendell, A., Norman, K. A., Mayes, A. R., & Montaldi, D. (2014). Individual difference in forced-choice recognition memory: Partitioning contributions of recollection and familiarity. *Quarterly Journal of Experimental Psychology, 67*(11), 2189–2206.

Mikami, A. Y., Szwedo, D. E., Allen, J. P., Evans, M. A., & Hare, A. L. (2010). Adolescent peer relationships and behavior problems predict young adults' communication on social networking websites. *Developmental Psychology, 46*, 46–56.

Miles, D. R., & Carey, G. (1997). Genetic and environmental architecture of human aggression. *Journal of Personality and Social Psychology, 72*, 207–217.

Milgram, S. (1963). Behavioral study of obedience. *The Journal of Abnormal and Social Psychology, 67*(4), 371–378. doi: 10.1037/h0040525

Milgram, S. (1964). Issues in the study of obedience: A reply to Baumrind. *American Psychologist, 19*, 848–852.

Milgram, S. (1974). *Obedience to authority: An experimental view.* New York: Harper & Row.

Miller, C. H., Hamilton, J. P., Sacchet, M. D., & Gotlib, I. H. (2015). Meta-analysis of functional neuroimaging of major depressive disorder in youth. *JAMA Psychiatry, 72*(10), 1045–1053. doi: 10.1001/jamapsychiatry.2015.1376

Miller, G. (2009). Neuropathology. A late hit for pro football players. *Science, 325*(5941), 670–672.

Miller, G. (2013). Neuroscience. The promise and perils of oxytocin. *Science, 339*(6117), 267–269. doi: 10.1126/science.339.6117.267

Miller, G. A. (1956). The magical number seven, plus or minus two: Some limits on our capacity for processing information. *Psychological Review, 63*, 81–97.

Miller, J. G. (1984). Culture and the development of everyday social explanation. *Journal of Personality and Social Psychology, 46*, 961–978.

Miller, M. E., & Bowers, K. S. (1993). Hypnotic analgesia: Dissociated experience or dissociated control? *Journal of Abnormal Psychology, 102*, 29–38.

Miller, M. N., & Pumariega, A. (1999). Culture and eating disorders. *Psychiatric Times, 16*(2), 1–4.

Miller, M., & Rahe, R. H. (1997). Life changes scaling for the 1990s. *Journal of Psychosomatic Research, 43*(3), 279–292.

Miller, N. E. (1983). Behavioral medicine: Symbiosis between laboratory and clinic. *Annual Review of Psychology, 34*, 1–31.

Miller, N. E., Sears, R. R., Mowrer, O. H., Doob, L. W., & Dollard, J. (1941). The frustration-aggression hypothesis. *Psychological Review, 48*, 337–342.

Miller, W. R., & Arkowitz, H. (2015). Learning, applying, and extending motivational interviewing. In H. Arkowitz, W. R. Miller, & S. Rollnick (Eds.), *Motivational interviewing in the treatment of psychological problems* (2nd ed.). New York: The Guilford Press.

Miller, W. R., & Rollnick, S. (2002). *Motivational interviewing: Preparing people for change* (2nd ed.). New York: Guilford Press.

Miller, W. R., & Rollnick, S. (2013). *Motivational interviewing: Helping people change* (3rd ed.). New York: The Guilford Press.

Milling, L. S., Gover, M. C., & Moriarty, C. L. (2018). The effectiveness of hypnosis as an intervention for obesity: A meta-analytic review. *Psychology of Consciousness: Theory, Research, and Practice, 5*(1): 29–45. DOI: http://psycnet.apa.org/doi/10.1037/cns0000139

Milner, B., Corkin, S., & Teuber, H. L. (1968). Further analysis of the hippocampal syndrome: 14-year follow-up study of H. M. *Neuropsychologia, 6*, 215–234.

Milner, J. (1992, January). Risk for physical child abuse: Adult factors. *Violence Update*, pp. 9–11.

Mineka, S., & Öhman, A. (2002). Phobias and preparedness: The selective, automatic, and encapsulated nature of fear. *Biological Psychiatry, 52*(10): 927–937. DOI: https://doi.org/10.1016/s0006-3223(02)01669-4

Miocinovic, S., Somayajula, S., Chitnis, S., & Vitek, J. L. (2013). History, applications, and mechanisms of deep brain stimulation. *JAMA Neurology, 70*(2), 163–171. doi:10.1001/2013.jamaneurol.45

Mischel, W. (1966). A social learning view of sex differences in behaviour. In E. E. Maccoby (Ed.), *The development of sex differences* (pp. 56–81). Stanford, CT: Stanford University Press.

Mischel, W., & Shoda, Y. (1995). A cognitive-affective system theory of personality: Reconceptualizing situations, dispositions, dynamics, and invariances in personality structure. *Psychological Review, 102*(2), 246–268.

Mishell, D. R. (2001). Menopause. In M. A. Stenchever, W. Droegemueller, A. L. Herbst, and D. R. Mishell. (Eds.), *Comprehensive gynecology* (4th ed., pp. 1217–1258). St. Louis, MO: Mosby.

Mitchell, D. B., Kelly, C. L., & Brown, A. S. (2018). Replication and extension of long-term implicit memory: Perceptual priming but conceptual cessation. *Consciousness and Cognition, 58*: 1–9. DOI: https://doi.org/10.1016/j.concog.2017.12.002

Mitchell, G. E., & Locke, K. D. (2015). Lay beliefs about autism spectrum disorder among the general public and childcare providers. *Autism, 19*, 553–561.

Mitchell, J. E., Roerig, J., & Steffen, K. (2013). Biological therapies for eating disorders. *International Journal of Eating Disorders, 46*(5), 470–477. doi: 10.1002/eat.22104

Mitchell, S. A., & Black, M. J. (1996). *Freud and beyond: A history of modern psychoanalytic thought* [Reprint ed.]. New York: HarperCollins.

Miyatake, A., Morimoto Y., Oishi, T., Hanasaki, N., Sugita, Y., Iijima, S.,... Yamamura, Y. (1980). Circadian rhythm of serum testosterone and its relation to sleep: Comparison with the variation in serum luteinizing hormone, prolactin, and cortisol in normal men. *Journal of Clinical Endocrinology and Metabolism, 51*(6), 1365–1371.

Moffic, H. S. (2003). Seven ways to improve "cultural competence." *Current Psychiatry, 2*(5), 78.

Mogil, J. S. (1999). The genetic mediation of individual differences in sensitivity to pain and its inhibition. *Proceedings of the National Academy of Sciences, USA, 96*(14), 7744–7751.

Mohammadzaheri, F., Koegel, L. K., Rezaei, M., & Bakhshi, E. (2015). A randomized clinical trial comparison between pivotal response treatment (PRT) and adult-driven applied behavior analysis (ABA) intervention on disruptive behaviors in public school children with autism. *Journal of Autism and Developmental Disorders, 45*(9), 2899–2907.

Moldofsky, H. (1995). Sleep and the immune system. *International Journal of Immunopharmacology, 17*(8), 649–654.

Molenberghs, P., Cunnington, R., & Mattingley, J. B. (2012). Brain regions with mirror properties: A meta-analysis of 125 human fMRI studies. *Neuroscience and Biobehavioral Reviews, 36*(1), 341–349. doi:10.1016/j.neubiorev.2011.07.004

Moll, H., & Tomasello, M. (2007). How 14- and 18-month-olds know what others have experienced. *Developmental Psychology, 43*, 309–317.

Möller, A., & Hell, D. (2002). Eugen Bleuler and forensic psychiatry. *International Journal of Law and Psychiatry, 25*, 351–360.

Molloy, K., Griffiths, T. D., Chait, M., & Lavie, N. (2015). Inattentional deafness: Visual load leads to time-specific suppression of auditory evoked responses. *Journal of Neuroscience, 35*(49), 16046–16054. doi: 10.1523/JNEUROSCI.2931-15.2015

Molofsky, A. V., Krencik, R., Ullian, E. M., Tsai, H. H., Deneen, B., Richardson, W. D.,... Rowitch, D. H. (2012). Astrocytes and disease: A neurodevelopmental perspective. *Genes & Development, 26*(9), 891–907. doi: 10.1101/gad.188326.112

Money, J. (1994). *Sex errors of the body and related syndromes*. Baltimore: Paul H. Brookes.

Monson, C. M., Resick, P. A., & Rizvi, S. L. (2014). Posttraumatic stress disorder. In D. H. Barlow (Ed.), *Clinical handbook of psychological disorders: A step-by-step treatment manual* (5th ed., pp. 62–113). New York, NY: Guilford Press.

Montesanti, S. R., Abelson, J., Lavis, J. N., & Dunn, J. R. (2017). Enabling the participation of marginalized populations: Case studies from a health service organization in Ontario, Canada. *Health Promotion International, 32*(4), 636–649. doi:10.1093/heapro/dav118

Montgomery, C., & Fisk, J. E. (2008). Ecstasy-related deficits in the updating component of executive processes. *Human Psychopharmacology, 23*(6), 495–511.

Montgomery, P., Spreckelsen, T. F., Burton, A., Burton, J. R., & Richardson, A. J. (2018). Docosahexaenoic acid for reading, working memory and behavior in UK children aged 7-9: A randomized controled trial for replication (the DOLAB II study). *PLoS ONE, 13*(2): e0192909. Published online at DOI: https://doi.org/10.1371/journal.pone.0192909

Moody, R., & Perry, P. (1993). *Reunions: Visionary encounters with departed loved ones*. London: Little, Brown.

Moore, T. E. (1988). The case against subliminal manipulation. *Psychology and Marketing, 5*, 297–316.

Moore, T. H., Zammit, S., Lingford-Hughes, A., Barnes, T. R., Jones, P. B., Burke, M., & Lewis, G. (2007). Cannabis use and risk of psychotic or affective mental health outcomes: A systematic review. *Lancet, 370*, 293–294, 319–328.

Moore-Ede, M. C., Sulzman, F. M., & Fuller, C. A. (1982). *The clocks that time us*. Cambridge, MA: Harvard University Press.

Moorhead, G., Neck, C. P., & West, M. S. (1998). The tendency toward defective decision making within self-managing teams: The relevance of groupthink for the 21st century. *Organizational Behavior & Human Decision Processes, 73*(2–3), 327–351.

Mora, G. (1985). History of psychiatry. In H. I. Kaplan & B. J. Sadock (Eds.), *Comprehensive textbook of psychiatry* (pp. 2034–2054). Baltimore: Williams & Wilkins.

Moran, K. M., Turiano, N. A., & Gentzler, A. L. (2018). Parental warmth during childhood predicts coping and well-being in adulthood. *Journal of Family Psychology, 32*(5), 610–621. DOI: http://dx.doi.org/10.1037/fam0000401

Moreines, J. L., McClintock, S. M., Kelley, M. E., Holtzheimer, P. E., & Mayberg, H. S. (2014). Neuropsychological function before and after subcallosal cingulate deep brain stimulation in patients with treatment-resistant depression. *Depression and Anxiety, 31*(8), 690–698. doi: 10.1002/da.22263

Moreland, R. L., & Zajonc, R. B. (1982). Exposure effects in person perceptions: Familiarity, similarity, and attraction. *Journal of Experimental Social Psychology, 18*(5), 395–415.

Morgan, C. A., Rasmusson, A., Pietrzak, R. H., Coric, V., Southwick, S. M. (2009). Relationships among plasma dehydroepiandrosterone and dehydro-epiandrosterone sulfate, cortisol, symptoms of dissociation, and objective performance in humans exposed to underwater navigation stress. *Biological Psychiatry, 66*(4), 334–340.

Morgan, C. D., & Murray, H. A. (1935). A method for investigating fantasies: The Thematic Appercetion Test. *Archives of Neurology and Psychiatry, 34*, 298–306.

Morii, M., & Sakagami, T. (2015). The effect of gaze-contingent stimulus elimination on preference judgments. *Frontiers in Psychology, 6*, 1351.

Morin, C. M., Bootzin, R. R., Buysse, D. J., Edinger, J. D., Espie, C. A., & Lichstein, K. L. (2006). Psychological and behavioral treatment of insomnia: Update of the recent evidence (1998–2004). *Sleep, 29*(11), 1398–1414.

Morishima, Y., Schunk, D., Bruhin, A., Ruff, C. C., & Fehr, E. (2012). Linking brain structure and activation in temporoparietal junction to explain the neurobiology of human altruism. *Neuron, 75*(1), 73–79. doi: 10.1016/j.neuron.2012.05.021

Morishita, T., Fayad, S. M., Higuchi, M. A., Nestor, K. A., & Foote, K. D. (2014). Deep brain stimulation for treatment-resistant depression: Systematic review of clinical outcomes. *Neurotherapeutics, 11*(3), 475–484. doi:10.1007/s13311-014-0282-1

Morita, K., Morishima, M., Sakai, K., & Kawaguchi, Y. (2013). Dopaminergic control of motivation and reinforcement learning: A closed-circuit account for reward-oriented behavior. *The Journal of Neuroscience, 33*(20), 8866–8890.

Morris, H., & Wallach, J. (2014). From PCP to MXE: A comprehensive review of the non-medical use of dissociative drugs. *Drug Testing and Analysis, 6*(7–8), 614–632. doi: 10.1002/dta.1620. PMID 24678061

Morris, J. S., Friston, K. J., Buche, L. C., Frith, C. D., Young, A. W., Calder, A. J., & Dolan, R. J. (1998). A neuromodulatory role for the human amygdala in processing emotional facial expressions. *Brain, 121*, 47–57.

Morris, M. W., & Peng, K. (1994). Culture and cause: American and Chinese attributions social and physical events. *Journal of Personality and Social Psychology, 67*, 949–971.

Morris, M., Nisbett, R. E., & Peng, K. (1995). Causal understanding across domains and cultures. In D. Sperber, D. Premack, & A. J. Premack (Eds.), *Causal cognition: A multidisciplinary debate* (pp. 577–612). Oxford, UK: Oxford University Press.

Morris, S. (2009, November 20). Devoted husband who strangled wife in his sleep walks free from court. Retrieved April 9, 2010, from http://www.guardian.co.uk/uk/2009/nov/20/brian-thomas-dream-strangler-tragedy

Morrow, C. E., Culbertson, J. L., Accornero, V. H., Xue, L., Anthony, J. C., & Bandstra, E. S. (2006). Learning disabilities and intellectual functioning in school-aged children with prenatal cocaine exposure. *Developmental Neuropsychology, 30*(3), 905–931.

Moruzzi, G., & Magoun, H. W. (1949). Brainstem reticular formation and activation of the EEG. *Electroencephalographs in Clinical Neurophysiology, 1*, 455–473.

Moscovici, S., & Zavalloni, M. (1969). The group as a polarizer of attitudes. *Journal of Personality and Social Psychology 12*, 125–135.

Motraghi, T. E., Seim, R. W., Meyer, E. C., & Morissette, S. B. (2014). Virtual reality exposure therapy for the treatment of posttraumatic stress disorder: A methodological review using consort guidelines. *Journal of Clinical Psychology, 70*(3), 197–208. doi: 10.1002/jclp.22051

Mowat, F. (1988). *Woman in the mists: The story of Dian Fossey and the mountain gorillas of Africa*. New York: Warner Books.

Mueller, K., Moller, H. E., Horstmann, A., Busse, F., Lepsien, J., Bluher, M.,... Pleger, B. (2015). Physical exercise in overweight to obese individuals induces metabolic- and neurotrophic-related structural brain plasticity. *Frontiers in Human Neuroscience, 9*, 372. doi: 10.3389/fnhum.2015.00372

Mufson, L. H., Dorta, K. P., Olfson, M., Weissman, M. M., & Hoagwood, K. (2004). Effectiveness research: Transporting interpersonal psychotherapy for depressed adolescents (IPT-A) from the lab to school-based health clinics. *Clinical Child and Family Psychology Review, 7*(4), 251–261.

Muhlberger, A., Herrmann, M. J., Wiedemann, G. C., Ellgring. H., & Pauli, P. (2001). Repeated exposure of flight phobics to flights in virtual reality. *Behaviour Research and Therapy, 39*(9), 1033–1050.

Mukamel, R., Ekstrom, A. D., Kaplan, J., Iacoboni, M., & Fried, I. (2010). Single-neuron responses in humans during execution and observation of actions. *Current Biology, 20*, 750–756.

Muller-Oerlinghausen, B., Berghofer, A., & Bauer, M. (2002). Bipolar disorder. *Lancet, 359*, 241–247.

Munoz, E., Sliwinski, M. J., Scott, S. B., & Hofer, S. (2015). Global perceived stress predicts cognitive change among older adults. *Psychology and Aging, 30*, 487–499.

Münsterberg, H. (1908). *On the witness stand*. New York: Clark, Boardman.

Münsterberg, H. (1913). *Psychology and industrial efficiency*. Boston & New York: Houghton Mifflin.

Murayama, K., Matsumoto, M., Izuma, K., Sugiura, A., Ryan, R. M., Deci, E. L., & Matsumoto, K. (2015). How self-determined choice facilitates performance: A key role of the ventromedial prefrontal cortex. *Cerebral Cortex, 25*, 1241–1251. doi: 10.1093/cercor/bht317

Murdock, B. B., Jr. (1962). The serial position effect in free recall. *Journal of Experimental Psychology, 64*, 482–488.

Murphy, C. C., Boyle, C., Schendel, D., Decouflé, P., & Yeargin-Allsopp, M. (1998). Epidemiology of mental retardation in children. *Mental Retardation and Developmental Disabilities Research Reviews, 4*, 6–13.

Murphy, L. R. (1995). Managing job stress: An employee assistance/human resource management partnership. *Personnel Review, 24*(1), 41–50.

Murray, S. L., Holmes, J. G., MacDonald, G., & Ellsworth, P. C. (1998). Through the looking glass darkly? When self-doubts turn into relationship insecurities. *Journal of Personality and Social Psychology, 75*, 1459–1480.

Muter, P. (1978). Recognition failure of recallable words in semantic memory. *Memory & Cognition, 6*(1), 9–12.

Muthuraman, M., Fleischer, V., Kolber, P., Luessi, F., Zipp, F., & Groppa, S. (2016). Structural brain network characteristics can differentiate CIS from early RRMS. *Frontiers in Neuroscience, 10*, 14. doi: 10.3389/fnins.2016.00014

Muzur, A. (2014). The nature of bioethics revisited: A comment on Tomislav Bracanović. *Developing World Bioethics, 14*: 109–110. doi: 10.1111/dewb.12008.

Nadeau, K. G., Quinn, P., & Littman, E. (2001). *AD/HD self-rating scale for girls.* Springfield, MD: Advantage Books.

Nagahara, T., Saitoh, T., Kutsumura, N., Irukayama-Tomobe, Y., Ogawa, Y., Kuroda, D.,... Nagase, H. (2015). Design and synthesis of non-peptide, selective orexin receptor 2 agonists. *Journal of Medicinal Chemistry, 58*(20), 7931. doi: 10.1021/acs.jmedchem.5b00988

Naifeh, J. A., Ursano, R. J., Kessler, R. C., Zaslavsky, A. M., Nock, M. K., Dempsey, C. L., ... Stein, M. B. (2018). Transition to suicide attempt from recent suicide ideation in U.S. Army soldiers: Results from the Army Study to Assess Risk and Resilience in Service members (army starrs). *Depression and Anxiety.* doi:10.1002/da.22870

Nairne J. S. (2015). Adaptive memory: Novel findings acquired through forward engineering. In D. S. Lindsay, C. M. Kelley, A. P. Yonelinas, & H. L. Roediger (Eds.). *Remembering: Attributions, processes, and control in human memory.* New York: Psychology Press.

Naitoh, P., Kelly, T. L., & Englund, C. E. (1989). *Health effects of sleep deprivation* (Naval Health Research Centre, Rep. No. 89–46), San Diego, CA: NHRC.

Najavits, L. M., & Anderson, M. L. (2015). Psychosocial treatments for posttraumatic stress disorder. In P. E. Nathan & J. M. Gorman (Eds.), *A guide to treatments that work* (4th ed., pp. 571–592). New York, NY: Oxford University Press.

Naqvi, R., Liberman, D., Rosenberg, J., Alston, J., & Straus, S. (2013). Preventing cognitive decline in healthy older adults. *Canadian Medical Association Journal, 185*(10) 881–885.

Narlikar, J. V. (2013). An Indian test of Indian astrology. *Skeptical Inquirer, 37.2.* Retrieved on July 7, 2018 at https://www.csicop.org/si/show/an_indian_test_of_indian_astrology

Narvaes, R., & Martins de Almeida, R.M. (2014). Aggressive behavior and three neurotransmitters: Dopamine, gaba, and serotonin—a review of the last 10 years. *Psychology & Neuroscience, 7*(4), 601–607. doi:10.3922/j.psns.2014.4.20

Nasar, S. (1998). *A beautiful mind: A biography of John Forbes Nash, Jr., winner of the Nobel Prize in economics 1994.* New York: Simon & Schuster.

Nathan, P. E., & Gorman, J. M. (Eds.). (2015). *A guide to treatments that work* (4th ed.). New York, NY: Oxford University Press.

National Academy of Neuropsychology. (May, 2001). NAN definition of a clinical neuropsychologist [Electronic version]. Retrieved April 13, 2010, from http://www.nanonline.org/NAN/Files/PAIC/PDFs/NANPositionDefNeuro.pdf

National Center for Complementary and Integrative Health [NCCIH]. (2018). Homeopathy. Retrieved from https://nccih.nih.gov/health/homeopathy

National Center for Education Statistics. (2017). Table 325.80 - degrees in psychology conferred by postsecondary institutions, by level of degree and sex of student: Selected years, 1949–50 through 2015–16. Retrieved from https://nces.ed.gov/programs/digest/d17/tables/dt17_325.80.asp

National Center for Health Statistics. (2015). Deaths: Final data for 2013. *National Vital Statistics Report, 64*(2), 1–119. Hyattsville, MD. Retrieved from www.cdc.gov/nchs/data/nvsr/nvsr64/nvsr64_02.pd

National Collegiate Athletic Association (2002). 2002 NCAA graduation rates report. Retrieved September 21, 2007, from NCAA—The National Collegiate Athletic Association: The online resource for the National Collegiate Athletic Association Web site: Retrieved from http://web1.ncaa.org/web_files/grad_rates/2002/index.html

National Commission for the Protection of Human Subjects of Biomedical and Behavioral Research. (2006). Fetal viability and death: United States. Retrieved April 26, 2013, from https://scholarworks.iupui.edu/bitstream/handle/1805/583/OS76-127_VII.pdf?sequence=1

National Heart, Lung, and Blood Institute. (2018). Overweight and obesity. Retrieved from https://www.nhlbi.nih.gov/health-topics/overweight-and-obesity

National Institute of Mental Health. (2019). Mental Illness. Retrieved from https://www.nimh.nih.gov/health/statistics/mental-illness.shtml

National Institute of Mental Health. (2018, May). Suicide. Retrieved from https://www.nimh.nih.gov/health/statistics/suicide.shtml

National Institute of Mental Health (NIMH) Genetics Workgroup. (1998). *Genetics and mental disorders* (NIH Publication No. 98-4268). Rockville, MD: National Institute of Mental Health.

National Institute of Neurological Disorders and Stroke. (2015). NINDS sleep apnea information page. Retrieved from http://www.ninds.nih.gov/disorders/sleep_apnea/sleep_apnea.htm

National Institute on Alcohol Abuse and Alcoholism (NIAAA). (2016). Alcohol facts and statistics. Retrieved from http://pubs.niaaa.nih.gov/publications/AlcoholFacts&Stats/AlcoholFacts&Stats.htm

National Institute on Drug Abuse (NIDA). (2002). Research report series—Prescription drugs: Abuse and addiction. National Institutes of Health (NIH). Retrieved July 19, 2008, from www.drugabuse.gov/ResearchReports/Prescription/prescription5.html

National Institute on Drug Abuse (NIDA). (2016). NIDA DrugFacts: Hallucinogens. Retrieved January 18 from https://www.drugabuse.gov/publications/drugfacts/hallucinogens

National Institutes of Health; National Heart, Lung and Blood Institute. (2011). *Your guide to healthy sleep.* NIH Publication No. 06-5271.

National Safety Council. (2015). Annual estimate of cell phone crashes 2013. Retrieved from http://www.nsc.org/DistractedDrivingDocuments/Cell-Phone-Estimate-Summary-2013.pdf

National Sleep Foundation. (2009). Can't sleep? What to know about insomnia. Retrieved May 5, 2010, from http://www.sleepfoundation.org/article/sleep-related-problems/insomnia-and-sleep

NCD Risk Factor Collaboration. (2017). Worldwide trends in body-mass index, underweight, overweight, and obesity from 1975 to 2016: A pooled analysis of 2416 population-based measurement studies in 128·9 million children, adolescents, and adults. *Lancet, 390*, 2627–2642. doi:10.1016/S0140-6736(17)32129-3

Neale, M. C., Rushton, J. P., & Fulker, D. W. (1986). The heritability of items from the Eysenck Personality Questionnaire. *Personality and Individual Differences, 7*, 771–779.

Neary, N. M., Goldstone, A. P., & Bloom, S. R. (2004). Appetite regulations: From the gut to the hypothalamus. *Clinical Endocrinology, 60*(2), 153–160.

Ne'eman, R., Perach-Barzilay, N., Fischer-Shofty, M., Atias, A., & Shamay-Tsoory, S. G. (2016). Intranasal administration of oxytocin increases human aggressive behavior. *Hormones and Behavior.* doi: http://dx.doi.org/10.1016/j.yhbeh.2016.01.015

Neimark, J. (1996). The diva of disclosure, memory researcher Elizabeth Loftus. *Psychology Today, 29*(1), 48–80.

Neimeyer, R. A., & Mitchell, K. A. (1998). Similarity and attraction: A longitudinal study. *Journal of Social and Personality Relationships, 5*, 131–148.

Neisser, U. (1982). Snapshots or benchmarks? In U. Neisser (Ed.), *Memory observed: Remembering in natural contexts* (pp. 43–48). San Francisco: W. H. Freeman.

Neisser, U., & Harsch, N. (1992). Phantom flashbulbs: False recollections of hearing the news about Challenger. In E. Winograd & U. Neisser (Eds.), *Affect and accuracy in recall: Studies of "flashbulb memories"* (pp. 9–31). New York: Cambridge University Press.

Neisser, U., Boodoo, G., Bouchard, T. J., Boykin, A. W., Brody, N., Ceci, S. J.,... Urbina, S. (1996). Intelligence: Knowns and unknowns. *American Psychologist, 51*, 77–101.

Nelson, C. A. (2011). Brain development and behavior. In A. M. Rudolph, C. Rudolph, L. First, G. Lister, & A. A. Gershon (Eds.), *Rudolph's pediatrics* (22nd ed.). New York: McGraw-Hill.

Nelson, D. B., Hanlon, A. L., Wu, G., Liu, C., & Fredricks, D. N. (2015). First trimester levels of BV-associated bacteria and risk of miscarriage among women early in pregnancy. *Maternal and Child Health Journal, 19*(12), 2682–2687.

Nelson, K. (1993). The psychological and social origins of autobiographical memory. *Psychological Science, 4*, 7–14.

Nelson, L. J., Padilla-Walker, L. M., Badger, S., Barry, C. M., Carroll, J., & Madsen, S. (2008). Associations between shyness and internalizing behaviors, externalizing behaviors, and relationships during emerging adulthood. *Journal of Youth and Adolescence, 37*, 605–615.

Nemeroff, C. B. (2016). Paradise lost: The neurobiological and clinical consequences of child abuse and neglect. *Neuron, 89*(5), 892–909. doi:10.1016/j.neuron.2016.01.019

Nestor, P. G., Kubicki, M., Niznikiewicz, M., Gurrera, R. J., McCarley, R. W., & Shenton, M. E. (2008). Neuropsychological disturbance in schizophrenia: A diffusion tensor imaging study. *Neuropsychology, 22*(2), 246–254.

Neto, F. (1995). Conformity and independence revisited. *Social Behavior and Personality, 23*(3), 217–222.

Newell, B. R., & Shanks, D. R. (2014). Unconscious influences on decision making: A critical review. *Behavioral and Brain Sciences, 37*(1), 1–19. doi: 10.1017/S0140525X12003214

Newman, J. D., Davidson, K. W., Shaffer, J. A., Schwartz, J. E., Chaplin, W., Kirkland, S., & Shimbo, D. (2011). Observed hostility and the risk of incident ischemic heart disease: A prospective population study from the 1995 Canadian Nova Scotia health survey. *Journal of the American College of Cardiology, 58*(12), 1222–1228. doi:10.1016/j.jacc.2011.04.044

Nicholson, I. (2011). "Torture at Yale": Experimental subjects, laboratory torment and the "rehabilitation" of Milgram's "obedience to authority." *Theory & Psychology, 21*(6), 737–761. doi:10.1177/0959354311420199

Nicholson, N., Cole, S., & Rocklin, T. (1985). Conformity in the Asch situation: A comparison between contemporary British and U.S. students. *British Journal of Social Psychology, 24*, 59–63.

Nickell, J. 1995. Crop circle mania wanes: An investigative update. *Skeptical Inquirer, 19*(3), 41–43.

Nickerson, R. S., & Adams, J. J. (1979). Long-term memory for a common object. *Cognitive Psychology, 11*, 287–307.

Niedermeyer, E. (2005). Historical aspects. In E. Niedermeyer & F. Lopes da Silva (Eds.), *Electroencephalography: Basic principles, clinical applications, and related fields* (5th ed., pp. 1–15). Philadelphia: Lippincott, Williams & Wilkins.

Nielsen, M., Suddendorf, T., & Slaughter, V. (2006). Mirror self-recognition beyond the face. *Child Development, 77*(1), 176–185. doi: 10.1111/j.1467-8624.2006.00863.x

Nielsen, T., Zadra, A., Simard, V., Saucier, S., Stenstrom, P., Smith, C., & Kuiken, D. (2003). The typical dreams of Canadian university students. *Dreaming, 13*(4), 211–235 DOI: 10.1023/B:DREM.0000003144.40929.0b

Nieto, F., Young, T. B., Lind, B. K., Shahar, E., Samet, J. M., Redline, S.,... Pickering, T. G. (2000). Association of sleep-disordered breathing, sleep apnea, and hypertension in a large, community-based study. *Journal of the American Medical Association, 283*(14), 1829–1836.

Nievar, M. A., Moske, A. K., Johnson, D. J., & Chen, Q. (2015). Parenting practices in preschool leading to later cognitive competencies: A family stress model. *Early Education and Development, 25*, 318–337.

Nihei, Y., Takahashi, K., Koto, A., Mihara, B., Morita, Y., Isozumi, K.,... Suzuki, N. (2012). REM sleep behavior disorder in Japanese patients with Parkinson's disease: A multicenter study using the REM sleep behavior disorder screening questionnaire. *Journal of Neurology, 259*(8), 1606–1612.

Nijenhuis, E. R. (2000). Somatoform dissociation: Major symptoms of dissociative disorders. *Journal of Trauma and Dissociation, 1*(4), 7–29.

Nikolajsen, L., & Jensen, T. S. (2001). Phantom limb pain. *British Journal of Anaesthesia, 87*, 107–116.

Nikolova, M., & Graham, C. (2014). Employment, late-life work, retirement, and well-being in Europe and the United States. *IZA Journal of European Labor Studies, 3*(1). doi:10.1186/2193-9012-3-5

Nisbett, R. E. (1972). Hunger, obesity, and the ventromedial hypothalamus. *Psychological Review, 79*, 433–453.

Nisbett, R. E., Aronson, J., Blair, C., Dickens, W., Flynn, J., Halpern, D. F., & Turkheimer, E. (2012). Intelligence: New findings and theoretical developments. *American Psychologist, 67*(2), 130–159. doi: 10.1037/a0026699

Nokia, M. S., Lensu, S., Ahtiainen, J. P., Johansson, P. P., Koch, L. G., Britton, S. L., & Kainulainen, H. (2016). Physical exercise increases adult hippocampal neurogenesis in male rats provided it is aerobic and sustained. *Journal of Physiology*. doi: 10.1113/JP271552

Nolen-Hoeksema, S. (1990). *Sex differences in depression.* Palo Alto, CA: Stanford University Press.

Nolen-Hoeksema, S. (2012). Emotion regulation and psychopathology: The role of gender. *Annual Review of Clinical Psychology, 8*, 161–187. doi: 10.1146/annurev-clinpsy-032511-143109

Nooyens, A. C. J., Baan, C. A., Spijkerman, A. M. W., & Verschuren, W. M. M. (2010). *Type 2 diabetes mellitus and cognitive decline in middle-aged men and women—The Doetinchem Cohort Study.* American Diabetes Association: Diabetes Care.

Norcross, J. C. (2005). A primer on psychotherapy integration. In J. C. Norcross & M. R. Goldfried (Eds.), *Handbook of psychotherapy integration* (2nd ed., pp. 3–23). New York: Oxford University Press.

Nordenskjold, A., von Knorring, L., & Engstrom, I. (2011). Predictors of time to relapse/recurrence after electroconvulsive therapy in patients with major depressive disorder: A population-based cohort study. *Depression Research and Treatment, 2011*, 470985. doi: 10.1155/2011/470985

Norenzayan, A., Choi, I., & Nisbett, R. E. (1999). Eastern and Western perceptions of causality for social behavior: Lay theories about personalities and situations. In D. A. Prentice & D. T. Miller (Eds.), *Cultural divides* (pp. 239–272). New York: Russell Sage Foundation.

Nosek, B. A., Greenwald, A. G., & Banaji, M. R. (2007). The Implicit Association Test at age 7: A methodological and conceptual review. In J. A. Bargh (Ed.), *Automatic processes in social thinking and behavior* (pp. 265–292). New York: Psychology Press.

Nosek, B. A., Spies, J. R., & Motyl, M. (2012). Scientific utopia: II. Restructuring incentives and practices to promote truth over publishability. *Perspectives on Psychological Science, 7*(6), 615–631. doi: 10.1177/1745691612459058

Nosich, G. M. (2008). *Learning to think things through: A guide to critical thinking across the curriculum* (3rd ed., pp. 2–16). Upper Saddle River, NJ: Prentice-Hall.

Novak, J. D. (1995). Concept maps to facilitate teaching and learning. *Prospects, 25*, 95–11.

Novak, M., Björck, L., Giang, K. W., Heden-Ståhl, C., Wilhelmsen, L., & Rosengren, A. (2013). Perceived stress and incidence of Type 2 diabetes: A 35-year follow-up study of middle-aged Swedish men. *Diabetic Medicine, 30*(1), e8. doi: 10-1111/dme.12037

Novella, S. (2007, November/December). The Anti-Vaccination Movement. *Skeptical Inquirer.* Retrieved May 21, 2010, from http://www.csicop.org/si/show/anti-vaccination_movement/www.guardian.co.uk/science/2007/feb/24/badscience.uknews

Novotney, A. (2013, March). I/O psychology goes to Mars. *Monitor on Psychology, 44*(3), 38.

Nurminen, L., Merlin, S., Bijanzadeh, M., Federer, F., & Angelucci, A. (2018). Top-down feedback controls spatial summation and response amplitude in primate visual cortex. *Nature Communications, 9*(1). doi:10.1038/s41467-018-04500-5

Nussbaum, A. D., & Dweck, C. S. (2008). Defensiveness vs. remediation: Self-theories and modes of self-esteem maintenance. *Personality and Social Psychology Bulletin, 34*, 599–612.

Nuttin, B., Wu, H., Mayberg, H., Hariz, M., Gabriels, L., Galert, T.,... Schlaepfer, T. (2014). Consensus on guidelines for stereotactic neurosurgery for psychiatric disorders. *Journal of Neurology, Neurosurgery, & Psychiatry, 85*(9), 1003–1008. doi: 10.1136/jnnp-2013-306580

Nyberg, L., & Tulving, E. (1996). Classifying human long-term memory: Evidence from converging dissociations. *European Journal of Cognitive Psychology, 8*(2), 163–183.

Oberman, L. M., & Ramachandran, V. S. (2007). The simulating social mind: The role of simulation in the social and communicative deficits of autism spectrum disorders, *Psychological Bulletin, 133*, 310–327.

Ocholla-Ayayo, A. B. C., Wekesa, J. M., & Ottieno, J. A. M. (1993). *Adolescent pregnancy and its implications among ethnic groups in Kenya.* In International Population Conference, Montreal, Canada: International Union for the Scientific Study of Population, 1: 381–395.

Ochsner, K., & Kosslyn, S. M. (1994). Mental imagery. In V. S. Ramaschandran (Ed.), *Encyclopedia of human behavior.* New York: Academic Press.

Ocklenburg, S., Beste, C., & Gunturkun, O. (2013). Handedness: A neurogenetic shift of perspective. *Neuroscience and Biobehavioral Reviews, 37*(10 Pt 2), 2788–2793. doi: 10.1016/j.neubiorev.2013.09.014

O'Connor, R. D. (1972). Relative efficacy of modeling, shaping, and the combined procedures for modification of social withdrawal. *Journal of Abnormal Psychology, 79*, 327–334.

Offit, P. A., & Bell, L. M. (1998). *What every parent should know about vaccines.* New York: Macmillan.

Ohayon, M. M., Priest, R. G., Caulet, M., & Guilleminault, C. (1996). Hypnagogic and hypnopompic hallucinations: Pathological phenomena? *British Journal of Psychiatry, 169*, 459–467.

Ohly, H., White, M. P., Wheeler, B. W., Bethel, A., Ukoumunne, O. C., Nikolaou, V., & Garside, R. (2016). Attention restoration theory: A systematic review of the attention restoration potential of exposure to natural environments. *Journal of Toxicology and Environmental Health. Part B: Critical Reviews, 19*(7), 305–343. doi:10.1080/10937404.2016.1196155

Öhman, A. (2008). Fear and anxiety. In M. Lewis, J. M. Haviland-Jones & L. F. Barrett (Eds.), *Handbook of emotion* (3rd ed., pp. 709–729). New York: Guiford Press.

O'Keefe, D. J. (2009). Theories of persuasion. In R. L. Nabi & M. B. Oliver (Eds.), *The Sage handbook of media processes and effects* (pp. 277–278). Los Angeles: Sage.

Olin, B. R. (Ed.). (1993). Central nervous system drugs, sedatives and hypnotics, barbiturates. In *Facts and comparisons drug information* (pp. 1398–1413). St. Louis, MO: Facts and Comparisons.

Ollendick, T. H., & King, N. J. (1998). Empirically supported treatments for children with phobic and anxiety disorders: Current status. *Journal of Clinical Child Psychology, 27*(2), 156–167.

Olsen, P. (1975). *Emotional flooding.* Baltimore, MD: Penguin Books.

Olson, H. C., & Burgess, D. M. (1997). Early intervention for children prenatally exposed to alcohol and other drugs. In M. J. Guralnick (Ed.), *The effectiveness of early intervention* (pp. 109–146). Baltimore: Brookes.

Olulade, O. A., Jamal, N. I., Koo, D. S., Perfetti, C. A., LaSasso, C., & Eden, G. F. (2015). Neuroanatomical evidence in support of the bilingual advantage theory. *Cerebral Cortex*. doi: 10.1093/cercor/bhv152

Olver, J. S., Pinney, M., Maruff, P., & Norman, T. R. (2015). Impairments of spatial working memory and attention following acute psychosocial stress. *Stress and Health, 31*, 115–123.

Oman, C. M. (1990). Motion sickness: A synthesis and evaluation of the sensory conflict theory. *Canadian Journal of Physiological Pharmacology, 68*, 294–303.

Onken, L. S., Blaine, J. D., & Battjes, R. J. (1997). Behavioral therapy research: A conceptualization of a process. In S. W. Henggeler & A. B. Santos (Eds.), *Innovative approaches for difficult-to-treat populations* (pp. 477–485). Washington, DC: American Psychiatric Press.

Open Science Collaboration. (2015). Estimating the reproducibility of psychological science. *Science, 349*(6251), aac4716. DOI: 10.1126/science.aac4716

Ophir, E., Nass, C., & Wagner, A. D. (2009). Cognitive control in media multitaskers. *Proceedings of the National Academy of Sciences of the United States of America, 106*(37), 15583–15587.

Organization of Teratology Information Specialists. (2017). MotherToBaby medications & more during pregnancy & breastfeeding: Fact Sheets. Retrieved on March 29, 2017, from https://mothertobaby.org/fact-sheets-parent/

Orr, E. (2018). Beyond the pre-communicative medium: A cross-behavioral prospective study on the role of gesture in language and play development. *Infant Behavior & Development, 52*, 66–75. doi:10.1016/j.infbeh.2018.05.007

Ortiz, E., & Lubell, B. (2017). Penn State fraternity death: Why did no one call 911 after pledge Timothy Piazza got hurt? Retrieved from http://www.nbcnews.com/news/us-news/penn-state-fraternity-death-why-did-no-one-call-911-n756951

Osborne, J. W. (2007). Linking stereotype threat and anxiety. *Educational Psychology, 27*, 35–154.

Osshera, L., Flegala, K. E., & Lustiga, C. (2012). Everyday memory errors in older adults. *Aging, Neuropsychology, and Cognition, 20*(2), 220–242. doi: 10.1080/13825585.2012.690365

Österman, K., Björkqvist, K., & Wahlbeck, K. (2014). Twenty-eight years after the complete ban on the physical punishment of children in Finland: Trends and psychosocial concomitants. *Aggressive Behavior, 40*(6), 568–581.

Oswald, I. (1959). Sudden bodily jerks on falling asleep. *Brain, 82*, 92–103.

Ottaway, N., Mahbod, P., Rivero, B., Norman, L. A., Gertler, A., D'Alessio, D. A., & Perez-Tilve, D. (2015). Diet-induced obese mice retain endogenous leptin action. *Cell Metabolism, 21*(6), 877–882.

Overeem, S., Mignot, E., Gert van Dijk, J., & Lammers, G. J. (2001). Narcolepsy: Clinical features, new pathophysiological insights, and future perspectives. *Journal of Clinical Neurophysiology, 18*(2), 78–105.

Overmier, J. B., & Seligman, M. E. P. (1967). Effects of inescapable shock on subsequent escape and avoidance behavior. *Journal of Comparative Physiology and Psychology, 63*, 23–33.

Owen, M. T., Easterbrooks, M. A., Chase-Lansdale, L., & Goldberg, W. A. (1984). The relation between maternal employment status and the stability of attachments to mother and to father. *Child Development, 55*, 1894–1901.

Ozer, D. J., & Benet-Martinez, V. (2006). Personality and the prediction of consequential outcomes. *Annual Review of Psychology, 57*, 401–421. doi: 10.1146/annurev.psych.57.102904.190127

Paap, K. R. (2014). The role of componential analysis, categorical hypothesising, replicability and confirmation bias in testing for bilingual advantages in executive functioning. *Journal of Cognitive Psychology, 26*(3), 242–255. doi: 10.1080/20445911.2014.891597

Paap, K. R., & Greenberg, Z. I. (2013). There is no coherent evidence for a bilingual advantage in executive processing. *Cognitive Psychology, 66*, 232–258. doi: 10.1016/j.cogpsych.2012.12.002

Paap, K. R., Johnson, H. A., & Sawi, O. (2014). Are bilingual advantages dependent upon specific tasks or specific bilingual experiences? *Journal of Cognitive Psychology, 26*(6), 615–639. doi: 10.1080/20445911.2014.944914

Palmatier, J. J., & Rovner, L. (2015). Credibility assessment: Preliminary process theory, the polygraph process, and construct validity. *International Journal of Psychophysiology, 95*(1), 3–13.

Palmer, S. E. (1992). Common region: A new principle of perceptual grouping. *Cognitive Psychology, 24*(3), 436–447.

Palmer, S., & Rock, I. (1994). Rethinking perceptual organization: The role of uniform connectedness. *Psychon Bull Rev, 1*(1), 29–55. doi:10.3758/BF03200760

Palva, J. M., Monto, S., Kulashekhar, S., & Palva, S. (2010). Neuronal synchrony reveals working memory networks and predicts individual memory capacity. *Proceedings of the National Academy of Sciences, USA, 107*(16), 7580–7585.

Pan, A. S. (2000). Body image, eating attitudes, and eating behaviors among Chinese, Chinese-American and non-Hispanic White women. *Dissertation Abstracts International, Section B: The Sciences and Engineering, 61*(1–B), 544.

Pan, H., Guo, J., & Su, Z. (2014). Advances in understanding the interrelations between leptin resistance and obesity. *Physiology & Behavior 130*, 157–169.

Pant, H., McCabe, B. J., Deskovitz, M. A., Weed, N. C., & Williams, J. E. (2014). Diagnostic reliability of MMPI-2 computer-based test interpretations. *Psychological Assessment, 26*(3), 916–924. doi: 10.1037/a0036469

Paparelli, A., Di Forti, M., Morrison, P. D., & Murray, R. M. (2011). Drug-induced psychosis: How to avoid star gazing in schizophrenia research by looking at more obvious sources of light. *Frontiers in Behavioral Neuroscience, 5*: 1. doi: 10.3389/fnbeh.2011.00001

Paredes, M., James, D., Gil-Perotin, S., Kim, H., Cotter, J. A., Ng, C.,... & Alvarez-Buylla, A. (2016). Extensive migration of young neurons into the infant human frontal lobe. *Science, 354*(6308): aaf7073. DOI: http://dx.doi.org/10.1126/science.aaf7073

Pargament, K. I. (1997). *The psychology of religion and coping: Theory, research, and practice*. New York: Guilford Press.

Pariyadath, V., Gowin, J. L., & Stein, E. A. (2016). Resting state functional connectivity analysis for addiction medicine: From individual loci to complex networks. *Progress in Brain Research, 224*, 155–173. doi: 10.1016/bs.pbr.2015.07.015

Park, J., Turnbull, A. P., & Turnbull, H. R. (2002). Impacts of poverty on quality of life in families of children with disabilities. *Exceptional Children, 68*, 151–170.

Parkes, C. M., Laungani, P., & Young, W. (1997). *Death and bereavement across cultures*. Routledge: New York.

Parkinson, W. L., & Weingarten, H. P. (1990). Dissociative analysis of ventromedial hypothalamic obesity syndrome. *American Journal of Physiology: Regulatory, Integrative, and Comparative Physiology, 259*, R829–R835.

Parsons, H. M. (1992). Hawthorne: An early OBM experiment. *Journal of Organizational Behavior Management, 12*(1), 27–43.

Partnership for Drug-Free Kids. (2014). The medicine abuse project: 2014 report. Retrieved from http://medicineabuseproject.org/assets/documents/MAP_2014_Report_final.pdf

Partonen, T., & Lonnqvist, J. (1998). Seasonal affective disorder. *Lancet, 352*(9137), 1369–1374.

Pashkow, F. J. (2011). Oxidative stress and inflammation in heart disease: Do antioxidants have a role in treatment and/or prevention? *International Journal of Inflammation, 2011*, Article ID 514623.

Passmore, H., & Howell, A. J. (2014). Nature involvement increases hedonic and eudaimonic well-being: A two-week experimental study. *Ecopsychology* (6), 148–154. doi:10.1089/eco.2014.0023

Patel, A., Yamashita, N., Ascaño, M., Bodmer, D., Boehm, E., Bodkin-Clarke, C.,... Kuruvilla, R. (2015). RCAN1 links impaired neurotrophin trafficking to aberrant development of the sympathetic nervous system in Down syndrome. *Nature Communications, 6*, 10119.

Paul, B. M., ElvevÅg, B., Bokat, C. E., Weinberger, D. R., & Goldberg, T. E. (2005). Levels of processing effects on recognition memory in patients with schizophrenia. *Schizophrenia Research, 74*(1), 101–110.

Paul, J. R., DeWoskin, D., McMeekin, L. J., Cowell, R. M., Forger, D. B., & Gamble, K. L. (2016). Regulation of persistent sodium currents by glycogen synthase kinase 3 encodes daily rhythms of neuronal excitability. Nature Communications, 7: 13470. doi:10.1038/ncomms13470.

Pauwels, L., Chalavi, S., Gooijers, J., Maes, C., Albouy, G., Sunaert, S., & Swinnen, S. P. (2018). Challenge to promote change: The neural basis of the contextual interference effect in young and older adults. *Journal of Neuroscience, 38*(13), 3333–3345. doi:10.1523/JNEUROSCI.2640-17.2018

Pavlov, I. P. (1906). The scientific investigation of the psychical faculties or processes in the higher animals. *Science, 24*, 613–619.

Pavlov, I. P. (1926). *Conditioned reflexes*. London: Oxford University Press.

Pavlov, I. P. (1927). *Conditioned reflexes: An investigation of the physiological activity of the cerebral cortex* (G. V. Anrep, Trans. and Ed.). London: Oxford University Press.

Pearson, J., & Kosslyn, S. M. (2015). The heterogeneity of mental representation: Ending the imagery debate. *Proceedings of the National Academy of Sciences of the United States of America, 112*(33), 10089–10092. doi:10.1073/pnas.1504933112

Pearson, J., Naselaris, T., Holmes, E. A., & Kosslyn, S. M. (2015). Mental imagery: Functional mechanisms and clinical applications. *Trends in Cognitive Sciences, 19*(10), 590–602. doi:10.1016/j.tics.2015.08.003

Pearson, J., & Westbrook, F. (2015). Phantom perception: Voluntary and involuntary nonretinal vision. *Trends in Cognitive Sciences, 19*(5), 278–284. doi:https://doi.org/10.1016/j.tics.2015.03.004

Peever, J., Luppi, P.-H., & Montplaisir, J. (2014). Breakdown in REM sleep circuitry underlies REM sleep behavior disorder. *Trends in Neurosciences, 37*(5), 279–288. doi: 10.1016/j.tins.2014.02.009

Peng, K., Ames, D. R., & Knowles, E. D. (2001). Culture and human inference: Perspectives from three traditions. In D. Matsumoto (Ed.), *The handbook of culture and psychology* (pp. 245–264). New York, NY: Oxford University Press.

Peng, L., Verkhratsky, A., Gu, L., & Li, B. (2015). Targeting astrocytes in major depression. *Expert Review of Neurotherapeutics, 1–8*. doi: 10.1586/14737175.2015.1095094

Pennsylvania State University. (2014). Why plagiarism is wrong. Retrieved from http://tlt.psu.edu/plagiarism/student-tutorial/why-plagiarism-is-wrong/

Peplau, L. A., & Taylor, S. E. (1997). *Sociocultural perspectives in social psychology: Current readings*. Upper Saddle River, NJ: Prentice-Hall.

Pepperberg, I. M. (1998). Talking with Alex: Logic and speech in parrots. *Scientific American Presents: Exploring Intelligence, 9*(4), 60–65.

Pepperberg, I. M. (2007). Grey parrots do not always "parrot": The roles of imitation and phonological awareness in the creation of new labels from existing vocalizations. *Language Sciences, 29*(1), 1–13.

Perls, F. (1951). *Gestalt therapy*. New York: Julian Press.

Perls, F. (1969). *Gestalt therapy verbatim*. Moab, UT: Real People Press.

Perrin, S., & Spencer, C. (1980). The Asch effect—A child of its time. *Bulletin of the British Psychological Society, 33*, 405–406.

Perrin, S., & Spencer, C. P. (1981). Independence or conformity in the Asch experiment as a reflection of cultural and situational factors. *British Journal of Social Psychology, 20*(3), 205–209.

Perry, G. (2013a). *Behind the shock machine: The untold story of the notorious Milgram psychology experiments*. New York, NY: New Press.

Perry, G. (2013b). Deception and illusion in Milgram's accounts of the obedience experiments. *Theoretical & Applied Ethics, 2*(2), 79–92.

Perry, G. (2014). The view from the boys. *The Psychologist, 27*(11), 834–837.

Perry, G. (2015). Seeing is believing: The role of the film obedience in shaping perceptions of Milgram's obedience to authority experiments. *Theory & Psychology, 25*(5), 622–638. doi:10.1177/0959354315604235

Perry, W. G., Jr. (1970). *Forms of intellectual and ethical development in the college years: A scheme*. New York: Holt, Rinehart, and Winston.

Peters, W. A. (1971). *A class divided*. Garden City, NY: Doubleday.

Peterson, C., & Park, N. (2010). What happened to self-actualization? *Perspectives on Psychological Science, 5*(3), 320–322.

Peterson, D. R. (1976). Need for the doctor of psychology degree in professional psychology. *American Psychologist, 31*, 792–798.

Peterson, D. R. (1982). Origins and development of the Doctor of Psychology concept. In G. R. Caddy, D. C. Rimm, N. Watson, & J. H. Johnson (Eds.), *Educating professional psychologists* (pp. 19–38). New Brunswick, NJ: Transaction Books.

Peterson, L. R., & Peterson, M. J. (1959). Short-term retention of individual items. *Journal of Experimental Psychology, 58*, 193–198.

Petit, D., Pennestri, M. H., Paquet, J., Desautels, A., Zadra, A., Vitaro, F.,... Montplaisir, J. (2015). Childhood sleepwalking and sleep terrors: A longitudinal study of prevalence and familial aggregation. *JAMA Pediatrics, 169*(7), 653–658. doi: 10.1001/jamapediatrics.2015.127

Petitto, L. A., & Marentette, P. F. (1991). Babbling in the manual mode: Evidence for the ontogeny of language. *Science, 251,* 1493–1496.

Petitto, L. A., Holowka, S., Sergio, L. E., & Ostry, D. (2001). Language rhythms in baby hand movements. *Nature, 413,* 35.

Petri, H. (1996). *Motivation: Theory, research and application* (4th ed.). Belmont, CA: Wadsworth.

Petrides, G., Tobias, K. G., Kellner, C. H., & Rudorfer, M. V. (2011). Continuation and maintenance electroconvulsive therapy for mood disorders: A review of the literature. *Neuropsychobiology, 64*(3), 129–140. doi: 10.1159/000328943

Petrova, P. K., Cialdini, R. B., & Sills S., J. (2007). Compliance, consistency, and culture: Personal consistency and compliance across cultures. *Journal of Experimental Social Psychology 43*: 104–111.

Petticrew, M. P., Lee, K., & McKee, M. (2016). Type A behavior pattern and coronary heart disease: Philip Morris's "crown jewel." *American Journal of Public Health, 102*(11), 2018–2025. doi:10.2105/AJPH.2012.300816

Pettigrew, T. F., & Tropp, L. R. (2000). Does intergroup contact reduce prejudice? Recent meta-analytic findings. In S. Oskamp (Ed.), *Reducing prejudice and discrimination: Social psychological perspectives* (pp. 93–114). Mahwah, NJ: Erlbaum.

Petty, R., & Cacioppo, J. (1986). *Communication and persuasion: Central and peripheral routes to attitude change.* New York: Springer-Verlag.

Petty, R., & Cacioppo, J. (1996). *Attitudes and persuasion: Classic and contemporary approaches* (Reprint). Boulder, CO: Westview Press.

Petty, R. E. (1995). Attitude change. In A. Tesser (Ed.), *Advances in social psychology* (pp. 194–255). New York: McGraw-Hill.

Petty, R. E., & Briñol, P. (2015). Processes of social influence through attitude change. In E. Borgida & J. Bargh (Eds.), *APA handbook of personality and social psychology, Vol. 1: Attitudes and social cognition* (pp. 509–545). Washington, DC: APA Books.

Petty, R. E., Wheeler, S. C., & Tormala, Z. L. (2003). Persuasion and attitude change. In T. Millon & M. J. Lerner (Eds.), *Handbook of psychology: Volume 5: Personality and social psychology* (pp. 353–382). Hoboken, NJ: John Wiley & Sons.

Pew Research Center. (2017). *Online harassment 2017.* Retrieved from http://www.pewinternet.org/2017/07/11/online-harassment-2017/

Pezdek, K., & Blandón-Gitlin, I. (2017). It is just harder to construct memories for false autobiographical events. Applied Cognitive Psychology, 31(1), 42–44. doi: https://doi.org/10.1002/acp.3269

Pezdek, K., & Hodge, D. (1999). Planting false childhood memories in children: The role of event plausibility. *Child Development, 70,* 887–895.

Pezdek, K., Finger, K., & Hodge, D. (1997). Planting false childhood memories: The role of event plausibility. *Psychological Science, 8,* 437–441

Pfeiffer, W. M. (1982). Culture-bound syndromes. In I. Al-Issa (Ed.), *Culture and psychopathology* (pp. 201–218). Baltimore: University Park Press.

Phan, T., & Silove, D. (1999). An overview of indigenous descriptions of mental phenomena and the range of traditional healing practices amongst the Vietnamese. *Transcultural Psychiatry, 36,* 79–94.

Piaget, J. (1926). *The language and thought of the child.* New York: Harcourt Brace.

Piaget, J. (1952). *The origins of intelligence in children.* New York: W. W. Norton.

Piaget, J. (1962). *Play, dreams and imitation in childhood.* New York: W. W. Norton.

Piaget, J. (1983). Piaget's theory. In W. Kessen (Ed.), *Handbook of child psychology: Volume 1. Theoretical models of human development* (pp. 103–128). New York: Wiley.

Pike, K. M., & Dunne, P. E. (2015). The rise of eating disorders in Asia: A review. *Journal of Eating Disorders, 3,* 33. doi:10.1186/s40337-015-0070-2

Pilon, M., Montplaisir, J., & Zadra, A. (2008). Precipitating factors of somnambulism: Impact of sleep deprivation and forced arousals. *Neurology, 70:* 2284–2290.

Pinares-Garcia, P., Stratikopoulos, M., Zagato, A., Loke, H., & Lee, J. (2018). Sex: A significant risk factor for neurodevelopmental and neurodegenerative disorders. *Brain Sci, 8*(8). doi:10.3390/brainsci8080154

Pinker, S. (1995). Language acquisition. In Gleitman and M. Liberman. (Eds.), *An invitation to cognitive science* (2nd ed., pp. 135–182). Cambridge, MA: MIT Press.

Pinker, S., & Bloom, P. (1990). Natural language and natural selection. *Behavioral and Brain Sciences, 13*(4), 707–784.

Pinsof, W. M., & Wynne, L. C. (1995). The efficacy of marital and family therapy: An empirical overview, conclusions, and recommendations. *Journal of Marital and Family Therapy, 21,* 585–613.

Pittenger, D. J. (2005). Cautionary comments regarding the Myers-Briggs Type Indicator. *Consulting Psychology Journal: Practice and Research, 57*(3), 210–221. doi: 10.1037/1065-9293.57.3.210

Plaks, J. E, Grant, H., & Dweck, C. S. (2005). Violations of implicit theories and the sense of prediction and control: Implications for motivated person perception. *Journal of Personality and Social Psychology, 88,* 245–262.

Platow, M. J., & Hunter, J. A. (2012). Intergroup relations and conflict: Revisiting Sherif's boys' camp studies. In J. Smith & S. Haslam (Eds.), *Social psychology: Revisiting the classic studies* (pp. 142–159). Los Angeles, CA: SAGE.

Plaut, D. C., & McClelland, J. L. (2010). Locating object knowledge in the brain: A critique of Bowers' (2009) attempt to revive the grandmother cell hypothesis. *Psychological Review, 117,* 284–288.

Pliatsikas, C., Moschopoulou, E., & Saddy, J. D. (2015). The effects of bilingualism on the white matter structure of the brain. *Proceedings of the National Academy of Sciences of the United States of America, 112*(5), 1334–1337. doi: 10.1073/pnas.1414183112

Plomin, R. (1994). The nature of nurture: The environment beyond the family. In R. Plomin (Ed.), *Genetics and experience: The interplay between nature and nurture* (pp. 82–107). Thousand Oaks, CA: Sage.

Plomin, R., & Deary, I. J. (2015). Genetics and intelligence differences: Five special findings. *Molecular Psychiatry, 20*(1), 98–108. doi:10.1038/mp.2014.105

Plomin, R., & DeFries, J. C. (1998, May). Genetics of cognitive abilities and disabilities. *Scientific American,* 62–69.

Plomin, R., & Spinath, F. M. (2004). Intelligence: Genetics, genes, and genomics. *Journal of Personality and Social Psychology, 86*(1), 112–129.

Plomin, R., DeFries, J. C., Knopik, V. S., & Neiderhiser, J. M. (2016). Top 10 replicated findings from behavioral genetics. *Perspectives on Psychological Science, 11*(1), 3–23. doi:10.1177/1745691615617439

Plomin, R., Owen, M. J., & McGuffin, P. (1994). The genetic basis of complex human behaviors. *Science, 264*(5166), 1733–1739.

Plotkin, S., Fine, P., Eames, K., & Heymann, D. L. (2011). "Herd immunity": A rough guide. *Clinical Infectious Diseases, 52*(7), 911–916.

Plug, C., & Ross, H. E. (1994). The natural moon illusion: A multi-factor angular account. *Perception, 23,* 321–333.

Plum, F., & Posner, J. B. (1985). *The diagnosis of stupor and coma.* Philadelphia: F. A. Davis.

Poeppel, D., Emmorey, K., Hickok, G., & Pylkkanen, L. (2012). Towards a new neurobiology of language. *The Journal of Neuroscience, 32*(41), 14125–14131. doi:10.1523/JNEUROSCI.3244-12.2012

Polce-Lynch, M., Myers, B. J., Kilmartin, C. T., Forssmann-Falck, R., & Kliewer, W. (1998). Gender and age patterns in emotional expression, body image, and self-esteem: A qualitative analysis. *Sex Roles, 38,* 1025–1050.

Polderman, T. J. C., Benyamin, B., de Leeuw, C. A., Sullivan, P. F., van Bochoven, A., Visscher, P. M., & Posthuma, D. (2015). Meta-analysis of the heritability of human traits based on fifty years of twin studies. *Nature Genetics, 47,* 702–709.

Polewan, R. J., Vigorito, C. M., Nason, C. D., Block, R. A., & Moore, J. W. (2006). A cartesian reflex assessment of face processing. *Behavioral and Cognitive Neuroscience Reviews, 3*(5), 3–23.

Pollack, M. H., Simon, N. M., Fagiolini, A., Pitman, R., McNally, R. J., Nierenberg, A. A.,... Otto, M. W. (2006). Persistent posttraumatic stress disorder following September 11 in patients with bipolar disorder. *Journal of Clinical Psychiatry, 67*(3), 394–399.

Pollitt, E., & Mathews, R. (1998). Breakfast and cognition: An integrative summary. *The American Journal of Clinical Nutrition,* V67: 804S–813S.

Pompili, M., Lester, D., Dominici, G., Longo, L., Marconi, G., Forte, A.,... Girardi, P. (2013). Indications for electroconvulsive treatment in schizophrenia: A systematic review. *Schizophrenia Research, 146*(1–3), 1–9. doi: 10.1016/j.schres.2013.02.005

Pormerleau, C. S., & Pormerleau, O. F. (1994). Euphoriant effects of nicotine. *Tobacco Control, 3,* 374.

Posada, G., Lu, T., Trumbell, J., Kaloustian, G., Trudel, M., Plata, S. J.,... Lay, K.-L. (2013). Is the secure base phenomenon evident here, there, and anywhere? A cross-cultural study of child behavior and experts' definitions. *Child Development, 84,* 1896–1905.

Posthuma, D., de Geus, E. J. C., & Deary, I. J. (2009). The genetics of intelligence. In T. E. Goldberg & D. R. Weinberger (Eds.), *The genetics of cognitive neuroscience.* Cambridge, MA: MIT Press.

Postman, L. (1975). Tests of the generality of the principle of encoding specificity. *Memory & Cognition, 3,* 663–672.

Potard, C., Kubiszewski, V., Camus, G., Courtois, R., & Gaymard, S. (2017). Driving under the influence of alcohol and perceived invulnerability among young adults: An extension of the theory of planned behavior. In *Transportation Research: An International Journal, Part F: Traffic Psychology and Behavior,* 38–46. Amsterdam, The Netherlands: Elsevier.

Poulin, M. J., Holman, E. A., & Buffone, A. (2012). The neurogenetics of nice: Receptor genes for oxytocin and vasopressin interact with threat to predict prosocial behavior. *Psychological Science, 23*(5), 446–452. doi: 10.1177/0956797611428471

Powell, R. A. (2010). Little Albert still missing. *American Psychologist, 65*(4), 299–300. doi: 10.1037/a0019288

Powell, R. A., Digdon, N., Harris, B., & Smithson, C. (2014). Correcting the record on Watson, Rayner, and Little Albert: Albert Barger as "psychology's lost boy." *American Psychologist, 69*(6), 600–611. doi: 10.1037/a0036854

Powers, M. H. (1984). A computer-assisted problem-solving method for beginning chemistry students. *The Journal of Computers in Mathematics and Science Teaching, 4*(1), 13–19.

Prakash, R. S., Voss, M. W., Erickson, K. I., & Kramer, A. F. (2015). Physical activity and cognitive vitality. *Annual Review of Psychology, 66,* 769–797. doi: 10.1146/annurev-psych-010814-015249

Pratkanis, A. R. (1992). The cargo-cult science of subliminal persuasion. *Skeptical Inquirer, 16,* 260–272.

Pratkanis, A. R., & Greenwald, A. G. (1988). Recent perspectives on unconscious processing: Still no marketing applications. *Psychology and Marketing, 5*, 337–353.

Pratt, J. A. (1991). Psychotropic drug tolerance and dependence: Common underlying mechanisms? In E. Pratt (Ed.), *The biological bases of drug tolerance and dependence* (pp. 2–28). London: Academic Press/Harcourt Brace Jovanovich.

Prendes-Alvarez, S., Schatzberg, A. F., & Nemeroff, C. B. (2015). Pharmacological treatments for unipolar depression. In P. E. Nathan & J. M. Gorman (Eds.), *A guide to treatments that work* (4th ed., pp. 327–353). New York, NY: Oxford University Press.

Preston, J. D., O'Neal, J. H., & Talaga, M. C. (2017). *Handbook of clinical psychopharmacology for therapists* (8th ed.). Oakland, CA: New Harbinger Publications, Inc.

Priester, J. M., & Petty, R. E. (1995). Source attributions and persuasion: Perceived honesty as a determinant of message scrutiny. *Personality and Social Psychology Bulletin, 21*, 637–654.

Prigerson, H. G., Bierhals, A. J., Kasi, S. V., Reynolds, C. F., Shear, M. K., Day, N.,... Jacobs, S. (1997). Traumatic grief as a risk factor for mental and physical morbidity. *American Journal of Psychiatry, 154I*, 616–623.

Pritchard, T. C. (2012). Gustatory system. In J. K. Mai & G. Paxinos (Eds.), *The human nervous system* (pp. 1187–1218). London, UK: Academic Press.

Prochaska, J. O., & Norcross, J. C. (2014). *Systems of psychotherapy: A transtheoretical analysis* (8th ed.). Stamford, CT: Cengage Learning.

Prot, S., Gentile, D. A., Anderson, C. A., Suzuki, K., Swing, E., Lim, K. M.,... Lam, B. C. P. (2014). Long-term relations among prosocial-media use, empathy, and prosocial behavior. *Psychological Science, 25*(2), 358–368.

Pryor, L., Strandberg-Larsen, K., Nybo Andersen, A. M., Hulvej Rod, N., & Melchior, M. (2019). Trajectories of family poverty and children's mental health: Results from the Danish national birth cohort. *Social Science and Medicine, 220*, 371–378. doi:10.1016/j.socscimed.2018.10.023

Przybylski, A. K., Deci, E. L., Rigby, C. S., & Ryan, R. M. (2014). Competence-impeding electronic games and players' aggressive feelings, thoughts, and behaviors. *Journal of Personality and Social Psychology, 106*(3), 441. doi: 10.1037/a0034820

Pulfrey, C., Durussel, K., & Butera, F. (2018). The good cheat: Benevolence and the justification of collective cheating. *Journal of Educational Psychology, 110*(6), 764–784. doi:10.1037/edu0000247

Pullum, G. K. (1991). *The great Eskimo vocabulary hoax: And other irreverent essays on the study of language*. Chicago: University of Chicago Press.

Purdy, D., Eitzen, D., & Hufnagel, R. (1982). Are athletes also students? The educational attainment of college athletes. *Social Problems, 29*, 439–448.

Puspitasari, A., Kanter, J. W., Murphy, J., Crowe, A., & Koerner, K. (2013). Developing an online, modular, active learning training program for behavioral activation. *Psychotherapy, 50*(2), 256–265. doi: 10.1037/a0030058

Putnam, A. L., Sungkhasettee, V. W., & Roediger, H. L., 3rd. (2016). Optimizing learning in college: Tips from cognitive psychology. *Perspectives on Psychological Science, 11*(5), 652–660. doi:10.1177/1745691616645770

Puts, D. A., Jordan, C. L., & Breedlove, S. M. (2006). O brother, where art thou? The fraternal birth-order effect on male sexual orientation. *Proceedings of the National Academy of Sciences, USA, 103*(28), 10531–10532.

Pyc, M. A., Agarwal, P. K., & Roediger, H. L. (2014). Test-enhanced learning. In V. A. Benassi, C. E. Overson, & C. M. Hakala (Eds.), *Applying the science of learning in education: Infusing psychological science into the curriculum*, pp. 78–90. Retrieved from the Society for the Teaching of Psychology web site: http://teachpsych.org/ebooks/asle2014/index.php.

Qin, J., Wang, H., Sheng, X., Liang, D., Tan, H., & Xia, J. (2015). Pregnancy-related complications and adverse pregnancy outcomes in multiple pregnancies resulting from assisted reproductive technology: A meta-analysis of cohort studies. *Fertility and Sterility, 103*, 1492–1508.

Quintero, J. E., Kuhlman, S. J., & McMahon, D. G. (2003). The biological clock nucleus: A multiphasic oscillator network regulated by light. *Journal of Neuroscience, 23*, 8070–8076.

Raaijmakers, J. G. W. (1993). The story of the two-store model of memory: Past criticisms, current status, and future directions. In D. E. Meyer & S. Kornblum (Eds.), *Attention and Performance. XIV (Silver Jubilee Volume)* (pp. 467–488). Cambridge, MA: MIT Press.

Raaijmakers, J. G. W., & Shiffrin, R. M. (1992). Models for recall and recognition. *Annual Review of Psychology, 43*, 205–234.

Raaijmakers, J. G. W., & Shiffrin, R. M. (2003). Models versus descriptions: Real differences and language differences. *Behavioral and Brain Sciences, 26*, 753.

Rachman, S. (1990). The determinants and treatments of simple phobias. *Advances in Behavioral Research and Therapy, 12*(1), 1–30.

Rachman, S. J., & Hodgson, R. J. (1980). *Obsessions and compulsions*. Englewood Cliffs, NJ: Prentice Hall.

Racine, M., Tousignant-Laflamme, Y., Kloda, L. A., Dion, D., Dupuis, G., & Choiniere, M. (2012). A systematic literature review of 10 years of research on sex/gender and pain perception - part 2: Do biopsychosocial factors alter pain sensitivity differently in women and men? *Pain, 153*(3), 619–635. doi:10.1016/j.pain.2011.11.026

Racsmány, M., Conway, M. A., & Demeter, G. (2010). Consolidation of episodic memories during sleep: Long-term effects of retrieval practice. *Psychological Science, 21*: 80–85.

Raffin, E., Richard, N., Giraux, P., & Reilly, K. T. (2016). Primary motor cortex changes after amputation correlate with phantom limb pain and the ability to move the phantom limb. *NeuroImage, 130*, 134–144. doi: 10.1016/j.neuroimage.2016.01.063

Rai, R., Mitchell, P., Kadar, T., & Mackenzie, L. (2014). Adolescent egocentrism and the illusion of transparency: Are adolescents as egocentric as we might think? *Psychological Studies, 67*(1), 58–66.

Raikkonen, K., Matthews, K. A., & Salomon, K. (2003). Hostility predicts metabolic syndrome risk factors in children and adolescents. *Health Psychology, 22*, 279–286.

Rainforth, M. V., Schneider, R. H., Nidich, S. I., Gaylord-King, C., Salerno, J. W., & Anderson, J. W. (2007). Stress reduction programs in patients with elevated blood pressure: A systematic review and meta-analysis. *Current Hypertension Reports, 9*, 520–528.

Rakoff-Nahoum, S. (2006). Why cancer and inflammation? Yale *Journal of Biology and Medicine, 79*(3–4), 123–130.

Ramachandran, V. S., & Blakeslee, S. (1998). *Phantoms in the brain*. New York: Quill William Morrow.

Ramdhonee, K., & Bhowon, U. (2012). Acculturation strategies, personality traits and acculturation stress: A study of first generation immigrants from transnational marital context. *Psychology & Developing Societies, 24*(2), 125–143.

Ramón y Cajal, S. (1995.) *Histology of the nervous system of man and vertebrates*. New York: Oxford University Press. English translation by N. Swanson and L. M. Swanson.

Ramos, M. R., Cassidy, C., Reicher, S., & Haslam, S. A. (2015). Well-being in cross-cultural transitions: Discrepancies between acculturation preferences and actual intergroup and intragroup contact. *Journal of Applied Social Psychology, 45*(1), 23–34.

Rangmar, J., Hjern, A., Vinnerljung, B., Strömland, K., Aronson, M., & Fahlke, C. (2015). Psychosocial outcomes of fetal alcohol syndrome in adulthood. *Pediatrics, 135*, e52–e58.

Ranke, M. B., & Saenger, P. (2001, July 28). Turner's syndrome. *Lancet, 358*(9278), 309–314.

Rao, S. C., Rainer, G., & Miller, E. K. (1997). Integration of what and where in the primate prefrontal cortex. *Science, 276*, 821–824.

Rapoport, J. L., Addington, A. M., Frangou, S., & Psych, M. R. (2005). The neurodevelopmental model of schizophrenia: Update 2005. *Molecular Psychiatry, 10*(5), 434–449. doi: 10.1038/sj.mp.4001642

Rapoport, J. L., Giedd, J. N., & Gogtay, N. (2012). Neurodevelopmental model of schizophrenia: Update 2012. *Molecular Psychiatry, 17*(12), 1228–1238. doi: 10.1038/mp.2012.23

Raposa, E. B., Bower, J. E., Hammen, C. L., Najman, J. M., & Brennan, P. A. (2014). A developmental pathway from early life stress to inflammation the role of negative health behaviors. *Psychological Science, 25*, 1268–1274.

Ratiu, P., Talos, I. F., Haker, S., Lieberman, D., & Everett, P. (2004). The tale of Phineas Gage, digitally remastered. *Journal of Neurotrauma, 21*(5), 637–643. doi: 10.1089/089771504774129964

Rauch, S. L., Shin, L. M., & Wright, C. I. (2003). Neuroimaging studies of amygdala function in anxiety disorders. *Annals of the New York Academy of Sciences, 985*, 389–410.

Raynor, H. A., & Epstein, L. H. (2001). Dietary variety, energy regulation and obesity. *Psychological Bulletin, 127*(3), 325–341.

Reason, J. T., & Brand, J. J. (1975). *Motion sickness*. London: Academic Press.

Rechtschaffen, A., & Kales, A. (1968). *A manual of standardized terminology, techniques, and scoring system for sleep stages of human subjects*. U.S. Department of Health, Education, and Welfare Public Health Service - NIH/NIND.

Reese, H. W. (2010). Regarding Little Albert. *American Psychologist, 65*(4), 300–301. doi: 10.1037/a0019332

Reger, G. M., Koenen-Woods, P., Zetocha, K., Smolenski, D. J., Holloway, K. M., Rothbaum, B. O.,... Gahm, G. A. (2016). Randomized controlled trial of prolonged exposure using imaginal exposure vs. virtual reality exposure in active duty soldiers with deployment-related posttraumatic stress disorder (PTSD). *Journal of Consulting and Clinical Psychology, 84*(11), 946–959. doi:10.1037/ccp0000134

Reichborn-Kjennerud, T. (2008). Genetics of personality disorders. *Psychiatric Clinics of North America, 31*, 421.

Reichborn-Kjennerud, T., Czajkowski, N., Neale, M. C., Orstavik, R. E., Torgersen, S., Tambs, K.,... Kendler, K. S. (2007). Genetic and environmental influences on dimensional representations of DSM-IV cluster C personality disorders: A population-based multivariate twin study. *Psychological Medicine, 37*(5), 645–653. doi: 10.1017/s0033291706009548

Reicher, S., & Haslam, S. A. (2006). Rethinking the psychology of tyranny: The BBC prison study. *British Journal of Social Psychology, 45*(Pt1), 1–40; discussion 47–53. doi:10.1348/014466605X48998

Reicher, S., & Haslam, S. A. (2014). Camps, conflict and collectivism. *The Psychologist, 27*(11), 826–829.

Reicher, S. D., Haslam, S. A., & Smith, J. R. (2012). Working toward the experimenter: Reconceptualizing obedience within the Milgram paradigm as identification-based followership. *Perspectives on Psychological Science, 7*(4), 315–324. doi: 10.1177/1745691612448482

Reinders, A., Quak, J., Nijenhuis, E. R., Korf, J., Paans, A. M., Willemsen, A. T., & den Boer, J. A. (2001, June). *Identity state-dependent processing of neutral and traumatic scripts in dissociative identity disorder as assessed by PET*. Oral presentation at the 7th Annual Meeting of the Organisation for Human Brain Mapping, Brighton, UK. *NeuroImage 13*(Suppl.), S1093.

Reiner, W. G. (1999). Assignment of sex in neonates with ambiguous genitalia. *Current Opinions in Pediatrics, 11*(4), 363–365.

Reisenzein, R. (1983). The Schachter theory of emotion: Two decades later. *Psychological Bulletin, 94*, 239–264.

Reisenzein, R. (1994). Pleasure-arousal theory and the intensity of emotions. *Journal of Personality and Social Psychology, 7*(6), 1313–1329.

Remini, L. (2015). *Troublemaker: Surviving hollywood and scientology.* New York: Ballantine Books.

Renneboog, B. (2012). Andropause and testosterone deficiency: How to treat in 2012? *Revue Médicale de Bruxelles, 33*(4), 443–449.

Renner, M. J., & Mackin, R. S. (1998). A life stress instrument for classroom use. *Teaching of Psychology, 25*, 47.

Rentfrow, P. J., & Jokela, M. (2016). Geographical psychology. *Current Directions in Psychological Science, 25*(6), 393–398. doi: 10.1177/0963721416658446

Rescorla, R. A. (1968). Probability of shock in the presence and absence of CS in fear conditioning. *Journal of Comparative and Physiological Psychology, 66*, 1–5.

Rescorla, R. A. (1988). Pavlovian conditioning—It's not what you think. *American Psychologist, 43*, 151–160.

Rescorla, R. A., & Wagner, A. R. (1972). A theory of Pavlovian conditioning: Variations in the effectiveness of reinforcement and nonreinforcement. In A. H. Black and W. F. Prokasy (Eds.), *Classical Conditioning II* (pp. 64-99). New York: Appleton-Century-Crofts.

Rethorst, C. C., Greer, T. L., Toups, M. S. P., Bernstein, I., Carmody, T. J., & Trivedi, M. H. (2015). IL-1b and BDNF are associated with improvement in hypersomnia but not insomnia following exercise in major depressive disorder. *Translational Psychiatry, 5*(8), e611. doi: 10.1038/tp.2015.104

Rettner, R. (2017). "52 Countries now ban spanking." *Livescience*, January 3. Retrieved on June 15, 2018, at https://www.livescience.com/57373-52-countries-ban-spanking-france.html

Reynolds, C. F., Frank, E., Perel, J. M., Imber, S. D., Cornes, C., Miller, M. D.,... Kuper, D. J. (1999). Nortriptyline and interpersonal psychotherapy as maintenance therapies for recurrent depression: A randomized controlled trial in patients older than 59 years. *Journal of the American Medical Association, 281*(1), 39–45.

Reynolds, J. A. (2002). *Succeeding in college: Study skills and strategies* (2nd ed.). Needham Heights: Allyn and Bacon.

Reynolds, R. M., Strachan, M., Frier, B. M., Fowkes, F. G., Mitchell, R., Seckl, J. R.,... Prices, J. F. (2010). Morning cortisol levels and cognitive abilities in people with Type 2 diabetes. *American Diabetes Association: Diabetes Care, 33*(4), 714–720.

Rezaei, N., Azadi, A., & Pakzad, R. (2018). Prevalence of andropause among Iranian men and its relationship with quality of life. *The Aging Male*. Published online on August 7, 2018. DOI: https://doi.org/10.1080/13685538.2018.1490951

Rezvani, A. H., & Levin, E. D. (2001). Cognitive effects of nicotine. *Biological Psychiatry, 49*, 258–267.

Rhodes, M. G., & Castel, A. D. (2008). Memory predictions are influenced by perceptual information: Evidence for metacognitive illusions. *Journal of Experimental Psychology: General, 137*(4), 615–625. doi: 10.1037/a0013684

Richard, O. D., Stewart, M. M., McKay, P. F., & Sackett, T. W. (2015). The impact of store-unit-community racial diversity congruence on store-unit sales performance. *Journal of Management.* doi: 10.1177/0149206315579511

Richards, C. F., & Lowe, R. A. (2003). Researching racial and ethnic disparities in emergency medicine. *Academic Emergency Medicine, 10*(11), 1169–1175.

Richardson, J., & Morgan, R. (1997). *Reading to learn in the content areas.* Belmont, CA: Wadsworth.

Rideout, V. J., Foehr, U. G., & Roberts, D. F. (2010). *Generation M2: Media in the lives of 8- to 18-year-olds:* Menlo Park, CA: Henry J. Kaiser Family Foundation.

Ridley, M. (1999). *Genome: The autobiography of a species in 23 chapters.* London: Fourth Estate.

Ridley, M. (2002). Crop Circle Confession. *Scientific American.* Retrieved February 17, 2010, from http://www.sciam.com/article.cfm?chanID=sa006&articleID=00038B16-ED5F-1D29-97CA809EC588EEDF

Rieber, R. W., & Robinson, D. K. (2001). *Wilhelm Wundt in history: The making of a scientific psychology.* New York: Kluwer Academic.

Rigby, C. S., Schultz, P. P., & Ryan, R. M. (2014). Mindfulness, interest-taking, and self-regulation: A self-determination theory perspective on the role of awareness in optimal functioning. In A. Ie, C. T. Ngnoumen, & E. Langer (Eds.), *Handbook of Mindfulness* (pp. 216–235). Cambridge, UK: Cambridge University Press.

Rijsdijk, F. V., Gottesman, I. I., McGuffin, P., & Cardno, A. G. (2011). Heritability estimates for psychotic symptom dimensions in twins with psychotic disorders. *American Journal of Medical Genetics Part B, Neuropsychiatric Genetics, 156B*(1), 89–98. doi: 10.1002/ajmg.b.31145

Rinne, J. O., Wesnes, K., Cummings, J. L., Hakulinen, P., Hallikainen, M., Hanninen, J.,... Rouru, J. (2017). Tolerability of ORM-12741 and effects on episodic memory in patients with Alzheimer's disease. *Alzheimer's & Dementia, 3*(1): 1–9. DOI: https://dx.doi.org/10.1016%2Fj.trci.2016.11.004

Ripolles, P., Biel, D., Penaloza, C., Kaufmann, J., Marco-Pallares, J., Noesselt, T., & Rodriguez-Fornells, A. (2017). Strength of temporal white matter pathways predicts semantic learning. *Journal of Neuroscience, 37*(46), 11101–11113. doi:10.1523/JNEUROSCI.1720-17.2017

Ritchey, M., LaBar, K. S., & Cabeza, R. (2011). Level of processing modulates the neural correlates of emotional memory formation. *Journal of Cognitive Neuroscience, 4*, 757–775.

Rizzolatti, G., Fabbri-Destro, M., & Cattaneo, L. (2009). Mirror neurons and their clinical relevance. *Nature Clinical Practice Neurology, 5*(1), 24–34.

Ro, E., & Clark, L. A. (2009). Psychosocial functioning in the context of diagnosis: Assessment and theoretical issues. *Psychological Assessment, 21*(3), 313–324.

Roane, B. M., Seifer, R., Sharkey, K. M., Van Reen, E., Bond, T. L., Raffray, T., & Carskadon, M. A. (2015). What role does sleep play in weight gain in the first semester of university? *Behavioral Sleep Medicine, 13*(6), 491–505.

Roberto, C. A., & Kawachi, I. (2014). Use of psychology and behavioral economics to promote healthy eating. *American Journal of Preventive Medicine, 47*, 832–837.

Roberts, G., Scammacca, N., Osman, D. J., Hall, C., Mohammed, S. S., & Vaughn, S. (2014). Team-based learning: Moderating effects of metacognitive elaborative rehearsal and middle school history content recall. *Educational Psychology Review, 26*(3): 451–468. DOI: https://doi.org/10.1007/s10648-014-9266-2

Roberts, L. (2018). Alarming polio outbreak spreads in Congo, threatening global eradication efforts. *Science, 361*(6397). doi:10.1126/science.aau6493

Robin, J., & Moscovitch, M. (2017). Familiar real-world spatial cues provide memory benefits in older and younger adults. *Psychology and Aging, 32*(3): 210-219. DOI: https://doi.org/10.1037/pag0000162

Robins, L. N. (1996). *Deviant children grown up.* Baltimore: Williams & Wilkins.

Robinson, F. P. (1946). *Effective study.* New York: Harper & Bros.

Robinson, J. W., & Preston, J. D. (1976). Equal status contact and modification of racial prejudice: A reexamination of the contact hypothesis. *Social Forces, 54*, 911–924.

Robinson, P. (1993). *Freud and his critics.* Berkeley: University of California Press.

Rodin, J. (1981). Current status of the internal-external hypothesis for obesity. *American Psychologist, 36*, 361–372.

Rodin, J. (1985). Insulin levels, hunger, and food intake: An example of feedback loops in body weight regulation. *Health Psychology, 4*, 1–24.

Rodin, J., & Langer, E. J. (1977). Long-term effects of a control-relevant intervention among the institutionalized aged. *Journal of Personality and Social Psychology, 35*, 275–282.

Roediger, H. L. (1990). Implicit memory: Retention without remembering. *American Psychologist, 45*, 1043–1056.

Roediger, H. L., & Karpicke, J. D. (2006). The power of testing memory: Basic research and implications for educational practice. *Perspectives on Psychological Science, 1*, 181–210.

Roediger, H. L., & McDermott, K. B. (1995). Creating false memories: Remembering words not presented in lists. *Journal of Experimental Psychology, 21*(4), 803–814.

Roediger, H. L., III (2000). Why retrieval is the key process to understanding human memory. In E. Tulving (Ed.), *Memory, consciousness and the brain: The Tallinn Conference* (pp. 52–75). Philadelphia: Psychology Press.

Roediger, H. L., III, & Guynn, M. J. (1996). Retrieval processes. In E. L. Bjork & R. A. Bjork (Eds.), *Memory* (pp. 197–236). New York: Academic Press.

Roethlisberger, F. J., & Dickson, W. J. (1939) *Management and the Worker.* Cambridge, MA: Harvard University Press.

Roffman, I., Savage-Rumbaugh, S., Rubert-Pugh, E., Ronen, A., & Nevo, E. (2012). Stone tool production and utilization by bonobo-chimpanzees (pan paniscus). *Proceedings of the National Academy of Sciences of the United States of America, 109*(36). doi: 10.1073/pnas.1212855109

Roffman, R. A., Stephens, R. S., Simpson, E. E., & Whitaker, D. L. (1988). Treatment of marijuana dependence: Preliminary results. *Journal of Psychoactive Drugs, 20*(1), 129–137.

Roffwarg, H. P., Muzio, J. N., & Dement, W. C. (1966). Ontogenetic development of the human sleep-dream cycle. *Science, 152*(3722), 604–619.

Rogers, C. R. (1951). *Client-centered therapy.* Boston: Houghton Mifflin Co.

Rogers, C. R. (1961). *On becoming a person: A therapist's view of psychotherapy.* Boston: Houghton Mifflin Co.

Rogers, R. W., & Mewborn, C. R. (1976). Fear appeals and attitude change: Effects of a threat's noxiousness, probability of occurrence, and the efficacy of the coping responses. *Journal of Personality and Social Psychology, 34*, 54–61.

Rogoff, B. (1994). Developing understanding of the idea of communities of learners. *Mind, Culture, and Activity, 1*(4), 209–229.

Roh, S. (2018). Scientific evidence for the addictiveness of tobacco and smoking cessation in tobacco litigation. Journal of Preventive Medicine and Public Health. Yebang Uihakhoe Chi, 51(1), 1–5. doi: 10.3961/jpmph.16.088

Rohrer, J. M., Egloff, B., & Schmukle, S. C. (2015). Examining the effects of birth order on personality. Proceedings of the National Academy of Sciences of the United States of America, 112(46), 14224–14229. doi: 0.1073/pnas.1506451112

Roid, G. H. (2003). *Stanford-Binet intelligence scales* (5th ed.). Itasca, IL: Riverside.

Romer, D., Reyna, V. F., & Satterthwaite, T. D. (2017). Beyond stereotypes of adolescent risk taking: placing the adolescent brain in developmental context. *Developmental Cognitive Neuroscience, 27*: 19. DOI: https://doi.org/10.1016/j.dcn.2017.07.007

Root, N. B., Rouw, R., Asano, M., Kim, C. Y., Melero, H., Yokosawa, K., & Ramachandran, V. S. (2018). Why is the synesthete's "a" red? Using a five-language dataset to disentangle the effects of shape, sound, semantics, and ordinality on inducer-concurrent relationships in grapheme-color synesthesia. *Cortex, 99*, 375–389. doi:10.1016/j.cortex.2017.12.003

Ros, T., Theberge, J., Frewen, P. A., Kluetsch, R., Densmore, M., Calhoun, V. D., & Lanius, R. A. (2013). Mind over chatter: Plastic up-regulation of the fMRI salience network directly after EEG neurofeedback. *NeuroImage, 65*, 324–335. doi: 10.1016/j.neuroimage.2012.09.046

Rosch, E. (1973). On the internal structure of perceptual and semantic categories. In T. E. Moore (Ed.), *Cognitive development and the acquisition of language* (pp. 111–144). New York: Academic Press.

Rosch, E. (1977). Human categorization. In N. Warren (Ed.), *Advances in cross-cultural psychology, 1* (pp. 1–72). London: Academic Press.

Rosch, E., & Mervis, C. (1975). Family resemblances: Studies in the internal structures of categories. *Cognitive Psychology, 7*, 573–605.

Rosch-Heider, E. (1972). Universals in color naming and memory. *Journal of Experimental Psychology, 93*, 10–20.

Rosch-Heider, E., & Olivier, D. C. (1972). The structure of the color space in naming and memory for two languages. *Cognitive Psychology, 3*, 337–354.

Rose, S., Kamin, L. J., & Lewontin, R. C. (1984). *Not in our genes: Biology, ideology and human nature*. Harmondsworth, UK: Penguin.

Rosen, L. D., Mark Carrier, L., & Cheever, N. A. (2013). Facebook and texting made me do it: Media-induced task-switching while studying. *Computers in Human Behavior, 29*(3), 948–958. doi:10.1016/j.chb.2012.12.001

Rosenbloom, T., Shahar, A., Perlman, A., Estreich, D., & Kirzner, E. (2007). Success on a practical driver's license test with and without the presence of another testee. *Accident Analysis & Prevention, 39*(6), p. 1296–1301.

Rosenfeld, J. P., Labkovsky, E., Davydova, E., Ward, A., & Rosenfeld, L. (2017). Financial incentive does not affect P300 (in response to certain episodic and semantic probe stimuli) in the complex trial protocol (CTP) version of the concealed information test (CIT) in detection of malingering. *Psychophysiology, 54*(5), 764–772. doi:10.1111/psyp.12835

Rosenfeld, J. P., Labkovsky, E., Winograd, M., Lui, M. A., Vandenboom, C., & Chedid, E. (2008). The Complex Trial Protocol (CTP): A new, countermeasure-resistant, accurate, P300-based method for detection of concealed information. *Psychophysiology, 45*(6), 906–919.

Rosenhan, D. L. (1973), On being sane in insane places, *Science, 179*, 250–258.

Rosenman, R. H., Brand, R. I., Jenkins, C. D., Friedman, M., Straus, R., & Wurm, M. (1975). Coronary heart disease in the Western Collaborative Group Study, final follow-up experience of 2 years. *Journal of the American Medical Association, 233*, 812–817.

Rosenthal, A. M. (1964). *Thirty-eight witnesses: The Kitty Genovese case*. New York: McGraw-Hill.

Rosenthal, R., & Jacobson, L. (1968). *Pygmalion in the classroom*. New York: Holt, Rinehart & Winston.

Ross, C. A., Ferrell, L., & Schroeder, E. (2014). Co-occurrence of dissociative identity disorder and borderline personality disorder. *Journal of Trauma & Dissociation, 15*(1), 79–90. doi: 10.1080/15299732.2013.834861

Ross, H. E., & Ross, G. M. (1976). Did Ptolemy understand the moon illusion? *Perception, 5*, 377–385.

Rostron, B., Chang, C. M., van Bemmel, D. M., Xia, Y., & Blount, B. C. (2015). Nicotine and toxicant exposure among U.S. smokeless tobacco users: Results from 1999 to 2012 National Health and Nutrition Examination Survey data. *Cancer Epidemiology, Biomarkers & Prevention*. doi: 10.1158/1055-9965.EPI-15-0376

Rothbaum, R., Weisz, J., Pott, M., Miyake, K., & Morelli, G. (2000). Attachment and culture: Security in Japan and the U.S. *American Psychologist, 55*, 1093–1104.

Rothenberg, A. (2001). Bipolar illness, creativity, and treatment. *Psychiatric Quarterly, 72*(2), 131–147.

Rothman, A. J., Gollwitzer, P. M., Grant, A. M., Neal, D. T., Sheeran, P., & Wood, W. (2015). Hale and hearty policies: How psychological science can create and maintain healthy habits. *Perspectives on Psychological Science, 10*, 701–705.

Rothstein, H. R., & Bushman, B. J. (2015). Methodological and reporting errors in meta-analytic reviews make other meta-analysts angry: A commentary on Ferguson (2015). *Perspectives on Psychological Science, 10*(5), 677–679. doi: 10.1177/1745691615592235

Rothstein-Fisch, C., & Trumbull, E. (2008). *Mangaging diverse classrooms: How to build on students' cultural strengths*. Alexandria, VA: Association for Supervision and Curriculum Development.

Rotter, A., Bayerlein, K., Hansbauer, M., Weiland, J., Sperling, W., Kornhuber, J., & Biermann, T. (2013). CB1 and CB2 receptor expression and promoter methylation in patients with cannabis dependence. *European Addiction Research, 19*(1): 13–20. doi:10.1159/000338642

Rotter, J. B. (1966). Generalized expectancies for internal versus external control of reinforcements. *Psychological Monographs, 80* [Whole no. 609].

Rotter, J. B. (1978). Generalized expectancies for problem solving and psychotherapy. *Cognitive Therapy and Research, 2*, 1–10.

Rotter, J. B. (1981). The psychological situation in social learning theory. In D. Magnusson (Ed.), *Toward a psychology of situations: An interactional perspective*. Hillsdale, NJ: Lawrence Erlbaum.

Rotter, J. B. (1990). Internal versus external control of reinforcement: A case history of a variable. *American Psychologist, 45*, 489–493.

Rotton, J., & Frey, J. (1985). Air pollution, weather, and violent crime: Concomitant time-series analysis of archival data. *Journal of Personality and Social Psychology, 49*, 1207–1220.

Rotton, J., Frey, J., Barry, T., Milligan, M., & Fitzpatrick, M. (1979). The air pollution experience and physical aggression. *Journal of Applied Social Psychology, 9*, 397–412.

Rouru, J., Wesnes, K., Hänninen, J., Murphy, M., Riordan, H., & Rinne, J. (2013, March 16–23). Safety and efficacy of ORM-12741 on cognitive and behavioral symptoms in patients with Alzheimer's disease: A randomized, double-blind, placebo-controlled, parallel group, multicenter, proof-of-concept 12 week study. Paper presented at American Academy of Neurology 65th Annual Meeting, San Diego, CA.

Rovet, J. (1993). The psychoeducational characteristics of children with Turner's syndrome. *Journal of Learning Disabilities, 26*, 333–341.

Rowan, J. (2001). *Ordinary ecstasy*. Hove, UK: Brunner-Routledge.

Rowe, D. C., Almeida, D. A., & Jacobson, K. C. (1999). School context and genetic influences on aggression in adolescence. *Psychological Science, 10*, 277–280.

Roysircar-Sodowsky, G. R., & Maestas, M. V. (2000). Acculturation, ethnic identity, and acculturative stress: Evidence and measurement. In R. H. Dana (Ed.), *Handbook of cross-cultural and multicultural assessment* (pp. 131–172). Mahwah, NJ: Lawrence Erlbaum.

Rozeske, R. R., Evans, A. K., Frank, M. G., Watkins, L. R., Lowry, C. A., & Maier, S. F. (2011). Uncontrollable, but not controllable, stress desensitizes 5-HT1A receptors in the dorsal raphe nucleus. *The Journal of Neuroscience, 31*(40), 14107–14115. doi: 10.1523/jneurosci.3095-11.2011

Rubia, K. (2018). ADHD brain function. In T. Banaschewski, D. Coghill, & A. Zuddas (Eds.), *Oxford textbook of attention deficit hyperactivity disorder* (pp. 64–72): Oxford University Press.

Rubinstein, M. L., Rait, M., & Prochaska, J. J. (2014). Frequent marijuana use is associated with greater nicotine addiction in adolescent smokers. *Drug and Alcohol Dependence, 141*: 159–162. DOI: https://doi.org/10.1016/j.drugalcdep.2014.05.015

Rubio-Fernandez, P., & Glucksberg, S. (2012). Reasoning about other people's beliefs: Bilinguals have an advantage. *Journal of Experimental Psychology: Learning, Memory, and Cognition, 38*(1), 211–217. doi: 10.1037/a0025162

Ruble, D., Alvarez, J., Bachman, M., Cameron, J., Fuligni, A., Garcia Coll, C., & Rhee, E. (2004). The development of a sense of "we": The emergence and implications of children's collective identity. In M. Bennett & F. Sani (Eds.), *The development of the social self*. New York: Psychology Press.

Rudd, P., & Osterberg, L. G. (2002). Hypertension: Context, pathophysiology, and management. In E. J. Topol (Ed.), *Textbook of cardiovascular medicine* (pp. 91–122). Philadelphia: Lippincott Williams & Wilkins.

Rudmin, F. W. (2003). Critical history of the acculturation psychology of assimilation, separation, integration, and marginalization. *Review of General Psychology, 7*, 3–37.

Ruff, R. M., Iverson, G. L., Barth, J. T., Bush, S. S., & Broshek, D. K. (2009). Recommendations for diagnosing a mild traumatic brain injury: A National Academy of Neuropsychology education paper. *Archives of Clinical Neuropsychology, 24*(1), 3–10.

Ruhe, H. G., Mason, N. S., & Schene, A. H. (2007). Mood is indirectly related to serotonin, norepinephrine and dopamine levels in humans: A meta-analysis of monoamine depletion studies. *Molecular Psychiatry, 12*(4), 331–359.

Ruhm, C. J. (2018). Drug mortality and lost life years amond U. S. midlife adults, 1999–2015. *American Journal of Preventative Medicine, 55*(1): 11–18.

Ruiz, S., Lee, S., Soekadar, S. R., Caria, A., Veit, R., Kircher, T., … Sitaram, R. (2013). Acquired self-control of insula cortex modulates emotion recognition and brain network connectivity in schizophrenia. *Human Brain Mapping, 34*(1), 200–212. doi: 10.1002/hbm.21427

Rumelhart, D. E., Hinton, G. E., & McClelland, J. L. (1986). A general framework for parallel distributed processing. In D. E. Rumelhart, J. L. McClelland, & the PDP Research Group (Eds.), *Parallel distributed processing: Explorations in the microstructure of cognition: Vol. 1. Foundations* (pp. 45–76). Cambridge, MA: MIT Press.

Rundus, D. (1971). An analysis of rehearsal processes in free recall. *Journal of Experimental Psychology, 89*, 63–77.

Running, C. A., Craig, B. A., & Mattes, R. D. (2015). Oleogustus: The unique taste of fat. *Chemical Senses, 40*(7), 507–516. doi: 10.1093/chemse/bjv036

Running, C. A., Hayes, J. E., & Ziegler, G. R. (2017). Degree of free fatty acid saturation influences chocolate rejection in human assessors. *Chemical Senses, 42*(2), 161–166. doi:10.1093/chemse/bjw116

Runyan, D. K., Shankar, V., Hassan, F., Hunter, W. M., Jain, D., Paula, C. S.,... Bordin, I. A. (2010). International variations in harsh child discipline. *Pediatrics, 126*(3), e701–711.

Ruscio, A. M., Borkovec, T. D., & Ruscio, J. (2001). A taxometric investigation of the latent structure of worry. *Journal of Abnormal Psychology, 110*, 413–422.

Russell, D. E. (1986). *The secret trauma: Incest in the lives of girls and women*. New York: Basic Books.

Russell, K. C., Gillis, H. L. L., & Kivlighan, D. M. (2017). Process factors explaining psycho-social outcomes in adventure therapy. *Psychotherapy (Chic), 54*(3), 273–280. doi:10.1037/pst0000131

Russell, R., Duchaine, B., & Nakayama, K. (2009). Super-recognizers: People with extraordinary face recognition ability. *Psychonomic Bulletin & Review, 16*: 252–257. DOI: https://dx.doi.org/10.3758%2FPBR.16.2.252

Russo, S. J., & Nestler, E. J. (2013). The brain reward circuitry in mood disorders. *Nature Reviews Neuroscience, 14*, 609–625.

Russo, S. J., Murrough, J. W., Han, M. H., Charney, D. S., & Nestler, E. J. (2012). Neurobiology of resilience. *Nature Neuroscience, 15*(11), 1475–1484. doi:10.1038/nn.3234

Rutherford, A. (2000). Mary Cover Jones (1896–1987). *The Feminist Psychologist, 27*(3), 25.

Ruzek, J. I., Eftekhari, A., Rosen, C. S., Crowley, J. J., Kuhn, E., Foa, E. B.,... Karlin, B. E. (2014). Factors related to clinician attitudes toward prolonged exposure therapy for PTSD. *Journal of Traumatic Stress, 27*(4), 423–429. doi: 10.1002/jts.21945

Ryan, R. M., & Deci, E. L. (2000). Intrinsic and extrinsic motivations: Classic definitions and new directions. *Contemporary Educational Psychology, 25*, 54–67.

Ryan, R. M., Chirkov, V. I., Little, T. D., Sheldon, K. M., Timoshina, E. L., & Deci, E. L. (1999). The American dream in Russia: Extrinsic aspirations and well-being in two cultures. *Personality and Social Psychology Bulletin, 25*, 1509–1524.

Ryan, R. M., Legate, N., Niemiec, C. P., & Deci, E. L. (2012). Beyond illusions and defense: Exploring the possibilities and limits of human autonomy and responsibility through self-determination theory. In P. R. Shaver & M. Mikulincer (Eds.), *Meaning, mortality, and choice: The social psychology of existential concerns* (pp. 215–233). Washington, DC: American Psychological Association.

Rydell, R. J., & Boucher, K. L. (2010). Capitalizing on multiple social identities to prevent stereotype threat: The moderating role of self-esteem. *Personality and Social Psychology Bulletin, 36*(2), 239–250.

Rysavy, M. A., Li, L., Bell, E. F., Das, A., Hintz, S. R., Stoll, B. J.,... Higgins, R. D. (2015). *The New England Journal of Medicine, 372*, 1801–1811.

Sabatini, E., Della Penna, S., Franciotti, R., Ferretti, A., Zoccoletti, P., Rossini, P. M.,... Gainotti, G. (2009). Brain structures activated by overt and covert emotional visual stimuli. *Brain Research Bulletin, 79*(5), 258–264.

Sacchet, M. D., Livermore, E. E., Iglesias, J. E., Glover, G. H., & Gotlib, I. H. (2015). Subcortical volumes differentiate major depressive disorder, bipolar disorder, and remitted major depressive disorder. *Journal of Psychiatric Research, 68*, 91–98. doi: 10.1016/j.jpsychires.2015.06.002

Sackeim, H. A., Prudic, J., Fuller, R., Keilp, J., Lavori, P. W., & Olfson, M. (2007). The cognitive effects of electroconvulsive therapy in community settings. *Neuropsychopharmacology, 32*, 244–254.

Sackett, P. R., Borneman, M. J., & Connelly, B. S. (2008). High stakes testing in higher education and employment: Appraising the evidence for validity and fairness. *American Psychologist, 63*(4), 215–227. doi: 10.1037/0003-066X.63.4.215

Sacks, O. (1990). *The man who mistook his wife for a hat and other clinical tales*. New York: HarperPerennial.

Safer, D. J. (2015). Recent trends in stimulant usage. *Journal of Attention Disorders*. Published online before print. doi: 10.1177/1087054715605915

Sagan, C. (1977). *The dragons of Eden: Speculations on the evolution of human intelligence.* New York: Random House.

Saha, S., Chant, D., Welham, J., & McGrath, J. (2005). A systematic review of the prevalence of schizophrenia. *PLoS Medicine, 2*(5), e141.

Sahin, M., & Sur, M. (2015). Genes, circuits, and precision therapies for autism and related neurodevelopmental disorders. *Science*. doi: 10.1126/science.aab3897

Saint-Georges, C., Chetouani, M., Cassel, R., Apicella, F., Mahdhaoui, A., Muratori, F.,... Cohen, D. (2013). Motherese in interaction: At the cross-road of emotion and cognition? (a systematic review). *PLoS ONE, 8*(10), e78103. doi:10.1371/journal.pone.0078103

Sakuma, A., Takahashi, Y., Ueda, I., Sato, H., Katsura, M., Abe, M.,... Matsumoto, K. (2015). Post-traumatic stress disorder and depression prevalence and associated risk factors among local disaster relief and reconstruction workers fourteen months after the great east Japan earthquake: A cross-sectional study. *BMC Psychiatry, 15*, 58. doi:10.1186/s12888-015-0440-y

Salamanca, J. C., Meehan-Atrash, J. Vreeke, S., Escobedo, J. O., Peyton, D. H., & Strongin, R. M. (2018). E-cigarettes can emit formaldehyde at high levels under conditions that have been reported to be non-averse to users. *Scientific Reports, 8*(1): 7559. DOI: http://dx.doi.org/10.1038/s41598-018-25907-6

Salamone, J. D., & Correa, M. (2012). The mysterious motivational functions of mesolimbic dopamine. *Neuron, 76*(3), 470–485.

Salend, S. J. (1987). Contingency management systems. *Academic Therapy, 22*, 245–253.

Salerno, J. M., Phalen, H. J., Reyes, R. N., & Schweitzer, N. J. (2018). Closing with emotion: The differential impact of male versus female attorneys expressing anger in court. *Law and Human Behavior, 42*(4), 385–401. doi:10.1037/lhb0000292

Salovey, P., & Mayer, J. D. (1990). Emotional intelligence. *Imagination, cognition, and personality, 9*, 185–211.

Sam, D. L., & Berry, J. W. (2010). Acculturation when individuals and groups of different cultural backgrounds meet. *Perspectives on Psychological Science, 5*(4), 472.

Samara, Z., Evers, E. A. T., Peeters, F., Uylings, H. B. M., Rajkowska, G., Ramaekers, J. G., & Stiers, P. (2018). Orbital and medial prefrontal cortex functional connectivity of major depression vulnerability and disease. *Biological Psychiatry: Cognitive Neuroscience and Neuroimaging, 3*(4), 348–357. doi:10.1016/j.bpsc.2018.01.004

Sana, F., Weston, T., & Cepeda, N. J. (2013). Laptop multitasking hinders classroom learning for both users and nearby peers. *Computers & Education, 62*, 24–31. doi:10.1016/j.compedu.2012.10.003

Sanbonmatsu, D. M., Strayer, D. L., Medeiros-Ward, N., & Watson, J. M. (2013). Who multi-tasks and why? Multi-tasking ability, perceived multi-tasking ability, impulsivity, and sensation seeking. *PLoS ONE, 8*(1), e54402. doi:10.1371/journal.pone.0054402

Sands, L. P., & Meredith, W. (1992). Intellectual functioning in late midlife. *Journal of Gerontological and Psychological Science, 47*, 81–84.

Sanes, J. N., Sabbah, S., Waugh, R., Worden, M. S., & Berson, D. M. (2019). Luxotonic signals in human frontal-polar cortex: A possible substrate for effects of light on mood. *Poster Presentation at Neuroscience 2018.* Retrieved from https://abstractsonline.com/pp8/#!/4649/presentation/20010

Sanes, J. R., & Jessell, T. M. (2013a). Experience and the refinement of synaptic connections. In E. R. Kandel, J. H. Schwartz, T. M. Jessell, S. A. Siegelbaum, & A. J. Hudspeth (Eds.), *Principles of neural science* (5th ed., pp. 1259–1283). USA: McGraw-Hill.

Sanes, J. R., & Jessell, T. M. (2013b). Repairing the damaged brain. In E. R. Kandel, J. H. Schwartz, T. M. Jessell, S. A. Siegelbaum, & A. J. Hudspeth (Eds.), *Principles of neural science* (5th ed., pp. 1284–1305). USA: McGraw-Hill.

Santhakumar, V., Wallner, M, & Otis, T. S. (2007). Ethanol acts directly on extrasynaptic subtypes of GABAA receptors to increase tonic inhibition. *Alcohol, 41*(3), 211–221.

Sanz, C., Andrieu, S., Sinclair, A., Hanaire, H., & Vellas, B. (2009). Diabetes is associated with a slower rate of cognitive decline in Alzheimer disease. *Neurology, 73*, 1359–1366.

Saper, C. B., Chou, T. C., & Scammell, T. E. (2001). The sleep switch: Hypothalamic control of sleep and wakefulness. *Trends in Neurosciences, 24*, 726–731.

Sapir, E. S. (1921). *Language: An introduction to the study of speech.* New York: Harcourt, Brace.

Sapolsky, R. M. (2004). *Why zebras don't get ulcers* (3rd ed.). New York: Owl Books.

Sarada, P. A., & Ramkumar, B. (2014). Positive stress and its impact on performance. Research *Journal of Pharmaceutical, Biological, and Chemical Sciences, 6*(2), 1519–1522.

Sarbin, T. R., & Coe, W. C. (1972). *Hypnosis: A social psychological analysis of influence communication.* New York: Holt, Rinehart, & Winston.

Sartorius, A., Demirakca, T., Bohringer, A., Clemm von Hohenberg, C., Aksay, S. S., Bumb, J. M.,... Ende, G. (2015). Electroconvulsive therapy increases temporal gray matter volume and cortical thickness. *European Neuropsychopharmacology, 26*(3), 506–517. doi: 10.1016/j.euroneuro.2015.12.036

Sartory, G., Cwik, J., Knuppertz, H., Schürholt, B., Lebens, M., Seitz, R. J., & Schulze, R. (2013). In search of the trauma memory: A meta-analysis of functional neuroimaging studies of symptom provocation in posttraumatic stress disorder (PTSD). *PLoS ONE, 8*(3), e58150. doi: 10.1371/journal.pone.0058150

Sastry, K. S., Karpova, Y., Prokopovich, S., Smith, A. J., Essau, B., Gersappe, A.,... Kulik, G. (2007). Epinephrine protects cancer cells from apoptosis via activation of cAMP-dependent protein kinase and BAD phosphorylation. *Journal of Biological Chemistry, 282*(19), 14094–14100.

Satterly, D. (1987). Piaget and education. In R. L. Gregory (Ed.), *The Oxford companion to the mind* (pp. 110–143). Oxford: Oxford University Press.

Sattler, J. M. (1977). The effects of therapist–client racial similarity. In A. S. Gurman & A. M. Razin (Eds.), *Effective psychotherapy: A handbook of research* (pp. 252–290). Elmsford, NY: Pergamon.

Savage-Rumbaugh, S., & Lewin, R. (1994). *Kanzi.* New York: Wiley.

Savage-Rumbaugh, S., Shanker, S., & Taylor, T. J. (1998). *Apes, language and the human mind.* Oxford, UK: Oxford University Press.

Savard, J., Ivers, H., Savard, M. H., & Morin, C. M. (2014). Is a video-based cognitive behavioral therapy for insomnia as efficacious as a professionally administered treatment in breast cancer? Results of a randomized controlled trial. *Sleep, 37*(8), 1305–1314. doi: 10.5665/sleep.3918

Scarpa, A., Raine, A., Venables, P. H., & Mednick, S. A. (1995). The stability of inhibited/uninhibited temperament from ages 3 to 11 years in Mauritian children. *Journal of Abnormal Child Psychology, 23*, 607–618.

Schachter, S., & Singer, J. E. (1962). Cognitive, social and physiological determinants of emotional states. *Psychological Review, 69*, 379–399.

Schacter, D. L., & Wagner, A. D. (2013). Learning and memory. In E. R. Kandel, J. H. Schwartz, T. M. Jessell, S. A. Siegelbaum, & A. J. Hudspeth (Eds.), *Principles of neural science* (5th ed., pp. 1441–1460). USA: McGraw-Hill.

Schafer, M., & Crichlow S. (1996). Antecedents of groupthink: A quantitative study. *Journal of Conflict Resolution, 40*, 415–435.

Schaie, K. W., & Willis, S. L. (2010). The Seattle longitudinal study of adult cognitive development. *Bulletin of the International Society for the Study of Behavioral Development, 37*, 24–29.

Schapiro, A. C., & McClelland, J. L. (2009). A connectionist model of a continuous developmental transition in the balance scale task. *Cognition, 110*(1), 395–411.

Scharnowski, F., Hutton, C., Josephs, O., Weiskopf, N., & Rees, G. (2012). Improving visual perception through neurofeedback. *The Journal of Neuroscience, 32*(49), 17830–17841. doi: 10.1523/jneurosci.6334-11.2012

Scheele, D., Striepens, N., Güntürkün, O., Deutschländer, S., Maier, W., Kendrick, K. M., & Hurlemann, R. (2012). Oxytocin modulates social distance between males and females. *The Journal of Neuroscience, 32*(46), 16074–16079. doi: 10.1523/jneurosci.2755-12.2012

Schilbach, L., Hoffstaedter, F., Müller, V., Cieslik, E. C., Goya-Maldonado, R., Trost, S.,... Eickhoff, S. B. (2016). Transdiagnostic commonalities and differences in resting state functional connectivity of the default mode network in schizophrenia and major depression. *NeuroImage: Clinical, 10,* 326–335. doi: 10.1016/j.nicl.2015.11.021

Schiller, P. H., & Carvey, C. E. (2005). The Hermann grid illusion revisited. *Perception, 34*(11), 1375–1397.

Schizophrenia Working Group of the Psychiatric Genomics, C. (2014). Biological insights from 108 schizophrenia-associated genetic loci. *Nature, 511*(7510), 421–427. doi: 10.1038/nature13595

Schlumpf, Y. R., Reinders, A. A., Nijenhuis, E. R., Luechinger, R., van Osch, M. J., & Jancke, L. (2014). Dissociative part-dependent resting-state activity in dissociative identity disorder: A controlled fMRI perfusion study. *PLoS ONE, 9*(6), e98795. doi: 10.1371/journal.pone.0098795

Schmitt, D. P. (2002). Personality, attachment and sexuality related to dating relationship outcomes: Contrasting three perspectives on personal attribute interaction. *British Journal of Social Psychology, 41*(4), 589–610.

Schmitt, D. P., Allik, J., McCrae, R. R., & Benet-Martínez, V. (2007). The geographic distribution of Big Five personality traits: Patterns and profiles of human self-description across 56 nations. *Journal of Cross-Cultural Psychology, 38*(2), 173–212. doi: 10.1177/0022022106297299

Schmitt, K. C., & Reith, M. E. A. (2010). Regulation of the dopamine transporter. *Annals of the New York Academy of Sciences, 1187:* 316.

Schmitz, C., Wagner, J., & Menke, E. (2001). The interconnection of childhood poverty and homelessness: Negative impact/points of access. *Families in Society, 82*(1), 69–77.

Schnabel, J. (1994). *Round in circles* (pp. 267–277). London: Hamish Hamilton.

Schneider, K. J., Bugental, J. F. T., & Fraser, J. F. (Eds.). (2001). *Handbook of humanistic psychology.* Thousand Oaks, CA: Sage.

Schneider, R., Grim, C., Rainforth, M., Kotchen, T., Nidich, S., Gaylord-King, C.,... Alexander, C. (2012). Stress reduction in the secondary prevention of cardiovascular disease: Randomized controlled trial of transcendental meditation and health education in blacks. *Circulation: Cardiovascular Quality and Outcomes.* 5:750–758.

Schneider, R. H., Staggers, F., Alexander, C. N., Sheppard, W., Rainforth, M., Kondwani, K., Smith, S., & King, C. G. (1995). A randomized controlled trial of stress reduction for hypertension in older African Americans. *Hypertension, 26*(5), 820–827.

Schneider, W., Dumais, S., & Shriffrin, R. (1984). *Automatic and control processing and attention.* London: Academic Press.

Schneider, W. J., & McGrew, K. S. (2012). The Cattell-Horn-Carroll model of intelligence. In D. P. Flanagan & P. L. Harrison (Eds.), *Contemporary intellectual assessment: Theories, tests, and issues* (3rd ed., pp. 99–144). New York, NY: Guilford Press.

Schneider, W. J., & McGrew, K. S. (2013). The Cattell-Horn-Carroll (CHC) model of intelligence v2.2: A visual tour and summary, from http://www.iapsych.com/chcv2.pdf

Schneidman, E. (1983). *Death of man.* New York: Jason Aronson.

Schneidman, E. (1994). *Death: Current perspectives.* New York: McGraw-Hill.

Schöls, L., Haan, J., Riess, O., Amoiridis, G., & Przuntek, H. (1998). Sleep disturbance in spinocerebellar ataxias: Is the SCA3 mutation a cause of restless legs syndrome? *Neurology, 51,* 1603–1607

Scholl, L., Seth, P., Kariisa, M., Wilson, N., & Baldwin, G. (2019). Drug and opioid-involved overdose deaths — United States, 2013–2017. Morbidity and Mortality Weekly Report (MMWR). (67), 1419–1427. doi: 10.15585/mmwr.mm675152e1

Schredl, M., Ciric, P., Götz, S., & Wittmann, L. (2004). Typical dreams: stability and gender differences. *The Journal of Psychology, 138*(6): 485–494. https://doi.org/10.3200/JRLP.138.6.485-494

Schredl, M., Ciric, P., Götz, S., & Wittmann, L. (2004). Typical dreams: stability and gender differences. *The Journal of Psychology, 138*(6): 485–494. https://doi.org/10.3200/JRLP.138.6.485-494

Schroeder, S. R. (2000). Mental retardation and developmental disabilities influenced by environmental neurotoxic insults. *Environmental Health Perspectives, 108*(Suppl. 3), 395–399.

Schroth, M. L., & McCormack, W. A. (2000). Sensation seeking and need for achievement among study-abroad students. *The Journal of Social Psychology, 140,* 533–535.

Schultz, D. P., & Schultz, S. E. (2004). *A History of Modern Psychology,* pp. 239–242. Belmont, CA: Wadsworth.

Schuwerk, T., Vuori, M., & Sodian, B. (2015). Implicit and explicit theory of mind reasoning in autism spectrum disorders: The impact of experience. *Autism, 19,* 459–468.

Schvey, N. A., Sbrocco, T., Stephens, M., Bryant, E. J., Ress, R., Spieker, E. A.,... Tanofsky-Kraff, M. (2015). Comparison of overweight and obese military-dependent and civilian adolescent girls with loss-of-control eating. *International Journal of Eating Disorders, 48*(6), 490–494. doi: 10.1002/eat.22424

Schwanenflugel, P., & Rey, M. (1986). Interlingual semantic facilitation: Evidence from common representational system in the bilingual lexicon. *Journal of Memory and Language, 25,* 605–618.

Schwartz, C. E., Kunwar, P. S., Greve, D. N., Moran, L. R., Viner, J. C., Covino, J. M.,... Wallace, S. R. (2010). Structural differences in adult orbital and ventromedial prefrontal cortex predicted by infant temperament at 4 months of age. *Archives of General Psychiatry, 67*(1), 78–84. doi: 10.1001/archgenpsychiatry.2009.171

Schwartz, J. H., & Javitch, J. A. (2013). Neurotransmitters. In E. R. Kandel, J. H. Schwartz, T. M. Jessell, S. A. Siegelbaum, & A. J. Hudspeth (Eds.), Principles of neural science (5th ed., pp. 289–306). USA: McGraw-Hill.

Schwartz, J. H., Barres, B. A., & Goldman, J. E. (2013). The cells of the nervous system. In E. R. Kandel, J. H. Schwartz, T. M. Jessell, S. A. Siegelbaum, & A. J. Hudspeth (Eds.), *Principles of neural science* (5th ed., pp. 71–99). USA: McGraw-Hill.

Schwartz, S. K. (2000). *Working your degree.* Retrieved March 6, 2010, from http://cnnfn.cnn.com/2000/12/08/career/q_degreepsychology/

Schweickert, R. (1993). A multinomial processing tree model for degradation and redintegration in immediate recall. *Memory and Cognition, 21,* 168–175.

Schwitzgebel, E. (1999). Representation and desire: A philosophical error with consequences for theory-of-mind research. *Philosophical Psychology, 12,* 157–180.

Scott, E., Zhang, Q.-g., Wang, R., Vadlamudi, R., & Brann, D. (2012). Estrogen neuroprotection and the critical period hypothesis. *Frontiers in Neuroendocrinology, 33*(1), 85–104. doi: 10.1016/j.yfrne.2011.10.001

Scott, K., De Jonge, P., Stein, D., & Kessler, R. (Eds.). (2018). *Mental disorders around the world: Facts and figures from the WHO world mental health surveys.* Cambridge: Cambridge University Press.

Scott, S. K., Young, A. W., Calder, A. J., Hellawell, D. J., Aggleton, J. P., & Johnson, M. (1997). Impaired auditory recognition of fear and anger following bilateral amygdala lesions. *Nature, 385*(6613), 254–257.

Scott, W. D. (1908). *The theory and practice of advertising.* Boston, MA: Small, Maynard, & Company.

Seedat, S., Scott, K. M., Angermeyer, M. C., Berglund, P., Bromet, E. J., Brugha, T. S.,... Kessler, R. C. (2009). Cross-national associations between gender and mental disorders in the World Health Organization world mental health surveys. *Archives of General Psychiatry, 66*(7), 785–795. doi: 10.1001/archgenpsychiatry.2009.36

Seehagen, S., Konrad, C., Herbert, J. S., & Schneider, S. (2015). Timely sleep facilitates declarative memory consolidation in infants. *Proceedings of the National Academy of Sciences of the United States of America, 112*(5), 1625–1629.

Segall, M. H., Campbell, D. T., & Herskovits, M. J. (1966). *The influence of culture on perception.* Indianapolis, IN: Bobbs-Merrill.

Segerstrom, S. C., & Sephton, S. E. (2010). Optimistic expectancies and cell-mediated immunity: The role of positive affect. *Psychological Science, 21*(3), 448–455.

Segerstrom, S. C., Taylor, S. E., Kemeny, M. E., & Fahey, J. L. (1998). Optimism is associated with mood, coping, and immune change in response to stress. *Journal of Personality and Social Psychology, 74*(6), 1646–1655.

Sehon, S., & Stanley, D. (2010). Applying the simplicity principle to homeopathy: What remains? *Focus on Alternative and Complementary Therapies, 15*(1), 8–12.

Sekar, A., Bialas, A. R., de Rivera, H., Davis, A., Hammond, T. R., Kamitaki, N.,... McCarroll, S. A. (2016). Schizophrenia risk from complex variation of complement component 4. *Nature, 530,* 177–183. doi: 10.1038/nature16549

Seligman, M. (1975). *Helplessness: Depression, development and death.* New York: W. H. Freeman.

Seligman, M. (1989). *Helplessness.* New York: W. H. Freeman.

Seligman, M. (1995). The effectiveness of psychotherapy: The *Consumer Reports* study. *American Psychologist, 50,* 965–975.

Seligman, M. (1998). *Learned optimism: How to change your mind and your life* (2nd ed.). New York: Pocket Books.

Seligman, M. (2002). *Authentic happiness.* New York: Free Press.

Seligman, M. E. P. (2005). Positive psychology, positive prevention, and positive therapy. In C. R. Snyder & S. J. Lopez (Eds.), *Handbook of positive psychology* (pp. 3–9). New York: Oxford University Press.

Seligman, M. E. P., & Csikszentmihalyi, M. (2000). Positive psychology: An introduction. *American Psychologist, 55*(1), 5–14. doi: 10.1037/0003-066x.55.1.5

Seligman, M., & Maier, S. F. (1967). Failure to escape traumatic shock. *Journal of Experimental Psychology, 74,* 1–9.

Selye, H. (1956). *The stress of life.* New York: McGraw-Hill.

Selye, H. (1976). *The stress of life* (Rev. ed.). New York: McGraw-Hill.

Selye, H. A. (1936). Syndrome produced by diverse nocuous agents. *Nature, 138,* 32.

Seo, D., Tsou, K. A., Ansell, E. B., Potenza, M. N., & Sinha, R. (2014). Cumulative adversity sensitizes neural response to acute stress: Association with health symptoms. *Neuropsychopharmacology, 39,* 670–680.

Sestieri, C., Shulman, G. L., & Corbetta, M. (2017). The contribution of the human posterior parietal cortex to episodic memory. *Nature Reviews Neuroscience, 18*(3): 183–192. DOI: https://doi.org/10.1038/nrn.2017.6

Shabani, K. (2016). Applications of Vygotsky's sociocultural approach for teachers' professional development. *Cogent Education, 3*(1). Retrieved on September 14, 2018 from https://www.tandfonline.com/doi/full/10.1080/2331186X.2016.1252177

Shackelford, T. K., Buss, D. M., & Bennett, K. (2002). Forgiveness or breakup: Sex differences in responses to a partner's infidelity. *Cognition and Emotion, 16*(2), 299–307.

Shadish, R., Cook, T. D., & Campbell, D. T. (2002). *Experimental and quasi-experimental designs for generalized causal inferences.* New York: Houghton Mifflin.

Shaffer, J. J., Peterson, M. J., McMahon, M. A., Bizzell, J., Calhoun, V., van Erp, T. G. M.,... Belger, A. (2015). Neural correlates of schizophrenia negative symptoms: Distinct subtypes impact dissociable brain circuits. *Molecular Neuropsychiatry, 1*(4), 191–200. doi: 10.1159/000440979

Shafton, A. (1995). *Dream reader: Contemporary approaches to the understanding of dreams (SUNY series in dream studies)* (pp. 40–46). New York: State University of New York Press.

Shakespeare, W., & Hubler, E. (1987). *The tragedy of Hamlet, Prince of Denmark.* New York: Penguin Group.

Shang, J., Fu, Y., Ren, Z., Zhang, T., Du, M., Gong, Q.,... Zhang, W. (2014). The common traits of the ACC and PFC in anxiety disorders in the DSM-5: Meta-analysis of voxel-based morphometry studies. *PLoS ONE, 9*(3), e93432. doi: 10.1371/journal.pone.0093432

Shapiro, A. K., & Shapiro, E. (1997). *The powerful placebo.* Baltimore: Johns Hopkins University Press.

Shapiro, F. (2001). *Eye movement desensitization and reprocessing: Basic principles, protocols, and procedures.* New York: Guilford Press.

Shapiro, F. (2012). *Getting past your past: Take control of your life with self-help techniques from EMDR therapy.* New York: Rodale.

Shapiro, K. L., Jacobs, W. J., & LoLordo, V. M. (1980). Stimulus relevance in Pavlovian conditioning in pigeons. *Animal Learning and Behavior, 8,* 586–594.

Sharma, R., Sahota, P., & Thakkar, M. M. (2018). Melatonin promotes sleep in mice by inhibiting orexin neurons in the perifornical lateral hypothalamus. *Journal of Pineal Research,* e12498. Epub ahead of publication. DOI: 10.1111/jpi.12498

Sharot, T., Delgado, M. R., & Phelps, E. A. (2004). How emotion enhances the feeling of remembering. *Nature Neuroscience, 7*(12), 1376–1380.

Shaw, N. D., Butler, J. P., McKinney, S. M., Nelson, S. A., Ellenbogen, J. M., & Hall, J. E. (2012). Insights into puberty: the relationship between sleep stages and pulsatile LH secretion. *Journal of Clinical Endocrinology & Metabolism, 97*:11, E2055–E2062.

Shean, R. E., de Klerk, N. H., Armstrong, B. K., & Walker, N. R. (1994). Seven-year follow-up of a smoking-prevention program for children. *Australian Journal of Public Health, 18,* 205–208.

Sheldon, K. M. (2012). The self-determination theory perspective on positive mental health across cultures. *World Psychiatry, 11*(2), 101–102.

Sheldon, S. H. (2002). Sleep in infants and children. In T. L. Lee-Chiong, M. J. Sateia, & M. A. Carskadon (Eds.), *Sleep medicine* (pp. 99–103). Philadelphia: Hanley & Belfus.

Shelton, J. (2004). *Homeopathy: How it really works.* Amherst, NY: Prometheus Books.

Shepard, R. N., & Metzler, J. (1971). Mental rotation of three-dimensional objects. *Science, 171,* 701–703.

Shepard, T. H., & Lemire, R. J. (2010). *Catalog of teratogenic agents* (13th ed.). Baltimore: Johns Hopkins University Press.

Shepherd, G. M. (2012). *Neurogastronomy: How the brain creates flavor and why it matters.* New York, NY: Columbia University Press.

Sherif, M. (1936). *The psychology of social norms.* New York: Harper & Row.

Sherif, M., Harvey, O. J., White, B. J., Hood, W. R., & Sherif, C. W. (1961). *Intergroup conflict and cooperation: The Robber's Cave experiment.* Norman: University of Oklahoma Book Exchange.

Sherlin, L. H., Arns, M., Lubar, J., Heinrich, H., Kerson, C., Strehl, U., & Sterman, M. B. (2011). Neurofeedback and basic learning theory: Implications for research and practice. *Journal of Neurotherapy: Investigations in Neuromodulation, Neurofeedback and Applied Neuroscience, 15*(4), 292–304.

Sherry, P., Gaa, A., Thurlow-Harrison, S., Graber, K., Clemmons, J., & Bobulinski, M. (2003). Traffic accidents, job stress, and supervisor support in the trucking industry. Paper presented at the International Institute for Intermodal Transportation, University of Denver, CO.

Shipstead, Z., Harrison, T. L., Engle, R. W. (2016). Working memory capacity and fluid intelligence: Maintenance and disengagement. *Perspectives on Psychological Science, 11,* 771–799. doi:10.1177/1745691616650647

Shokri-Kojori, E., Tomasi, D., Wiers, C. E., Wang, G. J., & Volkow, N. D. (2017). Alcohol affects brain functional connectivity and its coupling with behavior: Greater effects in male heavy drinkers. *Molecular Psychiatry, 22*(8), 1185–1195. doi:10.1038/mp.2016.25

Shokri-Kojori, E., Wang, G-J., Wiers, C. E., Demiral, S. B., Guo, M., Kim, S. W., & Volkow, N. D. (2018). β-amyloid accumulaton in the human brain after one night of sleep deprivation. *Proceedings of the National Academy of Sciences, 115*(17): 4483–4488. DOI: https://doi.org/10.1073/pnas.1721694115

Shore, L. A. (1990). Skepticism in light of scientific literacy. *Skeptical Inquirer, 15*(1), 3–4.

Shorter, E. (1997). *A history of psychiatry: From the era of the asylum to the age of Prozac.* New York: John Wiley & Sons.

Showalter, E. (1997). *Hystories: Hysterical epidemics and modern culture.* New York: Columbia University Press.

Shuglin, A. (1986). The background chemistry of MDMA. *Journal of Psychoactive Drugs, 18*(4), 291–304.

Shulman, S., Seiffge-Krenke, I., Scharf, M., Boiangiu, S. B., & Tregubenko, V. (2018). The diversity of romantic pathways during emerging adulthood and their developmental antecedents. *International Journal of Behavioral Development, 42*(2): 167–174. DOI: https://doi.org/10.1177%2F0165025416673474

Shungin, D., Winkler, T. W., Croteau-Chonka, D. C., Ferreira, T., Locke, A. E., Magi, R.,... Mohlke, K. L. (2015). New genetic loci link adipose and insulin biology to body fat distribution. *Nature, 518*(7538), 187–196. doi:10.1038/nature14132

Shweder, R. A., Haidt, J., Horton, R., & Joseph, C. (2008). The cultural psychology of the emotions. In M. Lewis, J. M. Haviland-Jones & L. F. Barrett (Eds.), *Handbook of emotions* (3rd ed., pp. 409–427). New York: Guilford Press.

Siegel, J. M. (2001). The REM sleep-memory consolidation hypothesis. *Science, 294,* 1058–1063.

Siegel, J. M. (2011). Neural control of sleep in mammals. In M. H. Kryger, T. Roth & W. C. Dement (Eds.), *Principles and practice of sleep medicine.* St. Louis, MO: Elsevier Saunders.

Siegel, S. (1969). Effects of CS habituation on eyelid conditioning. *Journal of Comparative and Physiological Psychology, 68*(2), 245–248.

Siegelbaum, S. A., Kandel, E. R., & Yuste, R. (2013). Synaptic integration in the central nervous system. In E. R. Kandel, J. H. Schwartz, T. M. Jessell, S. A. Siegelbaum, & A. J. Hudspeth (Eds.), *Principles of neural science* (5th ed., pp. 210–235). New York: McGraw-Hill.

Siegler, I. C., Costa, P. T., Brummett, B. H., Helms, M. J., Barefoot, J. C., Williams, R. B.,... Rimer, B. K. (2003). Patterns of change in hostility from college to midlife in the UNC alumni heart study predict high-risk status. *Psychosomatic Medicine, 65,* 738–745.

Siegler, R. S. (1996). *Emerging minds: The process of change in children's thinking.* New York: Oxford University Press.

Silva, D. (2017). Penn State fraternity death: Timothy Piazza's parents say son treated like 'road kill'. Retrieved from https://www.nbcnews.com/news/us-news/penn-state-fraternity-death-timothy-piazza-s-parents-say-son-n759426

Silva, K., Chein, J., & Steinberg, L. (2016). Adolescents in peer groups make more prudent decisions when a slightly older adult is present. *Psychological Science, 20,* doi: 10.1177/0956797615620379

Silva, M. N., Marques, M., & Teixeira, P. J. (2014). Testing theory in practice: The example of self-determination theory-based interventions. *The European Health Psychologist, 16,* 171–180.

Simeon, D., Guralnik, O., Hazlett, E. A., Spiegel-Cohen, J., Hollander, E., & Buchsbaum, M. S. (2000). Feeling unreal: A PET study of depersonalization disorder. *American Journal of Psychiatry, 157,* 1782–1788.

Simkin, D. R., & Black, N. B. (2014). Meditation and mindfulness in clinical practice. *Child and Adolescent Psychiatric Clinics of North America, 23,* 487–534.

Simner, J. (2013). Why are there different types of synesthete? *Frontiers in Psychology, 4,* 558. doi: 10.3389/fpsyg.2013.00558

Simner, J., & Carmichael, D. A. (2015). Is synaesthesia a dominantly female trait? *Cognitive Neuroscience, 6*(2–3), 68–76. doi:10.1080/17588928.2015.1019441

Simner, J., Mulvenna, C., Sagiv, N., Tsakanikos, E., Witherby, S. A., Fraser, C.,... Ward, J. (2006). Synaesthesia: The prevalence of atypical cross-modal experiences. *Perception, 35*(8), 1024–1033. doi: 10.1068/p5469

Simola, S. (2017). Managing for academic integrity in higher education: Insights from behavioral ethics. *Scholarship of Teaching and Learning in Psychology, 3*(1), 43–57. doi:10.1037/stl0000076

Simon, D. A., & Bjork, R. A. (2001). Metacognition in motor learning. *Journal of Experimental Psychology: Learning, memory, and cognition, 27*(4), 907–912.

Simon, S. L., Field, J., Miller, L. E., DiFrancesco, M., & Beebe, D. W. (2015). Sweet/dessert foods are more appealing to adolescents after sleep restriction. *PLoS ONE, 10*(2), e0115434. doi: 10.1371/journal.pone.0115434

Simpson, D. (2005). Phrenology and the neurosciences: Contributions of F. J. Gall and J. G. Spurzheim. *ANZ Journal of Surgery, 75*(6), 475–482.

Sin, N. L., Graham-Engeland, J. E., Ong, A. D., & Almeida, D. M. (2015). Affective reactivity to daily stressors is associated with elevated inflammation. *Health Psychology, 34*(12), 1154–1165.

Sindi, S., Kareholt, I., Solomon, A., Hooshmand, B., Soininen, H., & Kivipelto, M. (2017). Midlife work-related stress is associated with late-life cognition. *Journal of Neurology, 264*(9): 1996–2002. DOI: https://dx.doi.org/10.1007%2Fs00415-017-8571-3

Sing, T. L., Hung, M. P., Ohnuki, S., Suizuki, G., San Luis, B-J., McClain, M.,... & Brown, G. W. (2018). The budding yeast RSC complex maintains ploidy by promoting spindle pole body insertion. *The Journal of Cell Biology, 217*(7): 2425. DOI: http://dx.doi.org/10.1083/jcb.201709009

Singer, M. T., & Lalich, J. (1995). *Cults in our midst.* San Francisco: Jossey-Bass.

Singh-Manoux, A., Richards, M., & Marmot, M. (2003). Leisure activities and cognitive function in middle age: Evidence from the Whitehall II study. *Journal of Epidemiology and Community Health, 57,* 907–913.

Skinner, B. F. (1938). *The behavior of organisms: An experimental analysis.* New York: Appleton-Century-Crofts.

Skinner, B. F. (1953). *Science and human behavior.* New York: The Macmillan Company.

Skinner, B. F. (1956). A case history in scientific method. *American Psychologist, 11,* 221–233.

Skinner, B. F. (1961). *Cumulative record: Definitive edition.* New York: Appelton-Century-Crofts.

Skinner, B. F. (1971). *Beyond freedom and dignity.* New York: Alfred A. Knopf.

Skinner, B. F. (1974). *About behaviorism.* New York: Alfred A. Knopf.

Skinner, B. F. (1989) The origins of cognitive thought. *Recent Issues in the Analysis of Behavior,* Princeton, NC: Merrill Publishing Company.

Skolnick, A. (1986). Early attachment and personal relationships across the life course. In P. B. Baltes, D. L. Featherman, & R. M. Lerner (Eds.), *Life-span development and behavior (Vol. 7).* Hillsdale, NJ: Erlbaum.

Slade, E. P., Jahn, D. R., Regenold, W. T., & Case, B. G. (2017). Association of electroconvulsive therapy with psychiatric readmissions in us hospitals. *JAMA Psychiatry, 74*(8), 798–804. doi:10.1001/jamapsychiatry.2017.1378

Slater, A. (2000). Visual perception in the young infant: Early organisation and rapid learning. In D. Muir & A. Slater (Eds.), *Infant development: The essential readings*. Oxford, UK: Blackwell.

Slater M., Antley, A., Davison, A., Swapp, D., Guger, C., Barker, C.,... Sanchez-Vives, M. V. (2006). A virtual reprise of the Stanley Milgram obedience experiments. *PLoS ONE 1*(1), e39. doi:10.1371/journal.pone.0000039

Sleddens, E. F., Gerards, S. M., Thijs, C., de Vries, N. K., & Kremers, S. P. (2011). General parenting, childhood overweight and obesity-inducing behaviors: A review. *International Journal of Pediatric Obesity, 6*(2–2), e12–27.

Slipp, S. (1993). *The Freudian mystique: Freud, women and feminism*. New York: New York University Press.

Sloan, D. M., & Mizes, J. S. (1999). Foundations of behavior therapy in the contemporary healthcare context. *Clinical Psychology Review, 19,* 255–274.

Smedley, R. M., & Coulson, N. S. (2019). Genetic testing for Huntington's disease: A thematic analysis of online support community messages. *Journal of Health Psychology*. doi:10.1177/1359105319826340

Smith, A., & Anderson, M. (2018). *Social media use in 2018*. Retrieved from http://www.pewinternet.org/2018/03/01/social-media-use-in-2018/

Smith, A. R., Steinberg, L., Strang, N., & Chein, J. (2015). Age differences in the impact of peers on adolescents' and adults' neural response to reward. *Developmental Cognitive Neuroscience, 11*, 75–82.

Smith, J. D., Couchman, J. J., & Beran, M. J. (2014). Animal metacognition: A tale of two comparative-psychologies. Journal of Comparative Psychology, *128*(2): 115–131.

Smith, M. A., Roediger, H. L., & Karpicke, J. D. (2013). Covert retrieval practice benefits retention as much as overt retrieval practice. *Journal of Experimental Psychology: Learning, Memory, and Cognition*. doi: 10.1037/a0033569

Smith, T. C., Ryan, M. A. K., Wingard, D. L., Sallis, J. F., & Kritz-Silverstein, D. (2008). New onset and persistent symptoms of post-traumatic stress disorder self-reported after deployment and combat exposures: Prospective population based U.S. military cohort study. *British Medical Journal, 336*(7640), 366–371.

Smolen, P., Baxter, D. A., Byrne, J. H. (2006). A model of the roles of essential kinases in the induction and expression of late long-term potentiation. *Biophysical Journal, 90*, 2760–2775.

Snarey, J. R. (1985). Cross-cultural universality of social-moral development: A critical review of Kohlbergian research. *Psychological Bulletin, 97*(2), 202–232.

Snitz, B. E., O'Meara, E. S., Carlson, M. C., Arnold, A. M., Ives, D. G., Rapp, S. R.,... DeKosky, S. T. (2009). Ginkgo biloba for preventing cognitive decline in older adults. *The Journal of the American Medical Association, 302*(24), 2663–2670.

Snyder, C. R., & Lopez, S. J. (2005). The future of positive psychology. In C. R. Snyder & S. J. Lopez (Eds.), *Handbook of positive psychology* (pp. 751–767). New York: Oxford University Press.

Snyder, D. J., & Bartoshuk, L. M. (2009). Epidemiological studies of taste function: Discussion and perspectives. *Annals of the New York Academy of Sciences, 1170*, 574–580.

Snyder, H. R., Kaiser, R. H., Warren, S. L., & Heller, W. (2015). Obsessive-compulsive disorder is associated with broad impairments in executive function: A meta-analysis. *Clinical Psychological Science, 3*(2), 301–330. doi: 10.1177/2167702614534210

Snyder, M., Tanke, E. D., & Berscheid, E. (1977). Social perception and interpersonal behavior: On the self-fulfilling nature of social stereotypes. *Journal of Personality and Social Psychology, 35*, 656–666.

Snyder, T. D., & Dillow, S. A. (2010). Digest of education statistics 2009 (NCES Publication No. NCES 2010-013). Washington, DC: National Center for Education Statistics, Institute of Education Sciences, U.S. Department of Education.

Society for Industrial and Organizational Psychology [SIOP]. (2019). It's the same, only different - SIOP top 10 workplace trends 2019. Retrieved from http://www.siop.org/article_view.aspx?article=1894

Söderlund, J., Schröder, J., Nordin, C., Samuelsson, M., Walther-Jallow, L., Karlsson, H.,... Engberg, G. (2009). Activation of brain interleukin-1® in schizophrenia. *Molecular Psychiatry, 14*(12), 1069.

Sodowsky, G. R., Lai, E. W., & Plake, B. S. (1991). Moderating effects of socio-cultural variables on acculturation attitudes of Hispanics and Asian Americans. *Journal and Counseling and Development, 70*, 194–204.

Solomon, R. M., & Shapiro, F. (2008). EMDR and the adaptive information processing modelpotential mechanisms of change. *Journal of EMDR Practice and Research, 2*(4), 315–325. doi:10.1891/1933-3196.2.4.315

Somerville, L. H., Jones, R. M., Ruberry, E. J., Dyke, J. P., Glover, G., & Casey, B. J. (2013). The medial prefrontal cortex and the emergence of self-conscious emotion in adolescence. *Psychological Science, 24*, 1554–1562.

Soomro, G. M. (2001). Obsessive-compulsive disorder. *Clinical Evidence, 6*, 754–762.

Sorkhabi, N. (2005). Applicability of Baumrind's parent typology to collective cultures: Analysis of cultural explanations of parent socialization effects. *International Journal of Behavioral Development, 29*(6), 552–563. doi: 10.1177/01650250500172640

Sorrells, S. F., Paredes, M. F., Cebrian-Silla, A., Sandoval, K., Qi, D., Kelley, K. W.,... Alvarez-Buylla, A. (2018). Human hippocampal neurogenesis drops sharply in children to undetectable levels in adults. *Nature, 555*(7696), 377–381. doi:10.1038/nature25975

Spalding, K. L., Bergmann, O., Alkass, K., Bernard, S., Salehpour, M., Huttner, H. B.,... Frisen, J. (2013). Dynamics of hippocampal neurogenesis in adult humans. *Cell, 153*(6), 1219–1227. doi: 10.1016/j.cell.2013.05.002

Spangler, W. D. (1992). Validity of questionnaire and TAT measures of need for achievement: Two meta-analyses. *Psychological Bulletin, 112*, 140–154.

Sparing, R., Mottaghy, F., Ganis, G., Thompson, W. L., Toepper, R., Kosslyn, S. M., & Pascual-Leone, A. (2002). Visual cortex excitability increases during visual mental imagery—A TMS study in healthy human subjects. *Brain Research, 938*, 92–97.

Spaziani, M., Mileno, B., Rossi, F., Granato, S., Tahani, N., Anzuini, A.,... Radicioni, A. F. (2018). Endocrine and metabolic evaluation of classic Klinefelter syndrome and high-grade aneuploidies of sexual chromosomes with male phenotype: Are they different clinical conditions? *European Journal of Endocrinology, 178*(4): 343-352. DOI: https://10.1530/EJE-17-0902

Spearman, C. (1904). "General intelligence" objectively determined and measured. *American Journal of Psychology, 15*, 201–293.

Speca, M., Carlson, L. E, Goodey, E., & Angen, E. (2000). A randomized wait-list controlled clinical trial: The effects of a mindfulness meditation-based stress reduction program on mood and symptoms of stress in cancer outpatients. *Psychosomatic Medicine, 6*, 2613–2622.

Sperling, G. (1960). The information available in brief visual presentations. *Psychological Monographs, 74*(11), 1–29.

Speroff, L., Glass, R. H., & Kase, N. G. (1999). Recurrent early pregnancy loss. In *Clinical Gynecologic Endocrinology and Infertility* (pp. 1042–1055). Philadelphia: Lippincott Williams & Wilkins.

Sperry, R. W. (1968). Mental unity following surgical disconnection of the cerebral hemispheres. *The Harvey Lectures. Series, 62*, 293–323. New York: Academic Press.

Spiegel, D., Bloom, J. R., & Gottheil, E. (1989). Effects of psychosocial treatment on survival of patients with metastatic breast cancer. *Lancet, 2*, 888–891.

Sporns, O. (2014). Cost, efficiency, and economy of brain networks. In M. S. Gazzaniga & G. R. Mangun (Eds.), *The cognitive neurosciences* (5th ed., pp. 91–101). Cambridge, MA: The MIT Press.

Springer, S. P., & Deutsch, G. (1998). *Left brain, right brain: Perspectives from cognitive neuroscience* (5th ed.). New York: Freeman.

Squire, L. R., & Alvarez, P. (1995). Retrograde amnesia and memory consolidation: A neurobiological perspective. *Current Opinion in Neurobiology, 5*(2), 169–177.

Squire, L. R., & Kandel, E. (1999). *Memory: From mind to molecule*. New York: Scientific American Library.

Squire, L. R., & Kandel, E. R. (2009). *Memory: From mind to molecules*. Greenwood Village, CO: Roberts and Company Publishers.

Squire, L. R., Knowlton, B., & Musen, G. (1993). The structure and organization of memory. *Annual Review of Psychology, 44*, 453–495.

Squire, L. R., & Slater, P. C. (1978). Anterograde and retrograde memory impairment in chronic amnesia. *Neuropsychologia, 16*, 313–322.

Squire, L. R., Slater, P. C., & Chace, P. M. (1975). Retrograde amnesia: Temporal gradient in very long-term memory following electroconvulsive therapy. *Science, 187*, 77–79.

Stahl, S. M. (2013). *Stahl's essential psychopharmacology: Neuroscientific basis and practical applications* (4th ed.). New York: Cambridge University Press.

Stahl, S. M. (2017). *Prescriber's guide: Stahl's essential psychopharmacology* (6th ed.). New York: Cambridge University Press.

Standing, L., Conezio, J., & Haber, R. N. (1970). Perception and memory for pictures: Single-trial learning of 2500 visual stimuli. *Psychonomic Science, 19*, 73–74.

Stanovich, K. E., & West, R. F. (2000). Individual differences in reasoning: Implications for the rationality debate? *Behavioral and Brain Sciences, 23*(5), 645–665; discussion 665–726.

Steel, Z., Marnane, C., Iranpour, C., Chey, T., Jackson, J. W., Patel, V., & Silove, D. (2014). The global prevalence of common mental disorders: A systematic review and meta-analysis 1980–2013. *International Journal of Epidemiology, 43*(2), 476–493. doi:10.1093/ije/dyu038

Steele, C. M. (1992). Race and the schooling of Black Americans. *The Atlantic Monthly, 269*(4), 68–78.

Steele, C. M. (1997). A threat in the air: How stereotypes shape intellectual identity and performance. *American Psychologist, 52*, 613–629.

Steele, C. M. (1999, August). Thin ice: "Stereotype threat" and Black college students. *The Atlantic Monthly, 284*, 44–54.

Steele, C. M., & Aronson J. (1995). Stereotype threat and the intellectual test performance of African Americans. *Journal of Personality and Social Psychology, 69*, 797–811.

Steele, J., James, J. B., & Barnett, R. C. (2002). Learning in a man's world: Examining the perceptions of undergraduate women in male-dominated academic areas. *Psychology of Women Quarterly, 26*, 46–50.

Stefanovic-Stanojevic, T., Tosic-Radev, M., & Velikic, D. (2015). Maternal attachment and children's emotional and cognitive competencies. *Psihologijske Tema, 24*, 51–69.

Stein, H. T. (2001). Adlerian overview of birth order characteristics. Alfred Adler Institute of San Francisco. Retrieved June 16, 2004, at http://pws.cablespeed.com/~htstein/birthord.htm

Stein-Behrens, B., Mattson, M. P., Chang, I., Yeh, M., & Sapolsky, R. (1994). Stress exacerbates neuron loss and cytoskeletal pathology in the hippocampus. *Journal of Neuroscience, 14*, 5373–5380.

Steinberg, L., & Silverberg, S. B. (1987). Influences on marital satisfaction during the middle stages of the family life cycle. *Journal of Marriage and the Family, 49*, 751–760.

Steinke, E. E., Mosack, V., & Hill, T. J. (2018). The influence of comorbidities, risk factors, and medications on sexual activity in individuals aged 40 to 59 years with and without cardiac conditions: US National Health and Nutrition Examination Survey, 2011 to 2012. *The Journal of Cardiovascular Nursing, 33*(2): 118-125. DOI: https://doi.org/10.1097/JCN.0000000000000433

Steptoe, A., & Kivimaki, M. (2013a). Stress and cardiovascular disease: An update on current knowledge. *Annual Review of Public Health, 34*, 337–354. doi:10.1146/annurev-publhealth-031912-114452

Steptoe, A., & Kivimaki, M. (2013b). Stress and cardiovascular disease: An update on current knowledge. *Annual Review of Public Health, 34*, 337–354.

Steriade, M., & McCarley, R. W. (1990). *Brainstem control of wakefulness and sleep*. New York: Plenum.

Sterling, P. (2004). Principles of allostasis: Optimal design, predictive regulation, pathophysiology and rational therapeutics. In J. Schulkin (Ed.), *Allostasis, homeostasis, and the costs of adaptation*: Cambridge University Press.

Sterling, P., & Eyer, J. (1988). Allostasis: A new paradigm to explain arousal pathology. In S. Fisher & J. Reason (Eds.), *Handbook of life stress, cognition and health*: John Wiley & Sons.

Stern, W. (1912). *The psychological methods of testing intelligence* (G. M. Whipple, Trans.) (Educational Psychology Monograph No. 13). Baltimore, MD: Warwick & York, Inc.

Sternberg, R. J. (1986). A triangular theory of love. *Psychological Review, 93*, 119–135.

Sternberg, R. J. (1988a). *The triarchic mind: A new theory of human intelligence*. New York: Viking-Penguin.

Sternberg, R. J. (1988b). Triangulating love. In R. Sternberg & M. Barnes (Eds.), *The psychology of love* (pp. 119–138). New Haven, CT: Yale University Press.

Sternberg, R. J. (1996). *Successful intelligence: How practical and creative intelligence determine success in life*. New York: Simon & Schuster.

Sternberg, R. J. (1997a). Construct validation of a triangular love scale. *European Journal of Social Psychology, 27*, 313–335.

Sternberg, R. J. (1997b). The triarchic theory of intelligence. In P. Flannagan, J. L. Genshaft, & P. L. Harrison (Eds.), *Contemporary intellectual assessment: Theories, tests, and issues* (pp. 92–104). New York: Guilford Press.

Sternberg, R. J. (2005). The triarchic theory of successful intelligence. In *Contemporary Intellectual Assessment: Theories, Tests, and Issues*. New York: Guilford Press.

Sternberg, R. J. (2015). Successful intelligence: A model for testing intelligence beyond IQ tests. *European Journal of Education and Psychology, 8*(2), 76–84. doi: 10.1016/j.ejeps.2015.09.004

Sternberg, R. J., & Grigorenko, E. L. (2006). Cultural intelligence and successful intelligence. *Group Organization Management, 31*, 27–39.

Sternberg, R. J., & Kaufman, J. C. (1998). Human abilities. *Annual Review of Psychology, 49*, 479–502.

Sternberger, R. R., Turner, S. M., Beidel, D. C., & Calhoun, K. S. (1995). Social phobia: An analysis of possible developmental factors. *Journal of Abnormal Psychology, 194*, 526–531.

Stevens, C., & Neville, H. (2014). Specificity of experiential effects in neurocognitive development. In M. S. Gazzaniga & G. R. Mangun (Eds.), *The cognitive neurosciences* (5th ed., pp. 129–142). Cambridge, MA: The MIT Press.

Stevens, J. P., Wall, M. J., Novack, L., Marshall, J., Hsu, D. J., & Howell, M. D. (2017). The critical care crisis of opioid overdoses in the United States. *Annals of the American Thoracic Society, 14*(12): 1803–1809. DOI: https://doi.org/10.1513/AnnalsATS.201701-022OC

Stevens, J. S., Kim, Y. J., Galatzer-Levy, I. R., Reddy, R., Ely, T. D., Nemeroff, C. B.,... Ressler, K. J. (2017). Amygdala reactivity and anterior cingulate habituation predict posttraumatic stress disorder symptom maintenance after acute civilian trauma. *Biological Psychiatry, 81*(12), 1023–1029. doi:10.1016/j.biopsych.2016.11.015

Stevens, R. G., & Zhu, Y. (2015). Electric light, particularly at night, disrupts human circadian rhythmicity: Is that a problem? *Philosophical Transactions of the Royal Society B: Biological Sciences, 370*(1667): 20140120. DOI: https://dx.doi.org/10.1098%2Frstb.2014.0120

Stevenson, M. B., Roach, M. A., Leavitt, L. A., Miller, J. F., & Chapman, R. S. (1988). Early receptive and productive language skills in preterm and full-term 8-month-old infants. *Journal of Psycholinguistic Research, 17*(2), 169–183.

Stickgold, R., & Ellenbogen, J. M. (2008). Quiet! Sleeping brain at work. *Scientific American Mind, 19*(4), 23–29.

Stickgold, R., Hobson, J. A., Fosse, R., & Fosse, M. (2001). Sleep, learning and dreams: Off-line memory reprocessing. *Science, 294*, 1052–1057.

Stiff, J. B., & Mongeau, P. A. (2002). *Persuasive communication* (2nd ed.). New York: Guilford Press.

Stigler, S. M. (1997). Regression towards the mean, historically considered. *Statistical Methods in Medical Research, 6*(2), 103–114.

Stipek, D. J., Gralinski, J. H., & Kopp, C. B. (1990). Self-concept development in the toddler years. *Developmental Psychology, 26*(6), 972–977.

Stockhorst, U., Gritzmann, E., Klopp, K., Schottenfeld-Naor, Y., Hübinger, A., Berresheim, H.,... Gries, F. A. (1999). Classical conditioning of insulin effects in healthy humans. *Psychosomatic Medicine, 61*, 424–435.

Stoeckel, L. E., Garrison, K. A., Ghosh, S., Wighton, P., Hanlon, C. A., Gilman, J. M.,... Evins, A. E. (2014). Optimizing real time fMRI neurofeedback for therapeutic discovery and development. *NeuroImage: Clinical, 5*, 245–255. doi: 10.1016/j.nicl.2014.07.002

Stoesz, B. M., Hare, J. F., & Snow, W. M. (2013). Neurophysiological mechanisms underlying affiliative social behavior: Insights from comparative research. *Neuroscience and Biobehavioral Reviews, 37*(2), 123–132. doi: 10.1016/j.neubiorev.2012.11.007

Stoodley, C. J., & Schmahmann, J. D. (2009). Functional topography in the human cerebellum: A meta-analysis of neuroimaging studies. *NeuroImage, 44*(2), 489–501. doi: 10.1016/j.neuroimage.2008.08.039

Stoodley, C. J., Valera, E. M., & Schmahmann, J. D. (2012). Functional topography of the cerebellum for motor and cognitive tasks: An fMRI study. *NeuroImage, 59*(2), 1560–1570. doi: 10.1016/j.neuroimage.2011.08.065

Stowell, J. R., Kiecolt-Glaser, J. K., & Glaser, R. (2001). Perceived stress and cellular immunity: When coping counts. *Journal of Behavioral Medicine, 24*(4), 323–339.

Stratton, K., Gable, A., & McCormick, M. C. (Eds.). (2001a). *Immunization safety review: Thimerosal-containing vaccines and neurodevelopmental disorders*. Washington, DC: National Academies Press.

Stratton, K., Wilson, C. B., & McCormick, M. C. (Eds.). (2001b). *Immunization safety review: Measles-mumps-rubella vaccine and autism*. Washington, DC: National Academies Press.

Strauss, A. S. (2004). The meaning of death in Northern Cheyenne culture. In A. C. G. M. Robben (Ed.), *Death, mourning, and burial: A cross-cultural reader* (pp. 71–76). Malden, MA: Blackwell.

Strauss, C., Rosten, C., Hayward, M., Lea, L., Forrester, E., & Jones, A. M. (2015). Mindfulness-based exposure and response prevention for obsessive compulsive disorder: Study protocol for a pilot randomised controlled trial. *Trials, 16*, 167. doi: 10.1186/s13063-015-0664-7

Strawbridge, W. J., Cohen, R. D., Shema, S. J., & Kaplan, G. A. (1997). Frequent attendance at religious services and mortality over 28 years. *American Journal of Public Health, 87*, 957–961.

Strayer, D. L., & Drews, F. A. (2007). Cell-phone-induced driver distraction. *Current Directions in Psychological Science, 16*, 128–131.

Strayer, D. L., & Johnston, W. A. (2001). Driven to distraction: Dual-task studies of simulated driving and conversing on a cellular phone. *Psychological Science, 12*, 462–466.

Strayer, D. L., Drews, F. A., & Crouch, D. J. (2006). A comparison of the cell phone driver and the drunk driver. *Human Factors, 48*, 381–391.

Strayer, D. L., Turrill, J., Coleman, J. R., Ortiz, E. V., & Cooper, J. M. (2014). Measuring cognitive distraction in the automobile II: Assessing in-vehicle voice-based interactive technologies. AAA Foundation for Traffic Safety Fact Sheet. Retrieved from https://www.aaafoundation.org/sites/default/files/Cog%20Distraction%20Phase%202%20FINAL%20FTS%20FORMAT_0.pdf

Strehl, U., Birkle, S., Wörz, S., & Kotchoubey, B. (2014). Sustained reduction of seizures in patients with intractable epilepsy after self-regulation training of slow cortical potentials—10 years after. *Frontiers in Human Neuroscience, 8*(1), 604.

Strick, P. L., Dum, R. P., & Fiez, J. A. (2009). Cerebellum and nonmotor function. *Annual Review of Neuroscience, 32*, 413–434. doi: 10.1146/annurev.neuro.31.060407.125606

Stromeyer, C. F., III, & Psotka, J. (1971). The detailed texture of eidetic images. *Nature, 237*, 109–112.

Strunk, D. R., Brotman, M. A., & DeRubeis, R. J. (2010). The process of change in cognitive therapy for depression: Predictors of early inter-session symptom gains. *Behaviour Research and Therapy, 48*(7), 599–606.

Stubbs, R. J., van Wyk, M. C., Johnstone, A. M., & Harbron, C. G. (1996). Breakfasts high in protein, fat or carbohydrate: Effect on within-day appetite and energy balance. *European Journal of Clinical Nutrition, 50*(7), 409–417.

Stuss, D. T., Binns, M. A., Murphy, K. J., & Alexander, M. P. (2002). Dissociations within the anterior attentional system: Effects of task complexity and irrelevant information on reaction time speed and accuracy. *Neuropsychology, 16*, 500–513.

Su, L., Cai, Y., Xu, Y., Dutt, A., Shi, S., & Bramon, E. (2014). Cerebral metabolism in major depressive disorder: A voxel-based meta-analysis of positron emission tomography studies. *BMC Psychiatry, 14*, 321. doi: 10.1186/s12888-014-0321-9

Substance Abuse and Mental Health Services Administration. (2018). *Key substance use and mental health indicators in the United States: Results from the 2017 National Survey on Drug Use and Health* (HHS Publication No. SMA 18-5068, NSDUH Series H-53). Rockville, MD: Center for Behavioral Health Statistics and Quality, Substance Abuse and Mental Health Services Administration Retrieved from https://www.samhsa.gov/data/

Sue, D. W. (2010). *Microaggressions and marginality: Manifestation, dynamics, and impact*. Hoboken, NJ: John Wiley & Sons.

Sue, D. W., & Sue, D. (2016). *Counseling the culturally diverse: Theory and practice* (7th ed.). Hoboken, NJ: John Wiley & Sons.

Sue, S. (1977). Community mental health services to minority groups: Some optimism, some pessimism. *American Psychologist, 32*, 616–624.

Sue, S. (1992). Ethnicity and mental health: Research and policy issues. *Journal of Social Issues, 48*(2), 187–205.

Sue, S., Zane, N., & Young, K. (1994). Research on psychotherapy in culturally diverse populations. In A. Bergin & S. Garfield (Eds.), *Handbook of psychotherapy and behavior change* (pp. 783–817). New York: Wiley.

Suleiman, J., & Watson, R. T. (2008). Social loafing in technology-supported teams. *Computer Supported Cooperative Work, 17*, 291–309.

Suler, J. (2004). The online disinhibition effect. *Cyberpsychology & Behavior, 7*(3), 321–326. doi:10.1089/1094931041291295

Sullivan, D. R., Liu, X., Corwin, D. S., Verceles, A. C., McCurdy, M. T., Pate, D. A.,... Netzer, G. (2012). Learned helplessness among families and surrogate decision-makers of patients admitted to medical, surgical, and trauma ICUs. *Chest, 142*(6), 1440–1446. doi: 10.1378/chest.12-0112

Sullivan, P. F. (2005). The genetics of schizophrenia. *PLoS Med, 2*(7), e212. doi: 05-PLME-RIT-0198R1

Sullivan, P. F., Neale, M. C., & Kendler, K. S. (2000). Genetic epidemiology of major depression: Review and meta-analysis, *American Journal of Psychiatry, 157*, 1552–1562.

Sulloway, F. J. (1996). *Born to rebel: Birth order, family dynamics, and creative lives*. New York: Pantheon.

Sulpizio, S., Doi, H., Bornstein, M. H., Cui, J., Esposito, G., & Shinohara, K. (2018). fNIRS reveals enhanced brain activation to female (versus male) infant directed speech (relative to adult directed speech) in young human infants. *Infant Behavior & Development, 52*, 89–96. doi:10.1016/j.infbeh.2018.05.009

Sulzer, J., Sitaram, R., Blefari, M. L., Kollias, S., Birbaumer, N., Stephan, K. E.,... Gassert, R. (2013). Neurofeedback-mediated self-regulation of the dopaminergic midbrain. *NeuroImage, 75C*, 176–184. doi: 10.1016/j.neuroimage.2013.02.041

Suryani, L., & Jensen, S. (1993). *Trance and possession in Bali: A window on western multiple personality, possession disorder, and suicide*. New York: Oxford University Press.

Sutcliffe, N., Clarke, A. E., Levinton, C., Frost, C., Gordon, C., & Isenberg, D. A. (1999). Associates of health status in patients with systemic lupus erythematosus. *Journal of Rheumatology, 26*, 2352–2356.

Sutherland, P. (1992). *Cognitive development today: Piaget and his critics*. London: Paul Chapman.

Suzuki, T. N., Wheatcroft, D., & Griesser, M. (2016). Experimental evidence for compositional syntax in bird calls. *Nature Communications, 7*, 10986. doi:10.1038/ncomms10986

Svebak, S., Romundstad, S., & Holmen, J. (2010). A 7-year prospective study of sense of humor and mortality in an adult county population: The HUNT-2 study. *The International Journal of Psychiatry in Medicine, 40*(2), 125–146.

Swanson, H. (1994). Index of suspicion. Case 3. Diagnosis: Failure to thrive due to psychosocial dwarfism. *Pediatric Review, 15*(1), 39, 41.

Swayze, V. W., II. (1995). Frontal leukotomy and related psychosurgical procedures in the era before antipsychotics (1935–1954): A historical overview. *American Journal of Psychiatry, 152*(4), 505–515.

Sykes-Muskett, B. J., Prestwich, A., Lawton, R. J., & Armitage, C. J. (2015). The utility of monetary contingency contracts for weight loss: A systematic review and meta-analysis. *Health Psychology Review, 9*(4), 434–451. doi: 10.1080/17437199.2015.1030685

Szalavitz, M. (2009). Popping smart pills: The case for cognitive enhancement. *Time* in partnership with CNN. Retrieved May 5, 2010, from http://www.time.com/time/health/article/0,8599,1869435,00.html

Szell, M., & Thurner, S. (2013). How women organize social networks different from men. *Scientific Reports, 3*, 1214. doi: 10.1038/srep01214

Taglialatela, J. P., Savage-Rumbaugh, E. S., & Baker, L. A. (2003). Vocal production by a language-competent bonobo (*Pan paniscus*). *International Journal of Comparative Psychology, 24*, 1–17.

Tajfel, H., & Turner, J. C. (1979). An integrative theory of intergroup conflict. In W. G. Austin & S. Worchel (Eds.), *The social psychology of intergroup relations* (pp. 33-48). Monterey, CA: Brooks/Cole.

Tajfel, H., & Turner, J. C. (1986). The social identity theory of intergroup behaviour. In S. Worchel & W. G. Austin (Eds.), *The psychology of intergroup relations* (Vol. 2, pp. 7–24) New York: Nelson Hall.

Takahashi, A., Lee, R. X., Iwasato, T., Itohara, S., Arima, H., Bettler, B.,... Koide, T. (2015). Glutamate input in the dorsal raphe nucleus as a determinant of escalated aggression in male mice. *Journal of Neuroscience, 35*(16), 6452. doi: 10.1523/JNEUROSCI.2450-14.2015

Takeuchi, T., Ogilvie, R. D., Murphy, T. I., & Ferrelli, A. V. (2003). EEG activities during elicited sleep onset. REM and NREM periods reflect difference mechanisms of dream generation. *Clinical Neurophysiology, 114*(2), 210–220.

Takooshian, H., Bedrosian, D., Cecero, J. J., Chancer, L., Karmen, A., Rasenberger, J.,... Stephen, J. (2005). Remembering Catherine "Kitty" Genovese 40 years later: A public forum. *Journal of Social Distress and the Homeless, 14*(1–2), 72–85. doi:10.1179/105307805807066284

Talbott, G. D., & Crosby, L. R. (2001). Recovery contracts: Seven key elements. In R. H. Coombs (Ed.), *Addiction recovery tools* (pp. 127–144). Thousand Oaks, CA: Sage.

Tammen, S. A., Friso, S., & Choi, S. W. (2013). Epigenetics: The link between nature and nurture. *Molecular Aspects of Medicine, 34*(4), 753–764. doi: 10.1016/j.mam.2012.07.018

Tan, M. S., Yu, J. T., Tan, C. C., Wang, H. F., Meng, X. F., Wang, C.,... Tan, L. (2015). Efficacy and adverse effects of ginkgo biloba for cognitive impairment and dementia: A systematic review and meta-analysis. *Journal of Alzheimer's Disease, 43*(2), 589–603.

Tang, Y.-Y., Holzel, B. K., & Posner, M. I. (2015). The neuroscience of mindfulness meditation. *Nature Reviews Neuroscience, 16*, 213–225.

Tannenbaum, M. B., Hepler, J., Zimmerman, R. S., Saul, L., Jacobs, S., Wilson, K., & Albarracín, D. (2015). Appealing to fear: A meta-analysis of fear appeal effectiveness and theories. *Psychological Bulletin, 141*(6), 1178–1204.

Tanrikulu, I., & Erdur-Baker, O. (2019). Motives behind cyberbullying perpetration: A test of uses and gratifications theory. *Journal of Interpersonal Violence*, 886260518819882. doi:1.o0r.g1/107.171/0778/8068826206501581881199882

Tarescavage, A. M., Fischler, G. L., Cappo, B. M., Hill, D. O., Corey, D. M., & Ben-Porath, Y. S. (2015). Minnesota Multiphasic Personality Inventory-2—Restructured Form (MMPI-2-RF) predictors of police officer problem behavior and collateral self-report test scores. *Psychological Assessment, 27*(1), 125–137. doi: 10.1037/pas0000041

Tarescavage, A. M., Scheman, J., & Ben-Porath, Y. S. (2018). Prospective comparison of the Minnesota multiphasic personality inventory-2 (MMPI-2) and MMPI-2-restructured form (MMPI-2-RF) in predicting treatment outcomes among patients with chronic low back pain. *Journal of Clinical Psychology in Medical Settings, 25*(1), 66–79. doi: 10.1007/s10880-017-9535-6

Tarrier, N., & Taylor, R. (2014). Schizophrenia and other psychotic disorders. In D. H. Barlow (Ed.), *Clinical handbook of psychological disorders: A step-by-step treatment manual* (5th ed., pp. 502–532). New York, NY: The Guilford Press.

Tatke, S. (2012). Bystander effect typifies Indian psyche. The Times of India, July 15, 2012. Retrieved from http://timesofindia.indiatimes.com/city/mumbai/Bystander-effect-typifies-Indian-psyche/articleshow/14924402.cms

Taylor, B., Miller, E., Farrington, C. P., Petropoulos, M. C., Favot-Mayaud, I., Li, J., & Waight, P. A. (1999). Autism and measles, mumps, and rubella vaccine: No epidemiological evidence for a causal association. *Lancet, 353*, 2026–2029.

Taylor, C., Manganello, J. A., Lee, S. J., & Rice, J. C. (2010). Mothers' spanking of 3-year-old children and subsequent risk of children's aggressive behavior. *Pediatrics, 125*, 1057–1065.

Taylor, D. M., & Moghaddam, F. M. (1994). *Theories of intergroup relations: International social psychological perspectives* (2nd ed.). Westport, CT: Praeger.

Taylor, E. (2001). Positive psychology and humanistic psychology: A reply to Seligman. *Journal of Humanistic Psychology, 41*(1), 13–29. doi: 10.1177/0022167801411003

Taylor, S. E. (2006). Tend and befriend: Biobehavioral bases of affiliation under stress. *Current Directions in Psychological Science, 15*, 273–277.

Taylor, S. E., Klein, L. C., Lewis, B. P., Gruenewald, T. L., Gurung, R. A. R., & Updegraff, J. A. (2000). Biobehavioral responses to stress in females: Tend-and-befriend, not fight-or-flight. *Psychological Review, 107*(3), 411–429.

Teigen, K. (1994). Yerkes–Dodson: A law for all seasons. *Theory & Psychology, 4*, 525–547.

Temoshok, L., & Dreher, H. (1992). *The Type C connection: The behavioral links to cancer and your health*. New York: Random House.

Terman, L. M. (1916). *The measurement of intelligence*. Boston: Houghton Mifflin.

Terman, L. M. (1925). *Mental and physical traits of a thousand gifted children (I)*. Stanford, CA: Stanford University Press.

Terman, L. M., & Oden, M. H. (1947). *The gifted child grows up: 25 years' follow-up of a superior group: Genetic studies of genius (Vol. 4)*. Stanford, CA: Stanford University Press.

Terman, L. M., & Oden, M. H. (1959). *The gifted group at mid-life, thirty-five years follow-up of the superior child: Genetic studies of genius (Vol. 3)*. Stanford, CA: Stanford University Press.

Terracciano, A., Sutin, A. R., An, Y., O'Brien, R. J., Ferrucci, L., Zonderman, A. B., & Resnick, S. M. (2014). Personality and risk of Alzheimer's disease: New data and meta-analysis. *Alzheimer's & Dementia, 10*(2), 179–186. doi: 10.1016/j.jalz.2013.03.002

Tesler, N., Gerstenberg, M., Franscini, M., Jenni, O. G., Walitza, S., & Huber, R. (2016). Increased frontal sleep slow wave activity in adolescents with major depression. *NeuroImage: Clinical, 10*, 250–256. doi: 10.1016/j.nicl.2015.10.014

Tevis, M. (1994). "George I. Sanchez." In *Lives in education: A narrative of people and ideas*, 2nd ed., ed. L. Glenn Smith, Joan K. Smith, pp. 346–354. New York: St. Martin's Press.

Thase, M. E. (1999). When are psychotherapy and pharmacotherapy combinations the treatment of choice for major depressive disorders? *Psychiatric Quarterly, 70*(4), 333–346.

Thase, M. E., & Sachs, G. S. (2000). Bipolar depression: Pharmacotherapy and related therapeutic strategies. *Biological Psychiatry, 48*(6), 558–572.

The Associated Press (AP). (August 20, 2018). Europe sees sharp rise in measles: 41,000 cases, 37 deaths. *Medical Press: Diseases, Conditions, Syndromes.* Retrieved from https://medicalxpress.com/news/2018-08-europe-sharp-measles-cases-deaths.html

The College Board. (2011). Time management tips for students. Retrieved May 31, 2013, from http://www.collegeboard.com/student/plan/college-success/116.html

Thibodeau, P. H., & Boroditsky, L. (2013). Natural language metaphors covertly influence reasoning. *PLoS ONE, 8*(1). doi: 10.1371/journal.pone.0052961

Thibodeau, P. H., & Boroditsky, L. (2015). Measuring effects of metaphor in a dynamic opinion landscape. *PLoS ONE, 10*(7), e0133939. doi: 10.1371/journal.pone.0133939

Thibodeau, P. H., Hendricks, R. K., & Boroditsky, L. (2017). How linguistic metaphor scaffolds reasoning. *Trends in Cognitive Sciences, 21*(11), 852–863. doi:10.1016/j.tics.2017.07.001

Thiedke, C. C. (2001). Sleep disorders and sleep problems in childhood. *American Family Physician, 63,* 277–284.

Thomas, A., & Chess, S. (1977). *Temperament and development.* New York: Brunner/Mazel.

Thomas, E. F., McGarty, C., & Mavor, K. (2016). Group interaction as the crucible of social identity formation: A glimpse at the foundations of social identities for collective action. *Group Processes & Intergroup Relations, 19*(2), 137–151.

Thomas, M., Thorne, D., Sing, H., Redmond, D., Balkin, T., Wesensten, N.,... Belenky, G. (1998). The relationship between driving accidents and microsleep during cumulative partial sleep deprivation. *Journal of Sleep Research, 7*(2), 275.

Thomas, R. K. (1994). Pavlov's rats "dripped saliva at the sound of a bell." *Psycoloquy, 5*(80). Retrieved May 9, 2008, from http://www.cogsci.ecs.soton.ac.uk/cgi/psyc/newpsy?5.80

Thompson, W. W., Price, C., Goodson, B., Shay, D. K., Benson, P., Hinrichsen, V. L.,... DeStefano, F. (2007). Early thimerosal exposure and neuropsychological outcomes at 7 to 10 years. *The New England Journal of Medicine, 357*(13), 1281–1292.

Thoresen, C. E., & Harris, H. S. (2002). Spirituality and health: What's the evidence and what's needed? *Annals of Behavioral Medicine, 24,* 3–13.

Thorndike, E. L. (1911). *Animal intelligence: Experimental studies.* New York: MacMillan.

Thorndike, E. L. (1920). A constant error on psychological rating. *Journal of Applied Psychology, 5,* 25–29.

Thorndike, E. L. (1927). The law of effect. *The American Journal of Psychology, 39,* 212–222. DOI: http://dx.doi.org/10.2307/1415413

Thornton, A., & Hui-Sheng, L. (1994). Continuity and change. In A. Thornton & Hui-Sheng (Eds.), *Social change and the family in Taiwan* (pp. 396–410). Chicago: University of Chicago Press.

Thurstone, L. (1938). *Primary mental abilities.* Chicago: University of Chicago Press.

Tian, R., Hou, G., Li, D., & Yuan, T.-F. (2014). A possible change process of inflammatory cytokines in the prolonged chronic stress and its ultimate implications for health. *The Scientific World Journal,* 2014, Article ID 780616. doi: 10.1155/2014/780616

Tienari, P., Wynne, L. C., Sorri, A., Lahti, I., Läksy, K., Moring, J.,... Wahlberg, K-E. (2004). Genotype-environment interaction in schizophrenia-spectrum disorder: Long-term follow-up study of Finnish adoptees. *The British Journal of Psychiatry, 184,* 216–222.

Tobach, E. (2001). Development of sex and gender. In J. Worell (Ed.), *Encyclopedia of women and gender* (pp. 315–332). San Diego, CA: Academic Press.

Toga, A. W., & Thompson, P. M. (2003). Mapping brain asymmetry. *Nature Reviews Neuroscience, 4,* 37–48.

Toker, S., Shirom, A., Melamed, S., & Armon, G. (2012). Work characteristics as predictors of diabetes incidence among apparently healthy employees. *Journal of Occupational Health Psychology, 17*(3), 259. doi: 10.1037/a0028401

Tolman, E. C., & Honzik, C. H. (1930). Introduction and removal of reward and maze learning in rats. *University of California Publications in Psychology, 4,* 257–275.

Tomasello, M., Carpenter, M., & Lizskowski, U. (2007). A new look at infant pointing. *Child Development, 78,* 705–722.

Tomassy, G. S., Berger, D. R., Chen, H.-H., Kasthuri, N., Hayworth, K. J., Vercelli, A.,... Arlotta, P. (2014). Distinct profiles of myelin distribution along single axons of pyramidal neurons in the neocortex. *Science, 344*(6181), 319–324. doi: 10.1126/science.1249766

Tonnesen, S., Kaufmann, T., Doan, N. T., Alnaes, D., Cordova-Palomera, A., Meer, D. V.,... Westlye, L. T. (2018). White matter aberrations and age-related trajectories in patients with schizophrenia and bipolar disorder revealed by diffusion tensor imaging. *Scientific Reports, 8*(1), 14129. doi:10.1038/s41598-018-32355-9

Tor, P. C., Bautovich, A., Wang, M. J., Martin, D., Harvey, S. B., & Loo, C. (2015). A systematic review and meta-analysis of brief versus ultrabrief right unilateral electroconvulsive therapy for depression. *The Journal of Clinical Psychiatry, 76*(9), e1092–1098. doi: 10.4088/JCP.14r09145

Torgersen, S., Czajkowski, N., Jacobson, K., Reichborn-Kjennerud, T., Roysamb, E., Neale, M. C., & Kendler, K. S. (2008). Dimensional representations of DSM-IV cluster B personality disorders in a population-based sample of Norwegian twins: A multivariate study. *Psychological Medicine, 38*(11), 1617–1625. doi: 10.1017/s0033291708002924

Torrance, E. P. (1993). The Beyonders in a thirty-year longitudinal study of creative achievement. *Roeper Review, 15*(3), 131–135.

Torres, S. A., Santiago, C. D., Walts, K. K., & Richards, M. H. (2018). Immigration policy, practices, and procedures: The impact on the mental health of Mexican and Central American youth and families. *American Psychologist, 73*(7), 843–854. doi:10.1037/amp0000184

Townsend, S., Kim, H. S., & Mesquita, B. (2014). Are you feeling what I'm feeling? Emotional similarity buffers stress. *Social Psychological and Personality Science, 5*(5), 526–533.

Trace, S. E., Baker, J. H., Penas-Lledo, E., & Bulik, C. M. (2013). The genetics of eating disorders. *Annual Review of Clinical Psychology, 9,* 589–620. doi: 10.1146/annurev-clinpsy-050212-185546

Traffanstedt, M. K., Mehta, S., & LoBello, S. G. (2016). Major depression with seasonal variation: Is it a valid construct? *Clinical Psychological Science.* doi: 10.1177/2167702615615867

Trappey, C. (1996). A meta-analysis of consumer choice and subliminal advertising. *Psychology and Marketing, 13,* 517–530.

Trauer, J. M., Qian, M. Y., Doyle, J. S., Rajaratnam, S. M. W., & Cunnington, D. (2015). Cognitive behavioral therapy for chronic insomnia: A systematic review and meta-analysis. *Annals of Internal Medicine, 163*(3), 191–204. doi: 10.7326/M14-2841

Treadway, M. T., Buckholtz, J. W., Martin, J. W., Jan, K., Asplund, C. L., Ginther, M. R.,... Marois, R. (2014). Corticolimbic gating of emotion-driven punishment. *Nature Neuroscience, 17,* 1270–1275.

Treisman A. [M.] (2006). How the deployment of attention determines what we see. *Visual Cognition, 14,* 411–443.

Treisman, A. M., & Gelade, G. (1980). A feature integration theory of attention. *Cognitive Psychology, 12,* 97–136.

Treisman, M. (1977). Motion sickness: An evolutionary hypothesis. *Science, 197,* 493.

Tremblay, A., Doucet, E., & Imbeault, P. (1999). Physical activity and weight maintenance. *International Journal of Obesity, 23*(3), S50–S54.

Tremblay, P., & Dick, A. S. (2016). Broca and Wernicke are dead, or moving past the classic model of language neurobiology. *Brain and Language, 162,* 60–71. doi:10.1016/j.bandl.2016.08.004

Triandis, H. (1971). *Attitude and attitude change.* New York: Wiley.

Trojak, B., Sauvaget, A., Fecteau, S., Lalanne, L., Chauvet-Gelinier, J. C., Koch, S.,... Achab, S. (2017). Outcome of non-invasive brain stimulation in substance use disorders: A review of randomized sham-controlled clinical trials. *Journal of Neuropsychiatry and Clinical Neurosciences, 29*(2), 105–118. doi:10.1176/appi.neuropsych.16080147

Troncoso, X. G., Macknik, S. L., Otero-Millan, J., & Martinez-Conde, S. (2008). Microsaccades drive illusory motion in the enigma illusion. *Proceedings of the National Academy of Sciences, USA, 105*(41), 16033–16038.

Trumbull, E., & Rothstein-Fisch, C. (2011). The intersection of culture and achievement motivation. *eSchool Community Journal, 21*(2), 25–53.

Truong, K. D., Reifsnider, O. S., Mayorga, M. E., & Spitler, H. (2012). Estimated number of preterm births and low birth weight children born in the United States due to maternal binge drinking. *Maternal and Child Health Journal, 17*(4), 677–688.

Trut, L. M. (1999). Early canid domestication: The Farm-Fox experiment. *Science, 283.*

Trzaskowski, M., Harlaar, N., Arden, R., Krapohl, E., Rimfeld, K., McMillan, A.,... Plomin, R. (2014). Genetic influence on family socioeconomic status and children's intelligence. *Intelligence, 42*(100), 83–88. doi: 10.1016/j.intell.2013.11.002

Trzaskowski, M., Zavos, H.M., Haworth, C.M., Plomin, R., & Eley, T.C. (2012). Stable genetic influence on anxiety-related behaviours across middle childhood. *Journal of Abnormal Child Psychology, 40*(1), 85–94. doi: 10.1007/s10802-011-9545-z

Tsai, G. E., Condle, D., Wu, M-T., & Chang, I-W. (1999). Functional magnetic resonance imaging of personality switches in a woman with dissociative identity disorder. *Harvard Review of Psychiatry, 7,* 119–122.

Tsai, J. L., Simeonova, D. I., & Watanabe, J. T. (2004). Somatic and social: Chinese Americans talk about emotion. *Personality and Social Psychology Bulletin, 30*(9), 1226–1238.

Tucker, M. A., Hirota, Y., Wamsley, E. J., Lau, H., Chaklader, A., & Fishbein, W. (2006). A daytime nap containing solely non-REM sleep enhances declarative but not procedural memory. *Neurobiology of Learning and Memory, 86*(2), 241–247.

Tugade, M. M., & Fredrickson, B. L. (2004). Resilient individuals use positive emotions to bounce back from negative emotional experiences. *Journal of Personality and Social Psychology, 86*(2), 320–333.

Tukuitonga, C. F., & Bindman, A. B. (2002). Ethnic and gender differences in the use of coronary artery revascularisation procedures in New Zealand. *New Zealand Medical Journal, 115,* 179–182.

Tulving, E., & Thomson, D. M. (1973). Encoding specificity and retrieval processes in episodic memory. *Psychological Review, 80,* 352–373.

Tupak, S. V., Dresler, T., Badewien, M., Hahn, T., Ernst, L. H., Herrmann, M. J.,... Fallgatter, A. J. (2013). Inhibitory transcranial magnetic theta burst stimulation attenuates prefrontal cortex oxygenation. *Human Brain Mapping, 34*(1), 150–157. doi: 10.1002/hbm.21421

Tusel, D. J., Piotrowski, N. A., Sees, K., Reilly, P. M., Banys, P., Meek, P., & Hall, S. M. (1994). Contingency contracting for illicit drug use with opioid addicts in methadone treatment. In L. S. Harris (Ed.), *Problems of drug dependence: Proceedings of the 56th Annual Scientific Meeting.* (National Institute on Drug Abuse Research Monograph No. 153, pp. 155–160). Washington, DC: U.S. Goverment Printing Office.

Tversky, A., & Kahneman, D. (1973). Availability: A heuristic for judging frequency and probability. *Cognitive Psychology, 5*(2), 207–232.

Tversky, A., & Shafir, E. (1992). The disjunction effect in choice under uncertainty. *Psychological Science, 3*(5), 305–309.

Twenge, J. M., Joiner, T. E., Rogers, M. L., & Martin, G. N. (2017). Increases in depressive symptoms, suicide-related outcomes, and suicide rates among U.S. adolescents after 2010 and links to increased new media screen time. *Clinical Psychological Science, 6*(1), 3–17. doi:10.1177/2167702617723376

Twenge, J. M., Krizan, Z., & Hisler, G. (2017). Decreases in self-reported sleep duration among U.S. adolescents 2009–2015 and links to new media screen time. *Sleep Medicine, 39,* 47–53. DOI: 10.1016/j.sleep.2017.08.013

U.S. Department of Health and Human Services. (2010). *How tobacco smoke causes disease: What it means to you.* Atlanta, GA: U.S. Department of Health and Human Services, Centers for Disease Control and Prevention, National Center for Chronic Disease Prevention and Health Promotion, Office on Smoking and Health.

U.S. Department of Health and Human Services. (2014). *The health consequences of smoking—50 years of progress: A report of the Surgeon General.* Atlanta, GA: U.S. Department of Health and Human Services, Centers for Disease Control and Prevention, National Center for Chronic Disease Prevention and Health Promotion, Office on Smoking and Health (accessed October 5, 2015) at http://www.surgeongeneral.gov/library/reports/50-years-of-progress/full-report.pdf.

U.S. Department of Health and Human Services. (2018). *Physical activity guidelines for Americans.* Retrieved from https://health.gov/paguidelines/second-edition/pdf/Physical_Activity_Guidelines_2nd_edition.pdf

Umemura, T., Lacinová, L., Kotrčová, K., & Fraley, R. C. (2018). Similarities and differences regarding changes in attachment preferences and attachment styles in relation to romantic relationship length: Longitudinal and concurrent analyses. *Attachment & Human Development, 20*(2): 135–159. DOI: https://doi.org/10.1080/14616734.2017.1383488

Uncapher, M. R., Lin, L., Rosen, L. D., Kirkorian, H. L., Baron, N. S., Bailey, K., . . . Wagner, A. D. (2017). Media multitasking and cognitive, psychological, neural, and learning differences. *Pediatrics, 140*(Suppl 2), S62–S66. doi:10.1542/peds.2016-1758D

Uncapher, M. R., M. K. T., & Wagner, A. D. (2016). Media multitasking and memory: Differences in working memory and long-term memory. *Psychonomic Bulletin & Review, 23*(2), 483-490. doi:10.3758/s13423-015-0907-3

Underwood, M. K., Beron, K. J., & Rosen, L. H. (2009). Continuity and change in social and physical aggression from middle childhood through early adolescence. *Aggressive Behavior, 35*(5), 357–375.

Unger, R. (1979). Toward a redefinition of sex and gender. *American Psychologist, 34,* 1085–1094.

United Nations Office on Drugs and Crime (UNODC). (2014). World drug report. Retrieved from http://www.unodc.org/documents/wdr2014/World_Drug_Report_2014_web.pdf.

Unsworth, N., Fukuda, K., Awh, E., & Vogel, E. K. (2014). Working memory and fluid intelligence: Capacity, attention control, and secondary memory retrieval. *Cognitive Psychology, 71,* 1–26. doi: 10.1016/j.cogpsych.2014.01.003

Unsworth, N., Fukuda, K., Awh, E., & Vogel, E. K. (2015). Working memory delay activity predicts individual differences in cognitive abilities. *Journal of Cognitive Neuroscience, 27*(5), 853–865. doi: 10.1162/jocn_a_00765

Upthegrove, T., Roscigno, V., & Charles, C. (1999). Big money collegiate sports: Racial concentration, contradictory pressures, and academic performance. *Social Science Quarterly, 80,* 718–737.

Ursini, G., Punzi, G., Chen, Q., Marenco, S., Robinson, J. F., Porcelli, A.,… & Weinberger, D. R. (2018). Convergence of placenta biology and genetic risk for schizophrenia. *Nature Medicine, 24:* 792–801. DOI: http://dx.doi.org/10.1038/s41591-018-0021-y

Vadillo, M. A., Konstantinidis, E., & Shanks, D. R. (2016). Underpowered samples, false negatives, and unconscious learning. Psychonomic Bulletin & Review, 23(1), 87–102. doi: 10.3758/s13423-015-0892-6

Vail, A. (1976). Factors influencing lower class, black patients' remaining in treatment. *Clinical Psychology, 29,* 12–14.

Vaillant, G. E. (2002). Adaptive mental mechanisms: Their role in a positive psychology. *American Psychologist, 55,* 89–98.

Vainik, U., Baker, T. E., Dadar, M., Zeighami, Y., Michaud, A., Zhang, Y.,… Dagher, A. (2018). Neurobehavioral correlates of obesity are largely heritable. *Proceedings of the National Academy of Sciences of the United States of America, 115*(37), 9312–9317. doi:10.1073/pnas.1718206115

Valerio, S., & Taube, J. S. (2016). Head direction cell activity is absent in mice without the horizontal semicircular canals. *The Journal of Neuroscience, 36*(3), 741–754. doi: 10.1523/JNEUROSCI.3790-14.2016

Val-Laillet, D., Aarts, E., Weber, B., Ferrari, M., Quaresima, V., Stoeckel, L. E.,… Stice, E. (2015). Neuroimaging and neuromodulation approaches to study eating behavior and prevent and treat eating disorders and obesity. *NeuroImage: Clinical, 8,* 1–31. doi: 10.1016/j.nicl.2015.03.016

Valverde, R., Pozdnyakova, I., Kajander, T., Venkatraman, J., & Regan, L. (2007). Fragile X mental retardation syndrome: Structure of the KH1-KH2 domains of fragile X mental retardation protein. *Structure, 9,* 1090–1098.

Van de Castle, R. (1994). *Our dreaming mind.* New York: Ballantine Books.

Van de Garde-Perik, E., Markopoulos, P., de Ruyter, B., Eggen, B., & IJsselsteijn, W. A. (2008). Investigating privacy attitudes and behavior in relation to personalization. *Social Science Computer Review, 26*(1), 20–44.

van der Linden, S., Maibach, E., & Leiserowitz, A. (2015). Improving public engagement with climate change: Five "best practice" insights from psychological science. *Perspectives on Psychological Science, 10,* 758–763.

van der Merwe, A., & Garuccio, A. (Eds.). (1994). *Waves and particles in light and matter.* New York: Plenum Press.

Van der Stigchel, S., & Hollingworth, A. (2018). Visuospatial working memory as a fundamental component of the eye movement system. *Current Directions in Psychological Science, 27*(2): 136–143. DOI: https://doi.org/10.1177%2F0963721417741710

Van Dongen, H. P. A., Maislin, G., Mullington, J. M., & Dinges, D. F. (2003). The cumulative cost of additional wakefulness: Dose-response effects on neurobehavioral functions and sleep physiology from chronic sleep restriction and total sleep deprivation. *Sleep, 26,* 117–126.

van Duijl, M., Nijenhuis, E., Komproe, I. H., Gernaat, H. B., & de Jong, J. T. (2010). Dissociative symptoms and reported trauma among patients with spirit possession and matched healthy controls in Uganda. *Culture, Medicine, and Psychiatry, 34*(2), 380–400. doi: 10.1007/s11013-010-9171-1

Van Horn, J. D., Irimia, A., Torgerson, C. M., Chambers, M. C., Kikinis, R., & Toga, A. W. (2012). Mapping connectivity damage in the case of Phineas Gage. *PLoS ONE, 7*(5), e37454. doi: 10.1371/journal.pone.0037454

Varela, J. A., Wang, J., Christianson, J. P., Maier, S. F., & Cooper, D. C. (2012). Control over stress, but not stress per se increases prefrontal cortical pyramidal neuron excitability. *The Journal of Neuroscience, 32*(37), 12848–12853. doi: 10.1523/jneurosci.2669-12.2012

Varshney, M., & Nalvarte, I. (2017). Genes, gender, environment, and novel functions of estrogen receptor beta in the susceptibility to neurodevelopmental disorders. *Brain Sci, 7*(3). doi:10.3390/brainsci7030024

Vartanian, L. R. (2000). Revisiting the imaginary audience and personal fable constructs of adolescent egocentricism: A conceptual review. *Adolescence, 35*(140), 639–661.

Vecsey, C. G., Baillie, G. S., Jaganath, D., Havekes, R., Daniels, A., Wimmer, M.,… Abel, T. (2009). Sleep deprivation impairs cAMP signaling in the hippocampus. *Nature, 461*(7267), 1122–1125.

Verkhratsky, A., Marutle, A., Rodriguez-Arellano, J. J., & Nordberg, A. (2014). Glial asthenia and functional paralysis: A new perspective on neurodegeneration and Alzheimer's disease. *Neuroscientist.* doi: 10.1177/1073858414547132

Vernon, R. J. W., Sutherland, C. A. M., Young, A. W., & Hartley, T. (2014). Modeling first impressions from highly variable facial images. *Proceedings of the National Academy of Science, 111*(32), E3353–E3361. doi: 10.1073/pnas.1409860111

Vernon, S. W., & Roberts, R. E. (1982). Use of RDC in a tri-ethnic community survey. *Archives of General Psychiatry, 39,* 47.

Victor, T. A., Drevets, W. C., Misaki, M., Bodurka, J., & Savitz, J. (2017). Sex differences in neural responses to subliminal sad and happy faces in healthy individuals: Implications for depression. *Journal of Neuroscience Research, 95*(1–2), 703–710. doi:10.1002/jnr.23870

Villani, S. (2001). Impact of media on children and adolescents: A 10-year review of the research. *Journal of the American Academy on Child and Adolescent Psychiatry, 40*(4), 392–401.

Virkkunen, M., & Linnoila, M. (1996). Serotonin and glucose metabolism in impulsively violent alcoholic offenders. In D. M. Stoff, & R. B. Cairns (Eds.), *Aggression and violence* (pp. 87–100). Mahwah, NJ: Lawrence Erlbaum.

Visser, P. S., & Krosnick, J. A. (1998). Development of attitude strength over the life cycle: Surge and decline. *Journal of Personality and Social Psychology, 75*(6), 1389–1410.

Visser, P. S., & Mirabile, R. R. (2004). Attitudes in the social context: The impact of social network composition on individual-level attitude strength. *Journal of Personality and Social Psychology, 87*(6), 779–795.

Vitorovic, D., & Biller, J. (2013). Musical hallucinations and forgotten tunes—case report and brief literature review. *Frontiers in Neurology, 4,* 109. doi: 10.3389/fneir/2013.00109

Vogel, G. W. (1975). A review of REM sleep deprivation. *Archives of General Psychiatry, 32,* 749–761.

Vogel, G. W. (1993). Selective deprivation, REM sleep. In M. A. Carskadon (Ed.), *The encyclopedia of sleep and dreaming.* New York: Macmillan.

Vogt, B. A., & Palomero-Gallagher, N. (2012). Cingulate cortex. In J. K. Mai & G. Paxinos (Eds.), *The human nervous system* (pp. 943–987). London, UK: Academic Press.

Vokey, J. R., & Read J. D. (1985). Subliminal messages: Between the devil and the media. *American Psychologist, 40,* 1231–1239.

Volkow, N. D., Wise, R. A., & Baler, R. (2017). The dopamine motive system: Implications for drug and food addiction. *Nature Reviews Neuroscience, 18*(12), 741–752. doi: 10.1038/nrn.2017.130

von Bastian, C. C., Souza, A. S., & Gade, M. (2016). No evidence for bilingual cognitive advantages: A test of four hypotheses. *Journal of Experimental Psychology: General, 145*(2), 246–258. doi: 10.1037/xge0000120

Von der Beck, I., Oeberst, A., Cress, U., & Nestler, S. (2017). Cultural interpretations of global information? Hindsight bias after reading Wikipedia articles across cultures. *Applied Cognitive Psychology, 31*(3): 315–325. DOI: https://doi.org/10.1002/acp.3329

von Helmholtz, H. (1852). On the theory of compound colours. *Philosophical Magazine, 4*, 519–535.

von Helmholtz, H. L. F. (1863). *Die Lehre von den Tonempfindungen als physiologische Grundlage fur die Theorie der Musik* (1954, XX, trans. by Alexander J. Ellis). *On the sensations of tone as a physiological basis for the theory of music.* New York: Dover.

von Hofsten, O., von Hofsten, C., Sulutvedt, U., Laeng, B., Brennen, T., & Magnussen, S. (2014). Simulating newborn face perception. *Journal of Vision, 14*, 16.

von Stumm, S., & Plomin, R. (2015). Socioeconomic status and the growth of intelligence from infancy through adolescence. *Intelligence, 48*, 30–36. doi: 10.1016/j.intell.2014.10.002

Voogd, J., & Ruigrok, T. J. H. (2012). Cerebellum and precerebellar nuceli. In J. K. Mai & G. Paxinos (Eds.), *The human nervous system* (pp. 471–545). London, UK: Academic Press.

Voyer, D., & Rodgers, M. (2002). Reliability of laterality effects in a dichotic listening task with nonverbal material. *Brain & Cognition, 48*, 602–606.

Vrij, A. (2015). The protection of innocent suspects: A comment on Palmatier and Rovner (2015). *International Journal of Psychophysiology, 95*(1), 20–21.

Vygotsky, L. S. (1934/1962). *Thought and language.* Cambridge, MA: MIT Press.

Vygotsky, L. S. (1978). *Mind in society: The development of higher psychological processes.* Cambridge, MA: Harvard University Press.

Vygotsky, L. S. (1987). Thought and word. In R. W. Riebe & A. S. Carton (Eds.), *The collected works of L. S. Vygotsky: Vol. 1. Problems of general psychology* (pp. 243–288). New York: Plenum.

Wade, T. D., Gordon, S., Medland, S., Bulik, C. M., Heath, A. C., Montgomery, G. W., & Martin, N. G. (2013). Genetic variants associated with disordered eating. *The International Journal of Eating Disorders.* doi: 10.1002/eat.22133

Wagenmakers, E. J., Beek, T., Dijkhoff, L., Gronau, Q. F., Acosta, A., Adams, R. B.,... Zwaan, R. A. (2016). Registered replication report: Strack, Martin, & Stepper (1988). *Perspectives on Psychological Science, 11*(6), 917–928. doi:10.1177/1745691616674458

Wahlsten, D. (1997). The malleability of intelligence is not constrained by heritability. In B. Devlin, S. E. Fienberg, & K. Roeder, *Intelligence, genes, and success: Scientists respond to the bell curve* (pp. 71–87). New York: Springer.

Wakefield, A. J., Murch, S. H., Anthony, A., Linnell, J., Casson, D. M., Malik, M.,... Walker-Smith J., A. (1998). Ileal-lymphoid-nodular hyperplasia, non-specific colitis, and pervasive developmental disorder in children. *The Lancet, 351*, 9103.

Walker, L. J. (1991). Sex differences in moral reasoning. In W. M. Kurtines & J. L. Gewirtz (Eds.), *Handbook of moral behavior and development: Vol. 2. Research* (pp. 333–364). Hillsdale, NJ: Lawrence Erlbaum.

Walker, M. P. (2005). A refined model of sleep and the time course of memory formation. *Behavioral and Brain Sciences, 28*, 51–64.

Walker, P., Francis, B. J., & Walker, L. (2010). The brightness-weight illusion. *Experimental Psychology, 57*(6), 462–469. doi: 10.1027/1618-3169/a000057

Walter, C. (2008). Affairs of the lips. *Scientific American Mind, 19*(6), 24.

Wampold, B. E. (1997). Methodological problems in identifying efficacious psychotherapies. *Psychotherapy Research, 7*, 21–43.

Wampold, B. E. (2010). *The basics of psychotherapy: An introduction to theory and practice.* Washington, DC, US: American Psychological Association.

Wang, H. N., Wang, X. X., Zhang, R. G., Wang, Y., Cai, M., Zhang, Y. H.,... Zhang, Z. J. (2017). Clustered repetitive transcranial magnetic stimulation for the prevention of depressive relapse/recurrence: A randomized controlled trial. *Translational Psychiatry, 7*(12), 1292. doi:10.1038/s41398-017-0001-x

Wang, T., Shi, F., Jin, Y., Yap, P. T., Wee, C. Y., Zhang, J.,... Shen, D. (2016). Multilevel deficiency of white matter connectivity networks in Alzheimer's disease: A diffusion MRI study with DTI and Hardi models. *Neural Plasticity,* 2016, 2947136. doi: 10.1155/2016/2947136

Wang, Z., David, P., Srivastava, J., Powers, S., Brady, C., D'Angelo, J., & Moreland, J. (2012). Behavioral performance and visual attention in communication multitasking: A comparison between instant messaging and online voice chat. *Computers in Human Behavior, 28*(3), 968.

Ward, A. S., Li, D. H., Luedtke, R. R., & Emmett-Oglesby, M. W. (1996). Variations in cocaine self-administration by inbred rat strains under a progressive-ratio schedule. *Psychopharmacology, 127*(3), 204–212.

Ward, C., & Rana-Deuba, A. (1999). Acculturation and adaptation revisited. *Journal of Cross-Cultural Psychology, 30*, 422–442.

Ward, J., Mattic, K. R. P., & Hall, W. (1999). *Methadone maintenance treatment and other opioid replacement therapies.* Sydney, Australia: Harwood Academic.

Ward, M. M., Lotstein, D. S., Bush, T. M., Lambert, R. E., van Vollenhoven, R., & Neuwelt, C. M. (1999). Psychosocial correlates of morbidity in women with systemic lupus erythematosus. *Journal of Rheumatology, 26*, 2153–2158.

Ward, R. D., Gallistel, C. R., Jensen, G., Richards, V. L., Fairhurst, S., & Balsam, P. D. (2012). Conditioned stimulus informativeness governs conditioned stimulus-unconditioned stimulus associability. *Journal of Experimental Psychology: Animal Behavior Processes, 38*: 217–232.

Ware, M. A., Wang, T., Shapiro, S., & Collet, J.-P. (2015). Cannabis for the management of pain: Assessment of safety study (COMPASS). *The Journal of Pain.* doi: 10.1016/j.jpain.2015.07.014

Wartner, U. G., Grossmann, K., Fremmer-Bombik, E., & Suess, G. (1994). Attachment patterns at age six in south Germany: Predictability from infancy and implications for preschool behavior. *Child Development, 65*, 1014–1027.

Washburn, A. N., Hanson, B. E., Motyl, M., Skitka, L. J., Yantis, C., Wong, K. M.,... Carsel, T. S. (2018). Why do some psychology researchers resist adopting proposed reforms to research practices? A description of researchers' rationales. *Advances in Methods and Practices in Psychological Science, 1*(2): 166–173. DOI: https://doi.org/10.1177/2515245918757427

Washburn, M. F. (1908). *The animal mind: A text-book of comparative psychology.* New York: Macmillan.

Wasserman, E. A., & Miller, R. R. (1997). What's elementary about associative learning? *Annual Review of Psychology, 48*, 573–607.

Waterhouse, L. (2006a). Inadequate evidence for multiple intelligences, Mozart effect, and emotional intelligence theories. *Educational Psychologist, 41*(4), 247–255.

Waterhouse, L. (2006b). Multiple intelligences, the Mozart effect, and emotional intelligence: A critical review. *Educational Psychologist, 41*, 207–225.

Waterman, A. S. (2013). The humanistic psychology–positive psychology divide: Contrasts in philosophical foundations. *American Psychologist, 68*(3), 124–133. doi: 10.1037/a0032168

Watkins, C. E., Campbell, V. L., Nieberding, R., & Hallmark, R. (1995). Contemporary practice of psychological assessment by clinical psychologists. *Professional Psychology: Research and Practice, 26*, 54–60.

Watkins, C. E., Jr., & Savickas, M. L. (1990). Psychodynamic career counseling. In W. B. Walsh & S. H. Osipow (Eds.), *Career counseling: Contemporary topics in vocational psychology* (pp. 79–116). Hillsdale, NJ: Lawrence Erlbaum.

Watson, D. L., Hagihara, D. K., & Tenney, A. L. (1999). Skill-building exercises and generalizing psychological concepts to daily life. *Teaching of Psychology, 26*, 193–195.

Watson, J. B. (1913). Psychology as the behaviorist views it. *Psychological Review, 20*, 158–177.

Watson, J. B. (1924). *Behaviorism.* New York: W. W. Norton.

Watson, J. B., & Rayner, R. (1920). Conditioned emotional responses. *Journal of Experimental Psychology, 3*, 1–14.

Watson, J. C., Steckley, P. L., & McMullen, E. J. (2014). The role of empathy in promoting change. *Psychotherapy Research, 24*(3), 286–298. doi: 10.1080/10503307.2013.802823

Watson, J. M., & Strayer, D. L. (2010). Supertaskers: Profiles in extraordinary multitasking ability. *Psychonomic Bulletin & Review, 17*(4), 479–485.

Watson, N. F., Buchwald, D., Delrow, UJ. J., Altemeier, W. A., Vitiellow, M. V.,... & Gharib, S. A. (2017). Transcriptional signatures of sleep duration discordance in monozygotic twins. *Sleep, 40*(1), zsw019. DOI: https://doi.org/10.1093/sleep/zsw019

Waytz, A., Young, L. L., & Ginges, J. (2014). Motive attribution asymmetry for love vs. hate drives intractable conflict. *Proceedings of the National Academy of Sciences, 111*(44), 15387.

Webb, W. B. (1992). *Sleep: The gentle tyrant* (2nd ed.). Bolton, MA: Ander.

Weber, F., Chung, S., Beier, K. T., Xu, M., Luo, L., & Dan, Y. (2015). Control of REM sleep by ventral medulla GABAergic neurons. *Nature, 526*(7573), 435–438. doi: 10.1038/nature14979

Wechsler, D. (1975). *The collected papers of David Wechsler.* New York: Academic Press.

Wechsler, D. (2008). *Wechsler adult intelligence scale* (4th ed.). Bloomington, MN: Pearson.

Wechsler, D. (2012). *Wechsler preschool and primary scale of intelligence* (4th ed.). Bloomington, MN: Pearson.

Wechsler, D. (2014). *Wechsler intelligence scale for children* (5th ed.) Bloomington, MN: Pearson.

Wedding, D. (2005). Cross-cultural counseling and psychotherapy. In R. J. Corsini & D. Wedding (Eds.), *Current psychotherapies* (7th ed., p. 485). Itasca, IL: Peacock.

Weinberger, D. R. (1987). Implications of normal brain development for the pathogenesis of schizophrenia. *Archives of General Psychiatry, 44*, 660–668.

Weiner, B. (1985). An attributional theory of achievement motivation. *Psychological Review, 92*, 548–573.

Weiner, I. B. (1997). Current status of the Rorschach Inkblot Method. *Journal of Personality Assessment, 68*, 5–19.

Weiner, I. B. (2013). Applying Rorschach assessment. In G. P. Koocher, J. C. Norcross & B. A. Greene (Eds.), *Psychologists' desk reference* (pp. 148–152). New York, NY: Oxford University Press

Weiner, R. D. (2000). Retrograde amnesia with electroconvulsive therapy: Characteristics and implications. *Archives of General Psychiatry, 57*, 591–592.

Weis, S., Klaver, P., Reul, J., Elger, C. E., & Fernandez, G. (2004). Temporal and cerebellar brain regions that support both declarative memory formation and retrieval. *Cerebral Cortex, 14,* 256–267.

Weisman, A. (1972). *On dying and denying.* New York: Behavioral Publications.

Weiss, J. M. (1972). Psychological factors in stress and disease. *Scientific American, 26,* 104–113.

Weiss, N. H., Johnson, C. D., Contractor, A., Peasant, C., Swan, S. C., & Sullivan, T. P. (2017). Racial/ethnic differences moderate associations of coping strategies and posttraumatic stress disorder symptom clusters among women experiencing partner violence: A multigroup path analysis. *Anxiety Stress Coping, 30*(3), 347–363. doi:10.1080/10615806.2016.1228900

Weisse, C. S. (1992). Depression and immunocompetence: A review of the literature. *Psychological Bulletin, 111,* 475–489.

Weissman, M. M., & Klerman, G. L. (1977). Sex differences and the epidemiology of depression. *Archives of General Psychiatry, 34,* 98–111.

Welch, E., Ghaderi, A., & Swenne, I. (2015). A comparison of clinical characteristics between adolescent males and females with eating disorders. *BMC Psychiatry, 15,* 45. doi: 10.1186/s12888-015-0419-8

Wenneberg, S. R., Schneider, R. H., Walton, K. G., Maclean, C. R., Levitsky, D. K., Mandarino, J. V.,... Wallace, R. K. (1997). Anger expression correlates with platelet aggregation. *Behavioral Medicine, 22*(4), 174–177.

Wenzel, J. M., Oleson, E. B., Gove, W. N., Cole, A. B., Gyawali, U., Dantrassy, H. M, ... Cheer, J. F. (2018). Phasic dopamine signals in the nucleus accumbens that cause active avoidance require endocannabinoid mobilization in the midbrain. *Current Biology, 28*(9), 1392–1404. DOI: https://doi.org/10.1016/j.cub.2018.03.037

Werker, J. F., & Lalonde, C. E. (1988). Cross-language speech perceptions: Initial capabilities and developmental change. *Developmental Psychology, 24,* 672–683.

Wertheimer, M. (1982). *Productive thinking.* Chicago: University of Chicago Press.

Westen, D. (2005). Cognitive neuroscience and psychotherapy: Implications for psychotherapy's second century. In G. Gabbard, J. Beck, & J. Holmes (Eds.), *Oxford textbook of psychotherapy.* Oxford, UK: Oxford University Press.

Wetherell, J. L. (2002). Behavior therapy for anxious older adults. *Behavior Therapist, 25,* 16–17.

Wever, E. G. (1949). *Theory of hearing.* New York: John Wiley & Sons.

Wever, E. G., & Bray, C. W. (1930). The nature of acoustic response: The relation between sound frequency and frequency of impulses in the auditory nerve. *Journal of Experimental Psychology, 13*(5), 373–387.

Weyant, J. M. (1996). Application of compliance techniques to direct-mail requests for charitable donations. *Psychology and Marketing, 13,* 157–170.

White, G. L. (1980). Physical attractiveness and courtship progress. *Journal of Personality and Social Psychology, 39,* 660–668.

White, S. (2000). *The transgender debate (the crisis surrounding gender identity).* Reading, UK: Garnet.

Whiting, D. M., Tomycz, N. D., Bailes, J., de Jonge, L., Lecoultre, V., Wilent, B.,... Oh, M. Y. (2013). Lateral hypothalamic area deep brain stimulation for refractory obesity: A pilot study with preliminary data on safety, body weight, and energy metabolism. *Journal of Neurosurgery, 119*(1), 56–63. doi: 10.3171/2013.2.jns12903

Whorf, B. L. (1956). *Language, thought and reality.* New York: Wiley.

Wicker, A. W. (1971). An examination of the "other variables" explanation of attitude–behavior inconsistency. *Journal of Personality and Social Psychology, 19,* 18–30.

Widom, C. S., Czaja, S. J., Kozakowski, S. S., & Chauhan, P. (2018). Does adult attachment style mediate the relationship between childhood maltreatment and mental and physical health outcomes? *Child Abuse & Neglect, 76,* 533-545. DOI: https://doi.org/10.1016/j.chiabu.2017.05.002

Wiggert, N., Wilhelm, F. H., Derntl, B., & Blechert, J. (2015). Gender differences in experiential and facial reactivity to approval and disapproval during emotional social interactions. *Frontiers in Psychology, 6,* 1372.

Wild, C. J., Nichols, E. S., Battista, M. E., Stojanoski, B., & Owen, A. M. (2018). Dissociable effects of self-reported daily sleep duration on high-level cognitive abilities. *Sleep.* doi:10.1093/sleep/zsy182

Wiley, J., & Jarosz, A. F. (2012). Working memory capacity, attentional focus, and problem solving. *Current Directions in Psychological Science, 21*(4), 258.

Wilfley, D. E., & Eichen, D. M. (2017). Interpersonal psychotherapy *Eating disorders and obesity: A comprehensive handbook* (3rd ed., pp. 290–295). New York, NY: Guilford Press.

Wilhelm, I., Kurth, S., Ringli, M., Mouthon, A. L., Buchmann, A., Geiger, A.,... Huber, R. (2014). Sleep slow-wave activity reveals developmental changes in experience-dependent plasticity. *Journal of Neuroscience, 34*(37), 12568–12575. doi: 10.1523/JNEUROSCI.0962-14.2014

Wilhelm, I., Rose, M., Imhof, K. I., Rasch, B., Buechel, C., & Born, J. (2013). The sleeping child outplays the adult's capacity to convert implicit into explicit knowledge. *Nature Neuroscience.* doi: 10.1038/nn.3343

Wilkinson, D., Schaefer, G. O., Tremellen, K., & Savulescu, J. (2015). Double trouble: Should double embryo transfer be banned? *Theoretical Medicine and Bioethics, 36,* 121–139.

Williams, J. A., Bartoshuk, L. M., Fillingim, R. B., & Dotson, C. D. (2016). Exploring ethnic differences in taste perception. *Chemical Senses, 41*(5), 449–456. doi:10.1093/chemse/bjw021

Williams, J. F., & Smith, V. C. (2015). Fetal alcohol spectrum disorders. *Pediatrics, 136*(5), e1395–e1406.

Williams, M. E. (1995). *The American Geriatrics Society's complete guide to aging and mental health.* New York: Random House.

Williams, R. B. (1999). A 69-year-old man with anger and angina. *Journal of the American Medical Association, 282,* 763–770.

Williams, R. B. (2001). Hostility: Effects on health and the potential for successful behavioral approaches to prevention and treatment. In A. Baum, T. A. Revenson, & J. E. Singer (Eds.), *Handbook of Health Psychology.* Mahwah, NJ: Erlbaum, 661–668.

Williams, R. B., Haney, T. L., Lee, K. L., Kong, Y. H., Blumenthal, J. A., & Whalen, R. E. (1980). Type A behavior, hostility, and coronary atherosclerosis. *Psychosomatic Medicine, 42*(6), 539–549.

Willoughby, T., Good, M., Adachi, P. J. C., Hamza, C., & Tavernier, R. (2013). Examining the link between adolescent brain development and risk taking from a social-developmental perspective. *Brain and Cognition, 83,* 315–323.

Wilson, B. M., Mickes, L., Stolarz-Fantino, S., Evrard, M., & Fantino, E. (2015). Increased false-memory susceptibility after mindfulness meditation. *Psychological Science, 26*(10): 1567-1573. DOI: https://doi.org/10.1177/0956797615593705

Wilson, S. M., Darling, K. E., Fahrenkamp, A. J., D'Auria, A. L., & Sato, A. F. (2015). Predictors of emotional eating during adolescents' transition to college: Does body mass index moderate the association between stress and emotional eating? *Journal of American College Health, 63*(3), 163–170.

Wimber, M., Alink, A., Charest, I., Kriegeskorte, N., & Anderson, M. C. (2015). Retrieval induces adaptive forgetting of competing memories via cortical pattern suppression. *Nature Neuroscience, 18,* 582–589.

Winlove, C. I. P., Milton, F., Ranson, J., Fulford, J., MacKisack, M., Macpherson, F., & Zeman, A. (2018). The neural correlates of visual imagery: A co-ordinate-based meta-analysis. *Cortex, 105,* 4–25. doi:10.1016/j.cortex.2017.12.014

Winningham, R. G., Hyman, I. E., Jr., & Dinnel, D. L. (2000). Flashbulb memories? The effects of when the initial memory report was obtained. *Memory, 8,* 209–216.

Winslow, J. T., Hastings, N., Carter, C. S., Harbaugh, C. R., & Insel, T. R. (1993). A role for central vasopressin in pair bonding in monogamous prairie voles. *Nature, 365*(6446), 545–548. doi: 10.1038/365545a0

Winthorst, W. H., Roest, A. M., Bos, E. H., Meesters, Y., Penninx, B., Nolen, W. A., & de Jonge, P. (2017). Seasonal affective disorder and non-seasonal affective disorders: Results from the nesda study. *BJPsych Open, 3*(4), 196–203. doi:10.1192/bjpo.bp.116.004960

Winton, W. M. (1987). Do introductory textbooks present the Yerkes-Dodson law correctly? *American Psychologist, 42*(2), 202–203.

Wiseman, R. (2007). *Quirkology: How we discover the big truths in small things* (pp. 7–8, 28–29). New York: Basic Books.

Witt, W. P., Litzelman, K., Cheng, E. R., Wakeel, F., & Barker, E. S. (2014). Measuring stress before and during pregnancy: A review of population-based studies of obstetric outcomes. *Maternal and Child Health Journal, 18,* 52–63.

Wixted, J. T., Mickes, L., & Fisher, R. P. (2018). Rethinking the reliability of eyewitness memory. *Perspectives on Psychological Science, 13*(3): 324-335. DOI: https://doi.org/10.1177%2F1745691617734878

WLS-TV, Chicago. (2017, April 3). 2nd juvenile arrested in Facebook live gang rape of girl, 15. Eyewitness news, Chicago. Retrieved from http://abc7chicago.com/news/2nd-juvenile-arrested-in-facebook-live-gang-rape-of-girl-15/1831536/

Wolberg, L. R. (1977). *The technique of psychotherapy.* New York: Grune & Stratton.

Wolpe, J. (1958). *Psychotherapy by reciprocal inhibition.* Palo Alto, CA, US: Stanford University Press.

Wong, S. Y., Chung, R. Y., Chan, D., Chung, G. K., Li, J., Mak, D.,... Wong, H. (2018). What are the financial barriers to medical care among the poor, the sick and the disabled in the special administrative region of China? *PLoS ONE, 13*(11), e0205794. doi:10.1371/journal.pone.0205794

Wood, E., Zivcakova, L., Gentile, P., Archer, K., De Pasquale, D., & Nosko, A. (2012). Examining the impact of off-task multi-tasking with technology on real-time classroom learning. *Computers & Education, 58*(1), 365-374. doi:10.1016/j.compedu.2011.08.029

Wood, J. M., Lilienfeld, S. O., Nezworski, M. T., Garb, H. N., Allen, K. H., & Wildermuth, J. L. (2010). Validity of Rorschach inkblot scores for discriminating psychopaths from non-psychopaths in forensic populations: A meta-analysis. *Psychological Assessment, 22*(2), 336–349. doi: 10.1037/a0018998

Wood, J. M., Nezworski, M. T., & Stejskal, W. J. (1996). The comprehensive system for the Rorschach: A critical examination. *Psychological Science, 7*(1), 3–10, 14–17.

Woodhouse, A. (2005). Phantom limb sensation. *Clinical and Experimental Pharmacology and Physiology, 32*(1–2), 132–134.

World Health Organization. (2016). Mental disorders. Retrieved from http://www.who.int/mediacentre/factsheets/fs396/en/

World Health Organization. (2017). Global health observatory (GHO) data: Overweight and obesity. Retrieved from http://www.who.int/gho/ncd/risk_factors/overweight_obesity/overweight_adolescents/en/

World Health Organization. (2017a). *Depression and other common mental disorders: Global health estimates.* Retrieved from https://www.who.int/mental_health/management/depression/prevalence_global_health_estimates/en/

World Health Organization. (2018, 4/17/08). World health statistics data visualizations dashboard. Retrieved from http://apps.who.int/gho/data/view.sdg.3-4-data reg?lang=en

Wu, C-C., Lee, G. C., & Lai, H-K. (2004). Using concept maps to aid analysis of concept presentation in high school computer textbooks. *Journal of Education and Information Technologies, 9*(2), 10.1023/B:EAIT.0000027930.09631.a5

Wyman, P. A., Moynihan, J., Eberly, S., Cox, C., Cross, W., Jin, X., & Caserta, M. T. (2007). Association of family stress with natural killer cell activity and the frequency of illnesses in children. *Archives of Pediatric and Adolescent Medicine, 161,* 228–234.

Wynne, C. (1999). Do animals think? The case against the animal mind. *Psychology Today, 32*(6), 50–53.

Xie, L., Kang, H., Xu, Q., Chen, M. J., Liao, Y., Thiyagarajan, M.,... Nedergaard, M. (2013). Sleep drives metabolite clearance from the adult brain. *Science, 342*(6156), 373–377.

Yachison, S., Okoshken, J., & Talwar, V. (2018). Students' reactions to a peer's cheating behavior. *Journal of Educational Psychology, 110*(6), 747–763. doi:10.1037/edu0000227

Yaffe, K., Vittinghoff, E., Lindquist, K., Barnes, D., Covinsky K. E., Neylan, T.,... Marmar, C. (2010). Posttraumatic stress disorder and risk of dementia among U.S. veterans. *Archives of General Psychiatry, 67*(6), 608–613.

Yalom, I. (1995). *The theory and practice of group psychotherapy* (4th ed.). New York: Basic Books.

Yalom, I. D., & Leszcz, M. (2005). The theory and practice of group psychotherapy (5th ed.). New York, NY: Basic Books.

Yamaguchi, S., Isejima, H., Matsuo, T., Okura, R., Yagita, K., Kobayashi, M., & Okamura, H. (2003). Synchronization of cellular clocks in the suprachiasmatic nucleus. *Science, 302,* 1408–1412.

Yamamuro, K., Kimoto, S., Rosen, K. M., Kishimoto, T., & Makinodan, M. (2015). Potential primary roles of glial cells in the mechanisms of psychiatric disorders. *Frontiers in Cellular Neuroscience, 9,* 154. doi: 10.3389/fncel.2015.00154

Yang, C., Ba, H., Cao, Y., Dong, G., Zhang, S., Gao, Z.,... Zhou, X. (2017). Linking y-chromosomal short tandem repeat loci to human male impulsive aggression. *Brain, Behavior, and Immunity, 7*(11), e00855. doi:10.1002/brb3.855

Yang, C., Potts, R., & Shanks, D. R. (2018). Enhancing learning and retrieval of new information: A review of the forward testing effect. *Nature Partner Journals: Science of Learning, 3*(8). DOI: https://doi.org/10.1038/s41539-018-0024-y

Yang, Y., Raine, A., & Colletti, P. (2010). Morphological alterations in the prefrontal cortex and the amygdala in unsuccessful psychopaths. *Journal of Abnormal Psychology, 119,* 546–554.

Yarkoni, T. (2015). Neurobiological substrates of personality: A critical overview. In M. Mikulincer & P. R. Shaver (Eds.), *APA handbook of personality and social psychology, Vol. 4: Personality processes and individual differences* (pp. 61–83). Washington, DC: American Psychological Association.

Yavuz, E., Maul, P., & Nowotny, T. (2015). Spiking neural network model of reinforcement learning in the honeybee implemented on the GPU. *BMC Neuroscience, 16*(1), 181.

Ye, Y., & Lin, L. (2015). Examining relations between locus of control, loneliness, subjective well-being, and preference for online social interaction. *Psychological Reports, 116*(1), 164–175. doi: 10.2466/07.09.PR0.116k14w3

Yeager, D. S., Johnson, R., Spitzer, B. J., Trzesniewski, K., Powers, J., & Dweck, C. S. (2014). The far-reaching effects of believing people can change: Implicit theories of personality shape stress, health, and achievement during adolescence. *Journal of Personality and Social Psychology, 106,* 867–884.

Yerkes, R. M. (Ed.). (1921). Psychological examining in the United States Army. *Memoirs of the National Academy of Sciences, 15,* 1–890.

Yerkes, R. M., & Dodson, J. D. (1908). The relation of strength of stimulus to rapidity of habit formation. *Journal of Comparative Neurology and Psychology, 18,* 459–482.

Yeung, M. K., Lee, T. L., Cheung, W. K., & Chan, A. S. (2018). Frontal underactivation during working memory processing in adults with acute partial sleep deprivation: A near-infrared spectroscopy study. *Frontiers in Psychology, 9,* 742. doi:10.3389/fpsyg.2018.00742

Yip, Y. L. (2002, Autumn). Pivot–Qi. *The Journal of Traditional Eastern Health and Fitness, 12*(3).

Yopyk, D., & Prentice, D. A. (2005). Am I an athlete or a student? Identity salience and stereotype threat in student-athletes. *Basic and Applied Social Psychology, 27*(4), 329–336.

Young, J. E., Rygh, J. L., Weinberger, A. D., & Beck, A. T. (2014). Cognitive therapy for depression. In D. H. Barlow (Ed.), *Clinical handbook of psychological disorders: A step-by-step treatment manual* (5th ed., pp. 275–331). New York, NY: The Guilford Press.

Young, S. N. (Ed.). (1996). Melatonin, sleep, aging, and the health protection branch. *Journal of Psychiatry Neuroscience, 21*(3), 161–164.

Yu, C. (2008). Typical dreams experienced by Chinese people. *Dreaming, 18*(1), 1–10 DOI: 10.1037/1053-0797.18.1.1

Yuan, P., & Raz, N. (2014). Prefrontal cortex and executive functions in healthy adults: A meta-analysis of structural neuroimaging studies. *Neuroscience and Biobehavioral Reviews, 42,* 180–192. doi:10.1016/j.neubiorev.2014.02.005

Yule, G. (1996). *Pragmatics.* Oxford: Oxford University Press.

Zadra, A., Desautels, A., Petit, D., & Montplaisir, J. (2013). Somnambulism: Clinical aspects and pathophysiological hypotheses. *The Lancet Neurology, 12*(3), 285.

Zadra, A., Pilon, M., & Montplaisir, J. (2008). Polysomnographic diagnosis of sleepwalking: Effects of sleep deprivation. *Annals of Neurology, 63*(4), 513–519.

Zajonc, R. B. (1965). Social facilitation. *Science, 149,* 269–274.

Zajonc, R. B. (1968). Attitudinal effects of mere exposure. *Journal of Personality and Social Psychology Monographs, 9*(2), 1–27.

Zajonc, R. B. (1980). Feeling and thinking: Preferences need no inferences. *American Psychologist, 35,* 151–175.

Zajonc, R. B. (1984). On the primacy of affect. *American Psychologist, 39,* 117–123.

Zajonc, R. B. (1998). Emotions. In D. T. Gilbert & S. T. Fiske (Eds.), *Handbook of social psychology* (4th ed., Vol. 1, pp. 591–632). New York: McGraw-Hill.

Zajonc, R. B., Heingartner, A., & Herman, E. M. (1970). Social enhancement and impairment of performance in the cockroach. *Journal of Social Psychology, 13*(2), 83–92.

Zarate, C. A., Jr., Brutsche, N. E., Ibrahim, L., Franco-Chaves, J., DiazGranados, N., Cravchik, A.,... Luckenbaugh, D. A. (2012). Replication of ketamine's antidepressant efficacy in bipolar depression: A randomized controlled add-on trial. *Biological Psychiatry, 71*(11), 939–946. doi: 10.1016/j.biopsych.2011.12.010

Zarate, C. A., Jr., Singh, J. B., Carlson, P. J., Brutsche, N. E., Ameli, R., Luckenbaugh, D. A.,... Manji, H. K. (2006). A randomized trial of an N-methyl-D-aspartate antagonist in treatment-resistant major depression. *Archives of General Psychiatry, 63*(8), 856–864. doi: 10.1001/archpsyc.63.8.856

Zedler, B. (1995). "Mary Whiton Calkins." In M. E. Waithe (Ed.), *A history of women philosophers: Vol. 4* (pp. 103–123). Netherlands: Kluwer Academic Publishers.

Zeki, S. (2001). Localization and globalization in conscious vision. *Annual Review of Neuroscience, 24,* 57–86.

Zendle, D., Kudenko, D., & Cairns, P. (2018). Behavioral realism and the activation of aggressive concepts in violent video games. *Entertainment: Computing, 24:* 21–29. DOI: https://doi.org/10.1016/j.entcom.2017.10.003

Zentall, T. R. (2000). Animal intelligence. In R. J. Sternberg (Ed.), *Handbook of intelligence.* Cambridge, MA: Cambridge University Press.

Zhan, Y., Paolicelli, R. C., Sforazzini, F., Weinhard, L., Bolasco, G., Pagani, F.,... & Gross, C. T. (2014). Deficient neuron-microglia signaling results in impaired functional brain connectivity and social behavior. *Nature Neuroscience, 17,* 400–406. doi: 10.1038/nn.3641

Zhang, A., Ferretti, V., Güntan, I., Moro, A., Steinberg, E. A., Ye, Z.,... Franks, N. P. (2015). Neuronal ensembles sufficient for recovery sleep and the sedative actions of a2 adrenergic agonists. *Nature Neuroscience, 18,* 553–561. doi: 10.1038/nn.3957

Zhang, X., Cheng, X., Yu, L., Yang, J., Calvo, R., Patnaik, S.,... Xu, H. (2016). MCOLN1is a ROS sensor in lysosomes that regulates autophagy. *Nature Communications.* Published online June 30, 2016. DOI: 10.1038/ncomms12109

Ziegelmayer, C., Hajak, G., Bauer, A., Held, M., Rupprecht, R., & Trapp, W. (2017). Cognitive performance under electroconvulsive therapy (ECT) in ECT-Naïve treatment-resistant patients with major depressive disorder. *The Journal of ECT, 33*(2): 104–110. DOI: https://doi.org/10.1097/YCT. 0000000000000385

Zilles, K. (1990). Cortex. In G. Paxinos (Ed.), *The human nervous system* (pp. 757–802). San Diego, CA: Academic.

Zillmann, D., Baron, R., & Tamborini, R. (1981). Social costs of smoking: Effects of tobacco smoke on hostile behavior. *Psychology Journal of Applied Social, 11,* 548–561.

Zimbardo, P., Maslach, C., & Haney, C. (2000). Reflections on the Stanford Prison Experiment: Genesis, transformations, consequences. In T. Blass (Ed.), *Obedience to authority: Current perspectives on the Milgram paradigm* (pp. 193–237). London: Lawrence Erlbaum.

Zimbardo, P. G. (1970). The human choice: Individuation, reason, and order versus deindividuation, impulse, and chaos. In N. J. Arnold & D. Levine (Eds.), *Nebraska Symposium on Motivation, 1969.* Lincoln: University of Nebraska Press.

Zimbardo, P. G. (1971). The pathology of imprisonment. *Society, 9*(4–8), 4.

Zimbardo, P. G. (1972). Pathology of imprisonment. *Society, 9*(6), 4–8. doi:10.1007/BF02701755

Zimbardo, P. G. (2007). *The Lucifer effect: Understanding how good people turn evil.* New York, NY: Random House.

Zimbardo, P. G., & Hartley, C. F. (1985). Cults go to high school: A theoretical and empirical analysis of the initial stage in the recruitment process. *Cultic Studies Journal, 2,* 91–148.

Zisapel, N. (2001). Circadian rhythm sleep disorders: Pathophysiology and potential approaches to management. *CNS Drugs, 15*(4), 311–328.

Zlatin, D. M. (1995). Life themes: A method to understand terminal illness. *Omega: Journal of Death and Dying, 31*(3), 189–206. doi: 10.2190/E4BA-ML04-E2BK-7YJE

Zolotor, A. J., & Puzia, M. E. (2010). Bans against corporal punishment: A systematic review of the laws, changes in attitudes and behaviours. *Child Abuse Review, 19*(4), 229–247.

Zolotor, A. J., Theodore, A. D., Chang, J. J., & Laskey, A. L. (2011). Corporal punishment and physical abuse: Population-based trends for three- to 11-year-old children in the United States. *Child Abuse Review, 20*(1), 57–66.

Zorilla, E. P., Luborsky, L., McKay, J. R., Rosenthal, R., Houldin, A., Tax, A.,... & Schmidt, K. (2001). The relationship of depression and stressors to immunological assays: A meta-analytic review. *Brain, Behavior, and Immunity, 15*, 199–226.

Zreik, G., Oppenheim, D., & Sagi-Schwartz, A. (2017). Infant attachment and maternal sensitivity in the Arab minority in Israel. *Child Development, 88*(4): 1338–1349. DOI: https://doi.org/10.1111/cdev.12692

Zucchi, F. C. R., Kirkland, S. W., Jadavji, N. M., van Waes, L. T., Klein, A., Supina, R. D., & Metz, G. A. (2009). Predictable stress versus unpredictable stress: A comparison in a rodent model of stroke. *Behavioural Brain Research, 205*(1), 67–75.

Zuckerman, M. (1979). *Sensation seeking: Beyond the optimal level of arousal*. Hillsdale, NJ: Lawrence Erlbaum.

Zuckerman, M. (1994). *Behavioral expression and biosocial bases of sensation seeking*. New York: Cambridge University Press.

Zuckerman, M. (2002). Zuckerman-Kuhlman Personality Questionnaire (ZKPQ): An alternative five-factorial model. In B. De Raad & M. Perugini (Eds.), *Big Five assessment* (pp. 377–396). Seattle, WA: Hogrefe & Huber.

Zuo, L., & Cramond, B. (2001). An examination of Terman's gifted children from the theory of identity. *Gifted Child Quarterly, 45*(4), 251–259.

Zuvekas, S. H., & Vitiello, B. (2012). Stimulant medication use in children: A 12-year perspective. *American Journal of Psychiatry, 193*, 160–166.

Zvolensky, M. J., Schmidt, M. B., & Stewart, S. H. (2003). Panic disorder and smoking. *Clinical Psychology: Science and Practice, 10*, 29–51.

Name Index

A

á Váli Guttesen, A., 154
AAA Foundation for Traffic Safety, 420
Aarts, E., 610
Abad, V. C., 159
Abadinsky, H., 169
Abbas, A. I., 604
Abbott, L., 175
Abdolmohammadi, B., 291
Abdou, C. M., 465
Abe, K., 297
Abe, M., 399
Abel, E. L., 323
Abel, G. G., 252
Abel, T., PIA-14
Abela, J. R. Z., 588
Abelson, J., 422
Abrahamsen, A., 231
Abramson, L. Y., 498, 543
Accornero, V. H., 172
Accurso, E. C., 557
Achab, S., 67, 610
Acheson, D. J., 236, 237
Acosta, A., 387
Adachi, P. J. C., 473
Adam, K., 151
Adam, S., 354
Adamaszek, M., 76
Adams, D. B., 470
Adams, J. J., 257
Adams, R. B., 387
Adams, R. J., 328
Adams, S. A., 598, 599
Adams, W. G., 470
Addington, A. M., 563
Addis, D. R., 352
Addis, M. E., 587, 588
Ader, R., 409
Adler, A., 8, 493
Adler, S. R., 351
Adluru, N., 69
Adolphs, R., 77, 380
Advokat, C. D., 64, 602, 603, 604, 605
Aeschbach, D., 158
Afifi, T. O., 208
Agarwal, P. K., 246, 248
Agerup, T., 337
Ageta, H., 238
Aggarwal, N. T., 414
Aggen, S. H., 560
Aggleton, J. P., 470
Aghajanian, G. K., 606
Agresti, A., 35
Aguerrevere, L., 518
Aguiar, A., 333
Aguilar, D. D., 179
Aguilar-Gaxiola, S., 534
Ahlenius, H., 323
Ahlskog, J. E., 62
Ahluwalia, N., 377
Ahmed, L., 136
Ahn, W., 274
Ahtiainen, J. P., 89
Aiello, J. R., 442
Ainsworth, M. D. S., 336
Airasian, P. W., PIA-13
Aitchison, J., 275
Ajzen, I., 452

Akana, S., 376
Akerstedt, T., 151, 153
Akil, M., 62
Aksay, S. S., 608
Akula, N., 544
Alabi, N., 297
Aladdin, R., 151
Alamo, C., 604, 605
Albarracin, D., 453
Albazron, F. M., 67
Albert, D., 369
Albert, D. J., 470
Albert, S. M., 161
Albery, E., 585
Alborn, A. M., 89
Albouy, G., 89
Albus, M., 403
Aldag, J. M., 94
Alderfer, C. P., 370
Aldridge-Morris, R., 553
Alegria, M., 557, 598
Aleksejev, R. M., 220
Aleman, A., 511
Alessi, C., 161
Alexander, C., 427
Alexander, C. N., 427
Alexander, G., 470
Alexander, G. C., 177
Alexander, M. P., 236
Alfonso-Miller, P., 154
Alfredsson, L., 413
Algar, O., 323
Algoe, S. B., 94
Ali, M., 62
Alibiglou, L., 156
Aligne, C. A., 421
Alink, A., 257
Alkass, K., 88
Alkon, D., 260
Allen, D., 392, PIA-7
Allen, F., 172
Allen, G., 321
Allen, G. E., 289
Allen, J. J., 222, PIA-6, PIA-7
Allen, J. P., 468
Allen, K. H., 519
Allen, T., 511, 512
Allen, T. A., 506
Allenby, C., 67, 610
Alleyne, V. L., 430
Allik, J., 507
Alloway, T. P., 238
Alloy, L. B., 220
Allport, G. W., 504
Allsup, K., 352
Alm, H., 147
Almasy, S., 62
Almeida, D. A., 470
Almeida, D. M., 420
Almeida, O. P., 159
Alnaes, D., 565
Alonso, J., 535, 537
Alosco, M. L., 352
Alpert, N. M., 272, 273
Alston, J., 256
Altemeier, W. A., 153
Altimus, C. M., 541
Altschul, I., 208
Alvarez, J., 462

Alvarez, J. M., 462
Alvarez, P., 262
Alvarez, V. E., 291
Alvarez-Buylla, A., 57
Alzheimer's Association, 262, 263
Alzheimer's Disease Cooperative, 13
Alzheimer's Disease Neuroimaging
    Initiative, 70
Amabile, T., 44, 364, 403
Amano, K., 494
Amaral, D. G., 87
Amariglio, R. E., 13
Amat, J., 220
Amatya, D., 67
Ameli, R., 606
American Academy of Pediatrics, 320
American College of Obstetricians and
    Gynecologists, 324
American Counseling Association, 598
American Psychiatric Association, 292,
    293, 334, 377, 506, 532, 533, 536, 539,
    540, 541, 542, 545, 546, 547, 548, 550,
    551, 552, 554, 555, 556, 559, 560, 561,
    562, 578, 600
American Psychiatric Association
    Committee on Electroconvulsive
    Therapy, 608
American Psychological Association, 15,
    47, 585, 595, 596, 614, A-4, A-5, A-6,
    A-7, A-9
Ames, D., 263
Ames, D. R., 459
Ametaj, A. A., 580, 596
Amieva, H., 354
Amoiridis, G., 75
Amsterdam, B., 338
An, Y., 506
Anaki, D., 243
Anand, B. K., 375
Anastasi, A., 519
Ancoli-Israel, S., 154
Andersen, J., 412
Anderson, A. W., 77
Anderson, C. A., 222, 223, 469, 473,
    PIA-6, PIA-7
Anderson, J. W., 427
Anderson, L. W., PIA-13
Anderson, M., 467
Anderson, M. C., 258
Anderson, M. L., 584, 585, 596
Anderson, N. D., 352
Anderson, W., 579
Andersson, G., 602
Andreasen, N., 76
Andreski, P., 549
Andreu-Fernandez, V., 323
Andrews, C., 305
Andrews, J. D. W., 611
Andrieu, S., 412
Angelucci, A., 67
Angen, E., 427
Angermeyer, M. C., 540, 541
Angleitner, A., 509
Angus, L., 581
Ankarberg, E., 293
Ansari, A., 207
Anschuetz, B. L., 421
Ansell, E. B., 408
Anspaugh, D., 428

Anthony, A., 334
Anthony, J. C., 172
Antley, A., 446
Antonakis, J., 296
Antoni, M. H., 428
Antuono, P. G., 263
Anzuini, A., 320
Aoki, Y., 77
Apicella, F., 303
Applewhite, M., 449
Apps, M. A. J., 200
Araki, S., 293
Araque, A., 57
Arcelus, J., 557
Archer, J., 470
Archer, K., PIA-6
Archibald, L., 238
Arden, R., 299
Ardila, R., 429
Arendt, J., 149
Arevalo, J. M. G., 419
Arima, H., 470
Arkowitcz, H., 580
Arkowitz, H., 580
Arlotta, P., 58
Armitage, C. J., 587
Armon, G., 412
Armstrong, B. K., 453
Armstrong, N., 250
Armstrong, R., 174
Arnett, J. J., 350
Arnett, P. A., 560
Arnold, A. M., 255
Arnow, B., 602
Arns, M., 214
Aron, A., 35
Aron, E., 35
Aronson, E., 454, 466
Aronson, J., 299, 465
Aronson, M., 323
Arora, S., 297
Arulpragasam, A. R., 220
Asano, M., 104
Asarnow, L. D., 161
Asarnow, R. F., 562
Ascano, M., 320
Asch, S. E., 438, 439, 440, 444
Aserinsky, E., 153
Ash, M. G., 7
Asherson, P., 70
Ashida, H., 137
Ashmore, R. D., 466
Ashrafian, H., 297
Askren, M. K., 612
Asp, E., 80
Asplund, C. L., 381
Assaf, Y., 73
Assari, S., 557
Associated Press, 341
Athanasiou, T., 297
Athauda, G., 88
Athey, A., 154
Atias, A., 94
Atkinson, L. A., 150
Atkinson, R. C., 233, 238
Atladottir, H. O., 334
Aton, S., 152
Attia, E., 556
Auerbach, R. P., 537

NI-1

NAME INDEX

Auinger, P., 293, 421
Autenrieth, C., 412
Auveung, B., 334
Avis, D., 78
Avolio, B. J., A-12
Awh, E., 285
Axelrod, V., 136
Ayed, F. B., 179
Ayoub, C., 208
Ayoub, W. B., 178
Azadi, A., 351
Azmitia, M., 350

B

Ba, H., 429
Baan, C. A., 412
Babb, S. D., 173
Babcock, J. C., 593
Baberg, H. T., 172
Babiloni, C., 106
Bacchiochi, J. R., 518
Bachg, D., 409
Bachman, J., 178
Bachman, J. G., 177
Bachman, M., 462
Backenstrass, M., 499
Backer, B., 354
Backman, L., 242
Baddeley, A. D., 236, 237, 246, 250
Baddeley, J. C., 237
Badewien, M., 67
Badger, S., 350
Badrick, E., 412
Bae, A., 584
Baehr, E. K., 148
Baer, D. M., 213
Baez, S., 348
Bagby, R. M., 518
Bagiella, E., 418
Bahns, A. J., 467
Bahrick, H., 239
Bahrick, H. P., 251
Bai, Y., 208, 337
Bailer, U. F., 556
Bailes, J., 291, 610
Bailey, E., 612
Bailey, K., PIA-6
Baillargeon, R., 333
Baillie, G. S., PIA-14
Bains, G., 427
Bains, G. S., 427
Baiocco, R., 414
Baiz, D., 413
Bajo-Grañeras, R., 57
Baker, J. H., 557
Baker, L. A., 306
Baker, S., 428
Baker, T. E., 377
Bakhshaie, J., 546
Bakhshi, E., 213
Bakker, A. B., 421
Bakst, L., 511
Baldwin, G., 177
Balin, A. K., 354
Balkin, T., 151
Ball, B. H., 381
Ball, K., 352
Ball, T. M., 71
Balsam, P. D., 191
Baltes, P. B., 316
Bambico, F. R., 170
Bammer, R., 166
Banaji, M. R., 457
Bancroft, T., 334, 341
Band, E. B., 429
Bandstra, E. S., 172

Bandura, A., 195, 221, 222, 471, 472, 497, 518, 586
Banerjee, A., 26
Banich, M. T., 403
Banko, K. M., 371
Banks, C., 471
Banks, G. P., 610
Banos, R. M., 585
Banuazizi, A., 472
Banys, P., 170
Bao, X., 334
Baratta, M. V., 220
Barbosa, D. L., 587
Barbosa, P., 297
Barclay, N. L., 159
Bard, P., 386
Barefoot, J. C., 417
Bargh, J. A., 106, 147
Bargmann, C. I., 121
Barker, C., 446
Barker, E. S., 400
Barkley, R. A., 80, 98
Barlow, D. H., 580, 584, 590, 596
Barnes, A. M., 320
Barnes, D., 549
Barnes, D. E., 549
Barnes, G., 238
Barnes, J. C., 208
Barnes, T. R., 179
Barnes, V., 427
Barnett, R. C., 465
Barnett-Burns, S., 89
Barnyard, P., 239
Baron, J. N., 473
Baron, N. S., PIA-6
Baron, R., 469
Baron-Cohen, S., 334
Barondes, S. H., 544
Barone, E., 255
Baroni, A., 542
Barres, B. A., 57
Barresi, B., 81
Barrett, A., 387
Barrett, D., 443
Barrocas, A., 610
Barry, C. M., 350
Barry, K. L., 169
Barry, R., 469
Barsade, S. G., 296
Barsalou, L. W., 188
Barsh, G. S., 377
Bartal, M., 179
Bartels, A., 469
Bartels, J. M., 471
Barth, J. M., 382
Barth, J. T., 291
Bartholomew, K., 337
Bartke, A., 354
Bartlett, C., 473
Bartlett, D., 159
Bartlett, F. C., 250
Bartlett, N. R., 112
Bartol, T. M., 239
Bartolomei, F., 214
Barton, M. E., 274
Bartoshuk, L. M., 120, 121, 122
Bartz, J. A., 94
Bartz, P. J., 320
Basadur, M., 280
Bass, C., 67, 610
Bass, J., 593
Bassett, D. S., 84
Basten, U., 285
Bastidas, J., 88
Bastien, C. H., 159
Bastons-Compta, A., 323
Bateman, R. J., 13

Bator, R. J., 444
Batt, J., 427
Battista, M. E., 150, 153
Battjes, R. J., 583
Batton, D. G., 159
Bauer, A., 149, 263
Bauer, M., 544
Bauer, P. J., 264
Baumann, O., 76
Baumeister, D., 178
Baumert, J., 412
Baumgart, M., 263
Baumrind, D., 208, 352, 353, 446, 447, 448
Bautovich, A., 609
Baxter, D. A., 188
Bayerlein, K., 179
Bayliss, D. M., 237
Beach, S. R., 430
Beardsley, T., 299
Beary, J., 427
Beauchamp, G. K., 120
Beauregard, M., 214
Beaver, K. M., 208
Bechtel, W., 231
Beck, A. T., 543, 550, 588
Beck, H. P., 194
Beck, T. L., 414
Becker, A. E., 557
Becker, K. D., 595
Becker, R. E., 594
Beckers, J., 57
Beckman, M., 303
Bedrosian, D., 475
Beebe, D. W., 161
Beehr, T. A., 428
Beek, T., 387
Beekman, A. T., 602
Beer, J. M., 493
Beer, J. S., 382
Behar, C., 469
Behnaim-Luzon, V., 179
Behne, T., 303
Beidel, D. C., 545
Beier, K. T., 163
Bekesy, G. V., 118
Bekkering, H., 80
Belch, G. E., 453
Belenky, G., 151, 162
Belford, P., 443
Belger, A., 565
Bell, B. G., 380
Bell, E. F., 159, 324
Bell, L. M., 341
Bell, M. E., 376
Belletti, A., 302
Bellisle, F., 195
Bellocco, R., 153
Belsky, J., 337
Bem, D. J., 456
Bendell, A., 351
Bendlin, B. B., 69
Benedetti, F., 77
Benet-Martinez, V., 506, 507
Bengston, V. L., 348
Benington, J., 152
Benjafield, J. J. G., 489
Benjamin, S. L., 560
Benjet, C., 537
Benner, A. D., 543
Bennett, M. V., 57
Bennett, S., 207, 208
Benozio, A., 455
Ben-Poarth, Y. S., 517
Ben-Shakhar, G., 380
Benson, C. B., 324
Benson, H., 427
Benson, P., 334, 341

Bentley, K. H., 584, 590, 596
Benton, D., PIA-15
Benyamin, B., 317, 510
Benzinger, T. L., 13
Beran, M. J., 146
Berberich, J. P., 583
Berch, D. B., 352
Berent, S., 382
Berg, F., 556
Berg, R., 88
Berger, D. R., 58
Berger, H., 69
Berger, S. A., 251
Berghofer, A., 544
Berglund, P., 540, 541
Bergmann, O., 88
Beringer, L., 542
Berk, D., 426
Berk, L., 427
Berk, L. E., 304
Berk, L. S., 427
Berke, J., 178, 179
Berkowitz, F., 70
Berkowitz, L., 405, 469
Berlin, L. J., 208
Berman, A., A-9
Berman, M. G., 136, 612
Berman, Z., 73
Bermond, B., 386
Bernard, C., 411
Bernard, S., 88
Bernardo, L., 67, 610
Bernat, E., 106
Bernath, S. L., 134
Berndt, S. I., 377
Bernieri, F. J., 470
Bernstein, I., 158
Bernstein, M., 67, 610
Bernston, G. G., 380, 411
Beron, K. J., 353
Berresheim, H., 376
Berrocal, Y., 88
Berry, J. A., 152
Berry, J. W., 421
Berscheid, E., 467
Berson, D. M., 541
Berteretche, M. V., 195
Berthiller, J., 179
Bertollo, D. N., 609
Bertram, K., 297
Bertram, L., 263
Beste, C., 84
Betancourt, J. R., 599
Betancourt, T., 593
Bethel, A., 612
Bettler, B., 470
Beuriat, P. A., 95
Beutler, L. E., 588
Beyer, B. K., 18
Beyreuther, K., 121
Bhandari, A., 153
Bhatnagar, S., 376
Bhowon, U., 421
Bhupathiraju, S. N., 174
Bialas, A. R., 13, 564
Bialystok, E., 308
Bianchi, D., 414
Bianchi, R., 414
Bianchini, K., 518
Biederman, J., 542
Biel, D., 69
Biello, St. M., 150
Bieniek, K. F., 291
Bierhals, A. J., 409
Biermann, T., 179
Biesalski, H. K., 121
Biesanz, J. C., 456

NAME INDEX NI-3

Bietti, L. M., 414
Bigler, E. D., 69
Bijanzadeh, M., 67
Biller, J., 154
Binder, J. R., 260, 261
Bindman, A. B., 477
Binet, A., 285
Bingham, S., 350
Binkofski, F., 80
Binns, M. A., 236
Birbaumer, N., 126, 214
Bird, C. M., 261
Birkenhager, T., 262, 263
Birkle, S., 214
Birks, J., 255
Birmingham, K. Iles-Caven, 334
Birnbaum, R., 563, 564, 565
Bischoff-Grethe, A., 556
Bishop, J., PIA-12
Bishop, S. F., 170
Bisson, J., 596
Bittman, B. B., 426
Bivens, J. A., 304
Bixler, E., 157
Bizzell, J., 565
Bjerkedal, T., 317
Bjorck, L., 412
Bjork, E. L., 258
Bjork, R. A., 166, 167, 247, 257, 258
Bjork-Eriksson, T., 88
Bjorkqvist, K., 208, 216
Bjorner, J. B., 413
Black, M. J., 577
Black, N. B., 427
Blacker, C. J., 67, 152
Blackmon, L. R., 159
Blaine, J. D., 583
Blair, C., 291
Blair, R. J. R., 560
Blais, F. C., 159
Blaivas, M., 324
Blakeslee, S., 82
Blanchard, E. B., 586
Blanchard, M., 336
Blanchard-Fields, F., 458, 459
Blanchette-Sylvestre, M., 214
Blanco, C., 172, 173
Blanco-Elorrieta, E., 309
Bland, S. T., 220
Blandon-Gitlin, I., 252
Blaney, N., 466
Blanton, H., 465
Blass, T., 446
Blazer, D. G., 430
Bledsoe, C. H., 350
Blefari, M. L., 214
Blehar, M. C., 540
Bleiberg, K. L., 578
Bleich, A., 426
Bleuler, E., 561
Blitz, R., 323
Block, A., 517
Block, C., 405
Block, L., 589
Block, N., 146
Block, R. A., 191
Block, S. D., 355
Blommel, J. M., 442
Bloom, B. S., PIA-13
Bloom, J. R., 593
Bloom, L., 303
Bloom, P., 303, 305
Bloom, S. R., 375
Blount, B. C., 173
Bluher, M., 89
Blumenfeld, H., 291
Blumenthal, J. A., 417

Blumer, D., 542
Blunt, J. R., 248, PIA-14
Blyth, F. M., 94
Boals, A., 250
Bobb, S. C., 308
Bobe, L., 85
Bobulinski, M., 401
Bock, R., 320
Bockhacker, L., 552
Bodenhausen, G. V., 456, 457
Bodkin-Clarke, C., 320
Bodmer, D., 320
Bodrova, E., 333
Bodurka, J., 106, 494
Boehm, E., 320
Boes, A. D., 67
Bogdanov, M., 67
Boggs, D. L., 179
Bogle, K. D., 459
Bohringer, A., 608
Bohus, M., 552
Boiangiu, S. B., 350
Bokat, C. E., 231
Bolasco, G., 327
Boles, D. B., 382
Bolger, N., 94
Boll, T. J., 414
Bolliger, B., 404
Bolton, P., 593
Bolton, S., 332
Bonanno, G. A., 550
Bond, R. A., 439
Bond, T. L., 161, 378
Bondarenko, L. A., 149
Boniol, M., 179
Bonnelykke, B., 321
Bonsall, D. R., 150
Boodoo, G., 299
Boomsma, D. I., 89
Boor, M., 553
Booth-Butterfield, S., 453
Boothby, E. J., 147
Bootzin, R. R., 159
Bor, D., 104
Bordin, I. A., 216
Borgelt, L. M., 179
Borges, M. A., 246, 248
Borkovec, T. D., 547
Born, J., 152
Borneman, M. J., 290
Bornemann, M. A., 158
Bornheimer, L. A., 585
Bornstein, M. H., 303
Boroditsky, L., 305
Boronow, J., 587
Borra, R. J., 76
Bos, E. H., 541
Bosch, J. A., 411
Bosch, S., 273
Boseley, S., 334
Bossert, W., 441
Bosworth, H. B., 352
Botella, C., 585
Botteri, E., 412
Botwin, M. D., 505
Bouchard, C., 375, 509
Bouchard, M. B., 327
Bouchard, S., 159
Bouchard, T., 512, 531
Bouchard, T. J., 299, 317
Bouchard, T. J., Jr., 178, 317
Boucher, K. L., 465
Bouckaert, F., 608
Bourne, J. N., 239
Bourne, T., 324
Boutwell, B. B., 208
Bowden, C. L., 604

Bower, D., 19
Bower, J. E., 400
Bower, J. M., 76
Bowers, K. S., 167, 168
Bowes, C., 88
Bowlby, J., 578
Bowler, W. M., 421
Bowman, E. S., 251
Boxer, P., 222
Boyd, C. H., PIA-9
Boyd, L. A., 260
Boykin, A. W., 299
Boylan, J. M., 376
Boyle, A., 548
Boyle, A. E., 543
Boyle, C., 293
Boyle, M. H., 208
Boyson-Bardies, B., 302
Bracha, H. S., 563
Bradbury, T. N., 458
Braddock, J. E., 173
Braden, A. L., 214
Bradley, J. C., A-9
Bradman, A., 293
Brady, C., 147, 191
Brady-Smith, C., 208
Bramon, E., 543
Brand, B., 554
Brand, B. L., 553
Brand, J. J., 127
Brand, R. I., 417
Brandeis, D., 70
Brass, M., 80
Bratman, G. N., 612
Braun, S. R., 173
Bravo, M. J., 172
Bray, C. W., 118
Brazelton, T. B., 339
Brecher, M., 178
Breedlove, S. M., 13
Breier, A., 403
Breland, K., 211, 212
Breland, M., 211, 212
Bremmer, J. D., 70
Bremner, A. J., 136
Bremner, J. D., 554
Brems, C., 404
Brennan, J. F., 5
Brennan, P. A., 400
Brennen, T., 328
Brenner, J., 453
Breslau, N., 549
Breslow, R. A., 174
Breteler, M., 214
Breton-Lopez, J., 585
Brett, L. P., 194
Breuer, J., 577
Brewer, M. B., 462
Brick, J., 175
Briem, V., 147
Briggs, K. C., 518
Brigham, A., 574
Bright, S., 178
Briley, D. A., 512
Brinol, P., 451, 454
Britton, A., 412
Britton, S. L., 89
Broadbent, D., 236
Brobeck, J. R., 375
Broca, P., 81
Brocato, R. M., 442
Brodrick, J., 178
Brody, N., 299
Bromer, C., 239
Bromet, E. J., 540, 541
Brondolo, E., 418
Bronfenbrenner, U., 12

Bronkhorst, A. W., 236
Brook, J. S., 546
Brooks, J. G., 333
Brooks, J. L., 130
Brooks, M. G., 333
Brooks-Gunn, J., 208
Broshek, D. K., 291
Brotman, M. A., 543
Brouwers, S. A., 290
Brown, A. S., 240, 563
Brown, C., 598
Brown, C. A., 427
Brown, C. H., 606
Brown, G., 6
Brown, G. L., 470
Brown, G. W., 320
Brown, J., 238, 258
Brown, K. W., 427, 494
Brown, P. K., 113
Brown, R., 246, 303
Browne, D., 146
Browne, J. V., 327
Browne, M. N., 18
Brownstein, J. S., 153
Broyles, S., 106
Brozoski, D., 150
Brubaker, D. A., 587
Bruffaerts, R., 537
Brugal, M. T., 172
Brugger, S. P., 77
Brugha, T. S., 540, 541
Bruhin, A., 474
Brummett, B. H., 418
Bruni, O., 161
Brunner, E., 411
Bruno, A. M., 261
Brutsaert, D. L., 418
Brutsche, N. E., 606
Bryan, E. B., 322
Bryan, J., 208
Bryant, E. J., 378
Brymer, E., 613
Bu, G., 263
Buccino, G., 80
Buchanan, T. W., 77
Buche, L. C., 380
Bucher, B. D., 208
Buchmann, A., 89
Buchsbaum, M. S., 554
Buchwald, D., 153
Buck, L. B., 121
Buck, R., 387
Buckels, E. E., 442
Buckholtz, J. W., 381
Buckner, R., 511
Buckwalter, J. J., 354
Bucuvalas, M., 399
Bucy, P. C., 77
Budding, D., 76
Budnitz, D. S., 169
Buechel, C., 152
Buehler, C., 429
Bueno, O. F., 587
Buerger, K., 70
Buffo, P., 106
Buffone, A., 94
Bugaiska, A., 351
Bugental, J. F. T., 578
Buhle, J. T., 382
Buikema, A., 334, 341
Buis, T., 518
Bulgheroni, S., 76
Bulik, C. M., 557
Bullis, J. R., 580, 596
Bullock, T. H., 57
Bumb, J. M., 608
Bunge, M. B., 88

Buonano, F. S., 273
Buonocore, M. H., 236
Burchinal, M., 337
Burd, L., 324
Burger, J. M., 444, 446, 447, 493
Burgess, D. M., 293
Burgess, N., 262
Burgio, K. L., 587
Burguiere, E., 67
Burish, T. G., 590
Burke, D. M., 246
Burke, M., 179
Burks, N., 403
Burnay, J., 473
Burney, R., 427
Burns, J. F., 334, 341
Burrill, C., PIA-15
Burriss, R. P., 13
Burrows, C., 106
Burson, A., 612
Burt, S., 510
Burton, A., 255
Burton, J. R., 255
Busch, A. M., 587
Bush, D. E. A., 240, 260
Bush, G., 77
Bush, S. S., 291
Bush, T. M., 428
Bushey, D., 152
Bushman, B. J., 222, 470, 473, 474, PIA-6, PIA-7
Buss, A. T., 71
Buss, D. M., 14, 469, 486, 505, 507
Buss, R. R., 347
Bussa, B., 593
Busse, F., 89
Butcher, J. N., 517, 518
Butera, F., PIA-20
Butler, J. P., 153
Butner, J., 443
Butter, E. M., 430
Buttiglione, M., 106
Buysse, D. J., 159
Byers, A. L., 549
Byrd, R. S., 421
Byrne, J. H., 188

C

Caan, B. J., 428
Cabeza, R., 77, 352
Cabral, R. R., 599
Cabrera, H. F., 457
Cacioppo, J., 453, 454
Cacioppo, J. T., 4, 89, 380, 411, A-5
Cacioppo, S., 89
Cadden, M., 352
Caetano, C., 452
Caglio, M. M., 67, 610
Cahill, L., 241
Cai, M., 67, 610
Cai, Y., 334
Caims, P., 222
Cain, D., 578
Cain, M. S., PIA-6
Caird, J. K., 147
Cairney, S. A., 151
Cairns, E., 429
Cajal, S. R. y., 56
Calabrese, J. R., 604
Calamia, M., 518
Calder, A. J., 214, 380, 470
Caldji, C., 89
Caldwell, L. D., 430
Caley, L. M., 323
Calfa, G. D., 77
Calhoun, K. S., 545
Calhoun, V., 565

Calhoun, V. D., 214
Calkins, M. W., 6
Calvert, S. L., 474
Calvo, N., 308
Calvo, R., 354
Cam, C. A. N., 69
Camacho, E. M., 220
Cameron, J., 371, 462
Cami, J., 178
Campbell, A., 341
Campbell, D., 405
Campbell, D. T., 135, 601
Campbell, J. C., 405
Campbell, L. F., 595
Campbell, V. L., 520
Campo, R., 470
Campos, J., 336
Camposano, S., 273
Camus, G., 347
Canals, I., 323
Canas, A. J., PIA-14
Canli, T., 543
Cannon, W. B., 374, 386, 411
Cantu, R. C., 291
Cao, Y., 429
Cao-Lei, L., 400
Caparos, S., 136
Capell, A., 263
Capetian, P., 88
Cappo, B. M., 517
Caraballo, R. S., 173
Cardena, E., 553
Cardinali, D. P., 149
Cardno, A. G., 563
Cardoso, G., 534
Carducci, B., 531
Carette, B., 296
Carey, G., 470, 510
Carey, J. C., 320
Carey, S., 587
Caria, A., 214
Carli, L. L., 440
Carlsen, A., 104
Carlsmith, J., 455
Carlson, G. A., 542
Carlson, L., 427
Carlson, M. C., 255
Carlson, P. J., 606
Carmichael, D. A., 104
Carmody, T. J., 158
Carnahan, T., 472
Carnot, M. J., PIA-14
Carol, M., 427
Caroppo, P., 67, 610
Carpenter, L. L., 66
Carpenter, M., 303
Carpenter, P. A., 290
Carr, E. G., 208
Carrillo, M. C., 263
Carrion, V. G., 549
Carroll, B., A-9
Carroll, E. J., 521
Carroll, J., 350
Carroll, M. D., 377
Carruthers, M., 351
Carsel, T. S., 23
Carskadon, M. A., 154, 156, 161, 378
Carson, R. C., 467
Carter, C., PIA-12
Carter, C. S., 94
Carter, J. C., 66, 610
Caruso, D. R., 296
Carver, C. S., 428
Carver, L., 264
Carvey, C. E., 134
Case, B. G., 609
Caserta, M. T., 413
Casey, B. J., 346

Cassel, R., 303
Cassidy, A., 351
Cassidy, C., 421
Cassidy, J., 336
Casson, D. M., 334
Castel, A. D., 139
Castellanos, F. X., 77
Castelli, W. P., 417
Castillo, A., 428
Castillo, M., 208
Castillo, R. J., 531, 557
Castorina, R., 293
Catalan, J., 443
Catalino, L. I., 428
Catanzaro, S. J., 499
Cattaneo, L., 81
Cattell, R. B., 284, 504, 505
Caulet, M., 154
Cautin, R. L., 424, 520, 585, 596
Cavanaugh, A. M., 429
Cave, K. R., 137
Cebrian-Silla, A., 88
Cecero, J. J., 475
Ceci, S. J., 299
Centers for Disease Control and Prevention, 147, 173, 175, 177, 320, 341, 351, 540
Centerwall, B. S., 473
Cepeda, N. J., 257, PIA-6
Cerda, M., 179
Cermak, L., 231
Cerny, C. B., 428
Certain, R. D., A-9
Cervantes-Sandoval, I., 152
Cesar d'Ornano, A. M, 195
Cetkovich, M., 348
Cha, J. H., 459
Chabris, C. F., 273
Chace, P. M., 262, 263
Chahua, M., 172
Chaiken, S., 451, 452, 453
Chait, M., 279
Chaiyasit, W., 429
Chaklader, A., 156
Chakrabarti, B., 334
Chakraborty, M., 152
Chalavi, S., 88
Chambers, M. C., 25, 80, 97
Chan, A. K., 610
Chan, A. S., 71
Chan, C. J., 412
Chan, D., 421
Chan, R. W., 67
Chan, W. M., 88
Chancer, L., 475
Chandola, T., 412, 421
Chang, A., 543, 550, 565, 575
Chang, A.-M., 158
Chang, C. M., 173
Chang, E., 463
Chang, E. F., 236
Chang, I., 408
Chang, J. J., 216
Chang, Y. H., 302
Chant, D., 563
Chaplin, W., 418
Chaplin, W. F., 462
Chapman, R. S., 303
Charest, I., 256
Charles, C., 34
Charlesworth, W. R., 383
Charlton, B. G., 419
Charney, D. S., 154, 411
Chase-Lansdale, L., 337
Chatterjee, A. K., 153
Chatterji, S., 534
Chaudhury, S., 26
Chauhan, P., 337

Chauvet-Gelinier, J. C., 67, 610
Chavez, A., 565
Chedid, E., 70
Chedraui, P., 351
Chee, M. W. L., 152
Cheever, N. A., PIA-6
Chein, J., 369
Chen, B. R., 327
Chen, C. N., 557
Chen, H. J., 246
Chen, H.-H., 58
Chen, J., 89
Chen, J. Y., 305
Chen, L. Y., 263
Chen, M., 106, 174
Chen, M. J., 151
Chen, Q., 317, 337, 565
Chen, R., 323
Chen, S., 334
Chen, V. H. H., 442
Chen, X., 334
Chen, Y., 263, 458, 459
Chen, Z., 460
Cheng, E. R., 400
Cheng, X., 354
Cheng, Y.-P., 543
Cherry, E. C., 236
Cheryan, S., 20, 43
Chesham, R. K., 585
Chess, S., 335, 443
Chesson, A. L., Jr., 154
Chetouani, M., 303
Cheung, W. K., 71
Chey, T., 535
Cheyne, B., 405
Chhetry, B. T., 584
Chida, Y., 418
Chilcoat, H. D., 549
Chipping, J., 220
Chirillo, M. A., 239
Chirkov, V. I., 372
Chitnis, S., 66, 67
Chiu, C., 457
Chiu, C. Y., 442
Chiu, P. H.,71
Chiu, W. T., 534, 545
Cho, M. J., 584
Choca, J. P., 521
Choi, I., 459
Choi, S. W., 89
Choiniere, M., 126
Chomsky, N., 302, 306
Choo, W. C., 152
Chorley, D., 19
Chorpita, B. F., 595
Chosak, A., 557
Chou, S. Y., 377
Chou, T. C., 151, 154
Christensen, A., 593
Christensen, A. J., 414
Christianson, J. P., 220
Chu, J. A., 552
Chuhma, N., 169
Chunara, R., 153
Chung, G. K., 421
Chung, I. W., 584
Chung, R. Y., 421
Chung, S., 163
Church, A. T., 457, 507
Chwalisz, K., 386
Cialdini, R., 443, 444
Cialdini, R. B., 443, 444, 446
Ciardiello, A., 272
Cibelli, G., 106
Cicerale, A., 67, 610
Cieslik, E. C., 565
Cinnirella, M., 440
Cipriani, A., 606

Cirelli, C., 152
Ciric, P., 165
Citron, M., 264
Clancy, S. A., 254
Clandinin, M. T., 256
Clark, D. M., 596
Clark, F., 560
Clark, K., 6
Clark, L. A., 532
Clark, M., 6, 149
Clark, T. W., 177
Clarke, A. E., 428
Clarke, J., 466
Clarke, P., 411
Clarke-Stewart, K. A., 337
Clarkin, J. F., 595
Clarys, D., 351
Claypool, H. M., 456
Clayton, S., 104
Clement, K., 375
Clements, C. M., 220
Clemm von Hohenberg, C., 608
Clemmons, J., 401
Clough, P., 613
Clougherty, K. F., 593
Coccaro, E. F., 470
Coe, W. C., 168
Coelho, L. F., 587
Coenen, A., 214
Coffey, C. E., 543
Coffey, K. A., 428
Cohen, A. B., 460
Cohen, B., 350
Cohen, D., 303
Cohen, G., 257
Cohen, H., 156
Cohen, H. J., 430
Cohen, J. D., 64, 540, 543, 550
Cohen, L. G., 126
Cohen, L. J., 543
Cohen, N. J., 241, 350
Cohen, P., 546
Cohen, R. A., 256, 575
Cohen, R. D., 430
Cohen, S., 409, 410, 411, 413
Cohn, M. A., 428
Colbert, J., 203
Colcombe, S. J., 352
Colder, C., 172
Cole, A. B., 220
Cole, J., 159
Cole, S., 439
Cole, S. W., 419
Coleman, H. L. K., 421
Coleman, J. R., 147
Coleman, M., 334, 341
Coleman, R. M., 149
Coleman, T., 152
Coles, C., 172
Coles, C. D., 172
Coles, S., 323
Collado-Torres, L., 564, 565
The College Board, PIA-5
Collet, J.-P., 179
Colletti, P., 470
Colligan, J., 280
Colligan, R. C., 420
Collin, S. H. P., 262
Collins, A., 475
Collins, A. M., 243
Collins, C. J., 366
Colom, R., 237, 285
Columbo, J., 326
Columbus, C., 21
Comaty, J. E., 62, 64, 602, 603, 604, 605
Comer, J. S., 580, 596
Committee on Animal Research and Ethics, 48

Common Sense Media, Inc., 222
Conant, L. L., 260, 262
Condle, D., 554
Cone-Wesson, B., 172
Conezio, J., 248
Cong, X., 543
Conklin, L. R., 584, 590, 596
Connelly, B. S., 290
Conner, C. R., 247
Connor, S., 256
Conrad, R., 236
Constantine, M. G., 430
Consumer Reports, 595
Contractor, A., 430
Conway, A. R. A., 237
Conway, G., 320
Conway, M. A., 152, 257
Conway, P., 348
Cook, J. M., 467
Cook, K., 475
Cook, M., 196
Cook, T. D., 601
Coolidge, F. L., 164
Cooper, C., 255
Cooper, D. C., 220
Cooper, J. A., 220
Cooper, J. M., 147
Cooper, L. A., 598
Copersino, M., 179
Corballis, M. C., 84
Corbett, G., 580
Corbett, G. G., 305
Corbetta, M., 82, 260
Corcoran, K. A., 246
Cordova-Palomera, A., 565
Coren, S., 135
Corey, D. M., 517
Coric, V., 409
Corkin, S., 238, 241, 261
Cormier, J. F., 553
Cormier, K. A., 291
Cornes, C., 578
Corniola, M. V., 126
Corr, C. A., 355
Correa, M., 170
Corrigan, P. W., 614
Cortese, A., 494
Corwin, D. S., 220
Cosgrove, G. R., 609
Cosmides, L., 469
Costa, J., 414
Costa, P. T., 418, 505
Costa, P. T., Jr., 355, 507, 512, 510, 512, 518, 531
Costello, D. M., 543
Cote, S., 296
Cotet, C. D., 585
Cotter, J. A., 327
Cotton, S. R., PIA-6
Couchman, J. J., 146
Coughlan, B., 426
Coulson, N. S., 414
Couperus, J. W., 327
Coups, E., 35
Courage, M. L., 333, 338
Courtois, R., 347
Courtwright, D. T., 177
Couteur, D. G. L., 94
Coutinho, E. S., 585
Covino, J. M., 335
Cowan, N., 233, 235, 237, 239
Cowell, R. M., 148
Cowings, P. S., 128
Cowley, D. S., 606
Cox, C., 293, 413
Cox, G. R., 606
Craddock, N., 544
Crager, K. Jadliwala, 147

Craig, B. A., 121
Craighead, W. E., 587, 588, 606
Craik, F., 231
Craik, F. I., 308
Craik, F. I. M., 231, 240, 247, 351
Cramer, J. W., 320
Cramond, B., 294
Crandall, C. S., 467
Crane, J. W., 408
Craske, M. G., 588, 590, 596
Cravchik, A., 606
Crawford, S. L., 343
Creamer, M., 596
Creed, M., 67
Creelman, C. D., 106
Cremers, H., 511
Crespo-Facorro, B., 77
Cress, U., 251
Creswell, J. D., 427, 494
Crichlow, S., 440
Crick, F., 146
Cristea, I. A., 585
Critchfield, T. S., 203
Croarkin, P. E., 67, 152
Crone, N. E., 81
Crosby, L. R., 587
Cross, W., 413
Crossley, N., 76
Croteau-Chonka, D. C., 377
Crouch, D. J., 147
Crowe, A., 587
Crowley, A. E., 453
Crowley, J. J., 584
Crowley, M., 475
Crucian, G., 387
Cruikshank, K. A., PIA-13
Cruwys, T., 428, 447
Cruz, A., 473
Cruz, N., 317
Csikszentmihalyi, M., 279, 280, 281, 503
Cua, A. B., 354
Cuellar, N. G., 154
Cuevas, L., 237, 285
Cui, J., 303
Cuijpers, P., 537, 585, 587, 588, 602
Culbert, K. M., 557
Culbertson, J. L., 172
Cullen, K. E., 76
Culler, E., 246
Culver, N. C., 588
Cumming, R. G., 94
Cummings, J. L., 264, 543
Cummings, S. R., 350
Cunnington, D., 590
Cunnington, R., 80
Curry, M. A., 405
Curtis, K., 518
Curtis, R. C., 467
Curtis, R. G., 506
Curtis, R. H., 574
Cusato, B., 499
Cuthbert, B. N., 534, 575
Cutting, L. E., 77
Cwik, J., 549
Czaja, S. J., 337
Czajkowski, N., 560
Czeisler, C. A., 149, 150, 158

D

Dabbs, J. M., Jr., 470
Dadar, M., 377
D'Agata, F., 67, 76, 610
Dagher, A., 377
Daher, N., 427
Dahi, R. E., 153
Dahl, R., 293
Dahl, R. E., 161

Dahlstrom, W. G., 517
Daiello, L. A., 255
Daily, G. C., 612
Dalal, R., 459
Dale, A. M., 78
Daleiden, E. L., 595
Dalenberg, C. J., 252, 553
D'Alessio, D. A., 377
Dalgleish, T., 548
Dalhoff, K., 173
Dalia, C., 375
Dalix, A. M., 194
Dallery, J., 334
D'Allesandro, D. U., 588
Dallman, M., 376
D'Alton, M. E., 321, 322
Damasio, A. R., 64, 77
Damasio, H., 25
Damasion, A. R., 25
Damian, R. I., 493
Dan, Y., 163
Daneshvar, D. H., 291
D'Angelo, J., 147, 191
Dani, J., PIA-15
Daniel, R. P., 6
Daniels, A., PIA-14
Danso, H., 34
Darby, B., 443
Darby, D., 263
Dari, I., 179
Darley, J. M., 12, 475, 476
Darling, K. E., 426
D'Arrigo, S., 76
Darvill, T., 293
Darwin, C., 14, 382
Darzi, A., 297
Das, A., 324
Dasiewicz, P., 208
Dato, A., 375
Daum, I., 260
D'Auria, A. L., 426
Davare, M., 67
David, D., 585, 596
David, P., 147, 191
David, P. S., 351
Davidoff, J., 136
Davidson, K. W., 418
Davidson, R. J., 380, 382
Davies, I., 305
Davies, I. R. L., 305
Daviet, C., 595
Davis, A., 13, 564
Davis, C. J., PIA-14
Davis, G. C., 549
Davis, J., 606
Davis, J. O., 563
Davis, K. D., 291
Davis, K. F., 156
Davis, N., 77
Davis, O. S. P., 317
Davis, P., 20, 43
Davis, R., 297
Davis, R. L., 152
Davis, R. M., 151
Davis, S. F., A-5, A-6
Davis, T. E., 586
Davison, A., 446
Davydova, E., 70
Dawood, K., 13
Day, E., 462
Day, F. R., 377
Day, N., 409
Dayton, T., 277
de Bruin, A., 309
De Camp, J. E., 139
de Fockert, J., 136
de Fockert, J. W., 136
de Garde-Perik, Markopoulos, 452

de Geus, E. J. C., 297, 298
De Jaeger, X., 263
de Jong, J. T., 553
de Jong, P. T., 112
de Jonge, L., 610
De Jonge, P., 94, 535
de Klerk, N. H., 453
De La Cruz, G., 88
de la Torre, R., 178
de Lecea, L., 375
de Leeuw, C. A., 317, 510
De Leo, S. E., 327
de Leon, C. F. M., 414
de Los Cobos, J. P., 172, 173
de Mooij, S. M. M., 69
De Pasquale, D., PIA-6
de Ridder, S., 214
de Rivera, H., 13, 564
de Ruyter, B., 452
De Valois, K. K., 113
De Valois, R. L., 113
De Vos, M., 76
de Vries, N. K., 353
De Winter, F. L., 608
de Wolff, C. J., 370
De Wolff, F. A., 178
Dean, G., 18
Deary, I. J., 297, 298, 365
Deasy, C., 426
Debes, F., 293
Debiec, J., 240, 260
DeCasper, A. J., 328
Decedo, J. C., 241
deCharms, R., 370
Deci, E. L., 364, 370, 371, 473
Decker, K., 253
DeCoster, J., 456
Decoufle, P., 293
Defenderfer, J., 71
DeFour, D., 442
DeFreitas, M. R., 557
DeFries, J. C., 297, 298, 299, 510, 512, 531
Degenhardt, L., 179
Deger, M., 261
DeGrandpre, R. J., 497, 499
DeGuzman, M. C., 556
Dehaene, S., 106
deHalle, P., 302
Deinzer, R., 409
Deisseroth, K., 67
DeJong, W., 364, 44
DeKosky, S. T., 255
Del Giovane, C., 606
Del Prado, A. M., 457
Delagrange, P., 149
Delaney, A. J., 408
DeLaRosa, B., 67, 610
Deldin, P. J., 612
Deleuran, B., 334
Delfiner, R., 475
Delgado, M. R., 250
Della Penna, S., 106
Della Sala, S., 309
DeLong, M. R., 470
DeLongis, A., 403
Delrow, U. J., 153
Delva, J., 208
Dement, W. C., 150, 154, 156
Demerouti, E., 421
Demeter, G., 152
Demirakca, T., 608
Demiral, S. B., 153
Demler, O., 534
Demmig-Adams, B., PIA-15
Dempsey, C. L., A-9
Dempster, F. N., 258
den Boer, J. A., 554

Deneen, B., 57
Deng, L. X., 88
Deng, P., 88
Deng, X., 70
Denman-Brice, A., 238
Dennett, D., 146
Dennis, C. V., 88
Denny, L., 323
Denollet, J., 418
Denovan, A., 613
Densmore, M., 214
Denys, D., 66, 610
Department of Veterans Affairs
    Department of Defense, 585
Deppe, M., 85
Deregowski, J. B., 138
Derkits, E. J., 563
DeRubeis, R. J., 543
Desai, R. H., 260, 262
Desautels, A., 157
Deschamps, T., 70
Deshpande, P., 427
Deskovitz, M. A., 519
D'Esposito, M., 80
Despres, J. P., 375, 509
Desrocher, M., 242
DeStefano, F., 334, 341
Destiche, D. J., 69
Detera-Wadleigh, S. D., 544
Deutsch, G., 82, 84
Deutschlander, S., 94
Devanand, D. P., 608
Devitt, A. L., 246
Dewall, N. C., 430
Dewitt, M., 382
DeWoskin, D., 148
DeYoung, C., 511
DeYoung, C. G., 506, 507, 511, 512
Di Forti, M., 172
Di Martino, A., 77
Diamandis, P., 291
Diamond, L. M., 469
DiazGranados, N., 606
Diaz-Mataix, L., 240, 260
Dichgans, M., 70
Dick, A. S., 81
Dickens, W., 291
Dickens, W. T., 298
Dickerson, F., 587
Dickinson, T., 172
Dickinson-Anson, H., 241
Dickson, B. J., 261
Dickson, D. W., 291
Dickson, W. J., A-12
Didehbani, N., 67, 610
Diehl, R., 34
Diekman, A. B., 440
Diemer, E. W., 557
Diener, E., 386, 442
Dierker, L. C., 543
Diesendruck, G., 455
Diessmann, M., 261
Dietrich, K., 293
DiFrancesco, M., 161
Digdon, N., 194, 195
Dijkhoff, L., 387
Dijksterhuis, A., 494
Dijkstra, N., 273
Dill, D. L., 552
Dill, K. E., 473
Dillard, J., 443
Dillingham, T. R., 126
Dillow, S. A., A-5
Dima, D. C., 70
Dimidjian, S., 587, 588
Dimsdale, J. E., 172
Ding, D. C., 323

Ding, F., 148
Ding, M., 174
Ding, N., 302
Dinges, D. F., 151, 152
Diniz, J. B., 557
Dion, D., 126
Ditter, M., 88
Dixon, C., 548
Dixon, S. G., 284, 285
Doan, N. T., 564
Dobson, K. S., 587, 588, 589
Docherty, M., 222
Dodane, C., 303
Dodson, J. D., 416
Doege, T. C., 151
Doeller, C. F., 262
Doherty, M. J., 136
Doi, H., 303
Dolan, R. J., 380
Dolcos, F., 251
Dolinski, D., 447
Doliński, D., 446, 447
Dollard, J., 404, 469, 497
Dols, A., 608
Domagalski, T. A., 384
Domhoff, G. W., 164, 165
Dominey, P. F., 303
Domingo-Salvany, A., 172
Dominici, G., 608
Domjan, M., 499
Donaldson, Z. R., 94
DonCarlos, L., 161
Donchin, O., 67
Dong, C., 174
Dong, C. M., 67
Dong, G., 429
Donnelly, W. T., 159
Donnerstein, E., 222, 223, 473
Donohue, M. C., 13
Donohue, S. E., PIA-6
Donovan, J. J., 217
Doob, L. W., 404, 469
Dorahy, M. J., 553, 554
Dornbrot, D. E., 249
Doron, K. W., 84
Dorta, K. P., 578
Dotson, C. D., 122
Doubilet, P. M., 324
Doucet, E., 375
Doucette, J. T., 297
Douthitt, E. A., 442
Dove, A., 290
Downey, G., 474
Downs, J. F., 355
Dowrick, P., 334, 341
Doyere, V., 240, 260
Doyle, A. E., 542
Doyle, B. J., 410
Doyle, J. S., 590
Doyle, W. J., 410
Drager, B., 85
Draghici, A. M., 368
Dredze, M., 474
Dreher, H., 418
Drenth, P. J., 370
Dresler, T., 67
Drevets, W. C., 106, 494
Drews, F. A., 147
Dronkers, N. F., 81
Druckman, D., 166, 167
Drugan, A., 322
Drury, B. J., 20
Druss, B. G., 614
Du, L., 213
Du, M., 550
Du, V., 89
Duben, A., 469

Dubern, B., 375
DuBois, M. A. Shamasundara, 382
Dubowitz, H., 207, 208
Duchaine, B., 248
Duckworth, A. L., 291
Duclos, K., 152, 156
Dudai, Y., 260
Dudley, K., 339
Dudukovic, N. M., 256
Duering, M., 70
Duffy, A., 542
Duffy, J. F., 158
Duffy, V. B., 122
Duggan, M., 467
Duker, P. C., 208
Duku, E. K., 208
Dum, R. P., 76
Dumais, S., 249
Duman, R. S., 606
Dumas, J. A., 352
Dumont, F., 486
Dumoulin, M., 152
Duncan, R. M., 304, 333
Dunlop, B. W., 587–588, 606–607, 597
Dunn, B., PIA-14
Dunn, D. S., A-5, A-6
Dunn, J. C., 403
Dunn, J. R., 422
Dunne, P. E., 557
Dunner, D., 602
Dunsiger, S., 255
Dupuis, G., 126
Duran, R. E., 428
Durand, C., 302
Durbin, E., 335
Durrant, J., 207
Durrant, M., 4
Durso, F., 277
Durussel, K., PIA-20
Dussault, J., 375, 509
Dutt, A., 543
Duvillard, L., 67, 610
Duzel, E., 70, 238
Dwairy, M., 353
Dweck, C., 367
Dweck, C. S., 367, 457
Dyakonova, V. E., 250
Dyer, R. L., 147
Dyke, J. P., 346
Dykens, E. M., 293
Dyson, M. W., 335

E
Eadie, J. L., 177
Eagleman, D. M., 134
Eagly, A. H., 440, 451, 452, 453, 466, 475
Eaker, E. D., 417
Eames, K., 341
Earles, J. L., 248
Easterbrooks, M. A., 337
Eastern Virginia Medical School, 147
Eastman, C. I., 148
Eastman, K. L., 429
Eaton, N. R., 541, 575
Eaton, W. W., 334, 546
Ebbeling, C. B., 377
Ebbinghaus, H., 256–257
Eberly, S., 413
Ebesutani, C., 595
Eddy, J., 453
Edelmann, R. J., 384
Eden, G. F., 308
Edinger, J. D., 159
Edwards, C., 159
Eftekhari, A., 584
Egan, L. C., 456

Eggen, B., 452
Eghrari, H., 371
Egloff, B., 493
Egner, T., 382
Ehlers, A., 549, 596
Ehring, T., 549
Eich, E., 246
Eichen, D. M., 578
Eichenbaum, R., 241
Eickhoff, S. B., 543, 550, 565, 575
Eid, M., 366
Eiden, R. D., 172
Einstein, A., 502
Einstein, G. O., PIA-10
Eisenberg, D., 537, 614
Eisler, I., 593
Eitzen, D., 34
Ejaife, O. L., 414
Ekers, D., 587, 588
Ekman, P., 380, 383, 387
Ekstrom, A. D., 80
El Marj, N., 154
Elashoff, R., 593
Elbert, T., 126, 208
Eley, T., 510
Elgbeili, G., 400
Elger, C. E., 260
Elias, G. J. B., 66, 610
Eliassen, C. F., 427
Elkind, D., 347
Ellenberg, S., 575
Ellenbogen, J. M., 152, 153, 156
Ellilson, N. B., 467
Ellingsen, Ø., 427
Elliot, J., 463
Elliott, E., 367
Elliott, E. M., 237
Elliott, K., 595
Elliott, R., 581
Ellis, A., 590
Ellis, G., 334
Ellis, H. D., 382
Ellis, J. G., 159
Ellis, K. A., 263
Ellis, L. K., 403
Ellison, C. G., 430
Ellsworth, P. C., 467
Elmenhorst, D., 149
ElvevAg, B., 231
Ely, T. D., 549
Emeny, R. T., 412
Emmett-Oglesby, M. W., 172
Emmorey, K., 81
Emsell, L., 608
Ende, G., 608
Ende, N., 323
Endler, N. S., 608
Engberg, G., 563, 564
Engle, R. W., 237
Engle, W. A., 159
Engler, Y., 452
Englund, C. E., 152
Engstrom, I., 608
Enns, C., A-5
Enns, J. T., 135
Ensom, R., 207
Ephraim, P. L., 126
Epping-Jordan, M., 173
Epstein, L. H., 377
Epstein, R. A., 80
Erdley, C. A., 457
Erdur-Baker, O., 443
Erickson, K. I., 89, 352
Erickson, S. A., 418
Erikson, E. H., 8, 339, 353, 371, 494
Erikson, J. M., 339
Eriksson, J. G., 400

Eriksson, M., 400
Eriksson, P., 293
Eriksson, P. S., 88
Ernst, A., 88
Ernst, E., 425
Ernst, L. H., 67
Eron, L., 222
Eron, L. D., 473
Eschenbeck, H., 426
Escobedo, J. O., 173
Esfahani, N. E., 264
Eskenazi, B., 293
Eskkandar, E. N., 201
Eslick, A. N., PIA-6
Espeland, M. A., A-8
Espie, C. A., 159
Espinosa, A., 296
Esposito, G., 303
Essau, B., 413
Estrada, E., 285
Estreich, D., 442
Etkin, A., 382, 597, 543, 550, 565, 575
European Monitoring Centre for Drugs and Drug Addiction, 178
Evans, A. K., 220
Evans, B., 414
Evans, D., 594
Evans, D. A., 414
Evans, G. W., 421
Evans, I. D., 167
Evans, I. M., 587
Evans, J. G., 255
Evans, M. A., 468
Evans, P., 371
Evans, S. S., 587
Evans, W. H., 587
Evans, W. J., 350
Evens, A. C., 78
Everett, P., 25, 80, 97
Evers, E. A. T., 77
Everson, S., 4
Everson-Rose, S. A., 414
Evins, A. E., 214
Evrard, M., 252
Ewbank, M. P., 214
Ewers, M., 70
Exner, J. E., 520
Eyer, J., 411
Eysenck, H. J., 418, 518, 595
Eysenck, S. B. G., 518

F

Faasse, K., 586
Fabbri-Destro, M., 81
Faber, B., 563, 564
Fadiga, L., 80
Faedda, G. L., 542
Fagan, A. M., 13
Fagiolini, A., 399
Fahey, J. L., 420, 593
Fahlke, C., 323
Fahrenkamp, A. J., 426
Fairburn, C. G., 590
Fairchild, G., 214, 560
Fairhurst, S., 191
Fairman, B., 179
Falcone, M., 67, 610
Fallgatter, A. J., 67
Fallon, J. H., 241
Fan, Q., 77
Fan, X., 334
Fang, A., 557
Fanning, J. R., 470
Fanselow, M. S., 77, 380
Fantino, E., 252
Fantz, R. L., 326, 328

Faraone, S. V., 542
Farmer, A. E., 544, 563
Farmer, L. M., 188
Farooqi, I. S., 377
Farrar, S., 475
Farre, M., 178
Farrington, C. P., 334, 341
Farris, R., 257
Farthing, W., 146
Fasotti, L., 386
Fast, K., 122
Faubion, S. S., 351
Faurion, A., 195
Faust, M., 243
Fava, G. A., 602
Favot-Mayaud, I., 334, 341
Fawzy, F. I., 593
Fawzy, N. W., 593
Fayad, S. M., 66
Fayed, N., 554
Fazel-Rezai, R., 106
Fazio, R. H., 451
Fazio, S., 263
Fearn, M., 456
Fechner, G. T., 4, 105
Fecteau, S., 67, 610
Federer, F., 67
Fedoroff, I. C., 532
Fehr, E., 474
Feingold, A., 466
Feldman, D. H., 333, 348
Feldman, H. A., 377
Felician, O., 273
Feliciano, E. M. C., 153
Felsten, G., 612
Felten, D. L., 426
Feng, T., 179
Fenn, K. M., 251
Ferencz, E. A., 67
Ferguson, C. J., 222, 473
Ferguson, D., 473
Ferguson, J., 156
Ferguson, J. N., 94
Ferguson, N. B., 375
Ferguson-Noyes, N., 542
Fernald, A., 303
Fernandez, D. C., 541
Fernandez, E., 403
Fernandez, G., 260
Fernandez, M. I., 428, 454
Fernando, A. B., 380
Fernstrom, J. D., 121
Feroah, T. R., 150
Ferrari, M., 71, 610
Ferreira, T., 377
Ferrell, L., 553
Ferrelli, A. V., 155
Ferretti, A., 106
Ferretti, V., 149
Ferris, S. H., 13
Ferrucci, L., 506
Ferrucci, R., 76
Festinger, L., 454, 455, 464
Fevre, M. L., 399
Fiatarone, M., 352
Fiebach, C. J., 285
Field, J., 161
Fields, R. D., 57, 58
Fieux, S., 95
Fiez, J. A., 76
Fifer, W. P., 328
Figee, M., 610
Figueira, I., 585
Filippetti, M. L., 338
Filkowski, M. M., 610
Fillingim, R. B., 122
Fincham, F. D., 430, 458

Fine, M. A., 208
Fine, P., 341
Finger, K., 252
Finger, S., 81, 113, 510
Fingerhut, A. W., 465
Fini, M. E., 89
Fink, G. R., 80
Fink, M., 608
Finke, C., 264
Finke, R., 280
Finkel, B., 178
Finkel, D., 510
Finkelhor, D., 252
Finkelstein, J. D., 252
Finlay, B., 35
Fioriti, L., 260
Firman, N., 452
Fischer-Shofty, M., 94
Fischl, B., 78, 565
Fischler, G. L., 517
Fishbein, M., 452
Fishbein, W., 156
Fisher, C., 250
Fisher, E. M., 320
Fisher, L. D., 409
Fisher, P. L., 585
Fisher, R. P., 248
Fishman, I., 81
Fisicaro, S., 519
Fisk, J. E., 178
Fiske, S. T., 457
Fitzgerald, T. P., 153
Fitzhugh, E., 453
Fitzpatrick, M., 334, 469
Fivush, R., 334
Flaherty, J. A., 598, 599
Flanagan, D. P., 284, 285
Flanagan, M., 452
Flannery, D., 347
Flaskerud, J. H., 599
Flavell, J. H., 333
Flax, R., 442
Flegala, K. E., 247
Fleischer, V., 69
Fleming, J. E., 208
Fleming, M. F., 169
Flemons, W. W., 159
Flichtentrei, D., 348
Flinker, A., 81
Flint, J., 13
Floel, A., 85
Flor, H., 126
Flores, A., 413
Flores, J., 457
Floresco, S. B., 201
Florescu, S., 562, 563
Flores-Mendoza, C., 237
Florio, C. M., 517
Flynn, J., 291
Flynn, J. R., 298, 299
Foa, E. B., 584
Fodor, L. A., 585
Foehr, U. G., 222
Fogassi, L., 80
Fogerson, P. M., 541
Fois, G. R., 170, 172
Foland-Ross, L. C., 543
Foley, D., 351
Foley, K., 249
Folkard, S., 148, 149
Folkman, S., 402, 414, 426
Follett, K. J., 459
Folwarczny, M., 446, 447
Fonzo, G. A., 597
Foote, K. D., 66
Ford, A., 598
Ford, D. E., 598

Forder, J., 150
Forger, D. B., 148
Forman, E., 587
Forney, K. J., 556
Forrest, J. S., 178
Forrester, E., 585, 586
Fors, C., 151
Forseth, K. J., 246, 247
Forssmann-Falck, R., 384
Forster, H. V., 150
Forsyth, D. R., 476
Forsyth, J., 462
Forte, A., 608
Fortuna, L. R., 598
Fosket, J. R., 351
Fosse, M., 144, PIA-14
Fosse, R., 144, PIA-14
Fossey, D., 24
Foulkes, D., 155, 165
Fournier, G., 375, 509
Fournier, J. C., 71, 597
Fowkes, F. G., 412
Fox, M. C., 290
Fox, M. D., 67
Fox, M. J., 62
Fox, N. C., 13
Fragoza, R., 334
Fraley, R. C., 337
Franaszczuk, P. J., 81
Franciotti, R., 106
Francis, B. J., 139
Francis, D., 89
Franck, G., 164
Franco, A. R., 597
Franco-Chaves, J., 606
Frangou, S., 563
Frank, D. W., 381
Frank, E., 410, 578
Frank, E. Rabin, 410
Frank, G. K. W., 556
Frank, M. G., 152, 220
Frank, R., 25
Franke, R. H., A-12
Frankel, B. R., 592
Frankenhuis, W. E., 23
Franklin, C. A., 208
Franks, N. P., 149
Franscini, M., 89
Franson, K. L., 179
Fransson, E. I., 413
Frantz, S., A-55
Franzen, K. F., 173
Franzmeier, N., 70
Fras, I. A., 252
Fraser, C., 104
Fraser, J. F., 578
Fraser, S., 443
Frazier, J., 542
Frazier, J. A., 77
Frederick, D. A., 337
Fredricks, D. N., 324
Fredrickson, B. L., 417, 428, 429
Fredriksson, A., 293
Freed, F., 208
Freedman, J., 443
Freeman, A., 588
Freeman, D., 585
Freeman, I., 405
Freeman, J., 294, 585
Freeman, J. E., A-4
Freeman, W., 609
Freese, J., 493
Freire, E., 581
Fremmer-Bombik, E., 337
Frenda, S. J., 251
Freud, A., 8, 489

Freud, S., 8, 9, 162, 370, 469, 486, 487, 488, 489, 490, 491, 492, 493, 494, 545, 549, 576, 577
Freund, H. J., 80
Frewen, P. A., 214, 554
Frey, J., 469
Frey, L. M., 552
Fridlund, A. J., 194
Fried, I., 80
Fried, R., 542
Friedman, J. M., 377
Friedman, M., 417
Frier, B. M., 412
Friesdorf, R., 348
Friesen, W., 383
Friesen, W. V., 380
Frigge, M., 510
Frimer, J. A., 447
Frisen, J., 88
Friso, S., 89
Friston, K. J., 80, 380
Fritch, A., 126
Frith, C., 156
Frith, C. D., 80, 380
Frith, U., 334
Fritz, S., 473
Fritze, J., 323
Froh, J. J., 503
Frontera, W. R., 350
Frost, C., 428
Frost, W. N., 260
Frostegard, J., 411
Fruhmesser, A., 320
Fryar, C. D., 377
Frydenberg, E., 429
Fu, Y., 550
Fuchs, K. M., 321, 322
Fudge, J. L., 556
Fuentes, A., 242
Fujisaki, K., 297
Fukuda, K., 285
Fulcher, J. S., 383
Fulford, D., 88
Fulford, J., 273
Fuligni, A., 462
Fuligni, A. J., 152, 462
Fulker, D. W., 510
Fuller, C. A., 148
Fuller, R., 262
Furr-Holden, D. M., 179
Furumoto, L., 6

G

Gaa, A., 401
Gable, A., 334, 341
Gable, P. A., 456
Gable, R. S., 174
Gable, T. M., 420
Gabrelcik, J. C., A-9
Gabrieli, J. D. E., 166, 543
Gabriels, L., 610
Gade, M., 308, 309
Gado, M., 475
Gage, F. H., 88
Gage, P., 25, 80, 96–97
Gahm, G. A., 585
Gainotti, G., 106
Galaburda, A. M., 25
Galanaki, E. P., 347
Galante, M., PIA-20
Galatzer-Levy, I. R., 549
Gale, G. D., 380
Gale, J. T., 201
Galea, S., 179, 399
Galert, T., 610

Gall, C. M., 263
Gall, F. J., 510
Gallagher, D., 386
Gallese, V., 80
Gallistel, C. R., 191, 200
Gallo, J. J., 598
Galvin, J. E., 263
Gamble, K. L., 146
Gamble, K. R., 612
Gamwell, L., 530
Ganchrow, J. R., 328
Gandhi, A. V., 149
Gandhi, M., 502
Ganis, G., 273
Gano-Phillips, S., 458
Ganzel, B. L., 552
Gao, P. P., 67
Gao, S., 598
Gao, Y., 564, 565
Gao, Z., 429
Garb, H. N., 517, 519, 520, 521
Garber, J., 498, 543
Garcia, A. M., 308, 348
Garcia, J., 195
Garcia, L. F., 285
Garcia Coll, C., 462
Garcia-Campayo, J., 554
Garcia-Lago, E., 377
Garcia-Palacios, A., 585
Gard, T., 427
Gardner, E. P., 104
Gardner, H., 280, 283, 317
Gardner, J., 428
Gardner, R. J. M., 320
Garland, E. L., 382
Garlow, S. J., 610
Garner, M., 380
Garrison, K. A., 214
Garside, R., 612
Garuccio, A., 108
Gasecka, A., 89
Gaser, C., 77
Gass, M. A., 612
Gassert, R., 214
Gaucher, D., 447
Gaudiano, B. A., 575
Gautschi, O. P., 126
Gawronski, B., 348
Gay, P. E., 403
Gaylor, M., 493
Gaylord-King, C., 427
Gaymard, S., 347
Gazzaley, A. G., 80
Gazzaniga, M. S., 83, 84
Geary, D. C., 14
Geary, J. P., 373, 374
Geen, R. G., 473
Geher, G., 296
Gehrels, J., 154
Geier, J., 134
Geiger, A., 89
Gelade, G., 236
Gelder, M., 584
Gelenberg, A., 602
Gelfand, M. J., 529
Geliebter, A., 374
Gelkopf, M., 178
Geller, A. I., 169
Geller, B., 542
Gelman, S. A., 305
Genovese, C., 474–476
Gentile, D., 473
Gentile, D. A., 222, 223, 473
Gentile, P., PIA-6
Gentzler, A. L., 353
George, L. K., 430

Georges, F., 170, 172
Gerards, S. M., 353
Germi, J., 260
Gernaat, H. B., 553
Gersappe, A., 413
Gershoff, E. T., 207, 208
Gerstenberg, M., 89
Gert van Dijk, J., 159
Gertler, A., 377
Gertz, K. J., 214
Geschwind, D. H., 382
Geschwind, N., 382
Ghaderi, A., 557
Gharib, S. A., 153
Ghaziri, J., 214
Ghilotti, F., 153
Ghosh, S., 214
Giachero, M., 77
Giacobbe, P., 66, 610
Gianaros, P. J., 408, 411
Giancola, F., 349
Giancola, P. R., 470
Giang, K. W., 412
Gibbons, R. D., 606
Gibson, E. J., 343
Giedd, J. N., 563
Giesbrecht, T., 553
Gifford, R. K., 462
Gigerenzer, G., 251
Gilaie-Dotan, S., 136
Gilberg, C., 334, 341
Gilbert, B., 543
Gilbert, G., 214
Gilbert, S. J., 446
Gilbody, S., 587, 588
Gill, S. T., 18
Gillath, O., 337, 467
Gillen-O'Neel, C., 152
Gillespie, M. A., 366
Gillham, B., 405
Gilligan, C., 347
Gillis, H. L., Jr., 612
Gillis, H. L. L., 612
Gillund, G., 246, 248
Gilman, J. M., 214
Gilmour, J., 154
Gil-Perotin, S., 327
Gilreath, T., 179
Gil-Rivas, V., 412
Gilstrap, L. L., 252
Ginges, J., 460
Ginisty, A., 323
Ginther, M., 381
Ginzburg, K., 426
Giordano, P. J., 495
Giovanello, K. S., 352
Girardi, P., 608
Giraux, P., 126
Girden, E., 246
Girgis, Z. M., 447
Gitelman, D. R., 252
Gittelman-Klein, R., 521
Giuffreda, A., 179
Glangetas, C., 170, 172
Glaser, R., 409, 413, 426
Glass, R. H., 324
Glassman, W. E., 476
Gleaves, D. H., 553
Glei, D. A., 575
Glenn, A. L., 560
Glover, G., 346
Glover, G. H., 543
Glucksberg, S., 308
Glucksman, M. L., 11
Glynn, S. M., 587
Gmel, G., 324

Goate, A., 13
Godden, D. R., 245, 246
Gogol, M., 323
Gogtay, N., 563, 565
Goh, D., 493
Goin, M. K., 574
Goker, A., 443
Gold, E., 351
Gold, E. B., 351
Gold, J., 399
Gold, J. M., 562, 563
Goldberg, S. B., 592
Goldberg, T. E., 231
Goldberg, W. A., 337
Golde, T. E., 263
Goldfried, M. R., 581
Goldie, W. D., 194
Golding, J., 334
Goldin-Meadow, S., 367
Goldman, A. L., 565
Goldman, J. E., 57
Goldman, N., 148, 575
Goldman-Rakic, P. S., 260
Goldsmith, H. H., 336
Goldstein, N. J., 446
Goldstone, A. P., 375
Goleman, D., 151, 280, 296
Golestani, N., 308
Gollan, T. H., 308
Gollwitzer, P. M., 4
Golshani, R., 88
Gomes, T., 177
Gomez, F., 376
Goncalves, D. F., 263
Goncalves, R., 585
Gong, Q., 76, 550
Gong-Guy, E., 498
Gongvatana, A., 255
Gonsalves, B., 252
Gonulal, T., 333, 334
Gonzales, J. J., 598
Gonzales, P. M., 465
Gonzalez, J. S., 428
Good, M., 369
Goodday, S., 542
Goodey, E., 427
Goodglass, H., 81
Goodkind, M., 543, 550, 565, 575
Goodkind, M. S., 597
Goodman, E. S., 5
Goodson, B., 334, 341
Goodwin, R. D., 546
Goodwin, R. S., 179
Goodyer, I. M., 214, 560
Gooijers, J., 88
Goorsky, M., 339
Goossens, L., 89
Goovaerts, I., 418
Gordon, A. J., 179
Gordon, C., 428
Gordon, J., 339
Gordon, J. M., 179
Gordon, P., 532
Gordon, S., 557
Gorelick, D. A., 179
Gorman, J. M., 596
Gornik–Duros, M., 444
Gornitzka, G., 412
Gosselin, F., 77
Gosselin, R. E., 173
Gotlib, I. H., 71, 543
Gottesman, I., 563
Gottesman, I. I., 317, 563, 564
Gottfredson, M., 474
Gottheil, E., 593
Gottman, J. M., 469

Gotz, M., 57
Gotz, S., 165
Goudy, M. B., 36
Gough, H. G., 518
Gould, C. G., 306
Gould, J. L., 306
Gould, S., 178, 179
Gould, S. J., 299, 317
Gove, W. N., 220
Gover, M. C., 167
Goya-Maldonado, R., 565
Graber, K., 401
Grabowski, T., 25
Gračanin, A., 384
Grace, A. A., 563
Gradus, J. L., 549
Graham, C., 404
Graham, J., 344
Graham, J. R., 517, 518
Graham, P., PIA-14
Graham-Engeland, J. E., 420
Gralinski, J. H., 338
Granato, S., 320
Grandjean, P., 293
Grandner, M., 154
Grange, D. L., 593
Granholm, E., 562
Grant, A. M., 4
Grant, B. F., 171, 172, 173
Grant, H., 452, 457
Grant, M. C., 542
Graven, S. N., 327
Gravenstein, S., 409
Graves, W. W., 260, 261
Gray, J., 89, 411
Gray, J. R., 507, 511
Graybiel, A. M., 67
Grayson, A., 239
Green, A., 598
Green, B., 440
Green, D. M., 106
Green, D. W., 309
Green, M. F., 565
Green, R., A-9
Green, R. E., 291
Greenberg, L. S., 581
Greenberg, Z. I., 309
Greendale, G. A., 351
Greenwald, A. G., 106, 457
Greer, G. R., 179
Greer, T. L., 158
Greeson, J., 350
Gregory, R. L., 135
Gregory, S., 334
Greicius, M. D., 166
Gresham, L. G., 453
Greve, D. N., 335
Greve, K., 518
Grewen, K., 94
Griep, Y., 430
Gries, F. A., 376
Griesser, M., 307
Griffiths, T. D., 279
Griggs, E. M., 260
Griggs, R. A., 96, 194, 195, 447, 471, 472
Grigorenko, E. L., 317
Grilo, C. M., 557
Grim, C., 427
Grimaldi, D., 153
Grimbos, T., 13
Grimm, P., 121
Gripshover, S. J., 367
Griskevicius, V., 370, 371
Gritzmann, E., 376
Grob, C. S., 179
Grocer, S., A-5

Grof, P., 542
Grogan-Kaylor, A., 207
Groh, A., 260
Gronau, Q. F., 387
Groppa, S., 69
Grosenick, L., 67
Gross, A. M., 473
Gross, C. G., 411, 528
Gross, C. T., 327
Gross, J. J., 612
Gross, R. E., 66, 610
Grossman, K., 336
Grossman, M., 377
Grossmann, K., 337
Grossmann, K. E., 336
Grotta, A., 153
Grotz, C., 354
group, E., 77
Grove, W. M., 517
Groves, C. L., 222
Growdon, J. H., 238
Grubin, D., 380
Gruenewald, T. L., 429
Grumbach, M. M., 346
Grunbaum, A., 495
Grzyb, T., 446, 447
Grzybała, P., 446, 447
Gu, L., 57
Guardiola-Lemaitre, B., 149
Guedea, A. L., 246
Gueguen, N., 443
Guell, X., 76
Guger, C., 446
Guidi, J., 602
Guilford, J. P., 280, 282
Guilleminault, C., 154, 159
Gump, B. B., 417
Gunderson, E. A., 367
Gunderson, J., 126
Gunn, D. M., 237
Guntan, I., 149
Gunturkun, O., 84, 94
Gunzelmann, G., 152
Guo, J., 375
Guo, M., 153
Guoping, F., 67
Gupta, T., 403
Guralnik, O., 554
Gureje, O., 563, 563
Gurin, J., 595
Gurrera, R. J., 563, 565
Gurung, R. A., 139, A-5
Gurung, R. A. R., 429
Guskiewicz, K. M., 291
Guthrie, D., 339, 593
Guthrie, R. V., 5, 6
Guynn, M. J., 245
Gwaltney, J. M., 410
Gyawaii, U., 220
Gyulai, L., 604

H

Haan, J.,75
Haas, A. P., 557
Haas, B. W., 166
Haass, C., 263
Habas, C., 76
Haber, R. B., 235
Haber, R. N., 235, 248
Hachey, D. L., 377
Hackathorn, J., A-5
Hackett, R. A., 412
Hadad, M., 478
Haden, C., 334
Hadley, C. N., 403

Hafri, A., 80
Hagan, C. C., 214
Hagan, C. R., 553
Hagihara, D. K., 231
Hahn, J., 57
Hahn, K. S., 612
Hahn, T., 67
Hahnemann, S., 424
Haidt, J., 384
Haier, R. J., 285
Hailey, S. E., 147
Hains, S. C., 440
Hajak, G., 262
Hajcak, G., 596
Haj-Dahmane, S., 179
Haker, S., 25, 80, 97
Hakimian, S., 214
Hakulinen, P., 263
Halaas, J. L., 377
Halberstadt, A. L., 179
Halbesleben, J. R. B., 421
Hales, C. M., 377, 378
Haley, R., 203
Hall, A. P., 176
Hall, C., 164, 165
Hall, C. S., 164
Hall, H., 424
Hall, J. A., 457
Hall, J. E., 153
Hall, L. K., 237, 251
Hall, M., 152
Hall, S. M., 170
Hall, W., 177, 179
Hallahan, M., 459
Hallett, F., 322
Hallikainen, M., 263
Hallmark, R., 520
Hallquist, M. N., 168
Hallvig, D.,151
Halonen, J. S., A-5, A-6
Halpern, D. F., 291
Hamani, C., 66, 610
Hamby, S. L., 252
Hamilton, D. L., 462
Hamilton, J. P., 71, 543, 612
Hammen, C., 498
Hammen, C. L., 400
Hammes, W. P., 121
Hammond, T. R., 13, 564
Hampton, J. A., 274
Hamrick, M., 428
Hamza, C., 369
Han, G. H., 337
Han, J., 174
Han, M. H., 411
Han, Y., 208
Hanaire, H., 412
Hanasaki, N., 154
Hancox, J., 371
Handel, S., 236
Handelsman, D. J., 94
Handron, C., 20
Haney, C., 442, 472
Haney, T. L., 417
Hanges, P. J., 366
Hanlon, A. L., 324
Hanlon, C. A., 214
Hanninen, J., 263
Hannon, M. H., 2
Hansbauer, M., 179
Hansen, C. P., 401
Hansen, N. B.,598
Hansen, P. G., 442
Hanson, B. E., 223
Hanson, L. M., 430
Harbaugh, C. R., 94

Harbron, C. G., PIA-15
Harden, K. P., 512
Harding, H. P., Jr., 291
Harding, J. W., PIA-14
Hare, A. L., 468
Hare, J. F., 94
Hariz, M., 610
Harkins, S., 442
Harlaar, N., 299
Harley, V. R., 429
Harlow, H. F., 337, 338
Harlow, J. M., 96, 97
Harman, G., 458
Harmon-Jones, C., 456
Harmon-Jones, E., 456
Harms, P. D., 337
Harold, G. T., 458
Harorimana, D., 440
Harrington, J. R., 529
Harrington, K., 263
Harrington, M. E., 150
Harris, B., 194, 195
Harris, H. S., 430
Harris, K. F., 417
Harris, K. M., 239
Harris, R., 473
Harris, V. A., 459, 459
Harrison, P. J., 563, 564
Harrison, T. L., 237
Harsch, N., 250
Hart, J., Jr., 67, 610
Hart, P., 441
Hartfield, E., 467, 489
Hartley, B. L., 465
Hartley, C. F., 450
Hartley, T., 456
Hartung, P. J., 493
Harvard Medical School, 534, 536
Harvey, A. G., 161
Harvey, A. R., 88
Harvey, M., 597
Harvey, O. J., 465
Harvey, S. B., 609, 612
Haselton, P., 585
Hasin, D. S., 171, 172, 173, 179
Haslam, C., 428
Haslam, S. A., 421, 428, 447, 466, 471, 472
Hassan, F., 216
Hassan, S., 413, 449
Hastings, N., 94
Hatch, S. L., 612
Hattar, S., 541
Hattie, J., 332
Hauck, S. J., 354
Havekes, R., PIA-14
Havighurst, R. J., 354
Havlik, R., 351
Havranek, M. M., 404
Hawkins, J. B., 153
Hawks, S. R., 376
Haworth, C., 510
Haworth, C. M. A., 317
Hay, P., 590, 593
Hayat, S. Z., 70
Hayes, J. E., 121, 122
Hayes, J. P., 69, 352
Hayes, S. M., 352
Hayflick, L., 354
Hays, J. C., 430
Hayward, C., 546
Hayward, M., 585, 586
Hayworth, K. J., 58
Hazan, C., 337
Hazlett, E. A., 554
Hazrati, L. N., 291
He, J., 147
He, X. C., 323

Heath, A. C., 557
Heatherton, T. F., 161
Heavey, C. L., 593
Hebb, D. O., 368
Hecker, T., 208
Heden-Stahl, C., 412
Hedman, L. R., 147
Hedrick, M., 71
Heider, F., 458
Heider, K., 380
Heikkila, K., 413
Heil, G., 370, A-11
Heilig, M., 177
Heilman, K., 82, 387
Heilman, K. M., 82, 382
Heimberg, R. G., 590, 594, 596
Heimer, L., 87
Heine, S., 374
Heinemann, U., 121
Heingartner, A., 442
Heinicke, C. M., 339
Heinrich, B., 339
Heinrich, H., 213
Heishman, S. J., 179
Held, M., 262
Helias, M., 260
Hell, D., 561
Hellawell, D. J., 470
Heller, W., 588
Helmers, K. F., 352
Helms, J. E., 289
Helms, M. J., 417, 418
Helpman, L., 584
Hembree, E. A., 584
Hemingway, H., 411, 412
Henderson, C., 231
Henderson, R. K., 403
Henderson Slater, D., 126
Hendricks, R. K., 305
Hendricks, V. F., 442
Henin, A., 542
Henning, H., 121
Henningsen, H., 85
Henriques, B., 610
Henry, J. A., 178
Henry, P., 156
Henson, R. N. A., 69
Henter, I. D., 606
Hepler, J., 453
Heppner, W. L., 427
Herberman, R. B., 412
Herbert, J. S., 156
Herbert, T. B., 409
Herbst, J. H., 512, 531
Herder, C., 412
Hering, E., 113
Herlitz, A., 242
Herman, E. M., 442
Herman, L. M., 306
Hermenau, K., 208
Hernandez, D., 320
Hernandez, M., 542
Heron, M. J., 443
Herrero, J. L., 89
Herrick, K. A., 377
Herringa, R. J., 549
Herrmann, M. J., 67, 167
Herrnstein, R. J., 299, 317
Hersh, S. M., 471
Hershberger, S. L., 510
Herskovits, M. J., 135
Hertwig, R., 251
Hervais-Adelman, A. G., 308
Herxheimer, A., 148
Herzog, T., 459
Hess, T. M., 458, 459
Hesse, E., 336

Hetherington, A. W., 375
Hetrick, S. E., 606
Hewlin, P. F., 440
Hewstone, M., 462
Heyes, C. M., 219
Heymann, D. L., 341
Hicklin, J., 519
Hickok, G., 81, 246, 247
Hidalgo, L., 351
Higgins, E. T., 486
Higgins, R. D., 324
Higginson, A. D., 375
Higuchi, M. A., 66
Hildebrandt, G., 126
Hildreth, C. J., 410
Hilgard, E. R., 167
Hilgard, J. R., 167
Hilger, K., 285
Hill, D., 453
Hill, D. O., 517
Hill, E. S., 260
Hill, J. A., 324
Hill, P. C., 430
Hill, T. J., 350
Hillard, P. J. A., 161
Hiller, J. G., 412
Hillman, D. R., 159
Hillman, E. M. C., 327
Hilpert, P. L., 586
Hilsaca, K. F., 351
Hilton, J. L., 457
Hines, T., 18
Hinrichsen, V. L., 334, 341
Hinson, J. M., 151
Hinton, G. E., 231, 243
Hintz, S. R., 324
Hintze, J. M., 586
Hippocrates, 528
Hiripi, E., 556
Hirota, Y., 156
Hirsch, A., 120
Hirsch, J., 375
Hirshkowitz, M., 161
Hirst, W., 250
Hirtz, R., 67
Hirvonen, J., 179
Hisler, G., 153
Hismjatullina, A., 237
Hitch, G., 237
Hjern, A., 323
Ho, I. K., 414
Hoagwood, K., 578
Hobson, J. A., 156, 163, 164, PIA-14
Hoche, F.,76
Hochman, J., 251
Hodapp, R. M., 293
Hodge, D., 252
Hodge, H. C., 173
Hodges, J. R., 262
Hodgetts, S. I., 88
Hodgkinson, B., 594
Hodgson, B., 176
Hodgson, R. J., 589
Hodson, D. S., 350
Hoebel, B. G., 375
Hoeft, F., 166
Hofer, S., 414
Hoferichter, F., 366
Hoffmann, R., A-8
Hoffrage, U., 251
Hoffstaedter, F., 565
Hofman, A., 112
Hofstede, G. H., 13, 370, 384, 512
Hofstede, G. J., 13, 370, 384, 512
Hogg, M. A., 440
Hogg-Johnson, S., 238
Holahan, C. K., 294

Holden, C., 323
Hollander, E., 94, 554
Hollingworth, A., 237
Hollinshead, M., 511
Hollon, S. D., 587, 588, 595
Holloway, K. M., 585
Holman, E. A., 94, 412
Holm-Denoma, J. M., 161
Holmen, J., 427
Holmes, A., 511
Holmes, E. A., 273
Holmes, J., 77
Holmes, J. G., 467
Holmes, O. W., 425
Holmes, S., 351
Holmes, T. H., 400, 401
Holowka, S., 303
Holroyd, J., 167
Holt, L. H., 246, 248
Holt-Lunstad, J., 428
Holton, S. D., 590
Holtzheimer, P. E., 597, 610
Holzel, B. K., 427
Homa, D. M., 173
Hommel, B., 440
Hong, D., 320
Hong, J. P., 584
Hong, Y., 457
Hong, Y. I., 442
Honzik, C. H., 217, 218
Hood, D. C., 112
Hood, W. R., 465
Hooshmand, B., 351
Hopfinger, J. B., 236
Hopkins, J. R., 347
Horan, W. P., 565
Horhota, M., 458, 459
Horikawa, T., 165
Horn, J., 284
Horn, J. M., 493, 510
Horne, J. A., 156
Horner, A. J., 261
Horney, K., 8, 491, 493, 494
Hornung, J. P., 149
Horowitz, D. L., 463
Horrey, W. J., 147
Horstmann, A., 89
Hortacsu, N., 469
Horton, R., 384
Hosang, G. M., 70
Hoscheidt, S. M., 69
Hoshino, N., 308
Hosler, A. S., 543
Hothersall, D., A-12
Hotopf, M., 612
Hou, G., 411, 412
Houben, K., 377
Houben, S. T. L., 585
Houldin, A., 413
Houlihan, J. L., 404
Houshyar, H., 376
Houston, A. I., 375
Hovland, C. I., 191
Howard, D. C., PIA-10
Howard, D. V., 612
Howard, J. H., Jr., 612
Howard, R., 6
Howe, J. D., 214
Howe, M. L., 333, 338
Howell, A. J., 613
Howell, M. D., 177
Howes, O. D., 77
Hoyer, W. D., 453
Hoyt, W. T., 592
Hozel, B., 427
Hsu, B., 94
Hsu, D. J., 177

NAME INDEX NI-11

Hu, F. B., 174
Hu, P., 337
Hu, S., 128
Hu, X., 76
Hu, Y., 174
Hu, Z., 375
Hua, L., 147
Huang, B., 171
Huang, J. Y., 147
Huang, M. H., 351
Huang, S., 147
Huang, X., 263
Huang, Y., 89
Huang, Y. Y., 260
Hubbard, E. M., 104
Hubel, D. H., 134
Huber, B. R., 291
Huber, R., 89
Hubinger, A., 376
Hubler, E., 162
Hudak, M., 134
Hudgens-Haney, M., 381
Hudson, J. I., 556
Hudson, L., 20
Huesmann, L. R., 222, 473
Hufnagel, R., 34
Hugenberg, K., 457
Hughes, J., 583
Hughes, J. P., 377
Hughes, V. A., 350
Hui-Sheng, L., 469
Hull, A. J., 236
Hull, C. L., 365
Hull, J. G., 368
Hulvej Rod, N., 421
Human, L. J., 456
Hummer, R. A., 430
Hummer, T. A., 222, 223
Hung, M. P., 320
Hunsley, J., 518, 595, 596
Hunt, E., 283
Hunt, M., 574
Hunter, J. A., 466
Hunter, W. M., 216
Huonker, R., 67
Hur, K., 606
Hurford, J. R., 307
Hurlemann, R., 94
Hurley, D., 172
Hurley, S., 146
Hurvich, L. M., 113
Hussein, A. A., 381
Huttner, H. B., 88
Hutton, C., 214
Huynh, V. W., 152
Hvas, L., 351
Hviid, A., 334, 341
Hwang, C. S., 177
Hyde, J. S., 465
Hyde, M., 430
Hyde, T., 62
Hygge, S. A., 195
Hyman, I. E., 252
Hyman, I. E., Jr., 251
Hyman, S. E., 64, 540, 544, 550
Hyun, C. S., 593

I

Iacoboni, M., 80, 382
Iacono, W., 380
Iacono, W. G., 380
Ibanez, A., 308, 348
Ibanez-Reyes, J., 457
Iber, C., 154
Ibrahim, L., 606
Ibrahim, L. A., 606

Idel, H., 409
Iezzi, T., 126
Iglesias, J. E., 543
Ihori, N., 473
Iijima, S., 154
Ikeda, K., 121
Imaizumi, Y., 321
Imamizu, H., 76
Imbeault, P., 375
Imber, S. D., 578
Imhof, K. I., 151
Inagaki, R. K., 176
Incera, S., 309
Ing, L. P., 261
Ingaham, L. J., 563, 564
Innis, R. B., 179
Inokuchi, K., 238
Insalaco, G., 156
Insel, T. R., 94, 317, 534, 575
Institute of Medicine, 341
Ioannidis, J. P. A., 493
Iranpour, C., 535
Irimia, A., 25, 80, 97
Irmler, M., 57
Irons, G., 194
Irukayama-Tomobe, Y., 159
Irwin, A. R., 473
Irwin, M., 159
Isabel, J., 508
Isejima, H., 149
Isele, D., 208
Isenberg, D. A., 428
Isenberg, D. J., 440
Ishizawa, Y., 201
Isingring, M., 351
Ismail, H., 412
Isozumi, K., 156
Ispa, J. M., 208
Ito, T. A., 380
Itohara, S., 470
Itoi, E., 88
Ivers, H., 590
Iverson, G. L., 291
Ives, D. G., 255
Ivry, R. B., 76
Iwakabe, S., 599
Iwamasa, G. Y., 531, 532
Iwamoto, E. T., 172
Iwasato, T., 470
Iwawaki, S., 384
Izard, C., 93
Izuma, K., 371

J

Jackson, J. C., 529
Jackson, J. S., 465
Jackson, J. W., 535
Jackson, L. A., 468
Jackson, M. L., 152
Jackson, T., 126
Jacobs, E. A., 599
Jacobs, S., 409, 453
Jacobs, W. J., 196
Jacobsen, B., 563, 564
Jacobsen, R. K., 409
Jacobson, K., 560
Jacobson, K. C., 470
Jacobson, L., 32
Jacobson, N. S., 587, 588, 593
Jacobson, S. G., 112
Jadavji, N. M., 404
Jafarpour, A., 238
Jaffe, A. E., 564, 565
Jaganath, D., PIA-14
Jahn, D. R., 609
Jain, A., 334, 341

Jain, D., 216
Jalabert, M., 170, 172
Jamal, A., 173
Jamal, N. I., 308
James, B., PIA-6
James, D., 162
James, J. B., 465
James, W., 5, 146, 256, 365, 385
Jameson, D., 113
Jameson, M., 34
Jamieson, G. A., 167
Jamieson, J. P., 415, 416
Jan, K., 381
Jancke, L., 553, 554
Jang, K. L., 505, 512, 531
Janicki-Deverts, D., 410, 413
Janis, I., 440, 441
Janos, P. M., 294
Janowitz, H. D., 374
Jansen, A., 377
Janssen, S. M. J., 262
Janssens, L., 430
Jansson, L., 563, 564
January, D., 305
Jarosz, A. F., 238
Jarry, C., 351
Javitch, J. A., 62, 93
Jazayeri, M., 95
Jeffrey, R. W., 586
Jehn, K., 6
Jencius, M., 598
Jenike, M. A., 77
Jenkins, C. D., 417
Jenni, O. G., 89
Jensen, A. R., 317
Jensen, G., 191
Jensen, J., 612
Jensen, M. P., 214
Jensen, P. S., 542
Jensen, S., 553
Jensen, T. S., 126
Jeon, M., 420
Jerrett, D. J., 305
Jessell, T. M., 88
Jessen, F., 70
Jex, S. M., 428
Jha, S. K., 152
Jhamandas, J. H., 263
Jia, F., 213
Jiang, H., 166
Jiang, Y., 543, 550, 565, 575
Jin, R., 546
Jin, X., 413
Jin, Y., 69
Jobe, J. B., 352
Joel, D., 73
Johansen-Berg, H., 126
Johansson, P. P., 89
John, O. P., 510, 512, 531
Johns, H., 263
Johnson, B. N., 587
Johnson, C. D., 337, 430
Johnson, C. P., 334, 341
Johnson, D., 466
Johnson, D. J., 337
Johnson, H. A., 309
Johnson, J., 343, 546
Johnson, J. D., 222, 473
Johnson, K. A., 460
Johnson, K. O., 104
Johnson, M., 470
Johnson, M. E., 404
Johnson, P., 456
Johnson, R., 367, 466
Johnson, R. M., 179
Johnson, S. B., 414
Johnson, W., 317

Johnston, A. E., 291
Johnston, D., 57
Johnston, K. A., 147
Johnston, L., 178
Johnston, L. D., 177, 178
Johnston, W. A., 147
Johnstone, A. M., PIA-15
Joiner, T. E., 161, 540, 553
Joint Task Force for the Development
 of Telepsychology Guidelines for
 Psychologists, 597
Jokel, R., 70
Jokela, M., 506
Jones, A. K. P., 427
Jones, A. M., 585, 586
Jones, E. E., 458, 459
Jones, E. J., 599
Jones, G. W., 469
Jones, J., 450
Jones, J. L., 263
Jones, L., 560
Jones, M. C., 9
Jones, M. K., 195
Jones, P. B., 179
Jones, R. M., 346
Jones, S. K., 430
Jones-Hagata, L. B., 543, 550, 565, 575
Jonides, J., 136, 612
Jonval, L., 67, 610
Jordan, C. L., 13
Jorgensen, P. J., 293
Jorgensen, T., 409
Joseph, C., 384
Josephs, O., 214
Josephson, R., 57
Josephson Institute Center for Youth
 Ethics, PIA-20
Joswig, H., 126
Jourdan, D., 426
Jovasevic, V., 246
Judelsohn, R. G., 334
Julien, R. M., 62, 64, 602, 603, 604, 605
Junco, R., PIA-6
Juneja, M., 411
Jung, C., 8, 493, 506, 518
Jung, J., 171
Jung, R. E., 285
Juon, H. S., 532, 541
Just, M. A., 290
Justice, A. E., 377
Juurlink, D. N., 177

K

Kaas, J. H., 88
Kabani, N., 78
Kabat-Zinn, J., 382, 427
Kable, J. A., 172
Kachadourian, L., 172
Kadar, T., 347
Kadic-Maglajlic, S., 296
Kadipasaoglu, C. M., 246, 247
Kaemmer, B., 517, 518
Kagan, J., 335, 486, 519
Kagawa-Singer, M., 351
Kahali, B., 377
Kahan, M., 177
Kahn, I., 256
Kahn, V., 335
Kahneman, D., 272, 276
Kail, R., 237
Kainulainen, H., 89
Kaiser, R. H., 588
Kajander, T., 293
Kakko, J., 177
Kako, E., 305
Kales, A., 154, 157

Kalibatseva, Z., 532, 541
Kalisch, R., 382
Kalle, A., 612
Kaloustian, G., 337
Kalra, G., 350
Kamau, C., 440
Kamin, L. J., 299, 317
Kamitaki, N., 13, 564
Kamitani, Y., 165
Kammer, J. R., 543
Kan, C.-H., 428
Kandel, E., 260
Kandel, E. R., 62, 77, 87, 240, 260
Kandler, C., 509
Kane, M. J., 237
Kang, D., 153
Kang, H., 151
Kang, N., 148
Kanno, H., 88
Kanter, J. W., 587
Kanto, W. P., 159
Kaplan, D. M., 598
Kaplan, E., 81
Kaplan, G. A., 430
Kaplan, J., 80
Kaplan, M. F., 440
Kaplan, R., 612
Kaplan, S., 136, 612
Kaplan, S. L., 346
Kapoor, E., 351
Karantzas, G. C., 337
Karantzoulis, S., 263
Karau, S. J., 442
Kardum, I., 384
Kareholt, I., 351
Kariisa, M., 177
Karl, A., 126
Karlin, B. E., 584
Karlsson, H., 563, 564
Karmen, A., 475
Karney, B. R., 458
Karniel, A., 67
Karpicke, J. D., 245, 248, PIA-14
Karpova, Y., 413
Karsten, A., 303
Kasanin, J. D., 417
Kasch, K. L., 543
Kase, N. G., 324
Kasen, S., 546
Kasi, S. V., 409
Kasl, S. V., 417
Kaslow, N. J., 595
Kasoff, W. S., 66
Kass, A. E., 557
Kastenbaum, R., 355
Kasthuri, N., 58
Katigbak, M. S., 457
Katsura, M., 399
Katz, V. L., 324
Kaufman, C., 593
Kaufman, G., 452
Kaufman, J. C., 282
Kaufmann, J., 69
Kaufmann, T., 565
Kaul, J. D., A-12
Kavoussi, R. J., 470
Kawachi, I., 4, 412
Kawaguchi, Y., 201
Kaye, W. H., 558
Kazdin, A. E., 587, 596
Kearney, C. A., 602
Kearney, J., 586
Kecklund, G., 151
Keding, T. J., 549
Keel, P. K., 556, 557
Keeley, S. M., 18
Keenan, J. P., 273

Keesey, R. E., 375
Keidel, J. L., 261
Keillor, J., 387
Keilp, J., 262
Keirsey, D., 518
Keita, G. P., 541
Keith, T. Z., 285
Keleman, K., 260
Keller, C. J., 89
Keller, M. B., 602
Kellermann, T., 76
Kelley, K. W., 88
Kelley, M. E., 597, 610
Kellner, C. H., 608
Kelly, C. L., 240
Kelly, D. L., 179
Kelly, I, 18
Kelly, I. W., 18
Kelly, J. A., 454
Kelly, K. M., 610
Kelly, M. S., 610
Kelly, T. L., 152
Kemenes, G., 250
Kemenes, I., 250
Kemeny, M. E., 420
Kemper, K. J., 213
Kempermann, G., 88
Kempf, L., 365
Kendell, S. F., 178
Kendler, K. S., 217, 401, 544, 560, PIA-18
Kendrick, K. M., 94
Kenett, Y. N., 243
Kennedy, G., 429
Kennedy, J. F., 250
Kenny, A., 4
Kenrick, D. T., 370, 371
Kensinger, E. A., 238, 352
Keown, C. L., 81
Keown-Stoneman, C., 542
Keren, G., 426
Keri, S., 550
Kerig, P. K., 599
Kernberg, O. F., 595
Keromoian, R., 337
Kerr, N. L., 442
Kerr-German, A., 71
Kerr-German, A. N., 71
Kerridge, B. T., 171
Kerson, C., 213
Kersten, A. W., 248
Kerwin, D. R., A-8
Kesarwani, R., 263
Kesebir, S., 371
Kesler, S., 320
Kessler, R., 535, 536
Kessler, R. C., 534, 535, 537, 540, 541, 545, 546, 549, 556, A-9
Kettenmann, H., 57
Kety, S. S., 563, 564
Keulen, S., 76
Keyes, K. M., 179
Keyes, M., 317
Khademi, J., 216
Khalife, S., 606
Khayat, D., 195
Kiecolt-Glaser, J. K., 409, 413, 426
Kiejna, A., 556
Kielar, A., 70
Kiernan, P. T., 291
Kievit, R. A., 69
Kihlstrom, J., 389
Kihlstrom, J. F., 167, 250, 528
Kikinis, R., 25, 80, 97
Kilburn, J., 473
Kilgus, M. D., 574, 575
Killen, J. D., 546
Killgore, W., 154

Kilmartin, C. T., 384
Kilner, J. M., 80
Kilpatrick, D., 399
Kim, B. H., 366
Kim, C. E., 153
Kim, C. Y., 104
Kim, D., 440
Kim, H., 263, 327, 384
Kim, H. J., 532, 541
Kim, H. S., 428
Kim, J., 380
Kim, J. J., 89
Kim, K. C., 463
Kim, M., 137
Kim, P., 421
Kim, S., 20, 463
Kim, S. W., 153
Kim, U., 421
Kim, Y. J., 549
Kim-Fuchs, C., 412
Kimhi, Y., 334
Kimmel, R. J., 606
Kimoto, S., 57
Kim-Prieto, C., 459
Kimura, R., 263
Kinasz, K., 557
Kincade, M. J., 82
King, C. G., 427
King, J.-R., 106
King, M., 134
King, M. L., Jr., 463
King, M. W., 549
King, N. J., 586
King, R., 463
King, R. A., 173
King, S., 400
Kinge, J. M., 377
Kinney, D. K., 563, 564
Kinney, J., 239
Kinzie, D., 532
Kirby, J. S., 552
Kirby, K. A., 549
Kircanski, K., 586
Kircher, T., 214
Kirkby, K. C., 76
Kirkland, D., 280
Kirkland, S., 418
Kirkland, S. W., 404
Kirkorian, H. L., PIA-6
Kirmayer, L. J., 551
Kirsch, I., 166, 167, 168, 252, 499
Kirsten, J., 322
Kirzner, E., 442
Kishimoto, T., 57
Kishore, S., 585
Kitamura, T., 238
Kitaoka, A., 137
Kitayama, S., 373, 374, 384, 459
Kitsune, V., 70
Kittenis, M. D., 167
Kivimaki, M., 409, 412, 413
Kivipelto, M., 351
Kivley, L. S., 382
Kivlighan, D. M., 612
Klaver, C. C., 112
Klaver, P., 260
Klei, L., 334
Kleim, B., 549
Klein, A., 404
Klein, D. F., 546
Klein, D. N., 335, 602
Klein, L. C., 429
Klein, N., 213
Klein, S. B., 9
Kleindienst, N., 552
Kleineidam, C. H., 409
Kleinman, J. E., 62

Kleinot, M. C., 453
Kleitman, N., 153
Klemchuk, H. M., 427
Klerman, G. L., 541
Kliewer, W., 384
Kligman, A. M., 354
Kline, P., 504
Kling, J. M., 351
Kling, K. C., 465
Kloda, L. A., 126
Klopp, K., 376
Klorman, R., 586
Kluetsch, R., 214
Kluft, R. P., 553
Klump, K. L., 557
Klunder, A. D., 565
Klüver, H., 77
Knauer, R. S., 149, 150
Knecht, S., 85, 126
Knight, A., 462
Knight, J. A., 354
Knight, R. T., 81, 238, 246, 247
Knoblich, G., 152
Knopik, V. S., 293, 297, 298, 299, 510, 512, 531, 557, 564
Knoth, R., 88
Knowles, E. D., 459, 460
Knowlton, B., 240
Knuppertz, H., 549
Kobasa, S., 418
Kobayashi, K., 473
Kobayashi, M., 149
Kober, H., 382
Koberda, J. L., 214
Koch, C., 146
Koch, L. G., 89
Koch, S., 67, 610
Koegel, L. K., 213
Koelling, R. A., 195
Koenen-Woods, P., 585
Koenig, H. G., 430
Koerner, K., 587
Koerselman, F., 610
Koester, J., 57
Koestner, R., 371
Koh, J. K., 474
Kohl, S., 66
Kohlberg, L., 347, 348
Kohlenberg, R. J., 587, 588
Kohler, W., 7, 217, 218
Kohlmann, C.-W., 426
Kohout, J., A-5
Koide, T., 470
Koifman, B., 426
Koizumi, A., 494
Kok, B. E., 428
Kokkalis, J., 178
Kolachana, B. S., 62
Kolata, S., 238
Kolber, P., 69
Kolevzon, A., 94
Kollias, S., 214
Kolodny, A., 177
Kolt, G. S., 399
Komatsu, L. K., 274
Kompanje, E. J., 154
Komproe, I. H., 553
Kondel, T. K., 255
Kondwani, K., 427
Kong, A., 510
Kong, Y. H., 417
Konishi, H., 303
Konowal, N. M., 151
Konrad, C., 156
Konrad, K., 77
Konstantinidis, E., 494
Koo, D. S., 308

Koob, G. F., 170, 173
Koole, S. L., 602
Kopal-Sibley, D. C., 335
Kopp, C. B., 338
Koresh, D., 450
Korf, J., 554
Korkmaz, B., 334
Korn, S., 335
Korneev, S. A., 250
Kornhaber, M. L., 317
Kornhuber, J., 179
Kortenkamp, S., 387
Korzeniewska, A., 81
Kosslyn, S. M., 272, 273
Kotchen, J. M., A-8
Kotchen, T., 427
Kotchoubey, B., 214
Kotkin, M., 595
Koto, A., 156
Kotrcova, K., 337
Kotzot, D., 320
Kovacs, K., 173
Kozakowski, S. S., 337
Kozberg, M., 327
Kozel, F. A., 67, 610
Koziol, L. F., 76
Koziol-McLain, J., 405
Kraemer, H. C., 546
Kraff, M., 378
Kraha, A., 250
Kramer, A. F., 89, 352
Kramer, C., 323
Kramer, S. J., 403
Krapohl, E., 299
Krathwohl, D. R., PIA-13
Kratofil, P. H., 172
Kravits, S. L., PIA-12
Kreek, M. J., 177
Kreiner, P., 177
Kremers, S. P., 353
Krencik, R., 57
Kreutzer, M. A., 383
Kriegeskorte, N., 256
Kriegstein, A., 57
Kril, J. J., 88
Kristensen, P., 317
Kritz-Silverstein, D., 549
Kriwisky, M., 426
Krizan, Z., 153
Kroenke, C. H., 428
Krokoff, L. J., 469
Kroll, J. F., 308
Kroll, T., 149
Kronstein, P., 606
Krosnick, J. A., 454
Kross, E., 612
Krpan, K. M., 612
Krueger, R. F., 541, 575
Kruger, C., 553
Kruggel, F., 241
Krupnick, J. L., 599
Kruttner, S., 260
Kryger, M., 158
Krzyszycha, K., 446, 447
Kubic, L. S., 213
Kubicki, M., 563, 565
Kubiszewski, V., 347
Kubler-Ross, E., 354
Kudenko, D., 222
Kuhl, B. A., 256
Kuhle, C. L., 351
Kuhlman, S. J., 149
Kuhn, E., 584
Kuhn, H. W., 562
Kuhn, J., 66
Kuiken, D., 165
Kukal, D., 517

Kulashekhar, S., 237
Kulik, G., 413
Kulik, J. A., 428
Kulmala, J., 413
Kumar, S., 546
Kumari, M., 412
Kunkel, S. R., 417
Kuntay, A., 303
Kuntsi, J., 70
Kunwar, P. S., 335
Kuo, B. C. H., 430
Kuper, D. J., 578
Kupfer, D. J., 158
Kupper, A. E., 214
Kupper, N., 418
Kurdziel, L., 152, 156
Kuriki, I., 137
Kuroda, D., 159
Kurth, S., 89
Kurtz, J. E., 521
Kurtz, L. E., 94
Kuruvilla, R., 320
Kustermann, T., 70
Kutsumura, N., 159
Kvavilashvili, L., 249
Kwan, M. L., 428

L

la Fleur, S. E., 376
LaBar, K. S., 250, 380, 470
LaBerge, D., 236
Laberon, S., 354
Labkovsky, E., 70
Labouvie-Vief, G., 332
Lacayo, A., 172
Lacinova, L., 337
Ladda, R. L., 157
Lado, F. A., 89
Laeng, B., 328
LaFromboise, T., 422
LaGana, C., 586
Laghi, F., 414
Lagopoulos, J., 427
Lahti, I., 563
Lai, E. W., 421
Lai, H-K., PIA-14
Lai, M.-C., 334
Lajtha, A., 173
Laksy, K., 563
Lal, S., 6
Lalancette, M.-F., 439
Lalanne, L., 67, 610
Lalich, J., 450
Lall, G. S., 150
Lalonde, C. E., 302
Lam, B. C. P., 223
Lambert, M. J., 595
Lambert, N., 430
Lambert, R. E., 428
Lambie, A., 405
Lammers, G. J., 159
Lampe, C., 467
Lan, M. J., 67
Lana-Peixoto, Marco A., 154
Lance, C. J., 519
Landrum, R. E., A-5, A-6
Lane, R. D., 382
Laney, C., 251
Lange, C., 385
Lange, F. P., 273
Lange, S., 324
Langer, E. J., 403
Langone, M. C., 449
Lanius, R. A., 214, 554
Lanphear, B. P., 293
Lanteaume, L., 214

Laplante, D. P., 400
LaPointe, J. A., 519
Lapsley, D. K., 347
Laroi, F., 473
Larsen, J. T., 380
Larson, C. L., 380
Larson, D. B., 430
Larson, J. D., 237
Larue, V., 214
Larzelere, R., 208
LaSasso, C., 308
Lashley, K. S., 366
Laska, E. M., 609
Laskey, A. L., 216
Lasnik, H., 302
Latane, B., 12, 442, 475, 476
Lattie, E. G., 537, 614
Latzman, R. D., 29, 424, 519, 585, 596
Lau, A., 599
Lau, H., 156, 494
Laudenslager, M. L., 556
Laugero, K. D., 376
Laughon, K., 405
Launer, L., 351
Laungani, P., 355
Laurence, J. R., 166, 167
Laurent, E., 414
Lauriola, M., 368
Lauzon, N. M., 170
Lavergne, G. M., 470
Lavie, N., 279
Lavie, P., 158
Laviolette, S. R., 170
Lavis, J. N., 422
Lavori, P. W., 262
Lawrence, T. B., 6
Laws, G., 305
Laws, K. R., 178, 255
Lawton, E., 613
Lawton, R. J., 587
Laxpati, N. G., 66
Lay, C., 422
Lay, K.-L., 337
Laymon, M., 427
Layne, C., 593
Layne, R. M., 541
Lazar, S., 427
Lazarus, R. S., 389, 402, 414, 426
Lazzerini Ospri, L., 541
Le, B. N., 188
Le, C. P., 412
Le Grange, D., 557
Le Moal, M., 170
Lea, L., 585, 586
Leaderbrand, K., 246
Leary, M. R., 476, 502, 581
Leask, J., 235
Leavitt, L. A., 303
Lebedeva, N. M., 372
Lebens, M., 549
LeBlanc, S., 380
Lecca, S., 170, 172
Leccese, A. P., 178
Leckman, J. F., 293
Leclerc, C. M., 352, 458, 459
Lecoultre, V., 610
Leddy, J. J., 587
LeDoux, J. E., 64, 83, 106, 240, 260, 380, 381, 386, 389, 470, 550
Lee, A. D., 565
Lee, B. E., 598
Lee, C. M., 518
Lee, C. W., 585
Lee, D. J., 66, 610
Lee, F., 459
Lee, H. K., 541
Lee, J., 153, 429, 565

Lee, K., 419
Lee, K. L., 417
Lee, L., 152
Lee, M., 177
Lee, P. H., 511
Lee, R., 470
Lee, R. X., 470
Lee, S., 214, 535
Lee, S. J., 208
Lee, T. G., 80
Lee, T. L., 71
Lee, Y. M., 584
Lefevre, A., 95
Lega, B., 260
Legate, N., 317
LeGates, T. A., 541
Leggett, E. L., 367
LeGoff, D. B., 586
Lehnert, B., 108
Lehr, U., 417
Leib, R., 67
Leibel, R. L., 375
Leiderman, P. H., 337
Leiserowitz, A., 4
Leiter, J. C., 159
Lejuez, C. W., 368
Lemere, C. A., 263
Lemon, R. N., 80
Lemons, J. A., 159
Lemos, M. S., 364
Lena, M. L., 96, 97
Lenartz, D., 66
Lenhart, A., 467
Lensu, S., 89
Lenzenweger, M. F., 253, 595
Leon, P., 351
Leone, D. R., 371
Leong, A. T. L., 67
Leong, D. J., 333
Leong, F. T., 532, 541
Leong, F. T. L., 493
Leow, A. D., 565
LePort, A. K., 241
Lepper, M. R., 364
Lepsien, J., 89
Lerner, A. G., 178
Leroy, C., 421
Lesage, E., 200
Leslie, A. M., 334
Leslie, L. M., 529
Leslie, M., 295
Lester, D., 608
Leszcz, M., 592
Letenneur, L., 354
Leung, K., 351
Levant, I., 137
Leveck, M. D., 352
Levenson, J., 297
Levenson, R. W., 380
Levenstein, S., 409
Levesque, R. J. R., 175
Levi, E., 243
Levin, E. D., 173
Levin, I. P., 368
Levin, J., 70
Levin, K. H., 179
Levine, C. S., 376
Levine, M., 475, 477
Levine, S. C., 291
Levinson, S., 194
Levinton, C., 428
Levitsky, D. K., 427
Levy, B. J., 612
Levy, B. R., 417
Levy, K. N., 595
Levy, S. R., 457
Levy-Gigi, E., 550

Lewin, D. S., 161
Lewin, R., 306
Lewis, B. P., 429
Lewis, C., 82
Lewis, C. M., 317
Lewis, C. P., 67, 152
Lewis, D. K., 599
Lewis, G., 179
Lewis, H. C., 251
Lewis, J. E., 509
Lewis, J. R., 528
Lewis, P. A., 67, 152
Lewis, R., 429
Lewis, S., 443
Lewontin, R. C., 317
Li, B., 57
Li, C.-T., 179
Li, D., 411, 412, 612
Li, D. H., 172
Li, H., 213
Li, J., 334, 341, 375, 421
Li, L., 323, 324, 421
Li, R., 255
Li, S., 263
Li, X., 260
Li, X. Wang, 334
Li, Y., 89
Li, Y. J., 460
Li, Z., 323
Liang, D., 322
Liao, Y., 151
Libbrecht, N., 296
Liberman, D., 255
Lichstein, K. L., 159
Lieberman, D., 25, 80, 97
Lieberman, J. A., 604
Liebl, J., 88
Liechti, M. E., 178
Lievens, F., 296
Light, K., 238
Lilienfeld, S. O., 29, 167, 424, 519, 520,
   521, 553, 585, 596
Lim, B. C., 529
Lim, C. C. W., 562, 563
Lim, J., 152, 153
Lim, K. M., 223
Lim, L., 543
Lim, M. M., 94
Lim, Y. Y., 263
Lin, C. S., 70
Lin, L., 499, PIA-6
Lin, P. J., 275
Lin, S. Z., 323
Lincoln, A. J., 81
Lind, B. K., 351
Lindemann, B., 121
Lindquist, K., 549
Lindsay, E. K., 427
Lingford-Hughes, A., 179
Linkous, R. A., 442
Linnell, J., 334
Linnell, K. J., 136
Linnoila, M., 470
Linnoila, M. I., 470
Linville, N., 612
Linz, D., 222, 473
Lipsman, N., 66, 610
Lipson, S. K., 537, 614
Lipworth, L., 427
Lisanby, S. H., 608
Liston, C., 67
Little, T. D., 372
Littman, E., 517
Litzelman, K., 400
Liu, A., 78
Liu, C., 324
Liu, N. K., 88
Liu, S., 154

Liu, X., 220
Liu, Y., 334
Livermore, E. E., 543
Livesley, J. W., 560
Livesley, W. J., 505, 512, 531
Livingston, G., 255
Lizskowski, U., 303
Lo Bue, A., 156
LoBello, S. G., 541
Locantore, J. K., 352
Locascio, J. J., 238
Lock, M., 351
Locke, A. E., 377
Locke, E. A., 365
Locke, K. D., 334
Lockenhoff, C., 507
Lockhart, R. S., 231, 240
Lodder, P., 418
Lodge, D. J., 179
Loeber, R., 291
Loehlin, J. C., 510, 512, 531
Loewen, S., 333, 334
Loewenstein, R. J., 553, 554
Loftus, E., 248, 249, 250, A-1
Loftus, E. F., 188, 243, 251, 252, 553
Loftus, G. R., 188
Lohaus, A., 426
Lohman, E., 427
Lohmann, H., 85
Lohr, J. M., 167, 585
Loke, H., 429
LoLordo, V. M., 196
Lombardi, C., 159
Lombardi, D. A., 149
Lombardo, M. V., 334
Long, H. H., 6
Longo, L., 608
Longo, L. C., 466
Lonigro, A., 414
Lonky, E., 293
Lonnqvist, J., 541
Loo, C., 609
Loop, T., A-5
Lopez, R., 382
Lopez, S. J., 503
Lopez-Garcia, E., 174
Lopez-Munoz, F., 604, 605
Lopez-Quintero, C., 172, 173
Lord, T. R., 466
Lorenz, K., 469
Lorenzo, G. L., 456
Lotstein, D. S., 428
Loughead, J., 67, 610
Lovaas, O. I., 208, 213, 583
Lovegrove, M. C., 169
Lovett, S. J., 88
Lovibond, S. H., 472
Lowe, R. A., 477
Lowenstein, R. L., 553, 554
Lowery, R., 370
Lowry, C. A., 220
Lozano, A. M., 54, 610
Lu, A., 565
Lu, S., 323
Lu, S. Y., 69
Lu, T., 337
Lu, Y., 70
Lubar, J., 213
Lubell, B., 440
Lubinski, D., 512
Luborsky, L., 413, 595
Luchins, A. S., 456
Lucia, V. C., 549
Luck, S. J., 562, 563
Luckenbaugh, D. A., 606
Lucy, J. A., 305
Ludwig, D. S., 377
Ludwig, N., 94

Ludwig, N. N., 94
Luechinger, R., 553, 554
Lueders, A., 457
Luedtke, R. R., 172
Luessi, F., 69
Lui, M. A., 70
Lui, S., 76
Luigjes, J., 66
Lun, J., 529
Luo, L., 163
Luppi, P.-H., 156
Luria, A. R., 80, 256
Luscher, C., 67
Lusk, R., 442
Lustiga, C., 247
Lutgendorf, S. K., 419
Lutkenhaus, P., 336
Lutz, K. J., 350
Lutz, P. E., 89
Lutz, R. J., 453
Lutzenberger, W., 126
Ly, M., 69
Lydecker, J. A., 557
Lydersen, S., 337
Lydon, J. E., 94
Lyketsos, C., 255
Lykken, D. T., 512, 560
Lynam, D. R., 291
Lynch, G., 263
Lynch, M. E., 172
Lynn, S. J., 166, 167, 168, 553
Lynott, P. P., 349
Lyons, J. L., 70
Lyssenko, L., 552
Lyznicki, J. M., 151

M

Ma, J., 208
Ma, W. J., 371
MacCoun, R. J., 442
MacDonald, A. P., 367, 498
MacDonald, D., 78
MacDonald, G., 467
MacDonald, M. C., 236, 237
MacDougall, H., 334
Machnes, Z., 400
Maciejewski, P. K., 355
Mack, J. E., 252
MacKay, D. G., 246
MacKenzie, E. J., 126
Mackenzie, L., 347
MacKenzie, M. J., 208
MacKenzie, S. B., 453
Mackin, R. S., 401, 402
MacKinnon, C. D., 156
MacKisack, M., 273
Macknik, S. L., 134, 137
Maclean, C. R., 427
MacLeod, C. M., 256
MacMillan, H. L., 208
Macmillan, M., 96, 97
Macmillan, N. A., 106
Macpherson, F., 273
Macquet, P., 164
Macrae, C. N., 456, 457
Macropoulis, G., 203
Mactavish, E., 263
Madanat, H. N., 376
Madden, M., 467
Maddox, J., 425
Maddox, J. H., 608
Madore, K. P., 352
Madras, B. K., 179
Madsen, K. M., 334, 341
Madsen, S., 350
Maes, C., 88
Maes, M., 89

Maestas, M. V., 422
Magalhaes, A. C., 263
Magee, L., 590, 594, 596
Magee, W. J., 546
Maggioni, E., 77
Magi, R., 377
Magnussen, S., 328
Magoun, H. W., 75
Mahbod, P., 377
Mahdhaoui, A., 303
Mahler, H. I. M., 428
Mahoney, M. J., 503
Mahowald, M. W., 154, 158
Mahr, I., 170
Maibach, E., 4
Maibach, H. I., 354
Maier, S. F., 219, 220, 409
Maier, W., 94
Main, M., 336
Maislin, G., 152
Maitland, S. B., 242
Majda, B. T., 88
Mak, D., 421
Makhijani, M. G., 466
Makin, T. R., 126
Makinodan, M., 57
Malaktaris, A., 553
Malarkey, W. B., 409
Malhi, G. S., 427
Malik, M., 334, 412
Malinchoc, M., 419, 420
Maljkovic, V., 273
Malkani, R. G., 153
Mallis, M. M., 151
Malone, P. S., 208
Malouff, J. M., 585
Mamdani, M. M., 177
Manalo, S., 376
Mancuso, C., 255
Mandarino, J. V., 427
Mander, B. A., 150
Mandler, G., 249
Manganello, J. A., 208
Mangun, G. R., 236
Manheim, L. J., 366
Manji, H. K., 606
Mann, F. D., 512
Mann, J. J., 606
Manning, C. C., 447
Manning, R., 475
Mannix-McNamara, P., 426
Manoiloff, L., 308
Manos, R. C., 587
Mantione, M., 610
Manusov, V., 6
Maquet, P., 156
Mara, K. C., 351
Marcado, A. M., 409
March of Dimes Foundation, 324
Marconi, G., 608
Marco-Pallares, J., 69
Marcus, G. F., 231
Marcus, S. C., 609
Marder, E., 57
Marek, R., 517
Maren, S., 77
Marenco, S., 317
Marentette, P. F., 303
Margeta, M., 57
Margolin, S., 213
Margolskee, R. F., 121
Mark Carrier, L., PIA-6
Markman, E. M., 305
Markou, A., 173
Markowitz, J., 595
Markowitz, J. C., 578
Marks, D. F., 414
Markus, H. R., 373, 384, 439

Marmar, C., 549
Marmot, M., 352, 412, 421
Marmot, M. G., 411
Marnane, C., 535
Maroco, J., 414
Marois, R., 381
Marques, L., 557
Marques, M., 371
Marrone, O., 156
Mars, A. E., 334, 341
Marsden, K. E., 371
Marsella, A. J., 532
Marshall, G. A., 15
Marshall, J., 177, 333, 341
Marshall, S. W., 291
Marsiske, M., 352
Martelon, M., 542
Martin, B., 403
Martin, D., 609
Martin, G. I., 159
Martin, G. N., 540
Martin, J. A., 354
Martin, J. W., 381
Martin, L., 158
Martin, N. G., 557
Martin, R., 57
Martin, T. A., 518
Martin, W., 172
Martinet, L., 412, 413
Martinez-Conde, S., 134, 137
Martinez-Taboas, A., 553
Martins de Almeida, R., 470
Martinussen, R., 238
Martyn, A. C., 263
Martynowska, K., 446, 447
Marucha, P. T., 409
Maruff, P., 263, 414
Maruta, T., 419, 420
Marutle, A., 57
Marzetta, B. R., 427
Mas, A., 178
Mas, M., 178
Masaki, K., 351
Mash, E. J., 596
Maslach, C., 442
Masliah, E., 263
Maslow, A., 11, 369, 370, 500, 501, 502, 503, A-11
Mason, I., 153
Mason, N. S., 543
Massaro, D. W., 233
Massart, R., 400
Massazza, G., 67, 610
Masson, J. M., 495
Mastandueno, R., 348
Master, A., 20
Masters, J. C., 590
Masuda, M., 401
Masuda, T., 459
Matharan, F., 354
Matheny, J., 399
Mathews, R., PIA-15
Matsumoto, D., 598
Matsumoto, K., 371, 399
Matsumoto, M., 371
Matsuo, T., 149
Mattay, V. S., 565
Mattes, R. D., 121
Mattfeld, A. T., 241
Matthew, N., 334
Matthews, A., 291
Matthews, J. A., 552
Matthews, K. A., 152, 417, 418
Mattic, K. R. P., 177
Mattingley, J. B., 80
Mattox, S., 237
Mattson, M. P., 408
Matusch, A., 149

Matzel, L. D., 200, 238
Mauk, J. E., 334, 341
Maul, P., 201
Maurer, D., 328
Mavor, K., 464
Mawase, F., 67
Maxmen, J. S., 574, 575
Mayberg, H., 610
Mayberg, H. S., 597, 610
Mayer, B., 173
Mayer, J. D., 296
Mayer, L. E. S., 606
Mayer, R. E., PIA-13
Mayes, A. R., 351
Maynard, K. E., 417
Mayo, E., A-12
Mayo Clinic, 428
Mayo Clinic Staff, 158
Mayor, E., 414
Mayorga, M. E., 175
Mazziotta, J. C., 80
Mazzoni, G. A. L., 252
McAdams, D. P., 486, 495, 507
McAuley, E., 352
McAuliffe, S., 172
McAuliffe, T. L., 454
McCabe, B. J., 519
McCall, W. V., 66
McCann, S. J. H., 150, 506
McCarley, J. S., 147
McCarley, R., 163, 164
McCarley, R. W., 75, 563, 565
McCarroll, S. A., 13, 564
McCarthy, C. J., 532
McCartney, K., 337
McCarty, C. A., 429
McCauley, C., 441
McClain, M., 320
McClelland, D. C., 366
McClelland, J. L., 231, 243
McClintock, S. M., 610
McCormack, W. A., 368
McCormick, D. A., 149
McCormick, M. C., 334, 341
McCrae, R. R., 505, 506, 507, 510, 512, 513, 518, 531
McCrea, M., 291
McCullough, J. P., 602
McCullough, M. E., 430
McCurdy, M. T., 220
McDaniel, M. A., PIA-10
McDermott, J. F., 542
McDermott, K. B., 251
McDonald, G. P., 4
McDonald, W. M., 66
McDougall, T., 542
McDougall, W., 365
McElroy, S. L., 604
McEwen, B. S., 89, 250, 411
McEwen, C. A., 411
McFarland, S., 472
McFarlane, T., 532
McGarty, C., 464
McGaugh, J. L., 241, 250
McGhee, D. E., 457
McGill, A. E., 18
McGinn, L. K., 588
McGlinchey, E., 161
McGrath, C. L., 597
McGrath, E., 541
McGrath, J., 563
McGrath, J. J., 562, 563
McGrath, R. E., 521
McGraw, K., 126
McGraw, S. A., 351
McGreenery, C. E., 542
McGregor, D., A-11
McGrew, K. S., 284

McGue, M., 317, 510
McGuffin, P., 365, 563
McGuire, F., A-12
McGuire, L., 409, 413
McIntosh, A. R., 352
McIntosh, D. N., 412
McIver, D. J., 153
McKay, J. R., 413
McKay, P. F., 464
McKee, A. C., 291
McKee, M., 419
McKenzie, J. E., 606
McKinley, P., 418
McKinney, S. M., 153
McKinnon, A., 548
McLaughlin, A. C., 18
McLaughlin, S. K., 121
McMahon, D. G., 149
McMahon, F. J., 544
McMahon, M. A., 565
McMeekin, L. J., 148
McMillan, A., 299
McMillan, H. L., 208
McMonagle, T., 587
McMullen, E. J., 502, 581
McNally, R. J., 253, 399, 553
McNamara, J. M., 375
McNeill, D., 246
McPherson, J. M., 467
McRae, M. B., 430
McTigue, K. M., A-8
McWilliams, N., 578
Meador, B. D., 580
Meaney, M. J., 89
Mearns, J., 499
Mease, R. A., 260
Mechawar, N., 170
Mechelli, A., 76
Mechtler, K., 260
Medeiros-Ward, N., 279, PIA-6
Medical Economics Staff, 324
Medland, S., 557
Mednick, S. A., 335, 560
Meehan-Atrash, J., 173
Meek, P., 170
Meeks, T. W., 66
Meer, D. V., 565
Meesters, Y., 541
Meeter, M., 262
Mehler, P. S., 557
Mehrabian, A., 296
Mehta, A. D., 89
Mehta, S., 541
Meichenbaum, D., 590
Meijer, E., 380
Meikle, J., 334
Meille, V., 67, 610
Meineri, S., 443
Meiser-Stedman, R., 548
Mejia, O. L., 532
Melamed, S., 412
Melbye, M., 334, 341
Melchior, M., 421
Melero, H., 104
Melloni, L., 302
Melton, L. J., III, 350
Meltzer, J. A., 70
Meltzoff, A. N., 20
Melzack, R., 125
Mendes, W. B., 415, 416
Mendez, M. F., 252
Meng, X. F., 255
Meng, Z., 337
Menke, E., 421
Mennella, J. A., 120
Menon, T., 442
Menon, V., 166
Menzies, R. G., 195

Merckelbach, H., 553, 585
Meredith, L. S., 255
Meredith, W., 351
Merikle, M. P., 106
Merrill, R. M., 376
Merry, S. N., 606
Mervis, C., 275
Mervis, C. B., 274
Mesgarani, N., 236
Mesquita, B., 428
Messaritaki, E., 70
Messina, G., 375
Mesulam, M. M., 81, 252
Metcalfe, J., 246
Metz, G. A., 404
Metz, M., 260
Metzler, J., 272
Meusel, M., 173
Mewborn, C. R., 453
Meye, F. J., 170, 172
Meyer, E. C., 585
Meyer, G. J., 521
Meyer, J. S., 178
Meyer, L. H., 587
Meyer, O. L., 599
Meyer, R. P., 88
Meyer-Lindenberg, A., 565
Meyrick, J., 453
Mez, J., 291
Meziab, O., 549
Michael, R., 586
Michaels, J. W., 442
Michaud, A., 377
Michelini, G., 70
Mick, E., 542
Mickes, L., 252, 248
Micoulaud-Franchi, J. A., 214
Middleton, W., 553
Miech, R., 178
Mignot, E., 159
Migo, E. M., 351
Mihara, B., 156
Mikami, A. Y., 468
Mikell, C. B., 610
Mileno, B., 320
Miles, D. R., 470, 510
Milgram, S., 444, 445, 446
Milivojevic, B., 261
Miller, C. A., 260
Miller, C. E., 440
Miller, C. H., 71, 543
Miller, D. G., 251
Miller, E., 334, 341
Miller, E. K., 260
Miller, G., 94, 291
Miller, G. A., 70, 237
Miller, G. E., 410, 413
Miller, I. J., 122
Miller, J. F., 303
Miller, J. G., 459
Miller, K., 467
Miller, L. E., 161
Miller, L. S., 473
Miller, M., 401
Miller, M. D., 578
Miller, M. E., 168
Miller, M. K., 557
Miller, N. E., 404, 414, 469
Miller, N. F., 497
Miller, R. R., 191
Miller, W. R., 580
Milligan, M., 469
Milling, L. S., 167
Mills, M. E., 404
Milne, M., 428
Milner, B., 261
Milner, J., 208
Milovich, M. M., 471

Milstead, M., 347
Milton, A. L., 380
Milton, F., 273
Milun, R., 470
Mineka, S., 196
Miocinovic, S., 66, 67
Mirabile, R. R., 453
Miranda, M. C., 587
Mirani, J., 249
Misaki, M., 106, 494
Mischel, W., 344, 486, 506
Mishell, D. R., 351
Miskinyte, G., 323
Mitchell, A. J., 557
Mitchell, B. G., 178
Mitchell, D. B., 240
Mitchell, D. W., 326
Mitchell, G. E., 334
Mitchell, J. E., 606
Mitchell, K. A., 467
Mitchell, P., 347
Mitchell, R., 412
Mitchell, S. A., 577
Mitchum, A. L., 290
Mitroff, S. R., PIA-6
Miyagawa, T., 376
Miyake, K., 337
Miyamoto, Y., 376
Miyatake, A., 154
Miyawaki, Y., 165
Mizes, J. S., 583
Moffic, H. S., 598
Moghaddam, F. M., 463
Mogil, J. S., 126
Mohammadzaheri, F., 216
Mohammed, S. S., 240
Mohlke, K. L., 377
Moise, J. F., 473
Moise-Titus, J., 473
Molaison, H. G., 261
Molden, D. C., 367
Moldofsky, H., 151
Molenberghs, P., 80
Molina, V. A., 77
Moll, H., 303
Moller, A., 561
Moller, H. E., 89
Molloy, K., 279
Molodtsova, I., 372
Molofsky, A. V., 57
Molyneux, P. C., 150
Mommaas, M. A., 260
Mommersteeg, P. M., 418
Monda, M., 375
Monda, V., 375
Mongeau, P. A., 454
Moniz, A. E., 609
Monnais, L., 334
Monson, C. M., 585, 596
Montagna, P., 159
Montaldi, D., 351
Monteiro, P., 67
Montesanti, S. R., 422
Montgomery, C., 178
Montgomery, G., 156
Montgomery, G. H., 596
Montgomery, G. W., 557
Montgomery, P., 255
Monto, S., 237
Montplaisir, J., 156, 157
Moody, A., 88
Moody, R., 154
Moore, J. W., 191
Moore, T. E., 106
Moore, T. H., 179
Moore-Ede, M. C., 148, 149, 150
Moorhead, G., 441

Mora, G., 531
Moran, K. M., 353
Moran, L. R., 335
Moran, S., 283
Moratalla, R., 57
Moreines, J. L., 610
Moreland, J., 147
Moreland, R. L., 467
Morelli, G., 337
Morey, C. C., 237
Morgan, C. A., 409
Morgan, C. D., 520
Morgan, J. P., 178
Morgan, R., PIA-10
Moriarty, C. L., 167
Morii, M., 328
Morin, C. M., 159, 590
Moring, J., 563
Morishima, M., 201
Morishima, Y., 474
Morishita, T., 66
Morissette, S. B., 585
Morita, K., 201
Morita, Y., 156
Mormann, F., 146
Moro, A., 149
Morrell-Samuels, P., 306
Morris, H., 178
Morris, J. S., 380
Morris, M., 442, 459
Morris, M. W., 459
Morris, S., 158
Morrison, J. H., 411
Morrison, P. D., 172
Morrow, C. E., 172
Morse, C., 179
Morse, P. J., 337
Mortensen, K., 173
Mortensen, P. B., 334
Mortier, P., 537
Morton, D. L., 593
Moruzzi, G., 75
Mosack, V., 350
Moschopoulou, E., 308
Moscov, S., 339
Moscovici, S., 441
Moscovitch, M., 245
Mosely, W., 474
Moser-Mercer, B., 308
Moske, A. K., 337
Moskowitz, H. R., 122
Mosser, E. A., 149
Mößnang, C., 76
Mostert, P., 273
Mota, N., 208
Mota, N. P., 208
Motes, M. A., 67, 610
Motraghi, T. E., 585
Mottaghy, F., 273
Motyl, M., 23
Moussier, S., 471
Mouthon, A. L., 89
Movahedi, S., 472
Mowat, F., 24
Mowrer, O. H., 404, 469
Mowrer, R. R., 9
Moynihan, J., 413
Mozersky, R. P., 169
Mueller, K., 89
Mueller, U. J., 66
Mufson, L. H., 578
Muglia, P., 544
Muhlberger, A., 167
Muir, E. M., 88
Mukamel, R., 80
Mukherjee, S., 159
Muldoon, J., PIA-14

Muller, D., 382
Muller, R. A., 81
Muller, V., 565
Muller-Oerlinghausen, B., 544
Mullington, J. M., 152
Mulry, G., 454
Mulvaney, S., 389
Mulvenna, C., 104
Munafò, M., 13
Munif, D., 328
Munoz, E., 414
Munsterberg, H., A-12
Murakami, I., 137
Muralidhar, S., 380
Murata, K., 293
Muratori, F., 303
Murayama, A., 238
Murayama, K., 371
Murch, S. H., 334
Murdock, B. B., Jr., 247
Murphy, C. C., 293
Murphy, D. A., 454
Murphy, J., 587
Murphy, K. J., 236
Murphy, L. R., 421
Murphy, M., 263
Murphy, M. L. M., 411, 413
Murphy, T. I., 155
Murray, C., 299, 317
Murray, H. A., 520
Murray, J. E., 380
Murray, M., 414
Murray, M. A., 428
Murray, R. M., 172
Murray, S. L., 467
Murre, J. M. J., 262
Murrough, J. W., 411
Muscatell, K., 352
Musen, G., 240
Muszkat, M., 587
Muter, P., 248
Muthuraman, M., 69
Muzio, J. N., 150
Muzur, A., 322
Myers, B. J., 384
Myers, C., 260
Myers, I. B., 518
Myers, S. M., 334, 341
Mykletun, A., 612

N

Nadeau, A., 375, 509
Nadeau, K. G., 517
Nadler, J., 175
Nagahara, T., 159
Naganathan, V., 94
Nagasaka, T., 126
Nagase, H., 159
Naifeh, J. A., A-9
Nairne, J. S., 256
Naitoh, P., 152
Najavits, L. M., 584, 585, 596
Najman, J. M., 400
Nakamura, B. J., 595
Nakayama, K., 248
Nakonezny, P. A., 67, 152
Nalvarte, I., 429
Nam, C. B., 430
Nam, K. D., 459
Naqvi, R., 255
Narlikar, J. V., 18
Narvaes, R., 470
Nasar, S., 562
Nasca, R., 89, 411
Naselaris, T., 273
Naskar, S., 250

Nason, C. D., 191
Nass, C., PIA-6
Nathan, P. E., 598
National Academy of Neuropsychology, 291
National Center for Complementary and Integrative Health, 425
National Center for Education Statistics, A-5, A-6
National Center for Health Statistics, 263
National Collegiate Athletic Association, 34
National Commission for the Protection of Human Subjects of Biomedical and Behavioral Research, 324
National Heart, Lung, and Blood Institute, 426
National Institute of Mental Health, 533, 535, 536, 540, 575
National Institute of Mental Health Genetics Workgroup, 544
National Institute of Neurological Disorders and Stroke, 159
National Institute on Alcohol Abuse and Alcoholism, 174, 175
National Institute on Drug Abuse, 178, 604
National Safety Council, 279
National Sleep Foundation, 158
Navarro-Tapia, E., 323
NCD Risk Factor Collaboration, 378
Neal, A., 80
Neal, D. B., 404
Neal, D. T., 4
Neale, M., 6
Neale, M. C., 510, 544, 560
Nealey-Moore, J. B., 428
Neary, N. M., 375
Neck, C. P., 441
Necker, L. A., 129
Nedergaard, M., 148, 151
Neely, J. H., 258
Ne'eman, R., 94
Neiderhiser, J. M., 297, 510, 512, 531
Neimark, J., 249
Neimeyer, R. A., 467
Neisser, U., 250, 299
Nelson, C. A., 327
Nelson, D. B., 324
Nelson, D. J., 188
Nelson, K., 264, 334
Nelson, L. J., 350
Nelson, S. A., 153
Nemeroff, C. B., 549, 557, 606
Nenadic, I., 77
Neria, Y., 584
Nesselroade, J. R., 316
Nestler, E. J., 170, 411
Nestler, S., 251
Nestor, K. A., 66
Nestor, P. G., 563, 565
Neto, F., 439
Nettle, D., 23
Netzer, G., 220
Neuberg, S. L., 370, 371
Neugarten, B. L., 354
Neville, H., 88
Nevo, E., 306
Newberg, A., 606
Newell, B. R., 494
Newman, J. D., 418
Newman, J. P., 560
Newman, K., 474
Newschaffer, C. J., 334, 341
Newsom, J. T., 443
Neylan, T., 549
Nezu, A. M., 414

Nezworski, M. T., 519, 521
Ng, C., 327
Nguyen, T. T. I., 422
Nicassio, P., 159
NICHD Early Child Care Research Network, 337
Nichols, E. S., 150, 153
Nicholson, I., 448
Nicholson, J., 594
Nicholson, N., 439
Nicholson, R. A., 518
Nickell, J., 19
Nickerson, R. S., 257
Nicklas, E., 208
Nickless, A., 585
Nidich, S., 427
Nidich, S. I., 427
Nieberding, R., 520
Niedermeyer, E., 69
Nielsen, M., 338
Nielsen, S., 557
Nielsen, T., 165
Niemiec, C. P., 371
Nierenberg, A. A., 399
Nieto, F., 351
Nieuwenhuyse, B., 386
Nievar, M. A., 337
Nihei, Y., 156
Niibori, Y., 238
Nijenhuis, E., 553
Nijenhuis, E. R., 553, 554
Nikolajsen, L., 126
Nikolaou, V., 612
Nikolova, M., 404
Nilsson, L., 147, 242
Nilsson, L. G., 242
Nisbett, R. E., 291, 375, 459
Nishii, L., 529
Nisky, I., 67
Niwa, M., 297
Niznikiewicz, M., 563, 565
Nobrega, J. N., 170
Nock, M. K., 415, 415, A-9
Noesselt, T., 69
Nokia, M. S., 89
Nolen, W. A., 541
Nolen-Hoeksema, S., 541
Noordermeer, J. N., 260
Nooyens, A. C. J., 412
Norcross, J. C., 578, 579, 588, 596
Nordberg, A., 57
Nordborg, C., 88
Nordenskjold, A., 608
Nordin, C., 563, 564
Norenzayan, A., 459
Norman, K. A., 351
Norman, L. A., 377
Norman, T. R., 414
Northcraft, G., 6
Norwood, S. J., 66, 610
Nosek, B. A., 23, 457
Nosich, G. M., 18
Nosko, A., PIA-6
Nottelmann, E. D., 542
Novack, L., 177
Novak, J. D., PIA-14
Novak, M., 412
Novella, S., 334
Novotney, A., A-12
Nowell, C. J., 412
Nowotny, T., 201
Ntoumanis, N., 371
Nudds, M., 146
Nund, A., 151
Nurminen, J., 67
Nussbaum, A. D., 367
Nussbaum, A. M., 179

Nuttin, B., 610
Nuutinen, M. R., 220
Nyberg, L., 77, 241, 242
Nyberg, S. T., 413
Nybo Andersen, A. M., 421

O

Oakley-Browne, M., 546
Oathes, D. J., 543, 550, 565, 575, 597
Oberman, L. M., 81
O'Brien, L., 369
O'Brien, R. J., 506
Ocholla-Ayayo, A. B. C., 350
Ochsner, K., 272
Ochsner, K. N., 94, 382
Ocklenburg, S., 84
O'Connell, M., 4
O'Connor, E., 173
O'Connor, R. D., 586
Odbert, H. S., 504
Oden, M. H., 294, 295
O'Donnell, A., 594
O'Donnell, J., 148
Oeberst, A., 251
Offit, P. A., 341
Offord, K. P., 419, 420
Ogawa, Y., 159
Ogden, C. L., 377, 378
Ogedegbe, G., 462
Ogilvie, R. D., 155
Ogles, B. M., 595
Oglesbee, N., 612
Ogrocki, P., 409
Oh, J. M., 69
Oh, M. Y., 610
Ohashi, K., 542
Ohayon, M. M., 154
Ohly, H., 612
Öhman, A., 106, 195, 196, 381
Ohnuki, S., 320
Oikonomou, G., 149
Oishi, S., 371
Oishi, T., 154
Okamura, H., 149
O'Keefe, D. J., 453, 454
Oken, E., 153
Okoshken, J., 456
Okuda, M., 172
Okura, R., 149
Oleson, E. B., 220
Olfson, M., 262, 578, 609
Olin, B. R., 174, 175, 177
Olino, T., 335
Oliveira-Maia, A. J., 67, 610
Olivier, D. C., 305
Ollendick, T. H., 586
Olsen, P., 584
Olson, B. D., 486
Olson, H. C., 293
Olson, M. A., 451
Olulade, O. A., 308
Olver, J. S., 414
O'Malley, P., 178
O'Malley, P. M., 177, 178, 179
Oman, C. M., 127
O'Meara, E. S., 255
O'Neal, J. H., 64, 550, 602, 603, 604, 605, 606, 608
Ong, A. D., 420
Onken, L. S., 583
Onyango, G., 593
Onyemekwu, C., 382
Open Science Collaboration, 23
Ophir, E., PIA-6
Oppenheim, D., 337
O'Rahilly, S., 377

Oren, D. A., 540
Ormel, J., 535
Orr, E., 303
Orstavik, R. E., 560
Ortaldo, J. R., 412
Ortiz, E., 440
Ortiz, E. V., 147
Ortiz, F., 351
Ortiz, F. A., 457
Osborn, C. A., 252
Osborne, J. W., 464
Osman, D. J., 240
Osshera, L., 247
Ost, L. G., 586
Osterberg, L. G., 351
Osterman, K., 208, 216
Ostry, D., 303
Oswald, A. J., 428
Oswald, F. L., 366
Oswald, I., 154
Otero-Millan, J., 137
Otgaar, H., 585
Otis, T. S., 175
Ott, B. R., 255
Ott, U., 427
Ottaway, N., 377
Ottieno, J. A. M., 350
Otto, M. W., 399
Ouellet, M., 159
Overeem, S., 159
Overland, S., 612
Overmier, J. B., 219
Owen, A. M., 150, 153
Owen, M., 337
Owen, M. J., 365, 544
Owen, M. T., 337
Owens, J. F., 152
Oyffe, I., 178
Ozawa, H., 88
Ozer, D. J., 506

P

Paans, A. M., 554
Paap, K. R., 309
Pace-Schott, E., 163, 164
Pacilio, L. E., 427
Pack, A. A., 306
Padilla-Walker, L. M., 350
Pagani, F., 327
Pagano, B., 248
Pagano, J., 293
Page, M., 411
Paige, E., 403
Pakzad, R., 351
Pallanca, O., 214
Paller, K. A., 252
Palmatier, J. J., 380
Palmer, L. J., 159
Palmer, M. J., 452
Palmer, S., 130, 131
Palmer, S. E., 130
Palmieri, F., 375
Palomero-Gallagher, N., 77
Pals, J., 495, 507
Palva, J. M., 237
Palva, S., 237
Pan, A. S., 557
Pan, H., 375
Panno, A., 368
Pant, H., 519
Pantazis, G., 88
Pantev, C., 126
Paolicelli, R. C., 327
Papademetris, X., 511
Papadopoulos, L., 452
Paparelli, A., 172

Papini, S., 584
Paquet, J., 157
Parati, G., 159
Paredes, M., 327
Paredes, M. F., 88
Parente, F., 587
Pargament, K. I., 430
Parisi, P., 321
Park, E., 532, 541
Park, H., 459
Park, J., 421
Park, J. E., 584
Park, N., 371
Parker, K. P., 156
Parker, P., PIA-15
Parkes, B., 586
Parkes, C. M., 355
Parkinson, W. L., 375
Parner, E. T., 334
Parnham, T. C., 179
Parrish, T. B., 252
Parrott, D. J., 470
Parsons, H. M., A-12
Partnership for Drug-Free Kids, 147
Partonen, T., 541
Pascoli, V. J., 67
Pascual-Leone, A., 67, 273, 610
Pashkow, F. J., 410
Pashler, H., 257
Passamonti, L., 214
Passingham, R., 156
Passmore, H., 613
Pate, D. A., 220
Patel, A., 320
Patel, V., 535
Patihis, L., 251
Patnaik, S. Hu, 354
Patrick, B. C., 371
Patterson, J. M., 177
Patterson, M. L., 6
Paul, B. M., 231
Paul, E., 220
Paul, J. R., 148
Paul, S. M., 403
Paula, C. S., 216
Paulhus, D. L., 442
Pauli, P., 167
Paulus, M., 556
Paulus, M. P., 71
Pauwels, L., 88
Pavlov, I. P., 8, 188–193
Pawar, P., 427
Payne, J. D., 156
Pearse, D. D., 88
Pearson, J., 273
Peasant, C., 430
Pecoraro, N., 376
Pedersen, M. G., 334
Pedersen, N. L., 510
Pedersen, P. B., 13, 370, 384, 512
Pedrozo, A. L., 585
Peeler, C. M., PIA-9
Peers, T., 452
Peeters, F., 77, 382
Peever, J., 156
Peila, E., 67, 610
Pembrey, M., 334
Penaloza, C., 69
Penas-Lledo, E., 557
Penedo, F. J., 428
Peng, K., 459
Peng, K. K., 597
Peng, L., 57
Pennestri, M. H., 157
Pennings, E. J. M., 178
Pennington, N., 457
Penninx, B., 541

Pennsylvania State University, PIA-19
Penny, W., 238
Peplau, L. A., 12
Pepperberg, I. M., 306
Perach-Barzilay, N., 94
Perea, G., 57
Perel, J. M., 578
Peres, K., 354
Perez de los Cobos, J., 172, 173
Perez-Ara, M. A., 585
Perez-Tilve, D., 377
Perfetti, C. A., 308
Perfilieva, E., 88
Peris, T. S., 586
Perl, S., 88
Perlick, D. A., 614
Perlman, A., 442
Perloff, B. F., 583
Perls, F., 580, 582
Perrin, S., 439
Perry, G., 70, 447, 466
Perry, J. N., 517
Perry, N., 414
Perry, P., 154
Perry, W. G., Jr., 332
Pers, T. H., 377
Pescetelli, N., 106
Peters, J. F., 106
Peters, W. A., 463, 464
Peterson, C., 371
Peterson, D. A., 88
Peterson, D. R., A-4
Peterson, E. L., 549
Peterson, J. B., 507
Peterson, K. M., 352
Peterson, L. R., 238
Peterson, M. J., 238, 565
Petit, D., 157
Petitto, L. A., 303
Petri, H., 364, 365
Petrides, G., 608
Petrie, K. J., 148, 586
Petrofsky, J. S., 427
Petropoulos, M. C., 334, 341
Petrova, P. K., 444
Petrovitch, H., 351
Pettersson-Yeo, W., 76
Petticrew, M. P., 419
Pettigrew, T. F., 466
Petty, C., 542
Petty, F., 604
Petty, R., 453, 454
Petty, R. E., 444, 450, 451, 453, 454
Petukhova, M., 540, 545
Pew Research Center, 443
Peyton, D. H., 173
Pezawas, L., 565
Pezdek, K., 252
Pezzin, L. E., 126
Pfeiffer, N., 499
Pfeiffer, W. M., 551
Phalen, H. J., 384
Phan, K. L., 470
Phan, T., 429
Phelps, E. A., 106, 250, 380, 381, 389, 470
Phelps, J. A., 563
Piaget, J., 12, 274, 304, 330, 332, 333, 334
Pickar, D., 403
Pickering, R., 171
Pickering, T. G., 351
Pierce, W. D., 371
Piercy, F. P., 592
Pierrehumbert, J., 303
Pietrzak, R. H., 263, 409
Pike, K. M., 557
Pilling, S., 596
Pilon, M., 157

Pinares-Garcia, P., 429
Pine, D. S., 546
Pineda, J. A., 81
Pines, A., 172, 173
Pinker, S., 305, 306
Pinney, M., 414
Pinsof, W. M., 592
Pinto, C., 350
Pinto-Gouveia, J., 414
Pintrich, P. R., PIA-13
Piotrowski, N. A., 170
Pironom, J., 426
Pitman, R., 399
Pitman, R. K., 253
Pittenger, D. J., 518
Plake, B. S., 421
Plaks, J. E., 457
Planetta, P. J., 156
Plata, S. J., 337
Platow, M. J., 466
Platzman, K., 172
Plaut, D. C., 231
Plaut, V., 20, 43
Plaut, V. C., 20
Pleger, B., 89
Pliatsikas, C., 308
Plomin, R., 297, 299, 317, 365, 510, 512, 531
Ploner, C. J., 264
Plotkin, S., 341
Plotsky, P. M., 89
Plug, C., 136
Plum, F., 75
Podlogar, M. C., 553
Podolski, C. L., 473
Poe, G., 152
Poehlmann, K. M., 380
Poeppel, D., 81, 302
Polce-Lynch, M., 384
Polderman, T. J. C., 317, 510
Polewan, R. J., 191
Polk, R., 543
Pollack, M. H., 399
Pollitt, E., PIA-15
Pompili, M., 608
Pompili, S., 414
Pond, R., 430
Pope, H. G., Jr., 556
Popov, T., 70
Popova, S., 324
Porcelli, A., 317
Pormerleau, C. S., 173
Pormerleau, O. F., 173
Port, J. D., 67
Posada, G., 337
Posner, J. B., 75
Posner, M. I., 427
Possemiers, N., 418
Posthuma, D., 297, 298, 317, 510
Postle, B. R., 236, 237
Postman, L., 240
Potard, C., 347
Potenza, M. N., 408
Pott, M., 337
Potts, R., 248
Poudevida, S., 178
Poulin, M., 412
Poulin, M. J., 94
Powell, B., 493
Powell, J. W., 151
Powell, R. A., 194, 195
Powers, J., 367
Powers, M. H., 332
Powers, S., 147
Pozdnyakova, I., 293
Prado, V. F., 263
Prakash, R. S., 89

Prasad, G., 543
Prather, A. A., 411, 413
Pratkanis, A. R., 106
Prats, M., 348
Pratt, J. A., 169
Preacher, K. J., 467
Prendes-Alvarez, S., 606
Prentice, D. A., 465
Prescott, C. A., 401, PIA-18
Press, D. Z., 67, 610
Pressman, Y., 88
Preston, J. D., 64, 466, 550, 602, 603, 604, 605, 606, 608
Prestwich, A., 587
Preziosi, P., 255
Price, C., 334, 341
Price, C. S., 341
Price, L. H., 609
Price, R. B., 71, 597
Prices, J. F., 412
Priest, R. G., 154
Priester, J. M., 453
Prigerson, H. G., 355, 409
Pringle, P., 280
Pritchard, T. C., 121
Privado, J., 285
Proal, E., 77
Prober, D. A., 149
Probst, C., 324
Prochaska, J. J., 179
Prochaska, J. O., 578, 579, 588
Prokopovich, S., 413
Prosser, I. B., 6
Prot, S., 222, 223
Prowse, M., 427
Prudic, J., 262, 608
Pryce, C. R., 404
Pryor, L., 421
Pryor, T., 556
Przuntek, H., 75
Przybylski, A. K., 473
Psotka, J., 235
Psych, M. R., 563
Pulfrey, C., PIA-20
Pullikuth, A., 413
Pullum, G. K., 304
Pumariega, A., 557
Punzi, G., 317
Purdy, D., 34
Purves, D., 250
Puspitasari, A., 587
Putman, K. M., 380
Putnam, A. L., PIA-14
Puts, D. A., 13
Puzia, M. E., 216
Pyc, M. A., 245, 248
Pylkkanen, L., 81, 309

Q

Qi, D., 88
Qian, M. Y., 590
Qian, P., 323
Qin, B., 606
Qin, J., 322
Quadflieg, S., 456
Quak, J., 554
Quamme, J. R., 351
Quan, S. F., 154
Quante, M., 153
Quaresima, V., 71, 610
Quednow, B. B., 404
Quero, S., 585
Quesenberry, C., 428
Quested, E., 371
Quillian, M. R., 243
Quilty, L. C., 507

Quinn, P., 517
Quinn, P. D., 291
Quintana, S. M., 347
Quintero, J. E., 149
Quiroga, M. A., 237
Quist, E., 323

R

Raaijmakers, J. G. W., 240, 246, 248
Rabat, A., 152
Rabin, B. S., 410
Rachman, S., 550
Rachman, S. J., 589
Racine, M., 126
Racine, S. E., 557
Racsmany, M., 151
Radicioni, A. F., 320
Radmacher, K., 350
Radosevich, D. R., 257
Radua, J., 543
Radulovic, J., 246
Raffin, E., 126
Raffray, T., 161, 378
Rahe, R. H., 400, 401
Rai, D., 334
Rai, R., 347
Raikkonen, K., 418
Räikkönen, K., 400
Raine, A., 335, 470, 560
Rainer, G., 260
Rainforth, M., 427
Rainforth, M. V., 427
Rait, M., 179
Rajan, K. B., 414
Rajaratnam, S. M. W., 590
Rajeevan, N., 511
Rajendran, G., 238
Rajkowska, G., 77
Rakoff-Nahoum, S., 410
Ramachandran, V. S., 81, 82, 104
Ramaekers, J. G., 77
Ramdhonee, K., 421
Ramirez, V., 518
Ramkumar, B., 399
Ramnani, N., 200
Ramon y Cajal, S., 56
Ramos, M. R., 421
Ramsay, J. R., 67, 610
Rana-Deuba, A., 421
Randazzo, J., 297
Randi, J., 134, 425
Rangmar, J., 323
Ranke, M. B., 320
Ransom, B. R., 57
Ranson, J., 273
Ranson, S. W., 375
Rantanen, T., 413
Rao, S. C., 260
Rapoport, J. L., 563
Raposa, E. B., 400
Rapp, S. R., 255
Rapson, R. L., 467
Rasch, B., 151
Rasenberger, J., 475
Rasmussen, I., 427
Rasmusson, A., 409
Raths, J., PIA-13
Ratiu, P., 25, 80, 97
Rauch, S. L., 77, 550, 609
Raufelder, D., 366
Raulic, S., 263
Ravenell, J., 462
Raver, J. L., 529
Rayner, R., 9, 194, 550
Raynor, H. A., 377
Raz, N., 80, 352

Rea, C., 277
Read, J. D., 106
Realo, A., 507
Reason, J. T., 127
Reber, P. J., 252
Rechtschaffen, A., 154
Reddy, R., 549
Redline, S., 153, 351
Redmond, D., 151
Rees, G., 136, 214
Reese, E., 334
Reese, H. W., 194, 316
Regan, L., 293
Regenbogen, C., 76
Regenold, W. T., 609
Reger, G. M., 585
Regunath, G., 112
Rehm, J., 324
Reichborn-Kjennerud, T., 560
Reicher, S., 421, 466, 471, 472
Reicher, S. D., 447
Reid, K. J., 153
Reifsnider, O. S., 175
Reihman, J., 293
Reilly, K. T., 126
Reilly, P. M., 170
Reinders, A., 554
Reinders, A. A., 553, 554
Reis, H. T., 467
Reisenzein, R., 388
Reiser, B. J., 272
Reiss, A. L., 549
Reiss, P. C., 473
Reith, M. E. A., 172
Remini, L., 450
Ren, Z., 550
Rendsvig, R. K., 442
Renneboog, B., 351
Renner, M. J., 401, 402
Rentfrow, P., 506
Rentz, D. M., 13
Reppel, M., 173
Reschke, M. F., 128
Rescorla, R. A., 191, 193, 194
Resick, P. A., 549, 585, 596
Resnick, H., 399
Resnick, S. M., 506
Ress, R., 378
Ressler, K. J., 549
Rethorst, C. C., 158
Rettner, R., 216
Reul, J., 260
Revelle, W., 148
Rex, C. S., 263
Rey, M., 275
Reyburn, G., 214
Reyes, R. N., 384
Reyes Toso, C. F., 149
Reyna, V. F., 346
Reynolds, C. F., 409, 578, 602
Reynolds, C. F., III, 158
Reynolds, J. A., PIA-12
Reynolds, M. R., 285
Reynolds, R. M., 412
Reynoso, R., 149
Rezaei, M., 213
Rezaei, N., 351
Rezvani, A. H., 173
Rhebergen, D., 608
Rhee, E., 462
Rhodes, M. G., 139
Rice, J. C., 208
Rice, T. B., 150
Richard, N., 95, 126
Richard, O. D., 464
Richards, C. F., 477
Richards, D., 587, 588, 596

Richards, M., 352
Richards, M. H., 532
Richards, V. L., 191
Richardson, A. J., 255
Richardson, J., PIA-10
Richardson, W. D., 57
Richmond, S. E., 470
Richter-Levin, G., 550
Rideout, V. J., 222
Ridley, M., 19, 317
Rieber, R. W., 5
Riemann, R., 505, 509
Rieppi, R., 418
Riess, O., 75
Rietschel, M., 544
Rifas-Shiman, S. L., 153
Rigby, C. S., 317, 473
Riggio, L., 80
Rigotti, A., 378
Rijsdijk, F. V., 563
Rimer, B. K., 418
Rimfeld, K., 299
Rimm, D. C., 590
Ringel, N., 587
Ringli, M., 89
Rinne, J., 263
Rinne, J. O., 263
Riordan, H., 263
Ripolles, P., 69
Risley, T. R., 213
Ritchey, M., 380
Ritschel, L. A., 424, 585, 596
Ritter, B., 586
Rivero, B., 377
Riviere, J., 8
Rizvi, S. L., 585, 596
Rizzi, L., 302
Rizzolatti, G., 81
Rizzutti, S., 587
Ro, E., 532
Roach, M. A., 303
Roane, B. M., 161, 378
Robbins, A., 134
Roberto, C. A., 4
Roberts, B. W., 493
Roberts, D. F., 222
Roberts, G., 240
Roberts, L., 341
Roberts, R., 349
Roberts, R. D., 296
Roberts, R. E., 598
Robin, J., 245
Robins, L. N., 470, 561
Robinson, D. K., 5
Robinson, F. P., PIA-9
Robinson, J. F., 317
Robinson, J. W., 466
Robinson, L. K., 323
Robinson, P., 495
Robinson, S. L., 6
Robles, T., 409, 413
Roca, M., 554
Rocchi, R., 159
Rock, I., 130, 131
Rockenstein, E., 263
Rocklin, T., 439
Rockstroh, B., 70
Rodgers, M., 382
Rodin, J., 376, 403
Rodriguez, F. J., 112
Rodriguez, M. L., 88
Rodriguez-Arellano, J. J., 57
Rodriguez-Fornells, A., 69
Roeder, K. Devlin, 334
Roediger, H. L., 241, 245, 248, 251
Roediger, H. L., III, 245
Roefs, A., 377

Roelofs, J., 585
Roelofs, K., 511
Roerig, J., 606
Roest, A. M., 541
Roffman, I., 306
Roffman, J., 511
Roffman, R. A., 171
Roffwarg, H. P., 150
Rogalski, E. J., 81
Rogers, C. R., 11, 14, 500, 501, 502, 578, 579, 580
Rogers, J. H., 88
Rogers, M. L., 153, 540
Rogers, R. G., 430
Rogers, R. W., 453
Rogoff, B., 333
Roh, S., 172, 173
Rohrer, D., 257
Rohrer, J. M., 493
Roid, G. H., 286
Rollnick, S., 580
Romer, D., 346
Romero, C., 367
Romundstad, S., 427
Ronen, A., 306
Rooney, M., 405
Roos, S., 404
Roosevelt, E., 502
Root, N. B., 104
Rorschach, H., 520
Ros, T., 214
Rosato, F., 428
Rosch, E., 14, 274, 275
Rosch-Heider, E., 305
Roscigno, V., 34
Rose, J. S., 543
Rose, M., 151
Rose, S., 317
Rosen, C. S., 584
Rosen, K. M., 57
Rosen, L. D., PIA-6
Rosen, L. H., 353
Rosen, R., 158
Rosenbaum, M., 375
Rosenberg, J., 255
Rosenbloom, T., 442
Rosenfeld, J. P., 70
Rosenfeld, L., 70
Rosengren, A., 412
Rosenhan, D. L., 537
Rosenkranz, M., 382
Rosenman, R. H., 417
Rosenstock, S., 409
Rosenthal, A. M., 475
Rosenthal, R., 32, 413
Rosenthal, T. L., 195
Roset, P. N., 178
Rosner, B. A., 427
Ross, C. A., 553
Ross, D., 221, 471, 472
Ross, G. M., 136
Ross, H. E., 136
Ross, O. A., 291
Ross, S. A., 221, 471, 472
Rossi, B., 556
Rossi, F., 320
Rossini, P. M., 106
Rost, K. M., 598
Rostain, A., 67, 610
Rosten, C., 585, 586
Rostron, B., 173
Roszensky, R. H., 414
Roth, A., 426
Roth, R. M., 470
Rothbaum, B. O., 584, 585
Rothbaum, R., 337
Rothen, N., 104

Rothenberg, A., 542
Rothman, A. J., 4
Rothman, E. F., 179
Rothmond, D. A., 62
Rothstein, H. R., 222
Rothstein-Fisch, C., 373, 374
Rothwell, J., 67
Rotter, A., 179
Rotter, J. B., 367, 498, 499
Rotter, S., 260
Rotton, J., 469
Rouru, J., 263
Rouse, S. V., 517
Rouw, R., 104
Rovet, J., 320
Rovner, L., 380
Rowan, J., 578
Rowe, D. C., 470
Rowe, J. S., 442
Rowitch, D. H., 57
Roy-Byrne, P. P., 606
Roysamb, E., 560
Roysircar-Sodowsky, G. R., 422
Rozeske, R. R., 220
Ruan, H., 421
Ruan, Y., 88
Rubenstein, L. V., 598
Ruberry, E. J., 346
Rubert-Pugh, E., 306
Rubia, K., 77, 543
Rubin, M., 462, 584
Rubinstein, M. L., 179
Rubio-Fernandez, P., 308
Ruble, D., 462
Ruble, D. N., 344, 462
Rudd, P., 351
Rude, R. K., 505
Rudmin, F. W., 421, 422
Rudorfer, M. V., 608
Rueda, S., 473
Ruff, C. C., 474
Ruff, R. M., 291
Rugg, M. D., 260
Ruhe, H. G., 543
Ruhm, C. J., 177
Ruigrok, T. J. H., 76
Ruiz, S., 214
Rumbaugh, G., 260
Rumelhart, D. E., 231, 243
Rundus, D., 238
Running, C. A., 121
Runyan, D. K., 216
Rupprecht, R., 262
Ruscio, A. M., 546, 547
Ruscio, J., 547
Rushton, J. P., 510
Rusiniak, K. W., 195
Russell, D. E., 518
Russell, K. C., 612
Russell, N., 354
Russell, R., 248
Russo, N. F., 541
Russo, S. J., 170, 411
Rutherford, A., 9
Rutherford, E., 118
Ruzek, J. I., 584
Ryan, M. A. K., 549
Ryan, R. M., 364, 371, 372, 473
Rydell, R. J., 465
Ryff, C. D., 376
Rygh, J. L., 590
Rysavy, M. A., 324

S

Sabatinelli, D., 381
Sabatini, E., 106

Sabbah, S., 541
Sabo, B., 203
Sacchet, M. D., 71, 543
Sachs, G. S., 604
Sackeim, H. A., 262, 608
Sackett, P. R., 290
Sackett, T. W., 464
Sacks, O., 79
Saddy, J. D., 308
Saenger, P., 320
Safer, D. J., 172
Saffer, H., 377
Sagan, C., 154
Sagart, L., 302
Sagi-Schwartz, A., 337
Sagiv, N., 104
Sah, P., 408
Saha, S., 562, 563
Saha, T. D., 171
Sahin, M., 57
Sahota, P., 149
Sailer, S., 323
Saint-Georges, C., 303
Saitoh, T., 159
Saitoh, Y., 238
Sakagami, T., 328
Sakai, K., 201
Sakamoto, A., 473
Sakuma, A., 399
Salamanca, J. C., 173
Salamone, J. D., 170
Salas, D., 273
Saleem, M., 473
Salehpour, M., 88
Salend, S. J., 587
Salerno, J. M., 384
Salerno, J. W., 427
Sallis, J. F., 549
Salmon, D. P., 13
Salomon, K., 418
Salovey, P., 296
Salvaggio, A., 156
Sam, D. L., 421
Samara, Z., 77
Samet, J. M., 351
Sampson, N. A., 540, 545
Samuelsson, M., 563, 564
Sana, F., PIA-6
Sanaiha, Y., 263
Sanbonmatsu, D. M., 279, PIA-6
Sanchez, G., 6
Sanchez-Niubo, A., 172
Sanchez-Vives, M. V., 446
Sandhu, G., 337
Sandoval, K., 88
Sands, L. P., 351
Sanes, D. H., 67
Sanes, J. N., 541
Sanes, J. R., 88
Šantek, M., 384
Santhakumar, V., 175
Santiago, C. D., 532
Santorelli, S., 382
Santos, L. R., 456
Sanz, C., 412
Sanz-Vergel, A. I., 421
Saper, C. B., 151, 154
Sapir, A., 82
Sapir, E. S., 304
Sapolsky, R., 408
Sapolsky, R. M., 410
Sar, V., 553
Sara, L., 134
Sarada, P. A., 399
Sarbin, T. R., 168
Sareen, J., 208
Sargent, J. D., 368

Sartorius, A., 608
Sartory, G., 549
Sarvet, A. L., 179
Sasco, A. J., 179
Sastry, K. S., 413
Satija, A., 174, 302, 323
Sato, A. F., 252, 426
Sato, H., 399
Satterly, D., 347
Satterthwaite, T. D., 346
Sattler, J. M., 599
Sattler, K. M. P., 207
Saucier, S., 165
Sauer, H., 77
Saul, L., 482
Saults, J. S., 237
Sauv, Y., 255
Sauvaget, A., 67, 610
Sauvigne, K. C., 29, 519
Savage-Rumbaugh, E. S., 306
Savage-Rumbaugh, S., 306
Savard, J., 590
Savard, M. H., 590
Savickas, M. L., 493
Savitz, J., 106, 494
Savulescu, J., 322
Sawi, O., 309
Sayk, F., 173
Sbrocco, T., 378
Scacchi, P., 149
Scacchi Bernasconi, P. A., 149
Scaletta-Kent, J., 320
Scammacca, N., 240
Scammell, T. E., 151, 154
Scarpa, A., 335
Schachter, S., 387, 388, 389
Schacter, D. L., 240, 246, 253, 352
Schaefer, G. O., 322
Schaefer, N. K., 447
Schaeffer, D. J., 381
Schafer, M., 440
Schaffer, B., 583
Schaie, K. W., 316, 352
Schaller, K., 126
Schaller, M., 370, 371
Schapiro, A. C., 231
Scharf, M., 350
Scharnowski, F., 214
Schatzberg, A. F., 606
Scheele, D., 94
Scheman, J., 517
Schenck, C. H., 154, 158
Schendel, D., 293, 334, 341
Schene, A. H., 543
Schenk, D., 263
Schiffer, A. A., 418
Schilbach, L., 565
Schiller, P. H., 134
Schizophrenia Working Group of the Psychiatric Genomics, C., 13
Schlaepfer, T., 610
Schlagman, S., 249
Schlumpf, Y. R., 553, 554
Schmahl, C., 552, 554
Schmahmann, J. D., 76
Schmaling, K. B., 587, 588
Schmid, R. E., 155
Schmidt, K., 413
Schmidt, M., 155
Schmidt, M. B., 546
Schmitt, D. P., 467, 507
Schmitt, K. C., 172
Schmitt, N., 366
Schmitz, C., 421
Schmukle, S. C., 493
Schnabel, J., 19
Schneider, A., 164–165

Schneider, C., 339
Schneider, K., 581
Schneider, K. J., 578
Schneider, R., 427
Schneider, R. H., 427
Schneider, S., 156
Schneider, W., 249
Schneider, W. J., 284
Schneiderman, N., 428
Schneidman, E., 354, 355
Schnurr, P. P., 596
Schoenthaler, A., 462
Scholer, A. A., 486
Scholl, L., 177
Schols, L., 75
Scholz, J., 126
Schonfeld, I. S., 414
Schonherr, D. M., 66
Schottenfeld-Naor, Y., 376
Schraufnagel, C. D., 67, 610
Schredl, M., 165
Schroder, J., 563, 564
Schroeder, D. R., 351
Schroeder, E., 553
Schroeder, S. R., 293
Schroth, M. L., 368
Schuerman, J., 386
Schuetze, P., 172
Schugens, M. M., 260
Schulenberg, J., 178, 179
Schulenberg, J. E., 177, 178
Schulman-Olivier, Z., 427
Schultz, D. P., A-12
Schultz, P. P., 371
Schultz, S. E., A-12
Schulze, R., 549
Schulze, T. G., 544
Schumacher, J., 382
Schunk, D., 474
Schurholt, B., 549
Schutte, N. S., 585
Schuurman, R., 610
Schuwerk, T., 334
Schvey, N. A., 378
Schwab, E., 427
Schwabe, L., 67
Schwader, K. L., 147
Schwanenflugel, P., 275
Schwanenflugel, P. J., 275
Schwartz, C. E., 335
Schwartz, G. E., 382
Schwartz, J. E., 418
Schwartz, J. H., 57, 62, 93, 260
Schwartz, J. K. L., 457
Schwartz, S., 156
Schwartz, S. K., A-5, A-6
Schwartzman, D. J., 104
Schwarz, J., 151
Schwarz, N. F., 381
Schwarz, T., 499
Schwarzkopf, D. S., 136
Schweickert, R., 235
Schweitzer, N. J., 384
Schweitzer, P. K., 157
Schwitzgebel, E., 333
Schworm, W., 441
Schyns, P., 77
Scott, K., 535, 536
Scott, K. M., 540, 541
Scott, S. B., 414
Scott, S. K., 470
Scott, W. D., A-12
Sears, R. R., 294, 404, 469
Seckl, J. R., 412
Seedat, S., 540, 541
Seehagen, S., 156
Seeman, J., 578

Seeman, T. E., 419
Sees, K., 170
Segal, N. L., 166, 305
Segall, M. H., 135
Segerstrom, S. C., 420
Sehon, S., 425
Seibt, J., 152
Seidman, L. J., 77
Seidman, M., 452
Seifer, R., 161, 378
Seiffge-Krenke, I., 350
Seifritz, E., 404
Seim, R. W., 585
Seitz, R. J., 549
Sejnowski, T. J., 239
Sekar, A., 13, 564
Selcuk, E., 337
Seligman, M., 217, 219, 420, 543, 595
Seligman, M. E. P., 219, 291, 498, 503, 543
Selkoe, D. J., 263
Sellars, C., 560
Sellers, W., 427
Selye, H., 398, 399, 400, 408, 409
Seo, D., 408
Seong, S. J., 584
Sephton, S. E., 420
Sergio, L. E., 303
Serra, R., 456
Serrano-Blanco, A., 554
Sershen, H., 173
Sestieri, C., 260
Setchell, K. D. R., 351
Seth, A. K., 104
Seth, P., 177
Seubert, P., 263
Sevdalis, N., 297
Severin, D., 541
Seymour, B., 494
Seys, D. M., 208
Sforazzini, F., 327
Shabani, K., 333
Shackelford, T. K., 14
Shadish, R., 601
Shaffer, J. A., 418
Shaffer, J. J., 565
Shafir, E., 406
Shafton, A., 155, 156
Shahar, A., 442
Shahar, E., 351
Shahly, V., 556
Shakespeare, W., 162
Shamay-Tsoory, S. G., 94
Shan, L., 213
Shane, M., 511
Shang, J., 550
Shankar, V., 216
Shanker, S., 306
Shanks, D. R., 248, 494
Shao, W., 323
Shapiro, A. K., 595, 601
Shapiro, A. R., 550
Shapiro, E., 595, 601
Shapiro, F., 585
Shapiro, K. L., 196
Shapiro, P. A., 418
Shapiro, S., 179
Sharkey, K. M., 161, 378
Sharma, R., 149
Sharma, S., 89
Sharot, T., 250
Sharpe, D., 403
Shattuck, A., 252
Shaver, P., 337
Shaw, A., 443
Shaw, N. D., 153
Shay, D. K., 334, 341
Shean, R. E., 453

Shear, K., 546
Shear, M. K., 409
Shearer, D. K., 238
Sheeran, P., 4
Sheffield, J., 403
Sheffield, V. C., 112
Shehab, N., 169
Sheldon, K. M., 372
Sheldon, S. H., 156
Shell, P., 290
Shelton, J., 425
Shema, S. J., 430
Shen, D., 69
Shen, R.-Y., 179
Shen, Y., 543
Sheng, X., 322
Shenton, M. E., 563, 565
Shepard, R. N., 272
Shepherd, G. M., 121
Sheppard, W., 427
Sheppes, G., 550
Sheridan, J., 382, 409
Sheridan, J. F., 419
Sherif, C. W., 465
Sherif, M., 438, 465
Sherlin, L. H., 155, 213
Sherman, J. C., 76
Sherman, T., 562
Sherry, P., 401
Shestyuk, A. Y., 81
Sheth, S. A., 610
Shevrin, H., 106
Shi, F., 69
Shi, H., 323
Shi, S., 543
Shibata, K., 494
Shibuya, A., 473
Shields, D. C., 201
Shields, J., 563
Shiffrin, R. M., 233, 238, 240, 246, 248
Shih, P. C., 237, 285
Shimbo, D., 418
Shimp, T. A., 453
Shin, A., 153
Shin, J. H., 564, 565
Shin, L. M., 77, 550
Shin, S., 153
Shinohara, K., 303
Shipstead, Z., 237
Shirk, S. D., 427
Shirom, A., 412
Shlain, B., 177
Shoda, Y., 486, 506
Shokri-Kojori, E., 75, 153
Shore, L. A., 18
Shorter, E., 608
Shott, M. E., 556
Showalter, E., 553
Shriffrin, R., 249
Shuglin, A., 178
Shulman, G. L., 260
Shulman, S., 350
Shungin, D., 377
Shvil, E., 584
Shweder, R. A., 305, 384
Shyu, W. C., 174, 302, 323
Siciliano, R., 255
Siegel, C. E., 609
Siegel, J., 150
Siegel, J. M., 149, 156
Siegel, S., 191
Siegelbaum, S. A., 57, 62, 240
Siegler, I. C., 417, 418
Siegler, R. S., 333
Sigal, M., 178
Sigelman, J. D., 456
Sijbrandij, M., 602

Sikes, J., 466
Sikkema, K. J., 454
Silani, V., 159
Silove, D., 429, 535
Silva, D., 440
Silva, K., 369
Silva, M. N., 371
Silver, R. C., 412
Silverberg, S. B., 469
Silverman, W. K., 602
Silvers, J. A., 382
Simard, V., 165
Simeon, D., 554
Simeonova, D. I., 384
Šimić, M., 384
Simkin, D. R., 427
Simler, A., 273
Simmons, A. N., 556
Simmons, M. B., 606
Simmons, S. M., 147
Simner, J., 104
Simola, S., 456
Simon, D. A., 257
Simon, K. M., 588
Simon, N. M., 399
Simon, S. L., 161
Simon, T., 285
Simpson, D., 510
Simpson, E. E., 171
Simpson, L., 159
Simpson, P. M., 320
Sin, N. L., 420
Sinclair, A., 412
Sindi, S., 351
Sing, H., 151
Sing, T. L., 320
Singec, I., 88
Singer, B., 595
Singer, J. E., 387, 388, 389
Singer, M. T., 450
Singh, J. B., 606
Singh, K. D., 70
Singh, T., 173
Singh-Manoux, A., 352
Sinha, R., 408
Sirigu, A., 95
Sirko, S., 57
Sitaram, R., 214
Sivers, H., 543
Siy, J. O., 20
Skeen, P., 350
Skinner, B. F., 11, 14, 198, 199, 202, 203, 211, 213, 216, 497, 499, 531, 583, 591
Skirbekk, V., 377
Skitka, L. J., 23
Skladman, I., 178
Skolnick, A., 336
Skoner, D. P., 410
Skuse, D., 154
Slade, E. P., 609
Slade, M. D., 417
Slater, A., 328
Slater, P. C., 262
Slaughter, V., 338
Sleddens, E. F., 353
Sleeper, T., 150
Slipp, S., 491
Sliwinski, M. J., 414
Sloan, D. M., 583
Sloan, E. K., 412, 419
Sloan, R. P., 418
Slobin, D. I., 303
Slovic, P., 276
Smart, L. M., 381
Smedley, R. M., 414
Smith, A., 273, 467
Smith, A. J., 413

Smith, A. P., 410
Smith, A. R., 369
Smith, C., 165
Smith, J. D., 146
Smith, J. R., 447
Smith, K., 466
Smith, M., 560
Smith, M. A., PIA-14
Smith, P., 548
Smith, P. B., 439
Smith, R. P., 173
Smith, S., 427
Smith, S. M., 171
Smith, S. S., 560
Smith, T. B., 599
Smith, T. C., 549
Smith, T. W., 428
Smith, V. C., 175
Smith-Lovin, L., 467
Smithson, C., 194, 195
Smolen, P., 188
Smolenski, D. J., 585
Smoll, N. R., 126
Smoller, J., 511
Smyth, M. J., 412, 413
Snapp, M., 466
Snarey, J. R., 347
Snidman, N., 335
Snitz, B. E., 255
Snodgrass, M., 106
Snow, W. M., 94
Snyder, A. Z., 82
Snyder, C. R., 503
Snyder, D. J., 122
Snyder, H. M., 263
Snyder, H. R., 403, 588
Snyder, M., 464
Snyder, T. D., A-5
Society for Industrial and Organizational Psychology, A-12
Soderberg, P., 216
Soderlund, J., 563, 564
Sodian, B., 334
Sodowsky, G. R., 421
Soekadar, S. R., 214
Soininen, H., 351
Sokol, R. J., 323
Sokolov, A. A., 76
Soldatos, C., 157
Solomon, A., 351
Solomon, J., 336
Solomon, R. M., 585
Solomon, Z., 426
Somayajula, S., 66, 67
Somerville, L. H., 346
Somlai, A. M., 454
Sood, A. K., 419
Soomro, G. M., 548
Sordo, L., 172
Sorensen, E. R., 380
Sorensen, N., 293
Sorkhabi, N., 353
Sorrells, S. F., 88
Sorri, A., 563
Soto-Ortolaza, A., 291
Soubelet, A., 506
Southwick, S. M., 409
Souza, A. S., 308, 309
Spalding, K. L., 88
Spangler, W. D., 366
Spanlang, B., 585
Sparing, R., 273
Spaziani, M., 320
Spearman, C., 282, 284
Speca, M., 427
Speelman, E., 612
Speelman, L., 593

Speicher, C. E., 409
Spek, V., 418
Speliotes, E. K., 377
Spence, M. J., 328
Spencer, C. P., 439
Spencer, D. D., 380, 470
Spencer, M. B., 149
Spencer, R. M. C., 152, 156
Spencer, T. J., 77
Sperling, G., 234
Sperling, W., 179
Speroff, L., 324
Sperry, R. W., 83, 84
Spiegel, D., 166, 553, 554, 593
Spiegel-Cohen, J., 554
Spieker, E. A., 378
Spies, J. R., 23
Spijkerman, A. M. W., 412
Spinath, F. M., 297, 299, 365, 509, 512
Spitler, H., 175
Spitzer, B. J., 367
Sporns, O., 87
Spreckelsen, T. F., 255
Springer, J. A., 509
Springer, S. P., 82, 84
Spuhl, S. T., 304
Squire, L. R., 77, 87, 240, 260, 262
Srivastava, J., 147
Staal, W. G., 213
Stacy, B. A., 428
Staff, C. H., 156
Staggers, F., 427
Stahl, S. M., 64, 543, 550, 602, 603, 604, 605, 606, 607, 608
Standing, L., 248
Standing, L. G., 439
Stanhope, N., 257
Stanley, D., 425
Stanovich, K. E., 272
Stantoon, M. P., 154
Starace, N., 595
Staresina, B. P., 151, 154, 260
Stark, C. E., 241
Starr, L., 596
Stavropoulos, P., 553
Steckley, P. L., 502, 581
Steel, Z., 535
Steele, C., 20
Steele, C. M., 299, 464, 465
Steele, J., 465
Steelman, L. A., 384
Steelman, L. C., 493
Stefanovic-Stanojevic, T., 337
Stefansson, K., 510
Steffen, K., 606
Steier, P., 88
Stein, D., 535, 536
Stein, H. T., 496
Stein, M. B., 71, A-9
Stein-Behrens, B., 408
Steinberg, E. A., 149
Steinberg, L., 369, 469
Steiner, J. E., 328
Steinke, E. E., 350
Steinmetz, N., 152
Stejskal, W. J., 521
Stenholm, S., 413
Stenstrom, P., 165
Stephan, C., 466
Stephan, J. S., 260
Stephan, K. E., 214
Stephen, J., 475
Stephens, D., 370, A-11
Stephens, M., 378
Stephens, R. S., 171
Stepien, B., 260

Stepnowsky, M. A., 246, 248
Steptoe, A., 409, 412, 418
Steriade, M., 75
Sterling, P., 411
Sterman, M. B., 213
Stern, A. P., 67, 610
Stern, R. M., 128
Stern, W., 286
Sternberg, R. J., 282, 283, 284, 317, 468
Sternberger, R. R., 545
Sternfeld, B., 351
Stevens, C., 88
Stevens, J. P., 177
Stevens, J. S., 549
Stevens, R. G., 150
Stevenson, M. B., 303
Stewart, M. M., 464
Stewart, P., 293
Stewart, S. H., 546
Stewart, W., 425
Stewin, L. L., 150
Stice, E., 610
Stickgold, R., 152, 156, 163, 164, PIA-14
Stienen, M. N., 126
Stiers, P., 77
Stiff, J. B., 454
Stigler, S. M., 39
Stipek, D. J., 338
Stockhorst, U., 376
Stoeckel, L. E., 214, 610
Stoesz, B. M., 94
Stojanoski, B., 150, 153
Stolarz-Fantino, S., 252
Stoll, B. J., 324
Stollery, S. J., 560
Stone, E. M., 112
Stoodley, C. J., 76
Storr, C. L., 532, 541
Stout, J. C., 409
Stouthamer-Loeber, M., 291
Stowell, J. R., 426
Strachan, M., 412
Strachey, J., 8
Straif, K., 179
Strand, B. H., 377
Strandberg-Larsen, K., 421
Strang, N., 369
Stratikopoulos, M., 429
Stratton, K., 334, 341
Straub, R. E., 564, 565
Straus, R., 417
Straus, S., 255
Strauss, A. S., 355
Strauss, C., 585, 586
Strawbridge, W. J., 430
Strayer, D. L., 147, 279, PIA-6
Street, A. E., 549
Strehl, U., 213, 214
Striano, T., 303
Strick, M., 494
Strick, P. L., 76, 87, 470
Strickland, B. R., 541
Strickland, I., 560
Striepens, N., 94
Stroessner, S. J., 457
Stromeyer, C. F., III, 235
Stromland, K., 323
Strong, R. K., 470
Strongin, R. M., 173
Strunk, D. R., 543
Stubbs, R. J., PIA-15
Stuss, D. T., 236
Styne, D. M., 346
Su, L., 543
Su, Z., 375

Subramanyam, A., 350
Substance Abuse and Mental Health Services Administration, 534, 535
Suddendorf, T., 338
Suderman, M. J., 400
Sue, D., 421, 499, 532, 598, 599, 600
Sue, D. W., 421, 462, 499, 532, 598, 599, 600
Sue, S., 598
Suess, G., 337
Sugita, Y., 154
Sugiura, A., 371
Suh, L. S., 88
Suizuki, G., 320
Suleiman, J., 442
Suler, J., 443
Sullivan, D. R., 220
Sullivan, G. M., 584
Sullivan, H. S., 578
Sullivan, P. F., 317, 510, 544, 563
Sullivan, T., 430
Sullivan, W. C., 612
Sulloway, F. J., 493
Sulpizio, S., 303
Suls, J., 4
Sultana, A., 587
Sulutvedt, U., 328
Sulzer, J., 214
Sulzman, F. M., 148
Sumner, F. C., 6
Sun, N., 170
Sun, Q., 174
Sunaert, S., 88
Sund, A. M., 337
Sungkhasettee, V. W., PIA-14
Supina, R. D., 404
Sur, M., 57
Suryani, L., 553
Sutcliffe, N., 428
Sutherland, C. A. M., 456
Sutherland, G. R., 320
Sutherland, G. T., 88
Sutherland, P., 332
Sutin, A. R., 506
Sutton, N., 177
Sutton, R. M., 465
Suwanlert, S., 429
Suzuki, K., 223
Suzuki, M. B., 430
Suzuki, N., 156
Suzuki, T. N., 307
Suzuki, Y., 297
Svanborg, K. D., 177
Svebak, S., 427
Sveen, O. B., 586
Swain, J. F., 377
Swami, V., 337
Swan, S. C., 430
Swanson, H., 154
Swapp, D., 446
Swayze, V. W., II, 609
Sweeney, C., 428
Sweetnam, H., 255
Swendsen, J., 543
Swenne, I., 557
Swets, J. A., 106
Swing, E., 223
Swing, E. L., 473
Swinnen, S. P., 88
Syed, M., 350
Sykes, C. M., 414
Sykes-Muskett, B. J., 587
Symes, B., 421
Symmons, D. P., 220
Sys, S. U., 418
Szalavitz, M., 147
Szamoskozi, S., 585

Szell, M., 468
Szwedo, D. E., 468

T

Taconnat, L., 351
Tadrous, M., 177
Tafuri, D., 375
Taglialatela, J. P., 306
Tahani, N., 320
Tajfel, H., 462, 464, 472
Takahashi, A., 470
Takahashi, K., 156
Takahashi, R., 419
Takahashi, Y., 399
Takashima, N., 238
Takeuchi, T., 155
Takooshian, H., 475
Talaga, M. C., 64, 550, 602–603, 604, 605, 606, 608
Talavera, S. C., 173
Talbott, G. D., 587
Talos, I. F., 25, 80, 97
Talwar, V., 456
Tamaki, M., 165
Tamborini, R., 469
Tambs, K., 560
Tammen, S. A., 89
Tan, C. C., 255
Tan, H., 170, 322
Tan, L., 255
Tan, M. S., 255
Tan, S., 89
Tan, X. A., 426, 427
Tandon, N., 246, 247
Tang, X., 334
Tang, Y.-Y., 427
Tanke, E. D., 464
Tannenbaum, B., 89
Tannenbaum, M. B., 453
Tanner, G., 405
Tannock, R., 238
Tanrikulu, I., 443
Tanti, A., 89
Tanzi, R. E., 263
Tao, R., 564, 565
Tapia, G., 351
Tarescavage, A. M., 517
Tarrier, N., 590
Tartaglia, M. C., 291
Tatarko, A., 372
Tatke, S., 13
Tator, C. H., 291
Taub, E., 126
Taube, J. S., 127
Taveras, E. M., 153
Tavernier, R., 369
Tax, A., 413
Taylor, B., 334, 341
Taylor, C., 208
Taylor, C. B., 546
Taylor, D. M., 463
Taylor, E., 503
Taylor, J., 598
Taylor, R., 590
Taylor, S. E., 12, 420, 429
Taylor, T. J., 306
Taylor, W., 518
Teasdale, J. D., 498, 543
Teicher, M. H., 542
Teigen, K., 416
Teitelbaum, P., 375
Teixeira, P. J., 371
Tellegen, A., 317, 512, 517, 518
Temoshok, L., 418
Tenney, A. L., 231
Tenorio, G., 255

Terman, L. M., 286, 294, 295
Terracciano, A., 506, 507
Terry, G. E., 179
Tesler, N., 89
Teuber, H. L., 261
Tevis, M., 6
Thakkar, M. M., 149
Thase, M. E., 595, 604
Theberge, J., 214
Thelen, M. H., 553
Theodore, A. D., 216
Theorell, T., 413
Theriault, G., 375, 509
Therrien, Z., 595
These, M., 595
Thibodeau, P. H., 305
Thiedke, C. C., 154
Thierry, H., 370
Thijs, C., 353
Thiyagarajan, M., 151
Thogersen-Ntoumani, C., 371
Thomae, H., 417
Thomas, A., 335
Thomas, E. F., 464
Thomas, M., 151
Thomas, R. K., 191
Thomas, S. B., 598
Thomas, S. L., 473
Thompson, C. H., 6
Thompson, C. K., 81
Thompson, J., 134
Thompson, P. M., 83, 543, 565
Thompson, W. L., 272, 273
Thompson, W. W., 334, 341
Thomsen, M. B., 541
Thomson, D. M., 245
Thoresen, C. E., 430
Thorgeirsson, T. E., 510
Thorleifsson, G., 510
Thorndike, E. L., 14, 198, 498, 519
Thorne, D., 151
Thornton, A., 469
Thorsen, C., 334
Thorsen, P., 334, 341
Thurlow-Harrison, S., 401
Thurner, S., 468
Thurstone, L., 282
Tian, R., 411, 412
Tian, X., 302
Tienari, P., 563
Timaeus, I. M., 452
Timbo, B. B., 169
Timmerman, R., 323
Timoshina, E. L., 372
Timulak, L., 581
Tisdale, J., 88
Titchener, E., 5
Tivadar, R. I., 167
To, A., 67
Tobias, B., 389
Tobias, K. G., 608
Tobin, S. N. S., 354
Tobis, I., 389
Toepper, R., 273
Toga, A. W., 25, 80, 83, 97
Tojo, L. M., 178
Toker, S., 412
Tolman, E., 217, 218
Tolman, E. C., 217, 218
Tomasello, M., 303
Tomasi, D., 75
Tomassy, G. S., 58
Tomba, E., 602
Tomes, N., 530
Tomycz, N. D., 610
Tonegawa, S., 380
Toner, K., 502, 581

Tonnesen, S., 565
Tononi, G., 152
Tooby, J., 469
Tor, P. C., 609
Torgersen, S., 560
Torgerson, C. M., 25, 80, 97
Tormakangas, T., 413
Tormala, Z. L., 450, 451, 453
Torrance, E. P., 294
Torrens, M., 172
Torres, S. A., 532
Toscano, W. B., 128
Tosic-Radev, M., 337
Toups, M. S. P., 158
Tousignant-Laflamme, Y., 126
Townsend, S., 428
Towsley, S., 335
Tozzi, F., 544
Trabulsi, J. C., 120
Trace, S. E., 557
Tracey, I., 126
Tracy, D. K., 178
Traffanstedt, M. K., 541
Tran, K., 532, 541
Tranel, D., 77, 80, 380
Trapnell, P. D., 442
Trapp, W., 262
Trappey, C., 106
Trauer, J. M., 590
Treadway, M. T., 220, 381
Treccani, B., 309
Tregubenko, V., 350
Treisman, A., 236
Treisman, A. M., 236
Treisman, M., 127
Tremblay, A., 375, 509
Tremblay, P., 81
Tremellen, K., 322
Triandis, H., 450
Trifilieff, P., 260
Trivedi, M. H., 158
Trojak, B., 67, 610
Trojanowski, J., 446, 447
Trolle-Lagerros, Y., 153
Troncoso, X. G., 137
Tropp, L. R., 466
Trost, M. R., 443
Trost, S., 565
Trudel, M., 337
Trueswell, J. C., 80
Trumbell, E., 337
Trumbell, J., 337
Trumbull, E., 373, 374
Truong, K. D., 175
Trut, L. M., 508
Trzaskowski, M., 299, 510
Trzesniewski, K., 367
Tsai, G. E., 554
Tsai, H. H., 57
Tsai, J. L., 384
Tsakanikos, E., 104
Tsakiris, M., 338
Tsehay, A., 128
Tsou, K. A., 408
Tucholka, A., 214
Tucker, M. A., 156
Tucker, P., 149
Tucker-Drob, E. M., 512
Tugade, M. M., 429
Tukuitonga, C. F., 477
Tulving, E., 231, 240, 241, 245
Tupak, S. V., 67
Turecki, G., 89
Turiano, N. A., 353
Turkheimer, E., 291
Turnbull, A. P., 421
Turnbull, H. R., 421

Turner, H. A., 252
Turner, J. C., 462, 464, 472
Turner, R. B., 410
Turner, S., 596
Turner, S. M., 545
Turrill, J., 147
Tusel, D. J., 170
Tversky, A., 276, 406
Twenge, J. M., 153, 540
2018 Physical Activity Guidelines Advisory Committee, 378
Tyrrell, D. A., 410

U

Uchino, B. N., 428
Uckert, K., 369
Ueda, I., 399
Uitermarkt, B. D., 67
Ukoumunne, O. C., 612
Ullian, E. M., 57
Umemura, T., 337
Uncapher, M. R., PIA-6
Underwood, M. K., 353
United Nations Office on Drugs and Crime, 178
Unsworth, N., 285
Updegraff, J. A., 429
Upthegrove, T., 34
Urbina, S., 299, 519
Ursano, R. J., A-9
Ursini, G., 317
U.S. Department of Health and Human Services, 28, 173, 613
Uylings, H. B. M., 77

V

Vacharkulksemsuk, T., 428
Vadillo, M. A., 494
Vago, R., 427
Vail, A., 598, 599
Vaillancourt, D. E., 156
Vaillant, G. E., 428
Vainieri, I., 70
Vainik, U., 377
Valenstein, E., 82
Valentinova, K., 170, 172
Valera, E. M., 76, 77
Valerio, S., 127
Vallotton, C. D., 303
Valverde, R., 293
van Bemmel, D. M., 173
van Bochoven, A., 317, 510
van Buchem, M., 511
Van Craenenbroeck, E. M., 418
van Dam, R. M., 174
Van de Castle, R., 165
Van de Vijver, F. J. R., 290
van den Munckhof, P., 610
van der Linden, S., 4
van der Merwe, A., 108
Van der Stigchel, S., 237
van der Wee, N., 511
Van Dongen, H. P., 152
Van Dongen, H. P. A., 151, 152
van Duijl, M., 553
van Erp, T. G. M., 565
van Felius, R. A., 418
van Gerven, M. A., 273
Van Goozen, S. H., 560
Van Hemert, D. A., 290
Van Horn, J. D., 25, 80, 97
Van Horn, L., A-8
van Osch, M. J., 553, 554
Van Reen, E., 161, 378
van Roekel, E., 89

Van Straten, A., 587, 588
van Tol, M., 511
van Vollenhoven, R., 177, 428
van Waes, L. T., 404
van Wyk, M. C., PIA-15
Vande Voort, J. L., 67, 152
Vandell, D., 337
vanden Broek, W. W., 262
Vandenboom, C., 70
Vandenbulcke, M., 608
Vandenburgh, K., 112
Vangel, M. G., 76
Vanneste, S., 351
Vantilborgh, T., 430
Varela, J. A., 220
Varshney, M., 429
Vartanian, L. R., 347
Vasireddi, S. K., 260
Vasquez, M. J. T., 595
Vaughn, S., 240
Vavoulis, D. V., 250
Vecchio, F., 106
Vecsey, C. G., PIA-14
Vegunta, S., 351, 596
Veit, R., 214
Velikic, D., 337
Vellas, B., 412
Venables, P., 560
Venables, P. H., 335
Venkatraman, J., 293
Ventura, P., 585
Verceles, A. C., 220
Vercelli, A., 58
Verchinski, B. A., 565
Verdeli, H., 593
Verfaellie, M., 69, 352
Verges, B., 67, 610
Verhagen, M., 89
Verhoeven, J., 76
Verissimo, L., 364
Verkhratsky, A., 57
Vermetten, E., 554
Vernon, P. A., 512, 531
Vernon, R. J. W., 456
Vernon, S. W., 598
Verschuere, B., 380
Verschuren, W. M. M., 412
Verstappen, S. M., 220
Vervliet, B., 588
Vestergaard, M., 334, 341
Viberg, H., 293
Vicary, J., 106
Vichayapai, M., 20
Victor, T. A., 106, 494
Videnovic, A., 156
Vighetti, S., 67, 610
Vigorito, C. M., 191
Vik, A., 427
Vilhjalmsson, B., 510
Villani, S., 473
Villarreal, R., 499
Vincent, J., 443
Viner, J. C., 335
Vingerhoets, A. J. J. M., 384
Vingerling, J. R., 112
Vinnerljung, B., 323
Vinogradov, S., 88
Vion-Dury, J., 214
Virkkunen, M., 470
Visscher, P. M., 317, 510
Visser, P. S., 453, 454
Vitaro, F., 157
Vitek, J. L., 66, 67
Vitiello, B., 147
Vitiellow, M. V., 153
Vitorovic, D., 154
Vittinghoff, E., 549

Vlahov, D., 399
Vogel, E. K., 285
Vogel, G., 323
Vogel, G. W., 156
Vogt, B. A., 77
Vogt, D. S., 549
Vohs, K. D., 161
Voirin, N., 179
Vokey, J. R., 106
Volkow, N. D., 75, 153, 170
Vollenweider, F. X., 178
Vollset, S. E., 377
von Bastian, C. C., 308, 309
von Bonsdorff, M. B., 413
von Bonsdorff, M. E., 413
Von der Beck, I., 251
von Eisenhart Rothe, A., 412
von Helmholtz, H. L. F., 4, 118
von Hipple, W., 457
von Hofsten, C., 328
von Hofsten, O., 328
von Knorring, L., 608
von Stumm, S., 299
Vonderlin, R., 552
Voogd, J., 76
Voss, M. W., 89
Voyer, D., 382
Vreeke, S., 173
Vrij, A., 380
Vu, M. A., 352
Vul, E., 257
Vuori, M., 334
Vygotsky, L. S., 12, 14, 304, 333, 334

W

Wade, E., 246
Wade, T. D., 557
Waelde, L. C., 166
Waetjen, L. E., 351
Wagenmakers, E. J., 387
Wager, T. D., 382, 408
Wagner, A. D., 240, 256, PIA-6
Wagner, A. R., 194
Wagner, J., 421
Wahlbeck, K., 208, 216
Wahlsten, D., 317
Waight, P. A., 334, 341
Waite, L. M., 94
Wake, W. K., 317
Wakeel, F., 400
Wakefield, A. J., 334
Wald, G., 113
Waldfogel, J., 208
Waldman, I. D., 29, 519
Waldorp, L. J., 69
Wales, J., 557
Walitza, S., 89
Walk, R. D., 328
Walker, B., 411
Walker, B. N., 420
Walker, C., 88
Walker, L., 139
Walker, L. J., 348
Walker, M. P., 150, 156
Walker, N. R., 453
Walker, P., 139
Walker, R., 121
Wall, M., 179
Wall, M. J., 177, 549
Wall, P. D., 125
Wall, S., 336
Wallace, R. K., 427
Wallace, S. R., 335
Wallach, J., 178
Wallander, J., 337
Walsh, C. A., 208

Walsh, K., 594
Walters, E. E., 534, 546
Walther-Jallow, L., 563, 564
Waltkins, S. S., 173
Walton, K. G., 427
Walton, R. L., 291
Walts, K. K., 532
Wampers, M., 608
Wampold, B. E., 574, 595
Wamsley, E. J., 156
Wanderling, J. A., 609
Wang, B., 213
Wang, B. W., 178
Wang, C., 255
Wang, G. J., 75, 153
Wang, G. S., 179
Wang, H., 322, 541
Wang, H. F., 255
Wang, H. N., 67, 610
Wang, J., 220, 260, 334
Wang, J.-L., 468
Wang, M., 453, 458, 459
Wang, M. J., 609
Wang, N. Y., 598
Wang, P. S., 317, 535
Wang, S., 172, 173
Wang, T., 69, 179
Wang, X., 57
Wang, X. X., 67, 610
Wang, Y., 67, 263, 334, 543, 610
Wang, Z., 147
Wanitromanee, K., 429
Warburton, W., 222, 223
Ward, A., 70
Ward, A. S., 172
Ward, C., 421
Ward, J., 104, 177
Ward, M. M., 428
Ward, N. G., 574, 575
Ward, R. D., 191
Warden, M. R., 67
Ware, M. A., 179
Warner, K. L., 542
Warren, S. L., 588
Wartella, E., 222, 473
Wartner, U. G., 337
Wasch, H. H., 499
Washburn, A. L., 374
Washburn, A. N., 23
Washburn, M. F., 5, 6
Wass, C., 238
Wassef, A., 604
Wasserman, E. A., 191
Watanabe, J. T., 384
Waterhouse, L., 283
Waterman, A. S., 503
Waters, E., 336
Watkins, C. E., 520
Watkins, C. E., Jr., 493
Watkins, L. R., 220, 409
Watson, D. L., 231
Watson, J., 584
Watson, J. B., 9, 11, 14, 194, 216, 531, 550
Watson, J. C., 502, 581
Watson, J. M., 279, PIA-6
Watson, N. F., 153
Watson, R., 82
Watson, R. T., 442
Watts, J. W., 609
Waugh, R., 541
Waytz, A., 460
Webb, A. G., 352
Webb, W. B., 148, 151
Weber, B., 610
Weber, E., 104, 105
Weber, F., 163

Weber, G., 157
Webster, D., 405
Webster, D. W., 474
Webster, L., 587, 588
Wechsler, D., 282, 286
Wedding, D., 598, 599
Wee, C. Y., 57
Weed, N. C., 519
Weems, C. F., 549
Wegener, S. T., 126
Weidle, N. J., 169
Weihe, P., 293
Weiland, J., 179
Weinberger, A. D., 507
Weinberger, D. R., 62, 231, 317, 365, 564, 565
Weiner, B., 458
Weiner, I. B., 520, 521
Weiner, M., 70
Weiner, R. D., 608
Weingarten, H. P., 375
Weinhard, L., 327
Weinstein, M., 575
Weintraub, E. S., 341
Weintraub, S., 81
Weis, S., 260
Weise, S. B., 273
Weiskopf, N., 80, 214
Weisman, A., 355
Weiss, J. M., 404
Weiss, N. H., 430
Weiss, T., 67
Weisse, C. S., 428
Weissman, A., 322
Weissman, M. M., 541, 578
Weisz, J., 337
Weisz, J. R., 429
Weitzman, E. D., 149, 150
Weitzman, M., 421
Weizman, A., 178
Wekesa, J. M., 350
Welch, E., 557
Welham, J., 563
Wellings, K., 452
Wells, A., 585
Wen, X., 88
Wender, P. H., 563, 564
Wennberg, R., 291
Wenneberg, S. R., 427
Wenzel, J. M., 220
Werbel, A., A-9
Werker, J. F., 302
Wernicke, C., 14, 81
Wertheimer, M., 7
Wesensten, N., 151
Wesnes, K., 263
Wessely, S., 612
West, M. S., 441
West, R. F., 272
Westaway, D., 263
Westbrook, F., 273
Westbrook, G. L., 149
Westen, D., 590
Westenberg, H., 610
Westengard, J., 426
Westlye, L. T., 565
Weston, T., PIA-6
Wetherell, J. L., 587
Wever, E. G., 118
Weyant, J. M., 444
Whalen, P. J., 77
Whalen, R., 417
Wheatcroft, D., 307
Wheaton, F., 465
Wheeler, B. W., 612
Wheeler, D., 443

Wheeler, L. P. G., 88
Wheeler, S. C., 450, 451, 453
Whelton, W. J., 403
Whisenant, D., 154
Whitaker, D. L., 171
White, A., 174
White, B. J., 465
White, G. L., 466
White, M. P., 166, 612
White, R. F., 293
Whitehead, G. I., 447, 471
Whitfield-Gabrieli, S., 166
Whiting, D. M., 610
Whitman, C., 470
Whitney, P., 152
Whiton, K., 161
Whitten, W. B., 247
Whittington, C., 606
Whorf, B. L., 304
Wichers, M., 382
Wicker, A. W., 452
Widiger, T. A., 519
Widom, C. S., 337
Wiedemann, G. C., 167
Wien, S., 452
Wienbruch, C., 126
Wierenga, C. E., 556
Wiers, C. E., 75, 153
Wiesel, T. N., 134
Wiggers, K., 452
Wighton, P., 214
Wild, C. J., 150, 153
Wildermuth, J. L., 519
Wilent, B., 610
Wiley, J., 238
Wiley, K., 147
Wileyto, E. P., 67, 610
Wilfley, D. E., 578
Wilhelm, I., 89, 151
Wilhelm, K. P., 354
Wilhelmsen, L., 412
Wilkinson, C., 252
Wilkinson, D., 322
Willems, P. J., 370
Willemsen, A. T., 554
Willerman, L., 510
Willett, W., 174
Williams, A. O., 560
Williams, B., 549
Williams, J. A., 122
Williams, J. E., 519
Williams, J. F., 175
Williams, K., 442
Williams, K. D., 442
Williams, K. J., 465
Williams, M., 222, 542
Williams, M. A., 151
Williams, M. E., 350
Williams, M. J., 460
Williams, R. B., 417, 418
Willig, C., 414
Willig, J., 173
Willis, H., 462
Willis, S. L., 316, 352
Willoughby, T., 369, 473
Wilson, B. M., 252
Wilson, C. B., 334, 341
Wilson, K., 453
Wilson, N., 177
Wilson, R. S., 414
Wilson, S. M., 426
Wimber, M., 256
Wimmer, M., PIA-14
Windsor, T. D., 506
Winer, J. R., 150
Winkler, R., 409

Winkler, T. W., 377
Winlove, C., 273
Winlove, C. I. P., 273
Winograd, M., 70
Winslow, J. T., 94
Winstein, C. J., 260
Winthorst, W. H., 541
Winton, W. M., 416
Wiseman, R., 18
Wisenbaker, J. M., 275
Witherby, S. A., 104
Witt, W. P., 400
Wittchen, H. U., 540, 545, 546
Witte, O. W., 67
Wittmann, L., 165
Wittrock, M. C., PIA-13
Wixted, J. T., 248, 257
WLS-TV, Chicago., 475
Wohlfahrt, J., 334, 341
Wolberg, L. R., 574
Wolf, M. M., 213
Wolfs, R. C., 112
Wolkowitz, O. M., 403
Wolpert, B. J., 169
Wong, H., 178, 421
Wong, K. M., 23
Wong, M. Y., 208
Wong, S. Y., 421
Wong, W. W., 377
Wong-Kim, E., 351
Wood, E., PIA-6
Wood, J. M., 518, 519, 521
Wood, W., 4, 440
Woodall, C., 414
Woodhouse, A., 126
Woods, R. P., 80
Woodside, D. B., 66, 610
Woodworth, K. Y., 542
Woody, E. Z., 167
Woolley, J. D., 88
Worden, M. S., 541
World Health Organization, 378, 535, 540, 545
Worrell, G. A., 67, 152
Worthley, J. S., 246
Worz, S., 214
Wosinska, W., 444
Wozniak, J., 542
Wozniak, P. J., 604
Wright, C. I., 550
Wright, C. L., 586
Wright, J. W., PIA-15
Wu, C-C., PIA-14
Wu, E. X., 67
Wu, G., 324
Wu, H., 610
Wu, Y., 442
Wundt, W., 4, 5, A-11, PIA-13
Wurm, M., 417
Wyman, P. A., 413
Wynne, C., 219
Wynne, L. C., 563, 592

X

Xia, J., 322
Xia, Y., 173
Xie, L., 151
Xie, P., 606
Xiong, C., 13
Xu, H., 263, 354
Xu, J., 427
Xu, M., 163
Xu, Q., 148, 151
Xu, X., 76
Xu, X. M., 88

Xu, Y., 543
Xu, Z., 213
Xu, Z. C., 88
Xuan, Z., 179
Xue, L., 172

Y

Yachison, S., 456
Yaffe, K., 549
Yagita, K., 149
Yalom, I., 592
Yalom, I. D., 592
Yamaguchi, S., 149, 529
Yamamura, Y., 154
Yamamuro, K., 57
Yamashita, N., 320
Yamawaki, N., 246
Yamazaki, T., 76
Yan, G., 70
Yancey, D., 413
Yang, C., 248, 429
Yang, J., 263, 354
Yang, S., 541
Yang, Y., 470
Yantis, C., 23
Yap, P. T., 69
Yarkoni, T., 511
Yavuz, E., 201
Ye, Y., 499
Ye, Z., 149
Yeager, D. S., 367
Yeargin-Allsopp, M., 293
Yeh, M., 408
Yerkes, R. M., 416, A-12
Yeung, M. K., 71
Yeung, M. S., 88
Yip, Y. L., 429

Yokosawa, K., 104
Yokoyama, K., 293
Yoo, T., 366
Yoon, J. H., 88
Yopyk, D., 465
Yoshida, W., 494
Young, A. W., 380, 470, 456
Young, E. J., 260
Young, J., 595
Young, J. E., 590
Young, K., 598
Young, L. J., 94
Young, L. L., 460
Young, R., 328
Young, S. N., 149
Young, T., 112
Young, T. B., 351
Young, W., 355
Youngerman, B. E., 610
Yu, C., 165
Yu, H., 334
Yu, J. T., 255
Yu, L., 354
Yuan, P., 80
Yuan, T.-F., 411, 412
Yuan, W.-J., 421
Yukawa, S., 473
Yule, G., 302
Yule, W., 596
Yuste, R., 62

Z

Zadra, A., 157, 165
Zagalsky, R., 238
Zagato, A., 429
Zahn, T. P., 403
Zaiko, Y. V., 597
Zajecka, J., 602
Zajonc, R. B., 93, 389, 442, 467
Zaki, J., 94
Zalocusky, K. A., 67
Zammit, S., 179
Zammitti, E. P., 575
Zane, N., 598, 599
Zangwill, S. D., 320
Zarate, C. A., Jr., 606
Zaslavsky, A. M., 540, 545, A-9
Zavalloni, M., 441
Zavos, H., 510
Zedler, B., 6
Zee, P. C., 153
Zeighami, Y., 377
Zeki, S., 129, 469
Zeman, A., 273
Zendle, D., 222
Zentall, T. R., 219
Zetocha, K., 585
Zeveloff, J., PIA-20
Zhan, Y., 327
Zhang, A., 149
Zhang, B., 355
Zhang, E., 70
Zhang, H., 171, 323
Zhang, J., 69, 70
Zhang, R. G., 67, 610
Zhang, S., 429
Zhang, T., 550
Zhang, W., 550
Zhang, X., 354, 380
Zhang, Y., 377, A-8
Zhang, Y. H., 67, 610
Zhang, Y.-W., 263
Zhang, Z., 67, 610
Zhao, H., 153, 541

Zheng, H., 70
Zhou, H., 89
Zhou, X., 429, 606
Zhou, Y., 89
Zhu, Y., 150
Ziegelmayer, C., 262
Ziegler, G. R., 121
Zierer, A., 412
Zilles, K., 64, 78
Zillmann, D., 469
Zimbardo, P., 442, 471
Zimbardo, P. G., 442, 450, 471, 472
Zimerman, B., 542
Zimmer, L., 95
Zimmerman, G., 462
Zimmerman, J. C., 149, 150
Zimmerman, R. S., 453
Zipp, F., 69
Zisapel, N., 149
Zitman, F., 511
Zivcakova, L., PIA-6
Zlatin, D. M., 355
Zoccolotti, P., 106
Zoghbi, S. S., 179
Zolotor, A. J., 216
Zonderman, A. B., 506, 512, 531
Zorilla, E. P., 413
Zorumski, C. F., 66
Zreik, G., 337
Zucchi, F. C. R., 404
Zuckerman, M., 368, 399
Zuo, L., 294
Zupčić, M., 384
Zuvekas, S. H., 147
Zvolensky, M. J., 546
Zwaan, R. A., 387

Subject Index

A

ABA. *See* Applied behavior analysis
ABC model of attitudes, 451, 451*f*
Ablutophobia, 546
Abnormality. *See also* Psychological disorders
   changing conceptions of, 528–530
   defining, 528, 530
   diagnosing and classifying, 533–538
   models of, 530–532
   models to explain psychological, 530–532
Absolute threshold, 105, 105*t*
ACC. *See* Anterior cingulate cortex
Acceptance, 354
Accommodation, 133, 330
Acculturative stress, 421–422
Acetylcholine (ACh), 61–62, 62*t*, 263
Achievement tests, 291
Acrophobia, 546
Action potential, 59, 59*f*
Action therapy, 575, 588
Activation-information-mode (AIM) model, 164
Activation-synthesis hypothesis, 163–164, 163*f*
Activity theory, of aging, 354
Acute stress disorder (ASD), 544–545, 548
Adaptive behavior, 292
Adaptive forgetting, 256
Adaptive theory of sleep, 151, 152*f*
Adderall, 171
Addiction. *See* Psychoactive drugs
ADHD. *See* Attention-deficit/hyperactivity disorder
Adler's birth order theory, 493
Adler's superiority seeking motivation, 493
Adolescence, 346
   cognitive development, 346–348, 347*f*, 348*t*
   depression in, 543
   Erikson's identity *vs.* role confusion, 348
   moral development, 347–348, 348*t*
   parent-teen conflict, 348
   physical development, 346
   psychosocial development, 348–349
Adoption studies, 297–299, 510
   on schizophrenia, 563
Adrenal glands, 95
Adulthood, 350. *See also* Aging
   cognitive development, 351–352
   death and dying stages, 354–355
   late, 339*t*, 350, 353, 356
   physical development, 350
   psychosocial development, 352–353
Aerial (atmospheric) perspective, 132, 132*f*
Affect, 539
Affective component, of attitude, 451, 451*f*
Afferent (sensory) neurons, 87
AFTE. *See* Autogenic-Feedback Training Exercise
Afterimages, 113, 113*f*
Aggression, 404–405, 478

biology and, 470
media violence linked to, 472–474
in social interaction, 469–474
social learning explanations for, 470–474
Aggressive punishment, 207
Aging, 356
   brain changes, 351–352
   death and dying stages, 354–355
   memory changes, 351
   menopause, 350–351
   mortality despair, 353
   parenting, 352–353
   physical, 350
   physical and psychological theories, 353–354
   relationships, 352
   theories of physical and psychological, 353–354, 356
Agonists, 61, 64
Agoraphobia, 536*f*, 536*t*, 546, 547*t*
Agreeableness, 506, 511
AIM. *See* Activation-information-mode (AIM) model
Ainsworth's Strange Situation, 336–337
Alarm reaction, 408, 409, 422
Alcohol, 174–175, 180*t*
   aggressive behavior related to, 469
   blood alcohol level, 176*t*
Alcohol-use disorders, 536*f*
Algorithms, 276, 281
All-or-none, 59
All-or-nothing thinking, 550
Allostasis, 411
Allostatic load, 411
Allport's trait theories, 504
Alpha waves, 153, 155*f*
Altered identities, 552–554
Altered processes, 147
Altered state of consciousness, 146–147
Altruism, 472, 474
Alzheimer's disease, 13, 262–264, 351
Ambivalence, 336
American Academy of Sleep Medicine, 154
Ames Room illusion, 137
Amitriptyline (Elavil), 605
Amnesia
   anterograde, 240–241, 262
   biological causes of, 261–264
   infantile, 264
   organic, 261–264
   retrograde, 261–262
Amok (trancelike state), 553
Amphetamines, 171–172, 180*t*
Amygdala, 74*f*, 76*f*, 77
   emotion and, 380
Anal retentive personality, 490
Anal stage of development, 490, 492*t*
Analytical intelligence, 283
Andropause, 351
Anger, 354
Anhidrosis, 126
The Animal Mind (Washburn), 5
Animals. *See also* Cat experiment, of Thorndike; Dogs
   adaptive theory of sleep and, 152*f*

research on, 48
studies in language, 305–307
Anorexia nervosa, 377, 379, 555–557, 558, 606
ANS. *See* Autonomic nervous system
Antagonists, 61, 64
Anterior cingulate cortex (ACC), 200
Anterograde amnesia, 240–241, 262, 262*f*, 263
Antianxiety drugs, 64, 604, 607*t*, 611
Antidepressant drugs, 604–607, 607*t*, 611
Antipsychotic drugs, 602–604, 603*f*, 607*t*, 611
Antisocial personality disorder (ASPD), 559, 560
Anti-vaccination movement, 334
Anvil (incus), 117, 117*f*
Anxiety, 536*f*, 544–545
   basic, 493–494
   sexual disfunction and, 559
Anxiety disorders, 545–547, 547*t*, 551
   ASD and PTSD, 548–549
   causes of, 549–551
   generalized, 547
   obsessive-compulsive disorder, 547, 548
   panic, 546–547
   phobic disorder, 545–546
   symptoms, 547*t*
Apnea, 159
Apparent distance hypothesis, 136
Applied behavior analysis (ABA), 213, 583
Applied psychology, A-2
Applied research, 16
Approach-approach conflict, 405, 406*t*
Approach-avoidance conflict, 406, 406*t*
Aqueous humor, 109
Arachnophobia, 546
Arbitrary inference, 588
Archetypes, 493
Arousal, performance and, 416, 416*f*
Arousal theory, 368–369, 368*f*
ART. *See* Attention restoration theory
Asch's conformity study, 438–439, 439*f*
ASD. *See* Acute stress disorder; Autism spectrum disorder
ASPD. *See* Antisocial personality disorder
Assimilation, 329–330, 422, 423
Association areas, of cortex, 81
Ataque de nervios (attack of nerves), 550
Ativan, 174
Atmospheric perspective, 132, 132*f*
Attachment
   in infancy and early childhood, 335–336
   influences are, 337
Attention
   in observational learning, 223
   selective, 236
Attention restoration theory (ART), 612
Attention-deficit/hyperactivity disorder (ADHD), 98, 542
Attitudes, 460
   cognitive dissonance and, 454–456, 455*f*

formation of, 452–453
impression formation, 456–457
persuasion and, 453–454
social cognition, 454–456, 455*f*
Attribution
   fundamental, error, 458–460
   social cognition and, 458–460
Attribution theory, 458
Atypical antipsychotics, 602–603, 607*t*
Auditory association area, 80
Auditory canal, 117
Auditory nerve, 117*f*, 118
Authenticity, 579
Authoritarian parenting, 353
Authoritative parenting, 353
Authorities, 32
Autism spectrum disorder (ASD), 334, 340
   behavior modification and, 213
Autobiographical memory, 264
Autogenic training, 128
Autogenic-Feedback Training Exercise (AFTE), 128
Autokinetic effect, 136
Automatic coding, 249–250, 253
Autonomic nervous system (ANS), 86*f*, 89, 90–92
Autonomy, 371
Autosomes, 318
Availability heuristic, for problem solving, 276–277
Aversion therapy, 586
Avoidance-avoidance conflict, 405–406, 406*t*
Axon, 56–57
Axon hillock, 58–59
Axon terminals, 57

B

Babbling, 303*t*
Baby talk, 303
Bandura's aggression study, 472–473
Bandura's behavior therapy, 591*t*
Bandura's Bobo doll experiment, 221–223, 222*f*
Bandura's reciprocal determinism, 497–498, 497*f*, 500
Barbiturates, 174, 180*t*
Bargaining, 354
Basal ganglia, 74*f*
Basal metabolic rate (BMR), 375, 376, 376*f*
Basic anxiety, 493–494
Basic research, 16
Basic suggestion effect, 167
Basilar membrane, 117
Beck's cognitive therapy, 588–589, 591*t*
Behavior
   adaptive, 292
   as attitude component, 451*f*, 452
   attribution and causes of, 458
   disorganized or odd, 565
   of emotion, 382–384, 383*f*
   four ways to modify, 206*t*
   helping, 476–477, 476*f*
   religion encouraging healthy, 430

SI-1

SUBJECT INDEX SI-2

Behavior modification, 206t, 212–214, 583. *See also* Operant conditioning; Punishment
Behavior therapies, 583–588, 591t
Behavioral activation, 587
Behavioral assessments, 516–517, 521
Behavioral genetics, 317
   personality, 508–510
   twin studies, 508–510, 509f
Behavioral learning perspective, 496–499
Behavioral neuroscience, 56
Behavioral perspective, 11, 14t, 486
   of anxiety disorders, 550
   of dissociative disorders, 554
Behavioral psychology, 414
Behaviorism, 9, 531
Bell curve, 299
Benzedrine, 171
Benzodiazepines, 174, 180t, 607t
Beta waves, 153, 155f
Bias
   cognitive, 309
   confirmation, 279, 281
   cultural and, 289–290
   hindsight, 251
   observer, 24
Big Five personality dimensions, 505, 511, 512–513
Bilateral anterior cingulotomy, 609–610
Bilaterally transmitted, 79
Bilingualism, 308–309
Bimodal, 40
Bimodal distribution, 38, 38f
Binet's mental ability test, 285, 300
Binge drinking, 174
Binge-eating disorder, 377, 379, 556, 558
Binocular cues, 131, 133–134, 133f
Binocular disparity, 133–134
Bioethics, 322
Biofeedback, 128, 213
Biological models, for disorders, 531
Biological perspective
   of anxiety disorders, 550
   of personality disorders, 559
   on schizophrenia, 561–562
Biological preparedness, 196
Biological psychology, 56
Biology
   aggression and, 470
   of mood disorders, 543–544
   of personality, 508–510
Biomedical therapies, 575, 611
   ECT, 607–610
   emerging techniques, 610
   psychopharmacology, 602–607, 607t
   psychosurgery, 609–610
Biopsychological perspective, 13, 14t
   of abnormality, 532, 538
Biopsychosocial model, 532
Bipolar disorder, 536f, 536t, 537, 539–540, 541
Bipolar medications, 607t
Birth order theory, of Adler, 593
Black widow spider, 61, 62
Blind spot, 110, 110f
Blood alcohol level, 176t
BMR. *See* Basal metabolic rate
Bobo doll experiment, 221–223, 222f
Body movement and position, 126–128
Body temperature, sleep and, 149
Borderline personality disorder (BPD), 552, 559, 560
Bottom-up processing, 137
BPD. *See* Borderline personality disorder
BPS. *See* British Broadcast Company prison study
Brain, 86f
   activity during sleep, 155f
   adulthood changes in, 351–352
   anatomical directions, 73f
   association areas of cortex, 81
   cerebral hemispheres, 83–85, 83f, 84t
   cortex, 78–80
   hearing sense, 116–119
   hindbrain, 74–76
   infancy and early childhood development, 325
   lateralization, 79
   limbic system, 76–77
   lobes and cortical areas, 76f
   mapping function, 69, 70f
   mapping structure of, 69f, 74f
   motor and somatosensory cortex, 79f
   planes of section, 68f
   reward pathway of, 171f
   stimulation, 66
   structures, 73–85
   trephining, 528
Brain study
   invasive techniques, 66–67
   neuroimaging techniques, 68–71
   noninvasive techniques, 67
Brainstorming, 280t
Brightness, 108
Brightness constancy, 129
British Broadcast Company prison study (BPS), 472
Broca's aphasia, 81
Broca's area, 81
Brown eyes, blue eyes study, 463–464
Bulimia nervosa, 377, 379, 556, 558
Bupropion (Wellbutrin), 605
Burnout, 421
Bystander response, 475–476, 475f

C

Caffeine, 173–174, 180t
Cancer
   aging and skin, 351
   marijuana and, 179
   stress and, 412–413
Cannon-Bard theory of emotion, 386, 386f, 390f
Capacity, in memory, 237–238
Carpentered world, 135
Case studies, 25
Cat experiment, of Thorndike, 198–199
Cataplexy, 159
Catastrophes, 399–400
Catatonia, 562
Cattell-Horn-Carroll (CHC) theory of intelligence, 284–285, 284f, 300
Cattell's 16PF, 504, 516t, 518
Cattell's trait theories, 504
CB. *See* Cingulum bundle
CBT. *See* Cognitive-behavioral therapy
Cellular-clock theory, of aging, 354
Central nervous system (CNS), 86–89, 86f
Central sulcus, 79f
Central-route processing, 454
Centration, 331
CER. *See* Conditioned emotional response
Cerebellum, 74f, 75
Cerebral cortex, 74f
Cerebral hemispheres, 78, 83–84, 83f
Cerebrum, 78
Channels, 58
Character, 486
Characteristic adaptations, 511
CHC. *See* Cattell-Horn-Carroll (CHC) theory of intelligence
CHD. *See* Coronary heart disease
Chemical senses, 120–123
Child development. *See* Infancy
Child-directed speech, 303
Childhood development. *See also* Infancy
   anal stage, 490
   latency stage, 491–492
   phallic stage, 491
Children. *See also* Infancy; Parenting; Young adulthood
   coping, 429
   sleep disorders in, 154
Chinese Americans
   eating disorders of, 557
   emotions described by, 384
Chlorpromazine, 602, 609
Chromosomes, 318
   problems, 319–320
Chunking, 238
Cilia, 122
Cingulate cortex, 76f, 77
Cingulum bundle (CB), 565
CIPA. *See* Congenital insensitivity to pain with anhidrosis
Circadian rhythm, 148, 149
   disorders, 160t
Class-bound values, for effective psychotherapy, 599
Classical conditioning, 200t
   behavior therapies based on, 583–586
   elements of, 189
   human behavior applications, 194–196
   insomnia and, 158
   Pavlov and salivating dogs, 188–194
   reasons it works, 193–194
   spontaneous recovery, 210
   terminology chart, 189t
   therapies based on, 583–586
Claustrophobia, 545
Climacteric, 351
Clinical health psychology, 414
Clinical psychology, A-6
Closure, 130, 131f
CNS. *See* Central nervous system
Cocaine, 172, 180t
Cochlea, 117, 117f
Cochlear implant, 119, 119f
Coconut oil, memory effected by, 255
Cognition, 272. *See also* Thinking
Cognitive appraisal approach, 414–415
Cognitive arousal, performance and, 416, 416f
Cognitive biases, 309
Cognitive component, of attitude, 451f, 452
Cognitive development
   adolescence, 349
   adulthood and aging, 350–351, 356
   autism spectrum disorder, 334
   infancy, 329–334
   in infancy and early childhood, 340
   moral development, 347–348, 348t
   Piaget's formal operations, 346–347
   Piaget's theory, 329–333
   Vygotsky's theory of, 333–334
Cognitive dissonance, 454–456, 460
   attitude and, 455f
Cognitive learning theory, 216–220
   insight learning, 218–219
   Köhler's Smart Chimp, 218–219
   latent learning, 217–218
   learned helplessness, 219–221
Cognitive neuroscience, 12
Cognitive perspective, 12, 14t, 194
   of anxiety disorders, 550
   of dissociative disorders, 554
   personality disorders and, 560
Cognitive psychologists, 531
Cognitive reappraisal approach, 415
Cognitive theories
   of dreaming, 164
   of emotion, 387–390, 391
Cognitive therapies, 588–590, 591, 591t
Cognitive universalism, 305
Cognitive-behavioral therapy (CBT), 584, 589–590, 591t
   evaluation of, 590
Cognitive-mediational theory of emotion, of Lazarus, 389–390, 389f, 390f, 414, 423
Cohort effect, 316
Collagen, 354
Collective unconscious, 493
Collectivistic cultures, motivation in, 373
College, coping with stress in, 431–432
College Undergraduate Stress Scale (CUSS), 401, 402t
Color, 96
   afterimage, 113, 113f
   opponent process theory, 113–114
   perception, 112–115
   trichromatic theory, 112–113
Color blindness, 114–115
Color-deficient vision, 114, 114f
Columbine High School shooting, 473
Commitment, 468
Common factors approach, to therapy, 596
Common region, 130
Common sense theory, of emotion, 385, 385f, 390f
Communication
   animal, 305–307
   psychotherapy and style of, 599
Community psychology, A-10
Companionate love, 469
Comparative psychology, A-7–A-8
Compliance, 448
   cultural differences in, 444
   door-in-the-face technique, 443–444
   foot-in-the-door technique, 443
   lowball technique, 444
Compositional syntax, 306
Computed tomography (CT), 68, 69f
Concentrative meditation, 427
Concept maps
   adolescence, 349
   anxiety, trauma, and stress disorders, 551
   behavior therapies, 591
   behavioral and social cognitive learning perspectives, 500
   biological theories of personality, 514
   body senses, 128
   brain, 72, 85
   chemical senses, 123
   classical conditioning, 196
   cognitive learning theory, 221
   coping with stress, 431
   critical thinking, 32–33
   defined, PIA-14
   disorders of mood, 544
   dissociative disorders, 554
   dreams, 165
   eating disorders and sexual dysfunction, 560
   endocrine glands, 93–95
   exam studying, PIA-15
   forgetting, 259
   group therapy, 594
   hearing sense, 119
   how people think, 281
   humanistic perspective, 503
   hypnosis, 168
   infancy and childhood development, 340

information-processing model, 244
insight therapy, 581
intelligence, 300
language, 307
learning, 196
lectures, PIA-12
living brain, 72
long-term memories, 253
memory, 232, PIA-17
motivation understanding, 372
nervous system, 92
neurons and neurotransmitters, 65
neuroscience of memory, 264
observational learning, 223
operant conditioning, 214
perception, 138
personality assessment, 521
personality theories, 495–496
psychoactive drugs, 180
psychological disorders, 538
psychological research ethics, 48
psychology, 10, 17
science of seeing, 115
sensation, 107
sleep, 160
social influence, 448
social interaction, 477–478
stress and health, 422–423
student's ethical responsibilities, PIA-20
textbook reading, PIA-10
time management, PIA-7
trait theories, 517
writing papers, PIA-18
Concept prototypes research, 281
Conception of personality, 487–489, 488f
Concepts, 273–275, 281
Conclusions, drawing, 22
Concrete operations state, of cognitive development, 330t, 332
Concussions, long-term effects of, 291
Conditional positive regard, 501
Conditioned emotional response (CER), 195
Conditioned response (CR), 189–190, 190f
Conditioned stimulus (CS), 189, 190f
Conditioned taste aversions, 195, 196
Conditioning
 comparing operant and classical, 200t
 operative, 11
 in real world, 224
Conduction hearing impairment, 119
Cones, 110
 light absorbance from, 113f
Conflict
 parent-teen, 348
 stress and, 405–406, 406t, 407
Conformity, 438–440, 448
Congenital analgesia, 126
Congenital insensitivity to pain with anhidrosis (CIPA), 126
Conscience, 489
Conscientiousness, 505, 511
Consciousness
 altered states of, 146–147
 defined, 147
Conservation, 331
 experiment, 331f
Consolidation, 260
Constructive processing, of memories, 250, 251
Consumer psychology, 443
Consummate love, 469
Context-dependent learning, 245, 253
Contiguity, 130, 131f
Contingency contract, 587
Contingency-management therapy, 170

Continuity, 130, 131f
Continuous positive airway pressure (CPAP) device, for sleep, 159
Continuous reinforcement, 203
Contralateral organization, 78–79
Control, 20–21
 stress and lack of, 405–406
Control group, 30
Controlled processes, 147
Conventional morality, 348t
Convergence, 133, 133f
Convergent thinking, 279
Cooing, 303t
Coping strategies, 431
 culture and, 429–430
 emotion-focused, 426–427
 meditation, 427–428
 problem-focused, 426
 religion, 430
 social support as, 428–429
Coronal plane, 68f
Coronary heart disease (CHD), stress and, 411, 411f
Corporal punishment, banned, 216f
Corpus callosum, 74f, 78
Correlation coefficient, 27–28
Correlations, in scientific research, 26–28
Cortex, 78–81
 association areas of, 81
 structures under, 76–77
Corticalization, 78
Counseling psychology, A-6–A-7
CR. See Conditioned response
Creative intelligence, 283
Creativity, thinking and, 279–281
Critical periods, 323
Critical thinking, 18–19
Cross-sectional design, 316, 317t
Cross-sequential design, 316, 317t
Crying, 384
Crystal meth, 171–172
Crystalized intelligence, 284
CS. See Conditioned stimulus
CT. See Computed tomography
Cults, 449–450
Cultural bias, IQ tests and, 289–290
Cultural explanations, 532
Cultural idioms of distress, 532
Cultural perspective, of anxiety disorders, 550–551
Cultural relativity, 531
Cultural syndromes, 532
Culture
 American assumptions and psychotherapy, 599
 compliance in different, 443
 coping and, 429–430
 eating disorders and, 557
 fundamental attribution error and, 458
 hunger and, 372
 psychotherapy concerns with differences of, 598–600
 stress and, 421–422
 stressors of, 421–422
Culture-bound values, for effective psychotherapy, 599
Curare, 61
Curve of forgetting, 256–257, 257f
CUSS. See College Undergraduate Stress Scale
Cybertherapy, 597
Cynophobia, 545
Cystic fibrosis, 319

D

DA. See Dopamine
Dark adaptation, 112
Date rape drug, 174
Daydreaming, 147
DBS. See Deep brain stimulation
Death/dying, 356. See also Suicide
 in other cultures, 355
 stages of, 354–355
Decay, 58, 259t
Decibels, sound waves and, 117f
Decision making, 275–278, 281
 problems with, 278–279
Declarative (explicit) memory, 239, 241–242, 242f, 244, 261
Deep brain stimulation (DBS), 66, 610, 611
Defense mechanisms, psychological, 489, 490t
Deindividuation, 442–443, 448
Delta waves, 153, 154
Delusional experiences, 536f
Delusions, 561
Dementia, 352
 amnesia related to, 263
Dendrites, 56
Denial, 354
Denied past, 581
Dependent personality disorder, 559, 560
Dependent variable, 29
Depersonalization/derealization disorder, 554
Depressants, 171, 174–177, 180t
Depression, 354, 539–541
 causes of, 542–544
 helplessness and, 220
 stress and, 416
Depth of processing, 231
Depth perception, 131–134, 132f, 133f
Description, 20
Descriptive statistics, 36–42
 frequency distributions, 36–38, 36t
 measures of central tendency, 38–40
 measures of variability, 40–42
Desipramine (Norpramin, Pertofrane), 605
Desire, in observational learning, 223
Desired behavior, reinforcement of, 206
Developmental crises, of Erikson, 339t
Developmental psychology, A-7
Developmentally disabled. See Intellectual disability (intellectual developmental disorder)
Deviation IQ scores, 288–289
Devil's trident, 138, 138f
Dexedrine, 171, 180t
Diabetes
 pancreas and, 95
 sleep deprivation and, 152
 stress and, 412
Diagnostic and Statistical Manual of Mental Disorders, Fifth Edition, 292, 533
Diazepam (Valium), 64
DID. See Dissociative identity disorder
Difference threshold, 104
Diffusion, 58
Diffusion of responsibility, 476
Diffusion tensor imaging (DTI), 69, 565
Digit-span test, 237
Direct contact, 452
Direct instruction, 452
Direct observation, 516–517
Directive, 577
Disassociation, 167–168
Discipline, 215–216, 216f
Discrimination, 461–463, 477
Discriminative stimulus, 209–210

Diseases of adaptation, 409
Disorders of mood
 bipolar disorder, 541–542
 causes of, 542–544
 major depressive disorder, 539–541
Disorganized behavior, 565
Displaced aggression, 405
Display rules, 383–384
Dispositional cause, 458
Dispositional cause of behavior, 460
Dissociative amnesia, 552, 553
Dissociative disorders, 552–554
Dissociative fugue, 553
Dissociative identity disorder (DID), 553, 554
Distance counseling, 597
Distress, 398–399
Distributed practice, 257–258, 259
Disturbed or disorganized thought, 565
Disuse, 258, 259t
Divergent thinking, 280, 283
 stimulating, 280t
Dizygotic twins, 322f
DLPFC. See Dorsolateral prefrontal cortex
DNA (deoxyribonucleic acid), 320
Dogs, 274
 Pavlov's experiment, 188–194, 376
 Seligman's depressed, 219–221, 219f
Dominant genes, 318
 PKU and, 319f
Door-in-the-face technique, 443–444, 448
Dopamine (DA), 62, 62t
Dorsolateral prefrontal cortex (DLPFC), 73
Dot Problem, 278f
 solution, 280
Double approach-avoidance conflict, 406
Double takes. See Sensory memory
Double-blind studies, 32
Dove Counterbalance General Intelligence Test, 290
Down syndrome, 293, 320
Doxepin (Sinequan, Adapin), 605
Dreams, 155–156
 activation-synthesis hypothesis, 163–164, 163f
 AIM model, 164
 content of, 164–165
 Freud interpretation of, 162–163
 interpretation, 577, 581
 REM and, 155–156
Drive, 364
Drive-reduction theory, 365–366, 372
Drug dependency, 536f
 classical conditioning for, 196
Drug tolerance, 170
Drugs. See also Psychoactive drugs
 agonistic and antagonistic effects, 602–603, 603f
 antipsychotic, 602–604, 603f
 manufactured highs, 177–178
 nonmanufactured highs, 178–179
DTI. See Diffusion tensor imaging
Duck-billed platypus, 274
Duration, long-term memory, 239–240
Dweck's self-theory of motivation, 367–368

E

Ear
 canal, 117, 117f
 structure of, 117–118, 117f
Early childhood. See Infancy
Ears
 sound waves and, 116–118
 structure of, 117, 117f

Eating. *See also* Hunger
　motivation for, 374–378
　religion encouraging healthy, 430
Eating disorders, 555–558
　anorexia nervosa, 555
　bulimia nervosa, 556
　causes, 556–557
Ebbinghaus forgetting curve, 256–257, 257f
Ebbinghaus illusion, 135–136, 135f, 138
EBT. *See* Evidence-based treatment
Echoic sensory memory, 235, 244
e-cigarettes, 173
Eclectic, 574
Ecological validity, 287
Ecstasy, 178
ECT. *See* Electroconvulsive therapy
Educational psychology, A-8
EEG. *See* Electroencephalogram
Efferent (motor) neurons, 87
Ego, 488
Ego integrity parenting, 353
Ego movement, 8
Egocentrism, 331
Eidetic imagery, 235
Elaboration likelihood model, 454, 460
Elaborative rehearsal, 240
Electra complex, 491
Electroconvulsive therapy (ECT), 67, 607–610, 611
Electroencephalogram (EEG), 69–70
Electrostatic pressure, 58
Elemental connectedness, 130, 131f
Ellis REBT, 590
Embryo, 323
Embryonic period, 322, 322f, 323, 325
EMDR. *See* Eye-movement desensitization and reprocessing
Emerging adulthood, 349
Emotion, 379–380, 381f
　behavior of, 382–384, 383f
　Cannon-Bard theory, 386, 386f
　cognitive theories of, 387–390, 391
　comparison of theories, 390f
　early theories of, 385–387, 385f
　elements of, 380–384
　facial expressions of, 383f
　facial feedback, 386–387, 387f
　hunger and, 376
　labeling, 384
　Lazarus and cognitive-mediational theory, 389, 389f
　physiology of, 380–382
　range of, 539f
Emotional expression, 382–384, 383f
Emotional intelligence, 296–297
Emotion-focused coping, 425–428, 431
Empathy, 296–297, 579
Encoding, 230
Encoding failure, 257, 259t, 259
Encoding specificity, 245, 246
Endocrine glands, 93–98, 93f
Endogenous morphine, 63
Endorphins, 62–63, 62t
Enigma painting, 137, 137f
Enuresis, 160t
Environmental perspective, on schizophrenia, 562–563
Environmental psychology, A-10
Environmental stressors
　catastrophes, 399–400
　hassles, 402–403
　major life changes, 400–401
Enzymatic degradation, 64
Enzymes, 63–64
Epigenetics, 89
Episodic memory, 241–242, 242f, 244

biological bases of, 260–261
long term, 264
Equal status contact, 465–466
Erikson's generativity *vs.* stagnation, 352
Erikson's identity *vs.* role confusion, 348
Erikson's intimacy *vs.* isolation, 352
Erikson's psychosocial stages of development, 338–339, 339t, 340, 494
Escape, 407
Ethics
　of psychological research, 46–47
　of research, 446–447
　student responsibilities, PIA-19–PIA-20, PIA-19t
Ethnicity
　concerns with psychotherapy, 598–600
　depression prevalence by, 541
Eustress, 398–399
Event-related potentials, 69
Evidence, equality of, 18
Evidence-based treatment (EBT), 596
Evolutionary perspective, 13, 14t
Exam studying, PIA-12–PIA-15
Excitatory synapse, 61
Exercise. *See also* Physical activity
　for better sleep, 158
　for optimism, 420
Exhaustion, 408, 422
Expectancy, 498–499
Experimental group, 30
Experimental psychology, A-7
Experimenter effect, 31–32
Experiments, in scientific research, 28–31
Explanation, 20
Explanatory style, 419–420
Explicit memory, 240, 241–242, 242f
Exposure and response prevention (EX/RP), 585–586
Exposure therapies, 584–585
The Expression of the Emotions in Man and Animals (Darwin, C.), 386
EX/RP. *See* Exposure and response prevention
Extinction, 192, 192f, 587
　operant conditioning, 210
Extraversion, 506, 511
Extraverts, 506
Extrinsic motivation, 364, 371
Eye-movement desensitization and reprocessing (EMDR), 585
Eyes. *See also* Seeing
　light and, 108–110
　parts of, 109
　pathway of light, 111–112, 111f
　structure of, 108f, 109–110
　transduction of light, 110
Eyewitnesses, 248–249
Eysenck Personality Questionnaire, 518

F

Facial expressions, emotions and, 382–383, 383f
Facial feedback hypothesis, 386–387, 387f, 390f
Factor analysis, 504
False memory syndrome, 251–252
False positives, in memory, 248
Family, personality disorders and, 560
Family counseling, 592–593
Family studies, on schizophrenia, 563
Family therapy, 592–593
Farsightedness, 109, 109f
FASD. *See* Fetal alcohol spectrum disorders
Fear conditioning, 381
Feature detectors, 134

Feelings. *See* Emotion
Females, eating disorders in, 557
Fertilization, 321–322, 321f, 325
Fetal alcohol spectrum disorders (FASD), 323
Fetal alcohol syndrome, 293
Fetal period, 324, 324f, 325
Fetus, 324
Fight-or-flight system, 90–91
Figure-ground illusion, 130f
Figure-ground relationships, 129, 130f
Finding Meaning in Dreams (Domhoff), 164
Fish oil, memory effected by, 255
Five-factor model, 505
Fixation, 489–490
Fixed interval schedule of reinforcement, 203–204, 204f
Fixed ratio schedule of reinforcement, 204f, 205
Flashbulb memories, 249–250
Flat affect, 562
Flooding, 584
Fluid intelligence, 284, 285
Fluoxetine (Prozac), 605, 606
FMRI. *See* Functional MRI
fNIRS. *See* Functional NIRS
Foot-in-the-door technique, 443, 448
Forebrain, 76–77
Forensic psychology, A-9
Forgetting. *See also* Alzheimer's disease; Amnesia
　curve of, 256–257, 257f
　interference theory, 258, 258f
　reasons for, 257–258, 258f, 259t
Formal concepts, 274
Formal operations state, of cognitive development, 330t, 332–333
Four dimensions of cultural personality, of Hofstede, 512–513
Fragile X syndrome, 293
Fraternal twins, 297, 298f, 322f, 508–509, 509f
Free association, 577, 581
Free nerve endings, 124
Free-floating anxiety, 545
Free-radical theory, of aging, 354
Freewriting, 280t
Frequencies, 116
Frequency count, 517
Frequency distributions, 36–38, 36t
Frequency theory, 118
Freud's conception of personality, 487–489, 488f
Freud's division of personality, 487–488
Freud's psychoanalysis, 576–577, 581
Freud's psychodynamic therapy, 500, 554, 591t
Freud's psychosexual stages, 492t
Frontal lobes, 80. *See also* Motor cortex
Frontal operculum, 121
Frustration–aggression hypothesis, 404–405, 469
Fully functioning person, 502, 503
Functional fixedness, 278, 281
Functional MRI (FMRI), 70–71
Functional NIRS (fNIRS), 71
Functionalism, 6–7
Fundamental attribution error, 458–460
Future-ground, 129

G

G factor, 282
GABA. *See* Gamma-aminobutyric acid
Gall's theory of personality, 510–511
Gambling, slot machines, 205

Gamma-aminobutyric acid (GABA), 62, 62t
Gardner's multiple intelligences, 283, 300
Gardner's nine intelligences, 283, 283t
GAS. *See* General adaptation syndrome
Gate-control theory, 125–126
Gender
　concerns with psychotherapy, 598–600
　conformity and, 438
　hunger and, 376
General adaptation syndrome (GAS), 408–409, 408f, 422–423
General intelligence, 282
Generalization, 210
Generalized anxiety disorder, 536f, 536t, 547, 547t, 551
Generalized response, 191f
Generativity, 352
Generativity *vs.* stagnation, of Erikson, 352
Genes, 318
Genetics
　behavioral, 508–510
　mood disorders caused by, 544
　personality disorders and, 560
　problems, 319–320
　schizophrenia and, 564–565, 564f
Genital stage of development, 492, 492t
Genius, 293–294
Germinal period, 322, 322f, 323, 325
Gestalt principles of grouping, 129–130, 131f
Gestalt psychology, 7–8, 7f
Gestalt therapy, 580–581, 582, 591t
Getting Things Done (GTD) method, PIA-7
Gifted Children Growing Up (Freeman), 295
Giftedness, 293–294, 300
Gingko biloba, memory effected by, 254–255
Glial cells, 57
Glucagon, 374
Glutamate, 62, 62t, 121
Gonads, 95
Grammar, 302, 307
Grapheme-color synesthesia, 105f
Grasping reflex, 326f
Greece, motivation in, 370
Group behavior, 448
　social influence, 440–443
Group polarization, 441–442, 448
Group therapy, 592–594
　advantages, 593–594
Groups, in experiments, 30
Groupthink, 440–441, 441t, 448
GTD. *See* Getting Things Done (GTD) method
Gustation, 120–121
Gustatory cortex, 121, 121f

H

Habits, 497
Habituation, 106–107, 326
Hair cells, 117
Halcion, 174
Hallucinations, 154, 536f, 562, 565
　hypnogogic, 154, 156, 159
　hypnopompic, 156, 159
Hallucinogenics, stimulatory, 178
Hallucinogens, 171, 177–179, 180t
Halo effect, 518
Hammer (malleus), 117, 117f
Handedness, 84–85, 84t
Hardy personality, 418–419, 423
Harlow's Contact Comfort, 337–338

SUBJECT INDEX

Hashish, 178
Hassles, 402–403
Head injuries. *See also* Concussions; Traumatic brain injury
  amnesia and, 263
  long-term effects of, 291
Health
  aging and, 350
  allostasis and allostatic load, 411
  cancer, 412–413
  diabetes from stress, 412
  general adaptation syndrome, 408–409
  heart disease from stress, 411–412
  homeopathy, 424–425
  immune system and stress, 409–410
  stress and, 408–423
Health psychology, stress and, 413–414
Hearing impairments, 118–119
Hearing sense, 116–119
  pitch perception, 118
  sound transduction, 117–118
  sound waves and ear, 116–118, 117f
Heart disease, stress and, 411–412, 411f
Helping behavior, 476–477, 476f
Helplessness, 543
Hematophobia, 546
Hemp, 178–179
Heredity, 6
Heritability, 297
  and neuroscience of personality, 512
Hermann Grid, 134, 134f
Heroics, 222
Heroin, 176
Hertz (Hz), 116
Heuristics, 281
  for problem-solving, 276
Hidden observer, 167–168
Hidden past, 581
Hierarchy of fears, 583, 584t
Hierarchy of needs, of Maslow, 369–370
Higher-order conditioning, 193, 193f
Hindbrain, 74–76
Hindsight bias, 251
Hindu culture, death/dying ritual of, 355
Hippocampus, 74f, 76f, 77, 264
Histogram, 36, 36t
Hofstede's four dimensions of cultural personality, 512–513
Homeopathy, 424–425
Homeostasis, 365, 365f
Horizontal plane, 68f
Hormones, 93. *See also* Pituitary gland
  hunger influenced by, 374
  obesity and, 377
Horney's womb envy, 493–494
Hot flashes, 350
Howard, Ruth, 6
Human brain, 86–87
  anatomical directions of, 73f
  cortical areas of, 78f
  lobes of, 78f
  major structures of, 74f
  planes of section, 68f
  studying specific regions of, 66–67
Human brain function, mapping, 70f
Human development. *See also* Prenatal development
  building blocks, 318–320
  infancy and childhood development, 325–340
  nature and nurture, 316–318
  prenatal, 321–325
  research designs, 316, 317t, 320
Human factors psychology, A-11
Human Google, 256
Human sexuality

Freud's obsession with explanations of, 487
Humanism
  personality and, 500–503
  Rogers and, 500–502
Humanistic perspective, 11, 14t, 486
  current thoughts, 502–503
  personality and, 500–502
Humanistic therapies, 578–582, 591t
  evaluation, 581
Humans, ethics of research on, 46–47
Humors, 426, 528
Hunger
  hormonal influences, 374
  hypothalamus role, 375
  obesity and, 377–378, 379
  physiological and social components of, 374–376
  social components of, 376
  weight and metabolism influences, 375–376
Huntington's disease, 319–320
Hyperopia. *See* Farsightedness
Hyperpolarization, 59
Hypersomnia, 160t
Hyperthymesia, 256
Hypnic jerk, 154
Hypnogogic images/hallucinations, 154, 156, 159
Hypnopompic hallucination, 156, 159
Hypnosis, 166t, 167t
  consciousness affects from, 166–167
  false memory in, 251–252
  theories of, 167–168
Hypnosis in Therapy and Recovered Memories video, 167
Hypnotic susceptibility scale, 166, 166t
Hypnotized, 147
Hypothalamus, 74f, 76f, 77, 93f
  hunger role of, 374
  sleep and, 148–149
Hypothesis, 21–22

I

ICD. *See* International Classification of Diseases
Iconic memory, 234
Iconic sensory memory, 234–235
Id, 487
Ideal self, 501, 502f, 579
Identical twins, 321–322, 322f, 508–509, 509f
Identity *vs.* role confusion, of Erikson, 348
Illness
  sexual dysfunction and, 559
  stress duration and, 410, 410f
Illusion. *See* Perceptual illusions
Illusions of motion, 136–137
Imaginary audience, 347
Imipramine (Tofranil), 605
Imitation, in observational learning, 223
Immune system, stress and, 409–413
Immunizations, 340
Implicit memory, 240–241, 242f
Implicit personality theory, 457
Impression formation, 460
  implicit personality theories, 457
  social categorization, 456–457
Incentive approaches, 368
Incentives, 368
Independent variable, 29
Individual differences, in intelligence, 292–294, 300

Individualism/collectivism dimension, 512
Industrial-organizational psychology, A-11–A-12, A-11t
Infancy and early childhood
  attachment, 335
  attachment styles, 336–337
  autism spectrum disorder in, 334
  brain development, 327
  cognitive development, 329–334, 330t
  Erikson's theory, 338–339, 339t
  Freud on, 487–489
  motor development, 327, 327f
  oral stage of development, 490
  physical development, 325–328, 340
  Piaget's stages, 330t
  preoperational stage, 331
  psychosocial development, 335–339, 340
  reflexes, 326, 326f
  self-concept development, 338
  sensorimotor stage, 330
  sensory development, 327–328
  temperament, 335
  Visual Cliff experiment, 328, 329f
  Vygotsky's theory, 333
Infant-directed speech, 303
Infantile amnesia, 264
Infectious diseases, stress and, 413
Inferential statistics, 43–45
  correlation coefficient, 44–45, 45t
  statistical significance, 43–44
Infidelity, 14
Inflammatory response, 410
Information-processing model, 230
  three memory systems, 233–244
In-groups, 462
Inhibitory synapse, 61
Innate reflexes, 326
Insight, 218, 277–278
Insight learning, 218–219
Insight therapies, 575
  cognitive, 588–590
Insomnia, 158–159
Instinctive drift, 212
Instincts, 364–365, 372
Insulin, 374
Integration, 421, 423
Intellectual disability (intellectual developmental disorder), 292, 300
  causes, 293
Intelligence. *See also* IQ test
  bell curve misunderstandings, 299
  defining, 289
  emotional, 296–297
  giftedness, 293–294
  individual differences in, 292–297
  measuring, 285–286
  nature/nurture and, 297–299
  test construction, 286–291
  theories of, 282–285
Intelligence measures
  Binet's mental ability test, 285
  Stanford-Binet and IQ, 286
  Wechsler test, 286
Intelligence quotient (IQ), 286
  deviation, scores, 288–289
  score correlations by relationship, 298f
Intelligence theories
  Cattell-Horn-Carroll theory, 284–285, 284t
  Gardner's multiple intelligences, 283, 283t
  neuroscience, 285
  Spearman's G factor, 282
  Sternberg's triarchic theory, 283–284

Interaction with others, attitudes and, 453
Interference theory, 258, 259
Intergroup contact, 465
International Classification of Diseases (ICD), 533
Internet-based therapy, 597
Interneuron, 87
Interpersonal attraction
  liking reciprocity, 467
  online relations, 467–468
  physical attractiveness, 466
  proximity, 466
  similarity, 467
Interpersonal psychotherapy (IPT), 578, 581
Interposition, 132
The Interpretation of Dreams (Freud, S.), 162
Interval schedule, 203
Interviews, 517, 521
Intimacy, 352, 468
Intimacy *vs.* isolation, of Erikson, 352
Intrinsic motivation, 364, 371
Introversion, 504
Introverts, 506
Invasive brain stimulation, 66–67
Involuntary muscles, 90
Involuntary reactions, 8
Iproniazid, 604
Ipsilaterally transmitted, 79
IPT. *See* Interpersonal psychotherapy
IQ. *See* Intelligence quotient
IQ normal curve, 41, 41f
IQ tests, 282, 39t
  cultural bias, 289–290
  usefulness of, 290–291
Iris, 109
Irreversibility, 331
Isocarboxazid (Marplan), 604

J

James-Lange theory of emotion, 385–386, 385f, 390f
Japan
  motivation in, 370
  students and emotions, 384
Jet lag, 149
Jigsaw classroom, 466
Jim twins, 509–510
JND. *See* Just noticeable difference
Job stress, 421
Jones behavior therapy, 591t
Journaling, 280t
Jung's collective unconscious, 493
Just noticeable difference (JND), 104

K

"K," 606
Kanzi, chimpanzee, 306
Kenrick's motivation theory, 371
Ketamine, 606
Kinesthesia, 126–127
Klinefelter syndrome, 320
Kohlberg's three levels of morality, 347–348, 348t
Köhler's Smart Chimp experiment, 218–219
Korean cultural values, psychotherapy, 598
Kosslyn's fictional island, 272–273, 272f
Kübler-Ross's theory of death and dying, 354–355

L

Labels, of abnormalities, 537
Laboratory observation, 24
LAD. *See* Language acquisition device
Language, 301
   analysis levels, 301–303
   animals studies in, 305–307
   development of, 303, 303t, 307
   for effective psychotherapy, 599
   elements and structure of, 301–303
   thought relationship to, 304–305, 307
Language acquisition device (LAD), 302
Laser-assisted in situ keratomileusis (LASIK), 109
Latency stage of development, 491–492, 492t
Latent content, 577
Latent learning, 217–218, 217f, 218f
Lateral geniculate nucleus (LGN), 114
Lateral hypothalamus (LH), 375
Laughing, 427
Law, psychology and, A-9
Law of effect, 198
Law of infinitesimals, 425
Lazarus's cognitive-mediational theory of emotion, 385–387, 385f, 386f, 387f, 414, 423
Learned helplessness, 219–220, 543
Learning
   classical conditioning, 188–197
   cognitive learning theory, 216–221
   defined, 188
   neural bases of, 200–201
   observational, 221–223
   operant conditioning, 198–204
   punishment in operant conditioning, 206–209
   reinforcement, 199–206
Learning theories
   Bandura's reciprocal determinism and self-efficacy, 497–498
   Rotter's social learning theory, 498–499
Learning/performance distinction, 222
Lectures, PIA-11–PIA-12
LeDoux's emotion and amygdala work, 380–381
Left hemisphere, of brain, 84t
Leptin, 375
Lesioning studies, 66
Levels-of-processing model, 231
LGN. *See* Lateral geniculate nucleus
LH. *See* Lateral hypothalamus
Librium, 174
Licensed marriage and family therapists, 15
Licensed professional counselors, 15
Lie detector test, 380
Light, 107
   absorbance, from rods and cones, 113f
   color perception, 112–115
   eye and, 108–110
   mixing, 112f
   transduction of, 110
   visual pathway, 111–112, 111f
Light adaptation, 112
Light sleep, 154
Limbic system, 76–77, 76f
Linear perspective, 131, 132f
Linguistic relativity hypothesis, 304–305
Linking, PIA-16
Little Albert study, 9, 194
Little Peter study, 9
Lobes, 78, 78f
Lobotomy, 609
Loci method, PIA-16

Locus of control, 498, 499t
Longitudinal design, 316, 317t
Long-term information, 240–242
Long-term memory (LTM), 239–244
   organization, 243–244
   types of, 242f
Long-term memory (LTM) retrieval
   automatic coding, 249–250
   flashbulb memories, 249–250
   recall and recognition, 247–249, 248f
   reconstructive nature of, 250–253
   retrieval cues, 245–246
Long-term potentiation, 260
Love, 477
   components of, 468–469
Love triangles, 468–469
"Low road" and "high road," 381
Lowball technique, 444, 448
LSD (Lysergic acid diethylamide), 177–178
LTM. *See* Long-term memory

M

Magnetic resonance imaging (MRI), 68, 69, 69f
Magnetoencephalography (MEG), 70
Magnification, 550, 589. *See also* Minimization
Maintenance rehearsal, 238
Major depressive disorder, 539–542, 544
Major life changes, 400–401
Major repressive disorder, 536f, 536t
Males
   eating disorders in, 557
Manic, 541
Manifest content, 163
Manufactured highs, Maintenance rehearsal, 77–178
MAOIs. *See* Monoamine oxidase inhibitors
Marfan's syndrome, 319
Marginalized people, 422, 423
Marijuana, 178–179
Marjory Stoneman Douglas High School, Parkland, Florida, 317
Masculinity/femininity dimension, 513
Maslow's hierarchy of needs, 369–370
Maslow's humanistic perspective, 500–502
Massed practice, 257
Master gland. *See* Pituitary gland
Maturation, 188
Maze, typical, 217f
MBTI. *See* Myers-Briggs Type Indicator
McClelland's motivation theory, 366
MDMA, 178
Mean, A-5
Measures of central tendency, 38–40
Measures of variability, 40–42
Mechanical solutions, problem solving, 275–276
Media violence, aggression linked to, 222, 472–473
Median, 39
Medical marijuana, 179
Medical model, of psychological disorders, 528
Meditation, 427
Meditative state, 147
Medulla, 74, 74f
MEG. *See* Magnetoencephalography
Melatonin, 149
Memory. *See also* Forgetting
   adulthood and aging changes in, 351
   Alzheimer's disease, 262–264

   autobiographical, 264
   biological bases of, 260–261
   constructive processing of, 250
   echoic sensory, 235–236
   failure of, 261–264
   false memory syndrome, 251
   iconic sensory, 234–235
   improving, PIA-16, PIA-16f
   infantile amnesia, 264
   long-term, 239–244, 242f, 243f, 245–253
   models of, 230–232
   neuroscience of, 259–264
   in observational learning, 223
   organic amnesia, 261, 264
   reliability of, 253
   retrieval problems, 251
   sensory, 233–235
   short-term, 236–238
   sleep importance for, 152
   storage, 230, 284
   stress and, 399
   supplements for, 254–255
   three processes of, 230, 233f
   three systems of, 233–244
   three-stage process of, 233f
   trusting, 252
Memory retrieval
   cues, 245–246
   encoding specificity, 245
   problems with, 251
Memory trace, 258
Memory trace decay theory, 258, 259
Menopause, 350–351
Mental disorders, by country income level, 536f
Mental health, exercise for, 612–613
Mental illness. *See also* Abnormality; Psychological disorders
   reducing stigma of, 614
Mental imagery, 281
   sensory perception *vs.*, 273, 273f
Mental images, 272
Mental retardation. *See* Intellectual disability (intellectual developmental disorder)
Mental Rotation experiment, 273
Mental set, 278, 281
Metabolism, obesity and, 375
Metacognition, 139
Methamphetamine, 171
Methedrine, 171
Methods for remembering video, 247
Microsaccades, 137
   iconic memory and, 234
Microsleeps, 151–152
Middle age, 351, 356
Middle ear, 117
Milgram's experiment, 444–448, 445f
Military psychology, B-9
Milk letdown reflex, 94
Mind mapping, 280t
Mindfulness meditation, 427
Minimization, 550, 589
Minnesota Multiphasic Personality Inventory, Version II, Restructured form (MMPI-2-RF), 517–518
Minnesota twin study, 509–510, 512
Mirror neurons, 80
Miscarriage, 324
Misinformation effect, 251, 253
Mitosis, 321
MMPI-2-RF. *See* Minnesota Multiphasic Personality Inventory, Version II, Restructured form
MMR vaccine, autism and, 334

Mnemonic strategies, popular, PIA-16, PIA-16f
Mnemonics strategies, 247
Mnemonist, 256
Mode, 39–40
Modeling, 586
Models of abnormality
   biological, 530–531
   biopsychosocial perspective, 532
   psychological, 531
   sociocultural perspective, 531–532
Molly, 178
Monoamine oxidase inhibitors (MAOIs), 604–605, 607t
Monocular cues, 131
Monosodium glutamate (MSG), 121
Monozygotic twins, 321, 322f
Mood changes, 565
Mood disorders, 539–544
   causes of, 542–544
Mood-stabilizing drugs, 604, 607t, 611
Moon illusion, 136
Moral development, 348t
   adolescence, 347–348, 349
Moral dilemma, 347, 347f
Morale, A-10
Moro reflex, 326f
Morphemes, 302, 307
Morphine, 176
Motherese, 303
Motion parallax, 133
Motion sickness, 127–128
Motivation
   approaches to understanding, 364–366
   arousal approach, 368–369
   defining, 364
   drive-reduction theory, 365–366
   humanistic approaches, 369–372
   incentive approach, 369
   instincts, 364–365
   personality and nAch, 367
   psychological needs, 366–367, 372
   self-determination theory, 371–372
Motivation theories
   arousal theory, 368–369
   drive-reduction theories, 365–366
   Dweck's self-theory, 367
   Maslow's hierarchy of needs, 369–371
   of McClelland, 366
   self-determination, 371–372
Motivational interviewing, 580
Motor cortex, 79f, 80
Motor development, in infancy and early childhood, 327, 327f
Motor pathway, 89
Motor system (efferent), 86f
MRI. *See* Magnetic resonance imaging
MSG. *See* Monosodium glutamate
Müller-Lyer Illusion, 135, 135f
Multiple approach-avoidance conflict, 408, 408t
Multiple baby pregnancies, 322
Multiple births, 325
Multiple intelligences, 283, 283t
Multiple personality, 553
Multitasking, 181
   memory and, 279
Myers-Briggs Type Indicator (MBTI), 518
Myopia. *See* Nearsightedness

N

N1 sleep stage, 154
N2 sleep stage, 154
N3 sleep stage, 154
nAch. *See* Need for achievement

nAff. *See* Need for affiliation
Narcolepsy, 159
NASA. *See* National Aeronautics and Space Administration
National Aeronautics and Space Administration (NASA), 128
National Institutes of Health, on sleep apnea, 159
National Survey on Drug Use and Health (NSDUH), 534
Native Americans
 death/dying ritual of, 355
Natural concepts, 274
Natural killer (NK) cell, 412
Naturalistic observation, 24
Nature, 316–318, 320
Nature/nurture, 316–318
 intelligence and, 297–299
Navajo culture, death/dying ritual of, 355
NDRIs. *See* Norepinephrine-dopamine reuptake inhibitors
NE. *See* Norepinephrine
Near-infrared spectroscopy (NIRS), 71
Nearsightedness, 109, 109f
Necker cube, 129, 130f
Need, 365
Need for achievement (nAch), 366, 367
Need for affiliation (nAff), 366
Need for power (nPow), 366
Negative reinforcement, 201–202, 207t
Negative symptoms, 562
Negatively skewed distribution, 37
Neo-Freudians, 492–494
NEO-PI-R. *See* Neuroticism/ Extraversion/Openness Personality Inventory revised
Nerve hearing impairment, 119
Nerves, 57
Nervous system, 56
 central, 86–89
 functions of parasympathetic and sympathetic divisions, 90f
 overview, 86f
 peripheral, 89–92, 89f
Neural impulses, 58–60
Neurocognitive disorder, 262
Neurodevelopmental model, of schizophrenia, 563
Neurofeedback, 213
Neurogenesis, 88
Neuroimaging techniques, 68–71, 68f
 of psychotherapy, 597
 schizophrenia information from, 565
Neurons, 56–58, 56f. *See also specific types*
 neural impulses, 58–60, 59f
Neuropeptides, 62
Neuroplasticity, 88, 96–97
Neuropsychology, A-7
Neuroscience, 56, 300
 biology of personality, 510–511
 of memory, 259–264
 theories of intelligence, 285
Neurotic personalities, 494
Neuroticism, 506, 511
Neuroticism/Extraversion/Openness Personality Inventory (NEO-PI-R) revised, 518
Neurotransmission, 60–64
Neurotransmitters, 60–61
 as messengers of network, 61–63, 62t
Neutral stimulus (NS), 189–190, 190f
Newborns, vision of, 328
NIBS. *See* Noninvasive brain stimulation techniques

Nicotine, 173, 180t
Night blindness, 112
Night terrors, 157, 160t
Nightmares, 157
NK. *See* Natural killer (NK) cell
Nocturnal leg cramps, 160t
Nondeclarative (implicit) memory, 240–241, 242f, 244
Nondirective, 579
Noninvasive brain stimulation techniques (NIBs), 67
Nonmanufactured high, 178–179
Non-REM sleep (NREM), 153, 155f
Nonverbal intelligence assessments, 290
Norepinephrine (NE), 62t
Norepinephrine-dopamine reuptake inhibitors (NDRIs), 605
Normal curve, 37, 37f, 288, 288f
Norms, in testing, 288–289
Northern Cheyenne Native Americans, death/dying ritual of, 355
nPow. *See* Need for power
NREM. *See* Non-REM sleep
NRIs. *See* Selective norepinephrine reuptake inhibitors (NRIs)
NRIS. *See* Near-infrared spectroscopy (NIRS)
NS. *See* Neutral stimulus
NSDUH. *See* National Survey on Drug Use and Health
Nurture, 316, 320

O

Obedience, 448
 Milgram's research, 444–448, 447f
Obesity
 DBS for, 610
 hunger and, 377–378, 379
Object permanence, 330
Objective introspection, 5
Observational learning, 221–223
 attitude and, 453
 Bandura and Bobo doll experiment, 221–223, 222f
 four elements of, 223
Observer bias, 24
Observer effect, 24
Obsessive-compulsive disorder (OCD), 536t, 548, 551
Occipital lobes, 79
OCD. *See* Obsessive-compulsive disorder
OCEAN acronym, 505–506
Odd behavior, 565
Odontophobia, 545
Oedipus complex, 491
Oleogustus, 121
Olfaction, 122–123. *See also* Smell
Olfactory bulbs, 123
Olfactory receptor cells, 122–123, 123f
Olfactory sense, 122–123
Oligodendrocytes, 57
One-Session Treatment, 586
One-word speech, 303t
Online counseling, 597
Online interpersonal relations, 467–468
Online therapy, 597
Open-mindedness, 19
Openness, 505, 511
Openness/intellect, 506–507
Operant, 199
Operant conditioning, 11, 198–214
 applications of, 210–214
 behavior modification, 212–214
 biological constraints in, 211–212

 discriminative stimulus, 209–210
 extinction, 209, 210
 generalization, 210
 punishment in, 206–209, 206t
 reinforcement, 199–202, 200t
 shaping and modifying behavior with, 210–214
 spontaneous recovery, 210
 stimulus control, 209–210
 therapies based on, 586–587
 Thorndike and Skinner contributions, 198–199, 198f
Operant conditioning chamber, 199
Operationalization, 29
Opiates, 175–176, 180t
Opioids, 177
Opium, 176
Opponent-process theory, 113–114
Optic chiasm, 111–112, 111f
Optic disk, 110
Optic nerve, 110, 111f
Optical illusion, 109
Optimists, 419–420
Optogenetics, 66–67
Oral stage of development, 490, 492t
Organ of Corti, 117, 118
Organic amnesia, 261–264
Ossicles, 117
Otolith organs, 127
Outdoors/nature, for mental health, 612–613
Outer ear, 117
Out-groups, 462
Oval window, 117, 117f
Ovaries, 95
Overeating, 377–378
Overgeneralization, 550, 588
Overlap, 132
Ovum, 321
Oxytocin, 94

P

Pacinian corpuscles, 124
Pain, 124–125
 gate-control theory, 125–126
Pain disorders, 126
Pain nerve fibers, 124
Pancreas, 95
Panic attack, 546–547
Panic disorder, 536f, 536t, 546, 547t, 551
Papers, writing, PIA-17–PIA-18
Papillae, 121, 121f
Parallel distributed processing (PDP) model, 231, 244
Paranoid personality disorder, 559, 560
Parasympathetic division, 86f, 91–92
 of nervous system, 90f
Parenting
 authoritarian, 353
 generativity *vs.* stagnation, 352–353
Parent-teen conflict, 348–349
Parietal lobes, 79–80
Parieto-Frontal Integration Theory, 285
Paroxetine (Paxil), 605
Partial dopamine agonists, 603
Partial reinforcement effect, 202–203
Participant modeling, 586
Participant observation, 24
Passion, 468
Pavlov's dogs experiment, 188–194, 376
Pavlov's metronome/ticking sound experiment, 190–192, 190f
PCP, 178
PDP. *See* Parallel distributed processing (PDP) model

PE. *See* Prolonged exposure
Peak experiences, 370
Peg-word method, PIA-16
Perceived motion, 136f
Perception
 depth, 131–134, 132f, 133f
 Gestalt principles, 129–130, 131f
 influences on, 137–138
Perceptual expectancy, 137
Perceptual illusions, 134–138
 Ebbinghaus Illusion, 135–136, 135f
 Hermann Grid, 134, 134f
 moon Illusion, 136, 136f
 Müller-Lyer Illusion, 135, 135f
 perceived motion, 136–137, 136f
Perceptual set, 137
Performance, cognitive arousal and, 416, 416f
Perimenopause, 351
Peripheral nervous system (PNS), 86f, 89–92, 89f
Peripheral-route processing, 454
Perls Gestalt therapy, 591t
Permissive indulgent parenting, 353
Permissive neglectful parenting, 353
Permissive parenting, 353
Persistence, 407
Personal fable, 347
Personal unconscious, 493
Personality, 486
 behavioral and social cognitive view of, 496–500
 behavioral genetics, 508–510
 biology of, 508–511
 development stages, 489–492
 Freud's conception of, 487–489
 heritability current research, 512
 humanism and, 500–503
 of identical and fraternal twins, 509f
 informally assessing, 522
 learning theories, 497–499
 neuroscience, 510–511
 trait theories, 504–507
Personality assessment, 515–521, 516t
 behavioral assessments, 516–517
 interviews, 517
 personality inventories, 517–518
 projective tests, 519–521
Personality disorders, 558–560
Personality factors, in stress, 416–420
Personality inventories, 517–519, 521
Personality psychology, A-7
Personality theories, 486, 495–496
 Freud's influences, 493–494
 Neo-Freudians, 492–494
 psychodynamic perspectives, 486–495
Personality types, 417–418, 423
Personalization, 589
Person-centered therapy, 579, 582, 591t
Pessimists, 419–420
PET. *See* Positron emission tomography
Phallic stage of development, 491, 492t
Phantom limb pain, 126
Phantoms in the Brain (Ramachandran), 82
Ph.D., A-4
Phenelzine sulfate (Nardil), 604
Phenylketonuria (PKU), 319, 319f
Phi phenomenon, 136
Phobias, 194–195, 536f, 536t, 545–546, 549
Phobic object, 549
Phonemes, 302, 307
Photographic memory, 235
Photons, 108
Photoreactive keratectomy (PRK), 109

Physical activity, 378
Physical aging, 350
Physical attractiveness, 466
Physical dependence, 169–170
Physical development
    adolescence, 346, 349
    adulthood and aging, 350–351
Physiological psychology, A-7
Physiology of emotion, 380–382
Piaget's formal operations, 346–347
Piaget's stages of cognitive development, 329–333, 330t, 340
Pictorial depth cues, 131, 132f
Pineal gland, 93f, 95
Pinna, 117, 117f
Piriform cortex, 123
Pitch, perceiving, 118
Pituitary gland, 74f, 93, 93f
PKU. See Phenylketonuria
Place theory, 118
Placebo effect, 31–32
Placenta, 323
Plagiarism, PIA-19–PIA-20
Pleasure principle, 488
PNS. See Peripheral nervous system
Polygenic inheritance, 319
Polygon, 36, 36f, 37f
Polygraph test, 380
Pons, 64f, 64
Population, 26
Positive regard, 501–502
Positive reinforcement, 201–202
    for dissociative disorders, 554
Positive symptoms, 562
Positively skewed distribution, 40, 40f
Positron emission tomography (PET), 70
Postconventional morality, 348t
Posterior cingulate cortex, 260, 261
Posttraumatic stress disorder (PTSD), 536t, 536f, 548–549
    causes of, 548–549
    treatments, 584–585
Pot. See Marijuana
Poverty, stress and, 420–421
Power distance dimension, 513
Practical intelligence, 283–284
Pragmatics, 302–303, 307
Praise, as motivator, 373–374
Preconventional morality, 348t
Prediction, 20
Preferential looking, 326
Prefrontal lobotomy, 609
Pregnancy
    alcohol use during, 175
    preterm, 324
Prejudice, 461–463, 480
    equal status contact, 465–466
    origins of, 463
    overcoming, 463–466
    realistic conflict theory, 463
    scapegoating, 462–463
    social identity theory, 464
    stereotype vulnerability, 464–465
Prenatal development, 321
    fertilization, 321–322, 321f
    three stages of, 322–325, 322f
Prenatal hazards, 323–324
Preoperational state, of cognitive development, 300t, 331
Pressure, 403, 421
Preterm pregnancy, 324
Primary appraisal, 414, 415f, 418
Primary auditory cortex, 80
Primary drives, 365
Primary effect, 245

Primary reinforcers, 199–200
Primary visual cortex, 79
PRK. See Photoreactive keratectomy
Proactive interference, 258, 258f, 259t, 259
Problem solving, 275–278, 283
    problems with, 279
Problem-focused coping, 426, 429
Procedural memories, 264
Progressive muscle relaxation, 428
Projective personality tests
    problems with, 520–521
    Rorschach inkblots, 520
    TAT, 520
Projective tests, 519
Prolonged exposure (PE), 584
Proprioception, 127, 142
Prosocial behavior, 222–223
    helpful people, 478, 505t
    unhelpful people, 474–476, 505t
Prototypes, 273–274
Proximity, 130, 131f
    in interpersonal attraction, 466
Psychiatric social workers, 15, A-3
Psychiatrists, 15, A-3
Psychoactive drugs, 169–181, 180t
    dependence, 169–171
    depressants, 174–177
    hallucinations, 154, 156, 159, 536f, 562, 565
    physical dependence, 169–171
    psychological dependence, 170–171
    stimulants, 171–177
Psychoanalysis, 8, 492–494, 576–577
Psychodynamic approaches, 576–582
Psychodynamic perspective, 11, 14t
Psychodynamic perspectives, of personality, 486–489
    Freud and modern theories, 494–495
    Freud's conception of personality, 487–489, 588f
    neo-Freudians, 492–494
    personality development stages, 489–492
Psychodynamic therapy, 578, 591t
Psychodynamic therapy, of Freud, 494, 576, 591t
Psychological defense mechanisms, 489, 490t
Psychological dependence, 169–170
Psychological disorders
    anxiety, 544, 547t
    anxiety, trauma, stress, 544–551
    anxiety-related, 547–549
    biomedical therapies, 602–611
    bipolar disorders, 541–542
    causes of, 549–551
    dissociative, 552–554
    eating disorders, 555–558
    history of, 528
    labelling, 537
    major depressive disorder, 539–542
    models to explain, 530–532
    personality, 558–560
    prevalence, 534–538, 535f, 536f, 536t, 538
    schizophrenia, 561–565
    sexual dysfunctions and problems, 559, 605
    by year in United States, 535t
Psychological disorders treatment, 573–574
    behavior therapies, 582–592
    cognitive therapies, 582–591
    group therapy, 592–594
    humanistic therapy, 581–582

    psychotherapy, 576–578, 591t
Psychological models, for disorders, 531, 538
Psychological professionals, A-3–A-5
Psychological research, ethics of, 34–35
Psychological stressors, 403–407
    aggression, 404–405
    conflict, 405–407
    frustration, 404
    pressure, 403
    uncontrollability, 403–404
Psychological therapies, 574–575
    action therapies, 582–592
    biomedical, 602–611
    group, 592–594
    humanistic, 581–582
    psychodynamic approaches, 576–578
    psychotherapy, 595–600
Psychologists, 15, A-3, A-4f
Psychology. See also specific approaches
    bachelor's degree in, careers, A-5–A-6
    as career, A-3–A-5
    careers in, 15–16
    degrees, A-4–A-6, A-6f
    descriptive statistics, 36–42
    healthy, 339, A-8
    history of, 4–10
    influential approaches, 7–9
    interacting with other careers, A-8–A-10
    major theorists, 14t
    master's degree in, careers, A-5
    modern perspectives, 11–14, 14t
    professionals and specialization, 15–16
    research ethics, 46–47
    scientific approach goals, 19–23
    specialization areas, A-6–A-8
    statistics in, 45
    studies in, 82
    third force, 500–503
    timeline of, 5f
    work and, A-10–A-12
    work settings and subfields of, 15f
Psychoneuroimmunology, 409
Psychopathology, 538
Psychopharmacology, 607t, 611
    antianxiety drugs, 604
    antidepressant drugs, 604–607
    antipsychotic drugs, 602–604
    mood-stabilizing drugs, 604
Psychosexual stages of development, 489–492
Psychosocial development
    in adolescence, 346, 349
    adulthood and aging, 350–356, 359
Psychosocial stages of development, of Erikson, 338–339, 339t
Psychosurgery, 607–609, 610
Psychotherapy, 574–575
    characteristics of, 591t
    cultural, ethnic, and gender concerns, 598–600
    effective therapy characteristics, 596–600
    effectiveness studies, 596–600
    neuroimaging of, 597
    success of, 600
Psychotic experiences, 536f
Psy.D., A-4
PTSD. See Posttraumatic stress disorder
Puberty, 346
Punishment
    by application, 207
    defined, 206–207
    effective, 206–209

    modifying behavior with, 206t
    in operant conditioning, 206–209
    problems with, 207–208
    by removal, 207, 207t, 208
Pupil, 109

Q

Questions
    distinction between, 23
    textbook reading, PIA-9

R

Raccoon experiment, 211–212
Random assignment, 30
Randomization, importance of, 30–31
Range, 40
Rapid eye movement sleep (R, REM), 153, 155, 155f
Rapid-smoking technique, 586
Rat brain, 78
Rating scale, 521
Ratio schedule, 203
Rational emotive behavior therapy (REBT), 590, 591
Raven's Progressive Matrices, 290, 290f
RBD. See REM behavior disorder
RDoC. See Research Domain Criteria
Reading, textbooks, PIA-8–PIA-10
Real self, 501, 502f, 579
Realistic conflict theory, 463, 477
Reality principle, 488
REBT. See Rational emotive behavior therapy
Recall, 246–249, 253
Recall/review, in textbook reading, PIA-10
Recency effect, 247
Receptive-productive lag, 303
Receptor sites, 60f, 61
Recessive, 318
Recessive genes, PKU and, 319f
Reciprocal determinism, 497–498, 497f, 500
Reciprocity of liking, 477
Recitation, of textbook reading, PIA-9–PIA-10
Recognition, 246–249, 253
Reflection, 579–580
Reflex, 189
Reflex arc, 88
Reflexes, 9
    in infancy and early childhood, 325–329, 326f
Reinforcement, 586–587
    modifying behavior with, 206t
    in operant conditioning, 198–202
    positive and negative, 170
    schedules of, 202–206
Reinforcement value, 499
Reinforcers, 199–200
Relatedness, 371
Relationships
    adults forming, 350
    finding, in scientific research, 26–28
Relative size, 132, 132f
Reliability
    of memory retrieval, 243
    of tests, 287
Religion, coping and, 430–431
REM behavior disorder (RBD), 156
REM myth, 156
REM rebound, 156

Repetitive transcranial magnetic stimulation (rTMS), 67, 610, 617
Replicate, 23
Representative sample, 26
Representativeness heuristic, for problem-solving, 276
Research Domain Criteria (RDoC)
 matrix example, 534f
 project, 534, 575
Resiliency, 612–613
Resistance, 577
Resistance reaction, 408, 409, 432
Resting potential, 58
Restless leg syndrome, 160t
Restorative theory of sleep, 151
Results, reporting, 22
Reticular formation (RF), 74f, 75
Retina, 108f, 109
Retrieval, memory, 230, 232
Retrieval cues, 240, 245–246, 253
Retrieval failure, 253
Retroactive interference, 258, 258f, 259t, 259
Retrograde amnesia, 261–262, 262f, 264
Reuptake, 63, 63f
Reversible figures, 129
RF. See Reticular formation
Right hemisphere, of brain, 74f
Road rage, 420
Rods, 110
 light absorbance from, 113f
Roger's humanistic perspective, 500–502
Roger's person-centered therapy, 579, 591t
Rohypnol, 174
Role-playing, hypnosis as social, 167
Romantic love, 469
Rooting reflex, 326f
Rorschach inkblot test, 520
Rotter's social learning theory, 498–499, 499t, 500
rTMS. See Repetitive transcranial magnetic stimulation

S

S factor, 282
Sagittal plane, 68f
Sample, A-1
Sapir-Whorf hypothesis, 304
SARIs. See Serotonin antagonist/ reuptake inhibitors
Saturation, 108
Scaffolding, 333
Scapegoating, 462–463, 477
Scatterplot, 27, 28f
Schachter-Singer cognitive arousal theory (two-factor theory) of emotion, 387, 388f, 390f
Schedules of reinforcement, 199–202, 202f
Schemas, 329
Schizophrenia, 536t, 561–565
 causes of, 561–565
 genetics and, 564f
School psychology, A-8–A-9
School shootings, 462, 473–474
Schwann cells, 57
Scientific research, 17–32
 approach, 19–23
 controlling for effects, 31–32
 correlations, 26–28
 critical thinking, 18–19
 descriptive methods, 23–26
 experimental hazards, 31–32
 experiments, 28–31
 steps in, 21–23
SCN. See Suprachiasmatic nucleus
SDT. See Self-determination theory
Secondary appraisal, 415, 415f, 423
Secondary drives, 365
Secondary reinforcers, 199–200
Seeing, 107
 color perception, 103, 105f
 in infancy and early childhood, 325
 light and eye, 108–110, 108f
 nearsightedness and farsightedness, 109f
 visible spectrum, 108f
 visual pathway, 111–112, 111f
Selection, in experiments, 29
Selective attention, 236
Selective norepinephrine reuptake inhibitors (NRIs), 605, 607t
Selective serotonin reuptake inhibitors (SSRIs), 605, 605f, 607t
Selective thinking, 588
Self, 501
 of Dweck, 367
Self-actualization, 369
Self-actualization tendency, 501
Self-concept, 501
 in infancy and early childhood, 327
Self-determination theory (SDT), 371–378
Self-efficacy, 497–498
Self-fulfilling prophecy, 464
Self-help groups, 593
Self-perception theory, 456
Self-theory of motivation, of Dweck, 367
Seligman's depressed dogs, 219–221, 219f
Selye's diseases of adaptation, 411
Semantic memory, 241–242, 242f, 243, 264
 biological bases of, 260–261
Semantic network model, 243, 243f
Semantics, 302, 307
Semicircular canals, 127
Semipermeable membrane, 58
Sensation
 habituation and sensory adaptation, 106–107
 sensory thresholds, 104–106, 105t
 transduction, 104, 105f
Sensation seeker, 368
Senses. See also specific sense
 kinesthetic and proprioceptive, 126–127
 somesthetic, 124–125
 vestibular, 127–128
Sensorimotor stage, of cognitive development, 330, 330t
Sensory adaptation, 106–107
Sensory conflict theory, 127
Sensory development, in infancy and early childhood, 327–328
Sensory memory, 233, 233f, 244
Sensory pathway, 89
Sensory system (afferent), 86f
Sensory thresholds, 104–106, 105t
Separation, 422, 423
Separation anxiety, infant, 335
Serial position effect, 246–247, 247f, 253
Serotonin antagonist/reuptake inhibitors (SARIs), 605
Serotonin partial agonist/reuptake inhibitors (SPARIs), 605
Serotonin-norepinephrine reuptake inhibitors (SNRIs), 605, 607t
Sertraline (Zoloft), 605
Severe punishment, 208
Sex chromosomes, 318
Sex drive, 487
Sex-linked inheritance, 115
Sexual development, 346
 Freud's psychosexual stages, 489–492, 492t
Sexual dysfunctions and problems, 559, 605
Sexuality. See Human sexuality
Shape constancy, 129, 129f
Shaping, 210–211
Sheep brain, 78
Short-term memory (STM), 233, 236–238, 258
Sign language, animals learning, 305–307
Signal detection theory, 106
Significant difference, 44
Similarity, 130, 274f, 467
Single photo emission computed tomography (SPECT), 70
Single-blind studies, 32
Situation cause of behavior, 460
Situational cause, 480
Situational context, 529
Sixteen Personality Factor Questionnaire (16PF). See Cattell's 16PF
Size constancy, 129
Skewed distribution, 37, 38f, 40
Skin, 124–125
Skin receptors, 124–125
 cross-section, 123f
Skin sensory receptors, 124–125
Skinner behavior therapy, 591t
Skinner box, 199
Skinner's operant conditioning, 11, 198–214
Sleep
 biology of, 148–150
 brain activity during, 155f
 hypothalamus and, 148–149
 for mental health, 596
 patterns of infants and adults, 150f, 151
 reasons for, 161–162
 REM purpose, 153
 stages of, 153–156
 theories of, 151–152
 weight gain and, 161–162
Sleep apnea, 159
Sleep deprivation, 152–153
 fNIRS and, 71
Sleep disorders, 160t
 insomnia, 158–159
 narcolepsy, 159
 night terrors, 157
 nightmares, 157
 sleep apnea, 159
 sleepwalking, 157–158
Sleep paralysis, 155
Sleep seizure, 159
Sleep spindles, 152, 155f
Sleep-wake cycle, 148–150
Sleepwalking, 157–158
Smell, 120–122, 120f
 olfactory receptor cells, 122–123, 123f
Smokeless tobacco, 173
Smoking, marijuana, 171
SMS. See Space motion sickness
SNRIs. See Serotonin-norepinephrine reuptake inhibitors
Social anxiety disorder, 545, 547t
Social categorization, 456–457, 460
Social cognition
 attitudes, 450–453, 451f
 attribution, 458–460
 cognitive dissonance, 454–456, 455f
 impression formation, 456–457
 persuasion and, 453–459
Social cognitive learning perspective, 496–500
Social cognitive learning theorists, 497
Social cognitive theory, 463, 477
Social cognitive view, 495
Social comparison, 464
Social facilitation, 442
Social identity, 464
Social identity theory, 464, 472, 481
Social impairment, 442
Social influence, 448
 compliance, 443–444
 conformity, 438–440
 group behavior, 440–443
 obedience, 444–448
Social interaction, 461–466
 aggression, 472–474
 interpersonal attraction, 466–468
 overcoming prejudice, 465–466
 prejudice and discrimination, 461–463
 prosocial behavior, 474–477
Social learning, aggression explanations, 470–474
Social learning theory, 498–499, 499t, 500
Social loafing, 442, 448
Social networking, 467–468
Social phobia, 545
Social psychology
 social cognition, 450–453, 451f, 460
 social influence, 438–448
 social interaction, 461–478
Social Readjustment Rating Scale (SRRS), 400–401, 400t
Social role, 471–472
Social role-playing, hypnosis as, 168
Social-cognitive theory of hypnosis, 168
Social-support system, 428–429, 430
Sociocultural perspective, 12, 14t, 531–532, 553
Soma, 56
Somatic nervous system, 86f, 89–90
Somatic pain, 125
Somatosensory cortex, 78f, 79
Somesthetic senses, 124–126
Somnambulism, 157–158, 160t
Sound transduction, 110
Sound waves, 116–118
 decibels and, 117f
Source traits, 504
Space motion sickness (SMS), 127–128
Spare the rod, spoil the child, 215–216, 216f
SPARIs. See Serotonin partial agonist/reuptake inhibitors
Spatial neglect, 82
SPE. See Stanford prison experiment
Spearman's G factor, 282, 300
Special K, 606
Specific intelligence, 282
Specific phobia, 536f, 536t, 545–546, 547t
SPECT. See Single photo emission computed tomography
Sperling's iconic memory test, 234
Sperm, 321
Spinal cord, 86f, 87–88
Spinocerebellar degeneration, 75
Split-brain research, 83–84, 83f
Spontaneous abortion, 324
Spontaneous recovery, 191, 192f, 197
Sports psychology, A-9
SRRS. See Social Readjustment Rating Scale

SSRIs. *See* Selective serotonin reuptake inhibitors
Stagnated people, 352
Standard deviation, 40, 41t
Standardization, of tests, 287–288
Stanford prison experiment (SPE), 471–472
Stanford-Binet Intelligence Scales, Fifth Edition, 286
Stanford-Binet IQ, 286, 300
Startle reflex, 326f
State-dependent learning, 246
   encoding specificity, 245–246
Statistical significance, 43–44
Statistics, 35–36
Stem cells, 88, 323
Stepping reflex, 326f
Stereotype, 457
Stereotype threat, 299
Stereotype vulnerability, 464–465, 477
Sternberg's triangular theory of love, 468–469, 477
Sternberg's triarchic theory, 283, 300
Stigma, of mental health challenges, 614
Stimulants, 171–174, 180t
Stimulatory hallucinogenics, 178
Stimulus discrimination, 191
Stimulus generalization, 191, 191f
Stimulus motive, 368
Stimulus-response relationship, 9
Stirrup (stapes), 117
STM. *See* Short-term memory
STOP sign, 257f
Storage, 230
Strange Situation, 336–337
Stranger anxiety, 335
Street smarts, 283
Stress, 420
   cancer and, 412–413
   CHD and, 411, 411f
   children's health and, 413
   cognitive factors in, 413
   coping strategies, 425–428
   GAS and, 408–409, 408f
   health and, 408–425
   health psychology and, 413–414
   illness and duration of, 410f
   immune system and, 409–413
   obesity related to, 377
   personality factors in, 416–420
   physiological factors, 408–423
   social and cultural factors, 420–423
   stressors relationship to, 403–407
Stress disorders, 544–551
Stress hormones, 91
Stressors, 398–407
   culture, 421–422
   environmental, 399–403
   job, 421
   poverty, 420–421
   psychological, 403–406
   responses to, 411, 415f
   stress relationship to, 398–399
Stress-vulnerability model, 564, 565
String Problem, 278f
   solution, 281
Study skills, PIA-4, PIA-4t
Subgoals, 277
Subject mapping, 280t
Subjective discomfort, 538
Subliminal perception, 105
Subliminal stimuli, 105
Substance P, 125
Successive approximation, 211
Sucking reflex, 326f
Suicide, 540, 540f

antidepressants related to, 604–607
cults and, 449
Sultan, the chimpanzee, 218–219, 277
Superego, 489
Supertasters, 120
Supplements
   melatonin, 148
   memory effected by, 254–255
Support groups, 593
Suprachiasmatic nucleus (SCN), 149
Surface traits, 504
Surveying textbooks, PIA-9
Surveys, 25–26
Sweetness, 122
Sympathetic divisions, of nervous system, 90f, 90–91, 91f
Synapse, 60–61, 60f
Synaptic gap, 61
Synaptic vessels, 60
Synesthesia, 104, 105f, 177
Syntax, 302, 307
Systematic desensitization, 583

T

Task management, PIA-5–PIA-7
Task performance, 448
Taste, 120–123, 120f
   five basic, 121–122
Taste buds, 120–121, 121f
TAT. *See* Thematic Apperception Test
Tay-Sachs disorder, 319
tDCS. *See* Transcranial direct current stimulation
Telegraphic speech, 303t
Telepsychology, 597–598
Temper tantrum, 210
Temperament, 335, 486
Temporal lobes, 80
Tend and befriend theory, 429
Teratogens, 323–324
   common, 324t
Terman's "Termites," 294–295
Test construction, 300
   evaluating quality of, 286
   reliability and validity, 287
Testes (testicles), 93
Text anxiety, overcoming, 567
Textbook reading, PIA-8–PIA-10
Texture gradient, 132, 132f
Thalamus, 74f, 76–77, 76f
THC (tetrahydrocannabinol), 178
Thematic Apperception Test (TAT), 52, 520f
Theory, 20
The Theory and Practice of Advertising (Scott), A-12
Theory of mind, 334
Therapeutic alliance, 596
Therapy, 574
   characteristics of effective, 596–600
Theta waves, 153, 155f
Thinking
   concepts and prototypes, 273–275
   convergent, 279
   creativity and, 279–281
   divergent, 280
   language relationship to, 304–305, 307
   mental imagery, 272–273
   problem-solving and decisionmaking strategies, 275–278
   stimulant divergent, 279, 280t
Thirst, 77f
Thorndike's operant conditioning of, 198–199
Three colors theory, 112

Three Cs of hardiness, 418–419
Three levels of morality, of Kohlberg, 347–348, 348t
Thyroid gland, 93f, 95
Time management, PIA-5–PIA-7
Time-out tool, 213, 587
Timing, reinforcement of behavior and, 199–202
Tinnitus, 119
Tip of the tongue (TOT), 246, 253
Tobacco products, 173
Token economy, 212, 587
Tolman's maze-running rats, 217–218, 217f, 218f
Tongue, 120–121, 121f
Tonitrophobia, 546
Top-down processing, 137
Touch, 124–126
Tower of Hanoi puzzle, 241, 241f
Trait, 495
Trait perspective, 486, 506–507
Trait theories
   Allport, 504
   big five, 505–506, 505t
   Cattell and 16PF, 504
   current thoughts on, 506–507
   modern, 505–506, 505t
Trait-situation interaction, 506
Trancelike state (amok), 553
Transcranial direct current stimulation (tDCS), 67, 610, 611
Transcranial magnetic stimulation (TMS), 67
Transduction, 104, 105f
Transference, 577
Transorbital lobotomy, 609
Tranylcypromine sulfate (Parnate), 604
Trauma disorders, 544–547
   causes of, 542–544
Trauma-related disorders, 536t
Traumatic brain injury (TBI)
   amnesia and, 261–264
   IQ tests and, 282
Trephining, 528
Triage nursing, 76
Trial and error (mechanical solutions), 275–276
Triarchic theory of intelligence, 283–284
Trichromatic (three colors) theory, 112–113
Tricyclic antidepressants, 605, 611t
Tritanopia, 114
Truths, 18
Trypanophobia, 545
T-test, A-10
Turner syndrome, 320
Twin studies, 297–298, 298f, 318, 510f
   personality, 510–511
   on schizophrenia, 561–562
Twins, 321, 322f, 325
Two-factor theory, 387, 388f
Tympanic membrane, 117
Type 2 Diabetes, 412
Type A personality, 417, 418
Type B personality, 417–418, 423
Type C personality, 418, 423
Type D personality, 418, 423
Type H personality, 418–419, 423
Typical antipsychotics, 602–604, 607t

U

UCR. *See* Unconditioned response
UCS. *See* Unconditioned stimulus
Umami, 121
Umbilical cord, 323

Uncarpeted world, 135
Uncertainty avoidance dimension, 513
Unconditional positive regard, 501–502, 579
Unconditioned response (UCR), 189, 190f
   secondary reinforcers and, 199
Unconditioned stimulus (UCS), 189, 189f
   secondary reinforcers and, 199–200
Unconscious mind, 487
Uncontrollability, 403–404, 407
United States
   eating disorders in, 555–558
   obesity in, 377–378
   prevalence of mental illness, 535f
   psychological disorders, by year, 536t

V

Vaccinations, 341–342
   autism and, 329
Validity, of tests, 287
Validity scales, 518
Valium, 64, 174
Vaping, 173
Variable interval schedule of reinforcement, 203, 204–205, 205f
Variable ratio schedule of reinforcement, 205f, 205–206
Variables, in experiments, 29
Ventral tegmental area (VTA), 170
Ventromedial hypothalamus (VMH), 375
Ventromedial prefrontal cortex (vmPFC), 220
Verbal/rhythmic organization, PIA-16–PIA-17
Vestibular organ (semicircular canals), 117f
Vestibular sense, 127–128
Vicarious conditioning, 195
   attitude and, 450–453
Video games, violence in, 473–474
Videos
   Are Stereotypes and Prejudices Inevitable?, 461
   Assessing Treatment Effectiveness, 497
   Assimilation and Accommodation in Children, 33
   Behavior Therapy, 582–588
   Behavioral Genetics and Heredity, 510
   Bilateral Anterior Cingulotomy, 609
   Careers in Psychology, 16
   Cognitive Dissonance, 454
   Cognitive-Behavior Therapy, 590
   Conformity: The Asch Study, 439
   Conservation, 331
   Critical Thinking, 19
   Deciding to Help, 476
   Diagnosing and Classifying Disorders: The DSM, 533
   Diverse Perspectives, 11
   Effective Treatment of Panic Disorder using CBT, 590
   Electroconvulsive Therapy, 608–609
   Family and Twin Studies, 306
   Finding a Therapist If You Need One, 596
   Formal Operational Thought, 332
   Gardner's Theory of Intelligence, 283
   Gate Control Theory of Pain, 125
   GTD Method, PIA-7
   Health Psychology, 413–414
   How Much Sleep Do We Need?, 150
   How to Make Healthier Choices, 212
   Humanistic theories, 501
   Hypnosis in Therapy and Recovered Memories, 167

Intelligence Tests and Stereotypes, 299
Living with a Disorder: Schizophrenia, 562
"Low Road" and "High Road," 381
Maslow's Hierarchy of Needs, 369–371
Methods for Remembering, 247
Mind is What the Brain Does, 275
Mood Disorder: Depressive Disorder, 539
Negative Reinforcement, 201
Neuroscience of Memory: Long-Term Potentiation, 260
Neurotransmitters: Reuptake, 63f
Obedience to Authority, 447
Overview of Neuroplasticity, 88
Panic Attacks Impair Daily Functioning, 547
Parenting Styles, 352
Parts of the Brain, 73
Positive and Negative Symptoms of Schizophrenia, 562
Projective Tests, 520
Psychodynamic Therapy, 578
PTSD: The Memories We Don't Want, 549
Reasons for Forgetting, 256
Rods and Cones, 110
Schedules of Reinforcement, 202
Self-Determination Theory, 371
Seligman's apparatus, 219f
Sexual Problems and Dysfunction, 559
Shaping, 210–211
Smell and Taste, 120
Sternberg's Triangular theory of love, 468–469
Stress and Memory, 399
Study Methods, PIA-4
The Synapse, 60
Trait Theories of Personality, 504
What is Psychosurgery?, 610
Yoga and Meditation, 428
Violence. *See* Media violence
Virtual reality (VR) technology, 584
Visceral pain, 125
Visible spectrum, 108, 108f
Visual accommodation, 109
Visual association cortex, 79
Visual Cliff experiment, 329, 329f
VMH. *See* Ventromedial hypothalamus
vmPFC. *See* Ventromedial prefrontal cortex
Volley principle, 118
Voluntary muscles, 79
VR. *See* Virtual reality (VR) technology
VTA. *See* Ventral tegmental area
Vygotsky's theory of cognitive development, 333–334, 340

W

Waking consciousness, 146–147
Watson's behavior therapy, 591t
Wear-and-tear theory, of aging, 354
Web therapy, 597
Wechsler Adult Intelligence Scale, 286, 287t
Wechsler tests, 286
Weight gain, sleep and, 161–162
Weight set point, 375–376
Wernicke's aphasia, 81
Wernicke's area, 91
White matter, 69
Withdrawal, 169–170, 405
Women. *See also specific woman*
 alcohol effect on, 171
 emotional infidelity response of, 14
 psychology contributions of, 6–7
 Working backward heuristic, 277
Working memory, 236, 237

X

X. *See* Ecstasy
Xanax, 174

Y

Yerkes-Dodson law, 416
Young adulthood, 350, 356, 357, 546, 603

Z

Z score, 42
Zone of proximal development (ZPD), 333
ZPD. *See* Zone of proximal development
Zygote, 321, 325